ALIEN FRONT ONLINE

FOG MODE
Start an online game called FOGFOGFOG.

BANGAI-O

HIDDEN OPTIONS
Enter the name as **3 Groundhogs**. You will find the hidden options under Secret Garden in the options menu.

CRAZY TAXI 2

NO ARROWS
Hold START as the character select appears and press A.

NO DESTINATION MARK
Hold Y as the character select appears and press A.

EXPERT MODE
Hold Y + START as the character select appears and press A.

ALTERNATE VIEW
With controller C, hold START and press A, B, X or Y to change the view.

CHANGE ARROW COLOR:
With controller C, press L.

Alternate View

DAVE MIRRA FREESTYLE BMX

Enter PROQUEST mode to enter the following codes:

UNLOCK SLIM JIM
While in the Rider Select Screen, enter:

Down, Down, Left, Right, Up, Up, Y

UNLOCK ALL BIKES
While in the Bike Select Screen, enter:

Up, Left, Up, Down, Up, Right, Left, Right, Y

You will have to do this code for each of the riders.

UNLOCK ALL STYLES
While in the Style Selection Screen, enter:

Left, Up, Right, Down, Left, Down, Right, Up, Left, Y

You will have to do this code for each of the riders.

UNLOCK ALL LEVELS
While in the Track Select Screen, enter:

Left, Up, Right, Down, Left, Down, Right, Up, Left, Y

You will have to do this code for each of the riders.

Unlock All Bikes

Unlock All Styles

MAT HOFFMAN'S PRO BMX

X10 SCORE
Pause the game, hold L, and press X, B, B, Up, Down, Down.

DIVIDE SCORE BY 10
Pause the game, hold L, and press Up, Down, Up, B, B, X.

PERFECT BALANCE
Pause the game, hold L, and press X, Left, Up Right.

BALANCE METER
Pause the game, hold L, and press Left, B, X, Y, X, B, A.

BIG TIRES
Pause the game, hold L, and press Down, B, B, Down.

JUMP HIGHER
Pause the game, hold L, and press Up, Up, Up, Up.

SECRET CODES 2002

VOLUME 2

Dreamcast®	2
Game Boy® Color	12
Game Boy® Advance	37
Nintendo 64®	78
GameCube™	85
PlayStation®	94
PlayStation® 2	112
Xbox™	172

||||**BRADYGAMES**
TAKE YOUR GAME FURTHER™

THE GAMES

ALIEN FRONT ONLINE 3
BANGAI-O 3
CRAZY TAXI 2 3
DAVE MIRRA FREESTYLE BMX 3
MAT HOFFMAN'S PRO BMX 4
NBA 2K2 5
OOGA BOOGA 6
PHANTASY STAR ONLINE 7
RAINBOW SIX: ROGUE SPEAR 8
RAZOR FREESTYLE SCOOTER 8
TONY HAWK'S PRO SKATER 2 9

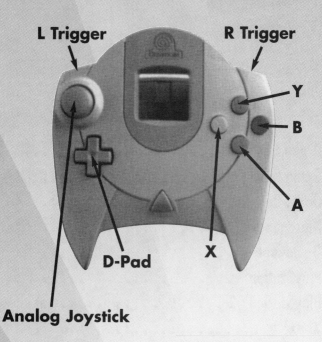

L Trigger

R Trigger

Y

B

A

X

D-Pad

Analog Joystick

UNLIMITED SPECIAL
Pause the game, hold L, and press Left, Down, Y, B, Up, Left, Y, X.

SLOW DOWN TIME
Pause the game, hold L, and press X, Y, B, A.

MORE TIME
Pause the game, hold L, and press X, Up, B, A.

ALTERNATE COLORS
Pause the game, hold L, and press Down, Down, Down, Down.

GRANNY
During Career Mode, retry any level 10 times in a row.

NBA 2K2

HIDDEN TEAMS
Enter **vc** as a code.

BIG HEADS
Enter **heliumbrain** as a code.

MONSTER PLAYERS
Enter **alienbrain** as a code.

ALTERNATE COMMENTARY
Enter **whatamisaying** as a code.

BALL CAMERA
Enter **betheball** as a code.

COOL LOOKS
Enter **radical** as a code.

HIP CLOTHES
Enter **the70slive** as a code.

TAUNT AFTER SCORING
Enter **sohappy** as a code.

SIGH MODE
Enter **Not so happy** as a code.

INFECTED PLAYERS
Enter **tvirus** as a code.

THE CURE!
Enter **The cure!** as a code.

WE'RE SCREWED EXTRA PLAYER
With the Hidden Teams code enabled, enter **Marrinson** as a code.

YO EXTRA PLAYER
With the Hidden Teams code enabled, enter **Stricker** as a code.

THE DOCTOR IS IN! EXTRA PLAYER
With the Hidden Teams code enabled, enter **Dobson** as a code.

I AM SEAMAN EXTRA PLAYER
With the Hidden Teams code enabled, enter **Aynaga** as a code.

IT'S A LIBRARY THING EXTRA PLAYER:
With the Hidden Teams code enabled, enter **Arnold** as a code.

RESET CHEATS
Enter **Sartorial** as a code.

OOGA BOOGA

MASTER CODE
Select Codes from the options menu and enter IGOTNOSKILLZ.

ALL TRIBAL MISSIONS
Select Codes from the options menu and enter IMINFRANCE.

BOARS
Select Codes from the options menu and enter PORKCHOP.

TIKIS
Select Codes from the options menu and enter IDOLATRY.

BIRDS
Select Codes from the options menu and enter AVIARY.

PLAY AS ABE
Select Codes from the options menu and enter AHOUSEDIVIDED.

PLAY AS DEATH
Select Codes from the options menu and enter SALMONMOUSE.

PLAY AS DISCODUDE
Select Codes from the options menu and enter DOTHEHUSTLE.

PLAY AS DWARF
Select Codes from the options menu and enter HEIGHTCHALLENGED.

PLAY AS LEPRECHAUN
Select Codes from the options menu and enter BLARNEYSTONE.

PLAY AS PIRATE
Select Codes from the options menu and enter WAREZWRONG.

PLAY AS SUPERGUY
Select Codes from the options menu and enter SECRETIDENTITY.

FIREBALL SPELL
Select Codes from the options menu and enter STRIKEAMATCH.

HOMING HEAD SPELL
Select Codes from the options menu and enter DODGETHIS.

LIGHTNING BOLT SPELL
Select Codes from the options menu and enter KILOWATTS.

LIGHTNING CLOUD SPELL
Select Codes from the options menu and enter STORMYWEATHER.

MINE SPELL
Select Codes from the options menu and enter KABOOM.

TORNADO SPELL
Select Codes from the options menu and enter BLOWHARD.

LEVEL 2 MASKS
Select Codes from the options menu and enter ICHEAT.

LEVEL 3 MASKS
Select Codes from the options menu and enter THEREFOREIAM.

LEVEL 4 MASKS
Select Codes from the options menu and enter SOVERYVERY.

LEVEL 5 MASKS
Select Codes from the options menu and enter WEAKANDSAD.

BOAR POLO MODE
Select Codes from the options menu and enter TRICKSHOT.

BOAR RODEO MODE
Select Codes from the options menu and enter SADDLEUP.

TRIBAL TRIAL MOVIE
Select Codes from the options menu and enter STRENGTHNO.

PHANTASY STAR ONLINE

Start a new game. While in the character creation mode, enter the following secret codes as your name to gain additional costumes. After the codes are entered, you can rename yourself as you wish. A happy sound will be played if you entered the code correctly.

UNLOCK ALTERNATE COSTUMES

Formarl:	DNEAOHUHEK
Fonewearl:	XSYGSSHEOH
Fonewm:	ASUEBHEBUI
Hucast:	RUUHANGBRT
Humar:	KSKAUDONSU
Hunewearl:	MOEUEOSRHUN
Racaseal:	NUDNAFJOOH
Racat:	MEIAUGHYSN
Ramar:	SOUDEGMKSG

RAINBOW SIX: ROGUE SPEAR

CHEAT MENU
During a game, hold A + B + X + Y + L and press Down.

RAZOR FREESTYLE SCOOTER

ALL CHARACTERS AND LEVELS
Pause the game, hold L and press Right, Down, Right, Left, Right, Up, Right, Right.

DARYL
Pause the game and press Left, Down, Left, Down, Right, Up, Right, Up.

HECTOR
Pause the game and press Left (x5), Right, Left, Right.

Daryl

BRITTANY
Pause the game and press Right, Left, Right, Right, Left, Right (x3).

TITO ORTIZ
Pause the game and press Down, Up, Right, Down, Up, Left, Down, Up.

CHIPPIE
Pause the game and press Up, Down, Down, Left, Right (x3), Down.

TIKIMAN
Pause the game and press Left, Down, Up, Left, Right, Up, Down, Left.

NORTON
Pause the game and press Left, Right, Up, X, Y, X, Up, Right.

Norton

TONY HAWK'S PRO SKATER 2

The following secret codes should be entered at the pause screen while in a game. **Hold the Left Trigger while entering the code.** If the code is entered correctly, you will see the Pause Menu shake.

For secret codes that affect gameplay by altering the environment or the skater, you can disable the option by re-entering the code. For example, if you enter the code for $5000, it won't take the money away again after re-entering the code.

ENVIRONMENTAL EFFECTS

DISCO LIGHTS
Down, Up, X, B, Up, Left, Up, A

MOON PHYSICS
A, X, Left, Up, Down, Up, X, Y

DOUBLE MOON PHYSICS
Left, Up, Left, Up, Down, Up, X, Y, Left, Up, Left, Up, Down, Up, X, Y

JET PACK MODE
Up, Up, Up, Up, A, X, Up, Up, Up, Up, A, X, Up, Up, Up, Up

Controls:

A = Jet Blast on or off

Y = Hover

L = Strafe left

R = Strafe right

Jet Pack Mode

PERFECT BALANCE
Right, Up, Left, X, Right, Up, X, Y

KID MODE
B, Up, Up, Left, Left, B, Up, Down, X

MIRROR MODE
Up, Down, Left, Right, Y, A, X, B, Up, Down, Left, Right, Y, A, X, B

SIM MODE
B, Right, Up, Left, Y, B, Right, Up, Down

SLO-NIC MODE
B, UP, Y, X, A, Y, B

BLOOD OR NO BLOOD
Right, Up, X, Y

SMOOTH SHADING
Down, Down, Up, X, Y, Up, Right

Smooth Shading

WIREFRAME MODE
Down, B, Right, Up, X, Y

FASTER SPEED
Down, X, Y, Right, Up, B, Down, X, Y,
Right, Up, B

Wireframe Mode

CAREER ENHANCEMENT

INSTANT $5000
A, Down, Left, Right, Down, Left, Right

100,000 POINTS IN COMPETITION
X, B, Right, X, B, Right, X, B, Right

CLEAR ENTIRE GAME WITH CURRENT SKATER
B, Left, Up, Right, B, Left, Up, Right, A, B, Left, Up, Right, B, Left, Up, Right

SKIP TO RESTART
X, Y, Right, Up, Down, Up, Left, X, Y, Right, Up, Down, Up, Left, B, Up, Left, Y

STATS

STATS AT 5
Up, X, Y, Up, Down

STATS AT 6
Down, X, Y, Up, Down

STATS AT 7
Left, X, Y, Up, Down

STATS AT 8
Right, X, Y, Up, Down

STATS AT 9
B, X, Y, Up, Down

STATS AT 10
A, Y, B, X, Y, Up, Down

STATS AT 13
A, Y, B, A, A, A, X, Y, Up, Down

UNLOCK CODES

UNLOCK ALL GAPS
Down, Up, Left, Left, B, Left, Up, Y, Y, Up, Right, X, X, Up, A

Trixie will become available to you in the character select screen.

Unlock All Gaps

UNLOCK ALL SECRET CHARACTERS
X, B, Right, Y, B, Right, B, Y, Right, X, Right, Up, Up, Left, Up, X

UNLOCK EVERY LEVEL
Up, Y, Right, Up, X, Y, Right Up, Left, X, X, Up, B, B, Up, Right

UNLOCK EVERYTHING (MASTER CODE!)
This code won't unlock Trixie. You will have to earn her by finding all the gaps or unlocking them all with a code.

A, a, a, x, y, up, down, left, up, x, y, a, y, b, a, y, b.

Once this is entered, end your run.

UNLOCK GYMNASIUM IN SCHOOL LEVEL
Grind the Roll Call! Opunsezmee Rail with about 1:40 on the clock to open the door to the gym.

THE GAMES

102 DALMATIANS: PUPPIES TO THE RESCUE 14
ACTION MAN 14
ATLANTIS: THE LOST EMPIRE 14
ARMY MEN 2 15
ARMY MEN: AIR COMBAT 16
ARMY MEN: SARGE'S HEROES 2 16
BLADE 17
BUFFY THE VAMPIRE SLAYER 18
CHICKEN RUN 18
DAVE MIRRA FREESTYLE BMX 19
DEXTER'S LABORATORY: ROBOT RAMPAGE 19
DONALD DUCK GOIN' QUACKERS 19
DRIVER 20
INSPECTOR GADGET 20
JEREMY MCGRATH SUPERCROSS 2000 21
M & M'S MINIS MADNESS 21
MAT HOFFMAN'S PRO BMX 21
MEN IN BLACK: THE SERIES 2 22
MONSTERS, INC. 22
MTV SPORTS: T.J. LAVIN'S ULTIMATE BMX 23
THE MUMMY RETURNS 23
NEW ADVENTURES OF MARY KATE AND ASHLEY 24
PORTAL RUNNER 24
POWERPUFF GIRLS: BAD MOJO JOJO 25
POWERPUFF GIRLS: BATTLE HIM 27
POWERPUFF GIRLS: PAINT THE TOWNSVILLE GREEN 28
POWER RANGERS: TIME FORCE 30
RAYMAN 30
ROAD CHAMPS BXS STUNT BIKING 30
ROCKET POWER: GETTIN' AIR 31
RUGRATS IN PARIS - THE MOVIE 31
SABRINA THE ANIMATED SERIES: ZAPPED! 31
SCOOBY-DOO! CLASSIC CREEP CAPERS 32
SHREK: FAIRY TALE FREAKDOWN 33

GAME BOY® COLOR

SPIDER-MAN 2: THE SINISTER SIX	.33
SPONGEBOB SQUAREPANTS: LEGEND OF THE LOST SPATULA	.34
TONY HAWK'S PRO SKATER 2	.34
WACKY RACES	.34
WENDY: EVERY WITCH WAY	.35
WWF BETRAYAL	.35
X-MEN: MUTANT ACADEMY	.35
X-MEN: MUTANT WARS	.35
X-MEN: WOLVERINE'S RAGE	.36
XTREME SPORTS	.36

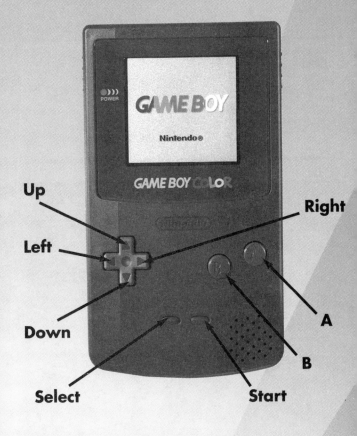

Up

Right

Left

Down

A

B

Select

Start

102 DALMATIANS: PUPPIES TO THE RESCUE

GARAGE LEVEL
Enter **Bone, Bone, Pawprint, Tank** as a password.

CAFETERIA LEVEL
Enter **Domino, Bone, Key, Paw Print** as a password.

CRUELLA — FINAL LEVEL
Enter **Toy, Bone, Bone, Bone** as a password.

ACTION MAN

ACCESS ALL LEVELS
Enter **7!B!** as a password.

ATLANTIS: THE LOST EMPIRE

LEVEL	PASSWORD
Submarine	DCNC
Cove	XDKV
Fire	CFCS
Ice	DHCV
Volcano	TJJT
Internal	JMFJ
Palace	QNFS

ARMY MEN 2

PASSWORDS

LEVEL	PASSWORD
1	Mortar, Tank, Mortar, Jeep
2	Jeep, Jeep, Mortar, Plane
3	Tank, Grenade, Tank, Mortar
4	Rifle, Mortar, Jeep, Plane
5	Mortar, Rifle, Plane, Jeep
6	Mortar, Grenade, Rifle, Chopper
7	Plane, Grenade, Rifle, Tank
8	Grenade, Mortar, Chopper, Mortar
9	Tank, Mortar, Rifle, Tank
10	Jeep, Chopper, Tank, Mortar
11	Rifle, Mortar, Grenade, Mortar
12	Jeep, Chopper, Grenade, Chopper
13	Plane, Plane, Grenade, Mortar
14	Plane, Rifle, Plane, Chopper
15	Rifle, Chopper, Chopper, Tank
16	Chopper, Chopper, Rifle, Grenade
17	Rifle, Tank, Plane, Mortar
18	Rifle, Rifle, Grenade, Jeep
19	Rifle, Jeep, Chopper, Grenade
20	Chopper, Grenade, Rifle, Jeep
21	Mortar, Grenade, Chopper, Jeep
22	Rifle, Tank, Chopper, Rifle
23	Plane, Jeep, Tank, Mortar
24	Chopper, Rifle, Jeep, Mortar
25	Tank, Grenade, Plane, Grenade
26	Plane, Tank, Rifle, Mortar
27	Tank, Tank, Jeep, Tank
28	Jeep, Tank, Jeep, Mortar
29	Chopper, Mortar, Chopper, Jeep
30	Tank, Tank, Grenade, Mortar
31	Chopper, Jeep, Grenade, Rifle

ARMY MEN: AIR COMBAT

PASSWORDS

LEVEL	PASSWORD
2	Box, Cross, Box, Box
3	Rocket, Rocket, Rocket, Cross
4	Patch, Rocket, Box, Box
5	Cross, Patch, Cross, Rocket
6	Helmet, Rocket, Patch, Helmet
7	Box, Cross, Rocket, Cross
8	Rocket, Patch, Cross, Helmet
9	Patch, Patch, Rocket, Rocket
10	Cross, Helmet, Cross, Helmet
11	Helmet, Patch, Cross, Helmet
12	Box, Cross, Patch, Patch
13	Rocket, Cross, Helmet, Helmet
14	Patch, Cross, Box, Patch
15	Cross, Box, Patch, Helmet
16	Helmet, Cross, Rocket, Patch

ARMY MEN: SARGE'S HEROES 2

PASSWORDS

LEVEL	PASSWORD
1	P2Z7Q4LB
2	C1F6Q3TP
3	V4R2B1JK
4	X6K2L1KT
5	S5H8L2RG
6	Y2C3T6BF
7	F1C4P9VP
8	VJC2PFHC
9	W3S4C75S

LEVEL	PASSWORD
10	M8R2X4LS
11	KBHD4V1D12 14NN6168
13	PDO1S4N5
14	BOT7V9CK
15	BDD61977
16	K4TLLC11
17	S6P8D2KG
18	77N5Y14N
19	Y2K4X8TP
20	825VN1N6
21	KFH1JGCO
22	T3F8ROZY
23	Y7C8R2N0
24	XW3L7B26
25	C2X3Q5TC
26	LV75HRR9
27	D2K7POS4
28	H4KXJ68D
29	1NSY1912
30	JYMCBB01

BLADE

GAME ENDING
Enter **9?!1N?BKT?51G** as a password.

BUFFY THE VAMPIRE SLAYER

PASSWORDS

LEVEL	PASSWORD
1	3NKFZ8
2	9MD1WV
3	XTN4F7
4	5BVPL2
5	9D6F0S
6	TSCNB4
7	CSJTQZ
8	BNPXZ9

CHICKEN RUN

INVISIBILITY

Enter **Crown, Bronze, Honor, Valor** as a password.

STAGE SKIP

Enter **Honor, Valor, Bronze, Silver** as a password. Pause the game and press SELECT to skip to the next stage.

UNLIMITED TIME

Enter **Diamond, Honor, Cross, Crown** as a password.

PASSWORDS

LEVEL	PASSWORD
2	Bronze, Cross, Crown, Bravery
3	Diamond, Bravery, Honor, Bronze
4	Cross, Bravery, Bronze, Bronze
5	Crown, Diamond, Crown, Honor
6	Valor, Diamond, Cross, Silver

DAVE MIRRA FREESTYLE BMX

FULL GAME

Enter **R6KZBS7L1CTQMH** as a password.

Full Game

DEXTER'S LABORATORY: ROBOT RAMPAGE

PLAY AS SUPER ROBOT

At the title screen, press A (x10), B (x10), SELECT. You will hear a sound if entered correctly.

DONALD DUCK GOIN' QUACKERS

LEVEL	PASSWORD
1-2	YMPHTM9
1-3	VNQJVPY
1-4	2ZSLXSW
1-5	PWYR3XD
2-1	1KC71PL
2-2	53YRKG0
2-3	42XQJJ8
2-4	4JD8JK[Diamond]
2-5	6G86G2W
3-1	ZD04XHV
3-2	V072VCK
3-3	1F871DF

DRIVER

CHEAT MENU

At the Main Menu, highlight Undercover and press Up, Up, Down, Down, Up, Down, Up, Down, Up, Up, Down, Down.

PASSWORDS

LEVEL	PASSWORDS
1	Face, Face, Face, Face
2	Tire Mark, Badge, Cone, Red Siren
3	Stop Light, Key, Key, Blue Siren
4	Cone, Cone, Cone, Badge
5	Key, Red Siren, Siren, Stoplight
6	Key, Badge, Tire Mark, Blue Siren
7	Badge, Cone, Badge, Red Siren
8	Red Siren, Badge, Key, Tire Tread
9	Cone, Blue Siren, Red Siren, Red Siren
10	Badge, Badge, Stoplight, Cone
11	Blue Siren, Key, Key, Key
12	Stoplight, Tire Tread, Red Siren, Badge
13	Key, Badge, Badge, Cone
14	Red Siren, Blue Siren, Red Siren, Blue Siren
15	Tire Tread, Key, Cone, Stoplight

INSPECTOR GADGET

PASSWORDS

LEVEL	PASSWORD
2	FH2KBH
3	FM!PQM
4	FRVTLR
5	FWQZ!?

JEREMY MCGRATH SUPERCROSS 2000

250CC CLASS
Enter **SHJBBCGB** as a password.

250CC Class

M & M'S MINIS MADNESS

LEVEL	PASSWORD
1-2	Yellow, Red, Blue, Blue, Green, Blue
1-3	Green, Blue, Yellow, Red, Yellow, Yellow
2-1	Green, Blue, Green, Red, Green, Yellow
2-2	Red, Yellow, Orange, Yellow, Brown, Blue
2-3	Brown, Green, Red, Blue, Orange, Blue

MAT HOFFMAN'S PRO BMX

FINAL STAGE
Enter the password **.N.3w.wl2w**.

MEN IN BLACK: THE SERIES 2

PASSCODES

LEVEL	PASSCODE
2	MTTH

3	STVN
4	SPDM
5	BTHH
6	BBYH
7	MRLL
8	MMDD

MONSTERS, INC.

LEVEL	PASSWORD
Himalayas Cave	SNOW
Himalayas Sled	SL3D
Monsters Inc 1	M1K3
Monsters Inc 2	P4PR
Monsters Inc 3	M1NC

LEVEL	PASSWORD
Monstropolis Day	D4Y-
Monstropolis Night	N1T3
Scare Floor	BDRM
Secret Lab 1	L4B-
Secret Lab 2	L4BB
Sulley's Apartment	SLLY
The Doorvault	V4LT

MTV SPORTS: T.J. LAVIN'S ULTIMATE BMX

PASSWORDS

LEVEL	PASSWORD
2	VBBCWBBBCX9
3	LBBBHBBBCX9
4	4BBCRBBBCX+
5	GHBFLBBBCX9
6	ZYBBHBCDFX7
7	QHBBNBCGYX5
8	8DVDBBCGYX7
9	DBBDZBCGYX+
10	XZBFWBCGYX4
11	N+BDMBC4YX7

DIRT TRACKS

Enter **6YBBQBBBCBF** as a password. You can find the dirt tracks in Practice mode.

THE MUMMY RETURNS

PASSWORDS

LEVEL	PASSWORD
1	71P 4KW
2	8K3 71J

LEVEL	PASSWORD
3	P3C 664
4	CXS 0N0
5	1N0 F1N
6	7B4 L6S
7	814 8W4
8	TNM N5Q
9	HTS 0ZX
10	1RD 10V
End	T64 15P

NEW ADVENTURES OF MARY KATE AND ASHLEY

LEVEL PASSWORDS

LEVEL	PASSWORD
Volcano Mystery	CBTHPM
Haunted Camp	GMQTCK
Funhouse Mystery	LHDDQJ
Hotel Who-Done-It	MDGKMQ

PORTAL RUNNER

PASSWORDS

LEVEL	PASSWORD
2	NBNT
3	FDRD
4	NVJV
5	NBRD
6	PDTG
7	NTGT
8	NBGL
9	PDJP
10	NVJC

LEVEL	PASSWORD
11	TJDH
12	VLGL
13	TJGL
14	VLJP
15	NTJV
16	NTTG
17	PBRD
18	TCVJ
19	VJDG
20	TGCF
21	NVLC
22	TGCG
23	VJGL
24	PBDP
25	NBDG
26	PDGK
27	PBGR
28	TGKR
29	VJNV
30	TCMT
31	VJRF
32	PCHS
33	TGMC
34	VJRJ
35	TGKB
36	NTRJ
End	PDND

POWERPUFF GIRLS: BAD MOJO JOJO

BUTTERCUP GRAPHIC
Enter **CHEMICALX** at the Enter Secrets screen.

BUBBLES GRAPHIC
Enter **BOOGIEMAN** at the Enter Secrets screen.

MAYOR GRAPHIC
Enter **BROCCOLOID** at the Enter Secrets screen.

BOOMER GRAPHIC
Enter **USESNIPS** at the Enter Secrets screen.

BUTCH GRAPHICS
Enter **BESNAILS** at the Enter Secrets screen.

BRICK GRAPHICS
Enter **TAILSRULE** at the Enter Secrets screen.

UNLIMITED SUPER ATTACK
Enter **GIRLPOWER** at the Enter Secrets screen.

UNLIMITED LIVES
Enter **DOGMODE** at the Enter Secrets screen.

UNLIMITED RED CHEMICALX
Enter **CHERRY** at the Enter Secrets screen.

UNLIMITED BLACK CHEMICALX
Enter **LICORICE** at the Enter Secrets screen.

UNLIMITED FLIGHT
Enter **IGOTWINGS** at the Enter Secrets screen.

MESSAGE AND PHOTO
Enter **BILLSGIRLS** at the Enter Secrets screen.

ANOTHER MESSAGE AND PHOTO
Enter **RICHARDKIM** at the Enter Secrets screen.

POKEY OAKS SCHOOL LEVEL
Enter **GOGETBUTCH** at the Enter Secrets screen.

ART MUSEUM LEVEL
Enter **DUST BOOMER** at the Enter Secrets screen.

BRICK TRADING CARD
Enter **BESTBUYPWR** or **ZORCH** at the Enter Secrets screen.

PRINCESS TRADING CARD
Enter **SEARS** or **FIZZAT** at the Enter Secrets screen.

POWERPUFF GIRLS TRADING CARD
Enter **CITYRULES** or **TOYSTOWN** at the Enter Secrets screen.

PROFESSOR UTONIUM TRADING CARD
Enter **ANUBISHEAD** or **TARGETGAME** at the Enter Secrets screen.

ROACH COACH TRADING CARD
Enter **ROACHCOACH** at the Enter Secrets screen.

ROWDYRUFF BOYS TRADING CARD
Enter **DOGGIEDO** or **EBWORLD** at the Enter Secrets screen.

SARA BELLUM TRADING CARD
Enter **GAMESTOP** or **SNOWPOKE** at the Enter Secrets screen.

SEDUSA TRADING CARD
Enter **SEDUSA** at the Enter Secrets screen.

UTONIUM CHATEAU TRADING CARD
Enter **TOWNSVILLE** at the Enter Secrets screen.

VOLCANO MOUNTAIN TRADING CARD
Enter **TOYSRUSCOM** at the Enter Secrets screen.

POWERPUFF GIRLS: BATTLE HIM

UNLIMITED RED CHEMICAL X
Enter **CANDYAPPLE** at the Enter Secrets screen.

UNLIMITED BLACK CHEMICAL X
Enter **MIDNIGHT** at the Enter Secrets screen.

UNLIMITED FLIGHT
Enter **JETFUEL** at the Enter Secrets screen.

UNLIMITED LIVES
Enter **UNDEAD** at the Enter Secrets screen.

UNLIMITED SUPER ATTACK
Enter **PHONECARD** at the Enter Secrets screen.

BLOSSOM GRAPHIC
Enter **MISSKEANE** at the Enter Secrets screen.

BUTTERCUP GRAPHIC
Enter **LUMPKINS** at the Enter Secrets screen.

BOOMER GRAPHIC
Enter **WANTSNIPS** at the Enter Secrets screen.

BUTCH GRAPHIC
Enter **SNAILSIAM** at the Enter Secrets screen.

BRICK GRAPHIC
Enter **ITOOKTAILS** at the Enter Secrets screen.

MAYOR GRAPHIC
Enter **MCCRACKEN** at the Enter Secrets screen.

TOWNSVILLE SKIES LEVEL
Enter **GOGETBUTCH** at the Enter Secrets screen.

UTONIUM CHATEAU LEVEL
Enter **BEATBRICK** at the Enter Secrets screen.

MESSAGE AND PHOTO
Enter **BILLSGIRLS** at the Enter Secrets screen.

ANOTHER MESSAGE AND PHOTO
Enter **RICHARDKIM** at the Enter Secrets screen.

ART MUSEUM CARD
Enter **MALPHS** at the Enter Secrets screen.

BOOGIEMAN CARD
Enter **HOTLINE** or **ELBO** at the Enter Secrets screen.

BOOMER CARD
Enter **ICEBREATH** or **BESTBUYHDQ** at the Enter Secrets screen.

CITY OF TOWNSVILLE CARD
Enter **TOYSPOWER** or **TALKING-DOG** at the Enter Secrets screen.

EVIL CAT CARD
Enter **POWERPUFF** at the Enter Secrets screen.

MAYOR CARD
Enter **TOYSTOUGH** or **TARGET-PUFF** at the Enter Secrets screen.

RAINBOW THE CLOWN CARD
Enter **MRSBELLUM** or **RICHMOND-VA** at the Enter Secrets screen.

TALKING DOG CARD
Enter **BIGBILLY** or **RUFFBOYS** at the Enter Secrets screen.

TOWNSVILLE ART MUSEUM CARD
Enter **MALPHS** at the Enter Secrets screen.

TOWNSVILLE CITY HALL CARD
Enter **PRINCESS** at the Enter Secrets screen.

UTONIUM FAMILY CARD
Enter **FLEETFEET** or **GOTOSEARS** at the Enter Secrets screen.

POWERPUFF GIRLS: PAINT THE TOWNSVILLE GREEN

UNLIMITED RED CHEMICAL X
Enter **RUBIES** at the Enter Secrets screen.

UNLIMITED BLACK CHEMICAL X
Enter **EBONY** at the Enter Secrets screen.

UNLIMITED FLIGHT
Enter **IFLYINSKY** at the Enter Secrets screen.

UNLIMITED LIVES
Enter **QUICKENED** at the Enter Secrets screen.

UNLIMITED SUPER ATTACK
Enter **POWERCALL** at the Enter Secrets screen.

BLOSSOM GRAPHIC
Enter **POKEYOAKS** at the Enter Secrets screen.

BOOMER GRAPHIC
Enter **SNIPSFORME** at the Enter Secrets screen.

BUBBLES GRAPHIC
Enter **UTONIUM** at the Enter Secrets screen.

BUTCH GRAPHIC
Enter **LIKESNAILS** at the Enter Secrets screen.

BRICK GRAPHIC
Enter **GOTMETAILS** at the Enter Secrets screen.

MAYOR GRAPHIC
Enter **OCTIEVIL** at the Enter Secrets screen.

MESSAGE AND PHOTO
Enter **BILLSGIRLS** at the Enter Secrets screen.

ANOTHER MESSAGE AND PHOTO
Enter **RICHARDKIM** at the Enter Secrets screen.

BONSAI GARDEN LEVEL
Enter **DUSTBOOMER** at the Enter Secrets screen.

UTONIUM CHATEAU LEVEL
Enter **BEATBRICK** at the Enter Secrets screen.

ACE CARD
Enter **WUNK** or **GOCIRCUIT** at the Enter Secrets screen.

BIG BILLY CARD
Enter **KABOOM** or **EBSTORE** at the Enter Secrets screen.

BROCCLOID EMPEROR CARD
Enter **MOJOJOJO** at the Enter Secrets screen.

BUTCH CARD
Enter **ROWDYRUFFS** at the Enter Secrets screen.

FUZZY LUMPKINS CARD
Enter **RZONE** at the Enter Secrets screen.

GRUBBER CARD
Enter **TOYSMAGIC** or **GRUBBER** at the Enter Secrets screen.

LITTLE ARTURO CARD
Enter **TOYSCIENCE** or **TARGETPOWR** at the Enter Secrets screen.

MS. KEANE CARD
Enter **FLEETFEET** or **SEARSRULES** at the Enter Secrets screen.

SNAKE CARD
Enter **SQUID** or **BESTBUYPUF** at the Enter Secrets screen.

TOWNSVILLE DUMP CARD
Enter **AMOEBABOYS** at the Enter Secrets screen.

ALL CARDS AND CHEATS
Enter **BILLHUDSON** at the Enter Secrets screen.

POWER RANGERS: TIME FORCE

LEVEL	PASSWORD
2	DBBR
3	GCB5
4	HCB9
End	PB3C or PC3B

RAYMAN

ALL LEVELS PASSWORD
Enter **CH5G4mSljD** as a password.

ACCESS ALL LEVELS
Pause the game and press A, Left, A, Left, A, B, Right, B, Up, B, A, Left, A, Down, A.

FILL ENERGY
Pause the game and press B, right, A, Up, B, Left, A, Down, B, Right.

Access All Levels

99 LIVES
Pause the game and press A, Right, B, Up, A, Left, B, Down, A, Right, B, Up, A, Left, B.

ROAD CHAMPS BXS STUNT BIKING

ALL MODES
Enter **QGF7** as a password.

ROCKET POWER: GETTIN' AIR

LEVEL SELECT

DIFFICULTY	PASSWORD
Easy	First Officer, Lars' red-haired friend, Ray, Sam's mom
Medium	First Officer, Lars' red-haired friend, Man with brown hair and glasses, Sam's mom
Hard	First Officer, Lars' red-haired friend, Lar's brown-haired friend, Sam's mom

RUGRATS IN PARIS - THE MOVIE

PASSWORDS

LEVEL	PASSWORD
2	QPRCHJNY
4	ZKHMRTBS

SABRINA THE ANIMATED SERIES: ZAPPED!

PASSWORDS

LEVEL	PASSWORD
1-2	Sabrina, Sabrina, Salem the cat, Jem
1-3	Sabrina, Salem the cat, Salem the cat, Red Head Boy
1-4	Sabrina, Harvey, Salem the cat, Harvey
2-1	Salem the cat, Cloey, Sabrina, Salem the cat
2-2	Harvey, Salem the cat, Red Head Boy, Red Head Boy
2-3	Harvey, Harvey, Red Head Boy, Sabrina
2-4	Harvey, Cloey, Red Head Boy, Salem the cat
3-1	Cloey, Jem, Jem, Harvey

LEVEL	PASSWORD
3-2	Jem, Harvey, Cloey, Sabrina
3-3	Jem, Cloey, Cloey, Salem the cat
3-4	Jem, Jem, Cloey, Salem the cat
4-1	Red Head Boy, Red Head Boy, Harvey, Cloey
4-2	Sabrina, Cloey, Jem, Salem the cat
4-3	Sabrina, Jem, Jem, Harvey
4-4	Sabrina, Red Head Boy, Jem, Cloey

SCOOBY-DOO!
CLASSIC CREEP CAPERS

PASSWORDS

Select CONTINUE from the main menu and enter the following passwords:

Chapter One: It's A Mystery!   Chapter Two: Boo's Clues!

It's A Mystery!

Boo's Clues!

Chapter Three: Chemo-Sabotage!   Chapter Four: Jailbreak!

Chapter Five: The Plan!   Chapter Six: Finale!

The Plan!

Finale

SHREK: FAIRY TALE FREAKDOWN

PASSWORDS

STAGE	PASSWORD
Village as Thelonius	LRSVGTLXM
Dungeon as Thelonius	YFSVGTLXK
Village as Shrek	SMHTVKCQR
Dungeon as Shrek	TQDFNHGGM
Swamp as Shrek	TFGKWLSJJ
Dark Forest as Shrek	KDNBQGKVY
Bridge as Shrek	KWJPYXCQC
Castle as Shrek	YNNHLBMBY

SPIDER-MAN 2: THE SINISTER SIX

INVINCIBILITY
At the title screen, press Up, Down, Right, A.

LEVEL SELECT
At the title screen, press B, A, Left, Down, Up, Right.

ONE HIT WITH WEB KILLS
At the title screen, press Down, A, B, A, A.

UNLIMITED WEBS
At the title screen, press Left, Down, B, Up.

TEDDY BEAR MINI GAME
At the title screen, press A, B, A, B, Down.

NIGHTMARE DIFFICULTY
At the title screen, press A, B, Select, Up, Right, Down.

PASSWORDS

STATUS	PASSWORD
Level 2 after defeating Mysterio	MP!63C
Level 3 after defeating Sandman	PL851D
Level 4 after defeating Vulture	MM947F
Level 5 after defeating Scorpion	TS6!96
Level 5-2 after passing the level to fight Kraven	TS6!9G
Level 6 after defeating Kraven	LR6!9G

SPONGEBOB SQUAREPANTS: LEGEND OF THE LOST SPATULA

LEVEL SELECT AND ALL ITEMS
Select CONTINUE and enter **D3BVG-M0D3**. Pause the game to find a level select.

TONY HAWK'S PRO SKATER 2

ALL BOARDS AND LEVELS
Enter **B58LPT GBBBBV** as a password.

WACKY RACES

ALL DRIVERS AND TRACKS
Enter **MUTTLEY** as a password.

All Drivers and Tracks

WENDY: EVERY WITCH WAY

STATUS	PASSWORD
50% completed	Star, Square, Square, Star
100% completed	Plus, Minus, Plus, Minus

WWF BETRAYAL

DEBUG MODE
Enter **4232** as a password.

X-MEN: MUTANT ACADEMY

APOCALYPSE
Press Right, Left, Up, Down, Left, Up, B + A at the title screen.

PHOENIX
Press Down, Right, Down, Up, Left, Right, B + A at the title screen.

Phoenix

X-MEN: MUTANT WARS

PASSWORDS

LEVEL	PASSWORD
2	0KNG6HWB
3	0LNG6HXQ
4	0LNF7HYP
5	0KPF7HZG
6	1KPF7H0D
7	1KPG7H19
8	1KPF7J2C
9	1KPF7J3L

X-MEN: WOLVERINE'S RAGE

LEVEL PASSWORDS

LEVEL	PASSWORD
2	Wolvie's Mask, Wolvie's Claws, X-Men Insignia, Wolvie's Torso
3	Wolvie's Claws, Sabertooth, Wolvie's Torso, Wolvie's Mask
4	Skull, Wolvie's Mask, X-Men Insignia, Wolvie's Claws
5	Cyber, Lady Deathstrike, Wolvie's Torso, X-Men Insignia
6	Wolvie's Mask, Wolvie's Torso, Wolvie's Head, Lady Deathstrike
7	Wolvie's Claws, Cyber, X-Men Insignia, Skull
8	Skull, X-Men Insignia, Wolvie's Claws, Sabertooth
End	Cyber, Skull, X-Men Insignia, Lady Deathstrike

ALTERNATE COSTUME

At the title screen, press Up, Up, Down, Down, Left, Right, Left, Right, B, A. You'll here Wolverine say, "All Right!"

XTREME SPORTS

CHEAT MENU

At the main menu, press Left (x5), Up (x5), Right (x5), Down (x5), Select (x5).

VIEW CREDITS

Enter your name as staff at the Sign-In. Exit the Sign-In and enter the Snack Hut to view the credits.

ALL COMPETITION MEDALS

Enter your name as **xyzzy** at the Sign-In. Exit the Sign-In, hold the A Button and press SELECT. Hold the A Button and press SELECT again to change the Medal count back to zero.

THE GAMES

ALIENATORS: EVOLUTION CONTINUES 39

ARMY MEN ADVANCE 40

ARMY MEN: OPERATION GREEN 40

ATLANTIS: THE LOST EMPIRE 41

BACKTRACK 41

BATMAN: VENGEANCE 42

BOXING FEVER 43

BRITNEY'S DANCE BEAT 44

CASTLEVANIA: CIRCLE OF THE MOON 44

DARK ARENA 44

DEXTER'S LABORATORY: DEESASTER STRIKES! 47

DOOM 48

DRIVEN 48

EARTHWORM JIM 48

ECKS V SEVER 49

E.T.: THE EXTRA-TERRESTRIAL 50

F-14 TOMCAT 50

FIREPRO WRESTLING 51

GRADIUS GALAXIES 52

GT ADVANCE 52

HIGH HEAT MAJOR LEAGUE BASEBALL 2002 53

INSPECTOR GADGET: ADVANCE MISSION 53

IRIDION3D 54

JACKIE CHAN ADVENTURES: LEGEND OF THE DARK HAND 54

JURASSIC PARK 3: PARK BUILDER 54

KAO THE KANGAROO 55

KONAMI COLLECTOR'S SERIES: ARCADE ADVANCED 56

LEGO BIONICLE 56

MEN IN BLACK: THE SERIES 57

MIDNIGHT CLUB: STREET RACING 58

MONSTERS, INC. 58

NBA JAM 2002 58

NFL BLITZ 20-02 59

PAC-MAN COLLECTION 59

PETER PAN: RETURN TO NEVERLAND 63
PITFALL: THE MAYAN ADVENTURE 63
PLANET OF THE APES 63
POWER RANGERS: TIME FORCE 64
RAMPAGE PUZZLE ATTACK 64
RAYMAN ADVANCE 66
READY 2 RUMBLE BOXING ROUND 2 66
ROCKET POWER: DREAM SCHEME 67
RUGRATS: CASTLE CAPERS 67
SCORPION KING: SWORD OF OSIRIS 68
SPIDER-MAN: MYSTERIO'S MENACE 71
SPONGE BOB SQUAREPANTS: SUPERSPONGE 72
SPYRO: SEASON OF ICE 73
STAR WARS: JEDI POWER BATTLES 74
SUPER BUST-A-MOVE 75
TETRIS WORLDS 75
TOM AND JERRY: THE MAGIC RING 76
TONY HAWK'S PRO SKATER 2 76
WILD THORNBERRYS: CHIMP CHASE 77

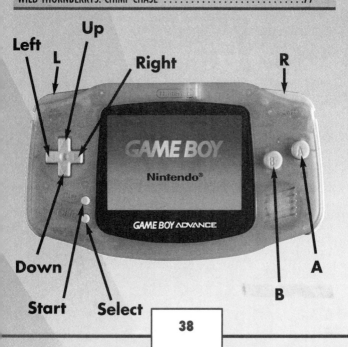

ALIENATORS: EVOLUTION CONTINUES

PASSWORDS

LEVEL	PASSWORD
2	MDKMZKCC

3	BHSZSKTC
4	ZKTSHKMC
5	JLPFDKHB
6	HMDBRKCB
7	GLDKLKZB
8	GLPKLKRB
9	GLDJBKKF
10	GLPJBKFF
11	GLDKBKZF
12	GLPKBKRF

13	GLDJLKHD

ARMY MEN ADVANCE

ALL LEVELS
Enter **NQRDGTPB** as a password.

PASSWORDS

LEVEL	PASSWORD
2	HJRDCHMC
3	GGRSGJMC
4	FSRSMKMC
5	DQRNBBMC
6	CSRJGCMC
7	BQRDMDPC
8	TJRDQFPC
9	SGRSCQPC
10	RJRNLRPC
11	QGRNRSPC
12	PSRJCTPC

ARMY MEN: OPERATION GREEN

PASSWORDS

LEVEL	PASSWORD	ALTERNATE
2	5VKPR6*B	K*67LZZM
3	5PK5LL*4	F58FWJ*N
4	Y8DTF4HK	3MC9TS15
5	62BVXHXY	3SXRLW0J
6	MQ5310VP	Y0V7G6ZM
7	SZQR6W1J	DLTYD4G7
8	44BQQCWH	NJ98C3XD
9	F4J1ZRWG	CG4PPSC6
10	FFOOWP36	5QFXBJJZ
11	*HBNVVV4	52CN4BBH
12	85M3QCF*	*BR53WWF

ATLANTIS:
THE LOST EMPIRE

PASSWORDS

LEVEL	PASSWORD
2	BMQDNPJS
3	BRZSGZDY

4	BVMJFYLG
5	B7JHPMHC
6	C6XQLVNF

BACKTRACK

ALL WEAPONS

During a game press SELECT, then press L, Right, B, L, R, Left. Now enter **WEAP** as a password.

All Weapons

All Weapons

AUTO AMMO

During a game press SELECT, then press L, Right, B, L, R, Left. Now enter **AMMO** as a password.

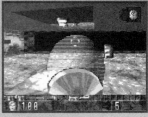

Auto Ammo

INVINCIBILITY

During a game press SELECT, then press L, Right, B, L, R, Left. Now enter **GOD** as a password.

BATMAN: VENGEANCE

PASSWORDS

LEVEL	PASSWORD
2	GOTHAM

3	BATMAN
4	BRUCE
5	WAYNE
6	ROBIN
7	DRAKE
8	BULLOCK
9	GRAYSON
10	KYLE
11	BATARANG
12	GORDON
13	CATWOMAN

LEVEL	PASSWORD
14	BATGIRL
15	ALFRED

Meanwhile, at the abondoned Gotham Chemical Plant, the hide-out of Poison Ivy!

BOXING FEVER

PASSWORDS

COMPLETE	PASSWORD
Amateur Series	90HG6738

Top Contender Series	H7649DH5
Pro Am Series	2GG48HD9
Professional Series	8G3D97B7
World Title	B3G58318
Survival Mode	G51FF888

BRITNEY'S DANCE BEAT

EVERYTHING
Enter the password **HMNFK**.

CASTLEVANIA:
CIRCLE OF THE MOON

MAGICIAN MODE
Complete the game. Start a new game and enter **FIREBALL** as the name.

FIGHTER MODE
Complete the game in Magician mode. Start a new game and enter **GRADIUS** as the name.

SHOOTER MODE
Complete the game in Fighter mode. Start a new game and enter **CROSSBOW** as the name.

Shooter Mode

THIEF MODE
Complete the game in Shooter mode. Start a new game and enter **DAGGER** as the name.

DARK ARENA

ALL CHEATS
Enter **S_X_N** as a password. This gives you Map, Invincible, All Weapons, All Keys, Unlimited Ammo and Level Skip.

INVINCIBLE
Enter **HLGNDSBR** as a password.

Invincible

ALL WEAPONS
Enter **THRBLDNS** as a password.

UNLIMITED AMMO
Enter **NDCRSDRT** as a password.

ALL KEYS
Enter **KNGHTSFR** as a password.

MAP
Enter **LMSPLLNG** as a password.

All Weapons

LEVEL SKIP
Enter **NFTRWLLH** as a password. Pause the game, go to the map and press SELECT to skip to the next level.

SOUND EFFECTS
Enter **CRSDR** as a password. At the Game Options, switch the Sound FX Off and then back on to hear a random sound effect.

Map

PASSWORDS

LEVEL	EASY	MEDIUM	HARD
2	CRSDRPLS	VWHTSRGH	LDNHGHNT
3	TKMWTHYB	TCRSDRLR	DBYFTHND
4	TTLLSFRT	DFRLMWTH	CSSRCNHT
5	STCRSTRD	LLYRMGHT	HNSWLLSN
6	NTLVMLNW	WRMRCHNG	TSTRSTLR
7	NTTRDTNY	TLNDFRFR	STNDRDSW
8	RQSTMWTN	MHMNNCNS	LLRSCRSS
9	GTSTNDBY	YWHLLRTR	LNDTBTTL
10	YRSDTFGH	NFRCHRSN	SRCNHRDS
11	TWTHYVRS	DMSSKWLL	WFLLWRWR
12	THYRCLLN	TKRRVNGN	RRKNGNWR
13	GHVTBTHR	PGNFRMTF	DNTFGHTW
14	HLYLNDHS	STWCHRST	CRRYSGNF
15	TBFRFGHT	NSRCMNGW	CRSSWRLR
End	GDFGHTBL	THSWRDSH	DSFNGLND

45

CHEAT MODE

Enter **NRYRDDS** as a password. This allows you to enter the following passwords. The previous passwords will not work.

EFFECT	PASSWORD
All Cheats	ALL
Invincible	HEALTH
All Weapons	WEAPONS

Unlimited Ammo	AMMO
All Keys	KEYS
Map	MAPS
Level Skip	SKIP
Sound Effects	SFX TEST
Disable Cheat Mode	PWORD

PASSWORDS

The following passwords can be used in Cheat Mode:

LEVEL	EASY	NORMAL	HARD
2	A	AA	AAA
3	B	BB	BBB
4	C	CC	CCC
5	D	DD	DDD
6	E	EE	EEE
7	F	FF	FFF
8	G	GG	GGG
9	H	HH	HHH
10	I	II	III
11	J	JJ	JJJ
12	K	KK	KKK
13	L	LL	LLL

LEVEL	EASY	NORMAL	HARD
14	M	MM	MMM
15	N	NN	NNN
End	O	OO	OOO

DEXTER'S LABORATORY: DEESASTER STRIKES!

ONE MORE TRY
Pause the game and press LLRR LRLL LRLL RRLL.

GET DOUBLE AMMO
Pause the game and press LRRR LLRR LLLL RLLR.

FAST DEXTER
Pause the game and press LRRR RLRL RRLL RLRR.

LESS DAMAGE
Pause the game and press LRRR RLLL RLLL LLLR.

LOW GRAVITY
Pause the game and press LLRR RRRR LLRR LLLR.

FAST ENEMIES
Pause the game and press LRRR RRLL LLRR RRLL.

SLIPPERY FLOOR
Pause the game and press LLRR RLRR RLLR RLLR.

STRONG ENEMIES
Pause the game and press LLRR RRLR RRLL LLLL.

CONTROLS ARE REVERSED
Pause the game and press LRRR RRRL RLLR RLLL.

DOOM

GOD MODE
Pause the game, hold L + R and press A, A, B, A (x5).

RADIATION SUIT
Pause the game, hold L + R and press B, B, A (x6).

LEVEL SKIP
Pause the game, hold L + R and press A, B, A, A, B, B, B, A.

INVINCIBILITY
Pause the game, hold L + R and press B, B, B, A (x5).

ADVANCE TEN LEVELS
Pause the game, hold L + R and press A, B, A, A, B, B, A, A.

BERSERK
Pause the game, hold L + R and press B, A, B, A (x5).

COMPUTER MAP
Pause the game, hold L + R and press B, A (x7).

ALL WEAPONS, ITEMS, KEYS
Pause the game, hold L + R and press A, B, B, A (x5).

DRIVEN

ALL CARS AND TRACKS
Select Top Secret Cars and enter **29801**.

MASTER CAR
Select Top Secret Cars and enter **62972**.

EARTHWORM JIM

LEVEL SELECT
Pause the game and press Right, R, B, A, L, L, A, R.

LEVEL CODES
Pause the game and enter the following to skip to that level:

LEVEL	CODE
Buttville	L, A, Up, R, A, R, A, SELECT
Down the Tubes	Up, L, Down, A, R, A
For Pete's Sake	R, L, R, L, A, R
Level 5	R, L, A, B, B, A, L, R
Snot a Problem	R, Up, SELECT, L, R, Left
What the Heck	SELECT, R, B, Down, L, B

ECKS V SEVER

JONATHON ECKS PASSWORDS

MISSION	PASSWORD
2	EXTREME
3	EXCITE
4	EXCAVATE
5	EXCALIBUR
6	EXTORT
7	EXPIRE
8	EXACT
9	EXHALE
10	EXHUME
11	EXHONERATE
12	EXPEL

SEVER LEVELS
VIOLATE

SEVER PASSWORDS

MISSION	PASSWORD
2	SEVERE
3	SURVIVE
4	SAVANT
5	SUFFER
6	SULPHER
7	SERVE
8	SEETHE
9	SEVERAL
10	SEVERANCE
11	SAVAGE
12	SACROSANCT

VULNERABLE	
VENDETTA	
VORACIOUS	
VINDICATE	
VESUVIUS	

E.T.: THE EXTRA-TERRESTRIAL

PASSWORDS

LEVEL	PASSWORD
2	Up, Up, A, Down, Down, B, R, L
3	Left, Up, Right, Down, L, A, R, B
4	A, Left, B, Right, L, Up, R, Down
5	L, R, R, L, A, Up, B, Left
6	L, Left, R, Right, A, A, B, A
7	B, R, B, L, A, Up, B, Up
8	Up, Up, A, Down, Down, Left, A, B
9	Right, B, B, Left, Up, R, R, L
10	Left, Left, A, L, Right, Right, B, R

F-14 TOMCAT

LEVEL	NOVICE	ACE
2	DHGJKLFF	XDFTRLFF
3	GSDFBFPT	KJTRDBPT
4	RRHCFDVM	RVBPZJVM
5	BPSXFDNF	BMNQYLNF
6	LDFSDTKQ	LFMSDNBQ
7	PXSBSZNJ	PGHPCZNJ
8	DKXZGZQK	DKDGBPQK
9	GKQBGHCT	GSYPZLCT
10	DTRHRPFJ	DCZXRPQR

LEVEL	NOVICE	ACE
11	WZPKJYZX	WRTNJYSX
12	JDZFLKFV	JDPQMLRT
13	SPNGDRRG	SPBXBMRG
14	SFGFJHDH	SPXPRGDH
15	LPFHPRFZ	LPFGNBGZ
16	TDKZXSHX	TQWJGZHN
17	DGBVKMNB	BGJKSZPQ
18	KJHGRJCB	PLMNHRTY
19	VBMQRWTP	GLMRTRRC
20	LKFDSPBV	NHDJPBCX

21	NHDCDKPM	LCMLFLTC

FIREPRO WRESTLING

EXTRA WRESTLERS

Select Edit/Edit Wrestler then select Name Entry. Enter **ALL** in the first line. Use the R and L buttons to move between lines. Enter **STYLE** on the left side of the second line and **CLEAR** on the right. Set Exchange to Off and Middle to the Square—this is the default. Press **START** and then move back up to the main menu. All of the wrestlers should now be selectable.

Extra Wrestlers

GRADIUS GALAXIES

ALL WEAPONS

Pause the game and press Up, Up, Down, Down, L, R, L, R, B, A.

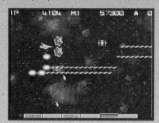

All Weapons

FAKE KONAMI CODE

Pause the game and press Up, Up, Down, Down, Left, Right, Left, Right, B, A. This will give you all weapons. But shortly after entering the code your ship will be destroyed.

GT ADVANCE CHAMPIONSHIP RACING

EXTRA MODE 1 (MINI CARS)
At the title screen, hold L + R and press Right + B.

EXTRA MODE 2 (F1 CAR)
At the title screen, hold L + R and press Left + B.

CREDITS
At the title screen, hold L + R and press Up + B.

ALL TRACKS
At the title screen, hold L + R and press Up/Right + B.

ALL CARS
At the title screen, hold L + R and press Up/Left + B.

ALL TUNE UPS
At the title screen, hold L + R and press Down/Right + B.

HIGH HEAT MAJOR LEAGUE BASEBALL 2002

HIDDEN PITCHES

As the pitcher, hold Left, rotate the D-pad clockwise and press B.

INSPECTOR GADGET: ADVANCE MISSION

PASSWORDS

LEVEL	PASSWORD
Statue Of Liberty: In The Statue	*7*MM14
Statue Of Liberty: The Flame Of Liberty	*3HMLI4
The Tower: The Tower Keeps Watch	R3*3M64
The Tower: The Lift	R7H3L64
The Tower: Higher Than Anything	*CH3L24
The Great Wall: At The Foot Of The Great Wall	*H*3M24
The Great Wall: On The Great Wall	R5*3MR4
Big Ben: The Palace	*3RM33P
Big Ben: The Top	RHRM37P
Egypt: The Valley Of The Kings	RC7M27P
Egypt: The Great Pyramid	*9R33XP

IRIDION 3D

ALL LEVELS
Enter *SH0WT1M3* as a password.

GALLERY OF RENDERS
Enter *G4LL3RY* as a password.

Gallery of Renders

PASSWORDS

STAGE	PASSWORD
2	BKMBVNG7L
3	BV0BBFGCH
4	D9DCBYZ7C
5	OLVCVYQGD
6	8M9CVYV3D
7	XVPDBP6FF

JACKIE CHAN ADVENTURES: LEGEND OF THE DARK HAND

ALL STAGES AND SCROLLS
At the title screen, hold R and press B, A, Left, Down, Up, Right or B, A, Up, Down, Left, Right.

JURASSIC PARK 3: PARK BUILDER

NO DINOSAUR DNA
Enter **Zero-Park** as a park name.

99,000,000 G
Enter **Bonus-Park** as a park name.

START WITH ALL SHOP ITEMS

Enter **Items-Park** as a park name.

HIGH OPINION FROM MEN

Enter **Men's-Park** as a park name.

HIGH OPINION FROM COUPLES

Enter **Love-Park** as a park name.

All Shop Items

KAO THE KANGAROO

PASSWORDS

LEVEL	PASSWORD
Deadly Waterfalls	Boxing Glove, Mushroom, Evergreen, Boxing Glove, Kao's Face
Mythical Caves	Mushroom, Evergreen, Fish, Boxing Glove, Kao's Face
Lost Village	Evergreen, Fish, Owl, Boxing Glove, Kao's Face
Ancient Ruins	Flag, Bomb, Kao's Face, Boxing Glove, Kao's Face
Bear Peak	Frog, Frog, Kao's Face, Boxing Glove, Kao's Face
Big Blizzard	Lamp, Palm Tree, Heart, Boxing Glove, Kao's Face
Crocodile Island	Heart, Palm Tree, Lamp, Boxing Glove, Kao's Face
Evil Descent	Owl, Butterfly, Bird, Boxing Glove, Kao's Face
Frozen Lake	Bird, Key, Frog, Boxing Glove, Kao's Face
Holy Temple	Bomb, Kao's Face, Boxing Glove, Boxing Glove, Kao's Face
Hunter	Palm Tree, Lamp, Frog, Boxing Glove, Kao's Face
Hypnodjin	Bomb, Flag, Coin, Boxing Glove, Kao's Face
Ice Caves	Key, Key, Kao's Face, Boxing Glove, Kao's Face
Island Shores	Coin, Heart, Palm Tree, Boxing Glove, Kao's Face
Lightning Speed	Palm Tree, Heart, Coin, Boxing Glove, Kao's Face
Little Valley	Butterfly, Bird, Key, Boxing Glove, Kao's Face
Megasaurus Ferocious	Fish, Owl, Butterfly, Boxing Glove, Kao's Face
Never-ending Slide	Flag, Coin, Heart, Boxing Glove, Kao's Face
Peril Desert	Heart, Coin, Flag, Boxing Glove, Kao's Face
Trade Village	Coin, Flag, Bomb, Boxing Glove, Kao's Face

KONAMI COLLECTOR'S SERIES: ARCADE ADVANCED

NEW CHARACTERS IN YIE-AR KUNG FU
At the Yie-Ar Kung Fu title screen press Up, Up, Down, Down, Left, Right, Left, Right, B, A, START. You will get the new characters at the end of a single player game or use them in two player.

IMPROVED GYRUSS
At the Gyruss title screen press Up, Up, Down, Down, Left, Right, Left, Right, B, A, START.

IMPROVED FROGGER
At the Frogger title screen press Up, Up, Down, Down, Left, Right, Left, Right, B, A, START.

IMPROVED SCRAMBLE
At the Scramble title screen press Up, Up, Down, Down, Left, Right, Left, Right, B, A, START.

EXTRA LIVES IN RUSH N'ATTACK
At the Rush N' Attack title screen press Up, Up, Down, Down, Left, Right, Left, Right, B, A, START.

NEW TIME PERIOD IN TIME PILOT
At the Time Pilot title screen press Up, Up, Down, Down, Left, Right, Left, Right, B, A, START.

LEGO BIONICLE

MINI-GAMES
Defeat the game with a character to get that character's mini-game. Alternatively, enter the following code as your name:

CHARACTER	CODE
Gali	9MA268
Lewa	3LT154
Onua	8MR472

CHARACTER	CODE
Kopaka	V33673
Pohatu	5MG834
Tahu	4CR487

MEN IN BLACK: THE SERIES

PASSWORDS

EPISODE	PASSWORD
3: Alien Technology Lab	HSDSHSBS

4: Rocket Silo	MXNMSNNG
5: MIB Safe House	THXBXSCK
6: Halloween In Manhattan	NNTNDWNY
End	NFNTMMDD

MIDNIGHT CLUB: STREET RACING

ALL CARS
Enter **AGEM** as a passcode.

COMPLETE GAME PASSCODES

CHARACTER	PASSCODE
Emilio	NIML
Larry	GTBP
Keiko	LGKG
All	LAPC

MONSTERS, INC.

PASSWORDS

DOOR	PASSWORD
3	LRB13G
4	4RB97C
5	7QCZB9

NBA JAM 2002

BEACH AND STREET COURTS
Select Season Mode and enter the password **LHNGGDBLBJGT**.

NFL BLITZ 20-02

EMERSON OGRES AND TEAM MIDWAY
At the title screen, press A, B, SELECT, Up, Right, Down.

MATCHUP SCREEN CHEATS
Use L, B and A to enter the following codes at the Matchup screen and then press Right.

CODE	EFFECT
432	Infinite Turbo
321	No Random Fumbles
313	Shadow Players
132	Ogre Field
225	Snow Field

PAC-MAN COLLECTION

APPENDIX FOR PAC-ATTACK
From the main menu, select Pac-Attack. Highlight Puzzle, hold Right and press A.

PAC ATTACK PASSWORDS

LEVEL	PASSWORD
1	STR
2	HNM
3	KST
4	TRT
5	MYX
6	KHL
7	RTS
8	SKB
9	HNT
10	SRY
11	YSK
12	RCF
13	HSM
14	PWW

LEVEL	PASSWORD
15	MTN
16	TKY
17	RGH
18	TNS
19	YKM
20	MWS
21	KTY
22	TYK
23	SMM
24	NFL
25	SRT
26	KKT
27	MDD
28	CWD
29	DRC
30	WHT
31	FLT
32	SKM
33	QTN

34	SMN
35	TGR
36	WKR
37	YYP
38	SLS
39	THD
40	RMN
41	CNK

LEVEL	PASSWORD
42	FRB
43	MLR
44	FRP
45	SDB
46	BQJ
47	VSM
48	RDY
49	XPL
50	WLC
51	TMF
52	QNS
53	GWR
54	PLT
55	KRW
56	HRC
57	RPN
58	CNT
59	BTT
60	TMP
61	MNS
62	SWD
63	LDM
64	YST
65	QTM
66	BRP
67	MRS
68	PPS
69	SWT
70	WTM
71	FST
72	SLW
73	XWF
74	RGJ
75	SNC

LEVEL	PASSWORD
76	BKP
77	CRN
78	XNT
79	RNT
80	BSK
81	JWK
82	GSN
83	MMT
84	DNK
85	HPN
86	DCR
87	BNS
88	SDC
89	MRH
90	BTF
91	NSM
92	QYZ
93	KTT
94	FGS
96	YLW
97	PNN
98	SPR
99	CHB
100	LST

PETER PAN:
RETURN TO NEVERLAND

PASSWORDS

LEVEL	PASSWORD
Jungle	RGCKYD
Beach	PGCMMD
Forest	CNCGKG
Ship	ZGWYCR

PITFALL:
THE MAYAN ADVENTURE

ALL LEVELS, ALL WEAPONS, MOVE ANYWHERE
At the title screen, press L, SELECT, A, SELECT, R, A, L, SELECT.

Use SELECT and R or L to highlight a level. Press Left to choose that level.

Hold SELECT and press the B Button during a game to get 99 of each weapon.

Hold SELECT and press in any direction during a game to move in that direction.

START AT LAKAMUL RAIN FOREST
Press A, L, A, R, A, L, SELECT, SELECT, START at the title screen.

9 CONTINUES
At the continue screen, repeatedly press START.

PLANET OF THE APES

PASSWORDS

LEVEL	PASSWORD
2	64N4HY
3	F5BMGF
4	B1SKZR
5	76FNHB

LEVEL	PASSWORD
6	P7GRXK
7	6B7VM#
8	QK6293
9	JDDUTJ
10	046PJ#
11	3#9QLS
12	C12KYY
13	CBCYPH

POWER RANGERS: TIME FORCE

FINAL BATTLE
Enter **8QSD** as a password.

Final Battle

RAMPAGE PUZZLE ATTACK

PASSWORDS

LEVEL	PASSWORD
Tokyo 1-1	GQGGHKGBHF

LEVEL	PASSWORD
Tokyo 1-2	LLMLMPLQMT
Tokyo 1-3	GJJBHKGBHF
Tokyo 1-4	BDFGCFBGCK
Tokyo 1-5	GSBBHKGBHF
Delhi 2-1	LPRQMPLQMT
Delhi 2-2	QKNLRTQLRP
Delhi 2-3	BFKGCFBGCK
Delhi 2-4	QBGLRTQLRP
Delhi 2-5	LQCQMPLQMT

Helsinki 3-1	GLSBHKGBHF
Helsinki 3-2	BGPGCFBGCK
Helsinki 3-3	GBLBHKGBHF
Helsinki 3-4	LQHQMPLQMT
Helsinki 3-5	QLDLRTQLRP
Paris 4-1	BKTGCFBGCK
Paris 4-2	LMLRMPLQMT
Paris 4-3	GJHCHKGBHF
Paris 4-4	BDDHCFBGCK
Paris 4-5	GSKCHKGBHF
Hollywood 5-1	LPQRMPLQMT
Hollywood 5-2	QKMMRTQLRP
Hollywood 5-3	BFJHCFBGCK
Hollywood 5-4	QBPMRTQLRP
Hollywood 5-5	LQBRMPLQMT
Washington D.C. 6-1	GLRCHKGBHF

RAYMAN ADVANCE

99 LIVES
Pause the game and press Left, Right, Down, Right, Left, R.

ALL MOVES
Pause the game and press Down, Left, Right, Left, Up, L.

INVINCIBILITY
Pause the game and press Right, Up, Right, Left, Right, R.

FULL HEALTH
Pause the game and press L, Down, Left, Up, Down, R.

99 Lives

READY 2 RUMBLE BOXING ROUND 2

MICHAEL JACKSON
At the main menu, highlight Arcade and press Left, Left, Right, Right, Left, Right, L + R.

RUMBLEMAN
At the main menu, highlight Championship and press Left, Left, Right, Left, Right, Right, Left, Right, Left, L + R.

SHAQ
At the main menu, highlight Survival and pres Left (x4), Right, Right, Left, Left, Right, L + R.

Michael Jackson

Shaq

ROCKET POWER: DREAM SCHEME

STATUS	PASSWORD
After Ocean Shores Beach	4GWD!KL1
Mad Town Complete	MFKGTB!R
Elementary School Complete	2V74BFDG
Town Square Complete	6!LN99V5
Neighborhood Complete	?FXX6BLJ
Spooky Woods Complete	2L!DZHS8

Power Hills Station

RUGRATS: CASTLE CAPERS

LEVEL	PASSWORD
2	QGPCJNWXGWCB
3	QQTKJYWLGKGF
4	CTKLJKGLSCQR
5	RLPTKKGLWKWP
6	FZLDVHMMDQRB
End	JSJRJKSLXCFJ

SCORPION KING: SWORD OF OSIRIS

PASSWORDS

Beat Intro

Beat Twin Anubis (no Runes)

Beat Twin Anubis with Rune 1

Beat Scarab (no Runes)

Beat Scarab with Rune 1

Beat Scarab with Rune 2

Beat Scarab with Runes 1 2

Beat Skull (no Runes)

Beat Skull with Rune 1

Beat Skull with Rune 2

Beat Skull with Runes 1 2

Beat Skull with Runes 1 3

Beat Skull with Runes 2 3

Beat Skull with Runes 1 2 3

Beat Skull Totems (no Runes)

Beat Skull Totems with Rune 1

Beat Skull Totems with Rune 2

Beat Skull Totems with Runes 1 2

Beat Skull Totems with Rune 3

Beat Skull Totems with Runes 1 3

Beat Gargoyle with Rune 1

Beat Skull Totems with Runes 2 3

Beat Gargoyle with Rune 2

Beat Skull Totems with Runes 1 2 3

Beat Gargoyle with Runes 1 2

Beat Skull Totems with Rune 4

Beat Gargoyle with Rune 3

Beat Skull Totems with Runes 2 4

Beat Gargoyle with Runes 1 3

Beat Skull Totems with Runes 1 2 4

Beat Gargoyle with Runes 2 3

Beat Skull Totems with Runes 3 4

Beat Gargoyle with Runes 1 2 3

Beat Skull Totems with Runes 1 3 4

Beat Gargoyle with Rune 4

Beat Skull Totems with Runes 2 3 4

Beat Gargoyle with Runes 1 4

Beat Skull Totems with Runes 1 2 3 4

Beat Gargoyle with Runes 2 4

Beat Gargoyle (no Runes)

Beat Gargoyle with Runes 1 2 4

Beat Gargoyle with Runes 3 4

Beat Gargoyle with Runes 1 3 4

Beat Gargoyle with Runes 2 3 4

Beat Gargoyle with Runes 1 2 3 4

Beat Gargoyle with Rune 5

Beat Gargoyle with Runes 1 5

Beat Gargoyle with Runes 2 5

Beat Gargoyle with Runes 1 2 5

Beat Gargoyle with Runes 3 5

Beat Gargoyle with Runes 1 3 5

Beat Gargoyle with Runes 2 3 5

Beat Gargoyle with Runes 1 2 3 5

Beat Gargoyle with Runes 1 4 5

Beat Gargoyle with Runes 2 4 5

Beat Gargoyle with Runes 1 2 4 5

Beat Gargoyle with Runes 3 4 5

Beat Gargoyle with Runes 1 3 4 5

Beat Gargoyle with Runes 2 3 4 5

Beat Gargoyle with Runes 1 2 3 4 5

Beat game with all Runes
(start at world 1 as Cassandra)

Beat Twin Anubisas Cassandra

Beat Scarab as Cassandra

Beat Skull Totems as Cassandra

Beat Skull as Cassandra

Beat Gargoyle as Cassandra

SPIDER-MAN: MYSTERIO'S MENACE

PASSWORDS

W7HV1 Fluid Upgrade + Armor Upgrade + Hammerhead Down + Docks and Factory open

W7HZZ	As above + Web Compressor
W7OZZ	As above + Big Wheel Down + Chemcorp open
080ZG	As above + Left Wrist Container
Z7OZk	As above + Heavy Impact
Z787k	As above + Rhino Down + Museum open
ZV87k	As above + Scorpion Down + Right Wrist Container
ZV7Z2	As above + Fire Suit
ZV3Z0	As above + Electric suit
HV37k	As above + Electro down + Amusement Park open
JV37H	As above + Belt
JV310	As above + Symbiote Suit
JV31-	As above + Mysterio Defeated

SPONGE BOB SQUAREPANTS: SUPERSPONGE

PASSWORDS

LEVEL	PASSWORD
1: Jelly Fields	BGNR
2: Sandy's Tree Dome	CLMB
3: Fish Hooks Park	KVNF
4: Downtown Bikini Bottom	WKGA
5: Cavernous Canyons	DFVJ
6: Thermal Tunnels	NGPS
7: Acrid Air Pockets	WMCV
8: Lava Fields	XNAD
9: Precipice Canyon	HPJQ
10: Desert Wasteland	QHDG
11: Kelpazoic Jungle	WFXM
12: Inside the Whale	MNTL
13: Road to the Bottom of Rock Bottom	QGAV
14: Lonely Souls	LXHK
15: Graveyard	HGCD
16: Last Stop	CNXK
17: Jelly Fields	LKKV
18: Man Ray's Lair	PVHS
19: Oil Rig	JAST
20: Canning Factory	WMBT

SPYRO: SEASON OF ICE

Enter the secret codes by pressing the buttons at the start screen—when Spryo is on screen and Press Start is flashing.

UNLOCK SPYRO'S WARP ABILITY
Left Right Right Left Up Left Left Right A   (LRRLULLRA)

UNLOCK SPYRO'S WARP ABILITY, UNLOCK ALL LEVELS
Down Up Down Left Right Up Left Up A   (DUDLRULUA)

SPARX GETS 99 LIVES WHEN STARTING A NEW GAME
Left Right Right Right Down Up Right Up A   (LRRRDURUA)

INFINITE HEALTH IN SPARX WORLDS
Down Up Up Down Left Right Right Left A   (DUUDLRRLA)

INFINITE WEAPONS IN SPARX WORLDS
Down Right Up Left Left Up Right Down A   (DRULLURDA)

MORE SPECIAL COMMANDS FOR SPARX
Right Up Right Left Down Up Left Down A   (RURLDULDA)

This activates special commands during Sparx worlds, which provides the following controls:

Up + SELECT	Gives Sparx an Invincibility Shield
Right + SELECT	Gives Sparx a Smart Bomb
Left + SELECT	Gives Sparx Rapid Fire
Down + SELECT	Gives Sparx Homing Bombs

L + SELECT Give Sparx all Keys

OPEN ALL PORTALS TO ALL WORLDS
Up Up Down Down Left Right Up Down A   (UUDDLRUDA)

STAR WARS:
JEDI POWER BATTLES

DARTH MAUL AND LEVEL SELECT
Enter the password **NMHOYQR**.

OBI-WAN PASSWORDS

LEVEL	PASSWORD
2	WFJ3BPG
3	XFJ3BYG
4	YFJ3B6G
5	ZFJ3BFH
6	0FJ3BPH
7	1FJ3BYH
8	2FJ3B6H
9	3FJ3BFJ
10	4FJ3BPJ

QUI-GON JINN PASSWORDS

LEVEL	PASSWORD
2	VHS3BPG
3	VMS3BYG
4	VRS3B6G
5	VWS3BFH
6	VOS3BPH
7	V4S3BYH
8	V8S3B6H
9	VCT3BFJ
10	VHT3BPJ

MACE WINDU PASSWORDS

LEVEL	PASSWORD
2	WB1BCPF
3	VCJMBFF
4	VC1MBPF
5	VCJNBYF

LEVEL	PASSWORD
6	VC1DBYF
7	VCGYCFH
8	VCXYCFH
9	VCDZCPH
10	VCVZCPH

DARTH MAUL PASSWORDS

LEVEL	PASSWORD
1	VMT3BYJ
2	VMT3D*K
3	VMT3GKL
4	VMT3JTL
5	VMT3L2L
6	VMT3N*L
7	VMT3QKM
8	VMT3STM
9	VMT3V2M
10	VMT3X*M

SUPER BUST-A-MOVE

EXTRA MODE

At the title screen press B, R, L, B. An icon will appear at the bottom right of the screen if entered correctly.

HIDDEN CHARACTERS

At the title screen press A, R, L, A. An icon will appear at the bottom left of the screen if entered correctly.

TETRIS WORLDS

POPULAR TETRIS

At the Main Menu, highlight Marathon, hold L and press SELECT. Find the Popular Tetris under the Marathon option.

TOM AND JERRY: THE MAGIC RING

PASSWORDS

CHAPTER	PASSWORD
2	3783
3	5423
4	5348
5	5126
6	8238
7	8143

TONY HAWK'S PRO SKATER 2

SPIDER-MAN

At the main menu or while paused during a game, hold R and press Up, Up, Down, Down, Left, Right, Left, Right, B, A, START.

Spider-Man

SPIDER-MAN WALL CRAWL

At the main menu or while paused during a game, hold R and press Right, A, Down, B, A, START, Down, A, Right, Down. Do a Wall Ride and Spidey will continue up the wall. Be careful, this may lock up your GBA!

ALL LEVELS AND MAXIMUM MONEY

At the main menu or while paused during a game, hold R and press B, A, Left, Down, B, Left, Up, B, Up, Left, Left.

All Levels

ALL LEVELS

At the main menu or while paused during a game, hold R and press A, START, A, Right, Up, Up, Down, Down, Up, Up, Down.

REPLACE BLOOD WITH FACES
At the main menu, hold R and press START, A, Down, B, A, Left, Left, A, Down.

ZOOM IN AND OUT
Pause the game, hold R and press Left, A, START, A, Right, START, Right, Up, START.

ALL CHEATS
At the main menu or while paused during a game, hold R and press B, A, Down, A, START,

Replace Blood with Faces

START, B, A, Right, B, Right, A, Up, Left. You will find the cheats in the Options menu.

NO TIME LEFT
At the main menu or while paused during a game, hold R and press Left, Up, START, Up, Right.

NO BLOOD
At the main menu or while paused during a game, hold R and press B, Left, Up, Down, Left, START, START. Re-enter the code to turn the blood back on.

JET PACK
Pause the game hold R and press Left, A, START, A, Right, Up, START. Hold B to fly, L and R to move left and right, and Up and Down to go forward and back.

WILD THORNBERRYS: CHIMP CHASE

LEVEL	PASSWORD
Jungle 2	4S7JXTJ3
Jungle 3	473H1SZD
Plains 1	B147T3B2
Plains 2	4DZZFB7F
Plains 3	Y5TSGWK2
Arctic 1	6GRHJ74W
Arctic 2	KF3W?6Jr
Arctic 3	MR8594NJ
Outback 1	8!YJCDH4
Outback 2	!!2VKJFS
Outback 3	NDC4SJ3S
Finale	M661M8LB

Nintendo 64®

THE GAMES

ARMY MEN: SARGE'S HEROES 2	.79
NFL BLITZ 2001	.80
READY 2 RUMBLE BOXING: ROUND 2	.82
SCOOBY-DOO! CLASSIC CREEPY CAPERS	.83
TONY HAWK'S PRO SKATER 2	.83
WCW BACKSTAGE ASSAULT	.84

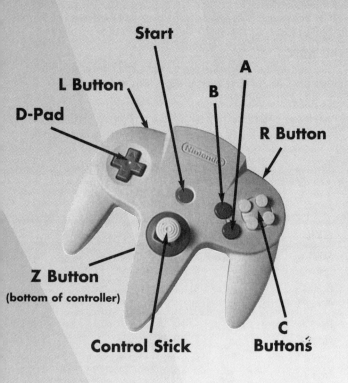

Start

L Button

D-Pad

B

A

R Button

Z Button
(bottom of controller)

Control Stick

C
Buttons

ARMY MEN: SARGE'S HEROES 2

PLAY AS PLASTRO
Enter **PLSTRLVSVG** as a code.

MINI MODE
Enter **DRVLLVSMM** as a code.

TIN SOLDIER
Enter **TNMN** as a code.

Tin Soldier

Play as Vikki

PLAY AS VIKKI
Enter **GRNGRLRX** as a code.

ALL WEAPONS
Enter **GBZRK** as a code.

MAX AMMO
Enter **SLGFST** as a code.

LEVEL PASSWORDS

Enter the following as codes to skip to that level:

LEVEL	CODE
2 Bridge	FLLNGDWN
3 Fridge	GTMLK
4 Freezer	CHLLBB
5 Inside Wall	CLSNGN
6 Graveyard	DGTHS
7 Castle	FRNKNSTN
8 Tan Base	BDBZ
9 Revenge	LBBCK
10 Desk	DSKJB
11 Bed	GTSLP
12 Town	SMLLVLL
13 Cashier	CHRGT
14 Train	NTBRT

LEVEL	CODE
15 Rockets	RDGLR
16 Pool	FSTNLS
17 Pinball	WHSWZRD

NFL BLITZ 2001

VERSUS CODES

To enter the following codes, the Z button is for the first slot, A button is for the second slot and the B button is the third slot. Then end it with a direction on the Control Stick.

EFFECT	CODE
Tournament Mode (in a 2 team game)	1-1-1 Down
Show Field Goal %	0-0-1 Down
Punt hang time meter	0-0-1 Right
Fast turbo running	0-3-2 Left
Huge head	0-4-0 Up
Super blitzing	0-4-5 Up
Hide receiver name	1-0-2 Right
Super field goals	1-2-3 Left

No punting	1-5-1 Up
No head	3-2-1 Left
Headless team	1-2-3 Right
Big head	2-0-0 Right
Big heads team	2-0-3 Right
Big football	0-5-0 Right

EFFECT	CODE
Tiny players team	3-1-0 Right

No first downs	2-1-0 Up
Allow stepping out-of-bounds	2-1-1 Left
Fast passes	2-5-0 Left
Powerup teammates	2-3-3 Up
Power-up offense	3-1-2 Up
Power-up blockers	3-1-2 Left
Power-up defense	4-2-1 Up
Target Receiver (no highlighting)	3-2-1 Down
Always QB	2-2-2 Left
Always receiver (requires human teammate)	2-2-2 Right
QB/receiver cancel always	3-3-3 Up
No interceptions	3-4-4 Up
No random fumbles	4-2-3 Down
Invisible (no effect)	4-3-3 Up
Turn off stadium	5-0-0 Left

| Weather: clear | 2-1-2 Left |
| Weather: snow | 5-2-5 Down |

The following codes require both teams to agree (enter the same code):

EFFECT	CODE
Smart CPU	3-1-4 Down
No CPU assistance	0-1-2 Down
Show more field	0-2-1 Right

Power-up speed	4-0-4 Left
No play selection	1-1-5 Left
Super blitzing	0-4-5 Up
Hyper blitz mode	5-5-5 Up

READY 2 RUMBLE BOXING: ROUND 2

MICHAEL JACKSON

Highlight the "Survival" option at the main menu, then press Left(2), Right(2), Left, Right, L + R. Alternately, successfully complete the game in arcade mode two times to unlock Michael Jackson.

SHAQUILLE O'NEAL:

Highlight the "Survival" option at the main menu, then press Left(4), Right(2), Left(2), Right, L + R. Alternately, successfully complete the game in arcade mode five times to unlock Shaquille O'Neal.

ZOMBIE BOXER:

Press Left, Up, Right, Down, R(2), L at the character selection screen.

SCOOBY-DOO! CLASSIC CREEPY CAPERS

UNLIMITED COURAGE FOR SHAGGY
During gameplay hold L and press C-Up, C-Left, C-Down, C-Up, C-Down, Up, Right, Down, Left, Up, Left, Down, Right, Up, Down.

LEVEL SKIP
During gameplay hold L and press C-Up, C-Down, C-Up, C-Down, Up, Down, Up, Down, Left, Right, Left, Right.

TONY HAWK'S PRO SKATER 2

10X POINTS
Pause the game, hold L and press C-Down (x4), C-Left, C-Right, Right.

STATS TO 10
Pause the game, hold L and press Down, Up, C-Up, C-Left, Down, Up, C-Up.

STATS TO 13
Pause the game, hold L and press C-Down, C-Right(2), C-Up, Up, Down, Right, Left.

JET PACK MODE
Pause the game, hold L and press Right, Up, C-Down, C-Up, C-Down, C-Left, C-Left, C-Right. Ollie to hover.

PERFECT BALANCE
Pause the game, hold L and press C-Down, Right, Down, C-Left, C-Down, C-Up, C-Right, C-Left.

UNLIMITED SPECIAL
Pause the game, hold L and press C-Left, C-Down, C-Up, Right, C-Right, Right.

ALL TAPES
Pause the game, hold L and press C-Right, Left, Up, C-Up, C-Up, Right, Down, Up.

THIN SKATER
Pause the game, hold L and press Left, C-Right, Right, Down, C-Down, Up, Up. You can repeat this code to make thinner.

TURBO MODE
Pause the game, hold L and press C-Left, C-Down, C-Up, Down, Up, Right.

MAXIMUM TURBO
Pause the game, hold L and press Down, Left, C-Up, C-Down, C-Left, Right, Up.**SLOW-NIC MODE**
Pause the game, hold L and press C-Up, Down, Left, C-Left, C-Down, C-Up, C-Right. Tricks will be in slow motion.

SIMULATION MODE
Pause the game, hold L and press Left, C-Right, Right, Down, C-Down, Up, Up.

SKIP TO RESTART
Pause the game, hold L and press C-Left, C-Down, C-Right, Down, C-Up, C-Up.

DOUBLE MOON PHYSICS
Pause the game, hold L and press C-Down, C-Left, C-Right, C-Left, Up, C-Down, Down, Right, C-Down, C-Down.

WCW BACKSTAGE ASSAULT

ALL HIDDEN WRESTLERS
At the main menu press C-Left, C-Left, C-Right, C-Right, C-Right.

SMALL WRESTLERS
At the main menu press R, R, L, L, C-Left, C-Right.

BIG WOMEN WRESTLERS:
At the main menu press R, R, B, B, L, L.

UNLIMITED STAMINA
At the main menu press R, R, B, R, R, B.

INDESTRUCTIBLE WEAPONS
At the main menu press L, R, L, R, C-Left, C-Left.

ALTERNATE GRUNTS
At the main menu press R, L, R, L, B, B.

THE GAMES

BATMAN VENGEANCE	.86
CRAZY TAXI	.86
DAVE MIRRA FREESTYLE BMX 2	.87
NHL HITZ 2002	.91
THE SIMPSONS: ROAD RAGE	.92
TONY HAWK'S PRO SKATER 3	.92
XGIII EXTREME G RACING	.93

Control Stick

Y   **Z**   **X**

L   **R**

A

Start

B

D-Pad   **C Stick**

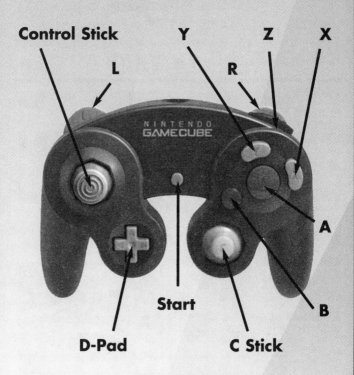

BATMAN VENGEANCE

UNLIMITED ELECTRIC BATARANGS AND BATARANGS

At the main menu, press L, R, Y, X.

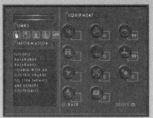

Unlimited Batarangs

CRAZY TAXI

PUSH BIKE

At the character select, highlight a driver, press L + R, L + R, L + R, then hold L + R + Up and press A.

ANOTHER DAY

At the character select press R and release it. Then, hold R and press A.

Push Bike

NO ARROWS

Hold R + START as the character select appears.

NO DESTINATION MARKERS

Hold L + START as the character select appears.

EXPERT MODE

Hold L + R + START as the character select appears and press A.

Expert Mode

DAVE MIRRA FREESTYLE BMX 2

UNLOCK MOST EVERYTHING
At the main menu, press Up, Right, Down, Left, Right, Right, Up, Down, Left, Right, Up, Left, Right, Right, Down, B.

MIKE DIAS
At the main menu, press Up, Left, Down, Right, Right, Left, Up, Down, Up, Right, B.

AMISH GUY
At the main menu, press Up, Left, Down, Right, Left, Left, Down, Up, Left, B.

Mike Dias

ALL BIKES
At the main menu, press Up, Left, Down, Right, Down, Down, Right, Down, Down, Left, B.

ALL THEMES IN PARK EDITOR
At the main menu, press Up, Left, Down, Right, Down, Up, Down, Right, Left, Left, B.

All Themes in Park Editor

SECRET OBJECTS IN PARK EDITOR
At the main menu, press Up, Left, Down, Right, Down, Up, Up, Down, Right, Right, B.

ALL MOVIES
At the main menu, press Up, Left, Down, Right, Left, Left, Right, Left, Up, Down, B.

AMISH GUY MOVES
At the main menu, press Left, Right, Up, Up, Right, Down, Right, Right, B.

All Movies

SLIM JIM MOVES
At the main menu, press Left, Right, Down, Left, Up, Left, Right, Left, B.

COLIN MACKAY

OPEN ALL...	AT THE MAIN MENU PRESS...
Bikes	Down, Down, Right (x5), Up, B
Levels	Up, Up, Right, Left, Up, Right, Right, Up, B
Moves	Left, Right, Right, Up, Left, Right, Right, Up, B
Outfit	Up, Down, Right, Down, Up, Right, Right, Up, B
Movies	Left, Left, Right, Right, Down, Down, Right, Up, B

DAVE MIRRA

OPEN ALL...	AT THE MAIN MENU PRESS...
Bikes	Down, Down, Up, Right, Up, Right, Up, Up, B
Levels	Up (x3), Right, Up, Left, Up, Up, B
Moves	Left, Right, Up, Up, Left, Right, Up, Up, B
Outfit	Up, Down, Up, Down, Right, Left, Up, Up, B
Movies	Left, Left, Up, Right, Up, Left, Up, Up, B

JOEY GARCIA

OPEN ALL...	AT THE MAIN MENU PRESS...
Bikes	Down, Down, Up, Right, Left, Left, Down, Right, B
Levels	Up (x4), Down (x3), Right, B
Moves	Left, Right, Up, Right, Down, Up, Down, Right, B
Outfit	Up, Down, Up, Left, Down, Right, Down, Right, B
Movies	Left, Left, Up, Up, Down, Right, Down, B

JOHN ENGLEBERT

OPEN ALL...	AT THE MAIN MENU PRESS...
Bikes	Down, Down, Left, Up, Left, Up, Left, Left, B
Levels	Up, Up, Left, Down, Right, Down, Left, Left, B
Moves	Left, Right, Left, Left, Down, Up, Left, Left, B

KENAN HARKIN

OPEN ALL...	AT THE MAIN MENU PRESS...
Bikes	Down, Down, Left, Up, Down, Right, Down, Down, B
Levels	Up, Up, Left, Left, Down, Up, Down, Down, B
Moves	Left, Right, Left, Down, Up, Down (x3), B
Outfit	Up, Down, Left, Down, Left, Up, Down, Up, B
Movies	Left (x4), Right, Right, Down, Down, B

LEIGH RAMSDELL

OPEN ALL...	AT THE MAIN MENU PRESS...
Bikes	Down (x3), Up, Left, Left, Down, Left, B
Levels	Up, Up, Down, Up, Left, Down, Down, Left, B
Moves	Left, Right, Down, Left, Left, Right, Down, Left, B
Outfit	Up, Down, Down, Left, Down (x3), Left, B
Movies	Left, Left, Down, Down, Left, Right, Down, Left, B

LUC-E

OPEN ALL...	AT THE MAIN MENU PRESS...
Outfit	Up, Down, Left, Down, Left, Right, Left, Left, B
Movies	Left, Left, Right, Right, Down, Down, Right, Up, B

MIKE LAIRD

OPEN ALL...	AT THE MAIN MENU PRESS...
Bikes	Down, Down, Right, Left, Down, Up, Up, Right, B
Levels	Up, Up, Right, Down, Down, Right, Up, Right, B
Moves	Left, Right (x3), Left, Right, Up, Right, B
Outfit	Up, Up, Down, Down, Left, Right, Right, Left, B
Movies	Left, Left, Right, Up, Up, Right, Up, Right, B

RICK MOLITERNO

OPEN ALL...	AT THE MAIN MENU PRESS...
Bikes	Down, Down, Up, Left, Right, Right, Left, Up, B
Levels	Up (x3), Down, Right, Right, Left, Up, B
Moves	Left, Right, Up (x3), Down, Left, Up, B
Outfit	Up, Down, Up (x4), Left, Up, B
Movies	Left, Left, Up, Down, Right, Left, Left, Up, B

RYAN NYQUIST

OPEN ALL...	AT THE MAIN MENU PRESS...
Bikes	Down (x5), Right, Up, Down, B
Levels	Up, Up, Down, Down, Left, Right, Up, Down, B
Moves	Left, Right, Down(3), Up, Up, Down, B
Outfit	Up, Down, Down, Left, Down, Up, Up, Down, B
Movies	Left, Left, Down, Right, Down, Right, Up, Down, B

SCOTT WIRCH

OPEN ALL...	AT THE MAIN MENU PRESS...
Bikes	Down, Down, Right, Up, Down, Down, Left, Right, B
Levels	Up, Up, Right, Up, Left (x3), Right, B
Moves	Left, Right (x3), Up, Down, Left, Right, B
Outfit	Up, Down, Right, Down, Up, Right, Right, Up, B
Movies	Left, Left, Right, Up (x3), Left, Right, B

TIM MIRRA

OPEN ALL...	AT THE MAIN MENU PRESS...
Bikes	Down, Down, Right, Left, Down, Right, Down, Up, B
Levels	Up, Up, Right, Down, Right, Left, Down, Up, B
Moves	Left, Right, Right, Up, Down, Up, Down, Up, B
Outfit	Up, Down, Right, Left, Left, Up, Down, Up, B
Movies	Left, Left, Right, Up, Down, Left, Down, Up, B

TODD LYONS

OPEN ALL...	AT THE MAIN MENU PRESS...
Bikes	Down (x4), Left, Right, Left, Down, B
Levels	Up, Up, Down, Up, Right, Right, Left, Down, B
Moves	Left, Right, Down, Down, Left, Right, Left, Down, B
Outfit	Up, Down, Down, Right, Up, Left, Left, Down, B
Movies	Left, Left, Down, Up, Up, Right, Left, Down, B

TROY MCMURRAY

OPEN ALL...	AT THE MAIN MENU PRESS...
Bikes	Down, Down, Left, Down, Right, Left, Up, Left, B
Levels	Up, Up, Left, Up, Up, Right, Up, Left, B
Moves	Left, Right, Left, Left, Up, Down, Up, Left, B
Outfit	Up, Down, Left, Down, Right, Left, Up, Left, B
Movies	Left (x3), Down, Up, Right, Up, Left, B

ZACH SHAW

OPEN ALL...	AT THE MAIN MENU PRESS...
Bikes	Down, Down, Left, Down, Up, Right, Right, Down, B
Levels	Up, Up, Left, Right, Down, Down, Right, Down, B
Moves	Left, Right, Left, Down, Left, Up, Right, Down, B
Outfit	Up, Down, Left, Right, Down, Down, Right, Down, B
Movies	Left (x3), Right, Left, Down, Right, Down, B

NHL HITZ 2002

CHEATS

After selecting your players, you will have a chance to enter codes by changing three icons with the X button, Y button and B button. Use the X button to change the first icon, the Y button for second and the B button for the third. You will then need to press in the direction indicated. For example, to enter the code for 1st to 7 Wins, you would press X three times, Y two times and B three times. Then press Left on the Directional pad.

EFFECT	CHEAT
Input More Codes	3 3 3 Right
Ignore Last Code	0 1 0 Down
1st to 7 Wins	3 2 3 Left
Win Fights For Goals	2 0 2 Left
No Crowd	2 1 0 Right
Show Hot Spot	2 0 1 Up
Show Shot Speed	1 0 1 Up
Rain	1 4 1 Left
Snow	1 2 1 Left
Big Puck	1 2 1 Up
Huge Puck	3 2 1 Up
Bulldozer Puck	2 1 2 Left
Hockey Ball	1 3 3 Left
Tennis Ball	1 3 2 Down
No Puck Out of Play	1 1 1 Down
Big Head Player	2 0 0 Right
Huge Head Player	3 0 0 Right
Big Head Team	2 2 0 Left
Huge Head Team	3 3 0 Left
Always Big Hits	2 3 4 Down
Late Hits	3 2 1 Down
Pinball Boards	4 2 3 Right
Domino Effect	0 1 2 Right
Turbo Boost	0 0 2 Up
Infinite Turbo	4 1 3 Right
No Fake Shots	4 2 4 Down
No One-Timers	2 1 3 Left

EFFECT	CHEAT
Skills Versus	2 2 2 Down
Hitz Time	1 0 4 Right

THE SIMPSONS: ROAD RAGE

HIDDEN CHARACTERS

Set the system date to the following to open the secret characters:

DATE	CHARACTER
Jan 1	Happy New Year Krusty the Klown
Oct 31	Happy Halloween Bart
Nov 22, 2001, Nov 28, 2002…	Happy Thanksgiving Marge
Dec 25	Merry Christmas Apu

TONY HAWK'S PRO SKATER 3

ALL CHEATS

Select Cheats from the Options menu and enter **MARKEDCARDS**.

MAX STATS

Select Cheats from the Options menu and enter **MAXMEOUT**.

Max Stats

All Movies

ALL MOVIES

Select Cheats from the Options menu and enter **POPCORN**.

XGIII EXTREME G RACING

ALL TRACKS
At the main menu press L, L, R, R, Z, Z, L+ R + Z.

All Tracks

INFINITE AMMUNITION
At the main menu press L, R, L, R, L + R, Z.

DOUBLE PRIZE MONEY
At the main menu press L, R , Z, L, R, Z, L + R.

INFINITE SHIELD
At the main menu press L + R, Z, L + R, Z.

WILL WIN THIS RACE
At the main menu press L + R + Z, L + R, Z, L + R + Z.

Will Win this Race

PLAYSTATION®

THE GAMES

007 RACING	95
ARMY MEN: AIR ATTACK 2	95
COOL BOARDERS 2001	96
DAVE MIRRA FREESTYLE BMX	96
FEAR EFFECT 2: RETRO HELIX	96
INCREDIBLE CRISIS	97
KNOCKOUT KINGS 2001	97
MAT HOFFMAN'S PRO BMX	98
NASCAR 2001	99
NCAA FOOTBALL 2001	100
NCAA GAMEBREAKER 2001	100
NFL BLITZ 2001	101
NFL GAMEDAY 2002	104
SIMPSONS WRESTLING	105
SNO-CROSS CHAMPIONSHIP RACING	106
SPIDER-MAN 2: ENTER ELECTRO	107
TONY HAWK'S PRO SKATER 2	108
TONY HAWK'S PRO SKATER 3	110
X-MEN: MUTANT ACADEMY 2	111

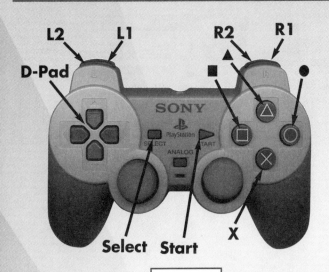

007 RACING

ALL CHEATS

Select Mission Mode and enter your name as **MMMQRRQ**.

ARMY MEN: AIR ATTACK 2

PASSWORDS

MISSION	PASSWORD
2	Up, X, ▲, Right, Left, ■, ●. X
3	▲, ●, Down, Left, ■, ■, Up, Up
4	X, Right, Left, X, ●, ■, ■, ▲
5	Down, Down, ●, ■, ●, ■, Right, X
6	▲, X, Up, Left, Right, Left, ●, ▲
7	Left, ■, Right, Down, ●, X, X, Right
8	▲, Right, ■, ■, ●, Down, Down, X
9	Up, X, ■, Left, Right, ●, Left, Left
10	▲, Up, ●, X, ■, Down, Down, Down
11	●, ●, Up, Left, Right, X, ▲, ■
13	Left, Left, ▲, ●, X, X, Down, Right
15	Left, Right, ●, X, ■, Down, Down, ●
16	▲, ●, X, Right, Right, ●, ■, Down
18	●, X, Right, ▲, ■, Up, X, X
20	Up, X, ●, Up, Left, ■, ●, X
21	Left, ●, ▲, Down, X, X, X, ●
22	▲, X, Down, Left, Right, X, ●, ■

COOL BOARDERS 2001

UNLOCK EVERYTHING
Select Career Mode and enter your name as **GIVEALL**.

DAVE MIRRA FREESTYLE BMX

UNLOCK SLIM JIM
At the Rider Select screen, press Down, Down, Left, Right, Up, Up, ●.

ALL BIKES
At the Bike Select screen, press Up, Left, Up, Down, Up, Right, Left, Right, ●.

ALL STYLES
At the Style Select screen, press Left, Up, Right, Down, Left, Down, Right, Up, Left, ●.

Unlock Slim Jim

FEAR EFFECT 2: RETRO HELIX

CHEAT MODE
First you must complete the game and start a new game. Once you have control of Hana, you should come to a console. Enter the following codes:

EFFECT	CODE
Big Head	10397
All Weapons	11692
Infinite Ammo	61166

ART GALLERIES

At the title screen, enter the following codes for the respective disc to open the Art Gallery. You can find the Art Gallery in the Extras section of the Options menu.

DISC	CODE
One	Left, Right, Up, Down, Down, ●
Two	Up, Up, R1, R1, R1, ■
Three	L1, R2, L1, R2, L1, ■
Four	●, ●, ■, L2, ■

INCREDIBLE CRISIS

CHANGE SIZE OF HEAD

Press Up or Down using the D-Pad of the second controller.

CHANGE SIZE OF CHARACTER

Press Left or Right using the D-Pad of the second controller.

KNOCKOUT KINGS 2001

HIDDEN BOXERS

Enter the following names in the career mode to unlock these hidden boxers:

ENTER THIS NAME	TO OPEN THIS HIDDEN BOXER:
100%	Full stats
BABY	Baby
BULLDOG	Bulldog
CLOWN	Clown
EYE	One Eye

ENTER THIS NAME	TO OPEN THIS HIDDEN BOXER:
GORE	Gorilla

Gorilla

NOLAN	Owen Nolan
FRANCIS	Steve Francis

MAT HOFFMAN'S PRO BMX

At the Pause menu (during a session in a level, press START), hold L1 and enter the following codes.

8 MINUTES ADDED TO YOUR RUN TIME
■, Up, ●, X

Entering the following codes will toggle the cheat on and off.

BIG TIRES
Down, ●, ●, Down

SPECIAL BAR ALWAYS FULL
Left, Down, ▲, ●, Up, Left, ▲, ■

GRIND BALANCE BAR
Left, ●, ■, ▲, ■, ●, X

PERFECT BALANCE
■, Left, Up, Right

ALL SCORES MULTIPLIED BY 10
■, ●, ●, Up, Down, Down

ALL SCORES DIVIDED BY 10
Down, Down, Up, ●, ●, ■

NASCAR 2001

CODES

Enter the Credits menu located in the Options menu and then select Development. Make sure to enter the codes after the movie and during the credits to access the following extras.

ENTER THIS CODE	TO ACCESS...
Hold L2 and press: ■, ●, ▲, X	Asher Boldt
Hold R1 and press ■, ▲, ■, ▲	John Andretti's Spare Car
Hold L2 and press ■, ●, X, Down, Up, Right, Left	KC Monoxide

Hold R2 and press ■, ●, X, Up, Down, Left, Right	Shorty Leung
Hold L1 and press ■, ▲, ■, ●, ■, X	Jocko Micaels
Hold R1 and press Left, ●, Up, Down, Right, Right, Right	Proving Grounds Track
Hold L2 and press ■, ● ■, Up, Up, Down, Up, Left, Right, X	Treasure Island Track

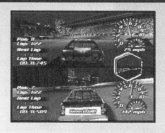

NCAA FOOTBALL 2001

CHEAT CODES

Select Game Settings/Secret Codes and enter the following:

EFFECT	CHEAT
Max Recruit Points	HEADCOACH
Maximum Attributes	BALLER
Always Catch Passes	HANDSOFGLUE
Quicker Players	SCRAMBLE
Slow Players	CEMENTFEET
Defense Always Intercepts	OSKIE
Reveal Plays	MINDREADER
Maximum Wind	SAFTEY
Faster Day to Night	DAYNIGHT
All Stadiums	OPENSESAME
The Juggernaut Team	BULLDOZER
Change Date	Y2K
View the Whole Poll	POPULARITY

NCAA GAMEBREAKER 2001

EASTER EGGS

Select Customize/Easter Eggs and enter the following:

EFFECT	CHEAT
All Blue Chips	MOTIVATE
Player Attributes at 99	BEAT DOWN
Better Walk-on Players	FRANKENSTEIN
Excellent Stats	Vers
Better Running	REAL ESTATE
Better Passing	GO DEEP
Stronger Defense	PHYSICAL
Strong Stiff Arm	HAMMER
Big Team Vs. Small Team	BIGandsmall
Credits	HOLLYWOOD

NFL BLITZ 2001

VS CHEATS

You must enter the following codes at the Versus screen by pressing the Turbo, Jump, and Pass buttons. For example, to get Infinite Turbo press Turbo (x5), Jump (x1), Pass (x4), and then press Up.

EFFECT	CODE
Tournament Mode (2-player game)	1,1,1 Down
Infinite Turbo	5,1,4 Up
Fast Turbo Running	0,3,2 Left
Power-up Offense	3,1,2 Up
Power-up Defense	4,2,1 Up
Power-up Teammates	2,3,3 Up
Power-up Blockers	3,1,2 Left
Super Blitzing	0,4,5 Up
Super Field Goals	1,2,3 Left
Invisible	4,3,3 Up

Invisible

No Random Fumbles	4,2,3 Down
No First Downs	2,1,0 Up
No Interceptions	3,4,4 Up
No Punting	1,5,1 Up
Allow Stepping Out of Bounds	2,1,1 Left
Fast Passes	2,5,0 Left
Late Hits	0,1,0 Up
Show Field Goal %	0,0,1 Down
Show Punt Hangtime Meter	0,0,1 Right
Hide Receiver Name	1,0,2 Right
Big Football	0,5,0 Right

EFFECT	CODE
Big Head	2,0,0 Right
Huge Head	0,4,0 Up

Huge Head

Team Tiny Players	3,1,0 Right
Team Big Players	1,4,1 Right
Team Big Heads	2,0,3 Right
Weather: Snow	5,2,5 Down
Weather: Rain	5,5,5 Right
No Hiliting on Target Receiver	3,2,1 Down
Red, White and Blue Ball	3,2,3 Left
Unlimited Throw Distance	2,2,3 Right
Deranged Blitz Mode (1-player game)	2,1,2 Down
Ultra Hard Mode (1-player game)	3,2,3 Up
Smart CPU Opponent (1-player game)	3,1,4 Down
Always Quarterback	2,2,2 Left
Always Receiver	2,2,2 Right
Cancel Always Quarterback/Receiver	3,3,3 Up
Show More Field (2-player agreement)	0,2,1 Right
No CPU Assistance (2-player agreement)	0,1,2 Down
Power-up Speed (2-player agreement)	4,0,4 Left
Hyper Blitz (2-player agreement)	5,5,5 Up
No Play Selection (2-player agreement)	1,1,5 Left
Super Passing (2-player agreement)	4,2,3 Right

TEAM PLAYBOOKS

EFFECT	CODE
Arizona Cardinals	1,0,1 Left
Atlanta Falcons	1,0,2 Left
Baltimore Ravens	1,0,3 Left
Buffalo Bills	1,0,4 Left
Carolina Panthers	1,0,5 Left
Chicago Bears	1,1,0 Left
Cincinnati Bengals	1,1,2 Left
Cleveland Browns	1,1,3 Left
Dallas Cowboys	1,1,4 Left
Denver Broncos	1,1,5 Right
Detroit Lions	1,2,1 Left
Green Bay Packers	1,2,2 Left
Indianapolis Colts	1,2,3 Up
Jacksonville Jaguars	1,2,4 Left
Kansas City Chiefs	1,2,5 Left
Miami Dolphins	1,3,1 Left
Minnesota Vikings	1,3,2 Left
New England Patriots	1,3,3 Left
New Orleans Saints	1,3,4 Left
New York Giants	1,3,5 Left
New York Jets	1,4,1 Left
Oakland Raiders	1,4,2 Left
Philadelphia Eagles	1,4,3 Left
Pittsburgh Steelers	1,4,4 Left
San Diego Chargers	1,4,5 Left
San Francisco 49ers	1,5,1 Left
Seattle Seahawks	1,5,2 Left
St. Louis Rams	1,5,3 Left
Tampa Bay Buccaneers	1,5,4 Left
Tennessee Titans	1,5,5 Left
Washington Redskins	2,0,1 Left

NFL GAMEDAY 2002

CODES

Select Code Entry from the options and enter the following:

CODE	EFFECT
5280 CLUB	Mile High Stadium
GRUDGE MATCH	GameDay stadium
989 SPORTS	989 team
RED_ZONE	Redzone team
ALL BOBO	Everyone named Bobo

BASKETBALL	Players named after NBA players
OVAL OFFICE	Players named after Presidents
EURO LEAGUE	Players named after NFL Europe players
EVEN STEVEN	Even teams
BIG PIG	Big football
TINY	Big players
MUNCHKINS	Small players
PENCILS	Thin and tall
ENDURANCE	More endurance
FATIGUE	Reduce fatigue
MR GLASS	Injured hamstring
MR FURIOUS	Hop-a-long

CODE	EFFECT
POP WARNER	Players float

LINE BUSTER	Better defensive line
SUPER FOOT	Better Running Back
FASHION SHOW	Cheerleader pictures after the game
CREDITS	Credits

SIMPSONS WRESTLING

ZERO HEALTH LOSSES
At the title screen press ●, R1, R1, R1, Right, Left.

INFINITE ENERGY
At the title screen press ●, R1, R1, R1, Down, Up.

MULTI-ROPE ATTACK:
At the title screen press ●, R1, R1, R1, Up, Down.

BIG APE ARENA
At the title screen press ●, R2, R1, ●, R2, R1.

BIG HEAD
At the title screen press ●, L1, L1, L1, Up, Down.

Big Head

BIG APE MODE
At the title screen press ●, L1, ●, R1, ●, L2, ●.

Big Ape Mode

NO OUTLINES
At the title screen press ●, Right, Up, Right, Down.

FLAT LAND
At the title screen press ●, L1, L1, L1, Left, Right.

Flat Land

BONUS MATCH
At the title screen press ●, Up, Up, Down, Down, Left, Right, Left, Right. Select Bonus Match Up at the main menu.

CREDIT GAGS
At the title screen press ●, L1, ●, L1, ●, R1, ●, R1.

MIRROR MATCHES
At the title screen press Up, Up, Down, Down, Left, Right, Left, Right, ●, L2, ●, R2, ●, L1, ●, R1.

BUMBLEBEE MAN
At the title screen press ●, Left, Up, Left, Down, R1.

MOE
At the title screen press ●, Left, Up, Left, Down, L1.

NED FLANDERS
At the title screen press ●, Left, Up, Left, Down, L2.

PROFESSOR FRINK
At the title screen press ●, Left, Up, Left, Down, R2.

DISPLAY COMPLETION DATE
At the title screen press ■, ●, L1, R1.

SNO-CROSS CHAMPIONSHIP RACING

These codes should be entered while at the main menu. Hold the R1 button, enter the code and then release the R1 button to finish the code.

RACE ON AN ATV
Up, Right, Down, Up, Right, Down

Race on an ATV

RACE ON A GOCART
Right, Right, Left, Left, Right, Right

UNLOCK SECRET CARTOON TRACK
Right, Up, Left, ●, ▲, ■

Choose the single-player mode and race on the Kiruna Track to see the cartoon landscape.

Race on a Gocart

UNLOCK THE SUMMER TRACK
▲, X, ●, ●, X, ▲

Choose the single-player mode and race on the Calgary Track to race along on the dirt track.

UNLOCK EVERY LEAGUE, SNOWMOBILE AND TRACK
Up, ▲, Up, ▲, Up, ▲

Secret Cartoon Track

LAUNCH THE DEMO MODE
Up, Up, Up, Down, Down, Down

SPIDER-MAN 2: ENTER ELECTRO

UNLOCK ALL CHEATS
Select Cheats from the Special Menu and enter **AUNTMAY**.

UNLOCK COSTUMES
Select Cheats from the Special Menu and enter **WASHMCHN**.

UNLOCK GALLERY
Select Cheats from the Special Menu and enter **DRKROOM**.

Unlock Costumes

UNLOCK TRAINING
Select Cheats from the Special Menu and enter **CEREBRA**.

UNLOCK LEVELS
Select Cheats from the Special Menu and enter **NONJYMNT**.

BIG FEET
Select Cheats from the Special Menu and enter **STACEYD**.

BIG HEAD
Select Cheats from the Special Menu and enter **ALIEN**.

DEBUG MODE
Select Cheats from the Special Menu and enter **DRILHERE**.

WHAT IF
Select Cheats from the Special Menu and enter **VVISIONS**.

VV HIGH SCORES
Select Cheats from the Special Menu and enter **VVHISCRS**.

LEVEL SELECT

MISSION: SPIDEY
THE CORKSCREW
SPIDEY VS. LIZARD
THE GAUNTLET
SPIDEY VS. SANDMAN AGAIN
KONICHI-WA SPIDER-SAM
ROCK OF AGES
SPIDEY VS. ELECTRO
THE BEST LAID PLANS

Unlock Levels

Big Head

TONY HAWK'S PRO SKATER 2

NEVERSOFT CHARACTERS
At the Main Menu, hold L1 and press Up, ■, ■, ▲, Right, Up, ●, ▲. This causes the wheel to spin. Then create a skater and give him the name of anyone on the Neversoft team. For example, name your skater Mick West and he'll appear. The best one is Connor Jewett, the son of Neversoft's President. (Don't change the appearance of the kid-sized skaters. It could crash your game.)

You must enter the following codes after pausing the game. While the game is paused, press and hold L1, and enter the codes.

JET PACK MODE
Up, Up, Up, Up, **X**, ■, Up, Up, Up, Up, **X**, ■, Up, Up, Up, Up

Hold ▲ to hover

Press **X** to turn on the Jetpack

Press forward to move forward

FATTER SKATER
X (x4), Left, X (x4), Left, X (x4), Left

Fatter Skater

THINNER SKATER
X (x4), ■, X (x4), ■, X (x4), ■

TOGGLE BLOOD ON/OFF
Right, Up, ■, ▲

SPECIAL METER ALWAYS YELLOW
X, ▲, ●, ●, Up, Left, ▲, ■

SUPER SPEED MODE
Down, ■, ▲, Right, Up, ●, Down, ■, ▲, Right, Up, ●

UNLOCK EVERYTHING
X, X, X, ■, ▲, Up, Down, Left, Up, ■, ▲, X, ▲, ●, X, ▲, ●

BIG HEAD
■, ●, Up, Left, Left, ■, Right, Up, Left

Big Head

ALL GAPS
Down, Up, Left, Left, ●, Left, Up, ▲, ▲, Up, Right, ■, ■, Up, X

This will give you Private Carrera.

ALL SECRET CHARACTERS
■, ●, Right, ▲, ●, Right, ●, ▲, Right, ■, Right, Up, Up, Left, Up, ■

MOON PHYSICS
X, ■, Left, Up, Down, Up, ■, ▲

DOUBLE MOON PHYSICS
Left, Up, Left, Up, Down, Up, ■, ▲, Left, Up, Left, Up, Down, Up, ■, ▲

$5000
X, Down, Left, Right, Down, Left, Right

100,000 POINTS IN COMPETITION
■, ●, Right, ■, ●, Right, ■, ●, Right

This will end the competition.

ACCESS ALL LEVELS
Up, ▲, Right, Up, ■, ▲, Right, Up, Left, ■, ■, Up, ●, ●, Up, Right

STATS AT 5
Up, ■, ▲, Up, Down

STATS AT 6
Down, ■, ▲, Up, Down

STATS AT 7
Left, ■, ▲, Up, Down

STATS AT 8
Right, ■, ▲, Up, Down

STATS AT 9
●, ■, ▲, Up, Down

STATS AT 13
X, ▲, ●, X, X, X, ■, ▲, Up, Down

STATS AT ALL 10S
X, ▲, ●, ■, ▲, Up, Down

SKIP TO RESTART
■, ▲, Right, Up, Down, Up, Left, ■, ▲, Right, Up, Down, Up, Left, ●, Up, Left, ▲

CLEAR GAME WITH CURRENT SKATER
●, Left, Up, Right, ●, Left, Up, Right, X, ●, Left, Up, Right, ●, Left, Up, Right

KID MODE
●, Up, Up, Left, Left, ●, Up, Down, ■

MIRROR LEVEL
Up, Down, Left, Right, ▲, X, ■, ●, Up, Down, Left, Right, ▲, X, ■, ●

PERFECT BALANCE
Right, Up, Left, ■, Right, Up, ■, ▲

SLO-NIC MODE
●, Up, ▲, ■, X, ▲, ●

WIREFRAME
Down, ●, Right, Up, ■, ▲

SIM MODE
●, Right, Up, Left, ▲, ●, Right, Up, Down

SMOOTH SHADING
Down, Down, Up, ■, ▲, Up, Right

DISCO LIGHTS
Down, Up, ■, ●, Up, Left, Up, X

TONY HAWK'S PRO SKATER 3

The menu will shake if the following are entered correctly.

BIG HEAD
Pause the game, hold L1 and press Up, ●, Down.

THIN SKATER
Press START to pause game play, then hold L1 and press X (x4), ■, X(x4), ■, X (x4), ■ to make your skater more thin. The pause menu will shake to confirm correct code entry. Note: Repeat this code to increase its effect.

FAT SKATER
Pause the game, hold L1 and press X (x4), Left, X (x4), Left, X (x4), Left.

PERFECT BALANCE
Press START to pause game play, then hold L1 and press Up, Down, Up, Up, ▲, X, ▲, ▲. The pause menu will shake to confirm correct code entry.

STUD MODE
Pause the game, hold **L1** and press ■, ▲, Up, Down, Right, Up, ■, ▲.

FULL SPECIAL
Pause the game, hold **L1** and press ▲, Right, Up, ■, ▲, Right, Up, ■, ▲.

10,000 POINTS
Pause the game, hold **L1** and press ■, ●, Right, ■, ●, Right, ■, ●, Right.

TURBO
Pause the game, hold **L1** and press press Left, Up, ■, ▲.

SLOW MOTION
Pause the game, hold **L1** and press Left, Left, Up, Left, Left, Up, X.

REVERSED LEVEL
Pause the game, hold **L1** and press Down, Down, ▲, Left, Up, ■, ▲.

X-MEN: MUTANT ACADEMY 2

UNLOCK EVERYTHING
At the title screen press SELECT, Down, R2, L1, R1, L2.

Unlock Everything

THE GAMES

18-WHEELER AMERICAN PRO TRUCKER 115

4X4 EVOLUTION 115

ARCTIC THUNDER 116

ARMY MEN RTS 117

ATV OFFROAD FURY 117

BALDUR'S GATE DARK ALLIANCE 118

BATMAN VENGEANCE 118

CART FURY 119

CRASH BANDICOOT: THE WRATH OF CORTEX 121

DAVE MIRRA FREESTYLE BMX 2 121

DEUS EX: THE CONSPIRACY 126

DRAKAN: THE ANCIENT GATES 126

DRIVEN 127

DYNASTY WARRIORS 3 128

ESPN NBA 2NIGHT 2002 129

ESPN NFL PRIMETIME 2002 129

FREQUENCY 130

GRAND THEFT AUTO III 131

HALF-LIFE 134

HEADHUNTER 135

HIGH HEAT MAJOR LEAGUE BASEBALL 2003 135

JEREMY MCGRATH'S SUPERCROSS WORLD 135

JONNY MOSELEY MAD TRIX 136

KINETICA 136

LEGACY OF KAIN: BLOOD OMEN 2 136

LEGACY OF KAIN: SOUL REAVER 2 136

LEGENDS OF WRESTLING 137

LEGO RACERS 2 137

LE MANS 24 HOURS 137

MAX PAYNE 138

MISTER MOSQUITO 138

MX 2002 FEATURING RICKY CARMICHAEL 139

MXRIDER 139

NAMCO MUSEUM 139

NASCAR HEAT 2002 139

NASCAR THUNDER 2002 140

NBA 2K2 142

NBA STREET 142

NFL BLITZ 20-02 144

NHL HITZ 20-02 148

PARIS-DAKAR RALLY 149

PIRATES: THE LEGEND OF BLACK KAT 149

PORTAL RUNNER 151

PROJECT EDEN 151

Q-BALL BILLIARDS MASTER 152

QUAKE III: REVOLUTION 152

REDCARD 20-03 152

SHAUN PALMER'S PRO SNOWBOARDER 153

SILENT SCOPE 2: DARK SILHOUETTE 153

SMUGGLER'S RUN 2: HOSTILE TERRITORY 154

SOLDIER OF FORTUNE 154

SPIDER-MAN THE MOVIE 155

SPLASHDOWN 157

SPY HUNTER 158

SSX TRICKY 159

STAR TREK VOYAGER: ELITE FORCE 159

STAR WARS: JEDI STARFIGHTER 160

STAR WARS: RACER REVENGE 161

STATE OF EMERGENCY 162

SUNNY GARCIA SURFING 163

THE SIMPSONS: ROAD RAGE 163

THUNDERSTRIKE: OPERATION PHOENIX 164

TIGER WOODS PGA TOUR 2002 165

TONY HAWK'S PRO SKATER 3 166

TOP GUN: COMBAT ZONES	167
TRANSWORLD SURF	167
TWISTED METAL: BLACK	168
WORLD DESTRUCTION LEAGUE: WAR JETZ	169
WORLD OF OUTLAWS: SPRINT CARS 2002	171
WORLD RALLY CHAMPIONSHIP	171

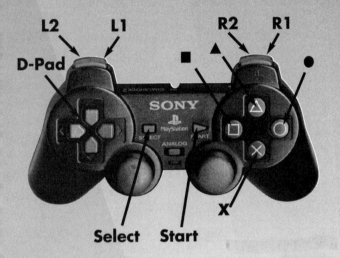

L2 L1 R2 R1

D-Pad ■ ▲ ●

Select Start

X

18-WHEELER AMERICAN PRO TRUCKER

NIPPON MARU

At the title screen hold **X** and press START. Continue to hold **X** to the Mode Select.

4X4 EVOLUTION

ALL TRUCKS

At any menu press L1, L2, R1, R2, L1, R1. This allows access to the cheat class of Ford Explorer Sport Tracs.

All Trucks

$1 MILLION IN CAREER MODE

At any menu press L2, ■, R1, ●, R1, L1, ●, L2, ■, R2, ■, R1.

$1 Million in Career Mode

WARP SPEED MODE

At any menu press L1, L2, R1, R2, ■, ■.

Warp Speed Mode

SLOW MOTION MODE

At any menu press L1, L2, R1, R2, ■, ●.

NORMAL SPEED MODE

At any menu press L1, L2, R1, R2, ●, ●.

ARCTIC THUNDER

NO DRONES
At the Mode Select, press ■, ■, ●, ●, L1, R1, START.

CATCHUP CODE
At the Mode Select, press ●, ■, ●, ●, ■, START.

RANDOM POWER-UPS
At the Mode Select, press R1, R2, ■, ●, R1, R2, START.

SNOWBALL POWER-UPS
At the Mode Select, press ■, ■, ■, L1, ●, START.

GRAPPLING HOOKS POWER-UPS
At the Mode select, press ●, ●, L2, ●, ●, L1, START.

Snowball Power-Ups

ROOSTER POWER-UPS
At the Mode Select, press R1, R2, L2, L1, ■, START.

SNOW BOMB POWER-UPS
At the Mode Select, press ●, ●, R1, R2, START.

BOOST POWER-UPS
At the Mode Select, press ●, R1(x2), ●, R2, START.

ACTIVATE CLONE
At the Mode Select, press L1, L2(x2), ●, L1, ●, START.

ALL INVISIBLE
At the Mode Select, press ■, ●, ■, R2, ●, ●, START.

All Invisible

NO POWER-UPS
At the Mode Select, press ■, ■, ●, ■, R2, ■, START.

SUPER BOOST
At the Mode Select, press ●, L1, ■, R2, ■, L2, START.

ARMY MEN RTS

STRONG PLAYER
During gameplay, hold R2 and press ■, ■, X, ▲, X, ■.

STRONG ENEMY
During gameplay, hold R2 and press ▲, ▲, X, ■, ▲, ▲.

DROP PARATROOPERS
During gameplay hold R2 and press ●, ■, ●, ■, ▲, ▲.

MORE FROM DUMPTRUCKS
During gameplay hold R2 and press ■, ■, ■, ▲, ●, X.

2000 ENERGY
During gameplay hold R2 and press ▲, ■, ●, X, ▲, X.

5000 PLASTIC
During gameplay hold R2 and press ▲, ●, ■, X, ▲, ■.

DIFFERENT COLORS
During gameplay hold R2 and press ■, ▲, ■, ■, X, ●.

ATV OFFROAD FURY

TOUGHER GAME
Select Pro-career and enter the name **ALLOUTAI**. This should send you back to the main menu.

ALL ATVS
Select Pro-career and enter the name **CHACHING**. This should send you back to the main menu.

ALL TRACKS
Select Pro-career and enter the name
WHATEXIT. This should send you back to
the main menu.

All Tracks

BALDUR'S GATE
DARK ALLIANCE

LEVEL WARP AND INVULNERABILITY
Hold L1 + R2 + ▲ + Left and press START during gameplay.

LEVEL 20 CHARACTER
Hold L1 + R2 + R3 + Left and press START during gameplay.

GAUNTLET MODE
Complete the game.

EXTREME MODE
Complete Gauntlet Mode.

PLAY AS DRIZZT
At the main menu, hold L1 + R1 and press ✖ + ▲. Or complete Extreme Mode.

BATMAN VENGEANCE

Enter the following codes at the Main menu.

ALL CHEATS
Press L2, R2, L2, R2, ■, ■, ●, ●.

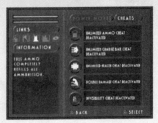

All Cheats

UNLIMITED BATCUFFS
Press ■, ●, ■, ●, L2, R2, R2, L2.

UNLIMITED BAT LAUNCHER
Press ●, ■, ●, ■, L1, R1, L2, R2.

UNLIMITED ELECTRIC BATARANGS
Press L1, R1, L2, R2.

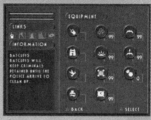

Unlimited Batcuffs

CART FURY

INFINITE CONTINUES
At the Cheats menu, L1, L2, L1, ■, ▲, ●.

UNLIMITED TIME
At the Cheats menu, ■, L1, R2, ●, ▲, R1.

INFINITE TURBO
At the Cheats menu, **X**, **X**, ■, ■, L2, L2.

LOW GRAVITY
At the Cheats menu, R2, R1, ■, ■, L1, L1.

JUMP
At the Cheats menu, L1, L2, L1, R2, **X**, **X**.

NIGHT DRIVE
At the Cheats menu, **X**, ●, ▲, L2, R2, L1.

Night Drive

TOGGLE FOG
At the Cheats menu, press R2, R1, **X**, ■, ■, ●.

BIG HEAD
At the Cheats menu, press ▲, ■, ■, L2, L1, R2.

ROCKET WHEELS
At the Cheats menu, L1, R2, ▲, ■, ■, ▲.

Big Head

ALL CARS

At the Cheats menu, press ▲, X, ▲, ■, L2, ▲. At the Select Driver screen press L1 to access the extra vehicles.

All Cars

ALL MOVIES

At the Cheats menu, press L1, ●, R2, X L2, ▲. This will open all of the movies in the Danny Sullivan Theater.

ALL TRACKS

At the Cheats menu, press R1, ▲, X, X, R2, L1.

DEATH CARS

At the Cheats menu, press L2, ■, L1, R2, R2, X. You will wipe out when you come in contact with another car.

DEATH WALL

At the Cheats menu, press X, ■, R2, ▲, R1, R2. This will cause you to wreck anytime you touch the wall.

Death Wall

PLAYER DEATH CAR

At the Cheats menu, press L1, ■, R1, R2, L2, L1. With this cheat you can take out the other cars. Caution: you will still wipe out when you accumulate enough damage.

MORE DRIVERS
Press R1 at the driver select.

DIFFERENT VEHICLES
Press L1 at the driver select.

CRASH BANDICOOT: THE WRATH OF CORTEX

QUICK TIME TRIAL IN WIZARDS AND LIZARDS

In the Wizards and Lizards level, pick up the clock and press Select. This will tele-port you to the end of the level.

DAVE MIRRA FREESTYLE BMX 2

UNLOCK MOST EVERYTHING

At the Main Menu press Up, Right, Down, Left, Right, Right, Up, Down, Left, Right, Up, Left, Right, Right, Down, ■.

MIKE DIAZ

At the Main Menu press Up, Left, Down, Right, Right, Left, Up, Down, Up, Right, ■.

AMISH GUY

At the Main Menu press Up, Left, Down, Right, Right, Left, Left, Down, Up, Left, ■.

ALL BIKES

At the Main Menu press Up, Left, Down, Right, Down, Down, Right, Down, Down, Left, ■.

Amish Guy

All Levels

ALL LEVEL

At the Main Menu press Up, Down, Down, Left, Right, Down, ■.

ALL THEMES IN PARK EDITOR

At the Main Menu press Up, Left, Down, Right, Down, Up, Down, Right, Left, Left, ■.

ALL OBJECTS IN PARK EDITOR

At the Main Menu press Up, Left, Down, Right, Down, Up, Up, Down, Right, Right, ■.

All Themes in Park Editor

All Movies

ALL MOVIES

At the Main Menu press Up, Left, Down, Right, Left, Left, Right, Left, Up, Down, ■.

MOVES

Enter the following at the Main Menu to unlock all of that characters moves:

CHARACTER	CODE
Amish Guy	Left, Right, Up, Up, Right, Down, Right, Right, ■
Colin Mackay	Left, Right, Right, Up, Left, Right, Right, Up, ■
Dave Mirra	Left, Right, Up, Up, Left, Right, Up, Up, ■
Joey Garcia	Left, Right, Up, Right, Down, Up, Down, Right, ■
John Englebert	Left, Right, Left, Left, Down, Up, Left, Left, ■
Kenan Harkin	Left, Right, Left, Down, Up, Down, Down, Down, ■
Leigh Ramsdell	Left, Right, Down, Left, Left, Right, Down, Left, ■
Mike Laird	Left, Right, Right, Right, Left, Right, Up, Right, ■
Rick Moliterno	Left, Right, Up, Up, Up, Down, Left, Up, ■
Ryan Nyquist	Left, Right, Down, Down, Down, Up, Up, Down, ■
Scott Wirch	Left, Right, Right, Right, Up, Down, Left, Right, ■
Slim Jim	Left, Right, Down, Left, Up, Left, Right, Left, ■
Tim Mirra	Left, Right, Right, Up, Down, Up, Down, Up, ■
Todd Lyons	Left, Right, Down, Down, Left, Right, Left, Down, ■
Troy McMurray	Left, Right, Left, Left, Up, Down, Up, Left, ■
Zach Shaw	Left, Right, Left, Down, Left, Up, Right, Down, ■

BIKES

Enter the following at the Main Menu to unlock all of that characters bikes:

CHARACTER	CODE
Colin Mackay	Down, Down, Right (x5), Up, ■
Dave Mirra	Down, Down, Up, Right, Up, Right, Up, Up, ■

Joey Garcia	Down, Down, Up, Right, Left, Left, Down, Right, ■
John Englebert	Down, Down, Left, Up, Left, Up, Left, Left, ■
Kenan Harkin	Down, Down, Left, Up, Down, Right, Down, Down, ■

CHARACTER	CODE
Leigh Ramsdell	Down, Down, Down, Up, Left, Left, Down, Left, ■
Mike Laird	Down, Down, Right, Left, Down, Up, Up, Right, ■
Rick Moliterno	Down, Down, Up, Left, Right, Right, Left, Up, ■
Ryan Nyquist	Down (x5), Right, Up, Down, ■
Scott Wirch	Down, Down, Right, Up, Down, Down, Left, Right, ■
Tim Mirra	Down, Down, Right, Left, Down, Right, Down, Up, ■
Todd Lyons	Down (x4), Left, Right, Left, Down, ■
Troy McMurray	Down, Down, Left, Down, Right, Left, Up, Left, ■
Zach Shaw	Down, Down, Left, Down, Up, Right, Right, Down, ■

LEVELS

Enter the following at the Main Menu to unlock all of that characters levels:

CHARACTER	CODE
Colin Mackay	Up, Up, Right, Left, Up, Right, Right, Up, ■.
Dave Mirra	Up, Up, Up, Right, Up, Left, Up, Up, ■
Joey Garcia	Up (x4), Down, Down, Down, Right, ■
John Englebert	Up, Up, Left, Down, Right, Down, Left, Left, ■
Kenan Harkin	Up, Up, Left, Left, Down, Up, Down, Down, ■
Leigh Ramsdell	Up, Up, Down, Up, Left, Down, Down, Left, ■
Mike Laird	Up, Up, Right, Down, Down, Right, Up, Right, ■
Rick Moliterno	Up, Up, Up, Down, Right, Right, Left, Up, ■
Ryan Nyquist	Up, Up, Down, Down, Left, Right, Up, Down, ■
Scott Wirch	Up, Up, Right, Up, Left, Left, Left, Right, ■
Tim Mirra	Up, Up, Right, Down, Right, Left, Down, Up, ■

Todd Lyons	Up, Up, Down, Up, Right, Right, Left, Down, ■
Troy McMurray	Up, Up, Left, Up, Up, Right, Up, Left, ■
Zach Shaw	Up, Up, Left, Right, Down, Down, Right, Down, ■

MOVIES

Enter the following at the Main Menu to unlock all of that characters movies:

CHARACTER	CODE
Colin Mackey	Left, Left, Right, Right, Down, Down, Right, Up, ▦
Dave Mirra	Left, Left, Up, Right, Up, Left, Up, Up, ▦
Joey Garcia	Left, Left, Up, Up, Down, Right, Down, ▦
Kenan Harkin	Left (x4), Right, Right, Down, Down, ▦
Leigh Ramsdell	Left, Left, Down, Down, Left, Right, Down, Left, ▦
Luc-E	Left, Left, Right, Right, Down, Down, Right, Up, ▦

Mike Laird	Left, Left, Right, Up, Up, Right, Up, Right, ▦
Rick Moliterno	Left, Left, Up, Down, Right, Left, Left, Up, ▦
Ryan Nyquist	Left, Left, Down, Right, Down, Right, Up, Down, ▦
Scott Wirch	Left, Left, Right, Up, Up, Up, Left, Right, ▦
Tim Mirra	Left, Left, Right, Up, Down, Left, Down, Up, ▦
Todd Lyons	Left, Left, Down, Up, Up, Right, Left, Down, ▦
Troy McMurray	Left, Left, Left, Down, Up, Right, Up, Left, ▦
Zach Shaw	Left, Left, Left, Right, Left, Down, Right, Down, ▦

COMPETITION OUTFIT

Enter the following at the Main Menu to unlock all of that characters competition outfit:

CHARACTER	CODE
Colin Mackey	Up, Down, Right, Down, Up, Right, Right, Up, ▦
Dave Mirra	Up, Down, Up, Down, Right, Left, Up, Up, ▦
Joey Garcia	Up, Down, Up, Left, Down, Right, Down, Right, ▦
Kenan Harkin	Up, Down, Left, Down, Left, Up, Down, Up, ▦
Leigh Ramsdell	Up, Down, Down, Left, Down, Down, Down, Left, ▦
Luc-E	Up, Down, Left, Down, Left, Right, Left, Left, ▦

CHARACTER	CODE
Mike Laird	Up, Up, Down, Down, Left, Right, Right, Left, ■
Rick Moliterno	Up, Down, Up (x4), Left, Up, ■
Ryan Nyquist	Up, Down, Down, Left, Down, Up, Up, Down, ■
Scott Wirch	Up, Down, Right, Down, Up, Right, Right, Up, ■
Tim Mirra	Up, Down, Right, Left, Left, Up, Down, Up, ■
Todd Lyons	Up, Down, Down, Right, Up, Left, Left, Down, ■
Troy McMurray	Up, Down, Left, Down, Right, Left, Up, Left, ■
Zach Shaw	Up, Down, Left, Right, Down, Down, Right, Down, ■

DEUS EX: THE CONSPIRACY

CHEAT MODE

During a game press SELECT to access the Goals/Notes/Images screen, then press
L2, R2, L1, R1, Start, Start, Start.

DRAKAN: THE ANCIENT GATES

INVINCIBILITY

Hold L1 + R2 + L2 + R1 (in order) and
press **X**, Down, ▲, Up, ●, Right, ■,
Left during game play.

FULL HEALTH AND MANA

Hold L1 + R2 + L2 + R1 (in order) and
press ▲, Down, ●, Left, ■, Right, **X**,
Up during game play.

Invincibility

MONEY

Hold L1 + R2 + L2 + R1 (in order) and press ●, ■, Right, Left, ✖, ▲, Down, Up during game play.

Experience

EXPERIENCE

Hold L1 + R2 + L2 + R1 (in order) and press ■, ▲, ●, ✖, Right, Down, Left, Up during game play.

Increase Spell Level

INCREASE SPELL LEVEL

Hold L1 + R2 + L2 + R1 (in order) and press Up, Down, Left, Right, Right, Left, Down, Up during game play.

DRIVEN

ALL DRIVERS

At the main menu, press Up, Down, Right, Right, Left, Up, Up, Down.

ALL TRACKS

At the main menu, press Up, Up, Left, Down, Left, Right, Right, Up.

ALL CHAPTERS IN STORY MODE

At the main menu, press Down, Left, Up, Right, Right, Up, Down, Left.

ALL CHAMPIONSHIPS IN ARCADE MODE

At the main menu, press Right, Left, Up, Right, Down, Down, Left, Left.

ALL CHAMPIONSHIPS IN MULTIPLAYER MODE

At the main menu, press Left, Down, Left, Up, Right, Left, Down, Right.

DYNASTY WARRIORS 3

Enter the following codes at the main menu.

ALL STAGES
Press R1, R2, L2, L1, ■, L1, L2, R2, R1, ▲.

ALL SOUND TESTS
Press L1, L1, R1, R1, L2, L2, R2, R2, ■, ▲.

All Stages

All Sound Tests

ALL MOVIES
Press ▲, L1, ▲, R1, ▲, ■, L2, ■, R2, ■.

EDIT INTRO
Press R1, ■, R1, ▲, R1, L1, ■, L1, ▲, L1.

BONUS MOVIE
Select Opening from the options. Highlight Replay and hold R1 + R2 + L1 + L2 and press **X**.

Edit Intro

ALL GENERALS
Press R2, R2, R2, L1, ▲, L2, L2, L2, R1, ■.

ALL SHU GENERALS
Press L1, ■, ▲, R2, L1, L2, L2, R1, ■, L1.

FC

ALL WEI GENERALS
Press L2, L1, ■, ▲, L1, L2, R1, R2, L1, L2.

All Shu Generals

ALL WU GENERALS
Press ▲, ▲, L1, ■, R1, R2, L1, L2, L2, L2.

All Wu Generals

ESPN NBA 2NIGHT 2002

Select Cheats from the Options and enter the following:

BIG HEAD
Enter the code **BIGHEAD**.

BIG HANDS
Enter the code **BIGHAND**.

BIG FEET
Enter the code **BIGFOOT**.

TINY PLAYERS
Enter the code **MINIMINI**.

PANCAKE PLAYERS
Enter the code **PANCAKE**.

INVISIBLE PLAYERS
Enter the code **INVISIBLE**.

BETTER PLAYERS
Enter the code **ABILITYBONUS**.

BETTER DUNKS
Enter the code **DUNKERS**.

BETTER SHOOTING
Enter the code **EXCELLENT**.

BALL TRAIL
Enter the code **BEFOREIMAGE**.

NO SPECTATORS
Enter the code **NOSPECTATOR**.

DARK
Enter the code **DARKNESS**.

ESPN NFL PRIMETIME 2002

ALOHA STADIUM AND PRO BOWL TEAMS
Enter the code **ALOHA**.

RELIANT STADIUM
Enter the code **HOWDY**.

WEATHER IN DOMES
Enter the code **SHAKE IT UP.**

FUMBLES
Enter the code **READY TO FUMBLE.** Press L2 for a fumble.

UNSTOPPABLE WITH BALL
Enter the code **CAN'T TOUCH THIS.**

BETTER JUMPS
Enter the code **SUPERMAN.**

SHOW EVERYONE
Enter the code **SHOW EVERYONE.**

CHANGE SCORING
Enter the code **SCOREBOX.**

FREQUENCY

Before entering the following codes, press Down, Right, Up, Left, Left, Up, Right, Down at the title screen:

AUTOCATCHER IN SOLO
Then during gameplay press Left, Right, Right, Left, Up.

MULTIPLIER IN SOLO
Then during gameplay press Right, Left, Left, Right, Up.

Autocatcher in Solo

BUMPER IN MULTI
Then during gameplay press Right, Left, Right, Left, Up.

CRIPPLER IN MULTI
Then during gameplay press Left, Right, Left, Right, Down.

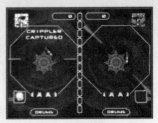
Crippler in Multi

FREESTYLER IN MULTI
Then during gameplay press Left, Right, Right, Left, Down.

NEUTRALIZER IN MULTI
Then during gameplay press Left, Right, Left, Right, Up.

Freestyler in Multi

GRAND THEFT AUTO III

VEHICLE CHEATS

BETTER VEHICLE HANDLING
R1, L1, R2, L1, Left, R1, R1, ▲

Enter this code while outside your vehicle. This code will make all vehicles handle better. When activated, enter L3 to cause the suspension to hop!

VEHICLE HEALTH CHEAT
R2, R2, L1, R1, Left, Down, Right, Up, Left, Down, Right, Up

This cheat must be done while inside the vehicle. Your car will still look damaged, but it will stop smoking and reach its 100% health status.

EXPLODE ALL VEHICLES
L2, R2, L1, R1, L2, R2, ▲, ■, ●, ▲, L2, L1

RHINO
●(x6), R1, L2, L1, ▲, ●, ▲

Explode all Vehicles

Invisible Car Chassis

INVISIBLE CAR CHASSIS
L1, L1, ■, R2, ▲, L1, ▲

FLYING VEHICLES
RT R2 ● R1 L2 DN L1 R1

Learn to fly the Dodo first, and then you'll understand how to fly in the vehicles. The Rhino is the easiest vehicle to fly, strangely enough. Use the turret for thrust as you aim it behind you and shoot.

Flying Vehicles

WEATHER CHEATS

FOGGY
L1, L2, R1, R2, R2, R1, L2, **X**

CLOUDY
L1, L2, R1, R2, R2, R1, L2, ■

RAIN
L1, L2, R1, R2, R2, R1, L2, ●

NORMAL WEATHER
L1, L2, R1, R2, R2, R1, L2, ▲

PEDESTRIAN CHEATS

PEDESTRIANS RIOT
Down, Up, Left, Up, **X**, R1, R2, L2, L1

This code is irreversible.

PEDESTRIANS OUT TO GET YOU
Down, Up, Left, Up, **X**, R1, R2, L1, L2

This code is irreversible.

Pedestrians Riot

PEDESTRIANS PACKING HEAT
R2, R1, ▲, **X**, L2, L1, Up, Down

This code is irreversible.

Pedestrians Packing Heat

OTHER CHEATS

WANTED LEVEL UP
R2, R2, L1, R2, Left, Right, Left, Right, Left

This will raise the Wanted Level by two each time you enter it.

WANTED LEVEL DOWN
R2, R2, L1, R2, Up, Down, Up, Down, Up, Down

This will bring the Wanted Level completely down to nothing.

WEAPON CHEAT
R2, R2, L1, R2, Left, Down, Right, Up, Left, Down, Right, Up

Continue to enter this code until you reach the maximum ammo amount (9999 for each weapon). When a weapon reaches its maximum ammo capacity, its ammunition supply becomes infinite. Regenerating your weapon power-ups at your Hideouts and then continually running through them can also help you reach this infinite ammo status. But first, you must collect Hidden Packages to make them appear.

CHANGE CHARACTER MODEL
Right, Down, Left, Up, L1, L2, Up, Left, Down, Right

This code is irreversible.

Change Character Model

HEALTH CHEAT
R2, R2, L1, R1, Left, Down, Right, Up, Left, Down, Right, Up

ARMOR CHEAT
R2, R2, L1, L2, Left, Down, Right, Up, Left, Down, Right, Up

MONEY CHEAT ($250,000)
R2, R2, L1, L1, Left, Down, Right, Up, Left, Down, Right, Up

UP THE GORE FACTOR
■, L1, ●, Down, L1, R1, ▲, Right, L1, ✕

This code makes victims lose body parts. You can pick-off limbs and heads with an aimed Sniper Rifle or M-16 shot.

SLOW-MOTION GAMEPLAY
▲, Up, Right, Down, ■, R1, R2

Enter this cheat three times for even more slowdown.

FAST-MOTION GAMEPLAY
▲, Up, Right, Down, ■, L1, L2

Enter this cheat three times for even more speedup.

SPEED UP TIME
●(x3), ■(x5), L1, ▲, ●, ▲

Enter this cheat a second time to return to normal time.

HALF-LIFE

The following codes will appear to the right if entered correctly.

SLOW MOTION
Go to the cheat screen and press Right, ■, Up, ▲, Right, ■, Up, ▲.

INFINITE AMMO
Go to the cheat screen and press Down, X, Left, ●, Down, X, Left, ●

XEN GRAVITY
Go to the cheat screen and press Up, ▲, Down, X, Up, ▲, Down, X

INVINCIBILITY
Go to the cheat screen and press Left, ■, Up, ▲, Right, ●, Down, X

INVISIBILITY
Go to the cheat screen and press Left, ■, Right, ●, Left, ■, Right, ●

ALIEN MODE
Go to the cheat screen and press Up, ▲, Up, ▲, Up, ▲, Up, ▲

HEADHUNTER

DEBUG MODE
During the game, hold R1 + ■ and press START.

HIGH HEAT MAJOR LEAGUE BASEBALL 2003

GAME EDITOR
Pause the game and press ■, ■, ●, ●, L1, R1. Then press R1 + L1 + R2 + L2.

JEREMY MCGRATH'S SUPERCROSS WORLD

ALL BIKES
Complete Career Mode on the Hardcore difficulty.

UNLIMITED TURBO
At the main menu press R2, L1, ■, ●, ●, ●. Re-enter the code to disable.

Unlimited Turbo

You Feel Lighter

YOU FEEL LIGHTER
At the main menu press Up, Up, Up, Up, R1, ■, ●. Re-enter the code to disable.

JONNY MOSELEY MAD TRIX

ALL SKIERS, OUTFITS, SKIS AND LEVELS
At the title screen press and hold L2 + L3 + R1 + Down + ■ + ● in order.

KINETICA

TURBO START
When Go appears, press Up + Gas.

LEGACY OF KAIN: BLOOD OMEN 2

BEGIN GAME WITH SOUL REAVER AND IRON ARMOR
At the main menu, press L1, R1, L2, R2, ■, ●, ▲.

LEGACY OF KAIN: SOUL REAVER 2

ALL BONUS MATERIALS
At the main menu press Left, ▲, Right, ▲, Down, ●, X.

All Bonus Materials

LEGENDS OF WRESTLING

ALL WRESTLERS
At the main menu, press Up, Up, Down, Down, Left, Right, Left, Right, ▲, ▲, ■.

LEGO RACERS 2

MARTIAN
At the main menu press Right, Left, Right, Up, Down, Left, Right, Up, Up.

MARS TRACKS
Pause the game and press Left, Left, Right, Right, Left, Left, Right, Right, Down, Left, Right.

WIDE ANGLE
Pause the game and press Left, Left, Left, Right, Right, Right, Up, Up, Up, Down, Down, Down, Left, Left, Left, Right, Right, Right.

LE MANS 24 HOURS

ALL CARS
Select Championship and enter your name as **ACO**.

ALL TRACKS
Select Championship and enter your name as **SPEEDY**.

ALL CHAMPIONSHIPS
Select Championship and enter your name as **NUMBAT**.

LE MANS
Select Championship and enter your name as **WOMBAT**.

CREDITS
Select Championship and enter your name as **HEINEY**.

MAX PAYNE

ALL WEAPONS AND FULL AMMUNITION
Pause the game and press L1, L2, R1, R2, ▲, ●, X, ■.

UNLIMITED HEALTH
Pause the game and press L1(x2), L2(x2), R1(x2), R2(x2).

LEVEL SELECT
Play through the first Chapter of the Subway. Then at the main menu press Up, Down, Left, Right, Up, Left, Down, ●. Now you can go to Load Level and pick where you want to go.

SLOW MOTION SOUNDS
Enter this code at the pause screen: L1, L2, R1, R2, ▲, ■, X, ●.

UNLIMITED BULLET TIME
To get unlimited bullet time, enter this code at the pause screen: L1, L2, R1, R2, ▲, X, X, ▲.

MISTER MOSQUITO

KANEYO MOSQUITO
At the character select, hold L1 and press Up, Right, Left, Down, ■, ■, R1, R1, R1.

KENICHI MOSQUITO
After entering the Mother Mosquito code, hold L2 and press Up, Right, Left, Down, ■, ■, R2, R2, R2 at the character select.

TWO PLAYER MINI-GAME
Turn on the system and hold START + SELECT on controller two.

RECKLESS CYCLIST GAME
At the title screen, rotate the Right analog stick 30 times clockwise.

MX 2002 FEATURING RICKY CARMICHAEL

ALL TRACKS

Select Two Player, hold R1 + L2 on the first controller and press Up, Down, Left, Right, ▲. Then hold ▲ + L2 + R2 + ✗ on the second controller.

MXRIDER

ALL TRACKS

Select Championship Mode, enter **IRATA** as the name and press select Done.

NAMCO MUSEUM

DISPLAY PLAY TIME FOR GALAGA ARRANGEMENT

At the Galaga Arrangement title screen, press Left, Right, Left, Right, Up, Down, Up, Down.

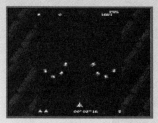

NASCAR HEAT 2002

CHALLENGE SKIP IN BEAT THE HEAT

At the main menu, press Up, Down, Left, Right, R1, Right, Left. Repeat as desired.

ARCADE STYLE BEAT THE HEAT MODE

At the main menu, press Up, Down, Left, Right, R1, Left, Right.

HARDCORE REALISM MODE
At the main menu, press Up, Down, Left, Right, R1, Up, Down.

CLEAN SCREEN DURING REPLAY
At the main menu, press Up, Down, Left, Right, R1, Down, Up. Press ● during the Replay.

SHOOT TIRES
In Single Race or Head-to-Head mode, enter the following cheats at the Race Day screen. Press Up to fire.

EFFECT	CHEAT
Shoot Tires in race	Up, Down, Left, Right, R1, Up, Up
Shoot Tires in practice	Up, Down, Left, Right, R1, Down, Down

NASCAR THUNDER 2002

EXTRA CARS
Select Create-a-car and enter the name as the following:

Dave Alpern

Buster Auton

Scott Brewer

Audrey Clark

Rick Edwards

Michelle Emser

Katrina Goode

Diane Grubb

Jim Hannigan

Troi Hayes

Crissy Hillsworth
Traci Hultzapple
Rick Humphrey
Kristi Jones
Joey Joulwan
Cheryl King
Mandy Misiak
Josh NeelonDave Nichols
Benny Parsons

Ken Patterson
Dick Paysor
Tom Renedo
Sasha Soares
Chuck Spicer

Daryl Wolfe

NBA 2K2

CODES

In the Options select Game Play. Hold Left on the D-pad + Right on the Left Analog Stick and press Start. This will create a new Codes option at the Options screen.

SUPERSTARS

Enter the code **MEGASTARS**. This will unlock the VC, Sega and NBA2K2 teams.

Codes

Superstars

NBA STREET

CHEATS

After selecting your players you will have an opportunity to enter codes. Use the ■, ▲, ●, X buttons to enter the following. The first number corresponds to the number of times you press ■, the second is for ▲, the third for ● and the last for X. After you enter these press any direction to enter the code. These numbers match up to icons on screen as follows

NUMBER	ICON
0	Basketball
1	Record Player
2	Shoe
3	Backboard
4	Bullhorn

For example for Big Heads the code is 4 1 2 1 or Bullhorn, Record Player, Shoe, Record Player. Here you would press ■ four times, ▲ once, ● two times and X one time. Then, press in any direction to activate the code. It will tell you if you have entered a code correctly.

EFFECT	CODE
No Cheats	1 1 1 1
ABA Ball	0 1 1 0
WNBA Ball	0 1 2 0
NuFX Ball	0 1 3 0
EA Big Ball	0 1 4 0
Beach Ball	0 1 1 2
Medicine Ball	0 1 1 3
Volleyball	0 1 1 4
Soccer Ball	0 2 1 0
Big Heads	4 1 2 1
Tiny Heads	4 2 0 2
Tiny Players	4 0 4 0
Casual Uniforms	1 1 0 0
Authentic Uniforms	0 0 1 1
ABA Socks	4 4 4 4
Athletic Joe "The Show"	1 2 0 1
Springtime Joe "The Show"	1 1 0 1
Summertime Joe "The Show"	1 0 0 1
Player Names	0 1 2 3
No HUD Display	1 4 1 2
No Player Indicators	4 0 0 4
No Shot Indicator	4 3 2 4
No Shot Clock	4 4 0 3

EFFECT	CODE
Unlimited Turbo	2 0 3 0
No Juice	1 4 4 3
Easy Distance Shots	2 1 3 0
Harder Distance Shots	2 2 3 0
Captain Quicks	3 0 2 1
Mad Handles	3 2 1 0
Mega Dunking	3 0 1 0
Sticky Fingers	3 4 1 0
Super Swats	3 3 1 0
Ultimate Power	3 1 1 0
Less Blocks	3 1 2 3
Less Steals	3 1 4 0
No 2-Pointers	3 3 0 3
No Alley-Oops	3 4 1 2
No Dunks	3 0 1 2
Less Gamebreakers	1 3 4 2
More Gamebreakers	1 4 3 2
No Gamebreakers	1 4 4 2
No Auto Replays	1 2 1 1
Explosive Rims	1 2 4 0

NFL BLITZ 20-02

HIDDEN CHARACTERS

NAME	PIN
LION	1963

NAME	PIN
PINTO	1966
ROBOTS	1970
DOLPHIN	1972

ROBOTR	1974
CLOWN	1974
TIGER	1977

VIKING	1977
EAGLE	1981
BEAR	1985

INDIAN	1992
COWBOY	1996
DEER	1997

NAME	PIN
VIKING	1997
HORSE	1999
RAM	2000
PIRATE	2001

RBL-DBN	9669

VERSUS CHEATS

At the versus screen use L2, R2 and **X** to enter the following cheats. For example, for Showtime Mode the code is 3 5 1 Right. Press L2 three times, R2 five times and **X** once then press Right to activate the code.

EFFECT	CODE
More Code Entry Time	2 1 2 Right
Tournament Mode	1 1 1 Down
No CPU Assistance*	0 1 2 Down
Showtime Mode	3 5 1 Right
Big Feet	0 2 5 Left

Power Loader	0 2 5 Right
Big Head	2 0 0 Right
Team Big Head	2 0 3 Right
Huge Head	1 4 5 Left

EFFECT	CODE
Classic Ball	0 3 0 Left
Weather: Clear	1 2 3 Right
Weather: Snow	5 5 5 Left
Weather: Rain	5 5 5 Right
Ground Fog	2 3 2 Down
Noftle	3 2 5 Up
No Punting	1 4 1 Up
No Highlight Target Receiver	3 2 1 Down
No Interceptions	3 5 5 Up
No Replays	5 5 4 Right
Fast Running Speed	0 3 2 Left
Fast Passes	2 4 0 Left
Super Blitzing	0 5 4 Up
Super Field Goals	1 2 3 Left
Allow Stepping Out of Bounds	3 1 1 Left
Always QB	2 2 2 Left
Always Receiver	2 2 2 Right
Extra Offense Plays	3 3 3 Down
Power-up Defense	4 2 1 Up
Power-up Linemen	5 2 1 Up
No Random Fumbles (If Teams Agree)	5 2 3 Down
Butter Fingaz	3 4 5 Up

Armageddon Team	5 4 3 Right
Bilders Team	3 1 0 Up
Brew Dawgs Team	4 3 2 Down
Cowboys Team	1 3 5 Left
Crunch Mode Team	4 0 3 Right

EFFECT	CODE
Gsmers Team	5 0 1 Up
Indians Team	0 4 5 Left

Midway Team	2 5 3 Right
Neo Tokyo Team	3 4 4 Down
Rollos Team	2 5 4 Up

NHL HITZ 20-02

CHEATS

After selecting your players, you will have a chance to enter codes by changing three icons with the ■, ▲ and ●. Use the ■ to change the first icon, the ▲ for second and the ● for the third. You will then need to press in the direction indicated. For example, to enter the code for 1st to 7 Wins, you would press ■ three times, ▲ two times and ● three times. Then press Left on the Directional pad.

EFFECT	CHEAT
Input More Codes	3 3 3 Right
Ignore Last Code	0 1 0 Down
1st to 7 Wins	3 2 3 Left
Win Fights For Goals	2 0 2 Left
No Crowd	2 1 0 Right
Show Hot Spot	2 0 1 Up
Show Shot Speed	1 0 1 Up
Rain	1 4 1 Left
Snow	1 2 1 Left
Big Puck	1 2 1 Up
Huge Puck	3 2 1 Up

EFFECT	CHEAT
Bulldozer Puck	2 1 2 Left
Hockey Ball	1 3 3 Left
Tennis Ball	1 3 2 Down
No Puck Out of Play	1 1 1 Down
Big Head Player	2 0 0 Right
Huge Head Player	3 0 0 Right
Big Head Team	2 2 0 Left
Huge Head Team	3 3 0 Left
Always Big Hits	2 3 4 Down
Late Hits	3 2 1 Down
Pinball Boards	4 2 3 Right
Domino Effect	0 1 2 Right
Turbo Boost	0 0 2 Up
Infinite Turbo	4 1 3 Right
No Fake Shots	4 2 4 Down
No One-Timers	2 1 3 Left
Skills Versus	2 2 2 Down
Hitz Time	1 0 4 Right

PARIS-DAKAR RALLY

ALL CARS
Enter ILUMBERJACK as your name.

PIRATES:
THE LEGEND OF BLACK KAT

CHANGE KATARINA'S OUTFIT
At the main menu hold L1 + L2 + Up + SELECT + L3 on controller one and R1 + R2 + ▲ + START + R3 on controller two. Press R3 on controller one to change the binary value. The different values correspond to the different outfits.

Enter the following codes during game play:

INVINCIBILITY FOR KATARINA
Hold R1 + R2 and press **X**, ●, L3, ▲, R3, Select, R3, L1, L2, ■.

INVINCIBILITY FOR THE WIND DANCER
Hold R1 + R2 and press SELECT, ▲, L1, **X**, R3, L2, ■, R3, ●, L3.

INFINITE ITEMS
Hold R1 + R2 and press ▲, L1, SELECT, L2, R3, L3, ■, **X**, R3, ●.

Gold

GOLD
Hold R1 + R2 and press ▲, R3, L1, ■, **X**, R3, SELECT, L3, ●, L2.

KATARINA'S NEXT SWORD
Hold R1 + R2 and press R3, SELECT, L2, L3, ■, **X**, L1, ●, L3, ▲.

Katarina's Next Sword

REVEAL BURIED TREASURE CHESTS
Hold R1 + R2 and press ●, **X**, ■, ▲, L1, SELECT, L3, L2, L3, R3.

REVEAL TREASURE CHESTS
Hold R1 + R2 and press R3, **X**, ▲, L3, ●, L1, SELECT, L3, ■, L2.

GALLEON
Hold R1 + R2 and press L2, ▲, R3, L3, **X**, ■, R3, SELECT, L1, ●.

ALTERNATE MUSIC
Hold R1 + R2 and press L1, **X**, ▲, L2, ■, ●, L3, SELECT, R3, L3.

HIGH PITCHED VOICES
Hold R1 + R2 and press R3, ●, SELECT, **X**, R3, ▲, L1, ■, L2, L3.

KANE'S HEAD AS POISON STATUS
Hold R1 + R2 and press ▲, L2, L1, ■, L3, **X**, L3, ●, R3, SELECT.

PORTAL RUNNER

LEVEL SKIP

Pause the game, hold L1 and press ●, Left, ●, Right, ●, ■, Left, Left, Right, R2.

FULL HEALTH

Pause the game, hold L2 and press ●, ●, ●, ■, ■, R2, R1, Up, ●, ■.

Level Skip

ALL MOVIES

At the main menu, hold L1 and press Left, Right, Left, Down, Up, Down, R1, ●, R2, ■.

PROJECT EDEN

CHEATS

During a game, press **X** to access the team screen. Rotate the Left Analog Stick clockwise three times and the counter-clockwise three times. A new icon should appear in the lower right corner. Select if for the following cheats:

Max Energy
Turn Invulnerability On
Turn Team Invulnerability On
Turn Team Invulnerability Off
Turn Infinite Weapon Energy On
All Weapons
Access All Levels
Skip Level

Q-BALL BILLIARDS MASTER

MORE GUIDELINE DETAIL

At the title screen, press Up, ▲, Down, ✗, Left, ■, Right, ●. Pause the game and select Options/System to change the guideline detail to high.

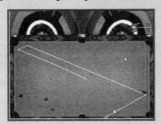

QUAKE III: REVOLUTION

LEVEL SKIP

During a game, hold L1 + R1 + R2 + Select and press ✗, ●, ■, ▲, ✗, ●, ■, ▲. You will automatically win the match.

REDCARD 20-03

ALL TEAMS, STADIUMS AND FINALS MODE

Enter **BIGTANK** as your profile name.

SHAUN PALMER'S PRO SNOWBOARDER

Highlight Options at the Main Menu and enter the following:

UNLOCK...	CHEAT
All Cheats	Hold Right + L2 and press ▲, ▲, ●, ▲
Max all Stats	Hold Right + L1 and press ▲, ▲, ●, ▲
All Boards	Hold Left + L2 and press ▲, ▲, ●, ▲

Secret Boarders	Hold Left + L1 and press ▲, ▲, ●, ▲
All Movies	Hold Left + R1 and press ▲, ▲, ●, ▲
All Levels	Hold Right + R1 and press ▲, ▲, ●, ▲

SILENT SCOPE 2: DARK SILHOUETTE

HEALTH TO TIME
In Arcade Mode, pause the game and press Up, Up, Down, Down, Left, Right, Left, Right, **X**, ●.

TIME TO HEALTH
In Arcade Mode, pause the game and press ●, **X**, Right, Left, Right, Left, Down, Down, Up, Up.

SMUGGLER'S RUN 2: HOSTILE TERRITORY

INVISIBILITY
Pause the game and press R1, L1, L1, R2, L1, L1, L2.

LIGHT CARS
Pause the game and press L1, R1, R1, L2, R2, R2.

NO GRAVITY
Pause the game and press R1, R2, R1, R2, Up, Up, Up.

Invisibility

SLOWER SPEED
Pause the game and press R2, L2, L1, R1, Left, Left, Left. You can enter this code up to three times from the normal speed.

FASTER SPEED
Pause the game and press R1, L1, L2, R2, Right, Right, Right. You can enter this code up to three times from the normal speed.

SOLDIER OF FORTUNE: GOLD EDITION

During a game press SELECT, then enter the following. Repeat the code to disable.

GOD MODE
hold R1 + L1 + R2 + L2 + ■ and press Left

AMMO
hold R1 + ■ and press Left

WEAPONS
hold L2 + R2 + ■ and press Left

COMBAT ITEMS
hold L1 + R1 + ■ and press Left

Combat Items

NO CLIPPING
hold L1 + L2 + R1 + ■ and press Left

NO TARGET
hold L1 + L2 + ■ and press Left

No Target

SPIDER-MAN THE MOVIE

UNLOCK EVERYTHING
Enter the code ARACHNID.

SMALL CHARACTER
Enter the code SPIDERBYTE.

BIG HEAD AND FEET
Enter the code GOESTOYOURHEAD.

Unlock Everything

BIG HEAD ENEMIES
Enter the code JOELSPEANUTS.

GOBLIN-STYLE COSTUME
Enter the code FREAKOUT.

Big Head and Feet

MARY JANE
Enter the code GIRLNEXTDOOR.

SCIENTIST
Enter the code SERUM.

POLICE OFFICER
Enter the code REALHERO.

Mary Jane

CAPTAIN STACEY
Enter the code CAPTAINSTACEY.

THE SHOCKER
Enter the code **HERMANSCHULTZ**.

THUG 1
Enter the code **KNUCKLES**.

THUG 2
Enter the code **STICKYRICE**.

THUG 3
Enter the code **THUGSRUS**.

UNLIMITED WEBBING
Enter the code **ORGANICWEBBING**.

ALL COMBAT CONTROLS
Enter the code **KOALA**.

MATRIX-STYLE ATTACKS
Enter the code **DODGETHIS**.

The Shocker

All Combat Controls

Level Skip

SUPER COOLANT
Enter the code **CHILLOUT**.

LEVEL SELECT
Enter the code **IMIARMAS**.

LEVEL SKIP
Enter the code **ROMITAS**. Pause the game and select Next Level to advance.

PINHEAD BOWLING
TRAINING LEVEL
Enter the code **HEADEXPLODY**.

FIRST PERSON VIEW
Enter the code **UNDERTHEMASK**.

First Person View

SPLASHDOWN

CHEAT SCREEN
Select Options, hold R2 and press Up, Up, Down, Down, Left, Right, Left, Right, ■, ●, ■, ●. You can now enter the following cheats.

Cheat Screen

ALL CHARACTERS
Enter **AllChar** as a code.

ALL COURSES
Enter **Passport** as a code.

ALL WETSUITS
Enter **LaPinata** as a code.

ENDING MOVIES
Enter **Festival** as a code.

Ending Moves

MAX PERFORMANCE METER
Enter **PMeterGo** as a code. You will still stall if you miss a buoy.

TOUGH AI
Enter **AllOutAI** as a code.

CPU CAN'T KNOCK YOU OFF
Enter **TopBird** as a code.

NORMAL AI ON HARD TRACKS
Enter **Hobble** as a code.

UFO GHOST IN TIME TRIAL
Enter **IBelieve** as a code.

F-18 GHOST IN TIME TRIAL
Enter **F18** as a code.

UFO Ghost in Time Trial

SPY HUNTER

SALIVA: YOUR DISEASE MOVIE
Enter the Agent name as **SALIVA**. The name will disappear. Now enter your name and select System Options at the next screen to access the movie.

SALIVA: THE SPY HUNTER THEME MOVIE
Enter the Agent name as **GUNN**. The name will disappear. Now enter your name and select System Options at the next screen to access the movie.

Saliva

MAKING OF SPY HUNTER MOVIE
Enter the Agent name as **MAKING**. The name will disappear. Now enter your name and select System Options at the next screen to access the movie.

SPY HUNTER CONCEPT ART MOVIE
Enter the Agent name as **SCW823**. The name will disappear. Now enter your name and select System Options at the next screen to access the movie.

Concept Art Movie

Early Test Animatic Movie

EARLY TEST ANIMATIC MOVIE
Enter the Agent name as **WWS413**. The name will disappear. Now enter your name and select System Options at the next screen to access the movie.

SSX TRICKY

UNLOCK EVERYTHING
At the main menu, hold L1 + R1 and press **X**, **▲**, Right, **●**, **■**, Down, **▲**, **■**, Left, **●**, **X**, Up. Release L1 and R1.

FULL STATS
At the main menu, hold L1 + R1 and press **▲**, **▲**, Right, **▲**, **▲**, Down, **X**, **X**, Left, **X**, **X**, Up. Release L1 and R1.

MIX MASTER MIKE
At the main menu, hold L1 + R1 and press **X**, **X**, Right, **X**, **X**, Down, **X**, **X**, Left, **X**, **X**, Up. Pick anybody, and he/she will be replaced by Mix Master Mike.

Mix Master Mike

Mallora Board and Outfit for Elise

MALLORA BOARD AND OUTFIT FOR ELISE
At the main menu, hold L1 + R1 and press **X**, **X**, Right, **●**, **●**, Down, **▲**, **▲**, Left, **■**, **■**, Up.

STAR TREK VOYAGER: ELITE FORCE

GOD MODE
Pause the game, hold L1 + L2 + R1 + R2 + R3 and press SELECT.

MAX HEALTH
Pause the game, hold L1 + L2 + R1 + R2 and press SELECT.

MAX ARMOR
Pause the game, hold L1 + R1 and press SELECT.

ALL WEAPONS
Pause the game, hold L1 + L2 + R1 + R2 + L3 and press SELECT.

FULL AMMO
Pause the game, hold R1 + R2 and press SELECT.

AUTO LOCK
Pause the game, hold L1 + L2 and press SELECT.

STAR WARS: JEDI STARFIGHTER

From the Options, select Codes and enter the following:

UNLOCK EVERYTHING
Enter the code **PNYRCADE**.

HEADHUNTER SHIP
Enter the code **HEADHUNT**. The display will read ??? if entered correctly.

Unlock Everything

INVINCIBLE
Enter the code **QUENTIN**.

NO HEADS UP DISPLAY
Enter the code **NOHUD**.

JAR JAR MODE
Enter the code **JARJAR**. This inverts the controls.

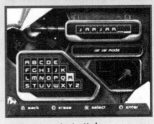
Jar Jar Mode

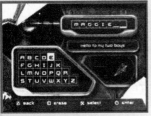
Message

DIRECTOR MODE
Enter the code **DIRECTOR**.

MESSAGE
Enter the code **MAGGIE**.

X-WING

Complete the bonus objective for Act 1: Mission 3.

TIE FIGHTER

Complete the bonus objective for Act 1: Mission 4.

ADVANCED ZOOMER

Complete the bonus objective on Act 2: Mission 3.

ADVANCED JEDI STARFIGHTER

Complete the bonus objective on Act 2: Mission 4.

SABAOTH FIGHTER

Complete the bonus objective on Act 2: Mission 5.

ADVANCED FREEFALL

Complete the bonus objective in Act 3: Mission 1.

ADVANCED HAVOC

Complete the bonus objective for Act 3: Mission 3.

REPUBLIC GUNSHIP

Complete the bonus objective for Act 3: Mission 5.

SLAVE 1

Complete all hidden objectives for Player One.

STAR WARS: RACER REVENGE

Before entering the following codes you must set a record and enter your name as **NO TIME**.

HARD MODE

At the main menu hold L1 + L2 + R1 + R2 and press ▲.

ALL TRACKS

At the main menu hold L1 + L2 + R1 + R2 and press Right, Left, Right, Left, ●, ■, ●, ■.

ART GALLERIES

At the main menu hold L1 + L2 + R1 + R2 and press Right, ■, Left, ●, Down, ✕, Up, ▲.

Hard Mode

Art Galleries

STATE OF EMERGENCY

The name of the code will appear if the following are entered correctly.

INVULNERABLE
Press L1, L2, R1, R2, **X** during game play.

UNLIMITED AMMO
Press L1, L2, R1, R2, **▲** during game play.

MISSION SKIP
Press Left, Left, Left, Left, **▲** during game play.

INFINITE TIME IN CHAOS MODE
Press L1, L2, R1, R2, **●** during game play.

LITTLE PLAYER
Press R1, R2, L1, L2, **X** during game play.

BIG PLAYER
Press R1, R2, L1, L2, **▲** during game play.

Invulnerable

Little Player

Punches Decapitate

NORMAL PLAYER
Press R1, R2, L1, L2, **●** during game play.

PUNCHES DECAPITATE
Press L1, L2, R1, R2, **■** during game play.

LOOTING ON THE RISE
Press R1, L1, R2, L2, **▲** during game play.

BULL
Press Right, Right, Right, Right, **X** during game play.

FREAK
Press Right, Right, Right, Right, **●** during game play.

SPANKY
Press Right, Right, Right, Right, **▲** during game play.

Spanky

SUNNY GARCIA SURFING

ALL SURFBOARDS
At the title screen, hold R1 + L1 and press Left, ●, Up, Down, ●, Left, Down, ●, X.

ALL SURFERS
At the title screen, hold R1 + L1 and press Left, ●, Up, Right, ●, Left, Left.

THE SIMPSONS: ROAD RAGE

HIDDEN CHARACTERS
Set the system date to the following to open the secret characters:

DATE	CHARACTER
Jan 1	Happy New Year Krusty the Klown
Oct 31	Happy Halloween Bart

Nov 22, 2001, Nov 28, 2002...	Happy Thanksgiving Marge
Dec 25	Merry Christmas Apu

SMITHERS
At the options screen hold R1 + L1 and press ▲, ▲, ■, ■.

NUCLEAR BUS
At the options screen hold R1 + L1 and press ▲, ▲, ■, X.

BOX
At the options screen hold R1 + L1 and press ▲, ▲, ■, ●.

Nuclear Bus

2D PASSENGERS
At the options screen hold R1 + L1 and press ●, ●, ●, ●.

MORE CAMERA OPTIONS
At the options screen hold R1 + L1 and press ▲, ▲, ▲, ▲.

2D Passengers

MORE MONEY
At the options screen hold R1 + L1 and press ■, ■, ■, ■.

NIGHT
At the options screen hold R1 + L1 and press X, X, X, X.

THUNDERSTRIKE:
OPERATION PHOENIX

MISSION SELECT
At the options, set Vibration to 1 and SFX and Music to 0. Then, hold L1 + L2 + R1 + R2 + ● + ■. The message Spooky Cat will appear if entered correctly.

TIGER WOODS
PGA TOUR 2002

UNLOCK EVERYTHING
Enter the password **ALLORNOTHIN**.

ALL COURSES
Enter the password **GIVEITUP**.

All Courses

GOLFERS

Enter the following passwords to access the corresponding golfer:

GOLFER	PASSWORD
Super Tiger Woods	2TREPUS01S

Cedric "Ace" Andrews	TSWERDNA120
Stuart Appleby	UYBELPPA160
Notah Begay III	DYAGEB04E
Brad Faxon	ENOXAF14D
Jim Furyk	OKYRUF05R
Lee Janzen	INEZNAJ11W

GOLFER	PASSWORD
Justin Leonard	RDRANOAEL130
Solita Lopez	GZEPOL10R
Colin Montgomerie	EYTNOM09E
Kellie Newman	SNAMWEN172
Jesper Parnevik	OKIVENRAP02U
Vijay Singh	SHGNIS03P
Moa "Big Mo" Ta'a Vatu	O1UTAVAAT06T

| Melvin "Yosh" Tanigawa | WAWAGINAT07I |
| Erika "Ice" von Severin | RVESNOV08G |

TONY HAWK'S PRO SKATER 3

ALL CHEATS

Select Cheats from the Options menu and enter **backdoor**. You can access the cheats from the pause menu.

ALL MOVIES

Select Cheats from the Options menu and enter **Peepshow**.

All Movies

OMPLETE GAME

Select Cheats from the Options menu and enter **ROADTRIP**.

ALL CHARACTERS

Select Cheats from the Options menu and enter **YOHOMIES**.

MAX STATS

Select Cheats from the Options menu and enter **PUMPMEUP**.

TOP GUN: COMBAT ZONES

ALL LEVELS AND PLANES
Enter **SHPONGLE** as your callsign.

TRANSWORLD SURF

UNLOCK EVERYTHING
During the game press SELECT, ■, Up, Up, ■, Down, Down, ■, Left, Left, ■, Right, Right, ■, Up, ■, Left, ■, Down, ■, Right, ■, Up, Up, ■, L1.

FULL SPECIAL
During the game press SELECT, ■, Up, ■, Down, ■, Left, ■, Right, ■, Down, ■, Up.

PADDLE FASTER
During the game press SELECT, ■, Up, ■, Down, ■, Left, ■, Right, ■, Down, Down.

SHARK SURFBOARD
During the game press SELECT, ■, Up, ■, Down, ■, Left, ■, Right, Right, ■, Down.

INVISIBLE SURFBOARD
During the game press SELECT, ■, Up, ■, Down, ■, Left, ■, Right, ■, Left, ■, Up.

NO HUD
During the game press SELECT, ■, Up, ■, Down, ■, Left, ■, Right, ■, Up, ■, Right.

No Hud

DIFFERENT COLORS

During the game press SELECT, ■, Up, ■, Down, ■, Left, ■, Right, ■, Down, ■, Left.

DISCO EFFECT

During the game press SELECT, ■, Up, ■, Down, ■, Left, ■, Right, ■, Down, ■, Right.

TURN THE SURF GREEN

During the game press SELECT, ■, Up, ■, Down, ■, Left, ■, Right, ■, Up, ■, Left.

DISABLE CODES

During the game press SELECT, SELECT, SELECT, SELECT.

TWISTED METAL: BLACK

Set the control option to Classic for the following codes.

WEAPONS INTO HEALTH

During a game, hold L1 + R1 + L2 + R2 and press ▲, X, ■, ●.

INFINITE AMMO

During a game, hold L1 + R1 + L2 + R2 and press Up, X, Left, ●.

INVULNERABILITY

During a game, hold L1 + R1 + L2 + R2 and press Right, Left, Down, Up.

GOD MODE

During a game, hold L1 + R1 + L2 + R2 and press Up, X, Left, ●.

MEGA GUNS

During a game, hold L1 + R1 + L2 + R2 and press X, X, ▲.

Mega Guns

KILLER WEAPONS ONE HIT KILLS

During a game, hold L1 + R1 + L2 + R2 and press X, X, Up. Now one shot kills. Re-enter the code to disable it.

ENHANCED FREEZE ATTACK

During a game, hold L1 + R1 + L2 + R2 and press Right, Left, Up.

WORLD DESTRUCTION LEAGUE: WAR JETZ

PASSWORDS

ARENA	PASSWORD
Panama 2	JBVKWNBBCBQM
Panama 3	MDKKWYFTKBQM
Australia 1	MHZKWTJMQBQM
Australia 2	ZBCKXPBHNBQM
Australia 3	LDRKXYFZTBQM
Thailand 1	ZHHKXJJTBBQM
Thailand 2	TBPKYZBVHBQM
Thailand 3	KFFPJRFNPBQN
Rhine River 1	YJVPJCJGVBQN
Rhine River 2	FCNPKXBVWBQN
Rhine River 3	PGDPKGFPDBQN
New York City 1	KKSPKRJHKBQN
New York City 2	VBFKPLHBWZBQN
New York City 3	WJYPLWFQGBQN
Antarctica 1	CMPPLHJJNBQN
Antarctica 2	RKFPMYBZHBQN
Antarctica 3	GNVPMQFSNBQN
San Francisco 1	TRLPMBJLVBQN
San Francisco 2	SVMPNFBFVBQN
San Francisco 3	RXDPNHFYDBQN
Valhalla 1	XBXPNGKRKBQN
Valhalla 2	LPXKVMCQZBQM
Valhalla 3	QSMKVSGKHBQM

SUPER CHEATS
Enter **SPRLZY** as a code.

ALL CHEATS
Enter **TWLVCHTS** as a code.

All Cheats

LEVEL SELECT
Enter **JMPTT** as a code.

Level Select

RAPID FIRE
Enter **FRHS** as a code.

SPEED SHOTS
Enter **NSTNT** as a code.

DUAL FIRE
Enter **NDBMBS** as a code.

SPIN SHOTS
Enter **DZZY** as a code.

SHIELDS ON ROLL
Enter **SCRW** as a code.

INVULNERABLE
Enter **DNGDM** as a code.

FAST PLANES
Enter **ZPPY** as a code.

BIGGER GUNS
Enter **HMMR** as a code.

BIGGEST GUNS
Enter **QD** as a code.

THICK ARMOR
Enter **MRRMR** as a code.

TOP GUN MODE
Enter **DH** as a code.

DOUBLE BUX

Enter **TWFSTD** as a code.

EXTRA 10 BUX
Enter **WNNNGS** as a code.

WEAPON UP AT 3
Enter **PYRS** as a code.

OVERLORDS
Enter **VRLRDS** as a code.

VALHALLA
Enter **WNRLFST** as a code.

GHOST MODE
Enter **SNKY** as a code.

SWITCH PLANE
Enter **NDCSN** as a code.

PLANE WINS
Enter **SMSHNG** as a code.

SHOW BOXES
Enter **BXDRW** as a code.

WAYPOINTS
Enter **WYPNT** as a code.

EVERY MOVIE
Enter **GRTD** as a code.

Every Movie

WORLD OF OUTLAWS: SPRINT CARS 2002

ALL DRIVERS
In career mode, enter your name as
MITYMASTA.

$5,000,000
In career mode, enter your name as
CHICMCHIM.

ALL TRACKS
In career mode, enter your name as
JOEYJOEJOE.

$5,000,000

WORLD RALLY CHAMPIONSHIP

From the main menu, select Extras then Secrets and enter the following:

EVERYTHING UNLOCK
Enter **OPENSESAME** as a code.

**INCREASED ACCELERATION
AND TOP SPEED**
Enter **EVOPOWER** as a code.

SPEEDED UP CODRIVER CALLS
Enter **HELIUMAID** as a code. This
gives your codriver a high pitched
voice.

REMOVED CAR SHELL
Enter **THATSSTUPID** as a code.

FLYING CAR IN REPLAY
Enter **FLOATYLIGHT** as a code.

OVERHEAD CAMERA
Enter **DOWNBELOW** as a code.

UPSIDE DOWN CAMERA
Enter **ONTHECEILING** as a code.

UNDERWATER VISUAL EFFECT
Enter **WIBBLYWOBBLY** as a code.

PSYCHADELIC VISUAL EFFECT
Enter **IMGOINGCRAZY** as a code.

XBOX™

THE GAMES

4X4 EVOLUTION 2	174
AMPED: FREESTYLE SNOWBOARDING	174
ARCTIC THUNDER	175
AZURIK: RISE OF PERATHIA	176
BLOOD WAKE	177
CEL DAMAGE	178
DARK SUMMIT	178
DAVE MIRRA FREESTYLE BMX 2	179
DEAD OR ALIVE 3	181
ESPN NBA 2NIGHT 2002	181
ESPN NFL PRIME TIME 2002	182
FUZION FRENZY	182
GAUNTLET: DARK LEGACY	183
MAD DASH	183
MAX PAYNE	184
NASCAR HEAT 2002	184
NASCAR THUNDER 2002	184
NBA 2K2	185
NBA INSIDE DRIVE 2002	185
NFL BLITZ 20-02	186
NFL FEVER 2002	188
NHL HITZ 20-02	190
PIRATES: THE LEGEND OF BLACK KAT	191
PROJECT GOTHAM RACING	192
RALLISPORT CHALLENGE	193
SPIDER-MAN THE MOVIE	193
SPYHUNTER	194
SSX TRICKY	194
STAR WARS: OBI-WAN	195
STAR WARS: STARFIGHTER SPECIAL EDITION	195
THE SIMPSONS ROAD RAGE	196
TONY HAWK'S PRO SKATER 2X	196
TONY HAWK'S PRO SKATER 3	197
TRANSWORLD SURF	197

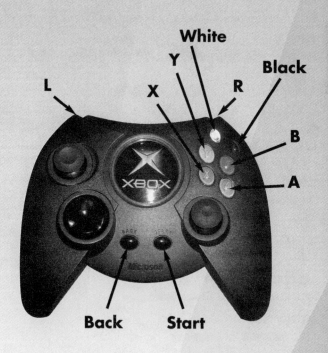

4X4 EVOLUTION 2

LEVEL SELECT

At the title screen or main menu press X, X, White, White, White, Y, Y, White, X, Y, Y, X, White.

MONEY

At the title screen or main menu press Y, X, White, Y, X, White, X, X, Y, White, X, Y.

REPUTATION

At the title screen or main menu press Y, Y, White, X, X, White, Y, Y, Y, X, X, X.

AMPED: FREESTYLE SNOWBOARDING

The following cheats are case-sensitive.

RAVEN

At the Cheat menu, enter **RidinwRaven**.

STEEZE

At the Cheat menu, enter **ChillinwSteezy**.

Steeze

ALL LEVELS

At the Cheat menu, enter **GimmeGimme**.

MEGA JUMPS

At the Cheat menu, enter **MegaLeg**.

FASTER SPIN

At the Cheat menu, enter **WhirlyGig**.

FREEDOM OF MOVEMENT

At the Cheat menu, enter **ZiPster**.

BOUNCY

At the Cheat menu, enter **MegabOUnce**.

BOARD THROUGH TREES

At the Cheat menu, enter **buzzsaW**.

Board Through Trees

ARCTIC THUNDER

NO DRONES
At the Mode Select, press X, X, Y, Y, White, Black, START.

CATCH UP CODE
At the Mode Select, press Y, X, Y, Y, X, START.

RANDOM POWER-UPS
At the Mode Select, press Black, R, X, Y, Black, R, START.

SNOWBALL POWER-UPS
At the Mode Select, press X, X, X, White, Y, START.

GRAPPLING HOOKS POWER-UPS
At the Mode Select, press Y, Y, L, Y, Y, White, START.

ROOSTER POWER-UPS
At the Mode Select, press Black, R, L, White, X, START.

SNOW BOMB POWER-UPS
At the Mode Select, press Y, Y, Black, R, START.

BOOST POWER-UPS
At the Mode Select, press Y, Black, Black, Y, R, START.

ACTIVATE CLONE
At the Mode Select, press White, L, L, Y, White, Y, START.

ALL INVISIBLE
At the Mode Select, press X, Y, X, R, Y, Y, START.

NO POWER-UPS
At the Mode Select, press X, X, Y, X, R, X, START.

SUPER BOOST
At the Mode Select, press Y, White, X, R, X, L, START.

AZURIK: RISE OF PERATHIA

GOD MODE

During a game press X, Black, White, R + L, click Left Analog-stick + Right Analog-stick. A sound will confirm correct code entry. Repeat this code to disable its effect.

LEVEL SELECT

During a game press Left Analog-stick Right + Right Analog-stick Left, Left Analog-stick Left + Right Analog-stick Right, A, B, click Right Analog-stick, click Left Analog-stick. Note: This will also allow you to change your stats and view all FMV sequences. However, you must power off the Xbox to exit an FMV sequence.

FULL POWER AND HEALTH

Hold Left and rotate the Right Analog-stick from Right counter-clockwise to Right Analog-stick Left. Release Left, then press A, X. You can now restore your health and elemental power.

SAVE

During a game press White, Up, Down, A, B, click Right Analog-stick during the "swing" animation. A click will confirm that the game has been saved. This may be done at any time during the game, but caution must be used when choosing a point to save. Avoid saving on moving platforms, areas where enemies respawn, while falling, or while dying.

GEM MODE

During a game press Right, Left, A, B, A, B, Right, Left. You can get Earth, Air, Fire, Water, and Obsidian gems by pressing A, B, X, Y, or Black. Any other button exits gem mode. You can increase your elemental power storage and get all the Obsidians through this mode. However, it is possible you might create more gems than supported and crash the game.

BIG HEADS:

During a game click Right Analog-stick, press R, Down, Up, A. A sound will confirm correct code entry.

AFRO

During a game press Down, Right, Black + White, click Right Analog-stick, click Left Analog-stick, press Left Analog-stick Right + Right Analog-stick Left, B, Y. A sound will confirm correct code entry.

ADJUST CAMERA

During a game press R, Down, Up, Down, Up, click Right Analog-stick, click Left Analog-stick. The game will stop, allowing the view to be altered. Press L or R to move the view up or down. Press Left Analog-stick or Right Analog-stick to move the view forwards and back. Press the D-pad to zoom in and out. Press A to view and remove the elemental power display. Press Back to resume the game.

ADJUST LIGHTING

During a game press A click Right Analog-stick, B, click Right Analog-stick, click Left Analog-stick. Darker areas will now be easier to see, at the expense of having less dramatic lighting. Repeat this code to return to normal.

BLOOD WAKE

ALL BOATS

At the title screen, press Up, Down, Left, Right, Left trigger, B, X, X, Right thumbstick, START.

ALL LEVELS

At the title screen, press X, Y, Up, Right, Left, Down, Up, Down, Left trigger, Left trigger, START.

All Boats

ALL BATTLE MODES

At the title screen, press Y, A, X, B, Left thumbstick, Right thumbstick, Black, White, Right trigger, Right trigger, START.

IMPORT BOAT

At the title screen, press Y, B, X, A, Left trigger, Right trigger, Left, Right, Left thumbstick, Right thumbstick, START.

Import Boat

INVULNERABILITY

At the title screen, press Left thumbstick, Right thumbstick, Down, Left, Down, Left, B, Y, START.

UNLIMITED AMMO

At the title screen, press Black, White, Left trigger, Right trigger, Right thumbstick, Right thumbstick, Y, X, START.

UNLIMITED TURBO
At the title screen, press Up, Up, Down, Down, Left, Right, Left, Right, B, A, START.

PUFFER FISH
At the title screen, press A, B, Black, White, Y, X, Right thumbstick, Right thumbstick, Left thumbstick, Left thumbstick.

BLOOD BALL MODE
At the title screen press X, Y, White, Black, B, A, Left, Up, Right, Down.

RUBBER DUCK MODE
At the title screen press Right thumbstick, Left thumbstick, Right Trigger, Left Trigger, Black, White, Up, Down, Left, Right.

CEL DAMAGE

ALL CARS, COURSES AND MODES
Enter **ENCHILADA!** as your name.

DARK SUMMIT

CHALLENGES COMPLETE
Press and hold Back + START and then press Y, L, X, B, R, A, R, Y.

LIFT POINTS
Press and hold Back + START and then press Y, L, X, B, R, A, R, A.

ALL BOARDERS
Press and hold Back + START and then press Y, L, X, B, R, A, R, B.

All Boarders

DAVE MIRRA FREESTYLE BMX 2

ALL BIKES

CHARACTER	CODE
Dave Mirra	Down, Down, Up, Right, Up, Right, Up, Up, X button
Ryan Nyquist	Down, Down, Down, Down, Down, Right, Up, Down, X button
Troy McMurray	Down, Down, Left, Down, Right, Left, Up, Left, X button
Mike Laird	Down, Down, Right, Left, Down, Up, Up, Right, X button
Tim Mirra	Down, Down, Right, Left, Down, Right, Down, Up, X button
Kenan Harkin	Down, Down, Left, Up, Down, Right, Down, Down, X button
Leigh Ramsdell	Down, Down, Down, Up, Left, Left, Down, Left, X button
Joey Garcia	Down, Down, Up, Right, Left, Left, Down, Right, X button
Rick Moliterno	Down, Down, Up, Left, Right, Right, Left, Up, X button
Todd Lyons	Down, Down, Down, Down, Left, Right, Left, Down, X button
John Englebert	Down, Down, Left, Up, Left, Up, Left, Left, X button
Scott Wirch	Down, Down, Right, Up, Down, Down, Left, Right, X button
Colin Mackay	Down, Down, Right, Right, Right, Right, Right Up, X button
Zach Shaw	Down, Down, Left, Down, Up, Right, Right, Down, X button

ALL LEVELS

CHARACTER	CODE
Dave Mirra	Up, Up, Up Right, Up Left, Up, Up, X button
Ryan Nyquist	Up, Up, Down, Down, Left, Right, Up, Down, X button
Troy McMurray	Up, Up, Left, Up, Up, Right, Up, Left, X button
Mike Laird	Up, Up, Right, Down, Down, Right, Up, Right, X button
Tim Mirra	Up, Up, Right, Down, Right, Left, Down, Up, X button
Kenan Harkin	Up, Up, Left, Left, Down, Up, Down, Down, X button
Leigh Ramsdell	Up, Up, Down, Up, Left, Down, Down Left, X button
Joey Garcia	Up, Up, Up, Up, Down, Down, Right, X button
Rick Moliterno	Up, Up, Up, Down, Right, Right, Left, Up, X button
Todd Lyons	Up, Up, Down Up, Right, Right, Left, Down, X button
John Englebert	Up, Up, Left, Down, Right, Down, Left, Left, X button
Scott Wirch	Up, Up, Right, Up, Left, Left, Left, Right, X button
Colin Mackay	Up, Up, Right, Left, Up, Right, Right, Up, X button
Zach Shaw	Up, Up, Left, Right, Down, Down, Right, Down, X button

ALL SIGNATURE TRICKS

CHARACTER	CODE
Dave Mirra	Left, Right, Up, Up, Left, Right, Up, Up, X button
Ryan Nyquist	Left, Right, Down, Down, Down, Up, Up, Down, X button
Troy McMurray	Left, Right, Left, Left, Up, Down, Up, Left, X button
Mike Laird	Left, Right, Right, Right, Left, Right, Up, Right, X button
Tim Mirra	Left, Right, Right, Up, Down, Up, Down, Up, X button
Kenan Harkin	Left, Right, Left, Down, Up, Down, Down, Down X button
Leigh Ramsdell	Left, Right, Down, Left, Left, Right, Down, Left, X button
Joey Garcia	Left, Right, Up, Right, Down, Up, Down, Right, X button
Rick Moliterno	Left, Right, Up, Up, Up, Down, Left, Up, X button
Todd Lyons	Left, Right, Down, Down, Left, Right, Left, Down, X button
John Englebert	Left, Right, Left, Left, Down, Up, Left, Left, X button
Scott Wirch	Left, Right, Right, Right, Up, Down, Left, Right, X button
Colin Mackay	Left, Right, Right, Up, Left, Right, Right, Up, X button
Zach Shaw	Left, Right, Left, Down, Left, Up, Right, Down, X button
Slim Jim Guy	Left, Right, Down, Left, Up, Left, Right, Left, X button
Amish Air	Left, Right, Up, Up, Right, Down, Right, Right, X button

RIDER COMPETITION OUTFITS

CHARACTER	CODE
Dave Mirra	Right, Right, Up, Right, Down, Down, Left, Left, X button
Ryan Nyquist	Right, Right, Down, Down, Left, Up, Up, Down, X button
Troy McMurray	Right, Right, Left, Up, Left, Left, Up, Left, X button
Mike Laird	Right, Right, Right, Up, Down, Down, Up, Right, X button
Tim Mirra	Right, Right, Right, Down, Down, Right, Down, Up, X button
Kenan Harkin	Right, Right, Left, Down, Up, Left, Down, Down, X button
Leigh Ramsdell	Right, Right, Down, Left, Up, Down, Down, Left, X button
Joey Garcia	Right, Right, Up, Down, Up, Right, Down, Right, X button
Rick Moliterno	Right, Right, Up, Up, Up, Right, Left, Up, X button
Todd Lyons	Right, Right, Down, Left, Left, Up, Left, Down, X button
John Englebert	Right, Right, Left, Right, Up, Up, Left, Left, X button
Scott Wirch	Right, Right, Right, Up, Left, Left, Left, Right, X button
Colin Mackay	Right, Right, Right, Left, Right, Up, Right, Up, X button
Zach Shaw	Right, Right, Left, Left, Down, Down, Right, Down, X button

DEAD OR ALIVE 3

EIN AND RANDOM SELECT

Finish Story Mode with all 16 characters. Use Hayate in Survival Mode or Mode. Enter **EIN** as your name.

ESPN NBA 2NIGHT 2002

Select Cheats from the Options and enter the following:

BIG HEAD
Enter the code **BIGHEAD**.

BIG HANDS
Enter the code **BIGHAND**.

BIG FEET
Enter the code **BIGFOOT**.

TINY PLAYERS
Enter the code **MINIMINI**.

PANCAKE PLAYERS
Enter the code **PANCAKE**.

INVISIBLE PLAYERS
Enter the code **INVISIBLE**.

BETTER PLAYERS
Enter the code **ABILITYBONUS**.

BETTER DUNKS
Enter the code **DUNKERS**.

BETTER SHOOTING
Enter the code **EXCELLENT**.

BALL TRAIL
Enter the code **BEFOREIMAGE**.

NO SPECTATORS
Enter the code **NOSPECTATOR**.

DARK
Enter the code **DARKNESS**.

ESPN NFL PRIME TIME 2002

ALOHA STADIUM AND PRO BOWL TEAMS
Enter the code **ALOHA**.

RELIANT STADIUM
Enter the code **HOWDY**.

WEATHER IN DOMES
Enter the code **SHAKE IT UP**.

FUMBLES
Enter the code **READY TO FUMBLE**.
Press Left Trigger for a fumble.

UNSTOPPABLE WITH BALL
Enter the code **CAN'T TOUCH THIS**.

BETTER JUMPS
Enter the code **SUPERMAN**.

SHOW EVERYONE
Enter the code **SHOW EVERYONE**.

CHANGE SCORING
Enter the code **SCOREBOX**.

FUZION FRENZY

FIRST PERSON MODE
Pause the game, hold L and press Y, B, Y, B. Repeat to disable.

MUTANT MODE
Pause the game, hold L and press Y, B, X, X. Repeat the code for Mutant Mode 2, again for Mutant Mode 3 and a fourth time to disable Mutant Mode.

First Person Mode

Mutant Mode

WELSH
Pause the game, hold L and press Y, Y, Y, Y. Repeat to disable.

SQUEAKY VOICES:
Pause the game, hold L and press Y, X, Y, Y. Repeat to disable.

GAUNTLET: DARK LEGACY

CHEAT CODES

Enter the following codes as your name. Note that you can only use one at a time.

EFFECT	CODE
10,000 Gold	10000K
9 Potions and Keys	ALLFUL

SECRET COSTUMES

Enter the following codes as your name. Each code unlocks a different costume.

CLASS	CODE
Dwarf	ICE600, NUD069
Jester	KJH105, PNK666, STX222
Knight	ARV984, BAT900, CSS222, DARTHC, DIB626, KAO292, RIZ721, SJB964, STG333, TAK118
Valkyrie	AYA555, CEL721, TWN300
Warrior	CAS400, MTN200, RAT333
Wizard	DES700, GARM00, GARM99, SKY100, SUM224,

MAD DASH RACING

ALL CHARACTERS

Pause the game, hold L and press X, B, Left, Y, Right, Right.

50 BALLS

Pause the game, hold L and press Up, X, B, Y, Left, Left.

ITEMS DON'T HIT

Pause the game, hold L and press X, B, B, Left, Left, Y, B.

FRUIT

Pause the game, hold R and press B, X, Left, Left, Y.

FLY AS ANY CHARACTER

Pause the game, hold L and press X, Y, A, Left, Left, Right, Right.

MAX PAYNE

CHEATS
During a game, press Back to access the menu. Hold L + R and press the Left Analog Stick + the Right Analog Stick, White, Black, Black, White, White, Black. A cheat option should appear on the menu.

NASCAR HEAT 2002

HARDCORE REALISM MODE
At the main menu press Up, Down, Left, Right, White, Up, Down.

WIRE FRAME CARS
At the main menu press Up, Down, Left, Right, White, Right, Left.

MINI CARS
At the main menu press Up, Down, Left, Right, White, Down, Up.

HIGH SUSPENSION
At the main menu press Up, Down, Left, Right, White, Left, Right.

CREDITS
At the main menu press Up, Down, Left, Right, White, Left, Left.

PAINTBALLS IN SINGLE RACE OR HEAD TO HEAD
At the Race Day screen press Up, Down, Left, Right, White, Up, Up. Press Up to fire a paintball.

NASCAR THUNDER 2002

EXTRA DRIVERS
At the driver creation screen enter the following names:

AUDREY CLARK	DAVE ALPERN
BENNY PARSONS	DAVE NICHOLS
BUSTER AUTON	DIANE GRUBB
CHERYL KING	DICK PAYSOR
CHUCK SPICER	JIM HANNIGAN
CRISSY HILLSWORTH	JOEY JOULWAN
DARYL WOLFE	JOSH NEELON

KATRINA GOODE	**RICK HUMPHREY**
KEN PATTERSON	**SASHA SOARES**
KRISTI JONES	**SCOTT BREWER**
MANDY MISIAK	**TOM RENEDO**
MICHELLE EMSER	**TRACI HULTZAPPLE**
RICK EDWARDS	**TROI HAYES**

NBA 2K2

CHEAT MENU

Select Game Play from the Options menu, hold Left on the d-pad and Right on the Left thumbstick. Then press START. A Codes options should appear at the options menu.

BONUS TEAMS

Enter MEGASTARS as a code. This will unlock the Sega Sports, Visual Concepts, and 2K2 teams in exhibition and street modes.

NBA INSIDE DRIVE 2002

Select Codes from the Options menu to enter the following. Re-enter the code to disable it.

EFFECT	CODE
Tiny Players	SMALLSHOES
Easy Three Pointers	THREE4ALL
Easy Alley Oops	IGOTHOPS
Accept All Trades	GIMMETHAT
Unlimited Turbo	CARDIOMAN

EFFECT	CODE
Chicago Skyline Stadium	WINDYCITY

8-Ball	GAMEOVER
ABA Ball	OLDSCHOOL
Beach Ball	SANDINMYSHORTS
Soccer Ball	HOOLIGAN
Volley Ball	SPIKEIT
WNBA Ball	GOTGAME
Xbox Ball	BACHMAN

NFL BLITZ 20-02

HIDDEN CHARACTERS

NAME	PIN
LION	1963
PINTO	1966
ROBOTS	1970
DOLPHIN	1972
ROBOTR	1974
CLOWN	1974
TIGER	1977

NAME	PIN
VIKING	1977
EAGLE	1981
BEAR	1985
INDIAN	1992
COWBOY	1996
DEER	1997
VIKING	1997
HORSE	1999
RAM	2000
Pirate	2001
RBL-DBN	9669

VERSUS CHEATS

At the versus screen use L, R and A to enter the following cheats. For example, for Showtime Mode the code is 3 5 1 Right. Press L three times, R five times and A once then press Right to activate the code.

EFFECT	CODE
More Code Entry Time	2 1 2 Right
Tournament Mode	1 1 1 Down
No CPU Assistance*	0 1 2 Down
Showtime Mode	3 5 1 Right
Big Feet	0 2 5 Left
Power Loader	0 2 5 Right
Big Head	2 0 0 Right
Team Big Head	2 0 3 Right
Huge Head	1 4 5 Left
Classic Ball	0 3 0 Left
Weather: Clear	1 2 3 Right
Weather: Snow	5 5 5 Left
Weather: Rain	5 5 5 Right
Ground Fog	2 3 2 Down
Noftle	3 2 5 Up
No Punting	1 4 1 Up
No Highlight Target Receiver	3 2 1 Down
No Interceptions	3 5 5 Up

EFFECT	CODE
No Replays	5 5 4 Right
Fast Running Speed	0 3 2 Left
Fast Passes	2 4 0 Left
Super Blitzing	0 5 4 Up
Super Field Goals	1 2 3 Left
Allow Stepping Out of Bounds	3 1 1 Left
Always QB	2 2 2 Left
Always Receiver	2 2 2 Right
Extra Offense Plays	3 3 3 Down
Power-up Defense	4 2 1 Up
Power-up Linemen	5 2 1 Up
No Random Fumbles (If Teams Agree)	5 2 3 Down
Butter Fingaz	3 4 5 Up
Armageddon Team	5 4 3 Right
Bilders Team	3 1 0 Up
Brew Dawgs Team	4 3 2 Down
Cowboys Team	1 3 5 Left
Crunch Mode Team	4 0 3 Right
Gsmers Team	5 0 1 Up
Indians Team	0 4 5 Left
Midway Team	2 5 3 Right
Neo Tokyo Team	3 4 4 Down
Rollos Team	2 5 4 Up

NFL FEVER 2002

ALL TEAMS AND STADIUMS

Create a new profile and name it **Broadway**.

Create a new profile and enter the name as follows:

TEAM	NAME
Chromides	Regulate
Commandos	Camo
Cows	Milk
Crocs	Crikey
DaRulahs	Tut
Gladiators	BigBacks
Hackers	Axemen
Monks	Robes
Pansies	Viola
Samurai	Slasher
Skeletons	Stone
Spies	Target
Tumbleweeds	Dusty
War Elephants	Horns
Wildcats	Kitty

BONUS STADIUMS

Create a new profile and enter the name as follows:

STADIUM	NAME
Abyss	Odyssey2
Millennium	Odyssey
New Seattle	SeaTown
Practice	Dome
Roman Coliseum	LionPit

NHL HITZ 20-02

CHEATS

After selecting your players, you will have a chance to enter codes by changing three icons with the X button, Y button and B button. Use the X button to change the first icon, the Y button for second and the B button for the third. You will then need to press in the direction indicated. For example, to enter the code for 1st to 7 Wins, you would press X three times, Y two times and B three times. Then press Left on the Directional pad.

EFFECT	CHEAT
Input More Codes	3 3 3 Right
Ignore Last Code	0 1 0 Down
1st to 7 Wins	3 2 3 Left
Win Fights For Goals	2 0 2 Left
No Crowd	2 1 0 Right
Show Hot Spot	2 0 1 Up
Show Shot Speed	1 0 1 Up
Rain	1 4 1 Left
Snow	1 2 1 Left

Big Puck	1 2 1 Up
Huge Puck	3 2 1 Up
Bulldozer Puck	2 1 2 Left
Hockey Ball	1 3 3 Left
Tennis Ball	1 3 2 Down
No Puck Out of Play	1 1 1 Down
Big Head Player	2 0 0 Right
Huge Head Player	3 0 0 Right
Big Head Team	2 2 0 Left
Huge Head Team	3 3 0 Left

EFFECT	CHEAT
Always Big Hits	2 3 4 Down
Late Hits	3 2 1 Down
Pinball Boards	4 2 3 Right
Domino Effect	0 1 2 Right

Turbo Boost	0 0 2 Up
Infinite Turbo	4 1 3 Right
No Fake Shots	4 2 4 Down
No One-Timers	2 1 3 Left
Skills Versus	2 2 2 Down
Hitz Time	1 0 4 Right

PIRATES:
THE LEGEND OF BLACK KAT

Enter the following codes during game play:

INVINCIBILITY FOR KATARINA
Hold L + R and press A, Y, Left thumbstick, B, Right thumbstick, Back, Right thumbstick, White, Black, X.

WIND DANCER INVINCIBILITY
Hold L + R and press Back, B, White, A, Right thumbstick, Black, X, Right thumbstick, Y, Left thumbstick.

INFINITE ITEMS
Hold L + R and press B, White, Back, Black, Right thumbstick, Left thumbstick, X, A, Right thumbstick, Y.

GOLD

Hold L + R and press B, Right thumbstick, White, X, A, Right thumbstick, Back, Left thumbstick, Y, Black.

KATARINA'S NEXT SWORD

Hold L + R and Right thumbstick, Back, Black, Left thumbstick, X, A, White, Y, Left thumbstick, B.

REVEAL BURIED TREASURE CHESTS

Hold L + R and press Y, A, X, B, White, Back, Left thumbstick, Black, Left thumbstick, Right thumbstick.

REVEAL TREASURE CHESTS

Hold L + R and Right thumbstick, A, B, Left thumbstick, Y, White, Back, Left thumbstick, X, Black.

ALL TREASURE CHEST KEYS

Hold L + R and press Y, Back, A, X, Right thumbstick, White, Left thumbstick, Black, B, Left thumbstick.

GALLEON

Hold L + R and press Black, B, Right thumbstick, Left thumbstick, A, X, Right thumbstick, Back, White, Y.

UNLIMITED WIND BOOST

Hold L + R and press Back, White, Right thumbstick, X, Left thumbstick, Y, Black, B, A, Left thumbstick.

ALTERNATE MUSIC

Hold L + R and press White, A, B, Black, X, Y, Left thumbstick, Back, Right thumbstick, Left thumbstick.

HIGH PITCHED VOICES

Hold L + R and Right thumbstick, Y, Back, A, Right thumbstick, B, White, X, Black, Left thumbstick.

KANE AS POISON STATUS

Hold L + R and press B, Black, White, X, Left thumbstick, A, Left thumbstick, Y, Right thumbstick, Back.

PROJECT GOTHAM RACING

ALL CARS AND COURSES

Enter your name as **Nosliw**.

RALLISPORT CHALLENGE

CLASSIC CLASS
Create a profile named **TheGoodStuff**.

EXPERT CLASS
Create a profile named **WheelToWheel**.

Expert Class

SPIDER-MAN THE MOVIE

UNLOCK EVERYTHING
Enter the code **ARACHNID**.

SMALL CHARACTER
Enter the code **SPIDERBYTE**.

BIG HEAD AND FEET
Enter the code **GOESTOYOURHEAD**.

BIG HEAD ENEMIES
Enter the code **JOELSPEANUTS**.

GOBLIN-STYLE COSTUME
Enter the code **FREAKOUT**.

MARY JANE
Enter the code **GIRLNEXTDOOR**.

SCIENTIST
Enter the code **SERUM**.

POLICE OFFICER
Enter the code **REALHERO**.

CAPTAIN STACEY
Enter the code **CAPTAINSTACEY**.

THE SHOCKER
Enter the code **HERMANSCHULTZ**.

Small Character

Scientist

THUG 1
Enter the code **KNUCKLES**.

THUG 2
Enter the code **STICKYRICE**.

THUG 3
Enter the code **THUGSRUS**.

UNLIMITED WEBBING
Enter the code **ORGANICWEBBING**.

ALL COMBAT CONTROLS
Enter the code **KOALA**.

MATRIX-STYLE ATTACKS
Enter the code **DODGETHIS**.

SUPER COOLANT
Enter the code **CHILLOUT**.

LEVEL SELECT
Enter the code **IMIARMAS**.

LEVEL SKIP
Enter the code **ROMITAS**. Pause the game and select Next Level to advance.

PINHEAD BOWLING TRAINING LEVEL
Enter the code **HEADEXPLODY**.

Pinhead Bowling

FIRST PERSON VIEW
Enter the code **UNDERTHEMASK**.

SPYHUNTER

ORIGINAL SPY HUNTER
Enter **OGSPY** as your name.

SSX TRICKY

MIX MASTER MIKE
At the main menu, hold L + R and press A, A, Right, A, A, Down, A, A, Left, A, A, Up. Pick anybody, and he/she will be replaced by Mix Master Mike.

MALLORA OUTFIT AND BOARD FOR ELISE
At the main menu, hold L + R and press A, A, Right, B, B, Down, Y, Y, Left, X, X, Up.

Mix Master Mike

STAR WARS: OBI-WAN

ALL LEVELS

Select New Game and enter **greytherat** as your name.

STAR WARS: STARFIGHTER SPECIAL EDITION

Unlock Everything

Enter **EUROPA** as a code.

BONUS FEATURE

Enter **NOHUD** as a code.

REVERSE CONTROLS

Enter **JARJAR** as a code.

DIRECTOR MODE

Enter **DIRECTOR** as a code.

Director Mode

SHIP GALLERY

Enter **SHIPS** as a code.

CONCEPT ART

Enter **PLANETS** as a code.

MORE CONCEPT ART

Enter **HEROES** as a code.

More Concept Art

SIMON DAY

Enter **SIMON** as a code.

VIEW CREDITS

Enter **CREDITS** as a code.

THE SIMPSONS ROAD RAGE

HIDDEN CHARACTERS

Set the system date to the following to open the secret characters:

DATE	CHARACTER
Jan 1	Happy New Year Krusty the Klown
Oct 31	Happy Halloween Bart
Nov 22, 2001, Nov 28,2002	Happy Thanksgiving Marge
Dec 25	Merry Christmas Apu

2D CHARACTERS

At the options screen, hold L + R and press X, X, X, X.

SMITHERS

At the options screen, hold L + R and press B, B, Y, Y.

NUCLEAR BUS

At the options screen, hold L + R and press B, B, Y, A.

MONEY

At the options screen, hold L + R and press Y, Y, Y, Y.

NEW CAMERAS

At the options screen, hold L + R and press B, B, B, B.

NIGHT MODE

At the options screen, hold L + R and press A, A, A, A.

TONY HAWK'S PRO SKATER 2X

ALL CHEATS

Pause the game, hold the Left Trigger, and then enter **SATURDAY BABY**, where "T" equals the White button. The screen shakes when entered correctly.

TONY HAWK'S PRO SKATER 3

ALL MOVIES
Enter the code **ROLLIT**.

TRANSWORLD SURF

BONUS BOARD
During a game press Back, Up, Down, Left, Right, Left, Up.

SHARK SURFBOARD
During a game press Back, Up, Down, Left, Right, Right, Down.

FULL SPECIAL METER
During a game press Back, Up, Down, Left, Right, Down, Up.

DIFFERENT COLORS
During gameplay, press Back, Up, Down, Left, Right, Down, Left.

GREEN SURF
During a game press Back, Up, Down, Left, Right, Up, Left.

NO HUD
During a game press Back, D-Up, D-Down, D-Left, D-Right, D-Up, D-Right.

DISABLE CODES
During a game press Back, Back, Back, Back.

DREAMCAST®

GAME BOY® ADVANCE

DOOM ©2001 Id Software, Inc. All Rights Reserved. Published and distributed by Activision Publishing, Inc. under license. Developed by David A. Palmer Productions.

EARTHWORM JIM © 2001 Interplay Entertainment Corp. All rights reserved.

F-14 TOMCAT © 2001 MAJESCO, INC.

FIREPRO WRESTLING © 2001 Spike

GRADIUS GALAXIES is a trademark of KONAMI CORPORATION. © 1985 2001 KONAMI & Mobile21 Co., Ltd. ALL RIGHTS RESERVED.

GT ADVANCE CHAMPIONSHIP RACING — Game & Software © 2001 MTO Inc. Exclusively licensed to & distributed by THQ Inc.

IRIDION 3D is a registered trademark of Majesco Sales, Inc. All rights reserved. © 2001 Majesco Sales, Inc.

JURASSIC PARK 3: PARK BUILDER Jurassic Park III is a trademark and copyright of Universal Studios and Amblin Entertainment, Inc. Licensed by Universal Studios Licensing, Inc. All rights reserved. The copyright to the code used to create this electronic videogame belongs to Konami Corporation. ©2001 KONAMI

LEGO BIONICLE: TALES OF THE TOHUNGA ©2001 The Lego Group. ©Lego is a trademark of the lego group. Developed by Saffire Corporation.

MEN IN BLACK: THE SERIES Game Design and Program © 2001 Crave Entertainment, Inc. All Rights Reserved. Men In Black: The Series © 2001 Columbia Pictures Industries, Inc. & Adelaide Productions, Inc.

MONSTERS INC. © 2001 Disney/Pixar THQ and its logo are trademarks and/or registered trademarks of THQ Inc. All Rights Reserved.

NFL BLITZ 20-02 © 2001 Midway Home Entertainment, Inc. All rights reserved.

PAC-MAN COLLECTION ™ & © 2001 Namco Ltd., All Rights Reserved.

PITFALL-THE MAYAN ADVENTURE © 1994, 2001 Activision, Inc. All rights reserved.

POWER RANGERS TIME FORCE © 2001 THQ Inc. ™ and © 2001 Saban.

RAYMAN ADVANCE © 2001 UBI SOFT Entertainment

READY 2 RUMBLE BOXING: ROUND 2 © 2000 Midway Home Entertainment Inc. All rights reserved.

ROCKET POWER: DREAM SCHEME © 2001 Viacom International. All rights reserved.

RUGRATS: CASTLE CAPERS © 2001 Viacom International Inc. All rights reserved.

"THE SCORPION KING: SWORD OF OSIRIS" interactive game © 2002 Universal Interactive, Inc. The Scorpion King and related characters are TM and © of Universal Studios. Licensed by Universal Studios Licensing, Inc. All rights reserved.

SPIDER-MAN: MYSTERIO'S MENACE ™ & © 2001 Marvel Characters, Inc. All Rights Reserved. © 2001 Activision, Inc. and its affiliates.

SPYRO: SEASON OF ICE © 2001 Universal Interactive, Inc.

STAR WARS: JEDI POWER BATTLES © 2002 LucasArts Entertainment Company LLC. © 2002 Lucasfilm Ltd. & TM or ® as indicated. All rights reserved.

TETRIS WORLDS © 2001 THQ

WILD THORNBERRYS: CHIMP CHASE © 2001 Viacom International Inc. All rights reserved.

GAME BOY® COLOR

102 DALMATIONS: PUPPIES TO THE RESCUE developed by Disney Interactive/Crystal Dynamics/Digital Eclipse, published by Activision. All rights reserved.

ACTION MAN ©2001 Infogrames Interactive, Inc. All Rights Reserved Used With Permission ©2001 THQ Inc. All Rights Reserved.

ARMY MEN 2 ©2001 The 3DO Company All rights reserved.

ARMY MEN: AIR COMBAT ©2001 The 3DO Company All rights reserved.

ARMY MEN: SARGE'S HEROES 2 ©2001 The 3DO Company All rights reserved.

BLADE developed by HAL Corp. and Avit Inc., published by Activision. All rights reserved.

BUFFY THE VAMPIRE SLAYER © 2000 Twentieth Century Fox Film Corporation. All Rights Reserved. Published and distributed by THQ Inc. © 2000 THQ Inc. All Rights Reserved.

CHICKEN RUN © 2000 THQ Inc. All Rights Reserved.

DAVE MIRRA FREESTYLE BMX™ Developed By Z-Axis. Acclaim ®, Dave Mirra Freestyle Bmx™ And Acclaim Max Sports TM & ©2000 Acclaim Entertainment, Inc. All Rights Reserved

DEXTER'S LABORATORY: ROBOT RAMPAGE © 2001 BAM! Entertainment. DEXTER'S LABO-RATORY is a trademark of Cartoon Network © 2000.

DONALD DUCK: GOIN' QUACKERS developed and published by Ubi Soft. All rights reserved.

DRIVER ©2000 Infogrames Entertainment S.A. All Rights Reserved.

INSPECTOR GADGET © 2001 Ubi Soft

JEREMY MCGRATH SUPERCROSS 2000 © 2000 Acclaim Entertainment, Inc.

M&M'S MINIS MADNESS © 2000 Majesco Sales, Inc. All rights reserved.

MAT HOFFMAN'S PRO BMX © 2001 Activision Inc. and its affiliates. All rights reserved.

MEN IN BLACK: THE SERIES 2 ™ © 2000 Columbia Pictures Industries, Inc. & Adelaide Productions, Inc. All rights reserved. Published by Crave Entertainment, Inc. © 2000 Crave Entertainment, Inc.

MEN IN BLACK: THE SERIES™ 2 ©2000 Columbia Pictures Industries, Inc. & Adelaide Productions, Inc. All rights reserved. Trademark: MEN IN BLACK™ Columbia Pictures Industries, Inc. Published by Crave Entertainment, Inc. ©2000 Crave Entertainment, Inc.

WENDY: EVERY WITCH WAY © 2001 Harvey Entertainment, Inc. Wendy, its logos, names and related indicia are trademarks of Harvey Entertainment, Inc. All Rights Reserved. Wendy : Every Witch Way TM & © 2001 TDK Mediactive, Inc. All Rights Reserved.

WWF BETRAYAL Betrayal Game and Software © 2001 THQ/JAKKS Pacific, LLC. World Wrestling Federation, its logos and all character likenesses are trademarks of World Wrestling Federation Entertainment, Inc. © 2001 World Wrestling Federation Entertainment, Inc. All Rights Reserved.

X-MEN: MUTANT ACADEMY Marvel Comics, X-MEN ™ & ©2000 Marvel Characters, Inc. All rights reserved. Activision is a registered trademark of Activision, Inc. ©2000 Activision, Inc.

X-MEN: MUTANT WARS X-MEN ™ & © 2000 Marvel Characters, Inc. ©2000 Activision, Inc. All Rights Reserved.

X-MEN: WOLVERINE'S RAGE developed by Digital Eclipse, published by Activision. All rights reserved.

XTREME SPORTS published by Infogrames. All rights reserved.

GAMECUBE™

GameCube™ is a trademark of Nintendo of America. All rights reserved. © 2001 Nintendo.

CRAZY TAXI © SEGA 1999, 2000. Acclaim® & © 2001 Acclaim Entertainment, Inc. Distributed by Acclaim Distribution. All Rights Reserved.

DAVE MIRRA FREESTYLE BMX 2 © 2001 Acclaim Entertainment, Inc. All rights reserved.

NHL HITZ 20-02 ©2001 Midway Home Entertainment Inc.

THE SIMPSONS ROAD RAGE © 2001 Twentieth Century Fox Film Corporation. All rights reserved. Fox Interactive, The Simpsons and their associated logos are trademarks of Twentieth Century Fox Film Corporation.

TONY HAWK'S PRO SKATER 3 © 1999-2001 Activision, Inc. and its affiliates. Published and distributed by Activision Publishing, Inc. Activision is a registered trademark and Activision O2, Tony Hawk's Pro Skater and Pro Skater are trademarks of Activision, Inc. and its affiliates. All rights reserved.

XGII EXTREME G RACING © 2002 Acclaim Entertainment, Inc. All rights reserved.

NINTENDO 64®

PLAYSTATION®

SNO-CROSS CHAMPIONSHIP RACING ® 2000 UDS. Published and distributed by Crave Entertainment, Inc. All rights reserved.

SPIDER-MAN 2: ENTER ELECTRO: MARVEL and Spider-man: TM and © 2001 Marvel Characters, Inc. All rights reserved. Published and distributed by Activision, Inc. and its affiliates. Activision is a registered trademark of Activision, Inc and its affiliates. Developed by Vicarious Visions. All rights reserved.

TONY HAWK'S PRO SKATER 2 is a trademark of Activision, Inc. © 2000 Activision, Inc and its affiliates. Tony Hawk is a trademark of Tony Hawk. All rights reserved.

X-MEN MUTANT ACADEMY 2 © 2001 Activision, Inc. All rights reserved.

PLAYSTATION® 2

PlayStation®2 is a registered trademark of Sony Computer Entertainment Inc. PlayStation and the PlayStation2 logos are registered trademarks of Sony Computer Entertainment Inc.

18-WHEELER AMERICAN PRO TRUCKER created by and produced by SEGA. Converted, Published and Distributed by Acclaim. Sega and 18 Wheeler are either registered trademarks or trademarks of Sega Corporation.

4X4 EVOLUTION © 2001 Terminal Reality, Inc.

ARCTIC THUNDER © 2001 Midway Home Entertainment Inc.

ARMY MEN RTS © 2002 The 3DO Company. All rights reserved.

ATV OFFROAD FURY© 2001 Sony Computer Entertainment America Inc. Developed by Rainbow Studios.

BATMAN VENGEANCE © 2001 Ubi Soft Entertainment is a trademark of Ubi Soft Inc. Ubi Soft and the Ubi Soft Entertainment logo are registred trademarks of Ubi Soft Inc. All rights reserved. BATMAN and all related characters, names and indicia are trademarks of DC Comics © 2001.

CART FURY © 2001 Midway Home Entertainment Inc.

CRAZY TAXI™ Created by and Produced by SEGA. Converted, Published and distributed by Acclaim. © SEGA 1999, 2000. SEGA and CRAZY TAXI are registered trademarks or trademarks of Sega Corporation. Acclaim® & © 2001 Acclaim Entertainment, Inc. All rights reserved.

CRASH BANDICOOT: THE WRATH OF CORTEX interactive game © 2001 Universal Interactive Studios, Inc. Crash Bandicoot and related characters TM and © Universal Interactive Studios, Inc. All rights reserved.

DAVE MIRRA FREESTYLE BMX 2 © 2001 Acclaim Entertainment, Inc. All rights reserved.

DRAKAN: THE ANCIENTS GATES © 2001 Sony Computer Entertainment America Inc. All rights reserved.

LEGAL

XBOX™

SECRET CODES 2002, VOLUME 2

Brady Publishing

An Imprint of Pearson Education
201 West 103rd Street
Indianapolis, Indiana 46290

ISBN: 0-7440-0169-2

Library of Congress Catalog No.: 2002135664

Printing Code: The rightmost double-digit number is the year of the book's printing; the rightmost single-digit number is the number of the book's printing. For example, 02-1 shows that the first printing of the book occurred in 2002.

05 04 03 02   4 3 2 1

Manufactured in the United States of America.

BRADYGAMES STAFF

Publisher	**DAVID WAYBRIGHT**
Editor-In-Chief	**H. LEIGH DAVIS**
Creative Director	**ROBIN LASEK**
Marketing Manager	**JANET ESHENOUR**
Licensing Manager	**MIKE DEGLER**
Assistant Marketing Manager	**SUSIE NIEMAN**

CREDITS

Senior Project Editor	**KEN SCHMIDT**
Project Editor	**CHRISTIAN SUMNER**
Screenshot Editor	**MICHAEL OWEN**
Book Designer	**KURT OWENS**
Production Designer	**TRACY WEHMEYER**

HARVEST

ııı ROB POBI

SIMON & SCHUSTER CANADA

New York London Toronto Sydney New Delhi

Simon & Schuster Canada
A Division of Simon & Schuster, Inc.
166 King Street East, Suite 300
Toronto, Ontario M5A 1J3

This Simon & Schuster Canada edition January 2015

SIMON & SCHUSTER CANADA and colophon are registered
trademarks of Simon & Schuster, Inc.

For information about special discounts for bulk purchases,
please contact Simon & Schuster Special Sales at 1-800-268-3216
or CustomerService@simonandschuster.ca.

Interior design: Lewelin Polanco
Cover design: PGB
Cover image: Shutterstock

Manufactured in the United States of America

3 5 7 9 10 8 6 4 2

ISBN 978-1-4767-2878-0
ISBN 978-1-4767-2872-8 (ebook)

It is an illusion that youth is happy, an illusion of those who have lost it. . . . [The young] must discover for themselves that all they have read and all they have been told are lies, lies, lies; and each discovery is another nail driven into the body on the cross of life.

—W. Somerset Maugham, *Of Human Bondage*, 1915

It is impossible to suffer without making someone pay for it.

—Friedrich Nietzsche, unpublished fragment from
Thus Spake Zarathustra, 1883–1885

HARVEST

TYLER ROCHESTER enjoyed walking home from school alone; it was a hard-won privilege that had taken negotiation and persistence. Of course, his parents had insisted on a few conditions—which he was old enough to know was just a fancy word for *rules*—but in the end he had won his independence. And any ten-year-old will tell you that independence is almost as good as cake—the kind with sprinkles.

Tyler was on his way home from the Damien Whitney Academy for Boys on the Upper East Side. Summer break was only a few days away and the city already felt like it was on fire so he allowed himself the luxury of opening the buttons of his school jacket. He also wanted to open his collar but he had spent a lot of time getting his tie just right, with a perfect knot, like Tom Cruise had done in that old movie *Mission: Impossible*.

The taxi dropped him off a block from his home. Tyler stopped for a Coke at the deli, taking a can from the fridge by the fruit stand. He paid the man at the register with his debit card and walked out into the heat.

Tyler Rochester never made it home.

Tyler Rochester had just become a statistic.

||| T W O

THE SUN was dropping over the Jersey shore, staining the atmosphere with the orange of late afternoon. The day had been cloudless and only the vapor trails over Newark marred the perfect blue of the sky. The wind was dead and the Hudson was in one of those rare states where it looked like a gently rolling field of dark, heavy oil. Manhattan, stretching ahead and to the left, glowed in the last breath of the afternoon.

Alexandra Hemingway made good time, the swing and grip of the paddle pushing her south, the tide donating a little extra speed. Every time her right arm came up, her shoulder blade clicked, a keepsake from David Shea.

The water headed out to sea, pulled by the unstoppable schedule of the moon. Today the garbage wasn't too bad—mostly the mundane detritus of coffee cups and plastic bags—but every now and then she had come across some pretty grim things in the water. Anyone who spent time on the river had. When she worked days, she'd often have an early-morning coffee with the rowers from Columbia; their superstition was that the season didn't officially start until they came across a body in the water. Business as usual in the Big Apple.

She had crossed under the George Washington Bridge a few minutes back and the further downstream she went, the greater her speed became. The GPS hooked onto her vest clocked her at nearly three knots faster than she had been just ten blocks back. As the outflow of the Hudson sluiced between New York and New Jersey, it picked up a lot of speed, the faster troughs sometimes moving at twenty-five knots down near Battery Park. To offset the heavy pull of the water she stayed close to shore. Inexperienced kayakers sometimes found themselves washed out past Red Hook and under the Verrazano—not the way she wanted to spend a Monday night.

She had grown up on the waves, her first solo foray out on Long Island Sound in the Laser her father bought her for her tenth birthday. Her passion for the sea had deepened with each new year until now, at thirty-seven, it felt like an integral part of her own biology. She was out here every night before her shift, rain or shine, pounding the water. It wasn't just a way to keep her body from atrophy, it was one of the few places where she could be alone—a near miracle in a city of thirteen million people.

And other than the morning Mank had been killed, she couldn't remember a time when she had needed to be alone in her own headspace as much as now.

Today wasn't about grief, at least not technically. But that morning the little stick had turned blue; then the clear solution in the comparative bottles had turned blue; and finally the meter had registered a plus sign. By the time she had chewed open the box of the fourth off-the-shelf home test, she was going through the motions out of nothing more than morbid curiosity.

She had squeezed in an emergency appointment with Dr. Sparks for confirmation. She was *with child*, in the parlance of Hester Prynne's time. *Knocked up*, as Phelps would say. *And out of work*, as her boss would soon be telling her.

She made the nearly hundred blocks from the GWB to the 79th Street boat basin in a little less than sixteen minutes, not a record in her scull but good time in the clumsy kayak. She was tall, a little over six feet, and she found most kayaks uncomfortable. Even though this was only her second run with the new fifteen footer, it already felt like an old friend—a good sign.

When she paddled into the marina, the carbon monoxide migration on the West Side Highway was clogged to walking speed in both directions; rush hour had started and people were heading home to suppers of booze, antacid, and reruns of *The Simpsons*.

Hemingway pulled up to the launch, took off her Ray-Bans, and hopped out into the mid-thigh water. It felt like it looked—warm and heavy. She removed the wheels from the mount holes on the back of the Prowler, lifted the stern, and placed the support posts into the scupper holes. Then she pushed the kayak up the slope to her truck.

———

Hemingway pulled the Suburban off the southbound West Side Highway, wove through the Tetris-like traffic blocking the intersection, and barreled east on 27th. She hit the brakes at a red light on the corner of 11th and the truck slid on the condensation that beaded the asphalt, coming to rest at a slight cant. The moon roof and windows were open and humidity misted the leather steering wheel. She thought about running the light to get the air flowing again but didn't want to get pulled over by a cop—things like that were bad for business. So she waited.

Two kids ambled across the lane. Gangly teens in the standard-issue streetwear of the uninventive: low-slung jeans, old-school Run DMCs without laces, caps locked on sideways. One wore a Knicks jacket, the other was in a Yankees jersey. It was too hot for the heavy clothing and Hemingway found herself pitying their need to conform. They had that loose-legged walk that speaks volumes to street kids. They crossed in front of her bumper, close enough that a pant leg brushed the fiberglass. The one in the Knicks jacket gave the kayak on the roof rack a once-over. He said something to his friend who turned back, his eyes sliding over the hood, past the windshield, to the top of the truck, as if he were staring at a spaceship.

Hemingway reached for the MP3 player, cranked the volume, and Andrew W.K. told her that it was time to party hard.

There was a shadow at the edge of her vision that set off a flash in her circuitry; before instinct converted to action the warm end of a muzzle pressed against her cheek.

"Out of the car, bitch," the voice behind the pistol said.

The flicker of the second guy pulsed in the rearview mirror, heading for the passenger's door.

She took her hands off the wheel in an *I'll-do-whatever-you-say* gesture that she punctuated by pounding down on the gas.

The big SUV lurched forward, tires screaming. There was a brief snap of time where the muzzle slid back and away from her cheek and she reached up for the wrist holding the pistol. She pounded down on the brake pedal with both feet, throwing her shoulders back into the seat.

The truck bucked and she slammed the wrist down into the doorframe. There was a snap of bone and the roar of the engine was overridden by a scream as the kid flew forward.

His pistol bounced off the dash and ricocheted into the back-seat. There was a single panic-stricken flash of teeth, then he spilled forward with another howl. She hit the gas and something solid thumped under her wheel and the truck jolted. Before the back wheel finished what the front hadn't, she stopped the SUV and tumbled out of the cab with her pistol clasped tightly in both hands.

The kid was sprawled out by the back tire, his leg twisted under the truck. His foot looked like someone had unscrewed it. Bones poked through the cuff of his jeans like pale splintered roots. His shoe lay ten feet away.

She spun her head, looking for the second kid. Traffic had stopped fifty feet back, silhouettes behind windshields dropping below dashboards.

Through the windows of the SUV she saw the second target coming up on the back right fender. A little chrome .32 glinted in his fist.

She crab scrambled sideways and stood up with her pistol leveled at the bumper he'd have to come around. She stepped back from the sweet spot in four long strides, bringing her sight up to adjust for the increased distance. When she reached the apex of the curve, and the barrel began to drop, she stopped. Held her stance. He rounded the back bumper, aiming too low; she was fifteen feet beyond where he expected her to be.

"Freeze, idiot," she said.

But he went for it.

She squeezed the trigger once and he doubled over and somersaulted in a single disjointed cartwheel, capped off with a high-pitched screech. His pistol clattered to the pavement under the cyclopic gaze of the traffic signal a few feet away. He hit the asphalt and his hands went to his groin. Someone to her right honked.

Hemingway stepped forward to the kid under the truck. He had crawled from beneath the frame and was gasping for breath, like a boated fish. She raised the pistol to his face. "You want it in the head or the heart?" She lowered her sights to the middle of his chest with the second part of the question. It did not sound rhetorical.

The kid looked up, barking out a plea between his jackhammer breaths. "No . . . please . . . Miss . . . I didn't . . . mean . . . no . . ."

Behind her, the low grunt of a wounded animal and the sound of a body dragging itself over asphalt. Metal scraping on street.

She turned.

Crotch-shot had crawled to his automatic, a black smear shimmering in his wake. He had wrapped his bloody fingers around the grip and was trying to lift it off the pavement. His arm moved as if he were suspended in acrylic; the gun looked welded to the road.

"Hey, fuckface," she said, and circled around the car, coming up on the kid's flank in her long-legged stride, gearing it up to a run.

She came at him from his left and he didn't see her coming; his attention was nailed to the pistol. She kicked the cap gun out of his hand and threw her foot into the wreckage that used to be his testicles.

He howled and puked a supper of what could only be beer and nachos all over his jacket. He collapsed back onto the pavement with a thud. It sounded like he cracked his skull.

Hemingway stood in the middle of the street, over the vomit-covered kid. She looked back at the one with the broken wrist and Captain Ahab foot. Then she checked her watch: her shift started in a few minutes. Someone honked again.

"You assholes made me late for work," she said to no one in particular. Then she pulled out her phone and dialed 911. "I should shoot you just for that."

A couple of tourists on the corner had their cell phones jabbed skyward in the universal YouTube salute. Hemingway raised her arm as if to wave. Then she smiled and gave them the finger.

III THREE

HEMINGWAY CLIMBED the steps in morose silence, wondering what she had done to deserve an attempted carjacking. The Suburban was ten years old and not particularly valuable, which was why she used it in the city, so what had that been about? It had to be the kayak. But those kids wouldn't know where to sell a kayak anymore than they would know where to sell weapons-grade plutonium. Maybe it was the heat. It was like the surface of the sun outside and the humidity was floating somewhere around a hundred percent—with conditions like that it wouldn't take much to set off the crazies in the city of the dead.

She thought that she had changed her karma or juju or whatever they were calling it these days. But it looked to be just more of the same: old-fashioned bad luck. It had started when Mankiewicz had been killed and for some reason hadn't let go. Not in three years.

Part of her thought that maybe it was some sort of Faustian bargain that she wasn't aware of—the bad-luck payoff for an unremembered wish. Only she had never asked for a thing. Except for Claire to come back when she was twelve. And then, twenty-two years later, the strength to walk into Shea's and finish what Mankiewicz had started. Not much in the way of a wish list. Not really.

The fates had given her Shea. And his men. When she had been done, four of them were dead and Shea was squirming around on the terra-cotta in his own blood and shit. She had stood over him while her chest made a weird sucking sound. She had raised the pistol, looked into the two rivets of fear that were his eyes, and scooped his brains out with her .357.

Of course it had all been captured by the surveillance cameras and there had never been any charges because video didn't lie.

Nicky, Shea's right-hand man, had put one into her shoulder as soon as she had gone in. She didn't remember much after that, except that she had shot at everything that had moved and more than a few things that hadn't. When it was all done, there were five dead men on the floor and walls and Hemingway had turned and walked out onto the sidewalk with only that weird whistling coming from somewhere in her body to let her know she was not yet dead.

The sucking chest wound was louder than the whine of the approaching sirens and when she stepped into the sun she realized that the side of her face was lit up with 50,000 volts of pain. She tried to open her mouth and all she heard was a scream that she was sure had come from somewhere deep inside.

She sat down on the curb, leaned up against a garbage can and stared down at the pair of pistols in her hands. Then she passed out with her shield hanging from her neck on a length of bloody chain.

When she woke up in the hospital, the shield was still

there but half her left lung and a portion of one shoulder blade was gone. Along with a whole lot of blood.

The first thing the doctor said was that her golf swing would never be the same. She tried to tell him that the only time she had held a club was when she had smashed Skippy Cooper's hand with a Callaway driver when he had tried to feel her up in the pro shop on the night of her sixteenth birthday. But when she had tried to open her mouth, she heard that scream again.

Someone—ballistics had never been able to figure out who, exactly—had put a round into her jaw. It had shattered most of the left ramus—a scratch that sixteen hours of reconstructive surgery and some titanium hardware had managed to correct; she hid a lot of the scar tissue with a pageboy haircut that added a little extra architecture to her already angular features. She had only lost one tooth, now replaced with a nice porcelain implant. But it had taken eleven weeks for the damage to heal to the point where she could chew bananas. Three more months until she was able to speak properly.

When she had finally walked out of Flushing Presbyterian she had a lunch box full of narcotics to help her deal with her repaired body; apparently sedated animals were easier to handle. She had walked away with remarkably few scars—a shiny fifteen-inch strip down her sternum where they had cracked her ribs; four melted patches of skin where lead had burrowed into her flesh; an extra angle to her jaw. She dumped the pills down the toilet when she got home—she had never been a big believer in crutches and she wasn't about to start. She hadn't taken so much as aspirin since. Fuck the doctors. And the five men who had tried to put her in the ground with Mank.

She made the top of the steps, walked into the detective's office, and the room erupted in cheers.

"Nice shooting, Hemi," Papandreou hollered from the far end.

"Did you have to get the guy in the nutsack?" Lincoln asked. "You're already on the Interweb—you flipped the bird at two German tourists."

"At least I smiled at them." And she went to her office.

Phelps was at his desk, his big feet up on the beaten oak, fingers knitted together on top of his head. "Hey, Hem, you okay?" He was trying to sound casual but she recognized concern in his tone. The father of two boys, she always felt she filled the space of de facto daughter in his life.

"You really worried?"

Phelps smiled, shook his head. "Not about you. But the kid you shot in the pills is another thing."

She shrugged and sat down. "It seemed like a good idea at the time."

"Yeah, well, don't it always?" Phelps dropped his feet to the floor, reached forward and picked up a mug with a happy face on the side. Took a sip. "You hungry?" he asked.

"Do you have to ask?"

Phelps stood up and fed one thick arm through a jacket sleeve. "Let's go get us some food."

———

They sat in their usual booth at the back of Bernie's. The diner was the best place in the neighborhood for sandwiches and coffee and its proximity to the precinct had made it a recession-proof success since 1921. At any given moment—night or day—there were a dozen cops sprinkled around the place, reading papers, writing notes, or simply avoiding going home to bad marriages.

Hemingway was downing the last bits of a chopped steak with mashed potatoes, peas, and gravy while Phelps looked on, astounded. "You know, Hemi, I been eating with you for almost seven years now and I still can't wrap my brain around how much food you can shovel away."

"*Shovel away*?" She smiled over a forkful of peas. "You're smooth with the compliments, Jon."

"I'm not kidding." Phelps shook his head. "In the Marines I never seen a guy eat like you. And there were some big motherfuckers in the war. That was back before they let chicks into the forces. At least in combat positions."

Hemingway washed the peas down with a slug of coffee and pushed her empty plate to the edge of the table. "Yeah, well, now they give us guns and shoes and the right to vote. It's a brave new world out there. The times they are a-changin'."

"Don't steal my generation's music, too."

It was then that her phone rang. She wiped her mouth with a napkin and answered with her usual, "Hemingway."

Michael Desmond, the dispatcher for the detective squads, identified himself. Then he told her what had happened.

She felt the chopped steak twitch in her guts. "Jesus. Sure. We'll be there in ten minutes."

When she hung up, Phelps was already on his feet. "Where we goin'?"

"East River Park."

"Who we got?"

She pulled a wallet out of her jacket. "Dead kid."

"Sure it's a murder?"

"Unless he chopped off his own feet, yeah."

THE BONES of the bridge filled the sky overhead and reflected off the windshield as Hemingway rolled past the police barrier. A uniformed officer in a yellow traffic vest waved her through the utility gate and she parked the Suburban on the grass at the edge of a small park under the shadow of the Queensboro. They sat in silence for a few seconds, each going through a personal checklist of preflight preparations. After a few ticks of the clock the internal monologues were done and they stepped out onto the manicured green.

The circus was in full swing on both sides of the yellow tape. Joggers took photos with their cell phones, excited that something was happening to break the monotony of the health train. A handful of news crews had set up camp at the tapelines on either end of the path, chattering into the cameras like pageant contestants, rictus grins and polished hair competing with non sequiturs for attention. The reporters were almost shouting to be heard over the traffic of the FDR a few yards away. Two of the borough's big forensic RVs were parked nose to nose, blocking off any chance of an errant camera—cell phone or news variety—from converting death into entertainment.

They headed for the Jacob's Ladder pulse of the photographer's flash behind the RVs, ignoring the white-haloed forms of the newspeople bottlenecked at either end of the footpath. The esplanade felt weird without joggers whipping by or Rollerbladers barking *Coming through!* They stepped off the thin strip of asphalt that cut through the imposed green space and Hemingway spotted a stone on the ground. She reached down, picked it up. It was smooth, the size of a robin's egg. She slipped it into her pocket.

Phelps watched her, used to the ritual, then headed toward the screens. "When you gonna get tired of doing your Virginia Woolf imitation?"

They walked the rest of the way in silence.

The boy lay on a tarp, eyes pointed at the sky, chin on chest, the pose reminiscent of Caravaggio's Crucifixion of St. Peter—only there was no tension in the muscles, no flex in the little neck. His clothes were filthy and ripped and stuck to his flesh, one jacketed arm under the railing, reaching for the East River. Queens beyond. He wore a school jacket and tie. His feet were gone.

Dr. Marcus was down on one space-suited knee, practicing his arcane arts on the child. Unblinking. Unmoving. A photographer moved around the tarp, snapping frames. Marcus looked up, nodded an unhappy greeting, and turned back to the body.

Someone came out of the darkness between the privacy screen and the RV and the eerie strobe of the photographer's flash gave the shape a jittery, unhealthy cadence. Three steps later it morphed into Walter Afonia—an old-timer doing the tail end of forty years at the Seventh, most of it in the detective squad.

"Hemingway, Phelps," he said in way of a greeting, then nodded at the boy on the plastic. "Kid's name was Tyler Rochester. Some jogger found him about a half an hour ago."

"The jogger?" Phelps asked.

"Dentist. Name's Zachary Gizbert. He was out here doing ankle training—whatever the fuck that means—and found the kid. Called it in on his phone and a car was here in a little over four minutes. A pair of patrolmen from the Ninth pulled the kid from the drink. He was against one of the pilings to the utility bridge." He nodded at the world beyond the screens. "Gizbert's back at the station giving a statement. Guy shit himself." Afonia paused, waiting for someone to crack a smile or tell a joke or cry. No one did. He continued with the same flat tone that had gotten them to this point. "Kid was dumped upriver. Tide's been going out for three hours."

Hemingway turned to Dr. Marcus. "What's TOD?"

Marcus looked up, nodded. "Two, two and a half hours."

Afonia moved in beside Marcus and looked down at the kid. "Tyler here made a call from his cell phone at six twenty-one to tell the housekeeper he was on his way home. He took a taxi up Fifth. Got off at the corner, stopped at a deli for a Coke. Paid for the cab and the soda with his debit card. Stepped back out onto the street and off the grid."

Hemingway stared down at the child, her interpretive software trying to convert the image of the dead boy into some sort of approachable geometry. "What about his cell phone?"

Afonia nodded like he was just getting to that. "Wasn't in his pockets. Good guess would be the bottom of the East River. If it's not, it's turned off."

"Anything unusual about the body?" she asked.

Afonia shrugged. "Someone took his feet off."

Hemingway looked off into the water washing by, thinking of kayaking on the other side of Manhattan a few hours back. The boy had been alive then. Now he wasn't. All in a few short hours.

Afonia looked down at the kid for a second. Then he swallowed and turned away from the body. "All I know is he disappeared sometime after buying a Coke at six forty-three p.m. and less than three hours later he washes up here. Kid's family lives up near you. You want this case, you can have it." Afonia fished around in his pocket, his hand coming out with a pack of Parliament Menthols. He offered one to each of them, then excused himself for a smoke in the darkness beyond the privacy screens.

Hemingway crouched down on her haunches beside the medical examiner. He didn't bother looking over; for him, a crime scene was not a place of greeting, it was a place of solemnity.

Clear polyethylene bags were secured over the boy's hands with cable ties. Inside the foggy plastic his fingers looked scrubbed and clean, in direct contrast to the filthy clothing and matted, tangled hair that knotted on his forehead. Tyler Rochester had been a good-looking kid who would probably have grown up into a handsome man. Only now he would stay ten forever.

After a few silent moments of magic with a black light, the ME said, "His feet were removed by a saw of some sort. Small, serrated blade. Not a bow saw. Something smaller. Hacksaw most probably." Then he leaned in and pointed at the boy's left eyeball. "There's a small puncture through the sclera, right here. I'm guessing premortem but it might have happened in the river. I'll have a better idea once I have the body back in the lab. Right now, that's all I can give you."

Hemingway looked out across the river, to the lights of

Queens on the other side, dappled with the unblinking eyes of apartment windows. Over there it looked alive. She turned back to the dead boy. Then to the medical examiner. "Defensive wounds?"

"His nails look pretty clean but I'll know a lot more when I get the swabs under a scope. Other than his feet there aren't any signs of a struggle."

The feet were enough.

Marcus stood up and pulled off his latex gloves. "The first cuts are tentative, unaligned. After an inch he hit his stride and did a clean job. But the killer didn't have any practical knowledge of anatomy. The cuts are too high—he went through the bottom flange of the tibia. Half an inch lower and he would have missed both the tibia and talus—it's mostly cartilage and it's a lot easier to saw through.

"I'll have blood work and a tox screen in a few hours. Come see me in three hours." He dropped his eyes to the stumps of the boy's legs, one sticking out of a cuff that the river had not been able to rinse of blood.

Afonia came back in.

"You can go home. We're taking the case."

Afonia blinked once then nodded. "I thought you would."

She turned to Phelps, "Call Papandreou and have him put a list together." She nodded at the dead boy without taking her eyes from Phelps. "Anyone who's walked. Countrywide."

The big cop reached for his phone. "Released in the last six months?"

"Make it twelve," she said, "I don't want to miss this guy because he controlled himself for six months and a day."

THE ROCHESTERS lived in a remodeled brownstone that had everything new money could buy. The home vibrated with the comings and goings of busy people.

A wiry man sporting a well-tailored suit and the fluid movements of a street fighter ushered Hemingway and Phelps into the library. He stood at the door as if an invisible fence prevented him from entering the space and introduced himself as Benoit. Then he told them that the Rochesters would be with them in a few minutes and asked if they wanted anything to drink. Phelps waved it away. Hemingway asked for a Perrier. Benoit disappeared.

Phelps finished casing the room and asked, "How much a place like this cost?" Like any good detective, curiosity was built into his genetic code.

"In this neighborhood? Maybe six mil." She glanced around the room, then amplified the result to include the rest of the brownstone. "The renovating about two. The furniture and paintings another three. Some of it's good." She leaned over and examined a bronze jaguar sitting on a painted Pembroke table. "Most of it's just all right."

"No shit?" Phelps jerked a thumb at the library walls. "I checked and the books are in Swedish and German. This isn't a library, it's a movie set."

She shrugged again. "They're supposed to look good, not be read."

"The rich *are* different."

She shook her head. "They're like everyone else: insecure."

The low hum of ambient noise beyond the doors of the library went silent and a few seconds later the Rochesters came in, followed by Benoit who had Hemingway's Perrier on a small silver tray.

Mr. Rochester clocked in at a fit sixty and had the sharp black eyes and firm handshake of a Wall Street poster boy. Mrs. Rochester was younger by two decades and had the unfocused eyes and loose body movements of a Xanax and vodka cocktail.

When everyone was clear on names, the Rochesters sat down and Hemingway nodded at Benoit as he brought her drink over. "Mr. and Mrs. Rochester, I have some very personal questions to ask and you may not want Benoit—"

Mr. Rochester held up his hand and shook his head. "He stays."

She took a breath and began. "We are sorry for what happened to your son. We want to find who did this and we want to do it quickly. In order to do that, we are going to have to reconstruct his routine. We have one objective: to find the person who did this."

Hemingway focused on Mrs. Rochester—the mother usually knew the routines, tradespeople, help, and schedules—but she was staring into the past, her mouth open, her eyes red and black from crying through her makeup.

Hemingway looked down at her notebook. "The first thing we need is a list of everyone that you can think of who might have had contact with Tyler. The school has given us a list of their teachers and personnel but we'll need to know his extracurricular life as well. Doctor, dentist, piano teacher, fathers of friends who have driven him home, any of your people; tutors; maintenance; cleaning crews; household staff; tradesmen—as comprehensive a list as possible."

Mrs. Rochester's head bobbed up, as if gravity had let go for a second. She tried to focus on Hemingway. "God, you don't think that it was someone he knows—*we know*—do you?"

Hemingway didn't look away. "We don't know."

The woman's mouth turned down and her eyes began ratcheting back and forth, as if the gearing had suddenly skipped. The tears very quickly started. "Why did this happen to us? All I wanted was a baby."

Her husband leaned over and put his arm around her. It seemed an awkward, unnatural gesture.

"Just a baby," she said, hugging herself and rocking slightly.

Hemingway thought of the cells dividing in her own body and she felt a flush of weird shame. "Have you, or any of your people, noticed anything unusual lately?"

Mr. Rochester turned to Benoit, the replicant, who simply shook his head and said in an even tone, "Nothing unusual."

"At what time did Tyler usually get home each day?" Hemingway kept her eyes locked on Mr. Rochester. A man like him would want to be certain that the detective investigating his son's murder had backbone; when they had shaken hands he had squeezed a little too tightly, one of those sexist tests men threw at her every now and then—probably his version of the acid test for competency.

It was Benoit who answered again. "He was usually in the elevator by four thirty-seven. Tonight he stayed late to use the library. Tyler is one of those rare children who likes books." He paused, then corrected himself. "*Liked* books." The man had a precise foreign accent that she couldn't quite place. It had a lilt of French to it but his Rs were a little hard.

"Did he walk to school unescorted every day?"

Benoit again. "Since January."

"And before that?" Hemingway kept her eyes locked on Mr. Rochester, ignoring Benoit.

Benoit opened his mouth and Phelps interrupted. "Mr. Rochester, you were his parents, *you* are the best source of information."

At that, Mrs. Rochester snorted. It was a loud farm girl guffaw. She stopped when her husband hit her with a hard stare.

"Unfortunately we have been occupied with other things as of late. Of everyone in his life, Benoit knew him best."

Hemingway's eyes flicked to Benoit; his face was still molded into that flat battlefield stare his type always had. His head rotated toward her, and she could almost hear the metallic click of gears and grease in the movement. "Until last week I followed him to and from school each day. I think he knew. I discussed it with his father, and Mr. Rochester agreed that he should spend the last month of the year learning what independence was. This was the first time he walked home without my presence."

And Hemingway recognized something else going on behind the flat eyes. She knew the type; Mank had been like that. If she really wanted to think about it, she was like that, too.

"Put a list together of everyone who saw him on a

regular basis. Highlight new people in his circles—the last six months or so."

Mrs. Rochester was nodding off into Mother's Little Helper Land again and Mr. Rochester looked like it was starting to sink in.

"All I wanted was a baby—" She sniffled, a loud inelegant pop, and wiped her sleeve across her nose. "How could someone do this to him?"

Mr. Rochester's face tightened.

Hemingway tried to get the interview back. The next question was a tough one, but standard operating procedure. "Is there anyone who would want to hurt you? Past business dealings, maybe?"

Mr. Rochester stared at her for a blank moment, and then his software was back up. He didn't hold up his hands and give her an emphatic *no fucking way* and he didn't think about it as if it had never crossed his mind, he simply stared at her and said, "Detective Hemingway, I can in no way think of anyone who would feel that something like this could be even remotely justified. This is beyond retribution, Detective. In any capacity." And for an instant his eyes found Benoit. They shook their heads in unison.

"Has anyone noticed anything out of the ordinary recently? Anything at all? A new delivery man, or florist, or car detailer? Any new spouses or boyfriends in your social circle? Anything at all might help, no matter how insignificant." Phelps kept his tone even, direct.

"What can you tell us about Tyler?" Hemingway automatically looked at Benoit but it was Mrs. Rochester who answered from behind some unseen curtain of communication.

"He was a good boy. Funny. Thick brown hair, big brown eyes . . ."

Hemingway remembered the boy's stare pointed up at the sky and the knot of hair on his forehead.

Mr. Rochester added, "He was gifted. Brilliant."

His wife waved it away as if that didn't matter. "He was the fastest runner in the hundred yard dash at the Randall's Island track-and-field day."

An image of the chop lines through his bones flickered in Hemingway's head.

Mrs. Rochester continued talking as the medication and misery gave her a momentary reprieve. "Loved baseball and eggs Benedict. He was my gift. And now he's gone."

Hemingway folded up her three by five, pocketed it, and nodded for Phelps to do the same. These people weren't going to be any help. Not yet. They were in the early stages of shock. Maybe tomorrow morning. Maybe tomorrow night. Maybe never. "We'll need to speak to you sometime tomorrow. If you think of anything in the interim, please let us know."

Mrs. Rochester repeated, "And now he's gone," then faded out again.

———

Benoit walked them to the door and Hemingway watched the way the rest of the people in the house shied away from him, the alpha among the omegas.

Benoit stopped in the foyer with them and asked, "What are the chances you'll find the man who did this?" There was no hope in his voice, no false buoyancy.

Hemingway did her best to sound confident but Benoit looked like the kind of guy who had well-honed bullshit detecting skills. Besides, they hadn't started to connect the dots yet. "We'll pick up a lot of evidence as we move upstream with this. We'll find this guy. I promise."

Hemingway held out her hand.

Benoit stared at it for a second before nodding perfunctorily and saying, "I hope you catch this guy before he sets his sights on another child. Have a good night, detectives."

Then he opened the door.

HEMINGWAY AND Phelps were in their booth at the back of Bernie's again. It was late. Bernie had put on his monthly Fiesta Night, ramping up the décor with greasy Mexican souvenirs hung around the joint like props in a film. The place had been packed with Corona-drinking cops with red eyes for most of the night. Now only stragglers remained.

Hemingway had talked Bernie into warming a Tourista Trio up for her—a culinary sculpture consisting of three burritos and three tacos on a bed of nachos and cheese topped off with fist-sized scoops of guacamole and sour cream. It was past its prime, and the cheese tasted like electrical cord, but she was grateful for the meal. Phelps was finishing a diet soda and a single soft-shell chicken taco adorned with lettuce and a little salt. Alongside the food their improvised office was littered with notes, case jackets, and photographs.

Hemingway knew who would be sitting where without having to look. Most cops were superstitious about things that civilians took for granted, including where to sit in a restaurant. Some chose defensive positions against walls and in corners; some stayed close to the coffee machine so they could order as fresh pots came off the burner; some sat near the windows to watch the world outside. According to the unwritten schedule, this was Hemingway and Phelps's booth every day from 6 a.m. until 3 p.m., from three to midnight it belonged to Donny Lincoln and Nick Papandreou, switching squatters' rights to officers Diego and McManus from midnight to 6 a.m. In a life filled with uncertainty, it was nice to have a table you could depend on.

Hemingway spotted Lincoln and Papandreou ambling over.

Phelps pointed at Hemingway's plate. "We're almost done."

Papandreou threw an orange file on the table, pulled up a chair, and nodded at Hemingway as she put a mouthful of nachos away. "You know, Hemi, for a woman you sure eat a lot of fuckin' food."

She wiped her mouth with a napkin and smiled. "I get that a lot."

"How's it going with your boat?"

The time Hemi spent out on the water was a rolling joke with some of the other cops. She smiled. "Still floating."

"You got a fridge on board? You know, for snacks and shit?"

Hemingway stabbed at the guacamole with her fork. "Sure. I keep Pop Tarts on board, just in case."

Papandreou tapped the orange folder. "Here's the list you asked for."

Phelps slurped the last of his soda out of the waxed paper cup, moving the straw around with his lips to vacuum the dregs, then reached for the file. "How many names you come up with?"

"You don't want to know."

Hemingway's fork stopped halfway to her mouth. She eyed the two cops, then put her fork down with a clang and wiped her mouth again. "Yes. I do."

"In the past twelve months, there have been eleven hundred and thirty-one men paroled countrywide who have violent and predatory histories with children. One hundred and eleven women. We ran the MO through the system and came up empty. Lots of child predators out there but none that seem predisposed to this kind of pathology." Papandreou jabbed a finger at the pile of files on the table. "A lot of bad people on the list but none of them seem right for the job."

Desmond, the dispatcher, came running into the diner. He looked angry which, along with the wet crescents staining the underarms of his suit, was the usual state of affairs with the man: bad news personified. He spotted Hemingway and headed over, eyebrows knitted together in an indignant V.

"Here's Desmond," she said, and pushed her plate away—Desmond was also a spitter.

"Whyintya guys fuckin' tell me you found them?" he snapped at Papandreou.

"We just got here."

Desmond fastened his eyes on Hemingway.

"What's up, Dezzy?"

Desmond's eyes stayed on her face for a moment, then focused on her plate, then looked back up to her eyes. "Where's your fuckin' phone?"

"In my jacket. Right here." She tapped the pile of linen beside her on the bench. She never carried a purse.

"You ain't fuckin' answerin'," Desmond snapped.

She pulled the iPhone out and scanned the screen. "It was on vibrate. Thirty-one messages."

Desmond turned to Phelps. "You, too, fat man?"

"This ain't fat, it's muscle," Phelps said. He eased his

mass back in the seat and his jacket fell open, exposing his substantial gut and an automatic in a shoulder holster. "My phone's in the car."

Hemingway's eyes shifted from Desmond to Papandreou to Lincoln to Phelps then back to Desmond. "Will someone please tell us what's going on," she said.

Desmond held out a dispatch sheet. "The medical examiner's office called. He wants to see you as soon as possible."

Phelps started to slide out of the booth. "What gives?"

Desmond threw his arms up in the air. "You'd know if you had your fuckin' phone with you."

Hemingway pushed the table away and stood up. "You can stop with the histrionics and get to the point."

"Marcus finished with the kid. The tox screens had a lot to say."

Hemingway was up now. "Such as?"

"Tyler Rochester was alive when someone chopped off his feet."

THE MEDICAL examiner's office was unusually busy for 1:30 a.m. Hemingway nodded a few hellos to personnel as she and Phelps worked their way through the hallways on their way to the lab, a bright space where the white-coated acolytes pried secrets from the dead.

Dr. Marcus was in his usual lab—a meticulously appointed subway-tiled space that contained a dozen glass booths, each with a single stainless steel table over an eighteen-inch square grate in the floor. Several of the cubicles were occupied, the inhabitants covered by opaque plastic sheets. When they walked in, Marcus looked up from a cup of coffee he was examining as if it held great cosmic meaning.

"Hemi, Phelps," he said.

No matter how many times Hemingway visited the morgue, it always seemed as if its walls off-gassed disinfectant and death.

After a thorough cleanup that involved changing his lab coat and gloves, Marcus walked them to the far end of the lab where the Rochester boy was laid out.

The boy was pale and bloodless. There was a cut on his

eyebrow that Hemingway hadn't seen down by the water because it had been hidden by his hair—a white gash filled with pale pink flesh, like a third eye not yet formed. His mouth was slightly open, the almost white tip of his tongue protruding between perfect teeth.

Tyler Rochester did not look like he was sleeping. Or in a coma. Or in God's arms. He looked like what he was: a dead child with no feet.

The sheet was folded down, covering him from mid-chest to where his legs stopped at the nub ends of bone. Hemingway took up position at the boy's side. Phelps, looking like he'd rather be anywhere else, stood on the other side of the body. It was clear that no one wanted to be here. The job of examining the dead always held a certain intrinsic sadness but seeing a child lying on the slab was tough for everyone, even Dr. Marcus, a man who had spent his career examining tragedy.

Marcus indicated Tyler Rochester's left eye. It looked like a dried-out cocktail onion pushed into his socket with a little too much force. "The boy had an anesthetic injected into his left eye. Downward trajectory—right-handed. Barbiturate-grade anesthetic. It will take another week for the lab to match the compound but I'd say something like thiopental. And at this point there is no indication of an analgesic, so he would have felt what happened to him." Marcus dictated from memory, ignoring the notes on the trolley.

"How long would it take for something like that to take effect?" Phelps's face was in work mode, an expressionless blend of angles.

Marcus's head bobbed back and forth as he calculated. "On a body mass like his? Twenty-five, maybe thirty seconds."

"Was he restrained?"

"No bruising under his throat, so he wasn't held from behind. No ligature marks on his wrists or ankles, so he wasn't cuffed or strapped down."

"And the kid would have felt this?" Phelps waved a hand over the space where the boy's feet should have been.

Dr. Marcus nodded. "Yes."

Hemingway ran a hand through her hair. "Have you figured out what he used to do this?"

"It was a hacksaw."

Hemingway took in a lungful of disinfectant-tainted air and tried to focus on the notes she was taking in her three-by-five. "You still think the killer lacks practical anatomical knowledge?"

Marcus nodded. "Like I said at the river, both feet were taken off too far above the ankle. Anyone with practice would know that half an inch down—between the tibia and talar head—is a lot easier to saw through because it's mostly cartilage and tendon. And if you look here, at the right ankle, you can see that he doesn't get the hang of the saw until an inch or so in."

Hemingway looked up from her three-by-five. She wanted to say that this didn't feel like the work of a first timer but kept it to herself. "He jabbed the kid in the eye, waited for him to drop, then went to work on his right foot?"

Marcus nodded. "The boy would have screamed, doubled over holding his eye. As long as the killer left him alone for thirty seconds, he probably wouldn't have run. He'd have wasted the last half minute of his life.

"The work was done on a smooth surface. The body was dumped in the water as soon as his feet were removed. There are some abrasions on the epidermal layer on the back of the ankles, near the cut line—the boy was dragged after his feet were taken off, dumped in the water while he was still alive."

"How long until he bled to death?"

Marcus shook his head. "The anesthetic slowed his heart rate, ergo his pulse. He didn't die of exsanguination. He drowned."

Hemingway looked down at the boy; he looked absolutely horrifying now. "How hard would it be to get a hundred-pound kid to a secluded spot by the river? An industrial lot, abandominium, grass yard? Go at sundown. Inject him. After he's out, place him on a wooden door or old tabletop. Maybe a sheet of plywood. Saw his feet off. Four minutes goes fast. Unless you're the one being sawed up." She stared down at the body for a few beats of her heart as the flowchart slowly came together. "If he had a lair, a place where he had taken the boy, there'd be tether marks on his hands. He would have a table for this—a surgeon's gurney or workbench. Something tailored to his needs."

"Maybe it's not part of his fantasy," Phelps suggested. "Maybe he's a sporting man. Maybe he gets his jollies from their helplessness—so helpless that they don't need restraints."

Hemingway nodded at that. "Maybe."

Dr. Marcus eyed her over the frames of his glasses. "There are no signs of a struggle. No defensive wounds. No ripped fingernails. There are a few cuts and contusions, most notably the one on his eyebrow, but that is postmortem, probably thumped his head on a rock in the river." He took his glasses off once again and went through the same ritual of cleaning his lenses with a static-free wipe, no doubt a nervous habit.

Hemingway wanted to tell the boy that she would find

his killer but she settled on reaching out and touching his hair, as if contact with him would somehow let him know what she was thinking. "What kind of a human being does this to a little boy?"

Marcus shrugged. "If I knew that, you'd be out of a job."

III EIGHT

HEMINGWAY PARKED in the garage and turned off the engine. The tired rattle of the big V-8 mimicked her own exhaustion and she sat there for a few seconds, trying to build up the steam she'd need to make it inside. After a few moments of nothing but the ticking of her motor offset by her own breathing, she grabbed the plastic bag off the passenger seat, checked both mirrors, and stepped out into the dark. She closed the door, leaving the truck with the kayak still strapped to the roof in the cool confines of the little garage behind her building.

She had owned this place for fifteen years. There was a bakery downstairs—one of those Italian bread places that had been there since the heyday of Ellis Island and was now in the hands of the fourth generation. Like everything else that the American Dream had changed, the children of the Arigo brothers didn't see their future in flour and eggs. When Joe and Sal eventually retired or died, a McDonald's or some other soulless corporate sound bite would move in and another piece of what had built America would be lost in the name of progress.

She walked out of the alley, around the building, her jeans sticking to her thighs with the humidity that had gotten worse in the past few hours. Tomorrow—today, technically—was going to be a stinker. One of those days where you wouldn't be able to tell if you were sweating or if you had pissed yourself. She couldn't remember it ever being so damp and wondered if this was one of those fabled hormone-fueled sixth-sense abilities that came along with her special condition.

No, *special condition* was a misnomer.

Life changer was more fitting.

Holy fuck. How had this happened?

At six weeks, her body had not yet changed, not outwardly. But the clockworks hadn't felt right for a week or two. There were no monster cravings—at least not yet—and she wasn't depressed or impatient or any of the other emotions she had seen chew her sister's pregnancies into nine-month bouts of hysterics. But the humidity was bothering her, and it never had before—Mother Nature was finally fucking with her.

She passed the antique store on the corner, then the bakery, and came to her door. She paused for a moment, her forehead on the painted surface. The day had been one of the toughest she had experienced in a while. The discovery she was pregnant, a carjacking, and a boy with no feet seemed like a triple play dreamed up by an epic sadist.

She reached into her pocket for her keys and touched the stone she had picked up on the esplanade near the dead child. She pulled out her keys, unlocked the door, and pushed it open. Her hair blew back in a gush of air-conditioning. She stepped inside and headed up the wide wooden staircase in the dark, her shoes clacking on the hardwood.

Hemingway dropped the plastic bag containing her breakfast onto the island, pulled a carton of whole milk out of the fridge, and poured a glass. She walked over to the wall of arched windows that framed a wedge-shaped view of the West Side Highway to her left, a broad swatch of the Hudson beyond to the right, and Jersey in the distance. The sight of the river brought her back to standing over the Rochester boy. The awkward way his arm had reached out for the river, as if he were pointing at the secrets they would find out there. His bloodless complexion, punctured eyeball and legs that terminated in lopped-off bone only hinted at the madness he had endured.

Her damp clothes were getting cold and the milk almost cracked her teeth but she stood there, looking out at the world. She had been a cop long enough to know they might never know who had killed the little boy. The stars just wouldn't align and they'd end up with a shelf full of boxes moldering away in the Pearson Place Warehouse Facility in Queens. Another cold case. Another child who would stay frozen in time forever. Another statistic.

The sound of footsteps echoed somewhere behind her in the vast space of the loft and she turned. Daniel came at her out of the dark, tired but smiling. "Hey, babe. Helluva day, huh?" He came over and kissed her. He tasted of toothpaste and smelled good.

"You have no idea."

He put his arms around her and she buried herself in his shoulder. "I saw you on the news. The carjackers this afternoon. And I assume the kid they found on the East Side was yours, too."

"Okay, so you have some idea."

He squeezed her for a minute; she knew she could fall asleep leaning against him. "I picked up some shumai and a six of Sapporo. It's in the fridge. Want me to heat up the dumplings and pour you a cold one?"

She thought about the baby inside her, about Tyler Rochester lying under the Queensboro Bridge, arm pointed out at the current, and decided that it was time to talk to Daniel. "Heat the dumplings but the beer can wait." She held up the milk.

He held her at arm's length and stared into her eyes. "Why don't you take a shower? The dumplings will be ready by the time you're done, then you can get some sleep."

"I have to talk to you."

He backed up and crossed his arms—they had had plenty of "talks" over the past two years and she had learned that his standard MO was to listen. Not that he was the strong silent type, but there was a certain fortitude necessary to deal with the kinds of problems she came with: the job; the way she dealt with the world; her family; the gun she kept under the pillow; the times she'd be gone for days on end, chasing down some depraved monster. Daniel's way of dealing with her was to listen. The last one—Mike—had opted for throwing shit and screaming. That had lasted for precisely one argument before she had tossed his ass out. Before that it had been Mankiewicz and that had always been—what was the word?—*broken* seemed to be the only thing that fit. Their relationship had never been built on a healthy foundation.

Daniel looked at her, his head cocked to one side the way Phelps often did, and she wondered if it was a trait common to the men she ended up with in one capacity or another—the ones she worked with and the ones she loved. She looked into his eyes, saw the trust in them, and dug down into herself for the courage to tell him. He was incapable of lying and that innate ability she had to read people had never detected so much as petty jealousy in him. If anyone could take this—and let her deal with it in a way that made sense to her—it was Daniel.

"I'm pregnant."

His mouth broke into a shy smile then quickly flattened out as he realized that her tone had not been as happy as it could have been.

She continued. "Six weeks."

"And?" He reached out and took her hand. There was nothing possessive about it. It was simply his way of saying he was there.

"And tonight I had to talk to the parents of a boy who had his feet sawn off while he was still alive."

Daniel kept his fingers pressed into her palm while he examined her. He didn't look judgmental or angry or confused. But it was obvious he was waiting for her to say something.

"And I don't know if this world needs another child. The good is bleeding out of our species and when I look at all the messed-up things that happen day in and day out, I wonder if it's fair to foist this upon another human being. The notion of any kind of a god is laughable when I see what happens to good people all the time. Fuck free will. Any kind of a god who cared about us wouldn't let the shit that goes on happen."

She paused, waiting for Daniel to say something. All he did was look at her and in that instant, she realized that she had found *him*—the one for her. She thought Mankiewicz was the one but, like so many other things, that had ended when Shea put him in the ground. Daniel had asked her to marry him three times and she had turned him down. It had not driven him away, or made him bitter. He seemed content just to be with her. He gave her space, and he appreciated his. "I love you," she said.

That made him smile. "I know." And that was it. Nothing about the baby. Or about the shitty condition of the world. Or about her doubts. "You want those dumplings?"

She nodded. "Why not?"

Daniel went to the kitchen, turned on the lights, and opened the fridge.

"It's not that I don't want your input. I do. Just not now. I need to know how I feel about things before I ask you how you feel about them."

With that he stopped and turned to her, the foil plate held in both hands. He looked like a long-haired Oliver Twist in a pair of boxers and a wifebeater. "Baby, you don't have to explain this to me. But let me know where you stand before you do anything"—he paused, then added the word—"*decisive*." He stared at her. "Is that fair?"

"You amaze me."

He smiled, put the dumplings into the oven. "That's me—amazing."

"How long until the dumplings are warm?"

"Twenty—twenty-five minutes."

"That's just enough time."

He pulled a plate from the cupboard. "Enough time for what?"

She headed for the bedroom. "You'll see."

He followed her. "At least we don't have to worry about you getting pregnant."

But at the back of her mind she couldn't forget that somewhere out there a child killer was alone in his head. Thinking bad thoughts.

And planning bad deeds.

TREVOR DEACON couldn't take his eyes off him. He wasn't handsome, at least not classically, but he had that unnamable quality Trevor had always been drawn to, the vibe of a young Montgomery Clift. Trevor stared at the photo, at the way he leaned against the fence, hands in the pockets of his gray flannel trousers, tie loose, top button undone. His jacket was over his shoulder—it was supposed to look casual, unpracticed, but Trevor knew better.

The boy was maybe ten years old.

Eleven tops.

Trevor stared into the dark eyes, rife with mischief. The boy would be his. Like the others, a gift.

Trevor used to hunt children through one of the big Internet auctions but that had become boring—like injecting vegetables with hypodermics down at the market, it was too easy. No sport. No challenge. No adventure. *No fun*.

With the auction, it had been easy to find them. He remembered the first; standing on the lawn, holding up a pair of deer antlers that had a starting bid of ninety-nine cents. VeryHappyWendy1977 had 629 feedbacks. Trevor had cycled through some of her completed auctions, and had been able to put a decent file together. The house was white stucco with a small mulberry beside the porch. In the background, behind one of the trees, he could see the spire of a church—this one pale green with a crystal ball at the transept of the cross. There was a number on a porcelain plaque beside the door: 15891. There was a car in the driveway, an old Volkswagen Jetta in white (she had been smart enough to blur the license plate with a basic spray paint command). She also mentioned her son, Franklin, as her reason to live. This, of course, had made Trevor very happy. He was sure that Wendy would be thrilled to know that someone was going to love her little boy for the rest of his life. VeryHappyWendy1977 would have to add a second *very* to her moniker.

The very first time Trevor Deacon had plugged into the collective database of the Internet, his world had forever changed. Since then, there had been no break from the voices in his head. No reprieve from the throbbing between his legs. And he had to keep the spider happy. Always the spider. Or else.

And so he had started hunting.

That first one had taken a little creative thinking, but not much. He had stared a little harder, connecting the dots that Wendy had been happy enough to supply. The child was wearing a Carlyle Academy shirt.

He had tapped into Google and found that Carlyle Academy was located in Staten Island. He found a directory of churches in the area, then Google-Earthed them one at a time until he found one that had a distinguished color to it—green. From there it hadn't been difficult to find 15891 Kottler Road. All because of this wonderful thing called the Internet.

The Internet had helped Trevor go from being a lonely, frightened, frustrated man to being a world-class lover. With the advent of cyberspace—thank you very much, Mr. William

Gibson, for that wonderful phrase—Trevor no longer had to make do with used-up teenagers. Now he got the good ones.

When it came to his boys, Trevor was a benevolent god, teaching them true love with a patience they could never have found out in the world. And like all pure sociopaths, Trevor took this responsibility very seriously. In the old days he had felt special, as if maybe he was one of the last members of a tribe that no one knew about. But now, with the digital world of bits and bytes swirling information around the globe at the speed of light, he had found others out there; like-minded souls he probably passed every day on the train and in the aisles of the liquor store where he bought his mother her Yukon Jack. But along with its blessings, the Internet had also brought about a lot more competition. It was social evolution, and only the smartest would survive.

The rest would be carted off to prison.

A story on the *Times* website had recently reported there were eight million Facebook users under ten years of age.

Then YouTube came along.

YouTubers loved uploading videos of cute kids with the looks he wanted. And it was easy to find them. All he needed as a starting point was a car license plate or a fridge magnet or a grocery bag in the background. Hell, it was amazing how many people had the local news on the TV in the back of their videos and photos. And nothing helped nail down a region like the local news. Why did people insist on leaving it out there for him?

Because they secretly wanted to help.

Trevor clicked back to the picture of little Bobby brown-eyes and staring into that smiling little face made him want it. But Trevor didn't want to use him up in his mind before he got to use him up in the garage; he'd have to make do with one of the others.

On the way to the garage he passed the birthday present his sole friend had given him—a photograph of a duck decoy floating in the current. As he walked by he reached out, brushing the back of his knuckles across the glossy paper. It was the only present he had ever received. As he walked by it he decided on Simon Becker.

He paused in front of the garage door, his hands out on the cold steel skin. The only thing he feared in the world lived in there. The door was riveted quarter-inch steel plate but it was an empty gesture—nothing could keep the spider in. Not if it wanted out. Some nights he'd be alone in his bed—maybe with one of them to keep him company—and he would hear it, the watermelon abdomen popping as it squished under the door. Trevor would freeze. He had read an article that said spiders hunted by carbon dioxide output, so he held his breath.

It would rattle the bedroom doorknob until its claws found purchase. Trevor never looked at it—never made contact with its million and a half eyes. He would lie still, shaking as it came snuffing over, its hairy legs rasping on the carpet. Then it would crawl up into bed with him.

One spiny appendage would wrap around him from behind. Then another. Pretty soon it would be spooning with him. Trevor would shut his eyes and pray. But it didn't do any good. The spider was too powerful to wish away.

When he woke the next morning, it would be gone, back under the garage door to live in the damp shadows of the garage. Waiting for him to feed it.

In the fifty-six years Trevor had lived here, he had never seen it in daylight. When he was a boy he had asked his mother about it. She had lied. There was no spider, she said. And the beatings had gotten worse. So he had stopped asking her about it.

The only thing that kept it away was screaming. *Their* screaming.

Trevor opened the two deadbolts, the padlocks, and the metal crossbar. He swung the door in, waiting for the bloated insect to launch at him from the shadows. But it didn't; somehow it knew he was working on getting another one and it would leave him alone for now.

The wire-caged bulb overhead did little to illuminate the gloom of the space. He walked over to the big coffin freezer, lifted the lid, and took one out. A perfect little foot, frozen solid, five neat little toes bunched up in what looked like a Babinski reflex because the boy had still been alive when he had sawed it off. He had a recording of the screams that he would play back sometimes; Simon Becker had had an amazing pair of lungs. He had one of Simon's feet put away at the back of the box, kept in waiting like a fat blue Mr. Freeze for the perfect summer afternoon. An afternoon like today.

It was small cold beautiful magic in his hand, with five little toes. It would help him forget the one he was working on. Until he was here. Chained down to the workbench. Screaming for him. For the spider.

Trevor sucked the frozen little toes, brittle and hard as china against his teeth, and wept with happiness.

Soon there would be more feet for the freezer.

Oh, thank Jesus for the Internet.

Thank Jesus and Mary and Joseph and God and William Gibson and Montgomery Clift and his mommy and the spider. Thank them all. For the Internet and all the little boys. The boys most of all. Above everything. Thank you thank you thankyou thankyouthankyou. THANK YOU.

Behind him the coffin freezer full of little feet sat silent, a larder waiting to be enjoyed.

As long as people kept posting photos of their children on the Internet, Trevor Deacon would be able to keep the spider away. And in the process, feed his freezer.

And feed it.

And feed it.

And feed it.

TYLER ROCHESTER'S fourth-grade picture had been destined to become part of the collective American consciousness from the moment someone with a hacksaw had fastened his sights on the boy. The information pipeline hammered every television, newspaper, magazine, tablet and smartphone with the boy's school portrait. The *Times* had carried a front-page piece on him, below a crisp image of the smiling face. Dark brown hair. Brown eyes. Blue jacket. White shirt. Striped school tie.

Hemingway threaded the Suburban through the staggered gauntlet of news vans. The main event was in front of the police station, a scattered collection of vehicles with one distinct purpose—to entertain. With the daunting task of feeding the twenty-four-hour news cycle, fact had already succumbed to fancy footwork and finger pointing. The reporters would camp at the precinct's doorway until the next tragedy scarred the American landscape and then they would move on.

Their first order of business would be to fault the police. Then, when they were done asking questions and pointing fingers, they would move on to the beefed-up police presence

at schools in the city, signing off with the old barn door analogy, asking if the extra security was too little, too late.

Hemingway had slept for two hours, then gone back to
the morgue to visit the Rochester boy before they released
him to the family. She had been in homicide for ten years,
promoted to violent homicide investigation almost seven
years back. Not a lot of time under her keel in one respect.
A lifetime in another. Many lifetimes, if she considered the
dead.

Child killings were the worst. It was one of those things
that always felt personal, no matter what you tried to tell
yourself.

As a detective, she was, if not used to, then at least familiar with the twisted pathologies of killers; this was going
to get worse before it got better. There would be no reprieve,
no reassignment. The only break would come when they
solved the case. Or it went cold. And if that happened, she'd
lose everything she had worked for. She'd lose the street time
and the exams and all the hard work—years of having to be
just a little more careful than the other cops, always having
to do something better than the men she worked with in order
to get equal credit. If she messed up the investigation, the
derogatory language would start. They'd call her scared or a
pussy; the hardened lowlifes in the department would call
her a bitch and a cunt. No way—she was not backing down.
She'd stick this out because that's what she did, what she had
always done. When the status quo were howling in pain, she
kept banging away at it. Another trait inherited from her
father.

The case would be media heavy to the end. When it came
to murders, the value the media puts on lives was directly
proportional to the entertainment value of the victim; it was
about ratings. Drifters and homeless people got the leanest

media coverage and, often, little in the way of investigative resources. The next layer up—another lost cause—were drug addicts. Then came the prostitutes, a layer of individuals no one cared about until the third or fourth victim. After that were drug dealers, followed by felons. The further up the social hierarchy you climbed, the closer you got to the American Gold Standard in murder victims: the rich white child.

She pulled into a reserved parking place and realized that her left hand was on her stomach. She stared at it for a while. Was she trying to feel a baby she wasn't sure she wanted? Or trying to shield it from the bad juju of the job? She rubbed her stomach, a new habit that felt oddly familiar. Then she grabbed her backpack and the Rochester file from the back and got out into the early morning.

She cut around back to avoid the news teams. She clocked through the gate and walked through the garage, nodding a good morning to Albert Chance, the car dispatcher. When she was inside she felt the familiar vibrations of the precinct, a building that never slept. But riding just below the familiar current of the place was a foreign species of white noise, that of interlopers.

The cops she passed on the staircase looked irritated, the natural defensive position of policemen under scrutiny. The morning was always busy as the collective mind of the hive geared up for the day but today it was in overdrive as the eye of the media dialed in on it. The usual hallway chatter was noticeably absent.

Hemingway climbed the back staircase to the top floor, doing the full five flights in a quick jog. With this case looming in front of her, she knew she would be doing little running and no kayaking. Spare time had just evaporated—what little would be left after the investigation was done chewing through her days would end up being spent on not enough sleep. And trying not to lose her mind. Stairs would be her only exercise for a while.

Phelps was at his desk, wearing another of his ubiquitous gray suits and a solid tie, this one a deep navy. He had a coffee in his hand and the same indignant look that the cops on the staircase had—siege mentality setting in as he prepared for battle.

"Detective Phelps," she said officially, handing him a paper bag.

"Hey, kiddo." He looked into the bag, finding four bagels stuffed with lox and cream cheese, all wrapped in wax paper. "Let me guess, one of these is for me, right?"

"Half of one." She winked.

He unwrapped a bagel and began fueling for the day. "You're the best."

She went to the window and looked out onto the street. From up here it looked worse than it had at street level—cameramen running around pulling establishing shots; reporters preening in handheld mirrors; yellow power cables reaching over the ground like tropical vines, feeding electricity to the lights. She put her hands into her pockets and felt the stone from last night. She wrapped her fingers around it. "You ready for this?" she asked.

Phelps took a slurp of coffee from his mug and shrugged. "I ain't never ready to deal with those pricks outside asking questions like 'did we find anything in the boy's ass?' I spoke to Dennet. He's making you PIO."

Being dubbed public information officer was a thankless job that every detective dreaded—it took time that wasn't available for people who didn't appreciate it. In the broadest sense, her job would be to feed the press tidbits of information meant to solicit their help whenever possible. But as the official talking head for the investigation she'd also be the official whipping post if things went screaming off the rails. Besides adding a lot of weight to her workload, it would also put her under a microscope, something she had learned to live with in the wake of the Shea investigation.

Her phone went off at her hip and she checked the message. "Dennet's here."

The noise five floors below rose in pitch as the captain's car pulled up in front of the precinct. From her bird's-eye perch she watched him step out into the glare of lights and he lit up like the Silver Surfer. She watched him shake his head, ignore shouted questions, disappear up the steps and into the building.

"Let's get this party started."

Phelps stood up, grabbed the second half of the bagel and lox he was working on, and pushed the paper bag across the desk. "Load up, you ain't gonna have time to eat after this."

"I hate the press." Hemingway kept her eyes on the group of reporters below. "Any suggestions?"

"With your education and family? Yeah. Go downstairs, resign, and become a Park Avenue plastic surgeon."

"I meant about the press."

"Just don't shoot anyone."

"Thanks."

They took the back stairs down to Dennet's office passing plainclothesmen and uniformed officers scuttling between floors, silent and on edge. Hemingway walked ahead of Phelps, a habit past the point of being unlearned; with Phelps in the back they both had a clear forward view—imperative in their line of work.

Ken Dennet was cornered in front of his office, trying to ease away from a duty cop hammering him with questions. When Hemingway and Phelps came out of the stairwell, he pointed at them, his thumb and forefinger miming a gun. "My appointment is here, we'll talk later." He ushered them into his office, waving Mike Babanel, the precinct's lawyer, over from a corner. When they were all safely inside, Dennet closed the door.

The captain dropped into his seat and stared at Hemingway. From down here the chatter of the media outside had the windows vibrating. "Where are you with the Rochester kid?"

No one wanted to hear that more killings were probably on the way. "We've gone through everyone who was even remotely connected with Tyler Rochester, from the school's personnel records to the Rochester family's list of help, through friends and business acquaintances. No red flags. We've hit all the registered sex offender lists—federal and state—and the recent parolee alerts. No one in any of the databases fits the MO."

Dennet looked up at the ceiling and the word *sonofabitch* came out of his mouth in a protracted hiss. "The good news is that the extra security we're putting on the street will help bolster public confidence. We've got a little over a week until the schools are out for the summer and anyone walks within two blocks of a schoolyard between now and then, I want them to see blue." Dennet leaned forward and pushed a security schedule across the desk. Hemingway picked it up and scanned it while he went on. "We've assigned a police officer to every school in Manhattan—our men are doing double shifts. After school's out, there's extra security around parks, day camps and anywhere else kids hang out."

"For how long?" Hemingway looked up from the three-page schedule, a stopgap measure to make the media think things were under control. Which they were. For now.

"Until you get a break or we arrest someone. I don't need to tell you that those news assholes outside aren't going to get tired, do I?"

The inference wasn't lost on Hemingway; for the three months the Shea investigation lasted, she had been under constant attack from reporters. "Nossir."

"Phelps tell you that you're public information officer on this?"

"Who do I clear my releases through?"

The captain reached for the coffee on the edge of his desk, took a slurp off the top, and nodded at Babanel on the sofa. "Mike will make sure you're golden." Then he made a point of looking at his watch and clapped his hands. "Okay, school duty starts. Go talk to Desmond downstairs—he's got the assignments. You'll handle the daily brief and we'll send a summary out to the other precincts. Then it's off to protect and serve the school children of this city—I want people to think that this is a police state. And above all, I don't want anyone else disappearing. One fucking kid goes off the reservation and those cocksuckers outside will do more harm than good. If you need help, or don't understand something, you ask. Clear?"

"Crystal, sir."

"Good. After school duty, you and Phelps hit the lists again. Do the rounds and ask questions. Find this guy."

HEMINGWAY AND Phelps had pulled duty at the Lyle School for Boys—one of Manhattan's oldest private educational institutions and a fixture of the Upper East Side. It served the same demographic as the Damien Whitney Academy for Boys where Tyler Rochester had gone. Maybe the man they were hunting had a taste for the neighborhood.

Phelps leaned against the hood of the cruiser, going at his fourth coffee of the day. He looked like he was oblivious to his surroundings but two tours on a sniper team in Vietnam had honed his observational skills to near clairvoyance; if anything within sight was anomalous, he'd spot it. Hemingway paced the sidewalk and watched the street, her hands on her hips, her jacket open. The final bell had rung ten minutes ago but there was a fifteen-minute override in place to help with latecomers. This made no sense to Hemingway— the Lyle School was not the kind of place where the students were late. Especially not after one of their kind had been splashed all over the news.

The cops weren't out for surveillance. They weren't out as a deterrent. They were there so it would look like the NYPD was on top of things. It was a PR move that Hemingway and Phelps resented because it pulled them away from the case. Now that the coroner's reports were finished, there were things to do, places to go, people to visit. Their window was floating by and they were making sweetfuckall in the way of headway because they were stuck here, making an appearance to appease the news cockroaches.

The heat was in a dancing mood again and the day was a sultry motherfucker. Hemingway wanted to take off her jacket but a white shirt rendered invisible by perspiration was no way to keep the boobage dialed down—something she never forgot on the job.

Her phone went off, startling her with its shrill chirp. She slid it from her pocket and answered the call. "Hemingway."

"Yeah, Detective Hemingway, this is Marvin Stapleton, I'm with the Nineteenth. We got a problem."

"What?"

"I'm at the Huntington Academy. Detectives Lincoln and Papandreou just left."

Hemingway knew the school; she had briefly dated a boy who had gone there. It was three blocks north, two east.

"And a kid got snatched."

She felt her stomach lurch and she regretted the second breakfast she had pounded down after the briefing.

"The perp killed a driver and took a boy."

"Rope it off. We'll be there in four minutes." She whistled for Phelps as she ran for the SUV.

TWELVE

STAPLETON HAD cordoned off the street and put up screens to conceal the mess from prying eyes. A single news team was already there, drawn by the scent of blood in the water. His cruiser was parked in the middle of the asphalt, beside the crime-scene screens, lights thumping like a heart. The Suburban slid around the corner in a four-wheel drift, tires smoking. Hemingway punched up the final hundred yards, screeched to a stop at the perimeter, got out, and ran under the tape with Phelps closing up her wake.

Officer Marvin Stapleton stood by the cruiser looking shell-shocked. Another man—the school's headmaster, Hemingway guessed—stood off to the side of the vehicle. He wore a good-quality suit and brogues.

"What happened?" was the first thing out of her mouth.

Stapleton jerked his head toward the wall of accident screens he had set up. "Driver for one of the kids is dead. Kid's gone."

"We know the name of the kid taken?"

Stapleton shook his head. "I called you as soon as I found out and been pulling out screens since."

Hemingway turned to Phelps. "Run the plate. Get us an

ID on this kid now." Her need-to-know programming was up and running and she ducked behind the screen.

It was a big Lincoln sedan, black, with tinted windows. The driver's door was open about a quarter of an inch. A puddle of blood had accumulated on the pavement under the sill, already scabbing over in the heat. She pulled a pair of latex gloves from a kit in her pocket and eased the door open. The stink of blood and shit rose out of the vehicle, made all the worse by the sour heat baking the street. Off in the distance the thrum of emergency sirens was nearly buried by the morning noise of the city.

A man in a black suit was sprawled across the front bench. He was a big man who had not yet been reduced by death. He was slumped sideways onto the passenger's seat, twisted and lying faceup. His left hand was on his throat, middle finger dipped into the long gash. Blood had pissed everywhere, splattering the steering wheel, dash, windows and carpets. His mouth and right eye were open. A jet of blood had squirted up onto his face and his left socket was a flat glistening puddle of red.

Hemingway scanned the interior. "What happened?" she asked Stapleton from the door of the vehicle.

The whir of emergency vehicles was gaining on the clatter of street noise, the distant Wagnerian thrum of police cars, fire trucks, and EMT vehicles: cavalry on the way.

Stapleton leaned in so he wouldn't give the news team at the fence ammunition and Hemingway gave him a point for that one. "Lincoln and Papandreou were here with me all morning. They had the back; I had the front. It's a big school, nearly six hundred students. The final bell rang and I saw Headmaster Sinclair outside," he nodded at the man in the suit standing at the edge of her vision. "He gave us the wave off and then I saw the car.

"It was just sitting here, idling in the drop-off zone. I came over. Rapped on the window. The sides are tinted but when I looked in the front . . ." He let the sentence die and swallowed loudly. "I saw."

Phelps was off his phone on the other side of the car, his body over the windshield at an odd angle as if it were electrified and he were afraid to touch it. He looked over the roof of the car at Hemingway. He, too, spoke softly. "Car is owned by a Jesse Grant."

Hemingway turned to the headmaster. "Do you know if you have a student by the name of Grant?"

He was rattled out of suspended animation. "Yes. Of course. Bobby Grant. Grade five. One of our brightest musicians—a pianist." His head ratcheted down to the car and his mouth went into a perfect O, making him look like an emoticon. "Is this the Grant boy's driver? Oh, Jesus."

Hemingway wondered how many black Lincolns turned up here every morning to drop off children. Since the recession, conspicuous consumption was out and low profile was in; a lot of the wealthier urbanites had traded their Bentleys and S-Class Benzes in for the less showy, and less costly, Lincolns.

"What's he look like?"

Sinclair's eyes scrolled up and to the right. "Ten years old. Brown hair, brown eyes. Thin. School uniform."

The description set off a tremor somewhere behind her eyes. She glanced up at the school and the windows were filled with the curious faces of hundreds of boys. Did any of them know how lucky they were?

Two patrol cars came around the corner, sirens blaring, pushing the early-morning pedestrians up onto the sidewalk. She was grateful that there wasn't much to attract tourists to this area at this time of day.

She grabbed the headmaster by the elbow and steered

him toward the school, gesturing Phelps over as chaperone for the man. "I need a picture of the boy and I need it right now."

Phelps took over steering duties and ran the headmaster across to the school.

The approaching police vehicles were a live presence that shook the earth, a cacophony of pulsing sounds and lights at the corner of the street. When they cleared the traffic lock, they barreled up the street in a cloud of scorched pavement and rubber that scared the news crew out of the way. The legion of flashing vehicles screeched to a halt. Doors opened. Officers spilled out onto the pavement and raced over.

"You see anything unusual?" Hemingway asked Stapleton.

He glanced at the car and shook his head. "Kids running up and down the street like they're on Broadway. The bell rang and they headed in. When the street was clear I saw the guy in the Town Car was just sitting there. That's it. No honked horns. No flurry of motion. No distraction—I watch for shit like that." He rolled up his sleeve, exposing an Airborne tattoo on his forearm. "Two tours in Iraq. You don't sneak up on me."

Hemingway glanced at the screens that hid the Town Car and thought, *Obviously.*

"Nothing unusual until I spotted the car idling here."

"How long was it running before you came over?"

He shrugged. "I don't know. Six, maybe eight minutes. It took me a few minutes to realize that it should have gone. It kind of fit in with all the kids in the formal wear. It belonged."

"They're not tuxedoes, they're uniforms." She turned away from Stapleton and wondered if the gap between detective and street cop had broadened since she had made it up through the ranks. She looked up and down the street, thinking that with a twelve- to fifteen-minute lead time the kid could be on the dark side of the moon by now. Or floating in the East River.

The uniformed cops closed in on her, a field of blue glittering with nickel and brass. She turned back to Stapleton. "They have a no-idling policy in front of the school?" She had done a lot of work with the board of education and in the big push to go green, a lot of schools had implemented a no-idling policy.

"The headmaster said they don't tell the parents how to behave because it would be 'counterproductive.'"

"You've got to be fucking kidding." Her eyes drifted over Stapleton's shoulder to the mouth of the street. Another cruiser rounded the corner, nearly taking out a cameraman. There were now six police cruisers, an ambulance, and a van from the fire department just over the tape. She was surrounded by uniformed police officers.

She took a breath and let it power her voice. "It looks like a little boy has been abducted. Brown hair and brown eyes. School uniform." Over the line, the reporters began chattering at the flurry of motion.

Her phone chirped and when she held it up she saw Bobby Grant's face smiling out at her—a citywide memo from Phelps. Within seconds all of the cops in front of her were staring at the same image on their own phones.

Bobby Grant looked so much like Tyler Rochester that they could have been brothers.

III THIRTEEN

THE REPORTERS had a hard time finding fault with the NYPD's reaction time. Under Hemingway's direction, the police had fanned out from the Town Car epicenter like an antivirus program, scouring every shadow and dark corner in the neighborhood. The smart money was on a vehicular abduction but they went on a thin wedge of hope that the boy had been taken by someone on foot. It wasn't the smartest line of reasoning, but sometimes the easy money pays off.

The police didn't find Bobby Grant. He had been pulled into a wormhole.

No witnesses. No surveillance photos or video. No sign of him at all.

Hemingway and Phelps ended up in the headmaster's office, fielding calls while appropriating files. The room smelled of mahogany and ancient pipe smoke and history. The sofas were tufted leather and the Persian carpet was worth more than many homes.

The first order of business was to make certain that the Grant boy had been in the car with the dead man. A call to

the home verified that he had left for school with Desmond—
the man with the slit throat cooking in the heat-baked Lincoln
outside. It seemed like a silly thing to have to verify but it
was entirely possible that the driver was there to either pick
up or drop off homework—something the headmaster said
happened from time to time.

It took another ten minutes of no news before Hemingway
succumbed to the grim truth that they had lost Bobby Grant.
And there had been three cops at the school—two if you
discounted Stapleton. She wasn't prone to claustrophobia and
she had never experienced a panic attack, but she suddenly
felt like she wasn't getting enough air. She nodded at Phelps,
who was standing over the headmaster's shoulder as they
went through attendance logs. "I'll be outside," she said, and
turned to the door. "Get a faxed release from the Grants and
a copy of the boy's file. And I want a list of everyone who
has stepped foot in this school. Then we go talk to the parents."

Phelps, who looked like he belonged behind a tractor
instead of a badge, nodded and by the way his eyes narrowed
he confirmed that he understood something was up with her.
Like many partnerships—business or personal—they had developed a silent communication that transmitted more than
language often did. "Sure."

She cut through the outer office and was met by the
worried stare of two secretaries. Once out in the hall she was
hit with more uncomfortable looks from faculty and students.

Hemingway had firsthand experience with the immutable
pain of having someone taken: her eight-year-old sister Claire
had been abducted from their beach house when they were
kids. The police were called. Private detectives hired. Armed
bodyguards for the rest of the children. Her first taste of *too
little, too late.*

Claire was found in a field in East Hampton three days

later; she had been beaten to death with a framing hammer. The killer was a nobody—just a bad man with worse ideas and poor self-control. The loss of Claire had manifested itself as a weird presence on the periphery of Hemingway's mind, always ready to remind her that things went off the rails more often than anyone wanted to admit.

Her parents had brought in counselors. Dr. Bryce, the family psychiatrist, had talked to her for a couple of years. She still talked to him every now and then. But all the therapy and role-playing and talking it out hadn't killed the feeling that the world was a place that couldn't be trusted, not in any real sense of the word. All because someone couldn't stop his id from grabbing the steering wheel and punching down on the gas.

She stepped through the double oak doors into the tiny courtyard. The heat hit her from the asphalt up. Before she was at the fence—twenty paces away—her head was shimmering. She took off her jacket and the movement made her shoulder blade click and she realized that this was going to get a lot worse before it got a little better—something about the way it was unfolding was more oppressive and threatening than the heat and the helplessness.

The forensics guys in their space suits had set up a clean tent around the car and even with the pumped-in air-conditioning she knew it had to be a million degrees under the plastic enclosure. Cops had come back from their search for the Grant boy. They milled about like extras in a film who hadn't been given any direction other than to look defeated. She cut through them and headed across the street.

As she moved, she consciously avoided turning her head toward the news cameras set up at either end of the street.

Papandreou stood beside one of the big panels that blocked the crime-scene tent from the cameras, sucking on a smoke and generally looking like he was trying out for an I-don't-give-a-fuck-athon. "Hemi," he said flatly.

"Where are we?"

Papandreou took a drag, blew the jet straight up into the lifeless air, and nodded at the screens. "They just pulled the guy out of the car. ME's still in the tent." Hemingway stepped around one of the protective panels. Behind the barriers, where the tiniest breeze couldn't reach, it felt like a foundry.

She recognized Mat Linderer outside the blue tent in his static-free suit, his attention nailed to a Panasonic Toughbook.

"Find anything?" she asked, simultaneously checking her watch.

Linderer looked up, then went back to his screen; everyone knew the clock was ticking. "Bunch of prints, looks like two sets. The majority belong to Desmond Grossman, our driver. A bunch of smaller prints that probably belong to the child are all over the back door and seat belt buckle on the right side. Both passenger doors were wiped clean."

Hemingway filed that one away. Whoever had killed the driver and—presumably—taken the child, had not only touched the car but had the presence of mind—or training—to wipe their prints off. Which meant they hadn't been wearing gloves. "The body tell you anything?"

"Single swipe with a very sharp blade across his throat. Nicked the top of the larynx. Severed both jugular and carotid. Didn't know it was coming is my guess."

"How's that possible?"

Linderer stopped in mid-keystroke and turned to her. "I collect the data, you answer the questions."

"I thought Friday was let's-be-a-prick day; today's only Tuesday."

Linderer stopped typing. "I didn't mean—"

"Yes, you did. We exchange ideas, that's what we do. You

want to be an asshole, do it on someone else's time. I know it's a hundred-and-fifty fucking degrees out here but we've got a missing child and we just pulled a human Pez dispenser out of the Lincoln. I would like to find this kid before someone does bad things to him, understand?"

"Yeah. Of course. I'm hot."

"We're all hot, Matty. This weather sucks. But you don't see me being a cunt, do you?"

He opened his mouth to protest but something stopped him. "I'm sorry."

"What else have you got?"

Linderer tapped the screen of the laptop. "When I model the blood spatter, Mr. Grossman in there had his pipe cut on a downward angle."

"You mean a downward stroke?"

He nodded and the collar on his space suit rasped in the lifeless air. "Yes, but the cut was in a straight line—there's no sweep to it. It was pulled across his throat from a low angle. The killer was probably kneeling on the pavement beside the car and when Grossman leaned over—probably to get something from the glove compartment—the door opened and he was hit with the blade."

"What was in the glove box?"

"Two Charleston Chews, a cell phone, a handgun, and three shots of Cialis."

"What kind of a pistol?"

"Small automatic. Beretta. He had a carry permit."

Hemingway was once again amazed at how quickly the forensics guys were able to turn someone's life into the past tense—it always struck her as abrupt.

Mr. Grossman hadn't known much about guns—a Beretta was as deadly as far as you could throw it. But it was expensive. For some, cost equated to value; the pistol had probably been purchased by someone who wanted the best but didn't know what to look for.

Linderer continued. "I'll have a full report once we get the car back to the lab but don't expect any surprises. Whoever did this knew what he was doing."

Phelps was suddenly there, straightening his tie. "I caught Dr. Grant at the office. A car is on the way to take him home." He held up his smartphone, the photo of Bobby Grant smiling out of the screen. "It's already on the news."

She took out her own phone and cycled to a photo of Tyler Rochester. She held it up beside the phone in Phelps's hand and stared at the pictures of the two children. It was impossible to miss the similarities.

"We've got one break," she said.

"Which is?" He pulled off his jacket and his shirt was stained with a deep shadow of sweat down the front and under both arms.

"We know his type."

ACCORDING TO Dr. Grant's files at both the DMV and city hall, he was two weeks shy of his sixty-first birthday. He looked like a mummified fifty, a benefit of being one of the city's most prestigious plastic surgeons. Mrs. Grant was twenty-five years his junior and had the classic look of a certain kind of second wife, replete with breast implants and a flat expression that differed from Tyler Rochester's mother in that it came from Botox, not booze and pills. The resemblance to a ventriloquist dummy was hard to miss.

Unlike the ministry of help at the Rochesters' townhouse, there was only one other person in the apartment—Mrs. Grant's mother, who looked in some strange way more suited to Dr. Grant than his wife. Everyone was holding up well considering their world had just been destroyed by a man with a razor blade.

Hemingway sat down in one of the wing chairs facing the sofa and explained that they had a few questions that they had to deal with now—things they needed in order to move forward with the investigation. She ran through the questions she had put to the Rochester boy's parents, focusing on new people in their son's life.

Mrs. Grant's mouth barely moved as she talked about her missing child. She began by saying that he was a good boy. Hemingway had interviewed many parents and they always began with that same heartbreaking expression. After that, Mrs. Grant went on in an orderly fashion, almost a summation of Bobby's life. He excelled at school, particularly science, taking MIT's Young Achiever's award this year for a robot he had designed and built that cleaned countertops using black light to target bacteria. She nodded at the piano in the corner of the living room, a shiny art deco Bösendorfer; she thought he played too much but when she approached the subject, he had reacted like most kids when told they had to cut back on video games. With pride she related how he had written two piano concertos over the winter and had a recital coming up at the Brooklyn Academy of Music in late July.

Bobby's driver, Desmond, had worked for them for six years now, driving the boy to and from school, to his extra-curricular activities and piano lessons from the first time he had stepped out of the apartment on his own. Dr. Grant had purchased the pistol they found in the glove box. It was clear to Hemingway that both Dr. and Mrs. Grant were upset about Desmond's death. They seemed like compassionate, decent people.

The deeper they got into the questioning, the tighter Dr. Grant's face got, until he stood up, nodded at the door, and told them that they would better serve his son if they were out trying to find him.

After cards were exchanged, Dr. Grant walked them to the elevator, telling them to do anything necessary. If they faced any budgetary restraints, they were to come to him. The bell pinged and the doors slid open. Phelps stepped into the car and as Hemingway turned to shake Dr. Grant's hand, he held it and looked into her eyes.

"After everything we went through to have Bobby, it will kill his mother if something happens to him. Find my son."

Hemingway did her best to look confident as she nodded. Then she turned and stepped into the elevator. As the doors slid closed, Dr. Grant stared at her, his face still locked in disbelief. On the descent to street level, something told her that he was still standing there, staring at the elevator doors, trying to figure out who he had to speak to in order to trade his soul for a time machine.

They moved through the lobby and out to the no-standing zone where she had parked the Suburban. When they reached the SUV, her phone chirped.

"Hemingway."

"Yeah, Hemi, it's Lincoln. I got you that appointment you wanted at the Manhattan office of the Department of Waterways and Estuaries. Your contact is Dr. Inge Torssen . . . Torssen . . . Torssensomethingorother. It's up near the Bronx—One Hundred and Forty-fourth on the West Side. Can you be there in fifteen minutes? This Torssen woman has a flight out of Newark in two hours and she won't be there for much longer."

"Fifteen it is," she said, hung up, and pulled a U-turn in a smoking arc of rubber.

FIFTEEN

DR. INGE TORSSENNSON was tall, blond, intelligent, and hypereducated. A quick Internet search showed that she had started her career as an undergrad at the Norwegian University of Science and Technology, studying particle theory under the loose rubric of general physics. She eventually moved to fluid dynamics, garnering a PhD in a branch of wave refraction from MIT. Her specialty was Doppler current profiling. She was at the Manhattan office of the Department of Waterways and Estuaries on a one-year sabbatical before accepting a professorship at UC Berkeley.

She had the stride of a wide receiver and as they descended into the basement of the building, Phelps whispered to Hemingway that he now understood why the Vikings had kicked so much ass.

"I've looked over the maps and times you forwarded and have come up with a few things that might help with your investigation." Her English was excellent but flowered with the soft consonants Scandinavians are famous for. At the end of the hallway she pushed open the double doors. The blast of humidity was a much heavier presence than the New York summer five floors up at street level. The walls were literally sweating.

The scale model of the Hudson River rolled to the far end of the room, a complicated pool under a domed ceiling that could have housed a fleet of jumbo jets. The shorelines of Manhattan, New Jersey, and Brooklyn were recreated in scaled detail, the earth, concrete, stone, grass and glass represented by a uniform brown resin. Wires, cameras, and sensors monitored every square inch of the man-made island, sending the stream of digital information to several computer stations positioned around the installment. Hemingway's eye was immediately drawn to the scaled-down Statue of Liberty, roughly the size of a Barbie doll, at the far end of the pool.

Beyond the diminutive Lady Liberty, a couple of modelers stood in thigh-high water at the Jersey docks, wearing waders and double filter particle masks. They were modifying the shoreline to post-Sandy specs and they looked like giants in an Asian science fiction film.

"I've reverse-engineered the boy's most probable path based on the drop times you provided. You have to understand that there are numerous variables involved, not just current. I've factored in salt flux, wind, and tide—but this is all very speculative. The body may have hung up in debris somewhere for a while. The good news, if you can call it that, is that the particular area of the river where he washed up is subject to extremely heavy currents that have established patterns." She walked them to one of the platforms at the far end, a steel balcony above the northeast corner of the island of Manhattan.

"If the boy was abducted between six twenty-one and six thirty-one p.m. on Monday, as you indicated, and his body was found at nine twenty-one by a jogger," she said, pronouncing it *yogger*, "we have a window of a little under two hours. You suspect that the boy's body was dumped at—or just after—sunset, which was eight twenty-two p.m. If he was put in the water at, say, any time between eight twenty-five and eight forty-five, with wind and current factored in, I'd estimate that he was put in the water somewhere here . . ." The laser pointer came to life in Torssennson's hand, the red dot of its eye zeroing in on a stretch of water that boiled and bubbled with the diminutive currents fed through the simulated topography. It was a stretch where the Hudson River cut between Randall's Island and Astoria.

The red dot crawled along the shorelines of Astoria, then crossed the channel, and negotiated the terrain of Randall's Island, once again crossing water—this time the Harlem River—hitting the shore of Manhattan at 120th Street. "I can't be certain where the boy was dumped, but it was above here," she said, circling a bubbling epicenter of foam at the southern tip of a stretch of scaled-down real estate stenciled with the words RANDALL'S ISLAND.

Hemingway knew that stretch of water; she had kayaked around it hundreds of times, and knew that fickle patch of roiling anguish had a reputation of being evil as far back as anyone in New York could remember. It was one of the few places on the river that the pleasure boaters avoided, especially the weekend sailors with the expensive nav systems on boats tattooed with monikers like *Daddy's Li'l Girl* and *My First Million*. Only the big river barges—laden with garbage or stone—negotiated its wrath.

Hemingway focused on the scaled-down current and eddies. "That's Hell Gate," she said.

Then her phone rang, something that surprised her; she figured that this far into the earth there wouldn't be any reception. She mimed an apology to Dr. Torssennson and went to the far end of the platform.

"Hemingway," she answered. Across Manhattan the men in particle masks were busy mixing whatever it was they used for landscaping material and the visual was so surreal that she wouldn't have been surprised to see a guy in a Godzilla suit somewhere off to their right. The office parties down here had to be YouTube worthy.

"Hemi, it's Lincoln. I just got a call from a retired judge who saw the Rochester boy's story on CNN this morning. Name's Jack Willoughby. Lives in Boca. He said there was a remarkable similarity between the Rochester case and one he presided over back in eighty-four."

She didn't get the flush of elation or the push of adrenaline that most people would have; years of following leads that enticed her down the road to nowhere had hardened her hope reflex. "That's three decades ago, Linc." She wasn't being negative, just pragmatic—according to Dr. Marcus, the Rochester boy had been taken apart by a nascent killer, not someone with a history for this kind of thing. And these guys had a window that usually closed in their late forties as their testosterone waned. Something about this didn't seem right. "Did you run a check on Willoughby?"

"Thirty-eight years as a trial judge in the city—solid record."

"What did he have to say?"

"He had a case where a twenty-eight-year-old male was pulled over for running a light in Queens. After a shouting match that made the duty officer suspicious, he checked the car and found a pair of children's feet in a grocery bag in the trunk. The perp ran but the car was registered in his mother's name and they picked the guy up at his home a few hours later."

At that her adrenaline kicked in. "And?"

"The prosecutor couldn't prove that the feet had come

from a murder victim; Deacon's lawyer argued that his client had purchased them from a man who worked in a medical supply warehouse. And the body of an eleven-year-old Indian boy had indeed gone missing from one such facility a few weeks before. The perp served six months for disrespectful treatment of human remains. Probation afterwards—judge couldn't remember the details but I'm looking into it now."

"We have a name? An address?"

"Name's Trevor Deacon, that's d-e-a-c-o-n. I checked— he's on Crestwood in Astoria. Hasn't moved in all this time."

She hung up and turned to Phelps. "Jon, it's go time."

"Whacha got?"

"We have a line on a perp with a similar MO. Retired judge called it in. The guy lives right there," she said, pointing to where Dr. Torssennson's pointer had just walked across the water. "In Astoria."

THE HOUSE was a little slope-roofed postwar with a garage, a small front yard taken up by an ancient elm, and a faded Post-it taped inside the screen door that told peddlers, Mormons, and Jehovah's Witnesses to take their business elsewhere.

Hemingway pulled up to the front of the house with two patrol cars as escort. She and Phelps hit the pavement and headed up the front steps while two of the patrolmen headed around back, guns out. The second pair of uniforms stood at the curb.

She and Phelps took up position on either side of the door. Thirty seconds after she pushed the bell, the front door opened and a small woman who had to be in her early eighties stuck her head out.

"Cantya read?" she rasped through a puff of tobacco smoke and jabbed a finger at the faded paper sign. "No Jesus. And no fuckin' Girl Guides." She stared at Hemingway for a second, then her eyes slid over to Phelps before coming back and settling on the undone top buttons of Hemingway's white cotton blouse. "Not if they know what's good for them."

Hemingway held up her badge, her other hand behind her, fingers wrapped around the rubber grip of her revolver. "We're looking for Trevor Deacon."

The old woman tightened her mouth around the cigarette and took a long haul, her lips wrinkled like an ancient, furry sphincter. "What'd he do this time?"

Hemingway took a step sideways so the woman would see the cruisers on the street. "Is Trevor Deacon here?"

From behind a cloud of smoke she seemed to teeter on the precipice of indecision for a few seconds before she nodded. "Yeah. He lives downstairs." She stepped out onto the porch in her ancient stained bathrobe and a pair of Pink Foil Nikes. "That's his door."

"Is he home?"

"How the fuckinell I know? I got X-ray vision I don't know about?"

Hemingway leaned down and looked the woman in the eyes. "Anyone else in the building?"

The old lady eyed her for a second. "Yeah, Elvis," she snapped, then tried to step back into the house and slam the door.

Hemingway grabbed her arm, swung her around, and Phelps had cuffs on her before her screaming started. Hemingway put her finger to her lips in a be-quiet gesture, and handed the old lady off to one of the uniformed officers. He dragged her down to the car, screaming that the cops were a bunch of assholes.

The two detectives ran through the upstairs part of the house, checking the rooms one by one. The door that led to the basement was boarded up. When they had finished, they headed down the steps outside. The old lady was still screaming inside the cruiser, every sentence accentuated with a subwoofer thud as she tried to kick her way out.

Hemingway looked for a buzzer at the basement door. The button had been taped over with another curled-paper ballpoint pen sign that read No SOLISSITERS. She pulled the screen open and knocked on the heavy multilock metal door— the kind designed to keep people out. Or in.

They waited.

She knocked again.

Phelps eased sideways, took off his sunglasses, and leaned into the window, cupping his hands to see into the dark.

Hemingway raised her fist to bang on the door again when Phelps let out a low groan. "Jesus, no!" he said, and pushed her aside.

He hammered the door with two good bottom-foot kicks and the impact barely registered.

"Phelps, what the—?"

But he already had his automatic out. He leveled it at the door and blew out the two padlocks. Then he kicked it in. It flew into the wall and bounced back.

He screamed, "Call EMS now!" to the cops at the curb.

Instinctively, Hemingway went in first, crouching low and taking the left flank like they had done a thousand times in drills and a few dozen on the job.

As she swung the muzzle of her pistol around, she saw why Phelps had blown out the locks.

Whatever it was now, at one time it had been a human being.

"This must be Elvis," Phelps said, and holstered his pistol.

BENJAMIN WINSLOW ticked off the final multiple-choice question, dropped his pencil, and raised his hand.

The scratch of graphite on paper around him ceased and a shuffle whispered through the lecture hall; he was the first one finished. *Again.* All three parts. Benjamin picked up his knapsack, walked to the front of the hall, and dropped his test paper and the Number 2 pencil onto the monitor's desk. He didn't bother nodding at the man; he often found the openmouthed look of awe annoying.

He pushed through the polished bronze doors and stepped out into the day. A photographer leaning against one of the massive limestone columns that flanked the door snapped a photo and gave him the thumbs-up. "Congratulations, kid. How's it feel to be a genius?"

"*Lorem ipsum,*" he said and headed down the steps before the guy figured out that he was being made fun of.

Benjamin took out his phone and dialed his father as he had promised.

He answered in one ring. "Dr. Winslow here."

"Hey, Dad, I'm done with the SATs."

"How'd you do?" his father said in his usual monotone.

Tests of all kinds had been a constant in Ben's routine ever since he could remember. Beyond his vast library of talent was an acute ability for predicting test results. But it wasn't much of a prediction; it was simply the ability to recall the number of questions he had known the answers to versus the number of questions he hadn't—simple math, really. "One of the multiple-choice questions in the reading section was interpretive so it depends on the test bias. Other than that, perfect." He got to the sidewalk and headed west, toward the park.

"Why don't you come to the museum? I've got to finish up some notes for tomorrow's lecture but I'll be done by the time you get here. We can walk down to the Garden Vegan and get a nice salad. Bean curd for the genius."

"How about a cheeseburger?"

"Kings don't dine on cheeseburgers, son." His father was quiet for a second and Benjamin wondered if he was angry. "Grab a cab."

Benjamin stopped at the curb and looked both ways before crossing Madison. "It's a nice day. I'd like to walk."

This time there was no pause. "We've talked about this. I don't want you walking through the park. It's filled with all manner of miscreants in the summer. Take a cab."

Benjamin wanted to tell his father that technically it was still spring but settled on, "Dad, I'm not a kid anymore."

"To a predator you're just a ten-year-old boy. Take a taxi."

I can take care of myself, he wanted to say but it came out as, "Yes, sir."

"See you soon, son." And his father hung up.

Benjamin reached around and put his phone into his

knapsack, then he headed across the street to the gauntlet of yellow taxis. This was ridiculous—who did his father think he was, a baby?

He got into the cab, smiled at the driver in the mirror, and said, "Central Park West between Eighty and Eighty-first, please. In front of the museum." Then he settled back for the ride across the park—a trip he would much rather have done on foot on such a nice day. What could happen to him out here?

III EIGHTEEN

HEMINGWAY STARED at Trevor Deacon. He had been a pedophile.

Had been.

Past tense.

Trevor would not be molesting children anymore. Trevor would not be doing much of anything anymore. What was left of him was neatly placed on the various pieces of furniture in the basement room, mostly the bookshelf and the old Telefunken record player/television combo under the window with the heavy bars.

His parts were all there, displayed like a collection of prized Franklin Mint plates. But the Franklin Mint wasn't going to be putting out decorative dinnerware to commemorate Trevor Deacon's accomplishments. Not now, not ever.

The forensics team was done with everything but the garage—the main body of the basement apartment was now open—so Hemingway busied herself learning what she could from Trevor Deacon's home. She stood with her hands in her pockets, her head tilted to one side as if she were scanning titles at the library, examining the demented performance art that looked like it had been lifted from a Rob Zombie story-board. Deacon's body had been reduced to its unarticulated components. Everything from his jaw to his feet was neatly placed in the cubbyholes of the teak shelving and on top of the stereo.

Hemingway was no stranger to violent death, and she was certainly no stranger to the closed-in world of the psychopath, but she needed to concentrate and with the old lady screeching through cigarette smoke from the door it was impossible to get a single thought going.

"Who's gonna clean this mess up?" she barked. "Me? Oh no. Not me. I've cleaned up after this piece of shit his whole life and I ain't gonna do it no more, I can tell you. He's a pig. And a sonofabitch. Just look at this place. It's a mess. A mess—"

Hemingway turned her head and nailed Papandreou with a hard stare. "Officer Papandreou, would you please escort Mrs. Deacon back out to the car. This is a crime scene." She turned back to the chunks of Trevor.

"Oh no you don't!" the lady screamed when Papandreou wrapped his fingers around her elbow. "I gotta keep my eyes on you sonsabitches. Last time you were here you ripped the place to shit. I ain't gonna clean up after you, neither. Take me upstairs, I ain't leaving my purse lying around with all you thieving cop assholes skulking around. I got experience with you guys."

Without taking his hand from her elbow, Papandreou said, "Mrs. Deacon, the last time we were here was 1984 and the police report said you opened the door and threw hot bacon grease at a police officer before he could open his mouth."

"I thought it was Trevor. I told the judge and he believed me. Check your fancy computers, ya dumb Greek cop bastard."

She turned her head back to the basement and barked, "You still ain't said—who's gonna clean this mess up?"

Hemingway resisted the temptation to walk over and slap the woman. "Nick?" she said, stretching it out to two irritated syllables.

Nick began pulling the old lady from the door. "We will have people come in and take care of that. But we have to record the evidence first. We can't do that with you standing here screaming. Let me take you upstairs and we'll get your purse. Then I'll have someone take you to the local precinct where a social worker will handle the logistics. You'll go to a hotel for a few days so we can catalog and clean up. While you're there, someone from social services will help you fill out the papers—as the victim of violent crime, you are enti- tled to compensation."

The old woman's eyes narrowed and her mouth pursed up again. "Compensation? How much compensation?"

"It depends on your current income but somewhere around six hundred dollars a month."

"Six hundred dollars a month! That sonofabitch over there is worth six hundred dollars a month! I wish he would have got this years ago." She picked up her pace. "Well, dipshit, you gonna take me to get my pension or not?"

Papandreou led Mrs. Deacon away and the rat-tat-tat of her voice was finally swallowed by the ambient noise in the apartment. Hemingway stepped back into character. Yester- day at this time, none of this had existed. Tyler Rochester had still been alive and the world was spinning happily on its axis. Less than a full turn of the planet later and little Tyler, a driver named Desmond, and a pedophile named Trevor Deacon had been turned into headlines. And then there was Bobby Grant—a child who looked so much like Tyler Roch- ester that they may as well have been brothers. Still missing.

Still gone. Still on his way to joining the others in the headlines unless they got lucky.

Deacon hadn't shown up on the predator list because he had never been registered on any of the databases. They were running down the case jacket but she already knew what they'd find. The guy had walked on a technicality and then got lost in the massive paperwork of the record-keeping engine. Three decades had gone by and he had slipped from communal memory because he had been careful. Until that judge had remembered him.

Of course, someone else had remembered Deacon as well: a guy with a saw and a lot of time to kill. What was the connection?

Hemingway turned back to the room—back to the task lighting and the strobe of the photographer's flash—and was grateful for the sudden silence. She walked around the space, a rec room turned apartment where Trevor had spent his life hiding from the world. His bed—an old iron frame—sat in the bedroom. The mattress, pillows, and sheets might have been another color yesterday—maybe white, maybe yellow—but were now a sopping mess of cracked red and black.

Deacon's torso lay on the bed. No arms. No legs. No head. No genitals. Just a big blood-spattered hairy roast waiting to go into the oven.

There wasn't much to look at in the rest of the apartment. There was an old Formica table with one chair, a toaster oven, a plaid sofa and the Cold War stereo/television combo. A coffee table with a book on birds and an ashtray on top. Not much of a place when you really looked at it.

The only thing that seemed new was the computer system set up near the fridge. Alan Carson, from the cybercrimes division, was in the process of dismantling Trevor's PC—a sleek red plastic tower with two forty-two-inch monitors.

Carson looked like a guy tinkering in his garage, not a man working a few feet from a chopped-up human being.

The forensics guys moved around in their space suits, hoods off now that they were done black-lighting the carpet and plucking samples with tweezers. The one thing that didn't make sense was that for a place so full of blood, there were no footprints or fingerprints, handprints, or glove smears. The only immediate evidence was on the Naugahyde covering of the single kitchen chair: a dried red crescent of blood that had come from the tip of a shoe.

But the crescent of blood frowned toward the back of the chair—an impossible position to tie your shoe, unless you had eight-foot legs.

He had stepped on the chair. Why?

The ceiling was barely seven feet tall and, with the exception of three ceramic sockets armed with bare forty-watt bulbs, was popcorn Sheetrock. Nothing had been taken down, nothing put up.

Carson looked up from the tower he was working on. "No hard drives." He pushed the Buddy Holly glasses up on his nose. "Panels were pulled, at least four hard drives gone. We can go after Internet records but if he pirated a neighbor's bandwidth it's gonna be tough."

If Deacon had been logged into the databases all those years ago—even on one of the "to watch" lists—there would have been a yard of ironclad conditions tacked on to his parole terms. Convicted pedophiles were not allowed within two hundred yards of anywhere children could be found, parks and schools in particular. They were not usually permitted to use the Internet; and if they were allowed to access the Internet, they had very strict access. Since Deacon had never been entered in the system, he had been completely unsupervised.

Mat Linderer from Dr. Marcus's office came over, sweating in his breathable antistatic suit. He had a wavy red line on his forehead where the sweatband had cut in and combined with the cornrows of a hair transplant, it looked like the top of his head had recently been sewn on. "Detective, there's not much here that looks out of place. Plenty of genetic material but most of it looks like it belongs to the vic. I found a pair of expensive telephoto lenses in the bottom drawer of the dresser." His tone was much friendlier than it had been that morning at the Huntington Academy.

"No camera?"

"No camera. But I did find this in the fridge." He held up a plastic Parkay container and peeled back the lid to show her the contents. It was lined with small clear polyethylene bags filled with a pink powder.

"What is it?"

Linderer shrugged. "I'll know when I get it back to the lab. Could be drain cleaner. Could be anthrax."

Hemingway took out her iPhone and snapped a picture for her files. "I want the results as soon as you've nailed them down."

He nodded, closed the lid, and eased it into a refrigerated cooler. "I'll call when I have something."

She walked over to a spot on the wall where four yellow pushpins were tacked to the fake paneling, the corner of a torn photograph hanging off one. The pins were spaced out for an eight-by-ten. What was missing?

Phelps, the Iron Giant, cycled slowly through the place, somehow managing to not be underfoot. Of all the people Hemingway had seen around crime scenes, no one had Phelps's uncanny ability to avoid being in the way. It was more than a skill, it was some kind of magical power.

Linderer waved him over and said, "I don't think this was a B and E but Detective Phelps's .45 did a lot of damage so I can't be sure. Both rounds went into the tumblers. But if the perp didn't break in, he was let in—those locks are very difficult to pick."

"The windows?" Hemingway asked, pointing at the two in the front and one in the bedroom. All three had heavy steel bars set into the sills. She had seen jail cells with leaner security.

Phelps, who had examined them carefully, said, "My grandson would have a hard time squeezing his skinny ass through there. No getting in."

"Or out," she added. "So whoever killed Trevor Deacon was let in and he locked the doors on the way out. Or had keys."

"We found one set of keys but not a second," Linderer said. "Everyone has a spare set."

Phelps pointed at the three steel doors to the basement: one that led upstairs to the boarded-over house passage; one for the garage; and one for the side entrance he had shot open. All the doors were secured with an array of security locks from the best manufacturers in the world. Thousands of dollars' worth of locks per door. "This guy liked his privacy."

Hemingway examined the door to the garage, painted over with the scribbly effigy of what could only be a spider, an image out of the dark recesses of Trevor Deacon's diseased mind. The forensics guys still weren't done in there but from the look she had seen on the face of the photographer, she knew it would be more of the same.

"What's with the spider?"

Phelps shrugged. "It's beyond me. Maybe he was a fan of *Charlotte's Web*."

Hemingway wasn't so sure.

With the thought still hanging over her, the task lighting from under the door blinked out and the door opened up. Two of Marcus's men came into the room, pulling off their hoods as they stepped over the threshold. They didn't look shaken—they were beyond being shocked on the job—but they did look upset.

Phelps headed into the garage. Linderer followed.

Hemingway stood at the threshold to the damp space under the house, examining the mad scribbled effigy of the spider, wondering how it had fit into Trevor Deacon's world.

Had it been his god?

His tormentor?

His confidant?

His lover?

From somewhere beyond Trevor Deacon's spider, Phelps said, "Hemi, there's something in here you should see."

She stepped through the steel door with the array of padlocks and security crossbars, past the arachnid sentinel, and into the gloom.

The garage was an ancient damp shadow that felt like the perfect place to keep a monstrous spider. The floor was patched and fissured and there was a filthy carpenter's bench in the middle of the room under the single bulb. Garden tools and lengths of welded chain hung from spiral nails planted in the concrete. The garage door was upholstered in pink insulation and part of the wall near the door was covered with moldy egg cartons—improvised soundproofing.

She passed another dark crescent of what could only be blood near the door—another shoe print like the one in the kitchen. It, too, had been covered with an evidence hood.

Phelps stood in the corner, beside an old coffin freezer. Linderer held the lid open with a rubber-gloved hand. Phelps was looking at her, not the freezer, and a feeble light that washed up onto his face gave his skin a yellow cast. Frozen vapor wafted over the lip of the appliance and slunk down to the floor.

She moved toward the light. Toward the open space that looked as if it were smoking. Her line of sight crawled over the lip of the metal box and she saw the neatly stowed plastic sandwich bags. It took a minute for her to figure out what she was looking at.

She closed her eyes, kept them shut for a second, then opened them, hoping that it had somehow taken on another form.

It hadn't.

Hemingway stepped toward the freezer, summoned by Trevor Deacon's madness.

She no longer felt Phelps or Linderer in the room. She could see them. But they were so far away that they could have been in another time zone.

The psychotic rendering of the spider on the door wasn't a representation of his god—it was something else, something a lot more basic; that drawing was Trevor Deacon's version of a BEWARE OF DOG sign.

Inside the freezer, stacked like dumplings, were dozens of little blue-white feet in Ziploc bags.

MARCUS SPENT a few seconds cleaning his glasses on the tail of his lab coat. Then he returned them to his nose, yawned, and pulled a file from a rolling trolley that sat in the aisle between the tables. He cracked the folder and read from the cover sheet. "Deacon, Trevor A., male, fifty-six years old. Case number 551.2101.677." The medical examiner peeled back the plastic sheet, bundled it into a sloppy knot, and put it in a bucket on the floor.

All the king's horses, all the king's men, and every forensic specialist in the land couldn't put Trevor Deacon together again. He was arranged in a more or less orderly anatomical position, except that his parts were not connected. His feet were at the end of the table, sitting on the soles, the sheared-through ankles pointing up at the ceiling like bloodless osso buco about to go into the oven. Deacon's head was in two parts, cut in half at the jaw. The top part of his skull sat at the head of the table, a meat helmet with slightly open eyes, one pupil dialed in toward his nose, cross-eyed in a way evolution had never intended.

Phelps stood on the other side of the stainless steel slab,

across from Hemingway. She knew that he would rather be somewhere else from the way his head was cocked to one side. Which was understandable—it was hard to gather any sympathy for the disassembled man laid out on the table like a set of wind chimes waiting to be strung together.

Examined from one angle, Deacon amounted to little more than another piece of human garbage subtracted from the cesspool of predators. Another broken person who did little other than transfer his own pain to the people he came in contact with. It wasn't hard to look at his remains and think that whoever had broken out the saw had done the human race a giant favor. But this was connected to Tyler Rochester and Bobby Grant; there was too much coincidence at play for it not to be. So they would be spending a lot of time thinking about the man on the slab before they put this one to bed.

"TOD was somewhere between midnight and two thirty a.m. last night." Dr. Marcus looked up. "And he did not die of natural causes."

Phelps snorted. Hemingway shook her head; this wasn't her first time in a lab, and certainly not her first time around a dead body, but she believed that a certain amount of respect was due the dead, even life's monsters. "What did he die of, Marcus?"

"Exsanguination."

"From one of these cuts?" Hemingway asked, sweeping her hand over the general area of the corpse.

The ME put the file down on the edge of the trolley, then picked one of Deacon's feet up. He pointed to the neat line of stump. "Sometime while his feet were being cut off is my guess."

At this Phelps said, "And he was alive when this happened?"

Marcus put the foot back in its place and as it touched the table, the flesh on the heel dented in, like a wax candle on a hot day. "Yes, he was."

Hemingway answered the sixty-four-thousand-dollar question. "This was done by the same guy who chopped up Tyler Rochester."

Marcus nodded. "This time the cut lines are straight, with very little travel. He's better than he was with Tyler Rochester. Smooth, long strokes and a lot of stamina. Taking a big guy like Deacon apart would have taken a good hour, maybe ninety minutes. But it's the same small-toothed saw—twenty-four teeth per inch."

"Same anesthetic?"

"The initial scan says yes. Again, thiopental with no analgesic is a fair guess. I'll know more in a couple of days when the tox screens come back but the MO is identical. If you look at his right eye you can see the damage where he was injected. A jab in the vitreous humor and then to work." Dr. Marcus paused, removed his spotless glasses, and cleaned them with a static-free wipe from a dispenser.

"Would it have taken thirty-five seconds to take effect, like the Rochester kid?" Hemingway asked.

"Longer if the same dosage was used; Trevor here was a big boy and he'd absorb it a lot slower. The effects might not even be as debilitating. But on top of the anesthetic I found heroin in his system. Heroin combined with something like thiopental would have made him a big, slow-moving target. Might have even killed him."

Phelps jammed his hands into his pants pockets and rolled up on the balls of his feet. "To get close enough to jab a guy like Deacon in the eye, it had to be someone he knew. Or at least felt comfortable enough to let in. The doors are fitted with back-locked Abloys and the bars on the windows are so close together a pygmy would have a hard time squeezing in."

Marcus readjusted the foot he had just put down, aligning it to some invisible grid that only he could see. "Even then, when someone jabs you in the eye with a hypodermic, a few seconds is enough time to take a swing. There were no defensive wounds. No tissue or fabric under his fingernails. Teeth were clean. No bruised knuckles. Nothing knocked over in the apartment. The only damage to the body was a broken toe on his right foot—probably when it hit the floor after it was removed. Technically it's postmortem even though he was probably alive when it broke."

Hemingway knew that this kind of work was nothing new but it took a special kind of someone to saw up a human being and place the parts around a room like accessories from Pottery Barn. And there had to be a purpose to the act. What had been the motivation?

"The similarities don't stop there," Marcus continued. "Like the Rochester boy, the inexperience in anatomy left some signature wounds. The right upper arm was cut an inch too far into the humerus then torqued to separate it from the body, like my grandkids do with chicken wings." He pointed to the corresponding joint but Hemingway didn't bother to lean in and examine it. "But he was already dead at that point."

The medical examiner went back to his notes and flipped through a few pages as if making sure he hadn't missed anything. "More than a little ironic that Mr. Deacon should meet his end by vivisection."

"Live by the sword." Phelps smiled and it was not a friendly expression. "Die by the sword."

||| T W E N T Y

AFTER FINISHING with Dr. Marcus, Hemingway and Phelps headed down to the sequencing and analysis labs, the backbone of the city's missing persons initiative. It was a maze of quarantined cubicles walled off from one another with frosted glass. Behind those walls was a twenty-four-hour horror show that never got canceled.

They moved past the sally port, through the main space, passing locked rooms where bodies in an advanced state of decomposition were being examined. In a discipline where DNA was now the defining factor in solving many cases, every effort was made to keep remains—or partial remains—from coming into contact with one another.

They found their way to Dr. Dorothy Calucci's lab. The two detectives had worked with her a year back on a case where a mother had locked her twin daughters in the oven as punishment for spilling milk on the floor. It had taken four screeching minutes for the girls to die. The mother was doing twenty-six years upstate but would be eligible for parole before she was thirty-five.

Calucci led the two detectives to one of the frosted rooms off the main lab where a few dozen stainless steel containers were distributed over as many tables. Each container was numbered and had a glass window in the hinged cover. Hemingway didn't have to look inside to know that they held children's feet, the handiwork of one Trevor Deacon.

Calucci lacked the bedside manner and dark humor of Dr. Marcus, a temperament a little more in tune with a case where the common element was live humans taken apart with a saw.

Calucci began the briefing without any greeting or salutation; she operated on the let's-not-waste-time frequency. "There were seventy-five feet in the Deacon house. Swabs determined that they belonged to boys. Sizing dictates that they were between eight and eleven years old. All of them were removed with a hacksaw or similar-type tool while the victims were alive. Out of seventy-five feet, there are thirty-one pairs and thirteen singles. So far we have identified six children—four pairs and two of the singles—by matching prints to online hospital registries that have been sistered to missing children networks. We expect to garner more matches through tissue samples submitted to the FBI's missing persons program within the CODIS database."

Hemingway didn't have to ask how long the process would take—as a lead detective in a squad specializing in child murders, she knew that nuclear DNA could be sequenced in about forty hours. Once sequenced and submitted to the FBI for identification, it took less than an hour for the software to find a match if there was one; there was no way to rush the process.

"We should start getting results Thursday morning." Calucci nodded at the protocols she had handed over. "You have six children identified there, detectives. The oldest case dates back to August 1992—a boy named Victor Roslyne. Disappeared on his way home from school."

Hemingway's pen stopped over the paper and she raised her eyes. "You mean to tell me that there are more than twenty years' worth of missing children's cases here?" she asked, indicating the stainless steel graveyard.

"So far, yes. There might be older cases but we won't know until we identify all of the victims. *If* we identify all of the victims."

Hemingway's focus wandered over the bins and she saw the diminutive feet beneath the clear windows. Staring down at the fruits of Trevor Deacon's labor, it was easy to understand Phelps's indifference up in Marcus's lab.

Hemingway wondered where, precisely, the system had failed—and it *had* failed. How else could you justify the disappearance and murder of at least forty-four children? Why hadn't Deacon been stopped years ago? How had his sickness managed to survive for so long? To flourish? Lincoln was hunting down the files now—they needed to know why this guy had walked.

Calucci continued with her briefing. "No heavy decomposition in any of the remains; they were frozen when fresh. There is a lot of cellular damage due to less than ideal freezing and improper storage conditions but we have usable DNA from all of the vics."

Hemingway scanned the forest of little feet then went to the files that Calucci had given her. "Are all six boys that you've identified from New York City?"

"Every one."

"Jesus," Phelps said in a low whistle. "This guy was a one-man plague."

Like Phelps, Hemingway knew the stats. Sixty-five

hundred children go missing in Manhattan and the surrounding boroughs each year: ninety-seven percent of those are runaways; a hundred and fifty cases turn out to be abductions by noncustodial parents or family members; and fifteen simply disappear from the known Newtonian universe. "Whoever killed this guy just reset the statistics." She tried to focus on the white field of her notebook instead of troughs filled with the screams of little boys. "Anything unusual with the remains?"

Calucci nodded and flipped through the sheaf of papers in her hand until she found what she was looking for. She folded back the page and handed the clipped bundle to Hemingway.

She read the page then looked up. "Are you sure?"

Calucci nodded. "On all of the single feet we found traces of competing DNA. I can black-light them if you want."

Phelps cleared his throat and held up his hand as if he were in grade school. "Can we have the dummy talk?"

Hemingway passed him the file. "Read."

He pulled out his glasses—cheap dollar-store grandpa deals—unfolded them, and plunked them onto the tip of his nose. For an instant he looked like he would begin with, "'Twas the night before Christmas," but the color quickly dropped out of his face. "You gotta be fucking kidding."

The grim line of Calucci's mouth barely moved. "It hasn't been matched to Trevor Deacon yet but there is no doubt that it's semen."

HEADMASTER FREYTAG stared at the boy, trying to figure out a way to bridge the communication gap. The headmaster had been at this a long time, and he had ushered the school through twenty-one years of minor catastrophes with a character that was strict, intelligent, and fair. But there were times when he needed to be creative. Maybe even a little vulgar. Times like now.

"Miles, do you know why you're sitting here?"

Miles Morgan shrugged as if it didn't make a difference. And in a way, it didn't. Like all the boys at the academy, Miles Morgan's future was written on watermarked paper. Whether he managed to finish his education at this institution or at another, he would walk into a life devoid of financial worries. He would spend his summers in Montauk, winters on Mustique. Except for the divorces coming his way, Miles Morgan would ride a worry-free wave to the cemetery.

But this was where Miles Morgan differed from the other boys at the school; he didn't care about any of that.

And Freytag found this refreshing.

Morgan followed his shrug with, "You're pissed about those four faggoty seventh graders."

Freytag sighed and leaned forward, his hands on the leather top of the desk. "Miles, you can't use language like that. Sexual orientation shouldn't be equated with weakness."

Morgan stared at him for a few seconds. "What?"

"You can't call someone 'faggoty'—it's not proper. Choose another term."

The boy shrugged again. "Can I call them assholes?"

Freytag wanted to sigh again but this time he held it in. "How about calling them bullies?"

Last Friday, four of the older boys had cornered Morgan in one of the bathrooms, thinking his heavy-lidded gaze revealed a victim in waiting. Their intentions were less than noble but fundamentally innocent—they tried to give him a wedgie. By the time a teacher had responded to the yells of terror and pain echoing from the bathroom, Miles Morgan had a broken finger and a crushed nose. But he had doled out nine lost teeth, one broken foot, one ruptured eardrum, one chewed-off nipple, two broken noses, and myriad cuts, contusions, and bruises—smiling a bloody smile the whole time. A younger boy, hiding in one of the stalls, had relayed the story—and the older boys had confessed; the only reason they hadn't been expelled was because Morgan thought the whole thing had been "a hoot."

"Bullies?" the boy asked. "Sure, bullies." He laughed, an inelegant, unselfconscious yodel.

"Miles, I know I don't have to tell you that fighting is not acceptable here at the school." Morgan didn't seem to grasp much; it didn't make the boy bad, of course, but it did make the job of explaining things to him somewhat difficult. "There are other ways to solve problems. It's not always necessary to—to . . ." he paused and scanned the report, ". . . bite someone's nipple off. There are ways of diffusing these situations."

Morgan yawned. "Yeah? Like how?"

"You can always try to talk your way out of trouble."

"I don't try to talk my way out of anything, sir."

Freytag thought of the newspapers, of the missing boys out there, and he wanted to impart some caution to Miles Morgan—it might help him at some point. "All I'm saying, Mr. Morgan, is that you can't always fight your way out of a bad situation."

Miles looked up and smiled. "Wanna bet?" he asked.

THERE WAS a commonality between the Rochester and Grant boys. On the surface, it was appearance, and while sometimes that might be enough, it wasn't here. Not with Trevor Deacon thrown into the mix. Hemingway didn't know what the link was, only that it existed out there in the mind of the man who had lopped off the feet of one child and abducted the other. They could have passed for brothers. This one had a very specific fantasy to feed. There was an exactness to it.

There had been no real cooldown period: fifteen hours could hardly be called downtime. These guys needed a refractory period to recharge the batteries. At least usually. But not this one. He was on a mission. This was not happenstance. This was not wrong place wrong time. There was planning behind this. Good old-fashioned analytical thinking.

Which translated to purpose.

And woven into the geometry of the problem, was Trevor Deacon, predator extraordinaire. Someone had jabbed old Trevor in the eye with a hypodermic, then gone to work on him with a hacksaw. Trevor's death had taken patience, a taste for inflicting star-spangled agony, and time. A boy and two grown men killed, another child missing. They had an overachiever on their hands.

How did Deacon fit in with Tyler Rochester and Bobby Grant?

The first thing they had looked into was the financial standings of the two families. The shortest distance between a murder and a motive was usually a dollar sign. Every large city had come across someone who wanted the police to think that they had a serial predator on their hands when in point of fact all they really wanted was one single victim dead, usually someone with a life insurance policy. But neither Tyler Rochester nor Bobby Grant had been insured and a cursory glance into their parents' financial holdings showed that money wasn't a problem for either family.

So who was doing this? Why was he doing it? And how was he picking his victims?

Where was the link?

She wanted to find it while there was still time to get to Bobby Grant. Not in a day, after he was dead. Not in a week after another—God forbid—boy had disappeared. Or washed up with his feet missing. No, Hemingway needed to see it now.

"You okay?" Phelps asked from his desk.

Hemingway looked up, blinked. "*What?* Yeah. Why?"

"You were grumbling. When you grumble, it usually means that you're going to shoot someone or stab them or some such shit."

Even in the cold of the air-conditioned office, she was sweating. She put her hand up under her collar and slid it over her shoulder, feeling the muscle just below the skin. Her fingers found the familiar disc of scar where a red-hot chunk of metal had exited her body and thunked into a barstool. It was burning.

She looked up and smiled at the expression painted on Phelps's face; he looked troubled.

She pulled her hand from under her shirt and her palm was moist and smelled of Irish Spring. How the hell could she be hot when it was sixty degrees in here?

"I'm good. Just trying to figure out what makes this fucker go ticktock."

"You know, for a woman educated at Yale, you sure sound like a cop most of the time." And he smiled a little, more of that fatherly approval coming out.

Alan Carson walked in, wearing Chuck Taylors and pressed jeans. He had the unmistakable air of nerd about him. His department was allowed a certain leeway in the unwritten dress code of the NYPD, mainly because they never interacted with the public. And they would have cried if they weren't allowed to wear their hipster-geek T-shirts and skinny jeans. "Beware of strangers bearing gifts."

"And it doesn't get stranger than him," Phelps mumbled to Hemingway. Like a lot of the old-timers, Phelps mistrusted both technology and the people who worshiped it.

"What do you have for me?" she asked Carson, ignoring Phelps.

He held up a portable hard drive. "I've got three years' worth of Trevor Deacon's Internet records here: every click-through in a thirty-six month period—more than ninety-one thousand pages. Some will be dead links but his entire online life is here."

"Anything interesting?" Phelps asked.

"Plenty to work with. But therein lies your dilemma— weeding out the relevant from the irrelevant." Carson slaved the hard drive to her computer. "Knock yourself out."

Hemingway opened Deacon's Internet log and it didn't take long to see that the man had spent a lot of time visiting school websites. She did a quick search and found that he had visited the Damien Whitney Academy for Boys and the Huntington Academy a little over three months back—Tyler Rochester's and Bobby Grant's schools.

The big question, of course, was could it be a coincidence?

"Once we identify the remains of his victims, we'll be able to cross-reference it with these websites." She lifted her head, waved Lincoln over.

"Yeah?" he asked. After their time at the Deacon house, Lincoln and Papandreou had spent the morning running down files on anyone associated with the Damien Whitney Academy for Boys and the Huntington Academy. They had not yet found a single thing to link Tyler Rochester to Bobby Grant.

"Do a search on these schools," she said, tapping the screen. "See if any children have gone missing in the past three years."

"Sure. Can you put it into a PDF?"

She looked up at Carson. "Can we?" Carson had a crush on her—it was one of those obvious things that, had she been of a different makeup, could have been the poor man's undoing. But she kept him at arm's length, always being polite because she didn't want him to think he had a chance with her.

Carson leaned over her shoulder and she heard him take in a breath of her scent. "Sure. Just . . . let . . . me . . ." His fingers tap-danced across her keyboard, then he stood up and nodded. "Done."

Lincoln thanked him and went to the printer.

"What was with this guy and the feet?" Carson asked.

"Feet are the most common nonsexual body part to be

fixated on. Research suggests that foot fetishism increases during times when sexual epidemics are an issue; by sexualizing feet, participants avoid diseases transmitted through regular sexual channels. With a guy like Deacon it was probably a further step in desexualizing his actions. He was probably taught that sex was a depraved act; by focusing on feet, he was able to live out his fantasies yet not bend the fundamental principles of the shame he had been taught—technically, it could be justified that the act isn't sex. We'll know more once the psychologist talks to his mother."

Carson's face squinched up but Phelps just nodded as if this were common knowledge. He had been hunting child predators since the mid-seventies and understood the power play at work in many of their minds, usually the result of some deep trauma inflicted upon them as children.

"Thanks, Al. I'll call you if I need anything."

Carson nodded and his eyes dropped to her chest for a split second. Then he flushed, brought his eyes up to hers, and nodded. "Sure. Anything at all. I'll let you know if I find anything else. This guy wasn't big on encryption."

When Carson was gone, Lincoln made smooching sounds. "He's got it bad for you, Hemi. I hear Club Med in my ears. Maybe Aruba. A hut on the beach. A hammock. You and Carson . . ."

"What are you guys? Twelve? I pity the women in your lives."

Lincoln smiled. "So do they."

She turned back to Trevor Deacon's life reduced to bits and bytes, a bread crumb trail that led back into his fantasies. No sane person would want to peek in there.

Her phone rang. "Hemingway."

"Detective Hemingway, Mat Linderer here. I have the results on that pinkish powder we found at the Deacon residence and I've analyzed the torn photograph corner you wanted me to check out. First the powder. It's—"

"Heroin," she interrupted.

There was a stunned moment of silence. "Um, yes."

"The autopsy," she explained. "What's the cut?"

"It's about thirty-five percent pure, sixty-five percent baby laxative."

"Low-end street grade."

"Yeah."

"Why is it pink?"

"The color was added *after* the manufacturing process—there's no molecular binding. It's a vegetable dye of some sort. My guess is it's not supposed to be there. Maybe it was smuggled in something red."

Hemingway added the information to her notes. "And the corner of that photograph?"

"Printed on a home printer, not commercial grade. I can tell you it's an HP—manufactured within the last twenty-one months due to the toner it takes; I found traces of their new magenta. The paper is by Fuji, and it's available everywhere. I can't tell you what the image was. Could be sky. Could be water. Could be a cloud or smoke or a reflection in wavy glass. I handed it over to our digital guys and they ran an image search on the web and it doesn't match anything that's out there. Deacon's thumbprint is on it. That's all I can give you."

"Thanks, Mat. Appreciated."

Hemingway put the phone in her pocket and lifted her head to see Phelps staring at her. She filled him in on the vegetable dye and the printer.

When she was done, Phelps reached over and lifted his own notes from under a cup of long-cold coffee. The chair squeaked under his considerable bulk. "How the hell did Deacon walk all those years ago?"

It was one of those things that made you wonder if the whole system wasn't completely broken, or corrupt, or both.

Phelps found the page he had been looking for. "As per Nick's findings. I haven't seen the files yet.

"The initial jacket from 1984 states that the arresting officer—a street cop named Ronald Weaver—deceased May twenty-third, 2004—made a wrongful search. And since they couldn't find a body, and the feet didn't match anyone who had been missing, they couldn't prove that it was murder. Deacon's attorney, Marcel Zeigler—deceased July 2010— alleged that Deacon had purchased the feet from a man who worked in a medical research facility, and that they came from a donor. They ran down all possible cadavers in storage, from medical supply companies to hospitals, schools, and private research labs. They couldn't positively match the feet to a donor, but the body of an eleven-year-old boy had been stolen a month previously. Zeigler made a reasonable argument that Deacon had unknowingly purchased the feet of a stolen cadaver. They clocked him on disrespectful treatment of human remains.

"Zeigler argued that Deacon was guilty of bad judgment, not murder. The judge bought the story and Deacon went home after a six-month vacation at a minimum-security facility upstate. Enjoyed shop class. Model guy all the way around." Phelps looked up, took off his glasses. "In the three years set by the parole board, he was never late for a meeting. Followed up with therapy. No felonies. No misdemeanors. Gold stars across the board. When parole was over, he dropped off the face of the earth and no one thought to look at him ever again."

Hemingway thought back to Deacon's garage. The memory of those frozen little feet, blue and brittle, had been popping up in her head all afternoon. "Did they ever ID the feet found in his car?"

"Before DNA by almost a decade. Blood-typed but no tissue sample. Incinerated as medical waste. Nope. Unsolved."

The sky was hazing over in late afternoon and Hemingway knew they had to get out there and do something. Even if it was empty motion, it had to be better than sitting in here second-guessing everything that made sense. Which was very little. "I hate the waiting," she finally said.

"You and me both, kiddo."

She looked at the conference table with the neatly stacked files, then at her computer screen, then back up at the clock. "I've gotta go," she said and stood up, pulling on her jacket. "I can't sit here."

Phelps began to rise, then his body locked in a half crouch, as if a silent message had been radioed in from headquarters. He lifted his head, looked at her face, took in her body language, and sat back down. He nodded once. "Say hi for me," he said, then turned back to his work.

WHENEVER SHE was here, it was as if she had never left. When she was away, she couldn't remember what the place looked like at all. And she knew it would always be like this.

Her shadow stretched over the grave and wavered on the headstone, a small rectangular chunk of black granite with the words MOSES MANKIEWICZ chiseled in tight, noncursive hammer strokes. He had chalked forty-one years up on the fuselage before being shot down. A long time compared to some, short compared to others. A fucking miracle when applied to Mank.

Hemingway stood there for a moment, the whir of traffic on the Jackie Robinson Parkway close enough that she could hear the ricochet of gravel off the curb just beyond the trees. Mank lay with his parents—they had died in a car accident when he had been six.

The headstone was small and simple, a totally incongruous monument to a man who had lived as large as Moses Mankiewicz. A man who had epitomized the saying that too much can never be enough.

A few small stones rested on the marker, left by her on

previous visits. She reached into her pocket and pulled out the one she had picked up on the esplanade last night, fifty feet from Tyler Rochester. She knelt down on the grass and put it on the edge of the granite slab. It wobbled for a second.

It took her a few minutes to build up the courage to talk to him—it always did. It seemed weird, foolish, even, that she was here. It was surprising that Phelps didn't say more about it. But when she needed to open up to someone, coming here seemed like a justifiable pilgrimage.

The sound of the cars faded away and she sat down on the grass, facing the headstone. Each time she came here she was surprised that it didn't destroy her. Wasn't that what was supposed to have happened? This was Shakespearean territory. Gabriel García Márquez, at least.

"Hey, Mank—" She stopped, pushed her hair away from her jaw with her finger and tucked it behind her ear. She liked to think of Mank looking up and seeing the new her. She had walked through fire and made it. He'd be proud.

"It's been a busy couple of days." She felt the tears getting ready and she stopped them, consciously pushing them back to where they would be forgotten, shut down for safekeeping. "I'm pregnant. Really pregnant. And I don't know what to do."

A warm dry wind fluttered her hair off of her ear and then went still. She pushed it back, took a breath, and wondered what she was doing here. She didn't need advice. She needed conviction. One way or the other. Something definitive. After that, it would all be fine. "Girly, huh?

"And there's this guy. He took a little boy last night. Name was Tyler Rochester. Kid walked off the face of the planet on the way home from school. Three hours later he's found in the East River. His feet were cut off." She went on, laying the case out piece by piece.

Mank had always been a great detective. His knack for figuring cases out had only been matched by his knack for getting into trouble. Real trouble. David Shea kind of trouble. Sometimes she came here and all they talked was shop. A one-sided conversation that always helped her see the method in the mayhem. With everything unfolding in her new life the way it was—with work and Daniel and the possibility of a baby—she worried that she might lose these times, another ill-fated long-distance relationship.

When she was done laying out the case, she went back to the baby, eventually getting around to Daniel. She didn't talk to Mank about him all that much—something about it felt like a betrayal—but she had talked about him at first, so Mank would get a feel for the guy.

She doubted that Mank would have given a shit anyway. He would want her to be happy. And he wasn't one for handing out judgment. *The guy treat you well? Yes. The sex good? Yes. You get butterflies in your stomach when he touches you? Yes. He put the seat down some of the time? All of the time. Open car doors for you? All the time. Then we're done here, sweetheart. Thank you. Good night. Please leave your 3-D glasses in the bin by the door on your way out.*

She never expected to have any kind of a therapeutic breakthrough when she was here, but something about the ritual was comforting. Even now, when she didn't really have the spare time to piss around playing Ouija phone with Mank, it did her good. And maybe that was the problem. She was here talking to a dead guy when back at home she had what was supposed to be the next phase of her life. No matter which way she turned it, it was a little self-destructive.

What would Mank have done if she had told him they

had been having a baby? He'd have laughed. Then hugged her. Then started calling her *Mother*. Never stopping to ask if it was something she wanted. And if she told him that she wasn't sure, the walls would get hit, plaster cracked, knuckles maybe even broken.

Mank had problems with his temper. He had never hit her, never even hinted at it, and after that first time, when she saw that his rage was focused at the world, she had never worried for herself again. He was nuts, but he was a good man. When he let go, he took it out on a wall or a fridge or the hood of a car. Sometimes on some poor schmuck who ended up in the hospital breathing through a tube, grateful that he hadn't been kicked into a vegetative state. Mank had been dangerous. The kind whose unsmiling mug shot showed up on the news every now and then accompanying a story about a cop who had crossed the line. But he never would have hit her.

And he had made a lot of enemies along the way. Enemies like David Shea.

One afternoon he had embarrassed Shea in front of his boys. And that had been the final *fuck you* Mank had ever handed out. The next morning his heart was no longer beating.

When it was over, and she was in the hospital staring up at the acoustic ceiling tile, calculating the number of holes per square foot, she realized that she had peaked. There was no greater test ahead of her.

And now she was pregnant.

Her hand was on the tightly clipped grass above where his chest might be. She closed her eyes, whispered the words, "Sorry, honey," and stood up. "I gotta monster to find."

She walked back to the truck, grudgingly leaving Mank back there in the ground. The sounds of the world slowly came back—first the wind; then the traffic on the expressway; finally her own footsteps.

Hers was the only vehicle in the parking lot. She opened it with the remote, climbed in behind the wheel, put on her seat belt, and began to cry.

HEMINGWAY, PHELPS, and an NYPD patrolman named Paul Kowalski headed upriver at a forty-knot clip. They had been combing an abandoned dock in Queens, not far from Trevor Deacon's residence, when the sun dropped behind the skyline of the city to the west. Hemingway watched it the last few minutes, wondering if the final gasp of daylight going out would be punctuated by the scream of a child.

Of course, she heard nothing but the indifference of the city.

Theoretically, it was too early in the investigation to discern patterns of behavior beyond broad generalities, but something told her that sundown was the witching hour. When the day had run out, so had Bobby Grant's time. She didn't know how she knew, only that she did.

The police boat was a twenty-foot Zodiac center console outfitted with a pair of 75 horsepower Mercs. Kowalski had the engines open and their wake spread behind in a mercurial jet stream, a deep white V that reached out for the shores of the river.

Phelps held on to a handle bolted to the side of the

console, the same even expression on his face that he wore throughout the almost seven years of their partnership. Even out here, on water that was piss hot, coupled with a wind that did nothing but magnify the humidity, he looked like he was fine, missing child notwithstanding. If she asked him how he was, he'd just shrug—the steam-driven Iron Giant in a suit, old school down to the soles of his shoes.

She licked a line of sweat from her upper lip and tried to focus on the shore zipping by starboard, an endless maze of jetties, parks, restaurants, condos, industrial buildings, and myriad places where you could dump a dead kid into the drink without being seen. Especially after dark. Patrolling the shoreline was a last resort but it was better than contacting psychics, if only marginally.

They were cutting due north, toward Hell Gate, fighting the outgoing tide. She was running on the belief that it was just a matter of minutes until another footless boy was surrendered to the East River. He was probably already out there, being drawn south by the careless hands of the current, heading for the Atlantic. She hoped she was wrong—she hoped that they'd get another day. But hope wasn't a strategy. Hope was passive.

The radio squawked to life, a single blurt that startled everyone in the Zodiac except for the Iron Giant.

"We found him," a nameless officer said, identifying his boat as an afterthought. "This is Search two-two-four-seven."

Hemingway checked the GPS and straight-lined their azimuth to 2247—a boat the roster said was piloted by a man named J. Smilovitch. The distance on the screen was an inch and a half—a little over half a mile west-southwest.

Kowalski keyed the mic. "This is three-one-one-five, we'll be there in two minutes." And he spun the wheel and opened up the throttle.

Hemingway took the mic. "This is Detective Hemingway. What *exactly* did you find?" she asked.

Through the distant static of radio contact Smilovitch said, "Someone's chopped off his hands. He looks awful. Just fucking awful—"

She thought back to Trevor Deacon, the child murderer extraordinaire who had taken the feet of at least forty-four children, forty-five including the pair found in his trunk. He hadn't been killed by an angry parent or a vigilante.

Trevor Deacon had been killed by a competitor.

THE DOCK at the police quay was lit up like a Hollywood premiere, the concrete span lined with officers. But they were not there to celebrate the launch of a studio production; they were there to welcome Bobby Grant. Hemingway was with the boy, his body cocooned in a polyethylene bag to keep new contaminants out and to lock in any evidence that had survived the waters of the East River.

Two of the ME's people climbed down into the boat, slid the folded tarp into a disaster bag, then strapped the lifeless child onto an aluminum stretcher. After he was on his way to the van, Hemingway and Phelps climbed out of the boat.

Dennet was waiting and he steered them through the throng of officers who parted in a sea of silent blue; even men who have seen death in all its permutations are humbled in the presence of a murdered child. The captain didn't ask any questions, didn't make any demands, he just pushed them toward the white NYPD Tahoe parked inside the fence, beside the medical examiner's van. Dennet got in the back with Hemingway; Phelps sat up front with the driver.

When the doors were closed and the engine started, the

captain opened the ceiling vent on his side of the backseat and waited until cold air was pumping out before he spoke. For a man under as much pressure as this case was bringing down, he seemed to be in a relatively calm mood. Of course all of that would change in a few minutes when he started yelling. The equation was pretty simple: bring back results, not more dead kids.

The driver followed the Econoline as it pulled through the gate out onto the Parkway.

When they were up to speed, Dennet turned to Hemingway and said, "Please tell me you are making headway. Please tell me you have leads. Please tell me that this thing isn't a scrub. We have two dead children, Alex. I don't need to tell you how bad this is going to look on the news. By the time we get to the station, it's going to be like the villagers outside of Frankenstein's castle." He paused and turned to the traffic outside the window.

The driver said, "We have two news vans following us."

Dennet waved it away. "Parasites. No marketable skills except frightening the uninformed. Christ, I remember when the news conveyed actual information via educated opinions. If we dug up Walter Cronkite and showed him what has happened to network news he'd ask to go right back to the dirt." He turned to Phelps in the front seat, then to Hemingway, the voice of the team. "Tomorrow morning we are going to hold a press conference. You are going to give these monkeys something that they can work with—and something they can work *on*. Let's use these people to our advantage. They like snooping, get them to work for us. I don't care how you do it, only that it gets done. I'll book it for eight a.m. so it'll make the morning cycle."

What could she give him? There were no concrete leads. When she thought about it, there was no concrete anything except those crescents of blood in Trevor Deacon's basement apartment. Man's size ten or ten and a half.

And two dead children. One with no feet. Another with no hands.

The Chevy hit 60th Street and cut east, leaving the white Econoline to go on to its destination.

"Where we going?" Hemingway asked.

Dennet didn't bother looking over. "To the Grant boy's apartment. You are going to tell two people that their son is dead. Then you are going to go to the morgue and walk through the autopsy with Marcus." He let out a sigh that might as well have been a curse. "And then you are going to go out there and find me the man who is chopping up these children."

SHE PULLED into the garage on autopilot—parking and getting out of the truck without exercising anything even remotely resembling concentration. She was halfway around the block when she realized she hadn't checked her mirrors before getting out and she hadn't checked the alley before leaving the garage; it was things like that that got people killed.

The trip to the Grants' apartment had been an exercise in agony. Mrs. Grant broke into hysterical weeping that her husband tried to quell but couldn't stop. The mother-in-law had collapsed into the sofa and stared ahead, comatose. Dr. Grant poured himself a drink but left it on the bar when Hemingway began to explain that they had fished his son from the river and someone had taken his hands off with a hacksaw.

The whole time Hemingway had talked to him, he stared at the Bösendorfer in the corner.

Dr. Grant made himself three drinks he never touched.

Of course, the time with the Grants was punishment from Dennet; a way to tell them to make inroads or they'd be doling out bad news to the parents of dead children until they stopped this guy.

Dennet had also been very clear that if they didn't make headway soon, they'd get pulled. The city would load more detectives onto the case. The FBI would be brought in. They'd be gone.

And all the bullshit she had put up with over the years would be relegated to the wasted effort bin. She'd end up in burglary or vice or some other career dead end where the intent was to push her into quitting. And then where would she be? What would she do?

After the Grants, she and Phelps had taken a ride to the grim land of the medical examiner to look at the boy. When they had walked in, the doctor was up to his elbows in the boy's chest, fishing out the mass of organs referred to as *the block* in-house. They wouldn't have tox screens back until the morning but it was the same perp; the boy's left eye was punctured and the bones in his wrists had the same twenty-four-teeth-per-inch saw marks.

And like Tyler Rochester, Bobby Grant had been alive when it had happened.

This time the killer had cut in the right place, putting the saw through the sweet spot between the ulna and the capitate. He was getting better at this.

Bad guy: *Four*.

Good guys: *Sweetfuckall*.

She rounded the corner and stopped. There was no traffic on Riverside and beyond that the Jersey shoreline glittered against the flat Hudson. She wondered where the monster was. What he was doing. What he was wearing. What he was thinking.

And who he was thinking about.

Hemingway stood on the sidewalk, staring out at the lights sparkling off the river. What had happened to all of Trevor Deacon's children? Had he released them into the arms of the river? If he had, why hadn't they been found?

Her hand went to her belly and she fell back into thinking that bringing a child into the world took a lot of guts, a bucketful of wishful thinking, and more than a bit of denial. Of course she had thought about all of this before—every time, in fact, she had seen one of life's discards in a parking lot or alley or any of the other places where people dumped the dead. But the exercise had crossed from academic to practical when she had peed on the little plastic stick yesterday morning and been rewarded with a big blue check mark.

Two dead children. A dead driver. A dead child murderer. There was a rhyme, a reason, to all of this. Some formula that she did not understand, could not see. Was the baby growing in her crippling her in some way or would the cellular revolution going on in her body add some vital insight?

Part of the solution?

Or part of the problem?

She unlocked the door and stepped into the entry. On her way up the stairs she passed the four equestrian portraits Mank had bought her the last time they had gone out. She paused for a second, thought back to the cemetery that afternoon, to the pebble she had laid on his gravestone. Then she turned away and walked into the loft.

The space was dark; Daniel wasn't home. Without turning on the light she went to the three big arched windows in front of the loft and stared at the distant shore of New Jersey. The only thing she was sure of was that this guy would keep going until she stopped him.

THE NEWSPEOPLE hummed like a horde of talentless vain insects. They laid cable, tested lights, ran through lead-ins, coiffed and primped and chattered into cameras. There was a sense of triumph in their actions, as if they had discovered something important even though all they would really do was fill time with empty speculation.

Hemingway and Phelps sat in Dennet's office, prepping for the press conference. Mike Babanel, the precinct's counsel, stood behind the captain's desk, looking like a leaner, balder Tom Hagen.

Dennet leaned forward and looked at Hemingway for a few seconds. "Are you ready for this?"

What could she say to that? "I can't wait."

Phelps stood against the wall that held the captain's citations and golf photos. The Iron Giant hadn't said much. Until now. "This could be putting you in his crosshairs, Hemi."

She just shook her head. "A six-foot chick with a gun isn't his type."

"The Grant kid's driver wasn't this guy's type, either." Phelps didn't sound convinced.

Babanel looked out the window, then at Hemingway. "Remember to think about your answers before you say anything. They are going to try to trap you. And remember that you will be on televisions all over the world. Those two things should help."

Had he said *help*? "Sure. Televisions all over the world. Think before I speak. Easy-peasy. What about swearing?"

Babanel, whose sense of humor was south of zero on the laugh-o-meter, shook his head. "Swearing's not recommended either, detective." He pointed to the document they had spent fifteen minutes going over. "Stick to the release and you are most of the way there. Answer seven questions. That's it. Keep the answers brief. Tell them that you will keep them informed of any breaks in the case, but that you need to be left alone so that you can pursue all relevant leads. When they ask 'What leads?' thank them for their time and leave the podium."

It made more sense to put Phelps out there; he had received every award, honor, medal, and citation there was—from the department and the city—some of them twice. The unsaid logic was that he was too valuable an asset to hang out for the vultures, while she was expendable. Focus would irrevocably shift to her; if someone had to be thrown to the dogs, she'd have the shortest fall and the largest impact. It was business, not personal.

And of course she had gone through this before. During the investigation into David Shea's death she had been hounded mercilessly; six weeks of intense scrutiny that ended as soon as she was found innocent.

She looked at Dennet, then Babanel, then turned around to see Phelps still leaning against the wall, looking like he'd rather be somewhere else. "Let the games begin," he said.

Standing in front of the podium brought her back to the weeks after Shea's death. She remembered the noise, the stench of hair spray, the forest of shiny-eyed idiots staring her down. But she had somehow forgotten how hot the lights could be. Or how loud the cameras were.

She stood on the front steps to the precinct with the morning sun bisecting the island from east to west. She tried not to wince into the bright halogen spots that came at her like a wall of headaches but she wasn't succeeding. But she wouldn't look down, or to the side—because that was negative body language.

". . . and last night we recovered the body of a second victim, ten-year-old Bobby Grant."

She paused as a murmur went through the crowd of reporters. She stared straight ahead.

"Like the first victim, Bobby Grant had been mutilated. I am unable to discuss or release the particular nature of his wounds at this juncture in time but I can say that his body was found in the East River by a police patrol."

And that was pretty much it—the department's peace offering.

"And if you can keep it civil, I'd be happy to answer questions." She stared into the lights, squinting to see hands.

She pointed and nodded.

Miles Rafferty: *Can you tell us if either of the boys were sexually assaulted?*

Hemingway wished she could shoot reporters based on nothing more than dislike. "Actually, that's something that we can neither confirm nor deny at this point because it still has bearing on the case." By wording it like that, the press could conjecture for days without figuring out if that had been a *yes* or a *no.*

She picked out another hand.

Donald Cox, CNN: *Can you be more specific in reference to the mutilations?*

Hemingway stared into the lights and shook her head. "Not at this time, no."

Edwin Choy, MSNBC: *Could you be more specific as to where Bobby Grant's body was found?*

At that she took a breath, and gave a general—and evasive—answer. "The body was found in the East River. I'm sorry I can't be specific because it still has bearing on the investigation." With that it sounded like they had something.

Another hand, this one belonging to Anderson Caldwell, fluttered in the dead air: *Did the two boys know one another?*

"That's a good question, Anderson, and one we're trying to figure out. It is possible that they crossed paths in some way but as of now it appears they did not know one another."

Jennifer Mann, Fox News: *Do you have any suspects?*

Babanel had said this was a given and prepped her. "We are investigating a lot of leads right now but I cannot at this time say whether or not we are considering any suspects."

Can I take that as a no?

"You can take that as neither a yes or a no. I am not being vague to hide information. I am being prudent in order not to jeopardize the investigation in any way. There is a difference."

Alistair Franklin, the *Washington Post*: *Do you think you have a serial killer on your hands?*

That was the one she was waiting for. She appreciated Franklin for wording it like he had—it allowed her to give a yes or no answer. "Yes, I do."

More camera flashes and hands and Horshack grunts.

Cameron Gillespie for *Nancy Grace*: *Do you think you will find the perpetrator?*

And at that Hemingway smiled. Now was the time to cash in on her past and maybe help the investigation go forward. She looked at Gillespie and paused, swiveling her head over the crowd. Then she took a breath, stared straight ahead, and slowly said, "I am going to find him and I am going to put him in prison."

While everyone was snapping photographs and yelling out questions, Hemingway leaned into the nest of microphones taped to the podium, and said, "If you would please calm down, Captain Dennet will fill you in on our plans—and recommendations—for keeping the school children of this city safe. He will run through the support networks that have been set up all over the city as well as our plans through the end of the school year on into the summer. Please check out the website at the bottom of your screen."

As she stepped away from the podium she saw Phelps look at his shoes and smile. "What?" she asked, and took her place beside him.

Still looking down, he said, "You know, for a chick, you got the biggest set of balls I ever saw."

"I get that a lot."

CAPTAIN DENNET got his wish; Manhattan looked like a police state. A pair of cruisers was assigned to every school on the island and surrounding boroughs. This blanket effort was extended to all institutions—public, private, male only, female only, coed—to keep the specter of favoritism from rearing its politically incorrect countenance. Those who criticized this overuse of manpower felt it would have been better utilized at schools where white ten-year-old boys were to be found—after all, that seemed to be the victim of choice. The champions of the citywide display of force said that even though the killer had chosen a certain demographic up until this point, there was nothing to say that he wouldn't change his taste, especially if another vast segment of school-age children were left unguarded. The logic, of course, went against all known research but the loudest voices got their way. Which meant that the NYPD had to be everywhere.

Hemingway and Phelps were assigned to the James Crichton Prep School in Morningside Heights. Papandreou and Lincoln were thirty-one blocks up, at the Esther Marring

School of New York—an all-black girls' school. The rest of the day's shift, culled from precincts as far south as Staten Island and as far north as the Bronx, were out en masse. They had a single message to convey: *we mean business.*

The news teams did their utmost to make the police look like the twenty-first-century equivalent of the Keystone Cops. They interviewed people on the street about security, as if the population had suddenly become surveillance specialists. They interviewed parents. Children. Registered sex offenders with computer-garbled voices and blotted-out faces. All in the name of constructive criticism.

They talked about Detective Alexandra Hemingway's oratory skills. Discussed her clothing. Brought up old news footage of the bloodbath she had left behind in David Shea's bar. Before and after photos of her where they discussed the scar tissue that made up the side of her jaw—as if she had chosen a bad pair of shoes, or worn stripes with plaid. They discussed the investigation into Shea's death and how Shea had killed her boyfriend, Moses Mankiewicz—a cop with a violent past.

They fixated on Hemingway's refusal to admit or deny that there were any suspects. Many hinted that this meant the police had a suspect, because that's what would bring in the ratings. But they were careful of being too certain of what they said, just in case they were wrong; no one wanted to risk damaging their imaginary integrity.

They focused on the easy money by generating fear.

They reported that attendance was down all over the city and that the poorer schools had higher absenteeism than the wealthier institutions. They went on that this was likely because the socioeconomically disadvantaged felt the police were there to protect and serve the rich, not everyone else.

And the higher attendance at the wealthier schools seemed to support these thin accusations.

The simple truth was that the rich believed their money bought them some kind of divine protection.

But belief often fails when tested against reality and at 8:13 a.m. another boy disappeared.

HIS NAME was Nigel Stuart Matheson. It was no surprise that he had brown hair and eyes. Or that he was thirteen days older than Tyler Rochester—three older than Bobby Grant. He was handsome. And wealthy. And gone.

Nigel disappeared while walking to school with a group of boys who lived in the same neighborhood—part of a strength in numbers program that many of the schools had adopted; a measure that made parents feel a little more secure. Everyone thought it was a good way to protect the children. After all, who would grab a child from a group?

One minute Nigel was there, waxing poetic about Curtis Granderson's strikeout record.

The next he was gone.

From the group.

From the street.

He came back in a big way: within fifteen minutes his picture was on every television and news website in the country. Smiling. Happy. Alive.

THIRTY

HEMINGWAY AND Phelps spent an hour individually in-terviewing the sixteen boys who had been with Nigel Mathe-son when he vanished.

After the first boy, Hemingway had to coach Phelps on his approach. These children were brought up to believe that they were special. They were taught that they were smarter and more gifted and when they looked at their lives they had to believe it. They would inherit the world and they knew it.

Phelps called them entitled little fuckers.

Hemingway just shrugged.

They were identical in dress and manner, and all had the easy comfort of certainty in who they were being groomed to replace. They were identical in their perfect hair, sly smiles, and blandness. Their versions of what had happened to Nigel Matheson were also the same.

They had passed a few other groups of schoolboys—one from Saint Dominic and another from the Jasper Collegiate Institute.

They crossed two intersections.

Went past a park.

Were captured by a surveillance camera inside the door of an apartment building.

He was there, among them.

Then he was not.

THE APARTMENT opened up onto a lush vista of Central Park that stretched away to the north. There was a big balcony with a stone railing where bronze hawks sat watch, a leftover from before urban renewal had destroyed most of the building's original charm. The space was a combination of chrome, leather, and plastic that had all the earmarks of a collection rather than being merely well decorated. Hemingway saw that most of the paintings were by the top black American artists, something not usually collected by whites.

Wendy Matheson was tall and graceful, with a fat-free body and natural beauty that resembled Hemingway's in some lateral way. Besides wealth and photogenic DNA, she did not appear mean, jealous, or hypocritical but it was obvious that Mrs. Matheson had always been very happy that life was about her.

Until now.

Mr. Matheson had been boarding a flight at LaGuardia when the school called. The NYPD offered to pick him up but he insisted on making his own way back. Until then, it was Hemingway, an uncomfortable-looking Phelps, and Mrs. Matheson.

Mrs. Matheson did not say much; she answered in mono-syllables and had the same distant expression of Mrs. Rochester, but none of the slurred speech.

As they talked, Hemingway's hand was on her stomach again—something she found herself doing too frequently now. Sitting there, staring down a woman whose son had just been taken, the gesture felt disrespectful, blasphemous.

They ran through the usual questions, from the basic to the invasive. With two boys down, Trevor Deacon dead, and the Grant boy's driver squirted all over the interior of the Lincoln, there wouldn't be a happy ending to the Nigel Matheson story unless they asked the tough questions.

They were at the point in the interview where they focused on lists and routine. The people Nigel Matheson spent time with and the places he went. They didn't bother asking about a life insurance policy.

They sacrificed poise and tact for truth and results. And it was obvious that Mrs. Matheson wasn't used to being hammered like this. Hers was a world of afternoons at Berg-dorf's and weekends on the ocean. The only time she bothered to look at a cop was if she was pulled over and even then she probably didn't pay much attention; to people like this, the police were something to be dealt with, not listened to.

After a few moments of listing Nigel's friends, she stopped in mid-sentence. At first Hemingway thought she had remembered something, an important detail or a signif-icant event. She looked up and said, "He was special." Her eyes went from Hemingway to Phelps then back to Heming-way again. Then she reached over and picked up a leather-bound book from the coffee table. "He wrote a play." And she began to sob.

Hemingway did something that was out of character but she couldn't stop herself. She went over to the sofa, sat down beside Mrs. Matheson, and put her arm around the woman.

"I'm sorry about this. I know that right now you can't believe me, but I know what you're going through. This isn't fair or right or anything else that makes sense. But now—I mean *right now*—we need you to be focused. Can you do that?"

Mrs. Matheson turned, buried her face in Hemingway's collar, and let out a scream so primal and rooted in anguish that it jolted Phelps in his seat.

Then she pushed herself up, wiped her nose in a handkerchief, and gave a single solid nod. "Okay."

Hemingway kept her arm around the woman. She felt the skin beneath the blouse, the muscle beneath the skin, the piston of her heart below that. Her whole body vibrated as if the molecules were on the verge of dispersing. "You want a coffee? Detective Phelps makes a great cup of coffee."

Mrs. Matheson seemed to actually consider the offer, then gave a soft, almost childlike nod. Her housekeeper materialized out of what appeared to be thin air, asked the detectives if they wanted some coffee as well, then disappeared.

"Look, Mrs. Matheson, we need—"

The front door kicked open, blowing Hemingway's question off the road.

Mr. Matheson barreled in, eyes red, tie in his fist. He ran to his wife, picked her up off the sofa and drew her into a hug. Over her shoulder he said, "I'm Andrew Matheson. What happened to my son?" He was tall, black, with close-cropped hair and the no-nonsense air of a man used to getting things done on a schedule.

"I'm Detective Alex Hemingway and this is my partner, Jon Phelps. Your stepson is missing, Mr. Matheson."

Andrew Matheson's face went brittle. "He's not my stepson, he's my son, detective."

Hemingway felt the saliva hit the back of her mouth in a surge of adrenaline. "Are you Nigel's biological father?" she asked.

"Of course not. Does it matter?"

Hemingway looked over his shoulder, at the family photograph on the console beside the Bang & Olufsen stereo. She focused on the boy between his parents.

Same as the others: brown hair, brown eyes.

White.

Dr. Grant said that after all the trouble they had gone through to conceive, this was going to destroy his wife.

Tyler Rochester's mother said that it had been hard to get pregnant. *Twice.*

Phelps said they could have been brothers.

All of a sudden she had it. "Mr. and Mrs. Matheson, I need you to tell me where you went for fertility treatment."

PHELPS TOOK the driver's seat and Hemingway strapped herself in, lit up the cherry, and pulled out her phone as they swung into traffic. They wound their way south and she cycled through her call log, looking for the Rochesters' number. She found it and dialed.

"Yes, hello. This is detective Alex Hemingway of the NYPD. I need to speak to Mrs. Rochester right now."

Pause.

"No, it's urgent."

Pause.

"Yes, very."

Pause.

"Sooner. Yes. Thank you."

She hung up and scrolled through her data for the Grants' number.

Dialed.

"Yes, this is Detective Alex Hemingway of the NYPD. I need to speak to Mrs. Grant immediately. It's urgent. Yes. Yes."

Phelps swung the big four-by-four around a double-parked

limousine and Hemingway suddenly wished she was driving. She hated the passenger seat. Always had.

"Yes, Mrs. Grant. I am very sorry to trouble you right now but I have an important question to ask you. It's personal and you have to keep it confidential—is that clear?"

Pause.

"Yes. I understand. Are you alone?"

Pause.

"Yes, I'll wait."

Pause. She covered the phone and said, "She's going to the bedroom." Pause. "Yes, I'm still here. Was Dr. Grant Bobby's biological father?"

She listened. Then punched the dashboard. "What was the name of the clinic you went to?"

Pause.

"Thank you."

She hung up. "Same fucking place—Park Avenue Clinic. Hit it."

And the big man in the gray suit flew the truck south on 7th Avenue.

THE SUBURBAN slid around the corner with the grace of a smoking cathedral. Hemingway kept one hand protectively over her stomach as she tried not lose the phone. "Nick, do we have anything on the Park Avenue Clinic? Or on a Dr. Sylvester Brayton who works there?"

"Park Avenue Clinic? What kind of a fuckin' name is—?"

"Jesus Christ, Nick, just do it without the commentary."

"Sure. Sorry. Okay . . . all right, the Park Avenue Clinic is a swanky place where a hundred grand buys you a bun for the oven—"

Hemingway closed her eyes and tried to push the blossoming headache away. "Forget the goddamned brochure stuff. Do we have anything in the system?"

"Let's see . . ."

Hemingway opened her eyes just as Phelps punched around a bus and missed clipping a taxi that had stopped on a stale yellow—possibly the only cab in history to not run a yellow.

Papandreou came back. "They're stock market country. They pay their taxes and look legit. One OSHA infraction during a renovation a few years back but that's it. Owned by big pharma."

Hemingway filed that away. "Now the doctor—Sylvester Brayton. B-R-A-Y-T-O-N."

There was the sound of fingers on a keyboard and he came back with, "Here we go. Brayton, Sylvester. Graduated George Washington School of Medicine. Then Johns Hopkins. On staff with the clinic as of a year before it opened its doors. Disappeared from staff rosters a little over a year ago."

Phelps slalomed through the tight crosstown traffic that seemed oblivious to the red flashing light clamped to the dash.

"Where is he now?"

The sound of typing was followed by, "I don't know."

"Nick, give me something."

More typing. "The guy just dropped off the face of the planet. No driver's license. No car registration. No cell phone contract." More typing. "Sweetfuckall. He just disappeared."

Hemingway ran through her conversations with the Grants and when she was done, Papandreou swore in Greek, a peculiar oddity; he was a fourth-generation New Yorker who didn't know a word of his ancestral tongue.

"We're on the way there right now. Find Brayton. And get a black-and-white to the clinic."

"Could be a coincidence," Papandreou said with no conviction at all.

This wasn't monkeys typing Shakespeare; Hemingway had already confirmed that two of the three victims were conceived at this clinic. There were no odds this good. "Get someone to the Rochester funeral—someone with a little tact— to find out about Tyler. I bet we're three for three." The dashboard clock gave them nine hours until sundown—nine hours that would sweep by like they had never been there at all. "And check out the other principals at the clinic. From the ground up. Find out if any of the MDs there have malpractice or ethics cases being reviewed—check with the medical board and the courts. If you find any cases, check out the plaintiffs. I'm guessing it's not a doctor—Marcus says whoever is taking these kids apart has no prior knowledge of anatomy."

"You think it's someone there?"

"I think it's someone everywhere. Do it. Put it all in motion."

THE PARK Avenue Clinic was a renovated brownstone sandwiched in between a law firm and a glass building that housed an art gallery. It had passed the status of clinic and entered into the realm of corporation more than two decades back and it wore its muscle proudly. There was valet parking and three limousines sat at the curb.

Phelps rammed the truck across two lanes, plugging a hole a Rolls had staked out with its massive gauche ass. The driver looked up, acknowledged the flashing bubble with a shake of his head, and pulled out into the cars heading downtown. Hemingway was on the curb before the Suburban came to a halt, her shield out, feet pounding the concrete. By the time she was at the front door to the building, Phelps was patiently bringing Dennet up to speed with that no-nonsense diction he was famous for. The next call would be to the District Attorney.

Hemingway yanked the big metal handle and the ten-foot polycarbonate door bowed out, then flew open.

The welcome desk was sculpted from a single chunk of volcanic rock, cut to show the negative space of a mother and child swallowed by the ash of Pompeii. The handsome woman behind the counter backed up when Hemingway came at her with the badge. Outside, the screech of a police siren stopped at the curb and the sound of car doors slamming punctuated her footsteps.

"Detectives Alex Hemingway and Jon Phelps, NYPD. I need to speak to your CEO right now."

The receptionist was mixed race but her dialogue was heavy Brooklynese. There was a tiny black microphone peeking out of the hair beside her ear. "May I ask what this is about?"

"You have ten seconds to get the CEO or director or whatever you call the head cheese down here. At the end of ten seconds, I am going get annoyed. You don't want me to get annoyed," Hemingway said.

The receptionist's eyes shifted from Hemingway's badge to the restructured line of her jaw, then back to the badge. She took a step back. "That would be Marjorie Fenton."

"Then phone her, sweetheart. You get Fenton down here right now." She leveled her finger at the microphone. "Ten seconds," she repeated.

It was then that a woman appeared beside them. Her face was a perfect blend of poised calm and subtextual annoyance. Five hundred pounds of security squeezed into two suits stood behind her. Whatever her title, there was little room for doubt that she was a major player in the clinic's ecosystem. "*I'm* Director Fenton, how may we help you—detectives, is it?" She was small, maybe five foot one. Close to sixty but could pass for fifty if the light and makeup were right. She put her hand firmly on Hemingway's elbow. "I am happy to make an appointment. We are terribly busy and can't operate with the police barging in and—"

Hemingway saw how this was going to go—or at least how Fenton imagined it would go—and she had no intention of letting the woman railroad her. "I am going to shut you up right now." At that, the wall of suit behind the woman flexed and Hemingway heard Phelps's shoes scrape the travertine behind her. She knew he had taken a step forward and that his hand was probably on the big automatic under his arm. For a man of his size, Phelps was able to move with surprising speed.

Hemingway continued in an even cadence. "You have heard about the two boys who were found in the East River? The other who was abducted this morning? Very shortly he is going to have parts of his body sawn off while he lies in the dirt somewhere, wondering why bad things are happening to him. If I don't get your help—and I mean *right fucking now*—I will go outside and call a press conference on the sidewalk. I will tell Wolf Blitzer and the rest of the cackling idiots that patients of this clinic are being murdered and yet you refuse to cooperate with us and I am going to emphatically state that the commonality between these victims is that they were all conceived here. You, Mrs. Fenton, can piss your retirement right down the toilet." Hemingway knew that this would all come out eventually anyway, but she was going for a knee-jerk reaction, not a rational response.

Fenton opened her mouth and Hemingway cut her off. Again.

"You may consider threatening me personally, but you'd be wasting your breath. I have a family attorney on retainer: Dwight Hemingway of Hemingway, McCrae and Pearson. They're a few blocks up, in nicer digs than this. I won't have to make meetings for three years, by which time the story of our little conversation here will be at the film stage and you will be on record as the director of Jeffrey Dahmer, Inc." Hemingway, almost a solid foot taller than the woman, pulled her elbow out of Fenton's grip and leaned over, her hands on her thighs as if reprimanding a child. "Now do you still want to play Queen Bitch with me?"

The door opened and the clink of cops in gear had everyone but Hemingway turn their heads. She kept her eyes locked on Fenton's, but this was a woman who gave nothing away. She just stared back, her expression frozen in the indifference that seemed to be her prime emotion.

Fenton turned to the receptionist. "Maya, we'll be in the big consultation room." Then she led the two detectives away.

Hemingway beckoned the two uniformed policemen to follow. Fenton moved fast in her heels and Hemingway recognized the rhythm of a runner in the way she timed her shoulders. The two security men and the two street cops closed up the rear. They rounded two ground-level corners and just before they came to an elevator, Phelps—still on the phone—said, "Yeah, we're there now," loud enough that Fenton shifted in her designer one-off.

They dropped into the building's guts in a backlit car, three of the walls decorated with Keith Haring acrylics—happy linear representations of parents and children with rays of goodness shooting out of their bodies. Hemingway's parents had a moderate collection of American modern, the brunt of their focus on Georgia O'Keeffe and Jacob Coleridge, but they owned a Haring or two; it didn't take a dealer's acumen to see that there had to be a million dollars' worth of canvas hanging on the walls. Money was evidently not an issue here.

That would change when the lawsuits started.

Hemingway was neither spiteful nor petty, and she wasn't holding Fenton at fault for her Sarah Palin imitation downstairs. She wondered if Fenton had an inkling of what was about to happen. Probably not—too much confidence in the way the world was supposed to treat her—which meant that Hemingway would have to bully her.

The elevator opened to a subterranean conference room that could have been under the White House if the president was into Ralph Lauren. The walls were paneled in bamboo and fitted with an array of multimedia presentation equipment, tools to help talk prospective parents out of their money. The table was a block of polished concrete and the chairs were high-backed leather deals that looked like they were lifted from a fleet of Bentleys. A heavy silver coffee service sat in the center of the table, along with sandwiches, muffins, and cookies.

They stepped out as a procession, Fenton doing her best to look authoritative. Hemingway was annoyed at the time they were losing and she could feel Phelps vibrating behind her like an angry infection. No doubt, this was one of those times when he would be silently lamenting the loss of the old days he always talked about, a time when the letter of the law hadn't been obscured by red tape and bureaucracy.

Fenton gestured to one side of the table and reached for the chair at the head but Hemingway grabbed it. Phelps dropped into the seat to her right. The two uniformed officers took up position at the door and Fenton was forced into one of the cheap seats with her security men behind her.

Fenton opened her mouth and Hemingway nailed her

again. "Mrs. Fenton, there is no discussion here. My patience and time is running out." She checked her watch. "You are almost at the end of my rope."

"Do I need counsel present?" Fenton didn't ask politely, courteously, or even as if it were any kind of a real possibility. She wanted to show she couldn't be pushed.

Hemingway turned on her predator face. "You know about Tyler Rochester and Bobby Grant?"

Fenton stared at her. "I read about it in the paper, yes."

"A third boy, Nigel Matheson, was abducted a few hours ago."

Fenton just stared, waiting.

"Bobby Grant and Nigel Matheson were conceived at this clinic and I expect to have the same news from the Rochester family in a few minutes. Dr. Brayton handled the pregnancies. Your clinic—or Dr. Brayton—are what links the victims. Very soon, the media will descend on this place and you can forget the right to a due process. You can forget the right to a fair trial. They will paint this institution black. And for just a second, I want you to imagine what the parents of the next child who turns up dead with his leg or his arm or his foot chopped off is going to do when they find out that we came to you." And she stopped cold to let that sink into Fenton's core reactor. "And you told us to go fuck ourselves." She looked into the points of anger that had replaced Fenton's eyes.

After a protracted pause, Fenton said, "First off, I do not know the name of every child we helped to conceive—the number now totals in the thousands."

"Would a doctor remember his patients ten years later?"

"I expect so, yes."

"So where is Dr. Sylvester Brayton?"

"Brayton left us a year ago and I am not in the habit of staying in touch with former employees. I heard he took a position somewhere in Europe."

"How long had Brayton been with the clinic?" Hemingway wanted to see if Fenton would be up front with information.

"I can't be certain, but an easy twenty years. Since before we opened this facility at least."

"Why did he leave?"

Fenton paused for a second. "We had mutually exclusive visions for the future of this clinic."

"So you won't tell me?"

Fenton shook her head. "I cannot discuss internal politics unless it has bearing on your case."

"Who picked up Brayton's patients?"

At that Fenton reached for the phone and punched in a four-digit extension number. "Yes, Maya, is Dr. Selmer back from Paris? Good. Could you please get him on the phone? Yes. Yes. Immediately. Then put him through."

Fenton hung up and looked at Hemingway. "Dr. Michael Selmer picked up Dr. Brayton's files. You have to understand that we are a fertility clinic, not a pediatrics ward. I doubt even Dr. Selmer will know that these boys were conceived here." She reached over and poured herself a cup of coffee. "What do you want from me, Detective?"

"That phone call to Selmer is a good start. Anything you can give me in the way of due diligence. I understand the doctor–patient privilege; I understand that we need a court order to access Dr. Brayton's files; I understand that we have to be very specific in our requests and that you can only release information that pertains to this case—we can't go fishing and we can't guess. But I am making the not-too-far-reaching assumption that these two—and soon to be three—children are not the only children at risk. There are more of Dr. Brayton's patients out there. Which means other children may be in danger. Until we have a court order in our hands, which will take—" She turned to Phelps and raised an eyebrow.

"Two hours," he said flatly.

"Since you cannot give me the names of Dr. Brayton's patients without breaking your fiduciary responsibility to this clinic and its patients, I expect you to get on the phone and contact each and every one of them. You will give them my coordinates and you will ask them to call me. You will be persuasive. They need to know that their children are in danger."

Fenton shook her head. "I don't have the legal authority to do that. They are Dr. Selmer's patients, not mine. Maya should have him on the phone any second." She pointed at the phone in the middle of the table beside the coffee and food.

The elevator opened and the receptionist came in. She was out of breath and held her pumps in her hand. "I can't find Dr. Selmer. I've called his apartment and he's not answering. I—"

Fenton pushed her chair back and stood up. "Did you call the doorman?"

Maya nodded, and with her mouth frozen in a perfect circle, she looked like an umlaut O come to life. "The doorman says there's no answer. He's not allowed to go in."

"Are you sure he's home?"

Maya nodded again. "He landed at nine thirty-five this morning. British Airways flight . . ." She pulled a crumpled sheet of paper from inside one of the shoes still dangling in her hand. ". . . flight two-two-nine-two. JFK. George, our driver, picked him up and dropped him off. Gate to apartment door. I called him. George left him at eleven oh five a.m. and the doorman says he hasn't left and no one answers his door. His car's in the garage."

Hemingway stood up. "We need an address."

||| THIRTY-FIVE

IT WAS earlier than yesterday; they had forced him to advance his schedule and from here on out time would be in short supply.

He looked down at the body; the best of what the boy was about was now missing.

He held him for a second, looked down on his face, on his features, and felt as if he were looking at part of himself. Nigel Matheson had been handsome. And talented. And many more things that no one could understand.

But all of those things were gone now. The handsomeness most of all.

He held him in the current as he said goodbye. He smiled down at the boy—his friend, really—and let go of his ankle, giving him up to the cold hands of the river.

Nigel Matheson floated out a few feet, scraped between the rocks and bumped the decoy that floated there. Then the current fastened its fingers on him and took him away.

He picked up the insulated knapsack with the Canadian flag sewn to it, the one he used to transport their parts. He slung it over his shoulder and scrambled up through the scrub.

DR. MICHAEL SELMER had an apartment on West 86th Street and Amsterdam. The doorman wore a green suit wired with ten yards of gold braid and looked like he had forgotten his tuba somewhere. His name tag read PEPE and after a few seconds of pressing his finger to the buzzer, he shook his head. "I told the lady on the phone—he ain't answerin'."

Hemingway let Phelps take this one; it was his turn to do some heavy lifting.

Phelps knocked and put his ear to the door. Then he leaned down and went to work on the lock. There was a soft click and he swung the door in.

They went through the apartment, weapons out, communication reduced to hand signals. Pepe stayed in the hallway.

The living room, dining room, kitchen, and study were empty.

Then Hemingway held up her hand and they listened. There was an odd, raspy sound coming from somewhere at the opposite end of the apartment.

They found him in the master bedroom.

He was asleep: plugs in his ears; a mask over his eyes;

mouth open to the ceiling; snoring a jet-lagged slumber. He wore silk pajama bottoms and nothing else.

Phelps reached out and touched his toe.

Selmer lifted straight off the bed in a screaming cat launch. He had the mask off and was up against the headboard in a single startled move. Then Pepe walked into the room and the fear in his face converted to confusion.

Hemingway had her badge out. "I'm Detective Hemingway and this is Detective Phelps. We need to speak with you."

He put his hand to his forehead and for a second it looked like he would faint. "Jesus Christ, why didn't you knock?"

———

A few minutes later they were in the living room, overlooking a church. Dr. Selmer still had his silk pajama pants on but had thrown a Paul Frank T-shirt over his chest. He had a coffee in his hands and looked like he was about to fall over, his squinty-eyed stare not dissimilar to the monkey logo. "Sorry, I took two Seconal about—" He checked the gold Cartier on his wrist, tried to focus, and gave up. "Hell, I don't know. Before I went to bed." He took a sip of his coffee and tried to follow Hemingway as she paced.

"Dr. Selmer, have you read the news?" she asked, indicating the iPad sitting on the coffee table.

He shook his head. Slurped more coffee. He clearly just wanted to get back to bed.

Hemingway stepped forward, yanked the iPad up off the exotic wood surface, and found the *New York Times* website. Then she handed him the tablet. "Maybe you should."

His eyes ratcheted down and he tried to focus on the print. When he couldn't, he reached for his glasses.

He scanned the screen and the tired look dropped away. Without taking his eyes from the screen he leaned forward and placed his mug down on one of the coffee table books neatly stacked on the table. He swiped through the content and what little color remained in his face drained away. He went to put the iPad back onto the coffee table but it slipped from his fingers and bounced on the floor. "Oh Jesus."

"So you recognize those names?"

He no longer looked like the drugged-out monkey on his T-shirt. "Before I say anything, what are you doing from a legal standpoint?"

Hemingway was glad he wasn't another Fenton. She ran through the chain of events, starting with her epiphany at the Mathesons' apartment and ending with her showdown with Fenton. "Our captain has this before the DA right now. From there it goes in front of a judge. We should have a court order giving us access to your files by the close of business today. Which is five hours closer to sunset and if this guy sticks to his routine, we'll find Nigel Matheson in the river just after sundown."

Selmer shook his head as he put it all through his processor. "This is bad."

"Your career?"

At that he laughed a single, derisive snort. "My career? When my name becomes associated with these horrors, what do you think will happen to me? I might as well move to Finland. My career, Detective Hemingway, is over.

"I am thinking about my patients—and they are my patients now, regardless of how they began their association with the clinic. Or with Brayton."

Something about the way he said the doctor's name set off some low-level alarm in her mind. "What can you tell us about Brayton?"

He shrugged. "Great doctor. Smartest guy in the room. A narcissist, but that's not uncommon in exceptional people."

"You know where he is?"

He shrugged again. "Scandinavia somewhere. Norway, I think."

She smelled bullshit behind it all.

"If the link between those three boys is Brayton, there are bound to be others. I can't tell you who they are. Not yet. Not legally. But I can put them in touch with you. I can warn them," he said, mimicking Hemingway's thoughts. He stood up. "I have to get to the clinic. To my files." He ran to the bedroom, pulling off his shirt. There was nothing sluggish about his movements now that the adrenaline had kicked in.

Hemingway stood up and her cell phone went off. She nodded at Phelps who went after the doctor and she answered her phone.

"Hemingway here."

"Hemi, it's Marcus. I found something you need to hear. The Rochester and Grant boys were half brothers."

"How is that possible? They were—" And then it hit her. "Sonofabitch, they had the same father."

"He's not hunting them because they're his type. He's hunting them because of who they are. It's not a phenotype; it's a genetic link."

THE ELEVATOR was large—an anomaly for Manhattan no matter what the price point. There were no Keith Harings hanging on the paneled walls but Dr. Selmer's parents had to be proud.

Selmer stood in a corner, staring at the floor. They would escort him to the clinic where he would begin calling the parents of other children who had been sired by the same donor. At least that was what he said the scope of his activities would be. Papandreou and Lincoln would stick with him until the footwork was done and they had a list of parents. Always the list.

Hemingway's phone made him jump.

She pressed it to her ear. "Hemingway."

"Hemi, it's Papandreou. It looks like they found Nigel Matheson in the East River."

She felt the air leave her lungs and she checked her watch. It wasn't yet 1 p.m. "What do you mean, 'looks like'?"

"It's hard to tell; the bottom of his face has been sawn off."

THIRTY-EIGHT

HEMINGWAY DROVE, Phelps rode shotgun. The lights and sirens were dialed to their apex as they pushed through traffic. The early-afternoon sun was behind the rolling sheet of clouds that stretched to the horizon but it still felt like the streets were heated to within a few degrees of combustion. A storm was coming and everyone hoped it would bring a brief respite from the heat and humidity.

She and Phelps had switched out with Lincoln and Papandreou who were now with Selmer at the clinic. They would act as chaperone until the court order came through. No one thought he would run but they were all concerned that Fenton would offer him a check to keep a united front for their house of secrets.

Hemingway pulled around a florist's truck, then rocked through a hole between two taxis, her tires screaming across the hot city pavement. Phelps held tight, his face the same impassive mask he had sewn to his skull whenever they were at work.

"He's early," she said, hating that she expected anything of this guy. There was an old cop rule that said the most you could count on from the other side was nothing. And even that was often hoping for too much.

Phelps shrugged, as if it all amounted to the same thing—which it did—another dead child.

A lane opened up in front of them and Hemingway pounded down on the gas. The truck lurched forward at nearly sixty miles an hour.

Rochester and Grant were half brothers.

They shared a parent.

A father.

A donor.

Which was as narrow a commonality as they could hope for. They had more than a lead—they had their case. She didn't know where it was yet, but the boys were the key. If they busted their asses, they'd find him. Hemingway didn't know how long it would take, only that it would get done.

THE BOY looked like a mechanic had taken his head apart to get at the transmission inside. Only there was no transmission. And there was no putting it back together again. He was waxy, lifeless, and horrifying.

Phelps looked down at the child, coughed once, then walked out of the room, leaving Hemingway and Marcus in silence.

Hemingway had seen a lot of damage done to the human body but she couldn't get used to what this guy seemed to feed on. There was no way to hammer this into any kind of comprehensible geometry. No. Way. At. All.

She looked down at the boy and gulped in a lungful of air. She could smell the river in him. "What am I looking at?"

Since Phelps's departure, the only noise had been the scratch of Marcus's pencil and the distant tidal force of her own heart. His pencil stopped and Hemingway looked up to see him staring at her. "His jaw was cut out," he said.

She forced herself to lower her eyes, to focus on the boy. "With our hacksaw?" It seemed a pointless thing to ask.

Marcus didn't add any body language to his response.

"Same saw. Same anesthetic. Same type of victim. Same injection point. Same everything. Except for the parts he took."

Hemingway tried to make sense of the ugly thing she was looking at.

"And he learned something from taking Deacon's skull apart. As opposed to going straight through like last time, he used two cuts, one straight back into the condyle, the second up from under his chin. Saved himself having to go through the ramus and spinal column."

"Was Matheson alive when this happened?"

Marcus waved the question away as if it were academic. "Of course."

Bobby Grant's half brother; Tyler Rochester's half brother.

Hemingway stared down at the boy. His lower jaw was gone and the meat on the skull above was swollen and distorted. The corners of his mouth were opened up to his temporomandibular joint. His top teeth and uvula hung in the wreckage of his face—a purple mass of bloodless anatomy that looked like it lived on the bottom of the ocean. Part of his larynx poked up through the top of his neck, like an exposed pupa. He looked worse than dead; he looked defiled.

For a second, Marcus put aside his professional demeanor and asked the question that was running through everyone's head. "Hemi, do you know the kind of person it takes to do something like this? What kind of experiences a human being needs to have under his belt to do this to a live child?"

Hemingway had no answer, she doubted anyone did. She stared at the boy. This hadn't been done by a human being at all.

The door to the lab opened and Phelps came back in. "Sorry about that," he said.

Marcus continued, business as usual. "Again, there are no defensive wounds. His hands are clean. Washed by the Hudson—true—but in good shape. No ripped nails, abrasions, cuts, bruises, lacerations, ligature marks, or fractures. I can see that on one victim. But all three? They don't fight and they don't see it coming." He looked up. "Our boys are comfortable around the killer."

"So was Deacon," she said.

DR. MICHAEL SELMER wasn't prone to greed and this had always made him suspect in the eyes of Director Fenton; there is nothing a medical corporation values less in an employee than moral rectitude, even in the abstract. The clinic and its principles were fundamentally positive but the ends-versus-means formula that was dictated by corporate survival often cast it in an unsympathetic light. Like now.

Selmer wasn't afraid of Fenton as much as he was worried about her. She wasn't evil, but she *was* devious. And tenacious—a trait worth ten times its weight in brains. In medicine it was all about staying power, and in his thirty-one years in the industry, he had never worked under anyone more driven than Frau Fenton.

She ran the clinic with relentless precision. She didn't outlaw the thieving of office supplies or begrudge her employees parking passes—no, if anything she was overly generous with benefits: Hermès briefcases each Christmas; a new Benz each spring. But there was a price for her love: you had to perform. Continually on. Continually perfect. Continually nervous.

This hypercompetitive atmosphere ensured that only the strongest survived and competitive mechanics had refined the clinic's personnel to the top stratum of American medicine. Which in turn attracted the top stratum of clientele. And the self-feeding machine acquired the finest research facility in reproductive endocrinology anywhere in the hemisphere.

Fenton had been waiting for him in the lobby and had insisted on walking him to his office. She had been alone, her two security baboons conspicuously absent. She had talked about loyalty. About the greater good. About finances and bright futures.

Before she left him at his desk, she pushed a copy of his contract into his hand, reminded him that he had a legal responsibility to the clinic and an ethical one to his patients. She didn't mention Brayton; she didn't need to. Then she had left him alone with his conscience.

Right from the start Brayton had been her golden boy, a handsome dark-haired wunderkind. He attracted all the right clients. All the right money. Until he had been found out.

As soon as Fenton left his office, Selmer had called his lawyer, his *personal* lawyer, not the clinic's people. Counselor Harwick had listened carefully, then told him that the press would catch on to this within twenty-four hours. He said Selmer could forget distancing himself from the great big mushroom cloud painted on the wall—it would make no difference that none of this was his fault.

He didn't ask Harwick about Brayton.

Harwick said the best path to a future was to have everything ready for the police when they arrived with the warrant. Legally, he couldn't tell Selmer to coach them ahead of time as to what portion of the files they'd be looking for, but he suggested that reaching out to the NYPD might not be the worst idea right now; being a live dog was better than being a dead lion. He closed by saying that in ten years Selmer would look back and tell him he had been right. Then he hung up.

He couldn't tell them about Brayton—he had signed a confidentiality agreement—but he could help protect the children.

The matter of confidentiality was largely one of interpretation and Selmer had a broad range of choices here, from helpful to near criminal. They could subpoena information they believed was there, but they could not come in like the gestapo and confiscate said information if he refused to hand it over. And they might not request the correct information.

Selmer worried about Frau Fenton, upstairs concocting a plan of defense with the clinic's battery of legal help. She wanted him to hold out until the last moment—the best thing for the clinic and maybe even for him, she had said. Which was bullshit.

She was worried that Brayton's indiscretions would be made public.

Brayton had crossed so many lines—ethical, moral and legal—that no one knew how far-reaching the consequences would be. He had been sent into exile. But he would be found—it was only a question of time. And when it all came out, the fires of hubris would burn the clinic to the ground.

He could call the parents, but he knew these people, knew the filters he'd have to go through. He was looking at three days if he was diligent. And they didn't have three days. So he went over his options. He could do this without breaking the law but he couldn't do this without violating the nonnegotiable tenets of medical practice. But he would never practice medicine again—so what did he care about doctor–patient confidentiality?

And of course he'd be sued after this. The Rochesters or

the Grants or the Mathesons would go after him in civil court and the litigious judicial system would take away everything he owned. But he wouldn't do jail time because he had done nothing illegal. Strictly speaking. So why not give it away with his head held high instead of letting them take it while he fought a losing battle?

Detectives Lincoln and Papandreou were in the lobby, as both protection and reminder that he was now under the eye of the law. If he walked out the front door, they would be with him. Which might be a good thing.

But Fenton would know. And she'd slap the lawyers on the NYPD faster than anyone could imagine. He'd go under glass and the bickering would start.

He looked at the spreadsheet, a list that had taken him a year to piece together. By law, the clinic was required to report this information to the Society of Assisted Reproductive Technology, under directives from the Centers for Disease Control. But government forms do not always ask the right questions.

It didn't take very long to see the pattern the police were onto: Tyler Rochester, Bobby Grant and Nigel Matheson had all been fathered by the same donor.

He wondered how long it would take them to figure out that the father was Dr. Brayton.

FORTY-ONE

HEMINGWAY AND Phelps threaded their way through traffic from the medical examiner's office downtown to the Deacon house in Astoria. Deacon and the boys were somehow linked; the question was how. Maybe they had missed something at the house.

When they pulled up outside, Phelps let out a protracted "Fuck me," stretching the first word into three syllables.

Without the cavalcade of police cars out front, it should have looked like any other house on the block. But the villagers had tried to exorcise the demons from its walls and it looked like the setting for a lynching. The big elm in the front yard was toilet papered and dozens of bicycle tires hung from the branches like black sightless eyes. The sidewalk was dotted with pentagrams laid out in bloody bright epoxy paint. The bricks and garage had been spray-painted with the words *monster*, *motherfucker*, and *beast*. The planters that had been by the door were smashed on the driveway. Evidently things were just hunky-dory in Walley World.

Hemingway maneuvered the two-ton SUV into the empty

space in front of Deacon's and they stepped out into the humidity.

A man in a wifebeater sitting on a stoop across the street yelled, "I wouldn't park there if I was you."

Hemingway crossed the street and pulled out her badge. "Yeah? Well you're not me, fuckface. And if anything happens to that truck while I'm inside, I'm going to come back here and kick the shit out of you. We clear, cupcake?"

The man spit into the brown bush beside the steps. "Yeah."

As they walked up to the door, Phelps said, "He's either a fuckface or a cupcake—he can't be both."

"What are you, the grammar police?" They approached the cracked concrete steps and Hemingway caught the movement of a shadow by one of the windows. "And what was with the Virginia Woolf reference the other day? You start reading them book things?" she asked, in a fake hillbilly accent.

"Discovery Channel."

The door opened before they had knocked. "You got my check?" Mrs. Deacon barked into Hemingway's face.

Phelps took a step back and Hemingway did her best to smile. "That's a different office than ours, Mrs. Deacon, and I'd—"

"The name's Bergen, lady. Deacon was that bastard's father. A bum. Like his kid. Knew it from the moment he was born. Didn't do nothin'. And now them people spray-painting bad words on *my* house, toilet papering *my* tree, like *I* had anything to do with the stuff what went on downstairs. How's I supposed to know, huh? Damn stupid people. They think I'm gonna move, they got another think-a-dink coming. Tryin' to scare an old lady in her golden years. That's just mean."

"Why aren't you in a hotel?"

"They let me keep my per diem—don't mind if I do—if

I stayed here. Don't need niggers going through my suitcase when I'm in the shower."

Hemingway closed her eyes, wondering where they made people like this. "We're here to look at your son's apartment," she said, trying not to sound angry.

The old woman's mouth pursed up, reprising its role as a furry sphincter. "I already told you people. I ain't been down there in years. Can't get there through the house—he had it locked up like the floor was paved in gold or some-thin'." And with that she slammed the door.

They turned and headed around to the basement entrance. On the bottom step Phelps leaned over and said, "I know hit men got bigger hearts than her."

What could she say to that? She had hunted these men long enough to know that for the most part monsters weren't born, they were made; it didn't take a lot of imagination to see how Deacon's mother could be worked into the flowchart.

Hemingway punched her code into the lock box, took out the big ring of keys, and opened the door—Phelps's entry shots were now repaired with a neat plywood patch fitted with new locks. They stepped under the bright yellow X of police tape into the gloom of Trevor Deacon's lair.

Just below the scent of disinfectant and ammonia was the stench of death and misery. It felt like a living presence. It wasn't the way Deacon met his demise—being sawn apart in his own bed—that rippled across the pond of her conscience; no, it was the thought of the children he had taken apart down here that made the place feel like a dark corner of the underworld.

They didn't know what they were looking for, only that it might be here, hidden in the gloom. The boys were tied to the clinic—which would probably be enough. But they still had a long way to go, and until it came together, they had to run down everything they had. And right now that meant Trevor Deacon's world.

She flicked on all the lights and even without Deacon's parts neatly displayed on the teak wall unit a feeling of sadness seemed to emanate from the very pores of the dwelling. It was difficult to imagine any happiness in this room. She couldn't picture anyone laughing or watching old movies or throwing birthday parties. But misery and mutilation and screams and loneliness were no stretch at all.

Hemingway laid the initial crime-scene photographs out on the table and they each took half, Phelps the kitchen/living room, Hemingway the bedroom and garage. The metal bed frame was still there, stripped down to the springs. It had once been a glossy white but was now a chipped dirty gray that cried rust at the rivets. She stood in the doorway and opened up her mind, willing herself into Trevor Deacon's headspace. It wasn't profiling or channeling or any of the populist ideas of how a detective worked, it was merely an effort to understand the man's thoughts and how he had acted on them. If she could see who he had been, she might get a line on his killer.

She stood at the foot of the bed and reached out, touching her fingertips to the cold metal. This was where Deacon had ended his time. The four main posts were scarred and scratched and she remembered the padlocks and lengths of chain in the garage, hanging on big spiral spikes. She wondered how many children had been in this room. And as much as she wished the bed could talk to her, she was grateful for its silence; she wasn't sure she could handle the things it had witnessed.

There were the children they knew of back in the medical examiner's office. But how many had been erased from the planet? How many would never be put to rest? They would remain ten-year-olds forever, grinning out from photographs on mantels and nightstands and websites for parents who hoped that they were out there somewhere. Lost, maybe, but alive. Growing up calling someone else Mommy. Not disassembled in a garage in Astoria.

What had Deacon done with their bodies? The forensics team had gone through the property with every available technology and found nothing. There was no backyard, the foundation had been scanned and there were no bodies set in the concrete. They had interviewed Deacon's coworkers and no one knew a thing about him. He hadn't owned a car in years and the neighbors said they never really saw him around much. He went to work, came home late, never spoke to anyone. It would take months, at least, to figure out how he had snatched the kids, where he had snatched them, why he had snatched them. But that shit could wait. What they needed right now was to find out who had killed him.

Other than the bed, the only furniture was a dresser that contained clothing and the two camera lenses Linderer had catalogued. They were hidden behind the shirts in the bottom drawer.

She pulled them out—both were Nikon telephoto lenses. One was a massive 500 mm affair that looked like the barrel assembly of a howitzer and the other was smaller but only marginally so. She was familiar with photography equipment and the lenses looked like the ones Daniel was always packing and unpacking for work. She dialed his number.

"Hey, baby," he answered. "All good?"

"Yeah. Look, can you tell me the price of a couple of lenses?"

"Maybe."

Hemingway picked up the box of the largest one, a beige cardboard carton with black writing. Deacon's name was on the box in felt tip marker. "Nikon f2.0, five hundred milli-meter."

"The sports guys use them for fieldwork. Ten grand new. Maybe five secondhand. What's this about?"

She didn't have time to explain. "Work. I can't talk about it."

"I see," he said, but it was clear he didn't.

She read the next box to him, "Nikon F2 in two hundred millimeter."

"Another sports lens. It's got a fixed focal length but it's perfect for low-light shots—say if you were shooting volley-ball in a gym. Five grand retail, three used."

"Thanks, baby, you're the best. I'll talk to you later." She hung up and pocketed the phone.

She took the lenses out of the boxes and Deacon's name was professionally etched into the focus ring that ran around the optics of each. The warranty registration cards were in both boxes, stamped by B&H Photo in Manhattan. She took a snapshot of each card with her phone and returned the lenses to their hiding spot.

Where was his camera?

Phelps was still going through the kitchen cupboards, working with slow precision.

The kitchen chair still had the protective box over the seat, the single crescent of dried blood from a shoe sole visible on the vinyl under the protective capsule. Man's ten or ten and a half.

The focal point of the room was still the spider scrawled onto the door to the garage, as haunting as when she had first seen it.

She opened the locks and stepped into the garage.

The space was as neat and sparse as it had been when Phelps had called her in to see the freezer full of feet. The single red crescent of the leather-soled man's shoe was there, under a protective polycarbonate box fastened to the floor with yellow tape.

The freezer stood in the corner. Unplugged. Door propped open. The lengths of welded chain still hung on rusty spiral spikes.

The workbench was back in the lab, secrets being pried from its wood. There were the feet of the children that they knew about of course. But what about children who hadn't shown up in the freezer? Maybe they'd be able to isolate their DNA from samples taken from Deacon's improvised operating table.

She held up the photo and the wood looked like it was swollen with old motor oil. So far they had identified thirteen different sources of DNA—and all had been matched to feet in Deacon's collection. Maybe that's all there were.

Had she really just thought that? *"All there were"?* Had she examined the remnants of the broken and ill and plain old evil for so long that she no longer thought in terms of right or wrong—only in terms of numbers?

Don't get all girly, she told herself. Do your job.

Her hip buzzed and she pulled her phone out. "Hemingway," she said automatically.

"Detective, this is Dr. Marcus. I've got news from the FBI's CODIS database on the Deacon victims."

"That was fast."

"We got lucky."

"How lucky?"

"They identified all but two of the boys. We don't have the case files yet but I can give you the dates they disappeared. The first case dates back to July of eighty-eight. It looks like Mr. Deacon was responsible for the disappearance of two children a year from that point on. There are holes in the schedule—I only have one child from 1994, 1997, and 2004 and there are no children for 2006. Other than that, it's pretty close to a schedule. I've e-mailed you the spreadsheet."

Hemingway pinched the bridge of her nose. "So the guy was active for a quarter century?"

"Whoever killed Trevor Deacon just cut down child abductions in New York City by eighteen percent."

Hemingway looked down at the empty space where the dirty, bloodstained workbench had sat. Whoever had killed Deacon seemed intent on carrying the torch, only at an accelerated rate. "Dr. Marcus, I appreciate it."

Back in the living room she paused in front of the four holes where the yellow pushpins had held a photograph. Less than twenty-one-month-old HP personal printer, Fuji paper, no discernible image, Deacon's thumbprint on the front surface.

She took out her phone and dialed the precinct, clicking through to the evidence department.

"Evidence, Rhea here," a man said in the bored tones of someone marking off time.

"Rhea, this is Hemingway. We found a Parkay container filled with baggies of heroin at the Deacon murder scene yesterday."

She heard the tap-tap-tap of fingers on a keyboard. "Yeah, got it here. Sixteen baggies, three grams a crack. Pink heroin. Never seen pink heroin before. What about it?"

"I need to check one out. Prep the paperwork and have it waiting for me."

"Hemi, this is a class A narcotic. You'll need to process the reqs and they gotta go through the prosecutor's office. After that you'll have to—"

"Call Dennet. If it's not ready when I get there in half an hour, I'm going to pull you through that little hole in the window on your cage. We clear?"

There was a moment of awkward silence followed by, "Sure thing, detective."

When she got off the phone, Phelps was staring at her. "You okay, Hemi?"

"Yeah, why?"

He stared at her for a moment.

"No reason." Then he opened the door and stepped into the light.

THE DISTRICT attorney was a man named Edward Schlesinger, a perfectionist extraordinaire. Hemingway, Phelps and Dennet stood off in the shadows, conserving energy and trying not to distract the man from his task. He was going over the warrant, ticking off points, underlining sections, and making corrections in the margins.

No one wanted an oversight rendering the investigation null and void. Not only did all the *t*'s have to be crossed and all the *i*'s dotted, but there had to be a scope of seizure that was defensible as legitimate and broad enough to net them the information they needed. There would be no going back to the judge for a second warrant because the first one had overlooked something. And since the DA was the man to defend the writ, he had to be certain that they hadn't missed anything.

The DA stopped, brought his pen up a paragraph, and reread a passage. He circled something in a broad flourish of his fountain pen, capped it, placed it on the leather surface of his desk, and leaned back in his chair. "We do not get a second chance at this, gentlemen—and lady," he added with a nod. "You are asking for a very limited scope of information in what could turn out to be a much larger picture. I'm not complaining—this makes my job of selling it to Judge Lester much simpler—but there are still a few areas where you're overreaching."

Hemingway stepped away from the bookcase and came over to Schlesinger's desk. He was a small man and sitting there, with Hemingway's six-foot frame towering over him, he looked positively tiny. But not the least bit uncomfortable; true to his ilk, he relished confrontation.

"Mr. Schlesinger, we know from the parents of the three murdered boys that they were conceived at the same clinic and their parents were treated by the same physician—Dr. Sylvester Brayton."

"And you are unable to find Brayton?" It was a good question.

It was Phelps who answered. "It's obvious he doesn't want to be found."

"Or that Fenton doesn't want him to be found," Hemingway said.

At that Schlesinger held up his hand. "This is exactly what I am afraid of, Detective Hemingway. We all want this to go well. Don't paint bogeymen on the wall unnecessarily."

Hemingway stared at him for a moment. "Something's wrong at the clinic. There's something that Fenton's not telling us."

"What do you know for sure?"

"That the parents of all three boys were patients of Dr. Brayton; we need to know the names of his other patients because they could be on a hunting list."

Schlesinger nodded. "Granted. But what does that give you? That gives you a doctor and three children. What you are requesting here is the identity of the donor. This man, whoever he is, has not been implicated in any crimes. By asking—"

"Not been implicated in any crimes? His children are being murdered—as far as I'm concerned, he's the only suspect we have."

"Yes, but how do I sell that to the judge? It's reaching."

Hemingway felt the room get a little smaller. "The one common link we have here is the donor."

"I agree. And I'm sure the judge will agree. But is it grounds for a warrant? The names of the boys I can sell; by all indications they are in imminent danger. But the donor has not been implicated in any of these crimes. There is no evidence to suggest that he knows anything about these children."

Hemingway stared at Schlesinger for a few moments and she felt the muscles of her jaw tighten. "Where else are we reaching?"

"You cannot ask for a list of all the couples who had a child fathered by this donor. Again, there's no evidence to suggest that they are all in danger. Not at this point."

"No offense, Mr. Schlesinger, but you're shitting me, right?"

Schlesinger steepled his fingers in what looked like a practiced pose. "I'm not the bad guy here, Detective Hemingway, I'm just telling you what the judge is going to tell me. If I can't defend every part of this request, the judge will dismiss it and what do we have then? Wasted time.

"So far you have three boys who were fathered by the same sperm donor. That's solid. But you can't ask for the names of all children fathered by this donor, because that's reaching. What about girls he fathered, if any? What about older children? Younger children? That clinic has been in business since . . ." He leaned forward, checked his notes. ". . . nineteen eighty-seven and Dr. Brayton practiced there since it opened its doors for business. Selmer came on board ten years back. This donor may have a history of providing sperm as long as that clinic has been around. Does that mean that children he may have fathered who are twenty-five years old are also at risk?" He opened his hands in a well-I'm-waiting gesture.

Hemingway's jaw clicked again. "No, it doesn't."

"No, it doesn't," he repeated, a lilt of condescension in his tone. "So we have to be narrow in our scope of request. Since all evidence points to boys with a very narrow range of age, I would like to propose an age limit." He leaned forward again, flipped through his notes. "All three boys were born in April and May ten years ago—they were all ten years and one to two months old. Would you be happy with a range of nine years and six months to ten years and six months?"

Hemingway stood up and backed away from the desk because in a second she was going to start swinging. "And what happens if a boy is found in the river who is aged ten years, six months and one day? Are you going to be the one who goes to his parents' home to explain they weren't warned that their son was on a psychotic hit list due to a decision you made?"

Schlesinger stared at her, his expression unreadable. "No, detective, that will be *your* job. *My* job is to go before Judge Lester and ask him to open the medical files that will help *you* solve these murders. Asking for every piece of paper in Dr. Selmer's files is a mistake."

Hemingway's jaw clicked again. "I'll settle for nine to eleven." It sounded like betting odds.

Schlesinger looked over at Dennet who shrugged. "Try," he said.

Schlesinger looked back up at Hemingway. "Okay, I'll try. And I'll be convincing."

Phelps came forward and threw a photograph onto the district attorney's desk. "Convincing's good," he said over the picture of Nigel Matheson laid out on the table at the morgue, his face opened like a mortar round had taken it apart. "Because this guy ain't fucking around."

||| FORTY-THREE

SELMER TURNED away from the electronic medical record and pressed his fingers to his eyes. He felt like his heart was pumping a viscid epoxy that was being rejected by his body. He concentrated on his breathing, taking deep gulps in through his nose and forcing them out through his mouth in a steady chug.

In.

Out.

In.

Out.

Over and over and over until he felt like his body was ready to breathe on its own again. He focused on his chest, ignoring the vomit he felt pushing at the back of his throat with its sour, coffee-tinted fingers. In a few minutes he felt better. Not perfect. But good enough, which was a minor miracle considering what he had just learned from the EMR of Tanya Everett.

He stood up, went to the fridge, and downed half a bottle of grapefruit Perrier. Selmer wanted to walk back to his desk, to look at the list with his notes scrawled in the margins, but he wasn't sure he'd be able to read it without feeling sick again.

He finished the water and dropped the bottle into the trash. Then he went back to his desk and looked down at the numbers.

He read the names over again, still making a conscious effort to oxygenate his blood.

The machinery of justice would roll over this place as soon as the ink from the judge's signature dried on whatever warrants the cops were smart enough to write up. Somewhere in his files was the information the police needed to find a man who took little boys apart with a saw.

But they didn't know about the girls.

The two detectives seemed bright and aggressive. But were they creative? Lateral thinkers? A court order could give them the information they requested but it wasn't the key to the kingdom. They could only ask for specifics, for information that they knew existed and that they believed would help them solve these murders. They couldn't fish.

They did not know about the girls. Ergo, they would not look into them.

Selmer looked at his wall of diplomas and citations and thank you cards and realized how deep inside the bubble he had become. Fuck it. His career was over anyway.

He swiped the pages of notes and the printed-out EMR into his messenger bag, slung it over his shoulder, and walked out into the hall.

The lawyers would do what they did, the media would do what they did, and he'd be able to hold his head high through the whole bloodletting even if he could no longer practice. It was just one of those things. Bad timing. Bad luck.

He knew that Fenton was upstairs, trying to slow the inevitable.

Fuck her and her little empire.

If he walked out the front with those two cops, she'd send one of the clinic's lawyers with him. If he protested, she'd have one waiting for him at the precinct. He had to do this the old-fashioned way.

Before he left his office he took a piece of the clinic's stationery to write Fenton a letter of resignation. The pen stayed poised over the paper for a second as he decided what to write. He finally settled on two words and an exclamation point.

Selmer took the small staircase at the back, the one they used to use back when they still hired people who smoked. He dropped down to the loading dock and out the back door, nodding a hello to a maintenance man in coveralls who was unloading paint from the trunk of an ancient, rust-riddled van—no doubt more beige and off-white for yet another useless "refreshing."

The dark pewter sky vibrated with the coming rain. He cut across the alley, walked past a hundred feet of Dumpsters and back doors, then stepped out onto the sidewalk. A man on the corner was screeching like Chicken Little, hocking umbrellas for five dollars apiece to a sweating populace who did their best to ignore him.

Selmer crossed between the cars waiting at the lights and the heat off the radiator grills warmed his pant leg. He looked up at the sky again; it was bending under the weight of the rain in its belly.

There was a throng of schoolboys in front of the electronics store, ogling the latest gadgets. The boys parted to let him through and he squeezed by, ducking into the parking garage. The attendant, Eddie, handed him his key without being asked and Selmer gave him a ten and a thank-you, realizing that he might never see Eddie again.

His leased Benz was on the second floor near the back. He threw his bag in the backseat, climbed in, drove down the ramp, and paused at the mouth of the garage.

By the time he got the car down to the entrance, the city looked as dark as the garage. The schoolboys ran by his grill and he thought of the boys who had died.

Maybe he could help stop it from happening again. He thought about how hard he had worked to get here. Then he thought about the note he had left for Frau Fenton. He was leaving with as much pride as he had started. Not a bad way to go, he thought, then pulled out into traffic.

Selmer hit a red light a block west of the garage and the schoolboys crossed in front of him, young and full of life.

Dr. Sylvester Brayton had sold the clinic's wealthiest clients on the idea of purchasing their sperm from a catalogue of rarefied samples. High IQs, handsome, healthy. Five hundred thousand dollars a crack.

The profiles were fake—Brayton had simply provided his own semen.

Fenton had figured it out that night at the opera. The next morning Brayton was gone. From the city. From the country. No doubt shuffled off to some dark corner of the globe in exchange for keeping quiet. A classic example of the win-win Fenton was always talking about.

Only it wasn't looking so win-win for Fenton now, was it? She looked like Charlie Sheen on a binge, spouting delusional rhetoric. Sure, Brayton was gone but his legacy would be around for a long time, like a curse lifted out of a fairy tale.

The heat came off the asphalt and licked up the side of the car.

He caught movement in the mirror, at the edge of his

peripheral vision. He glanced at the reflection and saw someone come around the back bumper.

It was stupid to dodge the lights at rush hour, almost
suicidal.

The engines around him changed pitch and he looked
up. The light was green.

Traffic began to move.

He took his foot off the brake and once again saw something at the edge of his sight—this time it was a face. He
turned. Recognized the face. Began the last expression that
would ever cross his features—a smile. There was a flash and
something whistled through his throat. He instinctively hit
the gas.

Blood spurted across the windshield and for a bright
panicked second he understood that he was already dead.

He lost consciousness and the Benz rolled west for half
a block before detonating a fruit stand and slamming into a
lamppost.

Then the sky opened up and the rain began.

FORTY-FOUR

THE OUTER office had been redecorated since the last time she had been here, the architectural symmetry of French Empire traded in for Midcentury Modern. The receptionist—a woman named Karen who had been here as long as Hemingway could remember—ushered her straight through the maze of cubicles to the big corner office. The plaque on the door read DWIGHT R. HEMINGWAY III.

When she walked in, the man behind the desk got up, came to her, and embraced her extended hand in both of his. Then he gave her a kiss on each cheek and held her at arm's length—something that seemed to be happening a lot lately.

"You look wonderful, Allie." He smiled as he spoke. "Radiant, even."

"Thanks, Uncle Dwight, but I'm a little old for compliments."

Her uncle laughed. "Ah, yes, Alexandra, the eternal pragmatist. The Hemingway women are never too old to be told they're beautiful—just look at your mother."

"How's Miles?" she asked. Even though she was here on

business, a certain amount of respect was due. Besides, a lot of her family information came from these moments.

"He's glad to be out of LA, I think. That series was killing him. Broadway's been good—"

"I've read the reviews."

"Well, we're spending time out in the country. If you ever want to get away from the Big Apple . . ." he let the sentence trail off.

"Uncle Dwight, I don't have a lot—"

"—of time." He nodded and mixed a smile in with the movement. "I know. What can I do for you?"

She hadn't seen him since last Christmas. He had taken her to lunch. They ate at Atelier, sitting at the family's usual table. The meal had started out full of awkward silences but eventually they found common ground and the afternoon disappeared over Scotch and catching up. He dropped her off at her place and she promised to keep in touch. To do this more often. But even as the Bentley pulled away, and he waved from the backseat, she knew they wouldn't. And here they were, more than six months later, and she hadn't so much as sent him an e-mail.

"This is all confidential," she said.

Uncle Dwight waved it away. "Everything we talk about is confidential, Allie." He was talking about her parents.

She was talking about a man who took children apart with a hacksaw.

"Have you heard about the boys we've found in the East River?"

He nodded and his handsome face tightened up. "Of course." He walked around his desk and sat down in the big leather chair. The skyline spread out behind him was wiped out by the thunderstorm hammering down. Every now and then the gray throbbed with lightning, as if a giant fuse had blown.

"We're lean on leads and I need a favor. A *big* favor."

He stared at her, his lawyer side trumping the uncle. Listen first; ask later.

She reached into her pocket and pulled out a padded envelope. She handed it across the desk. He peered inside then dropped it to the desk.

"That's heroin," she said.

"Okay."

"It's been colored with some sort of vegetable dye. I assume the color should make it easier to track down a point of origin."

"Okay."

"That heroin was found in the house of a man who murdered a lot of children." She handed a photograph of Trevor Deacon across the desk.

Her uncle didn't bother picking it up, as if contamination might be an issue.

"His name and address—including his former telephone number—are on the back. I don't care about the drugs, Uncle Dwight. As far as I'm concerned, they're a nonissue. Whoever sold them; whoever supplied them; whoever cut them—it doesn't matter to me. But I need to know about this man. I need to know where he went, what his habits are, and I've hit a wall. There's not a lot of pink heroin out there, so that's something."

Her uncle leaned back in his chair and crossed his arms over his chest. "I'm not that kind of a lawyer, Allie, you know that."

"Look, Uncle Dwight, I know the corporations you represent. I'm not asking for secrets. I'm not asking for names. You have my word—my *personal* word—that I want nothing from these people except information that will help me figure out Trevor Deacon's habits. You still represent Redfoot Industries?"

He nodded. It was a tentative, almost guarded, gesture.

"I don't care about Mr. Yashima's business dealings. But his beginnings are not as auspicious as his Wikipedia entry portrays. If anyone can find out where that comes from, it's him. I am asking *you* for the favor.

"I need to speak to the man—the actual street dealer—who sold this stuff to Deacon. I can't get down the food chain that quickly. All of Deacon's phone records and e-mail accounts are clean. I don't have any leads."

He stood up and turned to the rain beyond the window. For a few moments he stared out at the dark gray that had swallowed the skyline. When he turned back, his face was a mix of doubt and indecision. "These are not people that like questions, Allie. I can do this. But if you are lying to me, if anyone is prosecuted because of this, there will be repercussions. Do you understand what I am saying?"

"I promise this is not about drugs."

Her uncle dropped his eyes to the desk, to the photo and envelope she had given him. "Give me three hours," he said. Then he steepled his fingers and looked at her. "But I need something in return."

Here it is, she thought. "What?"

"Don't be so suspicious. I want you to call your father."

"I called him last month. He was out."

"That was the month before."

She thought about it for a second, then nodded. "You're right. It was."

"I'm not trying to get between you two because personally I don't see a need for it. You and he have a relatively good relationship. He worries about you. He'd just like you to be—"

"More like Amy."

Dwight shook his head. "That's not fair. To him *or* to you.

He doesn't want you to be anything like Amy. He has bound-less respect for you and for what you've done with your life. Sure, he would have wanted more grandchildren, but only if you wanted to have them."

She felt her hand head for her stomach and she con-sciously stopped it.

"He just worries about you being bombarded by the worst that humanity has to offer. Any father would be." He nodded at the envelope on the desk. "Maybe a career where you didn't carry around heroin."

"Is this you talking or him?"

"Both, I guess. But he misses you. So do I. I'm not asking you to take family vacations. I would just like a little—" he paused, which he rarely did "—*damage control.*"

She thought about calling him on that. Because they both knew it was bullshit. Her mother—her father's second wife—cared very little about anything except for her Bergdorf charge card and the bells and whistles that went along with being the wife of Steven Hemingway. It had always been that way and Hemi had long ago come to accept it. "Okay," she said after a moment of silence. "I'll call but I want him to stop sending me those checks. I'm fine. I don't need anything. When I needed help, he was there. I took the money for the down payment on my place."

"Which you *paid back.*"

"I don't want the money."

"What should he do with it? Burn it?"

She had thought about this one on the way up—as the family lawyer, Dwight knew what was going on. "It's not that I don't want any of the money, Uncle Dwight. I just don't want it now. I don't expect him to leave it to the church—it will probably end up being left to Amy and Graham and me.

When that happens, I'll worry about it. Until then, I haven't earned it."

At that, Dwight smiled. "It's not about you earning it. It's about your father wanting to give you something while he's still here. He doesn't send you any more money than he sends Amy. The difference between the two of you is that Amy cashes the checks."

"I'll call him."

"I'm flying out to the North Shore on Sunday. You want to come along?"

She pointed at the envelope on the desk. "I can't leave this case right now but I'll call him. Pinky swear. And as soon as I get a break, you and I will play a few rounds of tennis. How's that?"

He smiled and shook his head. "Why is it I always believe you when you lie to me? I always have."

She got up and came around the desk, gave him a hug and kissed him on the cheek. "Because I have good intentions."

"Evidently you've never heard about the road to hell."

She thought about the mutilated children they had found. "It's not a road, Uncle Dwight, it's a superhighway."

A VAST capillary system of interconnected hallways, corridors, and passages wormed through the earth beneath the American Museum of Natural History. If you didn't know where you were going, it could be an unsettling place to spend time. Benjamin Winslow had grown up in the subterranean world. His father had never really believed in babysitters and ever since he could walk, Benjamin had spent most of his nights and weekends here, three stories below the streets of the city, wandering the storage rooms while his father worked.

Mother Nature had let go outside and even here, burrowed deep in the earth, the boy could hear thunder pounding the city. The sound waves shook the bedrock and the foundation shuddered with each crack of electricity.

His father was an anomaly within the closed world of the museum. Most of the staff, including the department heads, lived under the continual threat of financial cutbacks. Where the other staff members were forced to deal with the endless internal politics of a massive institution, his father was beyond the petty pressures—and whims—of the museum chairs and departmental financial officers. He accomplished this by providing his own endowments for the department.

When the other departments in vertebrate zoology wanted to pursue research or acquire rare or exotic specimens, they had to deal with endless bureaucracy to make it happen. They had to beg, borrow, and steal. Not so the Department of Ornithology: when Dr. Winslow wanted something, he simply wrote a personal check for it. And received a tax write-off in the process. For this reason, the museum would never get rid of him.

Dr. Neal Winslow was monumentally wealthy; during the early part of the twentieth century, his grandfather's firm had been the largest manufacturer of surgical instruments outside of Germany. The postwar boom had grown the family fortune to a size where it could not easily be measured.

Benjamin walked by one of the storage lockers, a massive room the size of a gymnasium. He was friends with a lot of the museum's staff—most of them got a kick out of asking him questions they thought were difficult—and he had visited all of the storage rooms. They were lined with miles of steel shelving that reached up into the darkness, piled with the world's forgotten secrets.

Benjamin's favorite locker was the one that housed the specimens from the Department of Entomology—there were hundreds of thousands of drawers filled with glass-cased insects that he found absolutely fascinating. He knew more about certain species than many of the people in the department but a passion for invertebrate zoology had no practical application in his life so he had focused his attention on hyperbolic geometry and writing, two disciplines that got him the right kind of attention. Along with the paper the Harvard mathematics department had published, the school had been surprised by the six-volume, 1,200,000-word collection of biographies he had completed. It seemed that not many ten-year-olds were interested in the lives of Julius Caesar, Niccolò Machiavelli, Charles Darwin, Homer, Molière, and Nicolaus Copernicus. The newspaper coverage had started soon after that. And the scholarship offers.

Benjamin Winslow even had a Wikipedia entry; he loved being touted as a polymath.

Benjamin walked down the dark hallway that looked like it reached out into forever. Then he heard it, a soft scraping behind him. It wasn't much of a sound—hardly loud enough to qualify as noise, really—but it had been enough.

Benjamin spun around and saw the dark figure looming over him. Its arms came out and clamped on his shoulders. Then it squatted down and looked into his eyes.

"I've been looking for you, son. It's time to go. I have a schedule to keep to." His father didn't sound angry but his father never sounded angry.

"Sorry, Father. Of course."

Dr. Winslow patted him on the head. "Let's go home."

Benjamin hated going home early—more than anything else in the whole wide world.

FORTY-SIX

FOR THE first time in as long as Hemingway could remember, she was alone, something that rarely happened at the station and never happened during daylight hours. The rain filled the air with static that blocked out ambient noise. She stared out the window, watching the buildings across the street flicker through the heavy downpour.

Her corner of the floor was abandoned and quiet; Papandreou and Lincoln were at the clinic waiting for Dr. Selmer; and Phelps had gone for food when they came back from Uncle Dwight's. The DA was still with Judge Lester. The Matheson boy was with the coroner. Fenton was with her lawyers. All was at rest for the moment.

Except that he was out there, gearing up for another child.

She was tired but that was nothing new. Ever since the incident with Shea she had slept badly. She didn't suffer nightmares or have residual flashbacks, but for no reason she could understand, she never woke fully rested.

Hemingway didn't think about Shea anymore, not really. Along with the hospital and the surgeries and the physiotherapy, the memory of him had slowly faded away. Mank was a different story. He came back sometimes, mostly late at night when Daniel was asleep beside her and she was alone inside her head, staring at the shadows on the ceiling. She'd think of him, remember some little thing they had talked about, and she'd start to wonder what they might have had. She'd lie there in the dark and cry. But lately those moments were becoming rarer, and part of her worried that she'd forget about Mank altogether.

It wasn't fair to Daniel. She loved him; he loved her. What they had seemed to be right for both of them. And she felt safe with him, something she had never felt with Mankiewicz. And now they might be having a baby.

But it wasn't just a baby; it was a human life. From cradle to grave and all the pain in between. How could she bring a child into a world where the people who told you they had a handle on goodness tended to be the first to judge and to hate? Where genocide was taking place all over the world and torture was deemed okay by the government? Where a monster was out there sawing children up while their hearts were still beating?

She closed her eyes, focusing on the thrum of the rain against the world outside and the roof above her head, and everything else ceased to exist. She was back in the river, on the Hudson, feeling nothing more than the wind in her hair and the resistance of the water. She felt her body swaying a little, riding the swells in her kayak. She gripped the arms of the chair and the steel warmed to her touch like the carbon shaft of her paddle. For an instant she was under the George Washington Bridge, being pulled downriver by the tide, traffic rumbling across the spans high overhead.

And it all fell apart to the chirp of her cell phone.

"Hemingway."

"Allie, it's me."

Hemingway pinched the bridge of her nose to stave off the pounding she knew would soon start up in her head. She didn't want Amy and her neediness. Not now. "Amy, I'm at work and it's not a good day." Which was code for *fuck off*.

"I know. I saw you on the news this morning." Brief pause. "I've left Patrick. Left DC. I was hoping maybe we could talk. Help me get a little perspective. Have a drink."

That last part sounded like the goal. "Where are you?"

"I'm on the train right now but I'm staying at the Plaza."

Hemingway knew it was a mistake before she opened her mouth but it came out anyway. "Forget the hotel. Stay with Daniel and me. We can talk." Why had she done that? Daniel didn't like Amy.

Diagnosed as acutely narcissistic when she was sixteen, she had been a problem her entire life. She had always been theatric, very much to the detriment of herself and those around her. Every family has its tortured soul and Amy was the Hemingways'.

"Why don't you come to the hotel? We'll have a massage, order in some booze. I can tell you what happened."

She wouldn't make the mistake of inviting Amy to the loft again. "I'm on a tight schedule right now. Things are . . ."

The door blew open and Phelps came in. She knew something bad had happened when she saw his face. She said, "I gotta go," and hung up.

Phelps stared at her for a moment before speaking. "Someone cut Selmer's throat at a traffic light."

"Where the fuck were Papandreou and Lincoln?"

Phelps shrugged. "I don't know. Dennet caught me in the staircase. Nick and Linc are on the way in. Apparently Selmer gave them the slip."

"Why the fuck would he do that?" Hemingway couldn't

believe what she was hearing. She thought about what had happened and where it now put them. It took a few seconds for her to think of an upside. "At least now we get our warrant."

Phelps's eyebrows raised in a *how-you-figure-that?* expression that hung there for a bit. Then his face broke into a grin. "For a lady, you sure are smart."

"I get that a lot," she said.

THIS TIME they rolled into the Park Avenue Clinic with an army of cops and a docket full of warrants from the DA's office. Fenton was waiting for them, her two security boys flanking her like a pair of backup singers. Behind the backup singers stood the lawyers. No one looked happy, least of all Fenton.

"Nice to see you both again, detectives." If an electric fence had a voice, it would have sounded like her.

Phelps had the honor of handing over the sheaf of warrants the DA had secured, the only positive consequence of the death of Dr. Michael Selmer. Fenton didn't bother to look at them, she just handed them back to the lawyers.

Hemingway stepped into character. "Mrs. Fenton, Dr. Michael Selmer was murdered an hour ago. Someone cut his throat."

Fenton's expression twitched for a second, then snapped back to its former impassivity. "I didn't know."

Hemingway nodded at the warrants the lawyers were flipping through. "Those warrants entitle us to any and all computers, cell phones, fax machines, tablets, and other electronic devices that *may have* been used by Dr. Michael Selmer in the past twenty-four hours. We are also entitled to a list of any and all phone numbers that he may have used in this building within the same period, including fax numbers. The failure of anyone employed by this clinic to follow directives issued from any of our people will result in the charge of obstructing an investigation. Mrs. Fenton, would you please have someone show us to Dr. Selmer's office?"

Fenton stared up at Hemingway for a moment and her face had that same flat expression. Then she turned back to the wall of legal advice. They shook their heads in unison, and for a second it looked like the security men would break into a gruff harmony. Fenton rotated her gaze back up to Hemingway. "Please follow me," she said.

IT WAS well past supper and the precinct was set to its usual voltage in the ever-present battle of good versus evil. Once the rainstorm had finished throwing its tantrum, the heat had come back, baking the streets and sucking the rain back into the atmosphere. Before the puddles had gone, it was hotter and more humid than before the cloudburst. The air-conditioning did its best but the computer lab was stifling, the heat magnified by the red-hot processors humming within the server towers. There seemed to be a thousand little plastic fans spitting out air and even the Iron Giant looked irritated.

Alan Carson—the senior analyst from the cybercrimes division and the brains of their IT lab—had gone to work on Selmer's off-the-shelf encryption software. The clinic had provided all of the doctor's passwords but he had added a few of his own and it was chewing up time. Carson kept knocking back Yoo-hoos and throwing more horsepower at the problem.

Hemingway hated reducing anyone to a stereotype but there was no other way to look at the man. He was probably the same age as her—somewhere in the tail end of his thirties—but everything about him said teenager, from his black Chuck Taylors to his silly T-shirts. Probably had a doll collection at home—only he'd call them *action figures*. But he was good at his job—gifted, even—and never threw around any of the macho bullshit like some of the other cops. Besides, she got an admitted kick out of the crush he had on her. It was nice to cash in on free ice coffees every now and then. And the guy always remembered the sugar.

One of Carson's minions had hooked Dr. Selmer's hard drives up to a server. This computational life-support system was one of more than sixty such setups in the lab—now the second most well-funded sector in the department.

The goal was to retrace the doctor's last few virtual hours on the planet, an exercise that in the new digital world was usually more productive than retracing real-world hours. They had his phone records—both office and cellular—and Phelps and Hemingway were going over the list, running each number through the system and marrying it to a name.

Would someone he had called turn out to be the killer?

Until they knew, they'd keep digging into the patient files. That was the pressure point—everything met there. Somehow.

Between the time he had been dropped off and his final run-in with a razor-sharp piece of steel, Selmer had been a busy man. He made a total of one hundred and three phone calls. Of those, sixty-six were to residences in Manhattan, eleven were to directory assistance, and twenty-six were to out-of-state numbers, including three to Italy, two to Sweden, four to Australia and one to Mexico.

Hemingway went over the column of calls, short-listing anyone who was within driving distance of the clinic. The closer they got to Selmer's time of death, the shorter the distance had to be. There was still a chance that the killer wasn't any of these people but when you had nothing else to go on, you went with anything you could.

Carson punched the desk and howled, "Motherfucker!"

Phelps asked, "Motherfucker *good* or motherfucker *bad*?"

Carson flicked the screen. "I've cracked his off-the-shelf encryption. What do you want?"

Hemingway took up position over Carson's shoulder. "Start with the donor: bring up Tyler Rochester, Bobby Grant and Nigel Matheson's files." Her shirt was stuck to her body and the air held the hot oil smell of a tool shed. It was stiffling; how did Carson take this, day in, day out?

Carson clicked through the system, rapidly opening and closing fields. It took a few clicks for him to figure out how the patient files were organized but once he had it he went straight to Tyler Rochester's file. "Here you are. Donor 2309432. Guy was a Scandinavian atheist," Carson said.

At any other time, Hemingway would have smiled—for now, the reflex was turned off. "Check Bobby Grant's file."

Carson clicked around until he had the information up on the screen. "Here you go. Just like the Rochester kid. Another Nordic atheist and—" Carson pointed at the donor number: 4022393. "If they had the same father, how is that possible?"

Hemingway commandeered the mouse and clicked through to Nigel Matheson's file, reading the attributes of his donor: 3249023. "This guy came with the same options."

"He's a man, not a BMW," Phelps said.

Hemingway looked over at him. "This is marketed by men for women—trust me, there are options."

"You're a cynic," Phelps said.

She clicked around the page. "Height: six one; weight: a hundred and eighty-two pounds; hair color: brown; eye color: brown; complexion . . . blah . . . blah . . . blah. Here we go— religion: atheist; ethnicity: Scottish/Swedish; education level:

PhD; area of study: medicine/biology; blood type: O positive; CMV status: negative; pregnancies: n/a; accumulated number of pregnancies: n/a; IQ: Stanford-Binet (version five) score of one hundred and seventy-one." Hemingway turned to Phelps. "Still think these aren't options? And they're identical to the Rochester kid's." She nodded at the screen. "The donor number might be different but the rest of the information is identical. What do you make of that?"

"If it's the same donor, why give him different numbers?" Phelps sounded frustrated.

"Look at the donor numbers—they're all seven digits and they all contain zero, two, two, three, three, four and nine. Which is different," she said, and negotiated to a random file, "than the other donor numbers the clinic used—they are ten digits long. Didn't you see that when you were flipping through?"

Carson looked embarrassed. "I must have missed that."

"Why would he do that?" Phelps asked.

"He wanted people to think they were different donors."

"So what do we do?" Phelps asked. "If he lied about the donor identity, how can we find other children with the same donor?"

Carson raised his hand. "That's easy. I just enter the search parameters using the profile values that are specific—how many six foot one, hundred-and-eighty-two pound brown-eyed Scottish/Swedish atheists with a PhD in medicine and biology who have O positive blood and an IQ of one seventy-one can they have in the database? And I make sure the donor numbers contain those seven digits. Here, let me try something." He took back the mouse, set up a search with the donor's stats as parameters, and hit enter.

The results were instantaneous. "Here are the kids you're looking for," he said, raising his hand for a high five.

They ignored him, both leaning in to better see the data. After a few awkward seconds Carson lowered his hand. "Right back at ya."

Hemingway read the screen and shook her head. "Is this wrong?"

Carson ran the search again and the same total came up. "Nope. It's right. This guy fathered sixty-seven children."

SIXTY-SEVEN SUCCESSFUL pregnancies?" Hemingway asked. "You're kidding."

Carson flicked the screen again. "It's right there."

The more answers they found, the further they seemed to be from any kind of a solution. From a technical point of view it was progress; from a practical standpoint it was more work.

It was Phelps who spoke up. "It's actually very common. Fertility clinics are not subject to any kind of demographic responsibility. There have been multiple cases where kids who are dating find out they are related. Some donors father hundreds of children and usually in the same neighborhood— almost always in the same city. The Scandinavian countries have limited the number of times a doctor can use a specific donor in any given year. The UK is thinking about legislation."

Carson stared at him, his mouth open.

"Discovery Channel," he offered. "I started watching for Shark Week and it kind of became a habit. Ask me about Stonehenge."

"Or the Bloomsbury Group," Hemingway added.

Phelps shook his head. "You're mean."

She kept her eyes locked on the list of successful pregnancies. "And this should be criminal."

It was Carson who spoke. "Why? Look at this guy. Six one, PhD in medicine, Scandinavian, athletic, high IQ. Flip through their catalogue and I'll bet he comes with fucking cup holders and clear coat."

"Where's his name?"

Carson shrugged. "This is his donor profile, my guess is this is the preliminary stuff when you're trying to make a decision on which model to download. If you like what you read, it's probably on to . . ." He clicked around until he was back in the main directory then ran a search. "There's nothing on this guy in the system." He ran all the different donor numbers through the database. "Nada."

Phelps started up with his Discovery Channel education. "There should also be a profile detailing his hobbies, favorite food, allergies, medical background, and other assorted shit."

Carson smiled. "I'm sure that's exactly how it is worded on their website: check out your donor's food allergies *and other assorted shit.*"

And then Hemingway had another of her lightbulb moments. "It's him."

"Him? Him who, him?"

"Brayton. Jesus, just think about it. You guys are men. If you needed sperm, where's the first place you'd go to get it?"

Phelps closed his eyes and shook his head. Carson blushed.

"That's right. You've got your own dispenser." She went to the worktable and pulled Brayton's file out of a banker's box she had lugged over from the squad room. She read off her notes. "Height's right. Weight's right. Brown hair, brown eyes—check. Scottish-Swedish—mother's name was

Lindenberg—and Brayton could be Scottish. PhD in biology? Check. Very smart? Check. Like I said, options." She leaned forward, her face a few inches from the monitor, as if trying to smell out meaning in the lines of information. "Get me the names of all sixty-seven of this guy's children. If we don't figure this out soon, this is nothing more than a hunting list."

Carson wiped his palms on his thighs and reached for the keyboard. "You know, for a woman you can be pretty grim."

"I get that a lot."

III FIFTY

HEMINGWAY AND Phelps were on their way to visit the first family on their list—the Atchisons, parents of a ten-year-old boy named William. They lived on the Upper East Side.

Hemingway was calling Daniel to tell him not to expect her home. There were things they had to talk about and she didn't want him to think she was avoiding him.

He answered immediately. "Hey, babe."

"Hey yourself, Mr. Man. What's what?"

"Your sister's here." There was a pause. "She said *you* told her to come by."

Hemingway mouthed the word *fuck* without saying it out loud. "I might have."

"Yeah, well . . ." He let his voice trail off and she knew Amy was within earshot.

"She's with you now, right?"

"What are you, a detective?"

"Has she started drinking yet?"

"*Yet?*"

"I'm sorry, baby. She called me from the train, said she was checking into the Plaza. I told her to come by and she said she'd rather be at the hotel. I thought we had worked it all out."

"Yeah, sure." He didn't sound angry, just unhappy. The last time they had seen one another she called him a fag and a peasant, in that order. She had been pretty drunk and didn't remember it when Hemingway called her the next day but the damage had been done—Daniel had been raised with the belief that there was no greater sin than being a bad drunk. "I made the guest bed up for her. She told me that was *quaint*."

Hemingway flinched. Daniel had stayed as far away as he could from her family's money, and her sister took a spiteful joy in pointing out the financial shortcomings of their lives compared to hers. Not that Daniel gave a shit about money, but he hated being insulted—for all his Bohemian artsy fartsy weed-smoking patience he was still a proud man. That Daniel hadn't thrown her out was yet another testament to his goodness. "Sorry, baby. Can you take it for tonight? I don't know when I'll get back. If at all."

"That case? The one with the camera lenses you called me about?"

"Yeah. Can you cover for me? Be charming and shit."

"I won't be her punching bag." There was a pause on the other end of the line that ended with a deep breath and, "Okay. Sure."

"Thanks. I only have one sister."

"That's more than enough."

"You're a good man."

"You mean I'm a pushover."

"No. I mean you're a good man. Did you have plans for tonight?"

"Iggy has a gig downtown and I was going to head out with Matty to take some photos but that's kind of changed now."

"Go. Work. Have fun. She'll be fine by herself. Give her the spare key. We have lives to live, bills to pay. Get drunk, stay out all night, and keep your hands off the wimmens."

He laughed. "There ain't no wimmens but you, Allie."

Why did she hate it when her family called her that but loved it when it came from him? "Later, baby."

"Later," he said, and hung up.

She slipped the phone into her jacket pocket, and Phelps said, "Tell me, Hemi, how the hell does a guy like Brayton just disappear? He's making—what?—seven figures a year? Guy like that only disappears if he wants to disappear."

"You think he's hiding?"

Phelps shrugged. "Could be. If he's the donor, and if Fenton found out, I can see the logic in the decision. Would you want her on your ass? He's probably vacationing at Lake Vostok." When she looked over at him he said, "Discovery Channel."

If Brayton had indeed crossed all the lines they suspected—and Fenton found out—she would be a force to fear. "Think she has the balls to put him away?"

"Nothing would surprise me about that woman."

Her phone rang and she answered in typical Pavlovian form. "Hemingway."

"Detective, it's Dr. Marcus. I'm finished with Michael Selmer's body."

"And?"

"He was killed with a right-to-left sweep across his throat. Long, sharp blade. It was thin, so it's not a hunting or fighting knife. I'd say we're looking at either a fishing knife or one of those Japanese chef's knives. Single incision. He would have been unconscious almost immediately."

"No needle in the eye?"

"The MO matches the Grant boy's driver to a degree.

Something was removed from the car before your people got to the scene. The surveillance camera from the back door at the clinic showed that he left with a black leather bag—it looked like a Ghurka Express. It wasn't found in the car and there was a smudge of blood on the backseat, as if something were pulled from the car."

Selmer had printed up all of his files earlier in the day. There was a good chance that the killer might now have the same information as they did. "Thanks, Marcus. If anything else interesting comes across your table, I'm here."

"Not me. I'm going home. All work and no sleep makes me a cranky boy."

"You have any idea what I should be looking for in this guy?"

"Classic psychopath. Disarming. Friendly. Smart as hell. Manipulative and narcissistic. I can't see anyone with this kind of pathology living a totally normal life. The more murders he gets away with, the more his confidence grows. He is good at this. But he's running. The more you push, the sloppier he'll get."

Hemingway didn't agree. "I get the feeling he knows *exactly* what he's doing; I don't think *we're* pushing *him*, I think *he's* leading *us*."

"We're allowed to have our differences."

"Keep me informed." She hung up and the heavy summer smell of the city, that mix of exhaust and baked asphalt and electricity, hit her and took her back to that last summer with Mank.

They had moved in together. Stopped fighting. Things were going well. Or at least less shitty than they had been. She remembered their last night together. They had gone for a walk and ended up at a little Italian place in Morningside. It was good, maybe one of their best nights. They had walked slow, holding hands, ending up in an antique shop that for some reason was still open. Mank bought her those four equestrian portraits, the ones hanging at the top of the stairs. There were fireflies on the way up Amsterdam and Mank carried the paintings under his arm, wrapped in brown paper and twine. They bought a bag of plums from the fruit stand on the corner. They had gone to bed, made love and fallen asleep in a happy sweaty knot.

The next day Shea and that tumor of a sidekick, Nicky, had walked up behind Mank and put two rounds into his spine and two more into his brain as he lay screaming in pain on the pavement. There were three witnesses who identified Shea and Nicky. After the first witness didn't come home from work one afternoon, the remaining two decided that they had not seen a thing. Shea and Nicky walked.

After three weeks of sleepless nights and more tears than she thought she was capable of producing, she got into her car, drove across the Brooklyn Bridge, and paid Shea a visit.

The investigating officers put a lot of horsepower into tracing the anonymous call that had warned Shea. They chased it down to a prepaid AT&T cell phone, purchased five months before the shooting and prepaid for a year in advance. It had never been used except for that one time. Then it dropped off the face of the earth. The wiretap had recorded an electronic— not modified human—voice generated by an AT&T text-to-speech program available for free on the Internet.

Since there was no way to tie the call to Hemingway, and since her placing the call would have endangered her own life, all charges were dropped.

And it all came back because the city smelled like the last night she spent with Mank.

Her cell vibrated, signaling a text, and she snapped out of her memories, consciously removing her hand from her belly.

As Phelps pulled the heavy truck through traffic, she scanned the message, thinking it was from the medical examiner.

It read:

I'M NOT FINISHED.

BUT YOU ARE.

The message had come from Tyler Rochester's phone.

FIFTY-ONE

HEMINGWAY CALLED Carson on the car's wireless and had him slave Tyler Rochester's signal to the GPS function on her phone, remotely downloading the appropriate software patch. The process chewed up nearly four minutes including a phone reboot.

She checked the screen and held it up for Phelps to see. Then she asked the disembodied voice of Carson, "You certain?"

There was the distant tinny sound of keys being struck. "Absofuckinglutely. He's on a boat. The coordinates are right in line with the Staten Island Ferry. It just left the Whitehall Terminal. ETA St. George Terminal is twenty-two minutes."

"We'll be there in five," she said, and the big man in the gray suit punched his foot to the carpet and the Suburban rocketed south.

———

The collective hive of the NYPD had pulled together and when they arrived at Battery Park, a departmental boat was waiting for them. As they climbed aboard, the pilot told them they'd do it with a little over four minutes to spare. They had already called the captain of the ferry and told him to slow the boat down as much as he could—a maneuver that would get them two more minutes.

The inside of the St. George Ferry Terminal looked like a small-town airport in Cold War Eastern Europe, a dreary cavern of gray paint over concrete block. After the police boat docked, Hemingway and Phelps swept through the building with Frank Delaney, the head of security for the MTA South Ferry terminal. Delaney was a small wiry man who looked like a kid playing grown-up beside the two cops, but his thirty-one years of experience were evident in the way he had set things up. All the exits were manned and everyone in security had been told no one was to leave the building except through a single manned set of doors until one minute before the ferry docked. After that it was on a person-by-person basis and all passengers had to go through the cops.

As they ran through the building, Hemingway's stomach tightened up, rebelling after twelve minutes pounding the waves in the Zodiac. She wasn't normally prone to any kind of motion sickness but the mix of exhaust, heat, and an MSG-laden lunch seemed to be doing some previously unknown voodoo on her. She hoped she wouldn't have to chuck in a garbage can.

"You okay?" Phelps asked, trying not to sound concerned but unable to hide it.

"I'm not convinced that this is a good expenditure of resources."

The killer wouldn't be on the boat. She knew it and Phelps knew it. And Delaney probably knew it, too. Their killer wasn't the kind of guy to send a text from a ferry; ghosts didn't do things like that. He was long gone.

What was he up to? He didn't make a move that hadn't been rehearsed in his head a thousand times.

"You gonna have a lotta upset people coming off the ferry," Delaney said.

Hemingway made an effort to respect anyone who functioned under the umbrella of security—public or private—and she had a lot of respect for the MTA guys, who were continually bombarded with the sleaziest kinds of crimes. She had fought her way up to the rank of detective, busting her ass to overcome sexism and good old-fashioned ignorance, and she refused to dole it out to anyone else. Although many of the other detectives never actually expressed disdain for anyone of lower rank or station on the job, Hemingway had seen enough guys lose valuable allegiances due to mine-is-bigger-than-yours situations. Even Phelps, who she considered the last of the old-school gentlemen, sometimes pulled rank for no reason she could see. She thought of it as testosterone poisoning and ego massaging for the most part. But a man like Delaney could be their best asset—or their worst enemy—and she refused to lose a case because of ego.

They followed him to the ramp where the ferry would dock. Hemingway was glad that the running portion of the program was over but her stomach still felt like it was being squeezed by an oily fist.

Silty gray clouds deadened the Hudson as the sky geared up for more histrionics. The ferry was a few minutes out, a moving part in the much larger clockworks of the city behind it.

Hemingway leaned on the railing and took in a deep breath, hoping that the upset stomach wouldn't come back. She asked Delaney, "What did you tell the captain of the ferry?"

He shrugged. "Just what you told me to—to slow it down

as much as he could and to dock according to protocol. From there your people would run the show. Your uniformed officers will handle screening the passengers as they disembark."

It was time for a little diplomacy. "I know that technically this is an MTA affair, but we are looking for someone who is—"

"Above my pay grade?" he asked, smiling like this was one grand adventure.

Hemingway hadn't given Delaney any specifics but she needed him to understand that this guy was dangerous. "It's not a question of pay grade, it's about safety. I don't want you to lose any people because we downplayed the situation."

"This guy some terrorist asshole? I ain't never had a terrorist asshole on one of my boats."

"I'd take a terrorist over this guy anytime."

From where they stood, the city didn't look that far away unless you tried to see movement, then you realized how distant it was. There were no gulls riding the breeze and when she swiveled her head toward the dock cranes of Jersey the sky was empty of any movement except a few errant jet streams over Newark. She looked down at the water, at the garbage floating in the dark waters, and wondered if they'd get this guy before they found another boy floating out there.

Once again she found herself drawn back to wonder what had happened to Trevor Deacon's victims. Forty-four boys that they knew about—and probably more that they didn't—had been subtracted from society by that creep. Had they floated by here on their way out to sea? Would they ever know?

Standing there, watching the gentle slosh of the waves against the pilings, she felt her stomach tighten again, threatening to send their earlier lunch of dumplings and root beer scurrying for daylight.

"You sure you're okay?" Phelps asked from her right.

"Yeah. Fine. Fuck." She sounded irritated and immediately regretted it.

Delaney, sensing a weak spot in the conversation, jumped in. "You're the same Hemingway who shot those guys in Brooklyn a few years back, ain't ya?"

She nodded, hoping that he'd leave it at that; they rarely did and Delaney was no exception.

"That took some guts, detective. Walking in there and all. Musta seen that video a hunert times on the news. No bulletproof vest or nothin'?"

She shook her head but closed her eyes, hoping her stomach would settle down. If she waited him out he'd eventually change topics. They always did when faced with silence.

"They shoulda made you chief after that. How many guys—or ladies, excuse my French—can walk into a room full of armed assholes, draw second, and clean the place out? I been in security all my life and I ain't never seen anything like it. That was Dirty Harry kind of shooting." He leaned forward. "Don't take this the wrong way, but you got big balls for a lady."

With her eyes still closed she said, "I get that a lot."

Delaney pulled out a pack of cigarettes, held it up. "You mind?"

She opened her eyes, stared at him. Besides Phelps and the cops standing back in the shadows, the dock was empty. She couldn't very well protest on their behalf, even if it was a law—this was his turf and he was doing them a lot of favors. "Not at all." And that little voice that had not yet said anything—had only made its presence known by occasionally nudging her subconscious—reminded her that she was pregnant.

And it sunk in a little more. The irrevocability of the coming decision. Maybe she and Daniel would have the baby. Maybe a few. Raise a family and grow old and maybe nothing bad would ever happen to their children.

Why not?

Because that would take a commitment. A commitment to Daniel. A commitment to the baby. And, more importantly, a commitment to herself. Jesus, how did people say yes to this? A child wasn't like a house you didn't like or a marriage you no longer wanted to be in; there were no outs. It was a commitment until you stopped existing. Which in practical terms meant forever.

What kind of a choice was that?

She stepped sideways to avoid the smoke. It was a forgivable compromise. After all, how much carbon was she sucking down each and every day in the way of car exhaust?

Phelps pulled her aside and held up the schematics Delaney gave them. "We'll sweep the ferry from front to back. Delaney's guy says it's easy if we put men on the stairwells here, here, here, and here. And two more over here. It should be a ten-minute job."

Hemingway turned to the boat coming in. "He's not on the boat. He gave Tyler Rochester's phone to someone else. Maybe even a kid—wouldn't that be a sick fucking joke?"

"You want to call it off?"

"We can't do that on the off chance that he really is there and I don't want to send a bunch of cops onto the ferry unless they're in combat mode. It's all in or all out. This guy has killed enough people already."

The ferry was closing the gap and the faces of the people on board would soon be discernible.

"You can't be standing on the dock when the boat pulls in, Hemi. This guy knows you. Stay out of sight."

That Phelps was right didn't make it any easier—she was point man on this case and the idea of anyone else walking into her mess felt wrong. "I'll go wait inside."

Delaney, whose attention seemed to be nailed to his smoke, waved her over. "Come on, you can watch the whole thing on our security system." He dropped his cigarette over the railing and headed up the ramp.

III FIFTY-TWO

HE FACED the door, waiting for it to open. The noise—the hum of people, the sound of engines—did not exist. His focus was reduced to the bright polished bronze knob. He wanted to reach out, to touch it, but that was not part of the plan. He was to wait until she came through. He had played this moment out in his head and now was not a time to make adjustments—this was a time to act, not react. No changes could be made. No substitutions.

She would open the door and see him. Smile. Maybe even recognize him. He would smile back, because that was what should be done—what was expected. She would come to him. And he'd lift his arm.

She might see the blade.

There would be that tiny instant when she would flinch. Maybe step back.

Then her fingers would go to her throat.

She'd hit the floor.

And he would lean over her and watch her die.

Because that's what he did.

FIFTY-THREE

THE BOAT, though technically female following nautical tradition, floated under the moniker the MV *Andrew J. Barberi*. She was a big bitch, measuring more than three hundred feet in length with a width of almost seventy and tipped the scales at a solid 3,334 gross tons. Able to carry up to six thousand passengers through the worst that the Hudson had to offer at a respectable sixteen knots. Orange and yellow. Without grace. Or elegance.

Hemingway's focus shifted from one monitor to the next as she tried to see into the two-dimensional representations of the *Barberi*. Delaney stood at her side, chomping on an unlit cigarette, instinctively following Phelps and the uniformed officers as they wove through the 2,361 passengers.

The city had gone crazy with surveillance systems after 9/11 and the MTA was no exception; she was looking at millions of dollars' worth of paranoia.

Hemingway stayed in contact with Phelps through a headset Delaney had given her—more toys from the new antiterrorist budget. "Where is he?" she asked, and the image of Phelps on the monitor shrugged in response.

She slid her line of sight across the monitors, searching the crowd for someone—anyone—who might be their killer, looking for . . . What exactly *was* she looking for? Some looked tired; some looked pissed off; some looked high; some even looked happy.

But none of them looked like they got their jollies by taking little boys apart.

She watched Phelps set his shoulders and plow through the crowd, a pair of patrolmen in tow. She had come to love him in their almost seven years of protecting and serving. Not because he had adopted the role of surrogate father in her life. And not because he bought her shrimp shumai every Wednesday. But because he was a good man.

And he had never asked her about that phone call to Shea.

Phelps moved forward. His head swiveled back and forth on his stubble-dusted neck as his eyes took in the people and reactions around him. Down there, in the arena, Phelps would smell him out because that's what he had been designed to do.

Hemingway watched the monitors, wishing she were there with him. They had stared down everything from a Bell Atlantic employee with nine sticks of TNT strapped to his chest to a hostage taking at the Met, and sitting here looking at Phelps do this alone felt like some form of acute betrayal.

Phelps pushed through a throng of passengers, following the beacon on the screen of Hemingway's phone.

Hemingway's eyes slid from one passenger to another; none of them seemed to notice Phelps. They stared ahead, shuffling forward in uneven baby steps like cattle.

Phelps's voice came out of the speaker. "It's right here." He stopped and his head swiveled back and forth.

The two uniformed cops spun in place.

"We're right on top of the signal," he repeated.

"He's below you, Jon." She glanced sideways and Delaney nodded. "Or above you."

Delaney picked up a headset that was patched in but not being used. "Go to the far end of the deck. Take the stairs down. There's a pair of doors on the landing—on either side of the staircase. The codes are . . . ," Delaney reached into his pocket and brought up the notes he had jotted down before Phelps had gone on board. "Eight eight oh one three."

"Eight eight oh one three," Phelps repeated.

"Both doors go down to the maintenance corridor that leads to the engine room. If he's below you, he'll be in one of the tool rooms. They're marked in red. We don't have surveillance cameras down there." He kept the headset in his hand.

"Why not?" she asked.

"Passengers are not supposed to be down there. And we don't hire no terrorist assholes."

Phelps nodded and headed for the stairwell to the door that would take him to the engine level. She keyed the mic again. "Jon, be careful. If he's there, he's waiting for you."

Phelps nodded and she saw his head tilt to the side like it did when he smiled. The action said, *Don't worry about me, little lady.*

Phelps moved down the steps and stopped on the landing in front of the door. He reached out and grabbed the handle.

From her perch in the control room, Hemingway saw his fingers connect with the metal and twist. The door swung in. He stepped forward. And off the screen.

THE SOUND of the engines was no longer a subtle vibration that hit his inner ear but a full-blown presence that shook the floor. Phelps couldn't hear the men behind him or the sound of his own feet on the deck so he slowed down like he had learned back in the jungle all those lifetimes ago. The maintenance hallway was clean but hadn't been painted in years and grease and dirt had worked into the cracks. The engines superheated the air down here and the humidity was off the charts. The bright space of the stairwell behind them threw weird spidery shadows across the wall—a dark mass of arms and legs and heads that looked like a misshapen creature moving down a tunnel in search of prey.

Phelps took in the smell of diesel fuel and heat and solvents. And something else buried beneath it.

He reached into his coat and wrapped his fingers around the grip of his .45. He slid it out and swept his thumb down over the frame, knocking the safety out of its notch.

And then the engines stopped.

They came to the first door and Phelps reached out and touched the bronze knob. It was hot in his palm. He twisted his wrist, took a breath, held it and flung the door in, lining up on the opening with the big automatic.

It was a supply room, loaded to the ceiling with Styrofoam cups, cases of empty beer bottles, napkins and toilet paper.

They moved on.

The second door was stenciled with the words TOOLS/ROPES in a red Boston Traffic font. Phelps stepped in front of the metal portal and stopped dead center. He raised the pistol and gently turned the knob with his free hand.

Then he pushed the door in.

And found a room from hell.

THE DOOR swung in.

He was waiting for her.

He saw a shadow. Larger than himself. Coming through.

He reached out with the blade.

The shadow stumbled backward. Reached up. Gripped its throat.

Blood pissed out in a fan-shaped arc. Splattered the wall. The sill. Shoes.

PHELPS STUMBLED back.

And stared down at the destroyed architecture of the child.

Between his time in the jungles of Southeast Asia and four-plus decades as one of New York's Finest, he had seen the human body exposed to unimaginable indignities. But this tipped the scales in a whole new sport. Tyler Rochester's phone sat neatly on an overturned bucket beside the body. It was covered in bright happy stickers.

Phelps backed away from the door and keyed his mic. "He ain't here, Hemi. But he was. He left another one behind. He's been—" He paused as he tried to make sense of what he was looking at. "—Destroyed."

FIFTY-SEVEN

HE STEPPED over the body of Mrs. Atchison. Blood still thrummed out of her neck in a steady pulse but instead of the bright pyrotechnics of a moment ago it was now a thick diminishing throb. She was already brain dead. He moved cautiously by, lifting his feet over the blanket of red that had already filled the low points in the floor and was now reaching for the corners with thick rounded fingers.

He thought that she was alone with the boy but thinking something was not the same as knowing it. He checked the main floor. William was upstairs—he had seen him from the street, through the window of his bedroom. Now the boy was in the bath, singing and splashing while his mother bled out on the floor in the foyer.

On the other nights he had watched them from the park across the street, the housekeeper left at five; they were supposed to be alone now. But better safe than sorry.

He went through the house quickly, starting with the living room, the study, then on to the dining room and kitchen. A quick peek down the basement steps told him that the wine cellar was empty because there were no lights on. Besides, anyone in the basement would have heard Mrs. Atchison's body hit the floor and would have been drawn upstairs by the sound.

He went back to the foyer. She was dead now, sprawled out in an awkward pose that was almost comical because one of her hands was on her peepee. He smiled at that.

Then he walked up the stairs with the long filleting knife hanging from his hand.

The master bedroom, en suite, three guest bedrooms, main bathroom, and powder room were all empty. He went through the closets and even stooped to look under the beds.

William was in the tub, singing an old-fashioned song that he didn't recognize. The boy couldn't sing at all. But there was another thing that William did well and that's why he was here; to extract the boy's other gift.

After placing the filleting knife down on the antique console beside the bathroom door, he unslung the knapsack with the Canadian flag sewn to it and slid it to the floor. He removed the syringe from the plastic case in the side pocket and held it up to the light.

He didn't bother to tap out the bubbles but he did give it a quick check to make sure that it was still primed with anesthetic.

He reached out, placed one gloved hand on the bathroom door, and pushed it open.

William's singing echoed off the tiles. He was in the tub, head back, eyes closed, singing about being a lonely boy without a home. He had a wig of suds on his head.

Listening to whatever instinct was running through him, William opened his eyes. He saw the figure in the door. He smiled, maybe thinking for a split second that it was his mother.

And saw that it wasn't.

His smile grew puzzled. "What are you doing here? I thought that we were getting together tomorrow."

"I couldn't wait," he said, and stepped toward the boy in the tub.

FIFTY-EIGHT

BY THE time Delaney got Hemingway through the terminal, over the evacuating decks of the ferry, and down to Phelps, he was sitting on the bottom of the tight metal staircase to the maintenance corridor with his head in his hands.

"Don't go in there, Hemi." His voice sounded a little off in the confines of the space and she took it as echo. But what he said bothered her; in all their time together, he had never babied her, never tried to protect her from the sometimes horrifying realities of the work. If he had, they never would have made it as a team. That he was doing so now was unsettling.

Hemingway walked by, putting her hand on his shoulder as she passed. He was shivering, something that seemed impossible in the hundred-and-ten-degree heat that made the place feel like a terrarium. And then she realized the Iron Giant was crying.

The two uniformed cops leaned against the far bulkhead across from the stairwell. One looked like his brain was unplugged and the other had his eyes closed, fingers pressed to his sockets.

The hallway was tight and smelled like a hot engine after a day on the road. The space was lit with caged overhead bulbs that lent an extra air of malignancy to the stifling atmosphere and dark passage. She moved slowly toward the light spilling over the sill, across the floor, and up onto the wall in a flickering weak oval. It looked like a television was on in the room.

The engines were turned off and Manhattan-bound passengers would be taking another of the MTA's ferries, boarding at the secondary dock. The corridor was quiet and all she heard, other than the sound of her shoes on the boilerplate deck, was her heart chugging away in her ears.

She paused in front of the open door but didn't look in. Something else was mixed in with the smells of the engine deck and she recognized it as the stench of death. She turned slowly, swinging her eyes around, and focused on the dimly lit body spilled across the floor of the tool room.

The lubrication had left her sockets and she could not swivel her eyes. All she could do was stand there. Dumbly. Mutely. Staring at the dead child.

When the image had finally been absorbed, her CPU came back online and she ran down the hall, skidded to a stop at a garbage can, and threw up.

FIFTY-NINE

THEY STOOD on deck, staring at the city across the water. Phelps cradled a Styrofoam cup of coffee Delaney had been kind enough to provide and Hemingway sipped water she hoped would wash the taste of puke and Tic Tacs out of her mouth. They hadn't said anything for a few minutes and both were busy repairing their hard drives after what they had seen.

They were waiting for Marcus to finish in the tool room.

After what could have been an hour or a minute, Phelps asked, "How pregnant are you?" He took another sip of coffee, eyes still locked on the distant spires of Sodom and Gomorrah across the waves.

She thought about lying to him. She thought about asking him if he was nuts. She thought about punching him in the arm and saying, *Good one.* She even thought about crying. All she said was, "About six weeks."

Phelps pulled the cup away from his mouth and nodded a single, authoritative time.

"How'd you know?"

At that, he smiled. It was a shy, gentle smile and it always caught her off guard when he pulled it out during working hours. "I'm a detective, Hemi. I know you think I'm old and blind but I'm not that old *or* that blind."

That hadn't been an answer. At least not the kind she was looking for. "That doesn't explain the *how* part, Jon."

He took another sip of coffee. "You've been eating a lot lately—even for you." At that his smile broadened—her eating habits were a continual source of amusement to him; they had been since the first time they sat down to a meal together. "You keep your hand on your belly a lot. You're not touching alcohol. And you're glowing."

"Glowing? Did you say *glowing*? Now I know you're lying."

Phelps shrugged like it didn't matter one way or the other. "I remember how Maggie looked when she was pregnant with Francis. She had that same look you got now. I saw it again when Shane came along—hell, I knew she was pregnant before she did. And I seen Francis's wife when she was pregnant. I know what it looks like and it looks like you."

"That doesn't sound very scientific to me."

"What do you want me to do, lie?"

She took another swig of water and heard the clank of the gurney being wheeled over the steel deck on the way to the stairway to the basement. She thought about the boy in the tool room and she burped and tasted Tic Tacs again.

"And in all the time I've known you, nothing has made you throw up on the job."

"That was pretty bad, Jon."

"We've seen worse."

"When?"

"Remember the Dionne lady? That was worse. A *lot* worse."

She thought back to that one and the Tic Tacs spit a little

mint up the back of her throat again. "Isn't it supposed to be called morning sickness?"

"We got odd hours," he said. "Daniel know?"

He wasn't trying to walk her—he was pitching fastballs. "Yeah."

"You don't have to do anything you don't want to. Keeping it, not keeping it—it's up to you."

And now it was her turn to ask a question. "Why would you say something like that, Jon?" She hoped that hadn't sounded as accusatory to him as it had to her.

He paused this time, as if deciding if what he was going to say was a smart thing to do. "I was just wondering about Mank. I know you miss him."

"Of course I miss him—I was in love with the guy—but what the fuck does *that* have to do with anything?"

Phelps turned and looked at her—*really* looked at her. "Hemi, I don't stick my nose in where it doesn't belong. But we're friends. Hell, we're more than friends in many ways, and I want you to be happy. But I know you. I've watched you chew through a few guys in the past couple years. Mank's death killed a little piece of you. And that shit with Shea afterwards didn't help. You've always said you never wanted kids. I just assumed that you meant you didn't want kids right then. But maybe you never do. It's none of my business, except to be your friend. You love this Daniel of yours?"

She felt like he had just punched her in the stomach. "Yes. Yes, I do."

"You love him enough to have him in your life forever?"

Phelps was saying all the right things—all the things a friend would say—all the things that she had asked Mank at the cemetery yesterday. "I hadn't thought about it like that."

"Now who's lying? You know me—I'm not big on

handing out judgment—so this ain't about any kind of right or wrong. But you and I see the worst that people have to offer. We see the world as a broken damaged place full of broken damaged people who inflict the most frightening kind of pain on one another. That ain't an easy thing to forget.

"When Maggie got pregnant with Francis I had only been a cop for two years but that's long enough in this city. Hell, I think it's long enough in *any* city. I didn't want kids, not after what I seen in 'Nam and at work. But Maggie did. And you know what? My family helped me stay sane while I waded through all this shit over the years."

She jabbed a thumb over her shoulder, at the medical examiner's team fighting the stretcher down the stairs to pick up a child who had been defiled with a sharpened blade. "And what if something like that happens?"

"You know, after Shane was born I went to get a vasectomy. I was in the doctor's office and I was worried that I was making some kind of mistake. What if my children died? I talked to the doctor about it and he said one of the smartest things anyone has ever said to me in a time of crisis. He said, 'You can't plan your life on tragedy.'"

"Sure you can, Jon. Just ask the parents of that little boy downstairs. Ask them if bad things happen. They'll tell you that bad things happen all the time."

"Good things happen all the time, too. You got a guy who loves you and you love back. He ain't Mank and you know what? Good he ain't because you know and I know and everyfuckingbody knows that a life with Mank would have been a goddamned disaster. The only thing that guy could be counted on for was being angry. Everything else—as sunny as you want to paint it—was just wishful thinking."

He had never spoken to her like this, and she knew the

process had to be difficult for him. And he wasn't wrong—maybe that's all Uncle Dwight had tried to tell her. It was time to move on a little. Mank was dead. He wasn't coming back.

"I've been thinking about all those things, Jon. And I'm thinking myself into a hole. I don't know if I can do it." And that was as truthful as she was ever going to get with anyone.

Phelps took a deep breath of hot, heavy air. "I'm going to tell you one thing, and if you ever repeat it, to me or to anyone else, I'll never forgive you. When I was your age, I had a fourteen-year-old and a twelve-year-old. And I was never there, so Maggie raised our kids. I love Maggie with all my heart—she's the best thing that ever happened to me. And those boys. But she thinks that the South Pole is hot because people head south in the winter, she's convinced that Ikea is the capital of Sweden, and she hasn't read a single book that doesn't have pictures in it in the forty-one years we've been married. But I fucking love that woman. And she did a phenomenal job with those boys, all while taking care of her dying mother."

She focused on the new Manhattan skyline. The Freedom Tower still looked odd, foreign to her eye. She wondered how long it would take to become familiar.

"You got everything it takes to be a great mother, kiddo. And I don't just mean your family's money. Maybe I'm reaching, but your brother and sister have to get a very nice allowance to live those lives—so I assume that there's some there for you if you want it. And a child might be a good reason to want it. At least to pay for good schools and tennis lessons. Trips to Europe, maybe see a few museums. Braces and a fucking pony. Maybe you can give your kid a better life than most cops can. If you want to. If Maggie could do it, you sure can. I'm with you no matter what. You need someone to drive you to the clinic, and you don't want to tell Daniel about it, I'm there. This is your life. And that's all I am going to say about that. I am sorry if I hurt your feelings."

She had to pull her focus away from the city at that one. She turned, looked at him. He was a big, goofy-looking man who had been shot three times, stabbed once, had his nose broken more times than anyone could remember and had hands that looked like they were salvaged from a broken prizefighter. And she realized that in Daniel she had found a man who would measure up to Phelps, if not in battle scars, at least in caring. And the way they both cocked their head to one side when they were thinking or smiling. "Why is it that no matter how lousy I feel, you always manage to make everything seem just a little bit better?"

"Call it a gift." He nodded over her shoulder. "Speaking of gifts, here comes Dr. Death."

Dr. Marcus was in pants and shirtsleeves, the jacket and tie of earlier lost somewhere along the way. "Detectives," he said. "I am not in the habit of telling other people how to do their job, but you two need to make some headway and you need to do it fast."

"Same guy?" Hemingway asked, knowing it was a stupid question as soon as it was out of her mouth.

The medical examiner ignored her. "You have any suspects?"

"The only thing we're going on now is a connection to Dr. Brayton."

"Still haven't found him?"

Hemingway shook her head. "We've got it out to the FBI—if he's alive, we should know something soon."

"He your only suspect?"

There was no satisfactory way to answer that so neither cop said a word.

"I am going on the record as saying that I am sick and tired of looking at dead kids."

Hemingway ran a hand through her hair and straightened up, pushing the kinks out of her back. "Come up to the control room, you have to see the surveillance tapes. The Rochester boy's phone was programmed to send that text at a predetermined time. Did he set it before the murder or after? He had the processor in hibernation and the phone went on just before it sent me the text. And we damn well know he was here, on the boat, at the TOD."

"At around two p.m."

They walked across the yellow boilerplate ramp. The walk felt good. She felt her chest and head clearing out again. Her stomach, too.

The control room had seventy feet of river frontage with a clear view of Manhattan across the bay. How long had they been at this now? It felt like a lifetime.

Hemingway steered Dr. Marcus over to the back corner where Delaney was waiting.

"Show him," Hemingway said.

Delaney fiddled with a few buttons then paused to point out four monitors, "Here, here, here, and here." The displays flickered to life, showing the doorways on the passenger deck. "These are the doors to stairwells that drop to the engine deck." The time stamp started at 6:50. "This is ten minutes before the ferry's first cycle of the day." He hit a button.

The timer began spinning in hyperdrive. People danced by, paused in front of it—all in the jittery mercury-poisoned body language of fast-forward. The seconds on the counter turned into minutes turned into hours. No one said a thing as the past closed on a little boy's future—a little boy who was being strapped into a stretcher as they took a trip in the four-monitor time machine. The hours zipped by and not a single passenger—or employee—approached any of the doors.

1:30:21 . . . 1:34:30 . . . 1:38:15 . . . 1:41:10—Delaney cued back the knob and time slowed down.

"Right here," Hemingway said.

Delaney spun the dial down to real time and the seconds began ticking off in a familiar beat. A child approached one of the doors.

"That's the staircase between the main deck and the saloon deck—the same one Detective Phelps went down—the same one we've been using."

It was a boy. Dark brown hair, dark school jacket, light—probably white—shirt, school tie. He had a knapsack over his shoulder.

"That's the victim," Hemingway said.

Marcus moved closer to the screen, trying to see into the past.

The boy hunched in front of the door for a few seconds, his back to the camera, the knapsack jostling back and forth as he worked his hands. After a few seconds he put his shoulder to the door, turned the handle, and pushed into the staircase.

Delaney spun the knob and the clock began fast-forwarding again.

Eleven minutes later the boy was back at the same place and he entered the same door again. This time he wasn't carrying his knapsack.

Marcus held up his hand. "He went back up, then down again?"

Delaney pointed to a schematic. "There are some small grates at the end of the downstairs corridor here and here that lead to a pipe that runs up to an emergency hatch where the cars used to park before those terrorist assholes brought a war down on our asses. The hatches open up here and here. He had to have used one of them as a passage."

"And his killer?" Marcus asked.

Hemingway shook her head and went back to the monitors. "You can't open the escape hatch from the outside. Linderer said one of the hatches was opened—they aren't picked up by any of the surveillance cameras and they're not wired into any alarms because they can only be opened from belowdecks—MTA personnel only. We have the boy coming onto the ferry once, going through that door twice."

Marcus shifted his gaze to the schematics. "And you don't see his killer go down there at any point?"

"Like I said," Hemingway offered in what sounded like a defense to her. "A ghost."

The medical examiner stared at the screen for a few moments. "And we know it wasn't anyone on the crew." His people had black-lighted the staff and hadn't found a single trace of genetic material—whoever had taken that child apart would have lit up like phosphorescent plankton. And no one had been out of sight of the cameras long enough to have made the mess they were cleaning up downstairs.

It was Delaney who spoke. "None of my guys have records—as MTA employees they've had their assholes—excuse my French," he said sideways to Hemingway, "X-rayed. They're on camera all morning. They're good."

Hemingway waved it away. They were back to *ghost*.

Phelps pointed at the screen again. "Nowhere do we see anyone going in any of the access points to get to the basement. No one went through any of those doors. No one went down that corridor today."

Marcus shifted and a bead of sweat on his forehead shook loose and rolled down behind his glasses. He scooped it out of his socket with a finger that had just been probing a mutilated child, blinked, then squinted like a cartoon character.

"Carson will take apart all the footage that the MTA has for the past three days, to see if anything's been doctored."

Delaney shook his head. "That means they'd have to get by my people. And our surveillance system isn't online, it's autonomous. It ain't us. That video hasn't been touched. But knock yourself out."

"We have one crescent of blood downstairs. Looks like a size ten or ten and a half man's leather-soled shoe."

The same as the two back at the Deacon house, on both sides of a door guarded by a giant spider. "Anything different?"

Marcus looked down at Delaney who nodded his head. "I know, below my pay grade." He disappeared.

"I can't tell if the anesthetic was administered through either of the eyes for obvious reasons, but he's added a new tool to his repertoire."

"Which is?"

Marcus shrugged. "I won't know till I scope some metal I found in the spinal column, but it looks like a chisel. Probably driven by a hammer."

They still hadn't identified the victim. They had his school tie and Papandreou and Lincoln were running that down. The boy went to—or at least had a tie from—St. Mark's School for Boys on the Upper East Side. They'd start with the list of patient names they had culled from the Brayton/Selmer files.

From there they'd narrow it down to a student at St. Mark's. But they'd have to rely on DNA for the final say-so. They couldn't get an ID based on a photo of the remains—there was no legal way they could show pictures of this boy to anyone. And if they did, it wouldn't do any good; it was impossible to identify a child without a face.

"We gotta go." It was too hot in here and this wasn't even movement, let alone action.

On the way out they said goodbye to Delaney and thanked him for his help. Cards were exchanged, promises to phone if anything new was discovered were made, and the two cops headed for the staircase that led out to the terminal.

As they passed the ramp, Hemingway saw the guys from the medical examiner's office rolling the too-big stretcher over the painted boilerplate. It didn't look like there was anything under the plastic.

Hemingway and Phelps headed to the police boat. The air felt as oppressive as it had down in the basement with the dead child and she wondered if a trip on the water would help cool her off or make her feel worse. One thing was certain, the empty stomach was no longer agreeing with her. She looked up at the sky, wondering when it was going to let go again.

When they hit the steps down to the police Zodiac, Phelps stopped and turned back to her. "You do whatever you feel is the right decision. And I promise no one will think any different of you." Meaning: *me*. "Just make the right long-term decision, not the easy short-term one. And if that means you need a place to stay if it comes to that—me and Maggie got the guest suite out back. You can stay—for a reasonable rent—as long as you want. Babies. No babies. It's all the same to me."

She stared at him for a second, and realized that was the nicest thing anyone had ever said to her. "Thanks for worrying, Jon." Code for *I love you back*. "Now let's go get some food."

"You know, for a lady, you sure can eat."

"I get that a lot."

THEY WERE drilling through the Brayton/Selmer patient list. One call after another. Alphabetically. Some people were home. Some weren't. Black-and-whites had been sent out. The parents they reached had initial reactions ranging from horror to disbelief yet were all tinted with the same underlying timbre of fear.

Two parents had directed them to their legal representation and hung up. Hemingway was on her eighth family—the parents of Casey Dorf.

"The Dorf residence."

"This is Detective Alexandra Hemingway of the NYPD, may I please speak with Mrs. Angela Dorf?" They always started with the mother—it was only a matter of statistics until they came across a couple where the father had no idea he wasn't the child's biological parent.

A pause.

"This is Mrs. Dorf." The tone was suspicious.

"Mrs. Dorf, I need to talk to you about a very private matter and I need to make an appointment for a pair of local officers to come around and talk to you in person. Until that can happen, there are some things I need to warn you about. Are you in a position to speak freely?"

"Yes." Still suspicious. Maybe even more so.

"I need to talk to you about your daughter."

In a farmhouse somewhere in Connecticut, Mrs. Dorf gasped.

"Where is she right now?"

There was a long pause. "She's dead, Detective Hemingway. She died last summer."

"I'm, I'm sorry."

"Yes. Well. Of course you are."

"May I ask what happened?"

"Casey fell on the playground. Middle of the afternoon. Lots of children around. She was there and then she wasn't." And the tone of her voice said that the conversation was over. She hung up.

Hemingway wrote the word *deceased* beside the Dorfs' name. She lifted her head to find Phelps staring at her. He had a phone in his hand and his finger was on the cradle. "The Everetts' child, Tanya, died last year. Drowned at the beach in Greece—middle of the day."

Hemingway stared at him. It hit them simultaneously.

They rifled through Brayton's folders, looking for the same page in each. It took the better part of five minutes and when they were done, they went down the list pregnancy by pregnancy.

Of the sixty-seven children, there were fifty-nine boys and eight girls.

Two of the girls—a full twenty-five percent—were dead. Which was either a remarkable coincidence or a red flag.

It took Hemingway five more minutes to locate the next patient on the list, the mother of Stephanie Gordon. She had moved a few blocks down Fifth Avenue.

Hemingway asked to speak to Mrs. Gordon.

After a full minute of waiting, there was the sound of high heels on marble and Mrs. Gordon answered.

Hemingway introduced herself, then asked Mrs. Gordon about Stephanie.

There was the sound of a single deep breath, then Mrs. Gordon said, "My daughter is dead, Detective."

"I'm very sorry." She paused—the next part felt cruel. "May I ask what happened?"

There was another pause. "She was at a playdate with some other children. At the park—"

Hemingway didn't have to hear the last part to know what it was going to be.

"—in the middle of the day."

She thanked Mrs. Gordon and hung up.

Three out of the eight girls were dead. This was something much, much grimmer than bad luck.

She wrote the word *deceased* beside Stephanie Gordon's name before picking up the phone to call the mother of the next girl on the list.

THE BOY they had found on the ferry was named Zachary Simmons. He had been a brilliant painter. He was scheduled to start studies at the Sorbonne in mid-July, which would have been his tenth birthday.

Phelps and Hemingway suited up in silence, far too familiar with the routine of talking to the parents of dead children.

||| SIXTY-TWO

THE SUN had crawled below the skyline to the west. The air still felt like fluid and everything glistened but the rain had not come down. The offices were still sinister and if the garbage cans suddenly burst into flames, no one would have been surprised. It felt like hell. With bad coffee.

After talking to Zachary Simmons's mother, they had come back to the precinct, loaded up on coffee, and gone after the patients who had had baby girls.

Hemingway made the calls—a woman was less threatening than a man. At least that was the theory. She was met with anger, bewilderment, and hysteria.

They had the eight names up on the board.

They stood in front of it for a few moments, taking it in.

They now had another commonality: all of the female children from Brayton's files were dead.

Eight little girls had stopped being alive at some point last year.

All had died in freak accidents.

In most of the deaths there were dozens of witnesses.

Not one of the mothers so much as hinted at a suspicion

of foul play; the general consensus was the old wrong place, wrong time catchall.

Casey Dorf: *fell on a playground and died in the hospital two days later—June 24.*

Tanya Everett: *drowned while swimming at a beach in Greece—August 20.*

Stephanie Gordon: *fell off her bike in Central Park and broke her neck—July 22.*

Cynthia LaColle: *fell off her bike on the East Side Esplanade, driving her jaw up into her brain—May 27.*

Belinda Marsh: *fell off a swing, landed on a bolt that secured the iron base to the ground and it speared her in the throat; she bled to death in front of her mother—Sept 2.*

Heidi Morrison: *fell off the subway platform in front of a train—August 5.*

Tiffany Rostovich: *drowned in the bathtub at home—June 10.*

Pamela Zager: *died of an apparent heart attack in her sleep—July 8.*

Hemingway took out her pen and began a new page on her legal pad, arranging the deaths chronologically. "With the exception of Tanya Everett—who died fifteen days after Heidi Morrison, but thirteen before Belinda Marsh—these girls died exactly two weeks apart from one another."

"And then there were none," Phelps said.

||| SIXTY-THREE

HIS FATHER stood at the window, his eye fastened to the antique brass telescope, watching the birds in Central Park across the street. The only time his father seemed at peace was when he watched his beloved birds. He barely moved. Barely breathed. Barely seemed there at all. He could be found here every night, scanning the foliage for rare taxa.

What was it about them that fascinated him?

Like the birds he hunted, Benjamin's father was anomalous to the general population. Even in the world of academia, where eccentrics were the norm rather than the exception, his father was misplaced. He couldn't help his physical appearance—a car accident before Benjamin had been born had crushed parts of his spine and done irreparable damage. He walked with a pronounced, stooped-over gait that made him look like one of his avian subjects. Some of the boys at school laughed at his father, but that was to be expected from people who couldn't grasp the concept of fractions. Things would be better at Harvard. Hopefully.

Their apartment was unlike the home of any of the other children he went to school with. Whereas their parents decorated with porcelain vases, bronze busts, and modern art, his father had filled the house with glass-cased birds. Most of the boys he knew had stopped coming over because his house was simply "too weird," as they put it. It wasn't as if he had a lot in common with these boys in the first place, but it was interesting to interact with people his own age. Even if they couldn't read Homer in the original.

His father slowly swung the scope around, looking for wildlife where it shouldn't be. Sure, the park was filled with trees and grass and water, but it was artificial; everything was primped and manicured to within an inch of its life. Why would birds gravitate to the park when a ten-minute flight could carry them clear of the concrete landscape and put them in real nature? Maybe that was the origin of the expression "birdbrained," because they sure didn't seem to use their heads.

A few weeks back *Scientific American* had published an article comparing Benjamin to William James Sidis, the youngest child prodigy ever to be accepted to Harvard; Benjamin was younger than Sidis by a whole year.

He was also a lot smarter.

Benjamin was special. His father had always told him so. Which was why he loved him so much.

And Benjamin wanted nothing more than for him to stop.

HEMI FINALLY found Brayton. He had thrown a rope over a pipe in the basement of a rented apartment in Helsinki some eight months back. No note. No life insurance.

The body had been cremated.

Brayton's last employer had been a traveling clinic that served Lapland. The head doctor, Mika Jula, said that Brayton had been exemplary and wondered why he had chosen to work for so little when his skills would obviously be much more valuable elsewhere.

Jula had agreed to send a copy of the death certificate to Hemingway, and stressed that he wished there was more to share about Brayton.

Hemingway got off the phone and stared at Phelps. "Brayton's dead. Has been for months."

"Shit."

"Yeah. Shit. I'm hungry."

Phelps got up and started to put on his jacket. "Why am I the one always getting the food?"

Hemingway tapped her index finger to her temple. "Because I do all the thinking."

———

While Phelps was out hunting down more coffee and food, Hemingway called Marcus at home. She filled him in on Brayton then moved on to the eight dead girls. Lincoln and Papandreou were at the far end of the office, making calls to parents of the boys on the list.

She spent ten minutes laying out what she probably could have done in five—but she wanted no misunderstandings. When she asked him to start an inquest he didn't pause, didn't start any of the usual pissing contest conniptions he tended to do simply because he could; he just listened patiently. When she was done he asked if she'd send her notes over. He would need the night and some of the next morning to get his ducks in a row.

Hemingway understood: he'd have to mobilize massive amounts of manpower to open the deaths of these girls. Eight court orders. Eight sets of grieving, and not necessarily rational, parents. The newspapers. The injunctions. The scrutiny. Overnight seemed more than reasonable, it seemed like a gift.

Hemingway was not naive; Marcus also needed this mess behind him as soon as possible. The CSI effect had already gripped the talking heads and everyone was yakking about carpet fibers and DNA and all kinds of fancy shit they knew nothing about. People wanted answers; in lieu of answers, media-driven public opinion would accept scapegoats. His detractors were already spewing stupidity on the television, newspapers, and Internet. Marcus wanted this gone as much as she did.

There was no challenge in convincing him the girls hadn't died in random accidents. By the third girl he was a silent presence on the end of the line. And this didn't fit the MO of the ghost with the hypodermic and saw who had added a hammer and chisel to his toolbox.

He figured out the timeline as fast as she had.

"There were sixty-seven successful pregnancies in Brayton's files from the donor. We've lost four boys plus the Grant boy's driver, Dr. Selmer, and the eight girls."

"And the inimitable Trevor Deacon."

"Yeah. Deacon. I better get back to work. Call if you need anything, I'll be here all night."

"Maybe you should go home, get some sleep."

"That's not happening." Until they had a breakthrough, she'd be running on caffeine and adrenaline. "A cup of coffee and a sandwich and I'll feel a lot better." *Or at least less shitty.* She paused again, and realized that she felt like she had died and nobody had bothered to tell her about it. She hung up.

Before she had put the phone down, it rang again. She answered without checking the display.

The voice was reptilian. "Detective Hemingway, someone asked me to call you about a man who bought pink powder."

Trevor Deacon's drug dealer.

Hemingway snapped up. "Where can I meet you?"

There was a pause. "I'm not sure that's such a—"

"All I care about is information about the man you met. That's all. I can meet you anywhere."

Another pause. Then, "Twenty-seventh between Tenth and Eleventh there's a bar called Mitch's. Come alone. How long for you to get there?"

She checked her watch, looked outside and factored in traffic for this time of the night. "Give me half an hour." Then she hung up.

Phelps showed up with two paper bags stained with grease.

"Trevor Deacon's dealer just called. Twenty-seventh between Tenth and Eleventh."

Phelps put the bags down. "Haven't been there since it was gentrified. The Minnesota strip. Remember those days?"

"Before my time, Jon."

"Sorry, I keep forgetting that not everyone was around before the Internet."

Dennet marched in. He had a folder in his hand. "Where are you two going?"

Hemingway was in the midst of threading her arm through her jacket. "Got an appointment with Trevor Deacon's dealer."

"It can wait three minutes," Dennet said, putting the file in Hemingway's hand. Then he turned to Lincoln and Papandreou. "Linc, Nick, get over here."

They came over.

Dennet leaned forward, putting his knuckles on the table. "The Rochesters' attorney sent that over." He stood up, and began circling the table. "Ten years ago Brayton offered membership to an exclusive unique-donor fertility program at the clinic."

"Meaning?" Lincoln asked.

Hemingway opened the docket and took out a slick, leather-bound brochure with PAC embossed across the front in foil lettering. She scanned it.

"Instead of a patient picking a donor from a catalogue, which lacked exclusivity, Brayton offered an option where patients could purchase the proprietary rights to a donor."

Lincoln interrupted. "Some rich broad doesn't want to pick sperm out of a catalogue because some other woman might have used the same guy?"

Dennet nodded.

Lincoln shook his head in disgust. "Purchasing proprietary rights to a guy's sauce just ain't right."

Hemingway held up the folder. "This outlines Brayton's vision as one donor, one patient, one pregnancy."

"Which is bullshit," Phelps said. "We know the boys are half brothers."

Lincoln tapped his breast pocket. "But none of the parents did. This explains why."

Phelps was still sitting with his arms crossed. "What did he charge for this exclusivity?"

It was Dennet who answered. "Two hundred and fifty K for the donor, another two fifty for the paperwork and procedure."

Papandreou said, "Half a mil is a good motive for murder."

Hemingway headed for the door. "Linc, start looking at the parents. We'll be back in a few hours." Some people were paying a half a million dollars for something she wasn't sure she wanted for free. "What do you think, Phelps?"

The Iron Giant followed her to the door. "I think I shoulda stayed in school."

III SIXTY-FIVE

BENJAMIN WINSLOW lay on the bed, his face buried in the down pillow. He tasted blood from his cheek, feathers and tears. The apartment was silent except for the sound of his father showering.

Benjamin lay in the dark, hurting, crying, hoping for someone to come and take him away from this place.

Someplace beyond Harvard.

He'd even settle on the world swallowing him up.

As long as his father stopped touching him.

III SIXTY-SIX

IN ITS heyday it had been known as the Minnesota Strip, a place where kids from the sticks with no marketable skills could make it in the city. Twenty-seventh between Tenth and Eleventh used to be lined with boys, from young twinks up through the stereotypical Joe Bucks. Around the block, on Twenty-sixth, was where you could find *Coal Miner's Daughter* types competing with Pam Greer wannabes. This chunk of real estate had kept the porn industry saturated all through the VHS revolution.

Now it was just a section of town that gentrification had stripped of most of its character. Hemingway pulled the Suburban up to the curb, across the street from a bar sandwiched between an office supply store and a courier company. Mitch's Bar had been there so long it looked like a geological formation that had grown up from the bedrock. It reminded Hemingway of Bernie's; all that was missing were the ancient, greasy piñatas. There were places like it peppered through the city, holdovers that had survived a hundred years' worth of economic fluctuation. The street looked deserted and what little movement there was came from the dark humps of sewer rats milling around the base of a Dumpster down the street, big black shadows moving slowly in the heat.

Hemingway checked her cylinder, tucked the revolver into the holster at her waist, and said, "Wait here."

Phelps finished his coffee in one loud slurp. "I could use another coffee—this one's empty."

"I gave my word, Jon."

He was silent for a second. "Okay."

They stepped out onto the baked asphalt and the air tasted like a ticking engine. There was still no wind. No reprieve from the heat.

Phelps walked down the street, eying the dark corners and alleys. Hemingway walked into Mitch's alone.

The place was a bigger shithole inside than she had pictured, and she had a developed imagination. They served hobo juice for two bucks a bottle and Motörhead played out of one speaker, a machine-gun bass track that rattled the glasses. *The Rockford Files* was playing on a television suspended over the ancient feltless snooker table. There were no neon beer signs—this wasn't the kind of place beer company reps loaded up with free advertising—and she wasn't sure which was stronger, the smell of sweat or the stink of piss.

Two drunks were staring at empty glasses in a booth and an old woman at the bar looked like she had died in place a few days back but no one had noticed. The general population looked like they were hiding from something, life probably. Business as usual for the down and out.

"She okay?" Hemingway asked the bartender, a skinny kid with an open mouth in a stained Hertz Rent-a-Car T-shirt. He shrugged without taking his eyes off James Garner.

Hemingway found the dealer at the back, his hands on the plywood tabletop—a street fighter's signal that he meant no harm. As she walked up, he said, "You're here to talk to me."

She reached for the chair and he lifted his head. She froze for a second, something that rarely happened.

His face was tattooed with Gene Simmons makeup, bat wings that spread out from his nose, covering his cheeks and flaring up onto his forehead. Male pattern baldness had taken hold and he wore a greasy once-white T-shirt embellished with a rhinestone skull that had lost half its shine. The shirt rode up past his distended belly.

She sat down. "Thank you for meeting me. I'm Detective Hemingway."

"I'm Roy." He kept his eyes down, locked on the rings that sweating glasses had branded into the plywood. "You wanna buy me a drink? You don't hafta or nuthin' but it would be nice."

Hemingway waved at the bartender, signaling a round for Roy. He looked over, then turned back to the TV without acknowledging her.

"Ain't that kinda place," Roy said. "You gotta go to the bar."

Hemingway got up and walked over to the television. "Can we get a beer?" she asked.

The bartender shrugged. "You suck my cock if I bring it over?"

At that she stepped forward and grabbed him by the wrist, wrenching it around and forcing him off the stool. She cranked it again and he went to the floor. "How about I make you suck it yourself?" she said, twisting. "Or do you want to skip the dating so you can bring me a beer?"

"Yeah. Yeah. I was just being friendly. Fuck."

She let go and he fell over.

He stood up, massaging his shoulder. "No means no. I

get it." He walked over to the bar, capped a Pabst and brought it over, the swagger back in his step.

When the bartender had gone back to James Garner and friends, Roy took a draft and wiped the back of his hand across his mouth. "What you want?"

"I'm not wearing a wire. I'm not interested in any narcotics you may or may not have been involved with. And now that I've said that, it would be entrapment if I went back on my word. All I want to know about is—"

"Arnold Palmer," he said.

"Um, no, actually—"

"That's what he called himself. That guy on the news. Deacon." He pulled out the photo she had given to Dwight and slid it across the table. "He told me his name was Arnold Palmer."

"Where'd you meet him?"

He gave her a sad smile. "Staten Island Ferry."

And an image of the Simmons boy exploded in her head.

"I took it from Battery Park one night and he sat down beside me. Nobody sits down beside me except maybe fags and those hard-core hipster kids. At first I thought he was gay. He told me that he had been watching me. Following me, even. Knew what I did. Said he was a customer. I told him I didn't know what he was talking about. He knew what I had, where I picked it up, who I had picked it up from."

"When was this first meeting?"

"A year and a bit. May, I think. Met him about twice a month after that."

"On the ferry?"

"No. Never on the ferry. Mostly he just showed up sitting beside me on the subway or a park bench or buying beer. Weird guy." At that he stopped, looked up at her. "Weirder than me, I mean."

"You ever catch him following you?"

Roy shook his head. "Not once. Never saw him coming. He was a ghost or something."

"What can you tell me about him?"

"He liked watching kids. And I ain't just saying that because it was on the news. I met him at parks a lot. At first, I thought it was because he was trying to look like he fit in. I do lots of deals in pa—" He stopped, looked up at her. "Look, Detective, I ain't got a lot of skills. I can cook and that's about all I know. If this is about busting me, and I go to the joint, life ain't gonna be easy for a guy that looks like me, you know? How I know you ain't here to bust me?"

"All I can do is promise. If I was wearing a wire, I've been recorded telling you that I am not interested in your narcotics activity and if I later arrested you—or allowed this tape to be used to help arrest you—I would be breaking the law. It wouldn't hold up in court. You'd win."

"Not me. I don't win at nothing." He paused and took a sip of his beer. "I met him at Randall's Island a lot."

Hemingway remembered Dr. Torssennson's pointer crawling over the patch of earth where she figured Tyler Rochester had been dumped—Little Hell Gate was off the southern tip of Randall's Island.

Then she remembered the school schedules she had gone over with Phelps—the year-end track-and-field meet that was scheduled for next week—nine thousand private school boys on the same patch of earth. Randall's Island again.

"What's *a lot*?"

His eyes scrolled up as he retrieved the information from wherever he kept it. "Wednesdays for about two months. He liked baseball diamond forty-eight. It took a little while until I figured out that he liked looking at the kids. I ain't making excuses or nothing—I should have seen it right away—but my brain ain't wired to see that kind of stuff. Pickpockets, three-card monte—that kind of shit I can figure out. But people that like kids? Not part of my thinking. I may not be the most law-abiding guy out there, but some shit is broken. What I do, selling drugs, is pretty much all a guy that looks like me can do. Every now and then I get a job in some restaurant but something goes missing and they accuse me. Spago's ain't hiring a guy like me. So I deal a little tar cut with brown sugar or instant coffee. That's it. I never wrote a bad check. I don't steal. And I don't look at kids. It made me sick.

"I tried to shake the guy. I laid low for a while, changed my schedule, my routes. I thought he was gone. I hoped. Guy like him has a bad smell following him. Worse than failure, know what I mean? Didn't see him for a bit. Then one afternoon I'm sitting on a bench feeding pigeons an' he sits down beside me with a box of Chicken McNuggets. Said he was disappointed I didn't keep up my end of the friendship. Friendship? Jeezus, some people got a way with words. You could tell he thought of himself as some kind of supergenius—you know, the kind of guy thought he was so much smarter than everyone else. I told him the travel time uptown and across the bridge was killing me. I told him to find his own dealer up there. He was pissed. I think he liked that I sat there while he watched the kids. Made him feel like he had"—Roy looked at her—"a friend, I guess."

"He ever have anyone with him? A real friend, maybe?"

Roy laughed, a loud giggle that overrode James Garner getting his ass whipped by some truckers. "He didn't even like himself. No friends. Just a knapsack. Black, with a Canadian flag sewn on like he was pretending to be a tourist. And he had a camera. It was digital but it looked like one of those old big cameras, not like the small ones we got now. Had one of those—what do you call 'em? Telephoto lenses."

She thought about the lenses in Deacon's bottom drawer and the question of the camera came up again.

And Deacon's hard drives.

"I saw him talk to kids a lot. He'd mosey up to the sidelines of a game and snap a few photos, pretend like he belonged. And then he'd start talking to some lone kid. At first I thought he was just being friendly. And then I started to see how he looked at the kids and decided that I didn't need no more trouble than I got."

"You ever report him?"

"For what? Talking to kids? I never seen him do anything bad to the kids. He never even put a hand on their shoulder or nuthin'. All he did was talk to them."

"You ever hear what he discussed with them?"

He shook his head. "No. No. No. Whenever he did that, I split."

"Did he ever tell you anything about his life?"

Roy shook his head. "Said he had a nice house. Big car. Said he liked watching the kids because he was a sports fan. It was bullshit. You know how you can tell when people are bullshitting? They tell you they used to be this and they used to be that when all they are is a bum. I get a lot of that. I attract it like some kind of a magnet."

"Anything else you remember about him?"

At that Roy smiled. "He said that he was going to be famous someday."

Hemingway slid one of her cards across the table. "You think of anything else, you call me. I appreciate this."

"I was told to call you. I do what I'm told." Roy eyed the card for a moment, as if it held some great meaning.

"You have a number I can reach you at?"

Roy thought about it for a minute. Then he scribbled his number on a piece of cardboard he tore from a pack of cigarettes. "Yeah. Sure. We can have cocktails at the Ritz."

She stared at him for a moment, and her eyes unconsciously dropped to his belly It was pale. Hairy. She nodded a goodbye. "Thanks for everything." Then she walked past the old woman who still looked dead, past *The Rockford Files*, and into the night.

III SIXTY-SEVEN

LINCOLN AND Papandreou looked like they had been sleeping in their clothes and Hemingway couldn't decide if it was the heat or the hours that had done the damage. They limped across the street like a pair of broke-dick dogs and came into Bernie's.

Papandreou dropped into the booth and Lincoln grabbed a chair, swung it over to the table, sat down and threw his notebook onto the Formica. Then he reached for Hemingway's plate. "Leaving food behind? That ain't like you," he said, grimacing at the taste of the cold fries soaked in catsup.

"My stomach's acting up."

"I seen you eat a sandwich with bones in it once. You ain't got no stomach, you got a valve." Papandreou waved Bernie over, signaling for two coffees.

"How many of Brayton's patients did you get to?"

"Quite a few. You gotta meet the Borenstein woman."

Lincoln swung a fry around like an accusatory weapon. "The real prize is the Morgans. Totally fucking nuts."

"We're all nuts. It's part of the human condition."

Papandreou pulled the sugar dispenser over in preparation for the caffeine he had just ordered while Lincoln continued to pick at Hemingway's fries. "Then they're weird."

Phelps finished off his soda. "They're not weird, they're *eccentric*."

Bernie came over with their coffees. After he walked away, Papandreou upended the sugar dispenser into his. "No, Jon, they're fucking weird. One looks like some kind of freaking lesbian vampire, the other a redneck cop got lucky and inherited a bazillion dollars. Winslow is like that guy from *Psycho* with all the stuffed birds. Me? I collect shot glasses and back issues of *Popular Mechanics*. These folks? They collect weirdness."

Hemingway pushed her plate over so that it was in front of Lincoln; something about the congealing grease was beginning to turn her stomach. "As in?"

Lincoln shrugged. "It's not the shit we saw, it's the shit we didn't see. I don't know what it was."

"You're supposed to be a cop. Short-list it, Linc."

"Doris Borenstein. Fifty-three, married five times, looks like a taxidermied piranha–"

Hemingway held up her hand. "Don't do that."

Lincoln nodded an apology. "Sorry. Like I said, these people freaked us both out a little. Ms. Borenstein has no employment history and her name is listed as administrator or senior fundraiser for eleven charities—emphysema, MS, general big-time stuff like that. Nice apartment but she's cold as a mother-in-law's love."

Lincoln wiped the catsup and mayo off his fingers with a napkin and opened his notebook. "Next up we have Cindy and 'Ace' Morgan. Guy builds battleships and shit. Rich Texan. Their place is decorated like Keith Richards' bedroom. Gold leaf and leopard print and naked gold cherubs bolted to everything. He's seventy-five. Wears a cowboy hat and sounds like Ross Perot. His wife, Cindy, is thirty-five. Former veterinary technician and before that she was an 'Internet model.' They think this is all one big hoot, some kind of role-play or something. They thought we were fucking joking. And you should meet their kid, Miles. Christ, what a goof."

Lincoln flipped forward a few pages. "Then we get the McDaddy of them all, Dr. Neal Winslow—chief ornithologist for the American Museum of Natural History. Specializes in endangered and extinct taxa, most notably the—" he went back to his notes and haltingly read"—*Pinguinus impennis*, whatever the fuck that is. Some kinda bird, I guess.

"His kid Benjamin is some kind of genius. I mean totally off the charts. Smarter'n any of the other ones, and they're all weird little rain men. The kid's ten and has a full scholarship to Harvard. Wrote a collection of biographies of famous people just for the fun of it.

"Dr. Winslow is something else. Fifteen years ago he busted his back in a car wreck. Spine's held together with screws. Wife died seven years back—fell overboard on a cruise—inquest reported death by misadventure. Insurance never paid out because they couldn't rule out murder. Winslow didn't contest the judgment. Now he does Scouts with his kid. Owns a bunch of corporations. Lives in the Dakota. Plenty of zeros in the bank. Odd guy."

Papandreou nodded over his coffee. "Freak," he said. "Hunched over like some kind of bird."

Hemingway flicked Lincoln's notes. "What's wrong with you guys? His back was fucking broken. Don't be disrespectful." She leaned back in the chair and knitted her hands together on top of her head and she saw Lincoln's eyes automatically dial into her bust. "So what *don't* we know about these people?" she asked, taking her arms and crossing them in front of her chest.

Benjamin Winslow
Donor 9332042
Age: Ten years, three months, fourteen days

Dr. Neal Winslow was a single father.

His wife had promised him that it would be her job, her sole responsibility. He could pretend to be interested on birthdays and Christmas, maybe even Thanksgiving. Parent–teacher nights would, of course, be required at least once a year. He would never have to go to recitals or endure finding a piano teacher, or put thought into the child's schooling. She would handle all of it. He would be notified of events via a weekly memo. He wouldn't have to sleep with her. The details would be handled by medical professionals. And it would keep her happy. So he had agreed.

His wife went to a clinic specializing in such things. The child was born. And soon after, his wife disappeared from a cruise ship somewhere off the coast of Portugal. Her body was found three days later by fishermen, so badly bloated by the expanding gases in her system that they thought she was a blue crab–covered life raft.

Benjamin became his sole responsibility and he spent countless hours teaching his son, molding him. And by the time he was five, the boy could outpace his father at anything he took an interest in.

Benjamin had an aptitude not easily measured by standard testing methods but it was generally agreed that he had an IQ that topped 220. The boy excelled at multiple disciplines, not the least of which were mathematics and language. He was touted as a polymath, and Dr. Winslow nurtured his son's gifts.

Solomon Borenstein
Donor 2323094
Age: Ten years, one month, nine days

Five husbands littered Doris Bornstein's past, no small feat for a woman of forty-one years of age. Three had been rich, one had been nice and rich, and one was gay and rich. But they had all been smart. And good in bed. Except maybe for the gay one—unless he was high. But she had come to the table with her own money and had walked away from each without a battle. There had never been any forethought put into any of her divorces: one minute she was contented, maybe even a little happy, the next she was asking for a divorce. The first divorce was over poached eggs; the second, just after coming while he was giving it to her in the ass (the poor sonofabitch never even got to finish); the third, ten minutes after he bought her a nine-million-dollar beach house in Montauk; the fourth, during a Knicks game—she hated basketball—and the last one over a glass of wine on a British Airways flight.

Of course she was up front with numbers Two through Five about the way she had left the previous marriage(s). Like all men, each thought he was different than his predecessors. And they were, but only from one another. Three years was the average.

Solomon was conceived when she had been married to Herrik, her gay Norwegian god as she had called him. She had wanted a baby, he had wanted her to have a baby, but they had one rule—he didn't go near her vajayjay. So they had compromised and opted for a surrogate and a sperm donor. It was amazing what a socioeconomically disadvantaged woman would put her body through for a mere three hundred thousand dollars. Morning sickness and stretch marks? No alcohol or—God-fucking-forbid—drugs for nine months? It was absolutely unthinkable.

So Doris and Herrik had rented a womb, bought some sperm from the tall smart sexy donor that Dr. Brayton recommended, and settled in for the wonderful role of parenthood. Five months in—while they were on their way to London to see Van Morrison at the Royal Albert Hall—she looked over at Herrik and decided that the relationship had run its course. When they touched down at Heathrow, they each took a different car and had not spoken since.

Of course she loved her son, Solomon.

Miles Morgan
Donor 4032239
Age: Ten years, two months, three days

Forney Morgan, who everyone called Ace, had done it all himself. No rich daddy. No bank loans. No credit. And no fucking woman telling him what to do, how to do it, or how long he was allowed to do it for. Amen. Thank you. And fuck the cheese loaf on the way out the door.

Morgan Industrial was OPEC's leading manufacturer of petroleum barrels. He had started the business in his garage in Odessa, Texas—marking up outsourced barrels by a buck apiece. By the time Texas was producing nearly three million barrels a day he had gone from brokering to manufacturing. Now, at the Christmas end of his life, his interests had expanded to include shipbuilding—an endeavor that led him to Uncle Sam, for whom he was now producing nuclear submarines. Life was grand.

And then he found Cindy. Working in the veterinarian's office where he took Rumsfeld and Adolf—his Great Danes—

for their monthly checkup. She was twenty-three and had a big smile and an even bigger pair of tits. He had always been a boob monkey, ever since he could remember. It was good old-fashioned love at first sight.

She had agreed to a dinner. Over wine they found out that he was almost exactly forty years her senior. And besides her tits, she was fun to listen to.

She could also fuck the orange off a traffic cone.

They got married after a quick visit to the lawyer for a prenup that stated, should the best of intentions somehow not be enough, she would be taken care of and he would not lose enough to make him hate her, which seemed like a healthy compromise.

He didn't need any of the little blue pills to put the steel to her. When she clamped her cans together, stuck out her tongue, and licked one of her nipples, he almost ripped through his pants.

Two years in she asked for a baby. He thought about it and figured *what the fuck?* They tried. No pregnancy. She went to a doctor who specialized in correcting those kinds of women's problems. She checked out. And after two months of prodding, he had grudgingly gone to have the joystick examined. He knew what was up before the visit—an old motorcycle injury. He had been sixteen and the surgeon who had put him back together said that he might not have children. Turned out he was right; the boys just weren't swimming.

She had somehow gotten him to agree to the handsome spermcicle people. The joke had ended up being on her; instead of the Brad Pitt model she had ordered, the delivered product bore an undeniable resemblance to the Hamburglar, as if Ace himself had magically entered the very core of the child's being. Ace loved his son.

But the kid was a dolt. Yet somehow smart enough to realize that getting angry about it was a wasted effort.

He also had an unbelievably high pain threshold. Good old farm stock, Ace guessed.

Fuck Brad Pitt.

||| SIXTY-EIGHT

THEY WERE dealing with a breakfast of BLTs and NYPD travel mugs filled with the precinct's finest blend from the machine in the corner. Mother Nature had cranked the thermostat back up into the red zone and Hemingway's skin was having a hard time breathing.

Papandreou and Lincoln had come by to drop off their interview notes from a night spent running around the city, visiting Brayton's patients. After a quick rundown, they had left to get some much-earned sleep. True to habit, Papandreou had flicked the television on but left the sound off. Now, an hour later it was still flashing over Hemingway's shoulder as she put the breakfast away, wondering in some distant corner of her mind if she was having too much coffee for the baby.

Baby? There was no baby.

Not yet.

Not until she decided there was.

Keep telling yourself that, sister.

She took another bite of the sandwich.

Phelps chewed mechanically, his eyes focused on the television. She looked at her watch and figured that the local morning cycle had started, the newscaster delivering the night's mayhem with insincere gravity.

Without taking his eyes from the screen, he said, "Hemi, go home. Get some sleep." He looked ready for the trenches—fresh shaven and smelling of some not-too-bad cologne. "The world can get by without your help for a few hours."

‖‖ SIXTY-NINE

SHE WAS sound asleep, somewhere beyond the point where a phone call or human voice could penetrate, deep in a slumber only the incessant ringing of the doorbell could shatter.

She forced an eye open. Sat up. Looked around for a robe. Yanked it on over the nightie she had slept in.

She moved slowly down the stairs, coming to the main nave of the loft. The place was a mess and it looked like Daniel still hadn't come home. Her head felt like it was too small for her brain.

The bell jingled again and she rounded the banister to the staircase. She moved past the four equestrian portraits and almost slipped on the polished wood. She hitched the robe a little tighter. Opened the door.

She saw a smile. She smiled back. Something came at her. She never registered the blade whistling through her throat but she did feel the giddy high.

She saw her own blood spurt across the doorway.

Then she saw nothing at all.

PHELPS WAS still engrossed in the news. He had weathered so many media shit storms that he no longer took it personally. He thought most of the people on television were idiots anyway and he watched with the sound off, reading the chyron and the headlines. More than enough to get the gist of what they were saying.

He was no longer a young lion but he hadn't been hit by age as hard as a lot of his contemporaries. Many of them had opted out of active street duty years ago, deciding to spend the tail end of their careers perfecting their Microsoft Office skills. He had never felt the need to slow down. He liked what he did, was good at it, and rarely took his work home with him at night. Why fix what ain't broken?

Something flashed across the top of the screen and the announcer stared into the camera, looking graver than she had a second ago. They cut to a remote camera—a live report from the West Side.

The camera captured a body lying in a doorway, legs inside, torso, arms and head flopped out onto the limestone landing. There was a massive jet of what could only be blood sprayed across the white Sheetrock inside the entrance. The head was twisted on sideways, buried in a mess of black hair. A paramedic stooped and covered the body with a sheet.

Phelps recognized the door. He stood up, knocking his chair over.

Across the bottom of the screen the chyron read: *Detective Alexandra Hemingway of the NYPD murdered at her home.*

||| SEVENTY-ONE

PHELPS STARED at the television for a moment, mouth open, disbelief swirling around in his head like an angry weather system. "Hemi," he said slowly.

Hemingway looked up from her sandwich. The tremor of wrongness in his voice made her stop chewing.

"I think something very bad has happened."

She came around to his side of the conference table and looked up, eyes on the screen for a second—maybe two—before she said, "Oh, Jesus," and was gone.

Phelps grabbed his holster and ran after her.

||| SEVENTY-TWO

THE STREETS had not yet clogged up with the morning rush hour and Hemingway punched the big truck around the corner in a smoking drift that sounded like an angry *Tyrannosaurus rex*. The lights thumped and the sirens screeched and she had her foot to the floor as they drifted west, the city's architecture sliding sideways across the windshield.

Phelps was belted in, one hand on the holy shit handle, the other on the center console to keep him from slamming back and forth as she screeched through the corners and punched to the red line on the straightaways. A cruiser closed up their path; it had started out in the lead to clear the way but she had quickly grown tired of sitting behind it and had barreled past after two blocks.

Phelps hadn't so much as flinched. But he swore.

The ride usually took about twenty minutes at night, forty in traffic. Hemingway made it in seven.

They rounded the final corner in a swinging arc of smoke that scattered the reporters lined up at the edge of the road. She didn't slow, but hammered up the middle of the street, skidding to a stop a foot from the side door of the cruiser that blocked the road.

She ran through the tape, past the uniformed officer, through two more cops who tried to stop her, and pushed aside the EMT men crouching in her doorway. One tumbled back and fell down the stairs.

There was a white plastic sheet over the body that lay across her threshold. One of the EMT guys started back up the steps but Phelps stopped him.

Hemingway stood there, looking down at the sheet. The world went prismatic as tears filled her eyes. She closed them and the tears shook loose. She crouched down, reached out, and wrapped her fingers around the sheet.

There was nothing else in her focus except her fear.

She needed to see. Needed to know. And then she could fall apart.

She needed him. Loved him. He had been taken by a killer who enjoyed disassembling little boys.

Another bad man who wouldn't leave her alone.

She tightened her grip. The plastic was warm and humid, and her hand shook so badly that the sheet vibrated with her touch.

A big shadow that could only be Phelps blocked out the sun. She felt a hand on her shoulder.

Hemingway pulled the sheet back, and looked down at the twisted black blood-spattered grimace on her sister's face.

SEVENTY-THREE

PHELPS LED her to a cruiser where she took up position leaning against the grill. He pushed a cup of coffee into her hand and she stared at it for a moment as she tried to figure out what had happened. The initial fear and disbelief were replaced by an eerie sense of calm that she knew was a form of shock that would eventually come out in one big scream.

She had her back to the news cameras parked at the end of the block. She heard Phelps go back to the line, talk to the cops on the scene. He dipped his head into the ambulance. There was a commotion at the edge of her vision.

Phelps headed back and stood in front of her, shielding her from the cameras. "Okay. Look at me. I am going to tell you something and you have to act like I haven't said anything because it will be all over the news and you don't want this guy knowing any more about your personal life." He stepped in. "Okay?"

She was back in the present, back to the hot hood of the car and the too-warm coffee in her hand, and the sun already cooking the city. "What?"

He squared his shoulders. "Daniel's fine. He's the one who found her."

She stood up, searched over his shoulder. "Where?"

Phelps reached out, steadied her with a hand on each shoulder. "We walk over nice and slow. What would that film asshole you love so much say?"

"Bitch, be cool."

"Yeah, well, some people got no class."

"Where is he?" A tinge of hysteria had crept into her voice and she took a breath, willing the panic inside her to shrink.

"He's in the ambulance. He's fine but he's in shock."

She headed around Phelps, toward the ambulance. She was aware that the cameras were there but she was back in cop mode now. Long stride, hand on sidearm, her eyes hidden by her aviators.

Daniel was sitting on the edge of a stretcher, his head in his hands—just a skinny guy with long hair and too many holes in his jeans for a forty-five-year-old. There were bloody patches on his chest where he had wiped his hands. His camera bag sat on the floor beside him, the strap smeared with blood.

Until that second she forgot that he had gone out last night. Iggy, wasn't it?

Hemingway snapped her fingers at the tech and when his boots hit the street she climbed in and pulled the door closed behind her. She crouched in front of him, and the grip of her pistol clinked on the frame of the stretcher behind her.

Daniel looked up at her. He didn't smile, nod or acknowledge that he had even seen her. But he began talking, very matter-of-fact, a little too fast. "I was a few seconds late getting to her. Fifteen. Maybe twenty. I stopped at the diner to get a coffee. Came down the street. Passed some schoolkids. Guy walking his dog. When I got there she was still bleeding. Blood pissing out all over the place." Their eyes connected and they knew one another again. "I'm so fucking sorry, Allie. I tried, I really did."

The tears filled her eyes. She took a breath, pushed them back. Then unfolded from her crouch and sat down beside him. She put her arm around his shoulder. All she could think was had he been there, she might have lost him, too.

"I called nine-one-one. I wanted to call you but I couldn't remember your number. I tried to find it in my contacts but my hands were shaking so hard I dropped my fucking phone. And all of a sudden the police were here. And now you're here and I don't know what I saw but I want to unsee it."

"Daniel, it'll be fine. It's the adrenaline in your system. You're in shock. We'll get you some shots; B12 will help. You'll start shaking in a few minutes."

"In a few minutes?" He held up his hand—it was vibrating as if it were plugged into a hummingbird's central nervous system.

"You're going to be okay."

"Okay? Your sister is out there spilled all over our doorway—oh, sorry, *your* doorway—and you tell me it's going to be okay? No, Alexandra, it's not going to be okay. This is so fucking far from okay that it's in another language. Your sister is dead. I should have been here. You should have been here. How can we keep doing this? We never see each other. We never . . . Ah, fuck it." And he stopped, stiffened and slid into himself.

Phelps opened the door, stuck his head inside. "The medical examiner's people just showed up. And your sister has to leave." He jerked his head in the general direction of the cameras. "The less we give those assholes, the better."

Hemingway stood up, putting her hand on Daniel's shoulder. She gave it a squeeze. "Tell them what you saw, then we'll get you into a shower and bed."

Daniel waved her away. "Leave me alone."

She stopped to say something and then realized that she had nothing to offer. "I'll be outside if you need me."

But Daniel's head was back in his hands.

Hemingway and Phelps took up perch on the front bumper of the ambulance as the people who tended to these things came and went. They recorded, filmed, measured, black-lighted, dusted, collected, catalogued, and conversed.

It was slow in coming, but when it hit her it didn't feel all that different than the time she had been shot. There was that same weird burning in her chest, as if the machinery had stopped working, but none of the noise.

She had to call her folks. To tell them what had happened to their daughter. And for the second time in their lives, they would have to bury a child.

Hemingway pulled out her phone and stared at it for a while, trying to figure out how to handle this. It came alive in her hands, lit up with her parents' number in East Hampton; the summer cocktail circuit must have started.

She stared at it for one ring.

Two.

Then three.

Phelps pointed at her phone. "It's sooner or later, kiddo."

She accepted the call, took a deep breath, and pressed it to her ear. "Hemingway here." It was a lousy save, one that would only buy her a few seconds.

"Allie! We saw the news and we were so worried. Mom said it was some kind of mistake but I wasn't so sure. You know how I get. It's—"

Her father was yammering on, something that went against his Anglican poise. "Dad?"

"—a father thing. If you ever have children, then you'll know what I'm talk—"

"*Dad?*" A little louder.

And he stopped. "What?"

"Dad, it's Amy." She felt her voice waver just a little, but to a parent's ears it was enough.

There was a long pause. "Is she all right?"

"I'm sorry." And with that she held the phone out to Phelps.

They sometimes did this for one another, took up the slack. When Ernie, Phelps's brother, had lapsed into a coma after a fall, she had been the one to deliver the decision to not continue with mechanical assistance; Jon just couldn't say the words. At the time she hadn't understood what it meant to him. She did now. Some things have to be said to—and for—the people you love when they can't express themselves.

As he took the phone from her hands, her chest tightened. She leaned over and took a deep breath, grateful for the big sunglasses.

III SEVENTY-FOUR

PHELPS KEPT the front end of the Suburban at a single car length from the back bumper of the van carrying Amy's body to the morgue. On their left, the East River flashed between the traffic and the concrete as they headed south on the FDR.

Hemingway rode shotgun, her thoughts slowly and steadily creeping toward anger. Amy had died, and even though she could keep herself from crying, she couldn't keep the tears from forming. This was not allowed to derail her. Because that's what that prick out there wanted: for her to go away.

She would not let that happen.

No.

Fucking.

Way.

They already had him, they just couldn't see it. He was close, buried somewhere in the lives of these children. Now they knew it wasn't Brayton. But it was someone connected to him. They might already have spoken to him. Interviewed him. Shook his hand.

In that spooky way Phelps had of reading her thoughts,

he asked, "You gotta be all in or you gotta be all out. There ain't no middle position on this one, kiddo."

"We have him, Jon. Our perp is buried somewhere in the files and medical reports, in the hundreds of names we're looking into, in the way he's killed these people, and in the way I've pissed him off. I'm in. Until it's done."

Phelps pulled back as the van ahead took a tight right off FDR Drive, heading for home, the office of the underworld. "There's Amy's funeral, which means your parents. Daniel will need a little maintenance. And you got other shit on your plate, too."

Couldn't forget the baby.

She thought back to the ambulance, to the shell-shocked fear in Daniel's eyes. This had been his first real peek into her other life. It might have been too much. This luck had followed since forever, some kind of negative space in the universe that sucked in and destroyed the people she loved the most. Two sisters now. Mank. And everyone they had lost since Tyler Rochester had been found hugging a bridge piling in the East River.

"Your dance card's kinda full."

"Either my dance card's full, or I have a lot on my plate. It can't be both," she said, mimicking his tone in Deacon's driveway yesterday. "Do you really believe that?"

He shrugged. "Not really. No."

"Then stop being a prick. We go to the morgue. Then we go back to the office and finish up with the Brayton/Selmer list. Someone out there knows our ghost. We have a lot of people to visit."

"You need to sleep."

"Not as much as I need to find this guy."

III SEVENTY-FIVE

THEY STARTED with Doris Borenstein. She was the first of the morning and she had sandwiched them in between her beautician and her spiritual advisor, code words for plastic surgeon and psychiatrist.

A disembodied electronic voice asked them to hold their identification up to the camera. The man who let them in was ten percent larger than Phelps in every conceivable measurement and had a head that fit his shoulders like a five-gallon bucket slapped onto a snowman. He had pink eyes and white hair, a perfect albino. He introduced himself as Elio.

Doris Borenstein was a nervous woman. She was coiffed and perfect and looked like she had stepped out of the early seventies in a pair of bell-bottom linen trousers, a tailored button-down and a pair of sunglasses that would have done nicely as welding goggles. Her skin also looked three sizes too small for her skeleton.

Everything was carefully chosen and beautifully lit, including Doris Borenstein, who sat under a softened light that did a good job of masking her wrinkles. Elio hung back, mute, arms loose by his side. There was a large-caliber automatic in his belt that he didn't bother to hide.

"I apologize that I couldn't meet you later but my advisor only has one-hour slots available. Why, exactly, are you here?" she asked, hand held to her chest.

"First off, does your companion over there have a carry permit? I do not enjoy being uncomfortable."

Mrs. Borenstein smiled. It was an expression that belonged on a spider. "Elio is licensed to carry a concealed sidearm in nineteen states, branching out from his New York resident carry card. He has been in my employ for fourteen years."

Hemingway nodded but that didn't make her feel any more comfortable about the big sonofabitch standing there with a chrome Desert Eagle sticking out of his waistband.

"You spoke with Detectives Lincoln and Papandreou. Did they tell you that Dr. Selmer was murdered yesterday afternoon?"

"I heard. We are not required to like everyone we meet. I have a very biased opinion of anyone connected with that clinic. Especially considering what your two colleagues told me about Dr. Brayton's hit list. Incidentally, have you found him yet?" She looked from Hemingway to Phelps, then back to Hemingway.

"Dr. Brayton is dead. He committed suicide a few months back."

"Who says the police never bring good news?" Mrs. Borenstein smiled. "Now what, specifically, can I do for you?"

Hemingway looked up at Elio but spoke to Doris Borenstein. She didn't bother to ask if she wanted some privacy; Lincoln had underlined that she had insisted Elio stay in the room during questioning.

Hemingway chose her first question carefully, avoiding the subject of the girls. "Do you know anything that might help us? About the clinic; your son's siblings; Dr. Brayton—"

"—That reptile, Fenton?" Borenstein interrupted.

Hemingway waited.

"I am not a stupid woman. I love my son, he is a remarkable child. But that clinic misrepresented the package I purchased. Marjorie Fenton is not concerned with patient care, she is concerned with making money. She is a greedy little rug merchant and yes—I can't say that I'd be all that broken up if someone killed her as well. And that is not a threat of any kind—just wishful thinking."

"Please tell us about your son, Solomon."

At that she changed poses. "Solomon is a singer. Opera. The voice of an angel. If anyone ever took him," she turned her head and looked up at Elio, "I'd kill them and everyone they ever loved."

———

When they were back in the street, Phelps said, "That woman is trying to be Alexis Carrington."

Hemingway smiled and got in behind the wheel. "She's just bored."

Before pulling out into traffic she checked the patient list.

One down.

A million to go.

MARY ZRBINSKI attended to the general needs of the Atchison household. Her tasks ranged from picking up dry cleaning to arranging lifts to the airport. She made sure the cook had a well-stocked kitchen for the days he came in, and she made sure that William made his appointments. The Atchisons were decent people.

It was morning, the one day she came in at 10 a.m. as opposed to 7 a.m. She noticed that the black carriage lamps were still on as she came up the street. She put her key in the lock, pushed the door in, and stepped inside.

She closed the door and the stink hit her. What was that? She took a step and her feet went out from under her, wishboning her legs in a clumsy almost split that tore her skirt. Her head hit the hardwood and she lay there for a second.

The house was unusually quiet.

She pushed herself up and her hand slipped. The sensation of oil seeping through her clothes cooled her skin.

She fought to a sitting position.

Mrs. Atchison lay against the wall a few feet away. Blood was everywhere.

WHEN HEMINGWAY and Phelps pulled up to the Atchison house, a uniformed officer met them at the curb. A woman sat in the back of his cruiser, wrapped in a kit blanket, sobbing. The other officer squatted by the open door, talking to her.

"Dispatch said two? One a kid?" Phelps asked.

The Atchison house was on their list—they had been on the way here yesterday when Hemingway had received the text from Tyler Rochester's phone. She wondered if it was a coincidence. Either way, it was disturbing.

The cop nodded. "Maid came in for the day. Walked in and found the lady of the house at the front door. Called nine-one-one and we responded. Did a walk-through." He swallowed. "The kid's upstairs in the tub."

"You guys touch anything?"

The cop shook his head and swallowed again. "No light switches. Nothing."

Hemingway and Phelps headed into the house.

Mrs. Atchison was sprawled out on the floor. There were slip marks through the pudding-like scab, the sloppy hand-prints and thrash marks where the housekeeper had fallen.

The smell was so bad they had to breathe through their mouths.

They had their service pieces out; they had been at this too long to trust anyone else's work.

They moved around the stagnant puddle of Mrs. Atchison's blood, almost resorting to rock-climbing moves on the paneling to step over the mess on the floor. It seemed impossible that all this blood had fit into one person's body.

The ground floor was clear. As was the basement—a well-stocked wine cellar.

They moved up the stairs in file, Hemingway point.

Another wave of death hit them, this one mixed with the scent of lavender. They cleared the floor from front to back, quickly working their way to the bathroom. The door was ajar and a bright slash of light spilled out across the hallway.

They paused at the door, nodded a final *Are you ready?* to one another, then Hemingway reached out and pushed it in with the nose of her revolver.

Phelps staggered back and coughed, putting his hand to his mouth.

Hemingway stood in the doorway. There was no way to equate the mess she saw with a living, breathing child.

The boy lay in the bathtub, head back, tear streaks through the blood that spattered his face. His ribs were spread wide and he looked like a bloody cryptid insect in the process of becoming something else—his lungs had been lifted out and flopped back over his shoulders where they hung like scabbed bloated wings that had not yet formed. The rest of his internal organs were gone.

THEY SENT the Atchison boy off to the stainless steel table in Dr. Marcus's lab where he'd be reduced to evidence. The last two bodies should have given up more than the first two; they hadn't been scrubbed clean by the river.

Yet they were still shy on trace evidence. And completely lacking in suspects.

Something was bound to turn up; it was physically impossible for a person to enter a room and not leave a little of themselves behind. Hemingway and Phelps were becoming almost superstitious about this one, though: the only thing that denoted his passing were the dead children.

They had more interviews to do. New information to sift through. An ever-widening gene pool of potential killers; it felt like half the population of Manhattan was under suspicion.

Marcus had already signed out the autopsy reports on Brayton's eight dead girls. And then he had been interrupted with Hemingway's sister and William Atchison. One step forward, two steps back.

But Papandreou and Lincoln were out hunting down

whatever they could on the girls—half sisters in an equation no one understood.

Hemingway and Phelps still had patients to speak to. Parents to warn.

But how did you warn someone about this? You couldn't. Not really. There was no way to look the parents in the eye and tell them about bloody butterfly boy. That would be cruel. Hell, it would be more than cruel; it would be sadistic. But they needed to know their kids were in danger.

Hemingway was frustrated. "So he kills all of the female children first. Then he goes after the boys. Whoever is doing this had the information in Brayton's files before the first girl died. Before they took Selmer's bag out of the backseat of his car. It's someone who had access to Brayton's files at some point."

"Who has legal access to a doctor's files?" Phelps wondered aloud.

"Any of the nurses at the clinic. Receptionist. Cleaning staff. IT people. Maintenance. Movers. Shredding service. Delivery people. There are a thousand ways to get to a doctor's files if you're not interested in the legality of the situation. But everyone in the clinic—from the cleaning people to the guy who used to deliver the sandwiches at lunch to the coffee machine repair people—had been cleared. One guy with a twenty-year-old DUI and one with a domestic violence arrest—no conviction. Three people with parking violation problems. No one fits this."

At that Phelps looked over at her. "Hemi, when we find this guy, he's just gonna be some bum we've never heard of and no one ever paid attention to."

She wasn't so sure.

THE SKY had knitted over again in a gray foil, as if the storms of yesterday had come back to tease the city with the promise of rain. But the heat and humidity held on with sticky fingers and if Hemingway didn't get a shower soon, her blouse could be used as a biological weapon.

She hoped that the weather would stay ugly and they could forget about the final track-and-field day at Randall's Island. The place seemed tied to everything that had happened so far, from Deacon using it as a spectator and drug-buying hangout, to all the schools of the dead children using it as their physical education grounds.

Phelps's voice brought her back to the present. "There. Up ahead on the left. Green awning."

She glanced in her mirror, then over her shoulder, and cut across three lanes, pulling the truck into the fifteen-minute loading zone in front of the Fifth Avenue apartment.

After what felt like their hundredth ride of the day in a lushly appointed elevator, the apartment door was opened by a small woman in a perfectly tailored Chanel suit. She introduced herself as Carmen, said she was the Morgans' personal assistant, and that she would be happy to take their drinks request.

They thanked Carmen, told her that coffee would be fine and that they had very little time.

Lincoln hadn't been far off with his Keith Richards bedroom crack—the place looked like Donald Trump's with less restraint. Everything was animal print, gold leaf, and sparkled.

Carmen led them through a wall of floor-to-ceiling bronze-framed doors, out onto a stone terrace that wrapped around the corner of the building. The haze of Manhattan spread out like the world's largest canvas—the Morgans owned at least half of the top floor. They rounded the corner and Mr. and Mrs. Morgan were at a wrought iron table, wearing matching robes and having breakfast even though it was coming up on eleven o'clock.

"Mr. and Mrs. Morgan, I'm Detective Alexandra Hemingway. This is my partner, Detective Jon Phelps. Thank you for making the time to see us."

Everything about Mr. Morgan said self-made. He was a heavyset man who sported a pair of floral swim trunks and a diamond-encrusted Rolex that pinched his pink wrist. He stood up and shook hands. When he was standing he wasn't much taller than when he was sitting. "Glad to do it, detectives. Glad to do it. Call me Ace. The little lady's Cindy."

Mrs. Morgan was in her thirties and had the tight toned body of a gym bunny. Her skin was tanned the color of maple syrup and her blond locks were the best weaves that Hemingway had seen outside of *Charlie's Angels*. She giggled when she shook hands, and a good sixty carats of stones jingled on her wrist in a coil of tennis bracelets. Every movement she made seemed to be done with the intention of jiggling her breasts and it was obvious that even the Iron Giant had a hard time keeping his eyes off of them.

"You guys want some food? Bacon's flown in from Texas—double smoked. And we got some great cheese—smells like turds—but it's the best there is."

Phelps shook his head and gestured to Hemingway. "Detective Hemingway, are you hungry?"

She ignored him. "Thanks. No."

"Well, it's there if you change your mind. What's this shit with the kid?" Ace asked, and went back to eating.

The table was set with gold-plated flatware and water lilies floated in a low crystal bowl shaped like a woman's face. There were bagels and rolls and an assortment of fruit and cheeses that seemed to be there purely for presentation; Ace's attention was nailed to a plate piled high with bacon. A big cigar smoldered in an ashtray at the edge of the table.

Phelps smiled. It seemed like the Morgans were his kind of people. "As we went over on the phone, the boys who have been killed share the same biological father as your son. We think that Miles might be in danger."

At that Ace threw his head back and guffawed. "Shit, you haven't met little Miles." Mr. Morgan reached over and picked up his wife's cell phone in the rhinestone case on the table. He tapped the screen and said, "Oh Jesus fucking Christ, Cindy, what's with this password bullshit? I can't ever find my phone and you know I don't give a sweet flying fuck if you have a boyfriend just as long as he ain't got some disease that I can catch from your coochy-poochy. What's the fucking password?"

Cindy's nose crinkled up. "Don't swear so much, Daddy. It's two-two-two-two."

Ace smiled. "Sure you can remember that?" He punched it in.

"I think so."

A man in a black suit and tie showed up carrying a silver

service of coffee. He laid it down on an iron server and filled two cups for the detectives. Then he disappeared as silently as he had come.

Ace tapped around on the screen and returned the phone to the table. "Just don't sleep with any Democrats—I hate those fucking pussies. Fuck a real man, for Chrissake."

"Yes, Daddy," she said, and went back to picking at her low-fat cottage cheese.

Ace turned back to Phelps who had lost the look of comfort from a few minutes earlier. "All right, so we disagree that my son's in danger. I texted him—he should be here in a minute. What next?"

"Mr. Morgan—"

"Ace! I told you to call me Ace!"

"Ace. Yeah. Sure. We'll need a list of anyone your son knows—everyone from his hairdresser to—"

"Barber," Ace interrupted. "My kid does not go to a hairdresser, detective. He ain't no fag."

"We'd be grateful for a list of everyone in his life: his teachers; tutors; anyone who drives him around; friends he sees on a regular basis; parents of friends where he does sleepovers or playdates; stores you take him to; tradespeople you may have had in the house."

"Goin' back how far?"

"Three years would be good. Can you think of anyone who seems odd or suspicious?"

"All of her friends," Ace said, nodding at his wife. "They're a bunch of freaks."

Cindy slapped him on the arm. "Don't be mean, Daddy. You like Jezebel."

At that Ace nodded with the corners of his mouth turned down. "You got a point. I do like her." And he winked at Phelps.

Hemingway was about to stand up, to tell Phelps that they had to leave, when a little boy appeared at the edge of the table. He had come silently up on them and was standing there, arms crossed, staring at Ace. "You texted me, Father?"

She had yet to see one of Selmer's boys alive. Lincoln's comment about him being a goof was pushing it, but it was obvious that the kid wasn't like the other children on the list. He was heavy, stood with his mouth open, and had a dull expression on his face. Other than the brown hair and eyes, he didn't look like he had anything to do with Dr. Brayton's *Boys of Brazil* program.

Ace put a hand on the boy's shoulder. "This is Detective Phelps and his partner, Detective Hemingway."

The boy turned and extended his hand, first to Phelps, then to Hemingway. "Miles Morgan, a pleasure to meet you both." He had a good handshake but looked like he would rather be somewhere else.

Ace went on. "They tell me that there's a bad man out there running around killing little kids and that you might be in danger. Does that frighten you, son?"

The boy shook his head.

"And why not?"

With the speed of an adder, Miles Morgan's hand flashed up and he had a knife to Phelps's throat. It was an airframe knife with a black carbon blade that dented Phelps's skin. The boy backed up, flicked his wrist, and the knife was gone. "Though I walk through the valley of the Shadow of Death, I fear no evil because I am the meanest motherfucker in the valley, sir."

Phelps stared at the child.

Hemingway's hand was on her pistol. "Don't you ever draw a weapon on a police officer, Miles."

Miles looked her in the eyes. "I was answering his question."

"I don't care. You do that to a police officer and you can end up dead."

The boy looked over at his father, searching for some kind of qualifier to Hemingway's lesson.

"She might have a point, son."

And with that the boy smiled. "Is that all?"

"You ever get into any kind of trouble at school, Miles? Fighting?" she asked, looking at the bandage over his nose, his two black eyes.

"Fighting isn't trouble. Fighting's fun."

After Miles had walked away, Ace threw a few more strips of bacon down his throat, then opened up his hands. "When you want that list?"

Hemingway pulled out her three-by-five and a pen. "We can go over it right now. If you think of anything later, we can add it."

Ace eyed her for a second. "You know, you're pretty hot for a cop."

At that, Mrs. Morgan dropped her head and stared over the top of her sunglasses. She nodded. "You are."

Hemingway didn't bother smiling. "I get that a lot."

THEY SPENT the rest of the morning and all of the afternoon running down the balance of Brayton's patients. The ones who had moved away were interviewed on the phone and local PDs were sent out to do a formal report—if Tanya Everett hadn't been safe in Greece, this guy could go anywhere, even if the brunt of his focus seemed to be aimed on New York right now. Lots of new information came their way. More teachers. More tutors and drivers and butlers. More dead ends.

The last patient they saw was Dr. Neal Winslow, father of ten-year-old Benjamin. Benjamin was the oldest of Brayton's children by five days, and by all reports an exceptional child.

Dr. Winslow and his son lived in the Dakota facing Central Park. Signing in—even for the two detectives—was like going through airport security on Kentucky Derby weekend.

In the ride up in the elevator, a little old lady cradling a Pomeranian in one arm and a crocodile bag in the other eyed the two detectives warily, as if they might try to squeegee her dog. She got out on the third floor. They rode on to the seventh.

When they stepped out of the elevator Phelps looked around and whistled, taking in the unique architecture. "Who designed this place, Gomez Addams?"

Hemingway had been in the building before; she had dated a boy whose parents lived here back when she was in college—still did, as far as she knew—and the place hadn't changed at all. She rang the bell.

A thin man in a good English suit answered the door. He could have passed for a butler in an old Lon Chaney film. He stood in the doorway, leaning slightly forward as if he were caught in the midst of a bow. This had to be Dr. Winslow.

"I am Detective Alexandra Hemingway and this is my partner, Detective Jon Phelps. We called you earlier."

"Yes, you did," the man said. After a moment of what appeared to be indecision, he said, "Please come in."

As Phelps stepped over the threshold his mouth fell open. The apartment looked like a professionally curated museum. A pair of taxidermied birds the size of German shepherds flanked the door, glass eyeballs focused on infinity. And instead of the usual center table prescribed by most decorators, the entry was taken up with an Edwardian display case where six massive birds sat regally—and permanently—watching the door with imposed disinterest. They looked like a race of ancient penguins bred for fighting. Phelps paused in front of the case and it was obvious that he was wondering just what the hell he was looking at.

"*Pinguinus impennis*—the Great Auk," Dr. Winslow said lovingly. "The largest collection on the planet. Under one roof, at any extent. Declared extinct in 1844 but with unverified sightings up until 1852. Overpredated by man, of course."

He closed the door and walked past them, as if he had somewhere else to be. He moved deeper into the apartment.

The two detectives followed but Hemingway had a hard time not stopping to admire the birds that were everywhere.

Unusual taxidermied specimens filled most of the available space but somehow it didn't feel cluttered; the display cases were tastefully arranged as if at a good gallery, and the effect was mesmerizing. The hallway was lined with custom-made bronze and iron shelving filled with books on ornithology, mostly large leather-bound volumes.

On one of the shelves sat a common dove in a display case, a stained baseball beside it under the glass. The brass plaque read: MARCH 24TH, 2001—THROWN BY RANDY JOHNSON OF THE ARIZONA DIAMONDBACKS. THE ONLY FASTBALL TO KILL A BIRD. The piece hinted at a sense of humor lacking in the rest of the space.

They passed a King Island Emu, an ivory label stating that it was the last known member of its species—it had died in Paris in 1822. Most of the cases had similar labels, either LAST KNOWN OF ITS SPECIES or the more chilling, ONLY KNOWN OF ITS SPECIES, POSSIBLY A SUBSPECIES OR HYBRID. There was education and dedication behind the collection; this was a major passion that had taken generations to build.

There were none of the hand-tinted Audubon prints Hemingway expected. Instead, the walls were decorated with antique oil paintings of birds in atypical poses—cockfights and still lifes of hunting trophies. They passed a large canvas in a rocaille frame that depicted a sideboard piled high with dead pheasants. As they moved by, Phelps's body language became less fluid and Hemingway recognized the unease—this was not his kind of place.

A few of the smaller walls were decorated with framed photographs and Hemingway paused in front of a color print depicting a great blue heron with a frog in its beak, a duck decoy behind it, sun-bleached and weed-covered, riding the swirl between two rocks.

Dr. Winslow brought them to the living room, tastefully decorated with period Arts and Crafts furniture. The room was surprisingly dark for a building where properties started at twenty million a crack and she remembered that back in college she had been surprised that a place with such high ceilings could have such little ambient light.

A pair of telescopes stood at the window pointed out at the park—no doubt for bird-watching—one seemed to be tailored for a child. Several digital SLRs sat on a small table beside the telescopes, a collection of telephoto lenses neatly arranged like the spires of a small city. Like Daniel, Dr. Winslow was a Nikon man.

He gestured to two big Morris chairs and said, "How may I help you?"

Hemingway liked reducing people to stereotypes—it had helped her growing up and it was an invaluable skill as a detective; often, generalities were all there was to go on. Winslow had the air of a trust funder who had chosen the cloistered world of academia because it filled out the job requirement imposed by a certain kind of upbringing—old money that said a man had to fill his time with work. And with a passion as evident as his, it was easy to see that he wasn't bored.

"Dr. Winslow, first off we appreciate your taking the time to see us. We want to go over what you discussed with Detectives Lincoln and Papandreou yesterday."

The man nodded and closed his eyes. Hemingway had a hard time telling if the expression that came over his face was one of sadness or of being inconvenienced.

Hemingway glanced at her notes. "Did you suspect that Benjamin might not be as . . . unique as you had been promised?"

Dr. Winslow shook his head. "My wife handled the details. I had no expectations one way or another. Biology," he said, waving his hand through the air, gesturing to the dozens of cased birds, "has its limitations."

"Were you upset when you found out?"

Dr. Winslow thought about the question for a moment. "Detectives, when I was a child my mother purchased a dog. She bought it from the finest breeder in the country—a wonderful little whippet named Grosvenor. Around Grosvenor's first birthday he developed some health issues—health issues my mother had been told he would not have. The dog, it appeared, was guaranteed. The breeder said he would be happy to take Grosvenor back. He'd put the dog down and replace him with a pup from the newest litter. But my mother already loved that dog. Some things cannot be undone."

Hemingway found the comparison distasteful. "So you weren't upset?"

"I don't care how Benjamin came into my life, only that he has."

Winslow was one of two single fathers on the list. "Where is Benjamin now?" she asked.

"At school, of course."

"Did you think about keeping him home?"

He stared at her. "Keep Benjamin from school? No."

Hemingway thought about William Atchison cracked open in his tub. If Dr. Winslow had seen that, little Benjamin wouldn't be going anywhere until he was fifty. "You know about the boys who have been murdered in the past few days?" Winslow didn't look like the kind of guy who spent a lot of time in front of the television.

He nodded in that weird blinky fashion again and it made Hemingway uncomfortable.

"The link between the five victims is the donor—the same one as Benjamin's."

Winslow didn't say anything, he just stared at her as if awaiting the good news part of the conversation.

She continued. "We believe the killer may have had access to your file sometime in the past. We don't know how or when but it's one of the possibilities we are examining. Someone knows these boys share a father. We just don't know how."

At this he lifted his head, straightened his back as much as he could, and peered at her from under bushy eyebrows. "What about the opera invitation?"

"What opera invitation?"

He stood up and lifted a handsomely framed photograph from an oak sideboard, handing it to Hemingway. "Benjamin and I went in matching tuxedos. We had a lovely evening. We had punch and the music was wonderful." He sounded happy, childlike.

"When was this?"

Dr. Winslow picked up his iPad and clicked through his e-mail. Then he handed the tablet to Hemingway. "That's the invitation," he said. "May twelfth."

Hemingway looked at it. It was an invitation to an evening at the opera for friends of the clinic. It congratulated them on a happy nine years.

"I don't understand," she said.

"Instead of blind carbon copying everyone's e-mail address, they cc'd them. Everyone who was to get a nine-year invitation was probably on that e-mail list. Here, let me show you." He reached over and clicked on the address.

A list of e-mail addresses appeared. She read through

them, ignoring the cutesy e-mail handles and focusing on those with real names—she recognized at least thirty from Brayton's patients. The e-mail addresses for the Rochesters, Grants, and Simmonses were on the list.

She looked up at Phelps. Someone at the clinic had made a mistake and sent this out to all of Dr. Brayton's children. She counted the addresses—there were sixty-seven of them.

They had their hunting list.

Why hadn't anyone told her about this?

"Can you print this up?" she asked Dr. Winslow. "And please forward it to me—there might be something hidden in the metadata. You're not obliged to do so—I would need a court order to make you hand it over—but you would save us some time. It's your call."

Dr. Winslow waved it away. "Not a problem." He tapped in a command and walked out of his room, coming back in thirty seconds with a crisp full-color invitation printed on glossy paper. Then he handed the iPad to Hemingway. "Please forward it to yourself."

"Who sent the invitation?" Phelps asked.

Hemingway held up the tablet, touched her fingers to the screen, and magnified the text.

The e-mail had come from Marjorie Fenton.

HEMINGWAY CALLED CNN and the news teams descended on the clinic with a well-coiffed vengeance; all that was missing was the Reverend Samuel Parris, a bullhorn, and a gallows. Papandreou and Lincoln were across the street, Papandreou working on a hot dog while Lincoln cautiously sucked a Rocket Pop in a stooped over pose so he wouldn't drip red, white, and blue all over his shirt. When Hemingway pulled up in the Suburban, Papandreou chucked the last of the dog down and Lincoln tossed his Popsicle in the trash.

Hemingway plowed her way through the gauntlet of camera flashes, halogen lighting, and rhetorical questions. She yanked the door open and stepped into the skating-rink cold of the clinic. There wasn't a patient in sight.

Director Fenton was behind the receptionist's desk with her two security men, a troop of blue-suited lawyers behind her—they looked like Custer's boys just before the shit went down.

"Detectives," Fenton said as she checked her watch, "as of four minutes ago, the Park Avenue Clinic initiated bankruptcy proceedings. We have willfully placed a significant portion of our capital in escrow to go toward possible restitutions." The statement was practiced and vague.

"Mrs. Fenton, may we speak with you in private?"

Fenton's eyes twitched in their sockets and her mouth went flat, and for a second it looked like her operating system had crashed. Then her mouth opened very slowly and she said, "Yes, of course."

They followed her to the subterranean boardroom and Hemingway noticed that the artwork was gone; empty nails stuck out of the walls at every turn. Papandreou and Lincoln waited in the hallway with Fenton's legal counsel while Hemingway and Phelps talked to the woman. Fenton dropped into a chair and Hemingway perched herself on the edge of the table. Phelps leaned against the door, arms crossed, the Iron Giant at rest. Or waiting for an attack command.

"Mrs. Fenton, since I left here last time we have learned that Dr. Brayton has killed himself and you held an anniversary celebration last year for the patients."

Fenton just stared at her.

Hemingway's knuckles tightened on the edge of the desk and Fenton looked down at them, as if realizing for the first time that they were alone.

"If we had known about Brayton, we wouldn't have wasted valuable resources looking for him. And if you had told us about the opera, and that almost all of your patients had been there together, we might have been able to warn them. Two more children might be alive." And with that, Hemingway handed Fenton a photograph of the cryptid child from the bathtub.

The director looked at it for a second, then quickly turned away. Her jaw moved in its mounts and for a second it looked like she might gag.

"That's William Atchison. He was at the opera that night."

She stabbed another photograph into Fenton's hand, this one of the Simmons boy on the ferry. "And that's another patient of Dr. Brayton's—Zachary Simmons. He was at the opera as well." She followed these with the color copy of the invitation that Dr. Winslow had printed up for her. "You should have told me about this the first time I sat down with you." She wanted to knock this woman around.

At that Fenton held up a folder. Hemingway opened it. It was a clipping from the Style section of the *Times*, dated May 13 of last year. It was a photo taken in front of the Met, Dr. Brayton exiting a limousine. In front of him was a family, a little brown-haired boy in their midst. There was another to his left, and two more in the background. At first Hemingway thought you'd have to be blind to miss the similarity between the children but quickly realized that was what these women had ordered—what they had expected: handsome little men to be.

Fenton began to speak, and all the bite , all the swagger, had left her voice. She sounded tired. "I knew right there. At the opera. It was obvious that they were his. All of them. They were in different sections of the hall, so none of the parents caught on. But I didn't get to where I am by believing in coincidences. I called my lawyers that night. I had his samples destroyed and I fired him the next morning. He signed his life away to me; I could have put him in jail for the rest of his life. I honestly didn't know where he had gone—I wanted nothing more to do with the man. This clinic wasn't built on deceit and I find it very sad that this is its undoing. We have helped a lot of people build beautiful families over the years." Hemingway thought for the first time that Fenton sounded sincere. "I didn't know Brayton had killed himself but I can't say that I'm upset by it."

"Can you prove that Brayton is father of these children?"

Fenton nodded. It was a defeated gesture. "I have cheek swabs locked away."

"Whoever is killing these children has known about their connection to one another for a while. Who had access to your files—legally, ethically, physically? How are the files protected? We need to find this guy and we need to do it now. He's going through these children like some kind of a bad dream."

"From a legal standpoint, only those directly involved with a particular patient are supposed to access their files: it's not like a library where browsing and choosing is permitted.

"Actual access to a patient's record is restricted almost exclusively to physicians, health care providers, nurses, and medical assistants. A receptionist would potentially have access to, and occasionally handle, records, but would be technically prohibited from opening them. It's not in the job description. From there it gets worse."

Had she said *worse*?

"The number of people we employ in the billing department, the medical coders, and the records department is very robust. It's part of what makes—*made*—us efficient. These employees have access to a massive amount of information. When they come across any personal information while billing or filing they are supposed to read what was done, code it, bill it, and forget it. Half of the time they don't even read the patient's name, only their patient ID number.

"Our paper charts are kept in both the vault as well as a personal fireproof safe in each doctor's office. They are not left lying around. Our record and chart rooms are locked at all non-practice times but when the office is open, they are unlocked and available to our employees. Our medical records department physically stores all of our records. The runners who work there have total access to all of the patient records but they're not supposed to look inside them.

"Then things get a little more complicated. At the beginning of last year we transferred all of our patient files to electronic medical records—it's a new federal law. Access to electronic medical records is limited to authorized employees who need a password. Doctors and nurses are notorious for logging in and leaving their panels open because logging in and out all day long is annoying.

"There are complex security systems within the EMR networks but the measures are not infallible. There are apps that work from laptops, iPhones, iPads and other mobile devices. If a doctor were logged in and not physically with that device, it would be like leaving the file room open for anyone."

Hemingway thought of the text she had received from Tyler Rochester's phone; whoever was killing these children was comfortable around technology.

Fenton continued: "Anyone working in coding, billing, medical records, or medical transcription would have all the legal rights in the world to be looking into files. It's the cornerstone of their job. But there's a difference between legal and ethical. People check files all the time without any ethical reason whatsoever. Just not my people.

"Federal law mandates that patients' records be made available to them. If Jane Doe demands a copy of her medical record, she gets it. We return files to patients all the time. Once they are printed and released, who knows who has access to them?" She shrugged.

Fenton had just spread suspicion to most of the people in the country.

Her voice box started back up. "But none of this shifts

blame away from Dr. Brayton. We wouldn't be here if he hadn't been such a narcissist. I think what he did was unforgivable."

Hemingway looked down at the photo of William Atchison. "So does the guy who's killing these boys."

HEMINGWAY'S UNCLE had called; her parents would be at the Helmsley in a few hours and her brother was coming in from Los Angeles sometime during the night. Dwight—in his customary role as family mediator—wanted to know if she had a minute to drop by, if only to make an appearance.

She told him that she'd make it as soon as she could.

Papandreou and Lincoln still looked like tired, disheveled extras from a road movie. Phelps, on the other hand, was his same immutable self—hair combed, not so much as a yawn in the past twenty-four hours. Hemingway and Phelps had both managed to steal a shower; a change of clothes and freshly brushed teeth helped, at least until the heat needled back into everything.

"Okay." Hemingway held up her hand, indicating that it was time to focus on the pile of dead children and the collateral murders of five adults. "We need to figure out what's next on the flowchart."

Papandreou finished off a slurp on his drink and shook his head, the cream mustache making him look like that guy from Hall and Oates. "He ain't giving us time to breathe.

The more people he kills, the more people we have to interview. My brain's gonna explode and I haven't had ten
minutes to put any of this together."

Hemingway stared at him for a moment. "You don't get
to stomp your feet and say *not fair*. I'm really sorry that you're
tired and that you still can't see shit, but then I wonder how
the hell you became a detective in the first place. Did you get
anywhere with your interviews?"

Once the photograph of the opera became part of their
armament, Brayton's patients seemed more approachable, less
defensive, as if the police were now in on some grand little
secret that entitled them to civility. There was something
fundamentally wrong with a few of these people; this was
The Stepford Wives in wealthy Technicolor. They were so isolated, so used to things being done as—and when—they saw
fit, the thought of an interloper penetrating their cloistered
little terrarium was frightening.

Tyler Rochester's and Bobby Grant's deaths had made
little impact on many of the parents they had tried to warn;
that had been someone else's child, not *theirs*. Theirs was
special. She had never seen this level of worship to the cult
of children. It was beyond jaw-dropping, it was downright
disturbing.

"These people breathe a different oxygen than I do."
Lincoln pushed a stack of yellow interview jackets across the
table.

"Find anything we can use? Any video, photographs or
news footage? Tweets? Blogs? Cell phone pictures? Smoke
signals? Suicide notes? *Anything at all?*"

"We have the surveillance video of Heidi Morrison's death
from the MTA."

"And?"

"And nothing. She's standing on the platform with her

mother at the Hunter College station. Lots of kids milling about and just as the train pulls in she jumps out onto the track and gets grated by fifty tons of steel." He reached for his laptop, pried the top open, cued up a video, and let it play out.

A section of platform at the Hunter College station came to life. There was no sound.

The platform was molecularly packed, it was clearly rush hour; men in suits, corporate-looking women and schoolchildren made up the bulk of passengers.

"That's her," Lincoln said, indicating a smudge amid a sea of smudges that translated to the top of the girl's head. She was bouncing up and down—dancing. "And that's her mom." He indicated a woman to the smudge's left. Lincoln fast-forwarded through time.

Hemingway's focus stayed locked on the girl, now dancing in a manic pogo as the film played at thirty times normal speed.

The pulsing crowd slowed as Lincoln cued it up. The girl, still dancing, slowed down as well.

Interchangeable schoolboys ran through the frame, like fighter pilots dodging flak. An old lady eased her way from screen left to screen right, trying to get close to the tracks. A cop walked by. An old man with an umbrella came into the frame and leaned against a beam. Someone dropped a cup of coffee. Hemingway kept her focus on the girl.

For some reason the crowd moved to the left, like a flock of birds in flight, then back right as the lights of the approaching train became visible at screen left. People moved by her. Kids ran behind and around her. The old lady tried to strong-arm her way to the front of the queue.

All of a sudden the girl lurched forward, off the platform.

And the train rolled through.

"Rewind that."

Lincoln shrugged. "It won't do any good. Me and Nick watched it fifty freakin' times. She just flies off the platform like she's magnetic. No one pushed her. No one touched her."

"Just rewind it."

She watched it a few times and Lincoln was right: there was nothing to see. One minute the child was there, bopping up and down, the next she was under the train.

Lincoln reached over and tapped the files. "In every single instance we couldn't find a reason to be suspicious."

"Except?"

"Except those numbers don't make any kind of sense in the real world. A one hundred percent accidental mortality rate for eight ten-year-old wealthy American girls in one summer doesn't add up."

Hemingway stared at her notes. All they really had were names and times of death and—

Hemingway reached over for the photograph of the party that Dr. Winslow had given her. She stared at it for a second, then reached for her notebook. "Here we go. May twelfth last year. *Six o'clock at the Metropolitan Opera House at Lincoln Center. Evening dress. Cocktails followed by dinner and music. RSVP by April 29th.*"

She wrote *May 12* down at the top of the page, above the dates column. The party was held on May the twelfth."

"And?" Lincoln said, irritated.

"And those girls started dying exactly two weeks to the day later." She underlined the dates, one at a time. "It started with the party. It had to. It's someone who was there."

||| EIGHTY-THREE

IT WAS here somewhere.

But where—*exactly*—was here?

A room full of boxes—everything from protocols to autopsy reports, to the medical examiner's notes and crime-scene photographs, the FBI's CODIS returns and stacks of interview folders and known associates of everyone concerned.

Hemingway knew that it would come at them out of the blue. A criminal record. A text or an e-mail or a changed name. A parking ticket. A size ten or ten and a half leather-soled shoe that lit up in the lab. Someone with a faulty fuse box, an axe to grind, a debt to collect. Someone who listened to their Rice Krispies. Or God.

The news battalion camped across the street had fewer answers than the police did. They had thrown around so many bizarre scenarios that even the late-night shortwave conspiracy nuts thought they had lost their minds. The talking heads were calling it everything from payback for Area 51 experiments to biblical justice against mad science, and no one seemed to think his chatter was the least bit unethical.

The newspeople had become a pack of braying animals, and Hemingway wondered who would start the grassroots riot that was surely coming—it would start when someone finally stood up and made the ghost of the great Joseph N. Welch proud. An equivalent of, "I'm mad as hell and I'm not going to take this anymore!" might just do it.

Christ, she was tired. And amazed at the crap swirling around in her head. She needed to go home to get some sleep. Maybe talk to Daniel. And her folks. It was time for a little of the damage control Uncle Dwight had mentioned.

But first there was the case.

Out there, somewhere, was a very smart man with a saw who enjoyed doing terrible things to little boys.

In absolute terms, that was the effect, not the cause.

The cause was something much older—some deep childhood trauma that had melted the insulation off the wire. Bad home. Bad parents. No home. No parents. Evil done and evil now revisited. Somehow, doing those terrible things made him feel—*better* wasn't exactly the word; *less anxious* was probably closer to the truth. And there was a fantasy at play that she didn't know, couldn't understand. Some specific pathology that internally justified these monstrous acts. Some basic belief that she couldn't see but desperately needed to.

These boys were being destroyed by him.

Wrong—that was passive voice.

He destroyed them.

Active. And accurate.

There was planning behind it all. He had murdered eight girls on a clock that the Swiss could nail their train schedule to. And no one had noticed any of it happening. From a certain perspective, the whole thing tasted of black magic.

Had he been at the opera that night? Or was it some

random nut who had glommed on to some insane fantasy that involved cutting up these boys? It wasn't aliens or Jesus and it wouldn't turn out to be anyone who believed in those things; there was too much critical thinking in this for it to be someone who believed that the Force existed or Jonah had actually lived in the belly of a whale. There was too much creativity at work for it to be someone of such limited vision.

Lincoln and Papandreou were at the computer lab picking up the lists of family, friends, business associates, practitioners, employees, tradespeople, neighbors, and anyone else remotely acquainted with the victims and their parents. They would also have the same lists from fifty-one of the fifty-nine former patients of Drs. Brayton and Selmer who had been interviewed in the past day and a half. The computers would cross-reference the lists, narrowing their search. Then they would weed out the natural happenstance of six degrees of Kevin Bacon and find the real common link—some little piece of connecting tissue that would set the whole thing on fire.

Hemingway had dealt with dozens of families who had lost fathers and mothers and children to violent crimes over the years. When she took the academic exercise one step further, the murder of her own baby sister all those years ago had set her on this path; her own defining genesis had come out of a death. She remembered reading an old Russian proverb that said a tree can't grow healthy if the roots are sick.

And it was hard to get sicker than a nobody killing your baby sister for no other reason than it seemed like a good idea.

And now Amy was gone. She'd have to look her parents in the eyes knowing that it was her fault. Amy had been murdered because the killer had confused her with her sister. Which was understandable; when they were together, people often thought they were twins. Or had. Past tense again.

She needed to give the old power plant a rest; it was time for sleep.

Phelps came in with a pair of paper bags and held them up. "Coffee, shumai—the pink ones, right?—and sweet and sour soup. Breakfast, lunch, and supper all rolled into one."

She pulled her hand off of her stomach, pushed her chair back, and stood up. "I should marry you, Jon."

"I snore and watch fishing shows. It would get old real fast."

She smiled and it felt like it took all of her energy. "That's okay, I shoot people and never come home." And she realized that had sounded a little bitter.

As she took a Styrofoam cup from his hand she knew that she still had a big decision to make, one that would either allow or prohibit her intake of coffee—her favorite food group. And she'd have to make it soon, because there were tipping points for these things. There was a difference between unsure and irresponsible.

She stirred in a sugar. "What do you think makes this guy tick, Jon?"

"It's not ritualistic but it has purpose."

Hemingway thought about William Atchison. What had been done to him. "What kind of a purpose could drive a human being to do this? He's not angry, he's too controlled for that. He knows the difference between right and wrong, so he's not crazy. He sends me a text message, so he's confident. He knows we're coming for him, and he's hasn't run. So what could be driving this guy?"

Phelps pulled a coffee out of the bag and peeled the lid off. He raised it to his mouth and paused, staring at her above the rim of the Styrofoam cup for a few seconds. "What's the best motivator there is?"

And it hit her.

"*Fear,*" she said.

┃┃┃ EIGHTY-FOUR

HIS FATHER was waiting for him in the kitchen when he got home. He didn't look angry but he did look like something was wrong. Which was never a good thing.

Benjamin hoped it wasn't something he had done.

He came in, put his knapsack down on the bench by the back door, and took off his jacket. His father was sitting at the island with a Scotch in his hand, the kind he only took out when he was having one of his "moods." And lately, his moods were getting closer and closer together, as if he were plugged into a diminishing timer.

Benjamin thought of an innocuous greeting, something that wouldn't tip the scales one way or another. "Hello, Father."

His father looked down at him and his eyes had that faraway look that Benjamin didn't like. "Son. I need to talk to you."

He didn't sound angry, which was a good sign. But that distant stare wasn't going anywhere.

His father stood up from the island and he wobbled a bit.

Benjamin went to the sink and washed his hands, then

he dried them. He tried to act casual, as if nothing were wrong. But there was plenty wrong—he could tell. His stomach started to rock back and forth, something it always did before the bad things started to happen.

Benjamin stared up at his father, his hands clasped in front of him, and nodded. "Did I do something wrong, Father? Did my SAT scores come back?"

"What? No, son. No. Not at all." His father looked puzzled for a moment, then angry. "The police came by today. They wanted to talk to me."

Benjamin felt his legs go cold. He hadn't told anyone. Not a soul. He always kept the promises he made to his father. That was the Golden Rule: *Keep the secret.*

His father came forward and touched his cheek. Then he helped him climb up onto the island, on the cold stone by the sink.

He leaned in and whispered in Benjamin's ear. "They say you might be in danger. They said that you should be careful."

Benjamin didn't like hearing this. Not one little bit. "Ca-careful of what, Father?"

"Someone bad, son."

This sounded like a trick, so he chose the best answer he could; he was adept at making fast decisions. "I don't know anyone bad."

At that his father smiled and he knew he had said the right thing. "I know that, son. But there's a bad man out there, and he's hurting boys and they came by to warn me. I don't want to worry you—because there is nothing to worry about—but I wanted to tell you, just in case they ask. You tell them I told you, okay?"

Benjamin nodded because he knew that had been another trick question. "Yes, sir."

"The police don't know what they're talking about. You'll

be fine. After school's over next week we'll take a vacation. Maybe go back to Greece like last year—you'd like that, wouldn't you?"

Benjamin had liked Greece. And there were plenty of things that had occupied his father's time, lots of birds. "Of course."

For a second his father's focus seemed to go away, then snapped back like an elastic band. "Boys have been taken, Benjamin. When he's finished hurting them, he dumps them in the river."

"Why does he take them?"

"Because he's unhappy, son." At that his father looked down, at the floor. "You haven't spoken to anyone, have you? About . . ." he looked up at his son ". . . me?"

At that the needles in Benjamin's legs exploded and he thought he might pee himself. "Of course not, Father."

But his father did not look convinced. "This man has taken some of the boys we met at the opera last year."

"They seemed like a nice bunch of kids. Most of them, anyway. I didn't like Miles Morgan but I suppose he can't help himself. Not everyone can be like me."

His father smiled at that. "Son, you are singularly unique. I've always told you that. There's no one remotely like you out there." His father smiled, then kissed him on the cheek. "My little genius. Now go wash up."

At that his stomach started swinging again. "Yes, sir."

"And don't forget to wash your peepee."

||| EIGHTY-FIVE

THE PRESS were going absofuckinglutely apeshit. Every news outlet on the East Coast, from the little local cable stations that had avoided being plowed over by the Internet to the big boys who owned the airwaves from Chicago to Manhattan, were stationed in front of the precinct. The talking heads wanted justice; they wanted answers; they wanted a suspect; they wanted details. But mostly, they just wanted ratings.

Hemingway was in that place of uncomfortable limbo located behind the podium and in front of the bright lights. The heat had redlined and most of the newspeople looked like they were about to blow their radiators. Dennet thoroughly believed that with her sister's name indelibly recorded on the victim list, the reporters would grant her a degree of slack. Hemingway wondered if he really believed that or if it was just a clumsy attempt to blindside her; she knew the reporters would go after her like dingoes playing with a honey-covered baby.

Phelps stood behind to her right and she could feel his presence, a perfect mixture of sentinel, moral support, and guardian angel. She couldn't keep her eyes from dancing around the crowd—she was too tired to fight instinct—and she wouldn't be surprised if *he* was here in the room with her. It seemed like the kind of thing he might do.

She ran through the developments in the case and now that all of the relatives were notified she had been instructed to use names. Which meant that more newspeople were camped out on the sidewalk in front of the Rochesters, Grants, and the rest of the families—more bad luck they didn't need.

Hemingway recapped the timeline, starting with Tyler Rochester's disappearance. Trevor Deacon was added to the mix. She discussed where the bodies had been discovered. Confirmed their grievous injuries but left out lurid details. She didn't connect any of the dots for them. She didn't lead them through Deacon's involvement or tell them that the boys were half brothers. She neither confirmed nor denied the Park Avenue Clinic's position within the ongoing investigation. And she paused before reading her sister's name off of the list.

"Any questions?"

A forest of hands flicked toward the heavens.

At this point she reminded herself to keep the answers simple, monosyllabic if possible; the press conference would be followed with a brief and bloody biography of Detective First Grade Alexandra Hemingway and the armchair therapy would begin. Maybe they'd get someone like that Harvard psychiatrist Dr. Justin Frank to discuss her unaddressed rage and daddy issues. What pissed her off was that he'd probably be right.

"Yes?" she said, pointing at a reporter from ABC. She didn't really want questions—what she wanted was to fire a couple of rounds over the crowd and head for her Suburban.

"Are you certain that your sister's death is, in fact, part of the current spree of killings that you are investigating? Is there a chance that it is somehow payback for your having killed Irish mobster David Shea?"

The bitch had hit that one out of the park. No warm-up. No easing into it. Bang, straight into the cheap seats. "My killing of Shea was in self-defense. We fought. He lost. That's all. My sister's death is linked to the serial murderer we are now hunting."

A hand to her left—the *New York Daily News*.

She took it.

"Detective Hemingway, don't you feel that your close relation to the killer's last victim hinders your ability to stay objective?"

Hemingway sensed Phelps's presence behind her, ready to rip the microphones out by the roots and use them on the reporters like suppositories. She leaned forward, the mic an inch from her mouth, and clearly said, "No." *Good night and go fuck yourself.*

She nodded at a seasoned reporter from the *New York Times.*

"How many suspects do you have right now? And what do you feel the timeline will be on an arrest?"

The reporter was smart, a better caste of journalist when compared to most of the people lining the sidewalk in front of her. But that first question wasn't really a question, he knew that they didn't have a suspect; if they did, they would have released his name—or at least details about his arrest—by now. It forced her to admit that they were still paddling in a river of shit and the exercise had been geared to put her on the defensive. "As you know, we have not yet released the name of a suspect." *Because we don't have one.* "And as to the second question, the mountain of information we are carefully and methodically analyzing and cataloging is staggering. I can't give you a timeline because anything I say could be outdated in a few minutes or even a few seconds. I can promise that I'll be standing up here in the not-too-distant future giving you whoever is responsible for these deaths."

"That sounds like you have someone in mind."

No, it sounds like I wish I had someone in mind. "Like I said, I promise that not too long from now, we'll be having a much less one-sided conversation." She was pleased at how she had handled that.

Jennifer Krantz-Domingo-Gomez was in the front, her hand politely raised, no malice in her face. Hemingway knew the woman casually and she took a chance. "Yes, Jen."

Gomez, a little woman with a face like a candy you wanted to unwrap, smiled. "Have you collected any DNA or other forensic evidence during the investigation?"

Gomez just got on her Christmas list with that softball. "The medical examiner's office has handled itself with the usual proficiency and professionalism we have come to depend on. I can comfortably say that besides being in constant rotation with the FBI's CODIS program at Quantico, our own labs have done an exceptional job in processing evidence."

Her peripheral vision picked up movement to her left. "Yes, Pete," she said.

"Besides the FBI and their CODIS program, have you enlisted the help of outside agencies—on either a state or federal level? And if not, at what point in the investigation would you consider seeking their assistance?"

Shit. "The NYPD has the necessary resources and skill to deal with this. We will be making an arrest on this investigation and we will be making it as soon as humanly possible—without the help of the BCI or the FBI. If their presence would advance the investigation, they'd be here by now."

Sashi Numrta from *People* snapped her fingers. Without thinking about the action, Hemingway nodded at her.

The reporter blinked her eyes and turned on the charm. "Detective Hemingway, do you understand the concerns some have expressed over your handling of such a high-profile case when the shooting of David Shea is still fresh in everyone's mind? Are you uncomfortable with this or—?"

"No, I don't understand the concerns. I am a valuable asset to this force. Every single inquiry into the Shea incident found me faultless. Or maybe you haven't seen the footage."

Even the reporters laughed at that one—Numrta had hosted a miniseries on the shooting and those unbelievably long thirty-eight seconds of video had been played three dozen times over three nights. She was more than familiar with the video—she was probably the world's expert.

The only thing Hemingway remembered about that brief snippet of time was the noise—the sound of her heart thundering in her skull and the punch of gunfire. She remembered walking out into the sunshine and sitting down and not being able to breathe or scream and then passing out. "So I think that personal attacks and libelous accusations should be avoided."

"I wasn't accusing—"

"Next question," Hemingway said, cutting her off and nodding at another reporter.

"Detective Hemingway, as a police officer who makes roughly seventy-one thousand dollars a year, how is it possible that you own a building valued at over five and a half million dollars?"

"My finances are not up for discussion. I file my taxes every year on time and have a private firm handle the paperwork for me."

"I wasn't suggesting that your money is in any way ill-gotten—"

Had he said *ill-gotten*? What was this, Elizabethan England?

"—I thought that listeners would find it interesting that a woman who comes from such a wealthy background as yourself would make the decision to become a police officer."

Sonofabitch. He knew the story. Everyone knew the story. It had come out after Shea, when the media had taken her life apart with a scalpel, layer by layer. Maybe they were trying to convince the viewers that a real fucked-up human being was at the center of this story; nothing sells good television like the promise of weakness. "Do you have any questions about the investigation?"

The reporter shifted his feet and a few snickers echoed in the crowd.

"Next," she said.

A woman stepped forward, her pen pointed at Hemingway. "Detective Hemingway, with this many people dead in such a short period of time and no suspect in custody, are you worried about the possible damage to your career?"

At that Hemingway realized that they just wanted to film her losing her shit in time for the evening cycle. "To be honest, unlike yourself, I don't care about the ratings, I care about results. And if you'll excuse me, I have somewhere more productive to be."

EIGHTY-SIX

PHELPS RODE up in the elevator with her, his presence making her feel a little less vulnerable in what she knew was going to be an unpleasant reunion. She had gone over this meeting from every conceivable tactical angle and no matter how she approached it, she knew she'd walk away from this feeling worse than she already did.

"You'll do okay," Phelps said, his voice a full octave below the pitch of a diesel engine.

"That's one way to look at it." The reporters had acted like the mean kids from Willy Wonka, she hadn't talked to Daniel all day, and she was about to be ostracized from her family. She shrugged.

"Family's family," the big man said.

"You come from different people than I do, Jon." He rarely spoke of his family, but when he did, it was with fondness.

Phelps seemed to mull the statement over for a few nods of his head. "Yeah, I do. My old man chased work all over the place so he could feed us, dragging the family across the country. My mom looked forward to spending her golden years doing all the things he promised her she'd do before they reached the end of the rainbow. But on the day they handed him his gold watch he crawled into bed and stayed there, sleeping, being afraid and depressed. That whole time my mother sat downstairs with her suitcase packed, waiting to go on a safari she'd wanted her whole life. Six years later he had a heart attack and two weeks after that my mother bought herself a seniors group ticket to see Kenya, a place she had always dreamt of visiting with her husband. She had a stroke while packing her suitcase and died with her head on the carpet. She never got to see Africa. Everybody's broken, Hemi."

"I'm just not looking forward to it."

At that he just shrugged. "Ninety percent of the shit we worry about never comes true. The other ten percent? Fugged-aboudit."

She had never been tight with Amy, not in all the years they had spent as children at home, not through primary or high school, and by the time they had both shipped off to prep schools on opposite sides of the country the wedge had been so firmly entrenched in the real estate between them that it could never be mended. They saw one another at family gatherings and every couple of years Amy would call, usually when she was in the bag, under the pretense of patching things up. But in all those years they never got to the patching things up portion of the program. Amy usually slipped into some alcohol-fueled diatribe about how their parents had always paid more attention to Allie, and the conversation would usually go into a flat spin punctuated by the sound of a dial tone.

Amy had gone to therapy for a while but eventually, like every other time in her life when forced to take responsibility for her actions, she had simply walked away from the process. The unhappy girl burgeoned into someone whose insides were ugly and broken. And of course it was never her fault.

Their mother had always sided with Amy, maybe because she had recognized some of her own behavior and felt a need to justify it. And Hemingway believed that her father had as well. It all came down to Amy's being more fragile; she needed them to hold her hand through life. Eventually she had done well on paper—husband, children, nice house in the country and a respectable handicap at the golf club. But even with all the propping up, her life had never really gelled, and everyone shared the unspoken expectation that one day it would all just implode.

No one had thought she'd have her throat cut after being mistaken for her sister.

Hemingway remembered how she had collapsed in the living room and howled like a gored beast when Mank had been murdered. And although there were a lot of emotions at play here—anger, disbelief, pride, vengeance, rage—she would not—could not—let loss factor into it. Not yet. Of course, her parents would translate that into noncaring.

The elevator stopped and the bell pinged. Phelps stepped out and put his hand on the door to keep it from closing. "You coming?"

A man sat on a chair in the corner, facing the elevator doors, the staircase beyond. When Phelps and Hemingway stepped out, he stood up. There was a folded newspaper in his hand that looked like it had weight to it.

He was thin, Japanese, and wore a well-tailored suit and an open-collared shirt. As they walked over to him, he placed the paper down on the seat. There was the grip of an automatic in the folds of the newsprint.

He bowed, then extended his hand. "Alexandra, you have

my deepest sympathies. I am terribly sorry about your sister."
His English was perfect.

"Thank you, Mr. Ken. You know my partner, Detective Jon Phelps?"

Mr. Ken bowed a second time, and the ink under his collar flashed against the white fabric—irezumi ink; old time yakuza war paint. He had been a fixture in the family since before she had been born, working first for her grandfather, now for Uncle Dwight.

He gestured toward the door to the suite. "Your parents are expecting you." He dismissed them with a bow and went back to cradling his newspaper and watching the elevator and stairwell.

Hemingway paused at the door. "You sure you want to do this with me?"

"It's time you figured out I'll follow you anywhere."

She knocked.

Uncle Dwight answered the door. His tie was loose and he had a Scotch in his hand. He smiled when he saw her. "Allie, how are you?" He pulled her into his arms, holding the glass away from her shoulder.

She hugged him back and realized that the last time she had seen him felt like a thousand years ago. She could hear conversation off in the suite, some music, the clink of utensils on porcelain. The smell of flowers was almost overwhelming.

"You remember my partner, Jon Phelps."

The two men shook hands and Dwight kicked in with his considerable social skills. "Detective Phelps, thank you for coming. This is all informal, just a little get-together for family and close friends and as my niece's partner, you qualify as both."

"Mr. Ken is doing a nice job of intimidating people out there."

Dwight smiled at that. "He has that effect, yes." Then

Dwight grabbed her by the hand and led her off into the suite. "Your parents are in here," he said softly, "and they're looking forward to seeing you."

She knew Dwight, the family mediator, and figured that he was lying to her; he had probably said the same thing to them.

"Where's Miles?"

"He's on his way in from the country—I sent the jet. He should be here in an hour."

"Give him my best," she said, then spotted her father by the window, a whiskey tumbler in his hand, looking as if he had stepped out of a Ralph Lauren ad. Her mother was sitting in a silk wingback, two of her shopping friends by her side. A barman stood in the corner, a selection of crystal, ice, and booze out on a cart. A few other people stood around, talking, drinking, and looking like they were discussing tax loopholes. Conversation skidded to a stop.

Her father saw her and his face changed from a waxy disinterest to a smile. He came over and gave her a hug. He smelled as good as he looked. "Thank you," he whispered in her ear. "I was worried that you wouldn't come."

"She was my sister, Dad, and regard—"

"Because of your job," he said, cutting her off. "I know you're busy, Allie."

And with that she realized that she had been wrong—that she actually liked it when he called her that.

They unclenched and her father extended a hand to her partner. "Detective Phelps, thank you for escorting my daughter." They had met a few times over the years.

Phelps shook his hand and said something about it not being a problem.

The three of them went over to her mother. She was elegant and trim and her hand glittered with a fistful of diamonds.

Her pupils looked like pinpricks and her eyes could barely focus. "Hello, Allie. How nice of you to make the time."

There had always been tension between them and Hemingway assumed it had to do with her complete rejection of the country club friends, the shopping, and the men who looked like Brooks Brothers mannequins—all the keystones in her mother's soulless universe.

Hemingway ignored the jab and gave her mother a hug. "Hello, Mother. You remember my partner, Detective Jon Phelps."

Her mother looked Phelps over with the exaggerated body language of a drunk trying to look sober. "That's quite the suit, Detective," she said.

Phelps smiled, took her hand, shook it, and said, "Your daughter picked it out for me." Then he excused himself, probably to hunt down a club soda.

Hemingway made the rounds, shaking hands, air-kissing, and telling everyone that she wished she was seeing them under better circumstances. When she was finished, her father led her back to the front room and sat her down on one of the sofas.

"Graham's flying in from L.A. in a few hours, I know he'd love to see you."

She nodded but didn't say much.

"And Patrick's in a suite downstairs. He's pretty beat up about this." Patrick was Amy's husband. He wasn't a bad guy but there never seemed to be much to him and Hemingway felt that if he turned sideways, he'd disappear altogether. Had Amy said anything to their parents about the breakup? Had it been a real split or just another plea for attention? She was always breaking up with him.

Hemingway felt petty thinking about these things; it was time to move on.

Her father leaned in and put a hand on her shoulder. "How are you?"

"Don't worry about me. How's Mom?"

Her father shook his head. "No, Allie, I want to talk about *you*. How is Daniel? How is being a police officer?" He paused, and looked into her eyes. "Are you happy?"

"Dad, you have your hands full here. And I can't even begin to think about Amy. I'm tired and I need some sleep and—"

He cut her off. "And you are going to talk to me. Because life is short and I won't let you be a stranger anymore. I thought, and I suppose *still think*, that there's a different life waiting for you out there. One where you don't have to worry about—" He stopped cold and his eyes dropped to his drink for a second. "Having your throat cut when you answer the door."

She held up her hand. "I do this because it's what I was built to do. Can you imagine me sitting in Uncle Dwight's practice? Or in one of your companies? They'd laugh me out of the boardroom."

He cupped both her hands in his. "No, they wouldn't. They'd respect you because you are not a woman people can ignore. You are a good detective because that's what you've decided to be. If you decided to be a horse breeder or a rally driver or an astronaut, you'd be the best there is, because that's who you are."

She pulled her hands out of his. "I like what I do." But that wasn't entirely correct. There were plenty of negatives that went with the job. More than she could count if she bothered to think about it.

"But it's not good for you."

"This is why we don't talk."

And at that his face changed. "When Claire disappeared, I promised myself that I'd be there for you, take care of all of you. But I can't do that, I can't be everywhere all the time.

And what happened to Amy . . ." He stopped, and his lip trembled for a second, but he was able to push it back into himself. "What happened to Amy today was supposed to happen to you. Someone was out to hurt *you*, and I can't take that. I just want you to consider doing something else." He leaned over and kissed her on the cheek. "And if you can't consider doing something else, I want you to sit down with me and explain why you do this. Is that fair?"

She didn't know how to react to this. "Sure."

"Look, I know I don't say much, but if you solve every single murder of your career, it's not going to bring Claire back. Bad things happen and they're not your fault."

What about Amy's death? she wanted to ask. "Let me put this case to bed and we'll talk. If you want, we can take a vacation."

At that her father smiled. "Deal. But I pay. And we go somewhere nice. Maybe France. We can tour Burgundy in the fall, drink some wine, get to know one another."

Pregnant women don't drink wine. "France? That sounds great, Dad."

Someone back in the living room brayed with laughter and her father's eyes glanced over her shoulder. "I have to go back to those people and you have to get back to work. Or at least get some rest—you look tired. Beautiful, but tired." He leaned forward and kissed her again. "Please be careful."

She felt tears start with that one but held them off. "I'm good at what I do."

"So is this guy you're hunting." Her father stood up and pulled her to her feet. "Don't forget that."

As the elevator doors slid closed, Mr. Ken waved a good-bye, the newspaper still folded in his hand. As the car dropped into the shaft, Phelps said, "I don't like that guy."

At that, Hemingway smiled. "You're not supposed to."

THE POLICE tape was gone and the trauma-scene unit had cleaned up. Two uniformed cops sat in a cruiser out front—they'd be there until the case was over. Hemingway walked up to the car and leaned in the open window. She recognized the two officers from the precinct.

"Koombs, Dorsett. You can go home now."

Koombs, a little guy with big ears, shook his head. "Sorry, Detective. We got orders from Phelps. We are on you until you collar this guy."

Hemingway didn't like this—they would not have done this if she had been a man. "I'm lead detective on the case—I outweigh Phelps. Fuck off."

Koombs shrugged helplessly. "I can't."

"I'll call Dennet and have him pull you."

At that Koombs smiled, reached into his pocket. "Detective Phelps said you'd say that." He pulled out a folded sheet of precinct stationery and handed it over.

Hemingway opened it and read the short note. It was an order from Dennet for Koombs and Dorsett to watch over her residence until reassigned.

"Shit," she said.

"Sorry, Detective. Nothing personal."

She stood up and took in a deep breath, filling her chest and expanding her ribs. She looked up the street, then down, toward the water. It was empty. The guy wouldn't come after her again.

When she looked back at Koombs he was staring at her chest, grinning, those too-big ears lifted with his smile.

"Jesus," she said, and turned to leave. "Just don't get killed. I have that effect on the people around me."

"Phelps told us that, too," Koombs said.

The staircase was dark and she stood there on the threshold for a moment, trying to get her bearings. For the first time, the realization that her sister had been murdered came at her in a blast of air-conditioning that carried the smell of disinfectant.

As a precaution she went through all of the rooms in the apartment. Daniel was asleep in their bed, or at least pretending to be, his back to her.

She stood in front of the fridge for a few minutes, trying to decide if she was hungry. She settled on a glass of milk and a banana.

A new camera bag lay on the table, the tags clipped off, lenses and camera bodies halfheartedly jammed inside. She found Daniel's old bag in the garbage, the strap stained with a dark swatch of her sister's blood.

How had an evening at the opera mushroomed into a plague of visits by the Angel of Death? First the girls. Then the brown-eyed handsome boys started washing through Little Hell Gate. The Grant boy's driver. Deacon. Dr. Selmer. Mrs. Atchison. Amy.

But that's how things went: one minute all was well in the kingdom, the next fire rained down from the sky. That last night she took that walk with Mank through the East Side had been good, maybe the best night they ever had. A few short hours later it was blown away when Shea and Nicky had stepped from the shadows. The world didn't care about your plans because it was too busy turning. And the machinery seemed to be greased with blood.

She walked over to the window and took a sip of the ice-cold milk. She stared out at the street, at the cop car parked in front of her door, at the weird light on the asphalt. She could handle that it was not safe out there. It was, in fact, one of the few basic beliefs she held—it had taken hold the moment Claire had disappeared. But she couldn't handle that with a child. No how. No way.

So why did she even fantasize that she could have a baby? Maybe she'd get lucky, do something right, and her child would think of life as a gift, not a burden. But would that lessen her load? Would that help to quell the anxiety every time her child was out of her sight? What would happen if the kid was late coming home? Or at a sleepover? At school? She wasn't sure she could handle that. Day in, day out, year after year after year. You never stopped worrying about your kids, her father's talk was proof positive of that. Here she was, thirty-seven, and he still worried about her. And her particular background and pathology pretty much guaranteed that she'd never be at ease as a parent. Was the whole exercise worth it? She took a bite of the banana and turned away from the window.

Tomorrow promised to be worse than today; the final athletic day for sixty-two of the city's private boys' schools, a year-end showdown to weed out the trophy takers from the participation ribbon receivers. The buses would carry the boys from their various institutions to Randall's Island, the isolated chunk of real estate that did duty as recreational space for many of the city's schools. Dennet's bid to shut the event down had been quashed by the powers that be and Hemingway had resolved herself to a day of fruitless paranoia.

Sixty-two schools translated to a staggering eighty-nine hundred students; nine hundred and four who fell into the right age group; forty-one who shared a father. Forget ulcers, this kind of stress could cause cancer.

There was a lot that could go wrong, a lot that would be out of her hands, and again she wondered if she was being set up to take the fall. And with the paranoia came the realization that she needed some sleep. After a little food, she told herself.

She put the milk and banana down on the coffee table, sat down on the sofa, and fell asleep.

||| EIGHTY-EIGHT

PHELPS PICKED her up at 5 a.m., honking loudly and frightening the two patrolmen still out front. He brought coffee and bagels and drove slowly while she went through the process of waking up, bolstering her progress with slurps of caffeine.

Daylight was slowly seeping into the sky and the city was still magically silent except for early-morning delivery trucks. Phelps cut through the quiet streets toward Central Park. After crossing on 79th, he continued west until they found an on-ramp for the FDR.

"Sleep okay?" Phelps asked after she had absorbed a little of the coffee.

She thought about it. "Sat down on the sofa, and that's all I remember. You?"

"Me and Maggie are sleeping in the basement—much cooler than the rest of that place."

"Why don't you get an air conditioner, Jon?"

"Wife says it's cold enough all winter." He shrugged. "She's right."

She raised the coffee to her lips to take another sip and it hit her. "Jon, pull over!"

"There's no shoulder."

"Pull over. Now!"

Phelps flashed the lights and swung over to the rightmost lane. He glanced in the mirror and stopped the car. "What the fu—?"

Before the car came to a stop, Hemingway shoved the door open, stuck her head out, and threw up. Her stomach clenched a few times, forcing the coffee and bagel out between gasps for breath.

Then, as quickly as it came, it was over.

She pulled her head back inside, closed the door, and wiped her mouth with a napkin from the bagel bag. "This girly stuff sucks, Jon."

He looked at her, then down at the hand held protectively across her stomach. "I'm sure it does," he said, and checked his mirrors before he pulled back into traffic.

||| EIGHTY-NINE

SITUATED IN the East River, Randall's Island proper is separated from Queens by Hell Gate, and from the Bronx by Bronx Kill. Though technically deeded as part of Manhattan, it is separated from the city by the Harlem River and runs from roughly 100th to 127th Street.

Home to the New York City Fire Department's training facility, the New York City Department of Environmental Protection's wastewater treatment plant, the seventeen-floor Manhattan Psychiatric Center, a vast patchwork of sports fields and parkland, and roughly fifteen hundred full-time residents, Randall's Island was also one of the most coveted chunks of real estate in the Northeast. Nature lovers could visit the salt marshes and freshwater wetlands on either side of Little Hell Gate Inlet, and the sports minded could hit the batting cages or driving range.

Under the watchful eye of the Randall's Island Park Alliance, a vast chunk of the island's space had been allocated for sports and recreational purposes: there were sixty-three soccer, softball, baseball, field hockey, football and lacrosse fields; twenty tennis courts; and five miles of waterfront pathways. Major track-and-field events could be hosted at Icahn Stadium, a state-of-the-art facility that seated five thousand spectators.

Besides catering to the area's public schools, the island's recreational facilities also played host to the physical education programs of many of the approximately nine hundred private schools in the area. Schoolchildren can be found all over the island every day of the week.

———

As Phelps took the car off the Robert F. Kennedy Bridge and swung down onto Randall's Island, Hemingway marveled at the size of the place. She had paddled its shores when navigating her kayak past Little Hell Gate, and even visited it on a few occasions, but she had never looked at it as a reserve to hunt children. This morning it looked as large as a continent.

Phelps followed the Darth Vader instructions dictated by the GPS, driving past the psychiatric center and then swinging around to the tip of the island where a battery of police cars were ready for the day's task of keeping the children safe.

Lincoln and Papandreou were already there with the two dozen cruisers and an army of uniformed policemen, most drinking coffee. A few stood off from the crowd, smoking in little groups. Phelps parked off to the side and as Hemingway got out, more cars pulled up behind them.

The plan had come from her office and they had thrown it by both the State Association of Independent Schools, which oversaw the private schools, and the New York City Department of Education, which controlled the public schools—both bodies had rubber-stamped the idea of a police presence for the last games day of the year.

The plan was simple: there was one uniformed police officer assigned as security liaison to each school and it was their job to check the roster of each bus that left for Randall's Island; that same officer would ride with the last bus to the island and check return attendance at the end of the day when everyone packed up to head home. The math worked out to roughly one officer per seventy-five students plus the hundred extra policemen that would be manning crosswalks, parking lots, paths, the edge of wooded areas, bathrooms, on-ramps, off-ramps, and the island side of the footbridge that connected with Manhattan at 103rd Street.

But the real emphasis—the one Hemingway had tried to keep under the radar—was on the forty-one of Dr. Brayton's children who would be on the island today. Each had an officer assigned as a shadow—some uniformed, some plain-clothes. Hemingway had made the call, stressing that not focusing on these specific children was tantamount to negligence. This translated to forty-one shadows mixed in with the general population of police officers.

Along with the new day had come more heat. Papandreou wore a police T-shirt and jeans with white leather sneakers, Lincoln wore chinos and a Hawaiian shirt, and it was hard to decide who looked like more of a stereotype.

Phelps was in one of his many gray suits, this one a light summer wool. As usual he looked rested and ready. Hemingway had opted for jeans, engineer boots, and a cotton blouse. She couldn't remember when she had last worn girl shoes. Her badge hung from her neck on a beaded chain and her revolver was on her belt. She started to do the rounds.

She didn't like that she didn't recognize many of the cops who had pulled duty; the business of policing ran on respect and confidence, two things that were hard to come by when you hadn't worked with a person before. But she went through the group, introducing herself and trying to become familiar with as many as possible.

After half an hour of introductions, small talk, and more coffee, she got up on the gate of her Suburban. She went over handheld channels, protocol, and warnings. Then she went over the e-mail that outlined the parameters of their duties here.

By the time the coffee was gone, the sea of uniformed policemen and policewomen knew what was expected of them, but not what to look for; it was the old "anything out of the ordinary directive," which in New York City had a completely different set of boundaries than any other place on the planet. From the southwest corner of the island they dispersed to points northeast, heading out on foot, bicycle, golf cart, and car.

The buses started arriving around eight-thirty, filled with cheering bouncy children excited that summer vacation was almost here. Hemingway and Phelps made the rounds to the parking lots allocated to busses, intermittently checking attendance with the ride-along officers and making sure that the chaperones were up to speed.

Coaches and gym teachers lugged mesh bags of soccer balls, duffels of lacrosse sticks and baseball bats, and endless pieces of protective equipment. Everyone carried a water bottle. And the kids—from the grade school children to the high school seniors—bopped around with the boundless enthusiasm of youth.

After an hour of making the rounds, verifying that all was well, she headed back to the Suburban. They had a busy roster again today, and she probably wouldn't sleep for another thirty hours. Who said it was lonely at the top?

Hemingway saw Phelps moseying between two of the soccer fields on the way back to the SUV. He had a pair of old Wayfarers on and she wondered if he realized that fashion had come full circle and he was a style icon among the younger cops in the precinct; some of them sported thin ties and a flat top à la Chuck Yeager and it could be traced straight back to Phelps, an unwitting fashion plate in oxfords.

She nodded a hello and he waved back with a slow-handed boredom that said he had had enough, but she had learned a long time ago that you couldn't judge Phelps based on his enthusiasm.

He was probably right. After all, what kind of a self-destructive maniac would try to get through this kind of manpower?

The downside to such a massive display of force would be the news teams, contributing the usual more harm than good to the equation.

A breeze blew in off the river, smelling of salt and diesel and a general malaise that experience told her was a mixture of seaweed, garbage, and a long list of chemicals. She lifted her arms to get a little wind under her wings to cool her thermostat. As she stood there, enjoying the flutter of air against her clothes, Phelps came up.

"Hotter'n piss out here," he said, Oscar the Grouch with a badge.

"Eloquent."

"Fuck that noise. They don't pay me to be eloquent."

He turned to the south and stared out across the water at Manhattan's irregular skyline. Hemingway kept her arms spread and willed the wind to cool her; all it did was make her sweat a little more. Phelps was right—it was hotter than piss.

"What if he shows up here?" she asked.

Phelps unbuttoned his suit jacket and jammed his hands into his pockets. "He'd have to be insane to try and breach the security here. Anyone so much as goes close to one of these kids and he'll have a dozen cops bouncing up and down on his skull."

She closed her eyes and focused on the breeze and for some reason it smelled worse. "Okay, let's go get some food and head back to the precinct. I want to see what Carson and his übernerds have come up with."

As they swung around the asphalt of Wards Meadow Loop and back up to the Triborough hub, Hemingway surveyed the little uniformed specks mixed in among the frenetic flea circus of children. Even from a distance she could see the tension in the body language of the policemen, and she liked that. Nothing keeps a cop sharp like worry. And with nearly nine thousand kids on the island, forty-one who represented flesh-and-blood targets for a man with a saw, there was plenty to be worried about.

More than enough.

THE DAY was spectacular and he danced among the police officers and children. He did a little boogie at the edge of the field where Johnson's Academy and Maynard's Collegiate Institute were in the last quarter of the grade four tournament. He smiled and waved a good morning to the policeman to his left and the policeman waved back, like he had better places to be and bigger things to do than watch a bunch of kids kicking a ball around. And he couldn't argue with that; he had better things to do as well—Miles Morgan, for example.

He smiled at a couple of the chaperones and they smiled back. It was as if everyone were one big happy family. When he walked over to the water cooler, the lady in the MCI T-shirt asked him if he'd like a drink.

"Yes, please," he had said, because he assumed that was what she expected him to say. He took the plastic cup, nodded a thank you, and continued on his way.

He had been talking to a police officer a few minutes earlier, asking him what the big fuss was. Pedophile, he had answered. A real sicko, apparently. When the cop had excused himself to go to the bathroom, he had picked up his knapsack and headed out into the fields.

No one saw him. No one acknowledged him. He was invisible here, among his people.

It took fifteen minutes to make it to the lacrosse field where Miles Morgan was finishing his last game of the year—the last game of his life, really. Miles was like all of these boys—pretenders, ignoble blood and poor breeding. Worse than bastards. Sons of bitches.

He found the Morgan kid at the edge of one of the soccer fields. Three cops stood over by the goal, talking. The action over, everyone looked like they just wanted to cool down.

Miles was with some other boys, in the midst of a joke that involved several punches to the smallest one in the group. Miles picked him up in his peripheral vision and stopped, turned. He came over.

"You see all the cops?" he asked, once again demonstrating his finely tuned sense of observation. "Didn't think you were coming this week."

He shrugged and the knapsack with the Canadian flag sewn to it shifted on his shoulder. "When have I not come?" he asked.

Miles ignored the response. "Did you bring it?"

"Didn't I say I would?"

"You want to show me right here?"

They walked back between two buses.

He lowered his knapsack, pulled the two zippers, and pulled out a corner of the shadow box. Three hairy lifeless legs reached for the corner of the box, thick as pencils. "Biggest one in the world," he said, knowing the boy couldn't say no. They never did. "It feeds on birds."

"I can't pay you here. My money is in my shorts."

He pretended to think about this for a second. "I know a cool spot that's pretty private."

Miles Morgan's eyes narrowed. "I shouldn't."

"Why not?"

"Aw, man, they gave us this long-assed speech at school this morning. Said we need to stay in sight and to watch out for strangers. To keep on the fields where our classes are."

He shrugged. "What do you expect them to say? But all right, if you're scared to leave, I understand. If I was like you, I'd be scared, too." He zipped up the pack, stood up—subject closed.

The Morgan boy stopped him. "I really want it. And I'm not scared."

"Then I have the most private place in the world."

HEMINGWAY AND Phelps were in the cybercrimes lab with Carson, going through the endless data when her cell chirped. "Hemingway," she said automatically.

"Hemi, it's Nick. We lost Lincoln."

She felt something flutter in her stomach. "What the fuck do you mean *lost*?" At the edge of her peripheral vision Phelps stood up and reached for his coat.

Rising above Papandreou's voice was the static of cheering children. "Last time I saw him he was talking to the Morgan kid. Maybe five minutes ago. Morgan kid's gone, too."

She remembered Ace and Cindy's son—Little King Switchblade. "What happened?"

"I went for a squirt. I couldn't've been gone for more than five minutes. He was there when I left, standing by the buses watching a bunch of kids. Ten minutes later, he's AWOL. Poof."

She turned and headed out of the lab, Phelps holding the door for her. "Where are you?"

"Northeast tip of the island, the parking lot between softball fields fourteen and thirty-three."

Without asking, Phelps shoved a creased photocopy of a Randall's Island map in front of her face. She checked the top right-hand corner and located the two fields. "Below the wetlands?"

"Yeah."

"Where'd he go? Any holes?"

There was a pause and she could picture Papandreou standing on his tiptoes, squinting into the distance. "Everyone says they were doing their job but you know how it is. You close your eyes or turn your head, and they're gone. Hey— hold on. Yeah, you know what, he coulda gone that way, sorry—the only way I see out of here is under the railway bridge."

"You try his cell?"

"Yeah."

"And?"

"And he ain't answerin'."

"Find Lincoln and find that kid. We lose someone today, we lose this investigation to the Feds. And we'd deserve to." She checked her watch. "We'll be there in fifteen."

III NINETY-TWO

LINCOLN SCANNED the landscape for reporters; there weren't any—which was good. But he had lost the kid—Miles—which was bad; Hemingway would throw an Elizabeth Taylor if she found out. And where the fuck was Papandreou? He had gone for a piss—how long could that take, for Chrissake? He reached for his phone, then figured if Nick wasn't here, there was no point in making him run. He'd go after the little fuck himself.

Lincoln stepped up into one of the school buses, flashing his badge at the driver who was doing his best not to fall asleep. Lincoln grabbed the handle and swung out, using the added height of the steps to scour the landscape.

Where had that kid gone?

And then he spotted him, over near the trees, heading into the scrub on the way to the railway bridge. He caught a glimpse of the boy for a second just as he stepped into the bushes. Then he was gone.

"Thanks," he said to the driver, and went after the boy. He knew he could get the Morgan kid back before anyone noticed he was gone. He had to.

He moved quickly but didn't run—if any of the reporters caught sight of him, he didn't want to look like he was on a mission.

When he hit the trees he turned and looked back at the buses parked like a group of stagecoaches in Indian country. Papandreou still wasn't anywhere in sight. He looked ahead, toward the architecture of the bridge rising out of the earth, and figured that he could go get the kid and be back before Papandreou knew he was gone.

Like every other kid on the island, the Morgan boy was in blue shorts and a white shirt and he had never before noticed how many white plastic bags were strewn about. They all looked like the kid.

He cleared the trees and came into a field of uneven terrain strewn with rocks and construction castoffs. Sheets of plywood and concrete slag and roofing shingles littered the temporary construction yard and the railroad bridge stretched into the sky above. Lincoln could hear the children's shouting from behind the treeline and it sounded like a recording from a long-ago time. The Robert F. Kennedy Bridge was ahead, past the railroad bridge, and Lincoln headed toward it.

Miles Morgan was nowhere to be seen.

He threaded his way across the field, wondering what the fuck the kid was doing over here. If he wanted a smoke there were closer places. He cleared the railroad bridge and then came up on the cracked concrete foundation of the RFK. He looked back toward the sounds of cheering one last time, briefly considered calling Papandreou, then decided that he had come all this way on his own so a few more feet wouldn't matter. He stepped forward, under the RFK Bridge.

The shadow of the bridge rolled over him like a cloud bank. The heat didn't abate but the atmosphere changed and the humidity and stench beneath the concrete piling felt like a fever.

The walls of the abutment were spray-painted with graffiti that ran the gambit from sloppily scrawled FTWs and initials to multicolored masterpieces as long as motor homes. The garbage in there was the usual stuff of New York legend and it stunk of piss and damp earth and pigeon shit and the wind pulsed thorough but did little to improve the smell. The birds hidden in the overhead girders cooed like an eerie soundtrack and the sounds of the Triborough traffic rattling over expansion joints echoed down into the dark.

A handful of pigeons scattered and headed out into the sunlight.

The dark played with his head and the other side of the bridge looked like one of those mouse doors from the Tom and Jerry cartoons he had watched as a kid—a small arch not big enough to get a hand into. But it was a hundred feet high and probably fifty wide. And close. All he had to do was get there.

Lincoln moved slowly through the weird shadows, making a concerted effort to breathe through his mouth so he wouldn't have to smell the sour shit and mud and who knew what the fuck else that was rotting away down here.

He peered into the mottled gray geometry of shadow and the occasional glint of light off of broken glass. Where had the kid gone? Maybe it was time to call Papandreou. And say what? *Um, sorry, Nick, I lost a kid—yeah, the dull one.* No, that wouldn't work, they'd be laughing at him for days.

But something in here was wrong—he could feel it. He couldn't put his finger on the precise voltage of the problem, but he knew he had to be careful. He reached down and unclipped his service piece and the feel of the pistol in his hand triggered the combat mode setting in his brain. He moved forward, taking controlled breaths.

Water dripped. Pigeons whispered in the dark overhead. Cars rattled the concrete and steel. And the wind off the East River funneled through, stirring up dirt and dust that stung his eyes.

And then a soft voice to his right whispered, "Mister?"

He spun, leveling the pistol at the word. A child huddled at the wall. Miles Morgan.

Miles whispered again. "He's in here."

At that Lincoln spun his head, scanning the darkness. All he saw was shadow and garbage. And that arch that wasn't so far away but looked smaller and further away than it had a minute ago.

He reached for the boy. "Come here, kid."

The child's fingertips touched his.

Then he saw a second shadow come out of the dark off to his left. He swung the muzzle of his .38 around.

The figure stepped forward and when he saw who it was, he dropped his gun arm. "Jesus, you're gonna get shot sneaking around like that."

The figure twitched and Lincoln never really felt it. Not even the blood pissing down the front of his shirt.

He fell over in the filth and garbage under the Robert F. Kennedy Bridge.

And died.

III NINETY-THREE

LINCOLN WAS dead by the time Papandreou stumbled over him in the shadow of the bridge. His throat was open in a sharp V that went through muscle and flesh and nicked the bone behind. His pistol was in his hand. He hadn't fired a round.

A boy's shoe was found a few feet away and the impressions in the dirt suggested the boy had been squatting there when Lincoln had come across him. Lincoln had knelt down near the child, the boy had taken a step toward him, and it was at that point that his throat had been cut from the other side.

There were no other tracks; it was as if the killer and child had simply flown away.

The word *ghost* was not far from anyone's lips.

Papandreou was angry. "No way, Hemi. I've known Linc for twenty years and there's no fucking way some guy with a knife coulda taken him down if he had his pistol out. Lincoln was a shoot-first-and-ask-questions-later guy, you know that."

"Then what happened in there, Nick?"

Papandreou stared her in the eye for a second. "I don't know."

The commissioner pulled in an extra hundred uniformed officers and they were canvassing the island from one end to the other. Roadblocks were set up at all exits and every car checked and recorded, the driver's identification logged. Trunks were opened, duffel bags unzipped, coolers inspected. School buses were loaded back up with the kids and their chaperones and were leaving the island on a ramp denoted for their use; every bus was checked by a five-man police team before being allowed off the island and the name of every driver, teacher and chaperone was recorded. They would find Miles Morgan. After all, a ten-year-old boy didn't simply melt away.

Hemingway and Phelps were at the edge of the path, near the tall grass that separated the baseball diamond from the fire department's training facilities. The heat was stifling. The usual reinforcements had gathered their wagons and were doing their battlefield magic—three Econolines from the medical examiner's office, a fleet of police cars, and a division command post that was there to coordinate the search for the missing boy. The space-suited technicians from Marcus's office milled about in slow motion in the eerie light of the halogens and the scene under the bridge looked like a set from a science fiction film, all that was missing were massive egg pods.

Hemingway left Phelps and moved away from the whirr of the emergency teams, drawn toward the flow of the river at the northeastern corner of the island. She needed to clear her head.

As she walked across the baseball field the wind came in and picked up dust devils that swirled out over the water. The sound of cheering children had been replaced by the squawk of seagulls flailing in the sky above a garbage barge in the channel and the crack of flames from the fire department's training facility. A squad of firemen were going through exercises on the other side of the chain-link fence, and smoke and flames billowed out of the brick building like a medieval tower under siege. Dummies leaned up against the fence, fire scarred and dead looking. She headed for the water.

This one was the death of a thousand cuts. Kids and cops and family and strangers. When this case was over—when this guy was locked away in some concrete hole a thousand miles beneath the crust of the earth—she'd have time to think. Maybe take that trip with her father. Maybe head to Key Largo to spend a little time in the mangroves, kayaking and soaking up vitamin D and recalibrating her life. Maybe even go away with Daniel.

Maybe paint the guest room for a baby. Maybe not. The future was still wide open. At least for a few more days.

She stepped off the baseball diamond and cut through the line of police vehicles parked on the service road, walking into the high grass that crawled up a hill, then dipped down toward the water. The natural shoreline was a mix of brambles, shrubs, trees, and bushes woven into a tight green curtain below the broken dirt of the hill. She followed it until she found a cutoff down to the water and stepped off the road.

The path was a dirt rut that cut through the tall grass, worn smooth, the humps of big stones poking up. She recognized the double trail of a kayak trolley etched into the surface of the earth and the semicircles of toe prints from a shoe that had climbed up from the bank. There was a dock ahead—part of the training facility. The water's edge was littered with garbage and she stood there doing her best to clear her head and calm her breathing.

She watched the barge make its way south toward the swirling eddies of Hell Gate. The air above the boat was haloed with a cloud of seagulls that picked at its cargo and filled the air with white noise. The generating plant across the river in Astoria looked close enough to touch.

Like the birds over the barge, it was as if this bastard had wings. Like some great mythical bird with a razor-sharp beak—but instead of taking a titan's life, this fucker took whatever he wanted. If she hadn't lived it, she'd have thought it completely unimaginable.

Yet here she was.

At the shore of the river of the dead.

She spotted some humps in the water to her right, just under the fire department's dock, almost hidden in shadow. She focused on them for a few seconds, something about them incongruous. A swell from the barge came in and they rolled in the pitch, bobbing up and down. There was an instant as they peaked, then rolled slightly, and she realized that she was looking at the toes of feet pointing at the sky—one shoed, one not—and beyond that a human face riding in the waves.

A body.

A boy.

"Phelps!"

The sound was ripped away by the wind that carried the dust off the baseball diamond behind her.

The body bobbed in the water.

Another wave came in and it rocked once, almost flipped over, and shook loose from the reeds. It spun a quarter turn and edged out between the dock pilings, into the channel.

Another swell rolled in and kicked it free. It floated out, away.

Hemingway stumbled down the bank and jumped into the water. In a step she was up to her waist. She waded toward the boy but the hands of the current grabbed him and he moved out toward the channel.

"Phelps!"

She dove forward and swam for him with strong even strokes.

The current fastened its grip on the body and started pulling it down toward Hell Gate, toward the city beyond.

Her arms dug into the river with solid strokes but her boots dragged her back. She splashed through the chop, heading for the boy. She didn't look forward, didn't think about what she was doing, she just concentrated on her stroke. On moving. On making it.

The boy swung out with the current and she knew that if he made it into the fast water, she'd never catch him.

She put a final burst into her kick and lurched forward.

In a few more strokes her hand hit his stockinged foot. She grabbed it and tried to move sideways but he had just hit the fast water and it yanked her out.

In another second they'd both get sucked into the current. She swung out, into the heavy pull of the water and pushed the boy toward shore. It had no effect—it was like trying to push a concrete wall.

She pushed again.

Then again.

And finally they began to move.

The shore started to swing by at speed.

She gave one final burst of muscle, a mindless thrash that carried her out of the fast water to the slow draft of the shallows.

And then she was standing.

She had the boy by the ankle and had time to look at him now. It was Miles Morgan.

His chest was opened up and filled with water and swirling tendrils of flesh and artery and bone.

"Hemi!"

She looked up to see Phelps at the water's edge a hundred yards back. He stumbled along the rock-strewn terrain under the dock, heading for her.

She walked the boy in, eased his body up onto the bank where he would stay until the medical examiner's people got to him. As she dragged him out, the water in his chest sloshed out in a red burp and tentacles of vein spilled down his sides.

She dropped down on the bank.

The barge was past now and the final smash of its swells lapped at the shore. Fifty feet south a great blue heron eyed her suspiciously, then raised its beak disdainfully, turned, and flew out over the river.

She watched the bird for a few strokes of its wings, then turned to see Phelps come crashing through the scrub beside her. Behind him came a platoon of cops.

He saw the boy laid out on the rock, the yawning mouth of his opened ribs. "You okay?"

Hemingway coughed, wiped the back of a hand across her mouth, and nodded. "Perfect." Her eyes went back to the heron heading away. She thought about how an experienced cop like Lincoln had been taken down with a knife. About the corner of the photograph taken from Trevor Deacon's basement cell. She thought about Dr. Selmer's throat being cut at a stoplight and about the musical chairs game the boy on the ferry had played.

Hemingway pointed at the rocks she had just swum through. "Look."

Phelps followed her line of sight. He stared blankly for a few seconds then the deadpan expression dropped out of his features and he slowly shook his head.

About fifteen feet from shore were a pair of rocks. A duck decoy rode the water between them, defiantly facing the current. Its paint was battered and the plastic was sun bleached and dented. How it had gotten here was a mystery.

"Sonofabitch." He came over to her, helped her ashore. "You know, for a chick you're pretty smart."

At that, Hemingway smiled grimly. "I get that a lot."

III NINETY-FOUR

HEMINGWAY SWITCHED into the spare clothes she kept in the back of the Suburban, one of those old cop habits that she had picked up from Phelps. The clothes she had worn into the river went to the medical examiner's to be scanned for any trace evidence that might have come off Miles Morgan's body. They were on their way to the lab and the cherry blinked like a punk rock metronome. She slalomed through traffic in tight throws that pushed the big vehicle's center of gravity to its limit and when the big truck went up on two wheels Phelps tightened his grip on the holy shit handle.

Miles Morgan had been taken apart at the water's edge in a spot upriver from where he had been found floating in the reeds. Nothing but a burnt patch of red-black dirt by the water. The medical examiner called in another team, standard protocol to avoid contamination from Lincoln's murder; they came down the ramp as Hemingway and Phelps had raced up the other side toward the tollbooths.

Hemingway punched through holes in the traffic while Phelps called ahead to book the lab time they'd need. Then he gave Dennet a heads-up so he could put preemptive feelers out to the DA; if the science lined up like they believed it would, they'd have the ammunition for a warrant in a few hours.

The trip to the precinct took seventeen minutes, some sort of a minor miracle in the midday summer traffic. Hemingway stormed through the line of reporters, ignoring their questions, Phelps stuck to her side.

They ran up the five flights and she made it a full floor ahead of Phelps. The investigation room was stacked with countless bankers' boxes and Dennet was waiting for them. He was on the edge of the conference table, his hands in his pockets.

"What the fuck happened at Randall's Island, Alexandra?" Dennet never used her full first name. No one did. People called her Hemingway, Hemi, or Allie. Never Alexandra. Unless they were pissed.

"We have it, captain."

Dennet let out a breath like he had been kicked in the stomach. "Really? Because a few hours ago you had three hundred police officers at your disposal and what did that get us? Huh? Lincoln is lying in his own shit under a fucking bridge and another boy is on his way to the morgue. So it doesn't look like you have this. Not a little and not a lot."

She pulled the lid off of one of the boxes. "Give me an hour with the lab."

Dennet shrugged. "You can have all the time you need, but it won't do any good. Ace Morgan called in some heavy hitters from the Department of Justice and the FBI. The ink's not dry on the forms yet but I got a call from the New York Bureau office and they're in a meeting now. This goes to them before sundown. They'll keep you on as liaison but the horsepower will be coming from their people."

Phelps walked in and sat down, not huffing and puffing but looking like he needed rest.

Dennet didn't bother with a hello. He just stood there, his eyes on Hemingway.

She found the box she was looking for and pulled it out, opened it on the table, then snapped on her latex gloves and removed Dr. Winslow's invitation for the opera—the one he had printed up at home. She gently slid it into a large manila envelope. "Line up the DA—make sure he's available to file a warrant with a judge."

Dennet shrugged like it didn't matter one way or another. "You've got until the Feds take over. After that, you'll have to convince them."

She held up the envelope containing the invitation. "This is it, Ken."

He eyed her skeptically for a second before saying, "You have anything we can share with the press?"

She put the envelope under her arm and shook her head. "After I make the arrest."

"You want to tell me what you think?"

She came around the corner of the table and stopped. "Just make sure you line up the district attorney. We have this prick, all I need is the legal firepower to bring him in."

III NINETY-FIVE

HEMINGWAY PULLED the Suburban over in a no-parking zone, the cherry flashing, a wheel up on the sidewalk.

Mat Linderer came out the front doors of the Office of the Chief Medical Examiner. He looked odd out of the space suit Hemingway was used to seeing him in. "We'll be at the cybercrimes lab with Carson," Hemingway said, and gave him the envelope. "Call my cell when you know."

THE MASSIVE spreadsheet ran across the wall of monitors in a widening pool of information that had been correlated in every conceivable manner. Alan Carson plucked out the name Hemingway asked him about and loaded it into a deep web search field.

The first pass brought up nearly sixty-one thousand pages from around the world. Hemingway pushed her notes in front of him and said, "Can you narrow it to anything around—or after—these dates?"

"August twentieth last year? Sure." He negotiated through the search fields and punched in the new parameters. The results narrowed from sixty-one thousand pages to just under five thousand. He checked her notes again and began to dig.

At that point Hemingway's phone went off. "Excuse me," she said, and left Phelps standing over Carson's shoulder.

"Hemingway."

"Detective Hemingway, it's Mat Linderer from the OCME. I have your results. You were right—"

Hemingway felt her stomach jump the rails. She closed her eyes and concentrated on Linderer's voice.

"—both the invitation and the photograph tacked to the wall in the Deacon residence were printed by the same printer. The feed lines match and there's a pixel lag that is perfect. The paper is from the same manufacturer but a different batch."

Her stomach was back on track and she opened her eyes. "How long to get a report together? Something I can take to the DA."

"Give me five minutes."

She checked her watch. "You've got three. E-mail it to me."

Hemingway hung up and went back to Phelps and Carson. Carson nodded at the screen. "I can't find any record of his presence on any flights for the two weeks before the death, but I have this . . ." He used the cursor to highlight a foreign Google page.

She leaned forward and examined the screen. "It's in Greek."

"Let's run it through the translation software. It won't be perfect, but it will give you a pretty good idea of what it says." He hit a button and a new window opened up.

Both Hemingway and Phelps leaned forward. Both held their breath. Both read silently for a few seconds until Phelps finally said, "Sonofabitch. You were right."

On the morning of August 19th the year before, Dr. Neal Winslow had given a lecture at the Hellenic Ornithological Society regarding the reintroduction of shorebirds to reclaimed habitat. The lecture took place at a library in Athens.

The next morning nine-year-old Tanya Everett—one of Dr. Brayton's girls—drowned while swimming with friends, less than an hour from Athens.

Phelps shifted on his feet. "What do you think?"

"All this proves is that the photograph from Deacon's apartment was printed by the same printer as the invitation and that Winslow was in Greece when the Everett girl died. It doesn't prove that he killed anyone. It's all circumstantial."

"So what do we do?"

"Get his Internet records; his phone records; credit card statements; air miles card; health club membership—anything that we are allowed to get. We dig. It's there, somewhere."

"He said he didn't care where his son had come from. He said he hadn't known. The guy looked cool about all this," Phelps said.

"The man is fascinated by rare specimens, Jon—many the only known example of their kind. He values rarity. He wasn't satisfied with an off-the-shelf model. He lied to us."

SCHLESINGER DIDN'T look skeptical anymore than he looked convinced. He sat at his desk, arms folded, stare locked on Hemingway. "Are you sure?"

"We found two Nikon lenses in Deacon's bedroom. Winslow has a collection of similar lenses by his window, part of his bird-watching arsenal. We ran the warranty card found in Deacon's sock drawer and Winslow shops at the same store—B&H in Manhattan."

"Half the world shops there," Schlesinger said, sounding unconvinced.

She knew he was right; Daniel was there all the time.

Alan Carson stood in the corner, his arms folded across his chest. Babanel, the precinct's lawyer, sat on the sofa, his tie open, looking as hot as the rest of them. Dennet and Phelps stood by the door, like a pair of carvings. But the prize was the district attorney—if they had him, they had the warrant.

Hemingway slid a photograph across the table. "Brayton's eight girls began dying exactly two weeks after the opera, May last year. Dr. Winslow was deeply upset by this party."

"Motive?" Schlesinger asked.

"Wouldn't you be upset if you had ordered a prized purebred and you got a mutt?"

Schlesinger held up the file on Benjamin Winslow. "Kid's got an IQ over 200. Youngest person ever admitted to Harvard. Hardly a mutt."

"It's not about what he has, it's about what he was told he'd have. All of the Park Avenue Clinic's patients expected a certain amount of exclusivity. When Winslow found out his son wasn't as unique as he had been led to believe, it infuriated him.

"He decided to go after these children, beginning with the girls. Eight executions on a very precise schedule."

Schlesinger shook his head. "A man like Dr. Winslow is going to hire excellent counsel. The first thing they will ask will be his motive. And so will the judge when I present this to him. Why would he do this?"

Hemingway slammed her fist into the desk. "Because he's a sick fuck. Who knows why? His mommy didn't breastfeed him. Or his daddy did. We have him." She ground her finger into the report from the lab. "We have him cold."

The district attorney stared at her for a second, then asked, "Give me a chain of events that I can work with."

"I think Winslow and Deacon met on Randall's Island while Deacon was out there staring at kids. Winslow was chaperoning his son's class, something he did often. Both Deacon and Winslow carried expensive cameras with telephoto lenses. Winslow hunted birds, Deacon children. They struck up a conversation, maybe bought a coffee at the canteen at the same time. Became friends or at least buddies. Turns out they have a shared interest. Maybe Deacon pushed Winslow over to the dark side. But a learning process went on. Some sort of a team effort.

"Things soured at some point. Maybe they had their

eyes on the same boy and Winslow was a sore loser. He killed Deacon. We wondered how the killer got into Deacon's apartment with all those locks; Deacon let him in or he had his own keys. They had probably shared the garage for sessions."

Schlesinger nodded as if she had good points. "A buddy system?"

"Some serial killers work in pairs; usually weak people who find confidence in superior firepower. The core system always comes from a dominant partner with a particular fantasy that he or she imprints on the weaker. Winslow could have been the dominant one, the one who wanted to take it to the next level, to this weird parts-taking ritual of his, and Deacon balked. So he finished Deacon off.

"If Deacon had been doing this as far back as eighty-six, he had the automatic role of master. Winslow was a lot smarter than Deacon and maybe he got fed up and decided to mutiny."

Phelps stepped in, offering a little outside perspective. "Pairs of male killers feed off one another. That's what they do. With someone else to record it mentally, it goes from being a participatory activity to a spectator sport. One is always the boss—always maintains psychological control."

Schlesinger leaned over and picked up the photograph Phelps had taken with his cell phone out on Randall's Island. There was nothing interesting about it except the battered duck decoy, head dented, blind with sun-bleached glaucoma that had whited out its eyes.

Hemingway tapped the table. "I saw that same decoy and rocks in a photograph in Winslow's apartment. It was taken where I found Miles Morgan. Printed by the same machine that printed the torn photograph in Deacon's apartment."

Schlesinger's expression was still anchored somewhere in the land of necessary objectivity. "And his wife's death?"

Hemingway shrugged. "We don't know. It's been ruled an accident but who knows? If it was, maybe that's what kicked this whole thing off. He wouldn't be the first person to go off the deep end after the death of a spouse. If it wasn't . . ." She let it drop off.

Schlesinger leaned back in his chair and ran his eyes over the people in the room. "Which brings us back to motive. Without it . . ." He let the question float out into the air above his desk.

Hemingway figured it was time to drop the bomb. "We think we have video of Winslow on the ferry."

"When?"

"The day before the Simmons boy was murdered."

"Not very convincing."

"It is if it's a dry run. He was carrying a knapsack Deacon's drug dealer identified—it has a Canadian flag patch sewn on." She pushed another photograph across the table, this one lifted from a security tape on the ferry. It showed a stooped figure carrying a knapsack.

"That could be anyone." Schlesinger shook his head. "My grandfather."

"Dr. Winslow has a pronounced stoop from a spinal injury." Hemingway tapped the photograph. "It rained that day and he stayed on deck in his raincoat, looking down. Five feet from the escape hatch just off camera. There isn't a single shot of his face but the body language is easily identifiable. He headed across to Staten Island. The cameras picked up his knapsack, and we can clearly isolate the flag." She handed another photograph over. "And he's wearing open-laced oxfords with leather soles. We were able to run down an account he has at Brooks Brothers and his foot is listed as a size ten wide, which is why the lab wasn't certain if the footprints left behind at the crime scenes were ten or ten and a half. We get warrants for his home and office I bet we find the shoes and the knapsack. The murder weapon as well."

"What about the day the Simmons boy was murdered? Can you place him on the ferry?"

At that Hemingway shook her head. She knew it was a pull in the skein of the investigation but they'd figure it out. It was only a matter of time. "Not yet."

"Does he have alibis for the murders?"

"At this point, all we can say for sure is that he was at Randall's Island this morning. Chaperone for his son's class. We looked at some video footage at the time of Lincoln's death and he's nowhere to be seen."

Schlesinger's eyes shut down for a second as he went into thinking mode. "Okay, let me put warrants in front of the judge. Let's see what he says." He leaned back in his seat and knitted his fingers together on top of his head. "While I'm doing that, you bring him in for questioning."

HEMINGWAY AND Phelps flanked Dr. Neal Winslow's door with two uniformed policemen. Alfred, the building manager, was along to make sure they didn't cause any damage.

Phelps gave one grave robotic nod and pushed the buzzer. A long peal of songbirds broke out on the other side of the oak door.

Phelps rolled his eyes.

They waited thirty seconds.

No footsteps.

Phelps pressed his finger to the button again. Another peal of songbirds.

Followed by more silence.

"So you're not sure if he's home or not?" Phelps asked Alfred.

"We don't keep tabs on our residents; this is America."

Phelps rolled his eyes just as Hemingway's phone vibrated. She answered.

"Detective Hemingway, Ed Schlesinger. I just finished with Judge Lester and you have your warrants. I've e-mailed it to you."

"Thank you, sir." She hung up, fired up her e-mail, and held the warrant out for Alfred to read.

"Which means?" he asked.

"That we are going to open this door."

———

Hemingway, Phelps and the two uniformed officers swept through the place. Alfred stood by the door. When they finished, they met back in the living room, amid the glass-eyeballed birds.

Hemingway pulled out her phone and dialed Alan Carson. "Yeah, it's Hemingway, can you get a lock on Dr. Winslow's cell phone? I've got an arrest warrant for him."

"Hold on."

Hemingway nodded off the seconds while Phelps looked around.

He opened desk drawers, looked behind paintings, doing a fast inventory of the place. He quickly branched out from the living room, one of the uniforms following him.

Carson came back on. "He's moving too fast to be on foot right now. Fifth Avenue and East Sixtieth."

"Keep somebody on him. We're on the wa—"

From somewhere deep in the apartment, Phelps hollered, "Hemi!"

He was in the kitchen, standing in front of one of the floor-to-ceiling Sub-Zeros. The uniform was puking in the sink.

Phelps held a shoe by a lace and it dangled in his hand, spinning in the weird light cast up by the open freezer drawer. In his other hand he held a knapsack with a Canadian flag patch sewn to it.

Even from the other side of the room, Hemingway could see the dark crescent on the leather sole of the shoe.

But the big news was the freezer.

The cop was still letting go, his supper coming up in spasms.

Hemingway stepped forward and looked down into the lighted box.

Inside, neatly wrapped in cellophane, were parts of children.

NINETY-NINE

HEMINGWAY WAS still staring at the well-organized collection of hunting trophies when her phone rang. "Hemingway."

The cop was still vomiting in the background and she
stepped away from the noise. "Hemi, it's Dennet. A boy disappeared on the way home tonight. Driver dropped him off
in front of the building but the kid never made it upstairs.
Sol Borenstein."

Two blocks from Winslow's last reported location.

Hemingway and Phelps left the two uniformed officers
to wait for the medical examiner's people.

As she followed Phelps to the door, she grabbed the
photograph of the decoy bobbing in the current from the paneled wall.

HEMINGWAY SPOKE to Mrs. Borenstein on the phone. Elio had dropped Sol off at the front door—he needed to use the bathroom and couldn't wait for the ride up from the garage. Elio watched him run inside and assumed the doorman sent him off to the private resident's restroom behind the elevators. He figured the boy would meet him at the desk in the lobby.

Sol never made it inside.

He vanished between stepping through the front door and arriving on the other side.

Video from the surveillance camera showed the boy pulling the front door open, then looking off to his right. He smiled, waved, and stepped out of the frame.

Winslow's location was fed directly to the onboard laptop mounted to the dash of Hemingway's truck. Winslow was moving up Madison at twenty-seven miles an hour, between 71st and 72nd.

Hemingway and Phelps were three blocks down, at 68th. She didn't have the cherries on and didn't want to slow things down by being pulled over or—worse—alert Winslow up

ahead. But she had skipped a few lights that drivers punctuated with the standard *Fuck You!*

She caught up to him by 77th. Winslow's turn signal
blinked on at the 79th Street entrance to the park. It was an
easy car to spot, a black Bentley with heavily tinted windows,
detailed to the teeth. Hardly inconspicuous.

The black luxury sedan cut across Park Avenue southbound traffic in a gentle sweep and headed into Central Park.
The taxi up ahead balked at the amorphous opening and
Hemingway floored it, pulling the big four-by-four around
the cab in a fog of smoking rubber. She rocketed across the
southbound lane in a blare of horns, caught one final glimpse
of the museum off to her left, and was swallowed by the
shadows.

She gained on Winslow's Bentley, coming almost to its
bumper as they swung down, beneath the grass, then up past
the basketball courts.

Phelps fired up the dashboard cherry and the siren.

Winslow's Bentley continued on for a few seconds, then
the brake lights lit up. The car began to slow, to pull over.

The brake lights died, it lurched forward, then back to
the center of the lane.

"What the fu—?" Phelps had his hand out on the dash.

The car hung in front of them for a second, perfectly balanced like a graceful bird in flight. Then the driver hit the
brakes again and it veered sharply right, scraped the front
quarter panel on the stone wall, jogged left, then swung around
and impacted with the side of the tunnel.

The ass of the car swung out across the road.

Hemingway stomped down on the brakes with both feet.
The dinosaur roar of rubber on pavement echoed in the
tunnel and the Suburban slammed into the Bentley. The air
was filled with a thousand different sounds and the framed

photograph on the center console detonated against the windshield.

Hemingway heard nothing but a high-pitched squeal that she somehow knew was inside her head.

Phelps reached over, put his hand on her chest.

"I'm good," she said, but all she heard was the sound nailing into her brain.

She didn't hear the squeak of his hinge or any words he might have said.

She looked out the fragmented windshield. The nose of her truck was buried in the flank of the Bentley and the big sedan's windows had blown out. There was a boy in the backseat: Sol Borenstein. Splattered with glass. Seat belt holding his head up at an odd, lifeless angle. Blood everywhere.

She caught the stooped form of Dr. Winslow as he lurched out the far side of the vehicle. Phelps was off to her left, a prismatic smudge in her peripheral vision.

Winslow had the boy with him.

His son.

Benjamin.

Winslow was screaming but she couldn't hear him through the squeal that was still rocketing around her skull.

The photograph from Winslow's was folded in half on the dash, the glass disintegrated. A corner of the picture stuck out of the splintered edge of the frame.

There was a spine-jarring suction as her hearing rumbled back in one big pressurized thump that shook her head with subsonic boom.

And she heard the distant screech of sirens and Phelps yelling at Winslow.

"Winslow, put the knife down."

"I can't. I have to do this!"

"*Helllllllllp meeeee!*" the boy screeched. "Shoot him! Shoot him!"

Hemingway slapped at her buckle and the seat belt let go and slowly crawled back across her body. She reached out to steady herself on the dashboard and her fingers clamped down on the edge of the picture frame. The frame came apart and the photo fluttered loose, into her lap.

Across the back, in the precise well-trained script of a gifted ten-year-old, were the words:

For Daddy.
I love you.
Your secret keeper.
Benjamin

And all of a sudden she knew.

She fought her way out of the car and stood on the pavement on borrowed legs.

Dr. Winslow was on the other side of the Bentley, his hand in the air, a bloody blade in his fist. He had Benjamin clamped around the throat.

"This has to stop!" Whatever constraint he had left ruptured, and the knife flashed toward Benjamin's throat.

Hemingway screamed, "No!"

And her hearing went away again in a final, pneumatic snap timed to the flash of Phelps's pistol.

Winslow shuddered once as a cloud of red mist vapor-trailed out behind him. He stepped back clumsily, pulling the boy with him. His arm came down and the knife sang into his son.

Phelps fired again.

III ONE HUNDRED AND ONE

IT WAS hot and windless and with the gentle roll of the swell, the effect was hypnotizing. Hemingway pushed her Ray-Bans up on her nose and squinted into the light bouncing off the water to the south where the roiling patch of Hell Gate bubbled with the outgoing tide.

She was here to get a little perspective on what had happened.

And what was about to happen.

Big things. Forever things. No-turning-away-from things.

She had launched from Randall's Island, not far from where she found Miles Morgan's body floating in the shallows under the dock that day. At first her strokes were steady and purposeful—her shoulder clicking with each swing of her arm—but the further she got from land, the less she felt like paddling. Now she just rode the current, following the gentle pull of water on the hull.

It had all been there in front of them from the beginning but they hadn't seen it. Not really. Not for what it was.

Because it was unthinkable.

They had been right about one part, of course: Trevor

Deacon *had* run into a fellow enthusiast out on Randall's Island. The friendship had come up out of nowhere, one of those random pairings of fractured minds that come around more often than anyone really wants to believe.

Deacon had been near the trees, taking pictures, when someone came over to talk to him.

Benjamin Winslow was probably charming and friendly. But that wasn't what had won over Trevor Deacon—no, that had been accomplished with the photographs. In exchange for keeping them secret, all little Benjamin had wanted was to learn.

Deacon hadn't had a choice, not in any real sense of the word, because Benjamin's intelligence had only been surpassed by his sadism. Deacon quickly grew frightened of the child.

Then one night not too long ago he had squeezed between the bars of Trevor Deacon's windows and injected anesthetic into his eye while he slept. It was a battlefield anesthetic that he had stolen from an old field kit in the museum. Then he cut Deacon's feet off while he had still been alive. Just for kicks.

Phelps had said that his grandson would have a hard time squeezing his skinny ass through the bars. A hard time, sure, but not impossible.

By the time he was finished, Trevor had been reduced to the unarticulated parts. His body left on the bed.

Because a ten-year-old boy could not lift it.

And the shoe print on the chair? Benjamin had worn his father's size ten triple-E brogues from Church's. He used the chair as a ladder to reach the photograph he had given Deacon as a warning, taken at his dumping ground. He had given his father a picture taken at the same place. His dad had had it framed and put it up on the wall with the pictures of his other birds.

Benjamin had been set off by the picture that had captured Dr. Brayton and all the little handsome men to be that he had created. His own little biological empire. The photo had shown up in the *Times* the morning after the opera and that had been it, the fire had started.

Like his biological father, Benjamin Winslow had been a narcissist. And his practical father—Dr. Neal Winslow— had nurtured that in the boy. He had raised him as special. The boy had grown up alone, in a terrarium built for his uniqueness—like an exotic poisonous reptile kept for display. And he wanted no competitors in his little ecosystem. The only-child syndrome taken to an extreme conclusion.

He began with the e-mail list. It hadn't been hard to hunt them down. Not for a boy with his aptitude.

Benjamin had started with the girls because there were fewer of them. As he moved down the list he had discovered that he had an aptitude far beyond geometry and language.

Phelps had spoken with Dr. Winslow's travel agent and the trip to Greece last year had been his son's idea. The agent remembered Winslow insisting on the dates and saying that his son really wanted to go. Because he had known that Tanya Everett would be there. He had swum out with her and the rest of the children and pushed her under and held her down between his legs. The police in Greece weren't noted for their forensic prowess and the two hundred witnesses had negated any suspicion of foul play.

The others had been just as easy.

Heidi Morrison hadn't jumped in front of that train, she had been pushed. Benjamin hadn't been visible on the sur- veillance tapes because he was too short to be seen on the packed platform.

The boys?

They hadn't been abducted. They had been lured.

Benjamin had had no trouble moving among the boys because he was one of them. And in all the eyewitness accounts, children had been around. Even Daniel had passed the schoolboys that morning. The Grant boy's driver would never have suspected a child. Miles Morgan would have felt superior around Benjamin—but Benjamin Winslow had been way too smart for a boy like Morgan to deal with.

The kid had even outsmarted a good street cop like Lincoln.

Solomon Borenstein had walked away from the front door to his building because Benjamin had called him over to the car. And just like in Tanya Everett's death, Dr. Winslow had been used as a dupe. It had all gone wrong when little Solomon had started to cry and asked to go home. Dr. Winslow didn't understand what the problem was—he thought Solomon and Benjamin had a playdate.

Dr. Winslow saw his son slit the boy's throat in the rearview mirror. He had grabbed the knife. Fought with him. Crashed the car.

And lost.

They had been blind on so many fronts. The garage attendant where Dr. Selmer parked his car had said that kids had been around when Selmer left the garage—his throat had been cut less than two blocks away. At a downward angle. Because the killer was only four feet tall.

A ten-year-old killer had never factored into the equation.

Bobby Grant, the docile piano prodigy, watched Benjamin cut his driver's throat. After that, he would have listened to Benjamin—either he forced the Grant boy to come along or he told him that he had killed the driver to save him. Ten-year-old children believed things like that. Even gifted ones.

Benjamin had been walking with Nigel Matheson's group when he disappeared. He had pulled the boy down an alley and off the face of the earth with the promise of basketball tickets.

The toughest one to figure out had been Simmons on the ferry.

The surveillance film of the boy entering the staircase to the engine level, not coming out, then reentering it a second time had stumped them. They thought he had gone out through the escape hatch, then gone back in by the staircase.

Wrong again. Just another old magic trick, like Pepper's Ghost. Smoke and mirrors and getting the observer to use their own preconceptions to work against them. Everyone believes their own eyes. Even when they are lying.

There were two boys in the video.

Two boys who looked so much alike—dressed in their school jackets—that they were virtually indistinguishable.

First on the screen was Benjamin Winslow. He opened the door with the access code—the one he had seen a crewman punch in the day he had taken the ferry with his father—and descended the stairwell to the engine level to wait. He told Simmons to meet him there where he'd show him something special.

And when it was over he had gotten out exactly like Delaney had proposed—by crawling through the escape hatch that came out on the car deck. Then he had disembarked with the rest of the passengers. And a knapsack containing more hunting trophies.

Benjamin Winslow, for all his mathematical acumen and encyclopedic knowledge, had still only been a jealous ten-year-old boy.

And his diary had outlined the sexual abuse he had suffered for years. Monsters aren't born, they're made.

Dr. Winslow followed a strict vegan diet and had fresh meals delivered daily; he never used the freezer. Which was why Benjamin had been able to store his little museum of trophies in there for the few short days his killing spree had lasted.

It was amazing what a child had accomplished with nothing but determination and a hacksaw. They would be talking about that kid for years.

Hemingway checked her watch. If she wanted to make the clinic she'd have to start back now. And she had people to speak to. Forgiveness to ask. Amends to be made. There was her father. And Daniel. More of Uncle Dwight's damage control in action.

Maybe she'd take that vacation with her father and tour the vineyards of Burgundy. She took her hand off her stomach, picked up her paddle, and dug the blade into the water. Her shoulder clicked with the movement and the bow of the kayak started to swing around, away from the roil of Hell Gate.

And across the river of the dead.

ACKNOWLEDGMENTS

I have to thank Charles Shutt, MD, FACOG—dedicated doctor, passionate writer and bruddah—for helping me get the business end of the fertility clinic right. His input on medical records and EMR access was concise and thoughtful, and his explanation of the way the client-patient privilege actually plays out from a legal standpoint helped me dig my characters out of one of the holes I always seem to write them into. The true parts are his. The rest is mine.

I would also like to thank Detective Alfred King (retired) of the NYPD, who unknowingly had a part in writing this novel—I hope he doesn't mind seeing his name in print.

A
BOOKSHELF OF
OUR OWN

A
BOOKSHELF OF
OUR OWN

Works That Changed
Women's Lives

DEBORAH G. FELDER

CITADEL PRESS
Kensington Publishing Corp.
www.kensingtonbooks.com

CITADEL PRESS BOOKS are published by

Kensington Publishing Corp.
850 Third Avenue
New York, NY 10022

All Kensington titles, imprints, and distributed lines are available at special quantity discounts for bulk purchases for sales promotions, premiums, fund-raising, educational, or institutional use. Special book excerpts or customized printings can also be created to fit specific needs. For details, write or phone the office of the Kensington special sales manager: Kensington Publishing Corp., 850 Third Avenue, New York, NY 10022, attn: Special Sales Department, phone 1-800-221-2647.

First printing: January 2005

10 9 8 7 6 5 4 3 2 1

Printed in the United States of America

Library of Congres Control Number: TK

ISBN: 0-8065-2614-9

For Nina Louise

Nothing, I am sure, calls forth the faculties so much as the being obliged to struggle with the world.

—Mary Wollstonecraft, *Thoughts on The Education of Daughters*, 1797

CONTENTS

Foreword	00
Preface	00
The Tale of Genji, by Murasaki Shikibu	00
The Book of the City of Ladies, by Christine de Pisan	00
The Princess of Cleves, by Madame de La Fayette	00
A Vindication of the Rights of Woman, by Mary Wollstonecraft	00
Emma, by Jane Austen	00
Jane Eyre, by Charlotte Brontë	00
The Scarlet Letter, by Nathaniel Hawthorne	00
Madame Bovary, by Gustave Flaubert	00
Little Women, by Louisa May Alcott	00
Middlemarch, by George Eliot	00
Anna Karenina, by Leo Tolstoy	00
A Doll's House, by Henrik Ibsen	00
Tess of the D'Urbervilles, by Thomas Hardy	00
"The Yellow Wallpaper", by Charlotte Perkins Gilman	000
The Awakening, by Kate Chopin	000
The House of Mirth, by Edith Wharton	000
My Ántonia, by Willa Cather	000
Chéri, by Colette	000
A Room of One's Own, by Virginia Woolf	000
Gone with the Wind, by Margaret Mitchell	000

Gaudy Night, by Dorothy L. Sayers · 000

Their Eyes Were Watching God, by Zora Neale Hurston · 000

The Diary of a Young Girl, by Anne Frank · 000

The Second Sex, by Simone de Beauvoir · 000

Century of Struggle: The Women's Rights Movement in the United States, by Eleanor Flexner · 000

The Little Disturbances of Man, by Grace Paley · 000

The Golden Notebook, by Doris Lessing · 000

The Feminine Mystique, by Betty Friedan · 000

The Bell Jar, by Sylvia Plath · 000

Wide Sargasso Sea, by Kate Millett · 000

Sisterhood Is Powerful, compiled and edited by Robin Morgan · 000

The Female Eunuch, by Germaine Greer · 000

Black Women in White America, compiled and edited by Gerda Lerner · 000

From Reverence to Rape: The Treatment of Women in the Movies, by Molly Haskell · 000

Fear of Flying, by Erica Jong · 000

Against Our Will, by Susan Brownmiller · 000

Looking for Mr. Goodbar, by Judith Rossner · 000

The Woman Warrior, by Maxine Hong Kingston · 000

Of Woman Born, by Adrienne Rich · 000

The Women's Room, by Marilyn French · 000

Silences, by Tillie Olsen · 000

Women, Race & Class, by Angela Davis · 000

The House of the Spirits, by Isabel Allende · 000

Beloved, by Toni Morrison · 000

The Shawl, by Cynthia Ozick · 000

Backlash, by Susan Faludi · 000

The Beauty Myth, by Naomi Wolf · 000

Bridget Jones's Diary, by Helen Fielding   000

The Bitch in the House, compiled and edited by
    Cathi Hanauer   000

Honorable Mentions   000

Select Bibliography   000

Index   000

Foreword to come (2 pages)

PREFACE

Women's history is more than simply a catalog of the social and political events that have shaped women's lives over the centuries. There is a unique quality to every age in the history of women that can be understood and appreciated in the context of the fiction and nonfiction works of each era. *A Bookshelf of Our Own* attempts to present an overview of women's history from the perspective of literature written by and about women. I have chosen the authors and works featured in this volume because I think they offer valuable insights into the cultural and historical experience of women as they have been, as the epigraph to this book suggests, "obliged to struggle with the world."

The struggle of women to forge individual, social, and political identities, to gain equality, to demand and obtain respect, to love and be loved, to confront and challenge the circumstances that have constrained them, and to question, and sometimes reject, the lives they have chosen is evident in the works chronicled here; each character, subject, and author's perceptions and voice tells us something distinctive about women past and present. The authors' voices are not exclusively female: some of fiction's most extraordinary and memorable women protagonists were created by male writers and are discussed here in essays on four of the greatest nineteenth-century novels in world literature and one revolutionary play from the same century (Henrik Ibsen's *A Doll's House*). I have also included an Honorable Mentions list of fifty additional works for readers to consider. This list broadens the base of women's experience and includes more plays, as well as more fiction from the past twenty-five years. Poetry, that most singular of literary genres and the one that, as Russian poet

Yevgeny Yevtushenko put it, "ignores all frontiers," deserves a book of its own and thus has not been included, although a poem by Emily Dickinson appears to punctuate the essay on Charlotte Perkins Gilman's 1892 story of madness and enlightenment, "The Yellow Wallpaper." Due to obvious limitations of length, I have focused primarily on Western literature as it relates to women's history, but I nevertheless urge readers to seek out significant works by women authors from other cultures.

Although there are several remarkable women characters in classical literature, such as Medea, Antigone, and Hecuba, I have chosen to begin *A Bookshelf of Our Own* in the medieval period, with Murasaki Shikibu's *The Tale of Genji* and Christine de Pisan's *The Book of the City of Ladies*, the first major literary creations of women writers. Separated by culture and category, each work has its own special place in the history of women's writing. The *Genji* has the honor of being regarded as the first great novel in world literature; the fact that it was written by a lady of the Japanese court adds to its distinctiveness. Pisan's work, considered by some scholars to be the first true feminist treatise, is both a defense of women against the misogyny that was a feature of European life in the middle ages and a catalog of famous women whose attributes and contributions belie the then widely held notion of female inferiority.

Major novels by and about women would begin to appear in the eighteenth and nineteenth centuries. Prior to then, we have one groundbreaking novel, *The Princess of Cleves*, by Madame de La Fayette, which, although written in seventeenth-century France during the reign of Louis XIV and reflective of the Sun King's court, is set in the Renaissance at the similarly glittering court of Henri II, where "love was always allied to politics and politics to love." Madame de la Fayette offers readers an illuminating look at the concept of courtly love, as well as the morals and political maneuverings of the nobility. For a work of the eighteenth century, a time of political turmoil, revolutionary fervor, and the idea of inalienable rights in France, England, and the United States, I have chosen Mary Wollstonecraft's *A Vindication of the Rights of Woman*, which includes a call for the education of women that will produce individuals with reason, knowledge, and virtue. An insightful and important pronouncement of woman's rights, *Vindication* would become a foundation text in the struggle for women's liberation and gender equality.

By the nineteenth century, the novel had become the dominant form of Western literature. The century marked the emergence of women as strong, central protagonists in the novel, and for the first time in literary history, male novelists explored female consciousness in the context of a patriarchal society. Hawthorne's Hester Prynne, Flaubert's Emma Bovary, Tolstoy's Anna Karenina, and Hardy's Tess Durbeyfield challenged the expectations of the ways in which women were expected to conduct their lives, with ostracism and death as the inevitable punishments for such violations of convention. Unlike the characters mentioned above, Ibsen's Nora Helmer, in what is as much a polemic as it is a drama, decides her own fate when she ultimately rejects the role as a wife and mother that has kept her submissive, childlike, and irresponsible in favor of an uncertain new life of freedom.

During the nineteenth century, the voices of women writers were being heard as well, beginning with Jane Austen, whose social satires provide contemporary readers with a glimpse of the courtship manners and mores of her time, exemplified in this volume by Austen's 1813 novel *Emma*. With *Jane Eyre*, Charlotte Brontë would take the novel into the realm of interior consciousness, and by the 1860s and 1870s, George Eliot, then the dominant intellectual novelist in England, would add social awareness to psychological exploration, most notably in her masterwork *Middlemarch*. As the nineteenth century gave way to the twentieth, women writers offered provocative challenges to the male-dominated world view in works by Charlotte Perkins Gilman, Kate Chopin, Colette, Edith Wharton, and Willa Cather.

At the same time, women were working for equality and empowerment in the move toward suffrage. The history of the first wave of the women's movement is featured here in a profile of Eleanor Flexner's masterful *Century of Struggle: The Women's Rights Movement in the United States*. With the vote won for women in the United States and in England after World War I, an important political goal in the quest for equality had been realized. However, there was more work to be done if women were to achieve full creative and autonomous parity, as novelist and essayist Virginia Woolf made clear in 1929's *A Room of One's Own*. In Dorothy Sayers's 1936 novel, *Gaudy Night*, the central female character, Harriet Vane, is a best-selling detective novelist who questions whether it is possible for her to successfully combine creative autonomy with the commitment required for a successful marriage.

Virginia Woolf's call to women to achieve their full potential would be answered in the influential critical work *The Second Sex*, by Simone de Beauvoir, the novel *The Golden Notebook*, by Doris Lessing, and in Betty Friedan's *The Feminine Mystique*. Friedan's 1963 treatise on the discontent experienced by women because of their treatment as second-class citizens in post-World War II America served to launch the second wave of the women's movement. The women's liberation movement of the 1960s and 1970s resulted in a burgeoning of women's fiction and nonfiction by such writers as Sylvia Plath, Kate Millett, Germaine Greer, Molly Haskell, Erica Jong, Susan Brownmiller, Adrienne Rich, Tillie Olsen, Judith Rossner, and Cynthia Ozick, all of whom offer important perspectives on the social, political, psychological, and sexual status of women in the last decades of the twentieth century. The same decade also brought forth a multicultural perspective which added to the rich canon of women's writing and is represented here in works by Maxine Hong Kingston, Angela Davis, Isabel Allende, Toni Morrison, and Zora Neale Hurston, a once largely forgotten novelist of the 1930s and 1940s who received deserved recognition during the 1970s and whose novels continue to be taught in college courses on African-American literature, women's literature, and twentieth-century American literature.

The 1980s and 1990s saw the stirrings of a post-feminist consciousness in a reevaluation of the gains in equality made by women in the wake of the women's liberation movement. By the 1980s, women were earning graduate degrees and entering the work force as never before, while at the same time they were having children and endeavoring to balance the demands of the workplace with those of family life. The 1980s myth of the "super-woman" who could "have it all" was seized upon by the media, which, according to journalist Susan Faludi, mounted a "counterassault on women's rights, a backlash, an attempt to retract the handful of small and hard-won victories that the feminist movement did manage to win for women." Faludi explores this phenomenon in *Backlash: The Undeclared War Against American Women*, published in 1991. As examples of post-feminist literature, I have selected Cathi Hanauer's anthology of essays by women, *The Bitch in the House*, and the very entertaining *Bridget Jones's Diary*, by Helen Fielding. The experiences of new generations of women will determine how women's literature will evolve in the twenty-first century.

Readers will undoubtedly have their own choices for the works they feel best illustrate the history of women through the centuries. I have offered my choices for consideration in what is also a book about literature and the extraordinary pleasure, as well as the illumination, which can be derived from experiencing it. *A Bookshelf of Our Own* can serve as an introductory volume in the compilation of a library of writings on women that will hopefully grow and continue to instruct and entertain readers through the years with what Virginia Woolf called, "that complete statement which is literature."

Finally, I want to thank my editor, Margaret Wolf, for her support and her patience during the preparation of this book, and my husband, Daniel Burt, whose scholarly perspective was an invaluable resource in my own reconsideration of the works profiled here.

A
BOOKSHELF OF
OUR OWN

THE TALE OF GENJI

by Murasaki Shikibu

The first great novel in the history of world literature, *The Tale of Genji* is celebrated as one of the supreme masterworks of Japanese prose fiction and one of the most accomplished works of the imagination ever written. Adding to the novel's originality, as well as its significance in the history of women's literature, is the fact that it was written by a lady of the eleventh-century Japanese court.

Little is known about Murasaki Shikibu (c. 978–1031), the author of *The Tale of Genji*. Her father was a provincial governor and a member of the middle rank of the Japanese aristocracy. The name "Shikibu" ("Bureau of Ceremonial") designates a position once held by her father, and "Murasaki" ("purple") may have stemmed from the nickname of a female character in the *Genji*. Although her family was not prominent or powerful, it was distinguished by literary achievement. Murasaki Shikibu's great-grandfather helped compile the first imperial anthology of Japanese verse, and her father was a poet and scholar of Chinese classics, an essential qualification for a successful bureaucrat in the male-dominated public life of the time. As a child, Lady Murasaki's literary skills were evident but unappreciated. Her diary, in which she describes her experiences at court from late 1008 to early 1010, also records one method of childhood study, as well as the fact that her father, who noticed her capacity for learning, lamented that she had not been born a boy: "When my brother . . . was a young boy learning the Chinese classics, I was in the habit of listening to him and I became unusually proficient at understanding those passages which he found too difficult to grasp. Father, a most learned man, was always regretting the fact: 'Just my luck!' he would say. 'What a pity she was not born a man!' "

Around 998, Lady Murasaki was married to her cousin, a member of the imperial guard. Her only child, a daughter, was born in 999, and she was widowed in 1001 (some sources say 1011). In 1002 or 1003, she began the fictional narrative that would bring her notoriety and, it is thought, helped secure for her a position at court as lady-in-waiting to the Empress Shōshi. Despite the circumscribed and cloistered life of noblewomen during the period—they lived a sedentary life behind walls and screens, most had no public function, and their names were rarely recorded—it is not surprising that a woman did produce such a brilliant literary work as the *Genji*. Following Chinese tradition, only poetry, history, and philosophy were regarded as distinguished literary genres. Chinese art and culture was the exclusive province of men, who devoted themselves primarily to writing in Chinese, the official language of religion and government. The Japanese vernacular was left largely to women, with the result that women writers dominate the literature of the period and are credited with developing an indigenous literary style. There were two vernacular prose genres for women to choose from. One was the literary diary, a record of activities, observations, and feelings, of which Murasaki Shikibu's own diary is a leading example. The other available prose form was the *monogatari*, fanciful, often supernatural, storytelling derived from the folk tradition. Murasaki's great innovation was to combine both genres, creating a prose narrative infused with real situations and psychological insights. Murasaki Shikibu's literary talent was no doubt a major asset in her court service—she had the time and leisure to create her tale, together with access to the court world, both of which she used to full advantage in producing her epic. *The Tale of Genji* gradually evolved from chapter installments enjoyed by a small aristocratic audience into a narrative twice the length of Tolstoy's *War and Peace*, another novel renowned for its size as well as its brilliance.

Completed around 1013, *The Tale of Genji* is a massive fifty-four-chapter work that ranges over a period of seventy-five years and three generations, includes nearly five hundred characters, and chronicles the lives and careers of the nobleman Genji and his offspring. Genji is the son of the emperor and a "lady not of the first rank," who, as a consequence of her lover's indiscretion, is hounded to an early death by one of his senior wives. Beloved by his father and known as "The Shining Prince," Genji is in many ways a paragon of manly virtues, possessing wit, sophistication, and great physical attractiveness. At the beginning of the novel, the emperor wants to designate his son crown prince, but he lacks the political support to achieve this. In addition, a Korean soothsayer has warned that disaster will befall the country if Genji becomes emperor. Reluctantly, the emperor decides to reduce Genji to the status of mere subject, although he retains for him the rank of nobleman to ensure that he will have an official career. Thus dispossessed, Genji begins a lifelong quest to obtain compensation for his loss of royal rank. This takes the form of a search to find the perfect woman and to achieve redemption through love, even as he pursues affairs that challenge social mores and complicate his search for self-fulfillment. His early idealism is tested in his disastrous extramarital affair with his father's consort, which causes his exile, and in his relationship with the character Murasaki, who, like his mother, is a woman of unsuitable rank. Unlike a conventional romantic hero, Genji is humanized by his shortcomings and redeemed by his vulnerability and emotional needs.

In *The Tale of Genji* Murasaki provides intense and nuanced character portraits in which political pressure, custom, and individual identity join together to generate the novel's drama. An equally interesting facet of the novel is the author's penetration into the psyches of the various women whom Genji encounters. Rather than representing the expected fulfillment of love and redemption through their relationships with the highborn, captivating hero, Murasaki's women, bound by the customs and values of the author's time, suffer from their dependence on a man's unsteady devotion and are fearful of betrayal and abandonment. In the world of the *Genji* (which was the world of Murasaki Shikibu), women are expected to be submissive and to sexually acquiesce to the demands of men. But the author explores a psychological insight lurking behind the submissiveness: for example, the young

Murasaki finds Genji's sudden advances toward her "gross and unscrupulous" because she is disconcerted by the awakening of her sexuality in a situation that shows a man at his most selfish. Ultimately, Genji is the mirror through which Murasaki Shikibu's women see themselves; that the image is not necessarily the reality adds depth to the characters and situations.

After chronicling Genji's adventures up to his return to the city, restoration of his rank (his son becomes emperor, and Genji is promoted to government minister), Murasaki's death, and his death at the age of fifty-two, Murasaki Shikibu devotes the final thirteen chapters to the succeeding generation. The remainder of the novel focuses on the relationship between Kaoru, Genji's putative son, and Genji's grandson, Niou, as they compete for the affections of three sisters. The two young men "were thought by the world to be uncommonly handsome, but somehow they did not shine with the same radiance [as Genji]." The patterns of passion and betrayal established in previous generations by the emperor and Genji are repeated in the third generation but remain unresolved in the end, as the disaffected Niou and Kaoru fail to find the self-fulfillment that Genji has obtained.

Murasaki Shikibu's saga of Genji and his children offers the reader a true, deep understanding of human nature and experience in an open-ended, indeterminate manner that reflects human weakness as well as existential uncertainty and anxiety. It would take many more centuries for western writers to attempt what Murasaki accomplished in *The Tale of Genji* and to discover what she articulated in her epic: that the art of the novel "happens because the storyteller's own experiences of men and things, whether for good or ill—not only what he has passed through himself, but even events which he has only witnessed or been told of—has moved him to an emotion so passionate that he can no longer keep it shut up in his heart."

THE BOOK OF THE CITY OF LADIES

by Christine de Pisan

The Middle Ages in Europe, a period stretching roughly from 400–500 A.D. into the fifteenth century, was an era notable for a fear and mistrust of women inherent in Judeo-Christian tradition, which subscribed to the biblical assertion in Genesis that Eve was the perpetrator of Original Sin, and from medical science dating from the Greeks, which viewed females as anatomically defective males. These views were reflected in the literature of the age: medieval treatises, religious texts, romances, and *fabliaux* (a genre of short comic tales) portrayed women as lustful, treacherous, disobedient, garrulous, and inferior to men in every way. One woman who dared to directly confront the literary misogyny of the age was Christine de Pisan, whose discourse in defense of women, *The Book of the City of Ladies* (1405), is a masterpiece that some scholars have called the first true feminist treatise.

In an age when a woman's influence, limited at best, was generally characterized by her royal status (Eleanor of Aquitaine) or religious inclination (Joan of Arc, Hildegard of Bingen), Christine de Pisan stands out as a literary figure of remarkable depth. France's first woman of letters, Christine wrote poetry, biography, a book on etiquette for women, treatises on pacifism, the arts, government,

5

and war, and biblical commentary. She achieved renown for her writing during her lifetime and was the first medieval female author to earn a living exclusively from her work.

Born in Venice, Christine de Pisan (c.1364–c.1430) was the daughter of Tommaso di Benvenuto da Pizzano, a noted physician, astronomer, mathematician, and astrologer. Both of her parents were from prominent Italian families. When Christine was four years old, the family moved to Paris, where her father served as court astrologer to Charles V (1338–1380), although in her biography of Charles, she described Tommaso as "philosopher, servant, and counselor" to the king. Against the wishes of her mother, Christine was schooled by her father in Latin, philosophy, and various branches of science not usual in a medieval girl's education. At fifteen, according to the custom of the time, she was married to a man chosen by her father. Her twenty-five-year-old husband was Etienne de Castel, a courtier who became secretary and notary to the king. In 1390, after ten happy years together, de Castal suddenly died while on a trip to Beauvais in what may have been an epidemic of the Black Death. Left the sole support of three children, her mother, and a niece, Christine turned to writing to gain the patronage necessary for financial security.

To prepare for the task of earning a living by her pen, Christine embarked upon an extensive course of self-education. She studied history, science, and the art of poetry, and during this period she may also have worked as a manuscript copier. She began her career writing lyric poetry, composing *ballades* and *rondeaux* in the conventional forms popular at the time. The tone of her work was personal, with a poignant, emotive quality particularly evident in the poems about her widowhood. Christine's poetry gained favor with princes and nobles, and by the end of the decade she was earning a steady income. She began composing longer narrative poems, including fashionable "love debates" presented to a "court of love" for resolution, and the more serious *Long Road of Learning* (1403), a utopian dream-vision in which Christine visits the Court of Reason to discover who should rule a better world. Around 1400, she began writing long prose works, such as the biography of Charles V (1404), *The Book of Three Virtues* (1405), and *Christine's Vision* (1405), a cryptic semiautobiographical dream-vision that analyzes the ills of French society, not the least of which was its concept of womanhood.

Christine had previously criticized men's behavior toward women in *The Letter of the God of Love* (1399) and in attacks on Ovid and Jean de Meun, one of the authors of the hugely popular medieval romance, *The Romance of the Rose*. *The Book of the City of Ladies* may have had its origins in a series of letters Christine exchanged, between 1400 and 1402, with other leading intellectuals of the day debating the merits of *The Romance of the Rose*. This long poem expresses the concept of courtly love (a medieval philosophy of love and a code of rules for lovemaking) through the story of Amant ("Lover"), who attempts to pick a beautiful Rose guarded by such allegorical figures as Danger and Jealousy. Begun by Guillaume de Lorris around 1230, the poem was completed by Jean de Meung from 1275–80. Jean de Meun, sometimes referred to as the Voltaire of the Middle Ages, satirizes courtly love by making women personify its hypocrisy and falsity. His section is filled with attacks on women, whom he blames for humanity's departure from the ideal. Unlike her opponents, who considered Jean de Muen's *Rose* a work of the highest literary and moral merit, Christine criticized it as extremely vicious and vitriolic in its characterization of women and unChristian in its view of the relations between the sexes. Critic Rosalind Brown Grant has observed, "Christine sought to prove misogynists such as Jean de Meun wrong by arguing that what unites men and women as human beings—their rationality and possession of a soul—is more important than what divides them as sexes. . . . At the heart of Christine's defense of women, both in her letters on the *Rose* and in the *City of Ladies*, was her profound conviction that it is a *human*—and not a specifically *female*—trait to be prone to sin."

The Book of the City of Ladies is a biographical catalog, a genre from classical antiquity that celebrates the lives of famous men and women. In the allegorical framework of the dream-vision, in which Christine is the protagonist, she presents a catalog of renowned heroines from the past and present, including pagan, Greek, Roman, and biblical figures, as well as saints. Christine's vision comes to her as she is sitting in her study reading *Lamentations*, a thirteenth-century diatribe against marriage, which characterizes women as depraved and malicious, and vilifies them for making men so miserable. A depressed and weeping Christine wonders why men "are so unanimous in attributing wickedness to women" and why "we should be worse than men since we were also created by God." Three ladies personifying the virtues of

Reason, Rectitude, and Justice come to comfort her, and they suggest that she write a book refuting, point by point, misogynist accusations that women are evil. Reason tells Christine, "The female sex has been left defenseless for a long time now, like an orchard without a wall, and bereft of a champion to take up arms against in order to protect it." With the help of Reason, Rectitude, and Justice, the foundation, walls, towers, and streets of an allegorical "city of ladies" will be built to house illustrious women and defend them against the misogynists.

The City of Women is divided into three parts in which the Three Virtues give examples of renowned women in response to Christine's questions concerning the inferior political, social, and intellectual status of her sex. In Part I, Reason presents pagan women noted for their soldierly courage, artistry, or inventiveness; in Part II, Rectitude cites ancient Hebrew and Christian women celebrated for their gifts of prophecy, chastity, or devotion to family and country; in Part III, Justice recounts the steadfastness and religious devotion of the female saints. In the last chapter, Christine, seeking to dignify her female readers and to raise their self-esteem, addresses all women and informs them that the city is complete:

> All of you who love virtue, glory, and a good reputation can now be housed in great splendor inside its walls, not just women of the past but also those of the present and the future, for this city has been founded and built to accommodate all deserving women. Dear ladies, the human heart is naturally filled with joy when it sees that it has triumphed in a specific endeavor and has defeated its enemies. From now on, my ladies, you have every reason to rejoice—in a suitably devout and respectful manner—at seeing the completion of this new city. It will not only shelter you, or those of you who have proved your worth, but it will also defend you and protect you against your attackers and assailants, provided you look after it well.

The Book of the City of Ladies might have languished in obscurity were it not for the efforts of feminist scholars during the last decades of the twentieth century to recover previously unknown and unheralded literary works by women. Because of Christine's emphasis on the traditionally passive female traits of respectfulness, virtue, and devotion, there has been some controversy among scholars over whether *The Book of the City of Ladies* can be considered a true feminist text. Christine de Pisan was certainly not a feminist in the modern sense. She did not question the medieval hierarchical social order but sought to prove that women deserved to hold an honored place within it and that virtue and morality were not exclusively male preserves. *The Book of the City of Ladies* is a foundation text that marks the beginning of a canon of women's literature dedicated to elevating the status of women that would continue nearly four hundred years later with Mary Wollstonecraft's *Vindication of the Rights of Woman* and come to fruition in the equality-driven political and social women's movements of the nineteenth and twentieth centuries.

THE PRINCESS OF CLÈVES

by Madame de La Fayette

In 1678, during the reign of Louis XIV, a short historical novel titled *La Princesse de Clèves* appeared in Paris bookshops. Its author was anonymous, which was probably just as well, given that the novel, although set in the late sixteenth-century French court of Henri II, mirrored in many ways the court of the Sun King. *The Princess of Clèves* caused a sensation for its brevity, which was revolutionary in an era when historical romances (*romans*) were loosely constructed, episodic, and might run to seven thousand pages in length, as well as for the author's anonymity. A treatment of courtly love and the conflict between love and duty—a favorite seventeenth-century theme—*The Princess of Clèves* would go on to be considered the first classic French novel.

Madame de La Fayette (1634–1693) was born Marie-Madeleine Pioche de La Vergne. Her father, a military engineer, was a member of the minor French nobility. He died in 1649. Shortly afterwards, Marie-Madeleine's two younger sisters, left without dowries, entered a convent, as was a custom of the time. A year later, her mother married a more prominent nobleman, the Chevalier Renaud-René de Sévigné. The match allowed Marie-Madeleine's mother to secure for her daughter a place at court, as a lady-in-waiting to Anne of Austria, the widowed queen of Louis XIII and the regent for her son, Louis XIV, who had ascended the throne in 1643, at the age of five. Marie-Madeleine would also develop a lifelong friendship with her stepfather's niece-in-law, the Marquise de Sévigné, whose massive correspondence with friends and family would become renowned as a monument of French literature. Another friend was the young Henrietta of England, sister of the exiled Charles II, who would marry Louis' eccentric brother, Philippe, the Duc d'Orléans. Madame de La Fayette later wrote a biography of Henrietta, which was published after her death.

In 1655, Marie-Madeleine was married to Jean-François Motier, comte de La Fayette, a provincial nobleman with estates in the remote, mountainous region of the Auvergne in central France. Madame de La Fayette lived with her husband in the Auvergne until 1659, when, after producing the second of the couple's two sons, she returned to Paris. She would remain in the capital for the rest of her life, occasionally visited by her husband. She raised her children in Paris, became the hostess of a fashionable salon that attracted many of the leading intellectuals and writers of the day, and began her writing career. Her first publication, the only one to appear under her name during her lifetime, was a portrait of her friend, Madame de Sévigné, published in a collection titled *Divers Portraits,* in 1659. Her first fictional work, *La Princesse de Montpensier,* a depiction of court life during the reign of Charles IX, appeared anonymously in 1662, and she collaborated with her close friend La Rochefoucauld on the romance, *Zaïde,* set in ninth-century Spain, which appeared in 1670. In 1672, Madame de La Fayette began to research the historical background of *The Princess of Clèves*; she completed the novel six years later. It would be the last of her works published in her lifetime.

The Princess of Clèves begins: "The last years of Henri II's reign saw a display of opulence and gallantry such as has never been equaled in France. The King himself, charming to look at, the very flower of his race, was a great lover of women. His passion for Diane de Poitiers, Duchesse de Valentinois, had begun over twenty years before, but it was nonetheless dazzling. He excelled at all forms of sport; much of his time was given up to it; every day there was tilting at the ring, hunting, tennis, ballets, and the like." The physically well-favored, amorously inclined Louis XIV was soon to discard his second mistress for another "favorite," but the courtiers who frequented Versailles would have recognized their king, their sport, and their lavish milieu right away in these opening sentences. By chronicling the recent past rather than the present, Madame de La Fayette achieved a tactful, objective distance from which she could safely reflect the court world of Louis XIV in the reign of Henri II. To underscore *The Princess of Clèves*'s blend of fact and fiction, she called the novel a *histoire*, an ambiguous term which means both "history" and "story."

At the beginning of *The Princess of Clèves*, the author details the political and romantic rivalries at court, leading the reader to expect either the extravagances of the *roman* or the private scandals of the powerful. Instead, into this web of court intrigue comes Madame de Chartres, hoping to marry her beautiful young daughter to a high-ranking nobleman, preferably a prince of royal blood. The preliminary description of the intrigues at Henri's court provides the backdrop to the process of wooing that commences. Mademoiselle de Chartres, "one of the most eligible heiresses in France," has all the qualities of the romantic heroine: "She was absolutely dazzling. Indeed there was nobody to touch her, with her white skin, golden hair, classical features, and general aspect of sweetness and charm." In order to achieve an advantageous marriage in the complicated court network of political and romantic alliances, Madame de Chartres must guide her innocent sixteen-year-old daughter through a world in which glamour conceals motive and appearance disguises reality. She cautions her daughter not to be deceived by appearances, since what she will see is almost never real or true. The conflict between appearance and reality, the difference between the way people act and what they truly feel, generates the novel's drama. On the subject of love, Madame de Chartres is blunt: "She told [her daughter] that men were not very sincere, not very faithful, and not above deceit; she spoke of the unhappiness that love affairs can bring to a family, and then, on the other hand, she showed her the life of a good woman, happy, serene, and enjoying the particular glamour that attaches to noble birth when there is also virtue."

Mademoiselle de Chartres's character will be tested after marriage, as she accedes to her mother's wishes and agrees to wed the much-older prince of Clèves, whom she does not love. She tells the prince that she will try to love him, but that she feels no real passion for him or for any man. The new princess is dutiful toward her husband and maintains a spotless reputation in a court where, in the tradition of courtly love, extramarital attachments are the norm. The princess's behavior not only traduces this tradition, it cheats the courtiers out of the possibility of a new scandal to enjoy. One evening, at a court ball, the princess is ordered by the king to dance with a late arrival, the duc de Nemours. Described in the novel as "nature's masterpiece," the duke is the most handsome, gallant, and accomplished nobleman at court. He falls in love with the princess, and she, for the first time, feels passion for a man. The princess of Clèves is conflicted as she attempts to cope with her feelings for Nemours while recognizing her responsibilities to her husband. Her conscience will not allow infidelity, and, although she tries to hide her true feelings behind a decorous public mask, she experiences a split between her outward behavior and her inner desires. Driven to resolve this conflict, she confesses her feelings to her dying mother, who acknowledges that her daughter is "on the edge of a precipice." After her mother dies, the princess turns to her husband—the only authority figure available to her—and in the novel's most controversial scene, she courageously but naively confesses her attraction to the unnamed Nemours. Instead of receiving the emotional and moral support she so desperately needs, she is confronted with the prince's distrust and anxiety. Disappointed by his inability to provoke a passionate response from his wife, the prince is increasingly consumed by jealousy, insists upon knowing the name of his rival, and becomes obsessed with uncovering evidence of the princess' betrayal. Incapable of believing his wife's protestations of innocence, beyond what she feels for her would-be paramour, and convinced of her infidelity, the elderly prince languishes and dies.

The way is cleared for a happy romantic ending to the novel, since the princess of Clèves is now free to give in to her passion for Nemours. But this is no ordinary romance, and appearances, as Madame de La Fayette has cautioned the reader, are deceiving. The author has endowed her title character with qualities beyond that of any romantic heroine of the era, and she has presented moral dilemmas that make up the challenging, ambiguous world of the novel. The duc de Nemours prevails upon the princess's uncle to intercede on his behalf, and the uncle arranges a meeting between the two lovers. When Nemours declares that his love for the princess is "true and strong" and proposes an attachment, she is adamant in her refusal, stating:

> I confess . . . that my passions may govern me, but they cannot blind me. Nothing can prevent me from recognizing that you were born with a great susceptibility to love and all the qualities required for success in love. You have already had a number of passionate attachments; you would have others. I should no longer be able to make you happy; I should see you behaving towards another woman as you had behaved towards me. I should be mortally wounded at the sight and I cannot even be sure I should not suffer the miseries of jealousy. . . . I must remain in my present state and stand by the resolution I have taken never to abandon it.

The princess submits passion to the cold logic of reality. Nemours has deceived before; like all men, he will do so again. The princess of Clèves recognizes that she has a central duty to herself, not to her lover. She rejects marriage and gratified passion, and instead retires from the court and the world to her estate in the Pyrenees. The novel closes with a brief memorial to her life there: "She spent a part of each year in the convent and the rest of it at home but living in even greater austerity, with even more saintly occupations than in the strictest of orders. Indeed, her life, which was not a long one, provided an example of inimitable goodness." As for the duc de Nemours, he "did everything imaginable to make her change her mind. At last, after the passage of whole years, time and absence healed his grief and his passion died away."

The Princess of Clèves was an immediate success. Paris booksellers were unable to meet the demand, and provincial readers were forced to wait months for a copy. The novel sparked a search for the identity of its author, as well as a lively debate over its merits as a work of art and its truthfulness. Madame de La Fayette, after denying that she was the author, offered her own review of the novel, declaring it to be "most agreeable, well written without being extremely polished, full of wonderfully fine things that even merit a second reading." She praised the novel for its "perfect imitation of the world of the court and the way one lives there," but she was careful to add that it "should properly be regarded as a memoir." One of the great ethical debates of the era followed the novel's publication and concerned the scene in which the princess of Clèves tells the prince that she loves the duc de Nemours. The Paris journal *Mercure Galant* invited its readers to vote on whether the princess was right or wrong to confide in her husband. Opinion was overwhelmingly against her, thus blurring the distinction between art and life—as in so much popular fiction, past and present.

Considered the first psychological novel, *The Princess of Clèves* influenced later generations of French novelists, from Rousseau to Camus. Because it is a novel by a woman about a woman, it can also be regarded as a study in women's issues. *The Princess of Clèves*, with its focus on inner conflict, moral complexity, and human truth, has earned an honored place alongside the works of the great women novelists of the nineteenth century and beyond.

A VINDICATION OF THE
RIGHTS OF WOMAN

by Mary Wollstonecraft

Mary Wollstonecraft's feminist manifesto, *A Vindication of the Rights of Woman* (1792), is the first major pronouncement of women's rights, a foundation text in the struggle for women's liberation and gender equality, combining the force of the Declaration of Independence with that of the Emancipation Proclamation. In an era in which women had virtually no legal standing, in which their intellectual abilities were denied, and their roles and identities defined by the requirements of obeying and pleasing men, Mary Wollstonecraft argued that a woman was not a kind of superior domesticated animal but a rational human being. She insisted that women's mental and moral capabilities must be recognized and encouraged, and their independence and autonomy nurtured. In a revolutionary era in which despotism was challenged and the rights of man asserted, Wollstonecraft radically called for the extension of rights and liberties to women as well. Although others had written on behalf of women's rights before Wollstonecraft, her book is the first comprehensive argument affirming the necessity for women's education and diagnosing the social and moral implications of gender inequality.

Mary Wollstonecraft (1759–1797) was, in the words of her

friend and admirer the poet William Blake, "born with a different Face." During her brief, tempestuous life, she rebelliously refused to adapt herself to the conventional standards applied to women, contending with every limitation imposed on them. As Virginia Woolf observed in her memorial to the impact of Wollstonecraft's life and work, "Many millions have died and been forgotten in the hundred and thirty years that have passed since she was buried; and yet as we read her letters and listen to her arguments and consider her experiments . . . and realize the high-handed and hot-blooded manner in which she cut her way to the quick of life, one form of immortality is hers undoubtedly: she is alive and active, she argues and experiments, we hear her voice and trace her influence even now among the living." Mary Wollstonecraft first identified the challenges women faced and still face in reaching their full potential, and *A Vindication of the Rights of Woman* is an essential work that remains one of the most influential texts ever written in the history of women's liberation.

Wollstonecraft's theories on women's education and status were based significantly on her own experiences as a daughter, single woman, mistress, mother, and wife. In each role she defied conventions and challenged traditional assumptions. Her father, Edward, gave up his trade as a silk weaver and moved his wife and six children from London to Yorkshire, where he tried his hand at farming. From an early age, Mary cultivated her intellectual development although intellectual attainments were generally thought beyond women's capabilities. Edward Wollstonecraft's failure as a farmer caused him to become increasingly bitter and violent, and he began to drink and to abuse his family. As Wollstonecraft's husband and first biographer, William Godwin, writes, Mary "would often throw herself between the despot and his victim, with the purpose to receive upon her own person the blows that might be directed against her mother." Mary observed and experienced firsthand the unequal power dynamic between husband and wife, father and daughter, and it became clear to her that she would have to earn a living to support herself and her family. Characteristically, she chose self-reliance and independence over the security afforded by marriage. "I will not marry," Wollstonecraft declared, "for I do not want to be tied to this nasty world, and old maids are of so little consequence that, let them live or die, nobody will laugh or cry. It is a happy thing to be a mere blank and to be able to pursue one's own whims where they lead without having a husband and half a hundred children at hand to tease and control a poor woman who wishes to be free."

At the time, professional options for respectable women were few: a woman could work as a companion, a teacher, or a governess. Wollstonecraft tried all three. At nineteen, she left home to become the live-in companion of a Mrs. Dawson and accompanied her to the resort town of Bath, where Wollstonecraft was exposed to the superficial high life of the fashionable at leisure; she was both bored and appalled at the superficial and frivolous behavior of the fashionable ladies of the day. In 1783, Wollstonecraft interceded on behalf of her younger sister, Eliza, whose marriage was duplicating the pattern of domestic violence of their own family. With the aid of her close friend, Fanny Blood, Wollstonecraft took Eliza away from her husband, and the three opened a school in Newington Green. There she wrote *Thoughts on the Education of Daughters* (1787), in which she argued that a girl's intellect should be developed. This radical notion, which forms the core of the leading pedagogical ideas of *A Vindication of the Rights of Woman*, challenged the popular contention of French philosopher Jean Jacques Rousseau in his novel *Emile and Sophie: Or, a New System of Education* (1762) that rational pursuits belong to men alone and that women should be educated only in the ways and means of pleasing their husbands. The school eventually foundered, and Wollstonecraft next accepted a position in Ireland as a governess to the children of Lord and Lady Kingsborough. She entered service at the great Kingsborough mansion (as she later recalled from the perspective of a supporter of the French Revolution), "with the same kind of feeling as I should have if I was going to the Bastille." Her independence, rebelliousness, and her sensitivity to the inequities of wealth made her service as a governess intolerable, and she eventually left for London, where the publisher Joseph Johnson gave her lodging and sufficient editorial work reviewing and translating to support herself. Johnson encouraged Wollstonecraft to try to become a professional writer—a radical option for an eighteenth-century woman. In her own words, she aspired to become "the first of new genus," a woman writer who dared to grapple with the major issues of the day and refused to be relegated to the sphere of irrelevant frivolity and superficiality that was the common lot of other female writers then. While Wollstonecraft's contemporaries such as Fanny Burney and Jane Austen wrote anonymously, and subsequent writers such as

Anne, Charlotte, and Emily Brontë, as well as George Eliot, chose male pseudonyms to help assure that their work would be taken seriously, Wollstonecraft openly proclaimed her identity as an author and entered fully into the intellectual debates of the time, subjects no previous English woman had attempted in print before.

Wollstonecraft's mentor, James Johnson, was at the center of intellectual London, and his circle included the political theorist Thomas Paine, scientist Joseph Priestly, philosopher William Godwin, painter Henry Fuseli, and poet William Blake. Most were freethinking radicals, and Mary, who shared their interests in challenging orthodoxy, began expressing her views in Johnson's *Analytical Review.* The central event that absorbed Wollstonecraft and her circle was the French Revolution. At first, the English greeted the overthrow of an outdated despotic regime with enthusiasm. However, Edmund Burke's conservative treatise, *Reflections on the Revolution in France* (1790), which argued in favor of the English monarchical status quo over the upheavals in France, helped turn English opinion against the Revolution. Wollstonecraft's *A Vindication of the Rights of Men* (1790) was among the first rebuttals of Burke's position. In it, she challenged Burke's denial of the natural rights of man in favor of law, custom, and tradition. For Wollstonecraft, liberty and self-determination are basic attributes of human nature, and mankind's drive to resist subjugation and oppression is morally and religiously sanctioned. Wollstonecraft's treatise was her first popular success and one of the earliest political essays by a woman.

If the implications of the French Revolution provided the stimulus for *A Vindication of the Rights of Men,* they also formed the initial motivation for the similarly titled *A Vindication of the Rights of Woman.* Her essay is dedicated to the French diplomat and statesman Talleyrand, whose report, in 1791 on public education, given to the Constituent Assembly that was drafting the new French constitution, had restricted a proposed system of free education to men only. *A Vindication of the Rights of Woman* attempted to make a case why women must be included in a reformed educational system of an enlightened republic. As Wollstonecraft makes clear in her dedication: "Contending for the rights of woman, my main argument is built on this simple principle, that if she be not prepared by education to become the companion of man, she will stop the progress of knowledge and virtue; for truth must be common to all, or it will be inefficacious with respect to its influence on general practice." To make her case for the necessity of women being properly educated, Wollstonecraft begins by attempting to establish the key commonality between men and women that will drive the logic of her argument:

> In what does man's pre-eminence over the brute creation consist? The answer is as clear as that a half is less than the whole; in Reason.
> What acquirement exalts one being above another? Virtue; we spontaneously reply.
> For what purpose were the passions implanted? That man by struggling with them might attain a degree of knowledge denied to the brutes; whispers Experience.
> Consequently the perfection of our nature and capability of happiness, must be estimated by the degree of reason, virtue, and knowledge, that distinguish the individual, and direct the laws which bind society: and that from the exercise of reason, knowledge and virtue naturally flow, is equally undeniable, if mankind be viewed collectively.

If the essential attribute of human nature is reason, which is perfected by knowledge, then education is central to forming a virtuous individual and society. And if this is true for men, Wollstonecraft points out, it must also be true for woman. "For man and woman," she argues, "truth . . . must be the same. . . . Women, I allow, may have different duties to fulfil, but they are *human* duties, and the principles that should regulate the discharge of them, I sturdily maintain, must be the same." If the purpose of life for all mankind is the perfection of one's nature through the exercise of reason, then, according to Wollstonecraft, it is immoral to deny women the opportunity to gain both knowledge and virtue.

A Vindication of the Rights of Woman goes on to analyze the positives that flow from the education of women and the negatives that exist through women's exclusion from education's benefits. In their present state, women are "barren blooming" flowers due to a "false system of education, gathered from the books written on this subject by men who, considering females rather as women than human creatures, have been more anxious to make them alluring mistresses than affectionate wives and rational mothers; and the understanding of the sex has been so bubbled by this specious homage, that the civilized women of the present century, with a few exceptions, are only anxious to inspire love, when they ought to cherish a nobler ambition, and by their abilities and virtues exact respect." Women's typical education produces a "puerile propriety," an immature individual incapable of orderly thought and, therefore, easily influenced. Such training ill-equips women from being good wives or mothers. Marriage, Wollstonecraft argues, must be grounded on mutual respect, which can only be achieved when women are encouraged to develop their intellectual abilities; otherwise subordination, inferiority, and inequality are inevitable and ruinous in forming virtuous wives and mothers:

> Taught from their infancy that beauty is woman's sceptre, the mind shapes itself to the body, and, roaming round its gilt cage, only seeks to adorn its prison. Men have various employments and pursuits which engage their attention, and give a character to the opening mind; but women, confined to one, and having their thoughts constantly directed to the most insignificant part of themselves, seldom extend their views beyond the triumph of the hour. But were their understanding once emancipated from the slavery to which the pride and sensuality of man and their short-sighted desire, like that of dominion in tyrants, of present sway, has subjected them, we should probably read of their weaknesses with surprise. . . . It is time to effect a revolution in female manners—time to restore to them their lost dignity—and make them, as a part of the human species, labour by reforming themselves to reform the world.

To bring about this revolution Wollstonecraft proposes establishing government schools "in which boys and girls might be educated together" up to the age of nine. After that, "girls and boys, intended for domestic employments, or mechanical trades, ought to be removed to other schools, and receive instruction, in some measure appropriate to the destination of each individual, the two sexes being still together in the morning; but in the afternoon, the girls should attend a school, where plain-work, mantua-making, millinery, &c. would be their employment." Young people of superior abilities, male and female, would pursue their academic training together. "In this plan of education," Wollstonecraft asserts, "the constitution of boys would not be ruined by the early debaucheries, which make men so selfish, or girls rendered weak and vain, by indolence, and frivolous pursuits."

Wollstonecraft concludes her argument with an enumeration of the various follies and weaknesses that proceed when women are allowed to remain ignorant, and recommends corrections that extend beyond proper education. Women, Wollstonecraft argues, must be able to support themselves if a husband or family member cannot. Women also should have the full legal rights of citizens, including the right to own property, have custody of their children, and participate in governmental affairs. She ends with a plea and a warning:

> Let women share the rights and she will emulate the virtues of man; for she must grow more perfect when emancipated, or justify the authority that chains such a weak being to her duty. . . . Be just then! O ye men of understanding! and mark not more severely what women do amiss, than the vicious tricks of the horse or the ass for whom ye provide provender—and allow her the privileges of ignorance, to whom ye deny the rights of reason, or ye will be worse than Egyptian task-masters, expecting virtue where nature has not given understanding!

Initial reaction to Wollstonecraft's essay was generally temperate and favorable. Opinion, however, shifted markedly when the details of Wollstonecraft's subsequent life were made known following her death, in 1797. In 1793, Wollstonecraft visited Paris to observe firsthand the progress of the Revolution and its increasing violence during the Reign of Terror. There, she met a number of the Revolution's leading political figures. She also began an affair with American adventurer Gilbert Imlay, who deserted her after she gave birth to a daughter, Fanny. Despondent, Wollstonecraft returned to England and attempted suicide by jumping off London's Putney Bridge into the Thames. She was rescued by passersby. In 1796, she married philosopher William Godwin. One year later, Mary Wollstonecraft Godwin died within days of giving birth to a second daughter, Mary, who would later marry the poet Percy Bysshe Shelley and create a literary classic of her own, *Frankenstein*. To memorialize his wife, Godwin published *Memoirs of the Author of a Vindication of the Rights of Woman*, which revealed to the public that Wollstonecraft had borne a child out of wedlock, was deserted by her lover, attempted suicide, and engaged in sexual relations with Godwin before marriage. Many, scandalized by these revelations, found confirmation of the immorality and dangerousness of her ideas in her unconventional lifestyle. One writer declared, "Her works will be read with disgust by every female who has any pretensions to delicacy; with detestation by everyone attached to the interests of religion and morality, and with indignation by anyone who might feel any regard for the unhappy woman, whose frailties should have been buried in oblivion." Another would resort to verse:

> Whilom this dame the Rights of Women writ,
> That is the title to the book she places,
> Exhorting bashful womankind to quit
> All foolish modesty and coy grimaces,
> And name their backsides as it were their faces;
> Such license loose-tongued liberty adores,
> Which adds to female speech exceeding graces;
> Lucky the maid that on her volume pores,
> A scripture archly fram'd for propagating whores.

And he summed up his views in the following couplet:

> For Mary verily would wear the breeches
> God help poor silly men from such usurping b– – – – –s.

Wollstonecraft's impassioned argument on behalf of women's rights and aspirations, and her often rebellious attempt to live out the full implications of her ideas, would prove to be too far ahead of their time, too radical an assault on the accepted certainties of gender assumptions. It would take almost a century for Wollstonecraft's life and work to be rediscovered and appreciated during the pursuit of the women's rights goals she first articulated. As critic R. M. Janes has argued, "Wollstonecraft's particular contribution was to state and enact the major topics of feminist discourse. In the positions she articulated and the life she led, she touched upon almost every topic that has since been raised. Everything is there."

EMMA

by Jane Austen

Emma is not Jane Austen's most popular and endearing novel—that distinction belongs to her 1813 work, *Pride and Prejudice*, with its winning heroine and noble hero, and the satisfying resolution of their romantic dilemma. *Emma* features a noble hero (with a name to match his character—Mr. Knightley) and a gratifying romantic resolution, but it also possesses a more complex—and flawed—heroine in the title character, as well as more intricate situations that showcase the fullness of Austen's maturity as a novelist. Published in 1816, *Emma* is the fourth of Austen's six novels and the one that most demonstrates her exceptional skill as a social satirist, psychologist, and dramatist. It has also been chosen for this volume because it is considered to be the finest novel by one of the greatest novelists of all time.

Jane Austen (1775–1817) is the ideal example of the maxim that an author should write about what he or she knows best, and that everyday experience can be the source of great and enduring art. Austen was born into the English gentry class, whose customs she exclusively detailed in her novels. She was the youngest daughter of seven children of Reverend George Austen, the rector of Steventon in Hampshire, and Cassandra Leigh Austen. Jane

Austen and her older sister, Cassandra, were educated privately and at schools in Oxford, Southampton, and Reading. Austen grew up well read in English classics, prose, and poetry, was reasonable well versed in languages, and was also skilled in such traditionally feminine pursuits as music and needlepoint.

In 1801, George Austen, accompanied by his family, retired to Bath. After his death, in 1805, the family moved to Southampton to be closer to the two youngest Austen sons, who were in the navy. The Austens returned to Hampshire, in 1809, settling in the village of Chawton, where Jane remained until her death from Addison's disease at the age of forty-two. She shared a room with her sister all her life and had no personal acquaintance with any other important writers of the day. All her novels concern the central domestic drama of matrimony, but Austen never married, although her biographers have speculated that there were several romantic attachments and know of at least one marriage proposal. Rather than imitating her heroines and securing a husband and the property that went with him, Austen involved herself with her wide circle of friends and relatives, helped to run the family household (one of her duties was to oversee the sugar stores), and concentrated on her writing.

Jane Austen's writing career is divided into two distinct periods. Her earliest work, written in Steventon during the 1790s, includes fragments, satires, literary burlesques, and the first drafts of what would become her early novels: *Pride and Prejudice, Sense and Sensibility*, and *Northanger Abbey* (published posthumously). Then came a twelve-year lull, during which Austen wrote little. After the family's relocation to Chawton, Austen reworked her first three novels and composed her last three: *Mansfield Park, Emma*, and *Persuasion* (also published after her death). She wrote between domestic chores and social events at a tiny table in her drawing room. Austen chose for her subject the world she knew best and once told a niece who was thinking of writing novels, "Three or four families in a country village is the very thing to work on." Her novels—socially sophisticated, sharply rendered comedies of manners—were described by her as "the little bit (two inches wide) of Ivory on which I work with so fine a Brush, as produces little effect after much labour."

Emma, the longest of Austen's novels and the only one named for the central protagonist, is the most psychologically rich, with its closest focus on the inner development of its heroine. The novel depicts a year in the life of Highbury, a Surrey village in which nothing unusual generally happens beyond the natural cycle of births, deaths, engagements, and marriages, and the various unexceptional day-to-day occurrences of a self-contained, provincial community. Like all of Jane Austen's novels, *Emma* charts the progress of its protagonist to the altar, but unlike Austen's other novels, *Emma*'s heroine is unhampered by the lack of fortune and status, with only the disadvantage of her own immaturity to complicate her destiny: "Emma Woodhouse, handsome, clever, and rich, with a comfortable home and happy disposition, seemed to unite some of the blessings of existence; and had lived nearly twenty-one years in the world with very little to distress or vex her." Emma's mother is dead, her older sister is married and living in London, and her father is a hypochondriac and self-proclaimed invalid. Emma is the uncontested mistress of Hatfield, the most prominent household in Highbury, which she dominates. Only her sister's brother-in-law, Mr. Knightley, is willing to criticize her, and so Emma is afflicted with the "power of having rather too much her own way, and a disposition to think a little too well of herself."

The novel opens with Emma left on her own for the first time after her companion and former governess, Miss Taylor, marries the Woodhouses' neighbor, Mr. Weston, and leaves Hatfield. Emma flatters herself that she has successfully arranged the match, and she looks for another opportunity to try her hand at matchmaking. She befriends the impressionable Harriet Smith, "the natural daughter of somebody," and recklessly decides that she is the perfect mate for the local vicar, Mr. Elton. But to make the match happen, Emma must convince Harriet that her attachment to a local farmer, Robert Martin, is beneath her, and she intimidates Harriet into rejecting his proposal. Indulging in a romantic fantasy, Emma commits a series of social blunders that underscore her thoughtlessness, vanity, and snobbery. Her encouragement of Mr. Elton on behalf of Harriet is misconstrued by the clergyman as Emma's own interest in him, and she is comically blindsided by Mr. Elton's marriage proposal following a Christmas party that concludes the novel's first volume. Mr. Elton's drunken impertinence exposes Emma's errors of judgment in which the exaggerated sense of her own importance, together with her sense of infallibility and her snobbish prejudices, prevents her from correctly seeing the reality of social situations or the true nature of those around her. She ends this first stage of her development vowing never again to engage in matchmaking. Emma has played with love and romance by proxy through Harriet; however, the stakes will increase as she allows her own affections to be engaged and when she finds herself the victim of another character's scheming and manipulation.

Emma's superiority, assumed rather than earned, will also be challenged, as three newcomers arrive to help Highbury awake from its moribund routine, as well as to help Austen's heroine shed her complacency and complete her education. One is the estimable Jane Fairfax, the talented young niece of Miss Bates, a garrulous, slightly foolish Highbury spinster. Brought up and educated by Colonel and Mrs. Campbell as a companion to their daughter, Jane has returned to Highbury to visit her aunt and grandmother after Miss Campbell's marriage to Mr. Dixon. The modest Jane is Emma's equal (or superior) in everything but fortune; consequently she is not one of Emma's favorites. The second newcomer is Frank Churchill, Mr. Weston's son, who has arrived in Highbury to pay his respects to his father's new bride. The attractive and agreeably sociable Frank flirts with Emma, and the pair enjoys a secret joke at Jane's expense, alleging that she has had an unhappy love affair with Mr. Dixon, who seems to be the only possible source for the gift of a piano that Jane has received. The third character to arrive at Highbury is the former Augusta Hawkins, now married to Mr. Elton. An ill-bred parvenu, Augusta Elton challenges Emma for social dominance in Highbury and provides a mirror that reflects her own tendency toward vanity and snobbery: "Mrs. Elton was a vain woman, extremely well satisfied with herself, and thinking much of her own importance. . . . She meant to shine and be very superior, but with manners which had been formed in a bad school, pert and familiar." The bad breeding and behavior of both husband and wife is evident at the long-awaited ball at the Crown Inn, where they snub Harriet. Mr. Knightley forgoes his previous reluctance to dance and saves the embarrassed Harriet by becoming her partner (thus chivalrously living up to his name). It is a fateful moment for Emma, who acknowledges Mr. Knightley's superior nature and begins to see him as a potential romantic partner as well. The following day, Harriet is bothered by a band of gypsies (the novel's only melodramatic event) and is rescued by Frank Churchill. Harriet later confesses to Emma that she is now over

Mr. Elton and prefers someone more superior, leading Emma to think that she must mean Frank. Matchmaking yet again, Emma willingly accedes to her friend's preference.

As summer arrives, the complicated tangle of relationships reaches a critical point. Jane prepares to accept a governess position arranged by Mrs. Elton; Frank is inexplicably out of humor at the news; and Mr. Knightley decides to revive the social life of his estate, Donwell Abbey. A visit to Mr. Knightley's home stimulates a more ambitious picnic to Box Hill, where Frank caters to the worst of Emma's imperious tendencies by proposing a game in which each of the party is commanded to entertain her by saying one clever thing, "or two things moderately clever—or three things very dull indeed." The garrulous Miss Bates chooses the last, prompting Emma's unpardonably rude remark, "Ah! ma'am, but there may be a difficulty. Pardon me—but you will be limited as to number—only three at once." This witty remark at Miss Bates's expense crystallizes all of Emma's shortcomings and is the climax of the novel. Emma's deficiencies of character are made painfully clear to her in Mr. Knightley's later rebuke. Mortified by the hurt she has caused an old family friend who deserves her respect and compassion, and distressed at eliciting Mr. Knightley's poor opinion of her behavior, a repentant Emma visits Miss Bates the next day to apologize. This act of reformation, together with the acknowledgment of her error, paves the way for the comic conclusion of the novel, which depends on Emma's maturation.

In rapid succession, complication gives way to clarity, romance, and marriage. It is revealed that Frank has been secretly engaged to Jane all along, and his duplicity and manipulation are the final telling comparison with Emma's own behavior, which at times has also been far from open and honest. Emma's first thought, however, is for "poor Harriet," who is assumed to be in despair over the news. Instead, in the novel's great comic revelation, Harriet admits that, encouraged by Emma to aim for a husband of a higher station, she has set her sights on Mr. Knightley and not on Frank—it was Mr. Knightley's chivalrous behavior at the ball, not Frank's rescue of Harriet from the gypsies, that has engaged her affections. Emma is shocked into the recognition of her own blindness and folly: "With insufferable vanity had she believed herself in the secret of everybody's feelings; with unpardonable arrogance proposed everybody's destiny. She was proved to be universally mistaken. She had brought evil on Harriet, on herself, and she too much feared, on Mr. Knightley." Equally powerful is her realization "that darted through her with the speed of an arrow that Mr. Knightley must not marry anyone but herself." Initially misperceiving the other's feelings—Knightley, that Emma is in despair over Frank's engagement, and Emma over the presumed affection between Knightley and Harriet—the couple comes to a satisfactory understanding in the end, as Knightley proposes and Emma accepts. To add to the happy conclusion of reconciliation and unity, Harriet receives and accepts a second proposal from the hapless farmer, Robert Martin.

At his request, Jane Austen dedicated *Emma* to the Prince Regent (later George IV), who was a fan of the novelist. It sold quickly in its first edition of 1,500 copies, but a second edition was not published until 1833. Jane Austen herself had misgivings about her novel, fearing that "to those readers who have preferred 'Pride and Prejudice' it will appear inferior in wit, and to those who have preferred 'Mansfield Park' very inferior in good sense." Even more troublesome was her concern that she had created a heroine "whom no one but myself will much like." It is true that the most liked of Austen's heroines is undoubtedly Elizabeth Bennett, and *Pride and Prejudice* is the Austen novel most often read, as well as filmed—from the 1940 Hollywood version starring Greer Garson and Laurence Olivier to two miniseries as well as the 2001 comedy takeoff of the novel, *Bridget Jones's Diary*. But *Emma* has had its modern-day aficionados as well. During the 1990s, there were two well-executed versions of the novel: one a film starring Gwyneth Paltrow and the other a British miniseries. Perhaps the most artfully rendered and appealing film adaptation of *Emma* was Amy Heckerling's 1995 satire, *Clueless*, which updated Austen's novel to present-day Beverly Hills and changed Emma's name to Cher. This version speaks to the timelessness of the novel, which is, after all, essentially a story about a young woman who must learn painful lessons about human nature and bring her ego in line with reality in order to mature. Emma, like the reader, is schooled in the complicated matters of life and love, in which wisdom and clarity replace self-deception and confusion.

JANE EYRE

by Charlotte Brontë

Charlotte Brontë's novel of an independent-minded, principled young governess who comes to love her morally ambiguous, emotionally tortured employer, *Jane Eyre* (1847) is a romantic, psychological, and feminist classic that in fundamental ways revolutionized the art of fiction, with its assault on conventional nineteenth-century morality and its challenge to the novel's accepted methods of storytelling. The literary precursor of the modern gothic suspense novel, *Jane Eyre* also inspired such authors as Daphne du Maurier, whose best-selling *Rebecca* (*see* Honorable Mentions) began the twentieth-century genre of romance novels featuring an unassuming though plucky heroine and a dark Byronic bad boy ultimately redeemed by love.

Charlotte Brontë's life had a gothic quality that informed her work. Born in 1816, she was the third daughter of Patrick Brontë, the vicar of Haworth in the West Riding of Yorkshire, a picturesque but isolated region of impassable roads and desolate, windswept moors. After their mother's death, in 1821, the six Brontë children were cared for by an aunt and their puritanical, tyrannical father. Charlotte's biographer, English novelist Elizabeth Gaskell, wrote of Patrick Brontë, "He did not speak when he was annoyed or displeased, but worked off his volcanic wrath by firing pistols out the back door in rapid succession." After the two eldest Brontë daughters died of tuberculosis contracted at school, Charlotte and her sister Emily, also at school, were brought home. There, together with their younger sister Anne and brother Branwell, they were largely left to themselves. The major imaginative moment of their young lives occurred when their father brought home a set of wooden soldiers for his son. The toy soldiers became the *dramatis personae* in an ever-lengthening series of fantasy stories in which the children created the imaginary kingdoms of Gondal and Angria, and populated them with invented and historical figures. Charlotte's first stories, written in minuscule script in tiny homemade books, recorded the various lives and adventures of the characters in these fantasy kingdoms and provide an essential key to her artistic vision as a novelist.

The siblings' imaginative play continued well beyond childhood, but economic circumstances forced the Brontë children to abandon their fantasy empire of wish fulfillment to make their way in the world. Both Charlotte and Emily worked as teachers, and Anne became a governess. Branwell, whom it was hoped would succeed as a portrait painter, became instead the family disgrace, succumbing to drink and opium. To keep the family together, the sisters hatched a plan to open their own boarding school, and to perfect their French, Charlotte and Emily left Yorkshire to attend a school in Brussels. Left on her own when Emily's homesickness drove her back to Haworth, Charlotte developed an emotional attachment to the school's owner, whose wife quickly stepped in and stopped the infatuation. Charlotte returned to Yorkshire, where she and her sisters collaborated on a volume of poetry, published at their own expense under the names Currer, Ellis and Acton Bell. Only two copies were sold, and the sisters next turned to the commercial possibilities of the novel.

Charlotte Brontë's first attempt, *The Professor,* a one-volume realistic story based on her time spent in Brussels, was rejected by at least seven publishers. However, one sympathetic publisher suggested that "a work in three volumes would meet with careful attention," and she recast some of the elements of her childhood fantasy stories into a new novel in which she "endeavored to import a more vivid interest." In August 1847, a year after it was begun, *Jane Eyre* was published. The London season's literary sensation, a second edition of the novel was published three months after the first, and a third two months after that, an extraordinary success for the first book of an unknown author. *Jane Eyre* was published with the pseudonym Currer Bell to match Anne and Emily's Acton and Ellis Bell because, as Charlotte explained, "We had a vague impression that authoresses are liable to be looked on with prejudice." Anne's *Agnes Grey* and Emily's *Wuthering Heights* had been accepted for publication before *Jane Eyre*, but both novels did not appear until December 1847, when their publisher, hoping to profit from Charlotte's success, suggested in advertisements that their works were by one Mr. Bell, "the successful New Novelist." Anne's and Emily's novels, mistakenly believed to be the cruder, apprentice efforts of Currer Bell, were ignored. By 1848, *Jane Eyre* was a popular success. That same year, Branwell died, and at his funeral, Emily caught a cold that developed into tuberculosis. She died at the end of the year. Anne Brontë also died of tuberculosis, in the spring of 1849, leaving Charlotte alone. Charlotte wrote two other novels, *Shirley* and *Villette*, and in 1855, she married her father's curate. She died of tuberculosis while pregnant. Patrick Brontë survived all of his children, living to the age of eighty-four.

Jane Eyre, the story of a heroine, in Charlotte Brontë's words, "as plain and small" as herself, traces the title character's development from her troubled childhood to independence as a governess. In the care of her widowed aunt, Mrs. Reed, Jane is mistreated and neglected in favor of the three spoiled Reed children until her anger at her situation prompts a violent outburst that causes her to be delivered to the equally oppressive charity institution, Lowood Asylum. There, amidst the poor living conditions and repressive atmosphere, her rebellion recurs. Eventually she learns to harness her egoism and passion, which establishes the novel's dominant conflict between assertion and restraint, as well as love and duty. Jane makes friends at the school and eventually becomes a teacher there before accepting a position as a governess at Thornfield Hall, the country estate of Edward Rochester. Her task is to care for Rochester's illegitimate daughter, Adele Varens, a sweet, timid child. Despite Jane's homeliness and lack of status and sophistication, Rochester's brusque, cynical, world-weary manner, and a series of strange and alarming occurrences, including the sounds of maniacal female laughter, the burning of Rochester's bed, and the wounding of a mysterious visitor, Jane and Rochester develop a mutual regard for each other and eventually fall in love. Jane discovers that a disturbed woman lives on the locked third floor of the mansion; the night before her wedding to Rochester, the woman appears in her room. Rochester tells Jane that the woman is the household's unsavory seamstress, Grace Poole, but he has not told his bride-to-be the truth, and at the altar his sensational secret is revealed: concealed in Thornfield's attic is a madwoman named Bertha Mason, whom Rochester had married in the West Indies fifteen years earlier. Crushed by Rochester's deception, Jane departs Thornfield, and after nearly perishing on the moors is taken in by the Reverend St. John Rivers and his sisters. Jane calls herself Jane Elliott and returns to teaching. She rejects Rivers's proposal of a loveless marriage and a life as a missionary's wife. The claims of her former love prove stronger than her sense of duty to the honorable but emotionally shallow Rivers. After a telepathic vision in which she hears Rochester call her name, Jane returns to Thornfield to find the mansion burned, Bertha Mason dead, and Rochester blinded and maimed. With the moral and legal obstructions conveniently eliminated and Rochester sufficiently punished and penitent, the pair is reunited, and in one of most famous lines in fiction that begins the novel's final chapter, Jane records, "Reader, I married him." Rochester's sight returns and he is able to see the son born to him and Jane several years later.

In *Jane Eyre*, Charlotte Brontë recast the elements of the nineteenth-century gothic romance—its dark secrets, presentiments, coincidences, and eerie atmospherics—into a moral and psychological journey of a soul to fulfillment. At the center of the novel's drama is an unconventional heroine, never seen in fiction before. Jane is lowly and plain; she is forced to earn her living in a society of limited possibilities. Her hard-earned reward of the heart is played out against her struggle toward independence and emotional equilibrium. It is not surprising that Jane and her creator have been cited as early feminist models. Readers of today's romance novels would recognize a standard theme in Brontë's story of a lowly governess who falls in love with her wealthy employer, accepting him despite his rake's history and sensational secret. For the many nineteenth-century readers captivated by the novel, *Jane Eyre* was unique and daring, both for its story and its style, as well as for its intense exploration of the narrator's private thoughts and feelings (previously the province of poetry, not the novel). The popularity of Charlotte Brontë's first-person narrative of development was no doubt a factor in Charles Dickens's decision to launch his own first-person bildungsroman, *David Copperfield*, and influenced William Thackeray's similar attempt in *Pendennis*. For Thackerary, *Jane Eyre* hit even closer to home, when Charlotte Brontë, who greatly admired the novelist, dedicated the second edition to him. Thackeray was rumored to be Brontë's model for the character of Edward Rochester; it was also alleged that she was Thackeray's mistress.

Not all of the novel's first readers were delighted with the book, however. Jane's frank avowal of love for the morally suspect Rochester, as well as her rejection of the conventional role of the passive, relenting female in favor of independence and a self-determined morality, presented a challenge to Victorian orthodoxy and authority. Some found the book's sentiments, in the words of a contemporary reader, "un-Christian or worse." One appalled reviewer delivered the ultimate Victorian coup de grâce, charging that the book "might be written by a woman but not by a lady."

It is tempting for modern readers of *Jane Eyre* to filter their view of Charlotte Brontë's great work through celluloid and video images. The subject of at least thirteen film and television adaptations (one in every decade of the twentieth century since 1914), *Jane Eyre* shares—with Dickens's *David Copperfield* and *Great Expectations*, Flaubert's *Madame Bovary*, Hugo's *Les Misérables*, and Twain's *The Adventures of Huckleberry Finn*—the distinction of being one of the most often filmed novels. However, such adaptations should not replace or obscure the achievement of the original. The remarkable power of *Jane Eyre* derives as much from its intimate exposure of the narrator as from its melodramatic plot, with its sensational central secret and its deviations from reality through the heightened aura of the uncanny, which lends the novel a poetic, symbolic expressiveness. Rejecting the restriction of the novel to a surface imitation of life, Charlotte Brontë grafts onto her story a poetic method and intensity to achieve a depth of feeling and interior awareness in the stages of her heroine's moral and psychological development, linking each stage, as in a poem, through association, imagery, and symbolism. *Jane Eyre* brings to the reader the inner world of the psyche and the heart's private longing.

THE SCARLET LETTER

by *Nathaniel Hawthorne*

The great Victorian novelist Anthony Trollope once described the experience of reading Nathaniel Hawthorne: "He will have plunged you into melancholy, he will have overshadowed you with black forebodings, he will have almost crushed you with imaginary sorrows; but he will have enabled you to feel yourself an inch taller during the process." Hawthorne's genius, unique in American letters, is unfaltering in its moral seriousness; both bleakness and ecstasy can be experienced in his fiction. He addressed the Puritan obsession with the wages of sin, using it to focus it upon the hidden recesses of human nature, the consequences of moral transgressions, and the conflicts between authority, personal freedom, and responsibility. In *The Scarlet Letter* (1850), pride, guilt, retribution, and the alienation of the individual from society are explored in the story of Hester Prynne, who, despite the novel's setting in mid-seventeenth-century Puritan Boston, can be considered the first feminist central character in what is America's first great novel.

Nathaniel Hawthorne (1804–1864) was well versed in the culture of Puritan society. The Hathorne family (Hawthorne added the *w* after leaving college) could trace its ancestry to a member of John Winthrop's Massachusetts Bay Colony who moved to Salem, in 1636. One ancestor was a judge in the Salem witchcraft trials, and, according to family legend, one of the victims placed a curse on Judge Hathorne and all his descendants before her execution. Hawthorne's father was a ship's captain, and his mother was the daughter of Richard Manning, a blacksmith who became the proprietor and manager of the Boston and Salem Stage Company. When Nathaniel was only four, his father died in Surinam of yellow fever, and the family was absorbed into the large Manning clan. Nathaniel's childhood was spent between Salem and Maine, where the Mannings owned property, and he felt somewhat lost in the practical bustle of the large family. A sensitive child, Hawthorne decided by the age of seventeen that he would become a writer: "I do not want to be a doctor and live by men's diseases, nor a minister to live by their sins, nor a lawyer and live by their quarrels. So, I don't see that there is anything left for me but to be an author."

After graduating from Bowdoin College, Hawthorne returned to Salem, where, from 1825 to 1837, he lived a reclusive life, reading voraciously, particularly in the history of colonial New England, and emerging from his room only for evening strolls and occasional walking trips around Massachusetts. His first published work was the novel, *Fanshawe,* based on his experiences at Bowdoin, which appeared anonymously, in 1828. The novel was ignored and so dissatisfied its author that he would later seek out available copies to destroy. Hawthorne devoted the next twenty years to the shorter form of the prose tale and sketch. In the absence of an international copyright agreement, native novelists struggled in the marketplace because American publishers were able to pirate the best English writers, like Scott and Dickens, for free with impunity and therefore had no financial incentive to cultivate homegrown talent. But Hawthorne did find a market for his short fiction in New England magazines and newspapers, as well as in *The Token,* a Boston gift book annual, where most of the works collected in *Twice-Told Tales* (1837) first appeared. He worked hard at perfecting his craft, learning to project onto fictional characters and situations the moral and existential themes that fascinated him. Hawthorne's early tales, such as "The Gentle Boy," "Young Goodman Brown," "The Minister's Black Veil," "The Birthmark," "Ethan Brand," and "Endicott and the Red Cross," all illustrate a preoccupation with the psychological canons of the Puritan past—the ambiguity of sin, the conflict between heart and head, and the corrosive power of guilt—as well as the character types and settings that he would return to in *The Scarlet Letter.*

In 1842, Hawthorne married Sophia Peabody, and, unable to earn a sufficient income from his writing to support his growing family, he secured a position as an official at the Salem Customhouse from 1845 to 1849. Hawthorne's was a Democratic political appointment that he lost with the Whig election victory of Zachary Taylor. His dismissal, prompted by false allegations by Salem Whigs of "corruption, iniquity, and fraud," received national attention and contributed to the success he would later achieve with *The Scarlet Letter.* After losing his position, he returned to writing in earnest to make up for his lost income. In September 1849, he began *The Scarlet Letter* as a tale for a projected new volume to be titled *Old-Time Legends: Together with Sketches, Experimental and Ideal.* The novel's themes and situations reflect ideas recorded earlier in his notebook. Hester Prynne, his heroine, is anticipated in the entry: "The life of a woman, who, by the old colony law, was condemned always to wear the letter A, sewed on her garment, in token of her having committed adultery."

James T. Fields of Ticknor and Fields, the book's publisher, read the uncompleted manuscript and encouraged Hawthorne to expand the story and publish it as a separate work. It was finished in February 1850, and it became an immediate popular success, with the first edition of 2,500 copies selling out in three days. Two more editions appeared before the end of the year, and—although only 7,500 copies would be sold in Hawthorne's lifetime, earning him a grand total of $1,500—*The Scarlet Letter* has never gone out of print since it first appeared, becoming, along with *Moby-Dick* and *The Adventures of Huckleberry Finn*, an enduring classic and a continuing subject of serious critical literary scrutiny.

The Scarlet Letter centers on Hester Prynne, an attractive, apparently widowed young woman who has shocked and angered her rigidly Puritan community by taking a lover and bearing a daughter by him. Hester has been convicted of adultery—a crime against society that is punishable by death—but the Boston magistrates have decided to be merciful to her and have decreed that she stand before the townsfolk on the scaffold near the marketplace for three hours with her infant in her arms. To mark her as a sinner, she is also to wear on the bosom of her dress, embroidered in red cloth, the letter *A*—for "adulteress"—for the rest of her life. Governor Bellingham, Reverend John Wilson, and Reverend Arthur Dimmesdale, a young and eloquent minister, plead with Hester in vain to reveal the guilty man's identity. She refuses, much to the relief of Dimmesdale, since it is he who is Hester's secret lover. While standing on the scaffold, Hester sees a familiar figure on the edge of the crowd. The "stranger" is her elderly husband, Dr. Roger Prynne, who had sent Hester ahead of him from England two years earlier and had been presumed dead. The physician silently cautions her not to recognize him publicly and later, under the name of Roger Chillingworth, visits her in prison, where he demands to know the name of his wife's lover. Once again, Hester refuses to divulge his identity. Chillingworth vows to find the father of Hester's child and forces her to take an oath not to reveal to anyone that he is her husband. Shunned and ridiculed by the townsfolk, Hester lives in a lonely cottage by the seashore and supports herself and her daughter, Pearl, through her needlework. Her only companion is Pearl, a beautiful but willful and independent-minded child, who sometimes upsets her mother by the "freakish, elfish" look that comes into her eyes. Hester both loves and fears her bright, capricious child, but it is through Pearl that she demonstrates her own strength and independence, when she fights the authorities for the right to raise the child herself. She comes to see her daughter as a blessing rather than as an evil visited upon her by her sin.

Dimmesdale is unable to either confess or to accept his sin, and his health begins to fail. Tormented by guilt, he punishes himself by long night vigils, sometimes whipping himself, at other times fasting and praying for hours. Chillingworth, suspicious of Dimmesdale, moves into the reverend's house, ostensibly to provide medical assistance, but in reality to bait Dimmesdale into revealing his secret. Dimmesdale grows to fear and hate the physician, confessing as much to Hester when the two meet by chance one evening at the pillory scaffold. Later, Hester reveals Chillngworth's true identity to Dimmesdale, and the two make plans to leave Boston together with Pearl for a new life in England. However, Chillingworth books passage on the same ship, and Hester realizes that they can never escape him. After Dimmesdale gives a brilliant Election Day sermon, the crowd loudly cheers him in the marketplace. As the crowd begins to leave, Dimmesdale, by now weak and ill, ascends the scaffold with Hester's help and confesses that he is Pearl's father. He tears open his shirt and reveals a "red stigma" on his breast, which many of the townspeople later claim was a scarlet *A*. He then collapses on the scaffold and dies. Chillingworth, thus avenged, loses his purpose in life, and he dies within the year, leaving money and property to Pearl in England and America. Hester and Pearl leave Boston, but Hester later returns alone to the community and lives in the same small cottage by the seashore. It is thought that Pearl is happily married in Europe. Hester continues to wear the scarlet letter and work as a seamstress. Unhappy women troubled by affairs of the heart come to her for advice. After a long life, Hester dies and is buried beside Dimmesdale.

The power of *The Scarlet Letter* comes from Hawthorne's tight concentration on his four major characters—Hester, Dimmesdale, Chillingworth, and Pearl—in a series of striking tableaux that animate the novel's action and the characters' moral and psychological natures. Rather than explaining the causes of Hester's sin, Hawthorne focuses on its consequences by beginning the novel with the repentance extracted from her by the Puritan authorities. The nature of her sin is underscored by the multiple associations of the scarlet letter she is forced to wear as a public acknowledgment of her fallen nature. The scarlet letter becomes the novel's magnetic central symbol; it attracts the characters' reactions and is emblematic of each character's state of mind. For Hester, the letter is a sign of her human fallibility and her fate, which she freely chooses, acknowledges, and accepts. Ultimately, Hester, the fallen woman, is shown to be far more worthy of sympathy and respect than the narrow, intolerant Puritan community of the righteous. For Dimmesdale, the outward paragon of moral authority and saintliness, the scarlet letter is a symbol of his sinful nature and the guilty secret that he denies until the novel's climax, when he finally reveals his own "red stigma." The scarlet letter drives Chillingworth, the man of intellect and science, to hide his relationship to Hester and causes him to embark on a self-destructive pursuit of revenge, during which he is shown as more corrupt than the two lovers. The uncontrollable Pearl, who is brilliantly dressed in scarlet, is the living symbol of Hester's sin, condemned by the letter to an existence outside the human family until Dimmesdale's dying admission of his paternity.

When it was first published, *The Scarlet Letter* far surpassed any previous American novel and rivaled the greatest European works. It is the first undisputed American masterpiece, remarkable and unique for its intense moral and psychological exploration of four suffering souls in what was the dominant American culture of the early colonial era. Something of *The Scarlet Letter*'s power can be glimpsed in the reaction of Hawthorne's sensible wife after her husband finished the novel and read the last part of it to her: "It broke her heart," Hawthorne wrote.

MADAME BOVARY

by Gustave Flaubert

Subtitled *A Tale of Provincial Life*, Flaubert's masterpiece, published in book form in 1857, details the descent of his title character, desperate for sensation and deluded by romantic illusion, into tawdry affairs, finally destroyed by the conjunction of her nature and a repressive, inhospitable middle-class provincial environment. *Madame Bovary* is a must-read because it is one of the greatest and most original novels of all time and because, in Emma Bovary, Flaubert created a fascinating character whose psyche he painstakingly dissects and analyzes within the context of her constricted situation. It can also be argued that Flaubert, for the first time in fiction, presented readers with a female protagonist every bit as complex and dynamic as a central male character.

Considered a supreme example of the realistic novel, *Madame Bovary* is the artful product of a slow, meticulous writer intent on *le mot juste* and complete objectivity in telling his story. Flaubert devoted weeks to individual scenes and days to a single page; his fifty-six-month, seven-hour nightly struggle to complete *Madame Bovary* represents the birthing pains of a new kind of fictional narrative, one which earned Flaubert the accolade from Henry

James of the "novelist's novelist," and which gave the novel the respectability and seriousness in France formerly reserved for poetry, tragedy, and the epic.

Flaubert evolved his high standard for the novel, his advocacy of realism, and the novelist's strict artistic control over his material in a hard-fought struggle with his own divided temperament, which oscillated between romantic escape and the claims of a world that he often found disappointing and appalling. Flaubert's battle to shape the contradictory elements of romance and realism into an original work of art provides an interesting perspective on the dedication and craftsmanship involved in the development of what is often referred to today as a novelist's individual "voice."

Born in Rouen, Gustave Flaubert (1821–1880) came from the French bourgeois background that he analyzed so meticulously in *Madame Bovary* and found so limited and stultifying. His father was the chief surgeon at the Hôtel-Dieu hospital; his mother was the daughter of a small-town doctor. Possessing a precocious literary talent, Flaubert began writing romantic stories at the age of sixteen. His family, however, was determined that he should become a lawyer, and Flaubert spent a year at the University of Paris, where he studied little and failed his examinations. In 1844, a nervous collapse brought him back to the family estate at Croisset, near Rouen, where, after the death of his father in 1846, he lived with his solicitous mother and adoring, orphaned niece for the rest of his life, devoting his time exclusively to writing. Freed from the financial need to publish or the desire to court fame through gratifying conventional literary tastes, Flaubert began to evolve his narrative aesthetic, attempting to reconcile what he perceived was the duality of his nature: "There are in me, literally speaking, two distinct persons: one who is infatuated with bombast, lyricism, eagle flights, sonorities of phrase and lofty ideas; and another who digs and burrows into the truth as deeply as he can, who likes to treat the humble fact as respectfully as a big one, who would like to make you feel almost *physically* the things he reproduces."

Having finished an early version of what would eventually become *The Temptation of Saint Anthony* (1874) in 1849, which friends criticized mercilessly as romantically excessive, formless, and vague, Flaubert, at their suggestion, embarked upon a story of ordinary life, borrowed from the actual circumstances of the wife of one of his father's former medical students, whose love affairs and debts lead her to suicide. With a mixture of abhorrence for and fascination with this rather sordid story of provincial life, Flaubert began on St. Gustave's Day, September 9, 1851, the nearly five-year effort to penetrate imaginatively his characters and their environment. With a combination of compassion and satire, Flaubert mounted a withering indictment of his society's most cherished illusions: material satisfaction, faith in science and progress, religious consolation, and the ennobling power of love and passion. He aspired to write "a book about nothing," in which the trivial details of stultifying bourgeois life would replace the expected dramatic and romantic stimulus of other novels; it would be held together not by action but by ideas and sustained by his pursuit of *le mot juste,* in which every word, image, and scene contributed to an underlying pattern of meaning. Flaubert observed, "I am trying to be as buttoned up in this one as I was slovenly in the others and to follow a geometrically straight line. No lyricism, no commentaries, author's personality absent. It will make depressing reading. There will be atrocious things in it—wretched, sordid things." Flaubert's agonies of composition, which involved spending entire days finding the right phrase and eventually vomiting in a chamber pot after describing Emma Bovary's death by poison, suggest the novelist's attempt to subsume his entire personality in the artistic process, which more than justifies his later explanation of his protagonist's origin: "*Madame Bovary, c'est moi.*"

Emma Bovary, *née* Rouault, the character that inspired such unsettling devotion, is a convent-educated beauty with peasant roots, who has been deeply infected by the novels she has read and who dreams of the same idealized romantic fulfillment. Emotional rather than affectionate, sentimental rather than genuine, Emma is incapable of reconciling her desires and responsibilities, and becomes a martyr to her illusions, crushed when she attempts to act out her fantasies of passion and spirituality in a provincial world that only values the material, not the spiritual or the passionate that she craves. Wed to Charles Bovary, a widowed doctor of plodding mediocrity who adores her, Emma is disappointed in her marriage and unfulfilled in her expected role as wife and mother. Fueled by the stimulants of passion and the accoutrements of refinement that her limited means cannot sustain, she compensates with affairs with two men who fail her. Her first lover, Rodolphe, is a caddish libertine who exploits romantic clichés to gain Emma as his mistress but who refuses to assist her desired escape from her hateful life. Léon is Emma's pallid, timorous second lover, who seduces her not on horseback, like her previous chivalric parody, Rodolphe, but during a cab ride through the streets of Rouen. Inevitably, the prosaic, limiting reality of provincial life triumphs over her illusions and desires. Emma's life in the narrow confines of the town of Yonville is governed by the pedantic hypocrite Homais, Yonville's pharmacist, and the ineffectual parish priest, Father Bournisien, so lacking in his spiritual mission that he is incapable of recognizing even the proverbial cliché that men and women do not live by bread alone. Her dream world collapses from deceit and debt, and climaxes in suicide. In dying, Emma is finally given the ultimate opportunity of sacrificial martyrdom to become the romantic heroine that she had always aspired to be, but her death, like her life, is undermined by reality. Flaubert describes her death throes with an unflinching, clinical scrupulousness that subverts the sentimental. Emma's last vision is of a blind beggar, the novel's death's-head figure, who mirrors her own blindness and corruption, and her final dignity is undercut by those representatives of petit-bourgeois life, Homais and Bournisien, who guard her corpse. By the end, Flaubert has taken the reader simultaneously outward for a satirical portrait of mundane, provincial life that forms the environment with which Emma must contend, and inward to the formation of his protagonist's mental landscape, tracing the way in which thoughts, feelings, memories, and needs conspire to produce consciousness.

After completing *Madame Bovary* in 1856, Flaubert first brought out his novel serially in the *Revue de Paris*, reluctantly allowing some cuts to ward off the storm of controversy that promised to follow but resisting others, arguing to his editor, "You are objecting to details, whereas actually you should object to the whole. The brutal element is basic, not superficial . . . you cannot change the *blood* of a book. All you can do is weaken it." Charged with "outrage of public morals and religion" Flaubert faced a trial in which he bitterly predicted a guilty verdict, ironically finding in the trial "sweet recognition for my labors, noble encouragement to literature." Instead he was acquitted, and the novel became a notorious *succès de scandale*. He followed *Madame Bovary* with the lushly exotic *Salammbô* (1862), a historical novel set in ancient Carthage, *A Sentimental Education* (1869), in which his male protagonist develops a passion for an older married woman, the finished version of *The Temptation of Saint Anthony*, and *Three Tales* (1877), linked stories that described saints' lives. He died suddenly from a stroke, leaving unfinished the satiric novel, *Bouvard and Pécuchet*.

In writing *Madame Bovary*, Flaubert accomplished a revolution in the novel's subject matter and style. By presenting such a frank and unrelentingly realistic depiction of ordinary life, he replaced fictional idealization and falsification of character and scene with an accurate, authentic, and honest portrait of the ordinary and the ignoble. No previous novel had been so carefully designed with each part fitted into an elaborate whole; no female protagonist had been so carefully examined. A master craftsman, who insisted that the novelist should be "invisible and all-powerful: he must be everywhere felt, but never seen," Flaubert denied the reader direct, subjective narrative guidance; in doing so he raised the bar in the art of the novel by insisting that the reader play an active role in uncovering the patterns beneath the surface of things, subverting the expected fictional delights and substituting a coherent fictional universe held together by the force and clarity of the novel's vision. Flaubert's compassionate and objective penetration of human personality together with his technical skill has earned *Madame Bovary* its place as one of the most memorable and influential novels in world literature.

LITTLE WOMEN

by Louisa May Alcott

Louisa May Alcott's beloved novel of four adolescent girls growing up in nineteenth-century New England is traditionally considered a children's classic, although Alcott's sophisticated use of
language, frequent didactic narrative structure, and emphasis on
moral stricture can make it a challenging, culturally remote read
for many contemporary children—hence the adaptations published in recent years to make the story more accessible to young
readers. Some who choose to tackle *Little Women* (1868, 1869) at
an early age reexperience the novel at various times through the
years, enjoying it at different stages of their lives and intellectual
development. Originally written for young adolescent readers,
Little Women can, in fact, be appreciated as a women's novel and,
moreover, one with a feminist subtext; this is not surprising, given
that Alcott's lifelong heroine was proto-feminist writer Margaret
Fuller. Alcott's protagonists, the March sisters, and their wise,
principled mother represent five versions of nineteenth-century
womanhood, and the novel dramatizes the completeness and self-
sufficiency of their nearly all-female universe as it is eventually
joined by men who are happy to be educated in the domestic and
moral ideals of the household.

There are many telling similarities between the March family of *Little Women* and Alcott's own family. Like the spirited, literarily inclined Jo March, Louisa May Alcott (1832–1888) was the second oldest of four sisters. She would base the character of Jo on herself; the characters of Meg, Beth, and Amy March, as well as the girls' mother and father, were drawn from her sisters, Anna, Elizabeth, and Abbie May and her parents. Alcott's father, Bronson Alcott (1799–1888), one of the foremost intellectuals of his day, was variously a schoolmaster, educational innovator, school superintendent, transcendentalist, and traveling lecturer known later in his life as the celebrated "Father of Little Women." He founded the Temple School in Boston, and when that failed, he transferred his experimental educational methods to his children, teaching them at home in Concord, Massachusetts. In 1843, he founded a short-lived utopian community, Fruitlands, near Harvard, Massachusetts. The fits and starts of Bronson Alcott's career, together with his frequent absences on walking and lecturing tours, left the family in genteel poverty, which profoundly affected his children, especially Louisa, who would eventually become the family breadwinner. Louisa's mother, Abigail, known as "Abba," possessed the wisdom, strength, patience, and hopefulness necessary for marriage to an abstracted idealist who suffered from bouts of depression. When family fortunes were especially low, she worked at menial jobs to help support her family and for two years was a salaried city missionary to the poor in South Boston. Like Mrs. March, the much-loved and revered "Marmee" of *Little Women*, Abba Alcott kept the family together and exerted a powerful, steadying influence on her daughters. Louisa dedicated her books to her mother, describing her life in one inscription as "a long labor of love."

Louisa's decision to earn an income for her family was influenced in part by her desire to make life easier for her mother, "with no debts or troubles to burden her." To that end, she worked as a seamstress, domestic servant, governess, teacher, and companion, experiences she would later incorporate into her books. Beginning in 1851, with the publication of a poem in *Peterson's Magazine*, Alcott produced poems, serialized stories, and some children's tales, and was paid for her efforts. In December 1862, during the Civil War, she began service as an army nurse in Washington, D.C., but was invalided home with typhoid fever in January 1863. She recorded her nursing experiences in *Hospital Sketches*, which first appeared in the *Commonwealth* magazine in the spring of 1863, was published in book form soon afterwards, and received favorable reviews. In 1865, Alcott published her first novel, *Moods*, a romance. In his review of the novel, Henry James praised Alcott's understanding of men and women "with their every-day virtues and temptations," but felt that the author lacked an ability to "handle the great dramatic passions," and suggested that she could produce a very good novel "provided she will be satisfied to describe only that which she has seen."

In 1868, while living in Boston and working as the editor of a girls' magazine, *Merry's Museum*, Alcott was approached by Thomas Niles, Jr., of the Roberts Brothers publishing firm, with the suggestion that she use her powers of observation and sensitivity toward adolescents to write a domestic novel about young girls that would compete with the popular "Oliver Optic" series of boys' books. Using her own family as the foundation for her characters and situations, Alcott set to work on what would become the first part of *Little Women*, published in September 1868, after six weeks of writing.

Alcott incorporated into her novel the Christian moral precepts of John Bunyan's *Pilgrim's Progress*, a beloved book in the Alcott family. When *Little Women* opens, it is Christmastime and the March sisters—Meg, sixteen; Jo, fifteen; Beth, thirteen; and Amy, twelve—are in Bunyan's "Slough of Despond," lamenting the fact that they are poor (once wealthy, Mr. March lost his money "in trying to help an unfortunate friend"). Adding to the girls' sadness is the absence of their father, who is serving as a chaplain in the Civil War. The girls "played" at the story of *Pilgrim's Progress* when they were little; now Marmee suggests that they confront their own trials and tribulations, and make the pilgrim's progress toward "goodness and happiness" an actuality in their own lives: "Now, my little pilgrims, suppose you begin again, not in play, but in earnest, and see how far you can get before father comes home."

In this female-dominated household, with Marmee and Bunyan to guide them, the girls begin their journey toward maturity. Each has her particular burden: Meg, reduced to working as a governess for a rich family, longs for worldly comforts. Tall, awkward Jo, who has difficulty controlling her sharp tongue and short temper, is companion to the family's irascible Aunt March.

Jo's refuge is the attic, where she reads and writes, and cherishes dreams of literary success. Gentle Beth struggles with her painful shyness. Artistic Amy is affected and selfish.

The sisters begin their progress by resisting temptation. They use the dollar Marmee has given each of them to buy Christmas gifts for their mother, and they donate their delicious holiday breakfast to a poor German family that lives in town. On Christmas evening, after performing in a drama of Jo's devising, the girls are treated to a Christmas feast sent over to the March home by Mr. Laurence, the wealthy, somewhat gruff old gentlemen who lives in the large house next door. At a New Year's dance, Jo meets Mr. Laurence's orphaned grandson, the handsome and charming Laurie, who lives with his grandfather and has long wanted to meet the Marches. The temperamental and slightly spoiled Laurie benefits through his association with the warm, loving, principled March family and develops a close friendship with Jo.

During the course of the novel's first part, the sisters confront numerous challenges and sacrifices. Meg's vanity is tested when she spends a weekend with a wealthy school friend; Jo, in a fit of pique at her youngest sister, nearly causes Amy to drown in an icy pond; Beth must overcome her shyness to visit Mr. Laurence and play his beautiful piano; Amy disobeys at school and is humiliated by the unpleasant schoolmaster. When Mr. March becomes ill, Jo sells her beautiful long hair to help Marmee pay for the trip to Washington to nurse him. While she is away, Beth gets scarlet fever and, in one of the most affecting scenes in the novel, nearly dies. There is pleasure as well as pain: Beth recovers; Mr. March returns home on Christmas Day; and Meg falls in love with and becomes engaged to Laurie's tutor, John Brooke. Jo resents Brooke as an interloper who will take Meg away from the family, but she eventually learns to accept the situation.

Alcott ends the first part with the extended family grouped together in peaceful repose: "So grouped, the curtain falls upon Meg, Jo, Beth, and Amy. Whether it ever rises again depends upon the reception given to the first act of the domestic drama called 'Little Women.'" The novel was an immediate success, and in April 1869, after six weeks' work, Alcott published the second part of *Little Women*, called "Good Wives," which was also enormously popular. "Good Wives" contains the charm, humor, and family warmth of the first part, but it is frequently more sophisticated and serious in tone as Meg, Jo, Beth, and Amy leave their adolescence behind to confront in earnest their adult concerns. Meg marries and becomes the mother of twins. Jo is now selling stories to newspapers to supplement the family income and is mortified when Aunt March chooses the more refined Amy to accompany her to Europe. She goes to New York to develop her craft and to escape Laurie, who is in love with her. Jo becomes governess for Mrs. Kirke, who runs a boardinghouse, and befriends the kindly scholar, Professor Bhaer, one of the boarders. When she receives word of Beth's failing health, she returns home to care for her sister. Laurie proposes, but Jo refuses him, saying she does not think she will ever marry. (Alcott, who received letters from readers urging her to marry off Jo to her leading male character, wisely resisted such a simplistic plot resolution.) Beth dies, after a lingering demise portrayed in such an anti-melodramatic fashion that she almost seems to just retreat from life and fade away. Laurie and Amy fall in love and marry in Europe, and Jo, after suffering much loneliness despite her growing success as a writer and the comforting presence of her family, receives her reward in Professor Bhaer, whom she marries. When Aunt March dies, she leaves her home, Plumfield, to Jo, and the Bhaers open a school there for boys. The novel ends on Marmee's sixtieth birthday, during a jolly family apple-picking harvest. Jo, now thirty, has two sons, while Laurie and Amy have a baby daughter named Beth. The last sentiment belongs to Marmee, who, with her daughters gathered around her, "could only stretch out her arms, as if to gather children and grandchildren to herself, and say, with face and voice full of motherly love, gratitude, and humility: 'Oh, my girls, however long you may live, I never can wish you a greater happiness than this!' "

Alcott continued the story of the March family in *Little Men: Life at Plumfield With Jo's Boys* (1871) and *Jo's Boys* (1886), her last novel. The author of some 270 published works in every genre, Alcott became a celebrity on the strength of *Little Women*. Thanks to a new mass readership consisting of twelve- to sixteen-year-olds able to purchase inexpensively printed books, there was an even greater demand for Alcott fiction for young readers. Alcott obliged, producing such popular novels as *An Old-Fashioned Girl* (1870), *Eight Cousins* (1875), and *Rose in Bloom* (1876), all of which she described as "moral pap for the young." But *Little Women* in particular would not have remained as popular a book as it is today, spawned three movies and two miniseries based upon it, and prompted such critical debate over its merits and debits as a feminist novel, if it were simply a moral battering ram aimed at nineteenth-century girls. The novel may idealize the comforting coziness of nineteenth-century domestic life with, as one of the author's biographers put it, "the vividness of a Currier & Ives print," but in Meg, Jo, Beth, and Amy, Alcott created characters whose strengths and failings, struggles and triumphs are as easily recognizable to contemporary readers as they were instructive for young women marching toward a new concept called "feminism" more than one hundred years ago.

MIDDLEMARCH

by George Eliot

More than any other Victorian novelist, George Eliot (1819–1880) succeeded in transforming the novel, previously considered a lightweight form of entertainment, into a vehicle for the most subtle and profound social and psychological investigation. Insisting that the novel be the truthful and realistic examination of character, Eliot excluded from her fiction the idealization and exaggeration of other novelists, and instead offered an extensive study of culture and human behavior. Eliot's masterpiece is *Middlemarch* (1871–1872), a panoramic exploration of English society that is regarded by many critics as the greatest English novel. A detailed depiction of life in a provincial town during the 1830s, *Middlemarch* features an intriguing female protagonist of high intellect and idealism, whose dreams of defying the conventional values imposed upon her by society and attaining fulfillment in some heroic enterprise are shattered by a disastrous marriage.

George Eliot's life was anything but conventional. Born Mary Ann Evans in Warwickshire in the English Midlands, she was the youngest of five children of estate manager Robert Evans, a staunch political and Church of England conservative, who was distrustful of change and innovation. Mary Ann was a serious and studious child who read widely. While attending boarding school, she came under the influence of the charismatic, evangelical clergyman John Edmund Jones. To a precocious and thoughtful young girl like Mary Ann, Jones's dramatic preaching and message of personal salvation through faith and religious self-sacrifice struck a sympathetic chord. In 1841, she moved with her retired father to Coventry, where her family, concerned by her religious zeal, encouraged her friendship with the local progressive freethinkers Charles and Caroline Bray, hoping their influence would help moderate her almost fanatical piety. Instead, the philosophical rationalism to which she was exposed caused her to lose her religious faith entirely. In a confrontation with her family that would become a paradigm for similar scenes in her novels—conflicts between independence and duty, self and community—Mary Ann announced her refusal to attend church any longer. She eventually compromised, agreeing to go to church but refusing to give up her belief in a personal morality that was not based on the authority of religious faith.

After her father's death, in 1849, Eliot went to London, where she entered a wider circle better suited to her considerable intellectual gifts. She worked as an assistant editor of the progressive *Westminster Review*, wrote numerous book reviews, and mingled with the literary and somewhat bohemian circle surrounding the magazine. This included the critic and author George Henry Lewes, with whom Eliot fell in love and who returned her affection. The married Lewes was estranged from his wife but, under the restrictive divorce laws of the time, he could not divorce and legally remarry. The situation prompted the second and greatest personal crisis in Eliot's life. Defying convention and strong family disapproval, Eliot and Lewes established a home together, managing a happy, if secluded, life in London, ideal for their literary work. By the 1870s, Eliot was recognized as the most eminent novelist of her day and had achieved social respectability despite her unconventional life with Lewes.

It was Lewes who first encouraged Eliot to write fiction. She had always been an insightful thinker, but as she began her fiction she faced the challenge of animating her thoughts and creating believable characters and situations. She also set out to alter the basic formula of Victorian fiction—idealization and melodrama—to a careful analysis of realistic experience and diverse characters.

To avoid associating her work with other "lady novelists," whose sentimental and trivial fare ensured a lack of serious response, she chose the pseudonym George Eliot with her first fictional work, *Scenes of Clerical Life*, three stories that first appeared in *Blackwood's Magazine*. *Scenes of Clerical Life* attempted, in her words, "to do what has never yet been done in our literature . . . representing the clergy like any other class with the humours, sorrows, and troubles of other men." The book set the pattern for Eliot's subsequent novels: it insisted that ordinary life is the proper domain of fiction, showed tolerance and sympathy toward the characters, and dramatized lessons of human behavior through what she called "aesthetic teaching." Eliot's next effort was her first novel, *Adam Bede* (1859), which brought her acclaim and earned her a reputation as a major new writing talent. She quickly followed its success with two more novels, *The Mill on the Floss* (1860) and *Silas Marner* (1861).

Eliot had been drawing on her memories of Warwickshire for the settings of her first novels. When these sources began to run dry, she attempted a departure in *Romola* (1863), a historical novel set in fifteenth-century Florence. To research the novel, she traveled to Italy and studied the customs and values of that culture with the eye of a social scientist. With *Romola* Eliot learned to go beyond her memories and see an entire society as a complex whole. This experience deepened and broadened her scope as a novelist when she returned to more familiar English settings for her last three novels: *Felix Holt* (1866), *Middlemarch* (1872), and *Daniel Deronda* (1876). All three are novels in which Eliot attempted to display what she called the "invariability of sequence": the laws of social order and principles of moral conduct, including both the complex forces underlying characters' actions and the social, historical, and political climate in which her characters exist.

Eliot's original scheme for what she initially conceived of as a "novel called Middlemarch" began around 1869, and concerned a male protagonist, Tertius Lydgate, a doctor whose altruistic and scientific aspirations would be tested against the limitations of English provincial life. Eliot set his story during the period 1829–1831, the crucial years of the Catholic Emancipation, the death of George IV, the general election of 1831, and the passage of the first Reform Bill of 1832, in which traditional English authority and values were tested and out of which Eliot's contemporary world emerged. Eliot researched her subject in great detail so that she could recreate the past and gain a critical perspective on it, yet the project languished, and, in 1870, she turned to the story of another idealist, Dorothea Brooke, whose aspirations for a less constricted life would, like Lydgate's, be hampered by the demands of conventional society. Eliot decided to join her manuscript of "Miss Brooke" with the early "Middlemarch" material, and to reconstruct an entire social setting with four major plot centers: the story of Dorothea Brooke's unhappy marriage to the self-absorbed pedant Edward Casaubon, and her subsequent attraction to his relative, the artistic Will Ladislaw; Lydgate's marriage to the conventionally materialistic Rosamond Vincy and his professional life in Middlemarch; the story of Fred Vincy, a wastrel in search of a vocation, and his relationship with the sensible Mary Garth; and the circumstances surrounding the self-righteous businessman Bulstrode, whose secret and fall from grace in the Middlemarch community Eliot used to join the novel's many parts. Dorothea Brooke, Tertius Lydgate, and the rest of Eliot's wide cast of characters are all examined against a fully elaborate social hierarchy, from Middlemarch's gentry and farm families through the professional and laboring classes. All are related to a particular historical moment in which traditional values face the pressure of change in the reforming spirit of the age.

At the soul and center of *Middlemarch* are Dorothea and Lydgate. Dorothea is described as a "latter-born" Saint Theresa, "helped by no coherent social faith and order which could perform the function of knowledge for the ardently willing soul." She is a fervent neophyte and idealist in search of a great cause and the opportunity for self-expression. Instead of accepting the love of the kindly Sir James Chettam, she marries the middle-aged scholar Casaubon, whom she thinks is a kindred spirit but who, although he cares for her, fails to provide her with the expansion into the noble life of mind and spirit she seeks. The marriage falters, and the intellectually and emotionally rigid Casaubon is eventually undone by his jealousy of Dorothea and Will Ladislaw. Meanwhile, Lydgate's desire to advance medical science and to remain independent of materialistic concerns in order to do good works is similarly compromised by the petty and practical world of Middlemarch, as well as what Eliot calls his "spots of commonness"—his conceit and ambitions for social advancement that cause him to succumb to the superficial charms of the greedy Rosamond. He suffers financially and emotionally before attaining a respectable, successful career but ultimately regards himself as a failure. Dorothea finally accepts her love for Will Ladislaw in defiance of propriety, though her triumph of spirit and sense of satisfaction are muted after all that occurrs: "Certainly those determining acts of her life were not ideally beautiful. They were the mixed result of young and noble impulse struggling amidst the conditions of an imperfect social state, in which great feelings will often take the aspect of error, and great faith the aspect of illusion."

Middlemarch is a long and complex novel, which is sometimes shunned by readers seeking shorter and simpler fare. But Eliot's masterwork is well worth the time and patience for readers willing to experience what Virginia Woolf called "one of the few English novels written for grown-up people." A landmark achievement in the history of the novel, *Middlemarch*, in its subtlety and reach, provides a comprehensive and realistic vision of human nature that is as truthful today as it was in Eliot's time.

ANNA KARENINA

by Leo Tolstoy

One of the greatest novels ever written and one of the great tragic love stories in all literature, *Anna Karenina* (1877) traces the adulterous affair of the title character with the dashing Count Alexey Vronsky, which ends in Anna's destruction when she refuses to conform to the hypocritical values of upper-class morality. Providing a counterpoint to Anna's tragedy is the story of Konstantin Levin, a wealthy landowner, whose search for the meaning of his life is partially found among the peasants on his estate and through the attainment of a happy marriage. Tolstoy suggests the interconnection between his two protagonists with what has come to be one of the most famous opening sentences in literature: "All happy families are alike but an unhappy family is unhappy after its own fashion."

The quest for the significance and meaning of life, history's grip on the individual, the conflict between self-fulfillment and society, and the importance of the family are themes that Tolstoy emphasizes and explores in *Anna Karenina*, as well as in his first masterwork, *War and Peace* (1869). All are issues Tolstoy struggled with in his own life. Born in 1828 into a wealthy, noble family, Count Leo Tolstoy grew up on the family estate of Yasnaya

Polyana, south of Moscow. Both of his parents died when he was a child, and he was raised by relatives and educated by private tutors. After three years as a student at Kazan University, he returned home to manage the estate and to live an aimless and pleasure-seeking life in upper-class circles in St. Petersburg and Moscow. At the age of twenty-three, Tolstoy enlisted in the army as an artillery officer, and during the Crimean War he campaigned against the Caucasian hill tribes and helped defend Sevastopol. While in the army, he developed an addiction to gambling, as well as a determination to become a writer. His first works reflect his war experiences and his recollections of childhood. Tolstoy's early fiction, published in Russian magazines, announced the arrival of a promising new talent, part of the flowering of Russian fiction in the nineteenth century that included such literary masters as Turgenev and Dostoesvsky. Tolstoy traveled in Europe before marrying in 1862; he then settled down to raise a family of thirteen children and to reorganize his estate to reflect the principles of peasant reform, including land ownership and improved education for his serfs.

The conflicts Tolstoy explored in *War and Peace* and *Anna Karenina* sparked a personal crisis and the beginning of a quest for meaning; this led him to a renunciation of government, private property, and organized religion, and the discovery of a unique belief in primitive Christianity, together with a faith in simple peasant values that sprung from a close relationship to the land. He spent the rest of his life endeavoring to live according to his precepts, often to the consternation of his family, and writing books that embodied his philosophy. Despite his chosen role as holy man, sermonizer, and sage, Tolstoy produced some of his finest works during his later period, including "The Death of Ivan Ilyitch" and "The Kreutzer Sonata." Tolstoy's mysticism and asceticism attracted devoted followers but largely alienated him from his family. In 1910 he caught a chill and died in the house of a stationmaster while attempting to escape from his family's control during a journey to a monastery.

Tolstoy regarded *Anna Karenina*, a tightly constructed novel of deeper psychological insight than *War and Peace*, as his "first real novel." In 1870, he told his wife that he was intrigued by "a type of married woman from the highest society, but who had lost herself" and whom he intended to show as "pitiful and not guilty."

Two years later Tolstoy's core idea began to take shape after the death of a neighbor's mistress, Anna Pirogova, who had been abandoned by her lover and in despair committed suicide by throwing herself under a freight train. In 1873, armed with a first name for his protagonist and her violent end, Tolstoy began his five-year labor to finish *Anna Karenina*, with most of the novel serialized in the *Russian Messenger* between 1874 and 1877.

After *Anna Karenina*'s famous opening sentence concerning happy and unhappy families, Tolstoy begins with a disruption in the household of Anna's brother, Stiva Oblonsky, when his wife, Dolly, discovers that he has been having an affair. Anna, a warm, charming, vital woman loved and appreciated by her friends and family for her understanding and tactfulness, arrives in Moscow to restore domestic peace between her brother and his wife. From there, the novel explores the various social, psychological, and moral factors that destroy Anna's marriage to Alexey Karenin, a cold, ambitious government official by whom she has a son, and the conditions that ensure the sober, decent, and honest Levin's happiness as a husband to Dolly's sister, Kitty. Anna reconciles her brother and his wife, while her own marriage is threatened by her fateful encounter with the handsome, wealthy young cavalry officer, Count Alexey Vronsky, and the love for him that eventually consumes and dooms her. Initially, Anna and Vronsky are impediments to Kitty and Levin's marriage; at the start of the novel, Vronsky is Kitty's suitor, and he is the reason she rejects Levin's first proposal. The theme of love and marriage plays out through comparison between the two couples. Vronsky pursues Anna who tries to suppress her feelings for him and fails; she also fails in her struggle to reconcile with Karenin and to give up the man she loves. Kitty and Levin come together and marry as Anna and Vronsky, with their baby daughter, begin their version of married life in restless travel and social ostracism. Anna returns to claim her son, Seryozha, and to resolve the hopeless situation that has cut her off from society. However, her obsessive love for Vronsky has trapped her in an increasing dependency on him. Meanwhile, Kitty gives birth, and Levin witnesses a wider and richer basis for his relationship with his wife. Finally, Anna's passion, which unlike Levin's is not a means to a wider spiritual growth but exists as an end in itself, becomes the poison that destroys her. Suicide is Anna's only relief, as Levin's spiritual crisis in the face of the reality of death is resolved through the sustenance offered by family and country life; he is freed from the social and personal torments that punish Anna mercilessly.

Early drafts of *Anna Karenina* featured only the adulterous triangle of Anna, Vronsky, and Karenin, who, with his virtue besmirched because of his wife's lecherous and irresponsible passion, was marked for the tragic role. Tolstoy's uncompromising moral view concerning the sanctity of the family and the destructiveness of sexuality influenced his original decision to portray Anna as a fleshy she-devil whose lust he viewed as "terribly repulsive and disgusting." But Anna's hold on Tolstoy gradually forced a change in his view of her, which was reinforced by his incorporation of the parallel story of Levin and Kitty. The moral focus that Tolstoy derived from his own married life and spiritual struggles was deflected onto Levin, thus allowing Anna to become more than an archetype and a warning about the destructive nature of sexual passion. She emerged as a truly complex, sympathetic, and attractive character, whose deep capacity for love and defiance of convention, as well as her passion for Vronsky, is her downfall. In an upper-class social milieu that hypocritically tolerates adultery if it is discreetly pursued, Anna openly and honestly separates from her husband and goes off to live with her lover. Her society's penalty for such a breach of the rules is harsh: she is separated from her son and ostracized by her friends and acquaintances, while Vronsky retains the freedom to come and go as he pleases, just as he did before his affair. Anna is a victim of convention, trapped by the unfair divorce laws of the time, social hypocrisy, a weakness of character, and a sense of guilt, in a relationship that brings her misery rather than happiness, not because she has lost her love for Vronsky, but because that love has become her only focus. Increasingly jealous and demanding, fearful that she will inevitably lose Vronsky's love, and agonizingly torn between her lover and her son, she chooses death as her only escape. Anna Karenina would not be the first great fictional heroine to choose such a fate.

A DOLL'S HOUSE

by Henrik Ibsen

More than one literary historian has asserted that the precise moment when modern drama began was December 4, 1879, with the publication of Ibsen's *A Doll's House*; or, more dramatically, at the explosive climax of the first performance in Copenhagen on December 21, 1879, with the slamming of the door as Nora Helmer shockingly leaves her comfortable home, respectable marriage, husband, and children for an uncertain future of self-discovery. Nora's explosive exit ushered in a new dramatic era, legitimizing the exploration of key social problems as a serious concern for the modern theater, while sounding the opening blast in the modern sexual revolution. As Ibsen's biographer Michael Meyer has observed, "No play had ever before contributed so momentously to the social debate, or been so widely and furiously discussed among people who were not normally interested in theatrical or even artistic matter." A contemporary reviewer of the play declared, "When Nora slammed the door shut on her marriage, walls shook in a thousand homes."

Ibsen set in motion a transformation of drama as distinctive in the history of the theater as the one that occurred in fifth-century B.C. Athens or Elizabethan London. Like the great Athenian dramatists and Shakespeare, Ibsen fundamentally redefined the drama and set a standard that later playwrights have had to absorb or challenge. The stage that he inherited had largely ceased to function as a serious medium for the deepest consideration of human themes and values. After Ibsen, drama was restored as an important truth-telling vehicle for a comprehensive criticism of life. *A Doll's House* anatomized on stage for the first time the social, psychological, emotional, and moral truths beneath the placid surface of a conventional, respectable marriage while creating a new, psychologically complex modern heroine who still manages to shock and unsettle audiences more than a century later. *A Doll's House* is, therefore, one of the groundbreaking modern literary texts that established in fundamental ways the responsibility and cost of women's liberation and gender equality. According to critic Evert Sprinchorn, Nora is "the richest, most complex" female dramatic character since Shakespeare's heroines, and, as Kate Millett has argued in *Sexual Politics,* Ibsen was the first dramatist since the Greeks to challenge the myth of male dominance. "In Aeschylus' dramatization of the myth," Millett asserts, "one is permitted to see patriarchy confront matriarchy, confound it through the knowledge of paternity, and come off triumphant. Until Ibsen's Nora slammed the door announcing the sexual revolution, this triumph went nearly uncontested."

The momentum that propelled Ibsen's daring artistic and social revolt was sustained principally by his outsider status, as an exile both at home and abroad. His last deathbed word was "Tvertimod!" (On the contrary!), a fitting epitaph and description of his artistic and intellectual mind-set. Born in Skien, Norway, a logging town southwest of Oslo, in 1828, Ibsen endured a lonely and impoverished childhood, particularly after the bankruptcy of his businessman father when Ibsen was six. At fifteen, he was sent to Grimstad as an apothecary's apprentice, where he lived for six years in an attic room on meager pay, sustained by reading romantic poetry, sagas, and folk ballads. He later recalled feeling "on a war footing with the little community where I felt I was being suppressed by my situation and by circumstances in general." His first play, *Cataline,* was a historical drama featuring a revolutionary hero who reflects Ibsen's own alienation. "*Cataline* was written," the playwright later recalled, "in a little provincial town, where it was impossible for me to give expression to all that fermented in me except by mad, riotous pranks, which brought down upon me the ill will of all the respectable citizens who could not enter into that world which I was wrestling with alone."

Largely self-educated, Ibsen failed the university entrance examination to pursue medical training and instead pursued a career in the theater. In 1851, he began a thirteen-year stage apprenticeship in Bergen and Oslo, doing everything from sweeping the stage to directing, stage-managing, and writing mostly verse dramas based on Norwegian legends and historical subjects. The experience gave him a solid knowledge of the stage conventions of the day, particularly of the so-called "well-made play" of the popular French playwright Augustin Eugène Scribe and his many imitators, with its emphasis on a complicated, artificial plot based on secrets, suspense, and surprises. Ibsen would transform the conventions of the "well-made play" into the modern problem play, exploring controversial social and human questions that had never before been dramatized. Although his stage experience in Norway was marked chiefly by failure, Ibsen's apprenticeship was a crucial testing ground for perfecting his craft and providing Ibsen with the skills to mount the assault on theatrical conventions and moral complacency in his mature work.

In 1864, Ibsen began a self-imposed exile from Norway that would last for twenty-seven years. He traveled first to Italy, where he was joined by his wife Susannah, whom he had married in 1858, and his son. The family divided its time between Italy and Germany. The experience was liberating for Ibsen; he felt that he had "escaped from darkness into light," releasing the productive energy with which he composed the succession of plays that brought him worldwide fame. His first important works, *Brand* (1866) and *Peer Gynt* (1867), were poetic dramas very much in the romantic mode of the individual's conflict with experience and the gap between heroic assertion and accomplishment, between sobering reality and blind idealism. *Pillars of Society* (1877) shows him experimenting with ways of introducing these central themes into a play reflecting modern life, the first in a series of realistic dramas that redefined the conventions and subjects of the modern theater.

The first inklings of his next play, *A Doll's House*, are glimpsed in Ibsen's journal entry headed "Notes for a Modern Tragedy":

There are two kinds of moral laws, two kinds of conscience, one for men and one, quite different, for women. They don't understand each other; but in practical life, woman is judged by masculine law, as though she weren't a woman but a man.

The wife in the play ends by having no idea what is right and what is wrong; natural feelings on the one hand and belief in authority on the other lead her to utter distraction. . . .

Moral conflict. Weighed down and confused by her trust in authority, she loses faith in her own morality, and in her fitness to bring up her children. Bitterness. A mother in modern society, like certain insects, retires and dies once she has done her duty by propagating the race. Love of life, of home, of husband and children and family. Now and then, as women do, she shrugs off her thoughts. Suddenly anguish and fear return. Everything must be borne alone. The catastrophe approaches, mercilessly, inevitably. Despair, conflict, and defeat.

To tell his modern tragedy based on gender relations, Ibsen takes his audience on an unprecedented, intimate tour of a contemporary, respectable marriage. Set during the Christmas holidays, *A Doll's House* begins with Nora Helmer completing the finishing touches on the family's celebrations. Her husband, Torvald, has recently been named a bank manager, promising an end to the family's former straitened financial circumstances, and Nora is determined to celebrate the holiday with her husband and three children in style. Despite Torvald's disapproval of her indulgences, he relents, giving her the money she desires, softened by Nora's childish playacting that gratifies his sense of what is expected of his "lark" and "squirrel." Beneath the surface of this apparently charming domestic scene is a potentially damning and destructive secret. Seven years before, Nora had saved the life of her critically ill husband by secretly borrowing the money needed for a rest cure in Italy. Knowing that Torvald would be too proud to borrow money himself, Nora forged her dying father's name on the loan she received from Krogstad, a banking associate of Torvald.

The crisis comes when Nora's old schoolfriend Christina Linde arrives in need of a job. At Nora's urging, Torvald aids her friend by giving her Krogstad's position at the bank. Learning that he is to be dismissed, Krogstad threatens to expose Nora's forgery unless she is able to persuade Torvald to reinstate him. Nora fails to convince Torvald to relent, and, after receiving his dismissal notice, Krogstad sends Torvald a letter disclosing the details of the forgery. The incriminating letter remains in the Helmers' mailbox like a ticking time bomb as Nora tries to distract Torvald from reading it, and Christina attempts to convince Krogstad to withdraw his accusation. Torvald eventually reads the letter following the couple's return from a Christmas ball and explodes in recriminations against his wife, calling her a liar and a criminal, unfit to be his wife and his children's mother. "Now you've wrecked all my happiness—ruined my whole future," Torvald insists. "Oh, it's awful to think of. I'm in a cheap little grafter's hands; he can do anything he wants with me, ask me for anything, play with me like a puppet—and I can't breathe a word. I'll be swept down miserably into the depths on account of a featherbrained woman." Torvald's reaction reveals that his formerly expressed high moral rectitude is hypocritical and self-serving. He shows himself worried more about appearances than true morality, caring about his reputation more than his wife. However, when Krogstad's second letter arrives, in which he announces his intention of pursuing the matter no further, Torvald joyfully informs Nora that he is "saved" and that Nora should forget all that he has said, assuming that the normal relation between himself and his "frightened little songbird" can be resumed. Nora, however, shocks Torvald with her reaction.

Nora, profoundly disillusioned by Torvald's response to Krogstad's letter, bereft as it is of compassion for her heroic self-sacrifice on his behalf, orders Torvald to sit down for a serious talk, the first in their married life. She reviews their relationship. "I've been your doll-wife here, just as at home I was Papa's doll-child," Nora explains. "And in turn the children have been my dolls. I thought it was fun when you played with me, just as they thought it fun when I played with them. That's been our marriage, Torvald." Nora has acted out the nineteenth-century ideal of the submissive, unthinking, dutiful daughter and wife, and it has taken Torvald's reaction to shatter the illusion and to force an illumination. She goes on: "When the big fright was over—and it wasn't from any threat against me, only for what might damage you—when all the danger was past, for you it was just as if nothing had happened. I was exactly the same, your little lark, your doll, that you'd have to handle with double care now that I'd turned out so brittle and frail. Torvald—in that instant it dawned on me that I've been living here with a stranger . . ." Nora tells Torvald that she no longer loves him because he is not the man she thought he was, that he is incapable of heroic action on her behalf. When Torvald insists that "no man would sacrifice his honor for love," Nora replies, "Millions of women have done just that."

Nora finally resists the claims Torvald mounts in response, namely that she must honor her duties as a wife and mother, stating: "I don't believe in that anymore. I believe that, before all else, I'm a human being, no less than you—or anyway, I ought to try to become one. I know the majority thinks you're right, Torvald, and plenty of books agree with you, too. But I can't go on believing what the majority says, or what's written in books. I have to think over these things myself and try to understand them." The finality of Nora's decision to forgo her assigned role as wife and mother for the authenticity of selfhood is marked by the sound of door slamming and her exit into the wider world, leaving Torvald to survey the wreckage of their marriage.

Ibsen leaves his audience and readers to consider sobering truths: that married women are not the decorative playthings and servants of their husbands who require their submissiveness, that a man's authority in the home should not go unchallenged, and that the prime duty of anyone is to arrive at an authentic human identity, not to accept the role determined by social conventions. That Nora would be willing to sacrifice everything, even her children, to become her own person proved to be, and remains, the controversial shock of *A Doll's House,* provoking continuing debate over Nora's motivations and justifications. The first edition of 8,000 copies of the play quickly sold out, and the play was so heatedly debated in Scandanavia, in1879, that, as critic Frances Lord observes, "Many a social invitation in Stockholm during that winter bore the words, 'You are requested not to mention Ibsen's *Doll's House!*' " Ibsen was obliged to supply an alternative ending for the first German production when the famous leading lady Hedwig Niemann-Raabe refused to perform the role of Nora, stating, "I would never leave *my children!*" Ibsen provided what he would call a "barbaric outrage," an ending in which Nora's departure is halted at the doorway of her children's bedroom. The play served as a catalyst for an ongoing debate over feminism and women's rights. In 1898, Ibsen was honored by the Norwegian Society for Women's Rights and toasted as the "creator of Nora." Always the contrarian, Ibsen rejected the notion that *A Doll's House* champions the cause of women's rights:

I have been more of a poet and less of a social philosopher than people generally tend to suppose. I thank you for your toast, but must disclaim the honor of having consciously worked for women's rights. I am not even quite sure what women's rights really are. To me it has been a question of human rights. And if you read my books carefully you will realize that. Of course it is incidentally desirable to solve the problem of women; but that has not been my whole object. My task has been the portrayal of human beings.

Despite Ibsen's disclaimer that *A Doll's House* should be appreciated as more than a piece of gender propaganda—that it deals at its core with universal truths of human identity—it is nevertheless the case that Ibsen's drama is one of the milestones of the sexual revolution; it sounds themes and advances the cause of women's autonomy and liberation, echoing Mary Wollstonecraft's *A Vindication of the Rights of Women* and anticipating subsequent works such as Virginia Woolf's *A Room of One's Own* and Betty Friedan's *The Feminine Mystique.* The impact of Nora's slamming the door of her doll's house is still being felt more than a century later.

TESS OF THE D'URBERVILLES

by Thomas Hardy

Published in 1891, ten years before the end of the Victorian era, and set in Hardy's invented county of Wessex, *Tess of the D'Urbervilles* was considered controversial and unusual in its time because of its focus on rural characters and sexual frankness. The novel features one of Hardy's most compelling protagonists, Tess Durbeyfield, a young woman of beauty, strength, and passion, who is a tragic victim of her lower-class status and the double standards of Victorian morality. Critic Irving Howe observed that Tess "stands, both in the economy of the book and as a figure rising beyond its pages and into common memory, for the unconditional authority of feeling."

Thomas Hardy (1840–1928), one of English literature's longest-lived and most prodigious writers, was also one of the most influential. The last major Victorian novelist, Hardy is also the first major modern English novelist, and his work is a hybrid of nineteenth-century storytelling methods and modern ideas and concerns. He was the eldest child of Thomas and Jemima Hardy of Higher Bockhampton, Dorset, in southwest England. His father was a builder, country musician, and ballad singer who took his young son to village weddings and festivities. Through his father and his rural background, Hardy absorbed the rustic storytelling traditions he would draw upon for his novels. At eight, Hardy was sent to school in nearby Dorchester, and at sixteen he was apprenticed to an architect and church restorer. Thereafter, he would read and study on his own. In 1862, Hardy moved to London, where he was employed in an architect's office. He read Darwin and was greatly influenced by John Stuart Mill's *On Liberty*, which would become a source for his exploration of the conflict between the individual and society in his novels. Hardy also began to write poetry, which would remain his first love. He returned to Dorset in 1867, and in 1871, he produced *Desperate Remedies*, a novel that was published anonymously.

During the 1870s, Hardy published a series of conventional romances with rural settings—*Under the Greenwood Tree* (1873), *A Pair of Blue Eyes* (1874), and *The Hand of Ethelberta* (1876). He shifted from the comic to the tragic mode with *Far From the Madding Crowd* (1874) and *The Return of the Native* (1878), the first novels set in Wessex, Hardy's fictional equivalent of England's six southwest counties that formed a partly real and partly imagined landscape. By 1883, Hardy had moved permanently to Dorchester, the county seat of Dorset, and began producing his great masterpieces—*The Mayor of Casterbridge* (1886), *Tess*, and *Jude the Obscure* (1896). Thereafter, Hardy wrote poetry and produced *The Dynasts* (1904–1908), his three-part epic poem devoted to the Napoleonic era. His wife, Emma Gifford, died in 1912, and two years later he married his secretary, Florence Dugdale, who published a biography of the writer that was actually written by Hardy himself. Honored in later years for his longevity, Hardy was buried in Poet's Corner in London's Westminster Abbey, although he had designated that his heart should be interred in Emma's grave in Stinsford Churchyard in Dorset.

Hardy's decision to give up novel writing for poetry was fueled by the furor over his chosen subtitle for *Tess*—"A Pure Woman Faithfully Presented"—in which he asserted his heroine's essential virtue despite her seduction (or rape, which would have been considered just as worthy of moral condemnation), the birth of her illegitimate child, and the murder of her seducer. The novel, in fact, contained such uncomfortable truths that it effectively ended Hardy's career as a novelist. Begun in 1888, *Tess* was conceived as a full-frontal assault on Victorian hypocrisy regarding sexual matters. Hardy's subject was the fate of a ruined maiden, a popular theme of the English novel from Richardson's *Clarissa* through Scott's *Heart of Midlothian,* Dickens's *David Copperfield,* and Eliot's *Adam Bede,* as well as countless lesser works; these mainly supported the conventional view that once a seduction has occurred death or exile is the end of the matter, a climax to be avoided at all cost. Hardy would take an opposite view, arguing for interest in his heroine *after* her fall and shifting the focus from Tess's moral transgression to the circumstances that caused her fall as well as their wider implications.

In the original version published in volume form in 1891, Tess's doom is chronicled with a daring frankness and with her suffering unalloyed. Tess Durbeyfield is a young woman of humble birth and background. Dutiful and with an innate goodness and a fateful vulnerability, Tess is compelled by the economic collapse that threatens her family to claim an ancestral relationship with the well-to-do, parvenu D'Urberville family, who has, we learn, only adopted the name and has no connection to the Durbeyfields. The D'Urberville's rakish son, Alec, seduces Tess, who becomes pregnant. Ostracized by her neighbors both before and after the birth of her baby—whom she names Sorrow, and who dies after only a few months—she moves to a dairy farm many miles away from her home. Tess enjoys a brief respite at the farm, where she meets a minister's son, Angel Clare, an idealistic, supposedly progressive-thinking young man who plans to become a farmer. Tess eventually marries Angel—after the written confession of her past, slipped under his door before their marriage, goes under the carpet and is unseen. Upon listening to Angel's confession of an illicit affair in his own past, Tess, thinking she is likewise forgiven, speaks freely of Alec and her dead baby. Angel reacts with horror and abandons his wife. Despite Angel's freethinking opposition to orthodoxy, he is morally rigid and cannot accept the human, fallible Tess over the ideal figure he has created to love. Again on her own, dispossessed from the bower of bliss of the dairy, Tess finds herself in Hardy's version of the rural wasteland, condemned to grinding labor in a countryside devoid of comfort or community. Tess is again beset by Alec, now an itinerant preacher, and in despair of Angel's return to her, she finally agrees to live with Alec as his wife. Eventually a contrite Angel does return. Tess, overcome by her despair and resentment of Alec, stabs him to death. She rejoins Angel for a few days of happiness before the authorities close in on the couple, and Tess is executed for her crime.

The novel's final climactic scene at Stonehenge reflects Hardy's use of heightened effects to underscore and intensify his drama. Beyond the question of probability that these two fugitives should accidentally come upon Stonehenge on their final night together, Hardy's use of this setting seems symbolically appropriate. In a novel obsessed with the past—of past generations and actions—and natural or primitive instincts struggling against social morality, Tess's resting on a pagan altar prior to her societal sacrifice is fitting for the emblematic nature to which her drama has been raised. Yet Tess is not reduced merely to symbolic importance. Her resignation—"It is as it should be. . . . I am ready"—transcends the melodramatic extremes of sentiment and the overly expansive symbolic setting. Her humanity dominates the heavier strains of her implied martyrdom. At Stonehenge, Tess's character is not dwarfed by the monolithic stones or the cosmic symbolism, nor is it reduced by the machinations of plot. She has instead found a fit stage for her tragedy to be completed.

Hardy's tragic heroine is blighted by heredity and environment, betrayed by her lovers, and finally ground down by social laws and conventions. Yet, Hardy's provocative subtitle challenged contemporary readers to suspend conventional moral judgments in favor of the greater claims of Tess's suffering, integrity, and humanity. Hardy's defense of Tess is based on the contention that it is not circumstances but an individual's will that determines innocence or purity. Events are loaded against Tess from the start, and fate, as it is suggested through Hardy's theatrical plot, seems to conspire to ruin her. In her struggle against society's unnatural code that condemns her and the human condition that governs her, Tess is raised to the level of the heroic, the mythic, and the universal.

Hardy faced the challenge to gain an audience for his radical reinterpretation of the ruined maiden theme, and the censorship his novel eventually caused would contribute to his abandoning the novel form completely, after firing off a final vitriolic attack on Victorian complacency and hypocrisy in *Jude the Obscure*. Unwilling to forgo the lucrative market of serial publication, Hardy submitted his manuscript to two different magazine editors who contended that the book's "improper explicitness" made it unfit for family reading. Hardy eventually submitted a bowdlerized, sanitized version to a weekly newspaper—*The Graphic*—which accepted his story after Hardy had eliminated objectionable material and had rewritten sections in different colored ink so that the original version could easily be restored later. In the serial form, Tess's seduction follows a mock marriage ceremony, and no illegitimate child or its baptism are mentioned. Hardy, who eventually sought relief from censorship by abandoning the novel for poetry, bitterly and ironically contended, "If Galileo had said in verse that the world moved, the Inquisition might have let him alone." Although complaints continued about the book's indecency, and one bishop consigned the book to the flames, *Tess* was a popular and critical success in its day. It remains one of the supreme novels of the nineteenth century for its transcendent power and sheer grandiosity of vision.

"THE YELLOW WALLPAPER"

by Charlotte Perkins Gilman

Charlotte Perkins Gilman's short story, "The Yellow Wallpaper" (1892), a provocative and unsettling dramatization of a woman's despair and madness, can be described as the first feminist horror story and one of the fundamental fictions of gender studies. The most famous work of the American poet, novelist, and feminist theorist, "The Yellow Wallpaper" first appeared in the *New England Magazine* after a two-year effort to find a publisher. Editor Horace Scudder, who rejected the story for the *Atlantic Monthly*, justified his decision by declaring to the author that "I could not forgive myself if I made others as miserable as I have made myself [in reading your story]!" William Dean Howells, who would eventually include Gilman's story in his collection *Great Modern American Stories* (1920), initially regarded it as "too wholly dire" and "too terribly good to be printed." Reflecting the author's own experiences in being treated for depression, "The Yellow Wallpaper," depicting the nervous breakdown of a young wife and mother suffering what could later be diagnosed as severe postnatal depression, would be rediscovered by feminist scholars in the 1970s and proclaimed a masterpiece; it is one of the earliest and still one of the most effective psychological dramatizations of the impact of a woman's subjugation under a patriarchal system of control and repression.

Born Charlotte Perkins, in 1860, in Hartford, Connecticut, the author was the daughter of Frederick Beecher Perkins, a librarian and magazine editor who was the grandson of the noted clergyman Lyman Beecher, the father of *Uncle Tom's Cabin* author Harriet Beecher Stowe. Frederick Perkins abandoned his family when Gilman was an infant, and Gilman, her mother, and older brother depended mainly on the assistance of relatives and were forced to move to different residences at least once a year until Gilman was eighteen. Her mother attempted to toughen her daughter by showing her no signs of affection. As Gilman later observed in her autobiography, her mother, traumatized by her husband's desertion, believed that she should "deny the child all expression of affection as far as possible, so that she should not be used to it or long for it" and subsequently would not be hurt, as her mother had been. Ideas of women's empowerment and independence, however, came largely from Gilman's associations with her great-aunts, Harriet Beecher Stowe and Catharine Beecher. After home tutoring and training at the Rhode Island School of Design, Gilman worked as an art teacher, governess, and commercial artist, designing greeting cards and writing poetry. In 1884, she married artist Charles Walter Stetson, and, shortly after giving birth to their daughter, Gilman began suffering bouts of severe, debilitating depression. She eventually sought treatment from the eminent nerve specialist S. Weir Mitchell at his sanatorium in Philadelphia. Weir diagnosed Gilman with neurasthenia, or nervous exhaustion, and prescribed his "Rest Cure" of complete bed rest in total isolation, in which the patient was not allowed to read, write, talk to others, or even feed herself. After a month of this treatment, Weir sent Gilman home with the instructions to "live as domestic a life as possible. Have your child with you all the time. . . . Have but two hours' intellectual life a day. And never touch pen, brush or pencil as long as you live." As Gilman recalled in her autobiography, *The Living of Charlotte Perkins Gilman* (1935), "I went home, followed those directions rigidly for months, and came perilously near to losing my mind. The mental agony grew so unbearable that I would sit blankly moving my head from side to side—to get out from under the pain. Not physical pain, not the least 'headache' even, just mental torment, and so heavy in its nightmare gloom that it seemed real enough to dodge."

Dr. Weir's cure, particularly the limitation of her self-expression and the enforced isolation and inactivity, rather than helping Gilman recover her emotional equilibrium further exacerbated her instability and torment. She eventually took control of her own recovery and abandoned the rest cure. As Gilman observed in the essay "Why I Wrote 'The Yellow Wallpaper,' " "I cast the national specialist's advice to the winds and went to work again— work, the normal life of every human being; work, in which is joy and growth and service, without which one is a pauper and a parasite—ultimately recovering some measure of power." If inactivity was a contributing symptom of her mental anguish, Gilman self-diagnosed the root cause as her marriage. She separated from her husband, gaining a divorce in 1894, convinced that her marriage and its attendant stifling domesticity contributed to her breakdown. As Gilman recalled, "It was not a choice between going and staying, but between going, sane, and staying, insane." She described her four-year marriage as "this miserable condition of mind, this darkness, feebleness, and gloom" that threatened "utter loss." Gilman and her daughter moved to California and, as she observed, "The moment I left home I began to recover. It seemed right to give up a mistaken marriage."

Gilman supported herself by lecturing, editing, and teaching while beginning to publish the works that would gain her a reputation as one of the earliest feminist theorists and the leading intellectual in the women's movement in the United States at the turn of the century. She received her first widespread recognition for her satiric poem "Similar Cases," which argued the necessity for change in a healthy society. A collection of similarly satirical poems, *In This Our World,* appeared in 1893; many of the poems treated the restricted roles and emotional traumas suffered by women. A polemical analysis of the fate of women in America's male-oriented, capitalist society, *Women and Economics,* was published in 1898. Hailed as one of the key theoretical texts of the early women's movement, the book, which chronicles male dominance in modern society and the impact of economic dependence that made women slaves of men, would be translated into several languages. It established both Gilman's international reputation and suggested many of the central themes of her subsequent works, including *The Home: Its Work and Influence* (1903), *Human Work* (1904), *Man-Made World* (1911), and the feminist utopian novel *Herland* (1915). While these works retain a historical interest in reflecting early feminist ideas, it is the combination of the exploration of gender themes and controlled artistry that separates "The Yellow Wallpaper" from Gilman's other works and grants it a continuing relevance and significance.

Gilman would later describe her motive for writing and publishing "The Yellow Wallpaper," which appeared in book form in 1899, as a warning to others of the debilitating dangers of Dr. Weir's rest cure through a fictionalized version of her own "narrow escape." "The real purpose of the story," Gilman asserted in her autobiography, "was to reach Dr. S. Weir Mitchell, and convince him of the errors of his ways." However, the story achieves a much wider applicability, treating not just the psychological consequences of Weir's cure but the root causes for women's mental instability in the perceived connections between male dominance and female entrapment. Gilman's story, "with its embellishments and additions" to her actual circumstances—she confesses she "never had hallucinations or objections to my mural decorations"—conflates all male authority roles into the nameless narrator's physician husband, John, who supervises his wife's recovery from a nervous condition following childbirth. He has rented "ancestral halls for the summer," establishes a bedroom for his wife in the former attic nursery and playroom with bars on the windows, and prescribes complete isolation and rest in which, as the narrator reports, "I have a scheduled prescription for each hour of the day; he takes all care from me." Cautioned "not to give way to fancy in the least" but to maintain self-control, the narrator, whose "imaginative power and habit of story-making" are regarded as dangerous, is forbidden even to write; the story takes the form of secret diary fragments recording the progress of her cure, which proves to be far worse than the original complaint.

The locus of the narrator's increasing anguish and obsession in confinement is the room's decaying yellow wallpaper as it begins to mirror the narrator's condition and objectifies her increasing instability and mental deterioration. The wallpaper, with its "sprawling patterns committing every artistic sin," both intrigues and repels the narrator, forming a kind of hieroglyphic message or Rorschach test that the narrator begins to "read" and interpret. "It is dull enough to confuse the eye in following," she observes, "pronounced enough to constantly irritate and provoke study, and when you follow the lame uncertain curves for a little distance they suddenly commit suicide—plunge off at outragious angles, destroy themselves in unheard of contradictions." The wallpaper becomes a projection of the narrator's increasing feelings of desperate entrapment and alienation. Divided between an identity as her husband's good and dutiful patient and one that is increasingly suspicious of her husband's intentions and willfully defiant of his orders, the narrator sees in the pattern of wallpaper the bars of her psychological confinement, and in an emerging "sub-pattern" in the design, "a strange, provoking, formless sort of figure, that seems to skulk about behind that silly and conspicuous front design." The figure trapped within the wallpaper becomes the shape of a imprisoned woman "stooping down and creeping about behind the pattern," the narrator's double whom she tries to free: "I pulled and she shook, I shook and she pulled, and before morning we had peeled off yards of that paper." As "The Yellow Wallpaper" concludes, the narrator has become the imprisoned woman now freed from the paper, as John bursts into the locked room:

> "What is the matter?" he cried. "For God's sake, what are you doing!" . . .
> "I've got out at last," said I, "in spite of you and Jane. And I've pulled off most of the paper, so you can't put me back!"
> Now why should that man have fainted? But he did, and right across my path by the wall, so that I had to creep over him every time!

The meaning of "The Yellow Wallpaper" has intrigued readers since its initial publication. Originally interpreted as a horror story that records the stages of the narrator's descent into madness, the story has persisted as a chilling and expressive dramatization of a woman's psychosis of confinement and repression under a crippling patriarchal order. "It was not intended to drive people crazy," Gilman declared, "but to save people from being driven crazy." Gilman's therapeutic intention, to warn others of the debilitating consequences of Weir's rest cure, has been replaced in importance by the story's deeper appeal as a diagnosis of gender dynamics. Feminist critics have interpreted "The Yellow

Wallpaper" as a paradigm of male domination and female pathology and liberation. In this view, the narrator's madness becomes the means for her revenge upon and rebellion against patriarchal confinement. Beginning in total dependency and trust in her husband's judgment and power to cure her, the narrator increasingly violates his sanctions while suspecting his motives. Eventually liberating her trapped self, the narrator finds in her madness the freedom and power formerly denied her. The story, therefore, derives its considerable power by pushing gender politics to an extreme in which sanity and madness are reversed and authentic identity is reached in defiance of male authority. As Emily Dickinson, whose life was a study in female confinement and liberation, wrote:

> Much Madness is divinest Sense—
> To a discerning Eye—
> Much Sense—the starkest Madness—
> 'Tis the Majority
> In this, as All, prevail—
> Assent—and you are sane—
> Demur—you're straightway dangerous—
> And handled with a Chain.

THE AWAKENING

by Kate Chopin

Kate Chopin's frank exploration of a late nineteenth-century southern woman's quest for sexual and emotional fulfillment is a favorite text in women's studies and women's history classes. The novel, first published in 1899, was consigned to the literary oblivion reserved for women's literature until it was rediscovered in the 1950s. It received even more attention in the 1960s, when that decade brought about a new wave of feminist consciousness. Since its timely reevaluation by critics and scholars, *The Awakening* has been celebrated as an important literary document in the history of women's rights and is widely recognized as a classic of American literature.

The Awakening—arguably the last great nineteenth-century American novel and the first major novel of the twentieth century—is set in New Orleans and the resort of Grand Isle, locations Kate Chopin (1850–1904) knew well. Born Catherine O'Flaherty in St. Louis, Missouri, Chopin was the daughter of an Irish immigrant who became a successful businessman and married into a socially prominent French Creole family. When her father died suddenly in a railway accident in 1855, Chopin was raised in a matriarchal household run by her mother, her grandmother, and great-grandmother. She was educated at a Catholic girls' school, entered the fashionable world of the debutante upon graduation in 1868, and two years later married Oscar Chopin, a French Creole from New Orleans. Kate and Oscar would have five sons and a daughter, born between 1871 and 1879. The family lived in New Orleans, where Oscar worked as a cotton broker, and vacationed each summer at Grand Isle, an important setting for *The Awakening*. In 1879, to save money as a result of a poor cotton crop, the family moved to a plantation in French-speaking Cloutierville in north-central Louisiana, where Oscar ran a general store, and his wife often waited on customers, absorbing incidents and character types that she would eventually draw on in her novels and stories. Oscar died suddenly of malaria in 1882, leaving his family in debt. Chopin eventually moved her family back to St. Louis, beginning a period of self-assessment. It is during this period that Chopin declared that she "made her own acquaintance." She also studied Darwinism, and was impressed with the concept that women cannot avoid their "biological fates." At the age of thirty-nine, Chopin, who had always "scribbled," launched her writing career, motivated by her need to support her large family. She began to sell her short stories to leading periodicals, published her first novel, *At Fault*, at her own expense in 1890, and eventually brought out two well-received story collections, *Bayou Folk* (1894) and *A Night in Acadie* (1897), securing a rising reputation as a gifted and prolific writer of unsentimental southern regional life. Her work emphasized the nuances of human psychology and the various challenges faced by women. Chopin's early stories were received as "delightful sketches," but just below the surface of the southern belles and dutiful wives that comprised her characters was a rebelliousness that would become fully realized in *The Awakening*.

The Awakening, Chopin's second—and last—novel possesses a power that stems from the simplicity and economy of its story, as well as from the tragic momentum that it rapidly generates. The novel's protagonist, Edna Pontellier, is the twenty-eight-year-old wife of a wealthy, forty-year-old Creole businessman, Léonce Pontellier, and the mother of two sons. As the novel opens, Edna is vacationing with her family at a summer resort on Grand Isle in the Gulf of Mexico. Viewed conventionally, Edna's marriage is ideal. Léonce is judged by all as a model husband who has provided

Edna with a comfortable life of material ease and a place of distinction in society. For Edna, however, "a certain light was beginning to dawn" about the inadequacy of her existence. Her husband treats her as a "valuable piece of personal property"; submission to his will and sacrifice to the well-being of her children is all that is expected of her. Edna's gradual awakening is to an expanded sense of her individuality and sexuality, as well as to a corresponding need for autonomy. Experiencing an almost overwhelming aesthetic joy through music, reveling in the physical pleasure of swimming, Edna begins "to realize her position in the universe as a human being, and to recognize her relations as an individual to the world within and about her." Her recognition of herself as an individual rather than as a possession or in the role predetermined for her by her gender and class, as wife and mother, inevitably begins a process in which her relationship with Léonce deteriorates and her sympathy with the admiring Robert Lebrun grows into a passionate affection. Robert, however, is unable to cope with the implications of his feelings for Edna and flees to Mexico.

Returning to New Orleans, Edna translates her growing dissatisfaction with her life into the abandonment of her previous routine. She cultivates her aesthetic interest in painting and, in the eyes of her husband, neglects her assigned duties in his household: "Mr. Pontellier had been a rather courteous husband so long as he met a certain tacit submissiveness in his wife. But her new and unexpected line of conduct completely bewildered him. It shocked him. Then her absolute disregard of her duties as a wife angered him. When Mr. Pontellier became rude, Edna grew insolent. She had resolved never to take another step backward." Unable to comprehend or cope with the changes in his wife, Léonce follows the advice of the family doctor to bide his time, and he leaves on an extended business trip. While he is away, Edna moves out of their home into a smaller dwelling that she can finance independently, and begins an affair with the rakish Alcée Arobin. He gratifies Edna's heightened sexuality but proves to be as proprietary as her husband. When Robert suddenly returns and declares his devotion, it seems possible to Edna that she can attain both sexual desire and love; instead her hope for fulfillment is thwarted by Robert's inability to accept her autonomy. Left alone, without a satisfying role for her expanded sense of self, not as wife, mother, or lover, Edna can foresee only a succession of affairs and the scandal that will ruin her children. Instead, she acts to protect their reputation by ending her life in a way that could be viewed as accidental, by swimming out to sea and drowning.

The ending of *The Awakening* is, in the words of critic Barbara C. Ewell, "Perhaps the most ambivalent conclusion in all American literature." In it, Chopin connects Edna's self-sacrifice on behalf of her children with her desire to preserve the inviolability of her essential self that has been awakened. It is an ending that has been viewed both as a triumphant act of self-assertion, a liberation from the confines of unbearable constriction, and as a tragic failure, the self-deluded, regressive act of an individual unable to translate her desires and identity into any meaningful relationship in a world blind to the implications the novel has so effectively displayed. Chopin's novel marks out the battleground in an ongoing and escalating gender discussion, between individuality and defining roles, between self-assertion and determinism. Much of twentieth-century women's fiction will document the same or similar dilemmas and either come to the same conclusion or attempt to find a way for characters to, in a sense, regain the shore rather than feel forced to choose physical or emotional extinction.

When it appeared, *The Awakening* proved to be both the culmination of a decade of Chopin's artistic and intellectual development and the effective end of her literary career. Chopin advocates have attributed Chopin's silencing and even her early death to the hostile reaction *The Awakening* received. Many reviewers harshly attacked the novel, condemning it as vulgar, a judgment that recalls the public's reception to Flaubert's *Madame Bovary* (Willa Cather, in her review of *The Awakening*, called the novel a "Creole Bovary"). Edna Pontellier's behavior was judged immoral and her tragic end dismissed with a reassuring sense of good riddance. As one reviewer moralistically intoned, had Edna "flirted less and looked after her children more, we need not have been put to the unpleasantness of reading about her and the temptations she trumped up for herself." Libraries in St. Louis refused to carry the book, and Chopin was snubbed by a number of acquaintances. She earned few royalties from the novel. However, the novel was neither extensively banned nor uniformly condemned, as some later alleged. Chopin continued to write poems and stories up to her death, although her third collection of short stories was rejected by the firm that had published *The Awakening*. Declining health ultimately ended Chopin's career. Returning from a visit to the St. Louis World's Fair, she died of a massive cerebral hemorrhage at the age of fifty-four, in 1904.

Although never completely forgotten, Chopin's works were relegated after her death to the marginal category of the regionalist and local colorist. When her literary reputation was significantly resurrected in the 1950s and 1960s, *The Awakening* began to be reclaimed as an overlooked American masterpiece. Critics praised Chopin's considerable artistry and expressed an appreciation of her luminous, painterly style, her intricate weaving of images and symbols, and her brilliant psychological penetration. This positive critical attention secured for Chopin a place as a major literary figure and recognition for *The Awakening* as an essential American novel. The novel grew in importance as the momentum of the women's movement accelerated and gender issues prompted new literary assessments. *The Awakening* was heralded as a fundamental proto-feminist text, a powerful fictional rendering of the social, biological, and psychological dilemmas women face, as well as an exploration of the consequences of a raised consciousness. Written at the dawn of a new century in which women would struggle mightily toward freedom from gender-imposed restrictions, *The Awakening*, observed literary historian Larzer Ziff, "spoke of painful times ahead on the road to fulfillment."

THE HOUSE OF MIRTH

by Edith Wharton

Edith Wharton's *The House of Mirth* (1905) is, arguably, the first great novel by an American woman writer. Encouraged by her mentor Henry James to write about what she knew best—the complex web of elite New York society—Wharton, in treating the status of women in that world at the turn of the century, "emerged as a professionally serious, masterful novelist," in the words of biographer Cynthia Griffin Wolff. Her insider's tour of a "frivolous society" produced, as literary critic Diana Trilling wrote, "one of the most telling indictments of the whole of American society, of a whole social system based on the chance distribution of wealth, that has ever been put to paper." To a literary pantheon of American heroines that includes Hawthorne's Hester Prynne, James's Isabel Archer and Daisy Miller, Chopin's Edna Pontellier, and Dreiser's Carrie Meeber, Wharton added the complex and fascinating Lily Bart, whose gradual destruction in a society that knows the price of everything but the value of nothing, dramatizes cultural values, gender assumptions, and the inexorable pressures of conformity and cupidity. Drawing her title from *Ecclesiastes* 7:4, "The heart of fools is in the house of mirth," Wharton examines a uniquely American version of Bunyan's and Thackeray's

Vanity Fair, of the fashionable New York elite, whose showy brilliance conceals a moral vacuum, and whose refined manners disguise the most brutal betrayal and manipulation.

It is a world that Edith Wharton grew up in and whose values she was expected to accept and to abide by uncritically. Born in 1862, in a house near Washington Square in New York City, Edith Newbold Jones was the only daughter of socially prominent parents descended from aristocratic Old New York families. Her father's inheritance allowed the family to live, in Wharton's words, "a life of leisure and amiable hospitality." Educated by private tutors, she divided her time annually among New York, Europe, and Newport, Rhode Island. Edith delighted in reading and storytelling, and, at the age of fifteen, she secretly wrote a novella. A volume of her poetry was privately printed when she was sixteen. Her parents, fearing that their daughter was becoming unattractively bookish, rushed her debut into New York society prior to her seventeenth birthday to solidify her true vocation: to make a fashionable marriage. In 1885, she wed Edward Wharton, a wealthy Bostonian thirteen years her senior, and at the age of twenty-three she assumed her expected role as a young society hostess. The couple followed the fashionable migration according to the social seasons in New York, Newport, the Berkshires, and Europe. During her marriage to a man she discovered she had little in common, Wharton suffered periodic bouts of severe depression, culminating in a nervous breakdown, in 1898. The prescribed rest cure freed Wharton from her social obligations and allowed her to resume her creative writing. Wharton's first fiction did not appear until she was thirty, and she would later describe the experience of publishing her first collection of short stories, *The Greater Inclination*, in 1899, as an event that broke "the chains that had held me for so long in a kind of torpor. For nearly twelve years, I had tried to adjust myself to my marriage; but now I was over-mastered by the longing to meet people who shared my interests." Her decision to cultivate an unfashionable artistic and intellectual life as a writer marked a decisive break with the society in which she was raised, which viewed a professional writing career for a woman as scandalous. The testing of an individual's desires and principles against a rigidly unforgiving social conventionality, reflected in Wharton's own choice to break with precedent and propriety to become a writer, would establish the central theme of her works.

Wharton's first novel, *The Valley of Decision* (1902), is a historical novel set in eighteenth-century Italy. Wharton would later dismiss it as not a novel at all but "a romantic chronicle, unrolling its episodes like the frescoed legends on the palace-walls which formed its background." Henry James urged her instead to treat what she knew intimately, to "Do New York!" even if it meant that she "must be tethered in native pastures, even if it reduces her to a backyard in New York." The challenge Wharton faced in dealing with New York's *haut monde* in *The House of Mirth* was whether she could discover in its shallowness and trivialities deeper human significance and universal meaning. As Wharton remembered in her memoir, *A Backward Glance* (1934), she asked herself, "In what aspect could a society of irresponsible pleasure-seekers be said to have, on the 'old woe of the world,' any deeper bearing than the people composing such a society could guess? The answer was that a frivolous society can acquire dramatic significance only through what its frivolity destroys. Its tragic implication lies in its power of debasing people and ideals. The answer, in short, was my heroine, Lily Bart."

To underscore its human and universal significance, *The House of Mirth* required a sacrifice to the corrupted ideals of New York society; the novel dramatizes the fate of a beautiful and exceptional young woman of inadequate means who tries to maintain her tenuous social position among the fashionable who, in turn, are incapable of recognizing any values beyond the material and are not above betrayal to assert or protect self-supremacy. By birth Lily is accepted as a member of New York's ruling social aristocracy. Orphaned, she supplements a modest inheritance with an equally modest allowance from her staid Aunt Peniston. Her income is insufficient to sustain Lily among her fashionable social set. Raised to despise the "dingy" and trained as a decorative ornament for the discriminating, Lily, at age twenty-nine, feels the pressure to make an advantageous marriage. Without a husband of means, Lily feels vulnerable and powerless, and the novel traces her maneuvering in the marriage market as well as her susceptibility as a single woman to the self-interest of her purported friends.

The reader first meets Lily waiting for a train to take her to Gus and Judy Trenor's country estate, where she hopes to catch the wealthy but priggish Percy Gryce. A chance meeting with lawyer Lawrence Selden, whose limited means causes Lily to resist his evident attraction, leads to her agreeing to accompany him to his flat for tea, an impetuous act that seals Lily's future fate. Wharton would later attribute the popularity of *The House of Mirth* to her truth telling about a materialistically driven high society and her scandalous heroine:

> This supposed picture of their little circle, secure behind its high stockade of convention, alarmed and disturbed the rulers of Old New York. . . . Here was a tale written by one of themselves, a tale deliberately slandering and defiling their most sacred institutions and some of the most deeply revered members of the clan! And what picture did the writer offer to their horrified eyes? That of a young girl of their world who rouged, smoked, ran into debt, borrowed money, gambled, and—crowning horror!—went home with a bachelor friend to take tea in his flat! And I was not only asking the outer world to believe that such creatures were tolerated in New York society, but actually presenting this unhappy specimen as my heroine!

Lily is a breakthrough American fictional heroine, a headstrong and sensitive young woman who will battle through the novel her conflicting desires for wealth and power, as well as for independence, unselfishness, and responsibility. In characterizing Lily, Wharton evades the conventional idealization of female characters into clear categories of virtue and villainy, producing one of the first believably mixed female protagonists in American fiction.

Wharton's satiric point is made clear in Lily's material descent from a position of prestige and glamour to poverty and anonymity as a victim of a society that uses her and fails to appreciate or value her true worth. At the Trenors, Lily hesitates at snaring a husband, whom she does not love, for his money. Instead, she decides against her self-interest in favor of Selden and his appeal to her better nature beyond the contingencies of class and wealth. However, to meet her gambling and dressmaking debts, Lily turns to Gus Trenor for investment advice. She later discovers that her subsequent windfall carries the cost of becoming his mistress. Once her aunt learns of her debts, she disowns Lily. Finally, Lily's fate is sealed when Bertha Dorset, to conceal her own adultery, publicly implies that Lily has been having an affair with her husband. Lily is shunned and abandoned by her fashionable friends, whose hypocrisy is underscored when it is clear that Lily is tolerated only as long as she proves useful. Lily is forced to try her luck further down the social ladder by securing the patronage of the nouveau riche, but she proves to be a liability in gaining an entrée into high society. She then tries to become a milliner, but lacks the training and stamina to keep her job.

Unemployed and ill, now living in a dingy boardinghouse, Lily is tempted to retrieve her fortune and position by using the letters she has acquired proving the affair between Bertha Dorset and Selden, and to enjoy her $10,000 legacy from her aunt rather than to pay the debt she feels she morally owes to Gus Trenor. In the end, Lily resists both temptations, destroying the letters to protect Selden and discharging the debt to Trenor, which frees her. Lily thereby achieves a moral victory of self-worth and independence, despite her shabby surroundings and her death from an overdose of chloral, which she takes seeking relief from her misery in sleep. As Wharton shows in the career of Lily Bart and her circle, residents in the house of mirth are doomed by their virtues and rewarded by their vices. By possessing the moral scruples that make her ultimately incapable of the ruthlessness and selfishness that determine supremacy in her frivolous, corrupt society Lily is fated to fail. Yet she is also a victim of that society, unable to sustain and support an independent life for herself free of her materialistic dreams and the limited roles available to women during the period. Early in the novel, Selden asks Lily, "Isn't marriage your vocation? Isn't it what you're all brought up for?" To which Lily replies resignedly, "I suppose so. What else is there?" Ultimately, Lily fails to attain her marriage goal because her evident attractions—intelligence, originality, sensitivity, and morality—are insufficiently prized by a society for whom money is all. "I have tried hard," Lily confesses to Selden at their fateful last meeting, "but life is difficult, and I am a very useless person. I can hardly be said to have an independent existence. I was just a screw or a cog in the great machine I called life, and when I dropped out of it I found I was of no use anywhere else. What can one do when one finds that one only fits into one hole? One must get back to it or be thrown into the rubbish heap—and you don't know what it's like in the rubbish heap!"

Lily's inability to survive either in the debased world of fashion or in the grim reality of diminished expectations provides a cautionary, haunting indictment of the American dream of material success and power, and its cost. As the story of a woman's "great expectations," like Dickens's masterwork, Wharton's *The House of*

Mirth is a grand reversal of fortune, a contrary Horatio Alger story—from riches to rags—in which the heroine is cast out of the "inner paradise," and her fortune is lost rather than won. In terms of the view of society that Wharton presents, it is a fortune that is well lost with Lily's final achievement, and redemption in self-understanding and selfhood a priceless though fatal compensation.

MY ÁNTONIA

by Willa Cather

In 1918, the year *My Ántonia* was published, the world was about to enter a postwar era during which the nineteenth century would be left behind for the modern clamor of the twentieth. Willa Cather would later observe that the world "broke in two in 1922 or thereabouts." Philosophically and emotionally, Cather remained with those on the side of the divide allied with America's agrarian past and unwilling to embrace its urban, industrialized future. She had already demonstrated a remarkable talent for resurrecting the past and revivifying a region in her 1913 novel, *O Pioneers!* With *My Ántonia*, her most beloved work, Cather produced the last great celebration in the American novel of the frontier past and its heroic archetypal pioneers.

Born in 1873, Cather, like Jim Burden, the novel's narrator, came to Nebraska from Virginia as a child and lived on the prairie and in the town of Red Cloud (the Black Hawk of the novel). Cather left the prairie for schooling at the university in Lincoln, and subsequently pursued her professional career in the East. She made her home in New York, but she often went back to Nebraska and wrote much of her work at her summer home in New Brunswick, Canada, and in Jaffrey, New Hampshire, where she was buried after her death in 1947. Completely absorbed in her work, Cather remained single despite opportunities for marriage.

My Ántonia, published when Willa Cather was forty-five, was the author's fourth novel, but it was the first that most completely reflected her realization that "life began for me when I ceased to admire and began to remember." Cather was fascinated by the elemental landscape of the Nebraska prairie and by the intensity and idiosyncrasies of its inhabitants, particularly the immigrants who first carved lives from the unforgiving wilderness. In 1916, on a visit to her family in Red Cloud, Cather was reunited with her childhood friend, Annie Pavelka (formerly Sadilek), a Czech immigrant, whose father's suicide was one of the earliest stories Cather recalled as a child. Annie, now middle-aged, surrounded by her children at the center of a thriving domestic world, would serve as the model for Cather's protagonist and the means for her to process her memories of her Nebraskan childhood into a mythic expression of American life and character.

The biographical elements in *My Ántonia* certainly contribute to the emotional intensity and vividness of the novel. In the introduction, the narrator (presumably Cather herself) meets a childhood friend from Nebraska, Jim Burden, now a successful New York attorney in an unhappy marriage. The two recall their mutual friend, Ántonia, who continues to exert a powerful hold on their affection and imagination. Months later, Jim delivers a manuscript of his recollections of Ántonia, apologizing that his effort "hasn't any form," and adding, "I simply wrote down pretty much all that her name recalls to me." Jim's comments alert the reader to expect a novel that is not a conventionally plotted but is instead a series of episodes or, rather, images of Ántonia that demonstrates her impact. She is "my" Ántonia in the sense that she represents for Jim Burden his attempt to clarify his feelings about the past and its role in forming his present identity and fundamental values. The novel interweaves the life of its two central protagonists—Jim and Ántonia—with the logic of memory, in which years contract and scenes expand as the past is reassessed for significance. As Jim admits, "Ántonia had always been one to leave images in the mind that did not fade—that grew stronger with time. In my memory there was a succession of such pictures, fixed there like the old wood cuts of one's first primer." Ántonia is the means by which Jim can penetrate the past and unlock its treasures.

Cather once described her unconventional method in dealing with her heroine. She had placed an apothecary jar filled with flowers on a bare table and observed that "I want my new heroine to be like this—like a rare object in the middle of a table, which one may examine from all sides. . . . I want her to stand out—like this—like this—because she is the story." At the core of the book, therefore, is the symbolic center of gravity, Ántonia, whom Jim will come to appreciate as the organizing principle to redeem his past and sustain his present.

Cather's novel is set in the late nineteenth century, close enough in time for its first readers to recognize a way of life that was already beginning to diminish. Ántonia Shimerda, a farm girl from a family of Bohemian immigrants, is first encountered when ten-year-old Jim, an orphan, comes to live on his grandparents' farm on the Nebraska prairie. There, he confronts for the first time the prairie's vastness, an elemental and featureless landscape that seems to obliterate the individual, and that will make or break all its inhabitants. "There seemed to be nothing to see," Jim recalls. "No fences, no creeks or trees, no hills or fields. If there was a road, I could not make it out in a faint starlight. There was nothing but land: not a country at all, but the material out of which countries are made." Safely sheltered on his grandparents' well-regulated farm, Jim watches the challenges faced by Ántonia's family through a seasonal cycle that will cause Ántonia's father, a sensitive former musician ill-prepared and unhardened for the poverty and grinding work they face, to commit suicide. The forces that break her father, however, strengthen Ántonia. Generous, empathetic, and vital, Ántonia meets the challenge that defeats him. His death, however, sets in motion the different courses Jim and Ántonia will take. As she remarks to her friend, "Things will be easy for you. But they will be hard for us." Deprived by her father's death of any possibility of refinement and cultivation, Ántonia is forced to take on the heaviest farm chores. She will begin to recede from Jim's view, excluded from the possibilities that education and travel open up for him. Finally, the elemental relationship between Jim and Ántonia and the land that created a kind of vivid pastoral symbiosis in the opening chapters of the novel will also be tested as the scene shifts from the prairie to the town of Black Hawk.

With Jim's grandparents too old to take care of their farm, the

Burdens move to Black Hawk, where social custom and prejudice relegate Ántonia to the lowest rung of the social ladder as one of the "hired girls," the immigrant daughters forced off the farm to work as domestics for the more established citizens of Black Hawk. As pioneer life gives way to town life, there is a confusion of assessment that undervalues as primitive those who have tamed the landscape and created the conditions out of which the prairie towns were created. Although Jim's sympathy is clearly with the hired girls whose natural, instinctive openness and vitality contrast with the pinched and dreary lot of the more respectable, supercilious townspeople, his career as a student breaks his close association with Ántonia, who is increasingly glimpsed only through occasional reports from her friends. He learns that she has been deceived by a lover and left pregnant and unmarried. Meeting her again working in the fields, Jim finds that despite all that she has suffered, Ántonia retains her sympathy with others and affection for her life. Their meeting prompts Jim's crucial statements, "The idea of you is part of my mind," and "You really are a part of me," evidence that Ántonia has secured a symbolic place in Jim's imagination that the conclusion of the novel will help to clarify.

Twenty years later Jim sees Ántonia again. She is married to Anton Cuzak, a Czech farmer, and presides, Demeter-like, over a brood of sturdy, loving children and a prosperous Nebraska farm. Now toothless and gray-haired, she is "battered but not diminished," still luminous, possessing the "fire of life" that represents the indomitable spirit of the land itself. Jim's reunion with his childhood soulmate provides a vital linkage with his past and a return to his spiritual home. The luminous Ántonia, in turn, has been grandly appreciated as a principle of fertility and goodness, steadfastly joyous, nurturing, and essentially indestructible, an archetype of the noble pioneer woman. By recovering his prairie childhood through his connection with Ántonia—the organic product of the American landscape and character—Jim makes sense of his life, offering the reader a comparable lesson in extracting what is vital and enduring in the "precious, the incommunicable past."

The American novels following *My Ántonia* would increasingly deal with the betrayal and collapse of the American dream, the nation's frontier past and heroism becoming more an absence than a vital presence. Cather's novel succeeds as one of the greatest pastoral elegies in American literature, celebrating all that is elemental and archetypal through its heroine, Ántonia, one of a core group of essential female characters in American literature.

CHÉRI

by Colette

An important figure of early twentieth-century French literature, Colette has also gained critical acceptance and a well-earned renown within the genre of women's literature for her precise, beautifully crafted writing and sophisticated, sensitive treatments of human relationships. Colette's extraordinary ability to make the reader see, feel, and sense each moment of her characters' experiences is a central feature of *Chéri* (1920), probably her best-known novel. *Chéri* has been chosen for this volume because of the delicacy, sensuality, and eloquence of Colette's writing, and because it is a masterful description of the relationship between an older woman and a younger man.

Sidonie-Gabrielle Colette (1873–1954), nicknamed in her childhood "Chéri-Minet" or "Gabri," was born in the rustic Burgundian village of Saint-Sauveur-en-Puisaye, the daughter of Jules and Sidonie ("Sido") Colette. Her father, known as "The Captain," was a former officer in the Zouaves and had won a sinecure from Napoleon III as the town tax collector. Colette described her childhood and adolescence in the memoirs *My Mother's House* and *Sido* as one of almost "edenic" happiness, although she claimed somewhat dryly, "a happy childhood is poor preparation for human contacts." She was a child of France's *Belle Époque*, a period stretching roughly from 1871 to the start of World War I. During this time the arts and sciences flourished along with an urban cultural permissiveness that has identified the period as the era of the courtesan and the Moulin Rouge music hall, with its scandalous cancan dancers, as immortalized by the artist Henri Toulouse-Lautrec.

Beautiful, mischievous, and musically gifted, Colette received a girls-school education that stressed patriotism as well as the bourgeois notion that women should exert influence only in the domestic sphere of a solidly middle-class marriage. However, she was aware of an unconventional strain, as well as the failure of middle-class marriage, within her family: her mother had been previously and unhappily married to a wealthy landowner to whom she had twice been unfaithful, and after his death had married "The Captain," her second lover and the putative father of her first son. Colette's introverted half-sister, Juliette, thirteen years her senior, was prone to serious depression, which was made worse by an unhappy marriage to a well-to-do doctor. Juliette commited suicide in her forties. Colette's biographer Judith Thurman has observed, "One meets the shade of Juliette over and over in Colette's work. . . . She portrays depressed, abused, violent, and betrayed women—victims of their families, of their men, and of their own weakness—with an eloquence that belies her own distaste and detachment."

In 1893, the twenty-year-old Colette married the socially prominent and dissolute journalist, novelist, and music critic, Henry Gauthier-Villars, known in Parisian circles as "Willy." Fourteen years older than his country-girl bride, Willy introduced his young wife to figures of the bohemian Parisian high life and the *demimonde*. Willy's literary fame rested on putting his name to spicy novels and reviews penned by ghostwriters, and in the late 1890s, Colette joined his underground workshop with a memoir of her school days. The result was Colette's first work, *Claudine at School*, published under Willy's name, in 1900. The book, which revealed Colette's innate gift for narrative fiction, was an immediate success and led to several sequels in which Claudine grows up, marries, and, in the last of the series, *Retreat From Love* (1907), finds a much-desired independence in contented widowhood. In 1904, she produced a collection of short dialogues between a dog and a cat, *Creature Conversations*, the first of several works published under the name "Colette Willy." Colette would write about her years with Willy honing her craft in *My Apprenticeships* (1936). She separated from the unfaithful Willy in 1906 (the couple would divorce in 1910) and went on to marry the Baron Henri de Jouvenal, a politician and journalist, in 1912. She had a daughter, Colette (nicknamed "Bel-Gazou"), by Jouvenal, and divorced him, in 1925, because of his unfaithfulness and her affair with his adolescent son, Bertrand. In 1935, she embarked on her third, and happiest, marriage, to Maurice Goude-ket, a Jewish businessman and writer sixteen years her junior.

Faced with the need to earn money after her separation from Willy, Colette, while continuing to write, also pursued an adjacent career from 1906 to 1911 as a music-hall dancer and mime. This very public period of her life contributed to the notoriety for which she would become famous. She openly cohabitated with her lesbian lover, Missy de Belbeuf, the Marquise de Morny, and caused a huge citywide scandal when she and the marquise performed a love scene together in the pantomime, *Reve d'Egypte* (*Egyptian Dream*), at the Moulin Rouge in 1907. Colette's works during her music-hall years, which include *The Vagabond* (1910) and its sequel, *The Shackle* (1913), are set in the world of the popular French theater of the day and feature believable women characters who experience sexual desire and fulfillment, an uncommon ingredient in the fiction of the era. Colette left the theater after forming her liaison with the wealthy Jouvenal, and wrote news columns and reviews for the newspaper, *Le Matin*, even serving as a war correspondent during World War I.

Colette would mine her experience of the *Belle Époque*'s demimonde in *Gigi*, a series of five novellas, published in 1943, that would go on to become famous as a play and an Academy Award–winning musical, as well as, most notably, in *Chéri*. The novel of a young man barely out of adolescence engaged in an affair with a courtesan old enough to be his mother had its origins in eight disparate short stories Colette wrote for *Le Matin* before the war and integrated into book form in 1920. Colette drew her characters from people she had known, including her former lover and stepson, Bertrand de Jouvenal.

The action of *Chéri* begins in 1912, and concerns the six-year love affair between the forty-nine-year-old, still lovely courtesan, Léonie Vallon and the handsome twenty-five-year-old Fred Peloux, known as Chéri by his lover and his mother, also a courtesan and Léa's intimate friend. Léa and Madame Peloux have been financially successful in their chosen profession and are now able to live independent of their wealthy "benefactors." Both women, each in her own way, has been responsible for bringing up Chéri to take his place in society as a gentleman of leisure. The result is a beautiful young man who is also spoiled, childlike, irresponsible, vain, greedy, miserly, arrogant, and cruel.

The sensual, delicately nuanced quality of Colette's writing is evident in the opening pages of the novel. Having dallied together all morning, Chéri demands from Léa her glorious strand of pearls so that he can play with them. Léa hesitates—"There was no response from the enormous bed of wrought-iron and copper which shone in the shadow like a coat of mail"—but she indulges her lover and hands over the pearls. There is a suggestion that Léa does not want to call attention to the wrinkles on her neck by removing the necklace. Later in the scene, when she criticizes Chéri for "wrinkling" his nose when he laughs, he thinks, "My wrinkles, eh? Wrinkles are the last things she ought to mention." But it is Léa's age, as well as her beauty and charm, that is attractive to Chéri; she is his "nounoune," a nanny and mother, as well as a lover. By staying with her, the nearly inarticulate and puerile Chéri can remain a child. In contrast, Léa is worldly-wise, deliberate, and practical, able to identify her needs and satisfy them. She accepts with equanimity that, despite her battle against aging, their affair will eventually end.

Léa remains composed, even when she learns that a marriage of convenience has been arranged for Chéri to eighteen-year-old Edmée, a wealthy young woman of property who is pretty, quiet, and docile, with "a frightened conquered expression." Chéri promises to remain Léa's lover despite his marriage, and she submits to what is an expected and logical situation. However, after the wedding, Léa realizes that she loves Chéri with a passion stronger than any she has ever known. In despair at having to share him with a wife, Léa goes to the south of France. Mystified and discomfited by Léa's abandonment, Chéri turns on his wife, who suffers from his tantrums, accuses him of infidelity, and asks for a divorce. He refuses to divorce her and leaves home for six weeks, during which he lives with a bachelor friend and haunts Léa's vacant house in Paris. When he learns that Léa has come back to Paris, Chéri buys jewels for his wife and returns home.

In the third part of the novel the relationship between Léa and

Chéri comes full circle. Léa is aware that she has returned "a little thinner and mollified, less serene," and that, although she is still attractive, "it was necessary to drape prudently if not indeed entirely to hide her ruined throat, girdled with great wrinkles which the sunshine had not penetrated." After contemplating ways in which she can continue her profession for several more years, "an effort restored to her her common sense, filled her with lucid pride. A woman like me and not enough courage to know when to call a halt? Come, come, my fine friend, we've had our money's worth in our time." Léa is reconciled to a life of celibate independence, but a visit from Madame Peloux, who warbles on about her son and Edmée, makes her realize that she is not free of her love for Chéri. Late one evening Chéri arrives at Léa's flat, sullen and disheveled, and after quarreling for a time, the two rekindle their passion and for the first time declare their love for each other. In the morning, Léa, unknowingly watched by Chéri, makes plans for the two of them to leave Paris: "As yet unpowdered, a meager twist of hair on the nape of her neck, with double chin and ruined throat, she imprudently offered herself to the invisible eye." When Chéri rejects her plans for departure, Léa bitterly insults Edmée. The selfish Chéri rationalizes that he can no longer find in this resentful, aging woman his lovely, sophisticated, and dependable "nounoune." Léa realizes that the affair has ended, and she tenderly sends him away, granting him an adulthood in which she has no role.

In 1926, Colette published a sequel, *The Last of Chéri*, in which the title character is reunited with Léa after returning from service in World War I. He is appalled by his former mistress, now in her sixties, gray haired, matronly, and asexual, without any of her former sophisticated romantic charm. She chides Chéri for expecting life to be the same as before and adopts her earlier, maternal attitude toward him. Disillusioned with his life and in deteriorating mental and physical health, Chéri leaves his wife and takes up with Copine, another aging courtesan and a great admirer of Léa. He commits suicide in Copine's seedy apartment, which is festooned with photographs of Léa in her youth.

Chéri, which appeared at a time when Colette's penchant for the unconventional was well known, was criticized for its milieu, the world of the courtesan, and for its bad boy title character. At the same time, the novel was acclaimed for the lyrical eloquence of its prose. One of *Chéri*'s fans was novelist André Gide, who sent Colette a letter praising the work, in which he wrote, "What a wonderful subject you have taken up! And with what intelligence, mastery, and understanding of the least admitted secrets of the flesh!" But there is another important aspect of the novel. In *Chéri*, Colette dared to invert traditional gender roles by making her woman character not only older and a denizen of the *demimonde*, but also the stronger partner in their relationship. In Léa, Colette created a new female image, a sexually knowing, independent woman, who, because of her strength of character, transcends her need for her lover in order to give him the gift of liberation.

A ROOM OF ONE'S OWN

by *Virginia Woolf*

Woolf's powerful declaration of women's independence, autonomy, and artistry, *A Room of One's Own* is widely regarded as the first great achievement of feminist literary criticism that raised and helped to shape the central issues of the modern women's movement. As one of the groundbreaking literary modernists of the twentieth century, Virginia Woolf redefined the art of the novel, taking it from surface realism of external details to the deeper reaches of consciousness and the interior life. As an essayist and critic, Woolf demonstrated that a woman could formulate a new cultural understanding appropriate for dealing with the often neglected and misunderstood female perspective and the role woman writers ought to play in creative life. To capture the essence of Woolf's views on women, gender conflict, literary and cultural history, and the ways and means of creative criticism, *A Room of One's Own* is a foundation text, like Mary Wollstone-craft's *A Vindication of the Rights of Woman*, Simone de Beauvoir's *The Second Sex*, and Betty Friedan's *The Feminine Mystique*, works that remain powerful, compelling, and relevant.

Virginia Woolf was born in London, in 1882, the third child in a family of two boys and two girls. She was the daughter of the renowned Victorian critic, biographer, and scholar Sir Leslie Stephen, the author of the *History of English Thought in the Eighteenth Century* and the editor of the *Dictionary of National Biography*. Her mother, Julia, was a famous beauty and hostess of a distinguished literary circle that gathered at the Stephens' home. She died when Virginia was thirteen, and the loss contributed to the first of several emotional breakdowns that would recur throughout Woolf's life. In 1904, her father's death resulted in a second breakdown and a suicide attempt. When Virginia recovered, she moved with her brothers and sister to a home of their own in unfashionable Bloomsbury. There they formed the center of an eccentric and talented circle of artists, critics, and writers, including Lytton Strachey, Vita Sackville-West, E. M. Forster, and John Maynard Keynes, all of whom would become collectively famous as the Bloomsbury Group. In 1912, Virginia married Leonard Woolf, a critic and political writer. The following year she completed her first novel, *The Voyage Out*, which she had been working on for six years and which was published in 1915. Her second novel, *Night and Day*, appeared in 1919. Both are traditional in form and content; however, in the collection of stories that became *Monday or Tuesday*, Woolf began to experiment with a more daring, experimental form to render a character's stream of consciousness and the interior world of private thoughts and feelings. Her next novels, *Jacob's Room* (1922), *Mrs. Dalloway* (1925), and her masterpiece, *To the Lighthouse* (1927), are all written in Woolf's experimental style in which conventional plot is replaced by an emphasis on the inner, psychological states of her characters, and time and space reflect a deeply subjective, poetic vision. Woolf's later writing includes *Orlando* (1928), a mock biography of a character from Elizabethan times to the present in which the protagonist changes sexes to fit each age; *Flush* (1933), a biographical fantasy of the Brownings seen from the perspective of Elizabeth Barrett Browning's dog; a biography of the art critic Roger Fry (1940); and the novels *The Waves* (1931), *The Years* (1937), and *Between the Acts* (1941). During the 1920s and 1930s, Woolf also wrote several volumes of criticism, including *A Room of One's Own* (1929) and *Three Guineas* (1938), in which she expanded on her critique of artistic achievement and mounted a spirited campaign on behalf of women writers. In 1941, depressed over the outbreak of war and sensing the onset of another breakdown, Virginia Woolf drowned herself. Throughout a distinguished career as a novelist and critic, Virginia Woolf argued that the Victorian world that she was born into was obsolete, and that its patriarchal assumptions about the constricted roles women are assigned must be challenged by fresh ideas and new perspectives. None of her works better demonstrates this point than *A Room of One's Own.*

Originally entitled "Women and Fiction," *A Room of One's Own* grew out of two talks Woolf delivered at Cambridge University, in October 1928, one at Newnham College, the second at the all-women's Girton College (then the only college for women at Cambridge) before an audience, in Woolf's words, of "starved but valiant young women. . . . Intelligent, eager, poor; & destined to become school-mistresses in shoals." Woolf would later state that her motivation for her talk there was "to encourage the young women—they seem to get fearfully depressed." Mainly an argument for the financial independence and privacy necessary for female artistic achievement, backed up by a consideration of such women novelists as Jane Austen, the Brontës, and George Eliot, the talks would be expanded, in 1929, into *A Room of One's Own.* Woolf would add a fictional framework and scenes that contrast the lot of men and women at Cambridge and Oxford. She would imagine the fate of Shakespeare's sister and assert her conception of the androgynous state of mind, which she considered essential for the creation of great literature. Published by the Hogarth Press, the publishing firm Woolf ran with her husband, the essay, in which Woolf felt she would be "attacked for a feminist & hinted at for a Sapphist," is described on the dust jacket, likely composed by its author, as follows:

> This essay, which is largely fictitious, is based upon the visit of an outsider to a university and expresses the thoughts suggested by a comparison between the different standards of luxury at a man's college and at a woman's. This leads to a sketch of women's circumstances in the past, and the effect of those circumstances upon their writing. The conditions that are favourable to imaginative work are discussed, including the right relation of the sexes. Finally an attempt is made to outline the present state of affairs and to forecast what effect comparative freedom and independence will have upon women's artistic work in the future.

When *A Room of One's Own* appeared, in 1929, the fight to secure women's suffrage in both Britain and America, which had dominated women's rights activists for the previous seventy-five years, had been finally won. Despite enfranchisement, women, in Woolf's view, continue to be shut out of significant cultural institutions and suffer from various economic constraints that have prevented women from achieving their potential. Woolf's essay suggests that an entrenched patriarchal system impedes and silences a distinctive female voice and perspective. In the essay, Woolf assesses the impact of this system on female literary expression, providing the first conceptualization of literary history with gender as the key determinant. It is, in the words of critic Ellen Bayuk Rosenman, also the "first concentrated attempt to create a counter-theory to Victorian sex-roles," challenging the accepted notion of women's inferiority, dependency, and marginality.

The essay begins by responding to an unheard question: "But, you may say, we asked you to speak about women and fiction—what has that got to do with a room of one's own?" Woolf's thesis is that artistic genius and the ability of women to write great fiction requires freedom: "A woman must have money and a room of one's own if she is to write fiction." Living in a male-dominated world, lacking autonomy and economic independence, women are without the essential prerequisites to create important fiction. Women, according to Woolf, must be able "to think, invent, imagine, and create as freely as men do, and with as little fear or ridicule and condescension." In Woolf's famous formulation, five hundred pounds a year and a room of one's own makes genius possible for women. With them, "Food, house and clothing are mine for ever. Therefore not merely do effort and labour cease, but also hatred and bitterness. I need not hate any man; he cannot hurt me. I need not flatter any man; he has nothing to give me."

To explore the difference between this ideal and present and past reality, Woolf contrasts the possibilities and prospects faced by men and women at Oxford and Cambridge, Britain's training ground for society's movers and shakers. The woman visitor Woolf imagines is shooed off the grass, which is reserved for the male Fellows and Scholars of the colleges. Likewise, she is barred from a college's library without a male companion or sponsorship. The luncheon she receives from the all-male college is lavish and liberating, while her dinner at the all-women's college is meager and demoralizing. Symbolically, men are shown wielding significant power, controlling the means of education and culture, while women are pushed to the margins, excluded, and circumscribed. The contrast leaves the narrator with two linked questions: why are women so poor, and why have so few women written anything to rival male authors?

To answer the first question, Woolf shifts the scene to the British Library Reading Room, where research leads her to conclude that women's impoverishment has been caused chiefly by their childbearing and childraising responsibilities, which have impeded economic independence and caused dependency on males. The second question, concerning the paucity of women's literary achievement, is also connected with women's impoverishment—in their historical limited access to wider experience, the lack of a tradition of women's artistry to draw upon, and the cultural constraints that have silenced women's voices and obliterated their history. To make her point, Woolf surmises the likely biography of an imagined sister of Shakespeare who shared her brother's genius. Frustrated at every turn by gender constraints, Judith Shakespeare ends in suicide and obscurity, with her potential crushed by a lack of education, privacy, expectations, and freedom. To further her point, Woolf surveys literary history from a perspective that focuses on the deviation from the established gender norm in the achievement of Jane Austen, the Brontës, and George Eliot, none of whom had children, but all of whom were constrained by societal pressure that limited their experiences, autonomy, and possibilities.

In contrast to the fate of Judith Shakespeare and her sisters, a contemporary woman writer, one with five hundred pounds a year and a room of one's own, has, in Woolf's view, the potential for genius to flourish as never before. Freed from a battle of the sexes that dependency ensures, the liberated and autonomous woman writer may achieve an androgynous perspective that ultimately is required for literary greatness, in Woolf's view. "If we face the fact," Woolf concludes, "that there is no arm to cling to, but that we go alone and that our relation is to the world of reality and not only to the world of men and women, then the . . . dead poet who was Shakespeare's sister will put on that body which she has so often laid down."

A Room of One's Own remains a remarkable and provocative articulation of gender issues that resists the easy self-pity of victimhood based on male oppression; instead, it challenges women to achieve their full potential. The issues Woolf raises regarding the constraints women face in a patriarchal society, and the relation between sexual identity, literary expression, and achievement, remain vital questions with which women continue to wrestle.

GONE WITH THE WIND

by Margaret Mitchell

A *New Yorker* cartoon of the late 1930s depicts a teenage girl standing in front of a full-length mirror, one shoulder bared, one hand on her breast and the other hand on her forehead. A book lies open on the floor next to her. There is an expression of rapture on the teenager's face as she passionately exclaims, "I'm not afraid of you, Rhett Butler, or of any man in shoe leather!" *New Yorker* readers would have had no trouble identifying *Gone with the Wind* as the source of the caption and the theme of the cartoon. Within a year after its publication in 1936, Margaret Mitchell's sweeping epic of the American South during the Civil War and Reconstruction had sold over a million copies and become a cultural, as well as a publishing, phenomenon. The New York *Herald Tribune* reflected the excitement generated by the novel, when it proclaimed, "*Gone with the Wind* has come to be more than a novel. It is a national event, a proverbial expression of deep instinct, a story that promises to found a kind of legend."

Despite its enormous popularity and impact (helped, in great part, by the 1939 film version of the novel), *Gone with the Wind* has received relatively little literary attention, and its author has been largely consigned to the critical netherworld of the celebrity

romance writer. However, in *Gone with the Wind*, Mitchell produced more than just an iconic one-hit wonder that inserted
Rhett Butler, Scarlett O'Hara, and Tara into the collective consciousness and brought forth the modern romance genre. She
created an enduring woman-centered fiction that addresses important issues concerning the role of women—especially southern women—in nineteenth-century American society.

Margaret Mitchell (1900–1949) once said of her creation, "If
the novel *Gone with the Wind* has a theme, the theme is that of survival." The quote fits the era in which the novel was published—
the Great Depression of the 1930s—but it also reflects what
Mitchell, like other southerners, learned about the Civil War and
Reconstruction as a child. Born in Atlanta, a city to which she remained devoted throughout her short life, Margaret Mitchell was
the daughter of Eugene Mitchell, an attorney, and Maybelle
Stephens Mitchell, an active participant in the women's suffrage
movement. Her mother and father had been born during the devastating aftermath of the war, and Mitchell was exposed to local
history from her parents and older relatives who had experienced
the conflict. Her maternal grandmother showed her where Confederate forces had dug trenches in her backyard, and Maybelle
Mitchell took her daughter on tours of plantations ruined by
what she called "Sherman's Sentinels" or left to slowly decay after
Reconstruction brought poverty. Mitchell would later credit her
mother with fixing in her imagination the image of the South uprooted by Union troops. As Mitchell recalled, "She talked about
the world those people had lived in, such a secure world, and how
it had exploded beneath them. And she told me that my own
world was going to explode under me some day, and God help
me if I didn't have some weapon to meet the new world." Mitchell's
defensive weapon would become her writing, and her theme, how
individuals cope in order to survive and rebuild their lives.

Mitchell's first literary efforts, begun when she was a child,
were adventure stories, written mostly in the form of plays. She
continued her writing through her middle teen years at Washington
Seminary, a private girls' school near her home. While attending
the seminary, Mitchell attempted a novel that was similar in plot
to the kind of girls' series stories popular at the time. Called "The
Big Four," the novel was set in a girls' boarding school, concerned
the adventures of four friends, and featured a heroine named
Margaret who engaged in such valiant exploits as leading her

classmates through a fire. Mitchell considered the novel a failure but continued to write short fiction. She went on to Smith College, where she gained a reputation for her sense of humor and her flouting of campus rules, and fascinated her housemates with her stories of the Civil War. In the winter of 1919, Mitchell's mother died in the influenza epidemic that swept the nation, and Margaret returned home to run the household for her father and older brother, Stephens. In 1922, she married Red Upshaw, a some-time bootlegger, who raped and beat her. The couple divorced in 1924, and a year later Mitchell married the more stable and respectable John Marsh, a public relations manager.

From 1922 to 1926, Mitchell was a reporter and features writer for the *Atlanta Journal*, for which she wrote a series of articles on prominent Georgia women, and Confederate generals and their wives. In the first series, Mitchell featured women of force and power, such as Mary Musgrove, a Native American woman who was named empress of the Creek tribe despite having had three white husbands, and Lucy Mathilde Kenney, who disguised herself as a man in order to fight alongside her husband during the Civil War. Mitchell received much criticism from the paper's readers because she had favorably depicted strong women who did not fit the accepted standards of femininity. Deeply hurt by the criticism, she confined herself to writing lightweight fare for the *Journal*, including one article titled "Should Husbands Spank Their Wives?" In 1926, Mitchell gave up newspaper work, partly at the request of Marsh, who did not want her to work outside the home, and partly because she had ceased to find newspaper writing sufficiently challenging. She had also severely injured her ankle in an automobile accident and could not sit at a typewriter. She began a Jazz Age novel with a heroine named Pansy Hamilton and then completed a novella, set in the 1880s, in Clayton County, Georgia, where her ancestors had once owned a plantation (Clayton County would be the setting for much of *Gone with the Wind*). Titled "Ropa Carmagin," the novella was never published, and Mitchell later destroyed the manuscript.

While convalescing from her ankle injury, Mitchell read extensively in nineteenth-century Atlanta history. According to family legend, when few books remained at the local library that Mitchell had not read, her husband remarked, "It looks to me, Peggy, as though you'll have to write a book yourself if you're going to have anything to read." This began Mitchell's nearly ten-year labor to produce *Gone with the Wind*. She approached the project with a view toward clarifying the southern experience of the Confederate defeat, particularly from the perspective of its impact on women. It would become, of course, a romance novel as well as one author's depiction of history. Mitchell began her story with her heroine's climactic realization that would eventually appear in the book's final pages: "She had never understood either of the men she had loved and so she had lost them both." To reach this moment of insight, Mitchell centered her 1,367-page epic on the experience of her main female character, christened Scarlett, after Mitchell's publisher, Macmillan, objected to Pansy, her first choice for a name, because of its homosexual connotations.

The men Scarlett O'Hara loves and loses are Ashley Wilkes and Rhett Butler. The idealistic, dutiful, chivalric, handsome Ashley, who lives at the stately Twelve Oaks plantation, is the object of Scarlett's affections from the beginning of *Gone with the Wind*, when she is a green-eyed, sixteen-year-old spoiled and cosseted southern siren, to nearly the end of the novel, when Mitchell's heroine realizes at last that he has always been the wrong man for her. The right man is the attractive, roguish, cynical, sexually charismatic Rhett, a gambler, womanizer, and Confederate gun-runner, who nevertheless possesses a noble streak and a desire for respectability. Ashley is attracted to Scarlett but feels he is not strong enough for her; instead, he marries his female counterpart, gentle Melanie Hamilton. During the course of the novel, Scarlett will wed three times and be twice widowed. Her first husband is Melanie's brother, Charles, whom she marries to spite both Ashley and Melanie. Scarlett's second spouse is her sister's beau, shopkeeper Frank Kennedy, whom she weds for mercenary reasons. The third is, of course, Rhett, who loves her deeply. She will have a child by each of the men. Along the way, Scarlett flees burning Atlanta with Melanie and Melanie's newborn son in tow, faces poverty, disease, and death at Tara, the O'Haras' ruined plantation, kills a marauding Union soldier, and manages, with courage, fortitude, and not a little scheming, to amass a fortune and rebuild her home. By the novel's end, she has kept the fortune and the home, but has lost everything else of value to her.

Scarlett, one of the most recognizable heroines in American literature, is a morally mixed, deeply flawed protagonist, captivating and admirable in her passion and resilience, deplorable in her heartlessness and self-centeredness, and pitiable in her solipsism.

A complex mixture of modern and traditional values, and feminine and masculine traits, she is an alluring southern belle who is oblivious of people who do not contribute to her sense of entitlement. She is also an aggressive manipulator who rejects passive victimhood with a survivalist mentality that fuels her drive for mastery of her environment. Ultimately, Scarlett is doomed to exist between the conflicting poles of autonomy and dependence that Mitchell diagnosed as the central dilemma of southern women. Seen in this regard, *Gone with the Wind* offers a fascinating dramatization of gender roles and expectations, relevant not just to the period in the South before and after the Civil War, but increasingly valid to the book's first readers, struggling to survive the Great Depression while absorbing the values of the new emancipated woman of the post–World War I era.

The ambiguity of Scarlett's character is evident from the start, in the novel's memorable opening line: "Scarlett O'Hara was not beautiful, but men seldom realized it when caught by her charm as the Tarleton twins were." At once decorous and willful, Scarlett is a complex blend of her mother's carefully cultivated femininity and her father's aggressive masculinity, and the novel's events demonstrate how both are manifested in her defiance of convention and drive for independence and control. What ultimately dooms Scarlett are the traditional values of dependence on the old southern order and its definition of women that dominate here. She is pulled back from the equally iconoclastic Rhett by her obsession with Ashley, and she is stubbornly single-minded in her devotion to the antebellum values of security and protection, represented for her by Tara. She wants desperately to emulate her mother, Tara's gentle and pious chatelaine, and is distressingly aware that her turbulent character, fortified in part by the necessity to survive, forbids this. Scarlett is ultimately incapable of sustaining a meaningful role for herself beyond traditional gender expectations, yet she is unable to find contentment in independence. The failure of both the men and the women in *Gone with the Wind* to maintain the reassuring values of their formerly ordered society, however hard they may cling to these values, is the inevitable casualty of the changes brought about by the war and its disruptive aftermath.

The romance genre, and particularly historical romances, borrows much from Margaret Mitchell, particularly her survival plot in novels that endlessly test characters by circumstances and tangled relationships. Yet few characters in popular romances match the complexity of Scarlett O'Hara. In addition, most romance novels cannot resist the pleasing resolution that Mitchell's novel insistently avoids. *Gone with the Wind* features one of the most daring and unsettling conclusions in fiction. Scarlett is left alone, unsupported by Rhett, who walks out on her after uttering the immortal words, "My dear, I don't give a damn." But Scarlett refuses to give up: "With the spirit of her people who would not know defeat, even when it stared them in the face, she raised her chin. She could get Rhett back. There had never been a man she couldn't get, once she set her mind upon him." And so she falls back upon the twin consolations of Tara and the mantra that has helped to sustain her throughout the novel: "Tomorrow is another day," one of the working titles for the novel.

Despite her readers' continual pleas for a sequel to resolve the suspense over Scarlett's fate, Mitchell refused to comply and struggled to cope with "the hell on earth" that the book's popularity brought her until she was struck and killed by a taxi in Atlanta in 1949. More than fifty years after *Gone with the Wind* was first published, Alexandra Ripley, an author of historical novels and romances, took on the daunting task of continuing the saga of Scarlett and Rhett, and, in 1991, published *Scarlett*, a worthy effort, which, although it does not contain the complexity of Margaret Mitchell's novel, is recommended for its value as a sequel. In 2001, the southern stereotype set by *Gone with the Wind* was challenged in *The Wind Done Gone*, a novel by country western songwriter turned novelist, Alice Randall. Written to dispel the aura surrounding what Randall viewed as a racist cultural icon, *The Wind Done Gone* is the story of Scarlett seen through the personal diaries of Cynara, Scarlett's half-sister, the daughter of Gerald O'Hara and Mammy. It is undeniable that *Gone with the Wind* reflects the white southern point of view, and Randall deserves credit for confronting that fact. But *Gone with the Wind* nevertheless deserves its place as one of the defining popular literary expressions of the twentieth century. With Scarlett O'Hara, Margaret Mitchell offered her own unique point of view to create a riveting central female character and a view of one of America's defining historical tragedies through the lens of a female perspective that continues to express contemporary issues and concerns.

GAUDY NIGHT

by Dorothy L. Sayers

Equal parts detective novel, college novel, character study, and romance, *Gaudy Night* (1936), set at Shrewsbury, a women's college of Oxford University, is the third of four Sayers novels to feature the appealing Harriet Vane, who, like the author, is a best-selling detective novelist and an Oxford graduate. Created by Dorothy Sayers as a mate for her aristocratic, debonair sleuth, Lord Peter Wimsey, who had taken center stage in four previous detective novels and a short-story collection, Harriet is introduced in *Strong Poison* (1930), where she is on trial for the murder of her lover and is saved from the gallows by Wimsey's almost eleventh-hour apprehension of the real culprit. She next appears in *Have His Carcase* (1932), where Sayers provides her with a supporting role to Wimsey in the detection of the mystery. However, it is in *Gaudy Night* that Sayers gives Harriet the substance she deserves and demonstrates what a truly interesting character she is by placing her at the center of what is an intriguing and thought-provoking novel, as well an excellent detective story.

Dorothy L. Sayers once stated, "I am a writer and I know my craft." This was not an idle assertion. Sayers was a prodigious author, who, in addition to the mystery novels and short stories she produced during what has often been called the Golden Age of Detective Fiction, the period between the two world wars, published psychological novels, novels of manners, children's books, poetry collections, essays, literary criticism, and other nonfiction works. Sayers was also a dramatist, whose works, often with Christian themes, were produced by BBC radio, in London's West End, at festivals, and in the United States. Finally, she was a medievalist, who published translations of Dante, a twelfth-century Anglo-Norman romance, and *The Song of Roland*. This last métier was Sayers' favorite: "By instinct, preference, and training," she once declared, "I am a scholar—a medieval scholar."

Sayers began her scholarly training early. Born in 1893, in Oxford, she was the daughter of the Reverend Henry Sayers, Headmaster of Christchurch Cathedral Choir School. Her mother, Helen Mary Leigh, was the grandniece of *Punch*'s cofounder, Percy Leigh. Sayers grew up in Bluntisham-cum-Earith, a small parish in England's fen country, where her father had accepted a church living. When she was six, her father began to teach her Latin, a language in which, by the age of thirteen, she was proficient. She was tutored by a French governess and then spent two years as a boarder at the Godolphin School for Girls, where she distinguished herself academically. However, Dorothy was unhappy at the school. Tall, awkward, shy, bespectacled, and nearly bald after suffering several illnesses, including measles and pneumonia, she had few friends and threw all of her energies into academic work and preparations for obtaining a scholarship to Oxford. She won a Gilchrist scholarship and, in 1912, entered Somerville, a women's college at Oxford. Sayers flourished socially and academically at Somerville, and twenty years later described the impact of scholarly judgment and discipline she encountered there in a manner that would reflect a theme present in *Gaudy Night*: "The integrity of mind that money cannot buy; the humility in face of the facts that self-esteem cannot corrupt: these are the fruits of scholarship, without which all statement is propaganda and all argument special pleading."

In 1915, Sayers received first class honors in Modern Languages and a degree course certificate, the equivalent to women of the university's bachelor of arts degree. She would receive her master of arts in 1920, when Oxford finally granted that degree to women. After completing her studies at Oxford, she produced a small volume of poems, *OP I*, published in 1916 by Blackwell's, an Oxford publisher. After teaching at the Hull High School for Girls from 1916 to 1917, she settled in Oxford, where she pursued postgraduate studies at the university and worked for Blackwell's as a reader and editor. In 1918, she produced a second book of verse, *Catholic Tales and Christian Songs.*

Sayers' father left his parish in Bluntisham for an even poorer living in Christchurch, Wisbech, also in the fen country. Dorothy spent her vacations at the rectory there immersed in the writings of Conan Doyle, Edgar Wallace, and other authors of mystery fiction, not merely to while away pleasant hours, but also because, according to the fledgling author, "That is where the real money is!" In 1922, she moved to London, where she took a job as a copywriter at S. H. Benson, then the largest advertising agency in Great Britain. The following year, she published the first Lord Peter Wimsey detective novel, *Whose Body?*, which received favorable reviews and prompted Sayers to begin a sequel. In 1924, Sayers gave birth to a son, John Anthony, the result of an affair, probably with American writer John Cournos. The second Lord Peter mystery, *Clouds of Witness*, appeared in 1926; that same year, Sayers married Scottish-born journalist Captain Oswald Atherton Fleming. She continued to write about Lord Peter Wimsey, producing *Unnatural Death* (1927), *The Unpleasantness at the Bellona Club* (1928), and *Lord Peter Views the Body* (1928), a collection of twelve short stories.

Harriet Vane's entrance in *Strong Poison* was intended to signal the exit of Peter Wimsey as a character: Sayers planned to have him fall in love, marry, and then drop out of sight, leaving her free to develop other, more fully realized characters and social situations. But, like Sherlock Holmes, who was killed off by his creator, Arthur Conan Doyle, and then resurrected, Lord Peter proved too popular with readers to discard. Sayers also realized that it would be unconvincing for Harriet to immediately accept Wimsey's proposal of marriage. So Sayers delayed Lord Peter's exit and kept Harriet, in many ways Sayers' female alter ego, to provide an extra dimension to the series.

In the character of Peter Wimsey, Sayers created a detective who was an idealized English aristocrat-hero. The second son of the late Duke of Denver, Wimsey is rich, attractive (the late British actor Leslie Howard could have played the role to perfection), suave, elegant, sensitive, and humorous, with a quick mind and keen wit, and an abiding interest in sleuthing. He took first class honors in history at Balliol College, gained fame at Oxford as a cricketeer, is a connoisseur of food and wine, as well as a skillful amateur musician and a collector of incunabula. Wimsey served as an officer in World War I; his sergeant, Mervyn Bunter, became his valet and partner in detection.

Harriet Vane is the object of Wimsey's affection almost from the moment he first sees her in the dock. She is highly intelligent, thoughtful, fiercely independent, proud, and refreshingly forthright. Like Wimsey, she possesses a keen wit and a sense of humor. She is dark-haired and slim, with a low, attractive speaking voice. "So interesting and a really remarkable face," observes Wimsey's mother, the irrepressible Dowager Duchess, in *Strong Poison*, "though perhaps not strictly good-looking, and all the more interesting for that, because good-looking people are so often cows." In a country where class distinctions are paramount, Harriet's origins are solidly middle class. The daughter of a country doctor, Harriet was sent to Shrewsbury College, where she achieved first class honors in English. She was orphaned at twenty-three and, left penniless, was forced to earn a living and has worked hard at her chosen profession—writing detective thrillers. Described by one of Sayers' characters in the last Vane–Wimsey novel, *Busman's Honeymoon* (1937), as a "Bloomsbury bluestocking," Harriet has, like her creator, lived the London life of a post–World War I "New Woman"; her friends are bohemian, artistic, and unbound by social, sexual, and moral convention, and she has lived with a man without benefit of marriage. When she discovers that her lover, Philip Boyes, a very minor poet with a massive ego, only wanted to live with her to see if she was devoted enough to him to become his wife, she resents his dishonesty and breaks off the relationship. Harriet is then accused, tried, and acquitted of murdering Boyes with arsenic purchased while researching her latest book. She subsequently becomes a best-selling detective novelist, partly because of the notoriety she received after the trial.

By *Gaudy Night*, the thirty-one-year-old Harriet is ready to exchange the frantic existence of a best-selling London author for a celibate scholar's quiet life at her alma mater. Escape to Shrewsbury, she feels, would allow her to pursue more important work and at the same time relieve her of romantic complications—Lord Peter (now forty-five) has been assiduously but unsuccessfully wooing her for five years. Harriet is attracted to Wimsey, but she is unwilling to accept his love while she feels indebted to him for saving her life. "I could have liked him so much if I could have met him on an equal footing," she maintains. Bruised by her affair with Boyes, Harriet also doubts that a relationship based on honesty, equality, and independence can be achieved. In *Gaudy Night*, during the investigation of the mystery, Harriet attempts to resolve these emotional and intellectual issues.

Harriet has received an invitation to attend her ten-year college reunion, known as the Gaudy, at Shrewsbury College (based on Somerville). She feels intensely nostalgic for the three years she spent in pleasant and peaceful academic pursuit with schoolmates and dons, but at the same time she wonders if she can face these women after all that has happened to her. Nevertheless, she attends the Gaudy, where she is relieved to discover that both dons and classmates are only interested in her success as an author, not in her affair with Boyes nor her involvement in a sensational murder trial. She is reunited with the cheerful, kindly dean, Miss Martin, the stately warden, Dr. Baring, and several of her former tutors, including Miss Lydgate, a middle-aged English tutor of gentle aspect and great scholarly integrity, as well as the unpleasant Miss Hillyard, a bitter, contemptuous, antagonistic history don. Harriet also meets a visiting tutor, the brilliant Miss de Vine, a woman of "a penetrating shrewdness" and completely uncompromising scholarly integrity and detachment.

At the Gaudy, Harriet is heartened to find that her old friend and classmate, Phoebe Tucker, a historian wed to an archeologist, has blended career and family life in a happy marriage based on mutual respect and equality. She then encounters another schoolmate, a brilliant scholar, who has abandoned intellectual pursuits for the hardscrabble existence of a farmer's wife. The interchange between Harriet and her former schoolmate contributes to the uncertainty Harriet feels about marriage and highlights another issue explored in the novel: whether one should compromise or stifle one's natural talents and, as Miss de Vine, puts it, "persuade one's self into appropriate feelings." It also underscores the fact that, for the majority of educated women during Sayers' time, there was but one choice—marriage or a career. The Shrewsbury dons, all of whom are unmarried, illustrate this.

Harriet's enjoyable weekend is affected by two odd and discomfiting events. The first is the discovery by her of a paper blowing across the quad; when Harriet picks up the paper, she discovers a childishly rendered obscene drawing of a naked female figure "inflicting savage and humiliating outrage upon some person of indeterminable gender clad in a cap and gown." Then, during her journey back to London, she finds in the sleeve of her academic gown a crumpled paper with the scrawled message: "You Dirty Murderess, aren't you ashamed to show your face?" She has received similar letters since the trial and incorrectly assumes this one is meant for her as well.

Months later, Harriet receives a call from Miss Martin, who asks her to return to Oxford to help solve the mystery of a nocturnal college "poltergeist," who has been wantonly destroying college property and sending threatening notes to dons and students. The latest event, in many ways the most horrid from an academic viewpoint, was the destruction of manuscript sections of Miss Lydgate's monumental work-in-progress, "The History of English Prosody." Harriet goes to Shrewsbury to investigate and resides in the college under the pretext of doing research on the Victorian novelist, Sheridan LeFanu, and assisting Miss Lydate in the reconstruction of her manuscript.

During her investigation, Harriet carefully collects data, examines the alibis of everyone in college, including dons, students, and scouts (maids), keeps a detailed journal, and tries to make sense of the obscene drawings and anonymous threatening notes that mysteriously appear. The harassments and destruction of college property continue. Late one night, the mischief-maker removes the fuses in three residence halls, leaving the college in complete darkness and chaos while he or she wreaks havoc in the new library. In one bizarre occurrence, Harriet discovers swinging from the rafters in the chapel an effigy dressed in an evening gown. The dummy has been stabbed with a bread knife; under the knife is a quotation written in Latin. This points to the dons as likely suspects.

Tension and uneasiness rise among faculty, students, and staff as the harassments escalate. One Third Year student, a hardworking but emotionally fragile young women, receives thirty poison-pen letters predicting that she will fail her examinations and insinuating that she is going insane. After she attempts suicide, the dean and the warden agree with Harriet that, at this point, outside help must be obtained. At Harriet's request, Lord Peter comes to Oxford. He studies Harriet's dossier and considers the facts objectively. During a heated after-dinner discussion with the dons on the importance of intellectual integrity, Wimsey discovers that once, while teaching at another university, Miss de Vine learned that a male colleague had deliberately suppressed information that invalidated his research and the main argument of his thesis in order to obtain a professorship. When his dishonesty was exposed, the man lost his professorship and his M.A. degree, and committed suicide. Miss de Vine's story gives Wimsey a trail to follow, and he soon identifies and exposes the Shrewsbury prowler, though not before she tries her hand at outright murder.

All that remains is the resolution of the romance between Harriet and Wimsey. In the rarified atmosphere of Oxford, Harriet's attitude toward Lord Peter begins to change. The first hint of this change occurs before Wimsey arrives on the scene, when he writes to her with the caution that, despite the potential hazards of the investigation, she must not turn away from the task. Reflecting that "this was an expression of equality and she had not expected it of him," she considers, "If he conceived of marriage along these lines, then the whole problem would have to be reviewed in that new light." Later, Harriet is impressed by Wimsey's veneration of the pursuit of intellectual truth that Oxford represents and his understanding of the difficulties in reconciling scholarly and worldly values. During their time together at Oxford, he reveals his vulnerabilities as well as his strengths, his concerns, and his loyalties, and after five years, she is at last able to see him as a complete person and an equal, rather than merely a sophisticated, self-assured, imperious aristocrat. At the end of the novel, it is Miss de Vine who convinces her that with Wimsey, she "needn't be afraid of losing her independence; he will always force it back on you." She urges a still-ambivalent Harriet to "face the facts and state a conclusion. Bring a scholar's mind to the problem and have done with it." Facing the fact that she does love Lord Peter, Harriet accepts his proposal of marriage.

Sayers' skill in capturing the nuances of tone and personality is evident in *Gaudy Night*, and the novel contains several notable, sometimes humorous, characters and situations woven into the detection of mystery. There are the dons, of course, each eccentric, annoying, or endearing in her own academically ordered way; Harriet's former classmates, several of whom are comically preoccupied with their particular areas of interest and expertise (one woman is an expert in the life history of the liver fluke);

Reggie Pomfret, a Queen's student who develops a crush on Harriet; the current crop of Shrewsbury students, including the unhappy Violet Cattermole, who loses her fiancé to a seductive schoolmate after she is accused of sending one of the poison-pen letters; and Lord St. George, Wimsey's handsome, charming, and irresponsible nephew, who plays a major role in the outcome of the Vane–Wimsey romance.

Dorothy Sayers ended the Wimsey novels with *Busman's Honeymoon* (1937), subtitled "A Love Story With Detective Interruptions." In it, Harriet and Peter adjust to married life while investigating a murder in their honeymoon home. Sayers also featured the couple, along with characters from *Gaudy Night* and other Peter Wimsey novels, in a *Spectator* magazine series titled "The Wimsey Papers" (1939–1940), which dealt with issues pertaining to the newly declared world war. Author Jill Paton Walsh carried on the theme of the Wimseys' existence during the war in her mystery novel, *A Presumption of Death* (2002).

In *Gaudy Night*, the best of the Vane–Wimsey novels, Sayers felt she had come closest to producing the kind of fiction she had envisaged writing after *Strong Poison*—a "novel of manners instead of pure crossword puzzle." She succeeded in combining such a novel with the detective genre and in making a statement of paramount concern to her: the permanent value of intellectual integrity in an increasingly unstable world. *Gaudy Night* presents a fascinating glimpse of an Oxford women's college between the wars and places a winning heroine at the center of this well-ordered, often uncompromising academic universe, the better to emphasize—and resolve—her personal and professional dilemmas.

THEIR EYES WERE WATCHING GOD

by Zora Neale Hurston

College courses on African-American literature, women's literature, and twentieth-century American literature inevitably include what Zora Neale Hurston's biographer Robert Hemenway has called, "One of the most poetic works of fiction by a black writer in the first half of the twentieth century, and one of the most revealing treatments in modern literature of a woman's quest for a satisfying life." Hurston's remarkable novel narrating the search of Janie Crawford, the first great African-American woman protagonist, for identity in a racist and sexist society, extends the concept of race beyond the range of equality and prejudice into an expanded celebration of essential personhood that dissolves established distinctions. Hurston's lyrical, spiritualized consciousness transcends the conventional dichotomies of gender, race, and class, and gives the novel its power and undiminished capacity to unsettle and challenge.

A central figure of the Harlem Renaissance, Zora Neale Hurston was an innovator, a provocateur, and a contrarian. She was a pioneer in recording and incorporating black folktales and traditions into her work, invigorating American writing, as Mark Twain had done earlier, with the power and expressiveness of the vernacular. Hurston was born in 1891 (some sources say 1901), in Eatonville, Florida, the first incorporated all-black community in the United States. Her father, John Hurston, was the town's mayor and a Baptist preacher. The town's vibrant folk tradition with its frequent "lying" sessions of tall tales stimulated Hurston's anthropological and creative interests. When her mother died and her father remarried, Hurston was passed about from boarding school to friends and relatives. At sixteen she worked as a wardrobe girl for a traveling light-opera troupe. She quit the show in Baltimore and went to work as a maid for a white woman who arranged for her to attend high school.

From 1918 to 1924, Hurston studied part time at Howard University, in Washington, D.C., while working as a manicurist. Her first works appeared in the African-American magazine *Opportunity*, whose founder, Charles Johnson, encouraged her to come to New York City to develop her writing and to finish her college degree. While studying anthropology at Barnard College, Hurston wrote poetry, plays, articles, and stories, and, in 1925, received several awards given by *Opportunity* to promising black writers. She went on to study with the eminent cultural anthropologist Franz Boas and to conduct field research in Eatonville, Haiti, and Jamaica, which was incorporated in two important folklore collections, *Mules and Men* (1935) and *Tell My Horse* (1938). Her first novel, *Jonah's Gourd Vine*, appeared in 1934, and her masterpiece, *Their Eyes Were Watching God*, in 1937. Two final novels—*Moses, Man of the Mountain* (1939) and *Seraph on the Suwanee* (1948)—along with her autobiography, *Dust Tracks on the Road* (1942), failed to halt a declining reputation, and her later years were spent in extreme poverty and obscurity. She worked for a time as a maid, a librarian, and a columnist for the *Fort Pierce Chronicle*. She died indigent and was buried in an unmarked grave in Fort Pierce until writer Alice Walker, who was instrumental in restoring Hurston's reputation, had a headstone erected.

A complex woman, Hurston has been described by Robert Hemenway as "flamboyant yet vulnerable, self-centered yet kind, a Republican conservative and an early black nationalist." Some African-American critics reacted to her ideological independence and contrariness by complaining that the primitive, folk elements in her work were demeaning and one dimensional. Seeking acceptance by mainstream literary standards, some black writers feared that Hurston's evocation of the rural black experience marginalized African Americans and diminished wider acceptance of them. Others, like Richard Wright, author of *Native Son*, dismissed her work as outside the central protest tradition that he insisted serious black literature should embrace. In his review of *Their Eyes*, Wright ridiculed the novel as a "minstrel-show turn that makes the 'white folks' laugh." Even Ralph Ellison—in whom many subsequent critics have detected influences from Hurston in the expressionistic, folk-rich makeup of *Invisible Man*—complained about Hurston's "blight of calculated burlesque." Few initially credited Hurston's work as a major source of poetic and intellectual strength. However, as critic Judith Wilson has observed, Hurston "had figured out something that no other black author of her time seems to have known or appreciated so well— that our homespun vernacular and street-corner cosmology are as valuable as the grammar and philosophy of white, Western culture." It would take the women's movement of the 1970s, and the particular advocacy of Alice Walker, who was instrumental in reviving Hurston's reputation, to cause readers and critics to look again at *Their Eyes Were Watching God*, and to recognize it finally as a complex, groundbreaking work combining central issues of race, gender, and class in ways that had never previously been attempted in American literature.

Hurston's second novel was written in 1936, when the author was in Haiti doing fieldwork for her second folklore collection. The novel is suffused with the exoticism of the Caribbean setting, transposed to the American landscape of Hurston's youth. Hurston identified the central impetus in writing the novel as the failed love affair she had had, in 1931, with a younger West Indian student; in the novel she attempted to capture the "emotional essence of a love affair between an older woman and a younger man." Hurston's protagonist, Janie Crawford, seeks to discover her authentic self by rising above the restrictions imposed by others as well as the seemingly immutable laws of gender, economics, and race. As the novel opens, Janie has returned to her all-black Florida community after having buried her younger lover, Tea Cake Woods, and after standing trial for his murder. The black community does not know what has happened to Tea Cake, but they are affronted by forty-year-old Janie, who wears her hair swinging down her back like a much younger person, and who dresses as a man, in muddy overalls, although she is a woman of means. As far as the community is concerned, Janie is an older woman who should know better; she has undoubtedly been abandoned by her younger lover and has returned home in shame. Nothing could be further from the truth, as the reader discovers, when Janie confesses her full story to her best friend, Pheoby Watson.

Janie's story begins with her teenage sexual awakening, when she notices the organic process of bees pollinating a pear tree. The image suggests to Janie an exalted natural concept of marriage and marks the beginning of her quest for a human equivalent. "Oh to be a pear tree—*any* tree in bloom!" she exclaims. "With kissing bees singing of the beginning of the world!" Hurston writes: "She was sixteen. She had glossy leaves and bursting buds and she wanted to struggle with life but it seemed to elude her. Where were the singing bees for her?" Janie's vitality and desire for expansion will be countered by the restrictions of others with their very different concept of a woman's traditional role. Janie's poetry will be translated into prose; her sense of spirit compromised by hard, material facts. Her grandmother, a former slave, imposes on her granddaughter a marriage of security with an aging farmer, Logan Killicks, to prevent Janie becoming "de mule uh de world," the unavoidable fate of the unprotected black female. However, that is precisely what happens to Janie: as Mrs. Killicks, she exists to serve her husband's economic ambition, destined to drive a second mule and enhance his acquisitiveness. Janie runs away with the ambitious Joe "Jody" Starks, who is heading to the newly formed black community of Eatonville to make his fortune. Although Janie recognizes that Jody "did not represent sun up and pollen and blooming trees," he "spoke for far horizon," of an expansive opportunity, as compared to her restricted fate as Killicks's drudge. Jody pampers his "lady-wife" with new clothes and luxuries while restricting her direct involvement in the black community that he begins to dominate. Starks desires not a mule but a "doll-baby," a precious ornament to be admired as a sign of his distinction and power. Locked in a stagnant existence in which she "got nothing from Jody except what money could buy, and she was giving away what she didn't value," Janie's liberation comes following Starks's death, when Tea Cake Woods, eighteen years her junior, comes into her life.

Tea Cake, a musician and a gambler, is totally absorbed in the present and unfettered by social convention. Unlike Janie's first two lovers, he is also free from their class-consciousness and gender notions, uninterested in her inherited fortune from Starks and unconcerned by their age difference. Tea Cake is "a bee for her bloom," making Janie feel alive, vital, truly offering the unlimited horizon that Starks suggested but failed to provide. By loving her for what she is, neither as a mule nor a doll-baby but as an autonomous equal, he causes Janie to be reborn into a life that defies conventions of age and class. Janie, the former first lady of Eatonville, dons overalls to go "on the muck" with Tea Cake into the primitive depths of the Florida Everglades for the bean-picking season. As critic Mary Helen Washington has observed, "Here, finally, was a woman on a quest for her own identity and, unlike so many other questing figures in black literature, her journey would take her, not away from, but deeper into blackness, the descent into the Everglades with its rich black soil, wild cane, and communal life representing immersion into black traditions." But the couple's lyrical, pastoral Everglades honeymoon does not come without emotional and physical trials. Tea Cake fears that Janie will abandon him for a lighter skinned rival, and the couple is crucially tested in a hurricane. Here, Hurston suggests the significance of the novel's title—the hurricane is a sign of God's intention that must be anticipated and interpreted, an existential moment that forces self-definition. While trying to save Janie's life during the storm, Tea Cake is bitten by a rabid dog. In his subsequent derangement, his jealousy overpowers him and he tries to shoot Janie, who kills him in self-defense. As a key passage in the novel makes clear, the incident, though painful, makes a crucial spiritual point: "All gods dispense suffering without reason. Otherwise they would not be worshipped. Through indiscriminate suffering men know fear, and fear is the most divine emotion. It is the stones for altars and the beginning of wisdom. Half gods are worshipped in wine and flowers. Real gods require blood."

Janie's story now cycles back to the novel's beginning in Eatonville. As she confesses to Pheoby, "So Ah'm back home agin and Ah'm satisfied tuh be heah. Ah done been tuh de horizon and back and now Ah kin set heah in mah house and live by comparison." By embracing the intensity of experience that Tea Cake gave her, Janie Crawford has shaped a self-determined identity, one more organic, expansive, and vital than that restricted by race, gender, or class. As Janie explains in her final declaration, "It's uh

known fact, Pheoby, you got tuh *go* there tuh *know* there.Yo' papa
and yo' mama and nobody else can't tell yuh and show yuh. Two
things everybody's got tuh do fuh themselves.They got tuh go tuh
God, and they got tuh find out livin' fuh theyselves." Janie has
moved from dependency to self-reliance largely through embracing experience, by not settling for the commonly imposed definition of possibility as an African American or as a woman.

Their Eyes Were Watching God is a controversial novel that has
successfully resisted relegation to a narrow critical niche, whether
as an exclusively feminist or culturally centered text. Janie Crawford's story, along with the techniques used in its telling, would
prove to be a fountainhead for subsequent novelists such as Alice
Walker, Toni Morrison, and many others who have followed
Hurston's example in giving voice to the African-American experience from a long-overlooked woman's perspective.

THE DIARY OF A YOUNG GIRL

by Anne Frank

When Anne Frank began writing in the small red-and-white-checked diary, a birthday present for the new teenager, she observed that no one "will be interested in the musings of a thirteen-year-old schoolgirl." From 1942, when the Frank family and four other Jews went into hiding in the secret rooms in her father's Amsterdam business offices, until 1944, when they were discovered and sent to concentration camps, Anne used her diary to express her innermost thoughts and feelings, to grapple with the contradictory aspects of her personality, and to chronicle life inside *Het achterhuis* (the house behind), as she called their hiding place. Although she declared that, through her writing, "I want to go on living after my death!" Anne Frank could not have known that her diary would become the most influential and widely read human document to emerge from the Holocaust, one of the most enduring works of the twentieth century, and one of the most beloved autobiographies of all time. Anne Frank's death at Bergen-Belsen a month before the camp was liberated by Allied troops gives her diary an almost overpowering pathos and sadness over the waste of a life. Neither the facts of Anne Frank's fate, however, nor the particulars of her story should overwhelm an appreciation of her undeniable artistic achievement. Anne Frank crafted a great universal reflection of adolescence that expresses, as few works have done better, what the poet John Berryman has called "the conversion of a child into a person." Eleanor Roosevelt, who supplied the introduction to *The Diary of a Young Girl* when it was first published in the United States in 1952, rightly observed that the "diary tells us much about ourselves"; while critic Frederic Morton, discussing the impact of the diary on the world, has stated, "It may well be that the single most enduring thing to be born during the entire course of the Nazi nightmare was a book a young Jewish girl wrote in the occupied Holland of the early Forties." As a young woman's expression of the difficult process from childhood toward self-knowledge and maturity, Anne Frank's *The Diary of a Young Girl* is an essential and unavoidable work.

Annelies Marie Frank was born in Frankfurt, Germany, in 1929, the younger of Otto and Edith Frank's two daughters. Her father was a prosperous Jewish businessman who took his family to Amsterdam after Hitler came to power. There he managed a business selling pectin for canning and spices to Dutch housewives, leasing a warehouse and offices on the Prinsengracht, a canal/street in the old part of Amsterdam. There was little evidence to suggest that Anne was either interested in or capable of literary effort. Compared to her older sister, Margot, who was serious, well behaved, and an excellent student, Anne was recalled by a schoolmate as "interested mainly in dates, clothes, and parties." She was "a mischief maker who annoyed the neighbors with her pranks and continually was in hot water at school for her conduct." The talkative, extroverted Anne was nicknamed "Miss Chatterbox" and "Miss Quack-Quack," and her school compositions were judged by her teachers as "just ordinary, not better than average."

Anne Frank's maturity into an introspective and perceptive writer accelerated under the pressures of circumstances beginning with the German invasion of Holland and the imposition there of the same anti-Jewish laws that were in place in Germany. One of the first of her diary entries captured the growing threat felt by Holland's Jewish community: "After May 1940 good times were few and far between: first there was the war, then the capitulation and then the arrival of the Germans, which is when the trouble started for the Jews. . . . Jews were required to wear a yellow star; Jews were required to turn in their bicycles; Jews were forbidden to use streetcars; Jews were forbidden to ride in cars, even their own. . . . Jews were required to attend Jewish schools, etc. You couldn't do this and you couldn't do that, but life went on." Forbidden to own a business, Otto Frank turned over his firm to one of his employees while quietly making preparations to go into hiding. In July 1942, Margot Frank received a call-up notice from the Dutch Nazi organization, a euphemism for deportation to a labor camp. The Franks responded by making a final trek on foot from their home to their hiding place, to the so-called "Secret Annex" of Otto Frank's warehouse. Carrying luggage would have aroused suspicion, so each wore multiple layers of clothing, and Anne describes herself wearing "two vests, three pairs of pants, a dress, on top of that a skirt, jacket, summer coat, two pairs of stockings, lace-up shoes, wooly cap, scarf, and still more. . . . After we arrived at 263 Prinsengracht, Miep [Otto Frank's secretary and one of the group's protectors] quickly led us through the long hallway and up the wooden staircase to the next floor and into the Annex. She shut the door behind us, leaving us alone." For the next twenty-five months the Franks shared their cramped, secret rooms with Mr. van Pels, a coworker of Otto Frank, van Pels's wife, their teenage son, Peter (the Van Daans of the diary), and an elderly dentist, Fritz Pfeffer (Albert Dussel in the diary). Their links to the outside world were a radio and Otto Frank's loyal employees, who brought them food and supplies obtained with forged and illegally purchased ration cards, as well as news of the war and of their Jewish friends and neighbors who had been taken to concentration camps. Nearly daily roundups of Jews were observable from the windows of the Secret Annex. To avoid detection, the fugitives had to remain almost completely silent during business hours. As Anne observed, "We are as still as baby mice. Who would have guessed three months ago that quicksilver Anne would have to sit so quietly for hours on end, and what's more, that she could."

It was in this atmosphere of tense confinement and constant fear of detection that Anne experienced the first years of her adolescence. She found her refuge and future ambition to become a writer in her diary. Begun less than a month before being forced into hiding, Anne Frank's diary was initially conceived as a series of letters to an imagined friend named Kitty to whom Anne could confide her observations, thoughts, and feelings. "Writing in a diary is a really strange experience for someone like me," she noted. "Not only because I've never written anything before, but also because it seems to me that later on neither I nor anyone else will be interested in the musings of a thirteen-year-old schoolgirl. Oh well, it doesn't matter. I feel like writing, and I have an even greater need to get all kinds of things off my chest." With a growing facility and refreshing candor, Anne describes in her diary her life in hiding, her conflicts with the van Pelses and Pfeffer, her bodily changes and budding sexuality, her short-lived infatuation with Peter van Pels, her detached feelings toward her sweet but somewhat priggish older sister, her resentment of her mother, and admiration for her beloved father. Like most adolescents, Anne struggled to reconcile her "lighter, superficial self" with what she called "the deeper side of me." This self-analysis, recorded with remarkable precision and detail throughout the diary, traces Anne's development from an outgoing, vivacious child to an introspective, complex young woman. It is this introspection, and Anne's ability to objectify and to evaluate with complete honesty a young girl's feelings of longing and loneliness, that distinguishes her diary.

Throughout, Anne tries to make sense of the situation she finds herself in, alternating between feelings of despondency and hopeful idealism. In an entry from October 1943, she writes, "The atmosphere is stifling, sluggish, leaden. Outside, you don't hear a single bird, and a deathly oppressive silence hangs over the house and clings to me as if it were going to drag me into the deepest regions of the underworld. At times like these, Father, Mother and Margot don't matter to me in the least. I wander from room to room, climb up and down the stairs and feel like a songbird whose wings have been ripped off and who keeps hurling itself against the bars of its cage." Despite such despair, she often expresses a vitality and faith in her own and humanity's future. Through her writing, Anne would discover an ambition and a purpose. Inspired by a Dutch broadcast from London, in March 1944, that urged a future collection of diaries and letters to document the war experience, Anne began to revise her diary for future publication, confirming her aspirations as a writer. "I know what I want," she declared. "I have a goal, I have opinions, a religion and love. If only I can be myself, I'll be satisfied. I know that I'm a woman, a woman with inner strength and a great deal of courage! If God lets me live, I'll achieve more than Mother ever did, I'll make my voice heard, I'll go out into the world and work for mankind!" Anne's confidence in her abilities as a writer leads her to a faith in the future in the face of impending destruction, which she summarizes in the most quoted passage from her diary, written only weeks before she was taken: "It's utterly impossible for me to build my life on a foundation of chaos, suffering and death. I see the world being slowly transformed into a wilderness, I hear the approaching thunder that, one day, will destroy us too, I feel the suffering of millions. And yet, when I look up at the sky, I somehow feel that everything will change for the better, that this cruelty too shall end, that peace and tranquility will return once more. In the meantime, I must hold on to my ideals. Perhaps the day will come when I'll be able to realize them!"

Anne's last diary entry, August 1, 1944, records her ongoing struggle between hopefulness and despair: "I get cross, then sad, and finally end up turning my heart inside out, the bad part on the outside and the good part on the inside, and keep trying to find a way to become what I'd like to be and what I could be if . . . if only there were no other people in the world." On August 4, the security police raided the hideout based on information from an informant, the identity of whom has never been definitively proven. The Franks, van Pelses, and Pfeffer were transported by cattle car to Auschwitz where they were separated. A Dutch woman survivor who shared the same barracks with Edith Frank and her daughters later described Anne's courage, sensitivity, and empathy in the midst of the horror around her: "Anne was the youngest in her group, but nevertheless she was the leader of it. . . . She, too, was the one who saw to the last what was going on all around us. We had long since stopped seeing. . . . Something protected us, kept us from seeing. But Anne had no such protection, to the last. . . . She cried. And you cannot imagine how soon most of us came to the end of our tears." In the fall of 1944, as the Russians advanced on Auschwitz, Anne and Margot, along with thousands of other prisoners, were relocated to Bergen-Belsen. The following spring both died in a typhus epidemic that decimated the camp.

When Otto Frank, the group's only survivor, returned to Amsterdam, he received from Miep Gies Anne's diary, which had been discarded by the Nazis looking for valuables in the Secret Annex. He was shocked by what he read, admitting, "I never realized my little Anna was so deep." He edited and published an abridged version of his daughter's diary in 1947, called *Het achterhuis,* the title Anne herself had chosen for it. It would become a worldwide best-seller, translated into more than thirty languages and adapted into theatrical and film versions. In 1989, *The Diary of a Young Girl: The Definitive Edition* was published, which restores the portions of the diary that Otto Frank had deleted and includes the changes that Anne had edited out of the version that she made in preparation for publication after the war. It is now possible to read in full Anne Frank's extraordinary perspective as a young woman dealing with both the most natural process of adolescence and the most unnatural conditions of history, which was determined to destroy and deny the humanity that Anne Frank's diary indomitably asserts.

THE SECOND SEX

by Simone de Beauvoir

Any volume that discusses women's literature through the centuries would not be complete without the inclusion of Simone de Beauvoir's daring and controversial analysis of the role of women and the relationship between the sexes. First published in France, in 1949, and partially translated into English, in 1953, *The Second Sex* was a foundation text for the revived women's movement of the 1960s and 1970s, and remains one of the most influential works of the twentieth century. The impact of the book has been so great that the women who grew up in its wake have sometimes described themselves as "the children of Simone de Beauvoir."

Simone de Beauvoir (1908–1986) came to identify herself with feminism rather late in her life, as part of her ongoing support of a general spectrum of human rights. She once said that, when young, "feminism meant nothing to me." For her, the issue of women's equality was tied to a sense of self that was gradually extended, through intellectual and philosophical observation and discourse, to other women. Beauvoir's individualism began at a young age. She was born in Paris, the elder of two daughters of Georges and Françoise de Beauvoir, whose marriage had been arranged by Françoise's father, a wealthy banker who went bankrupt and was ultimately unable to pay his daughter's dowry. Beauvoir's father, who preferred pursuing success as an amateur actor to other pursuits, encouraged his daughter's early reading, but it was her strict Catholic mother, a person of unshakeable moral beliefs, who exerted the most influence on her and was most likely responsible for Beauvoir's lifelong interest in the questions of ethics. Early on, Beauvoir rebelled at her bourgeois upbringing and the social restrictions imposed upon her by her gender, proclaiming at the age of nineteen, "I don't want my life to obey any other will but my own." At the same time, unknown to her mother, she had rejected her religious faith, which she had once practiced intensely. Freed from the prospect of a stultifying middle-class marriage by her father's inability, because of his father-in-law's bankruptcy, to provide his daughters with a dowry, Beauvoir entered the Sorbonne, in 1928, with the intention of pursuing a career. A brilliant student, she earned her degree in philosophy at the Sorbonne, in 1929, becoming the youngest teacher of philosophy in France.

While at the Sorbonne, Beauvoir met fellow student Jean-Paul Sartre, whom she later described in the first volume of her autobiography, *Memoirs of a Dutiful Daughter* (1958), as "a soulmate in whom I found, heated to the point of incandescence, all of my passions. With him, I could always share everything." Their fifty-one-year liaison, which both viewed as essential and indestructible, precluded traditional notions of marriage, cohabitation, and children, and included a mutually agreed-upon concession for "contingent loves" of lesser importance. Beauvoir insisted that she and Sartre had "pioneered our own relationship—its freedom, intimacy, and frankness." As well known for their literary output and political commitment as they were for their unconventional relationship, Beauvoir and Sartre together formed the center of the postwar French left-wing intellectual and existential movements.

Beauvoir taught philosophy at several colleges until 1943, after which she devoted herself to writing full-time. There are signs that Beauvoir had begun to show some interest in women's issues during her year as a teacher in Rouen: she refused to spread propaganda on behalf of Marshal Pétain, France's minister of war, who wanted French women to bear more children to increase the nation's population, and she began to discuss with a teacher colleague the possibility of writing "a book about women." Before

The Second Sex, none of her books looked explicitly at the condition of women, although the three novels she had published—*She Came to Stay* (1943), *The Blood of Others* (1945), and *All Men Are Mortal* (1946)—all featured strong central female protagonists. Beauvoir seemed an unlikely spokesperson for the woman's perspective; prior to writing *The Second Sex*, she could recall no disadvantages or difficulties in her own life that she could relate to her gender. "Far from suffering from my femininity," she recalled, "I have, on the contrary, from the age of twenty on, accumulated the advantages of both sexes; after *She Came to Stay* those around me treated me both as a writer, their peer in the masculine world, and a woman; this was particularly noticeable in America: at the parties I went to, the wives all got together and talked to each other, while I talked to the men, who nevertheless behaved toward me with greater courtesy than they did toward members of their own sex."

For a period during the war, Beauvoir spent more time in the company of women, and by the war's end had observed that a great number of women suffered from the absence of men and were not willing, as she was, despite her attachment to Sartre, to seek an independent existence of their own. Beauvoir, looking for new approaches to her writing, had begun to think about issues of femininity, starting with questions pertaining to her own sense of being a woman. In her wartime journal, she wondered, "In what ways am I a woman, and what sort of woman?" After the war, when Sartre suggested she examine how being a woman had influenced her life and work so far, Beauvoir, using herself as a starting point but thinking and observing further, embarked on a study of women that, after two years' intensive research, would become *The Second Sex*.

Beauvoir divided the book into two sections. The first section, "Facts and Myths," is separated into three parts: "Destiny," exploring biological and psychological imperatives; "History," telling the story of women from the nomads through the French Revolution; and "Myths," which discusses women in the context of such authors as D.H. Lawrence, André Breton, and Stendhal. The second section, "Women's Life Today," shows how women develop during childhood and adolescence, the ways in which they have experienced different roles throughout their lives, and analyzes "The Narcissist," "The Woman in Love," and "The Mystic." Beauvoir concludes with a fourth part in "Women's Life

Today," titled "Toward Liberation," which looks toward the future and indicates how a woman can achieve independence through the establishment of an individual self.

Unmarried, childless, and free from domestic concerns and commitments, Beauvoir had experienced her independence and autonomy outside the conventional roles expected from women. Although she had little firsthand knowledge of the condition of women that she revealed in *The Second Sex*, Beauvoir's status as an outsider, assessing the relationship of the sexes from her anomalous position, provides much of the book's originality and genius. When Beauvoir began her study, she looked at the lives of women living "normal" married lives who, "in differing circumstances and with various degrees of success, had all undergone one identical experience: they had lived as 'dependent persons'. . . . I began to take stock of the difficulties, deceptive advantages, traps, and manifold obstacles that most women encounter on their path. I also felt how much they were both diminished and enriched by this experience. The problem did not concern me directly, and as yet I attributed little importance to it; but my interest had been aroused."

Beauvoir proceeded in her study, placing women's lives in the context of the existential and socialist philosophies to which she was committed, and her biological and historical research; she arrived at a central thesis that would come to resonate deeply with a generation of women ready to initiate and carry out a revived women's movement:

> Women lack concrete means for organizing themselves into a unit which can stand face to face with the correlative unit. They have no past, no history, no religion of their own; and they have no solidarity of work and interest as that of the proletariat. . . . The bond that unites [a woman] to her oppressors is not comparable to any other. The division of the sexes is a biological fact, not an event of human history. Male and female stand oppressed within a primordial *Mitsein*, and woman has not broken it. The couple is a fundamental unity with two halves riveted together, and the cleavage of society along the lines of sex is impossible. Here is to be found the basic trait of woman: she is the Other in a totality of which the two components are necessary to one another.

In Beauvoir's analysis, women accept their subordination and objectification for certain privileges and advantages bestowed on them as females but which are an evasion of full, adult, moral responsibility. For Beauvoir, the way out of this trap is for women to reject the feminine, the various modes that dictate dependence and subservience, and to choose an autonomous and independent life as a free and active person. As Beauvoir insists, "One is not born, but rather becomes, a woman. No biological, psychological, or economic fate determines the figure that the human female presents to society; it is civilization as a whole that produces this creature, intermediate between male and eunuch, which is described as feminine." She argues, "The emancipated woman wants to be active and refuses the passivity man means to impose on her. The 'modern' woman accepts masculine values: she prides herself on thinking, taking action, working, creating on the same terms as men." For Beauvoir, two keys to the safeguarding of women's freedom are paid work and contraception.

Beauvoir's solution to the objectification and subordination of women in *The Second Sex* can be seen as somewhat problematic in that the author's liberated woman who has left behind any traces of the feminine is in danger of resembling the free and independent male oppressor. Beauvoir also rejects any positives to be found in the experience of motherhood and marriage. However, the significance of *The Second Sex* rests more in its diagnosis of the problem rather than in its solution. As women's studies professor Mary Evans observed in her study of the author's works, *Simone de Beauvoir: Feminist Mandarin*: "Whether we agree or disagree with the conclusions of the book, its significance lies in de Beauvoir's success in placing on the intellectual agenda three crucial questions about the nature of relations between the sexes, namely, the problem of the origin of sexual difference, the nature and elaboration of sexual inequality and difference, and the issue of how men and women should live. These issues still dominate feminist discussion, and form an important part of debates in a number of academic disciplines and in psychoanalysis."

The Second Sex produced a firestorm of controversy upon its publication in France, and the book was both praised and excoriated. Beauvoir recalled that "some professors threw the book across their offices because they couldn't bear to read it." She was not surprised when the Catholic novelist, François Mauriac, attacked the book, but she was disappointed by the hostile reaction of her close friend, the novelist Albert Camus, who complained that Beauvoir had "made a laughing-stock of the French male."

By the time *The Second Sex* was published in its English translation, opinion was more temperate. Anthropologist Margaret Mead, writing about the book in the *Saturday Review of Literature*, held that "the book violates every canon of science and disinterested scholarship in its partisan selectivity," but praised the work's imaginative originality and granted that Beauvoir "provides a rare, exasperating, but unfailingly interesting experience." Philip Wylie, in the same magazine, wrote, "No one can leave her book unread and still be considered intellectually up-to-date. It makes a fresh contribution to awareness that cannot be missed any more than the contribution of Freud, say, or Einstein or Darwin—without the onset of a private cultural lag."

If *The Second Sex* provoked horrified gasps from traditionalists, it also generated the impassioned gratitude of women who had finally found in Beauvoir the first true explicator of their condition. In *Simone de Beauvoir on Women*, Jean Leighton observes that Beauvoir's "analysis of the subtle and insinuating way women are molded by society to accept their inferior role is masterful and devastating. Her perception of how the male-dominated culture tries to transform women into an 'object' who exists primarily to please men has had profound reverberations." *The Second Sex* ranks with Mary Wollstonecraft's *A Vindication of the Rights of Woman*, and Betty Friedan's *The Feminine Mystique* as one of the crucial documents on women's emancipation. Betty Friedan has called Simone de Beauvoir "an authentic heroine in the history of womanhood." Friedan's own groundbreaking work, which can be said to have launched the modern women's movement in America, would been inconceivable without the courageous examination of the status of women provided by Simone de Beauvoir in *The Second Sex*.

CENTURY OF STRUGGLE: THE WOMEN'S RIGHTS MOVEMENT IN THE UNITED STATES

by Eleanor Flexner

In 1959, during the so-called social doldrums before the acceleration of the second wave of the women's movement (the same year Barbie debuted), Eleanor Flexner produced a now-classic documentary history of the women's rights movement, *Century of Struggle*, that still serves as the best single-volume account of the struggle to win the right to vote in the United States. Writing in 1967 of her book, Flexner states:

> Ask students who invented the steamboat or the cotton gin, explored the sources of the Mississippi River, led the Populist Movement or the Progressive Party—and if they do not remember they will look for the answers in their history books. Ask them who founded the early women's college, who led the seventy-five-year campaign for their right to vote, who pioneered in protective legislation for working mothers, who developed the concept of settlement houses and social work among the underprivileged—ask them to identify Mary Lyon, Elizabeth Blackwell, Leonora Barry, Elizabeth Cady Stanton, Lillian Wald, Florence Kelley—and they will have to head for the nearest library.

Century of Struggle served then and now to dramatize a crucially important chapter of American history and to highlight the contributions of American women who have often been neglected or ignored. Progress by contemporary women toward equality and empowerment owe so much to these women, as Flexner rightly argues: "The history of women in this century continues to be relevant because even today almost every woman who seeks to widen her sphere of activity beyond her home encounters conflict." Compared to today, however, the crusading women of a Flexner's study "had to prove to others and to themselves as well, that a woman's brain was capable of the same kind of intellectual activity as a man's. They had to combat not only public prejudice but their own fears of being unladylike, of becoming unsexed creatures if they tried to be doctors or mathematicians. . . . No one really knew whether they might not sicken and die if they were exposed to logarithms—or physical education. It had to be proved, not once but over and over again, that they would survive—until these things were finally taken for granted." *Century of Struggle* supplies a detailed account of how far women had to go to secure equality, as well as the challenges that remain.

Born in 1908, in New York City, Flexner graduated from Swarthmore College in 1930, and did postgraduate work at Oxford. Her first book, *American Playwrights, 1918–38: The Theatre Retreats from Reality* (1938), reflects her theatrical activity during the Depression. Trade-union membership stimulated her interest in working conditions for American women that eventually led to *Century of Struggle.* A contributor to *Notable American Women, 1609–1950,* Flexner also wrote a 1972 biography of Mary Wollstonecraft. She died in 1995.

Century of Struggle, which concentrates on the nearly one-hundred-year effort to secure the vote for women in America, begins with a survey of the status of American women prior to 1800, to demonstrate the considerable gender obstacles women faced. As Flexner summarizes: "Married women could not sign contracts; they had no title to their own earnings, to property even when it was their own by inheritance or dower, or to their children in case of legal separation. Divorce, when granted at all by the courts or by legislative action, was given only for the most flagrant abuses." Moreover, women were restricted from educational opportunities to expand their possibilities beyond home and childcare. "It was almost universally believed," Flexner points out, "that a woman's brain was smaller in capacity and therefore inferior in quality to that of a man." Flexner locates the beginning of the women's movement to early educational reformers, such as Emma Willard, Frances Wright, Catharine Beecher, Mary Lyon, and Prudence Crandall, who challenged these restrictions and opened the door of educational opportunities for women. A second important factor in stimulating a women's movement in the United States, in Flexner's view, was the burgeoning antislavery campaigns of the 1820s and 1830s. "It was in the abolition movement," Flexner asserts, "that women first learned to organize, to hold public meetings, to conduct petition campaigns. As abolitionists they first won the right to speak in public, and began to evolve a philosophy of their place in society and of their basic rights. For a quarter of a century the two movements, to free the slave and liberate the woman, nourished and strengthened one another." Flexner celebrates contributions to both causes by such women as Sarah and Angelina Grimké, and labor activists such as Sarah Bagley of the Lowell, Massachusetts, mill workers who created the first women's trade unions.

The breakthrough came when Lucretia Mott and Elizabeth Cady Stanton, disappointed that women were excluded from the 1840 World Anti-Slavery Convention in London, began to conceive of a Women's Rights Convention. Announced for July 19, 1848, at the Wesleyan chapel in Seneca Falls, New York, the convention drew some three hundred participants who passed the Declaration of Principles asserting property and marriage rights for women, as well as the controversial, and by no means unanimous, claim that "it is the duty of the women of this country to secure to themselves their sacred right to elective franchise." The culmination of almost half a century of reform efforts, the Seneca Falls convention became the milestone and launching ground of the movement of women's rights in America. As Flexner declares, "Beginning in 1848 it was possible for women who rebelled against the circumstances of their lives, to know that they were not alone. . . . A movement had been launched which they could either join, or ignore, that would leave its imprint on the lives of their daughters and of women throughout the world."

Flexner goes on to chronicle the powerful alliance between Elizabeth Cady Stanton and Susan B. Anthony in directing the women's rights movement through the rest of the nineteenth century, as well as the intellectual progress of women, the growth of women's social organizations, and women in trade unions during the period as a context for considering the advancement of the suffrage movement following the Civil War. Flexner ably summarizes the dissension that widened the gap between the interests of African-Americans and women over the passage of the Fourteenth Amendment to the Constitution to enfranchise black males, which introduced the phrase "male citizens" for the first time in the Constitution, and thereby raised "the issue of whether women were actually citizens of the United States." *Century of Struggle* documents the hard-fought, state-by-state battle for voting rights for women and the seemingly impossible lobbying for a constitutional amendment.

Between 1896 and 1910, the period Flexner identifies as the "doldrums," no new woman suffrage states were won, and only six states even held referenda on suffrage, all of which were lost. The federal woman suffrage amendment, which had been introduced into Congress in 1878, and perfunctorily considered and dismissed annually ever since, seemed moribund. The aging Susan B. Anthony stepped down as president of the National American Woman Suffrage Association in 1900, and was replaced by Carrie Chapman Catt, a brilliant tactician who set out to organize grassroots suffrage support. Others, like Harriet Stanton Blatch, the daughter of Elizabeth Cady Stanton, and the militant Alice Paul increased the pressure for suffrage by marches and demonstrations. During World War I, Paul's Women's Party began daily, around-the-clock picketing of the White House, with banners referring to "Kaiser Wilson" and proclaiming "Democracy should begin at home." Arrests of picketers led to hunger strikes and force-feeding. Meanwhile, Catt and the NAWSA actively supported the war to demonstrate women's loyalty, while keeping pressure on states to consider suffrage referenda and supporting the federal amendment.

By the end of the war, NAWSA's painstaking work and the Women's Party's dramatic demonstrations had created a public climate favorable to passage of the federal suffrage amendment. On January 10, 1918, Jeanette Rankin of Montana, the first woman elected to Congress, introduced the suffrage amendment onto the floor of the House. As Flexner observes, "Endless lobbying and tallying by both suffrage groups had shown that the vote would be painfully close and that no one could foretell the outcome. It was with real anguish that the women keeping their tal-lies up in the galleries saw the hair-line finish and their supporters rounding up every possible vote." Four congressmen with determining votes came to the House from their sickbeds; one came from the deathbed of his suffragist wife. The final tally was 274 in favor of suffrage and 136 against. The amendment passed with only one vote more than the required two thirds.

It would take another year and a half to win over the Senate, which passed the Nineteenth Amendment on June 5, 1919. Flexner is particularly insightful in her chapter "Who Opposed Woman Suffrage" and in her account of the further delays obstructing ratification by the "antis," including southern white supremacists, liquor interests, anti-Bolsheviks, northern political bosses, and a National Women's Organization to Oppose Suffrage. On August 18, 1920, however, Harry Burn of Tennessee cast the deciding vote in favor of ratification, and the amendment carried 49 to 47, thus enfranchising twenty-six million American women after seventy-two years of struggle from the Seneca Falls convention. As Flexner points out, ninety-one-year-old Charlotte Woodward, the only surviving participant of the Seneca Falls convention, voted in the 1920 presidential election.

Having detailed the eventual triumph of women's suffrage in America, Flexner concludes with some sobering reflections. "Almost forty years after adoption of the Nineteenth Amendment," she observes, "a number of promised or threatened events have failed to materialize. The millennium has not arrived, but neither has the country's social fabric been destroyed." Flexner reminds her readers that the tireless campaigner for the vote Carrie Chapman Catt, in 1920, "warned suffragists that the franchise was only an entering wedge, that they would have to force their way through the 'locked door' to the place where real political decisions are made." From the perspective of 1959, Flexner sees scant evidence that the break-in and breakthrough has taken place. She points out that most working women remain at the bottom of the professional ladder, and political representation by women lags considerably behind the percentage of women in the population. Although improved and improving, women's progress to equality and power remains unfinished, with major obstacles still to be faced. The encouragement that Flexner offered her readers, in 1959, is no less needed today. "Whatever its hazards," Flexner concludes, "it is doubtful if the world which women face today can appear to them any more hostile or bewildering than that which confronted the early nineteenth century woman with aspirations. . . . Perhaps in learning more of the long journey these, and hundreds more, made into our present time, we can face our own future with more courage and wisdom, and greater hope."

THE LITTLE DISTURBANCES OF MAN

by Grace Paley

"In a world where women's voices have been routinely silenced,"
Jacqueline Taylor, in her critical study *Grace Paley: Illuminating the
Dark Lives,* asserts, "Grace Paley dares to create a voice that is
boldly female. In her three volumes of short stories, Paley manifests a willingness to speak the unspeakable. . . . Paley is an innovator, and her innovations often occur in relationship to the
particularly female consciousness she articulates. . . . Written in
colloquial language, her stories are deceptively simple; they seem
at first glance to be uncomplicated and even unadorned tales, but
closer inspection reveals their careful craft." Paley's friend and
fellow short fiction innovator Donald Barthelme declared her "a
wonderful writer and troublemaker. We are fortunate to have her
in our country."

A first-generation Jewish American and a New Yorker, Paley
derives her power as a writer by mining the rich core of her characters' ethnic and racial backgrounds, their idiomatic speech, and
the telling details of their unexceptional but instructive lives. She
has given voice to those who are often assumed to have little to
say and has investigated aspects of our world that, but for her,
would have gone beyond our notice. Although Paley's oeuvre is

thus far relatively small—three volumes of short stories, three collections of poetry, and a volume of essays—she is considered one of the most distinctive and important contemporary American writers. The world of her fiction is centered almost exclusively on the areas in New York City where she grew up and in Manhattan's Greenwich Village, where she raised her family and began her association with the various political groups that have directed her activism ever since. Yet there is little about her work that strikes the reader as narrow or dated. Paley has distilled significance from the local to reveal a complex, demanding world that resonates with universal human meaning. There is no better entrée to that world than Paley's first collection, *The Little Disturbances of Man* (1959), which established her reputation as a distinctive fictional voice.

The volume, like all of Paley's work, rests on a solid foundation of her own experiences and observations of the world around her. Born Grace Goodside in the Bronx, New York, in 1922, she was youngest child of Russian-Jewish immigrants. Her parents were Ukrainian socialists who immigrated to America after both had been arrested for participating in workers' demonstrations and after her father's brother had been killed by the czarist police. The family worked at menial jobs to allow Paley's father to attend medical school; after he became a physician, he set up a practice in the family's Bronx home. Paley grew up in a multi-language neighborhood in which Russian, Yiddish, and English blended together; the cadences of these languages would later inform her work.

To the great disappointment of her family, Paley showed little academic ambition. "I was a very good student up to the age of ten," she has recalled, "then my mind began to wander." She spent a year at Hunter College, another at New York University, and studied briefly at the New School for Social Research, taking a course in poetry with W. H. Auden. After reading her poetry, Auden urged her to abandon the artificiality of language she had derived from her reading for the more authentic vernacular that she knew firsthand. It would be a lesson she would take to heart when she began to write her stories more than a decade later.

In 1942, at the age of nineteen, Paley dropped out of college to marry Jess Paley, a motion picture cameraman, with whom she had two children. She devoted her time to her family and took occasional jobs as a clerical worker. On her many trips to Washington

Square Park near her Greenwich Village home with her children, Paley listened to other mothers talking about their lives. It struck her that no one was attempting to tell their stories. She began to write while immersed in her homemaking responsibilities. As her daughter later recalled, "She should have had a door to close and be behind it—but none of that happened; it wasn't like that. I don't know when she got the time, how she did it. She must have done it sometime—maybe it was while we were in day care. . . . It's not like my father took us to the park so she could work— none of *that* was going yet." As Paley recalled, "In 1954 or '55 I needed to speak in some inventive way about our female and male lives in those years." She began writing fiction because she was "thinking an awful lot about women's lives" and "wasn't able to get it into poems."

Paley's first story, "Goodbye and Good Luck," was inspired by a chance remark heard from her husband's aunt on a visit to the Paleys. The aunt said, "I was popular in certain circles, and I wasn't no thinner then," and Paley used both the comment and its ca- dences to reveal the life of the irrepressible Rose Lieber, who be- comes involved with a married actor in New York's Yiddish theater. Rose manages to accept all the many compromises and disappointments that life imposes with a grace and joy that re- deem her experiences. The story became the first work for *The Little Disturbances of Man,* a collection focused on the lives of or- dinary characters who are shown confronting the unexceptional but testing moments of experience. The title of the volume refers to those seemingly trivial and insignificant incidents that shape a life. The story, "An Interest in Life," from which the collection's title is drawn, concerns a husband's desertion of his wife and four children and opens with the matter-of-fact but chilling perspec- tive of the wife: "My husband gave me a broom one Christmas. This wasn't right. No one can tell me it was meant kindly." The story traces the wife's attempt to cope with her situation and place it into a context that will allow her to face her future. "The Loudest Voice," which draws on the Jewish immigrant experience and the challenge of assimilation, tells the story of a Jewish child who is recruited to play a prominent part in the school's Christmas pageant. The comically treated situation expands into a far-reaching and profound exploration of culture, identity, and compromises in a multiethnic community. In the two companion stories, "The Used-Boy Raisers" and "A Subject of Childhood," which are grouped under the title "Two Short Sad Stories from a Long and Happy Life," Paley introduces Faith Darwin, a recurring protagonist, who contrasts her identity as a wife, mother, and lover with the assumptions of the men in her life. It is one of the earliest dramatizations of the complicated emotional and psychological dilemma women faced in the pre-liberation era, balancing traditional gender roles and desired independence and autonomy. As Paley recalled, "I was a woman writing at the early moment when small drops of worried resentment and noble rage were secretly, slowly building into the second wave of the women's movement." What is most striking about *The Little Disturbances of Man* is Paley's articulation of those resentments and rages in the voice of characters whose voices had previously been silent or ignored.

In writing about Paley's work, novelist Jamaica Kincaid has observed, "Her prose is deceptively comforting. You are wired into the most simple, everyday language, just enjoying it, and then you find yourself in the middle of enormous questions or strange territory." The British novelist A.S. Byatt has commented that "we have had a great many artists, more of them women than not, recording the tragedies of repetition, frequency, weariness and little disturbances. What distinguishes Grace Paley from the mass of these is the interest, and even more, the inventiveness which she brings to her small world."

The Little Disturbances of Man heralded the arrival of a major writing talent, but it would be fifteen years until her next collection appeared. A contributing reason for the delay was Paley's increasing political activities during the 1960s and 1970s. She protested the Vietnam War as a founding member and later secretary of the War Resisters League, and campaigned in favor of draft resistance. In addition, she helped organize an artists' and writers' venture called Vietnamese Life, the goal of which was to share Vietnamese music, art, and culture with her Greenwich Village community. In 1969, she was part of a delegation that traveled to North Vietnam with the goal of bringing back three American pilots who had been shot down. Other issues that claimed Paley's attention were nuclear proliferation, women's rights, and human rights. As one of the White House Eleven arrested in December 1978, for displaying an antinuclear banner on the White House lawn, she was fined and given a suspended sentence. In 1980, Paley was awarded the Peace Award from the

War Resisters League for her activism. "I believe in the stubbornness of civil disobedience, and I'm not afraid of it," she has said.

Paley's political concerns, first introduced in *The Little Disturbances of Man*, become more central in *Enormous Changes at the Last Minute* (1974), her second collection. The collection brings backs characters from *The Little Disturbances of Man*, but it also employs a more open-ended experimental fictional technique and offers a darker vision of life. In one of her most anthologized stories, "A Conversation with My Father," Paley comments on her literary method. An ailing father requests from his daughter a simple story, "the kind de Maupassant wrote, or Chekhov, the kind you used to write." She wishes to please her father but cannot give him the straightforward, easily resolved story he desires. She reveals that she has avoided plot, "the absolute line between two points," in her writing, "not for literary reasons, but because it takes all hope away. Everyone real or invented deserves the open destiny of life."

Paley's third collection, *Later the Same Day* (1985), reintroduces characters from her earlier collections, such as Faith Darwin, who, in "Dreamer in a Dead Language," visits her parents in a nursing home only to discover that they are considering divorce. One of her strongest stories, "Zagrowsky Tells," concerns a bigoted Jewish pharmacist whose daughter gives birth to a child by an African-American father. Zagrowsky assumes responsibility for the care of his grandson, and his love for the child transforms him. It is one of the most hopeful stories in Paley's canon, with its affirmation firmly built on the actual world of mixed motives and ambiguous, complex individuals.

Throughout her life, Grace Paley has consistently chosen to explore complex issues, whether in her politics or in her writing. She has persistently insisted that both writing and action can produce the "little disturbances" and "enormous changes" she records in her stories. As she has observed, we all "have to remember, the world still has to be saved—every day." As her political activism attests, Paley has lived her life according to her conscience. She brings to her life and work the consciousness of herself as a Jew, a woman, a writer, and a citizen of the world. Nowhere is this consciousness more evident than in the voices of her characters—especially her women. They meet their challenges, from playground politics to global conflicts, with determination, wit, humor, and love. Paley has said, "People will sometimes ask, 'Why don't you write more politics?' and I have to explain to them that writing the lives of women is politics." *The Little Disturbances of Man* and Paley's subsequent collections make clear the truism that all politics is local, and that the opportunities for both revolution and reform come unexpectedly during the ordinary moments of one's life.

THE GOLDEN NOTEBOOK

by Doris Lessing

The Golden Notebook (1962) is one of the most influential and intense works of fiction to come out of the 1960s. It is not an easy novel to experience—divided into five sections, four of which contain subsections called "The Notebooks," it demands from the reader both an objective consideration of its construction and a visceral response to each of its parts. A profound and complex examination of a women's psyche, Lessing's masterpiece was published in 1962, just before the decade gave birth to a second wave of feminism (the following year saw publication of Betty Friedan's *The Feminine Mystique*), and has been read as a successor to the work of Simone de Beauvoir. At once a self-reflective text, a feminist manifesto, and an exploration of contemporary and British colonial culture, *The Golden Notebook* explores, as a *New Statesmen* reviewer observed, what it means to be "free and responsible, a woman in relation to men and other women, and to struggle to come to terms with one's self about these things and about writing and politics."

The fragmented style of *The Golden Notebook* and its humanistic vision reflects the circumstances in which Lessing grew up and how she has lived, as well as the way she has approached her writing. She was born in 1919, in what is now Iran, the elder of two children of a bank clerk who had lost a leg as a result of a wound suffered in the battle of Passchendaele during World War I. Lessing's father, Alfred Tayler, moved his family to an isolated area of Southern Rhodesia (now Zimbabwe), then a British colony. There, Tayler tried his hand at farming, at which he was unsuccessful, and the family lived in poverty for some twenty years. Lessing was educated at the Dominican convent school in Salisbury (now Harare) until she developed eye trouble at twelve or thirteen and returned home. From the age of sixteen until she went to London, in 1949, Lessing did secretarial work for, among others, the Southern Rhodesian Parliament and a Capetown newspaper. Lessing's first husband, Frank Wisdom, to whom she was married from 1939 to 1943 and by whom she had two children, held a civil service position in Salisbury. Lessing became involved in radical politics and, in 1945, married Gottfried Lessing, a German communist, with whom she had a son. After moving to London, Lessing was declared a Prohibited Immigrant and barred from Rhodesia until the advent of black majority rule, in 1980. Gottfried Lessing, who had immigrated to East Germany, where he became the commissar of trade and ambassador to Uganda, was accidentally killed, in 1979, during the revolt against Idi Amin. Lessing never remarried and, since 1949, she has lived with her son Peter Lessing in various residences in London.

Lessing had published four novels prior to *The Golden Notebook*. The first, *The Grass Is Singing* (1950), is set in Rhodesia and is the story of a white farmer's wife and her black servant, and the violent conclusion of their relationship. A candid presentation of apartheid, the novel presages the psychological insight, and political and social consciousness, Lessing would bring to her later works. She followed *The Grass Is Singing* with the first three novels that would become the "Children of Violence" series, a quintet published between 1952 and 1969, that traces the history of Martha Quest from her childhood in Rhodesia through postwar Britain to the year 2000. Critics found autobiographical parallels in the series, especially with the first novel, *Martha Quest*, an observation Lessing disputed, preferring to characterize "Child-ren of Violence" objectively as a "study of the individual conscience in its relations with the collective."

Lessing similarly objected to *The Golden Notebook* being read as an autobiographical confession, as well as a chronicle of contemporary "sex wars." Instead, she insisted that the novel be seen in the context of the great European works of the nineteenth century that attempted to synthesize the intellectual and moral climate of their times. "For me the highest point of literature," Lessing declared, "was the novel of the nineteenth century, the work of Tolstoy, Stendhal, Dostoevsky, Balzac, Turgenev, Chekhov." But Lessing was writing about a modern world dominated by fragmentation and chaos that resists such a straightforward synthesis and what D.H. Lawrence called "the old stable *ego* of the character." Lessing's solution was to turn the novel inside out, breaking up and realigning its component parts, shattering chronology and narrative sequence, and rendering her protagonist in multiple narrative voices and alter egos. For Lessing, *The Golden Notebook*'s "meaning is in the shape," and in her introduction, written in 1971, Lessing explains the plan of the novel:

> There is a skeleton, or frame, called *Free Women*, which is a conventional short novel, about 60,000 words long, and which could stand by itself. But it is divided into five sections and separated by stages of the four Notebooks, Black, Red, Yellow and Blue. The Notebooks are kept by Anna Wulf, a central character of *Free Women*. She keeps four, and not one because, as she recognises, she had to separate things off from each other, out of fear of chaos, of formlessness—of breakdown. Pressures, inner and outer, end the Notebooks; a heavy black line is drawn across the page of one after another. But now that they are finished, from the fragments can come something new, *The Golden Notebook*.

The Golden Notebook breaks up a conventional narrative describing Anna Wulf and her friend Molly Jacobs, set in London during the 1950s, with the intense interior views recorded in Anna's four notebooks, each concerned with a different aspect of her life (or its projection), so that a section of *Free Women* is followed by an excerpt from Anna's black, red, blue, and yellow notebooks. This pattern is repeated four times. A fifth "Golden Notebook" follows, recording Anna's breakdown and recovery, in which it is learned that she has been given the first line of *Free Women*—"The two women were alone in the London flat"—by her lover Saul Green. By the end of the novel, the reader reaches the present moment of the embedded novel's beginning, which is then concluded; it reaches, as well, the protagonist's developmental state that has allowed her to write the novel we have just read. The novel encompasses the widest possible exploration of its sexual, political, psychological, and authorial themes, depicting a protagonist in the multidimensional role of lover, mother, writer, individual, and political activist. "It is a novel about certain political and sexual attitudes that have force now," Lessing observed. "It is an attempt to explain them, to objectivize them, to set them in relation with each other. So in a way it is a social novel, written by someone whose training—or at least whose habit of mind—is to see things socially, not personally." Anna Wulf's inner crisis, her search for wholeness, mirrors a world in chaos in which identity is co-opted and undermined by various personal and social forces. The novel, within its unconventional style, articulates these points of pressure on its central protagonist and the process by which they operate and can be managed.

In the initial segment of "Free Women," Anna Freeman Wulf is a blocked writer visiting her friend Molly Jacobs. Both are technically "free women," since they are in between relationships, but beneath the surface they are both prisoners of forces that they cannot control. For Anna, her dilemma of balancing emotional and sexual fulfillment while retaining personal autonomy in the face of a world that seems bent on destruction has paralyzed her. As she tells her friend, "As far as I can see, everything's cracking up." The "Free Women" segment introduces simplified versions of the experiences and aspects of Anna's psychic distress that her notebooks will treat in complex detail. In order to cope with her existential crisis as a woman, intellectual, and activist, Anna compartmentalizes her life and reflections into her four color-coded notebooks. Lessing would explain that she divided Anna's reflections and different narrative forms into "four parts to express a split person. I felt that if the artist's sensibility is to be equated with the sensibility of the educated person, then it is logical to use different styles to express different kinds of people." When asked by Molly why she bothers with her notebooks, Anna responds, "Chaos, that's the point," meaning that collectively her experiences are spinning out of control and that keeping formlessness at bay by managing the parts might enable her to discover the whole truth about herself and her life, its purpose and point.

Anna's black notebook records her transactions with film and television agents who want to adapt her novel, *Frontiers of War.*

This prompts her to consider the experiences on which her novel was based: her own past in Rhodesia and her relationships with a group of communist intellectuals there during the war. These formative experiences, which she has converted into her successful first novel, now seem to her a distortion and a simplification of her past. What she perceives as an indulgence in nostalgia for death and destruction leads her to despair about the ability of writing ever to deliver the truth, which is the cause of her current writer's block. The red notebook treats Anna's disillusionment with the British Communist Party, based on the inability of either ideology or activism to cope with the conflicts Anna feels as an individual and a woman, and the moral collapse of the party as the news of the Stalinist purges come to light. If writing distorts the truth, political solutions equally fail to respond to personal and private imperatives or to halt violence and chaos; and the notebook breaks down into a series of newspaper clippings about such events as the execution of the Rosenbergs and the hydrogen bomb tests.

The yellow notebook shows Anna's response to her experiences in a narrative about a women's magazine writer named Ella, Anna's fictionalized alter ego, and her unsatisfying relationship with Paul Tanner, a married psychologist. It is an attempt to put Anna's public and private selves into fictional perspective. Ella is, therefore, a projection of Anna, whose self-destructive tendencies and emotional dependency on her lover, mirror her creation's dilemmas. The narrative eventually unravels into a series of story ideas, exploring various possible relationship scenarios. The blue notebook is a diarylike, more straightforward record of daily events, including Anna's psychotherapy sessions with her Jungian analyst, Mrs. Marks, who provides the basis of Anna's eventual recovery by having her relive her experiences. It also records her affair with the American writer Saul Green, which leads to the breakdown and recovery recorded in the final Golden Notebook. The reader now has the interior view and context to understand the character "Anna Wulf" introduced in the novel's opening pages. Alienated from her past, from her former political convictions, from those she has loved, Anna is unable to write or unify her world that has shattered into parts that do not cohere.

To achieve some psychic unity Anna and her lover go through a cathartic experience that expands the normal limitations of "individuality." She confronts the various selves that she has kept carefully separated in her notebooks, and, by risking madness, by recognizing a central principle that "we must not divide things off, must not compartmentalize," Anna moves from destruction toward control, from fragmentation to unity, encouraged by her lover to face their demons and confront their fears. "They 'break down,' " Lessing explains, "into each other, into other people, break through the false patterns and formulas they have made to shore up themselves and each other, dissolve." If the individual notebooks represent a defeat of integration and unity, the inner "Golden Notebook" shows the various elements of Anna's past and psyche reassembled. Anna refuses the role of victim (in love, politics, and art) and accepts the conditions of her past and present circumstances, breaking the spell that has incapacitated and silenced her. She provides the first sentence for Saul Green's next novel, and he provides the first line of hers, the initial sentence of the "Free Women" and *The Golden Notebook*. "Free Women," therefore, is a demonstration of what her experiences have taught Anna, converted into the simplified outline of her conventional novel. In it Molly deals with the pressures of her ex-husband and the suicide attempt of her son by remarrying. She urges her friend to begin writing again, but Anna opts instead for a life of service as "a matrimonial welfare worker." Anna, the author of "Free Women," has gained a foothold for her character and herself in the world of experience, and a tenuous control and victory over the forces of destruction and madness. Similarly, the pieces of Lessing's remarkable multidimensional responses to dissolution manage to cohere as "The Golden Notebook" gives way to *The Golden Notebook*.

The novel's contradictions and multiplicity, its evasion of simple categories and responses are central sources of its power, influence, and still vital relevance. One of the most ingenious, thorough, and honest explorations of identity, society, politics, and gender issues in literature, *The Golden Notebook* is acknowledged as a twentieth-century classic.

THE FEMININE MYSTIQUE

by Betty Friedan

An influential treatise on the status of women in post–World War II American society, *The Feminine Mystique*, published in 1963, is a must-read on anyone's short list of women's nonfiction. No other work in the history of feminist thought called for change in the position of women with as much reverberating success as Friedan's analysis of a postwar society that subordinated women and repressed their desires for greater opportunity and fulfillment beyond their expected roles as wives, mothers, and homemakers. *The Feminine Mystique* resonated deeply with American women and sparked a revolution that would result in the revitalized women's movement of the 1960s and 1970s.

The Feminine Mystique was born out of a postwar climate in which Americans, feeling a sense of displacement resulting from the upheavals of war and an awareness of a frightening new phenomenon called the "cold war," sought cultural stability and found it in idealized domesticity; in it men went to work, while most women, after either marrying right out of high school or college, or leaving careers to marry, put all their energies into rearing their children, keeping their husbands contented, and making sure their homes were tidy and attractive. However, despite the unprecedented economic progress that had purchased the American dream in suburban households with two-car garages and shiny new appliances, many women in the 1950s were beginning to experience a discontent so profound it could not be articulated.

One of these women was Betty Friedan, a freelance writer, wife, and mother of three children. Born Betty Naomi Goldstein in Peoria, Illinois, in 1921, Friedan was the oldest daughter in a family of two daughters and a son. Her parents had immigrated to the United States to escape the pogroms of Eastern Europe. Her father, Harry Goldstein, was a jeweler; her mother, Miriam Horowitz Goldstein, worked as a journalist after attending college but gave up her career when she married. Friedan was a gifted student who founded a literary magazine in high school, won a dramatic award (for a time she aspired to become an actress), and graduated as valedictorian of her class. She went on to Smith College, where she studied psychology and, after graduating summa cum laude, in 1942, won two research fellowships to the University of California at Berkeley. Unwilling to commit to a doctorate and a career as a psychologist, Friedan left Berkeley for New York City. The labor shortage caused by men who had left to fight in World War II gave Friedan the opportunity to find work there as a journalist, first for the Federated Press, a news agency for labor unions and liberal and radical newspapers, and then for the *U.E. News*, the official publication of the United Electrical Workers. In 1947, she married Carl Friedan, and a year later gave birth to the first of the couple's three children. The couple divorced in 1969.

In the 1950s, Friedan lost her job as a newspaper reporter after requesting her second maternity leave. She continued to write, however, submitting articles to women's magazines, whose messages of domestic fulfillment for women she would later use as sources for her assessment of a "feminine mystique." Dissatisfied with her primary role as wife and mother, Friedan began to explore the causes of her discontent. Her research revealed that women's magazines urged deference to men, the repression of ambition outside the home, and concealment of intellectual ability, while glorifying domesticity, so that women could become, as one *Ladies' Home Journal* article preached, "The fragile, feminine, dependent, but priceless creature every man wants his wife to be." Concurrent with this media viewpoint was the popular notion that the educational system was not adequately preparing women for their proper domestic roles. To that end, some colleges and universities featured a required course called "Marriage and Family Life Education," in which, Freidan would later observe in *The Feminine Mystique*, "the old role became a new science."

Friedan found disturbing the overriding message that women's contentment lay solely in domestic accomplishments. At the same time, she began to wonder whether other women shared her dissatisfaction with domesticity. In 1957, she sent out questionnaires to two hundred of her former Smith College classmates. The answers she received convinced her that she was not alone in suffering from a psychic distress she would come to define as "the problem that has no name." When Friedan and her Smith classmates met to discuss the questionnaire results during their 1957 college reunion, they canvassed Smith seniors about their aspirations. As Friedan later observed, "Try as we might, we couldn't get these fifties seniors to admit they had become interested in *anything*, at that great college, except their future husbands and children, and suburban homes. . . . It was as if something was making these girls defensive, inoculating them against the larger interests, dreams and passions, really good higher education can lead to."

Friedan next submitted an article to *McCall's* titled "Are Women Wasting Their Time in College?" in which she suggested that "maybe it wasn't higher education making American women frustrated in their role as women, but the current definition of the role of women." *McCall's* and *Redbook* rejected the article, and Friedan refused to allow the *Ladies' Home Journal* to print it after she saw that it had been rewritten to support the opposite viewpoint of her findings. She continued to research her subject, interviewing professional women and housewives on what she described as "the strange discrepancy between the reality of our lives as women and the image to which we were trying to conform." She then decided to expand the article into a book, which was published by W. W. Norton five years after Friedan signed her contract with them.

In *The Feminine Mystique*, Friedan aimed to heighten awareness about a woman's powerlessness within the family and in society, her limited opportunities for self-expression and fulfillment, and the negative stereotyping and discrimination career-minded women faced, as well as the unequal salaries earned by women who did work outside the home. Drawing her conclusions from her own experience and observations, and from the letters, interviews, and questionnaires she compiled from educated middle-class housewives who were struggling to find some meaning in their domestically ordered lives, Friedan diagnosed the anxiety and aimlessness experienced by American women as the product of a fantasy of postwar happy suburban female domesticity created and reinforced by educators, sociologists, psychologists, and the media. In the booming, if inflationary, postwar economic climate, advertisers in particular required a large class of consumers, and women, considered America's hyper-consumers, were encouraged in their roles as sex objects and domestic guardians whose longings could be fulfilled by buying the home and beauty products companies sold. According to Friedan, women accepted their social and sexual subordination in exchange for the material and psychological pleasures their passive femininity and protective, maternal roles as wives and mothers afforded them—but at the cost of feeling imprisoned and dehumanized in gilded suburban palaces.

After identifying and analyzing the dilemma of women trapped in the feminine mystique, Friedan called for a reassertion of female identity beyond that of domestic icon, consumer, helpmate, and caregiver. It was a call to activism that rejected the characterization of women as helpless victims and asserted the need for increased education and opportunities that would allow women to grow to their full potential. In her famous conclusion, Friedan writes somewhat prophetically: "Who knows what women can be when they are finally free to become themselves? Who knows what women's intelligence will contribute when it can be nourished without denying love? Who knows of the possibilities of love when men and women share not only their children, home, and garden, not only the fulfillment of their biological roles, but the responsibilities and passions of the work that creates the human future and the full human knowledge of what they are? It has barely begun, the search of women for themselves. But the time is at hand when the voices of the feminine mystique can no longer drown out the inner voice that is driving women on to become complete."

The Feminine Mystique was brought out in a modest first printing of two thousand copies. Over the next ten years it sold three million hardcover copies and many more in paperback, and has never gone out of print. Friedan received numerous letters from women who wrote that they had no idea, until they read her book, that other women shared their feelings. Women were not the only buyers of Friedan's book. As she recalls in her autobiography, *Life So Far*, "Many men whose wives had made those feminine mystique renunciations had bought the book for their wives, and encouraged them to go back to school or work." *The Feminine Mystique* also received a positive reception from such veterans of the first women's movement as historian and Women's Party member Alma Lutz, who declared that the book offered "a glimmer of hope that some of the younger generation are waking up."

Although the book was seen as a new unifying force in a second wave of twentieth-century feminism, it drew criticism, as well, for its focus on well-educated, middle-class and upper-middle-class white women, especially during the early 1970s, as the women's liberation movement was taking shape and the voices of African-American, working-class, and lesbian women began to be heard. However, the call for reform that *The Feminine Mystique* articulated and the movement that followed the book provided a flashpoint for debate on the status of all women, not just Friedan's target audience. Along with Simone de Beauvoir's *The Second Sex*, and such later feminist works as Germaine Greer's *The Female Eunuch* and Kate Millett's *Sexual Politics*, *The Feminine Mystique* is one of the most influential early texts on feminism, as well as a landmark work in the history of twentieth-century women's literature.

THE BELL JAR
by Sylvia Plath

The Bell Jar, Sylvia Plath's harrowing and mordantly funny account of a college woman's breakdown, suicide attempt, and recovery, was initially published in England, in 1963, just two weeks before Plath's suicide. Recognized as one of the most influential and powerful poets of the twentieth century and a writer who put at the center of her work the demands and limitations of being a woman—daughter, wife, career woman, and mother—Plath has been both mourned as a casualty in the pre-liberation gender wars and revered as an harbinger and early voice of the modern women's movement. Ellen Moers wrote in *Literary Women* (1976), "No writer has meant more to the current feminist movement," and Plath's life, death, and works continue to reverberate and fascinate. *The Bell Jar* has consequently assumed a central importance in helping to understand and interpret one of the most debated and controversial modern writers. However, it also deserves to be appreciated as more than an important autobiographical key to a literary and feminist icon. Critic Tony Tanner has called the novel, "Perhaps the most compelling and controlled account of a mental breakdown to have appeared in American fiction"; while other critics have commended Plath's ability to set intensely personal trauma within a wider social and cultural context. The book is a brilliant dramatization of the problems of growing up female in the United States during the 1940s and 1950s, a fictionalized version of the dilemma faced by women of the period, as anatomized by Betty Friedan in her groundbreaking study, *The Feminine Mystique,* which also appeared in 1963. *The Bell Jar* is one of the earliest novels to express rebellion against the conventional roles assigned to women, a forerunner of such later works as Erica Jong's *Fear of Flying* (1973) and Marilyn French's *The Women's Room* (1977). According to Charles Newman in *The Art of Sylvia Plath, The Bell Jar* is "one of the few American novels to treat adolescence from a mature point of view. . . . It gives us one of the few sympathetic portraits of what happens to one who has genuinely feminist aspirations in our society, of a girl who refuses to be an *event* in anyone's life." Newman goes on to assert that Sylvia Plath "remains among the few woman writers in recent memory to link the grand theme of womanhood with the destiny of modern civilization." Compared with other post–World War II American expressions of alienation and psychological crisis, such as J.D. Salinger's *The Catcher in the Rye* (1951), Ken Kesey's *One Flew Over the Cuckoo's Nest* (1962), Saul Bellow's *Herzog* (1964), and Philip Roth's *Portnoy's Complaint* (1969), *The Bell Jar* is the only one of these novels with a woman protagonist and one of the earliest modern novels of growth and development from a female perspective. Anchored by a satirical impulse to characterize the gender assumptions that blighted a young woman's aspirations in mid-century America and intimately informed by Plath's own experiences and traumas, *The Bell Jar* is a still-powerful, instructive, and universally relevant *Portrait of the Artist as a Young Woman.*

Described by its author as "an autobiographical apprentice work which I had to write in order to free myself from the past," *The Bell Jar,* initially published under the pseudonym Victoria Lucas to protect the identity and feelings of her family and friends, and withheld from publication in the United States until 1971, draws extensively on the details of Plath's background and biography. Born in 1932, in Jamaica Plain, Massachusetts, Plath was the eldest child of Otto and Aurelia Schoeber Plath. Her father had emigrated from Germany at the age of sixteen, earned a doctorate in entomology from Harvard, and had met her mother, an Austrian immigrant, while he was teaching at Boston University. Otto

Plath died suddenly, in 1940, when Plath was eight years old, and the trauma of his death would become a central theme in Plath's poetry and fiction. Many have speculated that Plath's determined assault on academic and artistic achievement became a way of gaining symbolic approval from her missing father. Plath began publishing poetry while a high school student and won a scholarship to the prestigious women's college, Smith, in 1950. During her junior year, she was selected as one of twenty coed guest editors for the college issue of *Mademoiselle* magazine. After returning home following a month in New York City, depressed over being rejected from a creative writing seminar at Harvard, Plath attempted suicide by taking an overdose of sleeping pills in the crawl space beneath her house. Found barely alive two days later, Plath became a patient in a mental hospital and began the therapy that eventually allowed her to return to Smith, in 1954. The circumstances leading up to and following her breakdown and suicide attempt would provide the narrative material for *The Bell Jar.*

Plath graduated *summa cum laude,* in 1955, and won a Fulbright fellowship to study at Cambridge University. There she met the aspiring English poet Ted Hughes, and they were married, in 1956. After living in Massachusetts, where Plath taught at Smith and worked as a secretary in the psychiatric division of Massachusetts General Hospital, the couple returned to England, in 1959. Her first volume of poetry, *The Colossus,* appeared in 1960, the same year she gave birth to a daughter, Frieda. In 1961, she began work on *The Bell Jar,* confiding to a friend that she had "been wanting to do this for ten years but had a terrible block about Writing A Novel. Then suddenly . . . the dykes broke." Plath labored to complete her novel while living in an isolated village in rural Devon, through her pregancy that resulted in the birth of a son, Nicholas, in 1962, and the breakup of her marriage when she learned that Hughes was having an affair. Despite ill-health, exhaustion from caring for her two infant children, and disillusionment over the collapse of her marriage, Plath managed to finish her novel—which she described to her brother as "a potboiler" that "no one must read"—began a second, and managed to write many of her greatest poems that later appeared in the posthumous collection *Ariel* (1965). Moving to a London flat in December 1962, Plath would write a final letter to her mother stating that "I have been feeling a bit grim—the upheaval over, I am seeing the finality of it all, and being catapulted from the cow-like happiness of maternity into loneliness and grim problems is no fun." On February 11, 1963, Plath committed suicide.

The issues that Plath struggled with throughout her life in the conflict between her artistic aspirations and the gender limitations imposed on her as a daughter, wife, and mother form the dramatic core of *The Bell Jar,* the story of approximately eight months in the life of nineteen-year-old Esther Greenwood, the novel's narrator. The plot of *The Bell Jar* closely follows the events of Plath's own life during 1953 to 1954, divided into three parts: reflecting her experiences living in New York City as a guest editor for a fashion magazine; her breakdown upon her return home that culminates in her suicide attempt; and her hospitalization, therapy, and eventual recovery. Like Plath (who wrote during this period of her life, "I am afraid of getting older, I am afraid of getting married. Spare me from cooking three meals a day—spare me from the relentless cage of routine and rote. I want to be free—free to know people and their backgrounds—free to move to different parts of the world"), Esther struggles with her aspiration to live an independent, fulfilling life as a writer and the shallow, restrictive reality she faces as a women of her time. It is her inability to integrate her experiences—with sex, work, and her relationships—with her sense of self and the gender role she is expected to accept that eventually leads to her breakdown.

Living in a New York City women's hotel and exposed to the glamorous lifestyle of editors of a popular fashion magazine, Esther finds herself feeling "very still and very empty, the way the eye of a tornado must feel, moving dully along in the middle of the surrounding hullabaloo." She is both attracted to the sophisticated adult world she is introduced to and repulsed by its tawdry shallowness. Esther is similarly divided between admiration for the sexually sophisticated Doreen and the simple innocence of the Kansan coed Betsy, whom Doreen dismisses as "Pollyanna Cowgirl." Esther finds herself torn between her desires for chastity and sex, feelings as seemingly mutually exclusive as her aspiration to become a poet and the expectations that surround her to become a dutiful wife, mother, and homemaker. On her last night in New York, after a series of disastrous encounters with men and disappointment over her future prospects, Esther climbs to the roof of her hotel and throws away her recently acquired fashionable wardrobe, symbolically rejecting the artificial identity imposed by her New York experience and underscoring her disillusionment and disorientation.

Returning to her surburban Boston home, Esther feels similarly trapped, limited to the world of "white, shining, identical clapboard houses . . . one bar after another in a large but escape-proof cage." Amid confused attempts to establish her career goals, sorting out her relationship with Buddy Willard and the double standard that allows males to explore their sexuality while females are expected to preserve their virginity, and a botched treatment of electroshock therapy, Esther grows increasingly dislocated and despairing. With her artistic dreams stymied, Esther finds the alternative route as a traditional wife and mother a life sentence of drudgery and subservience: "I saw the years of my life speed along a road in the form of telephone poles threaded together by wires. I counted one, two, three . . . nineteen telephone poles, and then the wires dangled into space, and try as I would, I couldn't see a single pole beyond the nineteenth." Esther imagines her despondency as a gigantic bell jar that descends upon her, suffocating her, imprisoning her, isolating her from others, and distorting her view of the world. "To the person in the bell jar," Esther observes, "blanked and stopped as a dead baby, the world itself is the bad dream." Her only way out is suicide, and after a series of often comic explorations of the means of self-destruction, Esther almost succeeds with an overdose of sleeping pills.

The final section of the book records Esther's painful recovery after surviving her suicide attempt. First placed in the psychiatric ward of a city hospital, she resists all efforts to help her. However, after she is moved to a private mental hospital, Esther makes progress in self-awareness under the care of an empathetic woman psychiatrist, who helps her come to terms with her feelings about her mother, her aspirations, and attitudes toward sexuality and self-worth. When allowed to leave the hospital for short excursions into Boston, she obtains a diaphragm and loses her virginity, an unpleasant experience with disastrous consequences. Esther survives that disillusionment, however, as well as the suicide of her friend Joan, and is finally brought to the point of expectantly awaiting her release from the asylum—"patched, retreaded and approved for the road." Central to Esther's recovery is her facing down and rejecting the identities imposed on her, accepting an imperfect but authentic self that allows her to break out of her disorienting, tortured confinement. "I felt surprisingly at peace," Esther realizes. "The bell jar hung, suspended, a few feet above my head. I was open to the circulating air." Although the novel ends with hope, with a sense of rebirth and engagement, Esther's future remains unsure, with the ominous threat of another breakdown still haunting her: "How did I know that someday—at college, in Europe, somewhere, anywhere—the bell jar, with its stifling distortions, wouldn't descend again?"

Plath, who in her own life was unable to prevent another descent of the bell jar, manages in her novel to present brilliantly the trauma of growing up female in pre-liberated America and the universal and timeless struggle of self-discovery.

WIDE SARGASSO SEA

by Jean Rhys

Wide Sargasso Sea (1966), Jean Rhys's final novel, published when she was in her seventies and twenty-seven years after her previous book, rescued a major twentieth-century author from obscurity and gained Rhys deserved international recognition. The author of five novels, three collections of short stories, and an unfinished autobiography, Rhys would be heralded by critic A. Alvarez as "one of the finest British writers of this century." Continuing her exploration of the alienated lives of isolated and marginalized women who dominate her works, *Wide Sargasso Sea* intensely and poetically explores cultural and gender alienation through an imaginative addendum to Charlotte Brontë's 1847 novel *Jane Eyre,* giving voice and understanding to the earlier novel's speech-less and raving madwoman in the attic. Rhys shifts the emphasis of *Jane Eyre* from the identity and romantic struggles of the plain governess Jane and her Byronic employer, Edward Rochester, to his marriage to the mad Bertha, a West Indian heiress whom he has secretly confined to the attic of Thornfield Hall. Bertha's identity and existence are the sensational secrets of Brontë's novel and the gothic stimulus of the novel's plot and resolution. The revelation of Rochester's bigamy at the altar during Jane and

Rochester's wedding separates the lovers and provides a seemingly insurmountable obstacle to their desires. Jane and Rochester are finally reunited and reconciled only after Bertha burns down Thornfield and dies, eliminating Rochester's marital impediment and causing his penitential but redemptive injury, the physical disfigurement that allows Jane to return to him and to confess: "Reader, I married him." As brilliant and compelling as Charlotte Brontë's novel is in its interior view of one of the first great fictional heroines, Jane Eyre's story also crowds from center stage an equally fascinating character whose motives and identity are subsumed by the monster's role Bertha is made to play in *Jane Eyre*. Rhys's *Wide Sargasso Sea* supplies what is missing from Brontë's novel: a biography of the first Mrs. Rochester and an account of the events that led up to her confinement in the attic rooms of Thornfield Hall. Rhys's novel, which she described as her "dream book which has often been a nightmare to me," becomes an encapsulated history of the West Indies and an intense critique of patriarchy and cultural imperialism from a female colonial sensibility.

Jean Rhys once observed that the only truth she knew was herself, and her life and works are thereby closely intertwined. Her background and heritage help to explain her fascination with outsiders, with alienated women protagonists caught between cultures, struggling to formulate a sustaining identity, as well as coping with the consequence of independence and autonomy. Rhys was born Ellen Gwendolyn Rees Williams, in 1890, on the Caribbean island of Dominica. Her Welsh father was a ship's doctor who had settled in Dominica toward the end of the nineteenth century. Rhys's mother was a third-generation Dominican Creole whose slaveholding family had experienced the hostility of their former slaves after emancipation when an estate house was burned down in the 1830s—the same experience suffered by the family of her protagonist, Antoinette Cosway, in *Wide Sargasso Sea*. The fourth of five children, Rhys was tall and thin, with fair hair and, in her words, "huge staring eyes of no particular colour." All of her brothers and sisters had brown eyes and brown hair, and her sense of physical alienation was exacerbated by her mother's declaration that black babies were prettier than white ones. Rhys recalled that she "prayed so ardently to be black." Like Antoinette in *Wide Sargasso Sea*, Rhys attended a convent school and gained her knowledge of the black culture of the islanders from servants.

At the age of sixteen, Rhys left Dominica for England and the start of a lifelong exile from her Caribbean home, returning only for a short visit, in 1936. Rhys attended a strict all-girls school in Cambridge and experienced the cultural shock of English public school life. A talented singer, Rhys passed the entrance examination for the Academy of Dramatic Art in London, but her family disapproved of her acting aspirations, and her financial support from her family came to an end, in 1910, with her father's death. She took a job in the chorus of a musical comedy and toured with a theatrical troupe for two years. She also posed as an artist's model, and her face was once used for a Pear's soap advertisement. Rhys began to write, in 1914, as a form of therapy to help her cope with a painful love affair as the mistress of a London stockbroker twenty years her senior.

In 1919, Rhys married the half-French, half-Dutch journalist Jean Lenglet, and the couple settled in Paris. Her writing came to the attention of English novelist and editor Ford Madox Ford who suggested "Jean Rhys" as her pen name. In 1922, Lenglet was arrested and imprisoned for fraud, leaving Rhys destitute. She managed to publish her first book, *The Left Bank, and Other Stories,* in 1927, and settled in England where she met literary agent Leslie Tilden Smith, whom she was to marry after divorcing Lenglet, in 1932. Her first novel, *Quartet,* appeared in 1928, to be followed by three more, *After Leaving Mr. Mackenzie* (1931), *Voyage in the Dark* (1934), and *Good Morning, Midnight* (1939). Reflecting her experiences in London, Paris, and Vienna, these novels all focus on the economic and emotional struggles of women protagonists in destructive relationships. Appreciated by a small cadre of fellow writers and reviewers for their understated, ironic, controlled artistry and candor in capturing female consciousness, her novels, however, failed to find a popular audience. During World War II, Rhys disappeared from the literary scene. Her books went out of print, and the few who had read and admired her work assumed she had died. Rhys's rediscovery began when actress Selma Vaz Dias solicited contact with the author through a magazine advertisement to get approval for a dramatic adaptation of *Good Morning, Midnight.* Rhys, who was living in Kent after the death of Smith in 1945, answered the ad, and cleared the way for *Good Morning, Midnight* to be performed as a dramatic monologue, in 1949. The actress' interest in her work became the impetus for Rhys to resume her writing career. She told Dias, "You've already lifted the numb hopeless feeling that stopped me writing for so long." Dias's adaptation would be subsequently broadcast on the BBC, in 1957, the year Rhys visited London to have dinner with the actress and talked about her plans for *Wide Sargasso Sea*. Rhys suffered a heart attack just before that novel was finished, and publication was delayed until 1966.

Taking its title from the huge mass of seaweed in the mid-Atlantic that tricks and traps ocean travelers with the appearance of solid land, *Wide Sargasso Sea* explores the stagnation and suspended animation that besets Antoinette Cosway, beginning with her childhood as the daughter of a West Indian plantation owner who has recently died, leaving his young wife and two children destitute on the isolated, decaying island estate of Coulibri. To save her family, Antoinette's mother attracts by her beauty a wealthy Englishman, Mr. Mason, whom she marries. Mason tries to revive Coulibri by importing cheap off-island labor, angering the estate's former slaves, and a mob burns down Coulibri, resulting in the death of Antoinette's feeble brother and the madness of her mother.

Following Antoinette's education at a convent school and the death of her mother and stepfather, Richard Mason, her stepfather's son by a previous marriage, arranges a match between Antoinette and an English gentleman, a younger son sent to the West Indies to help restore the family's fortune by an advantageous marriage. Although never named, the Englishman is identifiable by his circumstances as Edward Rochester. The second narrative section of *Wide Sargasso Sea* shifts from Antoinette's perspective, in part one, to Rochester's account of the couple's honeymoon on the isolated, seductive, but ultimately alien and terrifying island retreat of Grandbois. Here, Rochester's sexual repression and patriarchal gender assumptions, which reveal his will to dominate and punish, corrode his relationship with his bride. The dramatized conflict between reason and passion, order and chaos, English respectability and West Indian exoticism destroys the potential idyll of bride and groom, and sets in motion the events that will lead to Antoinette's confinement. Like the exotic natural beauty that surrounds them, both attracting and repelling Rochester by its excess, the passionate Antoinette profoundly unsettles the young Englishman, underscoring the guilt he experiences from his sexual desires and his fear of losing control. To try to win back her husband's affections, Antoinette solicits from her old black nurse, Christophine, a potion that succeeds both in enflaming Rochester's passions and exacerbating his abhorrence of his bride and her "primitive" island culture. To punish Antoinette, he has sex with a black servant so that his wife cannot fail to overhear them, and accepts the false accusations made by Daniel Cosway, a jealous and vindictive mulatto who claims to be Antoinette's half-brother, that Antoinette was sexually active before her marriage and that through her mother she is hereditarily insane.

Renaming Antoinette Bertha, after her mad mother, Rochester takes his wife to his English estate, and the narrative perspective returns to Antoinette's disoriented and confused mind as she attempts to understand her confinement in her attic room, attended by the servant Grace Poole, whose identity is the first clear indication that the narrative has joined the story of Brontë's *Jane Eyre*. As told in *Wide Sargasso Sea*, Antoinette's story contradicts Rochester's version as told to Jane Eyre. She, not Rochester, has married against her will in a conspiracy to gain her fortune. Deprived of her Christian name, exiled, and entrapped, Antoinette is a double victim of patriarchy and imperialism. Antoinette dreams of escape, comforted by a red dress that reminds her of her island home and her destiny, which she associates with the flames that destroyed that home. *Wide Sargasso Sea* ends, anticipating Antoinette's defiant act of setting the house afire that will claim her life. The novel concludes ambiguously, with Antoinette's suicide either a final defeat at the hands of a repressive society or a pyrric victory of self-assertion and vengeance on a victimizing ethos.

By filling in the gaps of Charlotte Brontë's novel and exposing its gender and cultural assumptions, *Wide Sargasso Sea* makes it impossible ever to read *Jane Eyre* in the same way again. Antoinette is revealed as a compelling, dark double to Jane Eyre. Like Jane, Antoinette is an orphan figure, neglected at home and abused by other children. Both are sensitive individuals who seek the consolation of love in their isolation and misery. However, unlike Jane, Antoinette is not rescued by a caring man with means but enslaved by him, and punished for her passion and identity as a cultural alien and sexual threat. Rhys's novel makes clear that Jane Eyre's ultimate victory at the expense of another woman should not stand unconsidered. Nor should the gender assumptions that drive the conventional romantic hero to enslavement and bigamy be so easily dismissed in the wish fulfillment of Brontë's happy ending. Rhys thoughtfully and poetically reopens consideration of a classic feminist text and forces a reassessment that unsettles and enriches by exploring an overlooked and neglected female consciousness.

SEXUAL POLITICS

by Kate Millett

Kate Millett's *Sexual Politics* (1970) is the rarest of all publishing phenomena: an erudite work of cultural and literary criticism that became a best-seller. Millett's Columbia University doctoral thesis examining gender politics in history and literature was the first scholarly justification for the modern women's liberation movement and became the manifesto of the movement as well as one of the seminal works of feminist criticism. As critic Maureen Freely observed, *Sexual Politics* "attacked the very people credited as authors of sexual liberation—Freud, D.H. Lawrence, Henry Miller, Jean Genet—and gave emerging 70s feminists the sexual metaphor that went on to define their politics for years to come." Selling more than 80,000 copies in its first year, *Sexual Politics* transformed its author from an anonymous artist and teacher to a feminist icon and media target who was hailed *and* reviled as the "Karl Marx of New Feminism" and the "Mao Tse-tung of Women's Liberation." *Time* magazine, which featured Millett on its cover, claimed that prior to *Sexual Politics* "the movement had no coherent theory to buttress its intuitive passions, no ideologue to provide chapter and verse for its assault on patriarchy"; while *Life* asserted that *Sexual Politics* was "to Women's Liberation what *Das Kapital* was to Marxism." In *Sexual Politics,* Millett set the boundaries and terms for subsequent feminist criticism and paved the way for the proliferaton of feminist scholarship worldwide.

Kate Millett was born in St. Paul, Minnesota, in 1934. After her father, a civil engineer, abandoned his family when Millett was fourteen, she and her two sisters were supported by their mother, who struggled to make ends meet selling insurance on commission, having been denied a guaranteed salary reserved for male salesmen. Millett earned her B.A. degree from the University of Minnesota, in 1956, and studied Victorian literature at Oxford University, becoming the first American woman there to receive a postgraduate degree with first class honors, in 1958. After teaching college English in North Carolina and to young children in Harlem, Millett moved to Japan, in 1961, to concentrate on sculpture. First becoming interested in gender issues after reading Simone de Beauvoir's *Second Sex* at Oxford, Millett would later credit this period of her life, experiencing Japan's extreme gender inequalities, with raising her consciousness as a woman. Millett met and married fellow sculptor Fumio Yoshimura, to whom *Sexual Politics* is dedicated, and returned with him to the United States to resume her teaching and artistic career. While a doctoral candidate at Columbia University, Millett taught part-time at Barnard College and increasingly began to get involved in social reform causes.

Her direct involvement with the emerging American women's movement was stimulated after attending a lecture during the winter of 1964 to 1965 titled "Are Women Emancipated?" Millett became a founding member of the New York chapter of the National Organization of Women (NOW), in 1965, and served as the chair of its education committee, from 1966 to 1970, producing the radical pamphlet, *Token Learning: A Study of Women's Higher Education in America,* in 1968. During the 1968 student strike at Columbia, Millett actively joined the protest on the student side and was fired from her teaching position at Barnard, an experience Millett would later say inspired *Sexual Politics.* Growing out of a paper Millett delivered at Cornell, her doctoral study was directed by Victorian literature scholar Stephen Marcus, whom Millett credits with supplying the necessary guidance to produce a rigorous academic argument. "I was trying for a combination of English critical writing, . . . and then threw in a bit of American plain talk too," Millett later recalled. Millett's work-in-progress was also criticiqued by her fellow members of the Downtown Radical Women, described by Millett as "a long-vanished . . . debating society where each detail of the theory of patriarchy was hatched, rehearsed, and refined upon again." The dissertation was awarded distinction, and it appeared to considerable media attention, in 1970, as *Sexual Politics*, having been accepted in a rough draft by Doubleday editor Betty Prashker.

Sexual Politics has been described by critic Muriel Hayes as "an impressively informed, controlled polemic against the patriarchal order, launched in dead seriousness and high spirits, the expression of a young radical sensibility, nurtured by intellectual and social developments that could barely be glimpsed even twenty years ago." In it, Millett shows her break with the dominant critical practices of the time, which eschewed extrinsic literary issues over the intrinsic qualities of a literary text; she chose instead to explore the cultural context in which literary works are conceived and produced. *Sexual Politics* begins by exploring the patriarchal assumptions underpinning the works of writers Henry Miller, Norman Mailer, and Jean Genet. Her explication of sexual descriptions in excerpts from each author's work reveals "notions of ascendancy and power played within them." Dominating Millett's interpretation is the radical notion that sexual relationships are expressions of political and "power-structured relationships, arrangements whereby one group of persons is controlled by another." Buttressing her analysis is a theory of sexual politics presented in the book's second chapter, which introduces her central thesis: "When one group rules another, the relationship between the two is political. When such an arrangement is carried out over a long period of time it develops an ideology (feudalism, racism, etc.). All historical civilizations are patriarchies: their ideology is male supremacy." The chapter goes on to outline the "techniques of control"—biological, sociological, psychological, economic, educational, and others—by which patriarchal values have been enforced and sexual relationships have been defined by male dominance and female subordination. Millett's theory of sexual politics formulates a useful set of analytical categories by which history and literature might be read in gender terms, while establishing key tenets of contemporary feminist literary criticism.

Having asserted a theory of sexual politics, Millett goes on in the third and fourth chapters to provide an historical analysis of the sexual revolution, during the period 1830 to 1930, in which patriarchal values were challenged, and the subsequent period Millett calls the "Counterrevolution," from 1930 to 1960, when patriarchal ideology reasserted its dominance and control. Arguing that a successful sexual revolution should accomplish complete economic independence for women and a redefinition of traditional family structures, Millett sees in the gains made by women in education, politics, and employment reform rather than revolution, while she shows how the objectification and subordination of women have continued through the institution of marriage and modern conceptions of romantic love. In the reactionary policies of Nazi Germany and the Soviet Union, Millett demonstrates how women have been coerced to serve the ends of the state, while she convincingly shows how patriarchal institutions and ideology affect the private lives of individuals. Dealing with the ideological forces opposing gender revolution, Millett harshly rejects Sigmund Freud's psychoanalytical theory as gender bias masquerading as science: "Although generally accepted as a prototype of the liberal urge toward sexual freedom, and a signal contributor toward softening traditional puritanical inhibitions upon sexuality, the effect of Freud's work, that of his followers, and still more that of his popularizers, was to rationalize the invidious relationship between the sexes, to ratify trational roles, and to validate temperamental differences." *Sexual Politics* establishes, therefore, a theoretical, historical, and psychological framework for an understanding of the working of a patriarchal ideology in modern civilization.

Sexual Politics concludes with chapters on the "counterrevolutionary sexual politicians"—D.H. Lawrence, Henry Miller, and Norman Mailer—writers, who, "after the usual manner of cultural agents, both reflected and actually shaped attitudes." Millett's critique of these writers, along with Jean Genet, who is treated for his "homosexual analysis of sexual politics," serves as a tour-de-force model of feminist criticism in which gender assumptions and bias are deciphered in each writer's works. Lawrence, in Millett's view, sentimentally celebrates virility and female passivity; while Miller and Mailer, both prisoners "of the virility cult" Lawrence promulgated, are indicted as misogynists who degrade women. Throughout this section of the book, Millett reveals her daring, iconoclastic interpretive and rhetorical skills that have made *Sexual Politics* a feminist classic.

Sexual Politics concludes with a postscript in which Millett optimistically forecasts the possibility of the revolution to overthrow the forces of patriarchy and social repression:

> As the largest alienated element in our society, and because of their numbers, passion, and length of oppression, its largest revolutionary base, women might come to play a leadership part in social revolution, quite unknown before in history. The changes in fundamental values such a coalition of expropriated groups— blacks, youth, women, the poor—would seek are especially pertinent to realizing not only sexual revolution but a gathering impetus toward freedom from rank or prescriptive role, sexual or otherwise. For to actually change the quality of life is to transform personality, and this cannot be done without freeing humanity from the tyranny of sexual-social category and conformity to sexual stereotype—as well as abolishing racial caste and economic class.
>
> It may be that a second wave of the sexual revolution might at last accomplish its aim of freeing half the race from its immemorial subordination—and in the process bring us all a great deal closer to humanity. It may be that we shall even be able to retire sex from the harsh realities of politics, but not until we have created a world we can bear out of the desert we inhabit.

An indictment and a rallying cry, *Sexual Politics* provoked a strong reaction from critics, both positive and negative, including a rebuttal from Norman Mailer in *The Prisoner of Sex* (1971). Millett would chronicle her attempts to cope with the pressure of her celebrity in *Flying* (1974), the first in a series of autobiographical books that include *Sita* (1977), *The Loony-Bin Trip* (1990), *A.D.: A Memoir* (1995), and *Mother Millett* (2001), which deal candidly with her loves, drug dependency, and family relations. Her other nonfiction works include *The Basement: Meditations on Human Sacrifice* (1980), *Going to Iran* (1981), and *The Politics of Cruelty: An Essay on the Literature of Political Imprisonment* (1994). As in *Sexual Politics*, all of Millett's subsequent work shows her interest in the relationship between the personal and the political, and the ways in which history, culture, and ideology shape human destiny. Candid, quirky, with a single-mindedness that characterizes the polemicist, Millett blazes trails and enables further exploration. Critic Martha Bridegam, in reviewing *Mother Millett*, offers useful advice that is equally relevant to *Sexual Politics* and all of Millett's writing: "Warts and all, this book belongs in your brain. You'll argue with Kate Millett as you read, but the important part is, you'll think."

SISTERHOOD IS POWERFUL: AN ANTHOLOGY OF WRITINGS FROM THE WOMEN'S LIBERATION MOVEMENT

Compiled and edited by Robin Morgan

There is perhaps no better time capsule for an understanding of the commitment and rage that fueled the second wave of the modern women's movement, during the 1960s and 1970s, than Robin Morgan's now-classic anthology of feminist manifestos, critiques, and position papers, *Sisterhood Is Powerful* (1970). Morgan, described by Alicia Ostriker as "one of the most honestly angry women since Antigone," masterminded what has been described by Kathleen Wiegner as "one of the first of the good anthologies of the women's movement" that, in the words of Paul Robinson, "profoundly affected the way that many of us think about women and the relations between the sexes." Although there is a strong hint of the mimeographed in the collection, hastily printed slogans, incitements, and morale boosts to be rushed to the frontline of a battle in progress, Morgan's feminist reader also includes several carefully considered justifications for the radical agenda that these committed feminists advocated. Its principal value today rests in its ability to reflect the sense of urgency and importance of a gender revolution that set out to rewrite the rules of gender etiquette and women's possibilities. Lacking a time machine with which to experience firsthand the turbulent gender conflicts of the 1960s, a reader is particularly well served by this anthology, both to help explain the past and to measure the losses and gains in the gender wars ever since.

Although "conceived, written, edited, copy-edited, proofread, designed, and illustrated by women," *Sisterhood Is Powerful* seems dominated by the shaping presence of one woman—its flamboyant editor, Robin Morgan, whose own feminist conversion and activist career typify much about her era. Born in 1941, Morgan grew up in Mount Vernon, New York, where she aspired to be a doctor and a poet. "The male-supremacist society destroyed the first ambition," she has observed, "but couldn't dent the second." Morgan had become a celebrity at an early age when she hosted her own radio program in the 1940s, "The Little Robin Morgan Show," and later, when she acted in the role of Dagmar on the popular 1950s television series *I Remember Mama*. Graduating from the Wetter School in Mount Vernon at the age of fifteen, Morgan was privately tutored in the United States and Europe, from 1956 to 1959, before attending Columbia University to cultivate her skills as a poet. During the early 1960s, she began publishing her poetry while working as a literary agent and freelance editor in New York City. Much of her focus began to be dominated by radical political activities centered around civil rights and opposition to the war in Vietnam. She contributed articles and poems to such underground journals as *Liberation, Rat, Win,* and *The Guardian*. In 1962, Morgan married Kenneth Pitchford, a poet and openly homosexual cofounder of the Gay Liberation Front. In 1968, Morgan came out publicly as a lesbian in *The New York Times*, but she and her husband had a son in 1969, and remained married until 1983.

Morgan's involvement with feminism was spurred by her disenchantment with the sexism she encountered among the radical left. As Morgan recalled in her memoir, *Going Too Far: The Personal Chronicle of a Feminist* (1977):

> There were the years in the New Left—the civil-rights movement, the student movement, the peace movement, and their more "militant" offspring groups—until my inescapably intensifying women's consciousness led me, along with thousands of other women, to become a refugee from what I came to call "the male-dominated Left" and what I now refer to as "the boys' movement." And it wasn't merely the mass epidemic of bursitis (from the continual

cranking of mimeograph machines) which drove us all out, but the serious, ceaseless, degrading and pervasive sexism we encountered there, in each man's attitude and in every group's structure and in the narrow political emphases and manhood-proving tactical styles themselves. We were used to such an approach from the Establishment, but here, too?

Morgan would include in *Sisterhood Is Powerful* a section entitled "Know Your Enemy: A Sampling of Sexist Quotes," with the following examples of the sexism of the New Left:

The only position for women in SNCC is prone—Stokeley Carmichael, 1966.

The only alliance I would make with the Women's Liberation Movement is in bed—Abbie Hoffman.

Active as a member of the New York Radical Women, Morgan participated with Kate Millet and others in developing much of the theoretical formulations of the contemporary women's movement. She became publicly identified as a radical feminist during the 1968 protest of the Miss America pageant, which many regard as the catalyzing event of the second feminist wave. Other public demonstrations sponsored by WITCH (Women's International Terrorist Conspiracy from Hell), the guerrilla theater, action-oriented group she founded, included protesting the New York Bridal Fair and "hexing" Wall Street. For Morgan sexual oppression became the core source for all gender, racial, and class inequity. "I believe that sexism is the root oppression," Morgan would assert, "the one which, until and unless we *uproot* it, will continue to put forth the branches of racism, class hatred, ageism, competition, ecological disaster, and economic exploitation."

Evidence of the widespread and interconnected social oppression of sexism in contemporary culture is evident in the various articles in *Sisterhood Is Powerful,* which join the issues of class, ethnicity, race, and social equality to the persistence of gender subordination. To combat it, Morgan, in her introduction, rejects the reformist feminist views of such groups as the National Organization for Woman (NOW), which she calls a "bourgeois feminist movement that never quite dared enough, never questioned enough, never really reached beyond its own class and race," for the revolutionary change fully implied by women's liberation. Less a coherent political or social philosophy, women's liberation, in Morgan's formulation, is an internal transformation that the anthology is intended to stimulate. "I hope this book means something to you," Morgan addresses her readers, "makes some real change in your heart and head . . . because *you* are women's liberation. This is not a movement one 'joins.' There are no rigid structures or membership cards . . . . It exists in your mind, and in the political and personal insights that you can contribute to change and shape and help its growth."

Morgan comments in her introduction about the origin and nature of *Sisterhood Is Powerful*. Its original title was to have been *The Hand that Cradles the Rock*, an "at-least triple entendre" referring to William Ross Wallace's 1865 poem, "What Rules the World," with its famous lines: "The hand that rocks the cradle / Is the hand that rules the world." However, that title had been previously used by humorist S. J. Perelman, who threatened an injunction if Morgan appropriated it. "So, we were forced to change the title," Morgan declares. "Not that I now mind, having convinced myself that Sisterhood must be *very* Powerful for us to have even survived, let alone finished this damned book." She lists the "reprisals" taken on the articles' authors and the setbacks encountered: "five personal relationships were severed, two couples were divorced and one separated, one woman was forced to withdraw her article, by the man she lived with; another's husband kept rewriting the piece until it was unrecognizable as her own; many of the articles were late, and the deadline kept being pushed further ahead, because the authors had so many other pressures on them—from housework to child care to jobs. More than one woman had trouble finishing her piece because it was so personally painful to commit her gut feelings to paper. We were also delayed by occurrences that would not have been of even peripheral importance to an anthology written by men: three pregnancies, one miscarriage, and one birth—plus one abortion and one hysterectomy." The format as well as the production of *Sisterhood Is Powerful* was affected by the gender of its creators. Morgan explains, "There is also a blessedly uneven quality noticeable in the book" that is markedly different from the "linear, tight, dry, boring, male super-consistency that we are beginning to reject. That's why this collection combines all sorts of articles, poems, graphics, and sundry papers. There are the well-documented, statistically solid pieces and the intensely personal experiences." As Morgan observes, "Women's liberation is the first radical movement to base its politics—in fact, create its politics—out of concrete personal experiences." It is "also the first movement that has the potential of cutting across all class, race, age, economic, and geographical barriers—since women in every group must play essentially the same role, albeit with different sets and costumes: the multiple role of wife, mother, sexual object, baby-producer, "supplementary-income statistic," helpmate, nurturer, hostess, etc. To reflect this potential, contributors from those different groups speak in this book—and frequently disagree with each other."

Arranged into six major divisions, *Sisterhood Is Powerful* begins with a documentary look at the status of contemporary women as wives, mothers, and workers, with articles on women in medicine, publishing, in the media, academia, factories, and offices. At every level, the writers find considerable evidence of gender oppression. If the first section looks at results, the second section, "The Invisible Woman: Psychological and Sexual Repression," examines causes, with articles such as "The Politics of Orgasm," by Susan Lydon, a section from Kate Millet's *Sexual Politics,* and the now classic essay by Naomi Weisstein, " 'Kinde, Kuche, Kirche' As Scientific Law: Psychology Constructs the Female." Included is Morgan's own "Barbarous Rituals," an itemization of a lifetime of conventional gender attitudes, values, and circumstances that defines being a women, from "kicking strongly in your mother's womb, upon which she is told, 'It must be a boy, if it's so active!' " to "getting older, getting lonelier, getting ready to die—and knowing it wouldn't have had to be this way, after all."

The third section of *Sisterhood Is Powerful* widens the focus to consider the perspectives of African Americans, high school students, and "colonized women"—Chicanas in the United States and the women of China. The fourth section collects ideological responses to sexism, including articles on the politics of housework by Pat Mainardi and "Female Liberation as the Basis for Social Revolution" by Roxanne Dunbar. The anthology closes with a collection of poetry by such writers as Marge Piercy, Rita Mae Brown, and Sylvia Plath, and a compilation of historical documents, including the NOW Bill of Rights and excerpts from the infamous SCUM (Society for Cutting Up Men) Manifesto, by Valerie Solanis. An appendix provides a bibliography, a listing of Women's Liberation Movement contacts, abortion counseling information, recommended "consciousness-raising" films, and a "Drop Dead List of Books to Watch Out For."

As much as there is a quaint obsolescence about a good deal of *Sisterhood Is Powerful*, with many of its positions and poses as defunct today as the listed phone numbers of its suggested women's liberation contacts, the spirit and force of the anthology still resonate. The apocalypse forecast by the overturning of sexism that is valiantly urged here may not have materialized, and the issues of feminism more than thirty years later may have grown too complex for such easy sloganeering, but what the second wave of the feminist movement set out to accomplish remains vitally compelling in the pages of *Sisterhood Is Powerful*. The truths that Robin Morgan and her earnest sisters expose and explore still provoke and still claim consideration.

THE FEMALE EUNUCH

by Germaine Greer

Of the books that defined and fueled the second wave of the women's movement in the 1960s and 1970s, such as Betty Friedan's *The Feminine Mystique* and Kate Millett's *Sexual Politics*, Germaine Greer's *The Female Eunuch* (1970 in England; 1971 in the United States) is perhaps the most rambunctiously iconoclastic. Witty, erudite, and irreverent, *The Female Eunuch* challenged conventional wisdom about feminism and gender assumptions. If her fellow feminist commentators and critics emphasized women as victims of male repression and culturally conditioned subordination, Greer, in surveying the problems of women's sexuality, psychological development, relationship with men, as well as their social and cultural history, identified "the castration of our true female personality" as "not the fault of men, but our own, and history's." Women, Greer argued, are complicit in their powerlessness by subscribing to a conception of female identity and sexuality that has been "misrepresented by being identified as passivity." Explaining the significance of her book's title, Greer, in her introduction, summarizes her thesis that women have been raised to endorse and live up to a stereotype of the "Eternal Feminine" that shares the characteristics associated with the castrate—

"timidity, plumpness, languor, delicacy and preciosity." Women, Greer declared, have abandoned their autonomy and considerable innate powers and accepted a contrary definition of femininity that has emphasized submissiveness and helplessness. The result is dependence, resentment, and lack of sexual pleasure and life fulfillment. *The Female Eunuch,* with an unprecedented frankness and candor about women's sexuality and desires, and an irreverent and contrarian stance that leaves few truisms held by either men or women unchallenged, served as a rallying cry and incitement for women to take back control of their bodies, their pleasures, their lives, and their relationships.

The author and her book broke the mold of what was expected of a feminist and a feminist text. When many feminists were characterized as dour manhaters, Greer provided a counter persona: feisty, vital, and unapologetically libidinous. *The Female Eunuch,* less a solemn argument than a string of explosive provocations, very much revitalized the gender debate. It was described as "women's liberation's most realistic and least anti-male manifesto," and its author was touted as a "dazzling combination of erudition, eccentricity and eroticism." Christopher Lehmann-Haupt, in a 1971 *New York Times* review titled "The Best Feminist Book So Far," contrasted it favorably to Kate Millett's *Sexual Politics,* calling *The Female Eunuch* "a book with personality, a book that knows the distinction between the self and the other, a book that combines the best of masculinity *and* femininity." *The Female Eunuch* became a much talked-about best-seller, and Greer, then a thirty-one-year-old Australian professor of literature at England's Warwick University, became an international media celebrity and feminist icon, gracing the cover of *Life* magazine along with the headline: "Saucy Feminist that Even Men Like." Despite such a superficial claim to importance, Germaine Greer and *The Female Eunuch* remains one of the defining works of the women's liberation movement and a still volatile polemic that rewrites the rules of female empowerment and women's identity.

Greer's take-no-prisoners style and maverick opinions that equally shocked the feminist faithful as well as the chauvinist opposition can be traced from her background, her involvement in the 1960s counterculture, and her somewhat late and accidental interest in feminism. Born in 1939, near Melbourne, Greer was educated at a convent school and completed an honors arts degree at Melbourne University, in 1959, before doing graduate work in Sydney. Greer's antiauthoritarian ideas were shaped by a group of freewheeling intellectuals who met for discussions at the Royal George Hotel. "When I first came to Sydney," Greer recalled, "what I fell in love with was not the harbour or the gardens or anything else but a pub called The Royal George, or, more particularly, with a group of people who used to go there every night . . . and sit there and talk." Greer earned a master's degree at Sydney University, in 1962, before going as a Commonwealth scholar to Newnham College, Cambridge, where she earned a doctorate, in 1967, writing her thesis on Shakespeare's early comedies. Richard Neville, editor of the underground magazine *Oz,* for which Greer would write, described her during her Oxford days as a "militant anti-authoritarian, trained in Australia" in which a "regular diet of reasoned anarchy, sexual precocity and Toohey's Bitter helped mould her unique shock style." Between 1967 and 1972, Greer lectured in English literature at the University of Warwick, was a self-styled "super-groupie" to jazz and rock musicians, and frequently contributed to a number of underground newspapers and magazines on themes of sexual liberation and anticensorship.

Greer came to her involvement in women's issues by chance, late in her intellectual development. Greer credits the genesis of *The Female Eunuch* to her agent, who urged her to develop a book marking the fiftieth anniversary of female suffrage. " 'You should write a book why female suffrage failed,' " Greer recalled her agent suggesting. "I remember losing my temper. I thought, 'What are we talking about! Women didn't get the vote until there was nothing left worth voting for. And what do you think the vote accomplishes anyway?' " A few days later, Greer had lunch with publisher Sonny Mehta, a friend from Cambridge, who wanted to pick her brain for prospective book ideas. Greer told him what her "dumb agent" had suggested and launched into a rant attacking the idea. When she had finished, Mehta told her, "That's the book I want," and despite Greer's conviction that such a book would never sell, they returned to Mehta's office where they agreed to a contract. She would spend much of 1969 in the Reading Room of the British Museum working on the book. "I showed the first chapters to Sonny and he said nothing," Greer recalled. "And I knew I hadn't done it. One day, I suddenly realized it had to be written in short chapters; otherwise nobody would read it because women don't have spare time and their concentration span is generally brief. So I began writing short chapters." When she showed what she had done to Mehta this time, he was "speechless as usual. But I could tell by the look in his eyes that I was doing the right thing now. It was only a matter of weeks after that and it was finished." Greer, who had up to then showed little evidence of having considered women's issues other than from her own perspective as a woman in the debate over sexual liberation, had produced one of the landmark books in the debate over women's identity and empowerment. With the 1970 publication of *The Female Eunuch* Greer would be hailed as "the high priestess of women's liberation in Britain," and her reputation would be further enhanced, in 1971, on a book tour of the United States that featured a highly publicized onstage debate in New York City with Norman Mailer.

The Female Eunuch is less a coherent, sequential argument than variations and multiple perspectives on Greer's central thesis of the denial and misrepresentation of female sexuality. Called by its author "part of the second feminist wave," *The Female Eunuch* differs in its mission and approach from the work of "old suffragettes" who, after gaining the vote, allowed their energy to be "filtered away in post-war retrenchments and the revival of frills, corsets and femininity after the permissive twenties, through the sexual sell of the fifties, ever dwindling, ever more respectable." Instead of reform and accommodation to accepted gender roles and rules, Greer argues for revolution. Criticizing Betty Friedan's National Organization for Women and other "organized liberationists," Greer charges that the liberation they promise is vacuous: "At worst it is defined by the condition of men, themselves unfree, and at best it is left undefined in a world of limited possibilities." Instead, Greer asserts that a woman who desires real and radical change should "begin not by changing the world, but by reassessing herself." *The Female Eunuch* offers such a reassessment.

The book is arranged into five major sections—*Body, Soul, Love, Hate,* and *Revolution*—that consider the physical and psychological conceptions of the female and a concluding series of provocative challenges to gender assumptions once the notion of passive femininity is rejected. In *Body* Greer anatomizes "the degree of inferiority or natural dependence which is unalterably female," as well as the ways in which women's physicality has been objectified with an emphasis on the passive, producing the stereotype of the feminine that Greer considers in *Soul*. Greer describes the stereotype she calls the "Eternal Feminine," as "the Sexual Object sought by all men, and by all women. She is of neither sex, for she has herself no sex at all. Her value is solely attested by the demand she excites in others. All she must contribute is her existence. She need achieve nothing, for she is the reward for achievement. She need never give positive evidence of her moral character because virtue is assumed from her loveliness, and her passivity." Greer goes on to trace the development of this stereotype from infancy and its conditioning. The castration of women leads to the distortion of the concept of *Love*, and this section surveys the ways in which the notion of the passive female is embedded in literature, marriage, and the nuclear family. In *Hate* Greer treats the consequences of the castrated female in sections on "Loathing and Disgust," "Abuse," "Misery," "Resentment," and "Rebellion."

The Female Eunuch concludes with a call for revolution and radical alternatives to the repression of the passive female. Violence in society is attributed to displaced male virility, and women are urged to "humanize the penis, take the steel out of it and make it flesh again. What most 'liberated' women do is taunt the penis for its misrepresentation of itself, mock men for their overestimation of their virility, instead of seeing how the mistake originated and what effects it has had upon themselves. Men are tired of having all the responsibility for sex; it is time they were relieved of it." Greer asserts that if women are "to effect a significant amelioration in their conditions it seems obvious that they must refuse to marry. No worker can be required to sign on for life: if he did, his employer could disregard all his attempts to gain better pay and conditions." Women must also "reject their role as principal consumers in the capitalist state," and Greer offers alternative cooperative models to undermine capitalism's competitiveness: women "could form household cooperatives, sharing their work about, and liberating each other for days on end." However, Greer argues, "The chief means of liberating women is the replacing of compulsiveness and compulsion by the pleasure principle." By reestablishing the preeminence of spontaneity and desire, woman, in Greer's view, can break the bonds of the female castrate and achieve a transformation in gender identity and women's prospects:

> To be emancipated from helplessness and need and walk freely upon the earth that is your birthright. To refuse hobbles and defor-

mity and take possession of your body and glory in its power, accepting its own laws of loveliness. To have something to desire, something to make, something to achieve, and at last something genuine to give. To be freed from guilt and shame and the tireless self-discipline of women. To stop pretending and dissembling, cajoling and manipulating, and begin to control and sympathize. To claim the masculine virtues of magnanimity and generosity and courage.

Greer's daring challenges to the status quo energize *The Female Eunuch*. If her solutions at times veer toward the outrageous and unrealistic, her framing of essential questions about the ways women are seen and see themselves remain on point and relevant. Provocation is in fact the point of *The Female Eunuch*, as Greer states at the outset: "This book represents only another contribution to a continuing dialogue between the wondering woman and the world. No questions have been answered but perhaps some have been asked in a more proper way than heretofore. If it is not ridiculed or reviled, it will have failed of its intention."

BLACK WOMEN IN WHITE AMERICA: A DOCUMENTARY HISTORY

Compiled and edited by Gerda Lerner

Concurrent with the revived women's movement of the 1960s and 1970s was a new sense of what came to be called "black pride," fostered in the wake of the civil rights movement and the turbulent sociopolitical climate of the late 1960s. At the same time, there was a new awareness of women's cultural experience that would result in the implementation of women's studies and women's history courses in American colleges. Gerda Lerner, now a professor emeritus at the University of Wisconsin, provided the framework for the development of women's history as a recognized field of study. In the mid-1960s, Lerner, a published author then in her forties and a graduate student in history at Columbia University, wrote her dissertation on women's history, a highly unusual choice at a time when the women's movement was still in its infancy. In 1968, a year after receiving her doctorate, Lerner began a twelve-year academic career at Sarah Lawrence College, where she began and directed the first program to offer a graduate degree in women's history. She would go on to organize programs designed to train future feminist historians and to earn a reputation as one of the world's foremost scholars in her field. Lerner published books and articles that would advance the concept that class and race were central to an understanding of the role gender had played in historical events and, in 1972, she produced *Black Women in White America*, a remarkable collection of writings, lectures, and speeches of African-American women from the time of slavery to the early 1970s.

In her preface, Lerner writes, "Seeing women cast only in subordinate and inferior positions throughout history and seldom, if ever, learning about female heroines and women of achievement, American girls are conditioned to limit their own life goals and self-esteem. Black women have been doubly victimized by scholarly neglect and racist assumptions. Belonging as they do to two groups which have traditionally been treated as inferiors by American society—Blacks and women—they have been doubly invisible. Their records lie buried, unread, infrequently noticed and even more seldom interpreted." In *Black Women in White America* Lerner helps to make amends for this lack of inclusion in the historical canon by chronicling the black experience from the perspective of African-American women through a variety of documents, including diaries, slave narratives, letters, and newspaper articles, over a period stretching from 1811 to 1971.

The voices in Lerner's compilation range from unknown slaves and well-known former slaves, such as Harriet Tubman and Sojourner Truth, to school founders like Mary Macleod Bethune, Lucy Laney, Charlotte Hawkins Brown, and Nannie Burroughs; the antilynching activist and suffragist Ida B. Wells Barnett; educator, suffragist, and first president of the National Association of Colored Women Mary Church Terrell; voting rights activist Septima Clark; civil rights leaders Fannie Lou Hamer and Ella Baker; congresswoman Shirley Chisolm; and many more women who may be less familiar but whose presence provides us with equally eloquent and important revelations concerning the African-American experience. Lerner has divided the book into ten chapters, with a general introduction for each and subsections that categorize the type of document and feature separate introductions where appropriate. These introductions furnish the essential historical and biographical context necessary for a complete understanding of the documents included in the volume.

Lerner begins her documentation with the voices of women slaves. She reminds readers that slavery was a "mutually reinforcing interplay of racism and economic motivation," which became increasingly oppressive over time. The essence of this institution "was that the slave was legally a chattel, a piece of property to be bought and sold and disposed of at the master's will." Lerner includes examples of bills of sale, as well as accounts of one women sold away from her children and another who shammed illness to stay with her husband. One moving account, taken from a slave narrative dated 1844, tells the story of Moses Grandy, a slave who witnessed his wife walking by him in chains. Although it is not told from a woman's viewpoint, it illustrates the cruelty of separation that was so devastating to both wives and husbands:

> Mr. Rogerson was with them on his horse, armed with pistols. I said to him, 'For God's sake, have you bought my wife?' He said he had; when I asked him what she had done, he said she had done nothing, but that her master wanted money. He drew out a pistol and said that if I went near the wagon in which she was, he would shoot me. I asked for leave to shake hands with her which he refused, but said I might stand at a distance and talk with her. My heart was so full that I could say very little. . . . I have never seen or heard from her from that day to this. I loved her as I love my life.

Also documented are accounts of the daily lives of women slaves and how they survived, the treatment of women under slavery, and stories of escapes to freedom, which include a narrative detailing an escape "conducted" by Harriet Tubman. Also included is a harrowing journal account by Frances Kemble, a distinguished British actress who had married a Georgia plantation owner, which narrates the frustration she feels at her inability to convince her husband to allow their female slaves the customary four weeks of rest after giving birth.

Once emancipation was achieved, education for African Americans became of paramount importance. Lerner's introduction to her second chapter, "The Struggle for Education," provides a history of this struggle and gives examples of black women who were the first to excel in the arts and the professions, such as the physicians Rebecca Cole and Susan M. McKenny Steward, attorney Lutie M. Little, sculptor Edmonia Lewis, and poet Phillis Wheatley. Lerner also points out that nineteenth-century black (and white) women "took up teaching, not as an avocation, but because it was, for a woman, the only respectable means of earning a living." The documents contained in the chapter highlight the efforts of black women teachers and school founders during Reconstruction and afterwards as they endeavored to teach the freedmen and to find innovative methods of instruction, worked to keep the schools they founded from failing through fundraising initiatives and considerable frugality, and faced the challenge of teaching in the "underfinanced, poorly equipped, and overcrowded" schools in the south during the Jim Crow era, a time of institutionalized racial segregation.

Teaching was not the only way in which African-American women earned a living. Lerner offers examples of twentieth-century women engaged in domestic work (Lerner names a figure of some 1,017,000), which includes accounts that reveal the exploitation of black domestics by white families—the poor wages paid to these workers and the punishing hours experienced by them—as well as pieces on the union organization of domestic workers in Atlanta and the Domestic Workers' Union. The writings and speeches of black women factory workers show that they fared little better, usually working longer hours and earning less than white women. Except for the southern tobacco and textile industries, where they were considered unskilled labor, African- American women were denied access to factory work until World War I. During World War II, writes Lerner, "black women worked in the war industries, entered the automobile, textile, electrical and transportation industries in large numbers, and worked in hospitals, schools and other institutional occupations. But the temporary gains of the war periods were quickly eroded in the postwar years, when black women were the first to be fired from wartime jobs and through economic need were forced back into domestic and other service jobs." Still, postwar union activity was present, primarily in the south, as examples of articles concerning rank-and-file workers and union organizers show. "The nation won't ever be free," asserted factory worker Luannna Cooper, in a speech given at a Progressive Party Conference in 1949, "unless people learn the truth. Speeches is all right but you might as well be asleep if you just have speeches. I tell you, black and white, we can't survive without the other. We got to organize."

In "A Woman's Lot," Lerner gives examples of what she calls "the special victimization," chiefly sexual, of African-American women, in documents dating from the nineteenth century through 1959. She describes the abusive treatment, including rape, of black women as "essential" to "the functioning and perpetuation" of an institutionalized racist system. In one account given to the national newspaper, *The Independent*, by "A Southern Colored Woman," in 1912, a black nurse asserts that she and other black women are little more than slaves, as well as the objects of lust: "On the one hand, we are assailed by white men, and, on the other hand, we are assailed by black men, who should be our natural protectors; and whether in the cook kitchen, at the washtub, over the sewing machine, behind the baby carriage, or at the ironing board, we are but little more than pack horses, beasts of burden, slaves!" (The theme of black women during the nineteenth and early twentieth centuries as little more than slaves despite emancipation is reiterated throughout the book.) Lerner also addresses and provides documentation of what she calls "the myth of the 'bad' black woman," sustained by a racism that mythologized the sexual potency of African Americans, both men and women. By this wayward definition, writes Lerner, "Every black woman was . . . a slut . . . therefore to assault her and exploit her sexually was not reprehensible and carried with it none of the normal communal sanctions against such behavior." Lerner advances this mythology to include the practice of lynching and highlights the efforts of antilynching activists, which includes an illuminating example from Ida B. Wells Barnett's celebrated *A Red Record*, her statistical survey of lynching.

The black family unit was a crucial component of survival for African-American women in a white-dominated society. In "Survival is a Form of Resistance," Lerner writes, "The black family established its own form of existence in response to the environment. Theirs was not the small and vulnerable nuclear family of white America, but the extended kinship system of rural folk and of the poor who cooperate that each child may live and survive. . . . Black women stood beside and with their men, doing their share and more, taking over when there was a need, seeing to it that the race survived." The struggles of black families are documented here. The chapter also includes a letter from Mrs. Henry Weddington, written to President Franklin Roosevelt, in 1941, in which she addresses the terrible labor situation among African Americans and writes in part:

> Why must our men fight and die for their country when it won't even give them a job that they are fitted for? They would much rather fight and die for their families or race. Before it is over many of them might. We did not ask to be brought here as slaves, nor did

we ask to be born black. We are real citizens of this land and must and *will* be recognized as such! . . . If you are a real Christian you can not stand by and let these conditions exist.

The last half of Lerner's compilation documents the experiences of African-American women in politics and government, benevolent societies and the national club movement, the Herculean struggle to deal with and overcome prejudice and racism before and during the years of Jim Crow, the battle to achieve integration, the fostering of black pride, and issues concerning black women and womanhood, which includes a 1970 *Washington Post* column by journalist Renee Ferguson on the subject of women's liberation and its meaning for black women. Regarding the entry of black women into political life, Lerner cites examples of clubwomen who were suffragists and the increased political activity of African-American women after passage of the nineteenth amendment. One of these post-suffrage women was Mrs. Robert M. Patterson, who ran as a Socialist candidate for the Philadelphia Assembly in 1922. In an article printed in *Women's Voice*, Mrs. Patterson called for greater opportunity for black women in public service: "In these times of unrest we need women of the type of Harriet Tubman and Sojourner Truth. Women of mental ripeness, courage and clearness of purpose and a burning spirit to dare and to do. . . ." Examples of calls for racial pride are given in documents dating from 1833 to a 1970 assertion of the necessity for black nationalism by Dara Abubakari (Virginia E.Y. Collins), a New Orleans grassroots com-munity leader and voting rights activist who gave up hope, writes Lerner, "that working from within the establishment can benefit black people." In a taped interview with Lerner, Abuba-kari compares the experience of African Americans to that of the Jews who achieved statehood with the creation of Israel and insists, "Black people have to get freedom for themselves; it cannot be given to them. . . . The only thing you can aspire to is nationhood."

The last voice in *Black Women in White America* belongs to Fannie Lou Hamer, who, in a 1971 speech given at the NAACP Legal Defense Fund Institute, speaks of the "special plight and role of black women" as a 350-year-old condition ripe for change:

We have a job as black women, to support whatever is right, and to bring justice where we've had so much injustice. . . . You see now, baby, whether you have a Ph.D., D.D., or no D, we're in this bag together. And whether you're from Morehouse or Nohouse, we're still in this bag together. Not to try to fight to try to liberate ourselves from the men—this is another trick to get us fighting among ourselves—but to work together with the black man, then we will have a better chance to just act as human beings and to be treated as human beings in our sick society.

Black Women in White America is essential reading for those interested in both black history and women's history. What makes the collection unique and so comprehensive is the presence of African-American women in an inspiring union of race, class, and gender. The voices in Lerner's extraordinary compilation speak to us with a directness that demands our empathy and our respect, and allows us to achieve an understanding of the struggles, the strength, the pride, and the sense of community that has historically defined the experience of African-American women in white America.

FROM REVERENCE TO RAPE: THE TREATMENT OF WOMEN IN THE MOVIES

by Molly Haskell

First published in 1973, Molly Haskell's pioneering discourse on the treatment of women in film arrived at a time when the revived women's movement, sparked by Betty Friedan's *The Feminine Mystique* and launched during the second half of the 1960s, had gained momentum, and literature examining the status of women began to proliferate. The era saw the burgeoning of women's studies as an academic discipline and the emergence of feminist film theory, which had its beginnings with *From Reverence to Rape: The Treatment of Women in the Movies*—since the 1970s a studied text in college film and women's studies courses.

Born in 1939, in Charlotte, North Carolina, Molly Haskell received her undergraduate degree from Sweet Briar College and then studied at the University of London and the Sorbonne. Before turning to film criticism, she worked as a public relations associate and at the French Film Office in New York. Haskell has reviewed movies for the prestigious film journals *Film Comment* and *Film Heritage*, for the *Village Voice*, *Vogue*, and *New York Magazine*, and has been a regular film reviewer for National Public Radio, as well as a member of the selection committee of the New York Film Festival and an associate professor at Barnard College. She has also written the "New Yorker" diary column for *The New York Observer* and taught writing at Marymount Manhattan College. Haskell's other books include *Love and Other Infectious Diseases: A Memoir* (1990), which chronicles her relationship with her husband, noted film critic Andrew Sarris, during Sarris's life-threatening bout with encephalitis, and *Holding My Own in No Man's Land: Women and Men, Film, and Criticism* (1997).

In *From Reverence to Rape* Haskell analyzes traditions of different types of women portrayed in American and European films. She explores the images of women created in film, the stars who filled those images or defied them, and the attitudes of their directors. Her focus is on the screen's heterosexual relationships, although, addressing the broader social context of the real world, she does ask, as have some questioning feminists since the beginning of the women's movement, "Is the separatism advocated by the lesbians and the manhaters (and which serves, like much movement rhetoric, to exalt rather than diminish men's power) the answer?" Nevertheless, Haskell's main argument in *From Reverence to Rape* is that heterosexual film relationships degenerated from reciprocal partnerships based on mutual growth and respect to unequal couplings in which women are portrayed as sex objects. Women viewers have accepted these relationships because, as Haskell suggests in her introduction, "Like recollections of old love affairs, the images of stars that stay with us are the triumphs rather than the disappointments. We remember them not for the humiliations and compromises they endured in conforming to stereotypes, but for the incandescent moments in which their uniqueness made mockery of the stereotypes."

For Haskell, literary heroines have fared little better than those on the screen; the majority of female central characters created by the world's most celebrated male and female novelists were socialized, as Virginia Woolf famously put it, to serve "as looking glasses possessing the magic and delicious power of reflecting the figure of man at twice its natural size." Traditional heroines were forced to use beauty, wit, charm, and, all too often, gentle passivity, to attain their main goal of experiencing love and marriage, not necessarily in that order. Haskell acknowledges the presence of strong, interesting heroines in fiction and movies, but at the same time she cites a prevailing nineteenth-century literary romantic sensibility and stereotyping in film, which, during the 1970s, deserved to be challenged in a new feminist climate. "Women," she writes, "have grounds for protest, and film is a rich field for the mining of female stereotypes." After asserting that the "big lie perpetrated by Western society is the idea of women's inferiority" and delving into the psychology that supports and challenges this notion in the context of male and female film roles, Haskell deconstructs movies and women's place within them by decade, from the 1920s to the 1980s (in the 1987 revised edition).

In her discussion of the movies of the 1920s, the last decade of silent films, Haskell acknowledges that the era is difficult to decipher because the prevailing cinema art form of the time has been largely lost to us. Cineastes have come to appreciate the silent comedy of Charlie Chaplin, Buster Keaton, and Harold Lloyd, and the epic morality films of Cecil B. DeMille, but, as Haskell observes, our historical view of women on screen during the 1920s has been shaped in great part by "the crystallized images posterity has given them, a sense of the archetypal forms without the variations," primarily the sexually predatory "vamps" (the exotic and sultry Pola Negri, "party girl" Joan Crawford, Clara Bow, who radiated a playful sexuality as the "It Girl," and even the early Greta Garbo) and the "virgins" (longstanding screen child-woman Mary Pickford, sweet-faced Lillian Gish, and gamin Janet Gaynor). A hallmark of the silent screen, with its reliance on the telling gesture, was the Victorian romantic and melodramatic tradition, in which love and marriage became the virgins' reward and the vamps' redemption.

The post–World War I, post-suffrage "new woman" became more evident in the films of the 1930s—an era that Haskell, as well as other film historians, have characterized as separated by the years before and after the Hays Office of the Motion Picture Producers and Distributors of America (MPPDA) created the Motion Picture Production Code, and the movie studios implemented what came to be known as the Hays Code in 1934, in an effort to impose standards of "good taste" in American films and to soften the stars' images after the sex and murder scandals of the 1920s. The female stars of the precode era, such as Greta Garbo, Marlene Dietrich, Mae West, Jean Harlow, Claudette Colbert, and Carole Lombard, brought a liberated, "salutary" sexuality to the screen, which the Hays Office, writes Haskell, "having assumed the mantle of our national superego," suppressed.

The dramas and comedies of the mid-1930s into the 1940s

featured professional and working-class heroines, played by such stars as Katharine Hepburn, Ginger Rogers, Rosalind Russell, Jean Arthur, and Barbara Stanwyck, "who were always doing something," observes Haskell, "whether it was running a business or running just to keep from standing still. But their mythic destiny, like that of all women, was to find love and cast off the 'veneer' of independence." In writing on Katharine Hepburn, that paragon of female screen independence and individuality, Haskell cites her feminist character in the 1936 flop *A Woman Rebels* as the role that labeled her "box office poison" until 1940 and her comeback in *The Philadelphia Story*; she points out that, although she played an influential and powerful political commentator romantically and complementarily paired with Spencer Tracy's earthy sportswriter in 1942's *Woman of the Year* (the couple's first film together), her character is ultimately castigated for her professional drive and lack of interest in home and family.

Haskell refers to Hepburn again, in concert with such leading ladies as Bette Davis, Joan Fontaine, Joan Crawford, and Gene Tierney, in a chapter devoted to the so-called "woman's film"—a genre that, like "women's fiction," observes Haskell, implies "a generically shared world of misery and masochism the individual work is designed to indulge." It is not a concept found in Europe, where, Haskell writes, "affairs of the heart are of importance to both men and women and are the stuff of literature." This matinee genre, with its weepy, soap-opera-like emphasis on romantic fantasy and sacrifice, "pays tribute at its best (and at its worst) to the power of the imagination, to the mind's ability to picture a perfect love triumphing over the mortal and conditional."

During the 1940s, the decade that ushered in the genre of *film noir* in the American cinema, "Woman," writes Haskell, "came down from her pedestal and she didn't stop when she reached the ground. She kept going—down . . . to the depths of the criminal world, the *enfer* of *film noir*—and then compelled her lover to glance back and betray himself." These characters were either treacherous, two-faced women (Mary Astor in *The Maltese Falcon*, Barbara Stanwyck in *Double Indemnity*) or morally ambiguous but essentially decent (Veronica Lake in *The Blue Dahlia*, Lauren Bacall in *The Big Sleep*). The *film noir* woman "was, in fact, a male fantasy. She was playing a man's game in a man's world of crime and carnal innuendo, where her long hair was the equivalent of a gun, where sex was the equivalent of evil. . . . She is to her thirties counterpart as night—or dusk—is to day." In addition to her discussion on *film noir* antiheroines, the war dramas featuring women nurses, and the screwball and pinup beauty-queen comedies of the 1940s, Haskell mentions examples of such "superwoman" characters as Rosalind Russell's Hildy Parks in Howard Hawks's *His Girl Friday* and what she calls "perfectly balanced" couples— Lauren Bacall and Humphrey Bogart in *To Have and Have Not,* and Hepburn and Tracy in *Adam's Rib.*

The postwar 1950s was marked by the demise of the Hollywood studio system and the emergence of television as a major influence. Haskell discusses the voluptuous, technicolor *femmes fatales* (Marilyn Monroe, Jane Russell, Ava Gardner, Kim Novak), the breathtaking beauties (Elizabeth Taylor, Grace Kelly), the musical comedy stars (Debbie Reynolds, Jane Powell, the early Doris Day, and Judy Garland), the "serious-artist actresses in black and white" (Anne Bancroft, Julie Harris, Patricia Neal, and Shelley Winters), as well as the ambiguous sexuality of plays by Inge and Williams on film, and the social realism and passive female sexuality in the films of directors like Elia Kazan. Of the fifties' "dumb" blond portrayers, Haskell spends time on Monroe but also singles out the "glowing" Judy Holliday, who, she writes, "stretches the stereotype . . . into her own doughy shape." She presents the dilemma of the aging female star in the context of fifty-three-year-old Gloria Swanson in *Sunset Boulevard* and the forty-year-old Bette Davis character in *All About Eve,* observing that the director (in the above cases, Billy Wilder and Joseph Mankiewicz, both in their forties) projects onto these women "the narcissism, the vanity, the fear of growing old which he is horrified to find festering within himself."

Haskell next takes on the European cinema, about which she suggests that, because of "centuries of tradition and all the forces of culture," the "myths and inventions made by man" is even more prevalent than it is in American film. "In America," she interestingly observes, "men and women are not so closely and inextricably, emotionally and ideologically, bound. A woman can more easily invent herself . . . and she is proportionately less venerated." The product of such male artist-directors as Ingmar Bergman, Federico Fellini, Bernardo Bertolucci, Luis Buñuel, Francois Truffaut, Roger Vadim, Jean-Luc Godard, and Jean Renoir, the actress in European films comes across "as the result of the 'higher' sensibility projected onto her by her director." In

contrast to the heroines in American movies, the female characters in European film, even at their most archetypical—"the waif,
the rebel, the discreet bourgeoisie, the older woman, and the
whore—seem to emanate not from their own desires, but from
those of the men who both worship and fear them."

Even while citing female stereotyping in American movies produced from the 1920s to the 1960s, Haskell acknowledges and
praises the mutual support and camaraderie that existed between
the spirited heroines of these films, relationships lost during the
"swinging sixties." (These virtues would be revived in the late
1980s and throughout the 1990s in one form, as a postfeminist
"sisters" genre—or, as some have called it, a "chick flick"—exemplified by such films as *Beaches*, *Steel Magnolias*, and *Thelma and
Louise*.) Haskell characterizes the years between 1962 and 1973
as "the most disheartening in screen history." The collapse of the
star system meant that women lost the economic leverage they
once had and, in a climate of increased sexual freedom and the
loss of a phony glamour imposed upon them by the studios, were
easily exploited. "The growing strength and demands of women
in real life spearheaded by women's liberation," writes Haskell,
"obviously provoked a backlash in commercial film: a redoubling
of Godfather-like machismo to beef up man's eroding virility
or, alternatively, an escape into the all-male world of the buddy
film. . . . With the substitution of violence and sexuality (a poor
second) for romance, there was less need for exciting and interesting women. . . ." Haskell cites the presence of a handful of "illustrious" women involved in the creative end of filmmaking
during this decade, but asks, "Where are the women to create
new fictions, to go beyond the inner space—as women are doing
every day in real life—into the outer world of invention, action,
imagination?"

When Haskell revised *From Reverence to Rape*, she added a
chapter entitled "The Age of Ambivalence," in which she explored women in film from 1974 to 1987. It was a period that reflected the ambivalence women were beginning to feel, having
pursued and won a certain level of equality, and now finding it a
challenge to balance work and career—"having it all." Movies of
this era tended to feature the "superwoman" or the "crazy
woman," observing that the latter included "neurotics, murder-
ers, *femmes fatales*, vamps, punks, misfits, and free-floating loonies
whose very existence was an affront, not only to the old, sexist de-

finitions of pliant women . . . but also to the upbeat rhetoric of the women's movement." These characters were "postfeminist types whose moves were orchestrated less by male needs than by some mysterious promptings of their own." Women moviegoers of the 1980s no longer expected films to reflect their lives, "no longer expected them to, nor looked for heroines who worked, married, divorced, thrashed out the conflicts between home and career." According to Haskell, the feminism served up in mainstream films was "shallow and formulaic"; during the eighties, television was the medium that responded best to the day-to-day working and family lives of women. Haskell ends the chapter with a catalog of women filmmakers whose diversity of experience and sensibility has affected the roles women play on screen—"their very diversity a guarantee against stereotype." For Haskell, women "want nothing less, on or off, the screen, than the wide variety and dazzling diversity of male options."

When *From Reverence to Rape* first appeared, Haskell was taken to task by hard-core cineastes who felt uneasy with the concept of movies as a social indicator and by feminists who thought that she had not been ideological enough. Some reviewers felt that she had been *too* ideological. But the significance of Haskell's comprehensive study cannot be disputed. It is still relevant today as film criticism and as social criticism. As a historical document, *From Reverence to Rape* joins *Sexual Politics* (1970), *Sisterhood is Powerful* (1970), and the iconoclastic *The Female Eunuch* (1970, 1971) as an example of the powerful, now classic literature on women published during the watershed years of the women's liberation movement.

FEAR OF FLYING

by Erica Jong

Perhaps no novel by a woman has generated more notoriety than Erica Jong's iconoclastic *Fear of Flying* (1973). Not since Chaucer's Wife of Bath, DeFoe's Moll Flanders, or Joyce's Molly Bloom had a heroine—this time the creation of a woman—spoken out so frankly and candidly about her sexual appetites, fantasies, and hangups while taking control of her life in ways that defied previous gender assumptions and the roles traditionally assigned to women. *Fear of Flying,* which Jong called her "emancipation proclamation," opened the floodgate for women writers to deal honestly with sex and gender anxieties. Isadora Wing's picaresque adventures in search of sexual fulfillment and self-definition became one of the biggest selling novels of the 1970s. During the women's liberation era, Isadora and Erica, who became synonomous, served as the poster kin for the movement. Both were either admired as feminist icons or reviled and dismissed as sex-obsessed and vulgar gender transgressors. Jong would later recall the cultural moment out of which *Fear of Flying* was created by stating that "something new was beginning to happen. Women were starting to write about their lives as if their lives were as important as men's. This took great courage. It meant going against all the parental and cultural admonitions of the time. I wrote *Fear of Flying* with heart in throat, terrified by my own candor." It is the novel's candor on such formerly taboo topics such as women's sexual fantasies that both electrified and outraged its audience.

Before *Fear of Flying* had even been published, shocked type-setters refused to work on the book; meanwhile galleys were quickly disappearing from editorial offices, being passed excitedly from friend to friend, everyone wanting to get an early look at the book that would eventually become a cultural phenomenon. When Jong wrote the novel, she was a young published poet and a graduate student studying eighteenth-century English litera-ture. Despite the prepublication buzz, her publisher did little to promote her first novel. The initial reviews were tentative, and sales were sluggish. However, the book began to sell and get talked about after John Updike's review in the *New Yorker* com-pared it to a female *Portnoy's Complaint* and *Catcher in the Rye*. Updike applauded the book's "cheerful, sexual frankness," calling it "the most uninhibited, delicious, erotic novel a woman ever wrote." Henry Miller would subsequently praise Jong as "more forthright, more daring than most male writers," and predicted that *Fear of Flying* "will make literary history, that because of it women are going to find their own voice and give us great sagas of sex, life, joy, and adventure." By the end of 1974, when the book appeared in paperback, sales had reached three million copies in the United States alone, and few people were unaware of Erica Jong or the novel that *Time* magazine had dubbed "an ICBM in the war between the sexes."

The identification between Isadora Wing and Erica Jong, and the autobiographical basis of *Fear of Flying*, are unmistakable and contribute to the novel's daring intimacy. Jong was born, in 1942, on Manhattan's Upper West Side. Her father was a Broadway musician who became "a traveling salesman of tchotchkes," and her mother was a painter whose artistic aspirations were sacrificed as a homemaker. "What I remember most about my mother," Jong recalled, "was that she was always angry," and that "my mother's frustrations powered both my femininism and my writing." Her mother's warning to her daughter, that fulfillment as an artist and a woman were contradictory, sets the underlying tension of *Fear of Flying*. It caused Jong to observe, "Womanhood was a trap. If I was too much like her, I'd be trapped as she was. But if I rejected her example, I'd be a traitor to her love. I feld a fraud no matter

which way I turned. I had to find a way to be like her and unlike
her at the same time. I had to find a way to be both a girl and a
boy." Jong, like Isadora, attended Barnard College as an undergraduate and did doctoral work at Columbia in eighteenth-
century English literature before concentrating on poetry. Also.
like her protagonist, Jong's first marriage to a fellow graduate student ended in divorce, and both subsequently married Chinese-
American psychiatrists, accompanying them to Germany during
their military service. Jong's first book of poetry, *Fruits & Vegetables,*
appeared to critical acclaim, in 1971. "I started with poetry," she
recalled, "because it was direct, immediate and short. . . . I went
on to fiction because fiction can contain satire and social comment and still tell stories." As Jong summarized in her memoir,
Fear of Fifty, these stories have dealt with sexual matters, societal
hypocrisies and taboos, as well as her own life, including the subsequent divorces of her second and third husbands, a volatile
combination that marked her as an easy target:

> I have lived as I chose, married, divorced, remarried, divorced, re-
> married and divorced again—and, still worse, dared to write about
> my ex-husbands! This is the most heinous of my sins—not having
> done these things, but having confessed to them in print. It is for
> this that I am considered beyond the pale. No PR can fix this! It's
> nothing more or less than the fate of rebellious women. They used
> to stone us in the marketplace. In a way, they still do.

Fear of Flying picks up the threads of Jong's autobiography, refracted through the lens of Isadora Wing, when her marriage to
her steady but uncommunicative and predictable psychoanalyst
husband, Bennett Wing, has grown stale, and marital sex has
turned as bland as Velveeta cheese: "filling, fattening even, but no
thrill to the taste buds, no bittersweet edge, no danger. And you
longed for an overripe Camembert, a rare goat cheese: luscious,
creamy, cloven-hoofed." As Isadora accompanies her husband to
a psychiatrists' convention in Vienna, her phobia about flying serves
as a metaphor for her fear of confronting her discontent and taking charge of her life. On the flight Isadora meditates on her frustrations that married life, society's prescription that women should
seek definition and fulfillment through a man, has left her sexually restless and, as "half of something else," incomplete. Isadora
confesses, "My response to all this was not (not yet) to have an af-

fair and not (not yet) to hit the open road, but to evolve my fantasy of the Zipless Fuck," a "platonic ideal" in which zippers fall away "like rose petals" and underwear blows off "like dandelion fluff." Isadora's fantasy of faceless, anonymous sexual encounters with strangers becomes a form of liberation—of desire free of guilt and remorse—to scratch the itch she feels for both sex and solitude:

> The zipless fuck is absolutely pure. It is free of ulterior motives. There is no power game. The man is not "taking" and the woman is not "giving." No one is attempting to cuckhold a husband or humiliate a wife. No one is trying to prove anything or get anything out of anyone. The zipless fuck is the purest thing there is. And it is rarer than the unicorn. And I have never had one. Whenever it seemed I was close, I discovered a horse with a papier-mâché horn, or two clowns in a unicorn suit.

Fear of Flying begins by reversing expected gender roles. While women have long been objectified by men, Isadora fantasizes about becoming the sexual aggressor with men now the objects of desire. Violating the traditional goal of female fulfillment in marriage, Isadora begins to wonder whether her itch might be satisfied by sex without responsibilities or consequences. Isadora's fantasized alternative comes in the form of British Laingian analyst Adrian Goodlove, who seems to answer Isadora's dream of liberating and uncomplicated gratification. Adrian, a self-proclaimed free spirit, urges Isadora to cast off her marital ties and live under the sway of immediate sensation, as outlined by his self-directed existential philosophy. He appears to be Isadora's unicorn, and her struggle between faithfulness to Bennett and her urge to fly with Adrian is finally resolved in his favor when Isadora agrees to accompany Adrian on a hedonistic romp through Europe. What Isadora discovers, however, is not liberation but a different kind of confinement. She has simply exchanged one defining man, her husband, for another, her lover, and her odyssey turns into "desperation and depression masquerading as freedom." Adrian, the priapic principle, is all attitude without substance and is frequently impotent. His no-rules philosophy that calls for casting off all ties and responsibilities turns out to be a fraud as he abandons Isadora in Paris, after two weeks, to meet his wife and children for a prearranged vacation in Brittany.

Having cast off her husband and in turn been cast off by her lover, Isadora is forced into a reassessment of motive and identity:

> I said my own name to try to remember who I was: "Isadora, Isadora, Isadora, Isadora . . . Isadora White Stollerman Wing . . . Isadora Zelda White Stollerman Wing . . . B.A., M.A., Phi Beta Kappa. Isadora Wing, promising younger poet, Isadora Wing, promising younger sufferer. Isadora Wing, feminist and would-be liberated woman. Isadora Wing, clown, crybaby, fool. Isadora, wit, scholar, ex-wife of Jesus Christ. Isadora Wing, with her fear of flying. Isadora Wing, slightly overweight sexpot, with a bad case of astigmatism of the mind's eye. . . . Isadora Wing whose mother wanted her to fly. Isadora Wing whose mother grounded her. Isadora Wing, professional patient, seeker of saviors, sensuality, certainty. Isadora Wing, fighter of windmills, professional mourner, failed adventuress. . . .

Isadora's litany of identity contradictions eventually helps lead her to a truth: "I was trapped by my own fears. Motivating everything was the terror of being alone." Underlying her relationship with husbands and lovers was a fear of facing herself, unsupported or unvalidated by a mate: "I wanted to lose myself in a man . . . to be transported to heaven on borrowed wings." Accepting this truth about herself, Isadora takes her first steps toward real flight and freedom as her own person, resolved to put an end to "this nonsense of running from one man to the next." Accompanying this realization is the actualization of her fantasy of the zipless fuck with a stranger on a train that is far closer to rape than a platonic ideal of uncomplicated, mutually empowering sex. Isadora thereby realizes that liberation is not a simple matter of exchanging the prescribed female role for that of the male aggressor. Although the novel's sexual candor got all the headlines, the thematic trajectory of *Fear of Flying* has less to do with zippers than with identity, the way gender assumptions constrain and limit. Jong has declared that *Fear of Flying* is "not an endorsement of promiscuity at all." It is instead "about a young woman growing up and finding her own independence and finding the right to think her own thoughts, to fantasize."

As the novel closes, Isadora, soaking in the bathtub of Bennett's London hotel room while awaiting his return and the uncertain resolution of their marital status, manages to lose her fear of being herself. Cleansed of guilt and remorse about her past and present, Isadora is reborn on her own terms—flaws, fantasies, and all. Jong would later write of the ending of *Fear of Flying*:

> In the days when *Fear of Flying* was written it was still a novelty for a heroine to reach out for independence and not die as a result of her hubris. In the great novels about women of the nineteenth century, *Anna Karenina* and *Madame Bovary*, death was the inevitable result of a woman's quest for life beyond the bourgeois sphere (which invariably took the form of a love affair—the only stab at independence available to most women). I felt considerable pressure to kill off Isadora at the end of *Fear of Flying*. I contemplated the heroine's suicide a la *Madame Bovary* or *Anna Karenina;* I also contempated capitulation to bourgeois marriage, an out-of-wedlock pregnancy, and a then-fashionable trek into the wilderness to join a (female) commune. Thank the Goddess, I opted for none of these. My deepest hunch as a novelist was to stick with what the character of Isadora would *really* do under the circumstances. She would go home—chastened, changed, empowered, and redeemed by her adventure—and life would go on.

For all its bluster and the shock value of a fully fleshed heroine with graphic appetites and psychosexual hangups, *Fear of Flying* makes its strongest claim by dramatizing a character's hard-fought struggle toward female independence and autonomy. Isadora Wing would become the prototype for a new kind of literary heroine—no-nonsense, self-possessed, and self-determining—whose conflicts and triumphs, her fears and her flights, continue to resonate more than thirty years later.

AGAINST OUR WILL

by Susan Brownmiller

Until the 1970s, rape victims who brought charges against their attackers were at the mercy of antiquated, insensitive legal statutes that made convictions difficult and of male judges and juries who tended to blame the victim for inciting the act or failing to prevent it. In 1906, for example, a Wisconsin court of appeals acquitted an accused rapist, despite evidence that the sixteen-year-old victim had screamed, tried to get away from her attacker, and was nearly strangled. The court ruled that because she did not testify that she had used her hands, feet, or pelvic muscles to demonstrate her lack of consent and because she was not bruised and had no torn clothing, any claim that she offered "utmost resistance" was "well nigh incredible." Forty-three years later little had changed as a Texas court acquitted an accused rapist, ruling that the victim's "feigned and passive resistance" did not constitute sufficient grounds for a case of rape.

More than any other writer, Susan Brownmiller helped to change our understanding of and response to rape in her groundbreaking book, *Against Our Will: Men, Women and Rape* (1975), which grew out of the first public rape victims' speak-out, held in 1971, at St. Clement's Episcopal Church, in New York City, which Brownmiller helped to organize. Reviewer Mary Ellen Gale called Brownmiller's long overdue history of rape and its cultural significance a work that "deserves a place on the shelf next to those rare books about social problems which force us to make connections we have long evaded, and change the way we feel about what know." A year following the book's publication, the first rape crisis center opened in Berkeley, California. Other centers followed in Michigan, Los Angeles, and Washington, D.C, and by 1980, there were over four hundred rape crisis centers nationwide. In 1975, the Michigan state legislature enacted the first comprehensive rape law reforms, specifically eliminating the physical resistance requirement and limiting the circumstances and extent to which a victim's sexual history could be introduced. In the years following, Michigan's rape laws would serve as models for other states. The transformation of our understanding of what rape is and how its victims should be treated can be traced directly to *Against Our Will*.

Born in 1935, in Brooklyn, New York, Brownmiller, after graduating from Cornell University, worked as an actress before beginning her career as a journalist, in 1959, as assistant to the managing editor of *Coronet*. During the 1960s, she worked as a national affairs researcher for *Newsweek*, a staff writer for the *Village Voice*, a reporter for NBC and ABC, and a freelance journalist writing increasingly on feminist topics. One of the first politically active feminists in New York City, Brownmiller helped found the New York Radical Feminists, in 1968, and as a member of that group took part in a number of public demonstrations, including a sit-in at the offices of the *Ladies' Home Journal*, in opposition to the magazine's demeaning treatment of women. A magazine article on Shirley Chisholm, the first black United States congresswoman, led to her first book, a biography of Chisholm for young readers, published in 1970.

Brownmiller calls her exploration of rape "a once-in-a-lifetime subject that had somehow crossed my path," and explains the genesis of *Against Our Will* in a personal statement that prefaces the book. In 1968, writing a magazine article on an interracial rape case, Brownmiller approached her subject "from the perspective of a woman who viewed a rape case with suspicion. . . . Although I conducted scores of interviews for that article, I did not seek out nor did I attempt to speak with the victim. I felt no kinship with her, nor did I admit, publicly or privately, that what had happened to her could on *any* level happen to me." In discussion with her feminist friends on the topic of rape, Brownmiller recalls denying that rape was a feminist issue at all: "Rape was a sex crime, a product of a diseased, deranged mind. . . . The women's movement had nothing in common with rape victims. Victims of rape were . . . well, what were they? *Who* were they?" Answers to these questions emerged gradually from listening to other women "who understood their victimization whereas I understood only that it had not happened to me—and resisted the idea that it could. I learned that in ways I preferred to deny the threat of rape had profoundly affected my life." The crystalization of this awareness came at the "Speak-Out on Rape" that Brownmiller helped to organize in 1971. While listening to rape victims tell their stories, Brownmiller had a significant "moment of revelation." "There, in a high school auditorium," she recalls, "I finally confronted my own fears, my own past, my own intellectual defenses. Something important and frightening to contemplate had been left out of my education—a way of looking at male-female relations, at sex, at strength, and at power." Brownmiller's view of both what rape is and its cultural significance had undergone a radical reassessment, and she concludes her personal statement by confessing that "I wrote this book because I am a woman who changed her mind about rape."

The result of four years of research and writing, *Against Our Will* provides the first comprehensive study of rape that traces its prevalence and significance in war from biblical times through the world wars to Vietnam. Brownmiller considers the origin and nature of American rape laws, the persistence of interracial rape in America from slavery onwards, and the prevailing psychological, legal, and cultural understandings of rape. "From prehistoric times to the present," Brownmiller asserts, "I believe, rape has played a critical function. It is nothing more or less than a conscious process of intimidation by which *all* men keep *all* women in a state of fear." For Brownmiller, rape becomes an instrument of patriarchal rule and a deadly and demeaning metaphor for male-female relationships. Central to her thesis is a paradigm-shifting redefinition of rape, in which Brownmiller argues that it is not a sexual act but an assertion of power based on an "anatomical fiat," the result of early man's realization that women could be subjected to "a thoroughly detestable physical conquest from which there could be no retaliation in kind." As Brownmiller asserts, "For if the first rape was an unexpected battle founded on the first woman's refusal, the second rape was indubitably planned. Indeed, one of the earliest forms of male bonding must have been the gang rape of one woman by a band of marauding men. This accomplished, rape became not only a male prerogative, but man's basic weapon of force against woman, the principal agent of his will and her fear. His forcible entry into her body, despite her physical protestations and struggle, became the vehicle of his victorious conquest over her being, the ultimate test of his superior strength, the triumph of his manhood."

Having speculated on rape's origin and gender implications, Brownmiller documents the persistence of rape as an instrument of power and control over women, which is shown as an ever-present aspect of warfare, uprisings, riots, and revolutions throughout human history. Brownmiller records rape atrocities from Troy to Vietnam and in Bangladesh, where a quarter of a million women, ravaged by their enemies, were cast out by their husbands as unclean. She treats rapes by whites and Indians throughout the settling of America, as well as by white slaveholders on their human property, and speculates on the connection among rape, marriage, and family life. "Female fear of an open season of rape," Brownmiller asserts, "and not a natural inclination toward monogamy, motherhood or love, was probably the single causative factor in the original subjugation of woman by man. . . . The most important key to her historic dependence, her domestication by protective mating." The price of such protection, Brownmiller argues was legal subordination: "Man's historic desire to maintain sole, total, and complete access to woman's vagina, as codified by his earliest laws of marriage, sprang from his need to be the sole physical instrument governing impregnation, progeny, and inheritance right." Rape was conceived as theft, a violation of property laws in which the male protector, not the woman victim, was traditionally compensated. At the time *Against Our Will* appeared, rape statutes still exempted a woman's spouse from the prohibition of forcible sexual intercourse. The legal protection of a husband's right of unconditional access to his wife's body "gives the lie to any concept of equality and human dignity. . . . A sexual assault is an invasion of bodily integrity and a violation of freedom and self-determination wherever it happens to take place, in or out of the marriage bed." Far from being psychopaths acting out aberrant urges, Brownmiller suggests that "men who commit rape have served in effect as frontline masculine shock troops, terrorist guerrillas, in the longest sustained battle the world has ever known." Rape must be understood, Brownmiller declares, as a persistent factor of our social order, a fundamental aspect of male-female relations, supported by a culture and a legal system that blames the victim and exonerates (and even glamorizes) the perpetrator. "As man conquers the world," Brownmiller states, "so too he conquers the female. Down through the ages, imperial conquest, exploits of valor and expressions of love have gone hand in hand with violence to women in thought and deed."

Against Our Will concludes by suggesting some means to break what poet Adrienne Rich would call a "rape culture," including ending the protection of husbands who force their wives to have sex, overturning employed standards of resistance and consent in dealing with rape, and striving for gender equality among law enforcement to encourage women to come forward to make sexual assault complaints that will be believed and taken seriously. "Once we accept as basic truth that rape is not a crime of irrational, impulsive, uncontrollable lust, but is a deliberate, hostile, violent act of degradation to intimidate and inspire fear, we must look toward those elements in our culture that promote and propagandize these attitudes. . . ." These include prostitution and pornography, which, Brownmiller asserts, contribute to "the false perception of sexual access as an adjunct of male power and privilege" and dehumanize women. The ultimate protection, she argues, for women against rape is self-defense and fighting back. "That is the activity we must engage in, together, if we—women—are to redress the imbalance and rid ourselves and men of the ideology of rape." Brownmiller ends *Against Our Will* with a challenge: "My purpose in this book has been to give rape its history. Now we must deny it a future."

LOOKING FOR MR. GOODBAR

by Judith Rossner

Judith Rossner's chilling and complex exploration of the descent of her central character, Theresa Dunn, into a sexual hell that ends with her murder at the hands of one of her bedmates is very much a novel of its time. *Looking For Mr. Goodbar* is primarily set in the Manhattan of the 1960s, the decade in which the sexual revolution and singles bars coexisted with the beginnings of the women's movement. It was published in 1975, at the height of what had come to be widely known as "women's lib," when drugs, rock 'n' roll, self-help, and a distaste for permanent commitment together with a fear of intimacy had been firmly ensconced in American culture, and the overheated "disco" era of Studio 54 and sex clubs like Plato's Retreat—all of which would help to define the 1970s as the "Me Decade"—was about to begin. *Looking For Mr. Goodbar* is one of the most important women's novels to come out of the 1970s, not only because it is an illuminating and cautionary tale of its time, but also because of Rossner's ability to make the reader feel the intensity of Theresa's thoughts, feelings, and experiences as she copes with her lack of self-esteem and a painful loneliness dating from childhood by rejecting love and companionship in favor of the promiscuous sexuality that will eventually cause her death.

Looking For Mr. Goodbar was Rossner's fourth novel. A native New Yorker, Judith Perelman Rossner (born in 1935) was early encouraged to become a writer by her mother, who was a teacher. At nineteen she dropped out of City College to marry Robert Rossner, a teacher and writer; the couple would have two children and later divorce. She worked in the advertising department of *Scientific American*, work she enjoyed but which she felt distracted her from the novel she was writing. She later opted for a less demanding job in real estate and finished her manuscript, which she did not publish. In 1966, she produced her first published novel, *To the Precipice*, the account of a Jewish woman raised in a New York tenement, who marries a wealthy gentile rather than commit herself to a self-made lawyer she has known from childhood and with whom she feels a more passionate attachment. The theme of separation and the conflict between selfishness and altruism is explored in *To the Precipice* and in Rossner's next two novels: *Nine Months in the Life of an Old Maid* (1969), the story of a self-absorbed insane woman who lives in isolation with her sister, and in *Any Minute Now I Can Split* (1972), a darkly comic tale of commune life. It is also seen in *Looking For Mr. Goodbar*. The genesis of Rossner's fourth novel was a piece she was asked to write for a women's issue of *Esquire* magazine on Roseann Quinn, a twenty-seven-year-old teacher who had recently been murdered by a man she had taken home with her from a singles bar. After *Esquire*'s lawyers decided not to let the story run, Rossner decided to write it as a novel.

Looking For Mr. Goodbar begins with the background of Gary Cooper White, the young drifter who has fled to New York to avoid arrest in Florida for armed robbery, and who has killed Rossner's protagonist after meeting her in a singles bar called Mr. Goodbar and taking her back to her apartment for sex. Rossner gives us White's taped confession while he is in police custody, then relates the story of the victim, Theresa Dunn, from her lower-middle-class Irish-American childhood in the Bronx to her murder on New Year's Day, 1970. Theresa, a first-grade teacher, has grown up with a sense of being damaged, both physically and emotionally. At four she contracted a mild case of polio, which was followed by scoliosis and surgery that resulted in a year spent in the hospital; this has left her overly sensitive about the worm-like scar on her back, her slight limp, and her weight. She has grown up with the belief that her parents do not love her, and she is emotionally detached from them, as well as from her outgoing, tomboyish younger sister, Brigid, who is happily married and has produced several offspring.

Theresa's closest family ties have been to her older siblings, Thomas and Katherine. She was especially fond of Thomas, who was eleven years older than her and her mother's favorite. It was Thomas who visited her in the hospital and read to her throughout her illness; his death in a training-camp gun accident at eighteen devastated the family. Theresa's relationship with Katherine, while close, is strained: she resents Katherine's beauty, the ease with which she obtains what she wants, and what Theresa feels is her status as their father's favorite. Theresa's family and the other characters in the novel are stereotypes that help to reveal the author's themes through her central character. Katherine, for example, typifies a certain kind of sixties woman: self-confident and sophisticated, she has aggressively taken part in whatever has been on offer in the New York bohemian world of the early-to-mid years of the decade and the hippie culture of the late sixties. Experimental, yet careful to make appropriate choices, Katherine has a gift for surviving and thriving that is lacking in her sister.

Theresa's first sexual experience is with her cynical City College English professor, Martin Engle, who takes an interest in her writing and hires her, ostensibly as a secretary, but in reality to seduce her. When she tells him, "I love you so much, Martin," he replies with his customary irony, "Ah, yes. . . . Love." Before she sleeps with Martin, Theresa envisions a romantic scenario concerning him that also contains a hint of her sexual predilection: "In her fantasies his wife had just died in an automobile accident and he had sent for her. He made love to her passionately after explaining that all love had gone from his marriage for years. Sometimes they played a game called Threshold of Pain, in which he and many assistants tested her to see where pleasure ended and pain began. . . ." During their affair, Martin fulfills a requirement that is important to Theresa in her romantic relationships: he talks to her. She values this quality in James Morrisey, her would-be fiancé and the only person to whom she can confess her love of teaching (she has difficulty sharing her feelings with her few women friends and avoids joining a women's "consciousness-raising" group).

When her affair with Martin Engle predictably ends, Theresa, disillusioned by love and fearful of rejection, turns to what becomes her drug of choice: sex. Finding bed partners in bars is all too easy, and she embarks on a series of casual one-night encounters with a variety of men, most of them nameless. The men we meet include Eli, a former Hassidic Jew who has changed his named to Ali, rejected his community, and lives in an untidy loft; and Victor, who is in New York on business, and with whom she shares a weekend of sex at his hotel. Theresa feels both comforted and constricted by her secret sexual roundelay and almost incredulous concerning the duality of her life:

> Actually, when she thought about it at all, she didn't really feel that she *had* a life, one life, that is, belonging to a person, Theresa Dunn. There was a Miss Dunn who taught a bunch of children who adored her ("Oh, that's Miss Dunn," she'd heard one of her children say once to a parent. "She's one of the kids. A big one.") and there was someone named Terry who whored around in bars when she couldn't sleep at night. But the only thing those two people had in common was the body they inhabited. If one died, the other would never miss her—although she herself, Theresa, the person who thought and felt but had no life, would miss either one.

Theresa's longest lasting and most sexually satisfying relationship is with Tony, an Italian-American garage attendant who makes love to her to the blare of rock 'n' roll. The couple never talks and never goes out, preferring instead to stay in bed. The one time Theresa ventures out with him as his girlfriend, it is to the Bronx for his mother's birthday. There, Tony physically attacks his mother's boyfriend and hits Theresa, thus essentially ending their relationship. With Tony gone, Theresa becomes closer to the patient, forbearing James, who loves her but who does not give her the sexual pleasure she craves. She cannot commit to him because she feels he does not see her realistically; that is, as the damaged person she truly is. When James gives her a ring at Christmas, Theresa has a panic attack, and he takes her home, where she voices her resentment of the ring as an emblem of ownership and control. However, after he leaves, she becomes distraught at the thought that she has lost him and admits to herself that "if James disappeared from her life he would leave an enormous gap that couldn't easily be filled."

All alone at New Year's, Theresa feels a sense of panic: "She felt as though she were walking a tightrope and certain moves would send her plunging, but she had no way of knowing exactly what they were." She resolves to begin a diary and starts to write, but her thoughts roll back to Martin Engle and she cannot get beyond the date: "How could you begin a diary not long before your twenty-seventh birthday without ever saying anything about what happened before? And what could she say about what had happened before? What was there to say about her life?" Overwhelmed by loneliness and feeling in desperate need of sex, Theresa visits Mr. Goodbar, where she picks up the man who will shortly murder her. Her last thoughts are calls for help from James and from Mommy and Daddy, who cannot save her now.

Looking For Mr. Goodbar was a best-seller praised by reviewers for its great sensitivity and skill. *The New York Times* book reviewer observed, "It is a measure to 'Mr. Goodbar's' richness and complexity that it can be viewed on many levels. Catholics might view it as a passion play: feminists might consider Theresa a political victim of rape." In truth, Theresa *is* a victim—of her childhood, her religion, and the culture of sexual freedom. Judith Rossner has masterfully evoked a culture that glorified sensation without understanding in a novel that calls into question the true meaning of "women's liberation."

THE WOMAN WARRIOR

by Maxine Hong Kingston

Maxine Hong Kingston's *The Woman Warrior* (1976) is one of the singular achievements of modern American literature. The first work by an Asian-American writer to gain widespread popularity and critical acclaim, it revolutionized accepted literary forms, creating a new genre that has been called "the creative memoir," and spawning an ongoing and important exploration of the American experience from personal, ethnic, cultural, and gender perspectives. Subtitled "Memoirs of a Girlhood Among Ghosts," *The Woman Warrior* presents the coming-of-age and coming-to-terms saga of an Asian-American woman's attempt to achieve an authentic identity and liberation against the cultural and gender restrictions imposed by the intimidating and threatening specters of both Caucasian-American life and her often mystifying and stultifying Chinese heritage. The work has been described as the first postmodern autobiography in which chronological, objective narrative is abandoned in favor of fragmented, subjective moments of illumination, mixing fact and fiction that blurs the distinction between biography and legend, reality and fantasy, truth and myth. A work of remarkable originality and popular appeal, *The Woman Warrior* has become one of the most assigned texts on contemporary college campuses, appearing on syllabi in course offerings in English, ethnic studies, women's studies, American studies, Asian studies, Asian-American studies, anthropology, sociology, history, and psychology. Clearly, the relevance and resonance of *The Woman Warrior* has exceeded the reach of the standard memoir of growth and development from a particular ethnic, cultural, historical, or regional perspective. As scholar Sau-Ling Wong has observed, "It is safe to say that many readers who otherwise do not concern themselves with Asian American literature have read [*The Woman Warrior*]." Through the remarkable poetic and vibrant quality of her prose, her daring, experimental mixture of fictional and nonfictional elements, and her balancing of rival cultural imperatives in pursuit of synthesis, Kingston has moved in *The Woman Warrior* from the particular to the universal, chronicling an Asian-American woman's personal and family story that is also a profound exploration of gender, cultural, and human identity.

Born Maxine Ting Ting Hong in Stockton, California, in 1940, the writer was the first of six American-born children of Chinese immigrants Chew Ling Yan and Tom Hong. Her father was trained in China as a scholar and teacher, and immigrated to the United States in 1925. Working as a laborer, he was eventually able to save enough to invest in a laundry in New York's Chinatown. Maxine's mother (Brave Orchid in *The Woman Warrior*) remained in China and was separated from her husband for fifteen years. During the interim, she trained in medicine and midwifery, and worked as a physician, a remarkable accomplishment for a Chinese woman of the time. She joined her husband in the United States in 1939 in Stockton, California, where Tom Hong had become the manager of an illegal gambling house owned by a wealthy Chinese immigrant. Maxine was named for an often lucky blond gambler. During World War II, the Hongs started a laundry in Stockton, where Kingston and her siblings were put to work as soon as they were old enough to help. The laundry became an informal Chinese community center where Kingston heard the "talk-stories" she would later draw on in her writing and characterized as "a tradition that goes back to prewriting time in China, where people verbally pass on history and mythology and genealogy and how-to stories and bedtime stories and legends. . . . [At the laundry] I would hear talk-story from everyone who came in. So I inherited this amazing amount of information, culture, history, mythology, and poetry." Speaking only Chinese until she

started school, Maxine failed kindergarten in part because she refused to speak. Gaining fluency and an increased mastery of expression in English, Kingston eventually excelled as a student,
publishing her first essay, "I Am an American" in *American Girl*,
in 1955, when she was still in high school. She attended the
University of California at Berkeley on a scholarship, graduating
in 1962 with a degree in English. The same year she married Earll
Kingston, an actor and fellow Berkeley graduate. Earning a
teaching certificate, Kingston taught English and mathematics in
a California high school for five years. Disillu-sioned with the
1960s drug culture and the ineffectiveness of the protest movement against the Vietnam War, the couple, with their young son,
left California, in 1967, en route to Japan. Stopping off in Hawaii,
they would remain there for the next seventeen years. Kingston
taught English, language arts, and English as a second language
at several high schools and business and technical colleges, and
for two and a half years she worked on the manuscript that would
become *The Woman Warrior.*

Kingston originally intended the work to be combined with the
stories that eventually made up *China Men* (1980) as "one big
book," exploring identity formation and cultural conflict faced by
Chinese Americans, based on her own experiences and her relationship with her mother and father and her relatives. Avoiding
the restrictions of "standard autobiography," which she identified
as dealing with "exterior things" or "big historical events that you
publicly participate in," Kingston concentrated instead on what
she called "real stories," narratives mixing facts and the imagination, dramatizing "the rich, personal inner life." Her publisher
insisted that the project be divided into two volumes and catego-
rized as nonfiction. *The Woman Warrior* was published in 1976, to
universal acclaim, winning the National Book Critics Circle
Award and establishing Kingston as a major writing talent. The
book was described by reviewer William McPherson as "a strange,
sometimes savagely terrifying and, in a literal sense, wonderful
story of growing up caught between two highly sophisticated and
utterly alien cultures, both vivid, often menacing and equally
mysterious." *The Woman Warrior* explores the forces of heritage,
family, and personal experience that impact the lives of women
and must be confronted before any genuine autonomy and liberation can be achieved. "Chinese-Americans," Kingston writes,
"when you try to understand what things in you are Chinese, how

do you separate what is peculiar to childhood, to poverty, insanities, one family, your mother who marked your growing with stories, from what is Chinese? What is Chinese tradition and what is the movies?" *The Woman Warrior* attempts to answer these questions, dealing in imaginative terms with the status of Asian women in America and the various burdens and responsibilities faced by all women.

Divided into five sections, each centered on a talk-story, *The Woman Warrior* provocatively begins with a family secret and a warning:

> "You must not tell anyone," my mother said, "what I am about to tell you. In China your father had a sister who killed herself. She jumped into the family well. We say that your father has all brothers because it is as if she had never been born."

Told to the narrator by her mother, Brave Orchid, as a "story to grow up on," the fate of "No Name Woman," who bears a child two years after her husband's departure for America, is intended as a sobering lesson to a maturing daughter of the dangers of unsanctioned sexuality and the consequences of a Chinese woman's transgressing the traditional gender rules—subservience to male authority and repression of personal desires—she is expected to obey. For her sexual indiscretion, the narrator's aunt provokes the community's wrath, and the villagers kill the family's livestock and destroy their possessions. A pariah who has caused her family shame and misery, No Name Woman gives birth unattended in a pigsty, kills herself and her newborn, and is sentenced by her own family to the anonymity of a nonperson; even her name is obliterated. This striking story establishes the costs and consequences of challenging the established, patriachal values of Chinese tradition, while the narrator's breaking the taboo of silence and imaginatively restoring aspects of her aunt's history and identity establish central themes of *The Woman Warrior*, including the repression faced by Chinese women and the harsh retribution suffered by transgressors, as well as the redemptive power of the imagination to restore the life of the voiceless and forgotten.

The second section, "White Tigers," recasts the legendary story of Fa Mu Lan—a woman warrior who takes her father's place in battle and avenges her family's wrongs that are carved onto her back—as an alternative Chinese myth in contrast to the

submissive, subservient female myth revealed by the fate of No
Name Woman. For the narrator, the thrilling adventures of a fantasized woman warrior invites a sustaining identification. Refusing
to be the passive victim of racist and sexist acts, the narrator, like
Fa Mu Lan, sees her writing as a different kind of fighting, declaring:

> The swordswoman and I are not so dissimilar. May my people un-
> derstand the resemblance soon so I can return to them. What we
> have in common are the words at our backs. The idiom for *revenge*
> are "report a crime" and "report to five families." The reporting is
> the vengeance—not the beheading, not the gutting, but the words.
> And I have so many words—"chink" words and "gook" words
> too—that they do not fit on my skin.

The middle chapter, "Shaman," presents a biographical sketch
of the narrator's mother, Brave Orchid, as the story of a modern
woman warrior. Like Fa Mu Lan, who went "away ordinary and
came back miraculous, like the ancient magicians who came
down from the mountains," Brave Orchid earns a medical degree,
bravely exorcises the malevolent "Sitting Ghost" that threatens
her school, and establishes a respectable career as a physician in
China before joining her husband in America. In contrast, "At the
Western Palace" presents the fate of Brave Orchid's sister, Moon
Orchid, a victim of sexual manipulation and submissiveness that
leads to madness. Moon Orchid has been left in Hong Kong by
her husband, who has come to America and bigamously married
a young assimilated Chinese-American woman. Brought to America
by her sister to reclaim her rights as her husband's first wife, Moon
Orchid's passivity, timidity, and subservience to established Chinese
values prohibits her reaching a positive settlement with her husband, and the radically different values she finds in America lead
to her gradual loss of sanity and self-identity, and eventual confinement to a mental asylum.

The silence and madness of No Name Woman and Moon
Orchid, therefore, stand in sharp contrast for the narrator to the
liberating possibilities of Fa Mu Lan and Brave Orchid; and the
conflict among competing gender and cultural assumptions are
applied in the book's concluding section, "A Song for a Barbarian
Reed Pipe," to the narrator's development through several events
in her childhood and adolescence. Silence and its cost is the dom-

inating theme of this portion of *The Woman Warrior* as the narrator recalls "the worst thing [she] had yet done to another person," cruelly trying to force a silent classmate to speak, a metaphor for the narrator's own inner trauma of inarticulateness, being suspended between the opposing ghosts in her life—her Chinese heritage and American life. "Once upon a time," the narrator recalls, "the world was so thick with ghosts, I could hardly breathe; I could hardly walk, limping my way around the White Ghosts and their cars." The narrator's haunting is a result both of her parents' refusal to acknowledge the reality of their American life and their imposition of the shadowy world of their Chinese past and childhood on their offspring. Regarded by the older generation of Chinese immigrants as not completely Chinese, at school the narrator finds herself insufficiently American; she is therefore alienated both from her ancestral past and her Amerian present. She is also female, judged inferior and a burden by Chinese standards, and an outsider by the dominating American patriarchy. The disjunction makes the narrator a double victim of the sexual stereotypes and racist stigmatism that threatens to destroy one's identity if one is unable to resolve these contradictions. As the narrator achieves the power to confront her mother for imposing silence on her, and is able to speak out against the various gender and racial forces that threaten her, she finds a new model, in the second-century Chinese woman poet Ts'ai Yen, to displace the swordswoman Fa Mu Lan. A prisoner of the barbarians for twelve years, Ts'ai Yen is able to recover her voice as she listens to the music of barbarian flutes and is inspired to write poetry that distills her experiences into an enduring voice that challenges her repression and achieves valuable communication:

> Ts'ai Yen sang about China and her family there. Her words seemed to be Chinese, but the barbarians understood their sadness and anger. Sometimes they thought they could catch barbarian phrases about forever wandering. Her children did not laugh, but eventually sang along when she left her tent to sit by the winter campfires, ringed by barbarians.

Ts'ai Yen is the final version of the woman warrior who, like the narrator, lives among people of a different race and offers the narrator, as a word warrior, a model for using self-expression as a means of reclaiming identity, liberation, and autonomy. By setting

Ts'ai Yen's story—along with those of No Name Woman, Fa Mu Lan, Brave Orchid, and Moon Orchid—in the context of her own experiences, the narrator ultimately achieves the means to exorcise her own ghosts, to find her own voice, and to achieve self-definition out of the various forces of gender and culture that silence, repress, and destroy. *The Woman Warrior* functions, therefore, both as a crucial record of Chinese-American experience and a dramatization of the process by which a woman, of whatever ethnicity, is forced to fashion an identity out of gender and cultural imperatives.

OF WOMAN BORN

by Adrienne Rich

Adrienne Rich, one of the most acclaimed contemporary American poets, is also an important prose writer, whose essays are collected in *On Lies, Secrets and Silence* (1979) and *Blood, Bread and Poetry* (1986), and whose most significant contribution to the debate over women's identity and empowerment is *Of Woman Born: Motherhood as Experience and Institution* (1976), one of the groundbreaking works in feminist theory. In it, Rich sets out to "examine motherhood—my own included—in a social context, as embedded in a political institution: in feminist terms." The result is one of the first attempts to understand motherhood as a cultural rather than a biological phenomenon, drawing an important distinction between "two meanings of motherhood, one superimposed on the other: the *potential relationship* of any woman to her powers of reproduction and to children; and the *institution,* which aims at ensuring that that potential—and all women—shall remain under male control." Rich calls institutionalized motherhood "a keystone of the most diverse social and political systems," which "has withheld over one-half the human species from the decisions affecting their lives; it exonerates men from fatherhood in any authentic sense; it creates the dangerous schism between 'private' and 'public' life; it calcifies human choices and potentialities. . . . It has alienated women from our bodies by incarcerating us in them." *Of Woman Born* traces the implications of this assertion and examines the role that motherhood has played in history and culture to shape the destinies of women.

Because *Of Woman Born* intentionally mixes personal testimony with research and theory, the biographical details of Rich's life and development are central to an understanding of the work. Born in Baltimore, Maryland, in 1929, Rich was the eldest of two daughters. Her father was a pathologist working as a professor and researcher at Johns Hopkins Medical School. Educated at home until the fourth grade and encouraged in her writing, her first book, *Ariadne,* was a three-act play and poems, privately printed when she was only ten. Rich would graduate with honors from Radcliffe College, in 1951, the same year that her first collection of poetry, *A Change of World,* was published in the prestigious Yale Series of Younger Poets. W.H. Auden, who selected Rich's collection for the series, declared that her poems "speak quietly but do not mumble, respect their elders but are not cowed by them, and do not tell fibs." In 1953, Rich married Alfred Conrad, an economics professor at Harvard University, and had three sons between 1955 and 1959. Preoccupied with her responsibilities as a wife and mother, Rich saw her writing languish; she broke her silence, in 1963, with the important collection, *Snapshots of a Daughter-in-Law.* "In the late fifties I was able to write," Rich recalls, "for the first time, directly about experiencing myself as a woman." The long title sequence was "jotted in fragments during children's naps, brief hours in a library, or at 3:00 A.M. after rising with a wakeful child" and explores for one of the first times in poetry the limitations faced by women in their restrictive domestic roles and in identities defined by masculine expectations. Rich's experience of motherhood would, as she declares in *Of Woman Born,* radicalize her and provide her with a central preoccupation in her poetry and prose.

When Rich's husband began teaching at New York's City College, the family relocated there, and Rich formed important relationships with fellow poets Audre Lorde and June Jordan. Rich also began her own teaching career, with stints at Swarthmore College, Columbia, Brandeis, and City College. In 1970, Rich's husband committed suicide, and, in 1976, Rich came out as a lesbian, beginning a long-term relationship with writer Michelle

Cliffe. During this period, Rich published some of her most important works, including *Leaflets* (1971), the National Book Award–winning *Diving into the Wreck* (1973), and *The Dream of a Common Language* (1977). Throughout, Rich captures in intense and striking images the challenges women face under a repressive social system that denies their human potential, while expressing the urgency to achieve a liberating and autonomous self-identity.

Many of the themes of Rich's poetry recur in *Of Woman Born*, which considers motherhood as the "experience by which women are expected to define themselves . . . and as an institution by which a male-dominated society controls and diminishes them." Calling motherhood "the great mesh in which all human relationships are entangled, in which lurk our most elemental assumptions about love and power," Rich surveys her subject from personal, anthropological, historical, and political perspectives, beginning with her own experiences as a mother of three boys. Relying on journal entries from the period, Rich, in powerful and candid language, records her ambivalence during her pregnancies and as the prime caregiver to her sons, in which she is "caught up in waves of love and hate, jealousy even of the child's childhood; hope and fear for its maturity; longing to be free of responsibility, tied by every fibre of one's being." Rich relates her guilt and anxiety over feeling inadequate as a homemaker and mother, and resentful that so much of her intellectual and artistic life was sacrificed to mind-numbing domestic chores. That she did not live up to the standard of the self-fulfilled, completed mother figure of myth led Rich to a realization: "I was effectively alienated from my real body and my real spirit by the institution—not the fact—of motherhood. This institution—the foundation of human society as we know it—allowed me only certain views, certain expectations, whether embodied in the booklet in my obstetrician's waiting room, the novels I had read, my mother-in-law's approval, my memories of my own mother, the Sistine Madonna or she of the Michelangelo *Pietà*, the floating notion that a woman pregnant is a woman calm in her fulfillment or, simply, a woman waiting. Women have always been seen as waiting: waiting to be asked, waiting for our menses, in fear lest they do or do not come, waiting for men to come home from wars, or from work, waiting for children to grow up, or for the birth of a new child, or for menopause." This insight leads Rich to consider how "the experience of maternity and the experience of sexuality have both been channeled to serve male interests." Patriarchy, she declares, "would seem to require, not only that women shall assume the major burden of pain and self-denial for the furtherance of the species, but that a majority of that species—women—shall remain essentially unquestioning and unenlightened." Patriarchal society idealizes woman as childbearer and enforces motherhood on many women who should never have had children; and it never prepares women for the contradictory emotions of loneliness and depression that is a consequence of the dissolution of sustaining kinship groups and the restriction of women from productive work outside the home. Patriarchal society, Rich asserts, has forcibly defined her and all women exclusively in maternal terms, with resistance against that restriction making her feel that she is "Kali, Medea, the sow that devours her farrow, the unwomanly woman in flight from motherhood."

A solution to this dilemma is the acceptance of a wider conception of women's identity, one in which motherhood is only "one part of the female process . . . not an identity for all time," and that alternative conceptions of maternity are possible. *Of Woman Born* juxtaposes the institution of motherhood under a patriarchal system with matriarchal systems of woman-centered beliefs and woman-centered social organizations. "Throughout most the world," Rich asserts, "there is archeological evidence of a period when Woman was venerated in several aspects, the primal one being maternal; when Goddess-worship prevailed, and when myths depicted strong and revered female figures. In the earliest artifacts we know, we encounter the female as primal power." As matriarchal society gave way to the patriarchal, women's power was restricted to childbearing alone, with women and motherhood controlled and domesticated. Woman "becomes the property of the husband-father," and a woman's value is defined exclusively by her ability to reproduce, particularly the sons who will inherit the patrimony. "Patriarchal man created—out of a mixture of sexual and affective frustration, blind need, physical force, ignorance, and intelligence split from its emotional grounding, a system which turned against woman her own organic nature, the source of her awe and her original powers."

In a review of obstetrics, Rich documents a demeaning process of control that dehumanizes women, in which childbirth is transformed from a natural process to a medical condition and the mother-to-be into a passive recipient of technology: "The loneliness, the sense of abandonment, of being imprisoned, powerless, and depersonized is the chief collective memory of women who have given birth in American hospitals." The institution of patriarchal motherhood both defines women exclusively as childbearers and limits their powers under a male-dominated birthing system. Rich similarly finds evidence of the patriarchy at work in the assumptions of child rearing in which women are expected to prepare their offspring to accept their appointed roles—males as active and aggressive; females as passive and subordinate.

Of Woman Born catalogs a number of suggested alternatives to the patriarchal institution of motherhood, "for the taking over by women of genetic technology; for the insistence on childcare as a political commitment by all members of a community," by the "return to a 'village' concept of community in which children could be integrated into the adult life of work; the rearing of children in feminist enclaves to grow up free of gender-imprinting," and a redefinition of fatherhood, "which would require a more active, continuous presence with the child." Many of these solutions, Rich writes, may be naïve and simplistic. Instead, she urges a fundamental "repossession by women of our bodies," which she states "will bring far more essential change to human society than the seizing of the means of production by workers." As Rich concludes:

> We need to imagine a world in which every woman is the presiding genius of her own body. In such a world women will truly create new life, bringing forth not only children (if and as we choose) but the visions, and the thinking, necessary to sustain, console, and alter human existence—a new relationship to the universe. Sexuality, politics, intelligence, power, motherhood, work, community, intimacy will develop new meanings; thinking itself will be transformed.
> This is where we have to begin.

THE WOMEN'S ROOM

by Marilyn French

One of the most influential novels of the modern feminist movement, Marilyn French's *The Women's Room* (1977) is a blistering
indictment of gender conflict in America from the 1940s through
the 1970s. The fictional counterpart to Betty Friedan's *The Feminine
Mystique*, *The Women's Room* supplies a collective biography of a
generation of American women, described by novelist Anne Tyler
as "expectant in the 40's, submissive in the 50's, enraged in the
60's" who "have arrived in the 70's independent but somehow
unstrung, not yet fully composed after all they've been through."
Anchored by the self-realization process of Mira—a woman whose
traditional upbringing leads to a conventional marriage that ends
suddenly in divorce, forcing a painful reassessment of the gender
assumptions that have dictated her and her peers' fates as women,
wives, and mothers—*The Women's Room* documents and dramatizes ordinary women's daily lives; this subject, rare in novels, presents the challenges and risks of women's liberation. A controversial
best-seller, *The Women's Room* was both praised for its uncanny,
unvarnished recognition of the actuality of contemporary women's
lives and decried as a polemical work of idealized female victims
and male villains, described by critic Libby Purves as "a pro-

longed—largely autobiographical—yell of fury at the perversity of the male sex," in which "the men in the novel are drawn as malevolent stick figures, at best appallingly dull and at worst monsters." Observing in her own defense, French has stated, "That infuriates me. Every time I see that I see orange. The men are there as the women see them and feel them—impediments in women's lives. That's the focus of the book. Aristotle managed to build a whole society without mentioning women once. Did anyone ever say: 'Are there women in [Joseph Conrad's] *Nigger of the Narcissus*?' " The often vitriolic defensiveness that characterizes much of the critical response to *The Women's Room* reflects the novel's still-threatening power to challenge preconceived assumptions. As reviewer Christopher Lehmann-Haupt observed, the novel "seized me by my preconceptions and I kept struggling and arguing with its premises. Men can't be that bad, I kept wanting to shout at the narrator. There must be room for accommodation between the sexes that you've somehow overlooked." Lehmann-Haupt is finally persuaded that "the damnable thing is, she's right." Reviewer Brigitte Weeks has praised the novel for forcing "confrontations on the reader mercilessly" and as a "wonderful novel, full of life and passions that ring true as crystal. Its fierceness, its relentless refusal to compromise are as stirring as a marching song."

Placing *The Women's Room* in the cultural context of its time, Susan Faludi has argued that it was strikingly different from the other "women's novels" of the 1960s and 1970s that attempted to present feminist themes. Portraying "a weepy, wispy lady flailing ineffectually at fate, breaking a few kitchen appliances perhaps, but never straying far beyond the picket gate (or the gate of the mental hospital)," conventional women's novels depicted women's restricted roles and their psychological cost though a protagonist who "analyzed her life, but she didn't act on her analysis in any politically meaningful way—and she didn't inspire you to act either." In Faludi's view, French's novel manages to do both:

The Women's Room played out its most important and formative role as an agent for social and political action. It helped inspire sisterhood, by bringing women from the suburbs together by disclosing their commonly held grievances. It offered a political framework, by uncovering the gears and pulleys, the subtle social engineering of the fifties, that tried to reduce women and men to two-dimensional roles. And it gave women that ingredient essential to all social revolutions, large and small—a feeling of hope. By showing women that the "problem" wasn't all in their heads, *The Women's Room* opened the minds of women to the possibility that their lives were subject to change.

An assault on conventional ideals and a call to action and revolutionary gender change, *The Women's Room* was designed to incite and motivate. "My goal in life," French has argued, "is to change the entire social and economic structure of western civilization, to make it a feminist world." In her extensive survey of patriarchy, *Beyond Power: On Women, Men, and Morals* (1985), French has defined feminism as "the only serious, coherent, and universal philosophy that offers an alternative to patriarchal thinking and structures." Feminists, she asserts, "believe that women are human beings, that the two sexes are (at least) equal in all significant ways, and that this equality must be publicly recognized. They believe that qualities traditionally associated with women— the feminine principle—are (at least) equal in value to those traditionally associated with men—the masculine principle—and that this equality must be publicly recognized. . . . Finally, feminists believe the personal is the political—that is, that the value structure of a culture is identical in both public and private areas, that what happens in the bedroom has everything to do with what happens in the board room, and vice versa, and that, mythology notwithstanding, at present the same sex is in control in both places."

Dramatizing what feminists believe and why, *The Women's Room* derives its considerable power from its reflections of French's own experiences, and the developmental process that took her from stay-at-home spouse during the 1950s to divorced, single mother and Harvard graduate student in the radical 1960s. Born in 1929, in Brooklyn, French earned a bachelor's degree from Hofstra College (now University), in 1951. She gave up a plan to pursue a graduate degree, however, to marry Robert M. French, Jr., with whom she had two children. Living in a suburban Long Island town and feeling entrapped as a housewife, French would later point to reading, in 1956, Simone de Beauvoir's *The Second Sex*, with its indictment of women's sacrifice of their potential, choosing to live vicariously through men as a determining force in the resumption of her academic career. French returned to Hofstra to earn her master's degree in 1964, and, in 1967, she divorced her husband and enrolled in the English graduate program at Harvard, where she received her Ph.D., in 1972. Teaching English at the College of the Holy Cross in Worcester, Massachusetts, from 1972 to 1976, French converted her doctoral thesis into her first book, *The Book As World: James Joyce's Ulysses,* in 1976, and a year later she brought out *The Women's Room.* The book's phenomenal commercial success allowed French to pursue writing full-time, and her subsequent works include the novels *The Bleeding Heart* (1980), *Her Mother's Daughter* (1987), *Our Father* (1994), and *My Summer with George* (1996), as well as the volumes of nonfiction, essays, and criticism *Shakespeare's Division of Experience* (1981), *Beyond Power* (1985), *The War against Women* (1992), and *From Eve to Dawn: A History of Women* (2002–2003), and the memoir *A Season in Hell* (1998).

All of French's works attempt to break conventions, to show the reality of women's lives through history, culture, and her own life. French explained in an interview that her intention in *The Women's Room* was to "tell the story of what it is like to be a woman in our country in the middle of the twentieth century." Using her own experiences in realizing and resisting the patriarchal values that restricted possibilities for women, *The Women's Room* attempts to document the workings of this male-dominated system as it affects ordinary women's lives. "I sometimes think I've swallowed every woman I ever knew," French has observed. "My head is full of voices . . . clamoring to be let out." Central to her purpose was the desire "to break the mold of conventional women's novel," which she has described as books that "deal with young unmarried women. The action is her choosing a husband, the only choice she has the power to make and the final choice of her life—thus they always end with her marriage." *The Women's Room* set out to continue women's stories beyond the altar into the sobering reality of their domestic lives. "Books, movies, TV teach us false images of ourselves," French has written. "We learn to expect fairy-tale lives. Ordinary women's daily lives—unlike men's—have not been the stuff of literature. I wanted to legitimize it and I purposely chose the most ordinary lives—not the worst cases." French focuses on the growth of her protagonist, Mira, from her upbringing and childhood, through her college experience, marriage, suburban lifestyle, and eventual radical reorientation of her life and values following her divorce. Mira's experiences are presented as representative of an entire generation of women coming to terms with the gender assumptions that have damaged them, and the novel equally treats the complementary stories of Mira's friends and peers, who respond in different ways to their circumstances as wives, mothers, and workers, to produce a panoramic group portrait. As one reviewer notes, "It is as if French had been taking notes for twenty years. Her dialogue, her characterizations, her knowledge of the changing relationships, sexual and otherwise, between men and women in a complex world of shifting values are all extraordinary." The novel's popularity and persistence are based, in the words of another, on the author's "genuine sympathy for other women caught in life situations, trivial or deadly serious, for which they were never prepared."

Submissive and repressed, Mira subordinates her intellectual potential and ambition to work menial jobs to support her stolid husband, Norm, through medical school. With the arrival of babies, Mira's world shrinks even further to her housekeeping and nurturing chores. With Norm's success comes the ideal house in the suburbs. French presents the details of suburban life, described by Anne Tyler as "balky ice-cube trays and Cub Scout meetings" that "interlace with adulteries, attempted suicides and enforced stays in mental institutions." Mira encounters Natalie, who copes with her homebound frustrations by continually redecorating; Martha, who fights her boredom with housework by going back to school and falling in love with one of her professors; and Lily, whose honest assessment of suburban women's maddening restrictions leads to her own confinement in an asylum. Norm eventually is unfaithful, and Mira breaks free from the suburbs to experience the turbulent sixties and seventies as an English graduate student at Harvard. There she encounters gender bias in academia as well as among the radicals who supposedly advocate enlightened liberation. Both take their toll on several more of Mira's peers, such as Val, Kyla, Grete, Ava, Clarissa, and Iso, who to a greater or a lesser degree are destroyed and damaged by a male-dominated/female-subordinated system. Mira eventually achieves her doctorate and winds up teaching at a coastal Maine community college where "she walks the beach every day, and drinks brandy every night, and wonders if she's going mad." The ultimate literary convention of the happy ending is avoided. As French has stated, "No one at all, lives happily ever after. A woman may endure, but suffering never ends."

Reflecting on her accomplishment in portraying the reality of women's lives during the period that created the modern women's movement, Marilyn French ably summarizes: "*The Women's Room* shows women's work for the tedious, draining, menial, and occasionally brilliant and creative thing it is; it insists on the centrality of women's work to the world at large and to women themselves. It shows the actual importance of men to a variety of women. It offers no finality, no promised Eden, but only endurance, survival." *The Women's Room* stands as one of the great breakthrough works in which centuries of conventions that have ruled the way women are portrayed are overturned for a sobering reality upon which self-realization and true liberation can be more securely based.

SILENCES

by Tillie Olsen

Silences, Tillie Olsen's 1978 collection of essays, talks, notes, and excerpts from the diaries, journals, and letters of a wide range of writers, past and present, has been called by Alix Kates Shulman a "classic of feminist literature." Described by its author as a work "concerned with the relationship of circumstances—including class, color, sex; the times, climate into which one is born—to the creation of literature," *Silences* describes the "thwarting of what struggles to come into being, but cannot" that has prevented writers, particularly women, from being heard. Although the author of only a single volume of acclaimed short stories, *Tell Me a Riddle* (1961), and an unfinished novel, *Yonnondio: From the Thirties* (1974), Tillie Olsen is greatly admired both for the artistry of her works and the obstacles she has had to overcome to produce them. Margaret Atwood has asserted that "few writers have gained such wide respect on such a small body of published work." Among her peers, Atwood declares, the word "respect" is simply inadequate to describe the feelings Olsen evokes: " 'Reverence' is more like it. This is presumably because women writers, even more than their male counterparts, recognize what a heroic feat it is to have held down a job, raised four children and still somehow managed to become and to remain a writer." A groundbreaking and foundation document of the modern women's movement, *Silences* deals with the ramifications and consequences of Olsen's determination to define herself as a "worker-mother-writer," and, as Atwood summarizes, "The exaction of this multiple identity cost Tillie Olsen 20 years of her writing life. The applause that greets her is not only for the quality of her artistic performance but, as at a grueling obstacle race, for the near miracle of her survival."

Olsen was born Tillie Lerner, in 1913, to Russian-Jewish immigrant parents in Nebraska. Both her parents had been involved in the 1905 Russian Revolution against the czar and had fled to America when the uprising failed. To support his family, Olsen's father worked as a farm worker, painter, paperhanger, candy maker, and packinghouse worker while maintaining his political commitment by serving as state secretary of the Nebraska Socialist Party. Educated through the eleventh grade in public schools in Omaha, Olsen read Rebecca Harding Davis's *Life in the Iron Mills* (1861) (*see* Honorable Mentions) as a teenager and was so impressed by its depiction of working-class life that Olsen vowed, as a youthful protagonist in an unpublished story proclaimed, "I shall write stories when I grow up, and not work in a factory." However, to supplement her family's income, Olsen left school early for work in a variety of menial jobs while becoming active in socialist politics. She was arrested, in 1931, for encouraging Kansas City packinghouse workers to unionize. By 1934, Olsen had moved to San Francisco and again was jailed for participating in the infamous Bloody Thursday Longshoreman's Strike of that year. In 1943, she married printer and union organizer Jack Olsen and raised their four daughters in a working-class section of San Francisco, supporting the family by taking jobs as a waitress, secretary, and laundress.

Having abandoned a novel about the Great Depression, *Yonnondio*, in 1937, Olsen did not take up writing again until the 1950s, when she enrolled in a writing class at San Francisco State University and won a Stanford University creative writing fellowship. She published the acclaimed short story, "I Stand Here Ironing," in 1956, followed by "Hey Sailor, What Ship?" in 1957. Both were collected with the title work to form the universally praised *Tell Me a Riddle,* in 1961, which established Olsen's reputation as one of the contemporary masters of short fiction.

Olsen's stories, expressed in a dialect-rich verisimilitude, focus on the perspectives of working-class characters, particularly women, whose stamina and endurance are tested under the constricting conditions of their unglamorous lives. As a mother of four children, forced for many years to work at low-paying jobs in addition to her ceaseless labor as a wife and mother, Olsen draws on her own experiences in her fiction to give voice to those whose lives and experiences have gone largely unrecorded. It is both the fate of her characters to be silenced by their circumstances and the near-fate of Olsen herself that she explores in *Silences*.

A miscellany of talks, essays, and excerpts, "garnered over fifty years, near a lifetime" in which the thought "came slow, hard-won," *Silences* opens with the title essay and its eloquent opening line: "Literary history and the present are dark with silences." Unlike natural silences—"that necessary time for renewal, lying fallow, gestation, in the natural cycle of creation"—the unnatural silences Olsen speaks of are the conditions that thwart literary creation, such as the economic conditions that silenced Herman Melville or the "censorship silences" that caused Thomas Hardy to abandon novel writing. The most tragic of these unnatural silences are all the "mute inglorious Miltons," individuals who may have had the genius but not the conditions necessary to enable them to produce literature. Members of the working class, condemned to the drudgery of subsistence, have been unable to express their lives creatively due to the conditions of their lives. "Substantial creative work demands time," Olsen asserts, "and with rare exceptions only full-time workers have achieved it. Where the claims of creation cannot be primary, the results are atrophy; unfinished work; minor effort and accomplishment; silences." Women face the additional burdens of motherhood and household responsibilities that restrict the time and autonomy necessary for creativity. To prove her point, Olsen notes that important nineteenth-century women writers—Jane Austen, Emily Brontë, Christina Rosetti, Emily Dickinson, or Louisa May Alcott—never married or had children. In the twentieth century, Olsen argues, most of the significant women writers still have not married or have remained childless. Almost no mothers have created enduring literature because, in Olsen's view, "More than in any other human relationship, overwhelmingly more, motherhood means being constantly interruptible, responsive, responsible," qualities antithetical to writing that requires "constant toil" rather than constant interruption. By class and gender restrictions, therefore, the working classes and women have been silenced.

Olsen next treats her own life and writing career to illustrate her point. "In the twenty years I bore and reared my children," she points out, "I usually had to work on a paid job as well, the simplest circumstances for creation did not exist." After her youngest entered school, Olsen squeezed time for her writing on the bus to her job, at night, during and after housework, trying to balance the impossible combination of "worker-mother-writer." "In such snatches of time I wrote what I did in those years, but there came a time when this triple life was no longer possible. The fifteen hours of daily realities became too much distraction for the writing. I lost craziness of endurance. . . . My work died. What demanded to be written, did not." Finally rescued by a grant to resume her work uninterrupted, Olsen writes, "This most harmful of all my silences has ended." As a survivor, Olsen closes with a warning that "we are in a time of more and more hidden and foreground silences, women *and* men."

The next essay in *Silences*, "One Out of Twelve: Writers Who Are Women in Our Century," considers why, even after considerable gains for women in the twentieth century, including "access to areas of work and of life previously denied; higher education; longer, stronger lives," women writers are accorded so little recognition and why there is only "one woman writer of achievement for every twelve men writers so ranked." The answer rests in a persistent gender bias in which women have been "excluded, excluded, excluded from council, ritual, activity, learning, language, when there was neither biological nor economic reason to be excluded." Olsen argues that all writers must be convinced of the importance of their ideas, and self-confidence, difficult for the working classes and for men not born into privilege, is "almost impossible for a girl, a woman." Women, moreover, are faced with the "sexist notion that the act of creation is not as inherently natural to a woman as to a man," and in the past have been forced to choose between artistic achievement and fulfillment as women. "More and more women writers in our century," Olsen observes, "primarily in the last two decades, are assuming as their right fullness of work *and* family life." Of this change she states, "I hope and fear for what will result. I hope (and believe) that complex new richness will come into literature; I fear because almost certainly their work will be impeded, lessened, partial. For the fundamental situation remains unchanged. Unlike men writers who marry, most will not have the societal equivalent of a wife—nor (in a society hostile to growing life) anyone but themselves to mother their children." Added to this central challenge faced by women writers is the persistent devaluation of women's achievement by a male-dominated critical establishment. Olsen argues that the solution to the imbalance between male and female writers of significance is to "read, listen to, living women writers; our new as well as our established, often neglected ones. . . . Read the compass of women writers in our infinite variety. . . . Teach women's lives through the lives of the women who wrote the books. . . . Be critical. Women have the right to say: this is surface, this falsifies reality, this degrades. . . . Help create writers, perhaps among them yourselves."

If the first essay of *Silences* deals with the factors that silence working class and women writers, and the second examines the ways to increase women's voices, the third essay, Olsen's afterword to Rebecca Harding Davis's *Life in the Iron Mills*, pays tribute to the life and achievement of a talented, influential, but neglected American woman writer who deserves to be heard. By treating Davis's career Olsen embodies and dramatizes her previous points about the circumstances that constrain women writers and the importance of Davis's perspective on aspects of women's lives that have often been overlooked. *Silences* concludes with quotations "selectively chosen for maximum significance" to illustrate her previously discussed themes. Dealing with the various forms of unnatural silences that have afflicted writers, both male and female, the section provides a valuable collection of commentary on the nature, pressures, and possibilities of breaking through the silences that have thwarted creative expression.

The impact of *Silences* has been significant. Written in the early days of the women's movement of the 1960s and 1970s, the book offered a new perspective on gender and creativity, and an empowerment of neglected perspectives. Not since Virginia Woolf's *A Room of One's Own* had a woman writer offered such a radical gender and class-based conceptualization of literary history and literary possibilities. Olsen's admonition to "teach books by women" has been answered by the increasing number of books by women now found in print and taught in college courses. New and neglected women writers, such as Rebecca Harding Davis, are silent no longer. *Silences* came at a decisive moment, articulating both the challenges and potential of the second wave of the women's movement. "Probably she is not the first," critic Annie Gottlieb has argued, "but to me Tillie Olsen *feels* like the first, both to extend 'universal' human experience to females and to dignify uniquely female experience as a source of human knowledge."

WOMEN, RACE & CLASS

by Angela Davis

An activist, scholar, educator, and one-time fugitive on the FBI's "Ten Most Wanted List," Angela Davis has lived a life in opposition, challenging the forces of social injustice wherever she has found them. Perhaps best remembered as a radical lightning rod of the 1960s and 1970s, the subject of "Free Angela" rallies around the world, Davis is also an important, influential social theoretician who has framed the debate over women's rights in daringly original and expansive contexts. One of the foundation texts of black feminist theory, Davis's *Women, Race & Class* (1981) explores the origins of the women's movement in America from the campaign to abolish slavery, and draws connections between sexism, racism, and classism in the subsequent battles over suffrage, equal rights, civil rights, and such contemporary issues as sexual assault and reproductive rights. As one critic has observed, the work "helped to establish the guidelines for critical analysis in current American feminist scholarship through its insistence on the investigation of the historically specific ways in which the inequalities of race, gender and class interact." It is a work that challenges preconceptions, overturns conventional understandings, and clears the ground for a new paradigm for understanding the complex, interconnected forces that must be op-posed in any serious effort to redress inequities and foment radi-cal change in women's lives.

Davis's experiences as a black woman and a radical during one of the most turbulent periods in American history has clearly shaped her works; a knowledge of these experiences provides the understanding essential for appreciating her perspective and achievement in *Women, Race & Class.* Born in 1944, in Birmingham, Alabama, Davis grew up in the segregated Jim Crow south. Her mother was an elementary schoolteacher, and her father owned a service station. When she was four years old, her family moved into a formerly all-white neighborhood that became known as "Dynamite Hill," after white supremacists bombed so many of the houses of newly arrived black families. Participating with her mother at civil rights demonstrations in Birmingham, Davis spent summers in New York City, where her mother studied to earn her master's degree. Davis gained scholarships to attend a private school in Greenwich Village and Brandeis University, where she majored in French literature. While studying abroad in Paris, Davis met students from Algeria and other African nations who had grown up under colonial rule; she began an intellectual search for a conceptual means to correlate her experiences with the burgeoning civil rights movement in the United States during the period and wider international historical and cultural devel-opments. The key was provided by Brandeis's Marxist philoso-pher Herbert Marcuse, who became Davis's mentor. "*The Communist Manifesto* hit me like a bolt of lightning," Davis re-membered in her autobiography. "I read it avidly, finding in it an-swers to many of the seemingly unanswerable dilemmas which had plagued me. . . . I began to see the problems of Black people within the context of a large working-class movement. . . . What struck me so emphatically was the idea that once the emancipa-tion of the proletariat became a reality, the foundation was laid for the emancipation of all oppressed groups in society."

After graduating from Brandeis, in 1965, Davis did graduate work in philosophy at the University of Frankfurt and finished her master's degree in philosophy under Marcuse at the University of California, San Diego, in 1968. Around the same time, Davis joined the Communist Party, the Student Nonviolent Coordinating Committee (SNCC), and the Black Panthers. Even among these radical groups, publicly committed to overthrowing traditional power hierarchies, Davis experienced sexism from the predominately male leadership: "I was criticized very heavily, especially by male members . . . for doing a 'man's job,' " she recalled. "Women should not play leadership roles, they insisted." Hired as an assistant professor of philosophy at UCLA, in 1969, Davis was fired by California Governor Ronald Reagan and the Board of Regents after word leaked out that she was a communist. Faculty members and the university president overwhelmingly condemned the dismissal, and Davis was reinstated by court order. However, when her contract expired the following year she was dismissed again. As she was fighting to regain her job, Davis organized a nationwide effort to free three prison inmates, known as the Soledad Brothers, who had been falsely accused of killing a Soledad Prison guard. In August 1970, a brother of one of the Soledad Brothers, using firearms Davis had purchased to protect herself from death threats, mounted a rescue and hostage taking at the Marin County Courthouse. The attempt was foiled in a firefight that claimed four lives, including that of a county judge. A federal warrant was issued for Davis's arrest, and she went into hiding. After a two-month search, during which Davis was placed on the FBI's "Ten Most Wanted List, " she was apprehended in New York and extradited to California, where she was imprisoned for sixteen months. Prosecutors accused Davis of masterminding the attack. Davis insisted on her innocence, claiming that she was a retaliatory target as a result of her political activism. Demonstrations of support took place around the world, and "Free Angela" buttons, bumper stickers, and billboards established a slogan that came to represent the plight of political prisoners worldwide. In 1972, after deliberating for thirteen hours, a jury of eleven whites and one Mexican American acquitted Davis on the three charges of murder, kidnapping, and conspiracy. Davis responded with a national lecture tour and her *Autobiography,* which appeared in 1974. Looking back on her time in jail and her trial, Davis has remarked, "That period was pivotal for me in many respects. I came to understand much more concretely many of the realities of the Black struggle of that period." Davis would embody her realizations into the call for a total reassessment of attitudes on race, class, and gender that she synthesized in *Women, Race & Class.*

Organized in a series of thirteen chapters that survey American history from slavery through modern times, *Women, Race & Class* offers an alternative and iconoclastic view of the intersection of race, class, and gender, which challenges standard versions and forces a reassessment of racism, classism, and sexism in America. Davis begins with a powerful account of slavery that contradicts the stereotype of most black women slaves as domestic servants. Davis shows instead that virtually all black women under slavery were field hands who worked side by side with men. Their experiences, in Davis's view, create a new paradigm for working women in America in which African-American women slaves "passed on to their nominally free female descendants a legacy of hard work, perseverance and self-reliance, a legacy of tenacity, resistance and insistence on sexual equality. . . ." She also skillfully draws the connection between the abolitionist movement and the burgeoning women's movement. The fight against slavery proved to be the training ground for the leaders of the women's rights movement such as Lucretia Mott, Elizabeth Cady Stanton, Susan B. Anthony, and others. However, Davis asserts that the solidarity and common cause between black liberation and women's liberation was short lived, undermined by racism and classism. Davis faults the framers of the landmark Declaration of Principles at the first Women's Rights Convention in Seneca Falls, in 1848, for ignoring "the circumstances of women outside the social class of the document's framers." Working women were not mentioned in the called-for reform in marriage, property law, and education, and black women were not in attendance at the convention.

Following the Civil War, the constitutional struggle to enfranchise black males widened the rift between race and gender among reformers, exposing the underlying racism of many women's rights leaders. Susan B. Anthony, for example, Davis points out, readily sought the support of southern white supremacists on behalf of the woman suffrage cause. While Elizabeth Cady Stanton, feeling resentful and betrayed by the enfranchising of black males over white women, is quoted declaring, "The representative women of the nation have done their uttermost for the last thirty years to secure freedom for the negro; . . . but now, as the celestial gate to civil rights is slowly moving on its hinges, it becomes a serious question whether we had better stand aside and see 'Sambo' walk into the kitchen first. . . . Are we so sure that he, once entrenched in all his inalienable rights, may not be an added power to hold us at bay?" Davis documents from many additional historical sources other instances of the racism that divided the movement for equal rights and the class bias that caused the early women's movement to ignore the plight of working women. Black women, in particular, she asserts, were left to struggle on their own, triply oppressed by their class, race, and gender.

For many in the women's movement of the nineteenth and early twentieth centuries, suffrage was the ultimate goal upon which women's liberation depended. Davis, however, makes clear that the vote was insufficient to resolve the oppression of workers, blacks, or women in America, and the nexus among race, gender, and class continues to qualify and complicate contemporary social justice issues. After a chapter on "Communist Women," which Davis devotes to profiles of neglected and forgotten women socialist reformers, *Woman, Race & Class* sets in perspective some contemporary social issues: rape, reproductive rights, and "women's work." In Davis's view, consideration of rape continues to rely on the myth of the black rapist; she argues that "the notion is accepted that Black men harbor irresistible and animal-like sexual urges, the entire race is invested with bestiality." In documenting the pervasiveness of this notion and its use to justify racial injustice, Davis asserts, "Racism has always served as a provocation to rape, and white women in the United States have necessarily suffered the ricochet fire of these attacks. This is one of the many ways in which racism nourishes sexism, causing white women to be indirectly victimized by the special oppression aimed at their sisters of color." Davis points out that the passage of the 1977 Hyde Amendment, mandating the withdrawal of federal funding for abortions, restricted reproductive rights on the basis of class privilege. "Black, Puerto Rican, Chicana and Native American Indian women, together with their impoverished white sisters, were thus effectively divested of their right to legal abortions." With class and race complicating the issue of reproductive rights, Davis suggests, "The abortion rights activists of the early 1970s should have examined the history of their movement. Had they done so, they might have understood why so many of their Black sisters adopted a posture of suspicion toward their cause. They might have understood how important it was to undo the racist deeds of their predecessors, who had advocated birth control as well as compulsory sterilization as a means of eliminating the 'unfit' sectors of the population." Davis concludes with a consideration of housework, childcare, and the economic and social factors that have continued to assign woman the role of "man's eternal servant," women being the "guardians of a devalued domestic life." Davis urges that housework should be "industrialized" and shifted from the private to the public sector. "For Black women today and for all their working-class sisters," she asserts, "the notion that the burden of housework and child care can be shifted from their shoulders to the society contains one of the radical secrets of women's liberation. Child care should be socialized, meal preparation should be socialized, housework should be industrialized—and all these services should be readily accessible to working-class people."

Although Davis can be charged with an overreliance on now-devalued communist theory to frame many of her arguments and solutions, *Woman, Race & Class* retains its importance and relevance in its repeated calls for inclusiveness in addressing issues of social justice, for a truly united black and women's liberation, and for a widened understanding of the complex interactions of race, class, and gender.

THE HOUSE OF THE SPIRITS

by Isabel Allende

It can be argued that the most distinctive, enduring methods and achievements of the novel in the second half of the twentieth century have been made by Latin American writers, beginning with Gabriel García Márquez's groundbreaking novel *One Hundred Years of Solitude*, published in 1967. It caused, in the words of fellow novelist Mario Vargas Llosa, "a literary earthquake in Latin America," the reverberations of which stunned the world. As critics in Europe and North America were lamenting the death of the novel in the face of the declining energy of literary modernism, García Márquez offered an invigorating renewal, synthesizing elements from Kafka, Joyce, Hemingway, Faulkner, and others from Hispanic oral and literary traditions with the novel's most basic resource—captivating storytelling. García Márquez fashioned an absorbing narrative that was simultaneously a family saga, historical chronicle, and universal symbolic myth. In combining everyday events with supernatural occurrences, he also pioneered the subsequently often imitated fictional technique of "magic realism." Among the writers who followed García Márquez's artistic lead, Isabel Allende became the first significant woman contributor to the so-called Boom of Latin American literature. Her remarkable first novel, *La casa de los espíritus* (1982), translated as *The House of the Spirits* (1985), established her distinctive voice and the reputation that would make her the best-known Latin American woman novelist, and perhaps the most widely read contemporary Latina writer in the world.

The House of the Spirits is an ambitious debut, weaving together family and national history derived from Allende's ancestors, background, and experiences. Allende was born in 1942, in Lima, Peru, where her father, a first cousin of the future socialist president of Chile Salvador Allende, was a Chilean diplomatic attaché. After her parents divorced when Isabel was two years old, she and her mother returned to Santiago and moved in with her maternal grandparents. They would serve as the models for the characters Esteban and Clara Trueba, and their home the central locale in *The House of the Spirits*. After her mother remarried, again to a diplomat, Allende accompanied her family on his assignments to Bolivia, Europe, and the Middle East. Returning to Chile when she was fifteen, Allende subsequently worked as a journalist, on television programs, and appeared in newsreels. She wrote a satirical column, "Los Impertinentes" (The Impertinents), for the radical women's magazine *Paula*, hosted a weekly television program, produced plays, and wrote short stories for children.

On September 13, 1973, Allende's life abruptly changed when her uncle and godfather, President Salvador Allende, was assassinated in a military coup, led by General Augusto Pinochet Ugarte, that toppled the elected socialist government and ushered in a period of brutal military repression. "I think I have divided my life [into] before that day and after that day," Allende would later recall. "In that moment, I realized that everything was possible—that violence was a dimension that was always around you." For the next fifteen months, at the risk of her own life, Allende assisted the victims of the Pinochet regime in escaping persecution, witnessing many of the events that she would later incorporate into her first novel. "Because of my work as a journalist," Allende wrote in an essay, in 1984, "I knew exactly what was happening in my country, I lived through it, and the dead, the tortured, the widows and orphans, left an unforgettable impression on my memory. The last chapters of *The House of the Spirits* narrate those events. They are based on what I saw and on the direct testimonies of those who lived through the brutal experience of the repression." In 1975, fearful that her life and family were in jeopardy, Allende left Chile for Caracas, Venezuela, with her husband and teenage children. Unable to resume her creative writing, she worked as a teacher and administrator before she was able to begin work as a reporter on one of Venezuela's leading newspapers.

The genesis for *The House of the Spirits* came in the form of a letter written to her nearly one-hundred-year-old dying grandfather, who had remained in Chile. "My grandfather thought people died only when you forget them," Allende observed. "I wanted to prove to him that I had forgotten nothing, that his spirit was going to live with us forever." Although the letter was never sent to her grandfather, who soon died, Allende's reclaiming her memories of her family and her country formed the core of her first novel. "When you lose everything, everything that is dear to you," she has written, "memory becomes more important." With *The House of the Spirits* Allende achieved "the recovery of those memories that were being blown by the wind, by the wind of exile."

Like García Márquez's *One Hundred Years of Solitude, The House of the Spirits* is a family saga with recognizable historical circumstances in an unnamed Latin American country. References to well-known incidents, however, such as the disastrous earthquake of 1933, the agrarian reforms of the 1960s, the election of Salvador Allende, and the death of poet Pablo Neruda, clearly locate the action of the novel in Chile. Both novels present a synthesis of realism and the uncanny, depicting characters caught between fact and fantasy, a world in which dreams, ghosts, and the irrational are grafted onto a panoramic documentation of modern Latin American history. However, Allende provides more than a worthy imitation of García Márquez's subject and technique. As reviewer Antony Beevor has perceptively observed, Allende has taken up García Márquez's genre "to flip it over." "The metaphorical house," Beevor argues, "the themes of time and power, the *machista* violence and the unstoppable merry-go-round of history: all of these are reworked and then examined from the other side—from a woman's perspective." Allende counters the male-dominated perspective of her fellow Latin American writers with, in the words of critic Bruce Allen, "an original feminist argument that suggests women's monopoly on powers that oppose the violent 'paternalism' from which countries like Chile continue to suffer." If historical fiction traditionally focuses on male protagonists and major events, *The House of the Spirits* redirects attention to the story of women's seemingly mundane lives and their transformative, heroic capacities. *The House of the Spirits* thereby deconstructs the traditionally dominating patriarchy of Latin American culture and substitutes a powerful, alternative female ethos in which recent Latin American history can be reimagined from a new visionary perspective.

Dedicated to her mother, grandmother, and "all the other extraordinary women of this story," *The House of the Spirits* reflects Chilean history during the first three-quarters of the twentieth century from the vantage point of four generations of women in the del Valle/Trueba family. Beginning with feminist matriarch Nívea del Valle, the novel concentrates on her descendents, Clara, Blanca, and Alba Trueba, the wife, daughter, and granddaughter of the domineering family patriarch Esteban Trueba. He is a self-made man who ruthlessly acquires land, wealth, and political power and combines both the character strengths and weaknesses that Allende shows as characterizing Latin American patriarchal society. Each of the extraordinary del Valle/Trueba women counterpoint and challenge his values, while his brutal, violent behavior, fear of change, and hypocritical double standard indirectly leads to his downfall.

Following the poisoning death of Nívea del Valle's beautiful daughter Rosa, Esteban, her fiancé, dedicates himself to restoring his family's estate, Tres Marías, while Rosa's clairvoyant and telekinetic sister Clara begins a nine-year-long silence, which is broken only when she announces that she will marry Esteban. Clara's uncanny sensitivity and empathy helps to humanize the driven Esteban, who has become the archetypal *patrón*, a feudal lord who determines his peasants' lives and rapes and impregnates the young women on his estate. After Esteban and Clara's daughter Blanca falls in love with Pedro Tercero García, the son of the estate's foreman, and Esteban learns of the affair, he strikes Clara, who has pleaded on behalf of the young couples' love. Clara responds to his action by leaving Tres Marías for her parents' home, vowing never to speak to her husband again. As Esteban successfully pursues a political career as a conservative senator, Blanca gives birth to Pedro Tercero's child, Alba. After

Clara dies, when her granddaughter is seven, Esteban concentrates on his beloved granddaughter's upbringing amid the growing political turmoil that challenges his reactionary views. Blanca resumes her relationship with Pedro Tercero, who has become a socialist revolutionary and political singer, while Alba becomes involved in student demonstrations on behalf of the insurgent populist movement that wins the national election despite the opposition of Esteban's conservative coalition of business interests, the military, the church, and CIA backing. Esteban supports the military coup that assassinates the new president and topples the elected government. He then is horrified by the political repression of the new regime and decides to help Blanca and Pedro Tercero leave the country. Alba is arrested and tortured by her grandfather's bastard son, Esteban Garciá, who has come to power under the coup. She is sustained by Clara's spirit, who urges her to counter her pain with the stories of her family and those of her ancestors. Released, a pregnant Alba forsakes vengeance and recrimination in the del Valle home of Nívea, Clara, and Blanca. Inspired by her grandmother's and mother's writings and her own memories, she reveals herself as the chronicler of her family's story, which becomes *The House of the Spirits*. Esteban dies in Alba's arms, invoking Clara's name and her spirit that has recalled him to his humanity:

> At first she was just a mysterious glow, but as my grandfather slowly lost the rage that had tormented him throughout his life, she appeared as she had been at her best, laughing with all her teeth and stirring up the other spirits as she sailed through the house. She also helped us write, and thanks to her presence Esteban Trueba was able to die happy, murmuring her name: Clara, clearest, clairvoyant.

Over the course of multiple life stories, *The House of the Spirits* has refracted Chilean history through the alternative perspective of the del Valle and Trueba women whose affirmation of love, spirit, and the future ultimately triumphs over the life-denying and destructive patriarchy typified by Latin American history and Esteban Trueba. The novel presents a series of strong women who oppose their male-dominated society with a visionary willfulness. Nívea del Valle fights for women's suffrage; Clara opposes her husband's dominance with a mystical sense of life's harmonies;

both Blanca and Alba break from the narrow and self-serving assumptions of their class and gender to embrace the greater good and liberating possibilities. *The House of the Spirits* supplies a moving and compelling treatment of female empowerment that opposes a cycle of violence and repression with cathartic and healing transcendence.

BELOVED

by Toni Morrison

One of the most emotionally compelling and intellectually complex treatments of the legacy of slavery ever explored in fiction, *Beloved* (1987) is thus far Toni Morrison's most ambitious and most fully realized novel, a masterpiece of almost unbearable power and seemingly inexhaustible cultural and psychological relevance. In this remarkable attempt to come to terms with the enormity of slavery and the American past, racial, personal, and national history comes together in an essential myth that probes a collective scar and suggests how healing can begin.

Beloved is Toni Morrison's fifth novel. She had published her first novel, *The Bluest Eye*, in 1970, when she was thirty-nine and had been working as a senior book editor at Random House since 1967. She had previously taught English courses at Texas Southern University and Howard University, where she had received her undergraduate degree in 1953; after graduation, she went on to obtain a master's degree from Cornell University. *The Bluest Eye*, a lyrical exploration of racial and gender identity, was followed by *Sula* (1974). Both novels were critically praised for their poetic prose, emotional intensity, and unique interpretation of African-American experience from the largely neglected woman's perspective. Neither book was a popular success and both novels were out of print when Morrison published *Song of Solomon* (1977), the breakthrough novel that established her reputation as a dominant voice in contemporary fiction worldwide. With *Song of Solomon,* Morrison extended her range, employing a male protagonist for the first time, Milkman Dead, whom critic Margaret Wade-Lewis has called "undoubtedly one of the most effective renderings of a male character by a woman writer in American literature." His quest to find a family legacy and to decipher his racial identity is a complex and resonant interweaving of myth and history that draws on black folklore, oral tradition, and classical archetypes. This expansiveness is continued in her next novel, *Tar Baby* (1981), in which Morrison continues an imaginative search for identity in the confrontation between blacks and whites, along with her characteristic fusion of realism with fantasy derived from the black American folktale, both of which are placed in a global setting that encompasses the entire African diaspora.

Tar Baby was a best-seller and prompted *Newsweek* to do a cover story on the writer. Ironically, Morrison felt at the time that her writing days were over. "I would not write another novel to either make a living or because I was able to," she later recalled. "If it was not an overwhelming compulsion or I didn't feel absolutely driven by the ideas I wanted to explore, I wouldn't do it. And I was content not to ever be driven that way again." The compulsion came reluctantly as Morrison began to confront the legacy of slavery, a subject obscured, in Morrison's words, by a "national amnesia." *Beloved* would become the deliberate act of reconstructing what has been forgotten, which the author defined as "a journey to a site to see what remains have been left behind and to reconstruct the world that these remains imply." In an act of bearing witness, of giving voice to the unspeakable, Morrison set out "to fill in the blanks that the slave narrative left," to "part the veil that was frequently drawn," in which the full ramifications of the slave experience could be probed, and its costs embodied in psychological, emotional, social, and cultural terms.

The inspiration for her story came from Morrison's editorial work on Middleton Harris's documentary collection of black life in America, *The Black Book.* Morrison became fascinated by a historical incident from a newspaper clipping contained in Harris's collection entitled "A Visit to the Slave Mother Who Killed Her Child." It concerns a journalist's report on a runaway slave from Kentucky, Margaret Garner, who, in 1855, tried to kill her children rather than allow them to be returned to slavery. Successful in killing one, Margaret Garner would provide the historical access point for Beloved, allowing Morrison to explore in fiction the conditions that could have led to such a horrific act and its consequences to the survivors.

Narrated in a series of flashbacks, assembled gradually from the limited perspective of its characters, *Beloved* opens in 1873, eighteen years after the defining trauma in the life of Sethe—a former slave on a Kentucky farm called Sweet Home. Sethe lives in an isolated house outside Cincinnati with her eighteen-year-old daughter, Denver, and the ghost of Sethe's dead baby girl, named by the inscription on her tombstone, "Beloved." The novel's present during the Reconstruction period is symbolically appropriate for a novel that will concern the search for wholeness, the effort to rebuild an identity, a family, and a community from one that has been shattered by the enormous human wastage and dehumanization of slavery. A clear chronology of events in Sethe's life emerges only eventually as numerous characters—Sethe's mother-in-law, Baby Suggs, the black river man Stamp Paid, and Sethe's fellow slave, Paul D., the last of the Sweet Home Men, and others—allow their experiences to be revealed, painfully, through the curtain of protective repression.

In 1848, the teenage Sethe is sold to Mr. Garner at Sweet Home as the replacement for Baby Suggs, whose freedom has been purchased by her son Halle, whom Sethe marries. When Mr. Garner dies, in 1853, the farm is placed in the hands of an overseer called "Schoolteacher," who transforms Mr. Garner's more benign regime with a brutal and calculated indifference to the humanity of the Sweet Home slaves. When one is sold, the rest plot their escape. On the eve of departure, the pregnant Sethe is attacked by Schoolteacher's two nephews. As one holds her down, the other submits her to "mammary rape," sucking the milk from her breasts. Unknown to Sethe, this violation is witnessed by Halle, who is incapable of assisting his wife. The event leads to his derangement and disappearance. Sethe sends her three children to join the emancipated Baby Suggs in Ohio and eventually reaches freedom there herself after giving birth to her daughter, Denver. The four other Sweet Home men are either brutally killed or imprisoned. Sethe enjoys only twenty-eight days of freedom before Schoolteacher arrives to take her back. Rather than allowing her children to be returned to slavery, Sethe tries to kill them. Three children are saved from death, but Sethe cuts Beloved's throat. Arrested and sentenced to hang, Sethe is pardoned due to the intervention of abolitionists and allowed to return to Baby Suggs's home at 124 Bluestone Road in Cincinnati, where she is shunned by the black community. The vengeful spirit of her murdered child also takes up residence, drives away Sethe's two sons, contributes to Baby Suggs's death after she despairingly retreats to her bed, and holds Sethe and Denver in her spell until the arrival, in 1873, of Paul D.

Paul D is able to expel the ghost, temporarily breaking the hold of debilitating grief and despair that has condemned Sethe and Denver to seclusion. Paul D offers the possibility of family and future, but neither he nor Sethe is truly ready to put the past behind them. As if to insist that both must confront that past, the ghost returns in bodily form as a young woman the age Beloved would have been had she survived, and she claims sanctuary. A sinister presence, Beloved's voracious obsession with food and Sethe's love splits the developing family apart. The revelation that Sethe has killed her daughter shocks Paul D and drives him away, leaving Beloved to claim complete dominance over Sethe as the physical embodiment of her uneasy conscience. Increasingly obsessed with righting the wrong to Beloved that cannot be corrected, Sethe loses her job as a cook and drops all contact with the outside world. Neglected and starving, Denver is forced to reach out to the larger community for assistance, an act that finally will break the hold Beloved has over Sethe. As the black women of the community who had previously ostracized Sethe for her murder now come to her assistance, a version of Schoolteacher's arrival at the house at 124 Bluestone is reenacted: the elderly Mr. Bodwin, who had gained Sethe's pardon in 1855, is mistaken by the deranged Sethe as a slave catcher. She is prevented from stabbing him with an ice pick, but her climactic gesture of striking out, not at the victims of slavery in her earlier assault on her children but at its presumed agent, does cause Beloved to vanish; it prepares the way for the novel's concluding reconciliation and affirmation. Sethe at first despairs at losing her child yet again, but her complete breakdown and retreat from life, following the previous example of Baby Suggs, is halted by the return of Paul D, whose acceptance of Sethe and the past asserts Sethe's ability to face the future. Contrary to Sethe's belief that her children were her "best things," that her all-encompassing love was the essential justification for her to kill them rather than allow them to be returned to slavery, Paul D insists, "You your best thing, Sethe. You are." The revelation he offers Sethe suggests that the past need not tyrannize but must be fully confronted, with wholeness being the result of self-respect *and* selflessness, of individual autonomy and participation in a sustaining wider human community.

Morrison was awarded the Pulitzer Prize for *Beloved*, 1988, and it is considered her masterpiece. In the novel Morrison buried a repressed, traumatizing past and then allowed it only gradually to emerge in disjointed, lethal images. In a present haunted by the past, a spirit from the host of the anonymous dead magically appears and compels an exorcism. Morrison's protagonists are left to celebrate their resilience and survival, yet what remains unresolved are the effects of the systematic cruelty and devastation of slavery upon the black community. In a work of shattering emotional intensity and historical synthesis Morrison has crafted one of the essential novels of the second half of the twentieth century.

THE SHAWL

by Cynthia Ozick

Dealing almost exclusively with the challenges faced by Jews in the modern world, Cynthia Ozick has turned her subject into a profound and universal exploration of the struggle for spiritual survival and affirmation in the face of seemingly insurmountable obstacles. Critic Diane Cole has asserted, "Few contemporary authors have demonstrated her range, knowledge, or passion," while Elaine M. Kauvar has described Ozick as a "master of the meticulous sentence and champion of the moral sense of art." The author of four novels—*Trust* (1966), *The Cannibal Galaxy* (1983), *The Messiah of Stockholm* (1987), and *The Puttermesser Papers* (1997)—Ozick has gained perhaps her most acclaim for her short fiction, collected in such volumes as *The Pagan Rabbi* (1971), *Bloodshed and Three Novellas* (1976), and *Levitation: Five Fictions* (1982). As critic Carol Horn has observed, "Her stories are elusive, mysterious, and disturbing. They shimmer with intelligence, they glory in language, and they puzzle." Two of her greatest achievements are the harrowing "The Shawl" and its sequel, the novella, *Rosa*, collected in the volume *The Shawl*, published in 1989. There are few better imaginings of the impact of the Holocaust or more striking introductions to this important writer's work.

Ozick was born in New York City, in 1928. Her parents, Russian-Jewish immigrants, were the owners of the Park View Pharmacy in the Pelham Bay section of the Bronx, where Ozick helped out by delivering prescriptions. At age five, Ozick was taken to Hebrew school by her grandmother, who was told by the rabbi not to bring her back because "a girl doesn't have to study." Ozick later traced the origins of her feminism to this experience and has expressed gratitude to her grandmother who rejected the rabbi's order and insisted that her granddaughter be allowed to stay in his class. Ozick would subsequently impress the rabbi with her "golden head," which quickly mastered her lessons. Attending public school in the Bronx, Ozick found it "brutally difficult to be a Jew" there; she remembers having stones thrown at her, being called a Christ-killer, and being publicly humiliated for refusing to sing Christmas carols. She excelled academically, however, at the all-girl Hunter College High School in Manhattan, where she mastered Latin poetry. She graduated from New York University, in 1949, and received a master's degree from Ohio State University, in 1950, writing a thesis entitled "Parable in the Later Novels of Henry James." Although Ozick has stated that her decision to become a writer dates "from the first moment of sentience," it was with her discovery of Henry James at the age of seventeen that she received the calling "to serve as a priest at the altar of literature."

In 1952, she married Bernard Hallote, an attorney. After a year in Boston, where Ozick worked as a department store copywriter, the couple moved into her parents' home in the Bronx. Ozick, using her childhood bedroom as a study, worked for a number of years on an ambitious philosophical novel called *Mercy, Pity, Peace, and Love*, which echoed James's *The Ambassadors*. She finally abandoned it and devoted seven years, from 1957 to 1963, to what would be her first published novel, *Trust*—a nuanced exploration of identity and self-discovery through the search for a biological father; in it Ozick's own unique voice and subjects began to emerge from the influences of James, E.M. Forster, and F. Scott Fitzgerald. "In writing *Trust*," Ozick has stated, "I began as an American novelist and ended as a Jewish novelist. I Judaized myself as I wrote it." She would evolve through her first novel the repeated theme that would dominate her subsequent work: the opposing claims of two dominating impulses, the pagan and the holy. As writer Eve Ottenberg has observed, Ozick's "characters struggle, suffer, perform bizarre feats, even go mad as a result of remaining or finding out what it means to remain—culturally, and above all, religiously—Jewish. . . . Her characters are often tempted into worshiping something other than God—namely, idols. And this struggle marks her characters with a singular aloneness—the aloneness of people who are thinking a great deal about who they are, and for whom thinking, not doing, is the most emotional and engaging aspect of their lives."

Ottenberg's characterization of the moral dynamic of Ozick's fictional universe is helpful for an understanding of *The Shawl*, which crystallizes many of Ozick's themes of Jewish identity, idolatry, isolation and community, and the crippling impact of the past. Both the story and the novella in it center on Rosa Lublin, a Polish Holocaust survivor who, in "The Shawl," witnesses the death of her baby daughter, Magda, in a Nazi concentration camp. Rosa's story is resumed thirty-five years later in *Rosa*. Now living in Miami, still unable to face the fact of her daughter's brutal murder, Rosa struggles to come to grips with her past and her present, providing the reader with an intimate and illuminating exploration of a psyche still haunted by a horrific experience, as she fights to cope with the costs and consequences of her memories.

Only eight pages long, "The Shawl" is one of the most powerful attempts to depict the horrors of the Holocaust in literature. On the march to a concentration camp, Rosa, accompanied by her teenage niece Stella, attempts to protect her infant daughter Magda by hiding her in her shawl. The shawl serves both as a protection for Magda, concealing her from the view of the Nazis, and as a pacifier, which the baby sucks after Rosa's milk dries up, silencing the cries that might give her away. After arriving in the camp, Rosa hears Magda's cry as she crawls, shawless, on the ground outside. Rosa runs back into the barracks to retrieve the comforting shawl to stifle Magda's cries and discovers that Stella has taken the baby's shawl to keep from freezing. Rosa seizes the shawl, hurries back to Magda, but it is too late. A German officer has picked up the baby and is headed to the electrified fence. Rosa's maternal instinct to save her child battles with her instinct for self-preservation, aware that she will be shot if she screams. As Magda is flung against the electrified fence to her death, Rosa stifles her cries by stuffing the shawl into her mouth:

All at once Magda was swimming through the air. The whole of
Magda traveled through loftiness. She looked like a butterfly
touching a silver vine. And the moment Magda's feathered round
head and her pencil legs and balloonish belly and zigzag arms
splashed against the fence, the steel voices went mad in their
growling, urging Rosa to run and run to the spot where Magda
had fallen from her flight against the electrified fence; but of
course Rosa did not obey them. She only stood, because if she ran
they would shoot, and if she tried to pick up the sticks of Magda's
body they would shoot, and if she let the wolf's screech ascending
now through the ladder of her skeleton break out, they would
shoot; so she took Magda's shawl and filled her own mouth with it,
stuffed it in and stuffed it in, until she was swallowing up the wolf's
screech and tasting the cinnamon and almond depth of Magda's
saliva, and Rosa drank Magda's shawl until it dried.

In language that is as precise as it is poetic, Ozick captures the
unimaginable horror of the Holocaust with a focus on the crippling paralysis and contradictions of the survivors.

To penetrate what Elie Wiesel has called "Rosa's dark and devastated soul," Ozick revisits her protagonist in *Rosa* some thirty-
five years later. Rosa and Stella have survived the camps and
made it to America, where Rosa operates an antique shop in New
York. Refusing to accept her daughter's death, Rosa creates a
bright future for Magda in her mind while turning the shawl that
protected her into a kind of holy relic, a means to evade the awful
truth of her experience. Infuriated when her customers show no
interest in the story of Jewish suffering she feels compelled to recount to them, unable and unwilling to adapt to life after her
traumatic experience, Rosa smashes up her store. Stella arranges
for her aunt's relocation to Miami Beach, where she lives in a
rundown retirement hotel. Resembling a "madwoman and a
scavenger," Rosa is disengaged from the life around her, rarely
venturing outside her tiny room, spending her time writing long
letters to her niece and to Magda, whom she imagines enjoying a
happy, productive life. She has requested that Stella send her the
shawl, and her niece responds: "Your idol is on its way. . . . Go on
your knees to it if you want. . . . You'll open the box and take it
out and cry, you'll kiss it like a crazy person. Make holes in it with
kisses. You're like those people in the Middle Ages who worshipped a piece of the True Cross, a splinter from some old outhouse. . . ." Like so many of Ozick's characters, Rosa copes with

reality as an idol worshiper, substituting a more pleasing or necessary myth for the truth.

On the day that *Rosa* begins, her routine and her increasing retreat into isolated fantasy is halted when she meets at the laundromat an old man with false teeth, a red wig, and a Polish accent. He introduces himself as Simon Persky, "a third cousin to Shimon Peres, the Israeli politician." Unlike Rosa's indifferent customers in New York, Persky is fascinated by Rosa's story and sympathetically claims kinship with her. Like her, Persky is a native of Warsaw, and he exposes the prejudices Rosa has long had about her Jewish identity. Rosa had been raised by assimilated Polish Jews, and everything about Persky—from the Yiddish paper he read, to his heavy accent, to what she imagines is the stink of the Warsaw ghetto that he must have inhabited—are objectionable characteristics she has rejected. However, in a series of ironically achieved insights, Rosa begins to see herself more clearly in Persky's reflection, including her own inadequate English, unkempt appearance, and old woman's odors. It is a shock of self-recognition that helps to break the spell of the past that has robbed Rosa of a present and future. When Magda's shawl arrives from Stella, its power as a relic that has imprisoned Rosa is broken. It is finally seen for what it is, a "colorless cloth" with "a faint saliva smell." As Rosa admits Persky to her room, and presumably to her reengaged life, the story concludes with an acknowledgement that the child who has haunted Rosa has finally been put to rest: "Magda was not there. Shy, she ran from Persky. Magda was away."

Rosa's recovery of herself in Ozick's view begins with facing the truth and accepting it in all its contradictions and ambiguities. Looking deeply beneath the exterior of a "madwoman and a scavenger," Ozick has uncovered an extraordinary character trying to cope with the unspeakable, unrelenting realities of modern existence. Ozick's remarkable volume justifies Elie Wiesel's description of *The Shawl* as "dazzling and staggering pages filled with sadness and truth."

BACKLASH

by Susan Faludi

Susan Faludi's *Backlash: The Undeclared War Against American Women* (1991) sets out to expose a troubling anomaly: why is it that, in the 1980s, after American women's apparent victories in the fight for equality, "another message flashes. You may be free and equal now, it says to women, but you have never been more miserable." Faludi identifies a persistent, media-driven "counterassault on women's rights, a backlash, an attempt to retract the handful of small and hard-won victories that the feminist movement did manage to achieve for women. This counterassault is largely insidious: in a kind of pop-culture version of the Big Lie, it stands the truth boldly on its head and proclaims that the very steps that have elevated women's position have actually led to their downfall." A controversial bestseller, *Backlash* has evoked comparisons with Simone de Beauvoir's *The Second Sex* and Betty Friedan's *The Feminine Mystique* as "feminism's new manifesto" in which, in the words of reviewer Laura Shapiro of *Newsweek,* "Once you've read this hair-raising but meticulously documented analysis, you may never read a magazine or see a movie or walk through a department store the same way again." The book made Faludi a sought-after guest on talk shows and a feminist spokesperson, though she rejected her elevation "as a sort of seer," preferring her role as a reporter and emphasizing the importance of her book as investigative journalism that corrects damaging falsifications. "To the extent that *Backlash* arms women with information and a good dose of cynicism," Faludi has asserted, "I think it will have served its purpose." She adds a secondary use for *Backlash*: "It's also very large, so it can be thrown at misogynists."

Susan Faludi was born in 1959, in New York City, the daughter of photographer Steven Faludi and Marilyn Faludi, a dynamic and outspoken woman who gave up her career ambitions to become a traditional housewife until she divorced her husband, in 1976. Faludi, who dedicated *Backlash* to her mother, has credited her mother's frustrations with her husband's "old-world belief that women should stay home, be decorative, make elaborate meals, and do all the traditional duties of wifedom," with teaching her about the circumscribed lives of women. "My mother has been cheated," she has said, "and the world's been cheated of her talents." Faludi's interest in journalism and her willingness to court controversy began in high school, when she surveyed her classmates on such hot-button topics as the Vietnam War, abortion, and the Equal Rights Amendment; for this she was accused of having "incited communism." As managing editor of the *Harvard Crimson*, Faludi reported on sexual harassment on campus, implicating a Harvard professor. Despite pressure from the professor and the administration to abandon the story, Faludi refused to back down, and the professor was eventually forced to take a leave of absence.

Faludi's first job after college was as a copy clerk for *The New York Times*, where her efforts to rise up in the ranks were rebuffed by a male reporter who told her that, because women were able to carry a baby for nine months, they were "biologically more patient," and she should defer to the more urgent need of male ambition. Faludi left *The Times*, in 1982, for a job with *The Miami Herald* and then a general reporting position at *The Atlanta Journal-Constitution*. After moving to the California, in 1985, Faludi worked for *West*, the Sunday magazine of the *San Jose Mercury News*, and, in 1990, became a staff writer for the San Francisco bureau of *The Wall Street Journal*. She wrote on how President Ronald Reagan's budget cuts impacted poor children and how companies in California's Silicon Valley were replacing older employees with younger, more cost-effective workers. In 1991, she won the Pulitzer Prize for her investigative reporting on the human cost of the $5.65 billion leveraged buyout of the Safeway Stores.

The genesis of *Backlash* began with Faludi's reaction to a 1986 study, featured as a cover story in *Newsweek*, that had been conducted by a research team from Harvard and Yale; it claimed that college-educated women at age thirty had only a twenty percent chance of getting married; by age thirty-five, the study found, their chances dropped to only five percent, and by age forty, the study asserted, a woman was "more likely to be killed by a terrorist" than find a husband. This so-called "marriage crunch" among women who had put off marriage for careers was widely reported, and its conclusion accepted that women would be wise to set aside their careers in favor of a quest for marriage. "What was remarkable to me," Faludi recalled, "was that there was so little interest in finding out whether the study was true or false. The story simply fit the notion of where women were at that point in history." Faludi investigated and discovered that the methodology used to generate the marriage study was flawed, and the study's unrepresentative sampling suggested that the report's conclusions were suspect. Despite contrary evidence, the myth of the marriage crunch and the warning to career women had taken hold. *Backlash* was written during an eighteen-month leave from Faludi's reporting assignments. During her leave she investigated the accuracy of other widely reported trend stories about women's status in the 1980s, including accounts of professional women leaving the workforce in large numbers to care for their homes and children, and increasing instances of single career women suffering from depression, nervous breakdown, and burnout. Faludi concluded that these were misrepresentations and misinterpretations, instances of a larger trend to discredit the women's movement. Faludi called these anti-liberation myths about single and working women are "the chisels of a society-wide backlash. They are part of a relentless whittling-down process—much of it amounting to outright propaganda—that has served to stir women's private anxieties and break their political wills." Describing her book's title, Faludi explains that

> *Backlash* happens to be a title of a 1947 Hollywood movie in which a man frames his wife for a murder he's committed. The backlash

against women's rights works in much the same way: its rhetoric charges feminists with all the crimes it perpetrates. The backlash line blames the women's movement for the "feminization of poverty"—while the backlash's own instigators in Washington pushed through the budget cuts that helped impoverish millions of women, fought pay equity proposals, and undermined equal opportunity laws. The backlash line claims the women's movement cares nothing for children's rights—while its own representatives in the capital and state legislatures have blocked one bill after another to improve child care, slashed bullions of dollars in federal aid for children, and relaxed state licensing standards for day care centers. The backlash line accuses the women's movement of creating a generation of unhappy single and childless women—but its purveyors in the media are the ones guilty of making single and childless women feel like circus freaks.

Backlash supplies a compendium of examples of the ways in which an attack on the women's movement and its achievements has been perpetuated in print, on television, in the movies, by the fashion and cosmetic industries, and in national politics. Faludi shows how the media and politicians present women's liberation as the source of women's problems, by distorting the facts and perpetrating myths that undermine equality and autonomy for women. "The backlash is at once sophisticated and banal," Faludi concludes, "deceptively 'progressive' and proudly backward. It deploys both the 'new' findings of 'scientific research' and the dime-store moralism of yesteryear; it turns into media sound bites both the glib pronouncements of pop-psych trend-watchers and the frenzied rhetoric of New Right preachers. The backlash has succeeded in framing virtually the whole issue of women's rights in its own language. Just as Reaganism shifted political discourse far to the right and demonized liberals, so the backlash convinced the public that women's 'liberation' was the true contemporary American scourge—the source of an endless laundry list of personal, social, and economic problems."

Backlash is particularly insightful (and entertaining) on how the depiction of women in the media helps to undermine gains made by the women's movement—by reporting dubious trends like the flight of women from the workforce to a more fulfilling life as homemaker or the mythical 1980s "baby boom" spawned by a "terror" of infertility and anxiety over the ticking biological clock. As Faludi concludes, the press was "not only dictating to women how they should feel, but persuading them that the voice barking orders was only their uterus talking." The demonizing of the single career woman, and the apotheosis of the post-liberation housewife, are ably demonstrated by Faludi on television and the movies. Faludi insightfully details how one of the most popular films of the 1980s, *Fatal Attraction*, was transformed from a story of how a married man must take responsibility for destroying the life of a single woman with whom he has an affair to the pathology of a single woman who must be killed to save a traditional household. "In the end," Faludi observes, "the attraction is fatal only for the single woman."

Backlash also features profiles of a number of antifeminists, including George Gilder, author of *Wealth and Power* and a former speechwriter for President Reagan, Allen Bloom, the author of *The Closing of the American Mind*, a book that decries feminism's supposedly pernicious influence in higher education, Robert Bly, author of *Iron John* and a founder of the men's movement in the United States, Sylvia Ann Hewlett, author of *A Lesser Life: The Myth of Women's Liberation in America*, and Michael Levin, author of *Feminism and Freedom*, a work that denounces feminism as an "antidemocratic, if not totalitarian, ideology." As Gayle Greene observed in her review of *Backlash*, "Faludi must be a crackerjack interviewer, letting subjects babble on until they blurt out marvelously self-incriminating revelations, offering up the real reasons they hate and fear feminists—motives that are self-serving, silly, often sinister—which Faludi simply, deadpan, recounts."

Backlash counters the myths by showing how contemporary women's anxieties and frustrations stem not from too much freedom and equality but from too little. Contrary to the backlash myths, Faludi demonstrates that women must still struggle for equality in politics, the workplace, at school, and at home, the real cause for women's discontent. The average women college graduate, Faludi demonstrates, still earns less than the average man with a high school diploma, and American women "face the worst gender-based pay gap in the developed world." This is exacerbated by insufficient childcare and family-leave policies. Women, Faludi shows, "still shoulder 70 percent of the household duties. . . . Furthermore, in thirty states, it is still generally legal for husbands to rape their wives; and only ten states have laws mandating arrest for domestic violence—even though battering was the leading cause of injury of women in the late '80s." While some of the statistics have changed in the years since *Backlash* was published, the need for countering misleading myths with truth remains fundamental. Women still are bombarded by contrary messages about marriage, motherhood, and careers, as well as new obstacles to achieving social justice and equality. *Backlash* helps its reader understand the ways in which popular culture and politics work out agendas that must be understood and confronted.

THE BEAUTY MYTH

by Naomi Wolf

Named by *The New York Times* as one of the seventy most influential books of the twentieth century, and hailed as "a provocative new feminist tract which should take its place alongside such polemics as Betty Friedan's *The Feminist Mystique*," Naomi Wolf's *The Beauty Myth: How Images of Beauty Are Used Against Women* (1991) suggests that the feminine mystique, which defined women by their domestic role, has been succeeded by a beauty mystique that dictates that women must be slim, young, conventionally good-looking, and subservient to men. As Wolf argues, "We are in the midst of a violent backlash against feminism that uses images of female beauty as a political weapon against women's advancement." The beauty myth, which promulgates an unrealistic (and unhealthy) ideal of female beauty, is "undermining—slowly, imperceptibly, without our being aware of the real forces of erosion—the ground women have gained through the long, hard, honorable struggle," according to Wolf. She asserts that the beauty myth has been one of the fundamental means of social control for men to secure patriarchal dominance. "I contend that this obsession with beauty in the Western world . . . is, in fact, the last way men can defend themselves against women claiming power." She suggests that the beauty myth is destroying women physically and psychologically. It is responsible for the rise of eating disorders, an increase in unneeded and dangerous cosmetic surgery, a general decline in women's self-esteem, with envy and competition growing among women, as well as a morbid fear of aging, and the addition of a "third shift"—after career and domestic chores—to overwhelm women with pursuing beautification at the expense of gaining real social power and achieving gender equality. As a result of the beauty myth, "in terms of how we feel about ourselves physically," Wolf concludes, "we may actually be worse off than our unliberated grandmothers."

The Beauty Myth offers a powerful and challenging way to view the cultural coding of beauty and its impact on women, raising awareness and provoking positive social change. "What I've tried to do," Wolf explained in an interview, "is make an argument so powerful that by the end the reader either has to find a situation we take for granted intolerable and take steps to change it—or kill the messenger."

The messenger was born in 1962, the daughter of academic parents in San Francisco, who grew up, in her words, "as a baby of the counterculture." The Wolf family lived in the Haight-Ashbury neighborhood, the epicenter of the free-love and "flower power" upheavals of the 1960s. As Wolf recalled in her book *Promiscuities: The Secret Struggle for Womanhood* (1997), "The city made us feel that we were not alive if we were not being sexual." During her teens, Wolf became obsessed with her body image and developed anorexia. "Adolescent starvation," Wolf writes in *The Beauty Myth*, "was for me a prolonged reluctance to be born into woman if that meant assuming a station of beauty." Despite serious health problems, Wolf excelled academically and graduated from Yale University in 1984. She became a Rhodes scholar, studying English at Oxford University and working on a doctoral thesis that focused on male and female writers of the nineteenth and twentieth centuries and how they "used beauty differently." In it, she demonstrated that "male writers often used beauty not to illuminate, but to silence women characters." Wolf's literary research became personal when she overheard a colleague say that she had won her Rhodes scholarship because of her looks. "I had an image of the documents I had presented to the committee—my essay, book of poems I had written, letters of recommendation—and the whole of it being swept away by that one sentence," she recalled in a 1991 interview. Although she never completed her Oxford degree, Wolf extended her research into the culturally inscribed standards of female beauty and their consequences, turning her thesis into *The Beauty Myth*, which created a sensation when it was first published in England in 1990, and in the United States in 1991.

Widely reviewed and discussed, *The Beauty Myth* was praised for raising important points and offering a new perspective on the obstacles faced by women in achieving good self-esteem and empowerment. As Caryn James observed in a *New York Times* review, "No other work has so forcefully confronted the anti-feminism that emerged during the conservative, yuppified 1980's, or so honestly depicted the confusion of accomplished women who feel emotionally and physically tortured by the need to look like movie stars." The book was also attacked for making sweeping generalizations at the expense of more objective, careful documentation. Some critics complained that Wolf's conception of the beauty myth confused a symptom with a cause. Betty Friedan criticized Wolf for dealing with the superficial rather than coming to grips with the modern-day political and social challenges that confront women; while Diane Johnson commented that Wolf "ultimately attributes all social evils . . . to the frenzied thrashings of threatened manhood, and here it is possible that she has not cast her net wide enough." Ironically, confirming Wolf's thesis that beauty is often used to silence women, the author's own good looks were held against her by several of the book's critics. As writer Lynn Darling observed, "The book that Wolf saw as 'a tribute to women's beauty and power' became, in flip media shorthand, a beautiful woman's condemnation of other women's attempt to be beautiful." Wolf remained undaunted by the controversy *The Beauty Myth* generated, confidently insisting to an interviewer, "I'm trying to seize this culture by its collar and say 'Stop! Look what you're doing!' To the extent that people get angry, I know I've done a good job."

The Beauty Myth mounts its case by identifying the pressures women face to look beautiful, in which an impossible ideal of eternal, youthful beauty has replaced the prefeminist goal of perfect domestic bliss. Women have left the home for careers, but little has changed to replace physical perfection as women's true source of fulfillment and constant anxiety. "The closer women come to power," Wolf asserts, "the more physical self-consciousness and sacrifice are asked of them." She summarizes the persistence of the beauty myth to undermine female empowerment: "During the past decade, women breached the power structure; meanwhile, eating disorders rose exponentially and cosmetic surgery became the fastest-growing medical specialty. During the past five years, consumer spending doubled, pornography became the main media category . . . and thirty-three thousand American women told researchers that they would rather lose ten to fifteen pounds than achieve any other goal." The beauty myth originates, according to Wolf, from men whose power is threatened by feminist gains, and it is internalized by women because the myth "exploits female guilt and apprehension about our own liberation." As Wolf explains, "The beauty myth of the present is more insidious than any mystique of femininity yet: A century ago, Nora slammed the door of the doll's house; a generation ago, women turned their backs on the consumer heaven of the isolated multi-applianced home; but where women are trapped today, there is no door to slam. The contemporary ravages of the beauty backlash are destroying women physically and depleting us psychologically. If we are to free ourselves from the dead weight that has once again been made out of femaleness, it is not ballots or lobbyists or placards that women will need first; it is a new way to see."

Wolf proceeds to show how the beauty myth operates in the workforce and the marketplace, draining time, attention, and money from women to satisfy what Wolf labels a Professional Beauty Qualification (PBQ) that has been added to their career aspirations. "For every feminist action," Wolf observes, "there is an equal and opposite beauty myth reaction. In the 1980s it was evident that as women became more important, beauty too became more important. The closer women come to power, the more physical self-consciousness and sacrifice are asked of them. 'Beauty' becomes the condition for a woman to take the next step. You are now too rich. Therefore, you cannot be too thin." The beauty myth is enforced by cultural ideals that profit a $20 billion-a-year cosmetics industry, a $33 billion diet industry, and a $300 million cosmetic-surgery industry (75 percent of whose patients are women), and a $7 billion pornography industry. Wolf draws a connection between women's subjugation to the beauty myth and a cult psychology that gives over personal power in order to achieve an illusive promise of thinness, youth, and an approved standard of beauty. Women, in Wolf's view, are complicit in their own objectification to male dictates. "Placing female pleasure, sex or food or self-esteem into the hands of a personal judge turns the man into a legislator of the woman's pleasure, rather than her companion in it," Wolf contends. " 'Beauty' today is what the female orgasm used to be; something given to women by men, if they submitted to their feminine role and were lucky." Wolf measures the cost to women of subscribing to the beauty myth in the rise of eating disorders, in the growing popularity of expensive and often dangerous cosmetic surgery, and in the unreasonable percentage of women's earnings spent on dubious cosmetics, dieting products, and impractical clothing. All contribute not only to a physical but a psychological torment of women, who find themselves chasing an unrealistic and unrealizable phantom of perpetual, perfect beauty.

Wolf concludes *The Beauty Myth* with an alternative set of choices proceeding from the rejection of the beauty myth and the release of a "feminist third wave." We must, Wolf concludes, "dismantle the PBQ; support the unionization of women's jobs; make 'beauty' harassment, age discrimination, unsafe working conditions such as enforced surgery, and the double standard of appearance, issues for labor negotiation; women in television and other heavily discriminatory professions must organize for wave after wave of lawsuits; we must insist on equal enforcement of dress codes, take a deep breath, and tell our stories." Seeing the beauty myth for what it is, Wolf insists, will break its power and allow for a reinterpretation of beauty that is "noncompetitive, nonhierarchical, and nonviolent." To achieve this goal, Wolf urges women to "be shameless. Be greedy. Pursue pleasure. Avoid pain. Wear and touch and eat and drink what we feel like. Tolerate other women's choices. Seek out the sex we want and fight fiercely against the sex we do not want. Choose our own causes. And once we break through and change the rules so our senses of our own beauty cannot be shaken, sing that beauty and dress it up and flaunt it and revel in it: In a sensual politics, female is beautiful."

BRIDGET JONES'S DIARY

by Helen Fielding

Bridget Jones's Diary by Helen Fielding records the romantic, professional, and personal trials and tribulations of a bright, klutzy, often neurotic, thirty-something single woman. Sound familiar? From *Friends,* to *Ally McBeal,* to *Sex in the City* the single woman in the postfeminist world seems ubiquitous, dominating the new genres of "chick lit" and "chick flicks." *Bridget Jones's Diary* (published in England in 1996 and the United States in 1998), though not the first novel to tackle the subject of the "singleton," defined and set the standard for the form. One of the most popular novels of the 1990s, *Bridget Jones's Diary* became a cultural phenomenon, with its heroine proclaimed an iconic, hapless but endearing everywoman, and her creator praised for seizing the comic zeitgeist of postmodern courtship, lifestyles, and the self-actualizing rituals of the urban hip. *Bridget Jones's Diary* is a witty, hilarious survey of contemporary mores and mantras that allows its readers vicariously to court social and relationship disasters with Bridget while seeing themselves reflected in the exaggerated lens of her manias and obsessions. Bridget's missteps and consumer- and media-driven angst certainly make us laugh and, although it is always dangerous to dissect a joke or to belabor the search for meaning in a work that its creator has insisted was motivated strictly by a spirit of fun, can still claim intriguing cultural significance. As Elizabeth Glieck observed in *The New York Times*, "People will be passing around copies of *Bridget Jones's Diary* for a reason: It captures neatly the way modern women teeter between 'I am woman' independence and a pathetic girlie desire to be all things to all men." The novel takes as its subject the peculiarly modern phenomenon of the nontraditional single household and post–women's liberation gender identity, and finds its humor in the disjunction between the female ideal and lifestyle rewards Bridget strives for and actuality, between the conception of the modern superwoman—self-possessed, empowered, fulfilled in the bedroom, nursery, and boardroom—and the reality that turns seekers of feminine perfection like Bridget into train wrecks of needy, self-absorbed inadequacy. "Women today are bombarded with so many messages," Fielding has observed, "like we should have Naomi Campbell's body and Madeline Albright's career. Here's someone saying, 'I can't be all these things!' but trying anyway." Therein lies both the fun of *Bridget Jones's Diary* and its extraordinary resonance among readers. "Bridget is groping through the complexities of dealing with relationships in a morass of shifting roles," Fielding has observed, "and a bombardment of idealised images of modern womanhood. It seems she's not the only one who's confused."

Fielding has deflected the suggestion that her protagonist is based on herself by calling Bridget "an imaginary amalgam of insecurities," contrasting herself with the Chardonnay-drinking, nicotine-addled, relationship-deprived Bridget by stating, "I don't drink, I don't smoke and am a virgin . . . yeah, right!" There are in fact sufficient correspondences between creator and creation to see Bridget at least as an alter ego. Born in 1959, in Yorkshire, Fielding is the daughter of a mill manager and a homemaker. After graduating from Oxford University, in 1979, she worked for a decade as a producer for the BBC before becoming a freelance writer. Her first novel, *Cause Celeb* (1994), is based on her experiences producing the Comic Relief charity telethon on behalf of African famine relief for the BBC. In 1995, an editor for London's *Independent* newspaper, where she was working as a feature writer, approached her to provide a weekly column based on her life as a single professional woman. She instead opted for the anonymity of a fictional persona. "You can be so much more honest if it's not supposed to be your own life," Fielding has explained. "You can shamelessly detail exactly what goes on in the three hours between waking up and leaving for work late." *Bridget Jones's Diary* debuted on February 28, 1995. After the first few columns, she thought, "This is self-conscious, stupid, who wants to read this? Then people started to say they liked it, and, being, as my agent says, as shallow as a puddle, I immediately admitted it was me since it was praise." Fielding drew on her own experiences and those of her single and married friends, for material to capture the 1990s London lifestyle. She also consulted some of her old diaries and duplicated her tendency to record caloric, alcohol, and nicotine intake that she uses to preface each diary entry as a gauge to Bridget's emotional states. A typical entry begins: "129 lbs. (excellent progress)—2 lbs. of fat spontaneously combusted through joy and sexual promise), alcohol units 6 (v.g. for party), cigarettes 12 (continuing good work), calories 1258 (love has eradicated need to pig out)."

To produce her novel, Fielding reformulated material from her columns into a year in the life of Bridget Jones with a romantic narrative structure echoing Jane Austen's *Pride and Prejudice*. Austen's sparkling courtship drama in which the sharp-tongued, quick-witted Elizabeth Bennet resists and later falls in love with the presumed arrogant Mr. Darcy is one of the most beloved romantic novels of all time, a realistic fairy tale in which a disadvantaged heroine manages to claim the hand of a gentleman of means and stature after the lovers readjust their distorted views of the other and of themselves. As a story that submits romance to the conditioning influences of family, class, economics, and identity, *Pride and Prejudice* is the perfect model for Fielding's purposes in which satire, love, and self-obsession are so inextricably mixed. Commenting on *Pride and Prejudice* and her borrowing from it, Fielding has observed, "I thought that it had been very well market-researched over a number of centuries." Bridget becomes a modern self-improvement-obsessed version of Elizabeth Bennet, starting the new year resolved to lose weight, stop smoking, get a grip on her drinking, learn to program her VCR, and develop "inner poise and authority and sense of self as a woman of substance, complete *without* boyfriend, as best way to obtain boyfriend." Despite her best intentions, she will through the course of the year consume 5,277 cigarettes, 3836 "alcohol units," gain seventy-four pounds while losing seventy-two, secure a boyfriend (the roguish Daniel Cleaver), lose him through his fecklessness, and finally gain another, Mark Darcy. She spends much of the year annoyed with Mark and humiliated in his presence.

Bridget begins her year in torment over her independent status as a single professional woman with a deep-seated need for fulfillment in a relationship, hoping to relieve the singleton's greatest fear of perishing "all alone, half-eaten by an Alsatian." Beset by the "Smug Marrieds" and family and friends who delight in making ticking biological clock sounds and impertinent inquiries about her love life ("We wouldn't rush up to *them* and roar, 'How's your marriage going? Still having sex?' "), the newly resolved Bridget first must endure a New Year's Day Turkey Curry Buffet at Geoffrey and Una Alconbury's suburban home, the first in a series of public disgraces that will test Bridget's "inner poise." There she encounters her intended setup, distinguished human rights lawyer Mark Darcy. The irony is not missed by Bridget: "It struck me as pretty ridiculous to be called Mr. Darcy and to stand on your own looking snooty at a party. It's like being called Heathcliff and insisting on spending the entire evening in the garden, shouting 'Cathy' and banging your head against a tree." Needless to say, the two do not hit it off. ("It's not that I wanted him to take my phone number or anything, but I didn't want him to make it perfectly obvious to everyone that he didn't want to.") Back at work as a publicist at a London publishing firm, Bridget conducts a protracted flirtation with her bad-boy boss, Daniel Cleaver, which features suggestive e-mails, a short skirt, and eventual sex but with insufficient follow-up phone calls.

By spring, however, Daniel assumes full boyfriend status. Instead of a summer of love, Bridget gets to watch cricket with Daniel in a baking apartment with curtains drawn. Even the promise of a romantic mini-break provides little fulfillment, other than watching Match of the Day inside their quaint room at an inn. Meanwhile, Bridget's ditzy mother, Pam, has rebelled against her suburban life as a homemaker, managed to wrangle a better job than Bridget's as a television presenter, and begun an affair with a shady operator named Julio. Humiliations continue when Bridget arrives at a Tarts and Vicars fancy-dress lawn party at the Alconburys in black lace stockings, suspenders, and a cotton rabbit's tail, having missed the message that the dress up has been canceled. Again Mark Darcy is in attendance, and they quarrel over his animosity toward Daniel. Returning from the party unannounced to Daniel's apartment, Bridget discovers his American lover. Inner poise gives way to disintegration: "I'm falling apart. My boyfriend is sleeping with a bronzed giantess. My mother is sleeping with a Portuguese. . . . Prince Charles is sleeping with Camilla Parker-Bowles. Do not know what to believe in or hold on to anymore."

Bridget breaks with Daniel and lands a new job on the current affairs television program *Good Afternoon!* where bad timing causes a live on-air spot of her sliding down a fireman's pole to show her trying to climb back up. Inexplicably, an invitation arrives for Bridget to attend the celebration of Mark Darcy's parents' ruby anniversary, where Bridget spends much of her time embarrassed by her family. Despite learning that Mark was not responsible for the invitation, Bridget does receive a date request from him and a major concession: " 'Bridget,' " Darcy declares, " 'all the other girls I know are so lacquered over. I don't know anyone else who would fasten a bunny tail to their pants . . .'" Mark sounds the novel's moral point that the imperfect Bridget is preferable to the lifeless paragons she aspires to become. This is a lesson that Bridget still must learn while reassessing her previous assumptions about Mark. To win him, Bridget tries to prove herself a stylish hostess only to endure the humiliation of a dinner party in which the soup turns blue, the tuna steaks mysteriously disappear, and the confit of oranges turns into marmalade. Her burgeoning relationship with Mark is further tested when Bridget's mother gets involved with Julio's phony time-share scheme, which bilks the savings of the Joneses and their friends, including Mark's parents. Mark's efforts to save Mrs. Jones make clear the points of both his worthiness and his willingness to accept Bridget as is—flaws, family, and all. Bridget, a Cinderella-also-ran, wins a Prince Charming after all, despite impossible obstacles, and in defiance of all her resolutions and self-help advice.

It is unclear as the novel concludes what, if anything, Bridget Jones has learned over the course of her year. Unlike Elizabeth Bennet, who realizes that she has been "blind, partial, prejudiced, and absurd" while recognizing the superiority of Darcy's judgment and experience and the expanded possibilities that his prospects offer, Bridget is, though rewarded in love, still far from stability and self-possession. The perfect harmony and blending of spirit and sense that delight the reader of *Pride and Prejudice* are beyond the reach of Bridget, and the reader suspects her battle with calories, cigarettes, alcohol units, and neuroses will delightfully continue (as indeed they do in Fielding's 2000 sequel, *Bridget Jones: The Edge of Reason*). As Bridget admits, "I am a child of *Cosmopolitan* culture, have been traumatized by supermodels and too many quizzes and know that neither my personality nor my body is up to it if left to its own devices. I can't take the pressure." It is Bridget's battles that endure and endear, not her victories.

Despite praise for the novel's spot-on accuracy in depicting how contemporary single women in their thirties actually think and feel, many have resisted Bridget as everywoman as cartoonish and a feminist betrayal. Alex Kuczynski has called Bridget "a sorry spectacle, wallowing in her man-crazed helplessness," who has been constructed "out of every myth that has ever sprung from the ground of *Cosmopolitan* and television sitcoms. To wit, that men are, in the words of one character, 'stupid, smug, arrogant, manipulative and self-indulgent'; that women are obsessed with boyfriends, diets and body hair, and that every emotional reversal is cause for a chocolate binge." In defense, it can be argued that Bridget is hardly presented as a role model but as a comic striver beset by the contemporary contradictions of gender in which female independence and autonomy battle with the need to be rescued and validated by a male. Imelda Whelehan, in considering the "chick lit" phenomenon of the 1990s, has observed that "its writers are a generation of women too young to be in the vanguard of the 1970s, and yet aware enough to have absorbed the cultural impact of *The Female Eunuch* and *Fear of Flying.* . . . These women are a part of a generation who felt that feminism did not speak to their needs and hadn't kept apace with its own victories. They perhaps even bought into the idea that it was feminism that had oppressed women by making them lose contact with the pleasures derived from celebrating femininity—dressing up, wearing makeup, and feeling glamorous. There was a significant feeling from the late 1980s onwards that feminism might be restricting women's choices, because it was mistakenly regarded as anti-sex and anti-glamour." Bridget may be a sorry excuse as a feminist, but her perspective on the gender battleground of the postfeminist world is as unavoidable as it is illuminating.

THE BITCH IN THE HOUSE

Compiled and edited by Cathi Hanauer

From 1854 to 1862, English poet Coventry Patmore (1823–1896) published *The Angel in the House*, a long and much-admired poetic sequence celebrating wedded love and the ideal of woman as domestic deity that dominated the nineteenth-century cultural imagination. Patmore's conception of the saintly female paragon, worshipped on her home-bound pedestal, would be later attacked by Virginia Woolf in a 1931 essay in which she states, "You who come of a younger and happier generation may not have heard of her. You may not know what I mean by 'the angel in the house.' She was intensely sympathetic. She was immensely charming. She was utterly unselfish. She excelled in the difficult arts of family life. She sacrificed herself daily. If there was chicken, she took the leg. If there was a draft, she sat in it. In short, she was so constituted that she never had a mind or a wish of her own, but preferred to sympathize always with the minds and wishes of others." In Woolf's view, for a woman to reach her potential, the myth of the all-sacrificing, subordinate woman—the angel in the house—must be killed. In the essay collection, *The Bitch in the House: 26 Women Tell the Truth About Sex, Solitude, Work, Motherhood, and Marriage* (2002), the angel is dead, replaced by her enraged alter ego, telling tales and naming names in the postfeminist gender wars.

The Bitch in the House was conceived and edited by Cathi Hanauer, a novelist (*My Sister's Bones*) and magazine writer who has been the book columnist for *Glamour* and *Mademoiselle*, and was the relationship advice columnist for *Seventeen*. "This book was born out of anger—specifically, my own domestic anger," she states in the introduction, "which stemmed from a combination of guilt, resentment, exhaustion, naiveté, and the chaos of life at the time." Hanauer, in her mid-thirties, moved with husband and two children, from their cramped New York apartment to their dream house in Northampton, Massachusetts, to enjoy the fruits of a less-stressed, egalitarian marriage and coparenting idyll. Hanauer had ostensibly achieved the mythical goal of "having it all." As she recalled, I "had everything I'd ever worked hard to have and everything I'd ever wanted—the husband, the kids, the job—and I found myself, rather than appreciating and being able to enjoy my life, sort of overwhelmed by the juggling act that my life had become. I was stressed out and tired, and I was basically a bitch in the house. And the more I talked to other women, the more I realized how many of us were feeling this way." As a means of understanding her frustrations in dealing with the gap between the contemporary woman's ideal of career-fulfillment, marriage, and motherhood and the often maddening reality, Hanauer solicited reflections on the current temperature of women from "mostly novelists and professional writers, but also a handful of other smart, thinking women who I knew had a story to tell. I requested of these potential contributors that they explore a choice they'd made, or their life situation—or their anger, if they felt it— in an essay; that they offer an interesting glimpse into their private lives, as if they were talking to a friend at a café." Contributors to *The Bitch in the House*, ranging in age from twenty-four to sixty-five, single, married, divorced, with children and without, candidly discuss the challenges they have faced and the revelations they have gained. The book's emphasis is less on self-help advice than on an at times brutally honest assessment of the expectations and disappointments that define a new, virulent strain of "domestic anger." Writers include Pulitzer Prize–winner Natalie Angier, poet Jill Bialosky, essayist Hope Edelman, fiction writers Ellen Gilchrist, Daphne Merkin, Elissa Schappell, and Helen Schulman, and memoirists Veronica Chambers and Vivian Gornick.

The result is a witty, intriguing, and often illuminating look at the lives and values of postfeminist lovers, wives, mothers, and independent women struggling to come to terms with gender expectations, both new and old, and the realities of women's lot in the post-liberation age.

This confessional exercise can be dismissed easily as the self-indulgent whines and gripes of those who seem to have it all and want even more. Such is the reaction of reviewer Joan Smith, who boils down the essence of *The Bitch in the House* to the generic, greedy refrain: "Why can't I have a gorgeous husband, fantastic sex, a fulfilling job, several adorable children, be a full-time mother and a have a few moments left over to write a bestselling novel?" However, *The Bitch in the House* manages to claim both relevance and importance by framing some of the possible terms of the next phase of feminism. As Maria Russo and Alexandra Wolfe write in their review of the collection, "The plight of the unhappy professional woman with children in her late 30's and early 40's has profound dimensions: Pulled between her biological and intellectual destinies, she essentially shortchanges her future if she doesn't pursue either one. But there are only so many hours in the day, so much emotional energy to go around, and part of her knows all too well that she's stuck in a zero-sum game. What sounds like a mere complaint about too many worldly burdens—by someone who's ridiculously privileged, as the human lot goes—is also an expression of a kind of post-feminist social and emotional reckoning." *The Bitch in the House* serves as *The Feminine Mystique* revisited forty years later. Betty Friedan similarly found herself discontented and frustrated conforming to the prescribed gender roles for women of her era as glamorized full-time housewives and mothers. She also surveyed other women to diagnose a common complaint, the "problem with no name" that Friedan labeled the feminine mystique, the myth of femininity—the pleasing of and subordination to men—as the ultimate goal of a woman's life. Nearly a half century later, from the chorus of voices Hanauer has collected in *The Bitch in the House*, it is apparent that the myth still lives and, in the words of writer Sandra Shea, "It's just been super-sized, to include children, a sensitive husband to co-parent them, and a fulfilling career. And women trying to reach these ideals are mad as hell at what they're finding instead." Hanauer's fellow "bitches" express their anger that the women's movement that Friedan and others touched off has done little to alter essential expectations that women can only be fulfilled with a mate, marriage, and motherhood, while adding to their burden new expectations for careers and the self-actualization that feminism has helped to foster. As Friedan herself pointed out in her book *The Second Stage* (1981), the feminine mystique has been succeeded by a "feminist mystique" of the superwoman who is expected to cope effortlessly with her relationships, career, and family. When women fail, guilt, resentment, and anger result, and the bitch in the house is unleashed.

Offering revealing examples of what happens when the post-feminist myth collides with reality, the collection is divided into four sections, treating relationships, marriage, motherhood, and general enlightenment. In the first, "Me, Myself, and I," writers take on the subject of women on their own, in and out of relationships. Mating remains the illusive goal for many of these women, despite the disillusionment several experience when lovers become roommates and solitude gives way to partnership. Daphne Merkin, whose "Memoirs of an Ex-Bride" compares her life before, during, and after marriage, captures the common feeling of the unattached woman from whose perspective "everyone else suddenly seems to be married—safely tucked in for the night in their tidy Noah's Ark of coupledom—while you're out in the lonely forest scavenging for a warm body to huddle up against." If single women seem ready to trade in their independence for coupledom, many of the married writers in the second section, "For Better and Worse," would gladly exchange their lives with them, resenting the compromises and sacrifices of married life and its costs in autonomy and passion. As several of the essayists make clear, domestic life remains, with all the consciousness-raising and gender enlightenment, grindingly routine, with a disproportionate burden still falling on the woman of the house. Add to the mix dual careers and kids, and things quickly turn toxic. Kristin van Ogtrop in "Attila the Honey I'm Home" identifies among married couples a "mobius strip of guilt and resentment, and more guilt because of the resentment" developing around the central dilemma of "who is doing more." Others, such as Hope Edelman and Laurie Abraham, explore the myth of coparenting; while Elissa Schappell in "Crossing the Line in the Sand: How Mad Can Mother Get?" confesses that "some days . . . all I do is yell at my kids, then apologize for yelling at them, then feel guilty for being such a lousy mother, then start to feel resentful about being made to feel like a bad mother." Susan Squire in "Maternal Bitch" is even more blunt: "If you avoid motherhood, you avoid activating the Bitch."

Three-quarters of the way through *The Bitch in the House* the venting about the flash points of being single, married, and with children gives way to perspectives gained and conclusions reached in the final section, "Look at Me Now." If the curse of many of the writers' lives is discovered to be unrealistic expectations about women's roles and responsibilities promulgated by both the feminine and feminist mystique, the concluding essays begin with an earned sense of compromises and self-acceptance needed to defuse the rage that results in the illusory pursuit of perfection as lover, wife, and mother. Nancy Wartik in "Married at 46" helps to clarify why one should marry and why one should not, particularly from the perspective of someone who has resisted coupledom to her mid-forties. Ellen Gilchrist's "Middle Way" offers a Zenlike armistice in the war between family and work. Advocating joy and patience with less rather than striving to have it all, Gilchrist provides the commonsensical observation that "I think I'm happy because I have quit trying to find happiness through other people. . . . Happiness is self-derived and self-created." Vivian Gornick's "What Independence Has Come to Mean to Me" assesses a lifetime alone that is sustained by a process of self-knowledge, and Pam Houston's "The Perfect Equality of Our Separate Chosen Paths" suggests that contentment rests not in fantasies subscribed to, such as a culturally shared timetable and proscription for women's happiness and fulfillment, but in the acceptance of limits and the small enjoyments—friends, family, health, and even pets—that sustain and redeem a life.

The Bitch in the House offers the reader an excellent opportunity to eavesdrop on the intimate revelations of contemporary women. If Woolf is right and the angel in the house must be conquered, it is no less true that the bitch in the house needs to be grappled with and her rage understood. Naming a problem is the first step in curing it, and *The Bitch in the House* helps to diagnose a "problem with no name" for the next wave of feminism to treat.

HONORABLE MENTIONS

Jane Addams, *Twenty Years at Hull House* (1910)
Dorothy E. Allison, *Bastard Out of Carolina* (1992)
Lisa Alther, *Kinflicks* (1976)
Julia Alvarez, *How the Garcia Girls Lost Their Accents* (1991)
Margaret Atwood, *The Handmaid's Tale* (1985)
Jane Austen, *Pride and Prejudice* (1813), *Persuasion* (1818)
Elizabeth Bowen, *The Death of the Heart* (1938)
Charlotte Brontë, *Villette* (1853)
Emily Brontë, *Wuthering Heights* (1847)
Rita Mae Brown, *Rubyfruit Jungle* (1973)
Pearl Buck, *Pavilion of Women* (1946)
Fanny Burney, *Evelina* (1778)
Anton Chekhov, *The Three Sisters* (1901)
Sandra Cisneros, *The House on Mango Street* (1991)
Laurie Colwin, *Happy All the Time* (1978)
Michael Cunningham, *The Hours* (1998)
Rebecca Harding Davis, *Life in the Iron Mills* (1861)
Daniel Defoe, *Moll Flanders* (1722)
Annie Dillard, *Pilgrim at Tinker Creek* (1974)
Daphne du Maurier, *Rebecca* (1938)
Charles Frazier, *Cold Mountain* (1997)
Betty Friedan, *The Second Stage* (1981), *The Fountain of Age* (1993)
Margaret Fuller, *Women in the Nineteenth Century* (1845)
Elizabeth Gaskell, *Wives and Daughters* (1866)
Carol Gilligan, *In a Different Voice: Psychological Theory and Women's Development* (1982)
Nadine Gordimer, *Burgher's Daughter* (1979)
Carolyn Heilbrun, *Writing a Woman's Life* (1988)
Lillian Hellman, *The Children's Hour* (1934)
Hayden Herrera, *Frida* (1983)
Henry James, *The Portrait of a Lady* (1881)

Jamaica Kincaid, *At the Bottom of the River* (1983)
Jhumpa Lahiri, *Interpreter of Maladies* (1999)
Clare Booth Luce, *The Women* (1937)
Mary McCarthy, *The Group* (1963)
Carson McCullers, *The Member of the Wedding* (1946)
Marsha Norman, *'Night Mother* (1982)
Joyce Carol Oates, *them* (1969)
Marjorie Rosen, *Popcorn Venus* (1973)
May Sarton, *The Magnificent Spinster* (1985)
Alix Kates Shulman, *Memoirs of an Ex-Prom Queen* (1972)
Jane Smiley, *A Thousand Acres* (1991)
Amy Tan, *The Joy Luck Club* (1989)
Anne Tyler, *Breathing Lessons* (1988)
Paula Vogel, *How I Learned to Drive* (1997)
Alice Walker, *The Color Purple* (1982)
Wendy Wasserstein, *The Heidi Chronicles* (1990)
Eudora Welty, *Delta Wedding* (1946)
Virginia Woolf, *Mrs. Dalloway* (1925)

SELECT BIBLIOGRAPHY

Aquiar, Sarah Appleton. *The Bitch Is Back: Wicked Women in Literature*. Carbondale: Southern Illinois University Press, 2001.

Arcana, Judith. *Grace Paley's Life Stories: A Literary Biography*. Urbana and Chicago: University of Illinois Press, 1993.

Auerbach, Nina. *Romantic Imprisonment: Women and Other Glorified Outcasts*. New York: Columbia University Press, 1985.

Bair, Deidre. *Simone de Beauvoir: A Biography*. New York: Summit Books, 1990.

Banner, Lois W. *American Beauty*. New York: Knopf, 1983.

Barlowe, Jamie. *The Scarlet Mob of Scribblers: Rereading Hester Prynne*. Carbondale: Southern Illinois University Press, 2000.

Beers, Patricia. *Reader, I Married Him*. New York: Barnes & Noble, 1974.

Bowlby, Rachel. *Virginia Woolf: Feminist Destinations*. New York: Blackwell, 1988.

Brabant, Margaret, ed. *Politics, Gender and Genre: The Political Thought of Christine de Pizan*. Boulder, Colorado: Westview Press, 1992.

Brownmiller, Susan. *In Our Time: Memoir of a Revolution*. New York: Dial Press, 1999.

Brumberg, Joan. *The Body Project: An Intimate History of American Girls*. New York: Random House, 1997.

Casagrande, Peter J. *"Tess of the d'Urbervilles": Unorthodox Beauty*. New York: Twayne, 1992.

Cohen, Marcia. *The Sisterhood*. New York: Simon & Schuster, 1988.

Danahy, Michael. *The Feminization of the Novel*. Gainesville: University of Florida Press, 1991.

Davis, Angela. *Angela Davis: An Autobiography*. New York: International Publishers, 1988.

Durbach, Errol. *"A Doll's House": Ibsen's Myth of Transformation.* Boston: Twayne, 1991.

Elbert, Sarah. *Hunger for Home: Louisa May Alcott's Place in American Culture.* Philadelphia: Temple University Press, 1984.

Erens, Patricia, ed. *Sexual Strategies: The World of Women in Film.* New York: Horizon, 1979.

Evans, Mary. *Reflecting on Anna Karenina.* New York: Routledge, 1989.

Evans, Sara M. *Born for Liberty: A History of Women in America.* New York: Free Press, 1989.

Fraiman, Susan. *Unbecoming Women: British Women Writers and the Novel of Development.* New York: Columbia University Press, 1993.

Freedman, Rita Jackaway. *Beauty Bound.* New York: Lexington Books, 1986.

Frye, Joanne S. *Living Stories, Telling Lives: Women and the Novel in Contemporary Experience.* Ann Arbors: University of Michigan Press, 1986.

Gilbert, Sandra M., and Susan Gubar. *The Madwoman in the Attic.* New Haven: Yale University Press, 1979.

——— *No Man's Land: The Place of the Woman Writer in the Twentieth Century.* New Haven: Yale University Press, 3 vols., 1988–1994.

Gordon, Lyndall. *Charlotte Brontë: A Passionate Life.* New York: Norton, 1995.

Gwin, Minrose. *The Woman in the Red Dress: Gender, Space, and Reading.* Urbana: University of Illinois Press, 2002.

Haight, Gordon S. *George Eliot: A Biography.* New York: Oxford University Press, 1968.

Hanson, Claire. *Hysterical Fictions: The 'Woman's Novel' in the Twentieth Century.* New York: St. Martin's Press, 2000.

Hanson, Elizabeth J. *Margaret Mitchell.* Boston: Twayne, 1990.

Heilmann, Ann. *New Woman Fiction: Women Writing First-Wave Feminism.* New York: St. Martin's Press, 2000.

Hemenway, Robert E. *Zora Neale Hurston.* Urbana: University of Illinois Press, 1977.

Horowitz, Daniel. *Betty Friedan and the Making of the Feminine Mystique.* Amherst: University of Massachusetts Press, 1998.

Isaacs, Neil David. *Grace Paley: A Study of the Short Fiction.* Boston: Twayne, 1990.

Jacobs, William Jay. *Women in American History.* Beverly Hills, California: Benziger Bruce & Glencoe, 1976.

Kaplan, Louise J. *Female Perversions: The Temptations of Madame Bovary.* New York: Doubleday, 1991.

Kaurar, Elaine. *Cynthia Ozick's Fiction: Tradition and Invention.* Bloomington: Indiana University Press, 1993.

Kawashima, Terry. *Writing Margins: The Textual Construction of Gender in Heian and Kamakura Japan.* Cambridge: Harvard University Press, 2001.

Kirkham, Margaret. *Jane Austen, Feminism and Fiction.* Atlantic Highlands, New Jersey: Athlone Press, 1997.

Larch, Jennifer. *Mary Wollstonecraft: The Making of a Radical Feminist.* London: Berg, 1990.

Lee, Hermione. *Willa Cather: A Life Saved Up.* London: Virago, 1989.

Levine, Linda Gould. *Isabel Allende.* New York: Twayne, 2002.

Macpherson, Pat. *Reflection on The Bell Jar.* New York: Routledge, 1991.

Maraini, Dacia. *Searching for Emma: Gustave Flaubert and Madame Bovary.* Chicago: University of Chicago Press, 1998.

Matteo, Sherri. *American Women in the Nineties: Today's Critical Issues.* Boston: Northeastern University Press, 1993.

Moglen, Helene. *The Trauma of Gender: A Feminist Theory of the English Novel.* Berkeley: University of California Press, 2001.

Morgan, Robin. *Going Too Far: The Personal Chronicle of a Feminist.* New York: Random House, 1977.

Nebeker, Helen. *Jean Rhys, Woman in Passage.* St. Albans, Vermont: Eden Press, 1981.

Orr, Elaine Neil. *Tillie Olsen and a Feminist Spiritual Vision.* Jackson: University Press of Mississippi, 1987.

Peters, Pearlie Mae Fisher. *The Assertive Woman in Zora Neal Hurston's Fiction, Folklore, and Drama.* New York: Garland, 1998.

Rosenman, Ellen Bayuk. *A Room of One's Own: Women Writers and the Politics of Creativity.* New York: Twayne, 1995.

Rothman, Sheila. *Woman's Proper Place: A History of Changing Ideals and Practices, 1870 to the Present.* New York: Basic Books, 1978.

Rupp, Leila J., and Vera Taylor. *Survival in the Doldrums: The American Women's Rights Movement, 1945 to the 1960s.* New York: Oxford University Press, 1987.

Sawaya, Francesca. *Modern Women, Modern Work.* Philadelphia: University of Pennsylvania Press, 2004.

Searles, Patricia, and Ronald J. Berger, eds. *Rape and Society.* Boulder, Colorado: Westview Press, 1995.

Shapiro, Anne R. *Unlikely Heroines: Nineteenth-Century American Women Writers and the Woman Question.* New York: Greenwood Press, 1987.

Showalter, Elaine. *A Literature of Their Own.* Princeton, New Jersey: Princeton University Press, 1977.

Smith, Sidonie. *A Poetics of Women's Autobiography.* Bloomington: Indiana University Press, 1987.

Spacks, Patricia Meyer. *The Female Imagination.* New York: Knopf, 1975.

Taylor, Barbara. *Mary Wollstonecraft and the Feminist Imagination.* New York: Cambridge University Press, 2003.

Templin, Charlotte. *Feminism and the Politics of Literary Reputation.* Lawrence: University of Kansas Press, 1995.

Thurman, Judith. *Secrets of the Flesh: A Life of Colette.* New York: Knopf, 1999.

Tidd, Ursula. *Simone de Beauvoir: Gender and Testimony.* New York: Cambridge University Press, 1999.

Tomalin, Claire. *The Life and Death of Mary Wollstonecraft.* New York: Harcourt, 1974.

Wallace, Christine. *Germaine Greer, Untamed Shrew.* Boston: Faber and Faber, 1998.

Ward Jouve, Nicole. *Female Genesis: Creativity, Self, and Gender.* New York: St. Martin's Press, 1998.

Willard, Charity Cannon. *Christine de Pisan: Her Life and Works.* New York: Persea Books, 1984.

Wilson, Anna. *Persuasive Fictions: Feminist Narrative and Critical Myth.* Lewisburg, Pennsylvania: Bucknell University Press, 2001.

Wolf, Cynthia Griffin. *A Feast of Words: The Triumph of Edith Wharton.* New York: Oxford University Press, 1977.

The Verse
by the Side
of the Road

FRANK ROWSOME, JR., formerly the Managing Editor of *Popular Science Monthly,* is also the author of *Trolley Car Treasury* and *They Laughed When I Sat Down.* He is currently Chief, Technical Publications Branch of NASA.

THE VERSE BY THE SIDE OF THE ROAD was first published in 1965.

The Verse
by the Side
of the Road

The Story of the Burma-Shave Signs and Jingles

By Frank Rowsome, Jr.

Drawings by Carl Rose

*A Dutton
Paperback*

NEW YORK
E. P. DUTTON

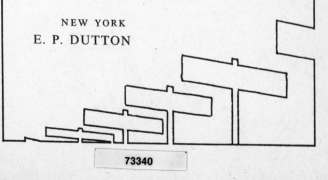

This paperback edition of
"THE VERSE BY THE SIDE OF THE ROAD"
First published 1966 by E. P. Dutton & Co., Inc.
All rights reserved. Printed in the U.S.A.

Copyright © 1965 by Frank Rowsome, Jr.
Reprinted by special arrangement with the
Stephen Greene Press, Brattleboro, Vermont

Published simultaneously in Canada by Clarke, Irwin and Company Limited, Toronto and Vancouver.

SBN 0-525-47191-X

Contents

1. Remember, Remember   1

2. On the Road to Red Wing   9

3. And Oh Louise   17

4. Don't Stick / Your Elbow / Out so Far   29

5. The Way It Worked   37

6. Free—Free—A Trip to Mars   49

7. An End to the Road Signs   59

     Appendix: Texts of All Burma-Shave Signs   71

1:

Remember, Remember

LIKE SO MUCH ELSE, the cars too were different in those days. The last of the spidery but agile Model T Fords had scurried off the production line in May 1927, having been overtaken in the national preference by the disk-wheeled Chevy. Its replacement, the Model A Ford—a nifty vehicle equipped with such elegances as windshield wings, four-wheel brakes, and an authentic gearshift lever sprouting from the floor—was now offered in colors other than black. It was unveiled nationally, in a masterly flurry of exploitation, on December 2, 1927, when thousands queued patiently outside showrooms for their first glimpse of the new wonder.

There were, in those springtime days of America's love affair with its automobiles, many other beloveds. There was the doughty Dodge, as reliable as an Airedale despite its willfully mixed-up gearshift pattern; the substantial Reo and Buick; the sprightly Pontiac and Overland; the Willys- and Stearns-Knights with their exotic sleeve valves; and the radical, warily regarded, air-cooled Franklin. For owners who disdained the commonplace there were ponderous Lincolns and Cadillacs; long-hooded Packards, special favorites with prospering bootleggers; and the lordly, spacious Pierce-Arrow, its wide-apart headlights staring with hauteur. For sportier tastes there were Kissels and Jordans, Auburns and Dusenbergs, Marmons and Templars, as well as the celebrated Stutz, a potent chariot that Cannonball Baker drove from city to city (making his runs in the after-midnight hours when traffic was lightest) at awesome averages of 55 and even 60 mph.

This was not, of course, the way most of us drove. Instead we climbed up—a two-stage ascent—into Old Betsy (very possibly a Studebaker or Nash, an Essex or Peerless) and set forth on our family Sunday-afternoon drive. We were perhaps headed for Nantasket Beach, or all the way around the lake, or out beyond Fort Loudon to

Mr. Welch's roadside stand where, among the brightly painted windmills, there would be an opportunity to buy some freshly picked corn or cucumbers. Because this trip might, with variation and caprice, amount to as much as sixty or sixty-five miles, we prudently stopped at Snow's Garage down on Village Avenue for gasoline, oil, and, if need be, free air and water.

Snow's had by now largely outworn its livery-stable origin. The red gasoline pump stood near the door, topped by a glass cylinder into which the fuel was pumped, thence to descend by gravity into the tank between the half-elliptic springs by Betsy's spare tire. Snow's also had a portable gasoline pump, a wheeled rectangular cart with a cranked pump, and this could be trundled out in the event that two cars needed fuel at the same time. If Betsy should need some oil, it was dispensed from a barrel into a quart measure and funneled into her engine. (Snow's newest and most formidable competitor, an oil-company gas station across the street, had already begun to serve up its beautiful dark-green oil in prefilled glass bottles, each with a screwed-on spout and carried out in a compartmented wire basket, like milk bottles.)

At the end of town, just before the sharp turn and the striped wooden barriers that guarded the railroad crossing, there was a red-and-green traffic light hung out over the intersection. Everyone in town was very pleased with that traffic light. Not for us the primitive pipe-and-painted-tin semaphores, dutifully swiveled by the policeman on duty. The red-and-green light symbolized the town's growth and importance, and the increasing flow of traffic coming through on State Route 31. We admitted, to be sure, that State 31 really wasn't at all like the celebrated Lincoln Highway, an awesome transcontinental artery, two lanes wide and with red-white-and-blue markers painted on its adjoining telegraph poles. It was said that along the Lincoln Highway you could often glimpse dusty,

3

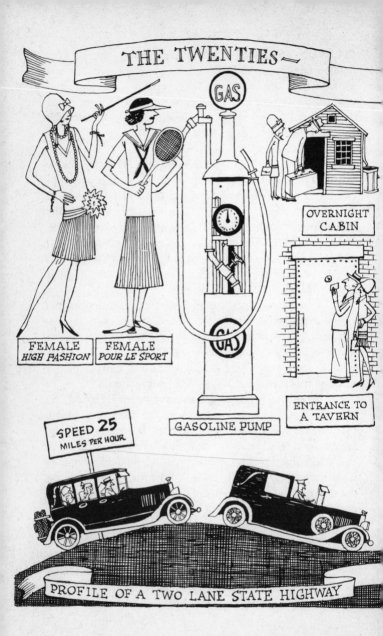

A PARTIAL PANORAMA

POPULAR BALLROOM DANCE

DEALER IN WINE & SPIRITS

MALE *COUNTRY CLUB ATTIRE*

MALE *WINTER PLUMAGE*

A PRESIDENT OF THE UNITED STATES

INCLUDING POPULAR CARS OF THE TIME

powerful cars with extra containers of fuel, oil, and water affixed to their running boards, and even with rope and axes for possible use during difficult passages coast to coast.

The highways, as well as the cars, were different and changing in the Twenties. Once out of town they still narrowed down to two lanes, narrow enough so that you warily surveyed each oncoming car for any tendencies toward road-hogging. Even when a two-lane road wasn't awkwardly narrow, drivers had to practice a routine now in relative disuse: the complex art of overtaking and passing another car. This was tricky, calling for skill, patience, resolution, and a knowledge of just how briskly Betsy could get out and around. Sometimes a driver misjudged and had to break off and tuck in behind, his face darkening with embarrassment and anger.

Curves there were in abundance in those days. Some rose naturally from the pre-automobile perambulations of roads. Even in the section-line Midwestern states, where curves were far less common, a sudden T-shaped corner (perhaps originating from property lines) could bring to a somnolent driver the humiliation of having to back out of an alfalfa field. Some curves were purely man made, arising from the parsimonious calculations of highway departments which held that the shortest bridge was the cheapest, even if it did mean a turn at each end. And curves occurred abundantly in the vertical plane as well, for this was long before earthmovers had developed their prodigious ability to cut and fill. Many small tads, perched back in the tonneau of the family touring car, would beseech a parent to drive *faster, faster* on the "roller-coaster road," sometimes called shoot-the-chutes or bump-the-bumps.

Often a picnic lunch was taken, with the food packed in advance, according to the custom of the Twenties, rather than, as now, with oddments flung into an aluminum ice chest. There were hard-boiled eggs (with a pinch of salt folded in a square of waxed paper); a shoebox of sandwiches, perhaps peanut butter and jam, or slices of corned beef, or ham and cheese. There'd also be soda crackers, a tin of deviled ham (with wonderful forked-tail red imps on the wrapper), and a jar of stuffed olives. There'd be a bag of potato chips, some cold roast chicken that had been located at the extreme back of the icebox, a supply of grapes or oranges and tangerines, cold milk in the Thermos, and bottles of ginger ale or grape juice for those grown up, or almost so. All this would be neatly stowed in a wicker hamper. When opened by the side of the road thirty miles from home, the hamper would be found to lack an opener for the deviled ham or the bottles. This lack would, among cries of recrimination, be ultimately remedied by use of the pliers and screwdriver from Betsy's toolbox, at the cost of no more than a spilled and fuzzing mouthful of ginger ale, and an injured expression on the face of the mother or aunt who had packed the lunch.

Those years of the Twenties were ones of continuous change. The roads grew steadily better, as did the cars. It was no longer necessary to carry elaborate kits for roadside tire repairs. And where the old car had had a natural cruising speed of about 35 mph and became excited at speeds above 45, displaying a disquieting tendency to lunge, the new Model A Fords or Chevys or Overlands were perfectly willing to lope all day long at 50, and had the brakes to suit. As the driving radius extended, it was no longer feasible to brag about a 225-mile day. More and more we took highway vacation trips. Roadside cabins began to appear—one- or two-room dollhouses arranged in an arc, with whitewashed stones outlining the curve of the driveway. They could be rented for two dollars or three dollars a night and were noticeably more convenient than tourist rooms, as well as cheaper than the Hotel Majestic downtown, where it was necessary to put on a necktie to confront the room clerk. Social historians should record the effect of cabins on, among other things, sports clothes, the practice of traveling with pets, and the growth of an additional meaning for the word "vacancy."

In times of continuous change it is difficult to recognize small beginnings. But in the fall of 1925, and again during the following year, one small beginning took place that would later catch the fancy of, and amuse, whole generations of highway-faring Americans.

2:

On the Road
to Red Wing

"My grandfather was an attorney in the early days of Minneapolis. In those times lawyers were short on education and long on enterprise, and Grandfather had each of these attributes. For a time he was the U.S. marshal here, with the duty of apprehending men who sold liquor to the Indians. In his law office he also manufactured a liniment—lawyers were into all kinds of things then, because in those days law practice wasn't as fruitful as it is now."

The speaker was Leonard Odell, a husky, broad-shouldered man in his late fifties, the president of the Burma-Vita Company, a division of Philip Morris, Inc. Odell was recounting the early beginnings of Burma-Shave to a recent visitor to the firm's plant on the western outskirts of Minneapolis. Beyond the executive-office walls, mixing and packaging machinery occasionally made staccato and profitable noises. Outside the window and beyond the freight siding Bassett's Creek and a city park could be glimpsed.

"He claimed he'd procured the liniment recipe from an old sea captain, and perhaps he did. Of course most all of those liniments came from sea captains; they traveled the world and encountered witch doctors and collected secret potions. Anyhow, Grandfather made it in his office up in the old Globe Building. It was a potent liniment both in action and smell. You could smell it on the ground floor when he was mixing it on the fifth floor, which probably didn't endear him to his fellow tenants. But he made it there for many years, selling it through a couple of drugstores in lower Minneapolis.

"His son, Clinton, was educated in law at the University of Minnesota, and he was a practicing attorney. Dad was also in the insurance business, and he was a very successful man. He founded the White-Odell agency, which, at one time, had more insurance on its books than

10

any other single agency in the United States. Dad was a *whale* of a salesman. He worked hard, probably too hard, because in 1920 he took sick—sciatic rheumatism, nerve disorders, couldn't walk. He was miserable. Took him pretty near three years to get the thing cured so he could walk again. He climbed out of his illness about 1923, when I was in high school and my brother Allan was at the University. The doctors told him he shouldn't try anything hard-driving again if he wanted to keep his health.

"Well, the family all had this liniment in their homes. I had an aunt who was burned severely on the hand about then with hot fat. In desperation she stuck her hand into this liniment, and in spite of what you might think, the pain stopped immediately. She had no blisters and no scars. It was a marvelous thing.

"So Dad, casting around for something to do, said maybe we can market this. My grandfather had had a stroke by then, and was confined to the house, and Dad was taking care of him. Dad made a royalty arrangement with him and we set out to sell it. We called it Burma-Vita. *Burma* because most of the essential oils in the liniment came from the Malay peninsula and Burma, and *Vita* from the Latin for life and vigor—the whole name meaning Life from Burma.

"Well, we sure starved to death on that product for a couple of years. With a liniment you have to catch a customer who isn't feeling well, and even when you do you only sell him once in a while. The wholesale drug company in town, the people that we got the ingredients from, kept reminding Dad that it would be better if we could find something we could sell everybody, all the time, instead of just hunting for people who were sick. They gave Dad some Lloyd's Euxesis to see what he thought of it.

"Now Lloyd's Euxesis, made in England, was the original brushless shaving cream on the world market. It was a sticky, gummy substance. Still, as an old traveling man, Dad could see the advantage of a brushless shaving cream. You didn't have to pack that wet brush in your grip, where it would mildew and get foul-smelling before you got home. (Remember how they used to get green at the base?)

"Some time before, Dad had heard about a chemist in town who had taken seriously sick, perhaps fatally, and had pulled up stakes for Arizona to see if he could recover. Dad was touched by the story, and in December he wrote him a note with a check for twenty-five dollars, and wished him a merry Christmas. Well, it was about a year later, in 1925, when we were close to the low ebb of all time with the liniment, when the door opened and in walked this chemist, Carl Noren. He said 'Here I am, and I'm well, and what can I do for you?'

"Dad said 'What do you know about a brushless shaving cream?' Carl said 'I never heard of one.' Dad tossed him a tube of Lloyd's Euxesis and said 'Can you make a better one than this?' Carl took a look at it and said 'Well, I can sure try—I used to be chief cosmetic chemist for the old Minneapolis Drug Company.' Then Carl picked up the phone and ordered the ingredients that he thought he'd need, and about three o'clock that afternoon batch number one of Burma-Shave came off the fire. It was, frankly, terrible stuff. We had formulations on and off the market about three times. It wasn't until we got to Formula One Forty-three that we came up with a good, stable product. Actually we'd gone by it and were up close to Formula Three Hundred, and then Dad discovered some of old One Forty-three left in a jar and got a real fine shave from it. That's how we discovered that, if you *aged* old One Forty-three for two or three months, you got a fine shave with it.

"All of us went out and tried to market it. My brother Allan was down in Joliet, Illinois, working with a program that we called Jars on Approval. You'd just walk into a man's office and say 'Here's a jar of Burma-Shave.' 'What's *that*?' he'd ask. You'd explain and tell him how to use it. You'd say 'Take it home and try it and if you like it, give me fifty cents when I come back next week. If you don't, just give me back what's left then and we'll still be friends.'

"Jars on Approval—if you want to starve to death fast, that's one way to do it. I guess Al was pretty discouraged. One day on the road between Aurora and Joliet he saw a set of small serial signs advertising a gas station: Gas, Oil, Restrooms, things like that—maybe a dozen of them—and then at the end a sign would point in to the gas station. Al thought 'Every time I see one of these setups, I read every one of the signs. So why can't you sell a product that way?'

"Well, it sounded good to me, and to everyone else. Except when he came home to tell Dad about his idea, Dad said 'The trouble with you is that you're homesick.' But Dad talked to some of the big advertising men here, and in Chicago—and they said that, year in and year out, it would never work. But Allan sold Dad on giving him two hundred dollars to try out his idea. I think Dad did it more to shut him up than anything else.

"We bought secondhand boards over at the Rose Brothers Wrecking Company. They had plenty of nail-holes in them and some were burned on one side. We sawed them up into thirty-six-inch lengths and painted them up, using a thin brass stencil and brush. They were pretty crude. These signs didn't have rhymes or jingles— just what you might call prose: SHAVE THE MODERN WAY / FINE FOR THE SKIN / DRUGGISTS HAVE IT / BURMA-SHAVE. It was getting on into the fall of 1925, and we had to hurry like the dickens to get them into the ground before it froze solid. We put them on two roads out of Minneapolis. One was Route Sixty-five to Albert Lea, and the other was the road to Red Wing. Maybe we had ten or twelve sets of signs on those two highways.

"By the start of the year we were getting the first repeat orders we'd ever had in the history of the company— all from druggists serving people who traveled those roads. As he watched those repeat orders rolling in, Dad began to feel that maybe the boys were thinking all right, after all. He called us in and said 'Allan, I believe you've got a real great idea here. It's tremendous. The only trouble is, we're broke.'

"With this, Dad did one of the greatest sales jobs I've ever heard of. He had a busted company, he had a product that most people had never heard of, much less believed in, and he had an advertising idea that ad men said wouldn't work. With these three things going for him, he incorporated and then went out and sold forty-nine percent of the stock in less than three weeks. This testified not only to his sales ability but also to the fact that he was a highly respected man that a lot of people had confidence in.

"So early in 1926 we set up our first sign shop. Using slogans and selling lines that Dad and Al thought up, we made a pile of silk-screen signs that weren't *quite* as crude as those first stenciled ones. And Al went out ahead and bought the locations, and I came along behind and dug the holes and tamped in the posts. Boy, did I learn this business starting from three feet under ground."

Leonard Odell walked over to the window, looking out over Bassett's Creek to the parkland beyond. "If you watch for a moment, you can almost always see a pheasant," he told his visitor. "There are thousands of them now. You know, Dad helped import the first pheasants into this state. He was a great conservationist. Made a hobby out of wildflowers, too. He was active in civic affairs and good politics. A hard-driving and conscientious man, with a lot of friends. After that spring we were on our way, and we had a lot of fun over the years. Boy, was Dad enthusiastic! He was a real stem-winder."

3:

And Oh Louise

THE ESSENTIAL SPIRIT of Burma-Shave—what made America first notice and later cherish the jaunty little signs—was of course their light-heartedness. Humor has always been infrequent in advertising, and in the years of the Depression it was so scarce as to be virtually a trace element. If one examines the newspapers and magazines of the period the nearest in the way of intentional humor one is likely to find is an occasional spasm of jocosity, as when an artist would depict a chubby, golden-ringleted female toddler, so busy holding her ice-cream cone above the leaps of a frisky puppy that her defective suspenders threaten to disclose her infant buttocks.

They were days when many advertisers preferred long blocks of copy, composed around the "reason why" principle. In drugstore products in particular, with business poor and competition fierce, many advertisers were aiming single-mindedly for the jugular. Listerine and Lifebuoy were instilling the thought that each citizen was needlessly malodorous; Absorbine Jr. was developing the concept that many apparently beautiful women had cracked and scabby toes; and numerous national advertisers, from Fleischmann's Yeast to Feenamint, were preaching the doctrine that infrequent and faulty bowel movements were both a national disgrace and a grievous personal failure.

It was upon this advertising scene—a lapel-grabbing, intensely serious hard sell—that the Odells arrived with their distinctive, often ironic humor: HE PLAYED / A SAX / HAD NO B. O. / BUT HIS WHISKERS SCRATCHED / SO SHE LET HIM GO. There was even an occasional note of irreverence toward other advertising: IT'S NOT TOASTED / IT'S NOT DATED / BUT LOOK OUT / IT'S IMITATED. The little signs first startled, then delighted, the highway traveler. Their unwillingness to be portentous, their amiable iconoclasm,

18

pleased people in the same way that *Ballyhoo* magazine briefly caught the national fancy, or that *Mad* magazine has recently charmed the young. The signs did not shout, and the only odors mentioned were pleasing ones: HIS FACE WAS SMOOTH / AND COOL AS ICE / AND OH LOUISE! / HE SMELLED / SO NICE. There was also an impious absurdity that was captivating, for no advertisers had ever spoken to us this way before: DOES YOUR HUSBAND / MISBEHAVE / GRUNT AND GRUMBLE / RANT AND RAVE / SHOOT THE BRUTE SOME / BURMA-SHAVE. There was unexpectedness about these flippant new signs; one would cruise a familiar highway and come upon, newly installed, a series such as: THE ANSWER TO / A MAIDEN'S / PRAYER / IS NOT A CHIN / OF STUBBY HAIR.

One aspect to the signs not evident at first was that several special advantages were concealed in an arrangement of six small messages planted one hundred paces apart. At 35 miles an hour it took almost three seconds to proceed from sign to sign, or eighteen seconds to march through the whole series. This was far more time and attention than a newspaper or magazine advertiser could realistically expect to win from casual viewers. Yet Burma-Shave almost automatically exacted this attention from virtually every literate passerby; as Alexander Woollcott once observed, it was as difficult to read just one Burma-Shave sign as it was to eat one salted peanut. Once the Odells had taught us that their signs were constructed with a jingling cadence, and were frosted with a topping of folk humor, we grew addicted to a degree that few advertisers have ever achieved for their copy.

Another advantage lay hidden in the spaced-out signs: they established a controlled reading pace, and even added an element of suspense. The eye could not race ahead and anticipate or spoil the effect, as it could on a printed page. Instead the arrangement, like the bouncing ball

19

in a movie group-singing short, concentrated attention on one sign at a time, building effects for the pay-off line, which was usually the fifth. The result was to deliver the message in much the style of a practiced raconteur who sets the stage for his snapper: PITY ALL / THE MIGHTY CAESARS / THEY PULLED / EACH WHISKER OUT / WITH TWEEZERS. Concentrating the effect in the fifth line was not simply a story-telling device; it also had echoes from childhood and even infancy when, perhaps to avert the threatened approach of bedtime, we begged (just once more) for a favorite rhyme or song: THE BEARDED LADY / TRIED A JAR / SHE'S NOW / A FAMOUS / MOVIE STAR.

Curious and wonderful results, unprecedented in the history of advertising, developed from these hidden characteristics of the six-line highway jingle. One was that people soon developed favorites, reading them aloud with even more savor than the first time they were encountered. The entire carload would chant as if a litany: BENEATH THIS STONE / LIES ELMER GUSH / TICKLED TO DEATH / BY HIS / SHAVING BRUSH. With many families the privilege of reading Burma-Shave signs aloud was a rotated honor, leading inevitably to sharp contention ("It is *so* my turn!"). There was also often someone assigned the duty of peering backward to capture and unscramble the signs that faced in the other direction, a task that required quick wit and a good memory: OF THEM FOR SEED / TO LEAVE ONE HALF / YOU DON'T NEED / WHISKERS / WHEN CUTTING.

Certain themes recurred through all the Burma-Shave jingles, like a motif for a French horn echoing through a symphony. One was the accept-no-substitutes theme. Substitution is an idea that eats corrosively into the mind of advertisers, most particularly those whose products are retailed in groceries and drugstores. The idea is embittering, like a plot from Greek tragedy: one has spent

20

money in building up a demand, and a customer wanders in off the street, maybe not having the name of The Product just right, and then a wretched clerk foists off on him a jar of The Competition, and all that fine money has gone to waste, and, worse, The Competition has rung up a sale, and is even started down the road of earning Product Loyalty for the stuff. It is a nightmare that can make advertisers writhe, and the Odells were no exception. But where conventional, printed-media advertisers would exhort Accept No Substitutes, making virtually no effect whatever on the glazed or unseeing eyes of their readers, the Odells contrived even here a note of gaiety: GIVE THE GUY / THE TOE OF YOUR BOOT / WHO TRIES / TO HAND YOU / A SUBSTITUTE. The intensity of hostility felt toward errant clerks is reflected in another jingle: THE GAME LAWS / OUGHT TO / LET YOU SHOOT / THE BIRD WHO HANDS YOU / A SUBSTITUTE. Occasionally one could detect a resolute effort to take a calm and rational view toward the matter: LET'S GIVE THE / CLERK A HAND / WHO NEVER / PALMS OFF / ANOTHER BRAND. A goaded-beyond-endurance patience was reflected this way: SUBSTITUTES / WOULD IRK A SAINT / YOU HOPE THEY ARE / WHAT YOU KNOW / THEY AIN'T.

The selling of a brushless shaving cream required the changing of settled habits. Gramps and Father had both used a badger-hair brush and perhaps a specially marked shaving mug; why should one change a time-honored and, indeed, traditionally masculine rite? Allan Odell approached the problem from a variety of ways: convenience, modernity, speed, improved results, and the elimination of a need, when traveling, to pack a wet brush. Sometimes the competitive arguments were graphic. Noting the growing acceptance of electric shavers, Clinton Odell himself tossed off a humdinger: A SILKY CHEEK /

SHAVED SMOOTH / AND CLEAN / IS NOT OBTAINED / WITH A MOWING MACHINE.

It was almost inevitable that competitive arguments inched close to the edge of propriety. For years Clinton recalled with wry amusement what happened when he, perhaps nodding for an instant, had approved a slightly distasteful jingle. As luck would have it, the jingle was installed directly across from a fashionable and dignified church in suburban Minneapolis. Bright new signs chanted the message SHAVING BRUSH / ALL WET / AND HAIRY / I'VE PASSED YOU UP / FOR SANITARY / BURMA-SHAVE. On the Sunday following the appearance of these unfortunate words, a party of stony-faced deacons assembled, marched across the street in their formal garb, and bodily plucked the motes from their eye.

Hairy brushes were by no means the sole competitors. Also striving for the favor of whiskery U.S. males were three other major brushless preparations, Mollé, Krank's Shave Cream, and Barbasol. Further, as soon as it grew

apparent that the creams were making inroads into the overall market, what the trade called the Big Soapers—Colgate, Palmolive, Williams, and the rest—promptly began to sell brushless creams of their own. And in the depression years, dozens of private brands appeared in the drug chains and the "pine board" (discount) stores. Being manufactured by regional cosmetic companies and bearing higher profit margins for retailers, these private brands added special meaning to Allan's preoccupation with substitution. In the heat of competition there would sometimes be a flash of tooth at the breezy little upstart. At one point Barbasol brandished its lawyers ominously over the jingle lines NO BRUSH / NO LATHER / NO RUB-IN. It was alleged that these words were the exclusive property of Barbasol, as evidenced by the nightly caroling over the American airwaves of the theme song of Singin' Sam, the Barbasol Man. Sam's song was "Barbasol, Barbasol—no brush, no lather, no rub-in—wet your razor and begin." "I don't think they really had a case," said Leonard Odell, "but we didn't bother to

fight them over it. By that time we were jingling so much we didn't need the line."

Procuring an adequate supply of jingles threatened for a time to be a serious problem. (At first they weren't even verses, just advertising admonitions. But as the Odell high spirits took over, and the advantages of rhyme became evident, the basic format was established.) Allan and Clinton composed all copy for the first few years. They gave birth to a few classics, notably EVERY SHAVER / NOW CAN SNORE / SIX MORE MINUTES / THAN BEFORE, and another of the early great ones: HALF A POUND / FOR / HALF A DOLLAR / SPREAD ON THIN / ABOVE THE COLLAR. Yet by the end of the Twenties it was painfully evident that their muse was growing haggard and scrawny. After a brief and unpromising dalliance with staff "jingle artists," Allan turned to the idea of an annual contest, with $100 paid for each verse accepted. When entries poured in by the thousands, it became excitingly clear that, thanks to industrious versifiers all over the country, the Burma-Shave muse was not only rejuvenated but, indeed, more fetching than ever.

Leonard Odell explained the contest mechanisms this way: "We were out for the best jingles we could get. Each year we advertised the contest over the radio, in magazines and newspapers, and in syndicated Sunday comic sections. We also made sure that people who had previously submitted winners were reminded of the new contest. At the beginning Dad was the principal screener. He'd go up to our summer camp with thousands of entries—we'd send more up to him each day—and for three or four weeks he'd scratch out the ones that had no possibilities, or that might have offended people. Then all of us would whittle away at his preliminary selection.

"After a while it got to be too much for Dad; some of the contests drew more than fifty thousand entries. We hired a couple of experts, women who worked as ad-

agency copywriters, to come in for a few weeks and filter
out the best ones. They were darned good at it, too, once
they got the hang of it. Not all of the entries were clean;
it was hard to believe that people would sit down and
write the things they did. Anyhow, after they'd picked
the top thousand, we'd make copies of them for the
company officers and the board of directors. Each of us
would pick the twenty or twenty-five best, and we'd meet

and find out that we'd picked different ones, and then the arguments began. We had a whale of a lot of fun— much more than in most directors' meetings. But we also took them very seriously, because jingles were our bread and butter. We'd just keep thinning them down, going back for more readings, trading favorites with each other, and meeting again. Sometimes it took us several weeks to agree on the next crop."

Quite naturally the disputations often turned on matters of taste. THE OTHER WOMAN / IN HIS LIFE / SAID "GO BACK HOME / AND SCRATCH YOUR WIFE" was regretfully vetoed for highway use, as was another on a reciprocal theme: MY MAN / WON'T SHAVE / SEZ HAZEL HUZ / BUT I SHOULD WORRY / DORA'S DOES. As senior officer, Clinton Odell served as a kind of Horatius at the bridge, vigilantly defending the American highway against anything off-color or scatological. LISTEN, BIRDS / THESE SIGNS COST / MONEY / SO ROOST A WHILE / BUT DON'T GET FUNNY had strong advocacy in committee, although it was never used. Another near miss: THE WIFE OF BRISTLY / BRUSHMUG ZAYMER / BOUGHT TWIN BEDS / WHO CAN BLAME HER?

Possibly one reason why these disputations arose was an awareness in the boardroom that the certified clean, boy-girl jingles were near the core of the most memorable Burma-Shave verse: SAID JULIET / TO ROMEO / IF YOU WON'T SHAVE / GO HOMEO. Often it was amiably suggested that Burma-Shave could facilitate courtship: WITH / A SLEEK CHEEK / PRESSED TO HERS / JEEPERS! CREEPERS! / HOW SHE PURRS. The same remedy was also prescribed for luckless males who didn't know any girls: HIS FACE / WAS LOVED / BY JUST HIS MOTHER / HE BURMA-SHAVED / AND NOW—— / OH, BROTHER! The grim possibility of a loveless life was sketched in one cautionary lyric: BACHELOR'S QUARTERS / DOG ON THE RUG / WHISKERS TO BLAME / NO ONE / TO HUG. A record of persistent failure with females might be accounted for this way: TO GET / AWAY FROM / HAIRY APES / LADIES JUMP / FROM FIRE ESCAPES.

Perhaps the all-time classic among boy-girl jingles, however, was a compact and metrically memorable verse from 1934. For reasons beyond easy analysis, it appears to have become engraved on the collective American memory: HE HAD THE RING / HE HAD THE FLAT / BUT SHE FELT HIS CHIN / AND THAT / WAS THAT.

4:

Don't Stick
Your Elbow
Out so Far

LEAFING THROUGH a list of old Burma-Shave jingles is also to leaf through almost unrecalled memories and associations. Suddenly you are driving to Maine again in that hot summer of 1932 and your companion, a radiant girl who is now a grandmother, is delighted north of Portland to come upon FOR PAINTING / COW-SHED / BARN OR FENCE / THAT SHAVING BRUSH / IS JUST IMMENSE. Or the half-recollected fact that the Burma-Shave people devoted many signs to the cause of highway safety comes back with a rush at the sight of REMEMBER THIS / IF YOU'D / BE SPARED / TRAINS DON'T WHISTLE / BECAUSE THEY'RE SCARED.

Public service, as it happened, was one of the major themes recurring in the complete canon. Two other themes, Allan Odell once told an advertising trade journal, are "straight advertising and exaggerated humor." Another way of putting it would be to classify the jingles as being either product advertising or public-service advertising, each category being served up in tones that ranged from the reasonably serious to the wildly rib-poking. And no matter how much the first five signs devoted themselves to the public weal, that sixth one always mentioned the

THAT SHAVING BRUSH / IS JUST IMMENSE / Burma-Shave

product. It was notable, in fact, that we were nationally conditioned to put it in even if it wasn't there, as various other advertisers who attempted to imitate the serial format ruefully discovered.

The first public-service jingle appeared in 1935, written by Allan. It managed deftly to combine a safety admonition with a plug for the product: KEEP WELL / TO THE RIGHT / OF THE ONCOMING CAR / GET YOUR CLOSE SHAVES / FROM THE HALF-POUND JAR. In 1937 a woman in Nebraska contributed a tersely macabre thought: DRIVE / WITH CARE / BE ALIVE / WHEN YOU / ARRIVE. In 1938 a man in Wichita received $100 for a lyric that would later recur in variant forms: DON'T TAKE / A CURVE / AT 60 PER / WE HATE TO LOSE / A CUSTOMER. The following year the safety theme came on strong, used in six of the twenty-one new jingles planted along the highways for 1939.

The moving force behind this trend was Clinton Odell. "Dad felt that we'd grown to be a part of the U.S. roadside," Leonard explained, "and had a duty to do what we could about the mounting accident rate. He figured that if people would remember our humorous messages,

31

they just might have more effect than routine do-this, don't-do-that safety advice. And of course we always had our name at the end of each set." It was a shrewd policy also in that it established the firm as being public-spirited, an attitude that could only be an asset in confronting the ominously growing anti-billboard forces. Throughout the country, regulation, special taxes, and outright prohibition of road signs were spreading; and it befitted Burma-Shave, which almost alone among businesses was solely dependent on road signs, to cultivate the reputation of being helpful as well as cheerful.

Several of that first large crop in 1939 managed to effect a jaunty tone with what could scarcely have been described as a droll theme. Wrote a woman from Illinois: HARDLY A DRIVER / IS NOW ALIVE / WHO PASSED / ON HILLS / AT 75. From Michigan came a variation on the hate-to-lose-a-customer concept: PAST / SCHOOLHOUSES / TAKE IT SLOW / LET THE LITTLE / SHAVERS GROW. (A decade later the idea was retooled this way: AT SCHOOL ZONES / HEED INSTRUCTIONS! / PROTECT / OUR LITTLE / TAX DEDUCTIONS.) Sardonic advice arrived from a New Jerseyite: AT CROSSROADS / DON'T JUST / TRUST TO LUCK / THE OTHER CAR / MAY BE A TRUCK.

The following year the number of highway-safety jingles had risen to seven out of twenty-two. The feat of linking shaving cream and highway safety was managed, at slight metric cost, by a Philadelphian who composed: ALWAYS REMEMBER / ON ANY TRIP / KEEP TWO THINGS / WITHIN YOUR GRIP / YOUR STEERING WHEEL AND / BURMA-SHAVE. As was perhaps inevitable, the boundary between the catchy and the grim was not easily established. Observed one plain-speaking lady: WHEN YOU DRIVE / IF CAUTION CEASES / YOU ARE APT / TO REST / IN PIECES. A distinctly gloomy prediction came from Indiana: DON'T PASS CARS /

  PAST

  SCHOOLHOUSES

  TAKE IT SLOW

  LET THE LITTLE

  SHAVERS GROW

  Burma-Shave

ON CURVE OR HILL / IF THE COPS / DON'T GET YOU / MORTICIANS WILL. A lady from Shamrock, Texas, won her $100 with a Cassandra-like forecast: DON'T STICK / YOUR ELBOW / OUT SO FAR / IT MIGHT GO HOME / IN ANOTHER CAR.

The basic problem was beautifully stated in a 1942 jingle: DROVE TOO LONG / DRIVER SNOOZING / WHAT HAPPENED NEXT / IS NOT / AMUSING. In time a variety of devices were used to adapt the somber aspects of safety to the genial Burma-Shave format. One such device was to employ the boy-girl theme so successful with other jingles: IF HUGGING / ON HIGHWAYS / IS YOUR SPORT / TRADE IN YOUR CAR / FOR A DAVENPORT. Or as a poet from the Southwest noted: TRAINS DON'T WANDER / ALL OVER THE MAP / FOR NO ONE / SITS ON / THE ENGINEER'S LAP. A matron of Birmingham, Alabama, evidently a spiritual daughter of La Rochefoucauld, composed what was clearly more an epigram than a jingle: A GIRL / SHOULD HOLD ON / TO HER YOUTH / BUT NOT / WHEN HE'S DRIVING.

A second adaptive device was to use Pearly-Gates imagery, for here familiarity from long use by humorists and cartoonists had leached away the grimness: AT INTERSECTIONS / LOOK EACH WAY / A HARP SOUNDS NICE / BUT IT'S HARD TO PLAY. From a lady of Issaqua, Washington, came this thought: GUYS WHOSE EYES / ARE IN THEIR BACKS / GET HALOS CROSSING / RAILROAD TRACKS.

Puns and wordplay, another Burma-Shave staple, also helped: HE SAW / THE TRAIN / AND TRIED TO DUCK IT / KICKED FIRST THE GAS / AND THEN THE BUCKET. Yet puns proved as unreliable for the Burma-Shave versifiers as they have been for the rest of mankind, being sometimes fine and sometimes ghastly: HER CHARIOT / RACED AT 80 PER / THEY

HAULED AWAY / WHAT HAD / BEN HUR. It was in fact with puns that the Burma-Shave editorial taste, ordinarily so finely attuned to the highway readership, proved sometimes uncertain: TRAIN APPROACHING / WHISTLE SQUEALING / PAUSE! / AVOID THAT / RUN-DOWN FEELING!

It would be inaccurate, however, to suggest that the overtones of highway safety gave serious problems to most jinglers. Often they selected naturally undistressing hazards: TWINKLE, TWINKLE / ONE-EYED CAR / WE ALL WONDER / *WHERE* / YOU ARE. A woman of Illinois earned $100 with her blithe inquiry: IS HE / LONESOME / OR JUST BLIND / THIS GUY WHO DRIVES / SO CLOSE BEHIND? Drunken driving came in for full attention, once with an intricate multiple pun: DRINKING DRIVERS / NOTHING WORSE / THEY PUT THE QUART / BEFORE THE HEARSE.

But trouble can lie in wait for the unwary, however well intentioned. In 1948 a jingle announced: THE MIDNIGHT RIDE / OF PAUL / FOR BEER / LED TO A / WARMER HEMISPHERE. No sooner was this rather undistinguished lyric erected about the country than a scorching letter arrived on the desk of the Burma-Shave board chairman. It was from a national association of beer haulers, and its gist, as the Odells recall, was "Doggone it, we've got about forty-one jillion members, and if you don't get that set of signs off the road pronto you're going to start losing a lot of customers, because beer-haulers shave just like everybody else." Since Clinton's policy was never to give offense, the midnight ride of Paul for beer disappeared as rapidly as the crews could replace it. Safety was furthered equally well by jingles that mentioned no commercial products: AROUND / THE CURVE / LICKETY-SPLIT / IT'S A BEAUTIFUL CAR / WASN'T IT?

The actual value of the highway-safety jingles was inherently unmeasurable, although it must have been substantial. A sheaf of praising letters and testimonials from safety officials and highway commissioners collected in the office, pleasing Clinton Odell greatly. He was also delighted to hear of a study on average highway speeds conducted by the University of Pennsylvania; it reported parenthetically that no phenomenon more reliably slowed down speeders than a set of Burma-Shave signs. This behavior was reflected in a 1955 jingle: SLOW DOWN, PA / SAKES ALIVE / MA MISSED SIGNS / FOUR / AND FIVE.

As Clinton interpreted it, public service extended beyond highway safety. A number of jingles on the prevention of forest fires were erected during the Fifties, spotted in locations where they could do the most good. Although of surely commendable intent, it was interesting and perhaps significant that they lacked the expected Burma-Shave zest: MANY A FOREST / USED TO STAND / WHERE A / LIGHTED MATCH / GOT OUT OF HAND. Something of this slightly devitalized quality had been evident earlier. In the months following Pearl Harbor, a number of sequences exhorting citizens to purchase bonds were quickly tooled up, and it was notable that they were marked more by laudable patriotism than by memorable concept and phrase: LET'S MAKE HITLER / AND HIROHITO / LOOK AS SICK AS / OLD BENITO / BUY DEFENSE BONDS. However, by evoking boot camps, basic training, and weekend passes, the main-line jingles quickly captured the essential Burma-Shave spirit: "AT EASE," SHE SAID / "MANEUVERS BEGIN / WHEN YOU GET / THOSE WHISKERS / OFF YOUR CHIN."

5:

The Way
It Worked

Fidelia M. Dearlove, for thirty-three years Allan Odell's secretary, did most of the paperwork on the road signs, and it was considerable. From her route lists, files, and pin-bristling maps, she could almost always tell what jingle was located where, when it had been inspected last, when the agreement with the farmer or landholder would expire, and when the crew in a truck would be along to change copy. to a sprightly new verse. With nearly seven thousand sets amounting to forty thousand individual signs scattered from Maine to Texas, and with twenty to twenty-five new jingles being installed regularly to replace an equal number already out, Miss Dearlove had a complex, ever changing situation to keep track of. What made it especially difficult was its dynamic quality: each day there would be mail or phoned reports from an advance man or the crews of installers on the road— they began in the south in winter and fanned out north as the weather bettered—reporting on departures from the original plan, or on new local sign taxes or other circumstances. It was no wonder that when some question about signs came up, almost everyone in the home office had the instinctive reaction of "ask Fidelia."

In the decade following the appearance of those first primitive signs on the roads to Albert Lea and Red Wing, Burma-Shave verses began to sprout like wildflowers. By the fall of 1926, with $25,000 spent on signs, they were dotted through Minnesota, Wisconsin, and Iowa; and sales had grown from virtually zero to about $68,000. In 1927, with an advertising appropriation of $45,000, signs had spread through most of the rest of the Midwest, and sales doubled. By 1929, with $65,000 spent on signs, the first exploratory tongues had reached both the Atlantic and Pacific coasts, with sales doubling once again. In 1930 the signs diffused through the South and New England. Carl Noren, risen to serving as a director of the Burma-Vita Company, was able to say with comfortable precision that "we never knew that there was a depression." During its peak times the company grossed more than $3,000,000 a year, demonstrating the greater effectiveness of cheerful jingles over the door-to-door appeal of Jars on Approval.

The only states that the roadside signs never formally appeared in were Arizona, Nevada, and New Mexico—deemed to have insufficient traffic density—and Massachusetts, deemed to present such obstacles as winding roads, excessive and obscuring foliage, and insufficient numbers of reasonably priced locations.

The first portent of a Burma-Shave invasion into new territory was the sight of the advance man, assigned to buy locations. He'd cruise along main, through highways, watching for spots that met his requirements: a straight and fairly level stretch, at road height, or no more than three or four feet lower, never higher. A place bearing other signs was to be avoided, particularly big billboards that could eclipse part of a series. The site should be visible for a considerable distance, it having been found that, if the set began just after a curve, some people would miss the first sign or two, an annoyance sufficient, in some cases, to generate testy letters of complaint.

Once a likely spot was identified, the advance man (who, like so many others connected with Burma-Shave, was likely to have a hearty, friendly personality) would approach the farmer owning the land, present him with a jar of the product, show him a sign, and begin negotiations: "How'd you like to have a set of these signs put up along the fence there?" This may not always have been the ideal opener, for it was recorded that exceptionally rustic farmers were known to counter warily: "How much is it going to cost me?" But in general a mutually agreeable deal could be concluded without difficulty, a year's lease of rights to install and maintain the signs

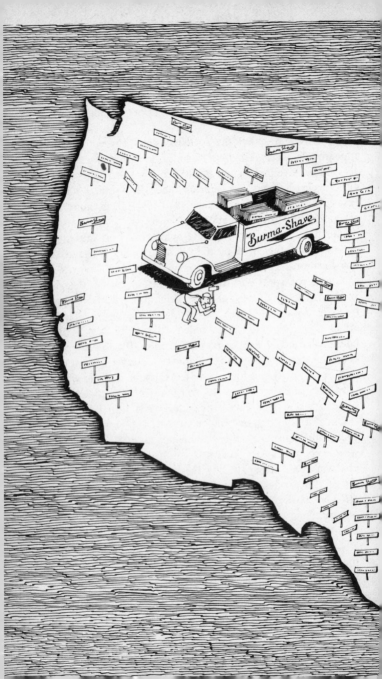

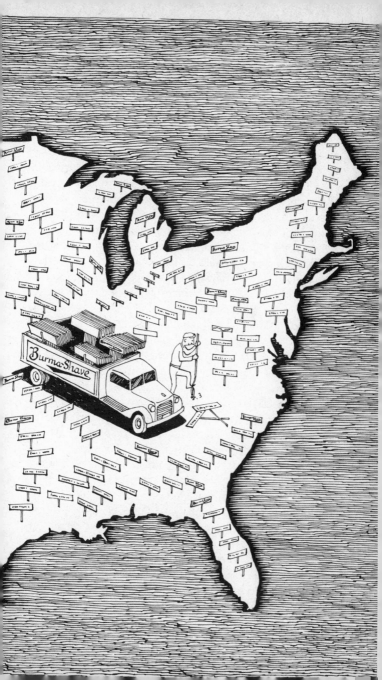

bringing the farmer from five to twenty-five dollars, depending on the desirability of the location. Occasionally a David Harum who owned a particularly choice spot, and who was resistant to the marked friendliness of the advance man, might get fifty dollars or even more a year, although such cases were rare.

Renewals were handled by mail; Fidelia worked out a system of sending out new contracts well in advance of expiration. If a farmer balked at signing, displaying inflated ideas of the site's value, she simply instructed a truck crew to remove the signs at their next passage. Mostly the relationship between farmers and Burma-Shave was an amiable one, with many leases extending for decades. "Oh, occasionally we'd get a man who'd pull down some signs to patch up his barn," noted John Kammerer, head of the company sign shop, "but it was mainly all the other way. The farmers were kind of proud of those signs. They'd often write us if a sign had become damaged, asking us to ship a replacement that they'd put up themselves. In the years when we brought old signs back here to the plant, when lumber was short, I'd sometimes see where they had repaired or repainted signs on their own hook, often doing a fine job of it, too."

Once the advance man had signed up the farmer, the two would pace off the location, tying bright strips of red or orange cloth to the fence to signal the spot for the installation crew following along behind. The crew, traveling in a 1½-ton truck jauntily painted with such admonitions as Cheer Up, Face, the War Is Over, would typically be manned by several husky Minnesota youngsters, appropriately muscled for the assignment of digging thirty-six postholes per day, each one no less than three feet deep. According to carefully fostered rumor, any indolent lad who found that digging to this depth through stubborn shale or past heavy boulders was excessively fatiguing, and who therefore covertly sawed off a foot or eighteen inches from the *bottom* of the post, was liable to summary discharge.

The company displayed a characteristic old-shoe informality in its sign operations. Periodic attempts to systematize it—special regional crews, a complex pattern of leaving trucks and gear in storage in remote parts of the country—were tried and discarded. Instead, the firm settled in to an informal but effective pattern. The dozen or so people in the sign shop, having pitched in during the cruelest part of the Minnesota winter to start production on the new crop of signs and having shipped off the first few hundred sets to regional warehouses, would then divide up in part to set out on the highways. They would be subdivided into several advance men, traveling solo, and three or four truck-borne pairs of installers, laden with signs and equipment, and all bearing Fidelia's latest route maps. With almost the dedication of Crusaders or seekers of the Holy Grail, they would often set out at the end of February and not return home to Minnesota until the ground froze around Thanksgiving. Each truck bore about forty sets of signs, perhaps six or seven working days' supply, after which it was necessary to put in at a regional warehouse and load up again.

There was much informal doubling of duties. The advance man would circle back after signs had been up in a new territory for a few weeks, paying sales calls on drugstores and wholesalers, and usually discovering that a pleasing demand had been generated. The muscular young installers—whom the Odells were accustomed to describe as qualified PhDs, the letters standing for Posthole Diggers—were also often pressed into service as the nucleus of a crew of "samplers," busily handing out small free tubes or jars at ball games, wrestling matches, and other convocations of males.

"We made a few mistakes," noted Burdette Booth, a shyly friendly man who has worked for Burma-Shave all his life. "Once in Los Angeles I had a crew giving out sample jars to men as they filed in to a wrestling match. Then everybody got mad at one of the wrestlers, and they started pitching those jars into the ring—they were just like *rocks,* perfect for throwing—and it was a wonder no one got klonked. After that I learned to sample as people were coming out of a gathering, not as they went in." In New York Leonard Odell learned the same lesson when a crew of his passed out sample tubes of Burma-Shave to baseball fans entering Ebbets Field. After the plate umpire made a call unfavorable to the Dodgers, much of the infield became so densely carpeted with tubes of brushless shaving cream that it was necessary to suspend play until the groundskeepers could tidy up.

Booth, who has served as installer, advance man, salesman, sampler, and plant engineer during his thirty-four years with the company, remembers each assignment as being a lot of fun, in different ways. "Of course you were away from home for long stretches. If I knew I'd be in an area for a while my wife would join me and we'd get a furnished room somewhere. Ohio was one state that I worked over real hard; I put up more than seven hundred sets of signs there. That could be real work—digging post-holes all day long. Sometimes when you came back to the cabin or motel after work, people would see the truck painted Cheer Up, Face, and they'd say 'So *you're* the Burma-Shave man!' They sort of thought of you as the Good Humor man, and expected you to be comical on the spot, which was not always easy with an aching back."

The signs themselves underwent continuous evolution. For the first five years they were one-inch pine boards, ten inches high and a yard long, dip-painted twice with the background color mixed with preservative. The lettering, a standard sign painter's Gothic, was applied by silk screen. Letters were four inches high unless the line doubled, when they were squeezed to three and one-fourth inches. To emphasize the new crop of jingles, signs alternated by years between red with white lettering and orange with black lettering. Signs were bolted to steel posts nine feet long. Depending on the length of the location, they were installed ten to twenty yards apart, usually inside the farmer's fence or stone wall. Since highway rights-of-way were narrow in the late Twenties, the signs were usually set back only fifteen or twenty feet from the road's edge.

But times have a way of changing. In 1931 the Odells hired John Kammerer, a young Minneapolis sign and silk-screen expert, to look into a little problem they were having in the paint shop with "bleeding, weeping, and running." The little problem was soon licked, but Kam stayed on for thirty-four years, absorbed in experimenting with and improving the signs. Learning that the steel posts rusted out prematurely in wet ground and near the coasts, Kam had them replaced with pressure-treated wood posts that did fine. Then it was noted that signs had a way of disappearing completely on dark nights if they were located near college towns. These depredations were greatly reduced after Kam had the boltholes counter-bored so that the nuts could be unscrewed only with a special wrench, and after he had crosspieces fitted to the bottoms of the posts as anchors. It was still quite possible for an energetic and larcenous lad to decorate his quarters with a Burma-Shave sign, but he now needed more tools and effort than would normally be brought to an impulse theft.

As roads grew wider and cars went faster, Kam and his crew worked steadily to keep up. In stages over the years the signs grew to twelve and then eighteen inches high and to forty inches in width, with corresponding increase of letter height. Posts were located farther back from the highway, as much as forty or fifty feet from the center line. And the distance between signs steadily lengthened until they were planted, the location permitting, as much as fifty yards apart.

Yearly alterations of color had seemed a good way to call attention to the new signs, but it was noticed that whenever people spoke of Burma-Shave signs, they invariably described them as red and white. Orange-and-black ones seem to have made no impression whatever on the public's retina, or at least on its memory. At this the company gave up, going almost exclusively to red and white. It made things simpler, especially as the early pattern of an annual change became increasingly difficult and expensive with thousands of sets of signs scattered around the country. So the company settled into a custom of inspecting each set each year, but replacing it only every other year.

Simplification was an excellent goal because, the company noted, things tended in general to get steadily more complicated. Several states passed laws taxing each working side of a sign, and since the words *Burma-Shave* normally appeared on the reverse of every sign, the tax load in these states abruptly doubled. The response was a special series of "bareback" signs. Again, South Dakota had a law reserving the color red for danger signs; another special series of white-on-blue signs was created for Fidelia's South Dakota route list, which also included part of Minnesota. And again, high taxes on signs and the growing scarcity of good locations, especially on the close-in approaches to such potentially lucrative concentrations of shavers as New York City, San Francisco, and Los Angeles, made the standard six-sign highway set relatively inefficient. For these troublesome roads the response was a special crop of bobtailed signs. They used three, two, or only one board, and the copy usually settled for a single rhyme or pun:

GOOD TO THE LAST STROP

COVERS A MULTITUDE OF CHINS

PAYS DIVIDENDS IN LADY FRIENDS

Still the basic six-sign set, freighted with puns and outrageous humor, remained spread over the American heartland. Experience accumulated for the sign shop and the installers. It was found, for example, that skunks, beavers, and woodchucks were generally less of a nuisance than college boys, although infrequently some rodent with an atypical taste for creosoted wood would gnaw down a sign. Cows as a rule made good neighbors, except that crews would sometimes find where cows had ruminatively rubbed the posts to a bright shine, tilting the set slightly askew in the process. Hunters, who appear to have an uncontrollable tendency to bag all highway signs, perforated many a Burma-Shave set, although usually with small effect. "One nice thing about a pine board," observed Kam recently, "is its ability to absorb gunfire. A drawback to the aluminum signs that we experimented with for a time was that bullet holes were much more conspicuous than with wood. Of course if a youngster with a twelve-gauge shotgun blasted away from a distance of ten feet, it wouldn't do any sign much good."

In the first decades the strangest natural enemies of Burma-Shave signs were horses. Signs in fields where horses were pastured would be found broken off forcibly at the attachment point. Although several jingles referred pejoratively to horses (e.g., OLD DOBBIN / READS THESE SIGNS / EACH DAY / YOU SEE, HE GETS / HIS CORN THAT WAY), the broken signs did not represent literary criticism. Study by Kam and his crew revealed that the signs were being installed at a perfect height to serve as horse back-scratchers. Throughout the country enterprising horses were discovering that, by sidling under an overhanging sign and humping slightly, a richly sensuous scratching could be achieved; and often, in some transport of equine ecstasy, the sign would snap. A partial remedy, quickly instituted, was to use ten-foot posts in place of nine-footers. It is not recorded how horses felt about this deprivation, although the damage was substantially decreased. A combination of uneven ground and tall, enterprising horses allowed it still to happen on occasion, but, as Kam noted a little sadly, "Our horse problem disappeared as, in fact, horses themselves disappeared from American farms. Tractors don't itch."

6:

Free—Free
A Trip to Mars

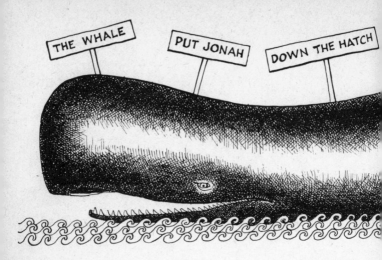

SELLING SHAVING CREAM by jingle may have been an odd way to make a living, but it had its compensations. For one thing, the mail was full of surprises, and Clinton Odell's don't-offend-people dictum meant that all complaints, however odd, had to be judiciously considered. Not all complaints were acted on, though. THE WHALE / PUT JONAH / DOWN THE HATCH / BUT COUGHED HIM UP / BECAUSE HE SCRATCHED drew criticism for irreverence as well as indelicacy, but the signs stayed up. On the other hand, to ease problems of lettering space for Kam's signs, a little simplified spelling was employed experimentally—e.g., *tonite, thot, sez*—but it took only a few reprimands in the mail from English teachers to bring that to a speedy end. And a minor classic of the Thirties, NO LADY LIKES / TO DANCE / OR DINE / ACCOMPANIED BY / A PORCUPINE, although it seemed wholly innocuous, drew an inflamed reproof composed on the letterhead of the Porcupine Club of Boston. We'll have you *know*, the executive secretary wrote in thin-lipped indignation, that

50

our fraternal organization gives *frequent* dances, attended by ladies who give *every* evidence of *enjoying* themselves. To Leonard Odell fell the task of sending a soothing response. After assurances of exceptional respect by the Burma-Vita Company for porcupines everywhere, he explained that in the New York Advertising Club he was personally a member of a subgroup called the Exalted Order of Goats, and that, speaking as an ex-Grand Odor, he had never felt badly about unfortunate references to namesakes. It was a repy that appeared to mollify the Porcupines.

The mail was unpredictable. WITH GLAMOR GIRLS / YOU'LL NEVER CLICK / BEWHISKERED / LIKE A / BOLSHEVIK, appearing in 1940, brought an especially testy complaint. It was postmarked from New York City, with an address from a locality near Union Square. Keep up this sort of thing, it rasped in Humphrey Bogart manner, and the old red herring will *really* get you. Allan held this letter for some days, eyeing it uneasily. It was evidently still on his mind a week later when, returning from lunch, he found a parcel on his desk bearing a similar postmark. As he was opening it gingerly, peering into a corner of its wrapping, he suddenly realized that it ticked ominously. It took only a few strides for him to race to the mixing room down the hall and plunge the package into a tank of water. This reaction virtually convulsed the office and factory staff, all covertly watching, who had collaborated in assembling the package, and in choosing an old alarm clock for the dangerous implications of its tick.

Burdette Booth also remembered a moment of surprise. "We were on the Texas route, changing copy and giving out half-ounce tubes as samples. In Austin we noticed that some cartons of samples were leaking—poor crimping on the tubes, maybe. I phoned Minneapolis and Al said to destroy them. 'Don't just leave them on the dump where someone might find them' he said. So early next morning, in a misty dawn, we stopped the truck on a bridge over a fair-sized river and pitched over the eight or ten leaky boxes. I knew the cartons would come apart and the tubes would sink.

"That afternoon in a town a hundred miles away I was parking the truck when I saw a Texas Ranger in the left-hand mirror. Then I saw another one in the right-hand mirror, and they both had their guns drawn. 'All right' they said, just like Gary Cooper. 'Get out slowly, with your hands high.' They made us unload the whole truck while they inspected the contents. What happened, I found out, was that a housewife had reported seeing two men on the bridge heaving a dismembered body into the river. So the authorities dragged the river but all they found was a piece of carton with *Burma-Shave* on it, and then they radioed out to pick us up. I explained what we'd done. 'All right, but don't do it again' the captain said, and we sure didn't. It's sweaty work unloading the whole truck while hard-eyed guys hold guns on you."

Something about the road-sign operation seemed to invite the unexpected. Leonard recalls a time in the Thirties, posthole-digging his way across New England, when he had just completed the laborious installation of OLD MC DONALD / ON THE FARM / SHAVED SO HARD / HE BROKE HIS ARM / THEN HE BOUGHT / BURMA-SHAVE. He was driving slowly past the signs to check them when he noticed from the mailbox, and verified from Fidelia's route list, that the farmer's name was in fact McDonald. "I didn't know what to do. I figured that we probably ought to take down the whole set, even though it was getting on toward dark. Finally we nervously hunted him up. He was a big man, kind of solemn. When I explained, he just looked at me for a long moment. Then he burst out laughing. Turned out that he got a big kick out of it, and of course the whole neighborhood did too."

In another case a young sailor sent in a long letter. His ship had just returned from an extended training cruise off Alaska, and he wished to relate a most remarkable occurrence, memorable to the several hundred young trainees aboard. They had been steaming above the Aleutians and, the weather being favorable, had passed through the Bering Strait into the Bering Sea. Those off duty had gathered on deck during the passage through the Strait, with Big Diomede Island on the portside and beyond it the mainland of Asia. Ice floes dotted the dark waters. As the ship nosed past a large floe, those on deck were flabbergasted to see a familiar row of small red signs strung along the ice. Binoculars revealed that all but the last sign—which clearly said *Burma-Shave*—were lettered eerily in the Russian alphabet. One sailor with a smattering of Russian announced that the jingle appeared to make some Cyrillic witticism about polar bears. The ship steamed slowly on, bearing several hundred baffled trainees. It was only later that the explanation circulated

53

through the ship's company: the signs had been planted, as an elaborate but thoroughly rewarding practical joke, by the crew of a helicopter flying ahead on ice reconnaissance.

The friendly relationship between Burma-Shave and the U.S. Navy was reflected later, during Operation Deepfreeze in Antarctica. Would the company care to contribute some signs, the Navy asked gravely, to sustain the morale of the men stationed on that remote subcontinent? Gosh, yes, Allan replied, enclosing a list of the sign sets then available. The three jingles chosen mirrored nicely the circumstances near the South Pole. One set was a public-service admonition on forest fires, and was erected on a road from the airbase at McMurdo Sound some thousand miles from the nearest combustible tree. A second set reflected the generally whiskery state prevailing: DEAR LOVER BOY / YOUR PHOTO CAME / BUT YOUR DOGGONE BEARD / WON'T FIT / THE FRAME.

MANY A FOREST / USED TO STAND / WHERE A

The third jingle chosen recalled, perhaps wistfully, the fact that human females were not permitted in Antarctica: USE OUR CREAM / AND WE BETCHA / GIRLS WON'T WAIT / THEY'LL COME / AND GETCHA.

It was characteristic of the luck of the Odells that photographs of the last series—erected in a howling wilderness with a snow tractor in the background and five politely interested penguins gracing the foreground—were picked up by United Press International and distributed to scores of U.S. newspapers. Even after allowing for the fact that Burma-Shave had become a sort of national institution, it was evident that Allan and Leonard had a knack for unpaid publicity that Barnum would have envied.

During the great days of radio, hundreds of "mention permissions" were granted to everyone from Amos 'n Andy to Jimmy Durante and Bob Hope. When television bloomed, it was not unnoticed that the signs could be as

GHTED MATCH   GOT OUT OF HAND   Burma-Shave

visual as the jingles had been oral. Many of the mentions on network air were brief (e.g., said Fibber McGee scornfully, "I've read better poetry than that on Burma-Shave signs with the last two posts missing"), but some were not, as in 1941 when Bob Hope devoted almost fifteen minutes to a Burma-Shave episode. Fred Allen had a particular fondness for gags built around the signs. One night on the Texaco Hour he devoted so much time to a skit titled "The Murder of the Burma-Shave Poet" that the Odells concluded that "we probably got more out of that network broadcast than Texaco did." Requests for permission to mention usually arrived by phone or telegram, with a note of urgency, and everyone in the office, down to the newest secretary, was authorized to issue permission "just so it was clean and wouldn't offend people."

Sometimes it was even possible to exploit a slightly misfiring jingle. In a time when retailing was being deviled by a fad for coupons, Allan wrote a satirical jingle: FREE OFFER! FREE OFFER! ! / RIP A FENDER / OFF YOUR CAR / MAIL IT IN FOR / A HALF-POUND JAR. While some 99 percent of those seeing this jingle interpreted it as satire, or at least as the light-hearted lunacy to be expected from Burma-Shave, the remaining 1 percent constituted a problem in cleanliness and rubbish disposal. Scores of fenders of notable decrepitude arrived at the plant by parcel post and express. Many enterprising people scavenged Minnesota junkyards, triumphantly bearing off rusty horrors that they lugged to the Burma-Shave offices. Others shipped in fenders forcibly detached from toy cars, which at least had the merit of depositing less dirt and rust. Each donor was greeted with simulated polite surprise, and courteously presented with a jar of Burma-Shave. As Leonard observed, it was one of those delightful little things that happen occasionally. Perhaps more to the point, by later relating the anecdote to the press, the Odells reaped far more value in publicity than the worth of the jars given out.

Once, however, the Odells met their match as amateur Barnums. Again the initiating jingle had been written by Allan, in this case the repeat of an earlier spoof: FREE—FREE / A TRIP / TO MARS / FOR 900 / EMPTY JARS. Although this offer seemed safe, the Odells had not reckoned on Arliss French, manager of a supermarket in Appleton, Wisconsin, one of a chain of Red Owl stores. Mr. French, widely known as Frenchy and no mean exploiter himself, took up the challenge with enthusiasm. He wired Burma-Shave that he was accepting their offer and where should the jars be shipped? After a bit of pencil-chewing, Allan wired back: If a trip to Mars you'd earn, remember, friend, there's no return.

But Frenchy was not easily put off; and besides, business in his store was being stirred up gratifyingly. He countered with a second publicized telegram: Let's not quibble, let's not fret, gather your forces, I'm all set. To this the Odells sent an almost obligatory response: Our rockets are ready; we ain't splitting hairs; just send us the jars—and arrange your affairs. They also sent Ralph Getchman, the general manager of Burma-Shave, to Appleton to see just what was going on.

As Leonard remembers it, "Ralph telephoned me soon: 'This boy's serious! He's got big reproductions of our signs running the full length of his store. He's putting full-page ads in the local paper saying Send Frenchy to Mars! In the store he's got jars heaped up in a huge pile. Any time people buy Burma-Shave he empties the cream into an ice-cream carton and keeps the jar. He's got some kind of rocket plane in the store that kids are swarming all over, and he's got little green men on the roof firing toy rocket gliders out over the parking lot.' I told Ralph the best I could think of for the moment was to send him to the Mars Candy Company down in Chicago for a weekend on the town, which was just barely good enough of an idea to get me off the phone.

"Meantime, though, the Red Owl chain was getting a big kick out of it, especially with the way the volume in the store was up. To help Frenchy they hired a publicity man named Moran, a fellow with a big red beard. He came to see us and said that we had a *great* idea going here. He'd discovered that there was a little town in Germany called Mars—spelled Moers actually, but pronounced Mars—population about a hundred and twenty-two, near Düsseldorf. He said that if we'd pay the plane fare, he'd take care of the rest, and that's how we did it. We decided to send Mrs. French along too, figuring that since she had eleven or twelve children maybe she could use a little vacation.

"So Frenchy showed up here with a bubble on his head, dressed in a silvery space suit with a big red owl on the front. They rented a Brink's armored truck to deliver the jars; it had a big sign on it, Sending Frenchy to Mars. We gave him some full jars that he could use in Mars to barter for goods and services. It made quite an affair for the TV and news photographers. The Frenches spent the night in Al's house, and he drove them to the airport in the morning. In Mars there was a three-day festival that was a dilly, with dancing in the streets and people coming in for miles around. The Frenches had a marvelous time, and when they got home they wrote us a wonderful letter. We still get Christmas cards from them.

"It was a real fun kind of thing," Leonard Odell concluded. "And syndicated right across the country."

7:

An End
to the
Road Signs

THE LITERARY QUALITY of the Burma-Shave verse was highly variable, not surprising, perhaps, considering that even Shakespeare did not attempt seven hundred sonnets. A minority of the jingles were—there is no other word for it—appalling: PEDRO / WALKED / BACK HOME BY GOLLY / HIS BRISTLY CHIN / WAS HOT-TO-MOLLY. Every now and then one moved beyond gaiety toward agitation: HE ASKED / HIS KITTEN / TO PET AND PURR / SHE EYED HIS PUSS / AND SCREAMED "WHAT FUR!" A few skirted the limits of felicity: HE LIT A MATCH / TO CHECK GAS TANK / THAT'S WHY / THEY CALL HIM / SKIN-LESS FRANK. There was, finally, a taste for the kind of whimsy that can sweep like a breeze across a grammar-school playground: HIS BRUSH IS GONE / SO WHAT'LL WE DO / SAID MIKE ROBE I / TO MIKE ROBE II.

At times numerous observers (including the Odells themselves) have dismissed the jingles as corny. This is an easy if not notably discerning assessment. Disregarding an occasional deviation, the jingles were in total a remarkable potpourri of folk humor, wit, and skillfully offbeat merchandising. While to dissect is sometimes to destroy, it is nevertheless possible to isolate certain of the elements that produced such generally pleasing and popular effects.

One characteristic, partly enforced by the format, was conciseness—an attribute that has been broadly popular from Aesop through Poor Richard to the fad for Confucius Say. The shortest full-sized jingle of record needed only seven words for its safety admonition: FROM / BAR / TO CAR / TO / GATES AJAR. Another notable compaction was: BROKEN ROMANCE / STATED FULLY / SHE WENT WILD / WHEN HE / WENT WOOLY.

Humor was, obviously, the second important characteristic. Those who undertake to analyze the complete canon will find that at least seven different strains of humor were employed. One was punning and wordplay, often enhanced by the serial effect: MY JOB IS / KEEPING FACES CLEAN / AND NOBODY KNOWS / DE STUBBLE / I'VE SEEN. Another was pure slapstick, in the mainstream of Buster Keaton and Red Skelton: SHE KISSED / THE HAIRBRUSH / BY MISTAKE / SHE THOUGHT IT WAS / HER HUSBAND JAKE. A pseudo-proverb was a favorite device, effective because the sententiousness associated with apothegms set up a nice contrast: WITHIN THIS VALE / OF TOIL / AND SIN / YOUR HEAD GROWS BALD / BUT NOT YOUR CHIN. (This jingle, incidentally, was a special favorite of the Odells'.) An irritable if not waspish wit was often used with telling effect, as in this highway-safety note: DON'T LOSE / YOUR HEAD / TO GAIN A MINUTE / YOU NEED YOUR HEAD / YOUR BRAINS ARE IN IT. The flirty-but-clean sex theme mentioned earlier was good for many a giggle, as was the use (rare among road signs) of topical themes: WE DON'T / KNOW HOW / TO SPLIT AN ATOM / BUT AS TO WHISKERS / LET US AT 'EM. Lastly, the sardonic and quietly sharp tongue often heard in country stores was basic: EVERY DAY / WE DO / OUR PART / TO MAKE YOUR FACE / A WORK OF ART.

A graduate-school dissertation recently prepared by George Odell, Allan's son, *The Burma-Vita Company and Its Relationship to Twentieth Century America,* makes a number of subtle observations about the corpus of the jingles. Their humor, George Odell notes, was often based on the image of the whisker, a concept faintly ludicrous to begin with, and certainly not as repulsive as many other drugstore advertising images. There was also the typically Western humor of exaggeration: WE'VE MADE / GRANDPA / LOOK SO TRIM / THE LOCAL / DRAFT BOARD'S AFTER HIM. This wide-swinging extravagance, traceable back past Mark Twain, Josh Billings, and Bret Harte, found sympathetic responses everywhere west of the Mississippi. The consistent use of slang and colloquialism, George Odell wrote, was comforting to viewers; it was reassuring to find a chatty, familiar jingle on a road many miles from home. Almost inevitably the impression was given that the company sure must be made up of friendly plain folks, very different from those other advertisers of drugstore products, who noisily threatened malodorousness, disease, and decay.

* * *

The commercial fortunes of the Burma-Vita Company can be read like tea leaves in the jingles themselves. For most of the first twenty years the company had at least one jingle per crop that engagingly bragged about the increased number of users. In 1947 came this spirited cock-a-doodle-doo: ALTHO / WE'VE SOLD / SIX MILLION OTHERS / WE STILL CAN'T SELL / THOSE COUGHDROP BROTHERS. But from then on there were notes of strain. In 1948, writing in a house organ called *The Burma Sign Post,* Allan reported slightly decreasing sales and greatly increasing costs, with company officers taking cuts in salary. Other omens followed. The bragging jingle of 1955 showed no increase: 6 MILLION HOUSEWIVES / CAN'T BE WRONG / WHO KEEP / THEIR HUSBANDS / RIGHT ALONG IN / BURMA-SHAVE.

This seven-year plateau was hardly promising in a time of national expansion. Other evidences piled up: increased re-use of existing, bought-and-paid-for rhymes; a tendency to choose the more hard-selling among these; a sharp drop in the ratio of public-service jingles; and then, most ominous of all, a four-year hiatus in which no new jingles whatever were erected. Although it was not visible from the texts of the verses, these were years in which the company was experimenting with alternative methods of advertising, such as radio and TV, as well as with economies of sign manufacture and maintenance.

Clearly the sales magic was slowly draining out of the sprightly little red signs. There were as many explanations as explainers. People were driving too fast to read small signs. Or the fun had gone out of the jingles themselves. Or it was all the fault of the superhighways with their sprawling rights-of-way and frequent exclusion of all commercial signs. Or it was urban growth and associated suburban spraddle. (Despite huge sampling drives, bus and car cards, and special signs on the feeder routes, large cities were a continuing problem that the Burma-Shave strategists never solved satisfactorily. This failure was serious because important marketing areas of the country were turning into supercities, accreting together more each year, like globules and curds on a slowly spreading puddle.)

Some mandarins of advertising had, quite naturally, a lucid if self-serving explanation: homemade, corny little signs, produced without benefit of agency commission, were no longer enough; now it was vital to portray graphically why the product was superior to its competitors, as by TV demonstrations. An opinion-polling marketing analyst made a depth study that was festooned with impressive garlands of statistical theory; the corporate image and possible future of Burma-Shave that emerged dimly from the welter of decimal places was, as is the custom with such studies, made up of equal parts of encouragement, discouragement, and enigma. Allan himself had a terser verdict: "Times change. If we were starting over now, I'm not sure the idea would work today."

It should not be thought that the Burma-Vita Company

had any intention of lurching blindly into bankruptcy. Impressive numbers of males were still purchasing jars, tubes, and their new aerosol siblings. Modest sidelines of after-shave and pre-electric lotions, deodorants, and even a tooth powder were adding to the gross. There was the memory of a mosquito repellent that had been discontinued only after a singularly mosquito-free summer, and a line of razor blades that had done just fine until the war had cut off supplies of adequate steel. Instead, the difficulty lay in the managerial implications of the situation: there were clear evidences that the road signs were not only growing costlier (some $200,000 a year by the 1960s) but also steadily less effective. Plainly it was expedient to divert more and more of this money into such standard advertising media as print, radio, and TV; and less of it into the fine goofy old road signs that had built and nourished the business.

This dreary if prudent course was already in effect when, on February 7, 1963, it was announced publicly that the Burma-Vita Company had been sold to Philip Morris, Inc. It would become an operating division of a subsidiary, American Safety Razor Products. Allan Odell, for fifteen years president and treasurer of Burma-Vita and in a sense its major creator, chose to enter semi-retirement although he would serve the new entity as a consultant; his younger brother Leonard would act as president of the new division. The two brothers were no longer young; and their father, Clinton, had died in 1958 at the age of eighty. "We were the last of the original Big Four to sell out," Leonard noted recently. The sale was a major milestone on the route that had begun, thirty-eight years before, on the road to Red Wing.

The Odells' decision to reduce gradually the number of road signs, replacing them with other advertising media, was ratified by the new owners. The action was, in fact, accelerated. It was determined that all signs were to be taken down as soon as practicable. One couldn't simply leave them up to fade into picturesque decay; and besides, counsel were of the opinion that if the signs stayed up, one might be held to continue to owe farmers rent money. So the trucks—still painted Cheer Up, Face—were sent out for the last time, fanning across the country on Fidelia Dearlove's routes. Crews unbolted the anti-college-boy attachment points and uprooted the posts, so that nothing visible remained of what had been. Only where the posts were so firmly embedded that extraction was virtually impossible did the crews saw them off flush with the ground, leaving the prescribed three feet of depth buried like an invisible marker. Farmers often seemed sad at the removal, and not just because of the cessation of rent checks. "It's sort of like losing an old friend," crews were told.

Characteristically, Allan and Leonard made the most of the elegiac spirit implied in such comment. Scores of newspaper feature writers and columnists proved eager to do pieces about the demise of Burma-Shave road signs; editorial writers fell into a mood of *Eheu! fugaces;* and the *Saturday Evening Post* ran a beautifully crafted article by William K. Zinsser that was later re-used in the *Reader's Digest.* At the Advertising Club of New York, a well-touted luncheon (with a jingle briefly erected outside along the dignified center mall of Park Avenue) was held for the joint purposes of saying farewell to the signs and of introducing Miss Nobu McCarthy, a Eurasian actress of exceptional charm hired to make Burma-Shave TV commercials. In general, farewells to the signs grew into a promotion that quite dwarfed such earlier triumphs as torn-off fenders and Frenchy's weekend in Mars.

It was also evident that all this was eyed with a certain tart envy within advertising and promotion circles; comment in the trade press noted that the Odells had "set off a wave of nostalgia" and that the "signs were having

as many retirements as an aging opera star." Probably the prevailingly wary attitude toward the Odells was most nicely expressed in 1964 by a man from the Washington *Star*. He described Leonard as a "genial, talkative man of fifty-seven with a highly suspect hayseed air. 'I'm just a country boy,' he will say disarmingly, but there is something about him that makes a city slicker count his fingers after a handshake."

On this occasion Leonard was in Washington to give a set of signs to the Smithsonian. The cultural-history section of that institution, alerted and possibly alarmed by all the publicity about the disappearance of the signs, had requested a typical set. After some thought the Odells chose their favorite about your-head-grows-bald-but-not-your-chin for permanent preservation. (There was, needless to say, no hesitancy about passing over hot-to-Molly or skinless Frank.) The presentation made a fine news story, and was comforting to all connected with the company. It remained for George Odell, Allan's son, to point out the special irony of preserving in the Smithsonian the advertising device of a firm that, in an earlier day, had plastered the country with: SHAVING BRUSHES / YOU'LL SOON SEE 'EM / ON THE SHELF / IN SOME / MUSEUM.

A question is often raised today as to whether the Burma-Shave road signs are actually all gone. Perhaps it is a quirk of memory or some persistence of vision, but many people will assure an inquirer that a set was noticed just a few weeks ago on the road to Chambersburg, or maybe it was that straight stretch just south of Winthrop. So far as is known, this is an illusion, a memory in masquerade. (Yet with some thirty-five thousand individual signs once planted about the nation, it is certainly not impossible for a few to have evaded the dismantling crews; so the chance of a few spectral sets, picked up in the headlights of certain older cars on misty nights, should perhaps not be wholly discounted.) But to the knowledge of the Burma-Vita Company, the only signs in existence today outside the factory are those donated to museums, or given to friends and gracing winding private driveways, and a few that have turned up, bearing outrageous price tags, in enterprising antique shops.

The question of the physical existence of a possible handful of remaining signs is scarcely worth a search program. Unlike the annual count of whooping cranes, this census would in the end be like one conducted to count the passenger pigeon or the great auk. More meaningful, perhaps, is the fact that the little red signs still exist, very much alive, in thousands of memories. The setting in each case is individual, although the memories have much in common. It may be that you are en route to Shady Grove by Pine Lake, driving a spunky Ford V-8 or a delightful Packard with bright red hexagons on its hubcaps. The sun is high, the sky blue, and drifting into the open car there is the warm tar smell from the road, blended with new honeysuckle. Then along the roadside this cadenced message unfolds:

IF YOU
DON'T KNOW
WHOSE SIGNS
THESE ARE
YOU CAN'T HAVE
DRIVEN VERY FAR.

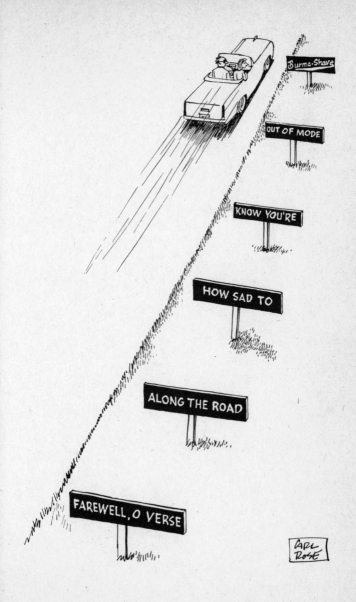

Appendix:

Texts of All
Burma-Shave
Signs

It HAS BEEN SAID that the most carefully perfected plan for the cataloging of a heterogeneous body of objects can never be more than partially satisfactory, and this is eminently true of the Burma-Shave jingles. The listing below, prepared from the company's own records and thus as complete and exact as is possible today, nevertheless presents various technical difficulties to a compiler. The Burma-Vita Company, although expert in the manufacture and sale of shaving cream, had neither a trained historian nor an archivist, and their records present several problems:

1. Texts of the very first sets of homemade signs, placed experimentally on the roads to Red Wing and Albert Lea, are lost. Testimony of participants indicates, however, that the texts used in 1927 were slight elaborations of the originals—i.e., that the earliest texts are contained within the 1927 series.

2. Variant forms of a number of jingles occurred when they were subsequently re-used. The commonest change was to revise the division of words among signs, but textual revision was not unknown. Note for example that in the "museum" jingle of 1930 the line *Way down East* recurs later as *On the shelf*.

3. Records on special jingles for regional tests or for such regionally marketed products as tooth powder, blades, or lotion were not always detailed. The special bobtailed jingles employed on the approaches to certain cities in 1939 and later are not identified by year of use, and were not always changed in annual or biennial cycles.

Finally, a note about editing. The texts here presented are precisely those in company records, shown unaltered. Changes made have been limited to the elimination of authors' names and addresses, of incomplete notations of sign colors used, and of identifying code numbers.   F.H.R. Jr.

SHAVE THE
   MODERN WAY
NO BRUSH
NO LATHER
NO RUB-IN
BIG TUBE 35¢
   DRUG STORES
BURMA-SHAVE

GOODBYE!
   SHAVING BRUSH
HALF A POUND
   FOR
HALF A DOLLAR
VERY FINE
   FOR THE SKIN
DRUGGISTS HAVE IT
CHEER UP FACE
   THE WAR IS OVER
BURMA-SHAVE

HOLLER
HALF A POUND
   FOR
HALF A DOLLAR
OH BOY!
SHAVING JOY
COMPLEXION SAVE
BURMA-SHAVE

SHAVE THE MODERN WAY
WASH THE FACE
APPLY WITH FINGERS
SHAVE
BIG TUBE 35¢
BURMA-SHAVE

ONE OF THE
   GREAT DISCOVERIES
GOODBYE! SHAVING
   BRUSH
OLD MEN LOOK YOUNGER
YOUNG MEN LOOK
   HANDSOMER
VERY FINE FOR THE SKIN
BURMA-SHAVE

TAKES THE "H"
   OUT OF SHAVE
MAKES IT
   SAVE
SAVES COMPLEXION
SAVES TIME & MONEY
NO BRUSH
   NO LATHER
BURMA-SHAVE

EVERY SHAVER
NOW CAN SNORE
SIX MORE MINUTES
THAN BEFORE
BY USING
BURMA-SHAVE

YOUR SHAVING BRUSH
HAS HAD ITS DAY
SO WHY NOT
SHAVE THE MODERN WAY
WITH
BURMA-SHAVE

TWO
HUNDRED
THOUSAND
MEN
USE
BURMA-SHAVE

HALF A POUND
FOR
HALF A DOLLAR
SPREAD ON THIN
ABOVE THE COLLAR
BURMA-SHAVE

1930

ONE POUND   85¢
HALF POUND   50¢
BIG TUBE   35¢
DON'T PUT IT OFF
PUT IT ON
BURMA-SHAVE

DOES YOUR HUSBAND
MISBEHAVE
GRUNT AND GRUMBLE
RANT AND RAVE
SHOOT THE BRUTE SOME
BURMA-SHAVE

SHAVING BRUSHES
SUCH A BOTHER
BURMA-SHAVE
LOOKS GOOD
TO
FATHER

EARLY TO BED
EARLY TO RISE
WAS MEANT FOR THOSE
OLD FASHIONED GUYS
WHO DON'T USE
BURMA-SHAVE

BE
NO
LONGER
LATHER'S SLAVE
TREAT YOURSELF TO
BURMA-SHAVE

UNCLE RUBE
BUYS TUBE
ONE WEEK
LOOKS SLEEK
LIKE SHEIK
BURMA-SHAVE

THO STIFF
THE BEARD
THAT NATURE GAVE
IT SHAVES LIKE DOWN
WITH
BURMA-SHAVE

SHAVING BRUSHES
YOU'LL SOON SEE 'EM
WAY DOWN EAST
IN SOME
MUSEUM
BURMA-SHAVE

FIVE
HUNDRED
THOUSAND
MEN
USE
BURMA-SHAVE

CHEER UP FACE
THE WAR IS PAST
THE "H" IS OUT
OF SHAVE
AT LAST
BURMA-SHAVE

HALF A POUND
FOR
HALF A DOLLAR
AT THE DRUG STORE
SIMPLY HOLLER
BURMA-SHAVE

SHAVING BRUSHES
YOU'LL SOON SEE 'EM
ON THE SHELF
IN SOME
MUSEUM
BURMA-SHAVE

SIX
HUNDRED
THOUSAND
MEN
USE
BURMA-SHAVE

1880 A.D.
STRAIGHT RAZOR AND
SHAVING SOAP
1930 A.D.
SAFETY RAZOR AND
BURMA-SHAVE

THE 50¢ JAR
SO LARGE
BY HECK
EVEN THE SCOTCH
NOW SHAVE THE NECK
BURMA-SHAVE

ARE YOUR WHISKERS
WHEN YOU WAKE
TOUGHER THAN
A TWO-BIT STEAK?
TRY
BURMA-SHAVE

MODERN MAN
SPREADS IT ON
PATS IT IN
SHAVES IT OFF
SEE HIM GRIN
BURMA-SHAVE

BUY A TUBE
USE IT ONE WEEK
IF YOU THEN WANT
YOUR MONEY BACK
SEND US THE TUBE
BURMA-SHAVE

HINKY DINKY
PARLEY VOO
CHEER UP FACE
THE WAR
IS THRU
BURMA-SHAVE

1931

EIGHT
HUNDRED
THOUSAND
MEN
USE
BURMA-SHAVE

TAKE A TIP
FOR YOUR TRIP
NO WET BRUSH
TO SOAK
YOUR GRIP
BURMA-SHAVE

FILM PROTECTS
YOUR NECK
AND CHIN
SO YOUR RAZOR
WON'T DIG IN
BURMA-SHAVE

THE ONE HORSE SHAY
HAS HAD ITS DAY
SO HAS THE BRUSH
AND LATHER WAY
USE
BURMA-SHAVE

IT'S A GOOD
OLD SPANISH CUSTOM
TAKE YOUR MUG
AND BRUSH
AND BUST 'EM
BURMA-SHAVE

NO MATTER HOW
YOU SLICE IT
IT'S STILL YOUR FACE
BE HUMANE
USE
BURMA-SHAVE

HELLO DRUGGIST
I DON'T MEAN MAYBE
YES
SIR!
THAT'S THE BABY
BURMA-SHAVE

HALF A POUND
FOR
HALF A BUCK
COME ON SHAVERS
YOU'RE IN LUCK
BURMA-SHAVE

GOLFERS!
IF FEWER STROKES
ARE WHAT YOU CRAVE
YOU'RE OUT OF THE
    ROUGH
WITH
BURMA-SHAVE

THO TOUGH
AND ROUGH
FROM WIND AND WAVE
YOUR CHEEK GROWS
    SLEEK
WITH
BURMA-SHAVE

SHAVING BRUSH
ALL WET
AND HAIRY
I'VE PASSED YOU UP
FOR SANITARY
BURMA-SHAVE

MAKES SHAVING
A
GRIN GAME
NOT
A SKIN GAME
BURMA-SHAVE

1932

POLITICAL PULL
MAY BE
OF USE
FOR RAZOR PULL
THERE'S NO EXCUSE
BURMA-SHAVE

LISTEN SHAVERS
KNOCK ON WOOD
WHEN OFFERED
SOMETHING
"JUST AS GOOD"
BURMA-SHAVE

```
_____(HEBREW)          A SHAVE
_____(CHINESE)         THAT'S REAL
_____(GREEK)           NO CUTS TO HEAL
THE BEST SHAVE            A SOOTHING
IN ANY LANGUAGE           VELVET AFTER-FEEL
BURMA-SHAVE              BURMA-SHAVE


THE CANNONEERS           THE TUBE'S
WITH HAIRY EARS          A WHOPPER
ON WIRY WHISKERS         35 CENTS
USED TIN SHEARS          EASY SHAVING
UNTIL THEY FOUND         LOW EXPENSE
BURMA-SHAVE              BURMA-SHAVE


BARGAIN HUNTERS          FROM NEW YORK TOWN
GATHER 'ROUND            TO PUMPKIN HOLLER
FIFTY CENTS              IT'S HALF A POUND
BUYS                     FOR
HALF A POUND             HALF A DOLLAR
BURMA-SHAVE              BURMA-SHAVE


FREE                     YOU'LL LOVE YOUR WIFE
ILLUSTRATED              YOU'LL LOVE HER PAW
JINGLE BOOK              YOU'LL EVEN LOVE
IN EVERY                 YOUR MOTHER-IN-LAW
PACKAGE                  IF YOU USE
BURMA-SHAVE              BURMA-SHAVE


FOR PAINTING             GIVE THE GUY
COW-SHED                 THE TOE OF YOUR BOOT
BARN OR FENCE            WHO TRIES
THAT SHAVING BRUSH       TO HAND YOU
IS JUST IMMENSE          A SUBSTITUTE FOR
BURMA-SHAVE              BURMA-SHAVE


WHEN THE JAR             LAWYERS, DOCTORS
IS EMPTY                 SHEIKS AND BAKERS
WIFE BEGINS              MOUNTAINEERS AND
   TO SING                  UNDERTAKERS
"FOR SPICES, JAM & JELLY MAKE THEIR BRISTLY
THAT JAR IS JUST            BEARDS BEHAVE
   THE THING"            BY USING BRUSHLESS
BURMA-SHAVE              BURMA-SHAVE
```

SEVERAL MILLION
MODERN MEN
WILL NEVER
GO BACK
TO THE BRUSH AGAIN
BURMA-SHAVE

1933

MOONLIGHT
AND ROSES
WHISKERS
LIKE MOSES
JUST DON'T GO TOGETHER
BURMA-SHAVE

THE MILLIONTH MAN
HAS JOINED
OUR RANKS
OF HAPPY SHAVERS
MANY THANKS!
BURMA-SHAVE

TRAVELERS!
ALL
YOU NEED IS
A RAZOR
AND
BURMA-SHAVE

LATE RISERS!
SHAVE IN JUST
2 MINUTES FLAT
KISS YOUR WIFE
GRAB YOUR HAT
BURMA-SHAVE

LITTLE SHAVERS
DON'T OVERLOOK
ILLUSTRATED
JINGLE BOOK
IN EVERY PACKAGE
BURMA-SHAVE

IT'S NOT TOASTED
IT'S NOT DATED
BUT LOOK OUT—
IT'S IMITATED
INSIST ON
BURMA-SHAVE

SHAVING BRUSH
WAS LIKE
OLD ROVER
WHEN HE DIED
HE DIED ALL OVER
BURMA-SHAVE

WISE OLD SANDY
SHOPPED AROUND
THIS IS WHAT
OLD SANDY FOUND
50¢ BUYS HALF A POUND
BURMA-SHAVE

THE ANSWER TO
A MAIDEN'S
PRAYER
IS NOT A CHIN
OF STUBBY HAIR
BURMA-SHAVE

SHAVING BRUSH
DON'T YOU CRY
YOU'LL BE A
SHOE DAUBER
BY AND BY
BURMA-SHAVE

WITHIN THIS VALE
OF TOIL
AND SIN
YOUR HEAD GROWS BALD
BUT NOT YOUR CHIN—USE
BURMA-SHAVE

EVERYTHING
IN IT
IS FINE
FOR THE
SKIN
BURMA-SHAVE

BRIDGE PRIZE
FOR MEN
JUST HALF A BUCK
TRY IT, HOSTESS
CHANGE YOUR LUCK
BURMA-SHAVE

RUDDY CHEEKS
AND FACE
OF TAN
NEATLY SHAVEN
WHAT A MAN!
BURMA-SHAVE

MUG AND BRUSH
OLD ADAM
HAD 'EM
IS YOUR HUSBAND
LIKE ADAM, MADAM?
BURMA-SHAVE

TO SHAVING BRUSH
I NEED
NOT CLING
I WILL NOT HUSH
OF THEE I SING
BURMA-SHAVE

FREE OFFER!
    FREE OFFER! !
RIP A FENDER
OFF YOUR CAR
MAIL IT IN FOR
A HALF-POUND JAR
BURMA-SHAVE

HE PLAYED
A SAX
HAD NO B.O.
BUT HIS WHISKERS
    SCRATCHED
SO SHE LET HIM GO
BURMA-SHAVE

THRIFTY SHAVERS
NOW ARE FOUND
BUYING SHAVES
BY THE POUND
ONE LB. JAR 85¢
BURMA-SHAVE

IF YOUR HUBBY
TRUMPS YOUR ACE
HERE'S SOMETHING
THAT WILL
SAVE HIS FACE
BURMA-SHAVE

(Regional Contest, 1933)

25 PRIZES
EVERY WEEK
THRUOUT THE FOOTBALL
    SEASON
YOU'LL FIND YOU'D
    RATHER
USE NO LATHER
B'GOLLY THERE'S A
    REASON
BURMA-SHAVE

78

PRIZE CONTEST DETAILS
MAY BE OBTAINED
AT FOOTBALL BROADCAST
EVERY SATURDAY
OVER WCCO
BURMA-SHAVE

HIT 'EM HIGH
HIT 'EM LOW
IT'S ACTION ROOTERS
    CRAVE
MILLIONS BOAST—
    MILLIONS TOAST
THE ALL-AMERICAN
    SHAVE
BURMA-SHAVE

HIT 'EM HIGH
HIT 'EM LOW
FOLLOW YOUR TEAM
OVER WCCO
AND WIN A PRIZE
BURMA-SHAVE

THERE'S FOOTBALL IN
    THE AIR
AND PRIZES FOR ALL TO
    SHARE
ACCEPT OUR INVITATION
WCCO'S THE STATION
(MANY PRIZES
GET YOUR SHARE)

1934

HE HAD THE RING
HE HAD THE FLAT
BUT SHE FELT HIS CHIN
AND THAT
WAS THAT
BURMA-SHAVE

THE ANSWER TO
A SHAVER'S DREAM
A GREASELESS
NO BRUSH
SHAVING CREAM
BURMA-SHAVE

EVERY DAY
WE DO
OUR PART
TO MAKE YOUR FACE
A WORK OF ART
BURMA-SHAVE

JONAH TOOK
NO BRUSH
TO MOP HIS FACE
WHERE JONAH WENT
HE NEEDED SPACE
BURMA-SHAVE

YOUR BEAUTY, BOYS
IS JUST
SKIN DEEP
WHAT SKIN YOU'VE GOT
YOU OUGHT TO KEEP
BURMA-SHAVE

WHEN CUTTING
WHISKERS
YOU DON'T NEED
TO LEAVE ONE HALF
OF THEM FOR SEED
BURMA-SHAVE

THE BEARDED LADY
TRIED A JAR
SHE'S NOW
A FAMOUS
MOVIE STAR
BURMA-SHAVE

THE GAME LAWS
OUGHT TO
LET YOU SHOOT
THE BIRD WHO HANDS
    YOU
A SUBSTITUTE
BURMA-SHAVE

BACHELOR'S QUARTERS
DOG ON THE RUG
WHISKERS TO BLAME
NO ONE
TO HUG
BURMA-SHAVE

THO LIVING COSTS
ARE UPWARD BOUND
FOUR BITS
STILL BUYS
HALF A POUND
BURMA-SHAVE

LATHER WAS USED
BY DANIEL BOONE
HE LIVED
A 100 YEARS
TOO SOON
BURMA-SHAVE

COLLEGE BOYS!
YOUR COURAGE MUSTER
SHAVE OFF
THAT FUZZY
COOKIE DUSTER
BURMA-SHAVE

THAT "PINK TOOTH-
    BRUSH"
IS A CURSE
BUT THAT PINK RAZOR'S
A DARN SIGHT WORSE
USE
BURMA-SHAVE

BRISTLY BEARD
OR SILKY FUZZ
JUST SHAVE 'EM BACK
TO WHERE
THEY WAS
BURMA-SHAVE

PITY ALL
THE MIGHTY CAESARS
THEY PULLED
EACH WHISKER OUT
WITH TWEEZERS
BURMA-SHAVE

BENEATH THIS STONE
LIES ELMER GUSH
TICKLED TO DEATH
BY HIS
SHAVING BRUSH
BURMA-SHAVE

EVERY SECOND
WITHOUT FAIL
SOME STORE
RINGS UP
ANOTHER SALE
BURMA-SHAVE

NOAH HAD WHISKERS
IN THE ARK
BUT HE WOULDN'T GET
    BY
ON A BENCH
IN THE PARK
BURMA-SHAVE

1935

HIS FACE WAS SMOOTH
AND COOL AS ICE
AND OH LOUISE!
HE SMELLED
SO NICE
BURMA-SHAVE

WATER HEATER
OUT OF KILTER
TRY THE BRUSHLESS
WHISKER
WILTER
BURMA-SHAVE

80

HELPS
YOUR BUDGET
HOLD ITS GROUND
HALF A DOLLAR
HALF A POUND
BURMA-SHAVE

CUTIE INVITED
VARSITY HOP
GUY FULL
OF WHISKERS
PARTY A FLOP
BURMA-SHAVE

DEWHISKERED
KISSES
DEFROST
THE
MISSES
BURMA-SHAVE

IT TOOK YEARS
TO PERFECT
FOR YOU
A BRUSHLESS CREAM
THAT'S GREASELESS TOO
BURMA-SHAVE

WITH 200 KINDS
FROM WHICH TO CHOOSE
2 MILLION MEN
PREFER
TO USE
BURMA-SHAVE

I JUST JOINED
THE YOUNG MAN SAID
A NUDIST CAMP
IS MY FACE RED?
NO! I USE
BURMA-SHAVE

AVOID THE STORE
WHICH CLAIMS
YOU SHOULD
BUY SOMETHING ELSE
THAT'S JUST AS GOOD
BURMA-SHAVE

20 MILES PER GAL.
SAYS WELL-KNOWN CAR
TO GO 10,000
MILES PER GAL
BUY HALF-POUND JAR
BURMA-SHAVE

IF YOU THINK
SHE LIKES
YOUR BRISTLES
WALK BARE-FOOTED
THROUGH SOME THISTLES
BURMA-SHAVE

YOU KNOW
YOUR ONIONS
LETTUCE SUPPOSE
THIS BEETS 'EM ALL
DON'T TURNIP YOUR NOSE
BURMA-SHAVE

GRANDPA'S BEARD
WAS STIFF AND COARSE
AND THAT'S WHAT
CAUSED HIS
FIFTH DIVORCE
BURMA-SHAVE

TUBE
IMMENSE
35 CENTS
EASY SHAVING
LOW EXPENSE
BURMA-SHAVE

KEEP WELL
TO THE RIGHT
OF THE ONCOMING CAR
GET YOUR CLOSE SHAVES
FROM THE HALF-POUND
    JAR
BURMA-SHAVE

BE A MODERN
PAUL REVERE
SPREAD THE NEWS
FROM EAR
TO EAR
BURMA-SHAVE

WHISKERS LONG
MADE SAMSON STRONG
BUT SAMSON'S GAL
SHE DONE
HIM WRONG
BURMA-SHAVE

AT XMAS TIME
AND BIRTHDAYS TOO
WE SOLVE
YOUR PROBLEMS RIGHT
FOR YOU—GIVE
BURMA-SHAVE

HALF A BUCK
HALF A POUND
NO SUBSTITUTE
IS EVER FOUND
FOR
BURMA-SHAVE

ENTHUSIASTIC USER
HENRY J. MC LASS
SPREADS OUR PRODUCT
ON THE LAWN
WHEN HE CUTS THE
    GRASS
BURMA-SHAVE

THE HAPPY GOLFER
FINDS WITH GLEE
THE SHAVE
THAT SUITS HIM
TO A TEE
BURMA-SHAVE

EENY-MEENY
MINY-MO
SAVE YOUR SKIN
YOUR TIME
YOUR DOUGH
BURMA-SHAVE

SHAVING BRUSH
IS OUT OF DATE
USE THE
RAZOR'S
PERFECT MATE
BURMA-SHAVE

IF SUBSTITUTION
HE SHOULD TRY
JUST LOOK THAT CLERK
RIGHT IN THE EYE
AND BELLOW:
BURMA-SHAVE

1936

RIOT AT
DRUG STORE
CALLING ALL CARS
100 CUSTOMERS
99 JARS
BURMA-SHAVE

TO GET
AWAY FROM
HAIRY APES
LADIES JUMP
FROM FIRE ESCAPES
BURMA-SHAVE

SPECIAL TREATMENT
EVERY HAIR
HOLDS IT UP
AND CUTS
IT SQUARE
BURMA-SHAVE

YOUR RAZOR
FLOATS THRU
THE HAIR
WITH THE
GREATEST OF EASE
BURMA-SHAVE

ED'S FACE
IS ROUGH
AND RUGGED
ED'S WIFE
DOESN'T HUG ED
BURMA-SHAVE

SHAVING BRUSH
& SOAPY SMEAR
WENT OUT OF
STYLE WITH
HOOPS MY DEAR
BURMA-SHAVE

TO EVERY MAN
HIS SHAVE
IS BEST
UNTIL HE MAKES
THE FINAL TEST
BURMA-SHAVE

GOLFERS!
HOLE IN ONE
IS QUITE A FEAT
UNLESS THAT HOLE
IS IN YOUR MEAT
BURMA-SHAVE

IF YOU
AND WHISKERS
DO HOBNOB
SOME SAILOR GOB
WILL STEAL YOUR SQUAB
BURMA-SHAVE

IF YOU'RE JUST
AN AVERAGE MAN
WANTING TO LOOK
THE BEST YOU CAN
USE
BURMA-SHAVE

THE CREAM
PRESERVES
PA'S RAZOR BLADE
THE JAR PRESERVES
MA'S MARMALADE
BURMA-SHAVE

FISHERMAN!
FOR A LUCKY STRIKE
SHOW THE PIKE
A FACE
THEY'LL LIKE
BURMA-SHAVE

SMITH BROTHERS
WOULD LOOK IMMENSE
IF THEY'D JUST
COUGH UP 50 CENTS
FOR HALF POUND JAR
BURMA-SHAVE

JIMMIE SAID A
NAUGHTY WORD
JIMMIE'S MOTHER OVER-
    HEARD
SOAPSUDS? NO!
HE PREFERRED
BURMA-SHAVE

CONGRESSMAN PIPP
LOST THE ELECTION
BABIES HE KISSED
HAD NO PROTECTION
TO WIN—USE
BURMA-SHAVE

CHEER CHEER
THE GANG'S
ALL HERE
RIDING ALONG
THREE MILLION STRONG
FOR
BURMA-SHAVE

LET'S GIVE THE
CLERK A HAND
WHO NEVER
PALMS OFF
ANOTHER BRAND
BURMA-SHAVE

HEAR ABOUT
THE JOLLY TAR
IT SMELLED SO GOOD
HE ATE
A JAR
BURMA-SHAVE

HIS TENOR VOICE
SHE THOUGHT DIVINE
TILL WHISKERS
SCRATCHED
SWEET ADELINE
BURMA-SHAVE

COOTIES LOVE
BEWHISKERED PLACES
CUTIES LOVE THE
SMOOTHEST FACES
SHAVED BY
BURMA-SHAVE

OLD MC DONALD
ON THE FARM
SHAVED SO HARD
HE BROKE HIS ARM
THEN HE BOUGHT
BURMA-SHAVE

FREE! FREE! !
A TRIP
TO MARS
FOR 900
EMPTY JARS
BURMA-SHAVE

AS YOU JOURNEY
DOWN THE YEARS
YOUR MIRROR IS
THE GLASS THAT CHEERS
IF YOU USE
BURMA-SHAVE

ALL THESE YEARS
YOUR SKIN
HAS DRIED
WHY NOT MOISTEN
UP YOUR HIDE
BURMA-SHAVE

1937

HOLLER!
HALF A POUND
FOR HALF A DOLLAR
ISN'T THAT
A CHEERFUL EARFUL
BURMA-SHAVE

DRIVE
WITH CARE
BE ALIVE
WHEN YOU
ARRIVE
BURMA-SHAVE

WEEK-OLD BEARD
SO MASKED HIS FACE
HIS BULL DOG
CHASED HIM
OFF THE PLACE
BURMA-SHAVE

LITTLE WILLIE
MODERN SOUL
BUSTED PAPA'S
BRUSH AND BOWL
NICE WORK WILLIE
BURMA-SHAVE

'MID RISING
TAXES
SOARING RENTS
STILL HALF A POUND
FOR FIFTY CENTS
BURMA-SHAVE

SUBSTITUTES!
SMOOTH GUYS SELL 'EM
EASY MARKS USE 'EM
WELL GROOMED MEN
ALWAYS REFUSE 'EM
BURMA-SHAVE

EVERY
SHEBA
WANTS A SHEIK
STRONG OF MUSCLE
SMOOTH OF CHEEK
BURMA-SHAVE

IF *HER* WHISKERS
SCRATCHED *YOUR* CHEEK
YOU WOULD
SEND HER OUT
TO SEEK
BURMA-SHAVE

THE CANNIBALS
TOOK JUST ONE VIEW
AND SAID
HE LOOKS TOO NICE
TO STEW
BURMA-SHAVE

YOU'VE LAUGHED
AT OUR SIGNS
FOR MANY A MILE
BE A SPORT
GIVE US A TRIAL
BURMA-SHAVE

IF HARMONY
IS WHAT
YOU CRAVE
THEN GET
A TUBA
BURMA-SHAVE

THE BURMA GIRLS
IN MANDALAY
DUNK BEARDED LOVERS
IN THE BAY
WHO DON'T USE
BURMA-SHAVE

KIDS! ATTENTION!
44 BEST JINGLES
USED SO FAR
IN JINGLE BOOK
WITH TUBE OR JAR
BURMA-SHAVE

MEN
WHO'VE TESTED
EVERY BRAND
ARE JUST THE ONES
WHO NOW DEMAND
BURMA-SHAVE

IT'S IN
THE BAG
OF EVERY MAN
WHO TRAVELS
LIGHTLY AS HE CAN
BURMA-SHAVE

FROM SASKATOON
TO ALABAM'
YOU HEAR MEN PRAISE
THE SHAVE
WHAT AM
BURMA-SHAVE

MY NECK WAS SORE
IN FRONT BEFORE
AND ALSO
SORE BEHIND
BEFORE
BURMA-SHAVE

STOMACH ACHE!
DOCTOR—
TOOTHACHE!
DENTIST—
WHISKERS!
BURMA-SHAVE

THE CROWD
YOU SEE
AROUND THAT STORE
ARE BURMA-SHAVERS
BUYING MORE
BURMA-SHAVE

BATHROOM SHELF
SURPRISES ME
FROM SHAVING CLUTTER
IT'S NOW FREE
I'M USING
BURMA-SHAVE

FINGERS WERE MADE
BEFORE BRUSHES—
USE 'EM
THEY'RE MUCH SAFER
YOU CAN'T LOSE 'EM
BURMA-SHAVE

SALESMEN, TOURISTS
CAMPER-OUTERS
ALL YOU OTHER
WHISKER-SPROUTERS
DON'T FORGET YOUR
BURMA-SHAVE

NO PULLING
AT THE WHISKER BASE
A SOOTHING FILM
PROTECTS
YOUR FACE
BURMA-SHAVE

PAPER HANGERS
WITH THE HIVES
NOW CAN
SHAVE WITH
CARVING KNIVES
BURMA-SHAVE

ROMANCES ARE
WRECKED
BEFORE THEY BEGIN
BY A HAIR
ON THE COAT
OR A LOT ON THE CHIN
BURMA-SHAVE

"THEY'RE OFF"
HE CRIED
AND FELT HIS CHIN
'TWAS JUST ANOTHER
EASY WIN FOR
BURMA-SHAVE

FIRE! FIRE!
KEEP COOL
BE BRAVE
JUST GRAB
YOUR PANTS AND
BURMA-SHAVE

A SILKY CHEEK
SHAVED SMOOTH
AND CLEAN
IS NOT OBTAINED
WITH A MOWING
    MACHINE
BURMA-SHAVE

CHEEK TO CHEEK
THEY MEANT TO BE
THE LIGHTS WENT OUT
AND SO DID HE
HE NEEDED
BURMA-SHAVE

HENRY THE EIGHTH
PRINCE OF FRISKERS
LOST FIVE WIVES
BUT KEPT
HIS WHISKERS
BURMA-SHAVE

DON'T TAKE
A CURVE
AT 60 PER
WE HATE TO LOSE
A CUSTOMER
BURMA-SHAVE

IF YOU HAVE
A DOUBLE CHIN
YOU'VE TWO
GOOD REASONS
TO BEGIN USING
BURMA-SHAVE

ON A HIGHWAY AD
HE SPIED IT
BOUGHT A JAR
NOW GLAD HE
TRIED IT
BURMA-SHAVE

RING OUT THE OLD
RING IN THE NEW
WHAT GOOD CAN
SHAVING
BRUSHES DO?
BURMA-SHAVE

SAY, BIG BOY
TO GO
THRU LIFE
HOW'D YOU LIKE
A WHISKERED WIFE?
BURMA-SHAVE

ARE YOU
AN EVEN-TEMPERED GUY
MAD ALL
THE TIME
BETTER TRY
BURMA-SHAVE

THE CREAM
ONE HEARS
THE MOST OF NOW
COMES FROM A JAR
NOT FROM A COW
BURMA-SHAVE

THE TIME
TO START
A REAL DISPUTE
IS WHEN YOU'RE
OFFERED A SUBSTITUTE
BURMA-SHAVE

RIP VAN WINKLE
SAID HE'D RATHER
SNOOZE FOR YEARS
THAN SHAVE
WITH LATHER
BURMA-SHAVE

OTHER THINGS HAVE
GONE SKY HIGH
HALF A DOLLAR
STILL WILL BUY
HALF POUND JAR
BURMA-SHAVE

TRAILER FOLK
HAVE LITTLE SPACE
FOR TOTIN' THINGS
TO FIX THE FACE
THEY USE
BURMA-SHAVE

BEFORE I TRIED IT
THE KISSES
I MISSED
BUT AFTERWARD—BOY!
THE MISSES I KISSED
BURMA-SHAVE

(Special Razor Blade
Promotion, 1938)

AFTER ONE TRIAL
YOU'LL WANT MORE
AT THE NEXT
GOOD DRUG STORE
15 FOR 25¢
BURMA-SHAVE
    BLADES

NO LADY LIKES
TO DANCE
OR DINE
ACCOMPANIED BY
A PORCUPINE
BURMA-SHAVE

HERE'S THE WINNING
SHAVING TEAM
THE PERFECT BLADE
THE PERFECT CREAM
BURMA-SHAVE BLADES
BURMA-SHAVE

IN EVERY
HALF A POUND
MY BOY
YOU GET A TON
OF SHAVING JOY
BURMA-SHAVE

SHARPEST BLADE
EVER MADE
COMFORT SPEED
GUARANTEED
15 FOR 25¢
BURMA-SHAVE
    BLADES

HERE'S SOMETHING
THAT COULD
EVEN SOAK
THE WHISKERS OFF
A RADIO JOKE
BURMA-SHAVE

HARDLY A DRIVER
IS NOW ALIVE
WHO PASSED
ON HILLS
AT 75
BURMA-SHAVE

DARLING I AM
GROWING OLD
NONSENSE!
DO AS YOU
ARE TOLD—GET
BURMA-SHAVE

A WHISKERED GENT
AT A BAZAAR
PAID FOR
A KISS
BUT GOT A JAR
BURMA-SHAVE

DRIVE LIKE
A RAILROAD ENGINEER
TAKE IT EASY
WHEN THE ROAD'S
NOT CLEAR
BURMA-SHAVE

MIRROR ON
THE BATHROOM WALL
WHAT'S THE
SMOOTHEST SHAVE
OF ALL?
BURMA-SHAVE

TRY A TUBE
THE CREAM
THAT'S IN IT
IS MAKING FRIENDS
A MAN A MINUTE
BURMA-SHAVE

SOAPS
THAT IRRITATE
THEIR MUGS
TURN JOLLY GENTS
TO JITTERBUGS
BURMA-SHAVE

PAST
SCHOOLHOUSES
TAKE IT SLOW
LET THE LITTLE
SHAVERS GROW
BURMA-SHAVE

MOM AND POP
ARE FEELING GAY
BABY SAID
AS PLAIN
AS DAY
BURMA-SHAVE

IF YOU DISLIKE
BIG TRAFFIC FINES
SLOW DOWN
'TILL YOU
CAN READ THESE SIGNS
BURMA-SHAVE

SHIVER MY TIMBERS
SAID CAPTAIN MACK
WE'RE TEN KNOTS OUT
BUT WE'RE TURNING
BACK
I FORGOT MY
BURMA-SHAVE

SPECIAL SEATS
RESERVED IN HADES
FOR WHISKERED GUYS
WHO SCRATCH
THE LADIES
BURMA-SHAVE

A PEACH
LOOKS GOOD
WITH LOTS OF FUZZ
BUT MAN'S NO PEACH
AND NEVER WUZ
BURMA-SHAVE

THE QUEEN
OF HEARTS
NOW LOVES THE KNAVE
THE KING
RAN OUT OF
BURMA-SHAVE

SPREAD IT ON
AND LIGHTLY TOO
SHAVE IT OFF
THAT'S ALL
YOU'RE THROUGH
BURMA-SHAVE

AT CROSSROADS
DON'T JUST
TRUST TO LUCK
THE OTHER CAR
MAY BE A TRUCK
BURMA-SHAVE

SHAVING BRUSHES
SOON WILL
BE TRIMMIN'
THOSE SCREWY HATS
WE SEE ON WIMMIN
BURMA-SHAVE

CHRISTMAS COMES
BUT ONCE
A YEAR
ONE SWELL GIFT
THAT'S ALWAYS HERE
BURMA-SHAVE

I PROPOSED
TO IDA
IDA REFUSED
IDA WON MY IDA
IF IDA USED
BURMA-SHAVE

CARELESS DRIVING
SOON WE HOPE
WILL GO
THE WAY
OF BRUSH AND SOAP
BURMA-SHAVE

CARELESS
BRIDEGROOM
DAINTY BRIDE
SCRATCHY WHISKERS
HOMICIDE
BURMA-SHAVE

(These special bobtailed jingles were employed in 1939 and later on the approach routes to a number of large cities, where locattions for full-length jingles were difficult to obtain. Each ended, of course, with the words *Burma-Shave*. They were displayed variously on two or three signs, sometimes even on a single extra-tall board.)

GOOD TO THE LAST STROP

COVERS A MULTITUDE OF CHINS

NIX ON NICKS

FOR FACES THAT GO PLACES

DON'T PUT IT OFF—PUT IT ON

SHAVE FASTER WITHOUT DISASTER

MAKES GOOD BECAUSE IT'S MADE GOOD

TAKES THE "H" OUT OF SHAVE

NO DIGGING IN ON TENDER SKIN

MAKES MISSES MRS.

BRUSH? NO! TOO SLOW

EQUIP YOUR GRIP

NO PUSHEE NO PULLY SMOOTH SHAVY
FEEL BULLY

BEARD UNRULY—MEET YOURS TRULY

AID THE BLADE

THOSE WHO CLICK—PICK

BETTER SHAVING AT A SAVING

START THE DAY THE MODERN WAY

50% QUICKER 100% SLICKER

YOU'LL ENTHUSE AS YOU USE

LOOK "SPIFFY" IN A "JIFFY"

NO SOONER SPREAD THAN DONE

SAVES YOUR JACK—HOLDS YOUR JILL

ROMANCE NEVER STARTS FROM SCRATCH

TRY OUR WHISKER LICKER

JOIN THE MILLIONS USING SOOTHING

A WORD TO THE WIVES IS SUFFICIENT

JUST SPREAD, THEN PAT—NOW SHAVE,
THAT'S THAT!

HOT TIP, PAL—MORE SMILES PER GAL

WON BY A HAIR THAT WASN'T THERE

PAYS DIVIDENDS IN LADY FRIENDS

IS YOUR FACE HER MISFORTUNE? TRY

IF GETTING UP GETS YOU DOWN—USE

WHEN YOU SHOP FOR YOUR POP

ONCE A DAY THE EASY WAY

NO TRICK TO CLICK IF QUICK TO PICK

OTHER DAYS—OTHER WAYS. NOWADAYS

DELUXE DE LOOKS WITH

HE'S NIFTY AND THRIFTY—LOOKS 30 AT 50

BEST REFERENCE—PUBLIC PREFERENCE

ECONOMIZE WITH THIS SIZE

A BETTER BUY—WHY NOT TRY

RIGHT ABOUT FACE

1940

SAID JULIET
TO ROMEO
IF YOU
WON'T SHAVE
GO HOMEO
BURMA-SHAVE

SUBSTITUTES AND
IMITATIONS
SEND 'EM TO
YOUR WIFE'S
RELATIONS
BURMA-SHAVE

WHEN YOU DRIVE
IF CAUTION CEASES
YOU ARE APT
TO REST
IN PIECES
BURMA-SHAVE

HE MARRIED GRACE
WITH SCRATCHY FACE
HE ONLY
GOT ONE DAY
OF GRACE!
BURMA-SHAVE

ALL LITTLE RHYMING
JOKES ASIDE
DON'T BE CONTENT
UNTIL YOU'VE
TRIED
BURMA-SHAVE

COLLEGE CUTIE
PIGSKIN HERO
BRISTLY KISS
HERO
ZERO
BURMA-SHAVE

YOU CAN'T REACH 80
HALE AND HEARTY
BY DRIVING 80
HOME FROM
THE PARTY
BURMA-SHAVE

BUY A JAR
TAKE IT FROM ME
THERE'S SO
MUCH IN IT
THE LAST HALF'S FREE
BURMA-SHAVE

HE'S THE BOY
THE GALS FORGOT
HIS LINE
WAS SMOOTH
HIS CHIN WAS NOT
BURMA-SHAVE

PUT YOUR BRUSH
BACK ON THE SHELF
THE DARN THING
NEEDS A
SHAVE ITSELF
BURMA-SHAVE

IT'S BEST FOR
ONE WHO HITS
THE BOTTLE
TO LET ANOTHER
USE THE THROTTLE
BURMA-SHAVE

DON'T PASS CARS
ON CURVE OR HILL
IF THE COPS
DON'T GET YOU
MORTICIANS WILL
BURMA-SHAVE

WITH GLAMOUR GIRLS
YOU'LL NEVER CLICK
BEWHISKERED
LIKE A
BOLSHEVIK
BURMA-SHAVE

A SCRATCHY CHIN
LIKE BRIGHT
PINK SOCKS
PUTS ANY ROMANCE
ON THE ROCKS
BURMA-SHAVE

ALWAYS REMEMBER
ON ANY TRIP
KEEP TWO THINGS
WITHIN YOUR GRIP
YOUR STEERING WHEEL
    AND
BURMA-SHAVE

GIVE HAND SIGNALS
TO THOSE BEHIND
THEY DON'T KNOW
WHAT'S IN
YOUR MIND
BURMA-SHAVE

THE BEARDED DEVIL
IS FORCED
TO DWELL
IN THE ONLY PLACE
WHERE THEY DON'T SELL
BURMA-SHAVE

SUBSTITUTES
WOULD IRK A SAINT
YOU HOPE THEY ARE
WHAT YOU KNOW
THEY AIN'T
BURMA-SHAVE

PRICKLY PEARS
ARE PICKED
FOR PICKLES
NO PEACH PICKS
A FACE THAT PRICKLES
BURMA-SHAVE

GUYS WHOSE EYES
ARE IN
THEIR BACKS
GET HALOS CROSSING
RAILROAD TRACKS
BURMA-SHAVE

A CHRISTMAS HUG
A BIRTHDAY KISS
AWAITS
THE WOMAN
WHO GIVES THIS
BURMA-SHAVE

JUST SPREAD
THEN PAT
NOW SHAVE
THAT'S
THAT
BURMA-SHAVE

1941

HERE'S
A GOOD DEED
FOR A SCOUT
TELL YOUR DAD
ALL ABOUT
BURMA-SHAVE

DON'T STICK
YOUR ELBOW
OUT SO FAR
IT MIGHT GO HOME
IN ANOTHER CAR
BURMA-SHAVE

THEY MISSED
THE TURN
CAR WAS WHIZZ'N
FAULT WAS HER'N
FUNERAL HIS'N
BURMA-SHAVE

SOLDIER
SAILOR
AND MARINE
NOW GET A SHAVE
THAT'S QUICK AND CLEAN
BURMA-SHAVE

TELL
THE DEAR
WHO SHOPS AROUND
THAT HALF A BUCK
BUYS HALF A POUND
BURMA-SHAVE

REMEMBER THIS
IF YOU'D
BE SPARED
TRAINS DON'T WHISTLE
BECAUSE THEY'RE
    SCARED
BURMA-SHAVE

SHE KISSED
THE HAIRBRUSH
BY MISTAKE
SHE THOUGHT IT WAS
HER HUSBAND JAKE
BURMA-SHAVE

WHEN BETTER
SHAVING BRUSHES
ARE MADE
WE'LL STILL SHAVE
WITHOUT THEIR AID
BURMA-SHAVE

HE USED
UMBRELLA
FOR PARACHUTE
NOW REJECTS
EVERY SUBSTITUTE
BURMA-SHAVE

WHEN JUNIOR TAKES
YOUR TIES
AND CAR
IT'S TIME TO BUY
AN EXTRA JAR
BURMA-SHAVE

GETS EACH
WHISKER
AT THE BASE
NO INGROWN HAIR
ON NECK OR FACE
BURMA-SHAVE

THE ANSWER TO
A MAIDEN'S PRAYER
IS A MAN
MOST ANYWHERE
USING
BURMA-SHAVE

IF MAN BITES DOGGIE
THAT IS NEWS
IF FACE
SCARES DOGGIE
BETTER USE
BURMA-SHAVE

RHYME AND REASON
EVERY SEASON
YOU'VE READ
THE RHYME
NOW TRY THE REASON
BURMA-SHAVE

AT INTERSECTIONS
LOOK EACH WAY
A HARP SOUNDS NICE
BUT IT'S
HARD TO PLAY
BURMA-SHAVE

WILD
DASHES
FROM BY-WAYS
CAUSE CRASHES
ON HIGHWAYS
BURMA-SHAVE

LIFE IS SWEET
BUT OH HOW BITTER!
TO LOVE A GAL
AND THEN
NOT GIT 'ER
BURMA-SHAVE

SUBSTITUTES
RESEMBLE
TAIL-CHASING PUP
FOLLOW AND FOLLOW
BUT NEVER CATCH UP
BURMA-SHAVE

TRAINS DON'T WANDER
ALL OVER THE MAP
FOR NO ONE
SITS ON
THE ENGINEER'S LAP
BURMA-SHAVE

FROM
BAR
TO CAR
TO
GATES AJAR
BURMA-SHAVE

WHEN PETER PIPER
PICKLE PICKER
KISSED HIS GAL
HIS BEARD
WOULD PRICK 'ER
BURMA-SHAVE

IF EVERY SIP
FILLS YOU
WITH ZIP
THEN YOUR SIPPER
NEEDS A ZIPPER
BURMA-SHAVE

BROKEN ROMANCE
STATED FULLY
SHE WENT WILD
WHEN HE
WENT WOOLY
BURMA-SHAVE

1942

PA LIKES THE CREAM
MA LIKES THE JAR
BOTH LIKE
THE PRICE
SO THERE YOU ARE
BURMA-SHAVE

STORES ARE FULL
OF SHAVING AIDS
BUT ALL YOU NEED
IS THIS
AND BLADES
BURMA-SHAVE

BROTHER SPEEDERS
LET'S
REHEARSE
ALL TOGETHER
"GOOD MORNING, NURSE!"
BURMA-SHAVE

PA ACTED
SO TICKLED
MA THOT
HE WAS PICKLED
HE'D JUST TRIED
BURMA-SHAVE

'MID RISING
TAXES
SOARING RENTS
STILL HALF A POUND
FOR FIFTY CENTS
BURMA-SHAVE

ICEMAN'S GRANDSON
NOW FULL GROWN
HAS COOLING SYSTEM
ALL HIS OWN
HE USES
BURMA-SHAVE

APPROACHED
A CROSSING
WITHOUT LOOKING
WHO WILL EAT
HIS WIDOW'S COOKING?
BURMA-SHAVE

IF YOU
DON'T KNOW
WHOSE SIGNS
THESE ARE
YOU CAN'T HAVE
DRIVEN VERY FAR

DROVE TOO LONG
DRIVER SNOOZING
WHAT HAPPENED NEXT
IS NOT
AMUSING
BURMA-SHAVE

LET'S MAKE HITLER
AND HIROHITO
LOOK AS SICK AS
OLD BENITO
BUY DEFENSE BONDS
BURMA-SHAVE

CAN'T SHAVE DAILY?
TENDER HIDE?
NOW BE HONEST
HAVE YOU
TRIED
BURMA-SHAVE

THERE'S NO WHISKER
IT WON'T SOFTEN
SHAVE 'EM CLOSE
AND NOT
SO OFTEN
BURMA-SHAVE

IF HUGGING
ON HIGHWAYS
IS YOUR SPORT
TRADE IN YOUR CAR
FOR A DAVENPORT
BURMA-SHAVE

SHAVING BRUSH
IN ARMY PACK
WAS STRAW THAT BROKE
THE ROOKIE'S BACK
USE BRUSHLESS
BURMA-SHAVE

A GIRL
SHOULD HOLD ON
TO HER YOUTH
BUT NOT
WHEN HE'S DRIVING
BURMA-SHAVE

MAYBE YOU CAN'T
SHOULDER A GUN
BUT YOU CAN SHOULDER
THE COST OF ONE
BUY DEFENSE BONDS
BURMA-SHAVE

OF ALL
THE DRUNKS
WHO DRIVE ON SUNDAY
SOME ARE STILL
ALIVE ON MONDAY
BURMA-SHAVE

"AT EASE," SHE SAID
"MANEUVERS BEGIN
WHEN YOU GET
THOSE WHISKERS
OFF YOUR CHIN"
BURMA-SHAVE

SUBSTITUTES
LIKE UNSEEN BARTER
OFTEN MAKE ONE
SAD
BUT SMARTER
BURMA-SHAVE

TRAVELING MEN
KNOW EASE
AND SPEED
THEIR SHAVING KITS
HOLD WHAT THEY NEED
BURMA-SHAVE

WHAT YOU SHOUTED
MAY BE TRUE,
BUT
DID YOU HEAR
WHAT HE CALLED YOU?
BURMA-SHAVE

BUYING DEFENSE BONDS
MEANS MONEY LENT
SO THEY
DON'T COST YOU
ONE RED CENT
BURMA-SHAVE

TO MOST BRUSH SHAVERS
IT'S QUITE CLEAR
THE YANKS AREN'T
        COMING
THE YANKS ARE HERE
USE BRUSHLESS
BURMA-SHAVE

1943

EVERY SHAVER
NOW CAN SNORE
SIX MORE MINUTES
THAN BEFORE
BY USING
BURMA-SHAVE

ONE POUND JAR   85¢
HALF POUND JAR   50¢
BIG TUBE   35¢
DON'T PUT IT OFF
PUT IN ON
BURMA-SHAVE

HALF A POUND
FOR
HALF A DOLLAR
SPREAD ON THIN
ABOVE THE COLLAR
BURMA-SHAVE

SHAVING BRUSHES
YOU'LL SOON SEE 'EM
ON THE SHELF
IN SOME
MUSEUM
BURMA-SHAVE

DOES YOUR HUSBAND
MISBEHAVE
GRUNT AND GRUMBLE
RANT AND RAVE
SHOOT THE BRUTE SOME
BURMA-SHAVE

IT'S A GOOD
OLD SPANISH CUSTOM
TAKE YOUR MUG
AND BRUSH
AND BUST 'EM
BURMA-SHAVE

EARLY TO BED
EARLY TO RISE
WAS MEANT FOR THOSE
OLD FASHIONED GUYS
WHO DON'T USE
BURMA-SHAVE

WITHIN THIS VALE
OF TOIL
AND SIN
YOUR HEAD GROWS BALD
BUT NOT YOUR CHIN—USE
BURMA-SHAVE

SLAP
THE JAP
WITH
IRON
SCRAP
BURMA-SHAVE

THE CANNONEERS
WITH HAIRY EARS
ON WIRY WHISKERS
USED TIN SHEARS
UNTIL THEY FOUND
BURMA-SHAVE

FILM PROTECTS
YOUR NECK
AND CHIN
SO YOUR RAZOR
WON'T DIG IN
BURMA-SHAVE

THO TOUGH
AND ROUGH
FROM WIND AND WAVE
YOUR CHEEK GROWS
    SLEEK
WITH
BURMA-SHAVE

1945

MANY A WOLF
IS NEVER LET IN
BECAUSE OF THE HAIR
ON HIS
CHINNY-CHIN-CHIN
BURMA-SHAVE

SHE RAISED CAIN
WHEN HE RAISED
    STUBBLE
GUESS WHAT
SMOOTHED AWAY
THEIR TROUBLE?
BURMA-SHAVE

BIG MISTAKE
MANY MAKE
RELY ON HORN
INSTEAD OF
BRAKE
BURMA-SHAVE

FROM STATISTICS
THAT WE GATHER
THE SWING IS TO
NO BRUSH
NO LATHER
BURMA-SHAVE

NO MAN CAN REALLY
DO HIS STUFF
WITH A FACE THAT'S
    SORE
OR A CHIN
THAT'S ROUGH
BURMA-SHAVE

FIRST MEN BUY IT
THEN APPLY IT
THEN ADVISE
THEIR FRIENDS
TO TRY IT
BURMA-SHAVE

IF THESE
SIGNS BLUR
AND BOUNCE AROUND
YOU'D BETTER PARK
AND WALK TO TOWN
BURMA-SHAVE

THIS IS NOT
A CLEVER VERSE
I TRIED
AND TRIED
BUT JUST
GOT WORSE

YOU CAN BEAT
A MILE A MINUTE
BUT THERE AIN'T
NO FUTURE
IN IT
BURMA-SHAVE

SLEEP IN A CHAIR
NOTHING TO LOSE
BUT A NAP
AT THE WHEEL
IS A PERMANENT SNOOZE
BURMA-SHAVE

99

LIFE WITH FATHER
IS MORE PLEASANT
SINCE
HE GOT THIS
BIRTHDAY PRESENT
BURMA-SHAVE

TO A SUBSTITUTE
HE GAVE A TRIAL
IT TOOK OFF
NOTHING
BUT HIS SMILE
BURMA-SHAVE

IT SPREADS SO SMOOTH
IT SHAVES SO SLICK
IT FEELS
LIKE VELVET
AND IT'S QUICK
BURMA-SHAVE

'TWOULD BE
MORE FUN
TO GO BY AIR
IF WE COULD PUT
THESE SIGNS UP THERE
BURMA-SHAVE

HIS LINE WAS SMOOTH
BUT NOT HIS CHIN
HE TOOK HER OUT
SHE TOOK HIM IN
TO BUY SOME
BURMA-SHAVE

DRINKING DRIVERS
ENHANCE THEIR
CHANCE
TO HIGHBALL HOME
IN AN AMBULANCE
BURMA-SHAVE

WHY DOES A CHICKEN
CROSS THE STREET?
SHE SEES A GUY
SHE'D LIKE TO MEET
HE USES
BURMA-SHAVE

THE CHICK
HE WED
LET OUT A WHOOP
FELT HIS CHIN AND
FLEW THE COOP
BURMA-SHAVE

TESTED
IN PEACE
PROVEN IN WAR
BETTER NOW
THAN EVER BEFORE
BURMA-SHAVE

BOTH HANDS
ON WHEEL
EYES ON ROAD
THAT'S THE SKILLFUL
DRIVER'S CODE
BURMA-SHAVE

1947

YOU'VE USED
OUR CREAM
NOW TRY OUR BLADES
PAIR UP THE BEST
IN SHAVING AIDS
BURMA-SHAVE

DON'T LOSE
YOUR HEAD
TO GAIN A MINUTE
YOU NEED YOUR HEAD
YOUR BRAINS ARE IN IT
BURMA-SHAVE

THAT SHE
COULD COOK
HE HAD HIS DOUBTS
UNTIL SHE CREAMED
HIS BRISTLE SPROUTS
    WITH
BURMA-SHAVE

THE WOLF
WHO LONGS
TO ROAM AND PROWL
SHOULD SHAVE BEFORE
HE STARTS TO HOWL
BURMA-SHAVE

AS YOU DRIVE
PLAY THIS GAME
CONSTRUCT
A JINGLE
WITH THIS NAME
BURMA-SHAVE

IF A GIFT
YOU MUST CHOOSE
GIVE HIM
ONE THAT
HE CAN USE
BURMA-SHAVE

WHEN THE STORK
DELIVERS A BOY
OUR WHOLE
DARN FACTORY
JUMPS FOR JOY
BURMA-SHAVE

JOIN
OUR HAPPY
BRUSHLESS THRONG
SIX MILLION USERS
CAN'T BE WRONG
BURMA-SHAVE

FAMOUS LAST WORDS
"IF HE WON'T
DIM HIS
I WON'T
DIM MINE"
BURMA-SHAVE

CAR IN DITCH
DRIVER IN TREE
MOON WAS FULL
AND SO
WAS HE
BURMA-SHAVE

SUBSTITUTES
THAT PROMISE
    PERFECTION
ARE LIKE
SOME CANDIDATES
AFTER ELECTION
BURMA-SHAVE

SANTA'S
WHISKERS
NEED NO TRIMMIN'
HE KISSES KIDS
NOT THE WIMMIN
BURMA-SHAVE

ALTHO
WE'VE SOLD
SIX MILLION OTHERS
WE STILL CAN'T SELL
THOSE COUGHDROP
    BROTHERS
BURMA-SHAVE

WE KNOW
HOW MUCH
YOU LOVE THAT GAL
BUT USE BOTH HANDS
FOR DRIVING, PAL
BURMA-SHAVE

IN CUPID'S LITTLE
BAG OF TRIX
HERE'S THE ONE
THAT CLIX
WITH CHIX
BURMA-SHAVE

THRIFTY JARS FOR
STAY AT HOMES
HANDY TUBES
FOR HIM
WHO ROAMS
BURMA-SHAVE

I USE IT TOO
THE BALD MAN SAID
IT KEEPS MY FACE
JUST LIKE
MY HEAD
BURMA-SHAVE

GRANDPA'S
OUT WITH
JUNIOR'S DATE
OLD TECHNIQUE
WITH BRAND NEW BAIT
BURMA-SHAVE

NO SOGGY BRUSHES
IN YOUR GRIP
YOU'VE ALWAYS
GOT A
FINGER TIP
BURMA-SHAVE

IF YOU WANT
A HEARTY SQUEEZE
GET OUR
FEMALE
ANTI-FREEZE
BURMA-SHAVE

SUBSTITUTES WOULD
HAVE THEIR PLACE
IF YOU COULD
SUBSTITUTE
YOUR FACE
BURMA-SHAVE

MAN PASSES
DOG HOUSE
DOG SEES CHIN
DOG GETS OUT
MAN GETS IN
BURMA-SHAVE

A GUY
WHO WANTS
TO MIDDLE-AISLE IT
MUST NEVER SCRATCH
HIS LITTLE VIOLET
BURMA-SHAVE

PRICES RISING
O'ER THE NATION
HERE IS ONE
THAT MISSED
INFLATION
BURMA-SHAVE

(Burma-Vita Tooth Powder Jingles)

THE FIRST
IMPROVEMENT
IN MANY A YEAR
FOR CLEANING TEETH
IS FINALLY HERE
BURMA-VITA TOOTH
    POWDER

SPEAKING OF
GREAT EVENTS
BURMA-SHAVE
PROUDLY PRESENTS
ANOTHER FINE PRODUCT
BURMA-VITA TOOTH
    POWDER

102

JUST MOISTEN
YOUR TOOTH BRUSH
DIP IN JAR
AND YOU'LL ENJOY
CLEANER TEETH BY FAR
BURMA-VITA TOOTH
    POWDER

DON'T WASTE POWDER
DOWN THE DRAIN
BY MISSING BRUSH
WITH FAULTY AIM
A DIP DOES IT
BURMA-VITA TOOTH
    POWDER

BETTER TOOTH CLEANSER
LOW EXPENSE
YOUR DRUGGIST
SELLS IT
40 CENTS
BURMA-VITA TOOTH
    POWDER

TOBACCO STAINS
AND STALE BREATH TOO
ARE TWO
OF THE THINGS
IT TAKES FROM YOU
BURMA-VITA TOOTH
    POWDER

1948

ROAD
WAS SLIPPERY
CURVE WAS SHARP
WHITE ROBE, HALO
WINGS AND HARP
BURMA-SHAVE

SPEED
WAS HIGH
WEATHER WAS NOT
TIRES WERE THIN
X MARKS THE SPOT
BURMA-SHAVE

HAT AND TIE
SMART AND CLEAN
SPACE BETWEEN
SPOILED THE SCENE
HE SHOULD USE
BURMA-SHAVE

WHY WORK UP
A DAILY LATHER
ONCE YOU'VE TRIED
WE'RE SURE
YOU'D RATHER
BURMA-SHAVE

THE BOY WHO GETS
HIS GIRL'S APPLAUSE
MUST ACT
NOT LOOK
LIKE SANTA CLAUS
BURMA-SHAVE

IF YOU THINK
SHE LIKES
YOUR BRISTLES
WALK BARE-FOOTED
THROUGH SOME THISTLES
BURMA-SHAVE

WITHIN THIS VALE
OF TOIL
AND SIN
YOUR HEAD GROWS BALD
BUT NOT YOUR CHIN—USE
BURMA-SHAVE

THE MORE
YOU SHAVE
THE BRUSHLESS WAY
THE MORE YOU'LL BE
INCLINED TO SAY—
BURMA-SHAVE

SUBSTITUTES AND
IMITATIONS
SEND 'EM TO
YOUR WIFE'S
RELATIONS
BURMA-SHAVE

IT'S NOT
HOW FAST OR SLOW
YOU DRIVE
THE QUESTION IS
HOW YOU ARRIVE
BURMA-SHAVE

HIGHWAYS ARE
NO PLACE
TO SLEEP
STOP YOUR CAR
TO COUNT YOUR SHEEP
BURMA-SHAVE

A MAN WHO PASSES
ON HILLS AND CURVES
IS NOT A MAN
OF IRON NERVES—
HE'S CRAZY!
BURMA-SHAVE

THE MINUTES
SOME FOLKS
SAVE THROUGH SPEED
THEY NEVER EVEN
LIVE TO NEED
BURMA-SHAVE

I'VE READ
THESE SIGNS
SINCE JUST A KID
NOW THAT I SHAVE
I'M GLAD I DID
BURMA-SHAVE

AT SCHOOL ZONES
HEED INSTRUCTIONS!
PROTECT
OUR LITTLE
TAX DEDUCTIONS
BURMA-SHAVE

WE DON'T
KNOW HOW
TO SPLIT AN ATOM
BUT AS TO WHISKERS
LET US AT 'EM
BURMA-SHAVE

REGARDLESS OF
POLITICAL VIEWS
ALL GOOD PARTIES
ALWAYS
CHOOSE
BURMA-SHAVE

PAPER HANGERS
WITH THE HIVES
NOW CAN
SHAVE WITH
CARVING KNIVES
BURMA-SHAVE

THE MIDNIGHT RIDE
OF PAUL
FOR BEER
LED TO A
WARMER HEMISPHERE
BURMA-SHAVE

WILD MEN PULLED
THEIR WHISKERS OUT
THAT'S WHAT MADE
THEM WILD
NO DOUBT—
BURMA-SHAVE

LOOK
DON'T LISTEN
POP IS TRYING
A SUBSTITUTE
INSTEAD OF BUYING
BURMA-SHAVE

A MAN
A MISS
A CAR—A CURVE
HE KISSED THE MISS
AND MISSED THE CURVE
BURMA-SHAVE

LITTLE BO-PEEP
HAS LOST HER JEEP
IT STRUCK
A TRUCK
WHEN SHE WENT TO
    SLEEP
BURMA-SHAVE

WHISKERS
EASY COME,
YOU KNOW
WHY NOT MAKE THEM
EASY GO?
BURMA-SHAVE

(Special Anti-inflation Signs, 1948)

BARGAIN HUNTERS
GATHER 'ROUND
FOR FIFTY CENTS
STILL
HALF A POUND
BURMA-SHAVE
NO PRICE INCREASE

FROM NEW YORK TOWN
TO PUMPKIN HOLLER
STILL
HALF A POUND
FOR HALF A DOLLAR
BURMA-SHAVE
NO PRICE INCREASE

OTHER THINGS HAVE
GONE SKY HIGH
HALF A DOLLAR
STILL WILL BUY
HALF POUND JAR
BURMA-SHAVE
NO PRICE INCREASE

A BIG
IMPROVEMENT
SINCE THE WAR
IS NOW ON SALE
IN YOUR DRUG STORE
BURMA-SHAVE
NO PRICE INCREASE

TUBE IMMENSE
STILL
35 CENTS
EASY SHAVING
LOW EXPENSE
BURMA-SHAVE
NO PRICE INCREASE

LEAP YEAR'S OVER
YOU'RE SAFE, MEN
ALL YOU COWARDS
CAN SHAVE AGAIN
WITH BRUSHLESS
BURMA-SHAVE

JUST THIS ONCE
AND JUST FOR FUN
WE'LL LET YOU
FINISH
WHAT WE'VE BEGUN
? ? ?

HE SAW
THE TRAIN
AND TRIED TO DUCK IT
KICKED FIRST THE GAS
AND THEN THE BUCKET
BURMA-SHAVE

WITH TELEVISION
ON THE SET
STARS ARE
RUNNING OUT
TO GET
BURMA-SHAVE

HEADLINE NEWS
FOR FACE
AND CHIN
NOW IMPROVED
WITH LANOLIN
BURMA-SHAVE

WITH
A SLEEK CHEEK
PRESSED TO HERS
JEEPERS! CREEPERS!
HOW SHE PURRS
BURMA-SHAVE

HIS FACE
WAS LOVED
BY JUST HIS MOTHER
HE BURMA-SHAVED
AND NOW—
OH, BROTHER

MEN
WHO HAVE TO
TRAVEL LIGHT
FIND THE HANDY TUBE
JUST RIGHT
BURMA-SHAVE

WHEN FRISKY
WITH WHISKEY
DON'T DRIVE
'CAUSE IT'S
RISKY
BURMA-SHAVE

SINCE HUBBY
TRIED
THAT SUBSTITUTE
HE'S 1/3 MAN
AND 2/3 BRUTE
BURMA-SHAVE

HIS BEARD
WAS LONG
AND STRONG AND TOUGH
HE LOST HIS
CHICKEN IN THE ROUGH
BURMA-SHAVE

HE ALWAYS USED
A STEAMING TOWEL
AND MUG AND BRUSH
AND LANGUAGE FOUL
'TIL HE TRIED
BURMA-SHAVE

IF YOU
MUST SAMPLE
HER "PUCKER PAINT"
BETTER DRIVE
WHERE TRAFFIC AIN'T
BURMA-SHAVE

IT GAVE
SWELL SHAVES BEFORE
NOW YOU'LL LIKE IT
EVEN MORE
THE NEW—IMPROVED
BURMA-SHAVE

PULL OFF
THE ROAD
TO CHANGE A FLAT
PROTECT YOUR LIFE—
NO SPARE FOR THAT!
BURMA-SHAVE

THO TOUGH
AND ROUGH
FROM WIND AND WAVE
YOUR CHEEK
GROWS SLEEK WITH
BURMA-SHAVE

IN SEVENTY YEARS
OF BRUSHIN' SOAP ON
GRAMPS COULDA
    PAINTED
THE PENTAGON
USE BRUSHLESS
BURMA-SHAVE

THESE THREE
PREVENT MOST
    ACCIDENTS
COURTESY
CAUTION
COMMON SENSE
BURMA-SHAVE

SAID ONE WHISKER
TO ANOTHER
CAN'T GET TOUGH
WITH THIS STUFF
BROTHER
BURMA-SHAVE

OLD DOBBIN
READS THESE SIGNS
EACH DAY
YOU SEE, HE GETS
HIS CORN THAT WAY
BURMA-SHAVE

TO SOOTHE
AND SMOOTH
YOUR TENDER SKIN
IT'S NOW IMPROVED
WITH LANOLIN
BURMA-SHAVE

ONE BURMA-SHAVE
THE SCHOOL BOY CRIED
AT LEAST
I'LL SMELL
AS IF I TRIED
BURMA-SHAVE

(Minnesota and
Wisconsin, 1949)

ASHES TO ASHES
FORESTS TO DUST
KEEP MINNESOTA
    GREEN
OR WE'LL
ALL GO BUST
BURMA-SHAVE

ASHES TO ASHES
FORESTS TO DUST
KEEP WISCONSIN GREEN
OR WE'LL
ALL GO BUST
BURMA-SHAVE

HIS CHEEK
WAS ROUGH
HIS CHICK VAMOOSED
AND NOW SHE WON'T
COME HOME TO ROOST
BURMA-SHAVE

TWINKLE, TWINKLE
ONE-EYED CAR
WE ALL WONDER
WHERE
YOU ARE
BURMA-SHAVE

ON CURVES AHEAD
REMEMBER, SONNY
THAT RABBIT'S FOOT
DIDN'T SAVE
THE BUNNY
BURMA-SHAVE

WHEN
SUPER-SHAVED
REMEMBER, PARD
YOU'LL STILL GET
    SLAPPED
BUT NOT SO HARD
BURMA-SHAVE

HIS BRUSH IS GONE
SO WHAT'LL WE DO
SAID
MIKE ROBE I
TO MIKE ROBE II
BURMA-SHAVE

THE PLACE TO PASS
ON CURVES
YOU KNOW
IS ONLY AT
A BEAUTY SHOW
BURMA-SHAVE

A WHISKERY KISS
FOR THE ONE
YOU ADORE
MAY NOT MAKE HER MAD
BUT HER FACE WILL BE
    SORE
BURMA-SHAVE

BURMA-SHAVE
WAS SUCH A BOOM
THEY PASSED
THE BRIDE
AND KISSED
THE GROOM

THESE SIGNS
WE GLADLY
DEDICATE
TO MEN WHO'VE HAD
NO DATE OF LATE
BURMA-SHAVE

IF YOUR PEACH
KEEPS OUT
OF REACH
BETTER PRACTICE
WHAT WE PREACH
BURMA-SHAVE

A GUY
WHO DRIVES
A CAR WIDE OPEN
IS NOT THINKIN'
HE'S JUST HOPIN'
BURMA-SHAVE

TO KISS
A MUG
THAT'S LIKE A CACTUS
TAKES MORE NERVE
THAN IT DOES PRACTICE
BURMA-SHAVE

THE WHALE
PUT JONAH
DOWN THE HATCH
BUT COUGHED HIM UP
BECAUSE HE SCRATCHED
BURMA-SHAVE

DOESN'T
KISS YOU
LIKE SHE USETER?
PERHAPS SHE'S SEEN
A SMOOTHER ROOSTER! !
BURMA-SHAVE

VIOLETS ARE BLUE
ROSES ARE PINK
ON GRAVES
OF THOSE
WHO DRIVE AND DRINK
BURMA-SHAVE

NO USE
KNOWING
HOW TO PICK 'EM
IF YOUR HALF-SHAVED
WHISKERS STICK 'EM
BURMA-SHAVE

CANDIDATE SAYS
CAMPAIGN
CONFUSING
BABIES KISS ME
SINCE I'VE BEEN USING
BURMA-SHAVE

HE TRIED
TO CROSS
AS FAST TRAIN NEARED
DEATH DIDN'T DRAFT
HIM
HE VOLUNTEERED
BURMA-SHAVE

MY JOB IS
KEEPING FACES CLEAN
AND NOBODY KNOWS
DE STUBBLE
I'VE SEEN
BURMA-SHAVE

HER CHARIOT
RACED 80 PER
THEY HAULED AWAY
WHAT HAD
BEN HUR
BURMA-SHAVE

(Burma-Shave Lotion Jingles, 1950)

SHE WILL
FLOOD YOUR FACE
WITH KISSES
'CAUSE YOU SMELL
SO DARN DELICIOUS
BURMA-SHAVE LOTION

IT HAS A TINGLE
AND A TANG
THAT STARTS
THE DAY OFF
WITH A BANG
BURMA-SHAVE LOTION

USE BURMA-SHAVE
IN TUBE
OR JAR
THEN FOLLOW UP
WITH OUR NEW STAR
BURMA-SHAVE LOTION

BRACING AS
AN OCEAN BREEZE
FOR AFTER SHAVING
IT'S SURE
TO PLEASE
BURMA-SHAVE LOTION

FOR EARLY
MORNING
PEP AND BOUNCE
A BRAND NEW PRODUCT
WE ANNOUNCE
BURMA-SHAVE LOTION

THE LADIES
TAKE ONE WHIFF
AND PURR—
IT'S NO WONDER
MEN PREFER
BURMA-SHAVE LOTION

HIS FACE
WAS SMOOTH
AND COOL AS ICE
AND OH! LOUISE!
HE SMELLED SO NICE
BURMA-SHAVE LOTION

1951

(Middle West and East)

I'D HEARD
IT PRAISED
BY DRUG STORE CLERKS
I TRIED THE STUFF
HOT DOG! IT WORKS
BURMA-SHAVE

SOAP
MAY DO
FOR LADS WITH FUZZ
BUT SIR, YOU AIN'T
THE KID YOU WUZ
BURMA-SHAVE

TRAIN WRECKS FEW
REASON CLEAR
FIREMAN
NEVER HUGS
ENGINEER
BURMA-SHAVE

SHE EYED
HIS BEARD
AND SAID NO DICE
THE WEDDING'S OFF—
I'LL *COOK* THE RICE
BURMA-SHAVE

ALTHO INSURED
REMEMBER, KIDDO
THEY DON'T PAY YOU
THEY PAY
YOUR WIDOW
BURMA-SHAVE

TRAIN APPROACHING
WHISTLE SQUEALING
PAUSE!
AVOID THAT
RUNDOWN FEELING!
BURMA-SHAVE

MY CHEEK
SAYS SHE
FEELS SMOOTH AS SATIN
HA! HA! SAYS HE
THAT'S MINE YOU'RE
    PATTIN'
BURMA-SHAVE

UNLESS
YOUR FACE
IS STINGER FREE
YOU'D BETTER LET
YOUR HONEY BE
BURMA-SHAVE

110

ANOTHER
RED SKIN
BIT THE DUST
WHEN PA TRIED
WHAT THESE SIGNS
    DISCUSSED
BURMA-SHAVE

THE BAND
FOR WHICH
THE GRAND STAND
    ROOTS
IS NOT MADE UP
SUBSTI-TOOTS!
BURMA-SHAVE

CAUTIOUS RIDER
TO HER
RECKLESS DEAR
LET'S HAVE LESS BULL
AND LOTS MORE STEER
BURMA-SHAVE

SPRING
HAS SPRUNG
THE GRASS HAS RIZ
WHERE LAST YEAR'S
CARELESS DRIVERS IS
BURMA-SHAVE

BIG BLUE TUBE
IT'S A HONEY
BEST SQUEEZE PLAY
FOR LOVE
OR MONEY
BURMA-SHAVE

PROPER
DISTANCE
TO HIM WAS BUNK
THEY PULLED HIM OUT
OF SOME GUY'S TRUNK
BURMA-SHAVE

SUBSTITUTES
CAN DO
MORE HARM
THAN CITY FELLERS
ON A FARM
BURMA-SHAVE

PAT'S BRISTLES
SCRATCHED
BRIDGET'S NOSE
THAT'S WHEN
HER WILD IRISH ROSE
BURMA-SHAVE

THE HOBO
LETS HIS
WHISKERS SPROUT
IT'S TRAINS—NOT GIRLS
THAT HE TAKES OUT
BURMA-SHAVE

A BEARD
THAT'S ROUGH
AND OVERGROWN
IS BETTER THAN
A CHAPERONE
BURMA-SHAVE

DRINKING DRIVERS
DON'T YOU KNOW
GREAT BANGS
FROM LITTLE
BINGES GROW?
BURMA-SHAVE

I KNOW
HE'S A WOLF
SAID RIDING HOOD
BUT GRANDMA DEAR,
HE SMELLS SO GOOD
BURMA-SHAVE

(West Coast and South)

THE WIFE
WHO KEEPS ON
BEING KISSED
ALWAYS HEADS
HER SHOPPING LIST
BURMA-SHAVE

LEAVES
FACE SOFT
AS WOMAN'S TOUCH
YET DOESN'T COST YOU
NEAR AS MUCH
BURMA-SHAVE

IS HE
LONESOME
OR JUST BLIND—
THIS GUY WHO DRIVES
SO CLOSE BEHIND?
BURMA-SHAVE

WE CAN'T
PROVIDE YOU
WITH A DATE
BUT WE DO SUPPLY
THE BEST DARN BAIT
BURMA-SHAVE

PEDRO
WALKED
BACK HOME BY GOLLY
HIS BRISTLY CHIN
WAS HOT-TO-MOLLY
BURMA-SHAVE

THE WOLF
IS SHAVED
SO NEAT AND TRIM
RED RIDING HOOD
IS CHASING HIM
BURMA-SHAVE

MISSIN'
KISSIN'?
PERHAPS YOUR THRUSH
CAN'T GET THRU
THE UNDERBRUSH—TRY
BURMA-SHAVE

RELIEF
FOR FACES
CHAPPED AND SORE
KEEPS 'EM COMIN'
BACK FOR MORE
BURMA-SHAVE

CLANCY'S
WHISKERS
TICKLE NANCY
NANCY LOWERED THE
    BOOM
ON CLANCY!
BURMA-SHAVE

HIS
TOMATO
WAS THE MUSHY TYPE
UNTIL HIS BEARD
GREW OVER-RIPE
BURMA-SHAVE

A CHIN
WHERE BARBED WIRE
BRISTLES STAND
IS BOUND TO BE
A NO MA'AMS LAND
BURMA-SHAVE

HEAVEN'S
LATEST
NEOPHYTE
SIGNALLED LEFT
THEN TURNED RIGHT
BURMA-SHAVE

BETTER TRY
LESS SPEED PER MILE
THAT CAR
MAY HAVE TO
LAST A WHILE
BURMA-SHAVE

TO STEAL
A KISS
HE HAD THE KNACK
BUT LACKED THE CHEEK
TO GET ONE BACK
BURMA-SHAVE

WE'VE MADE
GRANDPA
LOOK SO TRIM
THE LOCAL
DRAFT BOARD'S AFTER
    HIM
BURMA-SHAVE

"NO, NO,"
SHE SAID
TO HER BRISTLY BEAU
"I'D RATHER
EAT THE MISTLETOE"
BURMA-SHAVE

HIS ROSE
IS WED
HIS VIOLET BLEW
BUT HIS SUGAR IS SWEET
SINCE HE TOOK THIS CUE
BURMA-SHAVE

WHY IS IT
WHEN YOU
TRY TO PASS
THE GUY IN FRONT
GOES TWICE AS FAST?
BURMA-SHAVE

SHE PUT
A BULLET
THRU HIS HAT
BUT HE'S HAD
CLOSER SHAVES THAN
    THAT
BURMA-SHAVE

5-STAR
GENERALS
PRIVATES 1ST CLASS
SHOW EQUAL RANK
IN THE LOOKING-GLASS
BURMA-SHAVE

1953

(Middle West and East)

WHEN YOU LAY
THOSE FEW CENTS DOWN
YOU'VE BOUGHT
THE SMOOTHEST
SHAVE IN TOWN
BURMA-SHAVE

SUBSTITUTES
ARE LIKE A GIRDLE
THEY FIND SOME JOBS
THEY JUST
CAN'T HURDLE
BURMA-SHAVE

GUT RASIERT? ("IF YOU
    WANT A GOOD
    SHAVE?"—GERMAN)
————(CHINESE)
LA MEJOR AFEITADA
    ("THE BEST SHAVE"—
    SPANISH)
THE BEST SHAVE
IN ANY LANGUAGE
BURMA-SHAVE

WE'RE WIDELY READ
AND OFTEN QUOTED
BUT IT'S SHAVES
NOT SIGNS
FOR WHICH WE'RE NOTED
BURMA-SHAVE

IF CRUSOE'D
KEPT HIS CHIN
MORE TIDY
HE MIGHT HAVE FOUND
A LADY FRIDAY
BURMA-SHAVE

MEN WHO
HAVE TO
TRAVEL LIGHT
FIND THE 35¢ TUBE
JUST RIGHT
BURMA-SHAVE

FEEL YOUR FACE
AS YOU RIDE BY
NOW DON'T
YOU THINK
IT'S TIME TO TRY
BURMA-SHAVE

IT GAVE
MC DONALD
THAT NEEDED CHARM
HELLO HOLLYWOOD
GOOD-BY FARM
BURMA-SHAVE

IF ANYTHING
WILL PLEASE
YOUR JILL
A LITTLE JACK
FOR THIS JAR WILL
BURMA-SHAVE

A SHAVE
THAT'S REAL
NO CUTS TO HEAL
A SOOTHING
VELVET AFTER-FEEL
BURMA-SHAVE

THAT BAREFOOT
CHAP
WITH CHEEKS OF TAN
WON'T LET 'EM CHAP
WHEN HE'S A MAN
BURMA-SHAVE

AROUND
THE CURVE
LICKETY-SPLIT
IT'S A BEAUTIFUL CAR
WASN'T IT?
BURMA-SHAVE

IF HARMONY
IS WHAT
YOU CRAVE
THEN GET
A TUBA
BURMA-SHAVE

OUR FORTUNE
IS YOUR
SHAVEN FACE
IT'S OUR BEST
ADVERTISING SPACE
BURMA-SHAVE

THE BEARDED DEVIL
IS FORCED
TO DWELL
IN THE ONLY PLACE
WHERE THEY DON'T SELL
BURMA-SHAVE

THIS CREAM
MAKES THE
GARDENER'S DAUGHTER
PLANT HER TU-LIPS
WHERE SHE OUGHTER
BURMA-SHAVE

TOUGHEST
WHISKERS
IN THE TOWN
WE HOLD 'EM UP
YOU MOW 'EM DOWN
BURMA-SHAVE

NO MATTER
THE PRICE
NO MATTER HOW NEW
THE BEST SAFETY DEVICE
IN YOUR CAR IS YOU
BURMA-SHAVE

THESE SIGNS
ARE NOT
FOR LAUGHS ALONE
THE FACE THEY SAVE
MAY BE YOUR OWN
BURMA-SHAVE

HE ASKED
HIS KITTEN
TO PET AND PURR
SHE EYED HIS PUSS
AND SCREAMED "WHAT
    FUR!"
BURMA-SHAVE

THE HERO
WAS BRAVE AND STRONG
AND WILLIN'
SHE FELT HIS CHIN—
THEN WED THE VILLAIN
BURMA-SHAVE

THE SAFEST RULE
NO IFS OR BUTS
JUST DRIVE
LIKE EVERY ONE ELSE
IS NUTS!
BURMA-SHAVE

1955

DINAH DOESN'T
TREAT HIM RIGHT
BUT IF HE'D
SHAVE
DYNA-MITE!
BURMA-SHAVE

THO STIFF
THE BEARD
THAT NATURE GAVE
IT SHAVES
LIKE DOWN WITH
BURMA-SHAVE

TO CHANGE THAT
SHAVING JOB
TO JOY
YOU GOTTA USE
THE REAL MC COY
BURMA-SHAVE

HIS CROP OF
WHISKERS
NEEDED REAPING
THAT'S WHAT KEPT
HIS LENA LEAPING
BURMA-SHAVE

115

THE BLACKENED FOREST
SMOULDERS YET
BECAUSE
HE FLIPPED
A CIGARET
BURMA-SHAVE

THE BIG BLUE TUBE'S
JUST LIKE LOUISE
YOU GET
A THRILL
FROM EVERY SQUEEZE
BURMA-SHAVE

JAR SO BIG
COST SO SMALL
COOLEST
SMOOTHEST
SHAVE OF ALL
BURMA-SHAVE

THE MONKEY TOOK
ONE LOOK AT JIM
AND THREW THE
        PEANUTS
BACK AT HIM
HE NEEDED
BURMA-SHAVE

SLOW DOWN, PA
SAKES ALIVE
MA MISSED SIGNS
FOUR
AND FIVE
BURMA-SHAVE

SUBSTITUTES
CAN LET YOU DOWN
QUICKER
THAN A
STRAPLESS GOWN
BURMA-SHAVE

GRANDPA KNOWS
IT AIN'T TOO LATE
HE'S GONE
TO GIT
SOME WIDDER BAIT
BURMA-SHAVE

FOR SHAVING COMFORT
WITHOUT
A STING
THAT BIG BLUE TUBE
HAS EVERYTHING
BURMA-SHAVE

FREE—FREE
A TRIP
TO MARS
FOR 900
EMPTY JARS
BURMA-SHAVE

6 MILLION HOUSEWIVES
CAN'T BE WRONG
WHO KEEP
THEIR HUSBANDS
RIGHT ALONG IN
BURMA-SHAVE

A CHRISTMAS HUG
A BIRTHDAY KISS
AWAITS
THE WOMAN
WHO GIVES THIS
BURMA-SHAVE

TRY A TUBE
ITS COOLING
POWER
REFRESHES LIKE
AN APRIL SHOWER
BURMA-SHAVE

ONE SHAVE LASTS
ALL DAY THROUGH
FACE FEELS
COOL AND
SMOOTHER TOO
BURMA-SHAVE

TAKE
YOUR
TIME
NOT
YOUR LIFE
BURMA-SHAVE

WITHIN THIS VALE
OF TOIL
AND SIN
YOUR HEAD GROWS BALD
BUT NOT YOUR CHIN
BURMA-SHAVE

CATTLE CROSSING
MEANS GO SLOW
THAT OLD BULL
IS SOME
COW'S BEAU
BURMA-SHAVE

DOES YOUR HUSBAND
MISBEHAVE
GRUNT AND GRUMBLE
RANT AND RAVE
SHOOT THE BRUTE SOME
BURMA-SHAVE

1959

THE DRAFTEE
TRIED A TUBE
AND PURRED
WELL WHADDYA KNOW
I'VE BEEN DEFURRED
BURMA-SHAVE

MEN
WITH WHISKERS
'NEATH THEIR NOSES
OUGHTA HAVE TO KISS
LIKE ESKIMOSES
BURMA-SHAVE

THIS COOLING SHAVE
WILL NEVER FAIL
TO STAMP
ITS USER
FIRST CLASS MALE
BURMA-SHAVE

SAID FARMER BROWN
WHO'S BALD
ON TOP
WISH I COULD
ROTATE THE CROP
BURMA-SHAVE

DRINKING DRIVERS—
NOTHING WORSE
THEY PUT
THE QUART
BEFORE THE HEARSE
BURMA-SHAVE

DON'T
TRY PASSING
ON A SLOPE
UNLESS YOU HAVE
A PERISCOPE
BURMA-SHAVE

PASSING CARS
WHEN YOU CAN'T SEE
MAY GET YOU
A GLIMPSE
OF ETERNITY
BURMA-SHAVE

USE THIS CREAM
A DAY
OR TWO
THEN DON'T CALL HER—
SHE'LL CALL YOU
BURMA-SHAVE

DON'T LEAVE SAFETY
TO MERE CHANCE
THAT'S WHY
BELTS ARE
SOLD WITH PANTS
BURMA-SHAVE

THE POOREST GUY
IN THE
HUMAN RACE
CAN HAVE A
MILLION DOLLAR FACE
BURMA-SHAVE

AT A QUIZ
PA AIN'T
NO WHIZ
BUT HE KNOWS HOW
TO KEEP MA HIS
BURMA-SHAVE

IF DAISIES
ARE YOUR
FAVORITE FLOWER
KEEP PUSHIN' UP THOSE
MILES-PER-HOUR
BURMA-SHAVE

MANY A FOREST
USED TO STAND
WHERE A
LIGHTED MATCH
GOT OUT OF HAND
BURMA-SHAVE

HE LIT A MATCH
TO CHECK GAS TANK
THAT'S WHY
THEY CALL HIM
SKINLESS FRANK
BURMA-SHAVE

BABY YOUR SKIN
KEEP IT FITTER
OR "BABY"
WILL GET
ANOTHER SITTER
BURMA-SHAVE

THE ONE WHO
DRIVES WHEN
HE'S BEEN DRINKING
DEPENDS ON YOU
TO DO HIS THINKING
BURMA-SHAVE

1960

THIS CREAM
IS LIKE
A PARACHUTE
THERE ISN'T
ANY SUBSTITUTE
BURMA-SHAVE

TEMPTED TO TRY IT?
FOLLOW YOUR HUNCH
BE "TOP BANANA"
NOT ONE
OF THE BUNCH
BURMA-SHAVE

BRISTLES SCRATCHED
HIS COOKIE'S MAP
THAT'S WHAT
MADE POOR
GINGER SNAP
BURMA-SHAVE

DIM YOUR LIGHTS
BEHIND A CAR
LET FOLKS SEE
HOW BRIGHT
YOU ARE
BURMA-SHAVE

WE'VE MADE GRANDPA
LOOK SO YOUTHFUL
HIS PENSION BOARD
THINKS
HE'S UNTRUTHFUL
BURMA-SHAVE

THIRTY DAYS
HATH SEPTEMBER
APRIL
JUNE AND THE
SPEED OFFENDER
BURMA-SHAVE

USE OUR CREAM
AND WE BETCHA
GIRLS WON'T WAIT
THEY'LL COME
AND GETCHA
BURMA-SHAVE

OTHERS CLAIM
THEIR PRODUCT GOOD
BUT OURS
DOES WHAT
YOU THINK IT SHOULD
BURMA-SHAVE

HENRY THE EIGHTH
SURE HAD
TROUBLE
SHORT TERM WIVES
LONG TERM STUBBLE
BURMA-SHAVE

BEN
MET ANNA
MADE A HIT
NEGLECTED BEARD
BEN-ANNA SPLIT
BURMA-SHAVE

ANGELS
WHO GUARD YOU
WHEN YOU DRIVE
USUALLY
RETIRE AT 65
BURMA-SHAVE

DROWSY?
JUST REMEMBER, PARD
THAT MARBLE SLAB
IS DOGGONE
HARD
BURMA-SHAVE

FOREST FIRES
START FROM SCRATCH
SO THINK BEFORE
YOU TOSS
THAT MATCH
BURMA-SHAVE

STATISTICS PROVE
NEAR AND FAR
THAT FOLKS WHO
DRIVE LIKE CRAZY
—ARE!
BURMA-SHAVE

DEAR LOVER BOY,
YOUR PHOTO CAME
BUT YOUR DOGGONE
    BEARD
WON'T FIT
THE FRAME
BURMA-SHAVE

THIS WILL NEVER
COME TO PASS
A BACK-SEAT
DRIVER
OUT OF GAS
BURMA-SHAVE

1963

DON'T LOSE
YOUR HEAD
TO GAIN A MINUTE
YOU NEED YOUR HEAD
YOUR BRAINS ARE IN IT
BURMA-SHAVE

FILM PROTECTS
YOUR NECK
AND CHIN
SO YOUR RAZOR
WON'T DIG IN
BURMA-SHAVE

IF A GIFT
YOU MUST CHOOSE
GIVE HIM ONE
HE'LL LIKE
TO USE
BURMA-SHAVE

A SHAVE
THAT'S REAL
NO CUTS TO HEAL
A SOOTHING
VELVET AFTER-FEEL
BURMA-SHAVE

PEDRO
WALKED
BACK HOME, BY GOLLY
HIS BRISTLY CHIN
WAS HOT-TO-MOLLY
BURMA-SHAVE

IF HUGGING
ON HIGHWAYS
IS YOUR SPORT
TRADE IN YOUR CAR
FOR A DAVENPORT
BURMA-SHAVE

IF OUR ROAD SIGNS
CATCH YOUR EYE
SMILE
BUT DON'T FORGET
TO BUY
BURMA-SHAVE

IN CUPID'S LITTLE
BAG OF TRIX
HERE'S THE ONE
THAT CLIX
WITH CHIX
BURMA-SHAVE

WHEN THE STORK
DELIVERS A BOY
OUR WHOLE
DARN FACTORY
JUMPS FOR JOY
BURMA-SHAVE

A GUY
WHO WANTS
TO MIDDLE-AISLE IT
MUST NEVER SCRATCH
HIS LITTLE VIOLET
BURMA-SHAVE

EVERY DAY
WE DO
OUR PART
TO MAKE YOUR FACE
A WORK OF ART
BURMA-SHAVE

THRIFTY JARS FOR
STAY AT HOMES
HANDY TUBES
FOR HIM
WHO ROAMS
BURMA-SHAVE

WE DON'T
KNOW HOW
TO SPLIT AN ATOM
BUT AS TO WHISKERS
LET US AT 'EM
BURMA-SHAVE

IF YOU WANT
A HEARTY SQUEEZE
GET OUR
FEMALE
ANTI-FREEZE
BURMA-SHAVE

CAN'T SHAVE DAILY?
TENDER HIDE?
NOW BE HONEST
HAVE YOU
TRIED
BURMA-SHAVE

THE CHICK
HE WED
LET OUT A WHOOP
FELT HIS CHIN AND
FLEW THE COOP
BURMA-SHAVE

OUR FORTUNE
IS YOUR
SHAVEN FACE
IT'S OUR BEST
ADVERTISING SPACE
BURMA-SHAVE

*   *   *

A NOTE:

It was amazing — and gratifying — to see how people reacted to the first TV Theme Song book. Obviously I'm not the only one who remembers these "modern folk songs" fondly; in fact, this volume exists today because people insisted on more. Specifically, the most frequently requested additional themes were (can you guess?): *Rawhide, Gilligan's Island, Patty Duke,* and *Sugarfoot* (which surprised me). But everyone seems to have a special favorite. I hope yours is included. If not, well . . . there's always next time! Have fun and **sing out loud!**   JJ.

ACKNOWLEDGMENTS

- I've been very lucky to have had Bob Miller as my editor, friend, and supporter for the last five years. He and I both know that this book would never have been written if he hadn't insisted. For that, and for all of his help with all of my books, I'm grateful. Thanks, Bob — let's make it at least another five.
- The folks at Hal Leonard Publishing, particularly Mary Bultman (whose patience is astounding) and Glenda Herro, get a big kiss. Except Keith and Dave, who get *Rawhide* hand-shakes.
- Lloyd Jassin, my publicist at St. Martin's, has been a blessing and a good friend. Next time I go to Pittsburgh, I'm taking you with me, Lloyd. Keep up the great work!
- Thanks to Eric Lefcowitz for hanging in there.
- You're in here too, Sharon. Love American Style.
- 2nd Annual Citation for performance above and beyond the call of duty: Mary Kay Landon, Vicki Rombs, Lisa DiMona.
- Thank you Dan Acree for the fantastic publicity job.
- *Father Knows Best* is for Tom Shales. I didn't know there were lyrics either.
- *Davy Crockett* is for Douglas Durden, wherever she is.
- *Love Boat* is especially for Dick Bright, who epitomizes everything that's fun about TV Themes.
- Bill Frank at ASCAP and Charles Pavlosky at BMI came through again. You guys are terrific!
- My agents, Joyce (the Phantom) Cole and Jayne (First National) Walker, get a big hug.
- Thanks to Lonnie Graham for the pop culture psychology.
- Thanks to my two TV Theme experts: Steve Gelfand and Roger Dorfman. I was lucky to find you both.
- Rollin, rollin, rollin, thanks to Ron and Roland (as always).
- Special thanks to Arlene Muller for her kindness and assistance.
- Thank you Bob Denver and Jose Feliciano, and all the people who made the theme songs available to me: Rick Hansen. Michael Goldsen, John Gart, David Newell, J. R. Rogers, Joan Schulman, Paul Barry, Sidney Herman, Bob Wright,
- *Gidget* is for Jim Kerr. Now we can *both* sing it!
- Thanks to Andy Carpenter for his time and energy in helping me make choices. I appreciate it!
- Thanks to Josh Marwell for his enthusiasm and support.
- Harry Trumbore can be Top Cat this time.

Table Of Contents

S it-coms

The Patty Duke Show . . . . page 6
The Mary Tyler Moore Show . . . . page 8
Hogan's Heroes . . . . page 11
Love American Style . . . . page 14
The Love Boat . . . . page 16
The Odd Couple . . . . page 18
The Munsters . . . . page 20
M*A*S*H . . . . page 23
I Dream of Jeannie . . . . page 28
Cheers . . . . page 30
Gilligan's Island . . . . page 32
Father Knows Best . . . . page 34
Chico and the Man . . . . page 37
Gidget . . . . page 40
The Partridge Family . . . . page 42

W esterns

Rawhide . . . . page 44
Sugarfoot . . . . page 47
The Rebel . . . . page 50
The Lawman . . . . page 52
Davy Crockett . . . . page 56

M usic/variety

The Carol Burnett Show . . . . page 60
American Bandstand . . . . page 64
That Was The Week That Was . . . . page 67
The Tonight Show . . . . page 70

THE TV THEME SONG
SING~ALONG SONG BOOK
Volume 2

By John Javna

Designed by
Ron Addad & Roland Addad

Published by
Hal Leonard Publishing Corporation / St. Martin's Press
175 Fifth Avenue
New York, NY 10010

THIS BOOK IS WARMLY DEDICATED TO THE SALES FORCE OF
ST. MARTIN'S PRESS, WHO MADE TV THEMES, VOLUME 1,
A SUCCESS STORY

OTHER BOOKS BY JOHN JAVNA:

- *60s!* (with Gordon Javna)
- *How To Jitterbug*
- *The TV Theme Song Sing-Along Song Book*
- *Cult TV*

THIS BOOK WAS CREATED AND PACKAGED BY J-BIRD PRESS

TYPESETTING BY: KAZAN Typeset Services
PASTE-UP BY: Vicki Rombs

John Javna, professor of TV Theme-ology

THE TV THEME SONG SING-ALONG SONGBOOK, VOLUME 2

DESIGN BY: Ron Addad and Roland Addad (thanks, guys).
ISBN: 0-312-78218-7
Library of Congress Catalogue Number: 84-758771

First Edition
10 9 8 7 6 5 4 3 2 1

(Revised for volume 2)
Main entry under title:

The TV theme song sing-along songbook.

1. Television music — United States.   I. Javna, John.
M1527.7.T9 1984   84-758771
ISBN 0-312-78215-2 (pbk. : v. 1)
ISBN 0-312-78218-7 (pbk. : v. 2)

Table Of Contents

K ids shows

The Mickey Mouse Club . . . . page 74
Top Cat . . . . page 77
Winky Dink and You . . . . page 82
The Jetsons . . . . page 86
The Flintstones . . . . page 88
The Road Runner . . . . page 90
Woody Woodpecker . . . . page 92
Magilla Gorilla . . . . page 95
Scooby Doo, Where Are You? . . . . page 98
Yogi Bear . . . . page 100
Huckleberry Hound . . . . page 102
Looney Tunes
    (The Merry-Go-Round Broke Down) . . . . . page 104
Mister Rogers' Neighborhood . . . . page 107
Howdy Doody Time . . . . page 110

D rama/adventure

Zorro . . . . page 112
Baretta . . . . page 115
Mission: Impossible . . . . page 118
The Adventures of Robin Hood . . . . page 120

C ommercials

Roto-Rooter . . . . page 27
Brylcreem (A Little Dab'll Do Ya) . . . . page 55
Rice-A-Roni (The San Francisco Treat) . . . . . page 63
Chock Full O' Nuts . . . . page 72
Brush Your Teeth With Colgate . . . . page 73
Sometimes You Feel Like a Nut . . . . page 80
I Love Bosco . . . . page 85
Pepsi Cola (Pepsi's Got A Lot To Give) . . . . . page 123

Let's Play Telephone (Playing Themes on
    Your Push-Button Phone) . . . . page 125
The TV Theme Song Preservation Society
    Membership Information . . . . page 127
There's More! . . . . page 128

The Patty Duke Show

THE SHOW: How's this for a genetic miracle: Patty and Cathy Lane just *happen* to be identical cousins. But that's about all they have in common. Cathy, who's from Scotland, is living with her uncle's family in Brooklyn Heights, New York, while her parents are abroad. She's a shy, refined 16-year-old trying to adjust to the American way of life. Patty, on the other hand, is a typical American teenager who's in love with slumber parties, hot dogs, and rock' n'roll. Naturally everyone gets the look-alike cousins confused, even Patty's parents: Martin, a newspaper editor with the *New York Chronicle*, and Natalie. But the girls manage to use this to their advantage. Every time one of them gets into trouble (usually Patty), they switch identities and bluff their way out of it.

THE SONG: One of the best-remembered theme songs of the '60s. Favorite line: "a hot dog makes her lose control..."

Patty Duke was 17 years old when she first appeared as as Patty and Cathy Lane

Main Cast

Patty Lane: Patty Duke
Cathy Lane (her cousin): Patty Duke
Martin Lane (her father): William Schallert
Natalie Lane (her mother): Jean Byron
Ross Lane (her brother): Paul O'Keefe
Richard Harrison (her boyfriend): Eddie Applegate
Ted Brownley (Cathy's boyfriend): Skip Hinnant
J. R. Castle (Martin's boss): John McGiver
Sue Ellen (Patty's rival): Kitty Sullivan

INSIDE FACTS

PATTY DUKE'S AMAZING CAREER:

● At age 12, she starred as Helen Keller in the Broadway play, *The Miracle Worker*. She gave 994 live performances.
● Her 995th performance was in the film adaptation of the play.
● It won her an Oscar as Best Supporting Actress in 1962.
● In 1979 she won another award for the play: an Emmy (for the TV version). This time she switched roles — to Helen's teacher, Anne Sullivan.
● At 17, she was the youngest performer in television history to have a prime-time series named for her (1963).

TRIVIA QUIZ

THE SUBJECT IS...
DOUBLES

Patty Duke played her own cousin. Other TV actors and actresses have played their own relatives in regular series, too. Can you name the shows?
1. James Garner played the hero and his "Pappy" on ...
2. Carolyn Jones doubled as her sister Ophelia on ...
3. Max Baer, Jr. went in drag to play his character's sister on ...
4. Barbara Eden played the title character and her sister on ...
5. Elizabeth Montgomery caused trouble for herself as her cousin Serena on ...

ANSWERS

1. *Maverick*
2. *The Addams Family*
3. *The Beverly Hillbillies*
4. *I Dream of Jeannie*
5. *Bewitched*

The Patty Duke Theme ("Cousins")

Words: Bob Welles, Music: Sig Ramin

Meet Cathy who's lived most everywhere,
From Zanzibar to Berk'ly Square,
But Patty's only seen the sights
A girl can see from Brooklyn Heights,
What a crazy pair!

But they're cousins,
Identical cousins all the way,
One pair of matching book-ends,
Diff'rent as night and day.

Where Cathy adores a minuet,
The Ballet Russe and crepe suzette,
Our Patty loves her rock'n'roll,
A hot dog makes her lose control.
What a wild duet!

Still they're cousins,
Identical cousins and you'll find
They laugh alike, they walk alike,
At times they even talk alike,
You can lose your mind,
When cousins are two of a kind.

7

The Mary Tyler Moore Show

THE SHOW: In the seventies, when America's ideas about women were changing, Mary Richards was the perfect TV role model. Unlike other sitcom females, she wasn't married (or divorced). She didn't have kids. She wasn't young, glamorous, or goofy. Instead, she was capable and independent . . . and at work, she was the boss (except for Lou, of course). Mary had moved to Minneapolis to become an associate news producer at WJM-TV, the lowest-rated station in the Twin Cities. But even *she* couldn't help make them more successful: WJM was stuck with inept Ted Baxter ("Hi guys") as its anchorman. So in the end, she suffered the fate of every TV executive — in the last episode, she was fired along with the rest of the WJM staff . . . except Ted!

Almost everyone in the Mary Tyler Moore Show went on to star in their own TV series. Two of the alumni: Ed Asner (Lou Grant), and Valerie Harper (Rhoda)

THE SONG: Written and sung by Sonny Curtis, an original member of Buddy Holly's Crickets. It was released as a single twice — in 1970, and in 1980, when it was a minor country-western hit.

Main Cast

Mary Richards: Mary Tyler Moore
Lou Grant (her boss): Edward Asner
Ted Baxter (anchorman): Ted Knight
Murray Slaughter (newswriter): Gavin MacLeod
Rhoda Morganstern (Mary's friend): Valerie Harper
Phyllis Lindstrom (Mary's friend): Cloris Leachman
Sue Anne Nevins: Betty White
Georgette Franklin (Ted's girlfriend): Georgia Engel

Vital Statistics

Half-hour sitcom. CBS.
First aired: September 19, 1970
Most popular time slot: Saturday 9:00 – 9:30 PM (1972-76)
Last show: September 3, 1977
Ranked in a year's Top 25: 1971 (22); 1972 (10); 1973 (7); 1974 (9); 1975 (11); 1976 (19)

INSIDE FACTS

MARY'S STRANGE PATH TO STARDOM:

• Her first TV appearance was in a refrigerator ad. She played a 3″ tall pixie named Happy Hotpoint, who jumped out of an ice tray saying "Hi, Harriet. Aren't you glad you bought a Hotpoint?"

• Her next big role: a secretary named Sam in *Richard Diamond, Private Detective*. Her face was never seen — only her legs.

• Her *Dick Van Dyke* role came as a fluke: stumped in his search for the right actress to play Laura, producer Sheldon Leonard asked his partner, Danny Thomas: "Don't you know of any *more?*" Thomas remembered *Moore*, who had tried out for the role of the daughter on his sitcom.

• A 1969 TV special prompted CBS to offer her her own show.

TRIVIA QUIZ

A lot of people think they're experts on this show. Are you?
1. Name the address and number of Mary's apartment
2. What channel was WJM-TV?
3. Where did Rhoda work?
4. Where did Ted get his start?
5. How did Chuckles the Clown die?

ANSWERS

1. 119 North Weatherly, Apt. D
2. 12
3. Hempel's Department Store
4. A 5,000 watt radio station in Fresno, CA
5. An elephant shelled him

Love Is All Around

Words and Music: Sonny Curtis

9

Who can turn the world___ on with her smile,_____ who can take a noth-ing day___ and sud-den-ly make___ it all seem worthwhile?___ Well, it's you, girl, and you should know___ it, with each glance and ev-'ry lit-tle move-ment you show it. Love is all a-round, no need to waste ___ it. You can have the town; why don't you take___ it? You're gon-na make it af-ter all._____

Hogan's Heroes

THE SHOW: Described as "World War II with a laugh track, *Hogan's Heroes* was a funny sitcom in an unfunny setting: a German POW camp. But of course, this was no ordinary prison camp — it was Stalag 13. Headed by bumbling Col. Klink and his portly sidekick Sgt. Schultz ("I know nothing!"), Stalag 13 boasted that no one had ever escaped. The joke was that no one *wanted* to escape! Unknown to Klink, U.S. Air Force Col. Hogan and his band of fellow-prisoners were running a strategic undercover operation right under his nose. Using the name "Papa Bear," the prisoners aided the Allies by securing top-secret information and helping fugitives escape through underground tunnels. Among the heroes: wise-cracking English Cpl. Newkirk and French Cpl. LeBeau, who kept Sgt. Schulz quiet by stuffing him full of fancy French cuisine.

Bob Crane played Col. Robert Hogan for almost 6 years, longer than America was actually in World War II!

THE SONG: Military march. Lyrics were added later for a record: "Hogan's Heroes Sing the Best of World War II."

Main Cast

Col. Robert Hogan: Robert Crane
Col. Wilhelm Klink: Werner Klemperer
Sgt. Hans Schulz: John Banner
Cpl. Louis LeBeau (French): Robert Clary
Cpl. Peter Newkirk (English): Richard Dawson
Lt. Andrew Carter (American): Larry Hovis
Gen. Alfred Burkhalter: Leon Askin

Vital Statistics

Half-hour sitcom. CBS. 168 episodes.
First aired: Sept. 17, 1965
Most popular time slot: Friday, 8:30-9:00 PM (1965-67)
Last show: July 4, 1971
Ranked in a year's Top 25: 1966 (9), 1967 (18)

11

INSIDE FACTS
ABOUT THE ORIGIN OF HOGAN'S HEROES:

• It was created by Bernard Fein, a former cast-member of *The Phil Silvers Show* (*Sgt. Bilko*).

• He originally had it set in an American penitentiary.

• After trying to sell it for four years, he decided to quit show business, and boarded a plane for his hometown, New York City.

• On the plane, he saw someone reading *Von Ryan's Express*, a WW II novel. He flashed on the idea of changing the setting to a P.O.W. camp.

• He immediately flew back to Hollywood, and sold the idea in four days.

• Footnote: the authors of a successful play (and movie) called *Stalag 17* sued the creators of *Hogan's Heroes* for plagiarism and won.

TRIVIA QUIZ

Which star of Hogan's Heroes:
1. Really was a Nazi prisoner during World War II?
2. Fled his native Austria when Hitler invaded it?
3. Played Adolph Eichmann in a film about him?
4. Was mysteriously murdered in 1978?
5. Kissed lots of women on *Family Feud*?

ANSWERS

1. Robert Clary
2. John Banner
3. Werner Klemperer
4. Robert Crane
5. Richard Dawson

The Hogan's Heroes Theme Song

Words and Music by Jerry Fielding

1. He - roes, he - roes, hus - ky men of war, sons of all the he - roes of the war be - fore.
2. All good he - roes, love a good, big fight open up the bomb bays and bright - en up the night

We're all he - roes up to our ear - o's you ask the ques - tions, we make sug - ges - tions,
We ap - plaud the peo - ple who laud us, you pull the ros - es, we punch the nos - es,

that's what we're he - roes for.
that's what we're he - roes for.

What's ____ a he - ro do? Well we're not gon - na tell ya cos

we wish we knew. That's why we he-roes are so few. We've got a
slo-gan from Colo-nel Ho-gan and Colo-nel Ho-gan's a he-ro too,
Ne-ver flinch boys, ne-ver be a-fraid he-roes are not born, boys he-roes all are made.
Ask not why boys, ne-ver say die boys, an-swer the call, re-
mem-ber we'll all be he-roes for e-ver-more.

13

Love, American Style

THE SHOW: What was *Love, American Style* about? Well, it debuted in 1969, so the title wasn't exactly referring to the Cleaver family. But really, folks, it was all pretty innocent. Each program consisted of a bunch of cute one-act plays about love, with titles like "Love and the Practical Joker," "Love and the Legal Agreement," "Love and the Pill" (whoops — guess what *that* one was about . . .). But the real fun for viewers was seeing who the guest stars were each week. You never knew who'd show up — sometimes it was guys your parents would love, like Phyllis Diller and Red Buttons. But other

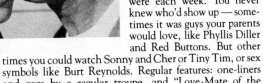

A typical "love-bird" scene from Love American Style

times you could watch Sonny and Cher or Tiny Tim, or sex symbols like Burt Reynolds. Regular features: one-liners and gags by a regular troupe, and "Love-Mate of the Week."

THE SONG: Sung by the Cowsills, it was released as a single — but failed to make the charts.

Main Cast

Regular Repertory Group:
Mary Grover, Richard Williams, Lynne Marta,
Bernie Kopell, Bill Callaway, Phyllis Elizabeth Davis,
Jaki DeMar, Stuart Margolin, Barbara Minkus
Tracy Reed, James Hampton, Buzz Cooper,
Clifton Davis, James A. Watson, Jr., Jed Allen

Vital Statistics

Hour, half-hour. ABC. 65 episodes.
First aired: Sept. 29, 1969
Most popular time slot: Friday, 9:00-10:00 PM (1970, 1971-74)
Last show: Jan. 11, 1974
Never ranked in the Top 25 shows of a year

INSIDE FACTS

"LOVE'S" CHILDREN:
• The pilot of *Happy Days* first appeared as a segment of *Love American Style*.
• It was called "Love and the Happy Day," and featured Ron Howard and Anson Williams as Richie and Potsie.
• *Love American Style* also spawned *The Love Boat*, which copied its format of celebrity skits about love, but tied them together with a uniform setting.
• Bernie Kopell, a member of the regular troupe, later became a regular on *Love Boat* as well.
• Stuart Margolin, another show regular, gained fame (notoriety?) as the unscrupulous "Angel" on *The Rockford Files*.
• 1971 regular Clifton Davis went on to star in his own ABC sitcom 3 years later: *That's My Mama*.

TRIVIA QUIZ

THE SUBJECT IS . . . LOVE

Like *Love, American Style*, these TV series had the word "love" in their titles. Name them.

1. Judy Carne and Peter Deuel starred as young marrieds who lived in a windowless apartment, 1966-71

2. David Birney was Jewish, and Meredith Baxter was Catholic, 1972-73

3. It starred Mr. and Mrs. Arnaz, 1951-57

4. Paul Sand played a bass violin as Robert Dreyfuss, 1974-75

5. Bob Cummings was a bachelor and professional photographer, 1955-59

ANSWERS
1. *Love On A Rooftop*
2. *Bridget Loves Bernie*
3. *I Love Lucy*
4. *Friends and Lovers*
5. *Love That Bob*

14

Love American Style

Words and Music by Arnold Margolin and Charles Fox

Love American style,
Truer than the red, white and blue.
Love American style,
That's me and you.

And on a star-spangled night, my love
You can rest your head on my shoulder.
While by the dawn's early light, my love,
I will defend your right to try.

Love American style,
Freer than the land of the free.
Love American style,
That's you and me.

We pledge our love 'neath the same old moon
But it shines red and white and blue now.
And in this land of hopes and dreams, my love,
All that I hope for 'tis of thee.

Love American style,
Truer than the red, white and blue.
Love American style, Truer than the red white and blue (fade)

15

The Love Boat

THE SHOW: Take a luxury cruise liner, fill it with love-starved celebrities, and what do you have? *The Love Boat*, TV's first floating singles bar. The action is hot and heavy on the deck of the Pacific Princess, with weekly guest stars (Carol Channing, Raymond Burr, etc.) falling in and out and in and out of love as they head for exotic ports all over the world. At the helm of the ship: fatherly Captain Stubing, patrolling his lively domain to make sure that everyone plays by the rules, and occasionally getting bitten by the love bug himself. In fact, the whole crew seems to plunge in with shipboard romances whenever they get the chance. But somehow sitcoms never seem to change. Even with all the cabin-hopping, it all comes off as good clean fun, and the Love Boat keeps sailing along.

Gavin MacLeod stars as Captain Stubing in one of America's most popular sitcoms ever

THE SONG: Performed by Jack ("Dear Heart") Jones, it was released at least twice as a single, but missed the Top 40. Written by Paul Williams, who authored "We've Only Just Begun," "Just an Old-Fashioned Love Song," etc.

Main Cast

Capt. Merrill Stubing: Gavin MacLeod
Vicki Stubing (his daughter): Jill Whelan
Burl "Gopher" Smith (Yeoman-Purser): Fred Grandy
Dr. Adam Bricker (ship's physician): Bernie Koppell
Isaac Washington (bartender): Ted Lange
Julie McCoy (cruise director, 1977-84): Lauren Tewes
Judy McCoy (cruise director, 1984 -): Pat Klous
"Ace" Evans (photographer): Ted McGinley

Vital Statistics

Hour-long sitcom. ABC. Current.
First aired: Sept. 24, 1977
Most popular time slot: Saturday, 9:00-10:00 PM
Last show: Still in first run.
Ranked in a year's Top 25: 1978 (14); 1979 (17); 1980 (24); 1981 (5); 1982 (14); 1983 (9); 1984 (12)

INSIDE FACTS

BACKGROUND INFO:

• *The Love Boat* was adapted from a novel called *The Love Boats*.
• The book was written by a former cruise hostess named Jeraldine Saunders, who based the story on her real-life experiences.
• Three pilot films were made before the idea was sold as a series. They aired as TV movies during the 1976-77 TV season.
• It has always been filmed on a real cruise ship, with passengers acting as extras.
• Before *Love Boat*'s premiere, it was difficult to get passengers to cooperate; they complained that the crew was in their way. This changed as soon as people began seeing themselves on TV.
• Its format was inspired by ABC's successful multi-story sitcom, *Love American Style.*

TRIVIA QUIZ

1. What are the "Love Boat Follies"?
2. Most of the episodes of *Love Boat* were filmed on two real cruise ships. One is the Pacific Princess. What's the other one?
3. Who played Marshall, Captain Stubing's brother?
4. For a sitcom character, what's unusual about Stubing's daughter Vicki?
5. *Love Boat* broke into the Top 20 in its first season, 1977-78. What was the #1 show that season?

ANSWERS

5. *Laverne and Shirley*
4. She's an illegitimate daughter
3. Gavin MacLeod
2. The Island Princess
1. A shipboard musical revue featuring the crew and big stars

The Love Boat   Words and Music by Charles Fox and Paul Williams

Love, exciting and new.
Come aboard, we're expecting you.

And love, life's sweetest reward,
let it float, it floats back to you.

The Love Boat
Soon will be making another run.
The Love Boat
Promises something for everyone.
Set a course for adventure,
Your mind on a new romance.

And love won't hurt anymore
It's an open smile on a friendly shore.
It's love.
It's love.

17

The Odd Couple

THE SHOW: When Felix Unger's wife threw him out of their apartment, Felix had nowhere to go — except 1049 Park Ave., the home of Oscar Madison. It seemed logical; Felix and Oscar were childhood friends, and Oscar had been living alone since *his* wife had told him to leave. So Felix showed up at Oscar's door, ready to move in. "Can two divorced men," asked the show's announcer at the beginning of each episode, "share an apartment without driving each other crazy?" Not these two. Felix, a professional photographer, was a neatness nut; Oscar, a sportswriter for the *New York Herald*, was a slob. Felix liked good wine and opera; Oscar liked cheap beer and gambling. And on and on. They put up with each other for five years. Then Felix and ex-wife Gloria remarried, leaving Oscar to mess things up in peace.
THE SONG: Originally the movie theme, with lyrics by the author of "Call Me Irresponsible," "High Hopes," and dozens more.

Jack Klugman and Tony Randall, two of America's favorite comedians, teamed up in The Odd Couple

18

Main Cast

Felix Unger: Tony Randall
Oscar Madison: Jack Klugman
Officer Murray Grechner (a friend): Al Molinaro
Speed (a poker-friend): Gary Walberg
Vinnie (a poker-friend): Larry Gelman
Roy (a poker-friend): Ryan MacDonald
Dr. Nancy Cunningham: Joan Hotchkiss
Miriam Wellby (Felix's girlfriend): Elinor Donahue

Vital Statistics

Half-hour sitcom. ABC.
First aired: September 24, 1970
Most popular time slot: Friday 9:30 – 10:00 PM (1971-73, 1974)
Last show: July 4, 1975
Never ranked in a year's Top 25 shows.

INSIDE FACTS

ABOUT THE ODD COUPLE:

● While a struggling N.Y. actor, Jack Klugman shared a $14/month apartment with Charles Bronson.
● His first TV series was in the "Harris Against the World" segment of *90 Bristol Court* in 1964-5.
● With a 5-pack-a-day cigarette habit, he developed throat cancer in 1975. A successful operation that saved his career inspired him to play a doctor — Quincy — in 1976.
● Tony Randall studied at Northwestern University to "correct" his native Oklahoma accent.
● After studying acting in N.Y.C., he landed a role in *Mr. Peepers*, a popular sitcom of the early '50s.
● This led to films like *Pillow Talk* and *Lover Come Back*, starring Doris Day and Rock Hudson.

TRIVIA QUIZ

1. Whose experiences inspired Neil Simon to write the play?
2. In real life, how did Miriam Wellby get her name?
3. What role did Klugman's wife play in the series?
4. What were the Pigeon sisters' first names?
5. Who played Myrna Turner, Oscar's secretary?

ANSWERS

1. His brother's
2. She was played by Elinor Donahue, who'd been on *Father Knows Best*, Robert Young, who'd been "Father," was currently starring as Marcus Welby. Tony Randall thought of it as a tribute to him
3. Oscar's ex-wife Blanche
4. Cecily and Gwen
5. Penny Marshall

The Odd Couple

Words: Sammy Cahn, Music: Neal Hefti

No matter where they go,
They are known as the couple.
They're never seen alone,
So they're known as the couple

As I've indicated
They are never quite separated,
They are peas in a pod.
Don't you think that it's odd?

Their habits, I confess,
None can guess with the couple.
If one says no it's yes,
More or less with the couple

But they're laugh-provoking
Yet they don't really know they're
  joking.
Don't you find when love is blind
It's kind of odd!

19

(REPEAT ALL VERSES)

Don't you think it's odd?
Don't you think it's odd?
Don't you think it's odd?

The Munsters

THE SHOW: Every day is Halloween at 1313 Mockingbird Lane, home of the ghoulish Munster family. The father, Herman (who works in a funeral parlor), is a "dead ringer" for Frankenstein; his wife Lily is a friendly lady vampire; Eddie, their son, is a werewolf; and 378-year-old Grandpa is Count Dracula. Actually, despite appearances, they're just an average American sitcom family. Mom, for example, cooks them all breakfast in the morning — in a steaming cauldron. And everyone looks up to Dad (who's over seven feet tall and so strong that he walks through walls). And of course they have pets — a bat named Igor, a prehistoric creature called Spot, and a raven that keeps repeating "Nevermore." Only Marilyn, their pretty niece, looks and acts human. But the rest of the family thinks she's monstrous, of course!

THE SONG: An instrumental on the show, the lyrics were written by the Munsters' producer, Bob Mosher and sung only once — on a kids' record. Later, Butch Patrick recorded a rock version with new lyrics. Title: "Whatever Happened to Eddie?"

Is it Frankenstein's monster? Nope — it's lovable Herman Munster!

20

Main Cast

Herman Munster: Fred Gwynne
Lily Munster (his wife): Yvonne DeCarlo
Grandpa: Al Lewis
"Eddie" Munster (his son): Butch Patrick
Marilyn Munster (his niece): Beverly Owen, Pat Priest

Vital Statistics

Half-hour sitcom. CBS. 70 episodes
First aired: September 24, 1964
Most popular time slot: Thursday 7:30 – 8:00 PM
Last show: September 8, 1966
Ranked in a year's Top 25: 1965 (18)

INSIDE FACTS

ABOUT HERMAN'S COSTUME:
● It took 2 hours to transform the bony 6'5", 180 lb. Fred Gwynne into Herman.
● His face was covered with grease, balloon rubber, and yellow-green makeup (even though the show was filmed in black-and-white).
● To make him look massive, he was given pants stuffed with foam in the legs, a shrunken jacket stuffed with foam in the shoulders and arms (it buttoned in the back), and 10-lb. boots with built-in 5" heels.
● The boots were designed to make it hard for Gwynne to walk in them, so he'd naturally have a clumsy, "lurching" walk.
● The costume was so hot that at first, Gwynne lost 10 lbs. sweating in it.

TRIVIA QUIZ

THE SUBJECT IS ...
THE MUNSTERS
1. What was the name of the funeral home where Herman worked?
2. What kind of milk did the Munsters drink?
3. What was Eddie's dog's name?
4. In what town did the Munsters live?
5. Who played Dr. Dudley, the Munsters' physician (hint: he played Uncle Arthur on *Bewitched*)?

ANSWERS

5. Paul Lynde
4. Mockingbird Heights
3. Woof Woof
2. Bat milk
1. Gateman, Goodbury, and Graves

The Munsters Theme

Words: Robert Mosher, Music: Jack Marshall

21

Mun - sters may shake your hand clam - mi - ly, but they're not ne - ces - sa - ri - ly
were - wolves and fiends shriek and howl a - bout, well the Mun - sters are out on the

dead. Be - hind their house you must - n't be a - fraid to
town. One night I dared peek thru their win - dow screen. My

see a fig - ure dig - ging with a spade. Per - haps some - one did - n't quite
hair turned white at such a cra - zy scene, be - cause ev' - ry eve - ning it's

make the grade with the Mun - sters, with the Mun - sters.
Hal - lo - ween, at the Mun - sters at the Mun - sters.

22

M•A•S•H

THE SHOW: Although it was often hilariously funny, M*A*S*H didn't gloss over the horrors of war like other "war comedies." It took us right into the operating room, where doctors and nurses of the 4077th worked furiously to save the wounded — and sometimes failed. Located a few miles from the front lines during the Korean War, this army hospital frequently resembled a 3-ring circus. The ringmaster (and top surgeon): Hawkeye Pierce, a reluctant draftee whose constant one-liners made him a sort of Groucho Marx with a scalpel. The supporting cast included more than 20 people in the show's 11-year run — which, by the way, was about 4 times as long as the actual Korean War.

M*A*S*H helped make Alan Alda one of America's most popular personalities

THE SONG: Originally the movie theme. Lyrics were written by the director's son, and sung in the film when a character was contemplating suicide.

Main Cast

Capt. Hawkeye Pierce: Alan Alda
Capt. John McIntyre (Trapper John): Wayne Rogers
Maj. Margaret Houlihan (Hot Lips): Loretta Swit
Maj. Frank Burns: Larry Linville
Cpl. Walter O' Reilly (Radar): Gary Burghoff
Lt. Col. Henry Blake: McLean Stevenson
Father Francis Mulcahy: William Christopher
Cpl. Maxwell Klinger: Jamie Farr
Col. Sherman Potter: Harry Morgan
Capt. B. J. Hunnicut: Mike Farrell
Maj. Charles Emerson Winchester: David Ogden Stiers

Vital Statistics

Half-hour sitcom. CBS.
First aired: September 17, 1972
Most popular time slot: Tues. 9:00-9:30 PM (1975-78)
Mon. 9:00-9:30 PM (;1978-83)
Last show: September 19, 1983
Ranked in a year's Top 25: 1974 (4); 1975 (5) 1976 (15); 1977 (4); 1978 (9); 1979 (7); 1980 (5); 1981 (4); 1982 (9); 1983 (3)

INSIDE FACTS

BACKGROUND INFO:
• M*A*S*H originated as a novel written by Maine physician J. Richard Hornberger, using the pseudonym Richard Hooker.
• He didn't want his honest account of Korean War experiences to damage his professional standing, so he didn't reveal himself until after the show was a hit.
• He was amused that the story was considered anti-war, since he was a conservative Republican.
• In 1970, director Robert Altman made a movie out of the novel.
• It was a smash, winning an Oscar for best script.
• On TV, its first-year ratings were erratic; CBS almost cancelled it mid-season.
• Alan Alda's father didn't want him to be an actor — he wanted him to be a *doctor*!

TRIVIA QUIZ

1. What does M.A.S.H. stand for?
2. Which discharge (give the number) did Klinger keep trying to get?
3. Who was Hot Lips married to?
4. How far was Toledo, according to a sign in the M*A*S*H camp?
5. What was Hawkeye's native state?

ANSWERS

5. Maine
4. 6133 Miles
3. Lt. Col. Donald Penobscott
2. Section 8
1. Mobile Army Surgical Hospital

Song From M*A*S*H* (Suicide Is Painless)

Words and Music: Mike Altman and Johnny Mandel

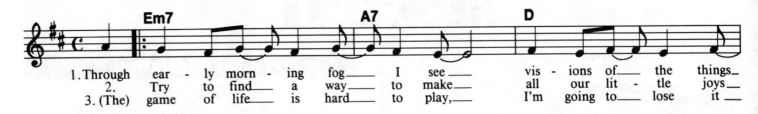

1. Through ear - ly morn - ing fog___ I see ___ vis - ions of___ the things___
2. Try to find a way___ to make___ all our lit - tle joys___
3. (The) game of life___ is hard___ to play,___ I'm going to___ lose it ___

24

___ to be. ___ The pains that are___ with - held___ for me.___ I
___ re - late,___ with - out that ev - er pre - sent hate,___ But
___ any - way,___ the los - ing card___ I'll some - day lay.___ So

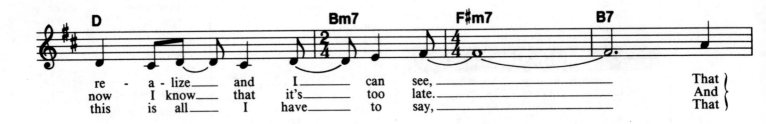

re - a - lize___ and I___ can see, _____ That }
now I know___ that it's___ too late. _____ And }
this is all___ I have___ to say, _____ That }

CHORUS

Su – i – cide___ Is Pain – less,   it   brings   on   man – y   chang –

– es,   and   I   can take___ or   leave___ it   if___   I   please___

25

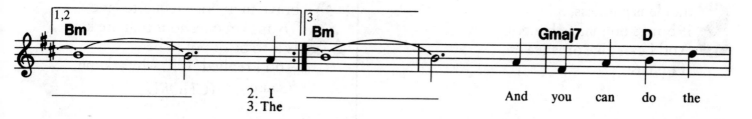

1,2

3.

2. I
3. The

And   you   can   do   the

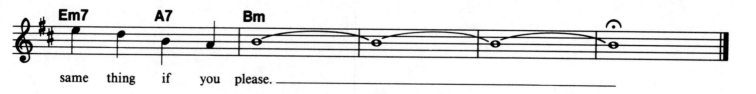

same   thing   if   you   please.___

The only way to win is cheat,
And lay it down before I'm beat,
And to another give a seat
For that's the only painless feat.
'Cause

26

CHORUS

Suicide is painless,
It brings on many changes,
And I can take or leave it
If I please

The sword of time will pierce our skins,
It doesn't hurt when it begins,
But as it works its way on in,
The pain grows stronger, watch it grin.
For   *(CHORUS)*

A brave man once requested me
To answer questions that are key,
Is it to be or not to be
And I replied "Oh, why ask me."
'Cause   *(CHORUS)*

AND
NOW...

A Song From A Sponsor

Roto-Rooter

When Ro - to Root - er comes, — That's when your trou - bles go, — When

27

Ro - to Root-er's here, — That's when your trou - bles dis - ap-pear. Call Ro - to Root-er,

that's the name, and a - way go trou - bles down the drain. — Ro - to Root - er,

sew - er ser - vice, Ro - to Root-er, Ro - to Root-er, Ro - to Root-er...

I Dream of Jeannie

THE SHOW: Astronaut Tony Nelson seemed out of luck when his space mission aborted and he parachuted to a desert island . . . until he uncorked an old bottle he'd found in the sand, releasing a beautiful genie named Jeannie. Grateful for her freedom, Jeannie granted Tony's wish to return to his home in Cocoa Beach, Florida. But that was just the beginning: Jeannie was so infatuated with her space hero that she decided to move in with him (just platonic, of course), turning his once-normal life into utter chaos. Only Tony's fellow-astronaut, Roger Healy, knew about Jeannie's magical powers (she could grant any wish with the blink of an eye). Everyone else thought he'd gone into orbit *permanently*. On Dec. 2, 1969, Jeannie got *her* wish when she and Tony were married. "Yes, master."

Larry Hagman and Barbara Eden, stars of I Dream of Jeannie

THE SONG: An instrumental on the show, but originally written with lyrics. Music by the composer of "The Good, the Bad, and the Ugly," "Hang 'Em High," and more.

Main Cast

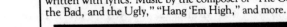

Jeannie: Barbara Eden
Capt. Tony Nelson (her "Master"): Larry Hagman
Capt. Roger Healy (Tony's friend): Bill Daily
Dr. Alfred Bellows (psychiatrist): Hayden Rorke
Amanda Bellows (his wife): Emmaline Henry
Gen. Wingard Stone (1st C.O.): Philip Ober
Gen. Martin Peterson (2nd C.O.): Barton MacLane
Gen. Winfield Schaeffer (3rd C.O.): Vinton Hayworth

Vital Statistics

Half-hour sitcom. NBC. 139 episodes.
First aired: Sept. 18, 1965
Most popular time slot: Sat. 8:00-8:30 PM (1965-66),
Mon. 8:00-8:30 PM (1966-67),
Tues. 7:30-8:00 PM (1967-68)
Last show: Sept. 1, 1970
Never ranked in the Top 25 shows of a year.

INSIDE FACTS

ABOUT THE "NAVEL CONTROVERSY":
- Although network censors had no objection to Barbara Eden's sexy costume or the fact that Jeannie was living with a man for whom she would do anything (anything?), they *did* object to her navel showing.
- The solution: she had to put a flesh-colored cloth plug in it so it wouldn't show while filming. A milestone in censorship!

ABOUT JEANNIE:
- Her birthday: April 1, 64 B.C.
- How she wound up in a bottle: she was imprisoned by Blue Djin, the most powerful genie, when she refused to marry him (a truly sore loser).
- Her rescue date: Sept. 18, 1965. That would make her 2,029 years, 5 months, and 17 days old when she emerged from captivity.

TRIVIA QUIZ

1. How did Tony find the bottle in which Jeannie was imprisoned?
2. How was he rescued from the desert island?
3. How did Jeannie get back to Florida with Tony?
4. What was Jeannie's sister's name?
5. To what rank was Tony promoted late in the show?

ANSWERS

1. He was looking for something with which to send an SOS
2. Jeannie blinked him a rescue helicopter
3. She blinked herself back into the bottle, and sneaked into his survival kit
4. Jeannie II
5. Major

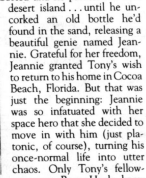

Jeannie, fresh as a daisy,
Just look how she obeys me,
Does things that just amaze me so.

She smiles, presto the rain goes,
She blinks, out comes a rainbow,
Cars stop, even the train goes slow.

When she goes by,
She makes sunshine on every rafter,
Sprinkles the air with laughter,
We're close as a quarter after three.

29

(There's no one like)
Jeannie, I'd introduce her
To you, but it's no use sir,
'Cause my Jeannie's in love with me.

She's in love with me!

Cheers

THE SHOW: Welcome to *Cheers*, America's favorite neighborhood bar. Pull up a stool, order yourself a drink, and relax. There are no celebrities here — just normal people with everyday problems. The owner/bartender is Sam Malone, a reformed alcoholic and former baseball player with the Boston Red Sox. His absent-minded old coach, Ernie Pantusso, used to help him out behind the bar. But Ernie passed away, leaving only Diane Chambers (Sam's ex-lover) and Carla Tortelli (with her houseful of kids) to wait on tables. Every week customers come and go at *Cheers*, but you can always count on seeing at least a few regulars whenever you drop in — usually wise-guy Norm, and Cliff, the mailman. *Cheers!*

Ted Danson, star of Cheers

THE SONG: Co-written and sung by Gary Portnoy, it was released as a single twice, in 1983 and 1984. In '83 it broke into the Top 100, but never became a hit. It is among the best-known themes of the '80s. Included by request.

Main Cast

Sam Malone (Cheers owner): Ted Danson
Diane Chambers (waitress): Shelly Long
Carla Tortelli (waitress) Rhea Perlman
Dr. Frasier Crane (Diane's fiance): Kelsey Grammer
"Coach" Pantusso (bartender): Nicholas Colasanto
Cliff Clavin (a patron): John Ratzenberger
Norm Peterson (a patron): George Wendt

Vital Statistics

Half-hour sitcom. NBC. Current.
First aired: Sept. 30, 1982
Most popular time slot: Thursday, 9:00-9:30 PM
Last show: Still in first run.

INSIDE FACTS

MISCELLANEOUS:
• *Cheers* was inspired by a real Boston bar named the "Bull and Finch."
• The show was created by the writers and producers of *Taxi*.
• Most of the cast were TV newcomers. Only George Wendt and Rhea Perlman had appeared in network sitcoms — Wendt in the short-lived *Making The Grade*, and Perlman in an occasional *Taxi*.
• Ted Danson got his start on TV in the soap opera *Somerset* in the '70s.
• Despite critical raves, *Cheers* received low ratings at first. NBC renewed it anyway.
• It went on to win an impressive batch of Emmy Awards, including Best Comedy Program, Best Actress, Best Script, Best Director, etc.

TRIVIA QUIZ

THE SUBJECT IS ...
TV HANGOUTS
Cheers is the name of a bar and a hang-out. Name the shows associated with these other hang-outs:
1. Kelsey's Bar
2. Arnold's Drive-In
3. The Pizza Bowl
4. Mel's Diner
5. The Longbranch Saloon

ANSWERS
1. *All In the Family*
2. *Happy Days*
3. *Laverne and Shirley*
4. *Alice*
5. *Gunsmoke*

Cheers (Where Everybody Knows Your Name)   Words and Music by Gary Portnoy and Judy Hart

Making your way in the world today
Takes everything you've got.
Taking a break from all your worries
Sure would help a lot.
Wouldn't you like to get away?

Chorus:

Sometimes you wanna go
Where everybody knows your name.
And they're always glad you came.
You wanna be where you can see
Our troubles are all the same.
You wanna be where everybody knows
   your name
You wanna go where people know
People are all the same.
You wanna go where everybody knows
   your name.

Climbing the walls when no one calls;
You've lost at love again.
And the more you're down and out,
The more you need a friend
When you long to hear a kind hello.
CHORUS

31

Gilligan's Island

THE SHOW: Skipper Jonas Grumby (you didn't know he had a name, did you?) and his sidekick, Gilligan, set sail on

the SS Minnow with a weird assortment of passengers: Thurston Howell III and his wife (wealthy snobs), Ginger Grant (a glamourous movie star), Roy Hinkley (a research scientist), and Mary Ann Summers (the girl-next-door). It was only supposed to be a three-hour tour. But then the weather started getting rough, the ship was tossed, and...well, you know the rest. Gilligan and the gang were shipwrecked on a tiny uncharted island in the South Pacific for three whole sea-

One of the funniest TV comedians of the '60s — Bob Denver

sons. There were lots of visitors, from cosmonauts to surfers, but somehow the cast never managed to escape. But the real mystery was: why did they pack all that luggage for a three-hour tour?

THE SONG: CBS thought viewers wouldn't understand what 7 people were doing on an island every week, and wanted the show to be about a charter boat instead. Producer Sherwood Schwartz's solution: this song.

Main Cast

Gilligan: Bob Denver
Jonas Grumby (the Skipper): Alan Hale
Ginger Grant (the movie star): Tina Louise
Mary Ann Summers: Dawn Wells
Roy Hinkley (the professor): Russell Johnson
Thurston Howell III (the millionaire): Jim Backus
Lovey Howell III (his wife): Natalie Schafer

Vital Statistics

Half-hour sitcom. CBS. 98 episodes.
First aired: Sept. 26, 1964
Most popular time slot: Saturday, 8:30-9:00 PM (1964-65)
Last show: Sept. 4, 1967
Ranked in a year's Top 25: 1965 (19); 1966 (22)

INSIDE FACTS

BACKGROUND INFO:

• It was inspired by Daniel Defoe's *Robinson Crusoe.*
• The name Gilligan was picked out of the Los Angeles phone book.
• Creator Sherwood Schwartz, who had a degree in psychology, wanted to create a microcosm of American society on the island.
• Each of the 7 characters was supposed to represent a segment of society: "a glamour girl, a country girl, an intellectual, a misfit, a resourceful bull of a man, and a wealthy couple."
• The pilot was filmed in six days on a Hawaiian island, at a cost of $175,000.
• CBS rejected the original pilot. Schwartz then re-edited it, adding a theme song that explained what they were doing on the island. That sold it.

TRIVIA QUIZ

1. What did Mary Ann do for a living before she was ship-wrecked?
2. Where did Gilligan sleep?
3. Gilligan's favorite rock group once landed on the island. What were they called?
4. What did the Skipper do to Gilligan when he got mad at him?
5. What was the Skipper's pet name for Gilligan?

ANSWERS

1. She was a clerk in a country store in Homers Corners, Kansas
2. In a hammock
3. The Mosquitoes
4. Hit him with his hat
5. "Little buddy"

The Ballad of Gilligan's Isle

By Sherwood Schwartz and George Wyle

Just sit right back and you'll hear a
    tale,
A tale of a fateful trip
That started from this tropic port
Aboard this tiny ship.

The mate was a mighty sailin' man,
The skipper brave and sure,
Five passengers set sail that day
For a three hour tour,
A three hour tour.

The weather started getting rough,
The tiny ship was tossed,
If not for the courage of the fearless
    crew,
The Minnow would be lost.
The Minnow would be lost.

The ship's aground on the shore of this
Uncharted desert isle,
With Gilligan,
The Skipper too,
The millionaire and his wife,
The movie star
And the rest
Are here on Gilligan's Isle

OR

The ship's aground on the shore of this
Uncharted desert isle,
With Gilligan,
The Skipper too,
The millionaire and his wife,
The movie star,
The professor and Mary Ann
Are here on Gilligan's Isle.

(*Note:* this ending was added later)

Father Knows Best

THE SHOW: Jim and Margaret Anderson and their three kids — "Princess," "Bud," and "Kitten" — were the classic American sitcom family of the 1950s. They lived at 607 South Maple Street in Springfield, U.S.A., where everything was as pure — and white — as *Ivory Soap.* Mom was the homemaker, Dad (a good-natured insurance agent) was the bread-winner, and the younger Andersons were all basically nice kids. They sometimes found themselves in trouble (nothing serious, of course), but their problems were just part of Growing Up, and provided great opportunities for Dad to show the world how understanding he was. After all, he *did* know best. This scenario may seem a little far-fetched today, but at the time it seemed Right . . . and for seven seasons we secretly wondered why *our* families weren't perfect too.

In the '50s, everyone wished they had a father like Robert Young.

THE SONG: An instrumental that played while the family made its appearance. These are the lyrics originally written for it. "Margaret, I'm home."

Main Cast

Jim Anderson: Robert Young
Margaret Anderson (his wife): Jane Wyatt
Betty Anderson (his daughter): Elinor Donahue
Bud Anderson (his son): Billy Gray
Kathy Anderson (his daughter): Lauren Chapin
Ed Davis (a neighbor): Robert Foulk
Myrtle Davis (his wife): Vivi Jannia

Vital Statistics

Half-hour sitcom. CBS. NBC. ABC. 203 episodes
First aired: October 3, 1954
Most popular time slots: Mon. 8:30–9:00 PM (1958-60),
Tues. 8:00–8:30 PM (1960-61)
Last show: September 17, 1962
Ranked in a year's Top 25 1958 (25); 1959 (14); 1960 (6)

INSIDE FACTS

A QUICK HISTORY:

• It debuted as a radio serial in 1949, on NBC.
• The radio show — also featuring Robert Young — was called *Father Knows Best?* The question mark was intentional.
• It's hard to believe, but after two years on CBS, the TV show was cancelled.
• Irate viewers flooded the nework with letters.
• The result: it was picked up by NBC for the following season, and aired at an earlier time so families could watch it together.
• At the height of the show's popularity, Robert Young decided he was tired of it, and quit.
• It was so popular that re-runs were shown in prime time for 3 more years.

TRIVIA QUIZ

1. What was Bud's real first name?
2. What insurance company did Jim Anderson manage?
3. When Betty and Bud each graduated from high school, where did they go to college?
4. In 1977, the cast got together again for *The Father Knows Best Reunion.* What was the occasion?
5. Elinor Donahue played "the girlfriend" in a '60s and a '70s sitcom. In one she was Ellie Walker, in the other Miriam Wellby. What shows?

ANSWERS

5. *The Andy Griffith Show,* and *The Odd Couple*
4. The Andersons' 35th wedding anniversary
3. State College, in Springfield
2. The General Insurance Company
1. James Anderson, Jr.

Waiting (Theme From "Father Knows Best")

Words: Leon Pober, Music: Don Ferris and Irving Friedman

Wait - ing _____ for love to find you _____ is

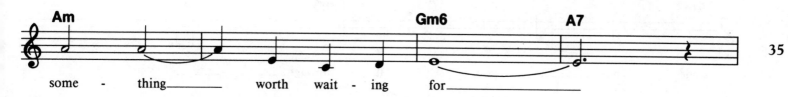

some - thing _____ worth wait - ing for _____

35

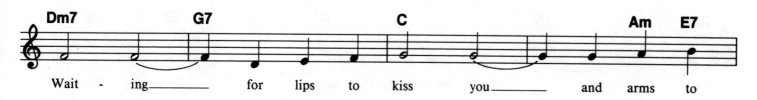

Wait - ing _____ for lips to kiss you _____ and arms to

hold you _____ for - ev - er - more. _____ Oh,

Wait - ing_____ may be so lone - ly_____ But

36

some - how_____ you see it through_____

Know - ing_____ some - where there's some - one Wait - ing

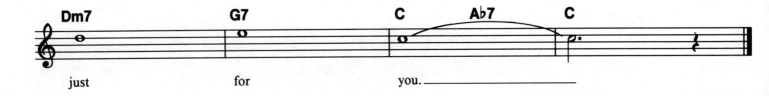

just for you._____

Chico and the Man

THE SHOW: Chico and the Man were TV's *other* odd couple. Chico Rodriguez was a fast-talking, street-wise Chicano; Ed Brown was a cranky old garage-owner in the Barrio of East Los Angeles. Somehow, Chico convinced Ed to hire him as a mechanic, and he moved into an old beat-up truck in the garage. Ed lived there too, so there was bound to be trouble. But even though they always seemed to be fighting, the pair gradually grew closer. In fact, Chico ("Looking good!") became a second son to widower Ed. Things really *were* looking good for this top-rated comedy. Then, half-way through the third season, tragedy struck: Freddie Prinze took his own life. But despite the star's sudden death, the program carried on. Ed adopted a new "Chico" — 12-year-old Raul — who lasted until the series was cancelled.

Freddie Prinze played Chico

THE SONG: Performed by Jose Feliciano, who composed it during a twenty-minute car ride on his way to a meeting with the show's producers — the meeting in which he was supposed to present the song!

Main Cast

Ed Brown (the Man): Jack Albertson
Chico Rodriguez: Freddie Prinze
Louie (the garbage man): Scatman Crothers
Della Rogers (Ed's landlord): Della Reese
Raul (adopted by Ed): Gabriel Melgar
Mando (Chico's pal): Isaac Ruiz
Reverend Bemis: Ronnie Graham

Vital Statistics

Half-hour sitcom. NBC.
First aired: Sept. 13, 1974
Most popular time slot: Friday, 8:30-9:00 PM (1974-76)
Last show: July 21, 1978
Ranked in a year's Top 25: 1975 (3), 1976 (25)

INSIDE FACTS

ABOUT THE "CHICO" CONTROVERSY
- From the outset, there were problems.
- Mexican-American groups protested the use of the term "Chico," which means "boy." They called it demeaning.
- They said the dialogue was racist, and threatened a boycott of the sponsor's products (a sample: the Man to Chico: "Get out of here and take your flies with you").
- They said it was unfair to portray Prinze as a Mexican-American, since he was, in fact, of Puerto Rican and Hungarian ancestry.
- They even complained about the theme song, which is a flamenco-style tune, saying it had nothing to do with Mexican-American music.
- The show was altered to accommodate them, but the theme stayed.

TRIVIA QUIZ

THE SUBJECT IS . . . VIEWER PROTESTS
Chico sparked a protest in 1974 from irate viewers. Here are other TV viewer/network confrontations. Can you name them?
1. Jews and Catholics protested the mixed marriage in this 1972 sitcom
2. Mexican-Americans protested this sombrero-wearing animated ad character in the late '60s
3. When NBC cancelled this series in 1968, it received the most protest letters in its history
4. When ABC interrupted this show to announce the safe return of an imperiled astronaut, it got a flood of irate phone calls

ANSWERS

1. *Bridget Loves Bernie*
2. *The Frito Bandito*
3. *The Monkees*
4. *Batman*

Chico And The Man (Main Theme)

Words and Music: José Feliciano

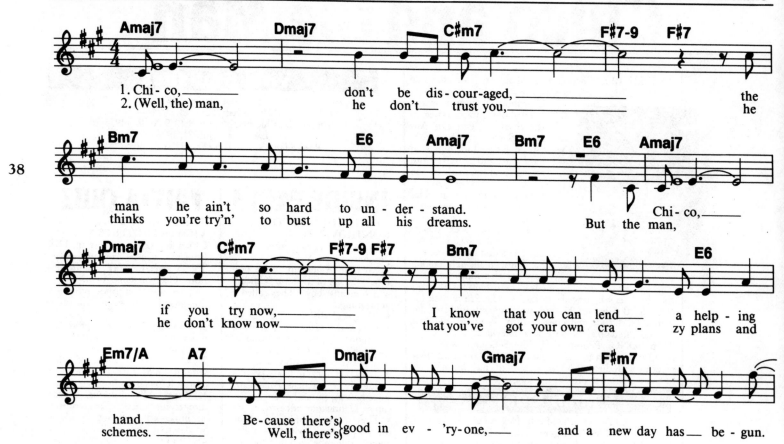

1. Chi - co,_____ don't be dis - cour - aged,_____ the
2. (Well, the) man, he don't_____ trust you,_____ he

man he ain't so hard to un - der - stand. Chi - co,_____
thinks you're try'n' to bust up all his dreams. But the man,

if you try now,_____ I know that you can lend___ a help - ing
he don't know now_____ that you've got your own cra - zy plans and

hand._____ Be - cause there's }
schemes. _____ Well, there's } good in ev - 'ry - one,___ and a new day has__ be - gun.

38

You can see the morn - ing sun____ if you try.____ And

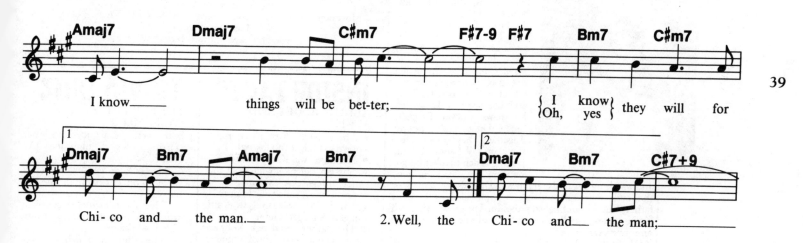

I know____ things will be bet-ter;____ {I know / Oh, yes} they will for

Chi - co and____ the man.____ 2. Well, the Chi - co and____ the man;____

yes they will____ for Chi - co and____ the man.____

39

Gidget

THE SHOW: "Everybody's goin' surfing, surfing USA." In the early '60s, surfing fever swept across America. But TV didn't catch the wave until 1965, by which time the Beatles had already overtaken the Beach Boys as trend-setters. TV's version: *Gidget*, a series about fun, fun, fun in the California sun. Like the popular movie, it chronicled the good-natured antics of Francine Lawrence (Gidget) and her surfer pals — Jeff Matthews (Moon Doggie), Siddo, Larue, and Treasure. Together, they frolicked on the shores of Santa Monica, playing Beach Blanket Bingo, hanging out, hanging ten, and watching assorted gremmies and hodads trying to shoot the curl. Parental guidance was provided by Gidget's father, Russell, an English professor. The show introduced future superstar Sally Field in the lead role, but wiped out after one year anyway.

Sally Field before her career really took off.

THE SONG: Recorded by Johnny Tillotsen, and co-written by Howard Greenfield, whose many credits include *Bewitched* and *Calendar Girl*.

Main Cast

Frances Lawrence (Gidget): Sally Field
Professor Russell Lawrence (her father): Don Porter
Anne Cooper (her sister): Betty Conner
John Cooper (her brother-in-law): Peter Deuel
Jeff Mathews (Moon Doggie): Steven Miles
Larue (Gidget's friend): Lynette Winter
Treasure (a friend): Beverly Adams
Siddo (a friend): Mike Nader

Vital Statistics

Half-hour sitcom. ABC. 32 episodes.
First aired: Sept. 15, 1965
Most popular time slot: Wednesday, 8:30-9:00 PM, Thurs. 8:00-8:30 PM
Last show: Sept. 1, 1966
Never ranked in the Top 25 shows of a year.

INSIDE FACTS
ABOUT GIDGET AND SURFING:

• There really was a surfer-girl known as Gidget (no joking).
• Her name was Kathy Kohner.
• She got her nickname from the other surfers. She explained: "I'm so small [they] called me 'Midget.' I got mad. So now it's Gidget. A girl midget. A gidget. Get it?"
• Her father, Frederick Kohner, wrote a book about her adventures, which was a best-seller in 1957.
• In 1959 it was adapted into a popular movie called *Gidget*, which gave surfing its first national exposure.
• In the film, Sandra Dee played the starring role.
• After she got the TV role, Sally Field revealed that she didn't know how to surf. She had to take lessons from surfer champion Darryl Stolper.

TRIVIA QUIZ
THE SUBJECT IS . . .
SALLY FIELD

Sally went from Gidget to other starring roles in film and TV. Name . . .

1. Her 2 Oscar-winning movies
2. Her convent name in *The Flying Nun*
3. The short-lived TV series in which she played a newlywed with E.S.P. (1973-74)
4. The film in which she co-starred with Burt Reynolds
5. The TV-movie for which she won an Emmy in 1977

ANSWERS

1. *Norma Rae*, and *Places in the Heart*
2. Sister Bertrille
3. *The Girl With Something Extra*
4. *Smokey and the Bandit*
5. *Sybil*

If you're in doubt about angels being
   real,
I can arrange to change any doubts you
   feel.
Wait 'til you see my Gidget,
You're headed for a big surprise.
The way she walks, the way she talks,
You won't believe your eyes.

No work of art can touch you
Like she'll touch your heart.
Everyone who sees her
Thereupon agrees her
Face can replace
The Mona Lisa.

41

If there's a phrase to praise her, it's hard
   to find.
Webster, indeed, would need a new
   book to bind.
Wait 'til you see my Gidget,
The dictionary's out of date.
Compared to her, the words that were,
are only second-rate.

She's got the smile and style that you
   can't resist,
The way she moves just proves angels
   do exist.
Wait 'til you see my Gidget,
You'll want her for your Valentine.
You're gonna say she's all that you
   adore,
But stay away, my Gidget is spoken for.
You're gonna find
That Gidget is mine.

The Partridge Family

THE SHOW: Gee whiz, those Partridges sure have a fun life, don't they? I mean, traveling around in their psychedelic bus, playing rock'n'roll all the time, just bein' stars. I'd give anything if I could do that! And anyway, their mom is so-o-o hip. My Mom wouldn't ever do what theirs does. I mean, wow, my Mom doesn't even know *how* to drive a bus, let alone sing in a rock band. And she's really uptight — not like Mrs. Partridge, who never really gets mad at the kids. She just kinda digs whatever's happening. You know, those guys sure got lucky when they made that record in their garage. I mean, to have a record company buy the song — and *then* to have it be a hit, too! I keep trying to get my brother to record us on his tape recorder, but he says he's too busy. Oh wow! Look, girls, like it's David Cassidy! He is *too* much! Isn't he dreamy? Far out! . . .

The Partridge Family catapulted David Cassidy to stardom

THE SONG: Sung by the Partridges while an animated egg cracked open and little birds paraded out.

Shirley Partridge: Shirley Jones
Keith Partridge: David Cassidy
Laurie Partridge: Susan Dey
Danny Partridge: Danny Bonaduce
Tracy Partridge: Suzanne Crough
Christopher Partridge: Jeremy Gelbwaks (1970-71), Brian Forster (1971-74)
Reuben Kinkaid (their manager): David Madden

Vital Statistics

Half-hour sitcom. ABC. 96 episodes.
First aired: Sept. 25, 1970
Most popular time slot: Friday, 8:30-9:00 (1970-73)
Last show: Aug. 31, 1974
Ranked in a year's Top 25: 1972 (16), 1973 (19)

INSIDE FACTS

THE PARTRIDGE CRAZE:
- They were described by a Screen Gems exec in 1972 as "the Partridge Family money machine."
- Their show, records, and licensed merchandise reportedly earned $11 million a year.
- Merchandise included bubble-gum cards, love beads, bumper stickers, astrological charts, lunch boxes, and lots more.
- A children's-wear manufacturer introduced a line of Partridge fashions.
- 200,000 people paid $2 each for membership in their fan club.
- *The Partridge Family Magazine* sold 400,000 copies a month.
- They sold millions of albums and had 7 Top 40 singles, in spite of the fact that none of them played on the records, and only David Cassidy and Shirley Jones even sang on them.

TRIVIA QUIZ

1. What did Shirley Jones have to learn to do for her role on the show?
2. What was the Partridges' dog named?
3. What was the Partridges' hometown in California?
4. What was Shirley Partridge's marital status?
5. The Partridge Family had 2 Top 10 hits besides "I Think I Love You." Name one

ANSWERS

1. Drive with a stick shift (to drive the bus)
2. Simone
3. San Pueblo — address (for fanatics): 698 Sycamore Road.
4. Widowed
5. "Doesn't Somebody Want To Be Wanted," (#6, 1971), "I'll Meet You Halfway (#9, 1971)

Come On Get Happy (The Partridge Family Theme)

by Wes Farrell and Danny Janssen

Hello world, hear the song that we're
singin',
Come on get happy.
A whole lot of lovin' is what we'll be
bringin'.
We'll make you happy.

We had a dream we'd go travelin'
together,
We'd spread a little lovin' then we'd
keep movin' on.
Somethin' always happens whenever
we're together,
We get a happy feelin when we're
singin' a song.

Trav'lin' along there's a song that we're
singin',
Come on get happy.
A whole lot of lovin' is what we'll be
bringin',
We'll make you happy.
We'll make you happy.
We'll make you happy.

43

Rawhide

THE SHOW: While Marshal Matt Dillon was patrolling Dodge City, and Ben Cartwright was taking care of business at the Ponderosa, trail boss Gil Favor and his trusty ramrod, Rowdy Yates, were out on the trail eating dust. Their endless mission: get a herd of cattle (or "beeves," as the cowhands called 'em) from San Antonio, Texas, to Sedalia, Kansas. It was tough work — but then, these guys were tough *men.* For seven years they hardly ever stopped, except to eat (grub was provided by that classic chuckwagoneer, Wishbone) or to meet some interesting new character who'd provide the story line for the week. Most of the time they kept "them dogies rollin'." An interesting sidelight: *Rawhide* was actually based on the 1860s experiences of a Texas trail boss, whose diaries provided the original inspiration for the show.

Keep them cameras rollin': Rawhide was Clint Eastwood's first starring role.

THE SONG: Sung by Frankie Laine, and written by the composers of *High Noon* and *When You Wish Upon A Star.* Reappeared as a dog food commercial in the '80s.

Main Cast

Gil Favor (the trail boss): Eric Fleming
Rowdy Yates (the ramrod): Clint Eastwood
Peter Nolan (the trail scout): Sheb Wooley
Wishbone (the cook): Paul Brineger
Hey Soos Patines (a drover): Robert Cabaj
Mushy (a drover): James Murdock

Vital Statistics

Hour-long western. CBS. 144 episodes.
First aired: Jan. 9, 1959
Most popular time slot: Friday, 7:30-8:30 PM
Last show: Jan. 4, 1966
Ranked in a year's Top 25: 1960 (18), 1961 (6), 1962 (13), 1963 (22)

INSIDE FACTS

CLINT EASTWOOD'S BIG BREAK:

- He had been "discovered" while he was working at a gas station in 1954 (he was also going to college).
- A screen test resulted in a Universal contract and several forgettable roles in forgettable movies.
- In 1956, he made his first TV appearance on *Highway Patrol.* He also made appearances on the syndicated *West Point* series.
- His big break came when, in 1958, he went to visit one of his wife's friends at CBS.
- While he was in the office, a CBS executive stopped in to visit the same friend.
- The executive knew that *Rawhide*'s producer was looking for an actor to play Rowdy, and, thinking Eastwood looked the part, invited him to read for it. He got the part. Instant star.

TRIVIA QUIZ

Clint Eastwood's role in *Rawhide* made him a star. Rowdy had a few pardners in that department — these 5 stars got "rollin' " as TV cowboys too. In what shows did they get their big breaks?
1. Steve McQueen
2. James Garner
3. Chuck Connors
4. Michael Landon
5. Lee Majors

ANSWERS

1. *Wanted: Dead or Alive*
2. *Maverick*
3. *The Rifleman*
4. *Bonanza*
5. *The Big Valley*

44

Rawhide

By Dimitri Tiomkin and Ned Washington

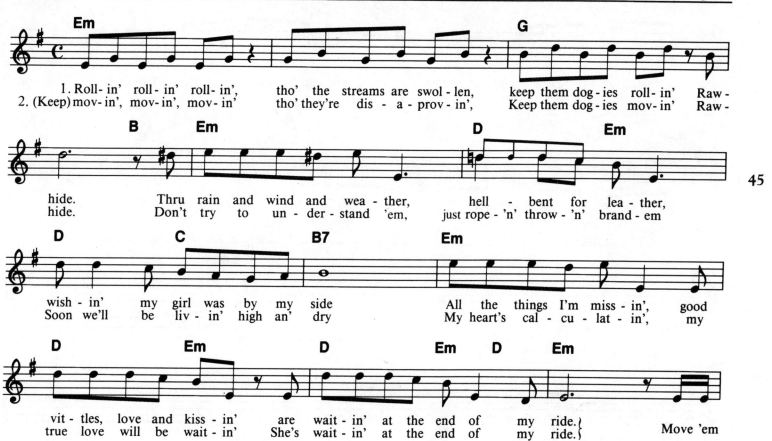

1. Roll- in' roll- in' roll- in', tho' the streams are swol- len, keep them dog- ies roll- in' Raw-
2. (Keep) mov- in', mov- in', mov- in' tho' they're dis - a - prov- in', Keep them dog- ies mov- in' Raw-

hide. Thru rain and wind and wea - ther, hell - bent for lea - ther,
hide. Don't try to un - der - stand 'em, just rope - 'n' throw - 'n' brand - em

wish - in' my girl was by my side All the things I'm miss - in', good
Soon we'll be liv - in' high an' dry My heart's cal - cu - lat - in', my

vit - tles, love and kiss - in' are wait - in' at the end of my ride.
true love will be wait - in' She's wait - in' at the end of my ride.

Move 'em

45

on, head 'em up, head 'em up, move 'em on, move 'em on, head 'em up, Raw - hide! Cut 'em

46

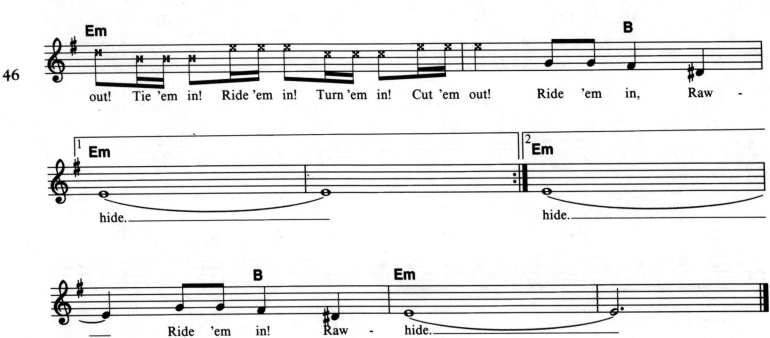

out! Tie 'em in! Ride 'em in! Turn 'em in! Cut 'em out! Ride 'em in, Raw -

hide._____ hide._____

_____ Ride 'em in! Raw - hide._____

Sugarfoot

THE SHOW: Tom Brewster was a peculiar western hero. He liked reading books, hated violence, and was terrible in gunfights (he could barely even shoot straight). In fact, he was so inept at traditional cowboy things that other cowboys had to invent a new term to describe him — "sugarfoot," one step lower than the lowly "tenderfoot." Brewster was an educated Easterner who was studying law with a correspondence school. He traveled west in the 1860s, full of dreams about the romance of the wild frontier, but kept finding trouble instead of adventure. And since he wasn't too handy with six-guns, all he could do was try to bluff his way out of dangerous situations. This method often flabbergasted his enemies. On the first episode of the show, for example, one villain (played by Dennis Hopper) asked him: "Whaddya tryin' to do, talk me to death?" And he was!

Will Hutchins starred as the bumbling cowboy, Sugarfoot.

THE SONG: Sung by a chorus over the credits, it is one of the best-remembered western themes. Included by request.

Main Cast

Tom Brewster (Sugarfoot): Will Hutchins

Vital Statistics

Hour-long western. ABC.
First aired: September 17, 1957
Most popular time slot: Tuesday 7:30 – 8:30 PM (1957-59)
Last show: July 3, 1961
Ranked in a year's Top 25: 1958 (24); 1959 (21)

47

INSIDE FACTS

ABOUT SUGARFOOT'S CRAZY SCHEDULE:

● Although it was in the Top 25 twice, *Sugarfoot* never aired as a weekly series. In fact, you never knew what you'd see in its scheduled time slot.

● In its first year, it alternated each week with *Cheyenne*, starring Clint Walker as Cheyenne Bodie.

● In the middle of the second year, Walker left *Cheyenne* and was replaced by Ty Hardin as Bronco Layne. But the show was still called *Cheyenne*, and it still alternated with *Sugarfoot*.

● In 1959, Walker returned and *Bronco* became a separate series. Now *Cheyenne* alternated with *Shirley Temple*, and *Bronco* switched off with *Sugarfoot*.

● In 1960, *Sugarfoot*'s last year, *Cheyenne*, *Bronco*, and *Sugarfoot* rotated in the same time slot.

TRIVIA QUIZ

THE SUBJECT IS ...
NAMES

Sugarfoot was one of many westerns whose title was the name of its main character. Here are 5 more. Name them.

1. A 6'7" half-breed drifter
2. A Pappy-quoting gambler
3. An ex-Confederate Army captain roaming the west
4. A New Orleans gambler/adventurer who used a little gun. His protection was Pahoo
5. He wore a derby hat, and carried a cane

ANSWERS

1. *Cheyenne* (Cheyenne Bodie)
2. *Maverick* (Bret and Bart Maverick)
3. *Bronco* (Bronco Layne)
4. *Yancy Derringer*
5. *Bat Masterson*

Sugarfoot   Words: Paul Francis Webster, Music: Ray Heindorf and Max Steiner

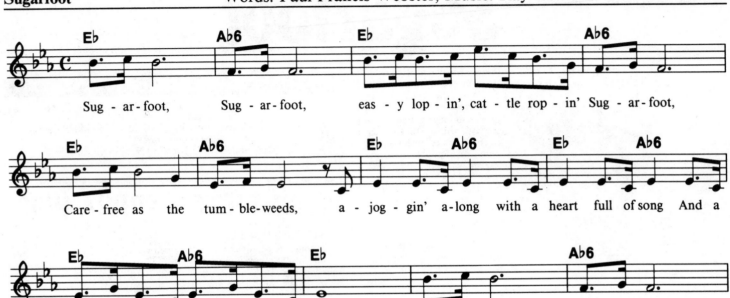

Sug - ar-foot,   Sug - ar-foot,   eas - y lop - in', cat - tle rop - in' Sug - ar - foot,

48

Care - free as   the tum - ble-weeds,   a - jog - gin' a-long   with a heart   full of song   And a

ri - fle and   a vol - ume of   the law.   Sug - ar - foot,   Sug - ar - foot,

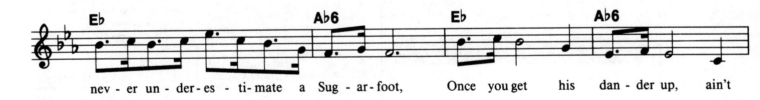

nev - er un - der-es - ti-mate a Sug - ar-foot,   Once you get   his   dan - der up,   ain't

no one who's quick - er on the draw. You'll find him, _____ on the side of law and

or - der, _____ From the Mex - i - cal - i bor - der, _____ to the roll - ing hills of 49

Ar - kan - saw; Sug - ar - foot, Sug - ar - foot, eas - y lop - in', cat - tle rop - in'

Sug - ar - foot, Rid - in' down to cat - tle - town, a - jog - gin' a - long with a

heart full of song And a ri - fle and a vol - ume of the law. _____

The Rebel

THE SHOW: Johnny Yuma, the angry young man with the Confederate Army cap perched on his head, "roamed through the west" after the Civil War. Just what he did there every Sunday night for two years is hard to recall. But presumably it was the standard western stuff — save ranchers threatened by bad guys, save women threatened by bad guys, save towns threatened by bad guys...you know. Actually, there *was* something a little different about this program: it was the first western to show that post-Civil War Americans were confused and angry. Johnny, described by one critic as

Nick Adams as Johnny Yuma, The Rebel.

"TV's first truly tragic hero," was plunged into an identity crisis by the South's humiliating defeat. As he made the rounds of the western settlements, he seemed to be looking for something — a place to settle down, a meaning to life, some peace of mind. No kidding! Apparently, there was no market for even a quasi-philosophical western, as *The Rebel* quickly disappeared. Great song, though.

THE SONG: Johnny Cash's first TV theme. Released as a single, it became a Top 20 Country/Western hit in 1961.

Main Cast

Johnny Yuma: Nick Adams

Vital Statistics

Half-hour western. ABC. 76 episodes.
First aired: October 4, 1959
Most popular time slot: Sunday 9:00 – 9:30 PM (1959-61)
Last show: September 24, 1961
Never ranked in a year's Top 25 shows.

INSIDE FACTS

ABOUT NICK ADAMS:
• This show was the second important "Rebel" in his career.
• The first was his screen debut in *Rebel Without A Cause*; he played a member of the gang that was out to get James Dean (Dennis Hopper was also in the gang).
• After *The Rebel*, Adams played another soul-searching character on a series called *Saints and Sinners* (1962-63).
• He portrayed a crusading newspaper reporter for the *New York Bulletin* named Nick Alexander.

MISCELLANEOUS:
• *The Rebel* was co-produced by Mark Goodson-Bill Todman Productions (*The Price Is Right, Family Feud*, etc.)
• It was one of the few shows they had ever handled that was not a game show.

TRIVIA QUIZ

THE SUBJECT IS . . . 1959
The Rebel debuted in the 1959-1960 TV season. Can you name the Top 5 shows in that season?
1. Matt Dillon had the #1 show
2. Ward Bond kept the settlers headed west in the #2 show
3. Richard Boone starred as Paladin in the year's #3 show
4. A comedian with a big nose co-starred with Marjorie Lord in the family sitcom that was #4
5. Freddie the Freeloader made frequent appearances in the year's #5 show

ANSWERS
1. Gunsmoke
2. Wagon Train
3. Have Gun, Will Travel
4. The Danny Thomas Show
5. The Red Skelton Show

Chorus:
Johnny Yuma was a rebel,
He roamed through the west,
Did Johnny Yuma THE REBEL,
He wander'd alone.

He searched the lands,
This restless lad,
He was panther quick and leather
    tough,
And he figured he'd been pushed
    enough,
THE REBEL, Johnny Yuma
CHORUS

He got fightin' mad
This rebel lad,
He packed no star as he wander'd far
When the only law was a hook and a
    draw,
THE REBEL, Johnny Yuma
CHORUS

51

He was fightin' mad,
This rebel lad,
With a dream he'd hold till his dying
    breath.
He'd search his soul and gamble with
    death,
THE REBEL, Johnny Yuma
CHORUS

The Lawman

THE SHOW: *The Lawman* was a product of the same TV factory that churned out *Cheyenne*, *Maverick*, *Bronco*, and *Sugarfoot* at the height of America's TV western craze in the late 1950s. Though not as well-remembered as its stable-mates today, it was surprisingly popular in its time (perhaps that's because it immediately followed *Maverick* on Sunday nights). The hero of the show was granite-jawed Dan Troop, U.S. Marshal in Laramie, Wyoming — a typical lawless frontier town. And the action was straight cowboy cops'n'robbers, with Troop and his trusty deputy Johnny McKay taking on bandits, rustlers and generic No-good Desperadoes. But the coolest things about Dan Troop were his neatly-trimmed mustache and his string tie. Viewers knew that any Marshal with that much style had to be indestructible; only the ratings could do *him* in.

John Russell played Marshal Dan Troop in The Lawman

THE SONG: Co-written by the team responsible for the themes from *77 Sunset Strip*, *Hawaiian Eye*, *Casper the Friendly Ghost*, and more. Immortal to those who watched the show, and one of the author's favorites.

Main Cast

Marshall Dan Troop: John Russell
Deputy Johnny McKay: Peter Brown
Lily Merrill (saloon owner): Peggie Castle
Jake (bartender): Dan Sheridan
Dru Lemp (cafe-owner): Bek Nelson

Vital Statistics

Half-hour western. ABC. 156 episodes.
First aired: October 5, 1958
Most popular time slot: Sunday 8:30 – 9:00 PM (1958-62)
Last show: October 9, 1962
Ranked in a year's Top 25: 1960 (15)

INSIDE FACTS

ABOUT THE STARS:
• John Russell starred in two other prime-time series besides *The Lawman*.
• His first role was in the 1955 syndicated show, *Soldiers of Fortune*. He played Tim Kelly, a mercenary adventurer.
• This show did so well that it attracted the attention of Warner Bros., which signed him up for *Lawman*.
• Six years after *Lawman* ended, he landed a role on the Robert Wagner series, *It Takes A Thief*, as Agent Dover.
• Peter Brown's next major TV role was on *Laredo*.
• It was a western that ran from 1965-67 on NBC. He played a Texas Ranger.
• Today, Brown is best known for his portrayal of Dr. Greg Peters in the soap opera, *Days of Our Lives*.

TRIVIA QUIZ

THE SUBJECT IS ...
LAWMEN
Like John Russell, these actors played classic western lawmen on TV. Name them:
1. James Arness (1955-75)
2. Henry Fonda (1959-61)
3. Hugh O'Brian (1955-61)
4. Gene Barry (1959-61)
5. Ray Teal (1959-73)

ANSWERS
1. Matt Dillon (*Gunsmoke*)
2. Marshal Simon Fry (*The Deputy*)
3. Wyatt Earp
4. Bat Masterson
5. Sheriff Roy Coffee (*Bonanza*)

Lawman (From the Warner Bros. series "LAWMAN")

Words: Mack David, Music: Jerry Livingston

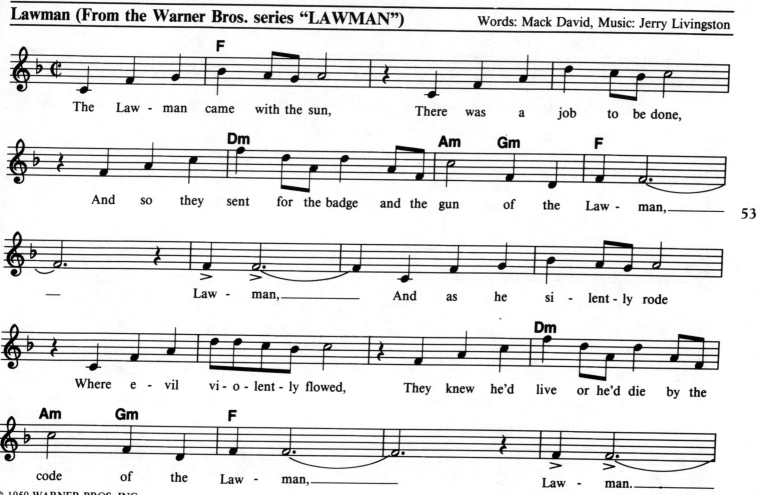

The Law-man came with the sun, There was a job to be done,

And so they sent for the badge and the gun of the Law-man,———

53

— Law - man,——— And as he si - lent-ly rode

Where e - vil vi - o - lent - ly flowed, They knew he'd live or he'd die by the

code of the Law - man,——— Law - man.———

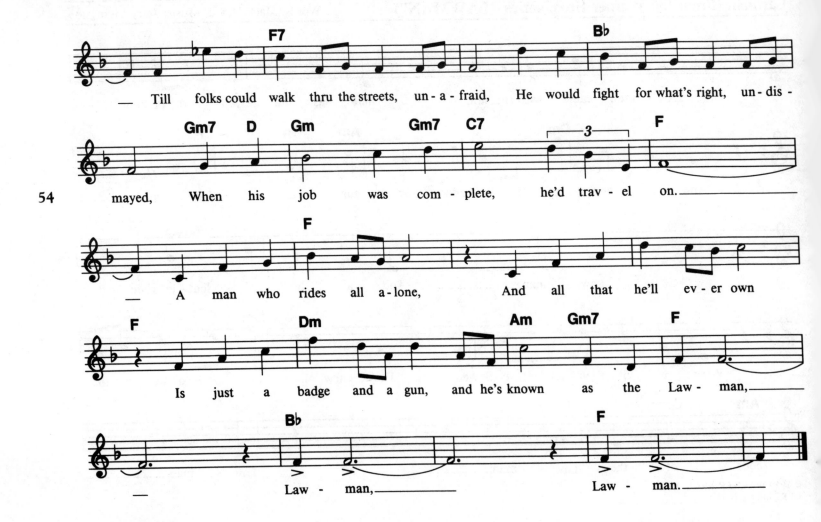

AND
NOW...
A Song From A Sponsor

Brylcreem, A Little Dab'll Do Ya　　　　　　　　　　　　Written by John P. Atherton

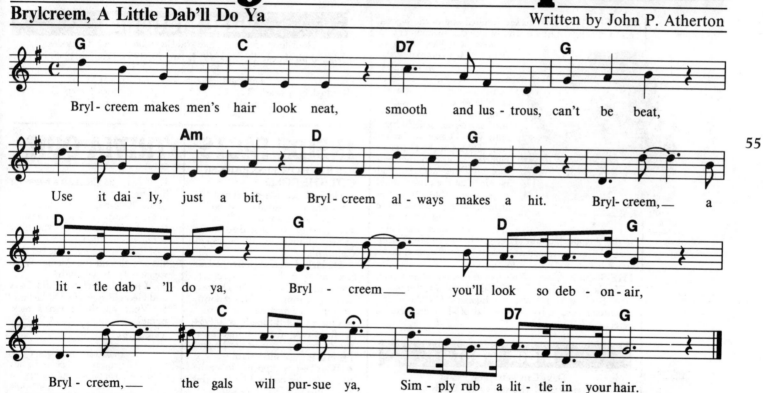

Bryl- creem makes men's hair look neat,　　smooth　and lus- trous, can't　be　beat,

Use　it dai- ly,　just a bit,　Bryl- creem al- ways makes a hit.　Bryl- creem,— a

lit - tle dab - 'll do ya,　Bryl - creem—　you'll look　so deb - on- air,

Bryl - creem,—　the gals　will pur-sue ya,　Sim- ply rub　a lit- tle in　your hair.

55

Davy Crockett

THE SHOW: *Davy Crockett* inspired one of the biggest fads of the 1950s; in a matter of months, merchants sold millions of dollars worth of *Davy Crockett* coonskin caps, bubble gum cards, rifles, fringed jackets, and other items. Its popularity was incredible — especially considering the show never even aired as a regular series! Originally Walt Disney had broadcast "Davy Crockett, Indian Fighter" as just another feature on *Disneyland*. He had no idea that the public would respond so enthusiastically — in fact, the final episode of the scheduled 3-part adventure, in which Crockett was killed

Actor/singer Fess Parker without his coonskin cap

at the Alamo, had already been filmed. To satisfy audiences, Disney resurrected Crockett for a few more episodes about his early days as a frontiersman.

THE SONG: A Top 20 hit four times in the same year, 1955! Parker's version hit #5, Bill Hayes' #1, Tennessee Ernie Ford's #5, and Walter Schuman's #14. An unprecedented record. It has 20 verses, all of which are included here.

Main Cast

Davy Crockett: Fess Parker
Georgie Russel (his sidekick): Buddy Ebsen
Polly Crockett (his wife): Helene Stanley
Mike Fink (his rival): Jeff York

Vital Statistics

Hour-long adventure, aired on *Disneyland*. ABC. 5 episodes.
Original air dates: Dec. 15, 1954; Jan. 26, 1955; Feb. 23, 1955; Nov. 16, 1955; Dec. 14, 1955
Time slot: Wednesday, 7:30 – 8:30 PM
Ranked in a year's Top 25: During original broadcast years, *Disneyland* ranked #6 (1954-55) and #4 (1955-56)

INSIDE FACTS

ABOUT HOW FESS PARKER GOT THE ROLE:
• He had decided to become an actor when he visited Hollywood in 1943 (while he was in the Navy).
• After WW II, he studied drama at the University of Southern California.
• He kicked around Hollywood for five years, making guest appearances on TV shows like *Dragnet*, and appearing in little-known, little-noticed movies.
• One of his B-films was a 1954 sci-fi feature about strange creatures who pop up near the Mojave Desert. It was called *Them*.
• Walt Disney happened to see the film, and decided to hire Fess (his real name) for *Davy Crockett*.
• The show made Parker "TV's first genuine overnight star."

TRIVIA QUIZ

1. What was Crockett's name for his rifle?
2. In 1962-63, Parker starred as Eugene Smith in a sitcom adaptation of a 1939 James Stewart film. What was it called?
3. Davy Crockett was the last man alive to defend the Alamo. What weapon was he left with?
4. What "bullet" trick did Davy and Georgie use to fool Mike Fink?
5. What was Mike Fink's nickname?

ANSWERS

1. Betsy
2. *Mr. Smith Goes To Washington.*
3. Out of bullets, he was using his rifle as a club
4. They made it seem like Davy could catch a bullet in his teeth
5. "The King of the River"

56

The Ballad Of Davy Crockett

Words: Tom Blackburn, Music: George Bruns

1. Born on a moun-tain top in Ten - nes-see, Green - est state in the
2. (In) eigh - teen - thir - teen the Creeks up-rose, add - in' red-skin ar - rows to the
3. Off through the woods he's a - march-in' a - long, mak-in' up yarns an' a

Land of the Free, Raised in the woods so's he knew ev 'ry tree,
coun - try's woes. Now, In - jun fight - in' is some - thin' he knows, so he
sing - in' a song, itch - in' fer fight-in' an' right - in' a wrong. He's

kilt him a b'ar when he was on - ly three. Da - vy,
should - ers his ri - fle an' off he goes. Da - vy,
ring - y as a b'ar an' twict as strong. Da - vy,

Da - vy Crock - ett, King of the wild fron - tier! 2. In
Da - vy Crock - ett, the man who don't know fear!
Da - vy Crock - ett, the buck - skin buc - ca - neer!

57

4. Andy Jackson is our gen'ral's name,
His reg'lar soldiers we'll put to shame,
Them redskin varmints us Volunteers'll tame,
'Cause we got the guns with the sure-fire aim.
Davy — Davy Crockett,
The champion of us all!

5. Headed back to war from the ol' home place,
But Red Stick was leadin' a merry chase,
Fightin' an' burnin' at a devil's pace
South to the swamps on the Florida Trace.
Davy — Davy Crockett,
Trackin' the redskins down!

6. Fought single-handed through the Injun War
Till the Creeks was whipped an' peace was in store,
An' while he was handlin' this risky chore,
Made hisself a legend for evermore.
Davy — Davy Crockett,
King of the wild frontier!

7. He give his word an' he give his hand
That his Injun friends could keep their land,
An' the rest of his life he took the stand
That justice was due every redskin band.
Davy — Davy Crockett.
Holdin' his promise dear!

8. Home fer the winter with his family,
Happy as squirrels in the ol' gum tree,
Bein' the father he wanted to be,
Close to his boys as the pod an' the pea.
Davy — Davy Crockett,
Holdin' his young 'uns dear!

9. But the ice went out an' the warm winds came
An' the meltin' snow showed tracks of game,
An' the flowers of spring filled with woods with flame,
An' all of a sudden life got too tame.
Davy — Davy Crockett,
Headin' on West again!

10. Off through the woods we're ridin' along,
Making' up yarns an' singin' a song,
He's ringy as a b'ar an' twict as strong,
An' knows he's right 'cause he ain't often wrong.
Davy — Davy Crockett,
The man who don't know fear!

11. Lookin' fer a place where the air smells clean,
Where the trees is tall an' the grass is green,
Where the fish is fat in an untouched stream,
An' the teemin' woods is a hunter's dream.
Davy — Davy Crockett,
Lookin' fer Paradise!

12. Now he'd lost his love an' his grief was gall,
In his heart he wanted to leave it all,
An' lost himself in the forests tall,
But he answered instead his country's call.
Davy — Davy Crockett,
Beginnin' his campaign!

58

13. Needin' his help they didn't
vote blind,
They put in Davy 'cause he
was their kind,
Sent up to Nashville the best
they could find,
A fightin' spirit an' a thinkin'
mind.
Davy — Davy Crockett,
Choice of the whole frontier!

14. The votes were counted an' he
won hands down,
So they sent him off to
Washin'ton town
With his best dress suit still his
buckskins brown,
A livin' legend of growin'
renown.
Davy — Davy Crockett,
The Canebrake
Congressman!

15. He went off to Congress an'
served a spell,
Fixin' up the Gover'ment an'
laws as well,
Took over Washin'ton so we
heered tell
An' patched up the crack in
the Liberty Bell.
Davy — Davy Crockett,
Seein' his duty clear!

16. Him an' his jokes travelled all
through the land,
An' his speeches made him
friends to beat the band,
His politickin' was their
favorite brand
An' everyone wanted to shake
his hand.
Davy — Davy Crockett,
Helpin his legend grow!

17. He knew when he spoke he
sounded the knell
Of his hopes for White House
an' fame as well,
But he spoke out strong so
hist'ry books tell
An' patched up the crack in
the Liberty Bell.
Davy — Davy Crockett,
Seein' his duty clear!

18. When he come home, his
politickin' done,
The western march had just
begun,
So he packed his gear and his
trusty gun,
And lit out grinnin' to follow
the sun.
Davy — Davy Crockett,
Leadin' the pioneer!

19. He heard of Houston an' Austin
an' so,
To the Texas plains he jest
had to go,
Where freedom was fightin'
another foe,
An' they needed him at the
Alamo.
Davy — Davy Crockett,
The man who don't know
fear!

20. His land is biggest an' his land is
best,
From grassy plains to the
mountain crest,
He's ahead of us all, meetin'
the test,
Followin' his legend into the
West.
Davy — Davy Crockett,
King of the Wild Frontier!

59

The Carol Burnett Show

THE SHOW: Carol Burnett is one of the great comediennes in TV history. For 11 seasons (incredible, isn't it?) she hosted a one-hour variety series in which she sang, danced, and played a wide range of characters — from Queen Elizabeth to a rag-tag cleaning lady. Of course she had a little help from her friends every week. Her regular ensemble, Harvey Korman, Vicki Lawrence (who looked just like Carol), Lyle Waggoner, and Tim Conway worked together so smoothly that they set a new standard for TV variety shows. And they enjoyed themselves so much that they often burst out laughing in the middle of skits. Among the show's most popular features: "Ed and Eunice," the constantly bickering couple, and "As the Stomach Turns," a parody of soap operas. Every show opened with a question and answer period, and ended with Carol tugging on her ear.

The inimitable Carol Burnett

THE SONG: Written especially as the show's closing theme by Carol's ex-husband and producer, Joe Hamilton.

Main Cast

Regular performers:

Carol Burnett	Tim Conway (1975-79)
Harvey Korman (1967-1977)	Dick Van Dyke (1977)
Lyle Waggoner (1967-1974)	Kenneth Mars (1979)
Vicki Lawrence (1967-79)	Craig Richard Nelson (1979)

Vital Statistics

Hour-long variety show. CBS.
First aired: Sept. 11, 1967
Most popular time slot: Monday, 10:00-11:00 (1967-71)
Last show: Sept. 8, 1979
Ranked in a year's Top 25: 1969 (24), 1970 (13), 1971 (25), 1972 (23), 1973 (22)

INSIDE FACTS

ABOUT CAROL'S CAREER:

• She became one of America's best known comediennes as a regular on *The Garry Moore Show*, from 1959-62.
• In her last year on the show, she won an Emmy for best performance in a music/variety series.
• After she left *Moore*, she tried her hand at films; her first movie: the forgettable *Who's Been Sleeping in My Bed*, with Dean Martin and Elizabeth Montgomery (1963).
• The next year, she hosted her first TV series. Called *The Entertainers*, it lasted less than one full season.
• *The Carol Burnett Show* ranks as the 8th-longest-running music/variety show in TV history, and the 3rd-longest show starring a woman (only Lucille Ball and Dinah Shore topped her).

TRIVIA QUIZ

Carol Burnett's supporting cast is almost as well-known as she is. Which one . . .
1. Was the bumbling Ensign Parker on *McHale's Navy*?
2. Had a #1 hit record the first time into a recording studio?
3. Starred in Mel Brooks' *Blazing Saddles*?
4. Co-starred in *Wonder Woman*?
5. Starred in the Broadway musical, *Bye Bye Birdie*?

ANSWERS

1. Tim Conway
2. Vicki Lawrence (*The Night The Lights Went Out in Georgia*)
3. Harvey Korman
4. Lyle Waggoner
5. Dick Van Dyke

It's Time To Say So Long

Words and Music: Joe Hamilton, Arranged by: Peter Matz

1. I'm so glad we had this time to-geth-er   Just to have a laugh or sing a
2. (There's a) time you put a-side for dream-in'   and a time for things you have to

song.   Seems we just get start-ed and be-fore you know it,   Comes the
do.   But the time I like the best is an-y eve-nin',   I can

time we have to say so long.   2. There's a
spend a mo-ment here with   you.   When the

time comes that I'm feel-in' lone-ly   When I'm feel-in' oh so blue   I just

61

AND NOW... A Song From A Sponsor

Rice-A-Roni

Rice - A - Ro - ni, the San Fran - cis - co treat!—

Rice - A - Ro - ni, it's fla - vor can't be beat — One

pan, no boil- ing, cook- ing ease, — a fla - vor that is sure to please, —

Rice - A - Ro - ni the San Fran - cis - co treat!—

63

American Bandstand

THE SHOW: In 1956, a Philadelphia disc jockey took over as the host of a local TV rock'n'roll show called

The immortal Dick Clark

Bandstand. His name was Dick Clark. Before long, his popularity had attracted the attention of ABC-TV's home office, and the network decided to broadcast the show nationally as *American Bandstand*. It was a wise decision; almost three decades later, Clark has become one of the best-known personalities in TV history, and *Bandstand* has literally become an American institution (the Smithsonian has enshrined the podium Clark used). The most popular part of *Bandstand* was always the dancers, who became celebrities in their own right for awhile. But teenage viewers were also attracted by the stars who showed up to lip-sync their newest releases, and by "Rate-A-Record," in which a panel of judges (teenagers, of course) would rate new singles on a scale of 35-98. How could anyone help but give *American Bandstand* at *least* a 92? After all, it's always had a good beat — and you can still dance to it!

THE SONG: Originally a hit for Les Elgart in 1954, it was adopted by Clark as his theme. Lyrics were added by Barry Manilow as a tribute to the influence of America's favorite dance party.

Main Cast

Host: Dick Clark

Vital Statistics

90-minute rock'n'roll dance party. ABC.
First aired: Aug. 5, 1957
Most popular time slot: Weekdays, after school.
Last show: Still rocking.

INSIDE FACTS

ABOUT THE PERFORMERS:

- Stars who made their TV debuts on *Bandstand* include: Bobby Darin, The Jackson 5, the Mamas and the Papas, the Osmond Brothers, Dionne Warwick, Isaac Hayes, and lots more.
- The only major rock acts of the '50s and '60s who *didn't* appear on the show were Elvis, Ricky, the Beatles, and the Stones

MISCELLANEOUS:

- In its first year as a national show, *Bandstand* announced a dance contest that brought 700,000 applications in the mail.
- The Beatles' "She Loves You" only got a 73 in "Rate-A-Record," so Swan Records passed up the chance to buy American rights to their other tunes.

TRIVIA QUIZ

If you were watching *American Bandstand* regularly in its early years, you heard these hit records played. Who was singing them?
1. "Puppy Love"
2. "Venus"
3. "The Loco-motion"
4. "Be My Baby"
5. "Will You Love Me Tomorrow"

ANSWERS

1. Paul Anka (1960)
2. Frankie Avalon (1959)
3. Little Eva (1962)
4. The Ronettes (1963)
5. The Shirelles (1960)

64

Bandstand Boogie

Words: Barry Manilow and Bruce Sussman, Music: Charles Albertine

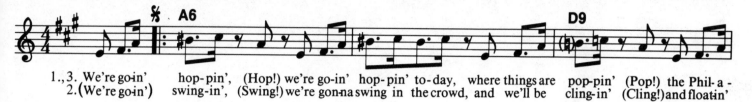

1.,3. We're go-in' hop-pin', (Hop!) we're go-in' hop-pin' to-day, where things are pop-pin' (Pop!) the Phil-a-
2.(We're go-in') swing-in', (Swing!) we're gon-na swing in the crowd, and we'll be cling-in' (Cling!) and floatin'

65

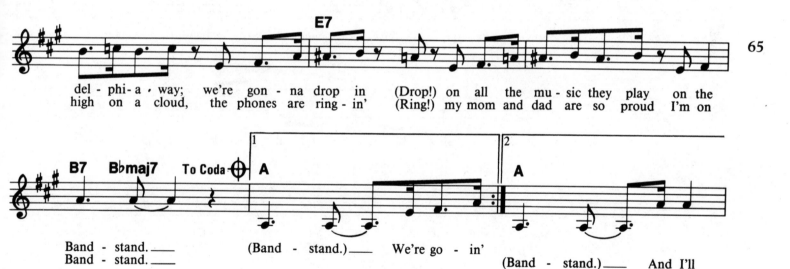

del - phi-a · way; we're gon - na drop in (Drop!) on all the mu - sic they play on the
high on a cloud, the phones are ring - in' (Ring!) my mom and dad are so proud I'm on

Band - stand. _____ (Band - stand.) _____ We're go - in'
Band - stand. _____ (Band - stand.) _____ And I'll

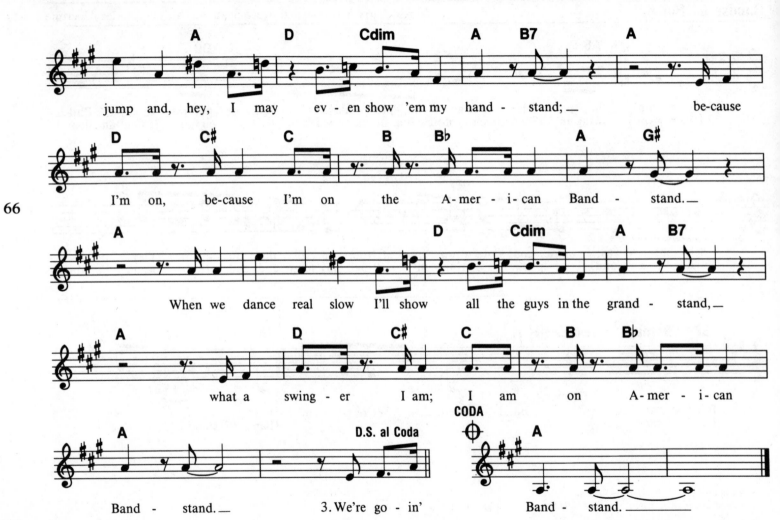

jump and, hey, I may ev - en show 'em my hand - stand; — be-cause

I'm on, be-cause I'm on the A- mer - i - can Band - stand. —

When we dance real slow I'll show all the guys in the grand - stand, —

what a swing - er I am; I am on A- mer - i - can

Band - stand. — 3. We're go - in'

Band - stand. —

66

That Was the Week That Was

THE SHOW: *That Was The Week That Was* (a.k.a. *TW3*) was the *Saturday Night Live* of the '60s: it was broadcast "live from New York," dealt with topical humor, and featured a regular ensemble of young comedy talent that included future stars David Frost, Alan Alda, Tom Bosley, and Buck Henry. Often very funny and always controversial, it was the first American show to feature cutting political satire. Each week, in a mock newscast (sound familiar?), they would parody current events. And in a revue-style format of short skits and musical numbers, *TW3* lampooned public figures from LBJ to the Beatles. One of *TW3*'s unforgettable segments: silent puppet plays about peace, freedom, and love, staged by Burr Tillstrom, creator of Kukla, Fran, and Ollie.

David Frost hosted TW3 in England and the U.S.

THE SONG: Sung at the show's open and close by Nancy Ames, a member of the cast who became a popular singer. The lyrics actually changed every week, as writers filled in the melody with references to the previous week's news.

Main Cast

Elliot Reid (1st host)	Henry Morgan
David Frost (2nd host)	Phyllis Newman
Alan Alda	Pat Englund
Tom Bosley	Buck Henry
Nancy Ames	Burr Tillstrom

Vital Statistics

Half-hour satire. NBC.
First aired: Jan. 10, 1964
Most popular time slot: Tuesday 9:30 – 10:00 PM (1964—65)
Last show: May 4, 1965
Never ranked in a year's Top 25 shows

INSIDE FACTS

ABOUT TW3's ORIGIN:
- It was based on a 1963 British series of the same name, hosted by 24-year-old David Frost.
- The English *TW3* attracted international publicity when a skit in which the Royal Family's barge sank ("And now the Queen, smiling radiantly, is swimming for her life. Her Majesty is wearing a silk ensemble in canary yellow...") prompted a debate in Parliament about banning the show.
- It was adapted to American concerns and aired as a 1-hour special in November, 1963, hosted by Henry Fonda.
- NBC got the greatest immediate response it had ever had for a show, mostly favorable.
- They decided to make it into a regular series a few months later.

TRIVIA QUIZ

THE SUBJECT IS...
THE CAST
Can you name the regular *TW3* cast-member who was also a regular on . . .
1. *The Steve Allen Show* (1961)
2. *I've Got A Secret*
3. *To Tell the Truth*
4. *M★A★S★H*
5. *ABC Stage 67*

ANSWERS
5. David Frost
4. If you don't know, ask someone
3. Phyllis Newman
2. Henry Morgan
1. Buck Henry

That Was The Week That Was

Words: Caryl Brahms and Ned Sherrin, Music: Ron Grainer

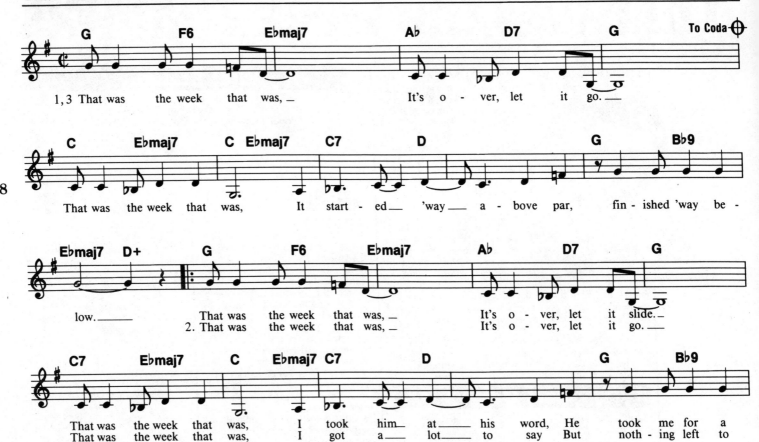

1, 3 That was the week that was, — It's o - ver, let it go. —

That was the week that was, It start - ed — 'way — a - bove par, fin - ished 'way be -

low. — That was the week that was, — It's o - ver, let it slide. —

2. That was the week that was, — It's o - ver, let it go. —

That was the week that was, I took him — at — his word, He took me for a

That was the week that was, I got a — lot — to say But noth - ing left to

69

The Tonight Show

THE SHOW: *The Tonight Show, Starring Johnny Carson,* is the king of the talk shows. But it's more than that; it's American pop culture in action. Since Carson took over as host in 1962, he has been a major influence in shaping American tastes. When, for example, he appeared wearing a Nehru jacket and turtleneck in the mid-'60s, clothing stores were swamped with people who wanted the outfit, too. When he played a game called "Twister" on the air with Eva Gabor in 1966, it took off overnight, becoming the most successful new game of the decade. When 2 of the Beatles wanted to announce their new Apple Records in 1968, the show they wanted to discuss it on was Carson's (surprisingly, Joe Garagiola was guest host that night. Lennon's first words: "Where's Johnny?"). By the late '70s, Carson had racked up more network hours than any performer in TV history, a record that continues to swell as his show goes on and on.

THE SONG: Co-written by Carson (a talented drummer) and singer/composer Paul Anka. There are no lyrics, but even if you don't read music you can sing it! Ready? And now . . . Here's Johnny!

More than a performer, Johnny Carson is a cultural force in America.

Main Cast

Host: Johnny Carson
Announcer/assistant: Ed McMahon
Band leader: Skitch Hendersen (1962-66)
Milton Delugg (1966-67)
Doc Severinsen (1967-   )
Tommy Newsom (1968-   )

Vital Statistics

90-minute, hour-long talk show. NBC.
First aired (starring Johnny Carson): Oct. 2, 1962
Most popular time slot: Weekdays, 11:30 P.M. – 1 A.M.
Last show: Still talking.

INSIDE FACTS

ABOUT JOHNNY'S CAREER:
- After hosting a local L.A. show called *Carson's Cellar* in 1953, and a summer game show in 1954, he got his big break.
- Working as a writer on *The Red Skelton Show* in the 1954-55 season, he was pressed into service as Skelton's one-time replacement when Skelton was injured during rehearsal.
- He did so well as host that he was given a prime-time summer variety show in 1955.
- He then moved to daytime, where he flourished in *The Johnny Carson Daytime Show* in 1956.
- His next program: ABC's game show, *Who Do You Trust?* It became the #1 daytime show.
- When NBC first offered him *The Tonight Show,* to replace Jack Paar, he refused. Then he reconsidered, and took the job.

TRIVIA QUIZ

Can you name some of the more memorable moments in *Tonight Show* history?
1. Ed Ames got one of the longest laughs during a tomahawk-throwing demonstration. What happened?
2. A marriage took place in 1969. Who got married on the show?
3. Carson joked about a shortage of what product, causing a buying panic?
4. Alex Haley, author of *Roots,* surprised Carson with what?
5. What happened when Peter O'Toole flew directly from the set of *Lord Jim* to the *Tonight Show?*

ANSWERS
1. He hit his target dummy exactly in the crotch.
2. Tiny Tim and Miss Vicki Budinger
3. Toilet paper
4. His genealogical chart
5. Exhausted, he became incoherent and had to be led off the stage by Carson

70

Johnny's Theme (The Tonight Show)

Paul Anka & Johnny Carson

71

AND NOW... A Song From A Sponsor

Chock Full o' Nuts Is That Heavenly Coffee

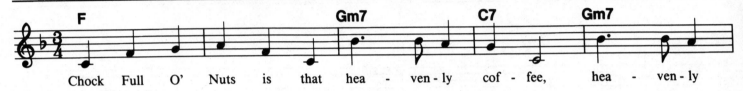

Chock Full O' Nuts is that hea - ven - ly cof - fee, hea - ven - ly

72

cof - fee, hea - ven - ly cof - fee, Chock Full O' Nuts is that hea - ven - ly

cof - fee, bet - ter cof - fee a mil - lion - aire's mon - ey can't buy.

A Song From A Sponsor

Brush Your Teeth With Colgate

Written by Robert Forshaw

Brush   your   teeth   with   Col - gate,   Col - gate   Den - tal   Cream,___   it   cleans   your

73

breath   (what   a   tooth - paste),   while   it guards   your   teeth._____

The Mickey Mouse Club

THE SHOW: Every day was special on *The Mickey Mouse Club:* Monday was "Fun With Music Day," Tuesday was "Guest Star Day," Wednesday was "Anything Can Happen Day," Thursday was "Circus Day," and Friday was "Talent Roundup Day." Hosted by Jimmie Dodd and "the Big Mooseketeer," Roy Williams, the program was a Walt Disney extravaganza of music, song, dance, cartoons, and adventure serials. The thread that held it together was the mouse-hatted Mouseketeers, many of whom starred in the serials. Among the most popular: "The Adventures of Spin and Marty," "The Hardy Boys," "Annette," and "Corky and White Shadow." The Mouseketeers were an extended family to kids everywhere. Everybody was on a first-name basis — Annette, Cubby, Doreen, Tommy, and Darlene were like TV friends. At the end of each show, they would sing their sad farewell. Why? Because they *liked* you.

Many young stars began their careers with The Mickey Mouse Club, including Tim Considine (Spin and Marty) and Don Grady (as a Mouseketeer), both of whom went on to star in My Three Sons.

THE SONG: With Mickey leading a parade of Disney cartoon characters, everybody sang along. Except Donald Duck.

Main Cast

Host: Jimmie Dodd
Co-host: Roy Williams
Some Mouseketeers: Annette Funicello, Darlene Gillespie, Carl "Cubby" O'Brien, Karen Pendleton, Tommy Cole, Bobby Burgess, Johnny Crawford, Lonnie Burr, Don Grady, Doreen Tracey, Cheryl Holdridge, Paul Petersen

Vital Statistics

Half-hour and hour-long children's show. ABC/Syndicated.
First aired: October 3, 1955
Most popular time slot: Weekday afternoons.
Last show: September 25, 1959/Still in syndication

INSIDE FACTS
ABOUT THE MOST POPULAR MOUSEKETEER:

• Over 3000 children tried out for Mouseketeer, but only 24 were selected in the first year.

• Of the 24, Annette Funicello was one of the last picked.

• Disney executives thought she was nice, but not especially talented. They expected Cubby O'Brien to be the star of the show.

• Within a few weeks she was getting more fan mail than any Disney star since *Davy Crockett,* surprising even Uncle Walt.

• Even during reruns she received over 1000 letters a week.

• 1959 was her last year as a Mouseketeer. That year she took a role in *The Danny Thomas Show* and had a part in *Zorro.*

• She went on to become a world-famous movie beach-bunny.

TRIVIA QUIZ

1. Which dancing Mouseketeer went on to star in Lawrence Welk's TV show (as a dancer, of course)?
2. What was the chant when it was time to show a cartoon?
3. Where did the Mouseketeers greet their guests on Talent Roundup Day?
4. How could you tell which Mouseketeer was which?
5. Which cartoon character gave lots of advice on the show?

ANSWERS

5. Jiminy Cricket
4. Their names were on their shirts
3. At a mock stage depot
2. "Meeska, Mooska, Mouseketeer Mousekartoon Time now is here"
1. Bobby (Burgess)

Mickey Mouse March

By Jimmie Dodd

Mick - ey Mouse Club! Mick - ey Mouse Club!

1. Who's the lead - er of the club that's made for you and
2. Here we go a - march - ing and a - shout - ing mer - ri -

me?}
ly:}
M - I - C - K - E - Y M - O - U - S - E!

{Hey, there! Hi, there! Ho, there! You're as wel - come as can be!}
{We play fair and we work hard and we're in har - mo - ny!}
M - I - C -

75

Bb   Bbm   F   C7   F   Bb   *(shout)* Mick - ey - Mouse!

K - E - Y   M - O - U - S - E!   Mick - ey Mouse!   Mick - ey

76

F   *(shout)* Mick - ey Mouse!   G7   C7   *(shout)*

Mouse!   For - ev - er let us hold our ban - ner high!   High!

Gm7   C7   F   Dm   G7

High!   High!   { Come   a - long   and sing   a song   and join   the jam - bor-
{ Boys   and girls   from far   and near,   you're wel - come as   can

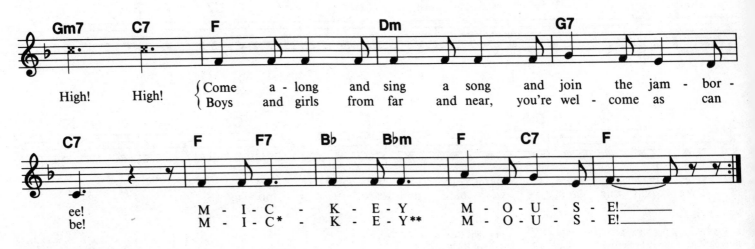

C7   F   F7   Bb   Bbm   F   C7   F

ee!   M - I - C - K - E - Y   M - O - U - S - E!____
be!   M - I - C* - K - E - Y** M - O - U - S - E!____

* *"See you real soon"*
** *"Why? Because we LIKE you!"*

Top Cat

THE SHOW: The story of a feline Sgt. Bilko and his loyal henchmen (henchcats?). In a lane behind police headquarters in Manhattan's 13th Precinct (right off Mad Avenue), a gang of alley cats have taken up permanent residence. Their leader: Top Cat (T.C. to his friends), a master con-artist and opportunist whose main concerns in life are harrassing assorted humans (like cops, milkmen, and garbage collectors) and coming up with sure-fire schemes to keep his gang safe and comfortable. He's got it down to a science: they always have milk, which they systematically swipe from doorsteps; in bad weather they take refuge in the basement of a nearby deli; and for money, T.C.'s always got a plan. The one thing he can't seem to lick is Officer Dibble, who's made a career out of trying to evict or arrest the gang. The other cats: slow (but not stupid) Benny the Ball, eager Choo-Choo, the brainless Brain, Fancy Fancy the fop, pseudo-intellectual Spook, Pierre, and Goldie. *Top Cat* was a prime-time flop, but kids love it in syndication.

Top Cat's voice was provided by Arnold Stang, perennial TV personality. Remember his ads for Chunky candy?

Main Cast

Character's voices:
Top Cat (T.C.): Arnold Stang
Choo Choo: Marvin Kaplan
Benny the Ball: Maurice Gosfield
Officer Dibble: Allen Jenkins

INSIDE FACTS

ABOUT T.C.'S CREATORS, WILLIAM HANNA AND JOSEPH BARBERA

- They created Tom and Jerry for MGM in 1940, in a cartoon called "Puss Gets the Boot." The unnamed cat and mouse were ignored by the studio until the cartoon appeared in movie theaters — where it was a big hit. In fact, it was nominated for an Oscar!
- They began working exclusively on Tom and Jerry, and over the next 15 years, won 7 Oscars.
- One of their most famous pieces: "Anchors Away," in which Gene Kelly's tap-dancing partner is Jerry the Mouse.
- When MGM closed its cartoon studios in 1957, Hanna and Barbera decided to open their own studio and produce low-cost animation for TV.

TRIVIA QUIZ

Test your knowledge of these other Hanna-Barbera shows and characters...
1. Pair of rascally mice
2. Bumbling marshal with sidekick Baba Looey
3. Series based on good-hearted little blue men
4. Penelope Pitstop was a part of these weekly cartoon car races
5. Series based on dot-gobbling video game

ANSWERS

1. Trixie and Dixie
2. Quick Draw McGraw
3. *The Smurfs*
4. *Wacky Races*
5. *Pac-Man*

Top Cat

Words and Music by William Hanna, Joseph Barbera, Hoyt Curtin and Evelyn Timmens

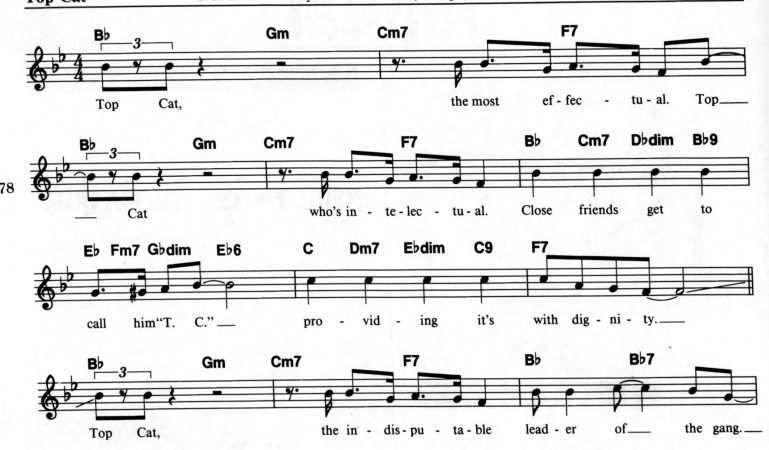

79

AND NOW... A Song From A Sponsor

Sometimes I Feel Like A Nut

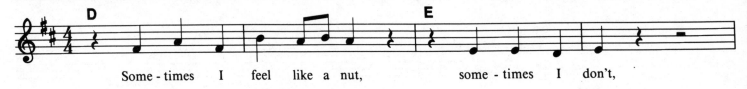

Some - times I feel like a nut, some - times I don't,

80

Al - mond Joy got nuts,_____ Mounds_____ don't,

Al- monds Joy's got cho - co - late, mmm,_____ Munch- y nuts too,_____

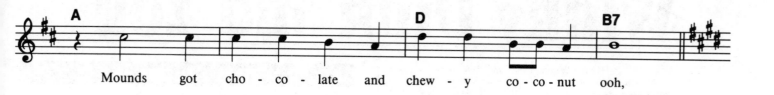

Mounds got cho - co - late and chew - y co - co - nut ooh,

Some - times I feel like a nut, Some - times I don't,

81

Al- mond Joy got nuts,_____ Mounds_____ don't,

Some - times I feel like a nut,_____ some - times I don't...

Winky Dink and You

THE SHOW: *Winky Dink and You* turned viewer participation into an art form — for kids, that is. Here's how it worked: Winky Dink was an animated cartoon boy (with a star for a head) who had adventures with his dog, Woofer. Whenever Winky got into a fix, the show's host, Jack Barry, would call on the audience to save him by drawing a bridge, a rope, or whatever he needed...right on the TV screen! In order to do this, kids had to have (and parents had to buy) a Winky Dink Magic Drawing Kit, which included a protective plastic screen that fit over the TV, crayons, and a cloth for erasing. Of course, a lot of kids who didn't own a Magic Screen ended up drawing directly on the TV (including the author — remember, Mom?). Other features: Jack Barry's inept assistant, Mr. Bungle, and a special coded message that was broadcast bit by bit throughout the show (if you didn't have the Kit, you couldn't decode the secret message). This probably wasn't many parents' favorite show, but kids loved it. It lasted for four years, and was revived briefly in the '60s.

THE SONG: A cult favorite today, it was a catchy tune that had kids singing along about their pal Winky in 1953.

Before Jack Barry became a famous game show host, he hosted Winky Dink and You

Main Cast

Host: Jack Barry
Assistant: Mike McBean
Orchestra: John Gart

Vital Statistics

Half-hour children's show. CBS. Syndicated.
First aired: Oct. 10, 1953
Most popular time slot: Saturday 11:00-11:30 A.M.
Last show: April 27, 1957. Syndicated 1969.

INSIDE FACTS

ABOUT THE HOST:

• Jack Barry began on TV as host of *Juvenile Jury*, a kids' game show, in 1947. It ran until 1955.

• His second regular TV job was on Joe Dimaggio's 1950 kids' show. Joe interviewed children while Barry assisted. His official title: "Club House Manager."

• Barry moved back to Host for his next outing. The show: *Oh Baby*, in which he interviewed babies. Their answers were dubbed in.

• He became a familiar face on adult game shows in the late '50s, hosting *The Big Surprise*, *High-Low*, *The $100,000 Surprise* (co-host with Mike Wallace), *Concentration*, and *Twenty-One*.

• The late '50s scandal in which quiz shows were exposed as frauds almost ruined his career. He couldn't work in TV from 1958-68.

• His comeback: *The Joker's Wild.*

TRIVIA QUIZ

THE SUBJECT IS... CARTOON BOYS

Winky was a popular cartoon boy. Can you identify these other classic TV cartoon boys?

1. On *Captain Kangaroo*, he wore a funnel for a hat
2. He was a dog's pet
3. A Japanese robot boy, he had built-in rockets in his feet
4. The red-haired teenage boy who jumped to TV from comic books and had a #1 record
5. A superstrong cave-boy

ANSWERS

5. Bamm-Bamm Rubble
4. Archie Andrews
3. Astro Boy
2. Sherman
1. Tom Terrific

82

Winky Dink and You

Words and Music: John Gart and John Redmond

Wink - y Dink _____ and you, Wink - y Dink _____ and me, al - ways have a

lot of fun to-geth - er, Wink - y Dink _____ and you, Wink - y Dink _____ and me,

we are pals in fair or storm - y weath - er. All the kids _____ who heard

Wink - y's mag - ic word, make a wish and then they all shout "Wink - o" what a big _____

83

sur - prise right be-fore_____ their eyes, wish - es do come true from say - ing "Wink -

84 o", prest - o, change - o, that's a thing of the past. Wink - o, Wink - o

works twice as fast, Wink - y Dink_____ and you, Wink - y Dink _____ and me,

al - ways have a lot of fun to - geth - er, Wink - y Dink_____ and you,

Wink - y Dink_____ and me, we are pals in fair or storm - y weath - er.

A Song From A Sponsor

I Love Bosco

Written by Joan Edwards & Lyn Duddy

85

I love Bos - co, it's rich and choc - 'la - ty, Choc - 'late flav - ored

Bos - co, is might - y good for me. Ma - ma puts it in my milk for

ex - tra en - er - gy, Bos - co gives me i - ron, and sun - shine Vit - a - min

D. Oh, I love Bos - co, That's the drink for me!

The Jetsons

THE SHOW: "Meet George Jetson . . ." and welcome to the 21st century, where the only thing that's changed since the prehistoric days of Fred Flintstone is technology; suburbia just keeps rollin' along. The breadwinner of the Jetson family is George, a computer digital index operator at Spacely Space Sprockets ("Yes, Mr. Spacely"); his pretty red-haired wife, Jane, is in charge of their home in the Skypad Apartments; Judy is a typical teenager who's in love with rock singer Jet Screamer and loves to dance the "solar swivel." And then there's Elroy, all-boy. Loves to tinker with his inter-galactic space

Penny Singleton is best known as the movies' Blondie — but she's been heard on TV since the '60s as Jane Jetson, George's wife.

set. The rest of the household includes their bumbling pet dog, Astro (who was almost replaced by a mechanical dog when he couldn't stop cat burglars), and Rosie the Robot, an out-of-date household helper the family can't bear to scrap. The Jetsons couldn't make it in prime-time, but as a Saturday morning show they have become a perennial. This was the first show ABC ever broadcast in color.

THE SONG: Not much to it, but it's easily one of the best-known themes on TV, judging by requests.

Main Cast

Characters' voices:
George Jetson: George O'Hanlon
Jane Jetson (his wife): Penny Singleton
Judy Jetson (his daughter): Janet Waldo
Elroy Jetson (his son): Daws Butler
Mr. Spacely (his boss): Mel Blanc

Vital Statistics

Half-hour animated cartoon show. ABC; Rerun on several networks. Syndicated.
First aired: September 23, 1962.
Most popular time slot: Saturday morning
Last show: Still in syndication
Never ranked in the Top 25 shows of a year.

INSIDE FACTS

ABOUT THE JETSONS' SPACE-AGE MACHINES

• One of *The Jetsons'* best features was their space-age gadgets. Here are a few:
• The Food-A-Rack-A-Cycle. A "push-button automat" that automatically delivered any kind of food the Jetsons selected.
• Their home in the Skypad Apartments, which could be "raised or lowered hydraulically to take advantage of the best weather."
• A Seeing-Eye Vacuum Cleaner, with two electronic eyes to search for dirt.
• A Reading Machine. Newspapers and magazines were delivered in micro-tablet form and inserted into the machine, which flipped the pages automatically. By pushing a button, readers could hear photographs talk.

TRIVIA QUIZ

1. What's the Spacely Space Sprocket slogan?
2. Jack Jetwash has a TV exercise program that helps housewives keep a part of their bodies in shape. Which part?
3. From what company did the Jetsons get Rosie?
4. Where does George walk Astro?
5. What's Mr. Spacely's first name?

ANSWERS

5. Cosmo G.
4. On a treadmill outside their apartment
3. The U-Rent-A-Robot Maid Service
2. Their fingers. From pushing all those buttons, 21st century suburbanites get "Push-button finger" if they're not careful
1. "Spacely Sprocket, easy on the pocket."

The Jetsons

Words and Music by Hoyt Curtin, William Hanna and Joseph Barbera

87

Meet George Jet - son.

Jane, his wife.

Daugh - ter Ju - dy.

His boy El - roy.

And Ro - sy, the Ro - bot Maid.__

The Flintstones

THE SHOW: When *The Flintstones* hit prime time in 1960, they started a national craze. TV had finally let cartoons out of the Saturday morning closet, putting them where "respectable" teenagers and adults could enjoy them openly. Everyone watched, and *The Flintstones* became the first cartoon show ever to rank in the top 25 shows of a year. It was essentially an animated version of *The Honeymooners*, with an obvious gimmick — it all took place in the Stone Age. The Flintstones lived in suburban Bedrock (pop. 2500) where Fred commuted to his job at the local quarries every day in his stone-wheeled car (which was foot-propelled). Wilma was the housekeeper, using prehistoric devices like a baby Mastodon vacuum cleaner and shopping for brontosaurus steaks at the supermarket. Next-door neighbors Barney and Betty Rubble shared in most of the adventures. Eventually both couples became parents, and Pebbles Flintstone and Bamm-Bamm Rubble became staples of the Hanna-Barbera Saturday morning cartoon entourage.

THE SONG: Easily the most famous TV cartoon song ever. Everybody likes to sing along with this one!

Alan Reed and Jean VanderPyl, the voices of Fred and Wilma Flintstone

Main Cast

Character's voices:
Fred Flintstone: Alan Reed
Wilma Flintstone: Jean VanderPyl
Barney Rubble: Mel Blanc
Betty Rubble: Bea Benaderet, Gerry Johnson

Vital Statistics

Half-hour animated cartoon show. ABC (1960-66). Syndicated.
First aired: Sept. 30, 1960
Most popular time slot: Friday 8:30-9:00 PM (1960-62)
Thursday 7:30-8:00 PM (1963-64)
Last show: Still in syndication
Ranked in a year's Top 25: 1961 (18); 1962 (21)

INSIDE FACTS

ABOUT ITS ORIGIN:

• When a survey showed that 65% of the audience for Hanna-Barbera cartoons were adults, the company decided to do a cartoon specifically aimed at them.
• Their first idea: a satire on modern suburban life, to be aired in prime time.
• The problem: they just couldn't make it funny enough.
• The magic moment: one of their cartoonists idly drew a picture of a suburban man in a convertible, and gave it a prehistoric look — the fins (this was the late '50s) were made of tree trunks, the roof was thatched.
• As everyone cracked up laughing, it suddenly dawned on them that they'd found the hook they were looking for — Stone Age suburbia!

TRIVIA QUIZ

1. Where did Fred work?
2. What was Fred's favorite meal?
3. Who was Fred's boss?
4. What was the name of the lodge Fred and Barney were members of?
5. Who was the lawyer who never lost a case, who appeared on the show?

ANSWERS

5. Perry Masonry
4. The Loyal Order of Water Buffaloes
3. Mr. Slate
2. Brontosaurus burgers and cactus juice
1. The Rock Head and Quarry Cave Construction Co.

(Meet) The Flintstones

Words and Music by Hoyt Curtin, William Hanna and Joseph Barbera

89

The Road Runner

THE SHOW: The theme song calls him "poor little Road Runner," but it's doubtful that Wile E. Coyote would call him that...*if* he could talk. Because, as anyone who's ever watched a Road Runner cartoon knows, the Road Runner always wins, and Wile E. always gets flattened, fried, or blasted (usually all three). Every cartoon is the same: the speedy hero (Accelerati Incredibus) is spied as he zooms along the road by his crafty — and hungry — natural enemy (Carnivorous Vulgaris), Wile E. Coyote (let's hear it for the underdog!). Wile E. receives a package from the Acme Corp. opens it, and surprise! It's an anti-Road Runner device, like a giant rubber-band slingshot rocket-sled missile with a bomb attached. Wile E. assembles it and painstakingly sets it in place, ready to spring the trap and catch his dinner. "Beep-beep!" The smiling Road Runner speeds along, spots the booby-trap, and darts out of danger in the nick of time. Wile E., meanwhile, plummets off a cliff as the bomb explodes in his hands. Some viewers complained of too much violence, but no permanent damage was ever done. Each time, the coyote would pop back up, ready to try again. And again. And again. "Beep-beep!"

THE SONG: Almost a tongue-twister, sung by a chorus as the bird zooms across the desert. "Beep-beep!"

Perhaps the most versatile voice talent in history, Mel Blanc provided the sound effects (Beep-Beep!) in Road Runner

Main Cast

Voice characterizations by Mel Blanc

Vital Statistics

Half-hour animated cartoon show. CBS. ABC.
First aired: Sept. 2, 1967
Most popular time slot: Saturday morning
Last show: Still running.

INSIDE FACTS
ABOUT THE CHARACTERS:

● They were created by Chuck Jones, who is also one of Bugs Bunny's "creators."
● They were introducd in a 1948 cartoon, "Fast and Furry-ous."
● Jones meant it as a parody, but since no one took it that way, he started doing Road Runner straight.
● The coyote was inspired by Jones' own ineptitude with tools.
● He introduced the Acme Corporation because he thought it would be funnier to have mail order gadgets than to see the coyote improvise traps.
● Jones tried giving Wile E. a voice for awhile, but audiences liked him better silent.
● Road Runner is one of the only cartoon characters to have a car named for him — the Plymouth Road Runner.

TRIVIA QUIZ
THE SUBJECT IS . . .
CARTOON BIRDS

Road Runner is a famous cartoon bird. Can you name these other cartoon birds?
1. The talking Magpies
2. Sylvester's desire
3. Donald's nephews
4. Chicken Hawk who doesn't know what a chicken looks like
5. Super-strong duck in diapers

ANSWERS
1. Heckle and Jeckle
2. Tweety Bird
3. Huey, Louie, and Dewey
4. Henery the Chicken Hawk
5. Baby Huey

90

The Road Runner

By Barbara Cameron

Road Runner, the coyote's after you.
Road Runner, if he catches you you're
through.

Road Runner, the coyote's after you.
Road Runner, if he catches you you're
through.

The coyote's really a crazy clown.
When will he learn that he can never
mow him down?
Poor little Road Runner never bothers
anyone.
Running down the road's his idea of
having fun.

Repeat CHORUS

91

Woody Woodpecker

THE SHOW: Woody Woodpecker was already a world-famous bird by the time he pecked his way onto television in 1957 — for seventeen years he'd entertained movie audiences by making trouble for Wally Walrus (and an assortment of other victims), and laughing maniacally whenever he succeeded ("Ha-ha-ha-HA-ha!"). But when he came to TV, several changes were made. First: TV censors insisted on editing out all scenes from his movie cartoons that included "tipsy horses, tobacco-spitting grasshoppers, and neurotic birds." Second: In order to appeal to new viewers, Walter Lantz (Woody's creator) made him cuter and friendlier than he'd been in films. Lantz also appeared on Woody's show as the host, demonstrating animation techniques and introducing other crazy creatures: Andy Panda, Chilly Willy, Gabby Gator, Space Mouse and Charley Bear. But of course Woody always got the last laugh. Ha-ha-ha-HA-ha!!!

Walter and Grace Lantz, the creator and voice of Woody Woodpecker.

THE SONG: A swing-era #1 hit for Kay Kyser's big band in the '40s (pre-TV) and a perennially popular kids' tune.

Main Cast

Host: Walter Lantz

Vital Statistics

Half-hour animated cartoon. ABC, NBC, syndicated.
First aired: Oct. 3, 1957
Most popular time slot: Determined locally
Last show: Still in syndication.

INSIDE FACTS

ABOUT WOODY:
● Walter Lantz's inspiration for creating him came from a real woodpecker that pecked on Lantz's roof until the roof needed replacing.
● When Lantz got frustrated trying to get rid of the bird, his wife suggested it would make a great cartoon character.
● He first appeared in 1940, in an Andy Panda cartoon called "Knock, Knock," and 6 months later was in a cartoon with his name as the title. Instant stardom.
● His voice was supplied by a woman — Gracie Stafford Lantz, the wife of his creator.

ABOUT THE SONG:
● It was introduced in a 1948 cartoon called "Wet Blanket Policy."
● It was the only Oscar nominee ever to originate in a cartoon short.

TRIVIA QUIZ

THE SUBJECT IS . . . CARTOON CREATORS
Woody is a Walter Lantz creation. Can you name the men who created these TV cartoon characters?
1. Fred Flintstone
2. Bullwinkle the Moose
3. Beany and Cecil
4. Mighty Mouse
5. Felix the Cat

ANSWERS
1. Hanna and Barbera
2. Jay Ward
3. Bob Clampett
4. Paul Terry
5. Otto Messmer, or Joe Oriolo (for TV)

The Woody Woodpecker Song

Words and Music by George Tibbles and Ramey Idriss

Ha ha ha ha ha, ha ha ha ha ha,— That's the Wood-y Wood-peck-er song.—

— Ha ha ha ha ha, ha ha ha ha ha,— He's a-

93

peck-in' it all day long.— He pecks a few holes in a

tree, to see, if a red-wood's real-ly red,— And it's

noth-ing to him— on the tin-i-est whim— to peck a few holes in your

Magilla Gorilla

THE SHOW: Magilla Gorilla, according to a 1964 Hanna-Barbera press release, was born in the small banana-mining town of Simian Springs, Africa. His parents were both professionals — his mother worked in the circus, and his father worked with Albert Schweitzer on several experiments — so it made sense for him to move to Hollywood to become an actor. He was discovered in Schwab's Drug Store, eating a banana split (that's what it says, anyway). In the show, Magilla is a crazy ape who's become a permanent resident of Mr. Peebles' Los Angeles pet shop (where he's on display in the store window). Peebles keeps trying to sell his gorilla, but buyers keep bringing Magilla back. Which makes Magilla — who's got a comfortable rocking chair and his own TV at the store — very happy, but keeps Mr. Peebles in a state of shock. Other characters on the show: Ricochet Rabbit (The Fastest Sheriff in the West), and two Pennsyltucky hillbillies, Punkin Puss and Mush Mouse.

TV veteran Howard Morris, whose credits include Ernest T. Bass on Andy Griffith and The Sid Caesar Show, was the voice of Mr. Peebles.

Main Cast

Characters' voices:
Magilla Gorilla: Allan Melvin
Mr. Peebles: Howard Morris
Ogee: Jean VanderPyl
Ricochet Rabbit: Don Messick
Droop-A-Long: Mel Blanc
Mush Mouse: Howard Morris
Punkin Puss: Allan Melvin

Vital Statistics

Half-hour animated cartoon show. Syndicated 1964. ABC (1966-67).
58 episodes.
First aired: 1964
Most popular time slot: Determined locally.
Last show: Still in syndication

95

INSIDE FACTS

MORE CELEBRITY VOICES BEHIND HANNA-BARBERA CARTOONS:
• In *The Pebbles and Bamm-Bamm Show*, which first aired in 1971, Pebbles' voice was supplied by Sally (*All In The Family*) Struthers, and Bamm-Bamm's by Jay (*Dennis the Menace*) North.
• Harvey (*The Carol Burnett Show*) Korman was the voice of The Great Gazoo, Fred Flintstone's space-man friend.
• When *I Dream of Jeannie* was adapted to a cartoon in 1973, her "master" became Corey Anders, a high school surfer. Corey's voice: Mark (Luke Skywalker) Hamill.
• In the 1972 series, *Jonny Quest*, Jonny's voice was provided by Tim Matheson, star of *Animal House*.
• Other H-B regulars included Dom Deluise, Ross Martin, Gary Owens, Henry Winkler.

TRIVIA QUIZ

Magilla is just one of several TV stars who might've come from Simian Springs. These others each starred in a TV show. Name the show.
1. Judy the Chimp
2. Enoch, Charlie, and Candy (3 show-biz chimps)
3. J. Fred Muggs
4. Chim (a chimp)
5. The Evolution Revolution (a chimp rock group)

ANSWERS

1. *Daktari* (1966-69)
2. *The Hathaways* (1961-62)
3. *The Today Show*
4. *Sheena, Queen of the Jungle* (1955-56)
5. *Lancelot Link, Secret Chimp* (1970-71)

Magilla Gorilla

Words and Music by Hoyt Curtin, William Hanna and Joseph Barbera

96

We've got a go-ril-la for sale, ___ Ma-gil-la Go-ril-la for sale ___ Won't you buy 'im take 'im home and try 'im. Go-ril-la for sale. ___ See in the win-dow Ma-gil-la Go-ril-la, full of charm and ap-peal, ___ hand-some, el-e-gant, in-tel-li-gent, sweet. He's real-ly i-

deal. Don't-cha wan-na l'il go-ril-la you can call your own,— A go-

ril-la who'll be with you when you're all a-lone.— Go-ril-la, Ma-gil-la Go-ril-

97

Spoken

-la for sale. How much is that go-ril-la in the win-dow? Take

our ad-vice, at an-y price a go-ril-la like Ma-gil-la is

might-y nice. Go-ril-la, Ma-gil-la Go-ril-la for sale. ___

Scooby Doo, Where Are You?

THE SHOW: As a hero, Scooby-Doo isn't exactly Lassie or Rin Tin Tin — he's closer to the cowardly lion in *The Wizard of Oz.* At the first hint of trouble, the large, lovable Great Dane runs in the opposite direction as fast as he can, leving his masters calling "Scooby-Doo, where are you???" Usually Scooby can be found with his head buried under his paws. Scooby and his four high-school pals — Freddy, Daphne, Velma, and Shaggy — spend most of their time cruising around in a vehicle called the "Mystery Machine," investigating and trying to solve mysterious supernatural puzzles. Somehow it's always Scooby — the cowardly canine — who accidentally stumbles on the key clue and uncovers the answer. Whatever Scooby's magic is, it works on real kids, too. He's the star of the longest-running TV cartoon series in history. His show has surfaced as *The New Scooby-Doo Movies, The Scooby-Doo/Dynomutt Hour, Scooby's All-Star Laff-A-Lympics,* and several other incarnations. And there'll undoubtedly be more from Hanna-Barbera.

Casey Kasem is a well-known announcer whose rock shows are seen coast-to-coast. He's also the voice of Shaggy.

98

Main Cast

Characters' voices:
Scooby Doo (a dog): Don Messick
Freddy (his friend): Frank Welker
Daphne (his friend): Heather North
Shaggy (his friend): Casey Kasem
Velma (his friend): Nichole Jaffe

Vital Statistics

Half-hour, one-hour, 90 minute & two-hour cartoon show. CBS. ABC.
First aired: September 13, 1969
Most popular time slot: Saturday morning
Last show: Currently in production

INSIDE FACTS
ABOUT HANNA-BARBERA STUDIOS:

• It is the largest animation studio in the world.
• In 1957, they introduced their first made-for-TV cartoon series, *Ruff and Ready.*
• Since then they have produced over 250 series, specials, and features.
• Most of their shows are still in syndication. They have been seen by an estimated 500 MILLION people in 80 countries!
• To see everything that the Hanna-Barbera Studios have ever produced, a person would have to watch TV 24 hours a day, every day, for 2 months!
• They have won 8 Emmy Awards, and William Hanna and Joseph Barbera have their own star on Hollywood's Walk of Fame.

TRIVIA QUIZ

THE SUBJECT IS . . . CARTOON DOGS

Scooby was one of a long line of TV cartoon dogs. Can you name these other 5?
1. A Shoeshine Boy who became a super-hero
2. Penrod Pooch battles crime disguised as . . .
3. Mr. Magoo's dog
4. Half of the *Oddball Couple*
5. Inventor of the Wayback Machine

ANSWERS

1. Underdog
2. Hong Kong Phooey
3. McBarker
4. Fleabag
5. Mr. Peabody (from *The Bullwinkle Show*)

Scooby Doo

Words and Music by Hoyt Curtin, William Hanna and Joseph Barbera

99

Yogi Bear

THE SHOW: If you're visiting Jellystone National Park, be sure to hold on to your pic-a-nic baskets! Because Jellystone is Yogi Bear's home territory — and Yogi ("I'm smarter than the av-er-age bear!") is always devising new schemes to separate campers from their lunches. His cautious accomplice and cavemate is little Boo-Boo Bear ("Hey Boo-BOO!"), who thinks Yogi is the greatest. And his nemesis — usually the only thing between Yogi and a full stomach — is Jellystone's Park Ranger, John Smith. Ranger Smith is determined to catch Yogi, making life more bear-able for park visitors, but most of the time Yogi manages to stay one step ahead of him, proving that Yogi is smarter than the av-er-age ranger, too. Also featured on the show: Snagglepuss, the cowardly lion, and Yakky Doodle, a goofy little duck. On the strength of Daws Butler's voice, Yogi has practically become an American institution.

Daws Butler, the incredible voice of Yogi, Huckleberry Hound, Snagglepuss, Mr. Jinks, Elroy Jetson, Cap'n Crunch, Quick-Draw McGraw, and dozens more

100

Main Cast

Characters' voices:
Yogi Bear: Daws Butler
Boo Boo Bear (his accomplice): Don Messick
Ranger Smith: Don Messick
Snagglepuss: Daws Butler
Yakky Doodle: Jimmy Weldon
Chopper: Vance Colvig

Vital Statistics

Half-hour cartoon show. Syndicated 1958. 123 episodes.
First aired: 1958
Most popular time slot: Determined locally.
Last show: Still in syndication

INSIDE FACTS

MISCELLANEOUS:

• Yogi's name was inspired by American pop culture hero Yogi Berra, an all-star catcher for the New York Yankees.

• He first appeared on the *Huckleberry Hound Show*, and became so popular that he was quickly given his own program.

• A measure of success: in 1960, a group called The Ivy Three released a novelty record called "Yogi" which reached #8 on the national charts. Sample lyrics: "I'm a Yo-gi. A Yogi bay-bee. Hey Boo-booooo."

• By 1964 he was popular enough for Hanna-Barbera to release a feature-length movie. The title: *Hey There, It's Yogi Bear.*

• He was revived in the '70s in *Yogi's Gang* and *Yogi's Space Race*, fighting pollution instead of snatching picnic baskets.

TRIVIA QUIZ

THE SUBJECT IS ...
BEARS
Yogi's one of TV's most famous bears. Name these other TV bears:
1. "Only YOU can prevent forest fires "
2. Featured on "The Life and Times of Grizzly Adams "
3. Co-starred with Dennis Weaver in a series named for him
4. Kermit's Muppet friend
5. A bunch of animated bears named Hair, Square, and Bubi

ANSWERS:
1. Smokey
2. Ben
3. Gentle Ben
4. Fozzy
5. The Hair Bear Bunch

Yogi Bear Song

Words and Music by William Hanna, Joseph Barbera and Hoyt Curtin

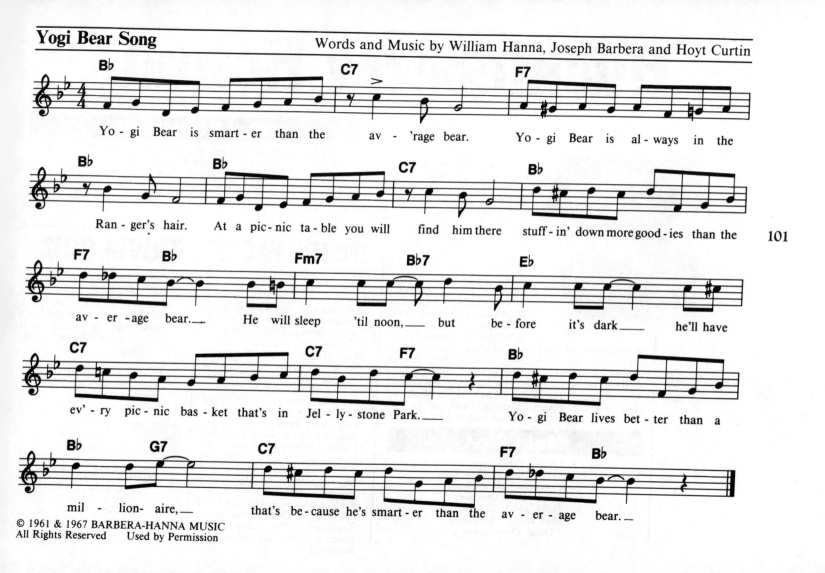

101

Huckleberry Hound

THE SHOW: Huckleberry Hound was TV's first original cartoon superstar. His syndicated show aired at 7:00 P.M., early enough for the kids to catch, but late enough for curious adults to watch too. And they did! Huck was a slow-moving, slow-thinking "canine Don Quixote" who turned up as a different character in every cartoon. In one episode he was in the French Foreign Legion. In another, he was the Purple Pumpernickel, a swashbuckling hero fighting a tyrant who wouldn't let his subjects pay their taxes with credit cards. In another adventure, he was a brilliant scientist who saved America from "an Idaho potato with an evil brain." Whatever the challenge, Huck always proved unstoppable, even if bricks fell on his head ("That smarts ") or he was clobbered by a falling tree ("Man, that was a right heavy tree ") Other characters featured: Yogi Bear, Hokey Wolf, and "those miserable meeces," Pixie and Dixie, taunting Mr. Jinks to distraction ("I hate you meeces to pieces!").

On Huckleberry Hound, Don Messick provided Pixie and Dixie's voices. Other voices: Boo-Boo Bear, Scooby-Doo, Ricochet Rabbit, and dozens more.

Main Cast

Characters' voices:
Huckleberry Hound: Daws Butler
Pixie (a mouse): Don Messick
Dixie (a mouse): Don Messick
Mr. Jinks (a cat): Daws Butler
Hokey Wolf: Daws Butler
Ding: Doug Young

Vital Statistics

Half-hour animated cartoon show. Syndicated 1958. 195 episodes.
First aired: 1958
Most popular time slot: Determined locally
Last show: Still in syndication

INSIDE FACTS

MISCELLANEOUS:
● Huckleberry Hound won an Emmy in 1959 for "Outstanding Achievement in the Field of Children's Programming" — the first animated cartoon to do so.
● It was also popular with adults, however. For example: scientists at the White Sands, N.M. Proving Grounds sent a letter to Hanna-Barbera asking that it be shown later in the evening, so they could see it, too.
● Another example: when the crew of a Coast Guard icebreaker stationed in Antarctica discovered an uncharted island in 1959, they voted to name it after their favorite TV character. — Huckleberry Hound!
● Huck was created to fit a voice invented by Daws Butler — "a Tennessee homespun guy who never got mad, no matter what happened."

TRIVIA QUIZ

THE SUBJECT IS ...
EMMY AWARDS
Huckleberry Hound won an Emmy in 1960 for excellence in children's programming. True or False: each of the following kids' shows has also won an Emmy.
1. *Lassie*
2. *Howdy Doody*
3. *Sesame Street*
4. *Ding Dong School*
5. *Kukla, Fran, and Ollie*

ANSWERS
1. True, in 1954 and in 1955
2. False. Surprisingly, it never did
3. Of course — many, beginning in 1969-70
4. Nope. Poor Miss Francis!
5. True, in 1953 and in 1970-71

102

Huckleberry Hound Song

Words and Music by Hoyt Curtin, William Hanna and Joseph Barbera

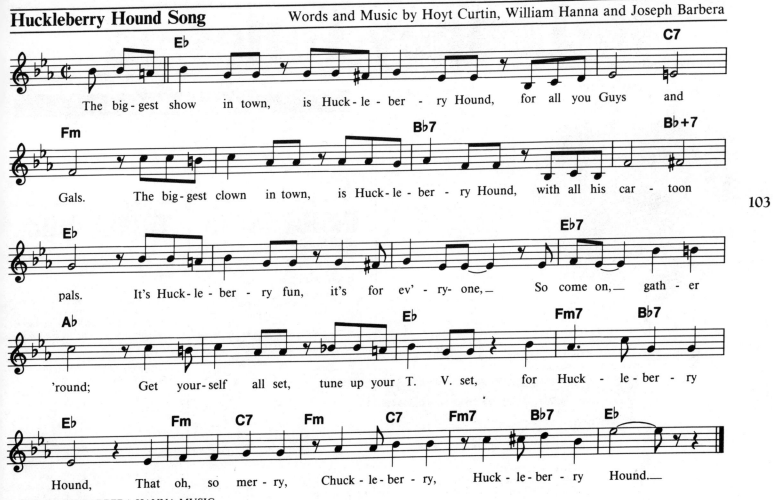

The big-gest show in town, is Huck-le-ber-ry Hound, for all you Guys and Gals. The big-gest clown in town, is Huck-le-ber-ry Hound, with all his car-toon pals. It's Huck-le-ber-ry fun, it's for ev'-ry-one,— So come on,— gath-er 'round; Get your-self all set, tune up your T. V. set, for Huck-le-ber-ry Hound, That oh, so mer-ry, Chuck-le-ber-ry, Huck-le-ber-ry Hound.—

103

Looney Tunes

THE SHOW: "Eh-h-h . . . What's up, Doc?" And here they are, direct from Hollywood, that zoo-full of zanies you've laughed at since you were old enough to turn on a TV! The "wascally wabbit"—Bugs Bunny, P-P-P-Porky P-P-P-Pig, "wabbit hunter" Elmer Fudd, Yosemite Sam ("Look out varmint, I'm a-warnin' yuh"), Sylvester and Tweety ("I tawt I taw a puddy-tat"), Speedy Gonzalez ("Arriba, arriba! Anda-lay, anda-lay!"), Daffy Duck ("Thufferin' thuccotash, that'th dethpicable!"), Foghorn Leghorn ("Now lissen heah, I say lissen heah boy!"), Henery the Chicken Hawk ("Are *you* a chicken?"), Pepe LePew ("Ooh, my leetle flower"), the Tasmanian Devil, Road Runner, Wile E. Coyote, and . . . "Th-th-th-th-th-that's all, folks!"

Cartoonist Bob Clampett, creator of Beanie and Cecil, fashioned Tweety Bird after a baby picture his father took of him.

THE SONG: Surprise! It's a pop tune from the '30s called "The Merry-Go-Round Broke Down," speeded up to sound as crazy as the characters!

Main Cast

All voice characterizations done by the amazing Mel Blanc.

Vital Statistics

Over 350 cartoon shorts. Syndicated, usually with Bugs Bunny or Road Runner as the headliner.

First aired in prime-time: Sept. 28, 1960

Most popular time slot: Saturday morning

Last show: It'll never happen.

INSIDE FACTS

MISCELLANEOUS:

- The name "Looney Tunes" was a take-off on Walt Disney's popular cartoon series, "Silly Symphonies."
- The first Looney Tune, "Sinking In The Bathtub," appeared in 1930. It featured a character called Bosko.
- In the 1935 cartoon, "I Haven't Got A Hat," a little-noticed pig named Porky appeared for the first time, stuttering his way through "The Midnight Ride of Paul Revere."
- In 1937, Daffy appeared in "Porky's Duck Hunt." In his second cartoon, Daffy sang "The Merry-Go-Round Broke Down."
- Bugs first said "What's Up Doc?" to Elmer Fudd in a 1940 cartoon, "A Wild Hare."
- Bob Clampett's '40s inspiration for the Tweety Bird was a baby picture of himself.

TRIVIA QUIZ

1. Which Looney Tune character bounces around, going "Hoo-hoo!"?
2. Pat Boone's last Top 10 hit, in 1962, was named after a Looney Tune character. Which one?
3. Which Looney Tune character was the first to star in an Oscar-winning cartoon, in 1947?
4. Which Looney character is known for saying "Of course you know this means war!"?
5. Which character's name was inspired by a Campbell's Soup Co. product?

ANSWERS

1. Daffy Duck
2. Speedy Gonzales
3. Tweety Bird ("Tweety Pie")
4. Bugs Bunny
5. Porky Pig (Campbell's Pork and Beans)

The Merry-Go-Round Broke Down

Words and Music: Cliff Friend and Dave Franklin

Intro: Ask me why I'm happy singing like a lark,
And I'll tell you of an old amusement park,
A "Merry-go-round" was there, I gladly paid the fare,
My baby rode around with me then suddenly...

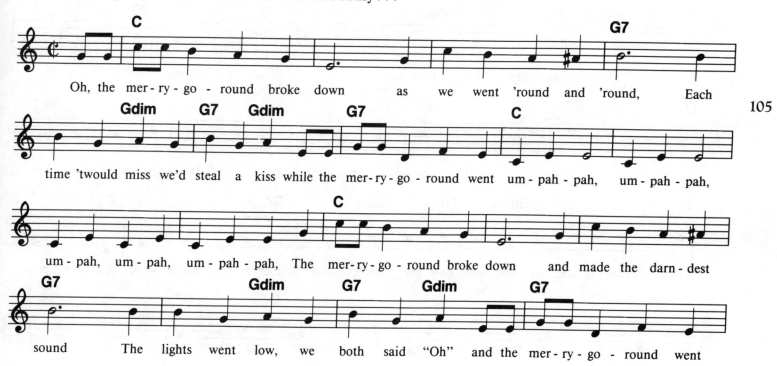

Oh, the mer-ry-go-round broke down as we went 'round and 'round, Each

105

time 'twould miss we'd steal a kiss while the mer-ry-go-round went um-pah-pah, um-pah-pah,

um-pah, um-pah, um-pah-pah, The mer-ry-go-round broke down and made the darn-dest

sound The lights went low, we both said "Oh" and the mer-ry-go-round went

106

Mister Rogers' Neighborhood

THE SHOW: As host of the longest-running children's program on PBS, the sweater-clad Fred McFeely Rogers has been a friend and neighbor to American youngsters for over 30 years. Speaking straight into the camera, Mister Rogers establishes a bond of trust rarely found on children's shows. Music is an important part of the rapport; songs like "What Do You Do With the Mad That You Feel" and "When A Baby Comes" help children deal with anger or jealousy. But mostly, Mister Rogers' Neighborhood is fun. Sometimes visitors like Rita Moreno or Marcel Marceau will drop by to say hello. And every day, there are visits to the Neighborhood of Make-Believe, whose residents include X the Owl, Cornflake S. Pecially, Daniel Striped Tiger, and Henrietta Pussycat.

THE SONG: One of today's best-known children's themes, it's written by Mister Rogers. Frequently requested by readers for inclusion in this book.

Mr. Rogers, host of one of America's best-loved children's programs.

Main Cast

Host: Fred Rogers
Lady Aberlin: Betty Aberlin
Handyman Negri: Joe Negri
Mr. McFeely: David Newell
Bob Dog: Bob Trow
Officer Clemmons: Francois Clemmons
Chef Brockett: Don Brockett

Vital Statistics

Half-hour children's show. NET (1967-70), PBS (1970-present)
First aired: May 22, 1967
Most popular time slot: Determined locally
Last show: Still in production/syndication

107

INSIDE FACTS

ABOUT MISTER ROGERS:
- He's a Presbyterian minister.
- In 1963, he made his TV debut on *Misterogers* from Toronto, Canada.
- When the show went national in 1968, the name was changed out of concern for children's reading skills.
- He was a pioneer in educational TV — in 1955 he created the first children's program on the first community-sponsored educational TV station in America (Pittsburgh's WQED).
- He's a composer and pianist, writing most of the songs sung on his program.
- He holds 14 honorary degrees from universities and colleges.
- He and Arnold Palmer were high school pals.

TRIVIA QUIZ

Fred Rogers is known and loved by millions of children. So were the hosts of these children's shows. What were their names?
1. *Ding-Dong School*
2. *Super Circus*
3. *The Magic Land of Allakazam*
4. *Wonderama*
5. *Learn To Draw*

ANSWERS
1. Miss Francis
2. Claude Kirschner
3. Mark Wilson
4. Sandy Becker, Sonny Fox, Herb Sheldon, or Bob McAllister
5. John Gnagy

Won't You Be My Neighbor?

1. It's a beau-ti-ful day in this neigh-bor-hood, A beau-ti-ful day for a neigh-bor. Would you
2. (It's a) neigh-bor-ly day in this beau-ty wood, A neigh-bor-ly day for a beau-ty, Would you

108

be mine?— Could you be mine?— 2. It's a be mine?— I have
be mine?— Could you be mine?—

al-ways want-ed to have a neigh-bor just like you!___ I've

al - ways want-ed to live in a neigh - bor-hood with you.___ So

let's make the most of this beau - ti - ful day, since we're to - geth - er we might as well say,

109

Would you be mine? Could you be mine? Won't you be my neigh - bor?

Won't you please, Won't you please? Please won't you be my neigh- bor? ___

Howdy Doody

THE SHOW: Howdy Doody ("Say kids — what time is it?") is one of the most celebrated children's shows of all-time. Hosted by Buffalo Bob Smith ("Y'know, kids — *you* can see *us* on your TV, but did you know that *we* can see *you* too? That's right! Ho-ho-o-o"), it was a circus-oriented puppet show set in the town of Doodyville. The star of the program was a freckle-faced marionette/boy named Howdy Doody who always wore bluejeans and a bandana, and was a Good Kid (sort of a juvenile pillar of the community). His nemesis was Mister Bluster, a scheming egomaniac who was also the town's mayor. And sometimes it was Clarabell, a seltzer-squirting clown who honked instead of talking. The rest of the Doodyville crowd was pleasantly strange: Flub-A-Dub, for example, was a lovably goofy creature made up of parts of 7 different animals; Dilly Dally was an inept handyman; Chief Thunderthud was a confused Indian chief who always said "Kowabunga;" etc. The show lasted for 13 years and 2343 performances!

THE SONG: To the tune of "Ta-Ra-Ra-Boom-De-Ay." More kids have sung along with this theme than any other kids' show!

The legendary Buffalo Bob Smith and friend

110

Main Cast

Buffalo Bob Smith: Bob Smith
Clarabell Hornblow (clown): Bob Keeshan, Bob Nicholson, Lou Anderson.

Vital Statistics

Half-hour and hour-long puppet show. NBC. 2,343 episodes.
First aired: December 27, 1947
Most popular time slot: Weekday afternoons and Saturday mornings.
Last show: September 24, 1960

INSIDE FACTS

ABOUT HOWDY DOODY'S ORIGIN:

• In 1945, Bob Smith was a New York radio host. His kids' show, *The Triple B Ranch*, featured a popular character named Elmer.

• Elmer always greeted the listening audience with a "Howdy doody!"

• It was such a popular phrase that when Smith moved to TV in 1947, he used it as the name of his new leading character.

MISCELLANEOUS:

• Smith's home-town was Buffalo, N.Y. — hence his nickname.

• There were actually two Howdy Doodys. The first one, who looked totally different than the second, only lasted a few weeks, disappearing when his creator left in a contract dispute.

• The original Clarabell was Bob "Captain Kangaroo" Keeshan.

TRIVIA QUIZ

1. What was Clarabell's way of communicating?
2. Who was Howdy's twin brother?
3. Who is the Doodyville wrestler trying to *finally* win a match?
4. What was *Howdy Doody's* original title?
5. What was Mr. Bluster's first name?
6. Mr. Bluster had a twin brother who lived in South America. What was his name?

ANSWERS

6. Don Jose Bluster
5. Phineas
4. *The Puppet Playhouse*
3. Ugly Sam
2. Double Doody
1. He honked a horn

It's Howdy Doody Time

By Edward Kean, Robert Smith and Henry Sayers

Buffalo Bob: Ho-ho-o-o! Well How-dy Doo-dy, boys and girls!
Howdy Doody: Howdy, Buffalo Bob!
Buffalo Bob: Well Howdy, Mr. Doody. And boys and girls at home in ALL our Peanut Galleries, LET'S GO-O-O!

It's How - dy Doo - dy time, It's How - dy Doo - dy time, Bob Smith and

How - dy Doo say How - dy Doo to you. Let's give a rou - sing cheer, cos How - dy

Doo - dy's here, it's time to start the show, so, kids, let's go!

111

Zorro

THE SHOW: Zorro was the Batman of the 1820s, a caped crusader who patrolled the countryside on a stallion named Tornado, fighting injustice and carving a "Z" wherever he went (to strike fear into the hearts of his enemies). The story: Don Diego de la Vega was a wealthy aristocrat studying in Spain. When he returned to his home in Monterey, California, he discovered that the cruel Comandante Monastario had overthrown the legitimate government there. Outraged, Don Diego (who had secretly become a master swordsman) disguised himself as Zorro to do battle with El Capitán and his fat, bumbling sidekick, Sgt. Garcia. Only Bernardo, his loyal "deaf-mute" servant, knew Don Diego's secret identity. Everyone else — especially his embarrassed father, Don Alejandro — thought he was a lazy "playboy." But we knew better, didn't we?

THE SONG: It was first recorded by none other than Henry Calvin — Sgt. Garcia! But it was a #19 hit for the Chordettes in 1959.

Guy Williams, before he grew a mustache and became El Zorro

Main Cast

Don Diego de la Vega (Zorro): Guy Williams
Bernardo (his servant): Gene Sheldon
Don Alejandro (his father): George Lewis
Captain Monastario (his enemy): Britt Lomond
Sgt. Garcia (the captain's ass't.): Henry Calvin

Vital Statistics

Half-hour adventure. ABC. 78 episodes.
First aired: Oct. 10, 1957
Most popular time slot: Thursday, 8:00 – 8:30 PM
Last show: Sept. 24, 1959
Never ranked in the Top 25 of a year.

INSIDE FACTS

ABOUT THE CHARACTER:
● Zorro first appeared in a short story by Johnston McCulley in 1919.
● His first appearance on-screen was in the 1920 movie, *The Mark of Zorro,* starring Douglas Fairbanks, Sr.
● In 1940, the film was remade with Tyrone Power in the starring role.
● Zorro means "fox" in Spanish.

ABOUT GUY WILLIAMS:
● He made an unsuccessful attempt to break into Hollywood in 1952.
● He returned to New York and became a male model instead.
● In the mid-50s he went back to California to try again.
● He won the role of Zorro because he was the only actor trying out for the part who could actually fence.

TRIVIA QUIZ

THE SUBJECT IS . . . HEROES ON HORSES

Zorro's horse, Tornado, was an important part of his image. Here are 5 more TV heroes who depended on their horses. Name the horses.
1. The Lone Ranger.
2. Gene Autry.
3. Jim and Joey Newton.
4. Little Joe Cartwright.
5. Hoss Cartwright

ANSWERS:

1. Silver
2. Champion
3. Fury
4. Cochise
5. Chub

112

Theme From Zorro

Words: Norman Foster, Music: George Bruns

113

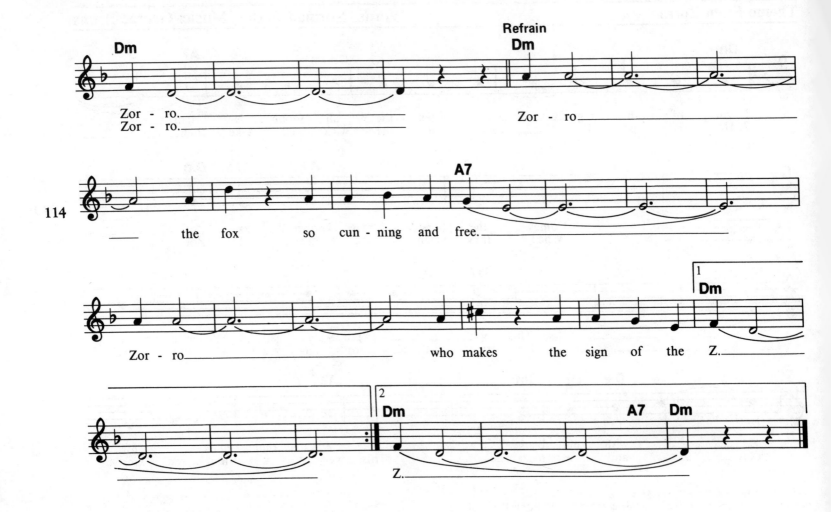

Zor - ro. Zor - ro.

Zor - ro

the fox so cun - ning and free.

Zor - ro who makes the sign of the Z.

Z.

Baretta

THE SHOW: Tony Baretta is one tough cop. I mean, this guy doesn't kid around — he's at war with everyone, from crooks to his stuffed-shirt superiors. And I'll tell ya sum-'thin' else — he knows the streets like the back of his hand, so don't try to pull a fast one on *his* beat! Baretta's an undercover cop who lives by himself (except for Fred, the Cockatoo) in a sleazy hotel called the King Edward, right in the middle of L.A.'s crime-infested 53rd Precinct. He grew up on this turf, so he knows how to fit in without being noticed. That makes it easier for him to swoop down unexpectedly and nail the law-breaking crumbs who are overrunning the city. No, he doesn't play by the rules. But as long as he gets results, Baretta couldn't care less who's upset. And in his words, "that's the name of *that* tune!"

Robert Blake, ex-Our Gang kid star, hit the streets in 1975 as Baretta

THE SONG: A #20 hit for the Rhythm Heritage in 1976 ("Don't do it"), but it was sung on the show by another artist — Sammy Davis, Jr.

Vital Statistics

Hour-long crime drama. ABC.
First aired: January 17, 1975
Most popular time slot: Wed. 9 – 10:00 PM (1975-77)
Wed. 10 – 11:00 PM (1977-78)
Last show: June 1, 1978
Ranked in a year's Top 25: 1976 (22); 1977 (9)

115

INSIDE FACTS

THE ORIGIN OF BARETTA:
- When Tony Musante chose to leave *Toma* after the 1973-74 season, ABC decided to replace him with Robert Blake.
- The proposed new title: *Toma, Starring Robert Blake.*
- But *Toma*'s ratings were low, so ABC opted for an entirely new name and location to give Blake the best shot at success.
- They moved it from New York to L.A., and gave the cop a new name — Baretta. It debuted in mid-season, and Blake won an Emmy.

ABOUT FRED THE COCKATOO:
- His real name was Lala.
- He had a stand-in (a stuffed bird) and a double who did flying stunts (named Weird Harold).
- His cage at Universal Studios was equipped with a burglar alarm.

TRIVIA QUIZ

THE SUBJECT IS ...
ONE-NAME COPS

Baretta was a cop known by one name. Name these other "one-name cop" heroes.
1. Raymond Burr in a wheel chair
2. Peter Falk in a raincoat
3. Mike Connors as a tough detective
4. Dennis Weaver as a displaced cowboy
5. Telly Savalas and his lollipops

ANSWERS

1. *Ironside*
2. *Columbo*
3. *Mannix*
4. *McCloud*
5. *Kojak*

Main Cast

Tony Baretta: Robert Blake
Billy Truman (his friend): Tom Ewell
Inspector Schiller: Dana Elcar
Lt. Brubaker: Edward Grover
Rooster (Baretta's informant): Michael D. Roberts
Fats (Baretta's informant): Chino Williams

Baretta's Theme (Keep Your Eye On The Sparrow)

Words: Morgan Ames, Music: Dave Grusin

1. Don't go to bed with no price on your head — (Don't do it)
2. Don't roll the dice if you can't pay the price —

Don't do the crime if you can't do the time —
Don't run your feet down a dead - end street — Keep your

eye ___ on the spar - row When the go -

ing ___ gets nar - row ___

3. Don't do me dirt or you're
4. Ain't gon - na fight with no

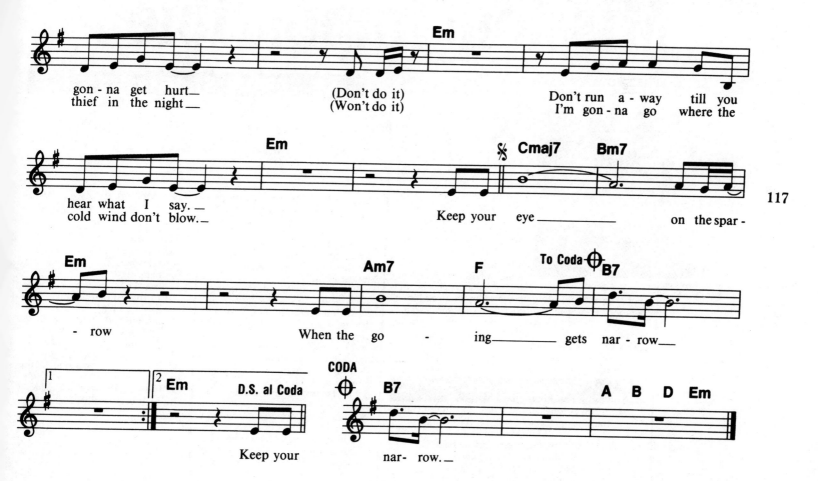

117

118

THE SHOW: "Good morning, Mr. Phelps . . ." At the peak of the '60s spy craze, secret organizations began popping up on TV. There was UNCLE & THRUSH; then CONTROL & KAOS; and finally, the IMF — Impossible Missions Force. Each week IMF leader Jim Phelps could be found in a deserted spot, searching for a bunch of photographs and an exploding tape recorder that would reveal his latest top-secret assignment. "Your mission, should you choose to accept it . . ." (and he always did) was usually to trick the ruler of some eastern European country or banana republic into sabotaging himself, using an incredibly complex "sting" operation. These wildly unbelievable maneuvers, executed by a team of hand-picked experts, never failed . . . proving that on TV, nothing is impossible.

Peter Graves starred as Jim Phelps, head of the I.M.F. (Impossible Missions Force).

THE SONG: Composed and performed in 5/4 time by Lalo Schifrin, the instrumental hit #41 on the charts in 1968. With lyrics, it's a complex and beautiful jazz vocal.

Main Cast

Dan Briggs (original I.M.F. leader): Steven Hill
Jim Phelps (replaced Briggs): Peter Graves
THE AGENTS:
Cinnamon Carter: Barbara Bain
Rollin Hand: Martin Landau
Barney Collier: Greg Morris
Willy Armitage: Peter Lupus
Paris: Leonard Nimoy

Vital Statistics

Hour-long adventure/spy drama. CBS. 171 episodes.
First aired: Sept. 17, 1966.
Most popular time slot: Sunday, 10:00-11:00 PM
Last show: Sept. 8, 1973
Ranked in a year's Top 25: 1969 (11)

INSIDE FACTS

MISCELLANEOUS:

● Bruce Geller, the show's creator, cited his favorite movie, 1964 Oscar-winner *Topkapi*, as the inspiration for M.I.

● There was little dialogue in the show. Suspense was built by cutting away from scenes to show "ticking bombs, ticking clocks, dripping water, etc."

● This was done as many as 100 times during one show!

● Dialogue was so sparse that in one show, Peter Graves fell asleep while he was in the middle of a scene.

● Graves was selected to replace Steven Hill as I.M.F.'s leader after the first season because Hill, an Orthodox Jew, refused to work after sundown on Friday and Saturday.

TRIVIA QUIZ

THE SUBJECT IS . . .
THE I.M.F.
Each member of the I.M.F. had a separate mission of his own. Can you name it?
1. Peter Lupus made his acting debut in this Annette/Frankie Avalon movie in 1964
2. Landau and Bain starred together in a sci-fi TV show (1975)
3. Leonard Nimoy hosted this documentary show (1976-82)
4. Peter Graves appeared in this movie spoof as a pilot
5. Greg Morris took a gamble as Lt. Nelson in this 1978-81 series

ANSWERS

1. *Muscle Beach Party* 2. *Space: 1999* 3. *In Search of . . .* 4. *Airplane!* 5. *Vegas*

Mission Impossible

Words: Fred Milano, Angelo D'Aleo, Music: Lalo Schifrin

Fly away, disappear.
I'll be there,
Waiting.

Run high, run low,
Don't stop, go
No matter where
You are bound
I'm around
Waiting,
Hypnotized
On a string,
Following,
Wanting.

Lead me there,
Anywhere.
I don't care.

Cannot stop and I won't stop
Till you're mine.
I keep on dreamin' of you,
No doubt about it
Took my head and made it spin
Somewhere where it's never been.

I'm in a desert,
The middle of nowhere.
With no shoes I calmly bear
Burning coals of fire,
But when I get through
That's when I'll begin to
Undertake a mission that's impossible.

It's said no one can tame you.
Don't give it a try.
You'll fall off if you get up that high.
And deep inside all of your beauty
There is no feeling.
They say you can't be made to laugh or cry.

No, I will have your love.
That's why I'm right. I'll have you.
Run or try to hide, I'll stay beside.
I'm gonna get you.
Get on a plane, go far away, but any day,
I'm gonna get you.

Don't be afraid if you may find
I'm on your mind
Don't try to fight it.
Love's a waiting fuse, you can't refuse
We're gonna light it.

119

The Adventures of Robin Hood

THE SHOW: In 1955, American TV imported a new kind of hero. Instead of cowboy boots, a 10-gallon hat, and a six-gun, he sported pointed slippers, wore a cap with a feather in it, and carried a bow and arrow. He was Robin Hood, the legendary British hero who "stole from the rich and gave to the poor." From their headquarters in Sherwood Forest, Robin and his gang (the Merry Men) waged a guerilla war on the illegitimate ruler of England, Prince John. The result: they became outlaws, relentlessly pursued by the evil Sheriff of Nottingham. Of course the peasants loved them; and so did Maid Marian, Robin's spy in the local government. It all sounds political, but *Robin Hood* was really just a great vehicle for adventure, archery exhibitions, and an outdoor barbeque every night. Hooray for the good guys!

THE SONG: As close to a traditional folk song as any TV theme ever came. Recorded by 6 different artists in the '50s.

Richard Greene played Sir Robin of Locksley, a.k.a. Robin Hood

Main Cast

Robin Hood: Richard Greene
Friar Tuck: Alexander Gauge
Little John: Archie Duncan
Maid Marian Fitzwater: Bernadette O'Farrell
The Sheriff of Nottingham: Alan Wheatley
Sir Richard the Lion-Hearted: Ian Hunter
Prince John: Donald Pleasance

Vital Statistics

Half-hour adventure. CBS. 135 episodes.
First aired: September 26, 1955
Most popular time slot: Monday 7:30 – 8:00 PM (1955-57)
Last show: September 22, 1958
Ranked in a year's Top 25: 1956 (20)

INSIDE FACTS

ABOUT THE SHOW:

- It was inspired by a 1938 movie (also called "The Adventures of Robin Hood") that starred Errol Flynn, king of the swashbucklers, at his peak. Co-stars: Olivia de Haviland, Basil Rathbone.
- Over 500 costumes were used in it, each checked for accuracy by the British Museum.
- It was filmed completely in England. Many of the scenes were actually shot in Sherwood Forest and in Nottingham.

ABOUT ROBIN HOOD:

- His exploits took place in the year 1191, A.D.
- He was featured in two more TV series: Mel Brooks' 1975 sitcom, *When Things Were Rotten*, and a cartoon called *Rocket Robin Hood*, which took place on Sherwood Asteroid.

TRIVIA QUIZ

THE SUBJECT IS...
MOVIE HEROES

Many TV heroes appeared in the movies first. Can you name these five:

1. He was played by William Powell in the movies, Peter Lawford on TV
2. Based on a comic strip by Alex Raymond, he was played by Buster Crabbe in film, Steve Holland on TV in 1953
3. In the movies, Elizabeth Taylor loved her. On TV it was Tommy Rettig (and others)
4. Film: Johnny Weismuller, TV: Ron Ely (and others)
5. He and Dale played themselves in movies *and* TV

ANSWERS
1. *The Thin Man*
2. *Flash Gordon*
3. *Lassie*
4. *Tarzan*
5. *Roy Rogers*

Robin Hood

Words and Music by Carl Sigman

Rob - in Hood, Rob - in Hood, ri - ding thru the glen. Rob - in Hood, Rob - in Hood,

with his band of men Feared by the bad, loved by the good, Rob - in Hood,

Rob - in Hood, Rob - in Hood.

1. He called the great - est ar - chers to a
2. He came to Sher - wood For - est with a
3. With Fri - ar Tuck and Lit - tle John they

ta - vern on the green, they vowed to help the peo - ple of the king. They
fea - ther in his cap, A fight - er nev - er look - ing for a fight. His
had a rog - uish look, They did the deed the oth - ers would - n't dare. He

121

han - dled all the trou - bles on the Eng - lish coun - try scene and still found plen - ty of time to
bow was al - ways read - y and he kept his ar - rows sharp. He used them to fight for what was
cap - tured all the mon - ey that the e - vil sher - iff took, And res - cued man - y a la - dy

122

sing.
right.
fair.

Rob - in Hood, Rob - in Hood, ri - ding thru the glen.

Rob - in Hood, Rob - in Hood, with his band of men. Feared by the bad,

loved by the good, Rob - in Hood, Rob - in Hood, Rob - in Hood.

A Song From A Sponsor

You've Got A Lot To Live Words by Batten, Barton Durstine & Osborn, Music by Joe Brooks

There's a whole new way of liv-in', Pep-si helps___ sup-ply___ the drive,___

123

___ it's got a lot to give___ to those who like to live___ 'cause Pep-si

helps 'em come a-live,_____ It's the Pep - si Gen-er-a-

tion com-in' at ya, go-in' strong,___ put your-self___

Let's Play Telephone!

A Modern Miracle

Hey, TV fans! Here's great news: now *you* can play TV themes (or at least parts of them) as *well* as sing them... even if you've never played an instrument before! All you need is a push-button phone.

That's right — now the miracle of modern electronics makes it possible for even the worst tone-deaf klutzes to be REAL MUSICIANS. And the best part is, you can do it anywhere, whenever the urge hits you — at home, in the office, even on the street.

Here's How To Do It

1. Pick up the phone (remember: it's got to be a push-button phone)

2. Call a friend (or an enemy, if you prefer). Say "Hey, remember the theme song from (your show here)?" Don't wait for an answer: "Well here it is!" And begin punching the appropriate buttons on your phone. If your friend isn't home, play the song anyway. The ringing provides an interesting background.

When To Do It

A few examples of prime times:

1. Let's say you're mired in a boring phone conversation with someone who just won't take the hint and let you hang up gracefully. No matter what the topic is, just interrupt and say: "Hey! I'll bet you can't guess what TV theme song this is . . ." and begin punching those buttons. That'll do the trick.

2. On the other hand, let's say you're on the phone with someone you're trying to impress (a prospective date, perhaps?) and one of those deadly lulls hits the conversation.

125

Don't get paranoid. Say "I'm really into music. In fact, here's a TV theme I just learned to play today" and begin punching buttons. It's always a hit.

126

If You've Got Perfect Pitch:

This may not be for you. The notes aren't exactly right (blame the phone company, not me). But as they say in the music biz, they're close enough for TV themes.

To Get You Started

Here are a few pointers:
1. Sometimes you've got to sing a note or two to fill in for notes that aren't on the phone.
2. Sometimes you can only play a part of a song. That's OK.
3. The numbers are grouped in beats. Two numbers together means you should play them fast.
4. These sample tunes work on Bell phones. I don't know if they work on others.

SAMPLE SONGS

EASY.

Opening four notes of *Mission: Impossible.*
3 – 3 – 9 #   (can be repeated)

Opening of *Peter Gunn*
3 – 3 – 63 – 93 – #9 (can be repeated)

INTERMEDIATE.

First 22 notes of *Robin Hood*
(Lyrics: Robin Hood, Robin Hood, Riding thru the glen.
Robin Hood, Robin Hood, with his band of men)
333 – 333 – 999 – 6 – 3
444 – 444 – # # # – 8 – 5

Looney Tunes. One note is slightly off.
2 – 0 – 9 – 6 – 2 – 1 (hold)
2 – 0 – 2 – 6 – 2 – 9 (hold)
9 – 9 – 2 – 6
2 – 9 – 2 – 6
2 – 2 – 2 – 6 – 9 – 0 (hold)

ADVANCED.

Popeye. Requires some singing.
3 – 999 – 6 – 3 9 (hold)
9 – #6# – (sing) – # 9 (hold)
9 – # – 6 – # – (sing) – (sing)
– 9 – # – 9 – 3 – (sing)
3 – 9 – # – 9 – 6 – (sing or 5) – (sing or 7)

Opening of *Bonanza*
3 – 333 – 333 – 333 – 3
(sing)
3 – 333 – 333 – 333
333 – 3369# (hold)

Patty Duke Show.
Begin with chorus: "Still they're cousins . . ."
000 – 4 (hold)   (last Chorus only)
0 404
0 – 2 – 6 – (sing) – 2
6 999 – 9 699
9 699 – 9 699
(sing: " you can lose your ") 6
0 – 0 – 4 (hold)
0 404 0 (hold)

Maverick verse
3 – 396 – 3
6 – 31
3 – 693 – – 1 (sing)
3 – 396 – 3616 (hold)
(sing: "Blowin' up a") 3 –
9 – (sing) (sing) – 6 – 3 (hold)

Now you're on your own!

TV Theme Song Fan Club

Now, here's the organization you've been waiting for: The Tuneful Viewer's Society for the Preservation of TV Theme Songs — **TV SPOTTS**, for short!

Help preserve the American folk music of the Electronic Era! Join with the tens of thousands of other Americans who are Singing Along, raising their voices together in a chorus of *Mr. Ed* and *Gilligan's Island.* Have an *official* "yabba-dabba-doo time" . . . .
Join **TV SPOTTS** Today!

IT'S FREE!
The best things in life ARE free, and **TV SPOTTS** is one of them. All you have to do to become a member — and get your FREE MEMBERSHIP KIT (including the official **TV SPOTTS** CARD!) — is send a self-addressed, stamped envelope to:

> **TV SPOTTS**
> 1201 Olympic Blvd.
> Santa Monica, CA 90404

You've got to include that stamped envelope, because there's no government funding (yet!) for the preservation of TV themes.

Your membership card will entitle you to call up local talk shows and demand that they devote a few hours to discussing your favorite music, to stand on street corners (like I do) with a guitar and serenade passers-by with the theme from *The Patty Duke Show* or *Love Boat,* to sing TV themes in the shower and ignore your neighbors banging on the wall demanding that you stop. And, it's also a great conversation piece or gift. Imagine your loved one's gleeful surprise upon receiving his/her own card in the mail. How thoughtful you are!

Now prestige can be yours . . . and it's free! Once we're established as a vital force in American pop music, who knows what we can do?

JOIN TODAY! Let your voice be heard, even if it's off-key!

John Javna
Choirmaster

There's More!

If you had fun with this book (and I know you did!), then here are some more books – and a record – you should know about!

128

THE TV THEME SONG SING-ALONG SONG BOOK, VOLUME 1. The book that brought TV Themes out of the closet. Same format, over 40 classic TV Themes, with Inside Facts, Trivia Quizzes, Commercials, etc. Includes: *Mr. Ed, The Beverly Hillbillies, Petticoat Junction, The Brady Bunch, Star Trek, Leave It To Beaver, The Addams Family, Green Acres,* and lots more! Only $5.95...A TV Theme Song-lover's Bible! From John Javna and St. Martin's Press.

THE TV THEME SONG SING-ALONG ALBUM, VOLUME 1. You asked for it — now HERE IT IS! Original recordings of 14 of the greatest TV Themes in history! Includes: *Star Trek, The Beverly Hillbillies, I Love Lucy* (sung by Desi Arnaz), *Perry Mason, Leave It To Beaver, Petticoat Junction, M*A*S*H,* and 8 more all-time favorites. If you love TV Themes, you've been waiting for this record! Only $8.98, from (guess who!) John Javna and Rhino Records.

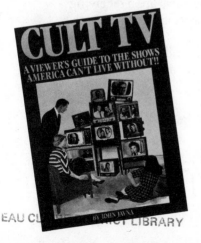

CULT TV. A Viewer's Guide To The Shows America Can't Live Without! Pictures, Trivia, Inside Stories, and 256 pages packed with everything you always wanted to know about your favorite TV shows, from *Star Trek* to *Perry Mason.* Includes: *The Addams Family, Sgt. Bilko, The Avengers, The Twilight Zone, Dr. Who, The Outer Limits, The Mary Tyler Moore Show, Saturday Night Live, Gilligan's Island, Batman, Taxi, Dragnet...*over 60 Shows in All! Fun for anyone who loves classic TV! Great bathroom reading (come on, admit it!) at $12.95, from John Javna and St. Martin's Press (of course).

ASK FOR THEM AT YOUR LOCAL BOOK AND RECORD STORES! If you can't get them there (but you probably can), send a check or money-order for the amount of each item, plus $1.50 for postage and handling (and 75¢ for each additional item) to:

THE TV THEME SONG EMPORIUM
1201 Olympic Blvd.
Santa Monica, CA 90404

And we'll rush them to you. Please allow 4–6 weeks for delivery. U.S. orders only.

WEAVING
WATER

© 2016, Annamarie Beckel

 Canada Council Conseil des Arts
for the Arts du Canada   Newfoundland
Labrador

We gratefully acknowledge the financial support of the
Canada Council for the Arts, the Government of Canada through the Canada
Book Fund (CBF), and the Government of Newfoundland and Labrador
through the Department of Business, Tourism, Culture and
Rural Development for our publishing program.

Cover Design by Todd Manning • Layout by Joanne Snook-Hann
Printed on acid-free paper

Published by
KILLICK PRESS
an imprint of CREATIVE BOOK PUBLISHING
a Transcontinental Inc. associated company
P.O. Box 8660, Stn. A
St. John's, Newfoundland and Labrador A1B 3T7

Printed in Canada

Library and Archives Canada Cataloguing in Publication

Beckel, Annamarie, 1951-, author
Weaving water / Annamarie Beckel.

ISBN 978-1-77103-092-2 (paperback)

 MIX
Paper from
responsible sources
FSC
www.fsc.org FSC® C011825

I. Title.

PS8553.A29552W43 2016   C813'.54   C2016-904039-9

WEAVING WATER

A NOVEL

Annamarie Beckel

*To Ineka —
With all best
wishes
Annamarie Beckel
January 2019*

kiLLick press
an imprint of Creative Publishers

St. John's, Newfoundland and Labrador, 2016

For Megan and Amy

A human being is a part of the whole, called by us "Universe," a part limited in time and space. He experiences himself, his thoughts and feelings as something separated from the rest – a kind of optical delusion of his consciousness. This delusion is a kind of prison for us.

Albert Einstein, a 1950 letter to Robert Marcus

We must be at our most skeptical when we evaluate arguments that confirm the extremely high opinion we have of ourselves.

Steven Wise, *Rattling the Cage*

CHAPTER 1

Beth sets the kerosene lamp on the kitchen counter above the junk drawer. Tries not to hear the melancholy plink-plink-plink of water dripping into the bowls and pans she's placed on the floor to catch the leaks. The lamp's soft glow illuminates the drawer's contents: matchbooks, candle stubs, scissors, ball of string, paper clips. She picks up a deck of cards, slides off the red rubber band, and releases the odour of must. The smell of old things in an old wooden drawer: Katherine's things.

When Beth and Alan first arrived at the cabin, there were shirts and dresses still hanging in the closet, white cotton socks and old-lady underwear rolled up and stuffed into a small bureau. The dead woman's clothes made Beth uneasy, and she and Alan packed them away in black plastic garbage bags to donate to the Salvation Army. They kept the furniture though, as well as the dishes and the pots and pans. Beth still isn't sure how she feels about that, but it made no sense to throw out what they can use.

The yellow lamplight casts shadows that shrink, waver, and then grow taller on the grey walls. Beth shuffles the cards and lays them out for a game of solitaire. Cringes when gusts of wind rattle loose shingles. She looks up to see rain streaming down the front window, and the eerie reflection of her own pale face bisected by the masking tape that covers the jagged crack. She tries to laugh at herself. She doesn't believe in ghosts. Of course she doesn't. But it was easier to laugh when Alan was here. He's gone now, back in St. John's. He took the black garbage bags with him.

And she's alone in a dead woman's cabin on a pond in the middle of nowhere.

~

Beth crouches down, pinches metal forceps to lift the crushed carapace of a beetle, teases apart slender, translucent fish bones and fragments of blue mussel shell. The black scat exudes an odour of fresh fish and musk. To her, not unpleasant. She finds an otolith, the tiny round bone from the inner ear that, under a microscope, will tell her the age and species of fish the otter ate. Probably trout, mud trout.

She pulls a labelled zip-lock bag from her backpack. Using the bag like a glove, she collects the scat, zips the bag, and tucks it into the cooler against the ice. Hopes the sample won't degrade too much for DNA analysis before she can get it back to the university. Genetic tests on scats will tell her how many river otters are in the group, how many males, how many females, and how closely related they are to each other.

The crows in a nearby birch caw raucously, like rowdy fans jeering a hockey referee's bad call. Beth hears mocking laughter, as if the crows know her research for what it is: picking through otter shit.

Wiping off the forceps, Beth reminds herself that river otters, like wolves and eagles, are an environmental success story, rebounding from small numbers to become plentiful again. And where reintroductions have been successful, it's research like hers that has made the difference.

Crows 1: Beth 1.

She hears the distant hum of a motor, a hum that grows steadily louder until it's a roar. A small boat rounds the point. The motor stops, creating an abrupt silence until the wake slaps rudely against the shore. Beth raises her binoculars: an Alumacraft, *Black Feather* painted in even letters on the bow. Who names an Alumacraft?

A lone fisherman stands, lights a cigarette, then fiddles with a fishing rod. After a few minutes, he casts. He looks toward Beth and nods. A flush rises into her cheeks. She lets the binoculars drop to her chest, packs up her research gear, and slides into her kayak.

~

The otters glide through the pond, propelling themselves with undulations of muscular bodies and thick, tapering tails. They stay near shore, their steady *uhn-uhn-uhns* like whispers through the grey mist that lies in a downy blanket atop the dark water. The oldest one lifts her head, smelling the air. She chirps to quiet the pups tussling in the water, then comes out on shore and sniffs at the place she marked with scat the night before. There's something new: the scent of human, female, sadness. She hurries back into the water and leads them all away.

~

Beth rises through the gossamer shroud of deep sleep, silky threads of a dream clinging: murky water, a tangle of weeds. She lies still in the dark. Hears snuffling noises just outside the window. *Mfuff-mfuff, mfuff-mfuff.* She stands, as quietly as she can, but the sagging springs groan, the sleeping bag rustles. The snuffling stops. There is only the wind shussing through spruce and fir. She tiptoes to the window. Sees a dark hulking shape near the base of a birch – the same spot where she left stale crackers the night before. She imagines the pink tongue curling around each salty square.

She feels an urgent need to pee, but she can't go to the outhouse with a bear in the middle of the path. She squeezes her thighs together. Why has she been so careless? She could have dumped the crackers down the outhouse hole. But no, she had to put them out for the jays and crows, and the red squirrel. She even spread peanut butter on a few. Stupid, stupid, stupid!

She knows a black bear isn't really *that* dangerous. Unless it has cubs nearby or it decides to come inside to search for more food. Did she lock the door last night? Does it matter? She assesses the dimensions of the window. Glances at the chair beside the bed. Calculates. If the bear heads for the door, she should be able to climb out the window – if she can get the screen out quickly enough. If she can't, she'll have to go right through it.

The alarm on her watch beeps, implausibly loud in the dark: 5:00. She scrambles to turn it off. Looks out the window again. The bear's head is raised, angled toward the cabin. Beth holds her breath and tries to ignore the pressure building in her bladder. Releases her breath slowly when the bear lowers its head to the crackers. The bear exhales a muffled *mfuff-mfuff*. Or a low woof?

She reaches for her glasses, slides them on, and sees what might be a long shaggy tail. Watches for another minute, waiting for more light. Groans. It's only a dog. A huge black Newfoundland.

Still in bare feet and T-shirt, she races outside. The broad head comes up and the dog gallops behind her, then waits by the outhouse door until Beth is finished. When she opens the door, the chocolate doggy eyes gazing up at her melt her resolve to be stern.

"Where'd you come from, buddy?" Her voice is raspy. These are the first words she's spoken aloud since Alan left three days ago. She does a quick inspection and determines that *it* is a *she*.

Feet wet and cold, Beth runs on her toes back to the cabin. The dog trots along behind her, pausing momentarily at the saltines, now just a few soggy crumbs. She tries to follow Beth right into the cabin, but Beth blocks her with a knee and closes the screen door.

"Go home now. Back to where you belong."

The Newfoundland plops down on the wide top step, chin on front paws. Stares through the screen. Beth can't close the door in her face. She has a soft heart. Mushy, really, when it comes to animals. Her father, a farmer, always told her she lacked iron.

Watching while Beth pulls on jeans, wool socks, and a sweatshirt, the dog lets out a small whine now and again. Very small, Beth thinks, for such a large dog. She considers letting the dog come into the cabin. Knows that would be a mistake.

She builds a fire in the cookstove, black soot smudging her hands and gathering in stark lines under her fingernails. Bursts of light from three different matches flare and die before the kindling catches and she can add more splits. She primes the pump and fills the metal percolator with water. All the while, the whimpers are growing more insistent. She adds coffee grounds to the pot. Spills some across the dark-red counter. Blames the dog. The dog has disrupted her morning routine. Beth places the coffee pot on the stove, adds more wood to the fire, and turns the rocking chair away from the screen door. She sits down and rocks with determination. Hopes the dog will leave.

In just three days alone, Beth has developed a morning ritual. She rises before daylight, builds the fire, then wraps herself in her sleeping bag while she waits for the coffee to perk. The living room window faces east, and she sits, cocoon-like, and waits for the light. When the sun edges over the spruce and fir ringing the pond, she takes up her journal and writes out her research notes: the weight of the pen in her hand, the physicality of holding a notebook balanced on one knee, the scent of real ink and real paper. It's the part of the ritual that makes her feel like her younger self, the self who was full of confidence and purpose, the self who believed she could do research that matters.

The first slow perks. Accompanied by snuffling and whining. Beth avoids looking toward the screen door.

The previous morning she had even dared to imagine herself as Thoreau or John Muir, thinking deep, complicated thoughts about wilderness and human nature. And then was grateful for her solitude: no witness to make her feel foolish.

It has come as a welcome relief to be alone and disconnected: no computer, no email, no Internet, and most important, no news. She's been worrying too much lately, about big problems she can do nothing about – climate change and the loss of more and more wilderness to oil and mineral extraction, the increasingly rapid pace of species' extinctions – and about personal problems she feels equally helpless to remedy. She's goddamn fifty-three. And all she has to show for it are a few minor papers from research she did twenty-five years ago. How the hell did that happen? And when?

She feels like a walking, talking cliché. She also feels cheated.

The coffee pot is perking madly now, close to boiling over, the heady aroma competing with the pungent smell of wood smoke. Beth lifts the pot from the stove and pours scalding coffee into a mug. Glances toward the door. The dog's nose is pushing in, creating a dent in the screen. The sunlight illumines a thin ribbon of drool.

She carries the mug outside. The dog stands, tail wagging, even as Beth nudges her off the top step. When she sits down, the dog settles on the ground beside her. A red squirrel dances in jerky bursts along the woodpile. It stops to release a chattering reproach at them – or maybe just at the dog for eating all the peanut butter crackers.

Beth rubs sleep from her eyes. Sighs. If she wanted a dog here while she was doing her research, she'd have kept Pirate, their three-legged black Lab, when Alan left.

She combs her fingers through the oily fur at the dog's thick neck. Finds a worn leather collar but no tags.

"What am I supposed to do with you?"

The dog lifts her ears and woofs, as if trying to answer Beth's question. She stands, nudges Beth's leg with her muzzle, then backs up and barks again.

When she was a kid, Beth watched *Lassie* re-runs religiously. She knows exactly what she's supposed to do right now: follow the dog wherever it wants to take her; someone might be in trouble. She suspects that's all nonsense. Besides, she doesn't want to follow the dog anywhere. She has work to do.

Newfoundlands are not supposed to bark much, but this one, woofing continuously now, seems inclined to be a breed non-conformist.

"Okay, girl, okay." Beth drains the mug, then goes inside and pulls on sneakers, layers a windbreaker over her sweatshirt. As soon as Beth steps outside, the dog bolts toward a narrow trail Beth hasn't explored yet. She assumes the path leads to the nearest cabin, the only cabin nearby and one of just eight or nine on the entire pond. Judging by her maps, the cabin is about five or six hundred metres to the north.

The trail is rocky and dark. The grey dawn can scarcely penetrate the closely spaced spruce and fir, whose damp fingers reach out to brush her shoulders and arms. The gaps between the branches are decorated with dewy spider webs – the Grinch's Christmas trees. The dog runs ahead but keeps coming back to make sure Beth is following.

In about ten minutes, they arrive at a clearing and a small cabin with dark-red clapboard. The door behind the screen door stands wide open. The dog runs forward and barks. Beth waits, but no one appears. She checks her watch: 6:12. Then climbs the steps and raps several times.

Leans close to the screen and cups her hands around her eyes. It's too dark to see anything but the vague outlines of a cookstove and a small kitchen table. An unlit kerosene lamp squats on the table.

Beth looks at the dog and shrugs. The dog scratches at the screen door, deeply marred below the handle, as if she does that often. The top step is hardly big enough for the two of them, and the squirming dog nearly pushes her off. She stares up at Beth.

"I can't just go in, can I?" She knocks again.

Ears forward, the dog continues to gaze up at her.

"Okay," Beth says, "but if we get in trouble, it's your fault." She opens the screen door; the dog squeezes through before Beth can grab her collar. She heads straight for the bedroom.

Stepping inside, Beth releases the door slowly so that it won't slam. Although it feels far too intimate, she peeks through the open door of the bedroom. A person lies supine on the bed, sleeping soundly. Or dead.

CHAPTER 2

Death by natural causes, Beth decides. No evidence of violence. Heart attack, probably. But she's never seen a dead person, except in a funeral parlour. The face is heavily lined, but has an odd waxy smoothness, as if the body has already been embalmed: a polished marble death mask framed by short white hair spiking out in all directions.

The dog nuzzles an exposed hand. The hand moves. Beth jumps back.

"Go away, Muin." A hoarse whisper.

The dog plants her front paws on the bed and licks the death mask, now fully mobile. Eyelids flutter open. Dark eyes stare at Beth for a long moment. "Oh, it's you."

Beth opens her mouth, then closes it. Cannot think of a single word to say.

"Guess I been away a while." A scrawny arm flings off the wool blanket. Thin legs clad in grey sweatpants, elastic at the ankles, swing around. Narrow shoulders stretch back, and long fingers tug at a grey T-shirt several shades lighter than the pants. "Bring the tobacco?"

Tobacco? Beth takes another step backwards. "I … I brought your dog back. She was over at my cabin this morning."

The dog trots out into the kitchen as if to demonstrate her inclination for wandering. The screen door creaks open then smacks shut.

"Morning? What day?"

Beth blinks, hard, as if she could make the scene disappear if she just closes her eyes tightly enough, then opens them again. "Monday," she says finally.

"Hmmm. Time for a cup a tea?" The bare feet slide into worn leather scuffs.

Beth shakes her head. "I just came over to bring your dog back."

"I believe she's chosen you." The dark eyes examine Beth more closely. "Not sure why though."

"What?"

"Sure, you don't understand now. But you will." A quick glance out the window, then back to Beth. "Where you living to?"

"The cabin near here. The one that belonged to Katherine Wells."

"You knew Katherine?" The question is abrupt, almost accusing.

"N-never met her," Beth says. "She was my husband's aunt, but he didn't know her very well. He inherited the cabin when she died."

The white eyebrows arch, as if he, or she, is expecting – no, demanding – more information.

"That was last winter," Beth explains. "A stroke. Apparently she died on the way to the hospital. But we didn't know any of that, or about the funeral, until a month later. We didn't even find out about the will until recently."

The hawk nose lends the face a severity Beth finds disconcerting. She swallows, then rattles on: "My husband thinks there might've been bad blood – or something – between his father and his aunt."

"I spect so."

"Cabin's in pretty rough shape," Beth says. "Could cost us more to repair than to build something new. Might have it torn down."

"Wouldn't do that."

"Why not?"

"Just wouldn't. It's a grand old place." Both hands push against bony thighs, and the person stands. "So we're neighbours then. But you can't stay? Even for a cup a tea?"

Beth hears longing, maybe even reproach. "Maybe a quick cup," she says. "But I can't stay long. I have work to do."

The hand that reaches out to Beth is large and weathered, the palm rough. "Mattie."

"Beth. Beth Meyer."

Mattie stretches, fingertips reaching toward the ceiling. Just a fraction taller than Beth's own five and a half feet, she notes, but far more spare.

"So," Beth says, "you were friends with Katherine?"

"Over forty years." Mattie looks at Beth sidelong. "Now she were always good for a cup a tea and a yarn."

Beth follows Mattie from the cramped bedroom into the kitchen, which smells of freshly split wood and dried leaves. Mattie pokes small birch junks and kindling into a cast-iron cookstove. Beth still can't tell if Mattie is a man or a woman, sixty or ninety. She looks for whiskers. Can't see any, but there's a pipe and a pouch of tobacco beside the kerosene lamp, and on the wall there's a gun rack that cradles a rifle and a double-barrelled shotgun.

Mattie strikes a match, filling the air with the chemical stink of sulphur. The dog scratches at the screen door. "Muin, you are a nuisance. Can you let her in?"

Beth goes to the door and pushes it open. "Moo ... what?" she says to Mattie.

"Moo-een." Mattie exaggerates each syllable, lips pulling forward then back, exposing a left front tooth that is chipped, almost in half, and a gap behind the eyetooth on the right. "Mi'kmaq for bear." Long fingers cup the dog's chin. "Looks like a bear, dontcha think?"

Beth bites down on her lip. "Guess so."

Mattie shuffles to the sink – mottled with black ovals where the white enamel has chipped away – and primes the pump. The squeaky complaints are loud in the quiet of the cabin. While Mattie fills the kettle and a bowl for Muin, Beth glances around the room: old black cookstove, kerosene lamp, two straight-back chairs at a small table, and an unfinished weaving in a large loom, the colours similar to those in the weaving that hangs in her own cabin. With the exception of the guns and the loom, the cabin is much like her own: no electricity or indoor plumbing, save for the hand-pump; a combined kitchen and living room; two small bedrooms. And yet, this cabin is somehow older, as if nothing has changed here for fifty years. Not a hint of anything modern, no telephone, not even an old transistor radio or plastic knick-knack. Bunches of dried plants dangle from hooks in the ceiling. Feathers of all sizes – mostly black, brown, and white, some mottled or striped – stand in a mason jar on the windowsill over the sink. In one corner, a rocking chair sits beside a half barrel filled with chunks of wood and antler. A few woodworking tools lie on a low shelf where a dozen carvings huddle together in an unlikely herd: a bear and several moose, a hare, perhaps a lynx, maybe an otter. Beth can't be sure without looking at them more closely. Below the carvings is a long shelf of clothbound books, a few with gold-embossed letters down their spines. They look old and tattered, like something you'd buy at a yard sale for a loonie each.

Mattie places the kettle on the stove. "What kinda work makes you wanna rush off so fast?"

Beth takes off her glasses, carefully wipes one lens on the bottom of her sweatshirt, then tries to clean the other one. Holds them up to the light. The lenses are smeared. As soon as she mentions otters, most people chuckle and tell her a joke: *That otter be otterly delightful. You otter be careful out there.* She slides on her glasses. "It's just preliminary," she says. "A small study on Medicine Rock Pond."

"What kinda study?"

12

"Ecological. The feeding habits of the river otters here."

"Hmmm. And how do you go about doing that?"

Beth shifts her weight from one foot to the other. "Collect their scats," she says finally, "and examine them for fish bones, broken shells, insect parts."

"I see. Gathering otter shit."

Beth sees the lips twitching, the smile held back. She braces for a stupid pun.

"You must be the lady my nephew seen yesterday," Mattie says. "Dan said you was watching him through spyglasses."

"I wasn't watching *him*. I was watching for otters."

"Said he thought you was uppity."

Uppity?

"No odds," Mattie says, waving a hand dismissively. "But you're some lucky you met me. I knows every otter on the pond. I can tell you exactly what they eat. Trout. Not much else here, except for a few clams and dragonflies. Stickleback or two. And every now and again they dip into the salty water and grab theirselves a lobster or whore's egg."

"Casual observations can be a good start," Beth says, crossing her arms, "but things do need to be verified scientifically. And if I can determine that there are enough otters here on this pond – and on the neighbouring ponds – to justify a full-fledged study, I'll apply for a grant."

"Somebody'd give you money to collect otter shit?"

"The Department of Environment and Conservation has designated river otters a VEC: a valued ecosystem component." Beth tries to speak with the weight and authority she believes her PhD should give her.

Mattie nods. "I see. A valued ecosystem component."

"A sort of 'canary in the coal mine' species," Beth explains. "Otters are top predators. They concentrate heavy metals and other contaminants in their tissues, so they're one of the first species affected by water pollution." She hears herself lecturing and clamps her mouth closed. Slides off her windbreaker and hangs it over the back of a chair. "So what do you do out here?"

"Not much. Bit of weaving, gardening, carving." Mattie turns toward the array of birdfeeders hanging just outside the living room window. A nuthatch clings, upside-down, to an empty suet feeder. "And I watch the birds and animals, specially otters."

The water is blurping away in the kettle. Mattie reaches up to a bundle of dried plants and pulls off some brown leaves. Crumbles them and tosses them into a battered metal pot. Pours in boiling water. "Tea'll be ready shortly, love." Mattie takes two thick ceramic mugs from the cupboard, sets them, and two spoons, on the table, then places a yellow sugar bowl between the mugs. Voluptuous pink roses bloom on one side, a brown crack trailing crookedly between them.

"I sees em all the time," Mattie continues. "Sometimes a loner, sometimes whole families. Usually five or six. Sometimes as many as eight or ten – a big ole family reunion right in front of the cabin." Mattie grasps the wooden handle of the teapot and pours, then sits down and gestures for Beth to sit as well. The dog circles under the table. When she finally settles, Beth has to move her feet aside to accommodate her bulk. A doggy odour, oily and a little fishy, wafts upward.

Mattie spoons sugar into the tea. "See the old grandmother most often."

"The grandmother? How do you know it's the grandmother?"

"Just do."

Beth decides to let that pass.

"She watches over the pond and everything that happens here."

Beth lets that pass too. "The dog doesn't scare them off?"

"Scare them?" Mattie reaches down to stroke Muin's head. "Only thing they want is to play with her."

Beth smiles. "Probably true. I'd sure like to know what all that play is about."

"No big mystery, love. They're just happier than most folks."

Beth runs a fingertip along the rim of the mug. Stops at the rough edge of a chip. *Happy* doesn't constitute much of an explanation for a scientist.

"How long have you lived here?" she asks.

"Hmmm. Must be eighty years or so by now."

"Eighty years?"

"Thereabouts."

"And you're out here all alone?" Beth says.

"Not hardly, girl. Haven't you noticed all the birds and animals?"

"Yes, but–"

"And there's Muin." At the sound of her name, the dog lifts her head, then lays it back down on Beth's feet.

"But there's no one else? No … spouse?" Beth asks, still unsure of gender.

"Buried a few in my time." Mattie jerks a thumb over a shoulder. "They're out back."

Beth flinches.

Mattie slaps a thigh and guffaws. "Gotcha, didn't I."

The flush starts at Beth's neck and proceeds to her scalp. Her ears burn.

"I knows you been wondering, but I likes to keep people guessing. I enjoys the torment." Mattie sits back in the chair. "Mattie is short for Matthew. Matthew MacKenzie." His eyes crinkle at the corners like an accordion. "And *no* spouse. How about yours?"

"Alan's a vet. He was here for a week, but he went back to St. John's on Friday. We have one daughter. In Vancouver, working in a lab." Beth brings the steaming mug to her lips to stop her flustered chattering. The tea is pale and smells like new-mown hay.

"Vancouver. That's grand." Mattie tastes the tea, grimaces. Stirs in another teaspoon of sugar. "So what do you do when you're not out chasing after otters?"

"Teach."

His face brightens. "Katherine was a teacher! History. Taught in Gander for years."

"I teach biology. At the university."

"University. Big stuff."

"Not really." She's been teaching for more than twenty years. She could do it blindfolded. She'd prefer, in fact, to do it blindfolded, then she wouldn't have to look at the bored faces. She still finds biology awesome, in the old sense of the word: inspiring awe. But she can't seem to convey that to her students. While she lectures, they stare out the window, check their cellphones, and type on their laptops what she's pretty sure are not biology notes.

"You say you see them a lot, the otters," Beth says. "Where do you think I'd be able to watch them?"

"Just a little ways down from Katherine's cabin. Near the old beaver lodge. You haven't seen em yet?"

"I've hardly been here a week. And I only started my project a few days ago."

"Maybe they're staying away for a while. Sure, they can be pretty cautious around anything new."

From the gentle way he says this, Beth suspects he's just being kind to the scientist who can't find her research animals. She pushes the tea away. Her skin feels hot, but also clammy. She pulls off her sweatshirt and lays it across her lap. Begins to fiddle with the metal turnkey on the kerosene lamp.

"So ..." She coughs into her hand. "If you've been here for eighty years, you must know the story on Medicine Rock Pond."

Mattie straightens. Eyes that were hazel just moments ago are now bright green with startling flashes of gold. "There's lotsa stories about the pond," he says cautiously.

"About the name, I mean."

His face relaxes. "Oh ... that. There's a rock at the outlet. Medicine Rock."

"Odd name."

"Might be Mi'kmaq. Might go all the way back to the Beothuk." Mattie shrugs. "Who knows? Long time ago, people would visit Medicine Rock to pray."

"People prayed to a rock?"

He laughs. "Don't be so foolish. Do people pray to a church? It's just the place where they go to feel close to their god ... or creator ... cosmic forces ... whatever you wanna call it." He clicks a thumbnail on the chipped front tooth. "I've often thought the world would be a better place if all of us had a Medicine Rock. A place to pray, not just for our own selves, but for the earth too."

"I'd say the earth needs our protection more than our prayers."

"Same thing, love. You don't pray for something you don't care about." Mattie picks up the pipe, which looks hand-carved, and opens the pouch of Amphora, stuffs tobacco into the bowl.

Beth lays a finger on the pouch. "When I first got here," she says carefully, "you asked if I'd brought tobacco. And then said something about the dog choosing me."

"Must've been dreaming." He talks around the pipe stem. "I gets a bit confused at times." He strikes a wooden match, holds it to the pipe, and inhales a few shallow draws, expels a cloud of grey smoke. The sweet aroma reminds Beth of her grandfather, of summer afternoons trailing behind him as they walked around the farm, of sitting quietly on the front porch, him rocking and smoking, her sipping lemonade. She fiddles again with the metal turnkey on the kerosene lamp.

"Careful," Mattie says, "gonna break that thing."

She pulls her hand away and tucks it into her lap. Looks down, and then up at Mattie. "So how do you know so much about the rock?"

Mattie takes the pipe from his mouth. "Been here a long time. Oughta know something by now." He sets the pipe in a stand. "And my nan was part Mi'kmaq."

"So you're Mi'kmaq yourself?"

"Not really." Mattie spreads his big hands on the table. "Mostly Irish and Scottish. Bit of French, Welsh, and English thrown in for good measure." He traces a purple vein under the tanned skin on the back of his hand, perhaps considering the mix of currents in that miniature river of blood. "Sure, I'm the mutt," he says. "It's Muin here that's the purebred." The dog's tail thumps against the floor. "How about you? What kinda mutt are you? Sure, you're not from around here."

"Minnesota farm girl. Mostly German, part Norwegian."

"Farm girl! That's grand. Tell you what: I'll help you with your otters if you helps me with my garden. Some kinda worm is eating my cabbages." He points at the tin pot. "More tea?"

"Thanks, but I really should be going." Beth stands. For just a moment, she is dizzy. She grabs the edge of the table. Her vision narrows then clears.

"But I have a story for you."

"I should get to work now."

Mattie touches the back of her hand. "We all live in stories, love. It's important to know which one you're in."

CHAPTER 3

Beth can feel his gaze on her back. Knows that if she were to turn around, she would see Mattie at the window. She hunches her shoulders against his scrutiny and steps onto the narrow trail.

We all live in stories. What story is she in?

Beth stops herself. She might pity his loneliness, but she doesn't have time to sit and listen to the rambling stories of an old man who *gets a bit confused at times,* who believes an old otter keeps watch over the pond. She has to confess to a certain curiosity though. Eighty years on the pond. Watching animals. Mattie probably does know a lot about the local wildlife. Could be useful to talk with him again – if she can just steer him away from his own homespun explanations and get him to speak plainly about what he's seen.

When she gets back to the cabin, Beth changes into shorts and sport sandals, stuffs her research gear into a backpack, tosses in bread and cheese and a water bottle. She looks up. Katherine's rocking chair. Her hands linger on the zipper of the backpack. Friends for more than forty years. Mattie must know a lot about Katherine too.

Anxious to get to work, she grabs an apple but skips breakfast. She has only a couple of weeks before she'll have to return to St. John's to prepare for the start of classes.

She stows everything in the kayak, including a small cooler for samples, and shoves off into a morning that is chilly and overcast. She paddles slowly along the shoreline and enters the small bay just south of the cabin, hoping to find the beaver lodge where Mattie said she could find otters. She lets the kayak drift and scans the water's edge with her binoculars. Finally spots the lodge, sticks bleached, almost hidden by encroaching grasses. She paddles closer. Plenty of droppings on the rocks nearby, some fresh, some old: an otter latrine. They're probably using the abandoned lodge for a den. In a few places, the grass is crushed where they've rubbed themselves dry.

How did she miss that before? She lands the kayak to examine the scats. Pulls out four zip-lock bags and labels each: *02 Aug 10: A5, latrine.* She collects four fresh samples and tucks them into the cooler. Still crouched, Beth counts the scats and records: *02 Aug 10: A5, abandoned beaver lodge (possible den), rubbing site (~3 m northeast of lodge), latrine (~2 m diameter, ~12 m northeast of lodge); 4 fresh scats, 8 old, 4-6 otters.* She photographs the lodge, the rubbing site, and the latrine.

The fir and spruce growing close to shore are dense. She guesses that if she were to come here at dawn and dusk, there's a good chance she could watch them, either from behind the trees or from the kayak. Just like Mattie said.

She lifts her cap to massage her forehead and then her temples. She has a headache and a vague light-headedness she's begun to blame on Mattie's tea.

Beth slides back into the kayak and continues south, slowly, binoculars swinging against her life-jacket. She follows the shoreline until it gradually bends east. The water is the colour of weak tea, but clear: she can see all the way to the rock and sand at the bottom, to the crushed red and blue Pepsi can, the silver Coors Light. She passes through patches of yellow water lilies and gently waving underwater grasses and weeds. Sees black ducks and sandpipers, a chattering kingfisher that swoops from one overhanging branch to the next, but no more signs of otters, no latrines or rubbing places.

After three more hours of slow paddling, she finds a single fresh scat on a flat rock about five kilometres of shoreline from the old beaver lodge. Before she collects the sample, she checks the landmarks against her map: the rock lies well within the one hundred metres of shoreline she's designated section F4. DNA tests will confirm it, but she'd be willing to bet the scat is from one of the animals active at the beaver lodge: otters have multiple dens within large home ranges. In this case, probably all of Medicine Rock Pond, which, despite its name, is more than fifteen hundred hectares. Even after twenty years in Newfoundland, Beth still has trouble using the word "pond" for such large bodies of water. Sixteen kilometres of shoreline: 160 one-hundred metre sections she's labelled A1, her cabin, counter-clockwise through P10.

The ocean is only four or five kilometres to the north, and connected to the pond by a river; it's likely that Mattie is right about that too: the otters are regularly going into the salt water to catch a lobster, mussel, or flounder. Beth puts the sample into the cooler, against the ice.

~

The sky is beginning to darken, but there will be dusky light for at least another hour. Beth slaps insect repellent onto her face and hands – for all the good it will do – tucks her journal and voice recorder into one pocket of her backpack, pencil and binoculars into another, and dons a cap. She paddles to the small bay south of the cabin, wedges the kayak's bow into a rock crevice about twenty metres from the beaver lodge. And waits.

Every now and then, the quiet is broken by the splash of a trout jumping, but Beth doesn't turn toward the sound. She hardly moves except to brush the pesky mosquitoes and black flies from her face and hands.

Half an hour later, she sees the "v" of a muskrat in the still water, its tail waving back and forth in a sensuous "s."

It emerges from the pond with a long cattail, sits on a rock, and manipulates the plant with its front paws until it can chew on the root. Beth congratulates herself on her stillness: the muskrat doesn't even know she's there.

When it's become too dark for observations, she pushes the kayak away from the rocks and starts back to the cabin. She rounds the point of the bay and sees the *Black Feather*, a small green light glowing on its bow. Beth hugs the shore, and when she is opposite from what must be Mattie's nephew, she grins and gives a hardy wave. *Uppity,* eh? He nods. Too dark to see whether he returned her smile or not.

Back at the cabin, Beth lights the kerosene lamp and records: *02 Aug 10: ~16°C, overcast, winds light, observed at otter spot 19:50 – 20:55, none observed.*

She taps the pencil on her journal. Too early to go to bed. She glances at the musty deck of cards and then at the unopened box on the table. One thousand pieces: the pleasure of sorting them by colour and shape, starting with edge pieces first; the simple satisfaction of fitting one piece to another until everything fits. Beth moves a folder of technical papers from the table to the kitchen counter, takes out her pocket knife, and slits the sides of the box.

~

One by one, the otters emerge from the lodge, called forth by the old female's chirps. Hidden in the long grasses, she has been watching and listening, sniffing the air. She smelled the human, then saw her bobbing on top of the water. Strong odour of plastic. She also caught the scent of the man and the boat's stink. She waited until they were gone, and the smells had softened, to call the others from the lodge. They hunt now in the shallows, whiskers detecting fish in the dark. The pups begin to wrestle, prompting adults to join in. *Uhn-uhn-uhn, uhn-uhn-uhn.*

~

Beth wakes early, while it's still dark. Decides to forego coffee. Also neglects to brush her teeth, wash her face, or comb her hair. She wants to be at the place she's designated the otter spot before dawn. She shines a flashlight on the plastic thermometer tacked outside the living room window: 14°C. Pulls a windbreaker over her fleece jacket. This time, she walks. By the time she arrives, the sky is just beginning to pale. She can tell by the absence of fresh scats that they didn't visit during the night.

There is no colourful sunrise: the sky simply lightens from a charcoal grey to a slightly less sullen shade. Beth sits on shore and waits. And waits. A slender mink appears at the water's edge, dark-brown fur glossy even in the overcast. With a weasel's humpback gait, it leaps from rock to rock, pauses to sniff at the otters' latrine, but doesn't linger. The mink is an interloper on its larger cousins' turf. It disappears into the woods.

Small raindrops begin to spot Beth's glasses. Her head aches, and she wishes that she'd taken the time to make coffee. Chilled, and wet, she walks back to the cabin, builds a fire, and fills the percolator. It's raining heavily now, and she rearranges metal pots and ceramic bowls to catch the drips from the leaking roof. She lights the kerosene lamp and looks at the thick folder of articles on the counter – mostly technical papers about DNA extraction from fecal samples, but also articles about the harmful effects of the effluent from oil refineries and tankers, about hydrocarbons, heavy metals, and organophosphates showing up in every corner of the globe. She lays a hand on the stack of papers: all those dire warnings, local and global. Decides that she just doesn't have the energy to read them this morning, not with a dull grey sky overhead.

In her worst moments, she can't help believing that people are a blight upon the earth: an aggressive invasive species heedlessly displacing all others. Wouldn't the earth be better off without them?

~

Late afternoon. Still raining hard and the wind is coming from the northeast at a pretty good clip. Cooped up in the cabin, Beth has tried to distract herself with the puzzle and, when that didn't work, with one of the mystery novels she brought with her. That didn't work either. She lays the paperback aside and stands. Every day her knees and hips remind her that she's getting older, that time is running out. And lately, she's been dogged by the suspicion that her so-called accomplishments – her doctoral thesis, her teaching, her scattered publications – are all second-rate. When she went to one of her younger colleagues to seek advice about her project, he'd actually raised his pale eyebrows.

"How long since you've done any field research?" he asked.

"I assisted Martin with his caribou project two years ago. Before that, I did some observations for O'Keefe when she was studying puffins. And for years I've been helping with marine mammal rescues."

"But when was the last time you headed up a research project?"

Beth stared out his office window, at an expansive view that included the university library and the clock tower. "Graduate school," she said.

"And that was?"

She tucked loose hair behind one ear. "Twenty-five years ago."

"Hard to get a grant when you don't have much of a track record." He turned back to his dual computer screens. "My advice is to start with a small request to a local agency."

Beth had settled on a preliminary survey she could complete in a few weeks – without any funding.

She begins to pace. Maybe Mattie and the crows are right: it's laughable. She counts eight long strides from one end of the room to the other, then five in the perpendicular. The count isn't accurate though because she has to step around the bowls and pans.

She grabs her wallet and windbreaker. She needs to get out of the cabin and the relentless drip of water. Beth makes a dash for the Toyota; the door creaks when she opens it. Inside, the stale air smells of spilt coffee.

Town is less than fifteen kilometres away, but driving over the rutted gravel roads and dodging water-filled potholes, she feels like it's at least fifty. The wipers are drumming at full speed. She leaves the radio off, keeping to her no-news rule.

About two kilometres after she finally reaches pavement, Beth spots the service station where she can buy gas and ice on her way out of town. A momentary pinch of guilt. She should call Alan. She hasn't talked to him since he left four days ago. She checks her watch: 16:42. He's probably still at the clinic tending to his four-legged patients. Maybe, on her way out of town, she'll give him a call.

She's tempted to go into the public library, still open on a grey Tuesday afternoon, and check her email, but decides not to break her no-email rule either. Beth passes the Bide-a-Wee, the town's shabby eight-unit motel, and the coffee shop where she and Alan had supper a week ago: seafood chowder that was mostly starchy cream and potatoes. The yellow glow from the front window looks cosy now, more welcoming. Maybe she'll treat herself to a piece of pie before she leaves town.

She pulls into the parking lot of a small grocery, the only grocery, her Toyota one of just two cars in the lot. Hunching against the wind and rain, Beth scuttles inside and grabs a plastic basket from the stack beside the economy bags of Purina and Rob Roy.

She walks slowly up and down the aisles; the only customer. The cashier, a stick-thin teenager wearing a white bib apron over tight jeans – who makes jeans for legs that skinny? – is stacking what looks like week-old iceberg lettuce into a cooler. The outer leaves are already tinged with rust. Overhead, a fluorescent light flickers, repeatedly, and Beth wonders how the girl can work here without going mad.

She scans the shelves for food that's easy to prepare: cans of sardines and Campbell's soups, boxes of crackers and Kraft Dinner, a small chunk of cheddar. Each can and box has a thin layer of gritty dust on top. She adds a loaf of whole-grain bread, some apples, batteries, wooden matches, emergency candles. And a bar of dark chocolate. If all else fails, at least she'll have chocolate.

While she stands at the checkout waiting for the cashier, Beth stares at the covers of the tabloids and magazines: *The National Enquirer, Globe, Us, People.* Doesn't worry about breaking her no-news rule.

The cashier finally comes, her bangs the same shade of red as a stop sign, fingernails enamelled a metallic blue. She glances at the groceries, then at Beth, then out the window, where the sky is cement grey. The Maple Leaf is straight out, snapping a tattoo. The edge of the flag is tattered.

The girl chews her gum thoughtfully. "Not great weather for camping, is it."

"No, it's not."

"Where you staying to?" She hasn't picked up a single box or can.

"The old Wells place."

The premature wrinkles between the girl's eyebrows deepen, then relax. "Oh, I remember her. She was nice. Cabin's out to Medicine Rock, right?" The cashier looks out the window and chews, gum snapping and popping. She turns back to Beth, blue-shadowed eyes wide. "You must be that lady who's here to collect otter poop!"

Beth marvels at the lightning speed of small-town communications. Who needs cellphones?

"Guess there's not much you can do on a day like today though." The cashier picks up a can of sardines and scans the barcode. The periwinkle fingernails click on the metal. "Tomorrow's not supposed to be much better. But you never know." She smiles encouragement. "No TV, no Internet," she says, "not even phone service out there. Nothin." Her eyes widen again at the horror of *nothin*.

"And that cabin's pretty far from everything," she continues. "Good thing Mattie MacKenzie's still out that way." The machine beeps as the girl scans another barcode. "Keeps mostly to herself though. Met her yet?"

"I met *him* yesterday."

The girl chuckles. "Must be up to her old tricks again. Some of the old-timers claim she's a witch. But I don't believe any of that old nonsense."

Beth pinches the bridge of her nose, squeezes hard. "Just a minute," she says. "I forgot something." She walks over to the stacks of dog food and grabs a box of Milk-Bones.

CHAPTER 4

She marches up the trail, light mist dotting her glasses. What in the world prompted her to buy dog treats? She doesn't need to appease anyone. She just wants to ask Mattie why *she* pretended to be *he*. She'd stewed on the possible answers to that question all night long: Poking fun. Pulling the leg of the uppity townie. Another story for Mattie to tell – just like telling everyone about the scientist who's come here to collect otter shit.

As soon as Beth steps into the clearing, Muin greets her with a series of low woofs. The dog runs toward her and prances clumsily around her legs, nudging the box of biscuits. "Okay, girl. Just a minute." Beth is glad now that she bought the Milk-Bones. Muin's not to blame. It wasn't the dog who made a fool of her.

Mattie appears at the screen door, opens it wide. "Come in, love. I'll make us some tea."

"I was in town yesterday. The clerk at Price Chopper asked about you."

"Me?" Mattie steps outside. She is wearing a red plaid shirt two sizes too big. The sleeves hang down to her fingertips.

"The clerk asked if I'd met *her* yet."

Mattie grins.

"Why did you do that?"

Mattie lowers herself to the front step, wraps her arms around her knees. "Simple really. I woke up from a long sleep feeling like a Matthew. Most mornings, I wake up feeling like a Matilda." She looks up at Beth. "Does it matter?"

29

Beth had asked herself exactly the same question on the long drive from town. What does it change? She couldn't think of a single thing.

"It matters because you pretended to be something you're not," Beth says.

"We all do that, love."

Muin pushes a wet muzzle against Beth's hand. She tears open the package and gives her a treat. It's gone before Beth can close the box.

"When you came by the other morning," Mattie says, "I was just coming back from a dream, a dream in which I was Matthew. I was still Matthew when Muin woke me up."

"But ... dreams are dreams," Beth says slowly, "and life is ..." She holds out her hands, palms up, box clamped under an elbow, "Life."

"Exactly! I knew you'd understand."

Beth's hands drop to her sides. Understand what?

"First time I clapped eyes on you, I knew you were a dreamer." Mattie peers into her face. "You were in the dream too, you know."

"You hadn't even met me yet."

"No odds. Seen any otters?"

Beth turns away and starts to pace. Muin follows the box of Milk-Bones.

On the drive from town, Beth had replayed their first conversation. Then, Mattie spoke with an accent so thick it almost sounded fake. This morning, the accent is gone, and Beth would swear the pitch of Mattie's voice is higher.

She stops pacing and turns to Mattie. "Is anything you told me true?"

"Everything's true ... one way or another."

"But have you really lived here for eighty years?"

"Yep."

"I mean in real life. Not in your dreams."

"Same thing." Mattie pulls at a stray thread on a button-hole. "You talk to them?"

"Who?"

Mattie rolls her eyes. "The otters, girl. You need to talk to them."

"But I haven't even seen any."

"That's why you need to ask them to show themselves. Tell them you mean no harm, that you just want to know a few of their secrets."

"Funny, we never learned that research technique in graduate school."

Mattie examines the foxglove blooming beside the step; the deep throats of the purple flowers are spotted red, like a spray of blood. She touches an oval leaf. "Well, now, there's scientific ways of knowing. Then there's the other ways."

Muin nudges the Milk-Bones. Beth doles out another biscuit but maintains her grip on the box. The dog could eat the whole package, cardboard and all, in a few slob-bery gulps.

Mattie snaps off a spike of the purple flowers and points it at Beth. "You can learn every little scientific fact about otters ... and still not know otters." She nods once, emphatically. "Unless you study them in other ways too."

"Like what? In dreams?"

"That's part of it."

Beth stares out across the pond, the same steel grey as the heavy overcast above. Maybe Mattie does consider herself a witch – all those dried plants hanging from the ceiling, the jar of feathers, the Matthew-Matilda busi-ness, foxglove and monkshood growing at her doorstep – decorative, but also poisonous. Maybe there really are spouses buried in the back. Mattie probably has skulls and jars of animal parts stored in the spare bedroom. Beth doesn't believe in witches or in any other such nonsense, but a shiver creeps across the back of her neck and up along her scalp. She pulls her turtleneck up to her chin.

"Come on in outta this drizzle," Mattie says. "I'll make us some tea. I have a story to tell you."

"No, I should get to work."

"No time for a story?" Mattie's lower lip pushes out. "Katherine always had time for a story." She throws up her hands. "But suit yourself."

"By the way," Beth says, "what you told me about the otters. Is any of that true?"

"Parts maybe." Mattie taps an index finger against her nose. "Or maybe not." She stands and steps into the cabin. Muin looks longingly at the Milk-Bones, then turns and follows Mattie. The screen door smacks shut.

~

Beth sits on shore at the otter spot, binoculars in her lap. She spent the day searching six more kilometres of shoreline, found two older scats but nothing new, nothing to collect.

The light is beginning to fade. She's been here for nearly an hour, and so far she's seen nothing but sandpipers, crows, and black ducks. She reaches out and picks ripening crackerberries off the low-growing plants, rolls the red berries in her palm. Tosses them, one by one, onto a flat rock. One red berry smacks against another and sends it bouncing along a crooked path. A silent game of marbles.

You need to talk to them. Mattie is off her rocker, a wingnut. For sure.

~

Her watch alarm beeps: 4:30. Beth hears the long warbling call of a loon, an echoing answer. She rises and builds a fire, pumps water into the percolator. It's early enough that she can make coffee and still be at the otter spot before the sun comes up. It's only a fifteen-minute walk through the woods.

32

When she gets there, Beth can tell from the fresh scats on the latrine that the otters visited during the night, so she's not hopeful she'll see them this morning. She waits anyway; at least she's brought coffee this time and it's not raining.

She sits down among the spruce and fir, arranges her journal and pencil, voice recorder and binoculars. Combs her fingers through her cropped hair. Feels the grease. She's long overdue for a swim and a shampoo. Her hands are dry, the skin rough, and her nails are ragged and outlined in black soot. She's not even sure she packed an emery board. Not like Alan. He always carries nail clippers and emery boards, a professional necessity. She wonders if he's still in bed.

The night before he left to return to St. John's, Alan cooked the trout he'd caught that day. She set the table and lit the candles. "Your dinner awaits," he said, words spoken with a mock English accent. Alan presented the fish with the flourish of a chef. He'd even garnished the plates with sprigs of pink clover. In the candlelight his face was pale, his peeling nose and blotchy freckles the only evidence that they'd just spent a week in the sun, kayaking, fishing, swimming.

He raised a finger and pointed, and Pirate gimped obediently to his bed in the corner, settled in with a groan, and fixed his gaze on their steaming plates.

Alan lifted a fork. "Wish I didn't have to go back." Poked at a boiled potato. "How long do you think it will take for you to get what you need?"

Beth reached for the pepper. "Depends on how long it takes me to find enough samples."

"I could come out next weekend and help."

She sprinkled pepper over her plate, then carefully lifted the backbone away from the fish. "Thanks, but two people bobbing around in kayaks might keep them away and then I won't get any observations."

"I could just go off and fish somewhere. Leave you to your work."

"Being able to focus on my research all day," she said slowly, "every day, means I can get back to St. John's that much sooner." She smashed a boiled potato with her fork. "And I need to know that I can still do this on my own."

"But I'm concerned about you kayaking by yourself."

"It's quiet water, Alan, and I'll wear my life-jacket. Promise." She closed her eyes, took a deep breath, and then said it quickly: "And I think I might need a little time to myself."

He looked out the window and pulled gently at the loose skin under his chin, then turned back to Beth. "For what?"

"Not sure." She tried to smile. "It's been more than twenty years since I've spent any real time alone."

"But I thought you were disappointed that Rachel didn't come home this summer."

"I am, but ..." She couldn't finish. Couldn't explain it, even to herself.

They bent over their plates and busied themselves picking bones from the delicate pink flesh. Pirate rose quietly from his bed and walked to the table, clicking nails and three-legged gait audible across the wood floor. With a tentative wag of his tail, he laid his head in Alan's lap and watched him eat. Alan scowled in feigned sternness and then slipped the dog the trout skin. He wiped his greasy fingers on a paper towel. "Call me every evening then?"

"There's no reception here, remember? I'll have to drive into town."

He blinked, his pale lashes barely visible. "Oh, right," he said, nodding. And the nodding annoyed her. She wished she could prod him into an argument, then she could yell at him. But for what? For agreeing with her?

Dinner over, they undressed and climbed into the creaking bed, both sleeping bags unzipped and spread under them and over them like blankets. They'd left the dishes for morning, even though it was only nine o'clock. Alan blew out the candle, then lay down facing her back. He touched her shoulder, and she turned to face him. He kissed her and stroked her breasts, murmured in her ear, "I'll miss you."

She felt her heart shrivel into something hard-shelled and miserly – because she didn't want to return his touch, or his words, but didn't have the courage to say so. She rubbed his chest and reached down to bring him to life, in a ritual that was no longer love-making but just sex.

When it was over, she rolled away from him and stared into the dark. She felt Pirate climb onto the bed and settle between them, a rustling of the sleeping bag then the soft, warm weight. Just before sleep, an image of water and limestone came to mind: the erosion of the bond between them like the steady, underground drip of water on stone, unseen and unremarked. Until this. Not a growing hatred or anger, or even dislike. But an absence, a worn-away hollow.

In the morning, Alan and Pirate left before she'd even gotten out of bed. A peck on her cheek, a slobbery lick to her nose, and they were out the door.

Beth slaps at a mosquito. She picks up the journal and pencil at her side, but then has to pause. Can't recall the date. Thinks it might be Thursday, the fifth, but isn't entirely sure. She scrawls a few notes: *5 Aug 10: ~16°C, clear and sunny, winds light, observed in A5, 5:20 – 7:18, fresh scat from 3-5 animals, none observed.*

None. *This all seems pointless – an animal behaviourist who can't find her animals. And what would it matter if I could?*

She stares at the stark words. Tries to erase them, but the hard eraser makes messy black smears. She crosses them out.

Beth collects three fresh samples, then walks back to the cabin and slips them into the cooler. She eats a quick breakfast of saltines and peanut butter, and re-heated coffee, then loads up the kayak and spends the rest of the morning paddling another few kilometres of shoreline. The sun is warm, almost hot, on her face, and she pictures Alan in his air-conditioned clinic, methodically washing his hands and cleaning his nails before entering an examining room, and then nodding patiently, face serious, while worried pet owners try to explain what they think is wrong with Bitsy or Fluffy or Max. She'll go into town later, she promises herself, pick up more ice and call him.

CHAPTER 5

About mid-day, having searched another four kilometres of shoreline, Beth heads toward the outlet, curious now whether she can identify Medicine Rock. The wind is calm, the paddling easy under a hazy sky.

Approaching the outlet, Beth studies the rocks. They're all different – rust-red, a dark red-black, various shades of grey, some with green or white striations – but none is particularly distinctive. They're millions of years old. Yet, sharply angled, they look new, not ancient, and they're jumbled together as if they were tossed there by a giant hand. Who decided to name one Medicine Rock?

Beth spots a red one that is darker than the others – almost maroon – and a bit bigger too. It stands upright and a little apart. She stares a few moments, squints, finally sees the craggy profile of a man's face. Maybe.

She beaches the kayak and pulls it up onto the rocky shore. A salmon leaps and falls back into the water with a soft splash. About thirty metres away, an eagle watches from a tall spruce. Probably looking for lunch, and Beth has interfered. She raises her binoculars and sees a mottled head and tail: an immature bird. The juvenile, now as large as an adult, spreads its great wings and lifts off.

She sits down beside the upright boulder she has decided is Medicine Rock and pulls a water bottle and bread and cheese from her backpack. She smells fresh water and the faint, sweet fragrance of the wild roses blooming at the edge of the woods behind her. A black and yellow swallowtail lands on the rock, opens and closes its wings, then flits away.

The place where they went to feel close to their god. Well, if she were forced to choose, she'd pick a big red rock beside tumbling water – in a place with eagles and salmon, wild roses and butterflies – over a cathedral any day.

Running a fingertip along a white vein in the rock, she wonders who came here long ago and to whom they prayed. And for what. *Please help us to find enough food for the winter. Please heal the sickness in my chest. Please let this baby be born healthy. Please let my wife – my husband, my mother, my child, my friend – live. Or die peacefully. Please. Please. Please.*

Heartfelt petitions. Not so different then from now. When she was a child she prayed, sometimes fervently, with a child's whole heart. She can't remember when she stopped. Probably when it became clear that no one was listening.

Beth touches the rock again. The surface is cold and rough.

Just what would she pray for if she thought someone were actually listening? A good life and good health for her daughter, her husband, and herself. Of course.

She lifts her face to the sun and closes her eyes. Hears water murmuring and gurgling as it flows around the rocks in its rush to the sea. She would pray for the earth, for the preservation of places like this one.

Her hand drops from the rock. But you can't just *decide* to hold on to childish delusions. No matter how much better they might make you feel.

Two years ago, Beth had actually tried, for Alice's sake. She even tried praying again. And then felt foolish for it. Because no one was listening then either. Her best friend suffered, in the worst kind of way, and Beth couldn't help her.

She swallows the last of her water and realizes she has to pee. There's just one small boat out on the pond, so she won't have to go far into the woods, but as soon as she steps in among the spruce and fir, she has an odd sense of being watched. She looks all around, sees no one, but walks in farther, until she begins to feel absurdly modest. She unzips her shorts and squats down in a thicket of tall ferns. Swats a mosquito from her bare thigh.

As she's zipping up again, she sees a glint. A beer can or discarded sausage tin? She steps closer: it's just a shallow pool of water reflecting the light. But beside the pool, half hidden by sphagnum moss, lie two small shells, cowry shells. Beth stoops to pick them up, but the shells are attached to each other by a corroded metal chain. She pulls, gently, so she won't break the chain, but then has to lift a rock to pull the shells and the chain free.

She doesn't know much about religious objects, but she's pretty sure she's found a rosary, an odd rosary of cowry shells, green glass beads, and bits of carved bone, which she can see now are crudely carved animals and birds. Beth picks shreds of moss off the carvings and, using a thumbnail, scratches soil and corrosion from the chain.

Rosary clasped in one hand, Beth walks back to the outlet. An aluminum boat sits on shore beside her kayak: the *Black Feather*. A man in hipwaders is standing in the fast-moving water. He draws back an arm to cast.

She shoves the rosary into her pocket. "Hi there," she calls out with false cheeriness. "Catching anything?"

"Few rises. Nothing big."

"I saw a salmon jump earlier. Great day," she offers, hoping she's now been friendly enough that she can leave without being called uppity.

He angles his head toward her. "Looking for otters?"

"Just doing a bit of research on the pond."

"Looking for otter shit is what I heard."

"There's a little more to it than that," she says.

"Is there now?" He casts the small fly out over the water, flicks the line, then pulls it in.

"You must be Mattie MacKenzie's nephew."

"Sort of."

"Sort of?"

"Grandnephew. My grandmother was her older sister – by almost twenty years." He shifts the fly rod to his left hand and steps toward Beth. Puts out his right. "I'm Dan. Dan Holloway."

"Beth Meyer."

He is just a few inches taller than Mattie and almost as spare. Under the bill of a red baseball cap, his eyes are the same hazel green. Hair, from what she can see of it, is dark, and generously flecked with silver.

"Mattie tells me you're from the university in St. John's."

In other words: *uppity*.

His gaze travels from her bare toes up to her face again. Beth, in her khaki shorts, black tank top, and sport sandals, suddenly feels both underdressed and over-dressed, as if she's just stepped out of an Eddie Bauer catalogue. She unties the chamois shirt draped over her shoulders and pulls it on.

"Said you were doing some kinda study on otters."

"Just a preliminary assessment, really. To see if I can do a real study here." She turns toward the kayak, says over her shoulder, "Was just taking a lunch break. I should get back to work."

"The shit always calls, doesn't it." Muttered, just loud enough for her to hear.

She spins around, intending a snappy retort, but comes up short: annoyed but empty-headed. Surprises herself then with a question. "Is she okay? Is she …?"

His smirk fades. "Cracked?"

"She doesn't have Alzheimer's or anything?"

"Nope. Sharp as a tack." He pulls a cigarette from his shirt pocket, sticks it between his lips and talks around it. "Just a bit nuts is all."

"How old is she anyway?"

Dan tilts his head, lips still gripping the cigarette. "Guess she must be in her mid-eighties by now." The cigarette bobbles.

"And she doesn't need some sort of caretaker, someone to help her out?"

"Nope." He flicks a lighter and cups his hand around the end of the cigarette. Exhales a cloud of grey smoke. "I pick up her groceries and cut wood for her. Do a few repairs around the cabin." He loosens a shoulder strap on the hipwaders. "My most important job is taking her weavings and carvings to a gallery in St. John's."

"Really?" Beth chews her bottom lip: Mattie an artist? "When I first met her," she says slowly, "she told me her name was Matthew." She expects Dan to grin just like Mattie did.

Instead, he takes a deep draw on the cigarette, exhales. "She does that sometimes."

"Seems a bit ... odd."

A salmon breaches, and they both turn to watch the disappearing ripples. Beth glances sideways at Dan. His face is angular and weathered, with the same prominent nose as Mattie's. Handsome, she supposes, in a craggy sort of way: the Marlboro Man.

"Matthew was her twin brother," he says. "Died long before I was even born. She claims to be living his life for him." He waves the cigarette dismissively. "Or something like that. I don't ask. Not my business." He looks at Beth, doesn't smile. "None a yours neither." He gently stubs out the cigarette and puts the unsmoked half into his pocket. Walks back out into the water.

~

Beth sips an indifferent merlot and studies the rosary by the yellow glow of the kerosene lamp. She's rubbed the chain with Brasso and scrubbed the dirt off the shells and beads, and the carved animals. The short length of chain for a cross is there, but the cross itself is missing.

After she'd left Dan to his fishing, she paddled back to the cabin and then drove into town, dutifully stopping at the pay phone to call Alan. She fingered the rosary while she waited: one ring, two, three, four, then the answering machine with her own chirpy voice asking her to "please leave a message."

"Hi, Alan," she said. "Everything's going–"

"Good to hear your voice ... finally. Glad I didn't miss you." He sounded out of breath. "I was just on my way out the door. Emergency surgery. How're things going?"

"I've collected samples from a few different sites on the pond."

"Great."

"Yeah, but I haven't seen them yet. Not sure I'll be able to get much in the way of observations."

"Observations don't matter that much, do they? Just as long as you can get enough samples."

"I guess. But I'd really like to watch them."

"Well, you said yourself they're elusive little buggers."

She scraped dirt off one of the small carvings. "What's the surgery?"

"Cat. Hit by a car."

She cringed.

"From the technician's assessment, it sounds like we won't be able to save it."

Beth envisioned his fingers running through his sandy hair, mottled now with grey.

"But I'll give it my best try," he said wearily. "Belongs to a little girl."

She could see his lined forehead, his fingers pulling at the loose skin under his chin, and knew that he would try his best. He always did. It's one of the things that made her fall in love. What were the others?

"I should get to the clinic," he said. "Thanks for calling. Good to know that you're okay and that you're getting some samples. Call me again tomorrow? I'll have more time then."

"Not sure I'll be able to get into town again."

"Okay. Well ... call me when you can."

"Good luck with the surgery."

Hasty goodbyes. No time to talk about Mattie and the odd he-she business. Or the rosary. Just as well. Too difficult to explain anyway.

She punched in the numbers and called her daughter. No answer, so Beth left a message: "Hi, Rachel, hope everything's good with you. I've started my research, and everything's going great. I'll call again soon. Love you."

Beth made it to the liquor store just before it closed and picked out three bottles of red wine. From there she went to the hardware and bought metal cleaner, an inexpensive scrub-brush, and four dust-covered wineglasses – three more than she needed, but it would be humiliating to purchase only one, like announcing to the whole town that the uppity scientist drinks alone.

She decided then to treat herself to supper at the Morning Glory. She grabbed a novel from the stash in the backseat and sat at the counter, one of only two customers, the other an elderly man tucked away in a corner booth. He nodded and tried to smile when she came in, but the right side of his mouth turned down; the whole right side of his face was slack, as if he'd suffered a stroke.

While Beth ate her salad and vegetable soup, she read the Agatha Christie mystery. And scrupulously avoided eye contact with the man's watery blue eyes, fearing that if she gave him an opening, he'd join her at the counter and regale her with stories of the olden days.

Driving back to the cabin in the golden light of a late-summer evening, Beth surprised herself with her eagerness to clean up the rosary, so eager, in fact, that she didn't bother to go out to the otter spot. Instead, she's spent the last two hours scrubbing and polishing. Beneath the corrosion, the chain is copper. A few of the green glass beads are cracked, and she can tell by the empty spaces on the chain that a few have broken away completely. It's the carvings that intrigue her. It looks as if there may have been ten when the rosary was intact; now there are only seven. The small chunks of bone appear to be a caribou or moose, a bear and a fish, an eagle, a loon, and an owl. If she turns one carving on its side and squints, it could be construed as an otter, or at least she'd like to think so. She lays the rosary aside, swallows the last of her wine, and gets ready for bed.

~

The old female catches a small fish. She chirps at a pup, who follows her out of the water. When she lets go of the fish, it bends and twists – silver flashes over the rocks. The pup paws at the fish and nips its tail, but it flops its way into the shallow water. The old female lunges and captures it again. Bites its head, hard, and leaves it for the pup.

Three of the otters come onshore and sniff at the marking place. Mixed among the scents of plants and rocks, earth and sweet water, are the lingering traces of a female mink, a male muskrat, and two crows, an old one and a fledging that have eaten a rotting fish. Of far greater interest is the strong musk of an unfamiliar otter, young and male but not a pup. Each of the three otters turns, treads both hind feet, and leaves scat over his scat, musk over his musk.

They re-enter the water and all of them swim to the lodge. One by one, they dive, surface inside, and shake water from their fur. They settle in to groom each other: a tangle of warm, wet bodies. The old female touches each one with her muzzle, sniffs each reassuring scent. All of them here. A chorus of *uhn-uhn-uhns* fills the dark, humid lodge.

CHAPTER 6

Rain drumming hard against the roof startles her awake before her alarm goes off. She hopes she's left the pans and bowls in the right places. She's given up putting them away in the cupboards.

Beth closes her eyes to recall her dream, the one that woke her in the middle of the night: A young man sits cross-legged before a fire. Black hair, sun-bronzed skin, blue baseball cap with a bright red C. His hands wield a long bone and a knife that glints in the firelight. She knows, in the way that dreamers know, that he is carving an otter. He doesn't speak or look up, but she also knows that his eyes are bright green and that he is handsome. She hears a branch snap. A bull moose is charging toward her, its broad antlers enormous. She tries to run, but the mud is deep; it sucks at her feet. When she finally pulls free, she crawls, on hands and knees, into the cover of trees and shrubs, and watches the moose through branches interwoven like a spider web. Broad wings sweep over-head, a dark shadow. *Hoo-hoo-hoooo, hoo-hoo.* Then she feels warm breath on her neck. *Mfuff-mfuff.* And turns her head slowly to see a black bear, its golden eyes peering into hers. She edges away, crab-walking backwards, and finds herself in murky water, floating. The sky is geometric patches of green – sage, moss, jade, emerald – that blos-som and disappear like patterns in a kaleidoscope. A loon calls in a prolonged, echoing tremolo.

Whiskers tickled her cheek, waking her. *Uhn-uhn-uhn, uhn-uhn-uhn.* The rosary. She dreamed of the ani-mals on the rosary.

Beth keeps her eyes closed to envision the handsome young man. She had wanted him to look at her. She lies still in the warm sleeping bag. It's been such a long, long time since she's felt anything remotely lustful.

~

After she returns from the outhouse, Beth checks the pans and bowls, empties some, moves others. Glances at the table. No rosary. She's sure she left it there, right beside the kerosene lamp and the scattered puzzle pieces. She searches all around the jar of Brasso, the scrub-brush and rags. Lifts the lamp. Nothing.

She builds a fire and prepares coffee, pumping water into the battered percolator. It's then that she sees the rosary on the windowsill above the sink. She doesn't recall putting it there. She rubs her temples. Maybe she had more wine last night than she thought. Beth picks up the rosary and looks again at the carving she thinks is an otter. Lays it back on the windowsill.

While she waits for the coffee to perk, she wraps herself in her sleeping bag and watches the grey morning light illuminate the weaving. She gives it closer attention now that she knows it's artwork worthy of a gallery. Beth studies how the changing light transforms the patterns and colours: azure water, a rose sky bleeding to violet and then to indigo, a row of dark-green spruce, grey rock. Feathers – blue jay and crow, or maybe raven – have been woven into the indigo sky. Embroidery, or maybe crewelwork, Beth isn't sure, overlays parts of the weaving.

Forty years of friendship. Did Katherine buy it? Or was it a gift from Mattie?

Beth pours coffee and turns the rocking chair toward what meagre light the rainy dawn has to offer. She's been alone for a week, but she's not lonely. Not yet anyway. In truth, she often feels most herself when she's alone: no one to worry about pleasing – or disappointing. As an only child on a farm, she'd spent most of her time alone, just her and Jax roaming the woods and fields. She was shy around other kids, often blushed when they spoke to her; sometimes, they called her stuck-up, but it didn't matter. She had the animals for company. She thought of them as friends, even the ones most people didn't like: crows, mice, bats, and barn owls. She'd loved waking up on a spring morning, traipsing downstairs still rubbing sleep from her eyes, and finding a newborn lamb standing in a cardboard box, bleating to break your heart. It became Beth's job to bottle-feed rejected lambs. Until she was nine. That fall, after the lambs had been loaded onto the truck, Beth's father took her along to the slaughterhouse. The next spring, she refused to feed the motherless lambs. Her dad told her she was too soft-hearted to be a farmer's daughter, muttered something about an absence of iron.

Beth hears a scrabbling at the door. A series of woofs. She groans, then throws off the sleeping bag. Cracks the screen door just wide enough to shake a finger. "Muin, go back to where you belong."

The dog uses her muzzle and then her massive head as a wedge to push her way in. Trots into the bedroom and sniffs at the bed. Comes back out, sits down by the counter, and stares at the box of Milk-Bones and then at Beth.

Beth shakes her finger again. "Don't even think about it. I will not reward this."

Muin circles and settles near the cookstove. The odour of wet dog fills the room.

"Okay, you can dry off, then it's back you go."

Muin looks at Beth as if gauging her seriousness. Beth wonders what she's thinking – what the dog knows. She doesn't look especially intuitive, or intelligent, but then Newfoundlands rarely do. And yet, they're one of the most dedicated and courageous of all rescue dogs, willing to swim untold distances through the coldest and roughest water to drag someone to safety. Blind instinct? Or something else? Just what's going on between those floppy black ears?

Muin lays her head on her front paws and closes her eyes, as if she knows Beth's mushy heart for what it is.

~

Three hours later, when the rain has slowed to a drizzle, Beth follows Muin up the trail to Mattie's cabin. The rosary is tucked in her pocket.

Mattie opens the door before Beth can even knock. "Give up being mad at me?"

"I wasn't mad," Beth says, "I was ... disappointed."

"Disappointed?"

"Okay, sure. I was pretty annoyed with your little trick."

Mattie chuckles.

"What? Are you someone different today?"

"Nope, still feeling like Matilda." She winks. "For now." She opens the door wider. "Tea?"

Beth steps into the cabin, Muin pushing in ahead of her. "Just water for me," she says.

"No tea?"

"Last time I came away with a headache."

"Nonsense. Just plain old Labrador tea. Harmless." Mattie pulls two mugs out of the cupboard. "But suit yourself. How about some Red Rose then?"

While Mattie prepares the tea – making a show of pulling the teabags from the box – Beth studies the unfinished weaving in the loom: a combination of cobalt, ochre, and ivory threads form an abstract pattern; woven within are real feathers – duck and gull? – and small pieces of driftwood. Dark green yarn has been wound around a spool. To be woven into the warp and weft, she guesses, although she can never remember which is which.

"Met Dan yesterday," Beth says. "He told me he takes your weavings to a gallery in St. John's."

"I'm just glad people like em. Helps pay the bills."

Beth points at what looks like a stylized spider web in one corner of the weaving.

"A nod to the master weaver," Mattie says before Beth can ask.

Mattie pours black tea into two mugs and brings them to the table, where a spike of foxglove stands in a mason jar. She sets the yellow sugar bowl between the mugs. "Haven't seen any otters, have you." It's a statement, not a question.

Beth straightens her glasses. "I've only been searching for a few days."

"They're keeping themselves away," Mattie says, sitting. "You try talking to them?"

"I haven't tried talking to animals since I was eight years old." Beth pulls out a chair and sits down. Muin leans against Beth's shins as she settles under the table.

"That's the trouble, see. Children know stuff we grown-ups forget." Mattie moves the jar and the spike of purple flowers from between her and Beth. "You scientists think seeing is believing. It's the other way around." She winks again. "Believing is seeing."

Beth snorts a laugh. "And that's exactly why people are always seeing spaceships and aliens, Sasquatch and other weird things. They already believe in them."

"So you don't believe in anything you can't see?"

"Of course there are things we can't see, but there's always some kind of evidence. You can't see gravity, but you can certainly see it at work."

Mattie stirs sugar into her mug. "You study animals. You believe they have souls?"

"I'm not even sure people have souls."

"What if it turns out that we all have souls?" Mattie puts her elbows on the table and interlaces her fingers. "And that we're accountable for how we've lived on this earth? For how we've treated its occupants? All of its occupants?"

"Accountable to whom?"

Mattie shrugs. She picks up a box of matches, slides it open, then shut again, the cardboard rasping. She taps the drawing of the glowering seal on the top. "It's us who need them, you know. Not them who need us. Maybe they don't want you watching em."

Beth takes a swallow of black tea, then reaches into her pocket and pulls out the rosary. She holds it out on her palm, green beads and chain dangling. "I found this yesterday. Near the outlet. About fifty paces back in the woods, just lying there beneath some moss."

Mattie touches one of the green beads. The muscles in her jaw tighten, but when she looks up at Beth, her expression is neutral.

"Any idea who it might have belonged to?" Beth says.

"Yours now."

"Mine?"

"You found it."

"But who do you think lost it?"

"How would I know?"

Beth rubs the small bone owl between a thumb and middle finger. "Maybe I should put it back where I found it." She lays the rosary on the table.

"Maybe you should." Mattie stands and goes to the loom, picks up a wicker basket and brings it back to the table. "I have a story for you."

"Mattie?"

"No worries. It's not long. And it's about studying animals." Mattie sits down and pulls a spool and a skein of dark-brown yarn from the basket.

Beth wraps her hands around the hot mug, watches steam rise in wispy curls.

Mattie begins to wind yarn onto the spool. "There was this youngster, see, who spent all his time outdoors, always out in the woods or by a pond or a river. His grandmother fretted about him getting lost or hurt. She prayed for him. The boy loved his nan, but like youngsters everywhere, he didn't have time for her worries. Or her prayers. He just wanted to be out in the bush, watching animals. He began carving them too, not from pictures or memory, but from the way he saw them. He could see their souls. Even carved his grandmother a rosary of animal souls."

Beth touches the carved otter, then glances toward the menagerie on the shelf.

Speaking softly, Mattie watches her fingers wind the yarn onto the spool. "After a while he begins trying to mimic Bear's huff-huff and her cub's bawl, Raven's deep cronk and Owl's hoo-hoo-hoo. He practices and practices, but only when he's alone, see, so the animals won't be confused." She looks up at Beth. "Or maybe he was afraid they'd laugh at him. Some folks worry about looking foolish, you know."

She pauses to untangle a knot. "When he finally thinks he's ready, he speaks. Raven hops closer, turns her head sideways, and peers at him with her black, black eyes. Bear and Owl stop what they're doing, and listen. The boy knows then that he can talk to them!" Mattie nods once, emphatically.

"One day he's out in the bush looking for a yellow moccasin flower to bring to his grandmother." She lays down the spool to pick up her mug. "Ever see one? Lovely. But not much smell to them."

"I've seen them," Beth says. "Usually in bogs."

"That's right. Too late in the year now though. All dried up." Mattie sips tea and turns to stare out the window at the birdfeeders, at the juncos and chickadees coming and going. She turns back and picks up the yarn and spool again, silently winding the yarn.

"What about the boy?" Beth asks, looking over the rim of her mug. "I believe you were trying to teach me how to talk to the otters."

"Hmmm. Where was I now?" Mattie rubs her nose. "Oh, yes. The boy goes farther and farther into the woods, into the bog, searching. Gets himself all turned around. Doesn't know which way to go. Gets scared then and runs one way, turns back, runs off the other way. Does this again and again, until there's no way he can retrace his path; he's trampled everything around him."

Beth pictures the sameness of bog all around, the black spruce and tamarack, the trampled moss. But if the boy was experienced in the woods? "What about the sun?" she says.

Mattie frowns as if she's annoyed. "Oh, it's cloudy, see. No sun. And it's beginning to get dark. The boy sits down on a log. He's worried now that he'll have to spend the night in the woods, and that makes him hungry, and scared. He's staring down at the moss now, feeling sorry for himself."

Her fingers stop moving between the yarn and the spool. She looks at Beth. "Then he hears a deep, gruff voice: 'Follow me, b'y.' He looks all around to see who spoke. Can't see anyone. He stands on the log. Still can't see anyone. Then he hears a rustling sound. A branch snaps. He turns and catches a glimpse of a big brown arse ambling off through the juniper: a moose. And he knows then that animals can talk to him too. And he can see that following the moose is the way he should go. Even finds three yellow moccasin flowers on his way home."

Beth arches an eyebrow. "And of course, Bullwinkle spoke with a Newfoundland accent."

"Was a Newfoundland moose, wasn't it." Mattie slaps the table, chuckling. "Don't be so foolish. The moose didn't say one word out loud. The boy heard it all in his head."

"Then why can't you just say that the boy imagined the words? That the moose just happened to be there? That's a simpler explanation."

"Simple isn't always right. Besides, that wouldn't make for a very good story now, would it." Mattie raises an index finger. "And I know you're wondering. It's a pirn, not a spool. That's the proper name."

"Dan told me you had a twin," Beth says quietly. "Was he the boy who carved the rosary?"

"It's just a story, love."

"Dan said he died young."

Mattie takes a deep breath, lets it out slowly. "Matthew drowned when he was just seventeen. In this pond."

Beth wants to ask how, but the sadness in Mattie's face stops her.

"We're very close," Mattie says. "Two halves of a whole." She drops the yarn and pirn into the basket. "What else Dan have to say?"

"That you ... live Matthew's life for him." Beth's voice rises on the word him, as if she is asking a question.

"Mostly in dreams." Mattie is staring at Beth, who nods as if she understands. But doesn't.

Beth coughs into her fist. "I had a strange dream last night." She tries to laugh, but her throat is too tight. "The animals on the rosary and a young man carving."

Mattie touches the back of Beth's hand. A touch like the flutter of moth wings – or the skitter of spider legs. "You should take it back to where it belongs."

Beth pulls her hand away.

"The rosary brought you that dream."

"I suppose you could put it that way," Beth says carefully. Muin rises from beneath the table, stretches, and lays her heavy head in Beth's lap. She strokes the oily black fur. "Most of the animals on the rosary were in the dream."

"That's not what I mean."

"What else is there?" Beth's fingers find a small knot behind Muin's ear. "Dreams are just a jumbled mix of the things we think about during the day."

Mattie picks up the rosary and examines each carved animal. "Don't you ever wonder if it's your dreams that are real? That it's your dreaming self that conjures your waking self into being?"

"All children think about that at one time or another."

"Maybe youngsters are more open to understanding possibilities."

Beth takes a long swallow of the cooled tea. Sets down the mug. "The weather's cleared. I should get going." She begins to stand, but stops halfway. Hanging from a hook by the door is a dirty blue baseball cap. With a faded red C. "Where did you get that?"

"What?" Mattie twists around in the chair.

"That blue cap."

"Matthew's had that forever. The Cubbies. Everybody's favourite losers. That's what he always says." She turns back to Beth. "Minnesota farm girl like you oughta recognize a cap from a Chicago team."

Beth knows she probably saw that cap on her first visit; it just didn't register until it showed up in her dream. But still.

Mattie holds out the rosary. "You best take this back to where it belongs."

CHAPTER 7

It's been raining on and off all day, and by late afternoon, Beth has spent nearly four hours cruising the shoreline and found only one fresh scat. She goes back to the cabin to change into dry clothes and then – unable to stomach the thought of another can of soup heated on the woodstove – decides to drive into town.

When she walks through the door of Price Chopper, she sees the same flickering fluorescent light and the same cashier with the bright red bangs, but today there are several other customers roaming the aisles. Beth picks up a package of coffee and a jar of peanut butter, then, while she waits for the cashier, studies the postcard rack. She spins it around: fishing boats, the triad of Newfoundland berries, icebergs, the classic photo of the little boy in kneepants standing between two enormous cod, a moose and her calf, and a sea otter floating on its back with an urchin on its chest, *You otter be here!* printed on the front. Beth sighs. There has never been a sea otter in Newfoundland. It's a Pacific species. What Newfoundland has are river otters that exploit marine food sources, a scientific inconvenience happily ignored by the makers of postcards and promoters of tourism. Beth lays the postcard beside her coffee and jar of Skippy. She'll send it to Rachel. She'll get the joke.

The cashier comes to the register. "How things going?" She leans forward, puts her hand to her mouth and whispers, "With the collecting, I mean."

"Fine," Beth says.

The girl picks up the postcard and scans the barcode. "Cute. I like otters."

Beth doesn't try to explain.

The girl's forehead furrows beneath the fringe of red bangs. "How do you get into your line of work? I mean, do you have to go to school to learn how to collect animal poop?"

Beth can feel the person waiting in line behind her come to attention. "Yes," Beth mumbles, "you do."

The girl's eyes widen. "Really? Like university?"

"Something like that."

"Wow! Who would think?" Still nodding in thoughtful wonderment, she places the coffee and peanut butter into a white plastic bag.

Beth grabs the bag and the postcard and walks to the post office. Inside, she goes to the counter against one wall and jots a quick note to Rachel, then steps to the main counter. The postmistress, her thinning hair dyed a severe black, turns around.

Beth lays the postcard on the counter. "Stamp, please?" She digs in her pocket for a loonie.

The postmistress picks up the postcard. "Cute," she says. She looks from the card to Beth, squinting over her glasses. "You must be that lady who's collecting otter … droppings."

Beth lays her coin on the counter and tries to smile.

~

As soon as she walks through the door of the Morning Glory, she sees Dan, and before she can turn around, he nods. It would be rude not to acknowledge him. *Uppity.* But Beth positions herself so that her back will be toward him when she slides into the booth.

She slips off her rain jacket. "Hi, Dan."

"Saw your kayak out on the pond earlier. How's the research going?"

"All right," she says. Then, having already heard enough comments about her collecting, she quickly adds, "Catch anything yesterday?"

"Nope. Midday's not the greatest time for fishing. But hey, I'll use any excuse to get out on the water." He gestures toward the other side of the booth. "Join me?"

Beth hesitates. She could claim she has something important to read, but all she's brought with her is an Agatha Christie novel. She hangs up her jacket and slides into the booth.

The teenage waitress drops a coffee-stained menu onto the Formica tabletop. With her swizzle-stick build and bright red bangs, she could be a sister to the cashier at the grocery.

Beth skims the menu. "What did you order?"

"Special."

"Which is?"

"The roast beef plate."

"Hmmm."

They both laugh. "Yeah," he says, "I wouldn't recommend it."

She finally settles on a grilled cheese sandwich and pea soup. Something she could have made on the woodstove, she thinks ruefully.

Dan sits back and lays an arm along the top of the cushion, taps his fingers on the red leatherette. "Stopped in this afternoon to see if Mattie needed anything. She said you'd been by."

"She happen to mention that I brought her dog back … again?"

"No, but then she wouldn't." Giving her a half-smile, he shakes his head. "She loves that dog. Lets her wander all over creation." He sits forward and folds his hands on the table. "She always went back and forth between their cabins … Mattie's and Katherine's. That's why she's over at your place all the time. It's her second home."

"Great. Does that mean I'll have to take her back to Mattie's every day?"

"Just let her be. She'll go back on her own. Eventually. She always goes where she likes." He picks up a water glass and takes a swallow. "Four or five years ago, she just showed up on Mattie's doorstep."

"No one claimed her?"

"I asked around, but nobody'd lost a Newfoundland. Vet thought she was a purebred, about one or two years old, but nobody knows for sure." He rotates the water glass in a puddle of condensation. "She can be a real pain in the ass at times, but she's company for Mattie. Specially now that Katherine is gone."

Beth decides he looks better without his hat, even if his forehead is divided in half – tan half stopping just above his eyebrows, pale half to the hairline, which hasn't retreated. He takes a pack of Macdonalds from his shirt pocket, lays it on the table, turns it up on one side, then onto the other. She folds down the corner of a napkin, once, then twice.

"So," she says into the silence, "Mattie says she's been on the pond for eighty years."

"Her whole life."

She folds the napkin a third time. "So, have you lived here your whole life too?"

"Only about five years or so." He taps the red and white pack of cigarettes on the table. "Recently anyway. Grew up here – in my grandma's house – across the pond from Mattie's. But soon as I could, I joined the army."

Beth smoothes the napkin. "And that would have been …?"

"1970." He laughs, just once. "I was joining up just about the same time the Yanks were coming here to stay out."

Beth does a quick calculation. If Dan was eighteen in 1970, he's somewhere around fifty-eight, four years older than Alan, although he doesn't look it. He has more hair, even if it is turning silver, and, despite the cigarettes, he looks very fit.

"What brought you back?" she says.

"Pretty simple, really. Nan left the cabin to Dad, and he left it to me. When I retired, I decided to come back. I like it here now. Mostly."

"Mostly?"

"Miss the city stuff sometimes, and the travelling. It's great in the summer, but I'm not sure I'll stay here year-round after ..." He rotates the glass again.

"Mattie dies?"

"She's pretty healthy, so that could be a long time yet."

"Nothing else to tie you here?"

Dan cocks his head. "You're full of questions."

"Scientist in me, I guess."

He gives her another half-smile. "No wife or kids, if that's what you mean."

"No, no, of course not," Beth says quickly, too quickly. "I didn't mean to pry."

He looks at her, a spark of devilment in his green eyes. "How about you?"

"Husband's a vet in St. John's," she says. "Our daughter Rachel is in Vancouver, working in a lab."

The waitress approaches, balancing a tray. As she's placing their plates and bowls in front of them, the old man with the drooping face steps slowly through the door.

Dan nods. "Hey, Clive. Why don't you join us?"

The old man shuffles toward them, props his cane on Dan's seat, leans both hands on the table, then slides into the booth beside Beth. Glances at Dan's plate; the left side of his face grimaces. When the waitress comes with the menu, he waves it away. "Just tea," he says gruffly.

Dan gestures toward Beth. "Beth, this is Clive Hiscock. Clive, this is Beth ..." He holds up his palms. "Sorry."

"Meyer." She can't remember Dan's last name either.

"From St. John's," he adds. "Here to do some research. On otters."

Clive turns a red-rimmed eye on Beth. It looks huge and watery behind the thick lens. His right eye stares off into space. "Otters, eh?"

"Just a preliminary study on Medicine Rock," she says.

"Clive's lived here near as long as Mattie," Dan says. "Maybe he knows something useful. And what he doesn't know, he'll be happy to make up."

The left side of Clive's mouth grins. "Never a word of a lie."

"Beth's staying at the old Wells place," Dan continues. He lifts his knife and fork and cuts through the mound of beef and mashed potatoes.

"Katherine Wells," Clive says slowly. "Passed now."

Beth's not sure if that's a statement or a question. "Last winter," she says. "She was my husband's aunt. She left him the cabin."

"Always liked Katherine." Clive's speech is very slow but only slightly slurred.

"Go on, b'y," Dan says. "Everybody knows you were in love with her."

Clive waves his good hand at Dan. "Don't be so foolish. She were a lovely, educated lady, teaching history to numbskull kids like you. Waste of her fine intelligence, I say."

Waiting for each of his words is agonizing.

"And Mattie sure enjoyed her visits." He tips his head toward Dan. "If you knows what I mean."

Dan points an empty fork at Clive. "Gossip. Small-town gossip."

"What would you know?" Clive turns his whole upper body toward Beth, nods sideways at Dan. "He were just a youngster when Katherine first come here. Then went off into the army when he was still a pup." He dabs at the right side of his mouth with a napkin, then winks at Beth with his good eye. "Live here long enough, you get to know things."

Dan shakes his head. "Clive, you're full of it."

Clive chuckles and points to his nose. "I knows what I knows."

The waitress brings a pot of hot water and a cup and saucer. Clive struggles to open the teabag, then drops it into the metal pot. Beth clasps her hands in her lap to keep herself from reaching out to help him.

"So, you're out there close to Mattie," Clive says, closing the lid on the pot. "Met the old witch yet?"

Beth recoils. Dan smirks. "First time Beth met Mattie," he says, "she thought Mattie was a man."

Clive guffaws, his whole body shaking.

"Mattie told me *she* was a *he*," Beth says. "I didn't necessarily believe it." She picks up a spoon and plunges it into the soup. "Actually," she says to Clive, "it was Dan who told me that Mattie had a brother who died young, that Mattie sometimes pretends to be him." She gives Dan a pinched smile. To hell with his *none a your business*.

"Drownded," Clive says.

"How?"

"Overturned a canoe. Didn't know how to swim, see."

Beth looks at Dan.

"Long before my time." Dan bends over his plate, forks mashed potatoes and gravy into his mouth.

"Let's see now," Clive continues, "guess I must've been about nine or ten." He pulls the teabag out of the pot. "I don't look it, my dear, but I'm eight years younger than Mattie. Damn smokes is what done it. You should quit," he says to Dan, "while you still got time."

He drops the sodden teabag onto the saucer. "Story

63

was that his pretty little girlfriend had something to do with it. She almost drownded too, but Mattie saved her."

"Really?" Beth stirs the now-cold soup. It has the texture of newly mixed cement.

"Yep. Mattie didn't become a witch till later." Clive chuckles again, then grows serious. "Might've been better if the girl had died. She lived like a zombie for years."

Dan looks up. "Her, I do remember. She was damn scary when I was a kid. She must've died what …? Forty years ago?"

Clive looks toward the ceiling and taps his fingers on the table. "Forty-eight," he says. "Katherine come here just two years after Emma died."

"And I guess *you* wouldn't forget that," Dan says.

Clive points to his temple. "I got a good memory." He pours the tea and adds sugar. Stirs, the spoon trembling in his hand.

Beth picks up half of the grilled cheese sandwich. "So the girlfriend lived for years after Matthew drowned?"

"If you can call that living," Clive says. "Her own people – fancy types from St. John's – wouldn't have nothing to do with her after. Damaged goods, see." He seems to be enjoying having an audience. He holds Beth in suspense while the cup makes a shaky journey to his lips.

"Way I heard it," he continues, after the cup has come to rest safely on the saucer again, "Emma's family never wanted her mixed up with Matthew at all. They was all high Anglican, see, and he were a Cat'lic." He leans toward Beth and whispers, "And there was a few said he might be part Micmac. Who knows? Don't matter much now, but it did then."

Dan shakes his head. "Clive, you'd make an epic out of a road-kill moose."

"I was there, b'y. You weren't even a thought yet." Clive passes a hand over his own damaged face. "Emma were in far worse shape than me. Staring straight ahead with those pale blue eyes. That's what I remember: the eyes. Like looking into the face of a ghost." He studies the painting behind Dan – a moose and her calf – as if it were a portrait of the dead woman herself.

"Emma's people probably gave her money," Clive says, "but Mattie was on her own. Can't begrudge her the bit of happiness she had with Katherine, I spose." He points at his ear with an index finger, makes little circles, slowly. "Even if she is cracked."

Clive dabs his mouth with a napkin, then fixes his good eye on Beth. "Be careful. Don't trust her." He places both hands on the table and pushes himself to his feet. Dan hands him his cane.

"You kids enjoy your supper, now," Clive says.

Beth waits until he is out the door. "Any truth to what he says?"

"Mattie likes to tease people, but she's not dangerous."

"What about the rest of it?"

Dan pushes his plate away. "Clive's an old busybody. Loves telling stories to anyone foolish enough to listen."

"That doesn't answer the question."

He shrugs. "Don't know. Don't care. Not my business." He picks up the cigarettes and drops the pack into his shirt pocket. "None a yours neither."

CHAPTER 8

Fingertips gritty and stinking of musty wood, Beth searches the contents of Katherine's junk drawer for something small and pointed. Katherine and Mattie. Dan didn't deny it. Maybe that's why Alan's family so rarely came out to the cabin when he was a boy, why Alan hardly knew his aunt. From what Beth can remember of Alan's father, he seemed like someone who'd have disapproved of something like that. A lot.

She grabs a paper clip and pushes the drawer, but the wood is warped and she has to jiggle the drawer from side to side to close it. She moves the kerosene lamp from the counter to the table, picks up the rosary, and sits down in the rocking chair. As soon as she gets it cleaned up, she'll take it back, although it seems a shame just to leave it to rot in the woods. She bends the paper clip open and pokes an end into the smaller links of the chain to clean out the last bits of dirt.

Her thoughts are scattering in a dozen different directions: Katherine and Mattie; Matthew's drowning and his damaged girlfriend; Mattie's heroism, both in saving the girl and then taking care of her for years; Clive. Dan. And not one of those directions has anything to do with her. Are, as Dan would say, *none a her business*. She drops her hands into her lap. She should forget all of them and get back to her research. She doesn't have time to waste. Beth lays the rosary beside the puzzle she's barely started and considers the stack of unread technical papers on the counter. She pushes herself up from the chair, packs her gear, and walks to the otter spot.

~

Beth sits on shore and watches the pink and lavender sky deepen through shades of violet. When she first arrived, several blue jays delivered a raucous scolding, and she wonders if the otters heard the birds, if they knew by their calls they'd seen something alarming, and so are now staying away.

She slaps at a stout buzzing around her ear. Can feel an itchy lump already rising. But at least she's warm and relatively comfortable. Not like when she did her doctoral research in Minnesota: she'd spent two frigid winters watching otters. There were mornings when clouds of steam rolled off their wet fur as they tumbled in and out of the river and onto the ice, feeding and wrestling, seemingly carefree, even when the mercury dipped to -30°C, and Beth, bundled in layers of down, had to keep her tape recorder tucked inside her parka, close to her body, just to keep the batteries working.

She would never admit it to any of her university colleagues, but she's always been a little enchanted by otters. To her, they have a *joie de vivre* that's rare among animals. They're like perpetual adolescents – complete with attitude. She knows that's anthropomorphic, but she's not sure how else to think about it. When she was in graduate school, scientific holy writ explained all animal behaviour as instinct and stimulus-response learning, à la B. F. Skinner. Talk of animal feelings was taboo. Now, most behaviourists acknowledge that animals think, that they feel pain, pleasure, anger, and fear, maybe even love and grief. Who's to say? It's impossible to know the mind of another person, let alone the mind of an animal.

She pulls at the grass, twists it into tufts, digs a finger into the dirt. She'd give almost anything to get inside an otter's head and that metre-long body, just for an hour, to learn how it senses and perceives its world, to know what it thinks and feels. They hear, see, taste, and smell – and possibly imagine – what people cannot. Some animals' sensory worlds are so rich they seem to have ESP. Beth thinks of it as ESSP, extra-sensitive sensory perception: dogs that can diagnose cancer in people more accurately than a pathologist, and detect blood sugar levels that are dangerously high or low, and sense chemical and electrical changes that signal an imminent seizure. Elephants have specialized organs in their feet that can sense seismic vibrations made by elephants miles away. Dolphins can recognize and remember the unique sound signatures of hundreds, maybe thousands, of other dolphins, and have sonic conversations that may be more complex than humans can ever fathom.

So just what are the otters saying to each other with their chirps and *uhn-uhn-uhns?* What can they perceive and understand that humans cannot?

Beth hears footsteps behind her, branches snapping. A moose? A bear? She turns her head very, very slowly. A sloppy wet tongue bathes her face. She releases her breath and pushes Muin away.

"Lovely evening," Mattie says, lowering herself to sit beside Beth. The tip of a black feather pokes out from her shirt pocket. She points at the binoculars. "Mind if I have a look?"

Beth lifts the binoculars from around her neck and hands them to Mattie, who puts them to her eyes and adjusts the focus. "Haven't seen em yet, have you," she says.

Muin noses at the backpack. Beth digs out a piece of cheese left from lunch.

Mattie scans the shoreline. "These are pretty damn good," she says. "You can see a lot." She lowers the binoculars. "But a lot you can't." She hands them back to Beth. "Talk to em yet?"

Beth offers the cheese to Muin.

"You should call their name."

"Their name?" Beth says.

"You know … address them. So they know it's them you're talking to." Mattie wraps her arms around her knees. "Course calling them by the name 'otter' might not bring em out. Sometimes you've got to call an animal by the name it's known for hundreds, maybe even thousands, of years." She strokes Muin's head, scratches behind her ears. "The old grandmother is the one you need to talk to. And maybe she doesn't know the name 'otter,' or thinks it's silly. Maybe she knows herself as *giwnig* or *edru*."

Beth hears *kee-o-nig* and *e-droo*. Mi'kmaq words? Or something else?

"Or maybe she wants to be called 'Grandmother.'" Mattie cups Muin's chin and speaks to the dog. "Or maybe she wants to be addressed as 'Valued Ecosystem Component.'"

"Very funny."

"You think I'm joking? Well … maybe just a little."

Muin picks up the backpack and lays it at Beth's feet. "Sorry, girl," she says. "No more cheese." A wet circle is spreading across the brown canvas. The dog sits down beside her. Beth drapes an arm around her and stares out across the water, watches an osprey. The hawk hovers, then glides closer to shore and hovers again. Dives. Flies off with a small fish in its talons.

"You're going about it all wrong, you know," Mattie says.

Beth tightens her arm around Muin.

"It's not more little facts we need. But a grand change in the way we think about animals. Nothing wrong with facts. They're just not enough." Mattie straightens her legs and leans back on her hands. She's wearing thick-soled hiking boots.

"What you scientists have got to understand," she continues, "is that the otter – and everything else – is a whole lot more than just facts." She leans toward Beth, her voice a whisper, as if she is confiding secrets. "The otter is special, see. Maybe even magical." Mattie holds up three fingers, points to each one in turn. "A creature of three worlds: water, earth, and air. The otter knows what's under the earth and what's under the water. All that lies beneath."

Muin snaps at a stout buzzing around her head. Misses. Beth lifts the binoculars and scans the darkening water.

Leaning back on her hands again, Mattie says, "She's a creature of that special time when day becomes night and night becomes day: a creature of transformation." She nods at Beth. "But she's a trickster too. Likes her games. So you gotta be careful."

"All great fun to speculate about," Beth says, "but everything you've said comes from mythology – ideas people have imposed on otters."

"Maybe." Mattie pushes herself up and rubs her hands together to brush off the dirt. "Maybe not." She puts her hands to her waist and stretches her shoulders back. "We should get going. These old eyes aren't what they used to be in the dark." She bends her neck from side to side, working out the kinks. "Why don't you come over for supper tomorrow?" she says. "Bound to be better than anything you can get at the Morning Glory."

"I should be out doing observations tomorrow evening."

"But you won't see anything."

"How do you know?"

"Just do," Mattie says. "So you might as well come over. Bout seven or so?" She turns to Muin. "Come on, girl."

Beth listens to their noisy retreat, then sits while the sky deepens from indigo to black. She watches the stars blink on, one by one.

It's all nonsense. She's not even tempted to call out their name.

~

Dark water ripples in front of her. A pup paddles at her side. The pup nudges her cheek with its muzzle, paws at her face, then grabs her around the neck. Quietly, they roll and tumble. The old female dives. Powerful stroke of tail, flick of back paws. Bubbles stream out behind her as she shoots through water the colour of night. The pup follows. When they rise up, she lifts her head and sniffs the air: fish and musk, earth and grass, the lodge, where the others are just beginning to stir.

The wind carries the lingering scents of dog and human. The dog and the old one are familiar. Safe. The scent of the new one is strong. Uncertain. Angry.

~

Beth takes out her journal and jots a few notes by the dim glow of a flashlight: *6 Aug 10: ~23°C, clear, winds light, observed at A5, 20:05 – 22:32; interrupted by Mattie ~20:30 – 20:45; none observed.*

She has been sitting still for nearly two hours since Mattie left. It's dark and there's no one around, so she strips down, lays her glasses and watch atop her clothes, and steps into the water before the mosquitoes can muster an attack. The rocks are slippery and the sudden cold makes her inhale sharply. Then she releases herself to the water, to its sensuous caress on her naked skin. She swims out from shore and slips beneath the surface. Shoots smoothly through dark water. Beth blows air out her nose and bends into a somersault, feels the giddy flip of her stomach. For a few otherworldly seconds, she is suspended, weightless and silent. She floats to the surface and gazes up at the stars. Locates the crooked W of Cassiopeia, Queen of Heaven.

A low *uhn-uhn-uhn* close to shore. Beth lies perfectly still. *Uhn-uhn-uhn, uhn-uhn-uhn.* Relaxed conversation.

At least two. She wants to raise her head and look, but she can't risk scaring them away. She's waited so long.

A high-pitched chirp. Another. If she didn't know better, she'd think the sounds came from a nocturnal bird.

A snort then. Her heart jumps. They've scented her.

Slowly, she brings her feet down and keeps her head low. She's rewarded with a glimpse of amber eyeshine, a grey muzzle, the arch of a tail. And then they are gone. The water forms silver wavelets around the shadow of their absence. Beth feels exhilarated – and bereft.

She swims to shore and uses her sweatshirt to dry off. Shivering violently now, she pulls and tugs at jeans and T-shirt, the dampness of her thighs like Velcro against the slide of denim. Wrestling her sweatshirt over her head, she steps into her sneakers, grabs her backpack, and runs to the cabin. She strips off her damp clothes and wraps herself in her sleeping bag.

As soon as she can grasp a pencil and hold it steady, she records: *6 Aug 10: Observed/heard at least two otters in A5, ~30 m northeast of beaver lodge, ~22:40 – 22:43. Judging by the grizzled muzzle, one is old. Heard grunts, two chirps, and a snort.*

Finally, she has seen them, if only for a few minutes. She lays the journal aside, then stands and picks up the kerosene lamp and her novel. Sees the rosary and decides to move it to the straight-back chair she's using as a nightstand so that she can look at the carving of the otter.

She strips down to a T-shirt and crawls into the sleeping bag, trying not to remember that this is where Katherine slept. She opens *Endless Night* and reads ... until she gets to the part about the old woman the villagers call a witch. She lays the novel aside, grabs the flashlight, and makes a final trip to the outhouse. Inside, the halo of light reflects off a large web spanning an entire corner. An orb-weaver, a filigree pattern of brown and white on her back, sits in the centre, waiting, as still as death. Beth stares at the enshrouded flies, caught and bound in silk. *Master weaver?* More like master predator.

~

The dreamer glides through pools lit by a silver moon. Amber eyeshine all around. Musk in her nose, smell of dank earth. She nestles into a cradle of thick roots, comfort of warm, wet fur all around. *Uhn-uhn-uhn, uhn-uhn-uhn.* Then she is hiding behind trees. From behind the web of branches, she watches her brother. He is pushing a rotary lawnmower across a vast expanse of green. The blades whir. A girl in a yellow sundress splashed with huge pink roses steps from the veranda. She is carrying a glass of lemonade. Cubes of ice clink as she steps across the new-mown grass. Her bare feet stain green.

She sees the girl through her brother's eyes: milk-white face shade-dappled by a straw hat, small swell of breast. Up close, the girl's eyes are a crystalline blue, a blue lighter than he's ever seen in anyone's eyes. He thinks that if he were to bring her wrist to his nose, her skin would smell as sweet as the roses on her dress. He tugs at the bill of his baseball cap, says his name, and when he takes the sweating glass from her hand, he wraps his tan fingers over her pale ones. The Kewpie-doll lips form an O of surprise, ivory skin flushes. The girl pulls her hand away, but when she turns to leave, she glances back and smiles.

The dreamer lets go of the branches. They snap back into place. She and her brother are close: two halves of a whole. The girl is an intruder.

CHAPTER 9

The alarm beeps. Beth turns it off and gives herself a few extra minutes. Dozes. Then slowly shakes herself awake and gropes for the matches, strikes one to light the lamp. Sees the green glint of the rosary on the chair beside the bed, the small bone carving of the otter.

She pulls on jeans and a sweatshirt and goes into the kitchen to make coffee. While she waits, she flips back to the notes she made the night before – just to confirm that she really did see them, that the otters weren't a dream or a phantom of her imagination.

Beth walks to the otter spot just as the sky is beginning to pale. It's unlikely they'll be back so soon, but she wants to take another look, then she'll be satisfied to search more kilometres of shoreline for scats.

She sits on shore and waits. Watches grey clouds creep in to smother the fragile sunrise, the pond's still surface reflecting both the innocent light and the sinister clouds. She listens to the morning chorus: a raven's deep quork, a chickadee singing its own name again and again, the jungle cackle of a northern flicker.

Her yawn brings tears to her eyes. She slept only a few hours the night before. Half awake, half asleep, a hazy dream of amber eyeshine and the smell of musk, all tangled around Clive's stories.

A high-pitched chirp, an answer. Beth raises her binoculars and spots four – no, five – in the water. She reaches into her backpack for her voice recorder and begins to dictate, quietly: "6:02. A5. Observing from fifteen metres. Five otters, swimming and wrestling about twenty metres northeast of beaver lodge. Chirping while wrestling."

When the otters emerge from the pond and chase each other, Beth can see that at least two are pups. The otters wrestle in twos and threes, in the water and out, tussling, grabbing, pretend biting, chirping. She soon loses track of who is who, but keeps dictating. Now and again, an otter abandons the wrestling to dive, sometimes surfacing with a fish in its mouth. The crunch of bones is audible in the morning stillness, and Beth wonders if she'll be able to hear it when she transcribes the recording.

"One adult is swimming to shore with a large fish. It comes out about six metres northeast of the latrine. A pup follows. The adult releases the fish – twenty to twenty-five centimetres long. The pup bites near the fish's tail. The fish wriggles free. The adult catches it again, bites its head, then goes back into the water, leaving the fish for the pup. This same adult, which is relatively small and slender, comes out on shore at the latrine, arches its tail, treads both hind feet several times, urinates – probably a female – and deposits black scat. It returns to the water."

Even when Beth is not whispering into the recorder, she leaves it running so she can time the behaviours. After another minute, two adults emerge from the water, shake, and then rub in the grass to dry themselves. They settle side by side to groom – themselves and each other – dark-brown fur glossy in the sun that's just beginning to emerge from behind the clouds. Beth can hear their steady *uhn-uhn-uhns*, which seem to be quiet assurances to each other that everything's okay – almost like cats purring. A wet pup approaches them and shakes water over them, but neither adult snarls or growls, or even harrumphs. They merely rearrange themselves to accommodate the pup, who has plopped down on top of them. One adult begins to groom the pup, nibbling at its head and neck.

Beth smiles. No curmudgeons in the otter world.

"One pup and one adult are still in the water about ten metres from shore, three metres apart. Adult periscopes. Snorts. All five look in the same direction, northeast."

Beth watches and listens, and after a long minute, hears the distant whine of a motorboat. By the time it rounds the point and enters the small bay, the otters are long gone.

The *Black Feather*. Beth steps back behind the trees before Dan can see her. No luck. He dips the bill of his cap toward her. She turns away, no nod, no wave. Doesn't give a damn about being called uppity.

~

She refills her mug with the last of the coffee in the percolator and sits down to expand on the notes she's just transcribed from the voice recorder: *7 Aug 10: ~16°C, overcast > pt. sunny, winds light, observed at A5, 5:30 – 6:18, 5 otters appeared near latrine at 6:02.*

Sixteen minutes. That's all she got. Damn. Why did Dan have to show up? Of all the places he could go to fish, why there?

She sits back in the armchair. Okay, okay. She shouldn't be angry with Dan. She and the otters don't own the pond. No curmudgeons allowed, she reminds herself. Then writes: *The 5 otters included at least 1 adult female (probably) and 2 pups. At 65-75 cm, the pups are about 2/3 as long as the adults and more slender. Probably 4-5 months old. The pups are now proficient swimmers.*

She suspects the old beaver lodge is the second natal den. The birth den would have been more secluded and higher in the watershed since pups can't swim when they're born. When they're about three months old, the mother moves them closer to the water to teach them to swim and to catch their own food.

Beth reconsiders a note she made from the voice recording: *The adult caught and released a large fish, 20-25 cm. The pup tried to grasp the fish by the tail, but lost it. The adult – the mother? – killed the fish and left it for the pup.* She taps the pencil against the page. It's likely that it was the mother who caught the fish for the pup, but she can't be sure. A few studies have shown that other adult females sometimes share food with pups, but no one knows whether these "helpers" are the pups' aunts or older sisters, or are completely unrelated.

Using a paring knife to sharpen the pencil, Beth lets the shavings fall to the floor. So many unknowns. No one even knows the role of the father in the wild. In captivity, the mother is so fiercely protective of her pups that when she gives birth, the adult male usually has to be removed from the enclosure – for his own safety. He can be put back in when the pups are three to four months old, and for the most part, adult males are gentle with pups. Yet radio-tracking of wild otters shows that adult males don't have much to do with pups. They remain solitary or live in all-male groups whose members share dens and may even hunt together – in a highly unusual social arrangement for a member of the weasel family.

Beth is hoping the DNA analyses will tell her the composition of her group, but she'd love to be able to identify who is who while she's watching them. But their ears are too small for coloured tags, they'd chew off any kind of wristband, and their necks are thicker than their heads, so collars would just slip off. And with no funding, Beth can't live-trap them to mark them or surgically implant radio-tracking devices. She doesn't want to do that kind of invasive research anyway.

She re-reads another note: *The 5 otters wrestled in 2s and 3s, in the water and out, frequently changing partners, chirping almost continuously.* Beth closes her eyes to imagine the exuberant physicality of wrestling – not so different from children chasing and tussling, playing so hard they have to stop just to catch their breath. But it's not just otter pups that wrestle and chase; adults do too, and not just with pups but also with each other. Otters are one of the superstars of animal play. They're like domestic dogs and cats who've been bred to behave like perpetual pups and kittens.

Closing the research journal, she lays it on the arm of the chair and drums her fingers on the cover. Just what is all that play about? She knows play makes endorphins flow, so it probably does feel good. Endorphins – opiates within the brain – are a gift of evolution: an opiate reward for performing a behaviour that increases the chances of surviving to reproduce. It's easy to see why endorphins would flow when animals are seeking food and sex, but not so easy to see when they appear to be wasting time and energy in play. And a behaviour with no purpose, no function, poses a serious problem for evolutionary theory. There's no reason for it to exist.

Beth pictures Mattie's slap of the thigh and guffaw, her easy dismissal of scientists who worry about such things. *No big mystery, love. They're just happier than most folks.* But the people who study play do worry; they spend considerable time at it. And so far, there's been lots of theorizing, but researchers aren't much closer to understanding play's purpose, especially among adult animals, than they were twenty-five years ago when Beth was writing her doctoral thesis and documenting lots of otter play but could only speculate about the reasons why.

She picks at the burgundy threads unravelling on the arm of the chair. Feel-good endorphins. She wouldn't mind a few of those right now.

Maybe that's what otters feel when they settle into one big otter-y pile to groom each other – simple physical contact that makes endorphins flow. Maybe they're like close friends, or a mother and daughter, lying on the beach together, talking, and then touching each other's hands and shoulders and hair in an intimate conversation that needs no words.

She thinks of Rachel – all grown up now and on her own – and feels the ache of her absence. This is the first summer she hasn't come home to work in Alan's clinic. Beth decides that she'll go into town this evening and call Rachel. She needs to hear her voice. She's like mama otter: *uhn-uhn-uhn*. She needs to hear that everything's okay.

Beth swallows the last of her coffee, gritty grounds on her tongue, the last dregs from the pot. Dan has probably left by now, she thinks. She can go back to the otter spot and collect some fresh samples. Since the otters were at the beaver lodge last night and then again this morning, they'll be on the move tonight. How did Mattie know that?

CHAPTER 10

Beth is standing on Mattie's doorstep before she even notices the black pickup in the driveway, rust eating away at the wheel wells. As soon as she opens the screen door, she sees Dan sitting at the table. He nods, but not warmly. Since she didn't acknowledge his greeting this morning, he's probably added stuck-up and humourless to the pool of adjectives he uses to describe her. Muin trots over to inspect her hands, and Beth wishes she'd remembered to bring treats. She retrieves a chair from the corner.

"Heard you were out watching this morning," Mattie says, dishing up salt fish and potatoes from the pots bubbling on the cookstove. From a cast-iron skillet, she spoons pork scrunchions and fat into a bowl. The windows are wide open, but the kitchen is hot and steamy. "What did you see?"

"There were five there before–"

"I showed up?" Dan lifts an empty fork in a salute. "Guess the otters and I both know where the best fishing is." His voice softens. "I'll try to stay away from there for a while. Don't want to get in the way of *research*."

"Thanks," Beth says, a little surprised at his easy concession.

Mattie sets three plates and the bowl on the table, hands both of them paper towels, then sits down opposite Dan. She wipes sweat from her brow with the back of her hand. "Glad to hear you've finally seen em. Call their name, did you?"

"No, I didn't." Beth picks up the bowl and spreads a spoonful of scrunchions and fat over her fish. She passes the bowl to Dan, then picks up a fork and stabs a boiled potato. "Did Dan tell you we saw Clive yesterday at the Morning Glory?"

Mattie snorts. "Saw? Or heard? Nobody can yammer on like Clive Hiscock." She spreads the scrunchions over her fish and potatoes, then turns to Beth. "Don't believe half of what he says."

Dan laughs. "He said the same about you. Even called you a witch."

"See what I mean?" Mattie says to Beth. "Born trouble-maker." She shovels potato into her mouth.

Muin settles under the table, resting her head on Beth's feet. Beth takes a small bite of fish, chews, and swallows. Mattie and Dan busy themselves pulling bones from the white flesh. Beth takes another bite, then another. All of them are concentrating on their plates.

Beth brings a paper towel to her lips and clears her throat. "He said that Matthew had a girlfriend?" Voice rising in a question.

Mattie stiffens. "The drowning wasn't her fault."

"He never said it was. He said that you saved her."

Mattie wipes her greasy fingers on a paper towel, doesn't look up.

"And that you took care of her for years afterwards," Beth adds.

Mattie lays down her fork, turns, and stares out the window. In that moment, she looks twenty years older. Beth sees, more than hears, the deep sigh. "Fed her and kept her clean," Mattie says. "Was the least I could do for Matthew."

Dan keeps his eyes fixed on his plate.

"Must have been hard," Beth says. "Clive said—"

With a loud scrape, Dan pushes his chair back from the table. "Tomorrow's supposed to be a grand day," he says. He leans back, propping the chair on two legs, and puts his hands behind his head, elbows out. "Wanna go fishing?"

Beth stops mid-chew. "With you?"

The right side of his upper lip curls, like an aging Elvis Presley. "Well now, I don't guess Clive'll be going out any time soon."

The blush starts at her kneecaps and proceeds to her hairline. She hopes her red face will be blamed on the heat in the kitchen. Flustered, she deliberates quickly. She's explored most of the pond in her kayak, but it could be useful to get a different view of things from a motorboat. Might also put to rest adjectives like stuck-up, humourless, and uppity.

"Okay," she says. "What time?"

"Five-thirty? Unless that's too early for a St. John's girl."

"Five-thirty's just fine. Maybe five would be better."

"Nope. Five-thirty's good. I'll stop by in the boat." Dan stands. "Thanks for supper," he says to Mattie. "If you need anything, just put out the flag." Then he is out the door, plate still half full.

The creak of the truck door opening is followed by a rattling slam. The motor turns over but doesn't catch until the third try. The gears grind as Dan backs out the driveway.

Mattie stands and puts her plate, and Dan's, on the counter. "Gone off for a smoke. Wish he and Matthew would stop that business." She takes two mugs from the cupboard. "Tea?"

"I really should be going. I need to get some ice. And I want to call my daughter. I haven't talked to her in days."

"Sure, you can spare a few minutes for a cup a tea." Without waiting for an answer, Mattie crumbles papery brown leaves and flowers and tosses them into the teapot. "So you saw five this morning?"

"An adult female, I think, and two pups, plus two others, but just for a few minutes."

Mattie pours boiling water into the pot. "What did you see?"

"Wrestling and grooming. Fishing. One of the adults caught a fish for a pup."

"That would be the old grandmother. Or the pup's mom or auntie."

"Mattie, I don't even know for sure that the one who caught the fish was a female. Or even that it was an adult. It wasn't much bigger than the pup."

"The old grandmother then. What did you hear?"

"Chirps and grunts. Snorts when they heard Dan's boat."

Mattie pours tea into the mugs. "Nothing else?"

"No," Beth says warily.

Mattie reaches into the cupboard for the yellow sugar bowl. Sets it on the table. Beth blinks. Pink roses. Just like the ones on the yellow dress in her dream. All afternoon, while she was out in the kayak, she'd recalled more fragments, but never enough to make any sense. She pushes her plate, and the uneaten food, aside. Mattie sets a mug in front of her. She leans away from it.

"Go on, girl. Nothing in there to hurt you." Mattie sits down, looks at Beth, then tips her head to the side. "You got something besides otters on your mind?"

"Not really." Beth picks up the mug and sips the dark tea. It tastes like sweet clover. Over the rim of the mug, she sees the blue cap hanging by the door. Feels spider legs creep across the back of her neck.

Mattie follows her gaze. "That cap is Matthew's favourite. I gave it to him when we were sixteen. Sent away for it. Mail order."

Beth takes another swallow of tea.

"Matthew's still here, you know," Mattie says. "Or maybe you believe that's just old foolishness."

Beth toys with the spoon beside the mug.

"And by taking that rosary, you brought him to you." Her lower lip pushes out. "Take it back yet?"

"I need to go now." Beth stands, but the room tilts. She sits back down and puts her elbows on the table, leans her face into her hands. The cabin feels hot and claustrophobic.

"It's like we all walk around with bags over our heads." Mattie's words are muffled by the cotton in Beth's head. "Can't see what's right in front of us."

Beth wishes she had a bag right now, because when she uncovers her eyes, the light is too bright. She peeks out through interlaced fingers.

Mattie gestures toward the bookshelf. "Sure, I've read about the Big Bang and evolution. They're probably true. But lots of other things are true too. Things you scientists call superstitions." She picks up the matchbox. Opens it and takes out a single match. "Every culture that's come before us has had some notion about ghosts." She strikes the match and watches it flare: yellow, ethereal blue at the base.

Beth catches a whiff of the acrid stink.

Mattie blows out the flame before it can burn her fingers. "Takes a lot of arrogance to dismiss all that as superstition just cause we don't understand it."

Beth lowers her hands. She's beginning to feel less dizzy. Was it the heat? Or the tea?

Mattie stands and goes to the basket beside the loom. She picks up a skein of ivory yarn and a pirn. Turns back to Beth. "Katherine was a lot like you. A hard-nosed history teacher. We had some good arguments." She chuckles. "Whenever I'd be getting on about ghosts, she'd say, 'You go on home now, Matilda, and send Matthew over. He's got better sense.'"

Beth stands. "I *really* need to go."

"But I've got a story for you."

"I need to get to town."

"Sure. Go on then. But it's a story about otters." Mattie brings the yarn and the pirn to the table.

Beth takes a deep breath and sits back down.

Mattie sits down across from Beth and begins to wind the yarn onto the pirn. "Matthew used to watch them for hours. Got so they knew him, and talked to him." She peers at Beth. "They gave him the greatest gift animals have to give: a whole new way of being alive to this world." Her eyes narrow. "And he got all that just from spending time with them. And listening."

Mattie sits back and clicks a thumbnail against her broken front tooth. "Seems to me you're watching, but you're not listening."

Without a word, Beth pushes herself up from the table and leaves.

~

As soon as the cool air hits her face and she breathes it in, her head clears, her thoughts unmuddle. She rubs her temples. She's been spending far too much time with someone who believes she knows everything there is to know about otters, who thinks Beth is going about her research all wrong.

Stepping onto the narrow path, she looks back over one shoulder, glad it's not dark yet – and then wants to slap herself. Getting spooked by a lonely old woman who believes in ghosts!

And yet she can't help marvelling at how Mattie manages to connect her nutty ideas into an illogical chain that ends with a conclusion Beth can agree with: Western society has become too arrogant about what it thinks it knows. Ghosts aside, Beth has always been annoyed by the smug – and erroneous – idea that humans occupy some sort of pinnacle, that evolution has been working toward some goal and humans are it. People forget that it's humans who decide what constitutes evolutionary success.

She pushes a branch out of her way. Well, if there's an apocalypse in the offing, she'd place her bet on cockroaches and rats.

Beth steps over raised tree roots and exposed rocks. She's just as impatient with the assumption that humans have arrived, at this point in the twenty-first century, at the *correct* world view, that radical changes in the way we think about ourselves and the world ended with the Copernican revolution in the sixteenth century, the Darwinian theory of evolution in the nineteenth, and theories of quantum physics in the twentieth. People talk with condescension about what humans believed just a few hundred years ago; yet these same people never seem to wonder what their descendants will shake their heads at. She suspects that future generations will be appalled at how the current one has treated the earth.

Her thoughts gain momentum as her feet stride along the path. Maybe people would be less arrogant if they understood that their own world view is shaped by the limits of their senses, literally, their view. We experience the world not as it is, she thinks, but the way our brains construct it. Mattie's not far off the mark to talk about everyone walking around as if we all have bags over our heads. Even when we're paying attention, we perceive only a small fraction of what's around us. How differently might we conceptualize the world if, like otters, our dominant sense were smell rather than vision? Beth smiles. *I smell what you mean. I can smell it in my mind's nose. I didn't even recognize him, he just didn't smell like the man I used to know.* We'd navigate by smell not sight, and instead of written language, we might have some sort of complex olfactory code for preserving information: libraries for odours. And if we had four digits on each hand and foot, then eight, not ten, would be the base for our numerical system. If, like migrating birds, we had a visual map of the earth's magnetic fields, or, like insects, we could see ultraviolet light and infrared, it would change the way we see each other, our artwork, our architecture, the way we travel – the way we live on this earth.

It's dusk by the time Beth arrives at the cabin. She has used her internal rant to distract herself from admitting just how unnerved she is by Mattie's talk of ghosts and the rosary. When she goes inside to grab her car keys and wallet, she can't help peering into every shadowed corner and hoping desperately, stupidly, that Matthew – or Katherine – doesn't put in an appearance. Beth is doubly eager now to hear Rachel's voice, to talk with someone who is sensible and rational, someone who would scoff at the very idea of ghosts.

CHAPTER 11

Driving as fast as she dares, Beth bumps along the pot-holed roads. When she finally arrives at the Irving – and the pay phone – she fishes a calling card from her wallet and punches in the numbers. The sanity of the woman's voice politely asking her to press 1 for English and then to enter her key code calms her. Step by step. Logical. The voice tells her, to the penny, how much money is left on the card, and then requests that Beth enter the phone number she wants to call: Rachel's. She listens to the tinny ring – five times – and then to Rachel's voice telling her that she's "busy right now. Leave a message if you want to."

Beth leans her head against the phone cubicle. Almost weeps. Rachel, where are you? I need to know that you're okay. To know that I'm okay.

Struggling to control her voice, she leaves a message: "Just calling to say hi, sweetheart. Hope everything's okay and that your lab work is going well. I'll try again soon. Love you." When she hangs up, she feels a familiar tightening in her chest, cords pulled taut. It's been more than a week since she last talked with Rachel. What if something's happened?

She smacks her forehead. "Stop," she says out loud. "Just stop." If anything serious were to happen, Alan would come out. It's only a four-hour drive. She doesn't need to worry.

But she can't stop herself. The umbilical cord still pulses with warm red blood.

Should she call Alan? Yes, no. Yes, no. She wishes she could call Alice. Alice would make her laugh at herself. But she can't. Her best friend is dead.

Beth punches in the calling card numbers again, follows the commands, then enters the number of her home phone. Alan picks up on the second ring: "Hello?"

"Hi," she says.

"Oh, hey. How's everything going?"

"Fine. Have you talked to Rachel recently?"

"Just yesterday."

Beth breathes out. "How is she?"

"Fine, as far as I know."

"Did you ask about her research?"

"Of course."

"How about that new guy she's seeing?"

"What new guy?"

Why does he always make her do all the worrying? "Alan, how do you know everything's okay?"

"Because she said so, Beth. How's *your* research going?"

Beth slides the calling card back into her wallet. "All right. I have quite a few samples now. In fact, I should make a trip into St. John's Monday or Tuesday to get them into a freezer."

"It'll be good to see you. Planning to stay overnight?" A brittleness in his words.

"Probably. I'll try to do some observations in the morning and then drive in while it's still light."

"So you've been able to watch them?"

"Some." Just sixteen minutes, but there's no need to explain about Dan and his stupid boat.

"Anything useful?"

"Pretty much the same stuff as when I did my thesis research."

"Well, you can't expect too much at this stage, right?" He hesitates. "I mean ... it's early yet."

"If I could just mark them," she says, "so I could know who was who, the observations would be a lot more useful."

"But that's hard to do, right?"

"Impossible without live-trapping them." Beth runs her finger down a row of numbered buttons, 1-4-7, then across, 7-8-9. "And I don't really want to do that."

"But maybe that's something you'll have to consider."

As if she hasn't already. She hears Pirate barking in the background. "How are things there?"

"Fine."

Fine. Everything's always *fine*. "Did the cat live?"

Silence. "No, she didn't," he says finally. "And I had to tell the little girl myself."

Beth visualizes him leaning against the stainless-steel refrigerator and staring down at the black and white tiles.

"I promised her that when the next litter of kittens comes in, I'll let her have first pick."

"That was nice, Alan."

"What else you gonna do?" He sighs. "In a weak moment, I even told her mom I'd do the neutering for free."

Beth smiles. "Always the astute businessman." Just like when he did the surgery, free of charge, for the stray dog who'd been caught in a leg-hold trap. And then adopted him. Her shoulders begin to loosen. "I met the neighbour."

"Neighbour? Just one?"

"An old woman and her dog. Claims she's lived on the pond for eighty years."

"Really! And she's there by herself?"

"Yeah. Maybe for too long. Seems a bit strange." Where to begin? There's no way to explain Mattie and the story about her twin. And the ghosts. Alan would think she's gone bonkers. Maybe she has. "She claims to know everything there is to know about otters."

"There you go," he says. "No need to mark them. Just talk to her."

"That's exactly what she said."

Alan laughs, then says, "That cabin's pretty isolated. I'm glad there's at least one other person out that way." He pauses. "Strange can be okay." He laughs again. "As long as she's not homicidal."

Beth laughs with him, then says, "It's good to talk with you, Alan, but I should get going. It's a long drive back to the cabin, especially in the dark."

"Promise me you'll be careful, Beth. I know you can handle a kayak. And it's quiet water, but …"

Beth waits, then speaks into the silence, "See you soon. Love you. Bye."

She drives around to the gas pumps. The buzz of the bright lights overhead is loud, drowning out all other night noises. The air around the lights is thick with insects. She lifts the nozzle, the gas fumes pungent, but familiar and almost pleasant.

Gas pumped, she goes inside and uses a credit card to pay the young man behind the counter for the gas and a bag of ice. His surliness, and his quickness to return to his small-screen TV, make it clear that he's not about to engage in conversation. Beth lingers anyway, looks longingly at a TV show she doesn't even recognize, listens to laughter that's not even real. She hates TV sitcoms, but she's reluctant to leave, to be alone again, in the dark.

"Something else?" he asks sharply.

She spins away and walks up and down the aisles, passing shelves of chips and snacks, refrigerators filled with soda pop and energy drinks, milk and beer. She studies the lip balms and the stale glazed doughnuts and blueberry muffins left from that morning – or maybe the morning before. Finally, she selects a pack of Dentyne and brings it to the counter. The young man flicks greasy hair out of his eyes and sighs hugely when he takes her coins.

It's dark now and Beth has to drive slowly, always on the alert for moose. She breaks her no-news rule and turns on the radio, but the announcer's cheerful voice only makes her feel more alone. She flicks it off.

Mattie's ghosts, she thinks. Nothing mysterious or scary about them. Not really. Mattie lost her twin when she was a teenager. She's lonely, especially now that she's lost Katherine too, and just trying to bring back the people she can't bear to live without.

Who would Beth bring back? Not her father, that's for sure. He was a harsh, unforgiving man when he was alive. She grew up believing that he didn't even like her all that much, that she was a disappointment to him. Her mother loved her though. She was kind-hearted and well-meaning, but ultimately, ineffectual. Beth doubts she'd have much wisdom to offer from the other side.

She peers into the darkness, headlights reflecting off pale birches. Knows there is a ghost she'd bring back if only she could: Alice, her best friend for more than twenty years. Gone now for two. God, how she misses her, not just their long conversations but also the times when they needed no words, when a single sidelong glance or raised eyebrow stood in for thousands. And the laughter, Beth misses the laughter. When Alice got going, she sounded like a donkey braying, incongruous for such an elegant, graceful woman. She'd try to stifle the guffaws, but her efforts only made them both laugh even harder, until their sides ached and tears ran down their cheeks. Alice was the sister Beth never had, and Beth still hasn't filled that void. Doubts that she ever can. And she's terrified that, in the end, she may have disappointed Alice too. Beth had taken her to the appointments, wept with her when her copper curls came out in handfuls, and sat with her. And sat with her, and sat with her some more. But it wasn't enough. Beth couldn't give her what she needed. When Alice asked, Beth couldn't let her go. And she wasn't there at the very end, when Alice needed her most.

Beth sees a sudden movement at the side of the road. A great-horned owl rises up before her. The broad wings span the width of the Toyota. A limp hare hangs in its talons, and, for a split second, the owl's yellow eyes stare into hers. Beth slams on the brakes, skids on the gravel, and comes to a grinding stop. Her mouth opens then closes, no sound, like in nightmares when her screams are stopped at the back of her throat. What is wrong with her? It's only an owl. But it isn't. It's the one thing Alice asked for that Beth could give her: A feather from her collection. A feather from the bird that can fly safely through the darkest night.

By the time she finally pulls into the driveway she has stopped shaking, but the headlights shining on the trees cast eerie shadows that dance over the red clapboard with every gust of wind. She reaches into the glove compartment. No flashlight. Of course not. Beth leaves the car idling, headlights on, and runs to the cabin. Unlocks the door. Inside, she fumbles around for matches and then lights a candle. She wrestles with the kerosene lamp until that's lit as well. She grabs the flashlight from the counter and runs back outside to turn off the car, and the headlights. Forcing herself to walk calmly, she returns to the cabin, hugging the bag of ice to her chest. Once inside, she locks the door and leans against it.

Beth drops the ice into the cooler with her samples and uncorks a bottle of wine. Tries to ignore how the lamp creates shadows that darken the corners and change the colours in the weaving: rose to blood-red, indigo to black. Her hand trembles as she lifts the glass to her lips. What a comfort Pirate would be right now. She thinks of Jax then, the collie-shepherd mix who was her childhood companion. That's another ghost she'd bring back. The old farmhouse and barn could be scary at night, especially the barn. Small animals crept or flew through the shadows, sheep shuffled in the straw, chewing their cud, breath steamy in the cold night air. But Jax was always right there with her, protecting her, loving her.

She takes a sip of wine. Maybe she should have kept Pirate here when Alan left, just for the company. But what would the old Lab do while she was out in the kayak? She'd hate keeping him closed up in the cabin all day. Besides, he's Alan's dog, not hers.

Scratching at the door. Beth freezes. Stares at the door for long minutes. Can hear nothing but her own heart: thump-thump, thump-thump, thump-thump. Too fast. Hears a bark, then a whine. She steps quickly to the door and cracks it open, sees the now-familiar chocolate eyes. Muin noses her way in and Beth stoops to hug her.

When the dog licks her face, Beth laughs and wipes away what could be a tear. "I don't know why you're here, girl, but I'm some glad you are."

Beth sits on the floor. Muin stretches out beside her. She keeps a hand in the warm fur, and when she finishes the glass of wine, she takes the dog with her to the outhouse. Then, settling in for the night, she pats the bed, encouraging Muin to jump onto it. Doesn't care that the dog's length and bulk push her to the edge of the mattress.

She checks, one more time, to make sure the flashlight is on the chair beside the bed, then leans in to blow out the lamp. Stops. No rosary. She moves the flashlight, her novel, and the lamp, then she stands. Muin jumps off the bed. Beth searches the floor all around the chair. Shakes out the sleeping bag and then the clothes on the floor. She sweeps the flashlight's beam and then her hand under the bed. Nothing. She sits back on her heels. Muin sits down beside her. Nothing is out of order, but the rosary is gone.

Holding the kerosene lamp like a torch, she goes out into the kitchen and living room. Muin follows. Beth checks the windowsills, moves both the rocking chair and the armchair, then the stack of articles on the counter and the bottles of insect repellent and sunscreen. Nothing. She even searches around the pans and bowls on the floor.

She pushes the jumble of puzzle pieces aside and sets the lamp on the table. She sits down in the rocking chair, elbows on her knees. Okay. What's logical? She's certain she didn't move the rosary from the chair beside the bed. And it couldn't have disappeared into thin air. Could someone have taken it? Matthew's ghost? Ridiculous! Mattie? She probably still has a key to the cabin.

Beth looks suspiciously at Muin. "Were you and Mattie here earlier tonight?" The dog's ears lift forward, her head tilts.

But that makes no sense ... unless Mattie somehow knows that Beth hasn't taken it back, and she's angry. *Take it back yet?* Beth never answered, so how could Mattie know? Rocking backwards, Beth picks at a splinter on the arm of the chair. Surely Mattie's not trying to make her believe her weird ideas about ghosts. Why? The splinter pricks her index finger, and Beth watches blood rise into a single bead on her fingertip. Maybe there is no rational explanation for what Mattie does. Beth looks to see if the blue baseball cap is hanging by the door. That would be just like her. Then she'd claim that Matthew's ghost left it there when he took the rosary. Beth sees only the empty hooks.

She blots the drop of blood with a tissue, then checks once again to make sure the door is locked. She takes the kerosene lamp into the bedroom and sets it on the chair. Placing the flashlight close at hand, she crawls into the sleeping bag and calls Muin onto the bed. Fully awake now, she picks up the novel and reads a few pages. When she realizes she has no idea what she's just read, Beth lays the book aside, blows out the lamp, and snuggles into Muin.

~

A slim crescent moon sits just above the horizon: silver light and shadows on dark water. Waves curl, then roll and crash against massive rocks, drowning out the sound of the otters' chirps and *uhn-uhn-uhns*. Two of them wrestle. Chirp. A pup joins in. Chirp. Poke to belly. Chirp. Nudge to cheek. Chirp. Paws grab. Turning. Twisting. Tumbling through foamy water.

Rocked back and forth by waves, they hunt then. Underwater, long whiskers detect movements of fish and lobsters. Sensitive paws probe rocks for mussels. When their bellies are full, they swim to the river and rinse their fur in water that does not taste or smell of salt.

CHAPTER 12

She is wearing the yellow sundress and sitting on a blanket spread over newly mown grass. The young man's lanky arm is draped around her shoulders, and they gaze out over silver water that glistens with reflected sunlight. From under the brim of her hat, she steals a shy glance at his face, and knows that he is only pretending not to see her looking. Without his blue cap, his hair has the ebony sheen of a raven's feather, a violet iridescence.

He turns to her and lifts the straw hat from her head. Lays it aside and pulls the pins from her hair, slowly. Kisses her face and her lips as he removes each tortoiseshell pin. One by one, he lays them carefully into the bowl of the hat. Platinum curls cascade down her back. He lifts the curls and kisses her neck, then gently pushes her down and lies beside her. He puts a hand to her narrow waist, slides it up to her breast. He unbuttons the top two buttons of her yellow dress. She lays her hand against his jeans.

The waves suddenly rise and sweep over them. Her mouth opens, but her scream is muffled by the water. She holds her breath and hears the echo of a scream. Flails in the murky water, knows that he can't swim. She tries to find him. Her lungs are bursting. She opens her mouth.

Beth wakes, gasping, the metallic tang of muddy water on her tongue. She swallows. Stares into the dark and waits for her heart to slow. Listens for Muin's soft breathing. She puts a hand to the dog's fur and then reaches to make sure the flashlight is still there. Her fingers find her watch: 1:12. She considers getting up and lighting the lamp, reading or working on the puzzle. She lies still in the dark and breathes, the warm weight of Muin's long body next to hers.

~

Staring straight ahead with those pale blue eyes. The face of a ghost. Dan's voice is soft. His green eyes are shadowed by a blue baseball cap. Beth is looking at his face through a spider web. She can hear the whir as the spider spins silk thread. Then, she and Dan are sitting on a blanket by a pond. She sees murky, roiling water. Remembers. But he puts an arm around her shoulders, gives them a reassuring squeeze. He kisses her neck. His fingers fumble at the snap on her jeans. He yells her name.

A loud banging startles her awake, someone shouting her name. Beth lies still. Dan! She leaps out of bed. Muin is already at the door.

"Just a minute," Beth calls out. She slides on her glasses and sorts through the mound of clothes on the floor for something reasonably clean. Hops to the door on one foot, still tugging at her jeans. Opens it to soft grey light and Dan's smirk.

"Guess five-thirty *is* too early for a St. John's girl."

"Forgot to set my alarm." Beth can't bring herself to look at his face, fears she'll blush scarlet and he'll know, somehow. "Just need to go to the outhouse, brush my teeth …" She bites her lip. "And make coffee?"

"No worries. Got a thermos in the boat."

Muin pushes her head out the door.

"What's she doing here?" Dan says.

"Showed up late last night. Think we should take her back before we go out?"

"No, she'll find her way home." He lifts his cap and pushes it farther back on his head, puts his hands on his hips. "But as soon as she sees the boat, she'll wanna come with us."

~

It's a perfect summer morning, cool and clear with just enough wind to keep the bugs away. The sky is deep rose where the sun is rising, apricot tinged with gold beyond.

For the first hour, while Dan fishes, Beth is content to sit, arm draped around Muin, and nurse the coffee Dan poured for her. It's heavy with cream and sugar, and Beth prefers black, but at least it's coffee.

He's already caught four good-sized trout and laid them in a cooler half-filled with ice. He's returned three smaller ones to the water. They've hardly spoken, but Dan seems comfortable with the silence. Beth is still avoiding looking into his face, but when his back is turned, she watches him, the clean, graceful movements of his shoulders and arms when he casts. She can't help comparing him to Alan. Dan is about the same height, but in better shape; he doesn't have that little paunch, and his face is tanned, not pasty. His prominent nose gives him a rugged, serious sort of look. But Alan is more intelligent, more interesting. Maybe. She doesn't really know that; she's just assuming. And Dan is certainly sexier, or at least in the dream he was.

When did Alan become unsexy? When did she and Alan become so ... boring? They didn't start out that way. She was working on her doctoral thesis in Minnesota when they met, Alan his veterinary training. They shared common interests in animals and the outdoors, a deep concern for the environment. There was lots of laughter, and teasing. Few fireworks though, no drama, no fighting. Theirs was a calm, solid kind of love. Or at least she thought so. After they married and finished school, they moved back to Alan's home province, to St. John's. To Beth, already pregnant, it seemed like a romantic adventure in an exotic locale – a fantasy that didn't outlast the pregnancy. Alan joined a veterinary practice; Beth started teaching at the university; Rachel was born. They were busy, doing all the things that young professionals with children do, but now they just seem ... boring. And somewhere along the way, they'd stopped laughing.

Beth studies Dan's back and wonders if she's missed something huge in her life. A grand passion. Or is that just in schmaltzy movies and novels?

After another half-dozen casts without a rise, Dan lays down the fly rod and pours coffee into the thermos lid, refills Beth's mug. He lights a cigarette. The three of them sit, staring out over the calm water. Dan has only to lean toward her and whisper: *Staring straight ahead with those pale blue eyes. The face of a ghost.* He has only to touch the waistband of her jeans ...

"Lovely morning," she says.

He nods. Takes a swallow of coffee, then a draw on the cigarette.

She wishes she'd remembered to bring her binoculars, then she could pretend to be scanning the shoreline. She thinks of the rosary then. In the bright light of day, its disappearance seems less ominous. "Does Mattie ever play tricks on you?" she asks.

"She does some odd things, but I wouldn't call them tricks." He takes another draw on the cigarette. "Why?"

"Just wondering. She seems like the kind of person who might." Beth snaps the lid of the plastic mug off, then back on. Off. On. "Does Mattie still have a key to Katherine's cabin?"

"Doubt it. Neither of them ever locked their doors." He cocks his head. "What? You worried that Mattie will come in uninvited?"

"No, no." She hesitates. Dan is looking at her, his head still canted to the side. She tries to speak casually, but her voice catches. "It's just that Mattie has said some strange things about Matthew and ghosts. It's giving me the creeps."

"Don't worry about it. Mattie's always getting on with stuff like that."

"But it seems important to her that I believe her."

"Trust me." Dan raises a hand, as if he were in a courtroom swearing an oath. "Mattie doesn't give a damn what you believe. She just enjoys tormenting people. Look at that whole Matthew-Matilda business."

"Yes, just look at that whole business. Doesn't that tell you something?"

"Go on, girl. After she says something weird, she just laughs and says it's probably all nonsense." He tosses the cigarette butt into the bottom of the boat. "She misses Katherine, so what's important to her now is having someone to talk to. She never cared whether Katherine believed her." He laughs. "And she knows I don't."

"I think," Beth says carefully, "that Mattie may have done something to try and *make* me believe her about Matthew's ghost."

"Like what?"

Beth looks at Muin, who returns her gaze, brown eyes innocent. "Taken something from my cabin," she says.

"Like what?" he repeats. He takes a mouthful of coffee.

"An old rosary that Matthew made."

He spews out the coffee. Wipes his mouth on his sleeve. "A rosary? That Matthew made?"

"Mattie said he made it for their grandmother when he was a boy."

"So why's it in your cabin?"

"I found it near Medicine Rock. When I showed it to Mattie, she said I should take it back."

"And you didn't?"

Beth runs a hand through her hair. Tugs at a brown and grey lock behind her ear. "Haven't had time."

"So why would Mattie steal it?"

"To take it back herself?" Beth says. "Or, more likely, to make me believe that Matthew's ghost took it. She said the rosary would bring him to me."

Dan shakes his head. "She says some pretty weird shit, but Mattie would never steal anything. And she sure as hell wouldn't go to the trouble of hiking all the way to your cabin just to take an old rosary. No matter who made it."

"Maybe you just don't know that side of her. You didn't even know about her and Katherine."

He lets out a long, exasperated sigh. "I knew. I just never thought it was any of my business." He swallows the last of his coffee and screws the lid back onto the thermos. "Listen, whatever happened, Mattie did *not* steal anything."

"Do you drink her teas?"

"Her teas? Sure." He squints at Beth. "What? You think there's something strange about them too?"

"Don't be ridiculous."

"Beth, I'm not the one being ridiculous."

"Never mind."

"No, tell me."

"Well …"

"Come on," he urges.

"I always feel dizzy and headachy when I drink them."

He puts a hand to his mouth and coughs, as if stifling a laugh. "No offense, but I think that's just you. And your imagination. It's just Labrador tea she gathers herself. And raspberry, maybe some rose hips." He touches the bill of his cap, pulls it lower. "You're letting her weirdness get to you. She'd love that."

Beth wishes she'd never mentioned it, any of it. Spoken out loud, everything does sound crazy, and now Dan probably thinks she's paranoid *and* a hypochondriac. She studies the soggy cigarette butts floating in the bottom of the boat. Small waves make little slapping sounds against the hull. She wishes she could think of something funny or interesting to say, something that doesn't make her sound like an idiot.

Dan lifts the lid of the cooler to check the trout. Muin puts her head in, sniffs. "Stop that now," he says, pushing her away. He closes the lid, his hand a dark tan against the stark white.

"So ..." Beth says. "Are you really part Mi'kmaq?"

He snorts a laugh. "A very, very small part. Might as well call myself Beothuk. That seems to be all the rage now." He takes off his cap, wipes his forehead with the back of his hand, and puts it back on. "Okay," he says, "so some great-great-grandmother, way back when, was half Mi'kmaq and half French. Myself? I'm a whole lot more Irish. Doubt that anyone in Dublin would consider me Irish, so I don't spect the folks in Conne River think I'm Mi'kmaq."

He shakes the thermos. "Coffee's near gone, so I guess it's time to head back. Wanna couple trout for your supper?"

"You caught them."

He looks into her face, hazel eyes assessing. "Could be you're spending too much time alone in that old cabin. Can make you think some strange stuff when you're not used to it. Why don't you come over for supper? I'm not a terrible cook."

Taking her stunned silence for a yes, Dan slides toward the small outboard. "I'll come over in the boat about five and get you." He raises an eyebrow. "Set your alarm this time."

"No, no, that's okay. It's just a short paddle across the pond."

"Suit yourself. Just look for the green bungalow directly east of your cabin. Tall junipers on either side of the deck." Dan starts the engine with one clean pull.

CHAPTER 13

Beth spots a red flag fluttering from a metal pole on the pier. She points, but Dan is already turning the boat toward Mattie's cabin. He cuts the motor and uses an oar to guide the boat into the pier. Muin jumps into the water and swims to shore, comes out and shakes herself off. Dan ties a rope to the flagpole, then turns and offers a hand to Beth, but she is already climbing the short ladder onto the pier.

Mattie appears on the front step. She is wearing the blue baseball cap. She dips the bill toward Beth and Dan. Muin gallops toward her.

"Seen the boat go out with Muin," Mattie says. "Thought you'd be stopping by."

"Here's your dog," Dan says. "Again."

"Any luck?"

"Nothing big," he says, "but enough for supper."

Mattie raises a finger. "Before I forgets, you should pick me up some dog food next time you're in town." She jabs the finger into his chest. "And none a that cheap stuff neither."

Dan glances at Muin. "No, we can't have that horse eating the cheap stuff."

"A bag of bird seed too. Black sunflower."

"Certainly. Can't have the hordes going hungry."

"Don't be saucy," Mattie says. "Time for tea?"

Before Beth can blurt out a no, Dan says, "Sure." When Mattie turns around, he leans toward Beth and whispers, "I'll watch her hands to see if she slips anything into your mug."

"Very funny," Beth says, turning toward the path to the outhouse. She thinks about making up an excuse and just walking back to her cabin, but then decides that she wants to ask Mattie about the rosary, in front of Dan. Then he'll see.

A few minutes later, she steps into the kitchen. Mattie has set out three mugs.

"Just water please," Beth says, sitting down.

"Oh, yes," Mattie says, "I keeps forgetting that I'm trying to poison you." She pours tea into two of the mugs.

Dan takes the third one to the sink and works the squeaky handle of the old pump. "Wonder when they'll get around to putting electricity out this way." He fills the mug with cold water.

"Don't need it, do we, Beth?"

"I'm not so sure about that. It would be nice to have an indoor bathroom and a refrigerator, a real stove."

"No need of it," Mattie says firmly. "Katherine and I don't want it."

Beth gives Dan an *I-told-you-so* look, but he is turned toward the rocking chair. The floor around it is littered with wood chips and shavings. A long, hollowed-out cylinder of wood and a knife lie on the bookshelf. "Carving this morning?" he says, sitting down at the table.

"Woke up as Matthew and felt like working on a flute." Mattie sets out the yellow sugar bowl. Muin is already ensconced under the table. To avoid her sprawled legs, all of them have to push back their chairs.

"What's this I hear about Matthew making some sort of rosary?" Dan winks at Beth. "Never thought he was all that religious."

"I'm not," Mattie says. "Made that for Nan when I was just a youngster." She jerks her chin toward Beth. "She found it. Or it found her." She tastes the tea, then adds more sugar. "But it's missing now, isn't it."

"Yes, it is," Beth says, looking straight at Mattie.

"Don't know why you thinks I took it," Mattie says.

"I never said that." Beth turns to Dan.

"I didn't say a word." He raises his hands, palms out. "I swear I didn't."

Mattie chuckles. "He didn't have to say nothing, love. What you thinks is as plain as the nose on your face." She grins. "Matthew's probably just having a bit of fun with you. He's got a sly sense of humour."

Beth folds her hands and lays them on the table. "Or maybe it's you who's having *a bit of fun* with me."

"That's just what I said."

"So you didn't come over to the cabin and take it?" Beth says. "You ... or Matilda or whoever?"

"Nope."

Beth stands. "I should get back to work."

Mattie raises her mug in a salute. "Yep, you got lotsa work to do yet."

Dan starts to rise. Beth puts out a hand, gesturing for him to stay seated. "Thanks," she says, "but I can find my own way home."

~

Beth rocks slowly, creaking forward, then back. Looks at the kerosene lamp, seeing it, not seeing it. Why would Dan lie? So that he and Mattie could share a good laugh at spooking the scientist? On the other hand, maybe it was just a lucky guess on Mattie's part. It's hardly a stretch that she would assume that Beth would know it was she who took the rosary. Beth rubs her palms on the rough fabric of her jeans, picks at a loose thread on the knee. Wishes she'd never found that stupid rosary. She'd be out in her kayak right now, doing what she should be doing: her research.

She decides to search the cabin one more time. Just to be absolutely sure. She looks first in the kitchen and living room, even though she's certain she left the rosary on the chair beside the bed. She looks at the table with the unfinished puzzle – a stereotypical mountain scene from the Canadian Rockies – then moves all the dishes, boxes, and cans off the counter and puts them away in the cupboard. She lifts the folder of scientific articles she hasn't read yet, then rifles through all the clutter: matchboxes, research journal, voice recorder, pens and pencils, insect repellent, sunscreen. Nothing. She checks both windowsills and all around the hand-pump and sink. Moves all the chairs and the table, as well as the bowls and pans she set out to catch the drips. She gets out the broom and sweeps the floor. Ends up with a pile of bread and cracker crumbs, wood debris, pencil shavings, and a fistful of black dog hair.

Beth carries the broom and the dustpan into the bedroom, pushes back the tan curtain hanging in front of the empty closet. Nothing but metal hangers on the wooden rod and a scattering of sand on the floor. She lets the curtain drop. Clears everything off the chair she's using as a nightstand: flashlight, matches, wineglass with a dried red circle in the bottom, paperback novel. She lifts the sleeping bag and shakes it, picks up all the discarded clothes from the floor, shakes out each piece, checks every pocket, and lays the clothes on the bed. She searches all around the chair, then kneels down and sweeps her arm under the bed as far as she can reach. Nothing but gigantic dust bunnies. She decides to move the bed. Pulls on one corner, then another, inching the heavy metal frame away from the wall.

Glint of green beads! Tucked into a dusty corner behind a metal leg. Beth picks up the rosary and, with a sick feeling in her stomach, knows that Mattie never took it at all. She has been a complete and total idiot.

She sits down on the edge of the bed and lets the beads and chain slide through her fingers. In her flustered hurry to grab her car keys and get into town last night, she must have knocked the rosary to the floor and kicked it under the bed. Beth puts a hand to her forehead, not sure whether she's more embarrassed or angry. Mattie wasn't assuming anything. Dan must have told her about Beth's suspicions, and in doing so, he has multiplied her humiliation tenfold.

Beth rubs a thumb over the small carving of the otter. She'd left Mattie's in a huff. Does Dan still expect her for supper?

She sits up straighter, rolls her shoulders back. She'll go. There will be those first awkward moments when she has to tell him that she found the rosary, but then she'll ask him again, and keep asking, until he finally confesses that he did tell Mattie.

Tomorrow, she'll have to go to Mattie and apologize.

~

The sun is high above, warming their fur as they rub themselves dry in the grass. Bellies full of fish, all six lie close to the lodge and to each other. Two begin to nibble through the fur on each other's head, shoulders, and back. A pup joins in. And then another adult, until finally, all six are grooming themselves and each other. Comfort in the touch. They listen to their own *uhn-uhn-uhns*, as well as to the long grasses rustling, the robins warbling, the juncos chirping, and to the jays and crows calling to each other. Nothing alarming in their calls.

The old female breathes in their familiar scents, the distinctive musk of each one and the fishiness of their muzzles. She breathes in the fragrances of earth, sky, and water, the smell of the lodge and the rocks and grasses around it. She detects the scent of the watcher. Knows by its faintness that she is far away. And yet her presence lingers.

CHAPTER 14

Precisely at 16:30, Beth slides into the kayak and heads east across the pond. She will not be late this time. The sky is overcast but there's no heavy wind to buffet her boat, and it will be light for another four hours. Plenty of time to have supper and then paddle back.

She's prepared her speech. Has pictured the scene a dozen different ways and practiced exactly what she will say: She's sorry. Yes, she jumped to silly conclusions. But then Mattie's very strange and says odd things. Even Dan admits to that.

Trying not to envision his self-satisfied smirk, she's given a lot of thought to how, without sounding whiny, she can confront him about telling Mattie – and then lying to her about it. He needs to apologize too.

Damn. Even her thoughts sound whiny.

Immersed in her own debate, she paddles steadily, hardly noticing the sky or the pond, but then she spots a pair of loons in the distance, a grey chick swimming between them, small for this time of year. She lays the paddle across the kayak and lifts her binoculars. Rising up from the water, one loon flaps checkerboard wings, throws back a sleek black head, and releases piercing warbles that reverberate across the pond. No matter how clichéd it may be, to her, the call embodies wilderness. Yet, even here, the human world intrudes: the snarl of a chainsaw and the monotonous low hum of a motorboat, beer and pop cans on the bottom of the pond, a yellow plastic bag waving gaily from a tall spruce.

Within thirty minutes, she sees the bungalow with the dark-green clapboard, a deck with sentinel larches on either side. No lawn, just trees and shrubs that almost hide the house. The *Black Feather* is tied up to the pier. Beth beaches the kayak, unzips her life-jacket, and tosses it into the cockpit.

Dan steps out onto the deck. He is drying his hands on a dish towel. "Wasn't sure you'd show up."

She walks up the path toward him. "I found the rosary," she says.

"Kinda thought you might."

"Listen, I'm really sorry that I said anything about it, that I even suggested that Mattie might have taken it. I'm—"

"No worries," he cuts in.

"I'm sorry," she insists, "but why did you have to tell her? Now I'll have to go to Mattie and apologize."

"I didn't."

"I bet you two had a good laugh about it."

"I swear, Beth, I didn't tell her a thing." He throws the dish towel over one shoulder and leans on the railing. "There's no easy way to explain this, but sometimes, Mattie just seems to know what you're thinking."

"What? She reads minds?"

"Don't have a better explanation."

He sweeps an arm toward the open patio door. "Let me show you around and then I'll start cooking."

Beth decides she'll let him change the subject. For now. Because she's not sure what her next question would be: Why are you lying to me? Or, What's your evidence that Mattie can read minds?

She slides off her wet sandals and leaves them by the door. When she steps inside, Beth has to hide her surprise. Given the state of Dan's battered pickup and his standard uniform of worn blue jeans, flannel shirt, and rubber boots, she'd expected a décor of shabby but functional.

Instead, she is greeted by neatness and quality. A real estate agent might describe the house as well-appointed: hardwood floors, tiled kitchen, large windows onto the pond, overstuffed sofa and chair in a colourful print that verges on tacky, but actually looks good with the latte-coloured walls. Tall bookshelves stand on either side of a stone fireplace, and a weaving incorporating Mattie's signature spider web and a stylized raven hangs over the mantel. There's also a black and white etching of a raven that looks to be Haida or Tlingit. A foot-tall carved raven perches on one of the bookshelves. Beth picks up the carving and runs a finger over the feathers. Turns it over: *Matthew MacKenzie.* She looks up at Dan.

"She signs all her carvings that way. I don't ask. Not my business." He slides the screen door shut.

Not my business. Dan's mantra. Maybe that's the only way to stay sane when you're dealing with Mattie.

Beth places the carving back on the shelf. In the quiet, she hears the refrigerator's hum start up. A refrigerator. With a freezer. She tucks her hair behind one ear. Smoothes the damp cloth of her shorts. Takes off her glasses and cleans each lens on the bottom of her shirt. Slides them back on. If she could just store her samples here she wouldn't have to drive them back to St. John's. Can she dare ask?

Dan lays a hand on the countertop that separates the living room from the kitchen. "Get you something? Beer? Wine? Rum and Coke?" He grins mischievously. "Or tea maybe?" She lets herself laugh with him. Decides that he looks more attractive when he's smiling. "Wine, please," she says.

"White or red?"

"White."

He opens the refrigerator and pulls out a bottle of wine and a Black Horse. "I just drink beer, but I picked this up in town today. George – the guy at the liquor store

– recommended it." He glances at the label. "A Chilean Chardonnay okay?"

"Perfect."

While he uncorks the wine, she scans the shelves of books: basic how-to's, detective novels and thrillers, some old classics, but also a few contemporary novels she recognizes as literary, which surprises her. And then she wonders why. Why has she assumed that Dan isn't a serious reader?

Grasping a beer in one hand, he gives her the glass of wine. His fingers, brushing hers, seem to linger. She glances up, but he's already turned away and is pointing the bottle toward the hallway.

"When I came back here I had the old place torn down," he says. "Then built this one. Did most of the work myself." He speaks with pride edged with uneasiness, as if embarrassed by his own enthusiasm. "Small, but it's all I need."

Beth follows him into a study. A heavy wooden desk with an old computer sits in front of the large window onto the pond. The desk is uncluttered, as if he doesn't use it much: no sticky notes, no office knick-knacks, not even a container for pencils and pens.

He opens the door across the hall. He has made what was probably designed to be a small bedroom into a cosy TV room. Two matching La-Z-Boys sit opposite a flat-screen TV. One chair looks well-used. A pile of *Maclean's* and *Canadian Geographic*, as well as a clean ashtray, sit on a small table beside it. The other La-Z-Boy still looks new.

"Mostly for news and hockey," Dan says. "A movie now and again." He steps away and opens the door to the bathroom. Spartan, but clean. Beth notes that there is only one toothbrush in the holder. The walls are blue-grey; cream tiles cover the floor and shower stall, which she contemplates with longing. She looks in the mirror and tries to straighten the collar of her wrinkled shirt. Wonders if she smells bad. She's gone swimming nearly every day, but hasn't showered for more than two weeks. Would it be too intimate to ask if she can shower here now and again?

She follows him back to the kitchen. She hasn't seen a photograph of him – or of anyone else – anywhere. "No dog or cat?" she says.

"Nope. Don't want the bother." He places a cast-iron skillet on the stove. "Just look at Mattie. She's always having to do something for that dog."

Yes, but? Beth thinks of Pirate and of how much she'd miss him if he weren't around. "Don't you ever get lonely out here?"

"Not really. Had my fill of people – and obligations – in the army. I came back here to relax and fish – not to have to do things I don't really wanna do." He turns on the burner and pours oil into the pan. "It's all I can do to keep up with what Mattie wants."

Dan spreads flour on a plate and sprinkles a few herbs from unmarked bottles onto the flour. He takes the gutted trout from the refrigerator and dips each one into the flour. Places the fish gently into the hot oil. "So how's the research going?"

"Okay. I've observed them a couple times near the old beaver lodge." She pauses. "Well … once, actually."

"When I showed up yesterday morning?"

"Yep." She sips the wine. "I probably should've gone out there again this morning instead of going fishing. Should be out there right now, I suppose."

"Hey, a scientist has to take it easy sometimes. You know what they say about all work."

"Guess so," she says. "But at least I have almost enough samples for an analysis of food habits. And for the genetic tests. Those will tell me who's in the group using the beaver lodge."

Dan flips one of the trout, bright pink flesh turning pale. "Just ask Mattie. She knows all that."

Beth smiles. "Or thinks she does." She clicks her fingernails against the chilled wineglass. Studies her bare toes and the lines of dirt that outline where her sandal straps go. "I've been keeping the samples on ice," she says carefully, "but I should get them into a freezer soon. Actually, I was planning to drive into the university tomorrow." She takes another sip of wine. "But if I could find a freezer here where I could store them ..."

Dan's eyebrows lift. He turns another fish. "You wanna store otter shit in my freezer?"

"I'd double-bag it."

He exhales through pursed lips. "For how long?"

"No more than a week," she says quickly. "Well, maybe just a little longer."

"Otter shit in my freezer," he says, shaking his head. "Don't you dare tell anyone. Clive'll never let me – or anyone else – forget it."

"I really appreciate this, Dan." She wants to hug him, but she's not sure he'd welcome it.

"And I want it triple-bagged." He turns the last trout, the hot oil sizzling. "Just another week? Then it's back to St. John's?"

"Guess so." But the thought of going back fills her with a familiar melancholy. She'll be returning to city dirt and city noise, and even worse, to the daily barrage of news – from CBC, *The Telegram*, her colleagues – about climate change, fracking near Gros Morne, chemical and oil spills, plastics showing up in every corner of the globe. And so few people who give a damn. She's begun to think that people just can't allow themselves to care – because they feel so helpless to do anything. She feels helpless. And hopeless.

Stop, she thinks. Just stop. She takes another sip of the chilled wine. "But I still need to get out to some other ponds yet," she says, "just to make sure there are enough otters in the area to justify a full-fledged study."

Nodding, but only half-listening, Dan lays out place settings on a table set near a window halfway between the kitchen and the living room. Beth watches as he puts out butter and fresh rolls from the grocery in town. She rubs the stem of the wineglass with her thumb. When she gets back to St. John's, she'll be taking up her life exactly where she left it: teaching Biology 1001, interminable staff meetings, as well as meetings of the Newfoundland and Labrador Environmental Network, which she'd joined in hopes of making a difference, but where she inevitably learns even more about all the environmental destruction going on around her.

And she'll be going back to Alan: same as always. *Fine.*

And Alice will still be dead.

Why can't she stop herself? Just for one evening? She upends her wineglass.

"I think they're ready," Dan announces. Deftly wielding a spatula, he lays the fish onto two plates. "A little skimpy, but if you'll get the potato salad and coleslaw from the fridge, there should be enough for the two of us."

Beth retrieves the salads, still in clear plastic containers bearing Price Chopper stickers. She holds them out in front of her, unsure whether to set the containers on the table or to put the salads into serving dishes. Opts for the former.

Dan refills her wineglass, grabs himself another beer, and they sit down. He jumps up again to get the salt and pepper and some paper towels to use as napkins.

Beth spoons potato salad onto her plate, then points the serving spoon toward the bookshelf. "So you like ravens?"

"Yep." Dan grinds pepper onto the steaming fish.

"There's some really interesting research coming out on how intelligent they are."

"Is there now?" He reaches for the tub of coleslaw, pauses, tub in mid-air. "Mattie's ideas might be pretty weird sometimes, but I think she's right about one thing: there's a lot more going on with animals and birds than scientists ever give them credit for." He buries a serving spoon in the coleslaw. "Or maybe, as a scientist, you don't believe that?"

"I agree there's a lot we don't know," she says carefully, "yet." She takes a forkful of trout. The flavour is delicate but savoury. Dan's a better cook than Alan.

"But you have faith that we will eventually," he says.

"I wouldn't call it faith."

He takes a swallow of beer. "What would you call it?"

She thinks a moment. "Confidence," she says. "I have confidence in the scientific method. And I'm agreeing with you: there's more going on than we've been able to figure out—"

"Tough to figure out if it turns out they're smarter than us."

She barks a surprised and abbreviated laugh. "This is starting to sound like a conversation with Mattie."

He teases out the backbone and accompanying small bones from the pale flesh. Doesn't look up.

"All right," Beth concedes, "I agree with you that there's probably more going on with animals and birds than most scientists think. But Mattie takes it way too far."

"How's that?"

"When she says the otters are waiting until I call them by their proper name to tell me their secrets. That the old grandmother watches over the pond."

The right side of his mouth turns up in a half-smile. "That's just Mattie." He scoops more potato salad from the plastic container. "Most of the time I don't even listen."

Not my business.

"And all that stuff about Matthew's ghost." He splits a roll with his fingers, butters one half. "That's just her way of coping. She never got over Matthew's death, and her way of dealing with it is to pretend he's still here. Keeps him alive for her, I guess." He bites into the roll.

"I get that. But it gives me the creeps when she says the rosary will bring him to me."

"Why are you even listening to that stuff? You're the one who's supposed to be the scientist."

"You truly didn't tell her that I thought she took it?"

"Christ, Beth. Why would I? She's tangly enough as it is."

"Then how could she know I couldn't find it?" She shakes her head. "Sorry, but I just can't buy that she's a mind reader."

"Can't explain it any better than that." Dan reaches for his beer.

"But then why—"

He clinks the brown bottle against her wineglass. "Here's to your otter shit," he says. "Hope you find what you're looking for."

CHAPTER 15

They are sitting at the table drinking coffee. They've talked mostly about the news, in a conversation that has been polite, but not much else. Dan has been guarded, and Beth has followed suit. Neither has mentioned Mattie again.

It came as no surprise that she'd missed nothing important in the national or international news. But what did startle her, when the reality sank in, is that it's been less than ten days since Alan left for St. John's. It feels like a month. She's known Mattie for less than a week, Dan for just a few days. What surprises her too, when she finally notices the cool breeze raising goosebumps on her forearms, are the dark clouds boiling in the west. Why has Dan said nothing? He must have seen the ominous sky.

She jumps up. "Oh my god! I've got to get going."

"You can't go out on the water in this," he says. "I'll drive you back." The words are hardly out of his mouth before the rain starts, fat drops hammering against the windows.

"You haven't had too much beer to drive?" Because she's certainly had too much wine.

"Nope." He closes the windows and the patio door, efficiently but not hurriedly.

"Can we load my kayak into the back of the truck? I'll need it first thing in the morning."

Dan peers out at the rain, which has become a deluge. "We'll get soaked." He glances at the clock over the sink: 7:12. "You could just wait until the storm passes. I can drive you and your kayak home then."

A move? Or is she just flattering herself?

~

Beth sits in the armchair and listens to water drip into the pans and bowls. She stares at a candle, at the small halo of light against the dark.

While she and Dan waited out the storm, they cleaned up the kitchen, and then, while he had a cigarette, she went into his office to check her email. She'd already broken her no-news rule. She drummed her fingers on the desk while she waited through all the beeps and buzzes of the dial-up connection, then she opened her inbox and scanned the scores of unopened messages – mostly spam and notices from the university she didn't even bother to open. Also three from Alan. But none from Rachel. True, she'd told her daughter she'd be out of touch for at least two weeks, but still.

She signed into Facebook. Saw that Rachel had posted a funny status about her lab work only hours earlier. Her daughter was fine. Fine without her.

Beth posted a cheery comment, then opened the first email from Alan, sent the day after he got back to St. John's: *Not sure when, or if, you'll get this. Hope the research is going well – and that you're getting the 'alone' time you need. Miss you. Love, Alan.*

She opened the second one, sent three days ago: *Sorry we couldn't talk long, but I'm glad to know you're okay and that you're getting some samples – and I hope by the time you read this that you've also been able to observe them – if only so you can come home sooner. I miss you. Pirate misses you. Love, Alan. P.S. The cat died. Too badly injured to save.*

Beth sat back in the leather chair. Pictured laundry piling up, the refrigerator empty, balls of dust and dog hair rolling like tumbleweed. Of course Alan misses her. Stop. She knows there's more to his missing her than just the chores going undone. And yet, sometimes, when he scowls just like her father used to, she suspects that she's disappointed him too, but she doesn't know how or in what way. Maybe he finds *her* boring.

She leaned forward and clicked on his third email, sent just last night, right after they talked: *I know you're probably not getting these, but it feels good to write them. I'm looking forward to seeing you. If you do get this, and if you can get away early enough, let's go out to India Gate for supper. And talk – about whatever it is you've been thinking about during all those hours alone. Love, Alan.*

She closed the messages without answering. Couldn't tell him by email that she's not coming home tomorrow. She'll have to do that over the phone. Beth ran her hands down the arms of the chair, felt guilty just for being at Dan's, like she'd been unfaithful, when, in truth, everything had been perfectly innocent. Disconcertingly innocent.

When he finally drove her home, Dan concentrated on the road, on the huge puddles and potholes. The truck rattled with every jarring bump, and the kayak, though tied securely, bounced around in the back. The trip around the bottom of the pond took nearly thirty minutes. They didn't talk much, just listened to the steady beat of the wipers, the right one leaving so much water on the windshield that Beth could hardly see the road.

By the time they arrived at Beth's cabin, the rain had slowed to a drizzle. Dan left the headlights on while she unlocked the door and went in to retrieve the samples, which she slid into another plastic bag. She handed them through the truck window, and Dan accepted the bag gingerly, grasping the top with just a thumb and forefinger.

They unloaded the kayak. He slid back into the truck and, with a simple "See ya," was gone.

Beth stares hard at the candle. She should be relieved that he spared her the embarrassment of having to ward off an unwanted advance, or even the suggestion of an advance. Instead, she has to confess to disappointment. *Here's to your otter shit. Hope you find what you're looking for.*

What is she looking for? Her project is beginning to feel like a last-ditch effort to rekindle the idea that she can still have a career, that she can still do research that matters. But she can't. No matter what research she does, she'll still be just as old, and the earth and all its wild places will still be imperilled.

Another depressing thought: she'll have to go to Mattie tomorrow and apologize.

~

She wakes, flat to the bed, palms pressed into the thin mattress, fingers gripping the edge. She'd been scaling a cliff above the ocean, the sunlight brilliant on the water. Someone she couldn't quite see was peering over the top, watching, only a bit of forehead and the bill of a blue baseball cap visible. Suddenly, the rope released from her harness. Her grip failed. Beth woke just before she hit the rocks below.

She sucks in air and listens to the wind shussing through the birches, the tap-tap-tap of rain hitting the leaves. Hopes the pans and bowls don't overflow.

~

She propels herself through dark water by languid undulations of body and tail. Paws grab her from behind, a whiskery snout presses into her cheek. A game. Rolling in black water. She turns and twists, releasing herself from the paws' grip. Swims. Swims hard, following a silver path laid down by the moon. Fish scatter, tinfoil bits of light. Heart thumping, muscles taut, she surfaces to breathe. Hears a flute: silver threads of moon woven through indigo sky.

Beth wakes, an image of dark-blue sky and moonlight fading, the silky slide of water soft on her arms. She can still hear the flute, the strains profoundly odd, more like the calls of birds and animals, or an infant's thin wails. The music stops. She gropes for her watch, stares at the green glowing numbers: 4:32. Who would be out with a flute at this hour? She sits up on the edge of the bed, slides on her glasses, and strikes a match to light the kerosene lamp. Carrying the lamp before her, she goes into the kitchen to light a fire and make coffee, quietly. Listens hard for the sound of a flute. In the bright light of Dan's kitchen, Mattie's ghosts had fled, but now? Now she wishes Muin would show up at the door.

~

Two cups of coffee, a clear head, and a golden sunrise have helped Beth to realize that she was still enmeshed in her dream, and not quite awake, when she heard the nighttime serenade. She sits up in her kayak and squares her shoulders. This morning, after she goes to the otter spot, she'll take the rosary back out into the woods and leave it where she found it. She will visit Mattie and offer an apology, and then be done with all these distractions. She won't even see Dan again. He showed her last night where he keeps the spare key. She'll put any new samples she collects in his freezer when he's not there. From now on, she's sticking to her research. She will make it something that matters.

Paddling steadily, she listens to the satisfying swish of water against the hull. Within minutes she is at the otter spot. She balances the paddle in front of her and lets the kayak drift. Waits, binoculars and voice recorder ready, and doesn't move. There is only the piping of shorebirds and the *peent-peent-peent* of a nuthatch. She hopes the jays and crows won't call out a warning.

The wild roses blooming on shore remind her of Rachel, beautiful but tough, nothing fragile about her. Of course Rachel doesn't need Beth's mothering the way she once did, and Beth has resolved to be glad that her daughter has become so competent and independent. There's a certain freedom in that. For both of them.

Maybe that's how an otter mother feels when she watches her pups become proficient at catching their own fish, when they're finally ready to leave her: a sense of accomplishment. But maybe there's an ache too. Maybe she recalls every pup she's ever birthed. Remembers the peculiarities of each cold black nose and silken head, each clumsy first swim.

Beth groans: she's being anthropomorphic. And sentimental.

The kayak bobs gently. She hears a raven's *cark-cark-cark*, but no chirps or soft grunts. There's hardly a ripple on the water.

Anthropomorphic and sentimental maybe, but Beth's pretty sure there's more to animal emotions than people want to believe. Most people – if they think about it at all – want to believe that pups are out of their mother's mind as soon as they're out of her sight, and that the pups forget their mother as well. But that belief is no less speculative than believing that the mother and pups remember each other. Neurologically, otters are very similar to dogs, and people want to believe their dogs still love them and remember them when they're out of sight. Otter pups stay with their mother for at least a year, maybe longer. Why, then, wouldn't an otter mother remember her pups? Or a pup its mother?

Horrible images spring to mind, and Beth is helpless to stop them: a young otter caught in a drowning set or a leg-hold trap. Do the other members of the group crowd around in panic and grief? Watch as their companion or child dies? A slow, painful death if it's a leg-hold trap. And if it's a nursing mother who's caught, the pups are left to starve. Beth can't even think about it without tearing up.

She lifts the paddle and quietly turns the kayak to keep herself facing shore. She scans the water's edge. Nothing. She should steel herself, go to Mattie, and get her apology over with. But then she sees a lone otter, swimming quietly along the shoreline. Funny how you never see them coming, Beth thinks. They just appear.

She notes the time: 6:42. Lifts the binoculars even though the otter is less than five metres away. Too close to use the voice recorder. It looks old, the muzzle silvery grey. The otter is swimming lazily. It turns toward the kayak and, paddling languorously with one back paw and guiding itself with a front paw, swims closer, so close that Beth can hear the water ripple against the kayak.

Slowly, she lowers the binoculars and stares into eyes that are round and dark behind a bulbous black nose that bears a small white scar. Long grey whiskers curve down into the water. The otter floats, staying in place with an occasional flip of a back paw, a gentle wave of a thick, tapering tail. And then quiet conversation: *uhn-uhn-uhn, uhn-uhn-uhn.*

Beth keeps her mouth closed and tries to mimic the sound deep in her throat: *uhn-uhn-uhn, uhn-uhn-uhn.* It doesn't come out right.

The otter periscopes, its head and neck coming high out of the water. Snorts an alarm.

Beth sits perfectly still. Doesn't look at her watch, but it feels as if they stare at each other for a full two minutes. What *is* that otter thinking?

Uhn-uhn-uhn, uhn-uhn-uhn.

Who is it talking to? This time Beth stays silent, just watching and listening. And then she hears it. *Hope.* The word is as clear in her head as if someone had spoken it aloud. The otter periscopes again, and this time, gives a high-pitched chirp and disappears beneath the water.

Beth waits a few minutes, then takes out her journal: *9 Aug 10: clear and sunny, winds light, ~17°C, observed at A5, 6:20 – 6:50. One otter appeared close to shore at 6:42 (about 5 m away), an old one with a grey muzzle and a small white scar between its nostrils; swam slowly along shore. Quiet series of grunts. Came to within 2 m of the kayak and ...* And what? Whatever she writes would be embarrassing if any of her colleagues were to read it: *The otter and I locked eyes. I felt like I was looking into the eyes of a sentient, intelligent being. I was on the verge of understanding something important about the way animals think and feel. I heard the word "hope."* Did she really hear that? Now she's not quite sure.

She writes: *It looked at me and grunted. I tried to imitate the sound. The otter periscoped and snorted, then watched me (~ 2 min), grunting quietly. Finally, it periscoped again, chirped, and dived.*

Beth slides the research journal into her backpack and lands the kayak near the latrine. She marks a thick plastic bag with the date and location. Collects one fresh sample, slides it into a second marked bag, and places it in the cooler.

CHAPTER 16

Mattie is sitting near the pond in the soft light of mid-morning. Muin is out in the water, but as soon as she sees Beth, she swims to shore and gallops toward her. When she is two feet away, the dog stops and shakes.

Beth brushes water off her shorts. "Sit, Muin." She pulls a Milk-Bone from her pocket.

Mattie pushes herself up from the deep chair. She is holding a long, hollow cylinder of wood and a knife. Shavings lie scattered on the grass. "Was just having tea," she says. "Want some? Plain ole black, right outta the box."

Beth can tell by the pitch of her voice, and the blue baseball cap, that she is Matthew this morning. "No thanks," Beth says. "I'm good." She gives Muin another treat and scratches her behind the ears. While she's still bent over, she says, "Listen, I'm sorry–"

"Found it, didn't you."

Beth straightens. "So Dan was by already this morning?"

"Nope." Mattie sits down and points the knife at the Muskoka chair beside her own.

"You sure?"

"I might be old, love, but I'm not senile. Not yet anyways." She rests the knife and the wooden cylinder in her lap.

Beth doles out the third, and last, Milk-Bone.

"Come on now," Mattie says, "sit down and stay a while."

"I took it back."

"Good."

Beth slides into the chair.

"Might be too late though." Mattie picks up the knife and taps the butt of the wooden handle on the arm of the chair. "You might've started something you can't stop."

Beth looks at her sidelong. "Like what?" she says quietly. Muin noses at Beth's pocket. Beth holds out her empty hands and lets the dog sniff them.

"Hard to know." Mattie points the knife toward the grass, and Muin circles and plops down. She takes off the blue cap and lays it on the arm of the chair, fingers lingering on the soiled bill. Her hands seem larger this morning, rougher. Beth blinks and looks away, toward the tall monkshood and evening primrose growing near the cabin, and then at the expanse of fireweed in the clearing, bordered by goldenrod and interwoven with vetch: a riot of purple, yellow, and pink.

Muin stands and puts her head in Beth's lap. "It's no small thing," Mattie says, "when an animal chooses you."

"Mattie, I don't know what that means."

"Simple. She wants to go with you when I cross over."

Muin's tail wags as if to confirm her choice.

"Are you telling me you're dying?" Beth says.

"Course I am. I'm old."

Beth leans forward. "What's the doctor say?"

"Don't need a doctor to tell me what I already know." She turns to Beth. "Looking forward to the rest, really. Though I'm sorry to leave Muin behind. Glad she's finally picked someone."

"I can't take your dog."

"You have to."

"But why me? Why not Dan?"

Mattie guffaws. "Don't be so foolish. Dan's a nice boy, but ..." She rubs her beaked nose with a thumb and middle finger. "When he was young, he looked just like Matthew, so I've forgiven him a lot." She lays a hand over Beth's. "No need to worry about it now, love. When the time comes, Dan'll give you a call."

"Don't I get a choice in this?"

"You don't want her?"

Muin looks up at Beth. "I'll leave you my number," she says.

Mattie shades her eyes with an open hand and watches a chattering kingfisher swoop from a nearby birch to a spruce overhanging the pond. "So what's new in the world of otters today?"

"Not much," Beth says. "Early this morning, I saw a lone otter near the beaver lodge."

The kingfisher plunges into the water and comes up with a small fish.

"The old grandmother," Mattie says.

"You can't know that."

"Had a scar on her nose, didn't she."

"That doesn't prove anything," Beth says. "In a few months – when the genetic tests are done – I'll know who's in the group."

"No need of all that. It's the grandmother, two of her daughters, and one daughter's pups. And sometimes a male, or another female, just passing through."

Beth presses her lips together. No point in arguing, especially with an old woman who's dying. Muin turns and presents her haunches for scratching.

"What else you see?" Mattie asks.

"The otter swam very close to the kayak and looked at me. That's about it."

"She's trying, love." Mattie tips the mug and studies what's left of the tea. "Course, your dreams'll help too."

"Dreams?"

Mattie puts on the blue cap, tugs on the bill. "Don't tell me you haven't been dreaming of em."

"The only thing I remember from my dreams," Beth says, "is climbing a steep cliff above the ocean. You released the rope from my harness and I fell."

Mattie laughs. "Weren't me, girl."

"And there was some odd flute music," Beth says, pointing at the cylinder in Mattie's lap.

"I plays the flute."

"You weren't out in the middle of the night, were you?"

"In my dream I was."

"That's not funny."

"Weren't meant to be." Mattie sits back in the chair and picks up the wood and the knife. "You're here to help her, you know."

"Who? Muin?"

A shaving falls to the ground. Beth hears a whisper. "Matilda, girl. Matilda."

~

The Toyota rattles over the washboard road. She stops at the Irving, then decides that before she calls Alan, she will try one more time to get Rachel. It's lunchtime here, early morning in Vancouver: Rachel should be getting ready for work. Beth enters her calling card number and, while she follows the verbal commands, studies the patterns in the dirt below the pay phone. People waiting – happy, angry, worried, hopeful – have used the toes of their shoes to build small mounds of dirt and pebbles. Beth places herself in the hopeful group and uses her whole foot, rotating from the heel, to leave a windshield-wiper pattern of scraped dirt bordered by ridges of grey pebbles.

She punches in Rachel's number. After five rings, Beth gets her voice mail. Why isn't she answering? Rachel always has her cellphone with her: it's like an added appendage. Beth places herself in the angry group now. Imagines Rachel hearing the phone, knowing it's her mother calling, and then ignoring the insistent rings.

Beth does her best to leave a cheery message: "Hi, sweetheart, hope everything's good there. My research is going really well. Hope to talk with you soon. Love you."

She steels herself to call Alan. Punches in the numbers of his cellphone and listens to the buzzing ring. Hopes he's busy with a patient and she'll get his voice mail.

"Hello?" Garbled, mouth full, probably eating lunch.

"Hi, Alan."

"Hi." A quick swallow. "How's it going?"

"Fine."

"You sound tired."

"No, not really." She pushes at the dirt and pebbles with her toe. "I found a freezer where I can store my samples." Shoves them into a narrow grey pile. "So I guess I won't have to make a trip back to St. John's after all."

"I was looking forward to seeing you. I was hoping we could go out to dinner."

She can see his face: brow furrowed, disappointed, but irritated as well.

He laughs once, harshly. "Where in the world did you find someone willing to store otter shit in their freezer?"

"Met an old guy at the Morning Glory. He's interested in my research."

"Well ... glad you found a freezer. I guess. Can't you still make the trip back?"

"I could ..." Beth leans her forehead against the phone, looks down at the ridge of gravel and dirt. "But driving back and forth would use up two whole days. If I just stay here, I can get the research done that much quicker."

Silence.

"Although to be honest," she adds quickly, "I'm not sure that any of it really matters."

"Of course it does, Beth. Scientists know almost nothing about the behaviour of otters. Except, of course, their extreme cuteness." Trying to lift her spirits. Maybe his own too.

"But does any of it matter?"

"Guess you *are* feeling worn out. Listen, you never know what's going to matter in the end. And studying otters isn't the most useless thing you could do. Some academics spend their whole professional lives studying ancient Byzantine dialects."

Thanks for that vote of confidence, Alan. "Easy for you to say," she argues, "you know your work is useful."

"People pay for it, yes. But does vaccinating people's dogs and cats, selling them flea collars and anti-dandruff shampoo, matter in the long run?"

She closes her eyes. "I don't know, Alan. Sometimes I feel like I don't know anything anymore."

"How much longer do you think you'll have to be out there?"

"I need to get out to at least a few other ponds to take samples, and I'm not sure how long that will take."

"I miss you, Beth."

"Me too." She flattens the mound of pebbles with her foot. "Well, I should be going now." A long moment of silence, some crackling on the line.

"Love you," he says.

"Love you too. Bye."

Love you. So easy to say to Rachel. A hesitation when it comes to Alan. When did *Love you* become a routine pretence with her husband, and not a real feeling? Maybe he feels the same way.

She slides back into the car. Slams the door harder than she needs to.

~

Beth sees the black pickup parked in front of the Morning Glory. She pulls in beside it, squeezes the steering wheel with both hands, hard, then releases it. Maybe she doesn't have to feel embarrassed around him. He never knew what she was thinking last night.

As soon as she steps through the door, Dan nods. She slides into the booth across from him.

"Special is cod." He looks at his half-empty plate. "Not

as good as my trout, but hey, what can you expect from amateurs?"

"Thanks for driving me home last night. Sorry it was such an ordeal."

"No worries."

The skinny waitress comes with the menu. "Special is pan-fried cod with boiled potatoes and coleslaw," she says. "Soup is turkey vegetable."

Beth doesn't even glance at the menu. "Just a bowl of the soup and a salad, please. Vinaigrette on the side. Thanks."

The waitress scribbles notes on her order pad and turns away.

"So you stopped by Mattie's this morning," Beth says.

"Nope." Dan looks up from his plate. "She tell you I did?"

"No, but when I went to see her, to apologize, she already knew I'd found the rosary."

He pushes at a boiled potato, then lays down his fork. "Like I told you, Mattie just knows things." He shrugs. "I've gotten so used to it, I hardly notice anymore when she answers my questions before I even ask."

"It's too strange."

"Not really. Might be simple ... the same way you know, and I know, the waitress will mess up something about your order."

"But that knowledge is based on experience. Mattie's is based on ... what?"   .

"She's had a whole lot more experience than the rest of us. And truth be told, it's not much of a mystery for her to figure out that you'd find that stupid rosary."

The waitress brings Beth's order: the iceberg lettuce is swimming in salad dressing. Dan looks at the salad, then lays a finger on the back of her hand. They both smile.

"Guess so," she says. Thinks, but doesn't say, But how did Mattie know that I'd lost it in the first place? She tastes the soup, adds salt and pepper. "She told me this morning that Muin has chosen me."

"For what?"

"Apparently she wants to go with me after Mattie dies."

He smirks. "Guess that lets me off the hook."

"Seriously, Dan. Is she dying?"

"Doubt it," he says. "Or not anytime soon. She's healthy as a horse." He leans back in the booth and takes a toothpick from his pocket. "So, push back any frontiers of science today?"

"Collected one fresh sample. I put it in your freezer with the others. Triple-bagged," she adds. "Hope that's okay."

"Anything to further the cause." His voice drops to a whisper. "Just don't talk about it too loudly."

Beth takes a spoonful of soup. It leaves a greasy film on her lips.

"By the way," he says, "there's a party tonight at the Bide-a-Wee. You should come and meet some of the local crowd ... if you're interested."

"Thanks, but I should go out and do observations. I already skipped them yesterday morning and last night."

Dan taps the toothpick on the table. "Come afterwards then. Probably won't even start till after eight. There'll be music."

"I'll see how things go." Beth takes a bite of the salad, winces at the tartness of the vinegar. Chews and swallows. "Do you fish on any ponds besides Medicine Rock?" she asks.

"I fish anywhere there's fish."

She holds up another forkful of lettuce, lets some of the salad dressing drip off. "So you would know which ponds around here have otters?"

"Most of em do."

"It could save me a lot of time," she says carefully, "if someone could tell me where I might be able to gather samples from otters who aren't part of the group on Medicine Rock." She watches his face. His frown is deepening. "To confirm that there are enough otters in the area for a real study," she explains quickly.

"If you wanna know about otters, you should come to the party tonight. A couple of the guys do some trapping. They know all about the otters around here."

"I guess." But she doesn't want to talk to anyone about trapping. She knows most of the trappers are just trying to make a few extra bucks, but she doesn't even want to think about it.

"Or just ask Mattie," Dan continues.

"Sure," Beth says, "and she'll give me some sort of answer, but I won't know what she means."

"True enough." He laughs.

Emboldened by his laughter, she puts a hand to her mouth and clears her throat. "I've been wondering ..." Beth's words are slow and cautious. "You said that you'd take any excuse to get out on the water. Would you be willing to take me to a few other ponds?"

Dan sighs. "Why not? I'd love to have more shit in my freezer."

CHAPTER 17

Beth drives past the Bide-a-Wee. She just wants to see who's there and then she'll head back to the cabin to finish the notes she jotted after her observations. It's a mild summer evening; about thirty people are standing around or sitting on lawn chairs on the small patch of grass under the motel floodlights. She spots Dan. Playing a fiddle. She brakes, turns around in the library parking lot, and goes back to the Bide-a-Wee.

When she steps out of the car, Beth nods to the few people she recognizes: Clive, the postmistress with the severe black hair, the clerk from the liquor store, and the surly boy from the Irving station. She seeks out the empty canvas chair beside Clive.

"How's the work going?" he says slowly.

"All right," Beth says, glancing toward the musicians. "Didn't know Dan could play. And aren't those the girls from the Morning Glory and Price Chopper?"

"Yep. And the guy with the accordion is their dad, Fred. Owns the Bide-a-Wee. His wife's birthday is the reason for the party."

Beth slides back in the chair. So the two skinny girls with the bright red bangs really are sisters, talented ones at that. The waitress from the Morning Glory is singing to her own guitar accompaniment, her sister adding the harmony. Surly Irving boy edges closer to them, no longer surly.

At a break in the music, Dan goes to a cooler and pulls out two Black Horse. He walks over to Beth, opens a bottle, and hands it to her. "Glad to see you could make it."

"You never told me you could play the fiddle," she says.

"Wouldn't take it on the stage."

"Hey, who's this?" says the accordion player, now standing at Dan's side.

"My new boss," Dan says. "I'm helping out with her research."

Clive waves his good hand at Dan. "Go on, b'y. What kinda help could you be?"

"Hey, I'm right there on the cutting edge. Taking her out tomorrow to scout out otters on some of the ponds around here."

Beth can almost see the synapses connecting behind Fred's eyes. "So you must be that lady who's collecting otter shit," he says.

She smiles wanly and nods.

"That otter be interesting," Fred says. "Otterly fascinating," he continues, grinning at his own puns. "You otter be careful out there."

Dan catches Beth's eye and grimaces.

The sisters start playing again, and Dan and Fred go off to join them. Beth tries not to notice the attractive, dark-haired, forty-something who reaches out to touch Dan's arm when he passes. Whatever she says makes him laugh.

Beth also tries not to see how people are assessing her. The young woman sitting on the other side of Clive whispers into his ear. He holds up his good hand and talks behind it. It won't be long until everyone knows that Beth is "that lady who's here to collect otter shit."

An older couple approach Clive, and when he begins to introduce them, Beth stands. It seems impolite to talk up to them, but she forgets their names almost immediately, can recall only that the woman is the town librarian.

"So you're the one doing that research?" the woman says. Her husband has already turned back to the musicians. "From the university?" she continues.

Beth nods.

The woman's lips pucker like she's just bit into a lemon. "Our tax dollars at work." She offers a plastic smile. "Where you staying to?"

"Old Wells place."

"Out near Mattie MacKenzie? Met her yet?"

"Time or two."

"She comes into the library now and again," the woman says. "Never has much to say though."

The postmistress joins them. "Hi, Dorothy," she says, then turns to Beth. "How's the collecting going?"

"All right." Beth wonders whether she remembers the postcard or if Clive's information has already spread that quickly.

"Must be lovely to spend all that time outdoors, out on the water. Not being stuck inside all day."

"It is, actually," Beth says, "especially when I get a chance to watch them."

Dorothy's lips pucker again. "But what about having to pick up their ... stuff? That can't be much fun. And what's the use of it all, really?"

The postmistress waves away the questions, and Beth likes her immediately.

"We see otters on our pond now and again," the postmistress says. "I think they're funny, but Harold, my husband, complains that they eat too many trout." She glances at Dorothy. "And leave their 'stuff' on the dock."

"Which pond?" Beth asks.

"Birchy. Just north of town a little ways."

"How many do you see?"

"Usually two or three. Sometimes as many as–"

"Beth's staying out to the old Wells place," Dorothy interjects. "Right there by Mattie's."

"That's good," the postmistress says. "If you need anything, Mattie'll help you out."

Dorothy frowns. "You think so, Agnes? She seems kinda crazy to me."

"What makes you say that?"

The librarian looks at Clive and then back to Agnes and Beth. "She always picks out the oddest books. Stuff no one else ever reads."

"And that makes her crazy?"

"Well, she keeps to herself out there in the woods. Hardly ever talks to anyone."

Agnes raises a painted black eyebrow. "Wish there was a few more folks kept their mouths shut till they had something to say." She turns back to Beth. "To answer your question," she says pointedly, "I sometimes see as many as six. But that's in the winter, when they're out on the ice."

Dorothy lays a hand on Agnes's arm. "What about her and Katherine?"

"What about them? Katherine was one of my favourite teachers. One of my son's too."

The librarian turns to Beth. "How's she seem to you?"

"Okay ... I guess."

"Sure, Mattie can be a little strange at times," Agnes says. "But then aren't we all?" She glances at Dorothy, then continues, "Long time ago, her brother drowned. She rescued his girlfriend, then took care of her for twenty years after. All alone out there in that cabin. That might make anyone a little cracked." She takes Beth's elbow and steers her away from the librarian. "Come on, let's get some of that birthday cake before it's all gone."

They step toward a table set near the motel's front entrance. In the middle, surrounded by other desserts, sits a huge chocolate cake covered with green candles and gaudy pink, blue, and yellow frosting. Beth opts for a small slice of cheesecake.

"Toppings are over there," Agnes says, pointing to a line of jars.

Beth spoons blueberry jam on the cheesecake and goes back to sit beside Clive. He studies her plate with his good eye. "Wouldn't eat that," he says. "That's Mattie's jam. Probably poison."

Beth's fork stops halfway between her plate and her mouth.

He slaps a thigh and guffaws. "Just tormenting you, girl. Go ahead. Enjoy."

Beth eats the cheesecake, wishing she had an espresso instead of a beer to wash it down. She watches the musicians play a set of jigs and reels. A few people are dancing. Beside her, a girl in a flouncy pink dress and sparkly pink sandals holds a plate with chocolate cake and ice cream; she leans back between her father's knees. Her small rosebud mouth, missing two front teeth, is ringed with chocolate. She bounces to the music, her gaze locked on the musicians. The plate begins to tip and, before Beth can say a word, the cake and ice cream slide down the front of the gauzy dress and the leg of Beth's khakis and plop onto the grass. The girl's lower lip trembles.

"No worries," Beth says, wiping at the dress and her own pants with a napkin. She twists around to smile an "okay" at the father and is startled by the severity of his scowl. He pushes the little girl away and steps to the table for more napkins. Fat tears roll down her cheeks.

"It's all right," Beth says. "We can clean this up and there's plenty of cake left. You can get more."

"No, she can't," her father growls, stooping to wipe at the mess on the pink dress.

Beth swallows. The harsh scowl, just like her own father's. A scowl, along with stony silence, covered all occasions, so that she could never be certain what she'd done wrong. Was it the muddy tracks on the kitchen floor, the glass of milk that slipped from her fingers, her running off to play with Jax when she'd been told to weed the peas? Was it because she was shy and scrawny, not chatty and pretty like her golden-haired cousin? Or was it because she wasn't a boy? The only thing Beth could be sure of was that she was a disappointment.

She goes to the dessert table, picks out a big piece of chocolate cake with thick multi-hued frosting. She brings it back to the girl. She wants to smash it into her father's pointy rodent face. Instead, she holds it out. "Here, sweetheart, there's plenty."

The little girl looks at her father uncertainly. His face still carries the same deep scowl, but he doesn't glance at his daughter, or at Beth. Beth sits down and rests a hand lightly on the girl's small shoulder. "It's okay," she says, "that stain'll wash out." The girl reaches timidly for the plate.

The girl's father doesn't say a word. Intimidation through silence. Beth knows all too well how that works.

While the little girl eats her cake, Beth smiles at her as often as she can catch her eye, then she helps herself to another beer and watches the musicians and dancers for another hour or so before she decides it's time to head back to the cabin. She can feel a headache starting, just above her left eye. She stands.

Dan raises a hand and shouts to her above the music. "Don't forget, boss. Seven tomorrow morning."

On the drive home Beth begins to see flashes of light at the periphery of her vision and knows that a migraine is coming on. Hopes she can make it back before it hits full force.

She's a little wobbly by the time she walks into the cabin. She rummages through her toiletry bag for ibuprofen, pops three with the water that's left in her bottle, then unwraps a Maxalt wafer from its foil pouch and places it on her tongue. Stumbles into bed and hopes the migraine will be gone by the time Dan comes to pick her up in the morning.

~

She startles awake, the sound of a gunshot ringing in her ears. She is curled into a tight ball and her cheeks are wet. Her head still throbs. In the dream she'd been wearing her favourite green overalls and standing in a field of newly mown hay, throwing a stick for Jax. He retrieved it again and again, dropping it at her feet. She threw it, hard, and he dashed off toward the setting sun, the light bright in her eyes. She called and called. Then the sharp crack of a rifle.

Beth straightens her legs and tries to relax. Begins to rock herself in the bed. It didn't happen that way. She hadn't been throwing sticks for Jax. Her dog got sick, eyes and nose running with slimy mucous like he had a bad cold. And then he just lay down and stopped wanting to go outside. She promised her dad she'd give him every dime of her babysitting money if he would just take Jax to the vet, but he wouldn't. The day he took his rifle down from the wall, she hugged Jax and wouldn't let go. Her father had to pry her arms away, and then he carried the dog outside. Ordered Beth not to follow. The sound of the gunshot split her heart wide open. A month later, when her mother offered to get her a new puppy, Beth refused. She hasn't owned a dog since she was twelve. Pirate is Alan's, not hers. She gropes her way into the kitchen for another Maxalt.

~

The night is black, a slender crescent of moon. She walks slowly, the scant light on the path like the beam of a small flashlight. The light veers off into the woods, and she follows, branches closing behind her. Thready clouds weave across the moon. Scarves of old man's beard draped on the spruce sway back and forth, back and forth, grey moans riding the wind. Ahead, she sees a shadow moving through the trees. She follows. The shadow stops, lays a hand on Medicine Rock. A gleaming rosary dangles from the wrist. An otter stands upright beside the rock, which suddenly flares as if lit from within. Glimpse of a yellow dress. The shadow turns, blue eyes hollow, and Beth knows that if she looks long enough, deep enough, she will see a sadness beyond measure, another heart split wide open. And then the shadow is gone. The otter comes down on all fours and slips into the water. The black sky swallows the light.

Dan is sitting on the edge of her bed, mouth opening and closing, but his words are muffled. She tries to tell him about the shadow, the hollow blue eyes, but he leaves. And then Mattie is there, spooning something hot and bitter into Beth's mouth. It dribbles down her chin.

She sits at the table. Mattie stands at the sink, her hand wielding a knife that flashes in the sunlight. A brace of rabbits, one of them a cold, iridescent blue-grey, lie on a large cutting board. Mattie picks up the unskinned rabbit. The shiny black eyes are wide open. The head wobbles. She slices the skin around the neck, then makes a slit down the length of the belly. She cuts off the feet, bones crunching. Slides off the skin as if undressing a baby. She cups a foot in her palm, turns and tosses it toward Beth. *Good luck. You'll need it. You've started something you can't stop.*

Mattie sits down at the table with Beth. Alice joins them, her bald head wrapped in a yellow scarf. They sort through puzzle pieces. Mattie and Alice click them into place, one after the other. Beth's pieces are large, like those of a child's puzzle. She cannot make them fit. She turns to Alice, but Alice won't look away from the puzzle.

And then she is sitting on shore, the trees and water wreathed in fog, but she can see a full moon just above the horizon. The sun is rising behind her. A high-pitched chirp and then an answer. The otters climb out of the water and come closer, not warily, but as if she is one of them. Six of them, continuous *uhn-uhn-uhns*. She tilts her head, surprised that she can understand them: *We are here. We are all here. Now.* And then they are gone. Silver rings in dark water. She turns toward the rising sun and sees the backlit shadow of a woman. The light behind her makes a halo of her copper curls. She drops a brown and white feather, then turns and walks into the light.

~

Beth awakens to chocolate brown eyes staring into hers, a slobbery kiss. How the hell did Muin get into the cabin? Her head still aching but no longer throbbing, she nudges the dog off the sleeping bag and stands. Looks down. She's still dressed. She reaches for her glasses. And then she remembers. Damn! Dan is supposed to pick her up at seven. She rushes out of the bedroom, stops short, hand clutching the door frame.

Mattie looks up from the puzzle. "So you're finally awake."

"What are you doing here?"

"Dan came to get me. Said he couldn't wake you up this morning, that you were talking gibberish. You had him worried, girl."

Beth looks out the window. Already late afternoon. She's slept fifteen, sixteen hours?

Mattie snaps a puzzle piece into place. "Must've been some party."

"Wasn't the party. It was a migraine."

"Dan says he'll come by tomorrow morning. If you're feeling better."

"I'll be fine," Beth says. "There was no need to worry, but thanks."

Mattie snaps another piece into place. "Hope you don't mind me working at this. Been a long day." She glances at the folder of technical articles. "And your reading material isn't exactly gripping." She waves a hand over the table. "Frustrating though. Pieces don't always fit where you think they oughta." She stands and stretches her arms above her head. "If you're sure you're okay now, we'll be going."

Muin is sitting, staring up into a corner of the kitchen. Her tail sweeps the floor, back and forth. She stands and barks, tail still wagging.

"Looks like you have a guest," Mattie says.

"What?"

Mattie nods toward the corner. "Sure, it's not one of mine."

Beth looks up but can see nothing but cobwebs and water stains. She puts a hand to her aching forehead, then squeezes the bridge of her nose. No, she will not start believing everything Mattie says. She and Clive are two of a kind. *Just tormenting you, girl.*

Mattie opens the door and Muin bounds off toward the path.

Beth makes coffee then, every movement in slow motion. While she waits, she sits and rocks, fragments of remembered dreams floating through the chemical soup still bathing her brain: Jax and a gunshot; Dan; Mattie butchering rabbits; talking otters; Alice in the sunlight.

After two more ibuprofen, coffee, and an hour of sitting, she's not feeling so bad anymore. She doesn't want to waste the whole day, so she packs up her gear.

Walking slowly through the woods to the otter spot, Beth pauses at a patch of plump pink and green blueberries. She picks the lone ripe one and pops it into her mouth: an explosion of sweet blue sunshine. And then she sees it. An owl feather, brown and white, cradled within the blueberry bushes. Beth picks it up and smoothes it, the sound like a whisper.

~

The old female is alone; the others are far away, hunting for fish and crabs. Long before she sees the human, she scents her. Hears branches snap, leaves rustle. She watches from the tall grass near the lodge, then quietly slips into the pond and swims closer, barely rippling the water. She lifts her head and sniffs the air. No scent of metal, only human and plastic. And the heavy odour of grief.

CHAPTER 18

Dan picks her up at seven, the *Black Feather* on a trailer behind the truck.

"Morning," she says, sliding into the front seat. A thermos and a metal travel mug clank together. Dan's mug is already ensconced in the cup-holder.

He looks her over, his eyes narrowed. "How you feeling this morning?"

"Fine. Just a bad migraine after the party."

"You looked like shit yesterday morning."

"Thanks." She tries to smile. "I appreciate your going to get Mattie, but that wasn't necessary. I'm all right."

His frown is sceptical. "Okay then. As long as you're sure you're up to it, we're off to One Gunshot."

"I'm fine. Really."

They've lucked out on the weather: overcast but not raining, the cloud cover hinting, teasing, that it might clear away later in the day.

Beth pours herself coffee, sweet and thick with cream, and for the next thirty minutes, while they bounce over rutted dirt roads, they exchange barely ten words, which is fine with her. She can use the rest. She stayed too long at the otter spot last night, and while she waited for otters who never showed, she smoothed the feather and remembered Alice. They'd met when Beth was five months pregnant, Alice four, stretched out on yoga mats beside each other, learning how to breathe. It was Alice who laughed first. And then neither of them could stop, not even when Alice started braying and the instructor scowled at them. All that breathing practice turned out to be useless for

Beth. Rachel was delivered by caesarean, but by then, Beth had gained her first, and most enduring, friend in St. John's – a bond formed initially by laughter and "not being from here." Alice could always make Beth laugh. It was one of the things Beth loved most about her. Alice could make any problem seem less serious.

Back at the cabin, Beth put the feather on the chair beside the bed. Hoped she would dream of Alice again. And this time, Alice would stay. But Beth slept without dreams.

On One Gunshot Pond, Beth wades into the cold water in her sandals to help Dan unload the boat from the trailer. Her feet are almost numb, the skin bright red, by the time she climbs into the boat.

They circle the perimeter twice, slowly. There are no houses on the pond, but the shoreline and the forest behind it are nearly identical to Medicine Rock: jumbled grey rock backed by thick spruce and fir, a scattering of birch and alder. On the second trip around, Beth finally spots a few droppings on a large rock. They look dry and bleached out, at least a week old. She takes samples anyway, just to make things look good to Dan.

They load up the boat and move on to Crawling Stone Pond, the trailer bumping and rattling behind the truck. The fir and birch are so close to the road that branches scrape both sides of the pickup. Even before they unload the *Black Feather*, Beth finds scats. Three fresh samples. She pulls plastic bags from her backpack and marks them: *11 Aug 10: Crawling Stone, north shore boat landing.* Stoops down beside black droppings filled with fish bones and insect parts. Dan watches from a distance and smokes. No questions. No apparent interest in her work, but at least he's kept his teasing comments to a minimum. He's kept all his remarks to a minimum. Doesn't seem annoyed at having agreed to take her around to these other ponds, just quiet.

They put the Alumacraft in the water. It's easy to see how the pond got its name. A rock island sits in the middle. As small waves slap up against it, the island appears to crawl closer to shore.

After just twenty minutes of scanning the shoreline with her binoculars, Beth sees more droppings on top of an old beaver lodge. She points and Dan guides the boat closer, cuts the motor, and lifts the prop. They step out into the shallow water and pull the boat up onto the rocky shore. Beth collects two more samples and slips them into the cooler with the others. She finds a latrine about seven metres from the lodge, but all the droppings are old. She counts them and estimates a group of three or four. She examines the beaver lodge more closely. All the sticks, their ends bearing the tell-tale marks of large incisors, are sun-bleached, nothing fresh and new, and there's a hole in the side of the lodge that no beaver would ever allow to go unrepaired. An abandoned lodge, similar to the one on Medicine Rock, a perfect otter den.

Dan grinds out a cigarette on a rock, tucks the butt into his pocket. "Lunchtime yet?" he says, grabbing his own cooler, a small red one, from the boat. They sit down on the flat-topped boulders near the beaver lodge. It's nearly noon, and, as promised, the clouds are starting to break up. Patches of blue sky peek through.

Beth pulls bread, cheese, and a water bottle from her backpack.

Dan opens his cooler. "Here," he says, "brought enough for two." He hands her a sandwich – sliced turkey, provolone, tomato on fresh rye bread – and a chilled bottle of Black Horse.

"Thanks," she says, tucking her own skimpy rations away in her backpack.

"So how many more ponds you wanna go to?"

She tries to read his voice, and his face, for irritation or impatience. Hears, and sees, just a casual question. "Another two or three?" she says. And maybe a stop by the ocean, she adds to herself, wondering just how far she can push his generosity.

Dan takes a bite of the sandwich, chews, and follows it with a swallow of beer. Gazes out over the water, which, with the sunlight, has gradually changed from grey to dark blue. Just down shore, six black ducks bob, all in a line; three tails point skyward, come down, three others go up.

"What, exactly, are you trying to accomplish?" he says.

"Well ..." Beth lowers her sandwich. "There's not a lot known about otters in the wild. Not really. The basic social unit is probably the female and her pups, but their social organization also seems to be pretty variable, more variable than most other members of the weasel family. You know, weasels, mink, marten, wolverine–"

"I know what weasels are." His head is tilted to the side, brow furrowed, but he's smiling.

"If the DNA analyses work," Beth continues, "and if I can get funding to collect samples over a large enough area and throughout the year – maybe two years – I should be able to learn something about the composition of otter groups, how they change seasonally, how far members of the groups travel and if their ranges overlap."

"And that would matter because ...?"

"By finding out what areas they use most often, I can identify the landscape features and micro-habitats that are important to their survival. Knowing more about them helps us to protect them." A pat answer. She wants that to be true, but she knows it's not, not if there's no political will to save wilderness and wildlife. Beth takes a bite of her sandwich.

"But people around here aren't much interested in protecting them," Dan says. "They trap them."

Beth wipes her mouth with the back of her hand. "This type of research helps us to understand not just the otters here but also other species, like the otters in South America and Africa that are endangered. There are thirteen otter species in the world and all but five of them are endangered. We need to study species that are doing well to understand why others are in trouble."

Dan takes a swallow of beer. "I don't mind, you know, taking you around to other ponds. But do you really think that anything you do can make a difference?"

She stops mid-chew. Swallows. "You never know what's going to matter in the end." Almost chokes on Alan's words.

"Sometimes you do." He looks toward the black ducks. "Might as well spend every day of our lives fishing. While we still can."

"So you don't think anything's worth the effort?"

"Can't see that it'll do much good." He spreads his arms. "Unless you can figure out a way to make saving all this profitable." He smiles halfway, a curl of the lip, and raises the brown bottle in a toast. "And then you'll be famous. Probably win the Nobel, the Pulitzer ... one a them big prizes."

~

It is early evening and the truck is approaching the "T" intersection at the bottom of Medicine Rock Pond. A left turn will take them to Beth's cabin, a right to Dan's house.

She's collected samples at five ponds. And finally screwed up the courage to ask Dan to take her out to the ocean. He agreed. Pretty readily, actually. But when the trips to the ponds took longer than they'd planned, they decided to leave the ocean sampling for another day. Beth is anxious to get the samples into Dan's freezer, but she hasn't decided yet whether or not she'll accept an invitation to his house. Will he even ask?

"Wanna see it?"

"What?" she says carefully.

"What's left of the big house Emma's family built. Not much there. Just the foundation and a stone fireplace, but a nice view of the pond."

She's tempted to tease him: *none a my business.* Instead, she says, "Okay."

He turns left at the "T" and after a few minutes, pulls to the side of the road and points. "That was the driveway."

They step down from the truck and pick their way along a narrow path through short, dense fir until they come to a wide opening with several enormous maples that must have been planted when the house was built. The light is golden, filtering softly through the trees. An old-fashioned rosebush covered with dark pink blooms stands by crumbling concrete steps. Beth touches the delicate petals, breathes in their spicy-sweet fragrance.

Dan stoops to clear away a patch of long grass. More crumbling concrete. He stands and sweeps his arm out and across. "Foundation was huge. Grandest house this pond has ever seen."

"Why'd they let it go to ruin?"

"After the accident, Emma's family never came out again. By the time they got around to putting it up for sale, the house was already rotting away." He pulls a cigarette from his shirt pocket. "Doesn't take long when nobody's keeping a place up." Flicks his lighter. "And people start scavenging."

She faces the pond; the remains of a stone fireplace and chimney stand to her right. She's probably looking through space that was once large glass windows onto an expansive view of the water. A clematis trails up the grey stone, the blooms a deep purple.

A loud *cronk-cronk-cronk* overhead, followed by a cacophony of caws. Beth looks up and sees a raven. Three crows – a murder – are harassing it. Dan is watching as well. When he walks down to the pond, she follows. There are a few old pilings in the water, all that's left of a pier.

Dan takes off his cap and wipes sweat from his forehead with the back of his hand. Puts the cap back on and chews his lower lip. Beth is sweating too, and the clear water looks inviting. She wishes she had the courage to suggest that they swim. Strip off their clothes and go into the cold water together. Naked. But she won't. A backbone of Jell-o. She wishes then that Dan would suggest it. If he would just ask, she would say yes.

"Look." He points with his cigarette. Out in the water, less than ten metres away, are three brown heads, three sets of small black eyes watching. Chirp. Chirp. Snort. And they are gone. Just gone.

"Well, there you go," Dan says, laughing. "Guess they're watching you as much as you're watching them."

The moment has passed. As they pick their way back to the truck, Dan tells her that he'll take her samples back to his freezer.

He drives to her cabin and drops her off. "See ya." And then he is gone. Just gone.

~

She huddles in a dark corner, peeking out from under a blanket. Watches as a slender young woman searches through the cabin. Her pale hair hangs loose, swings out when she turns. The rosary is woven around and through her fingers, dangling from her wrist. The green beads glow as if lit from within. She is wearing the yellow sundress with huge pink roses, and there is a dark purple bruise on her forehead.

With a wide sweep of her arm, the girl whisks carvings of ravens off the table. They clatter to the floor, then open their wings and fly to the window. Ebony feathers beat against glass: *thwump-thwump-thwump*.

The girl sees the puzzle. With thumb and middle finger, she flicks pieces off the table, slides an entire corner off the edge. She opens the journal then, grabs a pencil, and stabs the page. She throws the journal to the floor, opens a cupboard door, and there, in the dark, is the amber shine of animal eyes, low *uhn-uhn-uhns*, the smell of musk. She flings open another cupboard, pulls out pots and pans, tosses them. The crash and clank are deafening. In the quiet that follows, Beth hears beating wings and the distant strains of a flute. The girl stops and stands like a statue in a half-crouch, listening. She sees Beth then and bares her teeth in an ugly grimace, blue eyes filled with bright fury.

Beth cannot move, cannot scream.

She awakens in the dark, fading notes of a flute still in her ears. Beth lies still and waits for her heart to slow, its *thwump-thwump-thwump* like the ravens' wings against the glass. She sits up and reaches for her watch: 5:12. Light soon. Searches for the box of matches and lights the kerosene lamp. Carries it into the kitchen. The nightmare was so real she half expects to find everything in disarray, but all the cupboard doors are closed and the only bowls and pans on the floor are the ones she put there. The puzzle is spread out on the table, half finished, just the way she left it when she went to bed.

Beth builds a fire and prepares the coffee pot: a routine to calm her. But her hands are shaking. Coffee grounds scatter across the counter. She gathers them with a damp paper towel; a few catch under the counter's ridged metal border. She puts the percolator on the stove and sinks into the armchair. Her research journal is on the floor. Beth stares for a long minute, then finally reaches for it. Holds it in her lap and opens it slowly, but sees only her own handwriting. She rifles through the pages. Her own notes, all familiar, ending with last night: *11 Aug 10: clear and*

sunny, winds moderate, ~20°C, observed at A5, 19:42 –
21:50. None observed. No fresh scats on latrine.

She lays the journal on the arm of the chair, idly flips open the back cover. Blinks hard when she sees scribbles on the back page: *Matthew d 1943 at 17, b 1926. Emma d 1963.* Scrawled across the bottom of the page are a few characters she cannot make out. She holds the page closer to the lamp: *1944*, or at least she thinks so. Preceding the numbers are what appear to be two letters, what look like a *b* or an *h* and an *a* or a *d*. The script is in her own hand, and messy, as if she'd been writing quickly.

Beth wraps her arms around herself, hugging her own chest. She doesn't recall making these notes, but she must have. Probably jotted them down shortly after talking with Clive, or after one of her visits with Mattie, when she was trying to make sense of her stories.

She stares at the rivulets of water running down the windowpane. Above the drumming of rain on the roof and the steady plink-plink-plink into bowls and pans, Beth hears the first slow blurps of perking coffee.

CHAPTER 19

When the weather clears, Beth spends a couple of hours surveying more kilometres of shoreline, still puzzling about the scribbled notes in her journal. Mid-morning, she finds herself paddling past Mattie's cabin. She beaches the kayak beside the aluminum canoe, drops her life-jacket into the cockpit, and climbs the path to the cabin, journal in hand. Maybe Mattie will know something about the odd notes.

She raps on the door, but hears nothing: no chair scraping, no barks, no paws clicking across a wood floor. She walks around to the garden. No Mattie or Muin there either. Everything is eerily quiet, just the chickadees in the birches, cheerfully singing out their own name.

She knocks again, then tries the door. It's unlocked. She should go in and make sure that Mattie is okay. She quietly steps inside. The kitchen is tidy, no dirty dishes, nothing left on the counter. She peeks into the bedroom, but Mattie's not there either. She goes back into the kitchen. Touches the kettle. Then the woodstove. Both are cool. Mattie and Muin have been gone a while.

When she looks up, she sees the other bedroom door, the one that's always closed. She should check in there too. Just in case. She lays the journal on the kitchen table and puts her hand to the doorknob, envisions cobwebs and animal skulls, jars of animal parts. Pulls her hand away, then shakes her head at her own foolishness.

The door opens onto an old-fashioned guestroom. White muslin curtains with wide ruffles have been drawn back from the window, and the sun is pouring in: dust motes float through the light. A white chenille bedspread covers a double bed that sits on a white metal frame. A hooked rug, in shades of rose and burgundy, lies in the centre of the wood floor, and against one wall is a tall wardrobe. An old vanity with an oval mirror and crocheted doilies sits beside it. A porcelain ewer and basin rest primly on one of the white doilies; on the other is a wooden comb and brush set. On the nightstand, also painted white, are a candle, a wooden flute, and a ribbon necklace with a small bone carving of an otter, similar to the one on the rosary.

Beth touches the otter, then holds the necklace up to her throat and turns toward the mirror, the surface yellowed and wavy with age. She sees, with dismay, just how worn and old she looks. She puts the necklace back on the nightstand and steps closer to the mirror, takes off her glasses and tries to smooth the web of wrinkles around her eyes and mouth. She slides her glasses back on and pushes at her short, grey-streaked hair. Greasy. No wonder Dan has shown no interest.

Her attention is arrested then by the small weaving hanging beside the vanity: a deep rose sky blending to purple then to indigo; a white crescent moon; Mattie's signature spider web in one corner; and an otter, in rich shades of brown, standing. There's a small white scar on its black nose. At its feet is a rust-coloured rock overlaid with fine grey threads, almost like another spider web. Beth leans in closer, finally discerns that the threads could spell out the word "hope." Maybe.

She steps to the wardrobe, hesitates, then opens one tall door, then the other. Clothes hang neatly from wooden hangers. On the left are pants and shirts, denim and flannel. Dresses, for someone small and slender, hang on the right. Beth flips through them, gasps: the yellow sundress – with huge pink roses.

She hears a scrabbling at the door, Muin's low woof. She closes the wardrobe and steps out of the room, but her hand is still on the doorknob when Mattie and Muin come into the cabin. Mattie is carrying a small metal bowl heaped with blueberries.

"Fancy meeting you here." Mattie's face is neutral, unreadable.

Muin noses at Beth's hands, and she wishes she'd brought a Milk-Bone. Anything to create a distraction from Mattie's close scrutiny.

Beth tries to smile. "Just stopped in to say hi." She shoves her hands deep into her pockets. "When you didn't answer the door, I thought I should check and make sure you were okay."

Mattie sets the bowl on the table and picks up the kettle. "How about a cup a tea then?"

"No," Beth says. "No thanks. I really should get back to work now."

"But you just got here ... didn't you?" Mattie sits down at the table. At her right elbow is the yellow sugar bowl, the one with the pink cabbage roses. Beth stares. That's where the dream image came from. Has to be.

Muin settles at Mattie's feet. A large drop of clear drool hangs from the dog's mouth, momentarily suspended, then drops to the floor.

Mattie picks up Beth's journal. Holds it out. "Don't forget this then."

"Oh, yeah. Thanks." Beth reaches for the journal.

Mattie's grip is tight. "There's always a logical explanation," she says, letting the journal slide from her fingers. "Except when there isn't."

Beth hugs the journal to her chest. "For what?"

"Don't know. You tell me."

Beth steps toward the door, then spins back around. "I had a horrible dream last night." Her words come in a rush. "There was a young woman in my cabin, tearing everything apart."

Mattie's eyes widen, then she looks away from Beth, toward the window.

"She pulled everything out of the drawers and cupboards," Beth says. "When she saw me, she looked like she wanted to kill me."

Mattie watches two noisy blue jays come and then go. A nuthatch hangs upside down, poking at the feeder. She brings her fingers together, then moves them apart, as if playing the child's game of cat's cradle. "Strange dream," she says finally. "Guess you better get back to work now."

~

While the sun is still high and warm, Beth bathes in the pond, dips her head underwater to rinse the shampoo from her hair. She needs to get these distractions out of her head. She needs to focus on her research.

But what about that yellow dress? Or the bedroom set up for a couple long dead?

Stop. Focus. Otters.

Swimming out from shore, Beth breast-strokes slowly and keeps her eyes just above the water, trying to see the world from an otter's point of view. Just like her, they're a little near-sighted out of the water, so the view without her glasses might be fairly accurate, but they have small muscles in their eyes that reshape the lens for better vision underwater. That raw sensory input is manipulated by the brain into something the animal can understand.

So how might otter brains construct the world? At the most elementary level, they live in a world with no red. Blue, yellow, and green, but no red. So they don't even see the red of her kayak or the pink of the wild roses.

Pink roses. Jesus, don't go there again. Stop. Focus. Otters.

Certainly they would smell them though, far more strongly than people do. They can probably identify different bodies of water just by smell, and individual rocks and trees too, and whether a beaver lodge is occupied or not. She'd be willing to bet that an otter can tell from a single sniff of a scat just whose it is. And if it's a stranger's, the otter can probably know the stranger's age, sex, reproductive state, what it's eaten, its general health, and possibly a whole lot more.

She swims underwater and tries to spin as if she's an otter wrestling, but it makes her dizzy. She surfaces and rolls onto her back. She doesn't really have to stay here much longer. She's collected enough samples for an initial assessment of food habits. She just needs a few more fresh ones for the DNA tests, along with a trip to the ocean, to where the outlet of Medicine Rock Pond flows into the salt water. She'd also like to do a few more direct observations. They're not really part of this preliminary research, but watching them first-hand gives her a better understanding of them and their sensory world. Never mind what Mattie has to say about watching and not listening.

Beth swims back to shore. Thoroughly chilled now, she steps out of the water and wraps a towel around her. Uses a second one to dry her hair. She climbs the path to the cabin, damp feet picking up dirt and spruce needles along the way.

Muin is at the door, tail wagging as if welcoming her home.

"Go back to where you belong," Beth says in her teacher voice, mustering all the sternness she can. "I have work to do." She brushes off her feet, then opens the screen door and squeezes through. Muin settles on the step and watches her through the mesh.

Beth dries herself off and smoothes lotion everywhere she can reach. Smoothes an extra dollop onto her face and

ANNAMARIE BECKEL

around her eyes. Slips on khakis and a denim shirt. She hasn't eaten since breakfast and she's famished. She opens a can of sardines, but before she can fork even one piece of fish onto a cracker, the whining and scratching begin, and then the low woofs.

What does it mean when a dog has chosen you? But isn't it Mattie who's chosen Beth? Does it matter?

She opens the door. "Okay," she sighs, "you win." Muin sashays into the cabin.

Beth finishes her meagre supper, clears away the remains, and stuffs the journal into her backpack. When Muin shows no inclination for going back to Mattie's, Beth lets her come along to the otter spot. Truth be told, she's glad for the company. She's still a little unnerved by her dream and that spare bedroom with the yellow dress.

She sits down to wait, and Muin settles beside her, as if she's glad for the company too. Beth drapes an arm around her. The temperature is still mild, but the sky has become a sullen grey, and the air is too still. Although Beth has covered every square inch of herself with thick fabric or insect repellent, the mosquitoes and black flies still manage to find unprotected skin. She swats and squirms, binoculars and voice recorder at her side.

Muin stands, ears forward. After another minute, Beth hears the excited chirps, and spots them not far down the shore. She puts a hand to the dog's collar to keep her from rushing forward, then clicks on the voice recorder: "19:46, A5, at least three or four in the water, coming from the beaver lodge, now about thirty metres away, swimming toward me. At least one pup." She searches anxiously for the second one. It's not the trapping season, but there are other hazards for the young and unwary. When she finally spots it, she relaxes. "A second pup is swimming beside an otter with a grey muzzle."

Beth hears chirps coming from the opposite direction. Her jaw drops. Another four or five are swimming from the northeast. The groups are approaching each other. If they stay on course they will meet almost directly in front of her.

"Chirping from both groups is almost continuous now. The two groups merge, and at least four or five touch muzzles. They begin wrestling in twos and threes. Continuous grunting now, with occasional chirps from the ones that are wrestling."

They are behaving like they all know each other: a friendly flotilla of otters. Where did they all come from? With all the activity, Beth cannot begin to tell one from another. She slowly releases Muin's collar. It's as if the dog understands that she needs to keep still and quiet. Beth lets the binoculars fall against her chest, slips her camera from her backpack and tries to take photos. Manages a few in the fading light, then takes up her binoculars and voice recorder again.

"They are all swimming past me now, toward the beaver lodge. No aggressive behaviour. An old one comes out of the water at the latrine; it is small and slender. It stamps its back feet, leaves a black scat, and urinates." Beth can see that the grey-muzzled otter is most likely a female: *the old grandmother.*

"She is standing upright and looking in my direction." Beth doesn't move. Just stares for what feels like a full minute. Is the otter looking at her? Or at Muin? When the dog starts to move forward, Beth grabs her collar.

"The old female snorts, drops to all fours, and goes back into the pond."

Peering through the binoculars, Beth is finally able to count nine. Counts them again: two pups, seven adults – or sub-adults. She can't be sure. A small otter could be an adult female or a sub-adult male.

"At 19:57 two come out of the water about six metres northeast of the beaver lodge. They rub on the grass and then begin to groom themselves and each other around the head and neck. Two other adults come out at the latrine, alternate their back feet in a little dance, and leave scats, one after the other. The first one, by its urination pattern, appears to be a male; the second is a female, maybe. They return to the water."

Within a few minutes they are gone. Simply gone. Water sprites.

Muin lets out a whine. "Yeah," Beth says. "I wish they'd stayed longer too."

She notes the time: 20:02. Takes out three plastic bags and marks them: *12 Aug 10: A5*. Also writes on each bag: *old female?, male?, female?* With droppings this fresh, she can also collect anal gland secretions – their musk – but the samples should be frozen quickly to be useful. She'll have to drive over to Dan's. Tonight.

~

The otters tumble and roll through the water, aroused by the rich banquet of smells and the energy of newness. A female touches her muzzle to a male's, and knows he has just eaten trout and a beetle. But she detects another scent as well: he's the one she mated with last spring, just after she gave birth to two pups. She paws his face, chirps. They turn and twist in the water, lunge and feint, grab and spin.

The old female is more wary. She'd scented the dog. The dog is familiar, and harmless, but she'd also scented the watcher, faint sweet odours of excitement and joy riding the wind, traces of sour fear and sadness woven within.

CHAPTER 20

Beth sees the pothole too late. Clenches her teeth in anticipation of the jolt when her left front tire hits it. Muin's forefeet slide off the passenger seat.

"Sorry, girl."

She's going only 40 kph, but eases her foot off the gas and flicks on the headlights. She's been debating it, but still can't decide if she hopes Dan is there – or hopes that he's not. Catching herself, she refocuses her thoughts on otters: the two groups coming together amicably, then wrestling and grooming; no squabbles. *A big ole family reunion*, Mattie would say. Although in Beth's experience of family reunions, there's always been a squabble or two. But if an otter harboured hidden resentments or grudges, how would anyone know – except another otter? They never appear to be annoyed or worried. They always look content to be doing exactly what they're doing: otters being otters. To the unscientific eye, Mattie's not wrong: *They're just happier than most folks.*

Of course otter happiness wouldn't be the same as human happiness, Beth reasons, but she has to confess that she's been willing to describe otters, at least to herself, as possessing *joie de vivre*. What is *joie de vivre* if not happiness? Her thoughts take a cynical turn: Maybe otters feel *joie de vivre* because they don't form long-term pair bonds. Males and females can simply enjoy the physical imperative of the moment – and then go their separate ways. No worries about whether or not they're *fine* with their partners. A simple life. But maybe not. They live in their own world, with their own way of making sense of that world – a mental life just as complex as her own perhaps, just different.

She glances at Muin. The dog is staring out the windshield as if helping Beth to watch for moose. What kinds of thoughts are going through her head? What kinds of feelings? There's a news story that has taken up permanent residence in Beth's heart. The article was brief, only a few details reported for their oddness: A young man went out into the desert with his dog – and hung himself from a cottonwood tree. Wasn't found for six weeks. In all that time, the dog maintained vigil, leaving the body only long enough to find water. Beth cannot get that image out of her head: the dog waiting by the body, guarding its companion and friend for six long weeks, day and night. Waiting for what? Hoping for what? How long would the dog have stayed had the body not been discovered? Beth can't think about the story without tearing up. She doesn't wonder what the dog was thinking: she wonders what it felt. Love and loyalty and grief aren't thoughts, they're feelings, unfathomable feelings that go to the very core of who we are. And if animals can feel love and loyalty and grief, what else do they feel? Almost impossible to know. But just because animal feelings are hard to study – and inconvenient to acknowledge when people want to use animals for food and furs and research – doesn't mean they don't exist.

Animals have the same basic wiring as people. Why wouldn't they have the same emotions?

It's dark by the time Beth arrives at Dan's house. The black pickup's not in the driveway. Relief? Or disappointment?

Muin stands. Her tail, going full force, sweeps Beth's face.

"No, girl," Beth says, winding down both front windows halfway. "You stay here. I'll just be a minute." She grabs the plastic bags from the cooler, retrieves the house key from under a paving stone, but then finds the door unlocked. She slips into the kitchen and turns on a light, puts the triple-bagged samples into the freezer with the others. Now to escape before Dan returns. She's already been caught snooping once today.

She turns from the refrigerator and sees the wall phone. She could take just a few minutes to call Rachel and Alan while she's here. She reaches into her back pocket. No, she can't. She left her wallet and calling card in the cabin, and she certainly doesn't want strange long-distance charges to appear on Dan's phone bill. She could check her email though. Just five minutes. Five minutes and then she'll be gone.

She creeps down the shadowed hallway to the study, cracks open the door. Screams and jumps backwards. Mattie's broken-toothed grin, lit by the glowing screen, looks like a jack-o-lantern's.

"Didn't think I was that scary."

"What," Beth gasps, "are you doing here?"

"I could ask you the same question."

"I … I came over to put samples in Dan's freezer."

Mattie's brow furrows, then she laughs. "Otter poop in his freezer?"

"He knows all about it."

"I'm sure he does."

"So what *are* you doing here?" Beth says, still trying to catch her breath.

"He is my nephew, you know." Mattie turns back to the screen, closes a window with a click of the mouse, and the room becomes that much darker. She turns on the desk lamp. "I come here now and again to use the Internet. You can learn a lot from the Internet, you know."

She stretches her hands toward the ceiling, moves her head from side to side. "Long as you're here, you might as well stay for a beer. Dan's probably got some in the refrigerator. Or you could fix yourself a cup a tea. Plain black. On a real stove."

"No," Beth says, almost a whisper. "I should be going."

"But he'll be home soon."

Beth closes her eyes. "I really need to go."

"No time? Even for a beer or a cup a tea? You scientists sure work hard."

Beth hears barking. Mattie tilts her head.

"Muin came over to my cabin," Beth explains quickly. "And I didn't have time to bring her back before going out to do observations. I can leave her here, with you."

"Unless you need her."

"Why would I need her?"

Mattie pushes out her lower lip. "Just thought you could use some company. Guess Muin thought so too."

"I'm fine," Beth says, trying not to think about the dark cabin she'll be returning to.

"Okay then, leave her here." Mattie turns back to the computer. "Oh, and you might wanna use the bathroom before you go. I always do. Toilet flushes."

~

A slender crescent moon offers only scant light, and when she pulls up to the cabin, Beth grabs the flashlight from the glove compartment and points it at the door. Sees something white tucked in close to the latch. God, what now? She walks closer and grabs the piece of paper, unlocks the door and quickly locks it behind her. Lights the kerosene lamp and unfolds the note: WEATHER SHOULD BE GOOD TOMORROW. PICK YOU UP AT 7 TO GO TO THE OCEAN. Big block letters, almost a child's hand.

Note clutched in her fist, she looks all around the living room and kitchen, carries the lamp into both bedrooms. Nothing out of place, no drawers or cupboards ajar, but she wishes she'd kept Muin. She doesn't *need* her, it would just be nice to have company in the shadowy cabin.

Beth picks up the journal and settles into the armchair to transcribe her observations from earlier that evening. Pushes the switch on the recorder, rewinds, then plays the tape. She can hear the excitement in her voice when she describes the two groups coming together. Wrestling, chirping, almost continuous grunting: otter happiness.

By the time she checks and rechecks her notes, it's after midnight. She goes to the outhouse, then brushes her teeth over the sink. Strips down and crawls into her sleeping bag before blowing out the lamp. Every movement provokes a silky rustle from the sleeping bag and a groan from the sagging springs beneath the thin mattress. The floorboards creak, a curtain flaps softly at the window, paws skitter across the roof.

On the long drive back to the cabin, she'd come to terms with the idea of Mattie using a computer. Although it had surprised her at first, Beth can make sense of it. Mattie is certainly adventuresome enough to tackle a computer. What Beth had avoided thinking about, and what is now worming its way to the forefront, is her dream from last night and Mattie's spare bedroom. There is no making sense of that yellow dress. *There's always a logical explanation ... except when there isn't.*

Beth sits up, strikes a match, and re-lights the lamp, the oily odour of kerosene familiar now. She plumps the pillows behind her and reaches for the tattered copy of *Endless Night*. Reads. Until she comes to the part about the house being cursed. Where is Miss Marple? Beth wants Miss Marple right now, someone down to earth and entirely sensible. Someone who can always figure things out.

~

She wakes early, distressingly early. Longing in every inch of her body. She lies still and clamps her eyes shut, desperate to re-enter the dream, to finish what she and Dan had started. They'd been lying side-by-side, partly naked under a soft sun. He was kissing and touching her, fingers and mouth caressing her shoulders and breasts. Her hands were on him. Her jeans slid down her thighs. And then he was over her, his head haloed by the sun, and they were just about to … and she awoke.

She wills herself back to sleep. No use. She props herself on one elbow, gropes for the box of matches, and lights the kerosene lamp. At least she'd dreamed of nothing terrifying.

She pulls on a pair of jeans and sneakers and runs to the outhouse. When she returns, she builds a fire and pumps water into the percolator. She'd enjoyed this routine at first, but now she's tired of it. And looking forward to getting back to electricity, indoor plumbing, hot showers. But what about Alan? What about Dan? She feels tight cords forming a knot just behind her breastbone.

She wraps herself in the sleeping bag and sits down to wait for the coffee. Watches the dawning of what promises to be a bright, clear day, the first rays of sun already warm on her face. She feels lingering desire, a desire so strong her body aches.

CHAPTER 21

Precisely at 6:59, Dan knocks on the door. When she opens it, Beth avoids looking into his face. He glances around at the pots and bowls scattered throughout the living room and kitchen. "Guess the place could use some work."

She pulls on a jacket. "Not sure if we'll try to fix it up. Or tear it down and build something new, like you did." She grabs her backpack. "Although Mattie said we shouldn't."

"Don't worry about that," Dan says, stepping out the door behind her. "She just doesn't like change."

Beth locks the door, then slides into the pickup, pushing aside a stack of napkins and old invoices, a thermos and two travel mugs. On the third grinding attempt, the engine finally turns over. Dan looks over his shoulder as he backs up. No boat this time. They'll walk to the outlet. She wants to check out the entire area close to where the river from Medicine Rock flows into the ocean.

"Mattie said you stopped by last night." He laughs. "I warned her not to tell anyone about the shit in my freezer."

"Sure didn't expect to find her there."

"She paddles over once a week or so to use the computer."

"Paddles?"

"Her canoe." Dan speaks matter-of-factly, as if there is nothing remarkable about a woman in her eighties paddling thirty minutes across the pond – and back – in the dark. "When the weather's bad, I drive her. Or pick her up on the snowmobile."

"Mattie at the computer," Beth says. "Not an image I ever expected to see."

He punches in the lighter and pulls a cigarette from the pack in his shirt pocket. "Sure, she even has her own email account. I check it for her and let her know when there's anything from the gallery."

While they drive the now-familiar route into town, they chat about the news, which turns out, not surprisingly, to be no news. Dan flicks on the radio. After days of virtual silence, Beth finds the loud ads jarring: needles to the brain. But the coffee is a comfort. Beth wraps her hands around the travel mug.

Just beyond the town, the road twists and turns, but heads generally north. The landscape is rolling and thickly wooded with spruce, fir, and white birch. Dense thickets of alder grow close to the road, perfect hideouts for moose. They pass innumerable bodies of water, ponds at first and then the deeply indented, slender fingers of ocean, the rocky shoreline marked by tide-lines.

By water, Medicine Rock Pond is only four or five kilometres from the ocean. By car, it's nearly fifty, and after driving for almost an hour, Dan pulls into a roadside park: a wide beach and a few decrepit picnic tables, a green barrel trash can. As soon as she opens the door, Beth can smell the salt water, the wet kelp. The surf is gentle, the rhythmic rattle and click of rocks as waves sweep in and then retreat, turquoise water near shore, dark blue beyond. Standing tall and severe in the distance are steep grey cliffs streaked with amber and topped by a narrow swath of spruce and fir. An eagle soars near the cliff's edge.

"Outlet's a click or two that way." Dan points to the east. "Tide's going out, so we have plenty of time."

Beth is wearing heavy-soled hiking boots, but walking over the fist-sized rocks is precarious, the rocks sometimes rolling out from under her feet, potentially ankle-turning.

It's a sparkling summer day though, and she tries not to spoil it by noticing the makeshift fire pits surrounded by broken beer bottles and crushed cans, or the plastic bleach containers and lengths of brightly coloured synthetic rope strewn on the beach. She looks instead at pieces of driftwood and toward the gulls flying overhead. They make shallow dives, then rise up to drop sea urchins onto the larger rocks. Fragments of green and purple shell lie scattered everywhere. Terns dart past, screeching, their calls incongruous for such graceful birds: beautiful harpies.

Binoculars in hand, she sometimes walks beside Dan, but more often behind, looking for signs of otters. They walk slowly, conversation minimal, words often lost to the wind.

About a hundred metres before they reach the outlet, she finds a few older scats on top of a flat rock. She bends over them and probes with a piece of driftwood – dried fragments of lobster and mussel shell, slender fish bones, scales, a couple of otoliths. She pulls out plastic bags. The samples will be useful for food analysis but not for the DNA tests.

The outlet itself is broad, at least twenty-five metres across. Beth walks the near side, searching for fresh scats and hoping to find tracks in the scattered patches of wet sand. While she follows the river about fifty paces back into the woods, Dan stays out by the ocean. She is looking for signs of otters as well as a place to cross. Finds neither. And the flies in the woods are fierce.

She hikes back to where Dan is standing. "Looks like I'll have to wade across," she says. "Doesn't look too deep."

"Probably deeper than it looks."

Beth takes off her jacket and boots first, rolls up her socks and pushes them into the boots. Unzips her jeans and slides them off. She's worn her swimsuit under her clothes for just this possibility. She doesn't look at Dan or try to assess whether he's watching. She pulls sport sandals from her backpack, straps them on, then unbuttons her shirt.

"Guess you came prepared." He peers into the water.

"Careful of those rocks. They'll be slippery."

She holds her backpack over her head; she's already sealed her camera and voice recorder in plastic bags. She wades in. He's right: the rocks are slippery. She inhales sharply when the icy water reaches her thighs. She can feel the current pushing against her legs, but it's not strong. She takes a few more steps, wary of a deeper channel where the current might be stronger. The water is up to her waist now.

If she slipped and went under, would he come in after her? Rescue her and then, perhaps, kiss her? She considers slipping. On purpose.

Beth is now more than halfway across, and with every step the water becomes shallower. By the time she reaches the opposite shore she is shivering. She pulls a small towel from her backpack and drapes it across her shoulders.

It doesn't take long for her to find what she's looking for: fresh black scats, at least four, on top of a prominent rock. And near the rock is the perfect imprint of a small hind foot. The track shows all five toes and the webbing between them. She raises her arm in triumph.

Dan cups his hands around his mouth, shouts, "Long way to go just for otter shit."

Beth photographs the footprint and then bags the samples. She pulls her journal from its protective plastic bag and jots a few notes, walks about a hundred paces along the ocean and then back along the outlet until she comes to the trees – and the flies. Finds nothing more, but she's satisfied. She has what she came here for. The DNA analyses will confirm whether or not any of these scats are from the otters on Medicine Rock.

Steeling herself against the frigid water, she wades back across the outlet. When she reaches the other side, she dries herself off. This time, she knows Dan is watching, smoking and watching, a thumb hooked in his back pocket, cap tipped. "Get what you need?" he says.

"Think so. Can't be sure until I get the lab results back. And even if the DNA analyses work, the data won't be conclusive, only suggestive." She pulls her jeans over her damp swimsuit. It will be an uncomfortable ride back to the cabin. "Thanks for bringing me out here."

"Kind of interesting, being able to learn things from shit, I mean. And I don't know many women who'd hike for an hour, ford a river, and then let out a whoop when they found otter shit." He pushes his cap farther back on his head. "And I thought Mattie was strange."

Beth smiles and shrugs one shoulder. "It's just what I do." She sits down on a rock, brushes sand from her feet, and pulls on her socks and boots. "Found a nice track too. A small hind foot. Probably a pup." She stuffs the damp towel and sandals into the backpack.

They share a companionable silence on the hike back. Trailing behind him, Beth can feel sand inside her socks, rubbing under and around her toes. She walks slowly, still looking for signs of otters. And wonders why, even in his stained jeans, flannel shirts, and rubber boots, Dan looks better every time she sees him. She gazes toward the horizon, at the whitecaps in the distance. Knows that, with the help of her dream, she's well on her way to creating a schoolgirl crush on a man she hardly knows. She did that a lot in her teens and early twenties. Never mattered much that the boys, and then men, paid little attention to her. All she was after was the longing, the obsession. It was the intensity of the longing that made her feel alive.

She picks up a small, twisted piece of driftwood shaped vaguely like a bird's head. She knows next to nothing about the real Dan, the surly Dan of the curled upper lip, the *not-my-business* Dan. Maybe if she did, she wouldn't even like him. Maybe that's what she needs to do, find out more about him – before she makes a complete fool of herself and does something she can't undo. She tosses the driftwood into the water, sees a small white feather trapped between two rocks. She stoops to pick it up. Wishes she could talk to Alice. Alice would sort things out. She was a clinical psychologist, and whenever Beth asked for advice, Alice would pause, then say, *Do you want me to answer that as a therapist ... or a friend?* Alice wouldn't hesitate to point out just how stupid she's being. Beth holds up the feather, releases it to the wind.

When they get back to the pickup, Beth slips the samples into her cooler, then tucks her backpack down between her feet. "Thanks again. I really appreciate this."

"No problem."

CHAPTER 22

The drive back seems shorter, quieter. Dan leaves the radio off, but the silence is comfortable. Only vaguely aware of the passing landscape, Beth mulls a line of questioning that would be revealing but not intrusive. Before she can screw up the courage to ask him anything, however, they are approaching the "T" intersection at the bottom of Medicine Rock Pond. A right turn to Dan's, left turn to Beth's. She tugs at the damp swimsuit clinging to her midriff.

"I'm starving," he says. "How about some lunch? I'll drive you home after."

"Okay."

A right turn, then another fifteen minutes and they pull up to his house. Dan unlocks the door, then steps aside to let her go in first. She opens the freezer and slides in the samples, turns and says, apologetically, "Shouldn't be many more."

"Good. Don't wanna start confusing them with the sausage patties."

She grins. "You'd know that right away. They'd be crunchy." She turns toward the hall. "Mind if I use the bathroom?" She has dry underclothes in her backpack.

"Be my guest."

On her way back to the kitchen, they pass in the hallway. Dan touches her shoulder lightly, but keeps going.

Back in the kitchen, he opens the refrigerator and grabs the makings for sandwiches – sliced ham and turkey, bread, cheese, tomato, mayo – and the same cartons of coleslaw and potato salad from a few nights ago. Using his chin to hold the stack in place, he carries everything, along with two beers, to the kitchen table. Lifts an index finger to point at the cupboard. "Plates in there. Knives and forks in the drawer below." He sits down, opens a Black Horse, and gulps down half of it. He pulls out two slices of rye bread. As soon as Beth sets the plates and cutlery on the table, he grabs a knife and begins spreading mayonnaise.

"Starving," he repeats, grabbing slices of ham and slapping them onto the bread. "Looking for otter shit is tough work." He lays a slice of provolone over the ham.

Beth sits down across from him. He slides the packages of meat toward her. She reaches over them for a slice of cheese, lays it on the bread, adds tomato.

"Turkey? Ham?" he says.

"I generally try not to eat a lot of meat."

"You had a turkey sandwich just a couple days ago." A quarter of his is gone in one bite.

"I'm not a complete vegetarian," she says, levering the cap off the beer. "And I don't like being preachy about it."

"So you think people shouldn't eat animals?" He bites off another quarter of the sandwich.

"No, it's not that. Eating meat is part of who we are as predators." She takes a swallow of beer. "And I think hunting and old-fashioned farming can be all right. At least those animals get to have some kind of life. It's the factory farms that are awful."

"Okay, go ahead and be preachy, cause I'm not getting it." A third quarter of the sandwich disappears.

She places a slice of bread over the tomato and cheese, inhales slowly. "Animals on factory farms are treated like things that aren't even alive. Some of them live in tiny enclosures and never feel sunlight on their faces or grass under their feet. And ..." Beth looks up. He's not annoyed or scoffing, or even giving her a patronizing smirk. She continues: "And growing animals for meat takes a lot of grain and water. And energy. The single biggest way humans can reduce their carbon footprint is to cut back on the amount of meat they eat."

"No shit?" he says, then adds, "No pun intended." He finishes the last quarter of the sandwich and begins to construct another. "It'll take an awful lot of convincing to get people to eat less meat."

"The economy may do that all by itself. Meat will become too expensive. It'll be the food of the wealthy, a status symbol."

"Whoa! You're not too optimistic about the future, are you?"

She tilts her head to the side. "Who was it said that we might as well spend every day of our lives fishing?"

"Yeah, well. Fair enough."

Beth puts up a hand, palm out. "Okay, sermon over." Then opens the cartons of potato salad and coleslaw. "So now you know I'm an environmental pessimist, but that I'm also a woman who'll go to almost any length to collect otter scats." She chooses her words carefully. "But I know next to nothing about you."

"Not much to know. Born here, went away, came back. And you already know I like to fish. And can play the fiddle. Sort of."

Beth picks up serving spoons and puts them into the salads. "There's got to be more than that."

"Not really."

"Everyone's life is more complicated than that." She takes a bite of her sandwich.

"Not mine."

She wipes the corners of her mouth with a thumb and middle finger. "I don't believe that."

"I don't like complicated. I like simple." Dan slices a tomato.

"But what about all those years in the army?"

"Trust me. Nothing interesting there." He adds the tomato to his sandwich, slaps a piece of bread on top. He takes a long swallow of beer, finishing off the bottle, then goes to the refrigerator and pulls out another one. Holds it up. "Nothing environmentally destructive about drinking beer is there?"

Beth raises an eyebrow, then spoons potato salad onto her plate. "You were in the army for more than thirty years. Something interesting must have happened."

"Seriously, just routine work. Nothing remarkable."

"Nothing? In thirty years?"

He bites into the sandwich, chews, swallows. Beth folds her hands and lays them on the table.

"You're just gonna keep asking, aren't you?"

She nods.

"Okay," he sighs. "Once upon a time there was a wife. She didn't like the military life, all that moving around. Only lasted three years. And that's all there is to it." He finishes the sandwich and pulls the red and white pack of Macdonalds from his shirt pocket. "Mind?"

Beth does, but shakes her head no. Nibbles on a slice of cheese. "Children?" she asks quietly.

He lights a cigarette, sits back in the chair, and swings an ankle over one knee. He'd look relaxed if his foot weren't jiggling up and down. "Not from the marriage."

Beth looks at him sidelong.

Dan picks up the beer and rubs a thumb over the heavy-haunched workhorse on the label. "Wouldn't even know him if I passed him on the street." Picks at a corner of the label. "Look, I'm not big on talking about myself."

Beth takes a bite of potato salad and watches him while she chews.

"Kid must be at least … what? Almost forty by now. He was nineteen before I even knew he existed." He takes a long draw on the cigarette, exhales to the side. "If he hadn't run off, I wouldn't even know about him at all. All water over the dam now."

"What's his name?"

He squints at Beth. "You really wanna hear this?"

"Yeah, I do."

His foot jiggles up and down, up and down. "So Sharon, my girlfriend when I was eighteen ..." He laughs, but without humour. "Not even my girlfriend, really. More like a one-night stand. One last fling before I went into the army."

The ash is building up on the cigarette. Beth pushes an ashtray toward him.

"So Sharon tracked me down somehow, and some guy woke me in the middle of the night to tell me I had a call from Toronto. When I got to the phone, it took me a few minutes to even remember who she was." He takes a swallow of beer. "Anyway, she tells me I have a son who's now nineteen, and he's run off."

"And that's the first you knew of him?"

"Yep. And Sharon tells me she thinks he's run off to find me, his long-lost daddy." He shakes his head. "I was just thirty-seven or thirty-eight then, stationed in Cyprus. Don't know how she even tracked me down."

"So what happened?"

Dan uncrosses his legs, brings the jiggling foot to the floor. "He never contacted me. And Sharon never called again. End of story."

"You weren't curious?"

"Look, I never knew the boy, never even knew he existed." He scrapes a fleck of tobacco from his lower lip. "If he'd been younger, I'd've offered Sharon some money or something. Maybe even tried to meet him. But the kid was already nineteen. Didn't need a dad by then."

"But you might have grandchildren somewhere."

"So you think I should care about a son I never even knew I had? Never even wanted?"

"Well ... yes."

He puts his hands on his knees, leans forward. A thin contrail of smoke curls upward. "Not my business. None of them are my business." He stubs out the cigarette. "Now that you've got all your samples, I spose you'll be heading back to St. John's."

"I'm staying on for another couple of days. I'd like to get a few more observations."

"Planning to see Mattie again? She's gonna miss your visits."

CHAPTER 23

Awkward silences, punctuated by equally awkward conversation, on the drive to her cabin. But their combined efforts at chit-chat lead Beth to suspect that both of them are trying to apologize without having to say the words. When she slides out of the pickup, he leaves with a wave and a "See ya," but also a half-smile.

It's late afternoon. She should drive into town and call Alan, let him know she's planning to come home in a few days. Eventually, she'll also have to tell him that they might be inheriting a dog, a big dog. But no need to worry about that now.

She grabs her keys and locks the door. Slides into the Toyota. Stares out the windshield at the faded red clapboard, the crumbling window frames. Maybe what they have together is as good as it gets when you're fifty-three and married for twenty-five years. At least they don't hate each other and they don't have children somewhere they don't care about.

By the time she gets to the Irving, Beth has decided to call Rachel before she calls Alan. Her daughter picks up on the first ring. "Hi, Mom."

"Hi, sweetheart." Relief sweeps from Beth's forehead to her toes. "How are you?"

"Good. I'm standing in the checkout at Safeway right now. Sorry I couldn't answer when you called before. I was in the middle of experiments. And I couldn't call you back. What's with the no-reception thingy anyway?"

The chatter Beth loves. She smiles into the phone. Instant forgiveness.

"Oh, and thanks for the postcard," Rachel adds. "Cute. How's your stuff going?"

"Pretty well," Beth says. She can hear chaotic noise in the background, clanking carts, announcements of specials. "I think I've got enough to put together a decent research proposal."

"That's great, Mom."

"A lot depends on whether the samples are good enough for DNA analyses. Those can be tricky."

"How's the cabin?"

"Roof leaks and there's no electricity, but it's private and has a great view."

"Is there a beach? Can you swim?"

"It's rocky, but good for swimming. The water's clear."

"Cool. Maybe I'll have to come home next summer. Take some friends out there for a weekend."

Rachel, home for the summer. Beth closes her eyes and luxuriates in the thought for just a moment, then says, "How are things going with that new guy?" Her eyes snap open. What would she say if Rachel were to ask *her* that question?

"Over and out," Rachel says. "But that's okay. He wasn't all that great and I'm getting kind of tired of Vancouver anyway. Everything's so expensive. I might apply to graduate schools closer to home."

"That would be wonderful."

"Yeah, it'd be nice to be closer to you and Dad. Oh, I'm up to the checkout now. Gotta go. Love you."

"Love you too, sweetheart. Love you too."

Beth stands a while, cradling the phone. Then she squares her shoulders and calls Alan. As she waits through five long rings she makes patterns in the dirt at her feet. A Friday evening, he should be home. The answering machine comes on and she listens impatiently through her own message, then says, "Hi, Alan. Just me. Everything's fine."

She pauses, expecting him to pick up. When he doesn't, she continues: "Almost done here. Just want to get a few more observations. I'll probably head home Monday or Tuesday, but I'll call first, so you'll know when to expect me. Just talked to Rachel. She's thinking about graduate schools closer to home. Isn't that great? See you soon."

Just before the receiver hits the cradle, her hand stops short. She lifts the receiver back to her mouth. "Love you," she says quickly. "Bye."

~

13 Aug 10: A5, clear and sunny, winds moderate, ~18°C, 19:08 – 20:25. None observed. She flips the journal closed and stands. Rubs her aching hip and shakes out the tightness in her knees. She hadn't really expected to see them, not after seeing nine the evening before. They could be almost anywhere now. Might even be out at the coast, dining on flounder and crab, leaving more footprints in the sand.

No observations meant plenty of time to think. Too much time. And now, she wants to get back to the cabin before dark. If she didn't feel so silly – and if it weren't dangerous – she'd leave the lamp or a candle burning all night.

To distract herself while she was waiting, she'd begun to plan the house she and Alan could build to replace the cabin. Nothing fancy. Maybe something like Dan's, small but well-appointed: floor to ceiling windows onto the pond, a fireplace, a stove and refrigerator, an indoor bathroom. They could even ask Dan for advice. If she could just introduce him to Alan, that would put a quick end to her schoolgirl fantasies. Learning about his former wife, and the son he doesn't care about, the child of a girlfriend he can hardly remember, should have done it. But it hasn't. And she *will* ask the power company to bring in electricity. Then she can store her own samples in her own damn freezer. She won't need Dan at all.

~

The dog follows a faint but familiar scent, tracks it through dark trees skirting the pond. When she gets to the outlet, she smells the strong musk of otters – and forgets the other scent that brought her here, to the river. But the old female does not forget. The scent of the young woman is one she recognizes, a presence that has lingered here forever, searching, a presence who knows the otters, and the dog, intends harm to neither.

The dog bows down, resting her head on her large front paws. An otter pup approaches her, touches his muzzle to hers, then they leap up to chase each other, into the water and out, splashing, chirping, barking.

Later, worn out with chasing and wrestling, the dog sleeps among them, cradled by tree roots and warm wet fur. Sometime in the night, when it begins to rain, the dog wakes and remembers why she came here.

~

Beth is on her second cup of coffee when she hears tapping on the door. Opens it to find Mattie, rain streaming off her green slicker. She is holding her hands in front of her, rubbing them together. "Have you seen Muin?" she asks. Beth shakes her head.

"She's been gone all night," Mattie says. "I was hoping she was here, with you."

"Come in," Beth says, opening the door wider. "You're getting soaked."

Mattie steps inside. Her wet sneakers squish. Rain drips off the slicker and forms a puddle around her feet.

"Is there somewhere else she might wander off to?"

"No." Mattie's hands are still for a moment. "Well, yes. But this just feels different."

Just feels different. Beth's not sure how to weigh this, but Mattie seems genuinely worried.

"I better get back," Mattie says. "I left the flag up for Dan. As soon as the rain lets up, he'll go out fishing. I want him to go out in the truck and search. Or ..." She looks out the window at the Toyota. "If you would go out in your car then he can go out in the boat and search. If Muin's anywhere near shore, she'll come out when she hears the motor."

"But–"

"But what?"

"Never mind."

~

Bumping along the narrow dirt road, Beth tries to steer clear of the deepest ruts. Even so, the bottom of the car scrapes rock now and again. She's been driving slowly for hours, the radio off so she can listen for barking, although the wipers' smack-smack-smack drowns out all but the loudest sounds. Every few minutes, she stops the car, gets out, and calls. Waits hopefully for an answering bark. Sometimes, she can hear the distant whine of a motorboat and knows it's Dan. Who else would be out in this weather?

He'd answered her knock on the door in nothing but blue jeans. "More shit already this morning? Freezer's getting pretty full."

"Muin is gone. Has been all night. Mattie wants you to go out in the boat while I search by car." Beth could hear, and smell, coffee brewing.

He ran his hand through sleep-tousled hair. "But Muin's always gone."

"Mattie says this *feels different.*"

"What's that supposed to mean?"

"I don't know, but she seemed really agitated."

"Not a moment's peace," he sighed. "Not even on a Saturday morning."

Beth avoided looking at his bare chest. Even more spare than she'd imagined.

She glances at the gas gauge: half a tank. She can drive for hours yet. And she will. She'll stay out after dark if she has to. It surprises her just how much she cares about that goofy dog. Sure, Muin can be a nuisance, but she's also affectionate and lovable. And she's chosen Beth – whatever that means. But Muin's also a gorgeous purebred who's friendly with strangers. Someone might have decided to take her in. And keep her. Beth envisions her in a stranger's car, confused and already missing Mattie, wanting to come home. Sees, in her mind, Muin hurt, in pain and shivering, lying in a ditch somewhere with no protection from the rain. Beth begins to tear up. She can't even think about sitting at Mattie's table and not having Muin underfoot, of not smelling her distinctive doggy odour. She can't imagine how lonely Mattie would be without her. Just thinking about it makes her heart ache, which surprises her too – how much she's come to care about Mattie. She might be strange – and sometimes a little spooky – but she's never boring. What did Matthew mean? *You're here to help her.* Mattie seems pretty self-sufficient, so Beth can't see how she could help, except, perhaps, with her loneliness. Wait. Did she really just think that? Mattie as *he?* Beth hears a loud scrape. Cringes. And hopes she hasn't put a hole in the muffler or tailpipe.

She brakes. The road ahead is too deeply rutted for the low-slung Toyota. She studies the map on the seat beside her, a topographical map showing the old logging roads. If she's kept track of the twists and turns correctly, and the distance, she should be near the north shore of Medicine Rock Pond, just a little ways north and east of it. The trees are thick here, but the sky overhead has lightened and the rain has slowed to a drizzle. She'll get out and walk. She has to do something.

Beth pulls on her raingear, grabs a flashlight from the glove compartment, and slips it into the backpack along with the map. She slings the backpack over one shoulder and begins walking, but all she can hear is the swish-swish-swish of the raingear, so every minute or two, she stands still and calls: "Mu-u-e-e-n. Here, girl." Her breath makes white puffs in the air. It can't be more than ten or twelve degrees. "Here, Muin. Here, girl. Mu-u-e-e-n." She waits for an answering bark. Her hair is getting soaked, but she can't put her hood up. With the hood up, she won't be able to hear anything at all.

She comes across a pile of debris dumped at the side of the road: a threadbare, gold velour sofa; an ancient cabinet TV; an old grey computer monitor; a stained mattress; torn black garbage bags spilling out old issues of *Sports Illustrated,* phone books, and Sears catalogues. Who throws their trash out in the wilderness? She answers her own question: The same kind of person who'd steal a dog.

She continues walking for nearly an hour. Damp since early that morning, her clothes are sticking to her skin. The search is beginning to feel like looking for the proverbial needle in the haystack – despite Muin's size. Beth doesn't want to give up, but she's not sure this is the best way to find the dog – or even if she's still lost. Muin could be waiting at Beth's cabin right now. No, Mattie would be going back and forth between the cabins, if only to keep herself busy, and surely she and Dan have worked out what colour flag she'll put up if Muin returns. As long as Beth can hear the drone of the motorboat, she knows Dan's still out searching. So she'll keep searching too.

A quiet rustle, the snap of a twig. She stands still, heart and throat clenched tight. Hears it again, leaves and branches moving. She calls out, "Muin?" Then sees, up ahead, a furry black rump waddling off into the brush. Beth almost weeps. Any other time, she'd be thrilled to get a glimpse of a black bear, but not today.

She walks for another hour, keeping to the meandering road. No point in going off into the woods. It would just be harder to walk, and for all she knows, Muin is miles away. Or even in St. John's if someone has picked her up. Or dead. Beth balls her hands into fists to keep herself from crying. Her heart hiccups. Jax. She'd taken a hammer and nails and made a cross, painted it with the dates: '63 – '69. Put the cross and a handful of wild daisies on the grave. Beth swipes at tears.

She looks up and there she is, standing stock-still in the middle of the road – as if the massive dog had simply materialized out of wind and earth and rain. Beth drops to her knees and Muin bounds forward. Beth buries her face in the smelly wet fur. She puts her hands on either side of the broad head. "Muin," she says sternly, but can't continue the scolding. The dog licks the tears from her cheeks.

She pulls out the Milk-Bones she'd stuffed in her backpack, and while Muin chomps one down, Beth considers her next move. She should try to signal Dan, otherwise he'll be out searching the whole time she and Muin are walking back to the car and driving to Mattie's – more than two hours. But to signal him she needs to get out on shore.

She pulls out her map and compass. If they head south-southwest, they should come out on shore somewhere near Medicine Rock. Can't be much more than half a kilometre through the woods. She checks her watch: 15:32. Plenty of time to go to the pond, signal Dan, and get back to the car before dark. She folds up the map and steps into the woods. Muin happily follows, especially when Beth pulls out another Milk-Bone.

She holds the compass before her, on a south-southwest bearing. Within fifteen minutes they are standing on the north shore of the pond, just east of the outlet and

Medicine Rock, which, in the grey light and drizzle, looks almost black. She scans the pond. Dan's boat is nowhere in sight. She decides they'll wait there for an hour. If Dan hasn't shown up by then, they'll head back to the car. She pulls up her hood and sits down on a rock, calls Muin to her side, but the dog backs up and barks.

"What's wrong, girl?"

Muin runs toward the outlet, barks, and then comes halfway back. Beth pulls another treat from her backpack. Waves it. Muin won't come, even for the Milk-Bone.

Beth groans. Not another Lassie moment.

Okay, she could follow Muin for a short way. They'll be just as visible walking along the shore as they are sitting, maybe more so. She stands and walks toward Muin, who now trots along silently, leaping across the rocks, which, sharp-edged and slippery, are far more difficult for Beth to navigate. It takes her nearly ten minutes to cover the short distance to the outlet. Once there, Muin bolts straight back into the woods.

"Damn it, Muin. Come here." Beth can hear the dog crashing through the undergrowth. She stamps her foot. "Come here, Muin." Her love for the dog, and her relief at having found her, are quickly morphing into anger. She doesn't want to follow Muin and miss Dan, but she doesn't want to lose the dog either.

She lifts the binoculars and scans the pond. Still no Dan. She decides to go into the woods a short way, but not far, even if it means losing Muin. She'll stay near shore and signal Dan, and then both of them can search on foot together. At least they'll know the dog is somewhere nearby.

She calls for Muin again, then follows the answering bark into the dripping trees, gloomy with old man's beard. She spots her standing beside a small pile of rocks, near to where she found the rosary. Beth approaches slowly, calling to Muin. The dog stays put, looking alternately at

Beth and the cairn. That's how Beth sees it now, a cairn: grey and ochre rocks, all about the size of a grapefruit, piled knee-high.

"Good dog, good Muin," Beth croons until she is standing by the dog's side and has grabbed her collar. She turns toward the cairn. On the top stone, an ochre one, someone has painted a spider web. The paint has worn away and some of the lines are barely visible, but Beth can make out the word "hope" within the web.

Muin lifts her ears. A few moments later, Beth hears it too: the motorboat. They run toward shore. As soon as they emerge from the trees, Beth waves her arms wildly. She pulls the flashlight from her backpack, flicks it on, and waves that too, but Dan is turned away. Muin barks, but the outboard drowns out the sound. Beth adds jumping to arm waving.

Dan turns the boat in a wide arc. Finally spots them and steers the Alumacraft toward shore, cuts the motor and drifts in. Muin swims out to greet him.

"Where the hell have you been?" he says. The words are harsh, but Beth can hear his relief. Dan steps out of the boat and pulls it partway up on shore. Muin emerges from the water and shakes, and even in their raingear, Dan and Beth take a step back.

"This where you found her?" he says.

Beth points back across the woods. "Not far from here, but back on the old logging road."

"Doing what?"

"Nothing ... that I could see."

Dan tugs on the bill of his cap. "Well, at least you found her."

Muin has both front paws on the gunnel, ready to jump aboard.

"Okay, girl. Hang on a minute." He turns to Beth. "If you're okay to get back to your car on your own, I'll take Muin back to Mattie. I've never seen her like this."

Beth tucks damp hair behind one ear. "Got out here by myself. Guess I can find my own way back."

"Why don't you stop by Mattie's later? I'm sure she'll wanna thank you."

"Maybe. If it's not too late."

Muin jumps into the boat. Dan pushes it into the water and climbs in. "Thanks, Beth. Mattie's gonna miss you when you go."

And what about you, Dan? What about you?

CHAPTER 24

Now that she's no longer consumed with worry about Muin, the walk back to the car seems endless. She should have gone back in the boat and then asked Dan to drive her to the car. Still would have taken more than two hours, but at least she'd have company and a ride. But she has to consider: Dan never offered.

Beth trudges on, each step accompanied by the annoying swish of raingear. When she finally reaches the Toyota, she has to drive for nearly an hour, on bad roads skirting the pond, to get back to the cabin. It's nearly seven by the time she unlocks the door.

She changes into dry clothes. Looks with longing at the bed and thinks about just falling into it, but twenty minutes later, flashlight in hand, she is standing on Mattie's doorstep. She hears Muin's low woof, and when Mattie opens the door, Beth can see a pot of something bubbling on the cookstove. There are three places set at the small table: Dan and Mattie have waited supper for her. Muin nuzzles her hand and Beth feels tears welling. Hides her face by reaching for Muin's shaggy head. "What a bad dog you are."

"Come on now, sit down," Mattie says. "You must be gut-founded."

"I know I sure am," Dan says, rubbing his flat belly. "Mattie wouldn't even let me have a taste. Moose stew," he adds.

Beth breathes in the rich aroma and suddenly realizes that she is famished, emptied out by the whole ordeal. Mattie dishes up three large bowls, then sits down. Beth takes the seat across from Dan, while Muin settles in her customary place under the table. All of them move their feet aside, simultaneously, as if their steps were choreographed. Dan picks up a fork and digs into the stew.

"Dan says you found her not far from the outlet?" Mattie says.

"I was just walking and calling, and then there she was." Beth blows on a forkful of hot stew, takes a small bite – moose, carrot, potato, turnip, onion, and some subtle flavours she can't identify. She glances at the dried plants hanging from the ceiling, hesitates, then takes another bite. She is too damn hungry not to eat.

Dan sets down his fork and arranges, then rearranges, his knife and spoon. "Mattie," he says slowly, "it's time you started tying her up."

"No."

"Look, I can fix up a sturdy line between two trees. One that'll let her walk on a chain up and down the line."

Mattie shakes her head. "No. She's never run off before. Not like this. Must've had her reasons."

He picks up his fork and points it at Mattie. "That's exactly why she needs to be tied."

"She won't do that again."

"And how do you know that?" He looks as if he wants to poke her.

"Just know. That's all."

Dan lets out a beleaguered sigh. "Muin needs to be tied. I can't be chasing all around after that dog. And Beth won't be here to find her for you."

Mattie turns to Beth. "Where you going?"

"Don't change the subject." Glaring at Mattie, Dan shoves a huge bite of stew into his mouth.

"Where you going?" Mattie repeats.

"I've finished my research," Beth says. "At least for now. I'll be heading back to St. John's in a couple of days."

"You're not done here."

"Classes start soon. I need to get ready."

"But you're not done here," Mattie insists.

Dan shovels stew into his mouth, bites off thick chunks of buttered bread, keeps his eyes down.

"I've taken as many samples as I need to write a proposal," Beth says.

"That's not what I'm talking about." Mattie taps the back of Beth's hand with two fingers. "It's your other work."

"What other work?"

"You know."

"No, I don't," Beth says.

"You can be thick at times."

"Look who's calling who 'thick,'" Dan mumbles, around a mouth full of bread.

"You said that you came here to learn about otters." Mattie taps Beth's hand again. "Know anything more now than when you first came?"

Beth pulls her hand away. "Mattie?"

"Well, do you?"

Dan stands and tosses his napkin on the table. "Thanks for supper, but I need to get going." Points a finger at Muin. "*You* stay home." Muin scrambles out from under the table and follows him to the door. Dan lets the screen door slam behind him.

"I do have a job and a husband to get back to," Beth says.

"But you want to stay."

Muin turns her head toward Beth and whines. Mattie takes a bite of stew, chews slowly, swallows. "Nothing to feel guilty about. Everybody has those kinda thoughts one time or another. And he is a good-looking boy."

"Don't be ridiculous!" Heat rises up Beth's neck and into her cheeks. "He's just been helping with my research."

"That's good. Because whatever it is you're supposed to be doing here, it's not about Dan."

Beth stares at the bowl in front of her, takes a small bite of carrot but can hardly chew. When she finally allows herself to look up, the first thing she sees is Muin. She makes an effort to swallow and then clears her throat. "When I found Muin," she says, "and we walked out to the pond, she went straight to Medicine Rock. And then headed back into the woods. To the place where I found the rosary."

Mattie toys with a piece of turnip.

"She stopped beside a pile of rocks," Beth continues. "A cairn or a shrine of some kind. On one rock, someone had painted a spider web incorporating the word 'hope.' Looked a lot like your work."

"Did it now?" Mattie lays down her fork.

"Is it?"

Mattie pushes the bowl aside. Exhales through narrowed lips. "Was a time in my life, girl, when I needed to be reminded of hope, when every day was an act of faith." She taps her fingers on the table as if counting. "Must be what? More than sixty-five years now."

"When Matthew drowned?"

"Thereabouts."

"Why would Muin go there?"

At the sound of her name, the dog comes and lays her head in Beth's lap.

"She sees him. Follows him sometimes." Mattie looks toward the blue baseball cap hanging by the door, then back to Beth. "Muin and me ... we live with ghosts."

"Memories," Beth says gently. "You mean that you live with memories."

"I mean what I say."

"But ghosts are just products of our imaginations," Beth says, "our fears." She thinks of Alice. "Or our deepest desires."

"You sure of that?" Mattie puts an elbow on the table and rests her chin in her palm.

"Reasonably so."

Mattie picks up the box of matches. Slides it open and takes out one match. "Would you agree that scientists discover new stuff almost every day?"

"Sure."

"Stuff that sometimes changes the way we think about everything else?" Holding the match like a cigarette, Mattie points at the bookshelf.

"Yes," Beth says, a little more tentative now.

"For thousands and thousands of years, everybody knew about ghosts." Mattie strikes the match and lights the kerosene lamp. "Then, in the past two hundred years or so – yesterday, if you're Medicine Rock – a few scientists come along and say: Ghosts? What foolishness!"

She adjusts the height of the wick. "How long till some scientist discovers a ghost?" Pale light shadows the corners of her upturned lips. "Then we'll all be able to see em again."

~

Beth picks her way along the path. Every time she hears a rustle of leaves, she can't stop herself from shining the flashlight toward it. The minute she steps into the cabin, she lights the kerosene lamp and every candle she has – until the living room and bedroom are glowing with soft yellow light. An open bottle of pinot noir stands on the counter. She pours a glass, then checks to be sure the door and all the windows are locked. Checks again. Sits down in the rocking chair – Katherine's chair – and sees her own pale reflection staring back at her from the black window. Like someone outside looking in. Or a ghost. She turns the chair away from the window. Her toe beats a steady tattoo on the wood floor.

How long till some scientist discovers a ghost? She sips the wine. There's not one shred of scientific evidence, and it's likely there never will be, but she can't completely discount the possibility either. Lots of perfectly sane people harbour a vague belief in the possibility of ghosts, or in something loosely resembling the notion. Nothing scary about it. Not really.

Okay. So what about animals then? Considering the issue scientifically, if there are human ghosts, there's no biological reason why there wouldn't be animal ghosts. And that raises the question of souls. If we grant them to humans, there's no reason not to grant them to animals too. And what would that mean for how we think about, and treat, animals?

Mentally, she throws up her hands. Maybe otters do have souls. Maybe they've created some sort of otter god they worship. Maybe there are born-again pups. She should be laughing, but alone in the cabin, with shadowy light creeping up the walls, she's not amused by the thought of animal souls or animal ghosts. Or any other kind of ghost, for that matter.

Beth goes to the bedroom and grabs her novel. Sits down again in the rocking chair and reads a few pages – but can remember nothing. She lays the book aside. She doesn't need any more mystery anyway, certainly not a novel titled *Endless Night*. She moves the lamp to the table and sits down at the puzzle, one thousand pieces, still only half-finished. She picks up a blue piece that's mottled with white, tries at least six different ways to fit it into a snow-capped mountain. Sets it aside and picks up another piece, one that looks like it should be part of a spruce, but she can't make that one fit either.

Mattie's words niggle: *Know anything more now than when you first came here?*

How had she ever imagined that coming here and spending a few weeks studying otters would change anything? Seems naïve now, presumptuous and benighted. Especially in light of what she's managed to accomplish so far: to collect samples of otter shit no one but she really cares about; to become thoroughly spooked by a lonely old woman's ghosts and a yellow dress; and to invent a romantic fantasy to replace her tired old marriage. She cringes. Damn. She thought she'd been hiding her feelings, when all along she's been telegraphing everything like a moonstruck schoolgirl. She's let herself become a pitiful cliché.

The rain starts, pinging against the windows like a spray of BBs.

CHAPTER 25

She gets up, makes a fire, and prepares the percolator. Wraps herself in her sleeping bag and waits, watching the sun rise on a morning that is warm and clear, as if the rain the night before had washed the air.

A restless night, but no dreams. And sometime during all that tossing and turning, she decided that she has everything she needs to write a proposal. This morning, she'll check the otter spot one last time, then stop in to say goodbye to Mattie. She'll retrieve the frozen samples from Dan's and call Alan from the Irving. She can be in St. John's before dark.

~

Beth sees Mattie in the clearing, kneeling beside Muin, who is nose to nose with a small otter. Beth lifts the paddle and lets the kayak drift. Muin bends into a play bow: head down, hind-end up, front legs straight out. But the otter has seen Beth. It snorts, then galumphs down to the pond, thick tail bobbling, and enters the water with hardly a ripple. Muin follows at a gallop and plunges in. Chirping, the otter circles the dog, touches its muzzle to hers as if to start a game of wrestling, but then dives. Muin watches, ears forward, but when the otter fails to reappear, she swims out to Beth, who paddles to shore and beaches the kayak beside Mattie's canoe. Muin comes out of the pond and shakes, showering water in a wide arc: rainbow flashes in the morning sun.

Mattie straightens slowly, unfolding herself as she works out the kinks from hips and knees. She cups the dog's chin. "Guess the old grandmother's not in the mood for play this morning."

If Beth didn't know better, she'd think Muin looks disappointed. Maybe she is.

"Do they come here often?" Beth says.

"Often enough. That was the old grandmother. When I told her you were leaving, she said you can't. You have too much to learn yet."

"Indeed." Beth crosses her arms. "She have anything to say about what, exactly, I need to learn?"

Mattie chuckles. "Just playing with you, girl." She nods toward the cabin. "Time for a cup a tea?" She holds up a hand. "Or water? I got lotsa water."

Beth follows Mattie and Muin up the trail and into the cabin. There is a new weaving in the loom: loden, cobalt, mahogany, and ivory. It is less than a quarter finished, but Beth can see the stylized spider web in one corner. Just off centre, what looks like an otter's webbed foot is taking shape.

Mattie points her chin at the loom. "That's for you."

"Me?"

"For finding Muin."

"That's not worth a weaving."

"Is to me." Mattie pumps cold water into a jar. "But it won't be done for at least another week, so I guess you'll just have to stick around."

"I have to go back, Mattie. Classes start soon. But I'll be out this fall for a few weekends."

"I'm gonna miss our little chats." Mattie brings her mug and Beth's water to the table. "Talking with you is a lot like talking with Katherine."

Beth sits down across from Mattie and picks up the jar of water. Stares at the yellow sugar bowl, the pink roses, the brown crack trailing between them.

Mattie adds a spoonful of sugar to her mug. "I miss her, you know. The way you miss your friend."

Beth has never mentioned Alice, has she? She stands up. "Can we go outside?"

"Sure. It's a grand morning." Mattie grabs a dish towel. Outside, she wipes the rain off both Muskoka chairs, then settles into one, mug of hot tea resting on the arm. The fragrant steam smells of raspberries. Muin noses around in the grass where the otter was, then plops down near Beth's feet.

Mattie sips the tea, pursing her lips at the heat, then sets down the mug. "The old grandmother and I were having a chat before you got here. She says you're worrying about the wrong things."

"Hmmm. She happen to say what I should be worrying about?"

Mattie lifts her hands, palms up. "I'm just the messenger, love." She lays an arm on the chair and drums her fingers. "She could mean that you should stop worrying about whether or not what you do matters. And just do. You can't know what matters."

Beth rotates the jar, moving it out of the puddle of condensation. Alan's words. If only it were that simple.

"The earth is so much more than any of us can know," Mattie continues. "Everything is. Including otters. Which means you're wrong."

"About what?"

Mattie shrugs. "I'm wrong too. All of us are wrong. And most of the time we don't even know what we're wrong about." She puts a hand to her forehead to shade her eyes and watches a pair of loons and their chick swimming in the middle of the pond. "Could be that people trying to understand the world – I mean really understand it – is like Muin trying to understand long division. Might be something we just can't do."

The dog stands and puts her head in Beth's lap. Beth scratches her behind her ears. One of the adult loons releases an echoing yodel.

Mattie smiles. "But there's hope in that."

"Hope in ignorance?"

"No, not in ignorance. But in maybes. Possibilities."

Fingers buried in Muin's fur, Beth closes her eyes. Alice was full of maybes: *I'm not sure, but I wonder if ...* In the end, in those last horrible days, Alice had needed to believe in possibilities. Beth tried, but she could believe in nothing but her anger and her grief.

Mattie turns to Beth. "To lose hope is a failure of imagination."

"It might help our imaginations," Beth says bitterly, "if hope paid off now and again, if we got one shred of evidence that it matters."

"Maybe we do, but we just don't see it." Mattie takes a swallow of the cooled tea and watches the loons for a long moment.

Muin lifts her head. A few seconds later, Beth hears the crunch of gravel and then the creak of a truck door opening. The dog trots toward the pickup.

"Oh, hey," Dan says to Beth while he fends off Muin. "Didn't expect to find you here. Thought you'd be out collecting more *samples* for my freezer."

"Just stopped in to say goodbye."

"Don't forget your samples then. I don't wanna be left with a freezer full of otter shit." He turns to Mattie. "Anything you need in town?"

"Just the dog food and the bird seed."

"Okay then, see ya." He turns toward the truck, then spins back around. "Long as you're still here," he says to Beth, "wanna go fishing again?"

"I'd planned to pack up and leave today."

"Your loss." Dan looks up at the sky. "Great day. I'm gonna go out after supper and try for a salmon. Might even see otters. You never know."

Beth is listening hard, but can hear no innuendo. Doesn't see a smirk or even a knowing glance at Mattie.

"Okay," she says slowly. "I suppose I could stay on for one more day."

"I'll bring the boat around at seven."

She allows herself to look at Mattie only after Dan has left.

Mattie clicks a thumbnail against her broken tooth. "Long as you're staying, wanna help me pick some crackerberries?"

"I thought they made you sick."

"Guess you were wrong about that too."

CHAPTER 26

Beth tosses the line out over the water. Doesn't really care that she's not casting right. She only pretended to listen to Dan's careful instructions earlier. She wants to talk, but Dan is far more interested in fishing. Fishing in silence, apparently.

Beth is bone-weary of being alone with her own thoughts. She'd made a trip into town that afternoon and stopped at the Irving to call Alan. He didn't pick up. On a Sunday afternoon? She tried his cellphone. He didn't answer that either. But she didn't have the energy to worry about what that might mean.

She went to the liquor store and picked up another bottle of wine, as well as a six-pack of Black Horse, and some ice for the cooler, just in case. In case of what? She chose not to worry about that either.

Back at the cabin, Beth put the beer on ice, then went into the pond and bathed. Tried to wash the black soot from under her fingernails. She searched among her clothes for something reasonably clean and flattering. She doesn't own anything remotely sexy. Why would she want sexy? One more thing she chose not to worry about.

True to his word, Dan came by precisely at seven, and they've been fishing near the outlet for nearly an hour. So far, there hasn't been a single rise, salmon or trout. Beth pulls in her line, then holds the fly rod idly in one hand. "So what do you know about the cairn?" she says.

"What cairn?" Dan casts, then flicks the line.

"I found it yesterday, a pile of rocks about fifty paces back from Medicine Rock. Near where I found the rosary."

"Was hoping I'd heard the last of that damn rosary. Hasn't been stolen again, has it?" He says the words like it's a little joke between them. He pulls in the line in measured increments.

"I took it back to where I found it." She brushes a mosquito off her cheek. "But what about the cairn?" she says.

He examines the red and silver fly at the end of his line. "Never seen it. Never heard of it."

Not my business.

He reaches for his tackle box. "How do you know it's not just a pile of rocks? Not like there's a big shortage around here."

"No," Beth says. "They were piled there deliberately. All of them are the same size and the top one's been painted. The paint has worn away, but you can still make out the word 'hope.' Sort of."

Dan removes the fly from his line and clips on a small blue one with a bit of yellow feather.

He casts the new fly over the water.

"It's Mattie's work," she continues. "She said so last night, after you left. She told me she made it a long time ago, just after Matthew drowned. A memorial of sorts, I guess."

"There you go. No more to it than that." Dan's line goes taut. He pulls it firmly but gently. The fly releases, a long blade of grass snagged in the hook. His shoulders sag.

"Yesterday," Beth says, "when I found Muin, she was hell-bent on going there."

"No big mystery to that." Dan removes the grass from the hook and lets it drop into the water. "Mattie usually brings Muin along when she comes out to Medicine Rock."

"She comes out here?"

"Sometimes she canoes." He examines the blue and yellow fly. "Other times, I bring her out in the boat or on the skidoo. I go off and fish while she does whatever she does."

"Why didn't she say that last night, when I told her where I found Muin?"

"Cause Mattie is Mattie. She never keeps anything simple if she can make it complicated." He turns to the other side of the boat and casts again.

"But when she told me about Medicine Rock, she made it sound like it was just some old place people from long ago used to visit."

"Mostly is," he says. "I doubt that anyone but Mattie comes out to the rock anymore. But she always comes out here at least once around mid-August."

Beth tips her head, puzzled.

"Anniversary of Matthew's drowning."

"Oh." She wraps both hands around the fly rod. Fumbles a cast. She pulls the line taut, but knows by the feel of it that she hasn't caught a fish. The fly has hooked into weeds or a submerged log. Dan reaches for the line and tugs gently to work the fly loose.

Beth pulls in the line. "Mattie told me that Muin might have been following Matthew's ghost when she ran off."

"And you believed that?"

"Course not. I just find it all strange. And, to be honest, a little creepy."

"Strange. But not creepy. That's just Mattie."

"What about the spare bedroom then?" she says. "You can't tell me that's not creepy."

"What's creepy about the spare bedroom?"

"The wooden flute and the bone necklace on the nightstand? The clothes in the closet?"

"That's just Mattie's stuff." Dan looks at her sideways. "Why the hell were you in there anyway?"

She turns away. Fumbles another cast. The fly plops into the water less than two metres from the boat. "When I stopped by a couple days ago, I couldn't find Mattie. I was looking around to make sure she was okay."

"In the spare bedroom?"

Beth keeps her gaze on Medicine Rock. In the softening light and lengthening shadows, the face she'd imagined before, the old man's profile, has morphed into an old woman's. "Let's go ashore," she says. "I'll show you the cairn."

"Why?" He pulls a cigarette from the pack in his shirt pocket.

"You're not even curious?"

"Not really." But he slides the cigarette back into his pocket and stows their fly rods, tips up the prop and rows the short distance to shore. Beth helps him pull the boat partway out of the water. He reaches for a flashlight and waves it toward the woods. "Lead on, Macduff." Smirks. "I think there might've been a ghost there too."

"Very funny." She lays a hand on Medicine Rock and points. "About fifty paces straight back from Medicine Rock."

"That's not Medicine Rock."

"It's not?"

"It's that one over there." He points to a flat grey rock sitting squarely in the middle of the outlet. It has a few green and rust striations, but it looks like all the others, only larger.

"But there's nothing special about that rock," she says.

"Hey, I didn't name it."

Beth is disappointed, but she's not sure why. "Okay then," she says, "the cairn is about fifty paces back from this rock."

In just a few minutes they are standing beside the pile of rocks. Dan flicks on the flashlight and points at the painted rock on top. "It's Mattie's work, sure. But you already knew that."

Beth leans in closer. Tucked between the painted rock and the pale one beside it is a brown and white feather like the one on her nightstand. She reaches out to touch it, her chest squeezing her lungs so tight she can hardly breathe. Alice?

"All right, I've seen it," Dan says. "Can we go now?"

Hoo-hoo-hoooo, hoo-hoo. They both look up. A great horned owl is sitting in a spruce just a few metres away. The bird swivels its head and looks down on them with round yellow eyes that seem to have gathered within them every photon of available light. They shine brighter than the flashlight, which Dan has pointed at the ground. The bird ruffles mottled feathers and clacks its bill – a warning – then spreads wings that are nearly as broad as Beth is tall and glides silently into the dark.

"Well, there's your ghost," Dan says. He sets off toward shore.

Beth hesitates, debating whether or not to take the feather. Decides to leave it where it is. She's already taken enough from this place. She follows the bouncing light beam over the mounds of sphagnum and through the ferns and underbrush.

A high-pitched chirp.

"Stop," she calls out in a whisper, but Dan is already standing still. He turns off the flashlight. Beth can hear the steady *uhn-uhn-uhns*, but it takes a full minute for her eyes to adjust to the dark. She finally spots a small otter standing upright on the real Medicine Rock, muzzle silvery grey in the faint light.

"The old grandmother," she says softly.

The otter chirps again then drops down and slides into the pond. Disappears in a ring of dark ripples.

"Why here? Why now?" Beth says. "And standing on Medicine Rock of all places."

"It's just an otter, Beth. And it's here. Just like we are."

"But it's the same one that was at Mattie's this morning. It's like a sign … or something."

"A sign?" He laughs. "Now you're sounding like Mattie. Making something that's simple into some big complicated mystery." He takes a step toward her. He's standing so close she can smell his shirt: wool, dry leaves, wood smoke. "Look," he says more gently, "you've been spending way too much time with her."

Dan reaches out and gives her arm a squeeze. "Come on, let's go."

She feels the presence of his hand, then the absence.

He flicks on the flashlight, points it toward her. "Jesus, Beth, you look like you really have seen a ghost." He reaches out and squeezes her arm again. "Why don't you come back to the house for a while? Have a drink and calm down. I'll drive you home."

~

The old female swims to join the others. When they see the light beam, even the pups grow still. They sniff the air – strong scent of humans and fear. They hear voices above the sounds of the water churning around the rocks in the river. They touch each other's muzzles. *Uhn-uhn-uhn, uhn-uhn-uhn.* Growls of a motor, then a stink so strong they can taste the bitterness. The otters come out of the water and hide among the grasses and dark shadows. They begin to groom themselves and each other, comfort in the touch-touch-touching.

CHAPTER 27

Within twenty minutes, Dan is tying the *Black Feather* to the pier. He turns off the small light on the bow, and they climb out of the boat and walk around to the back of the dark house. He unlocks the kitchen door and flicks a switch. Beth blinks. The bright fluorescent light banishes any lingering sense of ghosts in a way that a kerosene lamp and candles can't.

He grabs a Black Horse and a bottle of white wine from the refrigerator. "You look like you could use this. Or maybe something stronger?"

She runs a hand through her hair. "No, wine is good."

He uncorks the bottle and pours, hands her the glass, then points his beer toward the living room. Beth sinks into the armchair. She sets the chilled glass on the end table, turns up the collar of her jacket, and wraps her arms around herself. Dan steps to the fireplace and opens the flue.

"Please don't bother," she says. "I'll be fine."

"No trouble. I'll just build a small one to take off the chill." He smiles. "And to scare off any ghosts."

"I feel pretty silly now."

"No worries. Mattie can have that effect on people." He adds kindling to the slender splits already in the fireplace. Flicks his lighter. The kindling smoulders, then flares. He feeds pieces of birch bark to the small flames. "Been a long time since she's had someone actually pay attention to what she says."

Beth watches the fire grow. Her shoulders begin to unhunch. "What's troubling," she says, "is that sometimes

– even though I can't follow her logic – I find myself agreeing with her. Maybe I'm getting to be as nutty as she is."

"Could be." He grins. "You do spend your days collecting otter shit."

Beth laughs. "And you let me store it in your freezer. So what's that say about you?"

He takes a swallow of beer. "Seriously, Beth, don't worry about trying to find logic in what she says. There is no logic. It's just senility talking."

"You don't really believe that."

"No, but she is a little unhinged." He adds a few more splits to the fire. "She likes to keep everybody off balance. I learned a long time ago not to listen to her." He pokes at the fire with a piece of wood. "Even Katherine ignored half of what she said. But she did have a way of keeping Mattie more … reasonable."

He steps out into the kitchen and turns off the fluorescent light, comes back to the fire and adjusts the small logs with the poker, adds a larger birch junk.

Beth takes a sip of wine and stares into the flames. She does feel silly now. She's allowed herself to get caught up in Mattie's strange web of beliefs about ghosts and animals who bring messages, to the point where she's beginning to see odd coincidences – the appearance of otters, owls, and brown and white feathers – the same way Mattie would. Dan's explanations are perfectly reasonable: As a teenager Mattie was derailed by her twin's drowning, and over the decades, she's become eccentric, fabricating the illusions she needs to survive.

"She'd love this," Dan says, poking at the fire. "Us talking about her."

"Hard not to."

"But you came back here so you could stop thinking about her and her creepy ideas." He points at her glass. "More wine?"

"Thanks."

While Dan fetches the wine, Beth goes to the bathroom. Finger-combs her hair and studies her face in the mirror. The light is harsh, highlighting wrinkles she doesn't want to see. Smile lines, Alan calls them, kindly. No, she will not think about him right now.

She returns to the living room and finds that Dan has placed her glass on the end table beside the sofa. Everything is perfect: wine, a crackling fire, soft light surrounded by a darkness that is warm and comforting rather than scary, Dan sitting on the sofa. Everything she would have imagined … if she had allowed herself to imagine it.

She unzips her jacket. "Lovely fire."

"Yep." His ankle rests on one knee, foot jiggling.

She takes off the jacket and lays it aside. He looks up at her from the sofa. She picks up the wineglass and sits down beside him.

"So you're heading back tomorrow?" he says.

"That's the plan."

He picks at the label on the Black Horse. "Not much point in hanging around any longer, I spose."

"Well, I can always use more observations." She runs her fingers up and down the stem of the glass. "And I might try to get out here a few weekends this fall. I'll probably need more samples."

"Guess there's always a need for more shit." Dan speaks the words gently, another joke between them. He finishes the beer and uncrosses his legs to set the bottle on the floor. "Beautiful time of year just to hang around and fish."

"Well … maybe I *could* stay on another day or two." She turns to face him. He leans closer, puts a hand to her chin and tips it up. She closes her eyes, then feels his hand drop. Her eyes spring open.

He scrubs his face with the hand that had cradled her chin. "Damn," he says softly. Sitting back, he swings his ankle back onto his knee, takes her hand in his, and looks down at their interlaced fingers. "I like you, Beth." His foot is going like a sewing machine. "But we're after different things."

She hugs the wineglass to a stomach that is doing somersaults. "I'm not after anything," she says quickly, stupidly.

Dan releases her hand, stands, and walks to the kitchen. "I like simple," he continues, "and you would make it" – he opens the refrigerator, a rectangle of light in the dark – "complicated." He grabs another beer. The refrigerator comes on, the hum loud in the silence. "I hate talking about this stuff," he says into the dark.

He levers the cap off, a soft pf-f-ft. Takes a long swallow, Adam's apple bobbing. He uses the back of his hand to wipe his mouth. "My idea of a great arrangement would be for you to come out here now and again. I could help out with your research, and we could have ... fun. No strings. But you'd want the strings. And that gets tangly."

He sits down beside her, a little farther away this time, and stares at the fire. "I don't wanna be a jerk, Beth." His face contorts in what could be an effort to smile. "Been there, done that. And there's probably a few women who would be glad to give me the T-shirt."

Beth looks up from her wineglass, sees Mattie's weaving above the mantle, the black outline of the raven just visible. "So ... basically, you want to live your life without complications."

"Easier that way. I've done complicated."

His eyes are narrowed, and she wonders who he's remembering: the girlfriend, the former wife, or someone else? She feels an odd alliance with these troublesome women.

"Might be easier," she says, "but kind of empty too."

"Beth, I'm not the one who's unhappy."

The fire has burned down to embers. Ugly goose-bumps are popping up on her forearms. She reaches for her jacket. "Maybe I should go now."

~

Wisps of fog drift past. They travel in silence through a dark tunnel of trees, two completely separate entities now, two different conversations in their heads. Beth stares into the black night. She's replayed what Dan said, several times, and has come to the odd conclusion that he's like an otter: wants to enjoy the physical imperative of the moment with no worries about what comes after. The comparison would make her laugh if she didn't feel like such a fool.

After a ride that seems to go on forever, they finally reach the cabin. Beth opens the door of the pickup. Dan reaches out to touch her arm. "I can still help out with your research, you know."

She looks away. The adult equivalent of *We can still be friends:* the mortification of a teenager. She slides out. "Thanks." But she's not feeling grateful for anything.

He keeps the headlights pointed toward the cabin until she unlocks the door. "See ya," he calls from the open window. "Have a safe trip back to St. John's." And then he is gone.

Beth turns the knob, too numb to be scared, but then she lights the lamp and holds it up like a torch. She carries the lamp into the bedroom. Sees the brown and white feather lying beside her paperback. Alice. Alice would have told her she was being an idiot. Alice would have saved her from humiliation.

CHAPTER 28

She is paddling through murky water as viscous as molasses, every stroke an effort. The blue cap shades her face from the bright sun overhead, but in front of her, grey fog swirls around a girl standing on a pier, a girl wearing the yellow dress. Another person, hair short and dark, and wearing a red plaid shirt, steps out of the fog, eyes and mouth tight with anger. Pushes the girl's shoulder. She cartwheels into the pond.

The dreamer tosses the paddle aside, stands, and jumps, tumbling through the thick fog. As soon as she hits the surface, the molasses water swallows her. She can no longer see the canoe. Or the girl in the yellow dress.

Her lungs are bursting. She has to breathe. She has to. She opens her mouth. Sweet, brown water pours in. Weightless, she floats, and watches the blue baseball cap drift from side to side, like a feather in a gentle breeze.

Beth awakens and tastes the sourness of last night's wine on her tongue, but something else too, something sweet. That goddamn yellow dress. That blue cap.

She lies still and listens to the rain drumming on the roof and the plaintive plink of water dripping into pans and bowls. Who will empty them when she goes back to St. John's? Because she's leaving today. For sure.

She gropes for the flashlight. Looks at her watch: 5:16. Slides on her glasses and lights the lamp. Sits on the edge of the bed and studies the clothes piled on the floor, finally pulls out a sweatshirt and jeans, then adds a rain jacket and sneakers before she runs to the outhouse. It's raining hard: big fat drops coming at a forty-five degree angle.

When she returns to the cabin, she builds a fire and prepares the coffee pot, then packs up the few boxes and cans left in the cupboards. She sits down in the rocking chair, listens to the perking coffee, and tries to forget the dream. She watches grey light seep into the cabin. Begins to realize there's a gaping hole in her chest, like a cartoon cannonball has been shot right through. She misses Alan. Why isn't he answering his phones?

A light tapping on the door. She jumps up. Has Dan come back to dump the frozen shit in her lap? She approaches the door cautiously. Cracks it open. It's Mattie, in a wide-brimmed rain hat, and Muin.

"Glad I caught you before you left." Mattie steps into the cabin and digs deep into the pocket of her slicker. "Thought you'd want this."

Wary, Beth takes a step back.

Mattie opens her hand to reveal a carving, just eight inches long, including the thick tapering tail. "Rowan," she says, holding out the otter on the flat of her hand, "wood of good fortune. Most folks call it dogberry."

Beth's touch is tentative, as if the wood might burn her. The otter is stylized, yet carefully detailed, down to a small scar on the tip of the nose. "It's ... it's beautiful."

Mattie lifts her hand higher. "Here, take her now."

Beth turns over the carving, sees the signature. *Matthew MacKenzie.*

"He made it for you." Mattie takes off her hat and hangs it by the door. Muin shakes, drops sizzling when they hit the stove.

Beth points to the percolator.

"No thanks. Never touch the stuff." Mattie winks. "Poison, you know."

"Water then?"

"No thanks." Mattie hangs her slicker beside the hat, then slips off her boots. Muin sniffs at the packed box on

228

the counter, at what's left of the carton of Milk-Bones Beth intended to take home to Pirate. Beth reaches into the box and offers one to Muin, who carries it over to the stove. The odour of wet dog replaces the aroma of coffee.

Mattie studies the puzzle still laid out on the table. "Not making much progress, are you?" She sits down in the rocker and folds her hands in her lap. "So … catch anything last night?"

Beth pours coffee into a mug and sinks into the arm-chair. She places the otter on the arm of the chair. "Not a thing," she says carefully.

"So things didn't go so good then."

"Not really."

"And otherwise?"

"Otherwise?"

"Just wondering." Rocking steadily, Mattie glances around the room. Muin's crunching is audible in the silence.

"What?" Beth blurts. "You put a love spell on me. Or a curse or something?"

Mattie chuckles. "That's a good one."

The idea is so ludicrous Beth can't stop herself from laughing with her, even though she half believes Mattie would try it. She almost wishes she had. Then none of it would be her fault. She wouldn't have to feel so stupid for indulging a teenage crush.

Muin rises from beside the stove and goes to Beth, turns and offers her hips for scratching. Beth buries her fingers in the dog's fur. The shaggy tail thumps against her legs.

"Sure," Mattie says, "you and him got things to work out, but I'm thinking you'll be okay. A lot of things aren't what they seem."

Beth knows, somehow, that Mattie is talking about Alan, not Dan. She studies the contents of her mug as if there might be leaves there she could read, but there is only opaque brownness. She can't predict the future. And neither can Mattie.

Mattie picks up *Endless Night,* fans the pages one way, then the other. "Good story."

"Haven't had time to finish it yet."

"Don't wanna spoil it for you, but when you're about halfway through, you think you've got it all figured out." Mattie lays down the book. "Then, at the end, you find out that nothing – not one thing – was what it seemed to be."

Beth looks over the rim of her mug. "At least Agatha Christie's always logical."

Mattie snorts. "You sound like Katherine." She studies the weaving. "All that logical stuff you and Katherine and Agatha like so much is just one part: the warp. The weft is the mystery. Leave out either one and the whole story unravels."

Beth rubs a thumb along the arched back of the carving. "I dreamed last night that I drowned."

"Spose you came close. Not a good idea, going out with him again."

"I jumped into the water to save a girl in a yellow dress," Beth says carefully. "Someone had pushed her off a pier."

Mattie stops mid-rock. "Come on, Muin. Time to go." She stands and pulls on her slicker and hat, ties the straps under her chin. "Guess you'll be heading back to St. John's as soon as this rain lets up."

Beth reaches awkwardly to hug her, then holds up the otter. "Thanks."

"I'm just the messenger, love."

After she closes the door behind Mattie and Muin, Beth places the carving on the table and goes to the bedroom to finish packing. Closes her eyes when she sees the feather on the chair. The owl had clacked its bill at her last night, warned her. She just didn't heed the warning.

She shakes out the sleeping bag and stuffs it into the sleeve, punching it harder than she needs to. When she pulls the drawstring tight, a familiar discontent takes hold: nothing between her and Alan has changed just because Dan rejected her.

The sleeping bag slips from her hands. The gaping hole in her chest is not from missing Alan, or from Dan's humiliating rejection, but from a different kind of absence.

CHAPTER 29

The heavy rain let up hours ago, but Beth has waited until mid-afternoon to drive into town. Because she doesn't know yet what to say to Alan, how to explain to him why she has to stay. She doesn't understand it herself.

Monday afternoon. She considers calling the home phone instead of the clinic or his cell, then she could just leave a message. She wouldn't have to answer his questions.

The light mist is just heavy enough that she has to keep the wipers on. When she gets to the Irving, she sees a small sign taped to the phone cubicle. She has to get out of the car to read it: *Out of Order.* A message from the universe. Her whole life is out of order.

She knows there's a pay phone outside the Morning Glory but worries that Dan might be there.

She cruises slowly past the library, the Bide-a-Wee, the churches, the liquor store, and Price Chopper. Doesn't see a phone cubicle anywhere. Turns around and goes back to the Bide-a-Wee. Every motel has a pay phone, doesn't it? Circling the parking lot, she almost wishes she'd see the black pickup parked behind the motel, in the middle of the day, out of sight. Then she'd have an easy story to tell herself about what kind of man Dan is. She could focus all the scattered energy of humiliation into outrage and disgust, could be grateful she'd dodged a tawdry affair. But she doesn't see the pickup. Or a phone.

Left with no other choice, she drives to the café. Slides out of the car and stands by the silver metal box. Mist dots her glasses. There is a small spider web in the bottom corner of the cubicle, the silk strands perfectly outlined with tiny drops of water. A struggling daddy-long-legs is enmeshed in the centre. Beth wants to pluck it from the web, to effect a rescue. She pulls at one long leg; it comes off in her fingers.

She leans her forehead against the phone, listens to the dial tone. Finally punches in the numbers of her calling card and the home phone.

Don't pick up, Alan. I don't know what to say. Please pick up. Please. I need you now.

The answering machine comes on. Tears well, but she's not sure if they're from relief or loneliness. "Hi, Alan. Things are–"

"Hi. Hope you're calling to tell me you're on your way home."

"Well ..." Beth almost sobs. "The research is going okay, but–"

"What's wrong?"

"Nothing," she says quickly. "There's just a lot to tell you." But how will she ever begin? More important, how will she end? "But everything can wait until I get home. I just wanted to let you know that I have to stay just a little longer. More research."

"More research? I thought you said you had enough to write your proposal."

"I still need just a few more samples. From out by the ocean," she adds. "Should be just a few more days."

"You sure there's nothing wrong?"

Beth can't discern whether it's suspicion or worry she hears in his voice. Maybe it's her own guilt whispering.

"You still there?"

"Yes." She watches the spider creep toward the daddy-long-legs still struggling to pull itself free. "What are you doing home on a Monday afternoon?"

"Knocked off work a little early."

"You feeling okay?"

"Just needed some time."

Time for what? "Alan ..."

"I miss you," he says.

She can hear the deep truth of it in his voice.

A long sigh. "But you need to do what you need to do," he says. "Stay as long as you need to. But no longer. Call me before you leave. And be careful on the drive home. And watch for moose."

She runs her fingertips along the ribbed metal cord tethering her to the phone. Comfort in the rituals, in the unneeded admonitions to be careful. But a genuine caring too.

"Promise me you'll be careful, Beth."

"I promise."

"Because I love you."

"I love you too." For the first time in a long time she feels like that could be true. She hangs up the receiver. A soft click in the cradle.

~

Beth picks up the carved otter and strokes the tapered tail. Thinks about walking to the otter spot just to get out of the cabin for a while. She's done enough thinking about Alan. She felt some clarity when she hung up the phone, but she still doesn't know how to explain to him the emptiness she feels. She can't explain it to herself.

The heavy overcast makes it seem later than it is. Only 16:05. Early for otters to be out and about, but she could go out in the kayak and look for signs, anything she might have missed in all her previous searches. She has to do something. She fills her water bottle at the pump and packs her backpack.

Paddling south from the cabin, she slows when she gets to the otter spot. Scans the shoreline: no fresh scats to indicate they've been here in the last day or two. She continues south around the small bay then heads out into the middle of the pond and circumnavigates two small islands. Finds nothing but the ever-present bare rock and scrubby spruce, sandpipers probing the shallows. When she crosses to the west shore, she spots some fresh scats and a small rubbing site about fifty metres north of Mattie's cabin. She lands the kayak and makes notes in her journal, but resists the temptation to take any samples. The last thing she wants is to have to go back to Dan's again.

Beth slides back into the kayak. Another hour of slow paddling and she is at Medicine Rock. The water in the outlet is high from all the rain, noisy as it pushes against and around the rocks. She lays the paddle across the bow and closes her eyes. Christ, was it just last night that she was here with Dan? It feels like a lifetime ago. She wishes it were a lifetime ago.

She lands the kayak near the tall maroon boulder she mistook for Medicine Rock. The overcast has descended as light fog. She can see only one clear boundary: a jade ribbon of spruce and fir separates grey sky from grey rock and grey water. Beth wipes her glasses on a corner of her shirt, slides them back on. The view doesn't change.

She walks back into the tangle of spruce and fir and, within a few minutes, finds herself standing before the cairn, staring at the ochre rock on top and the word "hope." Beth cannot reconcile the Mattie she knows now with the hopeless young woman, girl really, who built this cairn for her brother, and then sacrificed her entire youth to care for his damaged girlfriend. Mattie should be a tragic figure, but she's not, even after nearly seven decades of grieving. How could building a cairn and painting a rock have helped her?

Beth picks up the brown and white feather, smoothes it with a soft f-f-fth. She went to Alice's memorial service, even took charge of planning it, but none of that helped. All she could feel then – all she can feel now – are anger and loss. For Alice's suffering and for all the years stolen from their friendship.

When Beth finally looks up, she is surrounded by dense fog. She carefully places the feather between the two rocks, then turns and starts off toward Medicine Rock, listening hard for the sound of rushing water. Can't hear any, and the undergrowth and mounds of moss look unfamiliar. She turns and retraces her steps back to the cairn. Looks again at the ochre rock, the fragmented word, and the brown and white feather. She hears a chirp, an answer, and then a snort. She turns toward the sounds and begins walking. Everything looks just the same, the undergrowth, the mounds of moss, all unfamiliar, but before she's gone twenty paces she hears the river, and in another minute she is standing beside the kayak. She looks around, hoping to spot the otters, but she cannot see beyond a few metres, can hear nothing but churning water.

She rummages in the backpack for a flashlight, flicks it on, and secures it under the elastic cords on the bow to make the kayak more visible to anyone else caught out in the fog. If she hugs the shoreline, it will lead her right back to her cabin. Shoving off, she takes one last look at the real Medicine Rock. In the fog and twilight, it looks completely ordinary. Nothing special about it at all.

She paddles slowly through an eerie silence. The shorebirds have stopped piping. No chickadees, nuthatches, or juncos call out, no raucous jays or crows. No chattering red squirrels. No hum of a motor. Not even wind rustling birch leaves. Only the soft gurgle of water as it parts for the kayak and the paddle. She hugs the shore so closely the hull grazes barely submerged rocks. The loud scraping is unnerving. She feels alone, like the last living being on earth.

She hears it then: the faint sounds of a flute, a series of trills and twitters, repeated again and again. The

237

high-pitched notes are coming from in front of her. Abruptly, the music stops. Beth peers into the fog and can see a dim glow up ahead – like another kayak or canoe with a flashlight attached. She paddles cautiously toward the light. The soft glow becomes larger, then as suddenly as the music stopped, the light goes out. Beth stops paddling, drifts. Nothing now but dense fog. And dark silence.

The bow of the kayak bumps against the metal pole of a pier. Beth sees the stern of an aluminum canoe and looks up to the right. The soft glow is moving up toward what must be Mattie's cabin, and then it goes out again. Beth beaches the kayak beside the canoe and flicks off the flashlight, climbs the path. She hears Muin run to the door and bark, and when Mattie opens it, she is wearing the blue baseball cap.

Mattie takes a step back and opens the door wider. "You're shivering, love. Come in now and have a cup a tea. Kettle's already boilt."

"Thanks for the light," Beth says.

"Seen the kayak crossing the pond earlier. Thought you might need it."

"You weren't, by any chance, playing a flute?" The question, spoken aloud, sounds absurd.

Mattie laughs. "No, love."

"Matilda then?"

"She don't know how to play." Mattie sets a steaming mug on the table. "Come on now. Sit down. You looks half froze." She picks up a block of wood and sits down in the rocker. The floor around her is littered with curled shavings.

Still wearing her life-jacket, Beth sits down at the table. Muin settles beside her, the weight of her head on Beth's feet. Beth wraps her chilled hands around the mug. "I could have sworn I heard a flute."

Mattie flicks a shaving to the floor. "Probably did."

"No, must've been a bird, its song distorted by the fog. Could've been a winter wren, I suppose. Kind of sounded like one."

"You keeps getting in your own way." Mattie lays the wood and the knife in her lap and holds up a thumb and a forefinger, measuring off half an inch. "You needs that little bit a proof. When really, girl, it's all around us."

"Proof of what?"

"Mystery. Sure, for all your science, you wants to believe in mystery too."

Beth unzips the life-jacket and slides it off. "Dan says just the opposite. Tells me I'm creating a big mystery out of things that have a simple explanation."

Mattie snorts. "What's he know?" She interlaces her fingers, moves them apart. "Think about it. How many assumptions do you have to make for his version of things to work out?"

The kerosene lamp flares. The shadows on the wall lengthen.

"Not one of them assumptions can be proved," she continues. "But that don't bother you. Cause they're all *logical.* But making the single assumption that there's mystery in the world? *That* bothers you." She picks up the knife and the wood again. The blade glints in the lamplight.

"But once you open that door, you can believe in anything."

"Yep. Can't always know what's possible. Or impossible." Mattie waves the knife at Beth. "To make it easier, maybe you can just think of mystery as the stuff we don't know yet ... and maybe can't know."

Beth lifts the heavy mug. Sips the red tea. It tastes like rosehips. She watches the steam curl upward. "Dan showed me the real Medicine Rock last night," she says. "I didn't expect it to be so ... ordinary."

Mattie drops another shaving to the floor. "I don't really know why, but I'm guessing that's cause people long ago knew that mystery lives side by side with the ordinary." She shrugs. "Or maybe it's just cause they knew that every rock can be a Medicine Rock."

Muin stretches in her sleep, lets out a series of small woofs. She flicks her front paws as if she is dreaming of paddling through water.

"You like the carving?" Mattie says.

"I can't really see what you're working on."

"Not this one. The one Matilda brought over."

Beth runs a finger around the rim of the mug. Clears her throat. "It's beautiful," she says softly.

"She told me about your dream." Mattie angles the knife to make a deep gouge, the tip of her tongue showing at the corner of her mouth. "The one where I drownded."

Beth shifts in the chair. Pulls her life-jacket back on.

"She can't forgive herself for that." She looks up at Beth, eyes shadowed by the bill of the cap. "Maybe you can help her."

"Help her?"

Mattie lays the wood and the knife aside. "Matilda never meant no harm. Not really. I forgave her a long time ago, but Emma ...? She's another story."

"But I thought you saved Emma."

"Matilda did. Sort of. But only her and me, and Emma, knows the whole of it. And Emma can't forgive her."

"For what? I thought you took care of her for twenty years."

Mattie picks up the pipe and the pouch of tobacco. "It's a long story, love, so if you gots to rush off to collect more shit or something, now's not a good time."

"No, no, it's okay." Beth's words are tentative.

Mattie reaches into the pouch, takes out a big pinch of tobacco, and packs it into the bowl. "Emma's father thought I were plenty good enough to swing a hammer, plant a rosebush, or mow his grass ... but not near good enough for his daughter." She slides a match from the box. "Don't know how he found out about us, but when he did, he forbid her to have anything to do with me."

She strikes the match and holds it to the pipe, inhales a few shallow draws. The tobacco glows red. "So we was planning to run off." She shakes her head, slowly. "And damned if Matilda didn't want to come with us. Thought she couldn't live without me." Mattie pushes the cap to the back of her head. "And who knows? Maybe she were a little bit in love with Emma herself."

Beth pulls the life-jacket closer, zips it against the chill.

"We're two halves of a whole, see, so I knew exactly what she'd do." Her words are a cloud of grey smoke. "If we didn't agree to take her with us, she'd go to Emma and threaten to tell her father about us running off."

Beth takes a mouthful of tea, sweet and bitter.

"So when I seen she was gone," Mattie continues, "I went after her in the canoe. Seen them on the pier, arguing. And I guess you knows the rest."

Beth mis-swallows and nearly chokes.

"I jumped in after Emma. But I can't swim, see." Mattie's thin smile is wistful. "And Matilda wasted too much time trying to find me when she should've been looking for Emma. She didn't know Emma'd hit her head on the pier."

CHAPTER 30

Beth sits in the rocking chair and watches the sky, the clouds above the rising sun glowing pink and tangerine. A restless night, but at least there'd been no dreams of yellow dresses or blue caps. She spent hours, though, turning from one side to the other, punching the pillow, kicking off the sleeping bag then pulling it back on, all the while trying to puzzle out why Mattie told her about her role in the drowning. Sixty-five years of guilt? But Clive and Dan both claimed that Mattie rescued Emma, not pushed her.

Beth rubs her temples. Feels a headache coming on. So why did she dream it that way? And what in the world is she supposed to do to help?

~

She spends the morning in the kayak poking around the pond, trying to convince herself that she's doing something useful, that she has a reason to be here. By mid-afternoon she's famished. She paddles back to the cabin and checks the box of food she packed the day before: half a bar of dark chocolate, Skippy, a few saltines, a tin of sardines, rolled oats, and the box of Milk-Bones, nearly empty now. Cheese and bread in the cooler. Every bit of it unappetizing. She decides to drive into town.

On her way out of the cabin, Beth picks up the carving. She places the otter on the front seat of the Toyota and touches it now and again as she drives. She stops at the Irving to fill up the car and sees that the *Out of Order* sign is gone from the pay phone, but there's no one she wants to call. Not yet anyway.

Just as she's pulling out, Beth sees the black pickup approaching. Her stomach lurches. The truck comes closer. Dan nods. Beth lifts one finger from the steering wheel to acknowledge his nod. The truck passes, heading out of town.

So this is what her grand passion comes to? The lift of a finger, a nod. She almost laughs at herself. Almost.

She parks at the Morning Glory, and before she gets out of the car, she runs her fingertips over the carving, as if for good luck. Or a thank you. At least now she doesn't have to worry about running into Dan here.

She is just sliding out of the car when she hears the crunch of gravel behind her. The door of the black pickup creaks open. Dan leans out, holding the door between them like a shield. "Knew by all that shit still in my freezer that you hadn't left yet." He has one foot out of the truck, the other still in, as if he needs to be ready to pull his foot back in and slam the door, quickly.

"S-sorry," Beth says. "Just another day or two."

"No worries. Just teasing." He opens the hand gripping the steering wheel and then closes it again. Looks at his knuckles and opens the door a little wider. "Just wanted you to know that I meant what I said about helping with your research. That's the most interesting thing I've done since I came back here."

"Thanks," Beth says. "I guess."

"Almost makes me feel like I might be doing something useful." He looks away and adjusts his cap, as if embarrassed by his admission. "Even if I'm not, at least it's fun. And that counts for something."

"I guess."

"So you'll let me know when you come back this fall?"

"Sure."

"And if you get that grant, you'll be needing an assistant. Lots of ponds around here with otters. Good fishing too. I'd like to help keep it that way." He pulls his foot in and closes the door. Starts backing out, then rolls down the window. "See ya," he calls out.

Beth stands for a long minute and stares at the receding tailgate, trying to take in what just happened. So it comes to more than just the lift of a finger and a nod: it comes to one more person who gives a damn. Maybe that's not so bad.

She is smiling when she opens the screen door. Clive gives her a lopsided grin and a nod. Sliding into the booth, she glances at the congealed gravy on his plate. "That the special today?"

The left side of his mouth turns down. "Roast pork and mashed potatoes," he says slowly. "Wouldn't recommend it."

The skinny waitress brings a glass of water and a menu. "I'll just have the soup and a salad please," Beth says. "Vinaigrette on the side."

"How's things with the otters?" Clive articulates each word carefully.

"Good," she says. "I think I have what I need for now. Enough to write a proposal anyway."

"Proposal?"

"I'm hoping to get funding to do more research here."

"So you're planning to come back?" he says.

"Hope so," Beth says. "And even if I don't get funding, we'll still come out to the cabin now and again."

"How're you finding that old place?" He picks up his cup, hand shaking.

"Cabin needs repairs, but it's a beautiful spot."

"It is that." Clive lifts the cup to his lips. When he sets it down, tea slops onto the saucer.

"Guess we'll have to decide whether to fix it up," Beth says, "or tear it down and build something new."

"Hate to see that old place go."

"That's what Mattie said."

"Lotsa memories for her there."

"More than forty years of friendship," she says. "I guess it would be hard to see that go." She picks up the glass of water.

Clive fixes his one good eye on her. "Not just memories of Katherine," he says. "That's where Emma lived after. Where Mattie took care of her."

Beth almost drops the glass. Cannot stop the cascade of dream images: an angry young woman in a yellow dress searching the cabin, throwing pots and pans, stabbing her journal. A girl in a yellow dress tumbling from the pier.

"Too many memories maybe," he says. "Not long after Emma died, Mattie sold that cabin to Katherine. Moved into the one she's in now."

The waitress brings the order and sets down the bowls and cutlery. Beth stares at the bits of celery and onion floating amidst rice and small squares of chicken. "Did Katherine ever mention anything about ghosts in the cabin?" she asks quietly.

"Ghosts?" Clive frowns. "Katherine was a history teacher. She didn't go in for that kinda thing."

Beth picks up a fork and pokes at lettuce swimming in oily vinaigrette. "Did you actually see the accident? When Matthew drowned?"

Clive shakes his head. "Only ones actually seen it was Mattie and Emma's little sister, Lily. She come running outta the house when she heard the screams."

"How did it happen anyway?"

"Way I heard it, Matthew and Emma was out fishing. Or maybe they was just sneaking off for a little time together." Clive tries to wink his left eye. It closes only halfway.

"Both of them?"

"That's the way I heard it. Canoe overturned somehow

and Matthew drownded. Couldn't swim, see."

"Nothing else?"

His good eye stares off to the side. "Only that Mattie managed to save Emma. Now she could swim, but she'd hit her head somehow when the canoe overturned. That's what Lily saw. Mattie holding Emma in her arms."

"Why was Mattie even there?"

"Jealous, see. Probably spying on em."

Beth folds the corner of a napkin. "Do you remember anything about there being an argument between Mattie and Emma?"

"Never heard nothing about that," he says, "but Mattie being Mattie, she probably did fight with Emma." He pushes his heavy glasses up on the bridge of his nose. "I were just a youngster at the time, about the same age as Lily. Big news for a while, but then talk died down. As it always does."

He lifts the cup to his mouth. A brown drop falls from the cup to the table. He sets down the cup with a loud clink. "I do remember that only a handful of folks went to Emma's wake. Guess everybody felt like she'd already been dead for twenty years."

Beth stares at the drop of tea on the Formica tabletop. "Where was she waked?"

"In your cabin."

Clive reaches for his cane and pushes himself to his feet. "Well now, you have a safe trip back to the big city." He lifts a finger. "And watch for moose."

CHAPTER 31

Beth unlocks the cabin door, slowly, and wonders where, exactly, Emma was waked. Probably in the middle of the living room. Maybe under the weaving. She's always assumed Mattie made it for Katherine. Maybe she made it for Emma. A peace offering.

She turns away from the door, reminding herself, once again – just like she did a hundred times on the long drive from town – that it doesn't matter that Emma died in the cabin and was waked in the living room.

She looks at her watch: 18:42. Two hours until dark. She could leave for St. John's right now. She closes her eyes. No, she cannot let things she doesn't believe in send her scuttling back to the city. She'll sit outside and watch the sunset, then go to bed early. Pack up and leave first thing in the morning.

Beth goes inside and grabs a jacket and binoculars. Walks down to the water. The slanting light coming from behind her gilds the spruce and fir across the pond. To the north, loons call, probably the mated pair with their youngster. The yodels echo across the quiet water. She breathes deeply, pulling in the scent of fresh water and balsam.

Two ravens fly overhead, almost wingtip to wingtip. One veers away from the other and turns in a spiral. The other dips a wing, then it too spirals. It looks as if they are playing, delighting in the warmth and golden light of a summer's evening.

It looks as if. Always *as if.* Beth wishes she could know.

She hears a chirp, then another. Raises her binoculars and spots them about thirty metres away. Brown heads all in a line. With their tails arched and just breaking the water, they look like a multi-humped sea monster. They swim closer. Beth can hear their steady *uhn-uhn-uhns*. She scans the group for the two pups and the old scar-nosed female. One. Two. Three. All there, along with three others. They seem like old friends now, and Beth imagines that they've come to watch her. Maybe the otters have a whole catalogue of observations and they sit around debating why humans do what they do. *Uhn-uhn-uhn, uhn-uhn-uhn.* Good luck with that.

They approach to within a few metres. Beth knows they see her, undoubtedly smell her too, but they don't seem alarmed.

Uhn-uhn-uhn, uhn-uhn-uhn. Relaxed conversation. What *are* they saying?

Two otters, small but larger than the pups, come out of the water and stamp their back feet. Each leaves a black scat: gifts. More samples to collect if she wants them. She's so close she can smell the musk, and can tell by the way they urinate that both are probably females. Maybe Mattie is right: they're sisters, both daughters of the old grandmother. They slip back into the water and a pup and the old female come out. They begin to groom, themselves and then each other. The others dive and catch fish, eat them in the water, bones crunching. Two begin to wrestle, rolling and tumbling, splashing and chirping. A third joins in. Beth grins.

They do nothing out of the ordinary. No words come into Beth's head, and there are no strange behaviours or vocalizations: just otters being otters. No worries about their partners being fine or about accomplishing anything worthwhile in their lives. No worries about the fate of the earth. Who wouldn't feel *joie de vivre* when you're content just to be?

Beth lowers the binoculars. But she can't really know what they're thinking, whether they're worried or not. We're all trapped in our own heads. Can't even know each other's minds – Alan's, Dan's, Mattie's – let alone those of another species. Maybe otters do worry about the fate of the earth. Maybe animals know things we don't, things we cannot know and can never know.

The pup leaves the old grandmother, enters the water, and joins the wrestling. The old female turns toward Beth, stares at her for a full minute, then slowly approaches, moving her head up and down, sniffing the air. Beth can see her nostrils move. The otter puts her black nose to Beth's shoe, backs up and snorts, then leans forward and pokes the shoe with her muzzle. *Uhn-uhn-uhn, uhn-uhn-uhn.* Beth doesn't move, doesn't make a sound, but her heart is galloping. The otter takes a few steps forward and sniffs the back of Beth's hand. The long whiskers tickle. *Uhn-uhn-uhn, uhn-uhn-uhn.* Standing upright, she lays one webbed paw on Beth's shoulder and gently pokes her cheek with her silvery muzzle, the whiskers brushing Beth's face like a spider web. She sniffs at Beth's eye, her eyebrow, and then at her ear. *Uhn-uhn-uhn, uhn-uhn-uhn.*

For just a moment, Beth can see herself through the otter's eyes. Not her greying hair or her sunburnt nose, but the profound sadness and worry written in the lines around her mouth and eyes. Beth can smell it too, an acrid pungency like mildew. She wrinkles her nose against it, but then feels comfort in the paw on her shoulder, in the nuzzles to her ear. The taut cords behind her breastbone uncoil, and she feels light, as if she could float on the breeze like a feather. The pungent odour dissipates, replaced by the cinnamon sweetness of wild roses.

The old grandmother drops down and galumphs back to the water. And Beth is back in herself. Can smell only the otters' musk and the evergreen fragrance from the carpet of needles beneath her.

A minute later they all swim off in their sea-monster formation, disappearing into the dusk. Beth sits and watches until the last of the golden light has faded. She cannot take in what has just happened. It feels significant, full of meaning. But what meaning? She hears Mattie's voice whispering, but isn't sure if it's in her own head or in the wind or in the small wavelets caressing the shore: *A whole new way of being alive to this world.*

The sky darkens to indigo and a chill creeps into her joints and back. Beth rises awkwardly on legs gone numb and climbs the path to the cabin. When she reaches the door, she spins around and goes to the Toyota. Grabs the carving from the front seat.

Inside, she lights the lamp and places the carving on the table. She digs her journal out of her backpack. Picks up a pencil: *17 Aug 10: ~18°C, clear, winds light, observed from shore in front of cabin, A1, 18:46 to 20:50, 6 otters approached from south at 19:08.* She writes quickly, trying to capture every detail: *The old female touched my shoulder with a front paw and then sniffed my face and my ear, grunting the whole time.*

Beth taps the pencil on the page, chews the eraser, then writes: *Their visit felt like a blessing.* She draws a line through *felt*, replaces it with *feels.* Then crosses out the entire sentence. Writes: *THEIR VISIT IS A BLESSING.* She stares into the lamplight. Mattie's right: the otters are more than she can ever know, more than anyone can ever know.

She flicks through the journal, turning pages marred by dirty smudges and crinkled by drying raindrops. With a renewed sense of purpose, she begins to outline a research proposal. She wants nothing more right now than to be able to spend days and days just watching them, trying to learn some of what they know about being alive.

Beth works for more than an hour, until she comes to the bottom of the last blank page. She closes the journal, lays it on the table, and then checks to make sure the door is locked. She picks up the carved otter and places it on the chair beside the bed. Feels oddly comforted by the thought that the old grandmother is watching over her.

~

When she came close to the watcher, the old female could detect no scent of harm, only femaleness and sadness. The otters went away then, to fish and to play, but on their way back to the lodge, the old one returned to this place. She can still smell the strong scent of human, but also something high and sweet in the nose, the scent of now, the fragrance of joy.

The otters swim toward the lodge. The old female chirps. Her grey muzzle nudges a pup's belly, pokes his cheek. Paws reach to grab. The female pup joins them. They twist and turn in the water, rolling in somersaults. Then come onshore and chase each other over rocks. Over and around. And then back into the water.

The moon is high above. The old female rises up through ebony water, breaks through the surface of one world and into another. Silver drops fall from her whiskers. She's surrounded by shimmering ripples as five other heads surface. Amber eyeshine all around. They come out onto the grass and rub bellies and chins. Turn on their backs and rub themselves dry in this world of earth and rock and grass. They enter the lodge one by one, touch each other's muzzles. Scent of daughters, mothers, sisters, brother. Scent of one pup, two. *Uhn-uhn-uhn, uhn-uhn-uhn.*

CHAPTER 32

Beth awakens to the sounds of strong winds whipping through the birches. Woven within the wind, a sweet voice is singing a lullaby, the strains so faint she could not make out the words if the song were not so familiar: *Too-ra-loo-ra-loo-ral, Too-ra-loo-ra-li, Too-ra-loo-ra-loo-ral, Hush, now don't you cry.* The song she crooned to Rachel in the middle of sleepless nights.

Alert now, she lies perfectly still. Can hear only the wind and the creak of the rocking chair, back and forth, back and forth. She stands, heart thudding, and tiptoes to the doorway. The rocking chair is empty. But still rocking. The living room window is open and the wind is blowing against the back of the chair.

Beth breathes out and steps to the window. The chill wind makes her shiver. She lowers the sash. Lays a hand on the back of the chair, then sees the journal lying on top of the half-finished puzzle. The wind has flipped open the back cover. Beth reaches to close it, but sees the scrawls: *Matthew d 1943 at 17; b 1926. Emma d about 1962 or 63.* She still hasn't figured out when she wrote that. She holds the page closer to the window, turns it left and then right, upside down, and then finally, right side up again, until she's pretty sure the last few scribbles are *b* and *d, 1944.*

She looks out the window again and sees two women walking away. The wind is blowing one woman's long pale hair sideways. Her arms are wrapped around a bundle and she shakes her head to clear the hair away from her face; she is wearing the yellow dress with the huge pink roses. A tall woman with copper curls has an arm draped around the other's slender shoulders. She throws back her head and laughs, then turns and looks back over her shoulder.

Beth runs to the door and fumbles to unlock it. She throws it open, but they are gone. Simply gone. In bare feet and T-shirt, she runs toward the place where they disappeared, but it's Muin who emerges from the trees. She barks at Beth. Backs up and barks again.

"Is something wrong?"

Muin whines and then barks.

"Something with Mattie?"

Beth runs inside and pulls on clothes and shoes, then bolts out the door. Halfway to Mattie's, she stumbles on a root, falls, and scrapes her knee through her jeans. Muin comes back and pulls at her jacket. Beth is gasping by the time she reaches the cabin. She leaps up the steps and flings open the door. Mattie is slumped at the table, arms folded beneath her head.

Muin nudges Mattie's elbow. She slowly straightens.

"Oh my god," Beth wheezes, "are you okay?" Her heart is pumping so hard her chest hurts. Her side aches. "Is something wrong?"

"No, love, something is right."

Beth leans against the chair, still trying to catch her breath. She sinks down onto it.

Mattie turns and raises a finger. "I know."

"What?" Beth says cautiously.

Mattie rolls her shoulders and stretches as if just waking up. "Looks like you could use some tea," she says. She points her chin toward the counter. "And I've got some raisin squares going stale. Think you could choke one down?" She stands and shuffles to the counter. Muin follows. Mattie pulls a teabag from the Red Rose box, puts it into a mug, and pours in steaming water. She scoops a raisin square onto a plate, considers, then adds a second one before setting the plate and the mug on the table. Following the raisin squares, Muin sits attentively at Beth's knees.

Beth stares at the plate. Hears the wind testing the clapboard.

"What?" Mattie says. "You think there's poison in them too?"

"It's not that."

"What then?"

Beth rubs her scraped knee. "You said you know. What do you know?"

"What you learned from the otters last night."

"But how could you?"

"Just do." Mattie looks out the window, then back at Beth. "Your dreams don't belong just to you."

"I wasn't dreaming."

Mattie shrugs. "Asleep. Awake. It's all the same." She brings a mug to the table and sits down across from Beth.

Beth stares into the steaming tea. Wonders if she is in a dream. Maybe everything that happened last night, everything that's happening this morning is all a dream. She rubs her scraped knee again. It hurts. She lifts the mug. The hot tea scalds her lips. No, she is not in a dream. She wraps her hands around the mug, needs something solid to hold onto. She takes a small bite of the square and chews slowly. Muin whimpers, her gaze going back and forth between Beth's face and her plate.

Beth swallows. "The other night," she says, "why did you tell me what you did about the drowning?"

Mattie watches her over the rim of her mug. "I didn't tell you anything," she says quietly.

Beth runs her tongue over her teeth. "Mattie?"

Mattie sets the mug on the table and turns toward the birdfeeders just outside the window. "You'll have to ask Matthew."

"He said that I should help you. How?"

Muin goes to Mattie and licks her hands. Mattie stares at the birdfeeders, now occupied by two juncos, buffeted by the wind but clinging tight. Absently, her fingers work through the fur around the dog's ears. Three chickadees and a purple finch come and go. Muin looks at Beth, then back to Mattie. She circles and settles on the floor.

"I know what you've seen in your dreams." Mattie leans forward in the chair and puts her elbows on her knees. "That I'm no hero, that it's my fault they all died."

"All?" Beth takes a small bite of the raisin square.

Mattie closes her eyes, hands clasped so tightly her fingertips are red against her white knuckles. "One day – late winter it was – Emma just lay on her side all day, curled up and moaning." She opens her eyes and stares down at her hands. "I thought it was stomach cramps. So I made her some teas and bundled her up to take to the outhouse. That's when I saw she was all bloody down there. When I went to change the sheets, there she was." She rubs her hands together, pulls them apart. "I thought she was stillborn, but then she curled a tiny finger."

The square is a sweet gooey paste in Beth's mouth.

"Had to be a seven-month child at least, but no bigger than a newborn pup." Mattie leans her forehead into her clasped hands as if she is praying. "I washed her and bundled her. Even tried to squeeze milk from Emma's breasts and give it to her in an eyedropper, but she never took more than a few drops. I made weak teas of anything I could think of that might strengthen her." She holds out her arms like a cradle. "And I never stopped holding her."

Beth cannot move, even to take a swallow of tea to wash the paste from her mouth. The strange notes in her journal: *b* and *d, 1944.*

"She opened her eyes just once. Stared at me for the longest time, as if she knew everything: why she had no mama, no papa, why she was dying." Mattie shakes her head. "Only lived for three days."

"And you named her Hope," Beth says woodenly. "And she's buried under the cairn near Medicine Rock."

Mattie balls a fist, knocks it against the table. "If only I'd known earlier and been prepared, I might've been able to save her."

"She was too little, Mattie. You couldn't have saved her."

"Emma's belly was hardly swelled. She didn't even seem to know. When she was alive." Mattie smoothes the skin on her cheeks with both hands. "But after Emma died, she started visiting, angry I'd let her baby die."

She turns to Beth, and for the first time Beth sees fear and anguish in Mattie's eyes. "Or maybe she was just angry that I didn't let her and the baby drown with Matthew." Mattie looks away. "Or that I'd ever pushed her at all."

"And it was in Katherine's cabin that Emma came to you?" The question hangs in the air, a tangled thread. Beth watches Mattie, doesn't want to see the nod.

"Katherine never saw her." Mattie smiles ruefully. "She couldn't see ghosts."

"I think I heard her this morning," Beth says softly. She hears her own words as if they belong to someone else. "Rocking, and singing to the baby."

Mattie closes her eyes. "Maybe that poor girl is finally at peace."

"Was probably just the wind," Beth says in a rush.

"No, love. Wasn't the wind."

"I'm not sure."

"Yes, you are."

"But …" But what? She heard that lullaby. She heard Alice's braying laugh. She saw them.

"Don't be getting in your own way."

Mattie stands and Muin stands with her. She lifts the blue baseball cap from the hook beside the door. Settles the cap on her head, then sits down again. "You're not done yet, you know." It's as if she has gone out the door and Matthew has taken her place at the table. "You have more work to do."

"But what about Hope?" Beth says. "We were talking about Emma and Hope."

As if his hands were made of lead, Matthew lifts them and lays the weight of them on the table. "Matilda worked and worked to save my baby girl. Even when she knew she couldn't, she kept on trying."

"Why name her Hope then?"

"Matilda chose that name ... she had to."

"But she died."

He looks at Beth, his eyes a deep, unfathomable green. "So did Alice." He pushes the pouch of tobacco toward Beth. "You needs to take some of this to where it belongs." Taps a finger on the pouch. "And a bit of prayer wouldn't go astray."

"Prayer?"

"It's not what you think," Matthew says. "It's not about talking, it's about listening." He grasps Beth's forearm. "It's just like the otters, girl. You finally listened to em. Now listen to everything else you love."

He releases her arm and waves his hand in a wide arc. "To the water, to the sky, to the earth. To Rachel and Alan ... and Alice." He winks. "Muin too." He reaches down to cup the dog's chin. "You got things to say, dontcha, girl." Her tail wags.

"It's all one weaving, one story." He sits back in the chair and tugs at the bill of the cap. "Don't need to say one word. Just listen. And then put your hand to the weaving, girl. Every little thread matters."

~

Beth stands beside Medicine Rock, her own Medicine Rock. In the noonday light it's the old man's profile she sees. Clutched in her hand are the three tobacco ties Matthew made for her. Each tie contains a pinch of tobacco wrapped in yellow calico, bound with a length of pink yarn.

Tmawei, he called it. And *nechwa*. Didn't explain.

Just put it down by the rock, he said. And listen. Tis a prayer all by itself.

Beth closes her eyes and breathes in the sweet scent of wild roses. Water is grumbling and complaining as it churns around rocks in its rush to the sea. The rocks hold fast. When she opens her eyes, she sees the juvenile eagle watching her from a tall spruce. Beth has interrupted its pursuit of lunch yet again. But maybe not. Maybe the young eagle is here for the same reason she is. And doesn't understand it any better than she does.

She lays one tobacco tie at the base of the rock. For her love of the earth and all wild things.

She turns and walks toward the cairn. That's where she'll put down the second tobacco tie, beside Alice's feather. For Hope and for hope. For all that we do not know and for the hope that lies in the heart of that unknowing.

The third one she will keep. A prayer all by itself. A reminder that Alice is still with her. And that she is laughing.

When she returns to this place, she'll have the right words. Or maybe she'll just listen. Maybe it's enough just to be. Here. Now.

Uhn-uhn-uhn, uhn-uhn-uhn: We are here, we are all here. We are.

Acknowledgments

Thanks:

to the Newfoundland & Labrador Arts Council and to the City of St. John's for supporting this novel;

to Marnie Parsons for her careful and insightful editing;

to all the good folks at Killick Press. They've been a pleasure to work with;

to the host of people who read and commented upon seriously flawed early drafts: Katie and Ken Pittman, Amy and Megan Kratz, Debra Durchslag, Denise Wildcat, Anna Kate Newman, Mark Callanan, Pat Byrne, and the Wisconsin Train Wreckers Writing Group – Michele Bergstrom, Tom Joseph, David Brainard, Joey Wojtusik, Mark Gaedtke, and Tara Nolan;

to Sharon Bala, who deserves a special thank you for offering not one, but two thorough readings, perceptive commentaries, and a number of long, inspirational conversations while hiking and snowshoeing in Bowring Park and on the East Coast Trails.

"Our world is filled with storms. Turbulent problems assail the lives of many. In the midst of these storms, you need an anchor that can give you stability. Jesus is that anchor. He empowers and emboldens all who trust in Him. In *Anchored in Jesus*, veteran pastor Johnny Hunt shows us how to find firm footing in any instable environment. I highly recommend this book."

Steve Gaines, PhD
Pastor, Bellevue Baptist Church, Memphis, TN

"My dear friend Johnny Hunt has written a book on Jesus from his heart, not his head. In these days filled with storm and strife, waves and wind, we all need an anchor that will hold. This book will not only anchor you to Jesus but the *real* Jesus—not the Jesus of Hollywood but heaven; not the cultural Jesus but the biblical Jesus; not the Jesus many want Him to be but the Jesus we all need Him to be. Whether you are in a storm, going into a storm, or coming out of a storm, you need to read this book!"

James Merritt
Pastor, Cross Pointe Church, Duluth, GA
Author, *52 Weeks with Jesus*

"Johnny Hunt is a walking illustration of the transforming life of Jesus Christ. The very title of this book, *Anchored in Jesus*, personifies his life story and the living legacy of his testimony. To this day, through his writing, speaking, and leading, Johnny motivates thousands upon thousands of people to win with Jesus daily. Get this book, read it, and share another copy with a friend!"

Dr. Ronnie Floyd
President/CEO, Southern Baptist Convention Executive Committee

"It is fitting that Johnny Hunt would write a book entitled *Anchored in Jesus* because that is exactly where he has been through the decades I have known and loved him. These words are not just some type of theoretical treatise but have been practically beaten out on the anvil of his personal experience."

O.S. Hawkins
President/CEO
GuideStone Financial Resources

"I am always blessed and encouraged by the teaching ministry of my dear friend Johnny Hunt. This book does that once again. *Anchored in Jesus* teaches us just how all-sufficient and wonderful our Savior is. This book will stir your heart and inspire a greater passion for King Jesus."

Danny Akin
President, Southeastern Baptist Theological Seminary
Wake Forest, NC

"Pastor Johnny Hunt has always been about Jesus! I am thankful for his latest book, *Anchored in Jesus*, which reminds us that Christ is enough and He still is the same yesterday, today and tomorrow. May this book ignite our hearts like the disciples who walked the road with Jesus, saying, "Did not our heart burn within us while He talked with us on the road…?" (Luke 24:32). You can hear His voice as you read this book: 'You are anchored in *Me*!'"

Jeff Crook
Pastor, Christ Place Church, Flowery Branch, GA

"In this topsy-turvy world, everyone needs an anchor as the winds and waves of life howl about us. My friend and beloved brother in Christ shares why an anchor is critical, but even more critical, why that anchor must be Jesus. Johnny eloquently describes how 'the peace that surpasses understanding' can only be found moored to the anchor secured by none other than the Creator of those winds and waves."

Sonny Perdue
United States Secretary of Agriculture

"Pastor Johnny has mentored thousands of pastors, including me, in what it means to serve Jesus as a faithful shepherd. You won't find a man in our generation more committed to God's Word, God's people, and God's Great Commission."

J.D. Greear, PhD
Pastor, The Summit Church, Raleigh-Durham, NC
President, Southern Baptist Convention

"While I have never served on active duty in the military, I have pastored in a Navy town for 29 years. The Navy anchor symbolizes no drifting while in wind or waves. Johnny Hunt will help you stand firm against the drifting current of our culture in his book *Anchored in Jesus*."

Ted Traylor
Senior Pastor, Olive Baptist Church, Pensacola, FL

ANCHORED IN JESUS

Johnny Hunt

HARVEST HOUSE PUBLISHERS
EUGENE, OREGON

Cover design by BEMA Creative

Original Cover Art by Chris Moore / Bema Creative

Anchored in Jesus
Copyright © 2019 by Johnny Hunt
Published by Harvest House Publishers
Eugene, Oregon 97408
www.harvesthousepublishers.com

ISBN 978-0-7369-7835-4 (pbk)
ISBN 978-0-7369-7836-1 (eBook)

Library of Congress Cataloging-in-Publication Data is on file at the Library of Congress, Washington, DC.

Printed in the United States of America

19 20 21 22 23 24 25 26 27 / BP-GL / 10 9 8 7 6 5 4 3 2 1

CONTENTS

Introduction: The Power of Living Daily in Jesus 7

1. Anchoring in the Real Jesus 11

Part 1: Jesus, the Only True Anchor

2. A Messiah Who Changes Everything 25

3. A Lord Who Deserves Devotion 43

4. A Savior Like No Other 61

5. A High Priest Who Breaks the Mold 77

6. How to Abide in Jesus 95

Part 2: Transformed by Jesus

7. Changed from the Inside Out 113

8. Keep the Ball in Play 129

9. The Greatest Power in the World 145

10. Do You Look Like Your Father? 161

Part 3: Winning in Jesus

11. Fight the Good Fight of Faith 181

12. Do What You Were Called to Do 199

Epilogue: Play to Win 215

Notes 221

THE POWER OF LIVING DAILY IN JESUS

The careers of both architects and mariners rise and fall on anchors. An architect uses the term to refer to the strong foundation in bedrock required for any large structure. A mariner uses it to refer to a physical anchor that keeps a ship in place so that it doesn't drift into harm's way. I believe we can learn something crucial from both of them.

If we hope to live successfully as followers of Jesus, we need a solid foundation that anchors us to bedrock. If we hope to finish well, we need a strong anchor to keep us from drifting into trouble.

For the Christian, that anchor is Jesus Himself.

Getting anchored in Jesus keeps us from getting "tossed to and fro and carried about with every wind of doctrine, by the trickery of men, in the cunning craftiness of deceitful plotting." Getting anchored in Jesus enables us to speak the truth in love so that we "may grow up in all things into Him who is the head—Christ" (Ephesians 4:14-15).

Getting anchored in Jesus will enable you and me to produce healthy fruit that yields a life of positive influence and godly character. Don't let anyone deceive you: what happens in private inevitably becomes public. All of us are constantly engaged in an internal battle that sooner or later goes external: "For the flesh lusts against the Spirit, and the Spirit against the flesh; and these are contrary to one another, so that you do not do the things that you wish" (Galatians 5:17).

Do you know of any man who feels frustrated that he's not doing the things that he longs to do? I'm sure you do; maybe you're even that man. How, then, can you become the man that Jesus calls you to be? Is it even possible, given this fierce battle between flesh and Spirit? I know it's possible—but only as you and I yield more and more to the staggering power of Christ.

Paul describes our situation like this: "Walk in the Spirit, and you shall not fulfill the lust of the flesh" (Galatians 5:16). In other words, as we invite God's Holy Spirit to fill us—as we make it a daily habit to walk in Jesus and to be controlled by Him—our lives start changing in amazing ways.

Sounds simple enough, doesn't it? But we all know it's no easy struggle! If we want to "walk in the Spirit," it will mean the battle of our lives. More than one godly person has told me, "The Christian life is not just difficult, it's impossible." Only a consistent experience of "Christ in us" will enable us to enjoy the hope of glory.

My whole world changed as a young man when I discovered that Jesus made available to me everything I need to access the divine power it takes to live in Him. "Encouragement fuels enthusiasm," it's said, and I feel thrilled to know that the same Lord who has called me to a life of obedience has also furnished me with the grace and power I need to live out that calling. All of this makes me wildly enthusiastic about the future.

And it can do the same for you.

In my early years after coming to faith in Jesus, I started learning dozens of key principles about my newfound relationship with God. Before Christ, my life consisted mostly of gambling, drinking, cursing, fighting, and the like. There wasn't much else. Charles H. Spurgeon, a famous English preacher from the 1800s, once said that when God saved him, he lost 80 percent of his vocabulary. For me, the percentage was probably more like 90 percent. At the beginning, that meant my testimony for Christ focused primarily on what I had to quit.

In time, however, godly men challenged me to think less about what I had to give up and more about what I had received. They asked me what had I started doing *right*, through Christ's power? I can't begin to explain what a difference that simple change in perspective has made.

To this day, it amazes me that when Christ came to live in me, the old started dying and the new sprang to life. I can personally testify that Jesus quite literally changes our desires. We start *wanting* to do what pleases Him. It's as though new sap starts coursing through our veins. God prunes off the old leaves and makes room for fresh growth.

Today my life is all about what I am becoming in Christ—the internal godliness, the external righteousness, the fruit of His Spirit—none of which I can produce on my own. It is no longer mostly about what I give up, but vastly more about what I have gained and about what I pursue.

Oh, how I want to become like Jesus! That's my goal, the end-game. Beyond question, the ultimate challenge of a life anchored in Jesus is becoming more like Christ.

Years ago, Eddie Carswell of Newsong wrote a chorus that I think captures it wonderfully:

Jesus, be Jesus in me,
No longer me, but thee,
Resurrection power, fill me this hour,
Jesus, be Jesus in me.[1]

Do you want that? I know I long to become more like Jesus, to increasingly reflect Christ in my day-to-day life. What other life is worth pursuing for any man who claims to follow Jesus? In fact, it's the *only* life worth seeking.

May God help you and me to pursue Jesus, to allow Him to transform us, and to fight the good fight in His power. And may His Spirit remind us daily that *everything* begins when we make sure we're anchored in Jesus.

1

ANCHORING IN THE REAL JESUS

At the end of the day, nothing is more important than knowing Jesus and being known by Him.

That's especially important today, because we live in an era of multiplying counterfeits. Counterfeit money, counterfeit designer brands, counterfeit identities, even counterfeit extra virgin olive oil (no, really). It's estimated these counterfeits cost the world economy hundreds of billions of dollars each year. None of these counterfeits, however, comes even close to the havoc created by counterfeit faith.

Never in history have we seen as many counterfeit versions of Jesus as we see today. If a church preaches a biblical truth that offends some people, they simply leave and look for a place that makes them feel more comfortable. Often that involves a counterfeit Jesus.

Does a holy, sin-hating Jesus offend you? Then seek a Jesus who never does anything to offend anyone. Is a fire-and-brimstone Jesus more your style? Lucky for you, it's not hard to find a group that fixates on divine judgment. Want a Jesus who promises you wealth and comfort? You can find that kind of counterfeit Christ nearly anywhere.

Of course, in order to embrace these counterfeits, we have to lay aside our Bibles. We have to exchange the real Jesus of Scripture for a counterfeit who will allow us to adopt a skewed belief to match our ungodly behavior.

Never before have I seen such a smorgasbord of "Jesus options" as I see today. And never in history have we more desperately needed to anchor ourselves in the real Jesus and His unchanging character as described in His eternal Word. Jesus is *the* greatest revelation of God, while the Bible is the second greatest revelation of God (next only to Jesus Himself). If you want to get anchored in Jesus, make sure you steer clear of some common counterfeits.

The "No Offense" Jesus

Many churches today invite you to come to their worship services, where you'll never have to worry about feeling offended or being made to feel bad. They champion the counterfeit Jesus who will never tell you anything you don't want to hear. These churches encourage you to define the truth as you see it and to apply that truth in a way that never requires you to change anything you do.

These groups have forgotten the word *repentance*—yet the real Jesus said, "Unless you repent you will all likewise perish" (Luke 13:3). Preachers of this counterfeit Christ must remain vigilant, because to maintain the lie they must skip or jump over countless obvious truths in Scripture. The mantra for these organizations when challenged on their teaching is, "Well, that's your interpretation."

Keep in mind, though, that the Bible was written in the language of the common man so that *everyone* could understand God's simple truths. Author Randy Alcorn often says, "A moment after we die we will know exactly how we should have lived." A proper perspective of death has a way of giving great clarity to how a man should live!

Clear, convicting biblical messages have often pointed out some sin in my own life. At these times, I begin to feel a sense of shame, guilt, and fear. Yet I'm so grateful that as I humble myself and repent of my sin, I receive God's unconditional forgiveness, mercy, and compassion. While many today look for a Jesus who will never make them feel guilty, I know that if I lack the capacity to sense any guilt, I will never experience divine conviction that leads me to seek God's grace. In His mercy, God loves me as I am; but He loves me too much to leave me as I am. God-prompted guilt can cause me to say, "Lord, please forgive me. I am wrong." I then move toward the person I sinned against and seek his or her forgiveness.

God used Holy Spirit-induced guilt to inspire the psalmist to write:

> Search me, O God, and know my heart;
> Try me, and know my anxieties;
> And see if there is any wicked way in me,
> And lead me in the way everlasting.
> (Psalm 139:23-24)

Thank God that the Holy Spirit convicts me of my guilt and offers me the grace of God. In the very first Sunday night service I ever attended, the Spirit convicted me of my sin, I was converted to Jesus, and became a follower of Christ.

The "Forget the Old Testament" Jesus

The morning after I came to faith, my wife purchased for me my first Bible. From day one, I fell in love with God's Word. It was all new to me, so revealing and refreshing. I soon read, in what many consider the greatest book of doctrine and theology in the entire Bible, something Paul wrote about the power and authority of Scripture:

> Now we know that whatever the law says, it says to those
> who are under the law, that every mouth may be stopped,
> and all the world may become guilty before God. There-
> fore by the deeds of the law no flesh will be justified in His
> sight, for by the law is the knowledge of sin.
>
> But now the righteousness of God apart from the law
> is revealed, being witnessed by the Law and the Proph-
> ets, even the righteousness of God, through faith in Jesus
> Christ, to all and on all who believe. For there is no differ-
> ence; for all have sinned and fall short of the glory of God
> (Romans 3:19-23).

By studying passages like these as a newborn Christian, I began
to grow in and through the Word. I am so grateful to God for the
Bible. I remember writing in the flyleaf of my first Bible, "The Bible
will keep you from sin and sin will keep you from the Bible." The
B-I-B-L-E, yes, that's the book for me!

I learned that Jesus is concealed in the Old Testament and
revealed in the New Testament. So many Old Testament passages,
beginning with Genesis 3, speak of God's provision for my sin
through the coming of the Messiah, Jesus Christ our Lord. I began
to memorize many great Old Testament passages, such as Psalm 22
and Isaiah 53. In texts like these, our faithful God reminded His
ancient people that from *their* race Messiah would come to redeem
anyone who placed his or her faith in Him. Every Christmas, my
spiritual walk received deep encouragement as we read Old Testament prophecies, given hundreds of years before the birth of Jesus,
that found their fulfillment in Christ. The New Testament then
reached back to the Old Testament to name the individuals through
whom Messiah had come.

Who does not feel blessed to hear the great, ancient stories of
God's victories as He fought for His people? Paul even tells us that

the Rock that followed the Israelites in the wilderness was Christ Himself (1 Corinthians 10:4). Bottom line, I thank God for my Bible, both the Old and the New Testaments.

Yet here we are in the twenty-first century, with increasing numbers of contemporary "churches" attacking the Old Testament, sowing doubt and confusion among God's people. Never forget that the Jesus we worship as our Savior and Messiah repeatedly gave His full, unequivocal approval to *all* of the Old Testament. How blessed we are to know that Jesus frequently pulled from the Old Testament, even using the story of Jonah to picture His own resurrection. Scripture—which in Christ's day included only the Old Testament, since the New Testament had yet to be written—"cannot be broken," Jesus insisted (John 10:35). He made it clear that what the Old Testament declares, God declares (see Matthew 22:30-32). The Bible knows *nothing* of a Jesus who rejected the Old Testament. Instead, He often says things like this:

> "Do not think that I came to destroy the Law or the Prophets. I did not come to destroy but to fulfill. For assuredly, I say to you, till heaven and earth pass away, one jot or one tittle will by no means pass from the law till all is fulfilled" (Matthew 5:17-18).

So then, if Jesus publicly declared such a wholehearted commitment to the entire Bible, how can we do otherwise? We can't, if we want to be fully anchored in Him.

Does this mean I understand everything God did in the Old Testament? Hardly. Nevertheless, I have no problem believing that the God of the Old Testament is the God of the New Testament. Jesus referred to His Father as the God of Abraham, Isaac, and Jacob, and the apostles did the same, even after Pentecost (Luke 20:37; Acts

3:13)—and of course, the God of Abraham, Isaac, and Jacob is the God of the Old Testament.

While we may see more examples of judgment in the Old Testament, over and over again that same God of judgment displays incredible acts of mercy and forgiveness. We see our heavenly Father extending His power against His own people in severe acts of discipline, and then as they repent, He uses that same hand of power to judge the pagan nations that abused them.

The "Spirit Trumps the Word" Jesus

I have come to see that God the Holy Spirit and the sacred Scriptures never disagree. They speak with one voice, the voice of Almighty God.

Have you ever heard someone say that the Holy Spirit told them to do something totally contrary to Scripture? I have—and rest assured, the Holy Spirit said no such thing. He never speaks in opposition to the very Word He inspired. Why would He? When we believe the Lord is leading us, and we think we have heard His small, still voice, the guidance we believe we have received can always be confirmed with Scripture.

To be controlled by the Spirit is to walk according to the Word. To be filled with the Spirit is to obey God's Word. While the Word of God without the Spirit of God is powerless, the Spirit of God without the Word of God is directionless. To be filled with the Spirit and to be filled with the Word is to find yourself anchored in Jesus.

The "Doctrine Doesn't Matter" Jesus

In our day, many professing Christians have very little commitment to Bible doctrine. Such a lack of commitment causes many of them to drift into the dangerous waters of confusion and counterfeit teaching. Consider that the Bible teaches the *doctrine* that Jesus is "full of grace and truth" (John 1:14). Now, is He full of both grace and truth all the time, or is He full of grace sometimes and full of truth at other times?

The Bible makes it clear that Jesus is *always* full of *both* grace and truth. That is why the Scripture teaches us to speak "the truth in love" (Ephesians 4:15). We must never separate these two. God's imperative to us always includes both.

Remember when Jesus predicted Peter's denial, even when the big fisherman brashly declared his undying commitment? In that prophecy, Jesus spoke the truth in grace. He spoke grace in forewarning Peter of his denial, and truth in His insistence that everything would turn out just as He said (even though His words stung).

But let's make the question even more dramatic. Was Jesus *still* full of grace when He told His best friend, "Get behind Me, Satan!" (Matthew 16:23)? Doesn't that sound awfully harsh? Yes, it does—but being gracious does not necessarily mean being nice. The Bible reminds us, "Faithful are the wounds of a friend, but the kisses of an enemy are deceitful" (Proverbs 27:6). It also says, "Rebuke a wise man, and he will love you" (Proverbs 9:8b).

When Scripture teaches us that Jesus is "full of grace," it means that He will *always* do for us whatever we need to bring us closer to His likeness. Whether we need encouragement, rebuke, hope, or conviction, the grace of Jesus will supply it. Jesus is an absolutely faithful friend. For that reason:

- Jesus loves us, but He refuses to flatter us.
- Jesus loves us like we are, but He loves us too much to leave us as we are.
- Jesus tells us the truth, even when it hurts, in order to help us.

Everyone needs a faithful friend—and you and I can have no

closer friend than Jesus. *That's* grace. He was (and is) always full of grace, but that doesn't mean He always seems nice while He's blessing us with that grace (see Romans 11:22). Getting anchored in Jesus means getting anchored in sound doctrine (see 1 Timothy 1:8-11; 6:3-5; Titus 1:7-9; 2:1-5).

The "I Don't Care How You Act" Jesus

As we become anchored in Jesus, the Lord is faithful to convict us of wrong and to expose our sin in order to get His grace and truth into us. As this truth gets assimilated into our lives, it becomes part of our DNA. And when that begins to happen, our behavior starts to resemble our beliefs.

As you journey along with me in *Anchored in Jesus*, we will see how each chapter deals with subjects that came straight from the heart and mouth of Jesus. Many times, the Holy Spirit later inspired Christ's followers to further develop the truths they heard that had so transformed them. The real Jesus, in whom we need to get anchored, issued both warnings and encouragements so we would know how to cooperate with His Spirit to see our lives transformed.

When I first became a Christian, I spent most of my early years thinking about the changes that had come into my life and all the vile things that I no longer did. As I began to grow, however, my attention shifted. I began to focus more on the good, new things Jesus had brought into my life.

I discovered that His grace gave me the power to obey and even the power to change my desires. I now *wanted* to do those things that please Him. Soon I began displaying the fruit of a new life in Christ. Jesus helps us to become godly.

No wonder Paul encouraged new converts to follow him *as he followed Christ.* He told them, "Imitate me, just as I also imitate Christ" (1 Corinthians 11:1). A Christian anchored in Jesus starts to become increasingly like Christ. Paul named Christlikeness as his most prized goal (see Philippians 3). To become godly is to have the fruit of Christ's life habitually displayed in your life. Oh, how I desire to be a godly man!

Let's Get Oriented

Allow me to give you a quick overview of what you'll find in *Anchored in Jesus.* I find that it helps me to grasp an idea or set of concepts when I can picture what's coming, and I hope what follows will help you to get oriented in our journey together.

In Part 1, we will focus on Jesus Himself. Enough of the counterfeits! What does the real Jesus look like, and how does He instruct us to live in this world for our benefit and His Father's glory? We'll spend some time appreciating four beautiful portraits of our Lord as painted in the New Testament: Messiah, Lord, Savior, and High Priest. To wrap up the section, we will hear from Jesus Himself on how to "abide" in Him—an indispensable key for any man who wants to grow in Christ and live out his purpose in life.

In Part 2, our focus will turn to developing the kind of "fruit" that Jesus wants all of His followers to produce. That process begins *internally* and then shifts to the *external* qualities and actions through which others can see the glory of God in us. The fruit of the Spirit in our lives makes this possible—and only Jesus can produce that fruit.

As we yield our lives to Christ's control, He manifests His life in us and through us. It's important to remember that spiritual fruit does not grow for our benefit, but for those to whom we minister. It's *Christ's* life, reproduced in *us*, for *His* glory. Others see our good works (our fruit) and glorify our Father in heaven (see Matthew 5:16).

As we live in a day of counterfeits, it should not surprise us that plastic fruit seems to be everywhere. The counterfeit is easy to produce and in some ways resembles real spiritual fruit. Genuine spiritual fruit, however, lasts even in difficult times, while counterfeit fruit dries up and blows away. The fruit of the Spirit takes time and discipline to grow and make our life greener. Jesus ministers to others through the fruit He develops in us.

I would guess that three of the most used words in the Christian faith are *love, joy,* and *peace.* When the *love* of John 3:16 becomes a reality to us, we experience the *joy* of John 15—a joy that remains. The Bible tells us we can enjoy "peace with God" through faith in Jesus Christ, leading to the "peace of God" (see Romans 5:1-5). *Peace* is an inner serenity that controls us, regardless of our outward circumstances. God demonstrated His *love* toward us while we were yet sinners, sending His Son to earth to provide a way for us to enter His presence. At the cross, the war ended and God's *peace* came. As a result of Jesus' work on Calvary, and through faith, we can experience God's *joy* deep within. More hymns and songs have been written about these three words—*love, joy,* and *peace*—than any others found in Scripture.

Since these gifts are all anchored in Jesus, when we get anchored in Him, He gives us the ability to live differently with others. As His love increasingly takes root in us, related traits blossom in us, such as patience, kindness, goodness, faithfulness, gentleness, and self-control. Just as Christ showed patience with us, so we can now show patience with others. We, too, can pass over someone's mistreatment of us and show them kindness instead. In fact, when we get anchored in Jesus, we can actually do good deeds for them. The question *What would Jesus do?* takes on more significance as we seek to treat others as Jesus has treated us. We, too, can show mercy even when mercy is not extended to us. How is this possible? Jesus makes it happen.

I call the trait of "self-control" the Biggy, because I desperately need it, especially whenever the wheels come off. My temper, attitude, and desires all require self-control. Again, I cannot make myself the man Jesus calls me to be. Only as His fruit grows in me can I become who He desires me to be. The word *temperate* in 1 Corinthians 9:25 describes the key attribute that puts self-control on display: "And everyone who competes for the prize is temperate in all things. Now they do it to obtain a perishable crown, but we for an imperishable crown. Therefore I run thus: not with uncertainty. Thus I fight: not as one who beats the air. But I discipline my body and bring it into subjection, lest, when I have preached to others, I myself should become disqualified" (1 Corinthians 9:25-27). By getting a handle on self-control, we prepare ourselves to become powerhouse men of God.

In the third and final section of *Anchored in Jesus*, I want to encourage all of us to fight the good fight of faith. Pursue with energy and diligence whatever path God has called you to follow! The Lord wants you and me to play to win, and so to close this book, I attempt to spur us on to the high calling Jesus has in mind for each of us.

Position over Location

To the Christian, location is not nearly as important as position. The apostle Paul often would introduce his writings with words like this: "To all the saints in Christ Jesus who are in Philippi." Note "in Christ Jesus" (position) and "in Philippi" (location). The *real* comes when we are in Christ Jesus. Nothing trumps being in Jesus and anchored in Him.

I have always loved the book of James, written by the Lord's half-brother. Many scholars refer to James as the "practical theologian" of the New Testament. He challenges us to be "doers of the word" (James 1:22) and insists that each believing man must be a doer who

acts (James 1:25). I have tried hard to follow James's counsel in my
own life and ministry, but I know I still often find it easier to focus
on what I do more than on who I am and to whom I belong.

When we anchor ourselves in the real Jesus of Scripture, however,
the "doing" tends to follow a lot more naturally from the "being."
When we get anchored in Jesus, our character becomes more consistent, changing us forever. As a result, Galatians 2:20 gets increasingly fleshed out in our lives:

> I have been crucified with Christ; it is no longer I who live,
> but Christ lives in me; and the life which I now live in the
> flesh I live by faith in the Son of God, who loved me and
> gave Himself for me.

The lives we live now, anchored in Jesus, grow out of the faithfulness of God. His attributes increasingly become our attributes.
What an amazing thought! As a Christian man, don't you want that?
I long for Paul's words to be true of me so that I will "walk worthy of
the Lord, fully pleasing Him, being fruitful in every good work and
increasing in the knowledge of God" (Colossians 1:10).

Anchoring ourselves in Jesus is the *only* way to make that happen. And the best approach I know of to firmly set that anchor in
place is to secure it in the powerful, unchanging, sovereign character of the Lord Jesus Christ Himself. Let's begin the initial part of
our journey, therefore, by lingering over the Bible's wonderful portrait of Jesus as the Messiah, the Son of God.

Part 1

JESUS, THE ONLY TRUE ANCHOR

2

A MESSIAH
WHO CHANGES
EVERYTHING

In late 2017, Netflix announced it would create a ten-episode television series called *Messiah*. The streaming service said the show would chronicle "the modern world's reaction to a man who first appears in the Middle East, creating a groundswell of followers around him and claiming he is the Messiah. Is he sent from God or is he a dangerous fraud bent on dismantling the world's geopolitical order?"[2]

What comes to mind when you hear the word *Messiah*? The word itself means "anointed one" and originally referred to someone anointed with oil and set apart for some special task. Over time, it came to refer to a unique servant of God, sent by the Lord Himself to set the world aright. The Old Testament has scores of prophecies about this Messiah, whom Christians believe appeared on earth in the first century in the person of Jesus Christ (the word *Christ* is the Greek form of the Hebrew title *Messiah*).

The producers of the series *Messiah* asked, "What if someone showed up in 2018 amid strange occurrences and was thought to be the Messiah? What would society do? How would the media cover him? Would millions simply quit work? Could governments collapse? It's a series that could change everything."[3]

The series hadn't yet aired by the time I wrote this book, so I don't know if it could really "change everything." But I do know that the real Messiah did indeed change everything—and He's still changing everything today.

The Glory of the Heavenly Messiah

Jesus was no ordinary Messiah. In fact, Scripture claims that Jesus came to earth from heaven at the command of His heavenly Father. For that reason, the New Testament often identifies Jesus as "the [Messiah], the Son of God" (e.g., Matthew 16:16; 26:63; Mark 1:1; John 11:27). John even says he wrote his Gospel "so that you may believe that Jesus is the Christ [Messiah], the Son of God, and that by believing you may have life in his name" (John 20:31 ESV). For good reason, therefore, the apostle Paul could call Jesus "the Christ, who is God over all, blessed forever" (Romans 9:5 ESV).

One of Jesus' favorite titles for Himself was "the Son of Man," and He left little doubt about His place of origin: "No one has ascended to heaven but He who came down from heaven, that is, the Son of Man." A little later He declared, "He who comes from above is above all" (John 3:13,31). And in case anyone misunderstood, He would say even more explicitly, "I have come down from heaven, not to do My own will, but the will of Him who sent Me" (John 6:38). When some religious leaders grumbled about His claim, He declared, "As the living Father sent Me, and I live because of the Father, so he who feeds on Me will live because of Me. This is the bread which came down from heaven…He who eats this bread will live forever" (John 6:57-58).

While Jesus often used metaphorical language, He made this point crystal clear: Jesus is the Messiah, the "Mighty God" of Isaiah 9:6. I wonder if the apostle Paul had Isaiah's text in mind when he described Jesus as "being in the form of God" (Philippians 2:6). The word *being* stresses the essence of a person's nature, his continual state or condition. In fact, Jesus has *always* been God; at no time was Jesus *not* God. He is God today and at no moment in the future will He ever cease to be God. Jesus is eternally God.

See Jesus, See God

The apostle John tells us, "No one has seen God at any time. The only begotten Son, who is in the bosom of the Father, He has declared Him" (John 1:18). Jesus came in the flesh to explain, declare, and make known who God is. If you want to know what God is like, then look at Jesus. If you want to know what God says to humanity, then listen to Jesus. If you want to know how God represents Himself to the world, then observe the life of Christ.

One day, Jesus and a disciple named Philip had a short conversation about this very issue.

> Philip said to Him, "Lord, show us the Father, and it is sufficient for us."
>
> Jesus said to him, "Have I been with you so long, and yet you have not known Me, Philip? He who has seen Me has seen the Father; so how can you say, 'Show us the Father'? Do you not believe that I am in the Father, and the Father in Me? The words that I speak to you I do not speak on My own authority; but the Father who dwells in Me does the works" (John 14:8-10).

To know Jesus is to know God. No wonder that when Jesus spoke to the Pharisees, He could say, "Most assuredly, I say to you, before Abraham was, I AM" (John 8:58). Jesus used the special covenant name of God to refer to Himself, translated "I AM" (*eimi* in Greek, *YHWH* in Hebrew). Grammatically, it makes no more sense in English than in Greek to say, "Before Abraham was, I AM." It would make much more sense to say, "Before Abraham was, I existed," but Jesus cared much more about theological truth than about grammatical accuracy. He fully intended to declare, "I am God Almighty, the *Yahweh* you know from the Old Testament" (John 8:57-59). Jesus is the eternal Son of God, the "Mighty God" of Isaiah 6:9.

When you look at Jesus, you're looking into the face of God. Paul called Jesus "the image of the invisible God, the firstborn over all creation" (Colossians 1:15). The Greek word translated "image" is the term from which we get our English word *icon*, which refers to a copy or a likeness.

Ancient people used the word *image* to describe an engraving on wood, an etching in metal, the brand of an animal hide, an impression in clay, or an image stamped on some other medium. When Jesus arrived in this world, the planet had "God" stamped all over it.

Do you know that God's image is stamped on *your* soul? You'll never find real meaning in life until you understand that you were not merely made *by* God; you were made *for* God. He wants you to represent Him to this world! *You* are God's icon to reach a planet estranged from Him.

The Hope of the Promised Messiah

We live in a world that desperately needs hope. On our diseased rock, death reigns, evil often triumphs, and hope too often seems absent. Since God knows our desperate condition better than we do, almost from the very beginning He has laced His Word with shining markers of hope. And the brightest, most dazzling of all those markers were His repeated promises of a coming Messiah.

God delivered the very first such marker immediately after Adam and Eve sinned. After the Lord pronounced their sentence, He also gave the guilty couple a bright beacon of hope. He told the serpent who had deceived them,

> "I will put enmity between you and the woman,
> and between your offspring and her offspring;
> he shall bruise your head,
> and you shall bruise his heel."
> (Genesis 3:15 ESV)

Bible scholars often call this verse "the first mention of the gospel," because in veiled form it prophesies both the defeat of Satan and the triumph of the Messiah through the cross.

Over the centuries, the Lord added promise after promise and detail after detail regarding this coming Messiah, always pointing to the day when He would provide salvation for His people and redemption for His creation. By the time of Jesus, the Jewish people had a heightened expectation for Messiah's arrival, even wondering whether John the Baptist might be the predicted one (see John 7:40-43).

Soon after Jesus began His public ministry, the crowds who heard His words, observed His behavior, and gasped at His miracles began to wonder, *Could this be the Messiah?* Some said yes, some said no, and most didn't dare to commit themselves one way or another. The Gospel of John offers some good snapshots of the situation:

- "Andrew...found his own brother Simon, and said to him, 'We have found the Messiah'" (John 1:40-41).
- "Do the rulers know indeed that this is truly the Christ [Messiah]?" (John 7:26).
- "When the Christ comes, will He do more signs than these which this Man has done?" (John 7:31).

- "Still others asked, 'How can the Messiah come from Galilee? Does not Scripture say that the Messiah will come from David's descendants and from Bethlehem, the town where David lived?' Thus the people were divided because of Jesus" (John 7:41-43 NIV).

In fact, both the law and the prophets had for centuries witnessed to the coming Messiah. Although neither the common people nor their scholars had a clear picture of the Messiah, their Bibles contained all the information required to identify Him. The problem was that the Old Testament presents what *seems* like two contrasting pictures of the Anointed One. While some texts depict Him as a conquering king, others portray Him as more of a suffering savior. How could both be right?

More than a Historical Curiosity

I've visited Israel many times, and on one trip I wanted to go up to the Temple Mount. I arrived on a Friday, during the Muslim observance of Ramadan. From noon to 2:00 p.m., about 300,000 Muslims took over the sacred space for their call to prayer. For centuries, Muslims have controlled Temple Mount, building on it both the Dome of the Rock and the al Aqsa mosque. Archaeologists don't know exactly where Herod's temple used to stand, but they know it was on Temple Mount. During feasts like Ramadan, however, Jews can't pray up there, lest they spark a riot.

So, where do observant Jews go to pray? They head to the Wailing Wall, one level down. So that's where we went too. I visited the Wailing Wall and prayed Bible promises.

What's so special about the Wailing Wall? When the Romans destroyed Jerusalem in AD 70, they left only the Wailing Wall standing. It's a retaining wall that helps keep Temple Mount in place. The

Romans left it standing simply to say, "Take a look, and don't ever forget who we are and what we can do to you."

Many Jewish people today look back to the time of Nehemiah and believe that the restorer of Jerusalem's walls will one day build another wall and another temple. Praying at the Wailing Wall gives them hope that Messiah is coming. As Christians, of course, we believe that Messiah already has come, and that one day He will come again.

I mention the Temple Mount because I see it as much more than a historical curiosity. Did you know that the cross of Jesus stood just north of the temple altar? And did you know that Temple Mount and Mt. Moriah are closely connected? Further, did you know that when Abraham tried to offer Isaac as a sacrifice, as recounted in Genesis 22, he did so on Mt. Moriah?

Abraham provides an amazing picture of the God who would sacrifice His only Son to satisfy the demands of His holy nature—except that in Abraham's case, God intervened and provided another sacrifice, a ram caught in a thicket. Abraham therefore called the place "The LORD Will Provide," and the text in Genesis adds, "And to this day it is said, 'On the mountain of the LORD it will be provided'" (Genesis 22:14 NIV).

More than two thousand years ago, through a virgin birth, God the Son clothed Himself in human flesh and came into this world to become our sacrifice. Unlike with Isaac, however, God did not spare Jesus, but allowed Him to fully taste death for all of us.

Don't make the common mistake that it was God the Father who tipped His wrath on His hapless Son. Jesus, as the second Person of the Trinity, controlled the lever that tipped that awful divine wrath on Himself. No one took Jesus' life; He laid it down freely, of His own accord. No wonder the prophet Isaiah, writing six hundred years before the birth of Jesus, said of Him, "He was wounded for our transgressions…by His stripes we are healed" (Isaiah 53:5). We are healed by the stripes of Jesus, the Messiah—the One Isaiah would also call "Everlasting Father" (Isaiah 9:6).

After Jesus rose from the dead, the apostles and their associates looked back to these ancient Hebrew prophecies to prove that Messiah *had* come in the Person of Jesus. Luke tells us that an educated believer named Apollos "vigorously refuted his Jewish opponents in public debate, proving from the Scriptures that Jesus was the Messiah" (Acts 18:28 NIV). Peter went even further, pointing to the Second Coming of Christ when he told the crowds, "Repent, then, and turn to God, so that your sins may be wiped out, that times of refreshing may come from the Lord, and that he may send the Messiah, who has been appointed for you—even Jesus. Heaven must receive him until the time comes for God to restore everything, as he promised long ago through his holy prophets" (Acts 3:19-21 NIV). Peter's hope remains our own hope to this very day.

The Grace of the Suffering Messiah

The New Testament's classic passage on Jesus the Messiah is found in Philippians 2:5-11. In those cherished verses, and in unforgettable language, the apostle Paul lays out for us the staggering lengths and agonizing depths that Jesus went to in order to be our Messiah. He writes that Christ Jesus:

> Who, being in very nature God,
>   did not consider equality with God something to be used to his own advantage;
> rather, he made himself nothing
>   by taking the very nature of a servant,
>   being made in human likeness.
> And being found in appearance as a man,

he humbled himself
by becoming obedient to death—
even death on a cross!
(Philippians 2:5-9 NIV)

Theologians refer to these verses as the *kenosis* passage, a Greek term referring to the "self-emptying" of our Lord in the incarnation. Jesus "emptied" Himself of many of His divine prerogatives in order to serve and minister to others on earth as the Messiah. The eternal God, Jesus, willingly chose to clothe Himself in human flesh, thus becoming Immanuel, "God with us." Jesus lived among us as the God-man.

Paul tells us that even though Jesus was God, He did not consider equality with God something to use for His own advantage. Jesus didn't clench His hands around His divine prerogatives and refuse to give them up. Though Christ had all the rights, privileges, and honor of deity, He refused to cling to those rights. Instead, for our sake, He willingly gave up many of them for a season.

Let's be clear: Jesus did *not* empty Himself of deity, nor did He exchange His deity for humanity. He emptied Himself of many outward, invisible manifestations of the Godhead, but not of His divine nature or attributes. Instead, Jesus willingly set aside many of His divine privileges. Let me suggest just five examples of this "emptying."

First, of His own free will Jesus left the throne room of heaven, where for ages upon ages multitudes of angels had cried out to Him, "Holy, holy, holy is the LORD God Almighty." He took up residence in a virgin's womb, clothed Himself in human flesh, and was born into a world that despised Him and ultimately killed Him. Now, think about that.

Jesus grew tired, just like us—yet He remained fully God.

He grew hungry, just like us—yet He remained fully God.

He grew thirsty, just like us—yet He remained wholly God. Amazing!

Second, Jesus willingly submitted Himself to the sovereign will of His Father. He told the crowds, "The Son can do nothing of Himself, but what He sees the Father do; for whatever He does, the Son also does in like manner" (John 5:19).

Third, Jesus at times divested Himself of important information that God the Father clearly possessed. In speaking about the time of His Second Coming, for example, He declared, "But of that day and hour no one knows, not even the angels of heaven, but My Father only" (Matthew 24:36).

Fourth, Jesus sacrificed for a time His eternal riches. Although He was rich, He became poor so that you and I might be rich (see 2 Corinthians 8:9).

Fifth, as the only human who never sinned, Jesus took our place on the cross, placing on Himself the penalty for our sins. At the moment of that terrible exchange, the Father turned His face away from His Son, because at that instant His Son bore the sins of the whole world. Jesus fully experienced the abandonment and despair that inevitably results from the outpouring of God's wrath against sin. "[God] made Him who knew no sin to be sin for us, that we might become the righteousness of God in Him" (2 Corinthians 5:21).

We will never be able to fully grasp how much Jesus gave up when He took on human flesh. At the same time, however, He didn't give up everything. This is why Jesus could still walk on water, because only God can walk on water. This is why Jesus could say to a terrible storm, "Be muzzled" (the original Greek term), and the sea would instantly grow calm. This is why He could say to a deceased little girl, "Arise," and she would immediately come back to life. He was human *and* God at the same time. And so on the Mount of Transfiguration, the very essence of Jesus began to shine forth, His face dazzling as the sun. Why? Because He's the God-man!

God took the deficit in my spiritual account and transferred it to Jesus' account, and then He took the assets in Christ's account and put them in my account. From me, Jesus got only sin; from Jesus, I got only riches. Think of that the next time you remember the moment you came to faith in Jesus.

I once told a well-to-do man, "I would love for you to come and visit with us at our church." I'll never forget his shocking response. In all my years of ministry—and I've been at this for more than forty years—I'd never heard anyone say anything like it.

"I bet you would," he replied. "A lot of people would like to have me and my money in their church."

I honestly couldn't care less what any man has in the way of worldly wealth. When a man comes to God, he has absolutely *nothing* to bring, except for his sin. No man can ever truthfully say, "When I came to Jesus, I gave up an awful lot."

No, he didn't.

But by God's grace, *Jesus* did.

The Peace of the Reigning Messiah

While the *kenosis* passage describes the self-emptying of Jesus, it doesn't leave Him there. Thank God! To the contrary, it exalts Him as the One whom God anointed as King of kings and Lord of lords. The passage continues:

> Therefore God exalted him to the highest place
>   and gave him the name that is above every name,
> that at the name of Jesus every knee should bow,
>   in heaven and on earth and under the earth,
> and every tongue acknowledge that Jesus Christ is Lord,
>   to the glory of God the Father.
> (Philippians 2:9-11 NIV)

In this remarkable passage, Paul tells us that God exalted Jesus to the highest place—but the apostle's statement jars me. How do you exalt *God*? How can you lift up the Highest even higher? How can you raise up someone who already occupies the summit?

At Christmastime, I've heard people ask, "What kind of gift do you give someone who already has everything?" We usually ask the question with tongue in cheek, but in this case, I'm not asking a tongue-in-cheek question. How does God exalt *God*?

I'm not sure I know the answer to my question, but I do know God's exaltation of Jesus did not involve Christ's nature or His eternal place within the Trinity. It's not as though when Jesus came to earth, He left a vacant seat that someone else could fill!

Just before His arrest and crucifixion, Jesus prayed what we call His "high priestly prayer." In it He said, "And now, O Father, glorify Me together with Yourself, with the glory which I had with You before the world was" (John 17:5). While such a request staggers me, Jesus' return to the same glory He shared with the Father before His incarnation did not require a further exaltation but a restoration.

So again, how does God exalt God?

I think the answer involves Christ's status as the God-man. It appears that God gave Jesus privileges after His ascension that He did not have prior to the incarnation. Let me suggest three examples.

First, if Jesus had not lived among us as a man, He could not have fully identified with those He came to save. The book of Hebrews tells us that Jesus, the God-man, can fully "sympathize with our weaknesses" (Hebrews 4:15). If you've ever wondered, *Can God really understand what's going on in my life?* the answer is yes! Jesus, who became one of us, can perfectly sympathize with our weaknesses.

Second, as a man, Jesus overcame every temptation thrown at

Him. In the desert, Satan told Jesus, "Listen, you've not eaten in forty days. Why not turn these stones into bread? You're hungry, aren't you?" When that temptation failed, the devil tried again: "If you're really God, then jump from the pinnacle of the temple. Hey, the angels of God wouldn't let God dash His foot against a stone, would they?" That approach failed too. Finally, the devil tried the biggest temptation of them all. "Bow down and worship me," he said. "Do you see all these vast lands? They're all under my control. If you will bow down and worship me, I will give you all of them." Jesus resisted that temptation and every other one He ever faced.

This is why we can never say to God, "Lord, you just don't know how strong a temptation this is!" Yes, He does. He endured *far* stronger temptations than any of us ever will, and yet He never once gave in to a single one. For that reason, God has highly exalted His Son and given Him a name He shares with no one, anywhere.

Third, do you know one of the greatest things Jesus accomplished as a man? He came to earth, where Satan ruled, and defeated hell. John tells us that Jesus came to "destroy the works of the devil" (1 John 3:8). Through His work on the cross, Jesus defeated death and the grave. I've lost count how many times I've visited the cemetery, and barring a miracle, I'll be back many times more. But when Jesus went to the cemetery, He kicked the end out of the grave and made a tunnel out of it.

Jesus alone conquered sin. And because of that ultimate triumph, God has exalted Him to the highest place. At the name of Jesus, every knee will bow and every tongue confess that Jesus Christ is Lord, to the glory of God the Father.

One day, Hitler will bow at the feet of Jesus and say, "Jesus Christ is Lord."

One day, Antichrist will bow at Jesus' feet and say, "Jesus Christ is Lord."

One day, every atheist who ever lived will bow at the Messiah's feet and say, "Jesus Christ is Lord." No, this is no "God delusion"; it's God who became man.

The entire intelligent universe is destined one day to worship Jesus Christ as Lord, from angels in heaven to demons in hell, from men in coal mines to astronauts in orbit, from obedient believers on the earth to lost men and women in hades. *Everything* that has breath will one day acknowledge Jesus Christ is Lord, to the glory of God. *How* they acknowledge Him, however, will differ radically.

Some will confess Him as Lord with overflowing, grateful hearts. His peace will rule their cleansed souls as they delight in His reign as Prince of Peace, of whom it is said, "Of the increase of His government and peace there will be no end" (Isaiah 9:7). Others will confess Him as Lord while overcome with abject terror and soul-crushing regret. But however they do it, everyone, everywhere, one day *will* confess that Jesus Christ is Lord.

I sat with a lady one night who, I learned, was just a few months older than I am. "Pray for me," she said. "All I want to do is to go to be with Jesus. I am ready to close my eyes for good." She said it with as much of a smile as someone in great pain can manage.

What gives a woman such confidence and peace, knowing that even as she closes her eyes in death, she'll wake up and see *Him*? That woman knew Jesus is alive. She knew Him as her Messiah. And she willingly, eagerly, and joyfully counted Him as the King of kings and Lord of lords—*her* King and *her* Lord.

Does that kind of peace reign in your own heart?

The only person worthy of ultimate exaltation chose a life of utter humility. The Lord Jesus Christ abandoned His golden throne in favor of a dirty sheep pen. He took His majesty and placed it in the midst of madness. In Jesus, glorious deity entered the world on the floor of a filthy stall.

And now He calls us to follow His example.

A Call to Servanthood

No greater example of a servant exists than the Lord Jesus Christ. If it ever becomes your sincere desire to say, "I want to be as much like Jesus as I possibly can," you will become a *great* servant.

God never calls any Christian to a life of self-centeredness. The Christian life is not about what you can get but about what you give. It's a life of self-surrender to the will of God, to the needs of your fellow man, and to the example of Jesus Christ.

John 13 may give us the best illustration of a genuine servant. It describes Jesus washing the feet of His disciples, a dirty job typically reserved for lowly servants.

Foot washing was a normal practice in the ancient Middle East. When a guest came in off the dusty roads, custom dictated that someone waiting at the door should wash the visitor's feet. Jesus broke from custom, however, when He chose to do the work Himself. His action staggered His disciples because they considered the job too menial for anyone but a servant. And yet the Lord Jesus, God in the flesh, demonstrated that *no* service to a fellow human is too low.

After He finished His unsettling object lesson, Jesus told His men,

> "You call me 'Teacher' and 'Lord,' and rightly so, for that is what I am. Now that I, your Lord and Teacher, have washed your feet, you also should wash one another's feet. I have set you an example that you should do as I have done for you. Very truly I tell you, no servant is greater than his master, nor is a messenger greater than the one who sent

him. Now that you know these things, you will be blessed
if you do them" (John 13:13-17 NIV).

Did you catch that last phrase? "*If* you do them." God blesses us
when we serve others, not merely when we talk about serving them,
study serving them, or encourage others to serve them.

Somehow, in the twenty-first century, we talk about theology far
more than we do something practical with it. We lack what I'd call
"theological pragmatism."

I not only want people to know the gospel, but I long for them to
embrace the Christ and undergo a radical personal transformation.
More than anything, I want that radical personal transformation to
begin with me.

The Only Way to Know God's Will

"Let this mind be in you," Paul tells us, "which was also in Christ
Jesus" (Philippians 2:5). Elsewhere the apostle declares, "We have
the mind of Christ" (1 Corinthians 2:16).

And what is "the mind of Christ"? In essence, it's a submissive
attitude. God has given us the mind of the Messiah so that we can
submit ourselves to live the way He would have us to live. To have
the mind of Christ is to display in your life the attitude that Christ
exhibited while He walked this earth.

The life of Jesus teaches us that the only way we will *ever* know
the will of God for our lives is to realize that when we became Christians, we surrendered our rights. The only right we have now is to
live out God's perfect will for us. His will trumps ours. Jesus habitually chose to submit His will to that of His Father, for our benefit.
So, if He was willing to do that for us, then how could we refuse to
do the same for Him?

Remember that Jesus laid aside His privileges to benefit others.

Our Messiah did not consider any treasure too great to be surrendered. He laid aside His glory, His comfort, His reputation, and the infinite honor due His name in order to win our salvation. In doing so, He did not think of Himself but of others. This is the mind of Christ.

Let this mind be in you.

A LORD WHO DESERVES DEVOTION

When I fly, I often pray, "Lord, please put me beside someone who needs to know about the love of Christ." That prayer has brought me lots of divine appointments! When I feel drained after a long trip, however, sometimes I say, "Lord, please put me in a seat with nobody around me. I'm tired and I want to rest."

Several years ago, right before Mother's Day, I felt exhausted after spending some extended ministry time in Colorado Springs. I'd had a short night, my flight was late, and I didn't get to bed until 1:40 a.m. I had a board meeting scheduled for 7:00 a.m. the next day—and you know why they call them "board," don't you?

As I sat at the window, completely spent, I thought, *I'm going to doze a little and then I'll be able to enjoy my family when I arrive home tomorrow evening.*

When the flight attendant came by to serve beverages, she looked at me and said, "You mean to tell me that we're not going to get to hear you preach a Mother's Day message on Sunday morning?"

Although I didn't recognize her, she clearly recognized me, and so she continued: "My daughters enjoy hearing you preach, and they've never really enjoyed preachers. You keep their attention."

The young woman sitting in the seat next to me overheard our exchange and immediately chipped in, "It's no coincidence that the Lord has put me beside a preacher!"

I thought, *This is gonna be interesting.*

It turned out that my seatmate had moved from Detroit to Colorado Springs. As a young girl, she'd dreamed of working for James Dobson—but clearly, her life didn't match the type of witness his ministry deserved.

For the next hour, I described how Jesus Christ can make a difference in a person's life. Toward the end of our conversation, I told her, "Before you get off this plane, you need to get right with God. You need to ask Christ to forgive you for where you've drifted." I recommended a wonderful church in Colorado Springs, and then I added, "Go back and finish your education. I encourage you to follow the dream that God placed in your heart. I hope that one day I'll see an article from Focus on the Family that you helped write."

Do you know why I still remember this encounter from all those years ago? I remember it because it illustrates for me a single potent truth that plays out in two very different ways.

The Devotion of a Heart Submitted to Christ

How we respond to the lordship of Jesus Christ puts us in one of two seats, seats that move us toward two very different destinations. Peter says it like this: "But in your hearts revere Christ as Lord. Always be prepared to give an answer to everyone who asks you to give the reason for the hope that you have" (1 Peter 3:15 NIV).

Christian men need a holy, humble heart for Christ as Lord. The apostle here gives us a picture of a heart over which Christ rules. The verse reminds me of Matthew 6:33, where Jesus said, "But seek first the kingdom of God and His righteousness, and all these things shall be added to you." When Christ is Lord, He's King in your life. And when He's King, you don't have to worry about what you'll eat or what you'll wear; when you put Him first, He'll take care of it all.

Somehow, though, we tend to get this all turned around, just as that young lady did on the plane so many years ago. We think that if we submit to the lordship of Jesus Christ, He'll make us do the very thing we detest the most. So we refuse to surrender.

But in this passage, Peter gives us a biblical snapshot of the joy-filled, surrendered servant. He pictures for us the devotion of a life in which Christ rules as Lord. Did you know that to revere Christ as Lord takes personal devotion on your part? This passage helps to explain how the contemporary American church got to where it is. Sadly, we really don't understand lordship.

Peter insists that every Christian man is to give Jesus a special place in his heart. The word translated "revere" means to turn *everything* over to Christ. Suppose someone were to ask you, "Is Jesus Lord of your life?" To answer yes would mean that you have allowed Christ to rule in your heart, that you have given Him free access to every area of your life. You have turned everything over to Him and you live only to please and glorify Him. It means that if anything in your life conflicts with who Jesus is and what He stands for, then God will reveal that to you, you will repent of it, and you will say with passion, "I want to please God more than anything." To call Christ "Lord" means to fear displeasing Jesus infinitely more than you fear what men might do to you.

In some older translations, the word translated "revere" is rendered "sanctified." The underlying Greek term was used in pagan religions to refer to the act of setting apart a building as a temple, thus designating it as religious in character, to be used for worship. In a similar way, we are to set aside our hearts to Christ. We designate our lives as temples to be used for the Lord's purposes. We are to live for the Lord's pleasure, according to His design.

My, You Look Different

When you submit yourself to Christ's lordship, your life will look distinctly different from men who don't belong to Christ. To "revere" or "sanctify" Jesus in your heart means that you live to honor Him, to acknowledge Christ as the Holy One in your life. You give first place to Him, willingly choosing to obey Him in everything.

"Lord" is the English translation of the Greek term *kyrios*, which in this passage refers to Jesus as Yahweh of the Old Testament. Peter was exhorting his fellow Christians to set apart the Lord Jesus as Yahweh. They were to consider Jesus as very God, giving first place to Him in their hearts, obeying Him before anything or anybody else.

Have you set aside Christ as the Lord of your life? Have you committed yourself to live in obedience to Jesus Christ?

This is crucial because the Christian faith makes no sense unless we first set apart Jesus Christ as Lord of our lives—nor will the Christian lifestyle *ever* work. Most church attenders today feel miserable because they have never sanctified Jesus as King over everything in their lives. They have divided loyalties, as though one foot stood on dry pavement and the other on ice. Any foot disconnected from Christ as Lord skates on a banana peel. Life is slippery, and Peter is telling us that men need to set apart Jesus as Lord in a distinct, definite act of the will.

My life purpose is to follow Jesus Christ as the very Lord of *everything* in my life, for His eternal purposes. Everything I am, everything I have, must be surrendered to Him. It bears repeating: the Christian life makes sense in no other way, nor does it work.

Jesus Himself highlighted this issue through a pointed question He asked His disciples. "Why do you call me 'Lord, Lord,'" He wondered aloud, "and not do the things which I say?" (Luke 6:46).

If we call a person "Lord," our obedience is expected. If you were to call me "Lord," not only would I own you, but I would own everything you have. I'd be the owner, the master. Giving lip service to Christ's lordship is totally insufficient...and yet I fear that the average church attender today does exactly that. Genuine faith, however, *always* produces obedience. It cannot do otherwise.

How do you know if Jesus is Lord of a man's life? You can see that the man obeys Christ. It really is that simple.

Good Tree, Bad Tree

How can we tell a good tree from a bad tree? Jesus told us, "Every good tree bears good fruit, but a bad tree bears bad fruit" (Matthew 7:17 NIV). Jesus gave us this saying to describe the difference between a genuine disciple and a phony one. In speaking this way, He had less interest in agriculture than in salvation-culture.

Every now and then, a woman will say to me, "I don't know if my husband's saved or not. But he's a bad dude." Well, Jesus told us that bad trees bear bad fruit. He went even further when He said, "A good tree cannot bear bad fruit, and a bad tree cannot bear good fruit. Every tree that does not bear good fruit is cut down and thrown into the fire. Thus, by their fruit you will recognize them" (Matthew 7:18-20 NIV).

If someone were to show me a piece of tree bark and ask if I could identify the type of tree it came from, I'm pretty sure I'd fail. If somebody were to bring me a leaf and ask me to identify the tree from the leaf, I doubt I'd do much better. But bring me an apple, and I'll tell you it came from an apple tree. Bring me a lemon, and I'll tell you it came from a lemon tree. Bring me a peach, and I'll tell you it came from a peach tree. Jesus did not tell us we will know men by their bark or by their leaves but by their *fruit*. Jesus is telling us, "Who really belongs to Me? Look at the fruit the man's life produces. An apple tree produces apples. It's just like that."

If it's an olive tree, it will produce olives.

If it's a Christian, it will produce obedience to Jesus as Lord.

So let me ask: Is Jesus *your* Lord? Do *you* obey Him? What kind of fruit are you producing?

One of the evidences that Jesus Christ became Lord of my life is that He began to develop me—not all at once, but over time. I hope that I have the proper bark and the right leaves, but I pray in the name of Jesus that my life increasingly bears the fruit of the lordship of Jesus Christ.

Further and Further

Jesus went even a step further. He made a statement that I guarantee made His disciples a little nervous. He told them, "Not everyone who says to me, 'Lord, Lord,' will enter the kingdom of heaven, but only the one who does the will of my Father who is in heaven" (Matthew 7:21 NIV).

Merely saying "Jesus is my Lord" doesn't make it so. Jesus insisted that not everyone who speaks the words has really submitted to Jesus as Lord. It's not the people who *call* Jesus "Lord" who enter the kingdom of heaven, but only the people who *do* the will of God.

Are *you* doing the will of God?

Look around and you'll see countless people *not* doing the will of God, who nevertheless claim to know Jesus as Lord. But how can He be their Lord of everything if they never give Him any of their finances? How can He be their Lord when they never give Him any of their time? How can He be their Lord and yet they keep all their talents for themselves? Show me who you serve with your talents, and I'll show you the Lord of your life. Everybody worships someone or something, but not everybody worships at the same throne.

As if all this weren't enough, Jesus went even further. He told His startled men, "Many will say to me on that day, 'Lord, Lord, did we not prophesy in your name and in your name drive out demons and in your name perform many miracles?' Then I will tell them plainly, 'I never knew you. Away from me, you evildoers!'" (Matthew 7:22-23 NIV).

On the day of judgment, Jesus will tell these men—religious guys who called Him "Lord" but who didn't bother to obey Him—"I never knew you. Depart from me, you lawbreakers!"

The barrenness of this sort of "faith" demonstrates its true character. The faith that *says* but does not *do* is really unbelief…which means that, according to God's Word, our churches overflow with unbelieving men. These guys acknowledge with their lips that Jesus Christ is Lord, but their lives prove their barrenness. Their actions deny the God who died to save them. Christ is to be preferred above all else!

Peter calls baptism a sign of a good conscience toward the lordship of Christ (see 1 Peter 3:21). So if that's true, then how under heaven can somebody say, "Jesus Christ is Lord," and then say, "Nope" when Jesus calls him to be baptized?

Paul instructs us to set aside a proportional amount of our income to give to God's work on the first day of the week (see 1 Corinthians 16:2). How, then, can someone say, "Jesus is Lord," but "Nope" to supporting the ministry of the church?

"We could use your help here to serve the Lord," a church elder says to a man one day.

"Sorry, ain't got time."

"Do you see that man over there?" whispers the Spirit. "I'd like you to ask him how he's doing."

Uh, no. Evangelism isn't my gift.

The Bible says that when Jesus is Lord, He's preferred. He's Lord of our life, and if we have anything left over, we might serve somewhere else; but our service starts with Him. He should never get our leftovers. Life is full of decisions, and the question is often, Who are you going to serve?

If you have a choice between a tee time at 9:00 a.m. on Sunday morning or going to worship the Lord with His people, what do you choose?

If you have a choice between going to the beach and honoring Christ by serving with God's people, what do you prefer?

You can't call Jesus "Lord" and take a vacation from Him.

Enthrone Jesus

I love how the hymn "At the Name of Jesus" puts it: "In your hearts, enthrone [Jesus]; there let Him subdue all that is not holy, all that is not true." The heart is the central part of a man's existence, which is why God's Word says, "Above all else, guard your heart, for everything you do flows from it" (Proverbs 4:23 NIV). A heart controlled by Christ pursues all that is holy and true.

Can you sing with a clear conscience and a full heart the words of this famous hymn?

> All hail the power of Jesus' name, let angels prostrate fall.
> Bring forth the royal diadem and crown Him Lord of all.
> O that with yonder sacred throng we at His feet may fall.
> We'll join the everlasting song and crown Him Lord of all.

Jesus *is* Lord. But is He *your* Lord? And does the fruit of your life show it? The night I came forward at church to get saved, I said, "I want to give my heart and life to Jesus Christ." I'll never forget that night. I didn't know it, but I was sanctifying the Lord God in my heart. I was setting aside Jesus as Lord of my life.

I didn't come forward thinking, *Man, I am on my way to hell* (even though I was). I didn't walk to the front thinking, *I am scared! Let's get this contracted, secure my membership, get me in that tank before I go to hell.* None of those thoughts swam in my head. I had been told that Jesus Christ was in the life-changing business, and I thought that if He could change my life and change my want-to's and desires, then I was a candidate. And He made good on His word! He changed my life.

Did I miss hell? Oh, yes! Did Jesus forgive my sins? Oh, yes! Did He cleanse me? Oh, yes! But bottom line, He brought me into a relationship of obedience to God. When I devoted myself to Him, He did some things in my life in a single week that some men still haven't done fifteen years after they got saved. The question is, how devoted are we to Christ as Lord? He can do a lot in a very short time if the devotion is real.

An Artificial Distinction

The issue of Christ's lordship is a major problem in the church today. Somehow we've created an artificial distinction between trusting Christ as Savior and confessing Him as Lord. We've made two experiences out of just one.

The result? We have a host of men in our churches who have "accepted Christ" in order to miss hell and gain heaven, but who seem completely unconcerned about obeying the Lord.

Listen, salvation is not a cafeteria line where we can take the Saviorhood of Jesus Christ and pass on His lordship. We're not free to take what we want and leave the rest. We cannot get saved on the installment plan, with fingers crossed and inner reservations, as though one could take Christ on layaway. We have only one option: We receive Jesus as Lord or we reject Him.

My favorite verse in the whole Bible is Romans 10:13, which says, "For 'whoever calls on the name of the LORD shall be saved.'" When I put my faith in Christ many years ago, I did not understand lordship, but I received Him as Lord nonetheless. I didn't know the Bible, since I'd never owned one, but I believed all of it. How is that possible? Well, I don't understand electricity, but I believe in light switches. I don't understand automobiles, but I drive one.

Once we receive Jesus as Lord, our options end. We're no longer our own; He's bought us at the price of His own shed blood (see 1 Corinthians 6:20).

On January 7, 1973, I devoted my life to Jesus Christ as Lord. On that day, He saved me and I became part of the family of God. My salvation had nothing to do with my later call to preach. On the day of my salvation, Jesus made me into a Christian, not a preacher. Preachers can go to hell; Christians don't. On the day I received Jesus as Lord, my options ended. I'd been bought at a price.

I belong to Him, and that makes all the difference.

The Development of a Disciple's Heart

One little saying has made a lot of people uncomfortable: "If He's not Lord of all, He's not Lord at all." While I agree wholeheartedly that Jesus is Lord of all, I will also insist that He prepares us, over time, to understand what lordship entails.

Jesus knows we can't "get it" all at once. That's why He once told His men, "I have much more to say to you, more than you can now bear" (John 16:12 NIV). Jesus didn't tell them everything they needed to know in one big download. Did they need to know those things?

Absolutely. But He prepared them to receive it all. They had to be *developed* as disciples.

The night I came to Jesus Christ, I didn't know my Bible. I didn't understand lordship. Despite that, the Bible was still true and lordship was a reality. So how did the reality come to be true in my experience?

From that night on, God began to develop me. He started to take me from Point A to Point B and beyond. Peter gets at this truth when he writes, "Always be prepared to give an answer to everyone who asks you to give the reason for the hope that you have" (1 Peter 3:15 NIV). God instructs us to be "prepared" to speak to others about the difference it makes to have Christ as Lord. And how do we get prepared? I think it's crucial to understand that while *lordship is positional, preparedness is progressive.*

There's only one way to accept Jesus, and that's as Lord. You can't receive Him for what He is not! He *is* Lord, and that's how I received Him. How could I ask Him to become less so that I could become more? That's just crazy.

My development as a believer looks a lot like my development as a human. I was born into this world as a child, but I didn't remain a child. Just so, while I didn't understand anything about "lordship" when I became a Christian, today I'm still wearing the same skin in which God birthed me. It's stretched a lot, though! God is developing me.

This is why I study my Bible diligently. This is why I gather with God's people for worship every Sunday. This is why I take advantage of training opportunities. I want to progress. I want God to develop me. I want Him to take me from Point F to Point G to Point H and beyond.

Be Prepared to Give an Answer

For what purpose is God developing me? Peter says the Lord wants to prepare me, in part, so that I can give an answer to anyone who wants to know what makes my life so different.

The Greek word translated "answer" means to provide a credible explanation of some personal conviction. The Christian discipline of apologetics refers to the marshaling of evidence from all possible sources to declare the validity of claims to Christian truth.

We have a reliable Bible, an inerrant, good, perfect Word from Almighty God Himself. Our faith is defensible, so that we can speak with both integrity and authority. Regardless of who wants answers, we can speak God's Word to them with confidence.

When the Bible says, "Always be prepared to give an answer," it's picturing something similar to a defense presented in court. The phrase is used to describe an attorney who talks his client out of a charge brought against him. It means to answer back, to give a defense. The underlying Greek word more literally could be translated "talk off from." OK, Peter, talk off from what? Talk off from the lordship of Christ.

Ever since Jesus became my Savior, I've been "talking off from" His lordship. When the young lady on the plane realized she was sitting beside a preacher, I began to "talk off from" the lordship of Jesus Christ. I began to give a defense of the Christian's need for Christ to be Lord.

The word *defense* (*apologia*) doesn't mean to apologize. I never apologize for being a Christian! The word means "to defend." If you're going to give a credible answer, you must understand what you believe and why you are a Christian. You also must be able to articulate your belief. The Bible instructs us to do this humbly, thoughtfully, reasonably, and biblically.

When I first became a Christian, I thought I was supposed to tell everybody about Jesus. I'd go to work and say, "Mr. Solomon, I got saved and Jesus Christ changed my life." He would respond, "Well, Johnny, I'm a Jew." I didn't even know what a Jew was. So I would say, "It doesn't matter. He'll save anybody." I knew it made no difference who you were or what you'd done. I shared the gospel with everyone I knew, because I didn't know any better.

Afterwards, I'd often go to a friend, Alfred Joyner, for advice. He discipled me before people saw discipleship as cool. Alfred was a truck driver, not a pastor. I would come to Alfred and say, "I talked to Mr. Solomon today, and here's what he said." Alfred would then take his Bible, turn to a particular passage, and read verses like Romans 10:10-13 to explain to me that Jesus came to save Jew and Gentile alike. Before too long, I had a good answer to give. I could "talk off" from the Bible about the lordship of Jesus Christ to anybody God might put in my life.

A year and a half after I became a Christian, do you know what people started calling me? "Preacher." They gave me that title before I was one. In fact, although I wasn't yet a preacher, I was a witness. I had learned some things about developing my walk with Jesus.

God also sent me another discipler named Mitchell Bennett. I can still remember the color of shirt he wore when I asked him specific questions. He would say, "Johnny, the Bible speaks to that." I didn't know it, but God was taking me from Point A to Point B and beyond. He was developing me.

The moment I put my faith in Christ, Jesus became my Lord positionally. I've never had more of Jesus than the night I received Him. We don't receive Him on installment plans; we get all of Him, all at once. When Jesus Christ is Lord, that's the top rung of the ladder. No one gets more or higher or better than that. Positionally, you have it all from the beginning. But developmentally, you can grow over time.

And God *expects* you and me to grow.

A Suffering World Needs Hope

It helps me to recall that *suffering* provides the context for Peter's first letter. As we Christians suffer in a fallen world, the apostle expects that observers will note the remarkable optimism and hope we have. And so he writes, "In your hearts revere Christ as Lord. Always be prepared to give an answer to everyone who asks you to give the reason for the hope that you have" (1 Peter 3:15 NIV).

We need to be ready always to give a defense. A defense to whom? To everyone. That's inclusive, relating to all life circumstances. We are witnesses, not prosecuting attorneys. That's why it's so important to shore up our witness with a life that backs up our defense. In a loving and respectful manner, we're to present an account of what we believe and why we believe it.

Several years ago, the community where I used to live asked if my wife and I would host an open house in order to raise money to help needy children. We considered it a wonderful cause and so said yes. A lot of people came through our home.

Visitors went upstairs, around the house, and then exited from our basement, where I had a pool table. On the pool table I had placed stacks of my life story, *From the Poolroom to the Pulpit*, with a sign next to them that said, "Take one. Free gift." People took hundreds of copies.

Those in charge of the event later told me, "Mr. Hunt, the most common statement we heard about your home was, 'It was amazing what we did not see: liquor cabinets. And it was amazing what we did see: pictures of Christ, a lot about the family, and needlepoints that referred to eternity.'"

In this suffering world, people *will* ask about the reason for our hope. How do they know we have a hope? They know it because those with hope act differently than those without it. They respond differently to pain and hardship. Believers might be dying, too, but they have joy, real joy, wonderful joy. And why do they have that joy? They have it because they put the Lord Jesus on the throne of their heart.

When people observe you, do they see a difference? Do they see something they want but don't yet have? The absence of hope in the lives of unbelievers causes them to inquire about the reason for the hope they see in believers. The victorious life of a disciple of Jesus prompts sincere questions from those who don't yet know the Savior.

When a man asks you why you have hope, be ready to give him a reason for what you believe. Be prepared to explain how the hope you have in Christ enables you to live as you do.

What Was That Book?

I boarded a plane one day for a one-hour flight home. I happened to be sitting at the bulkhead, so I had to stow my stuff overhead. I grabbed my Bible and a copy of Oswald Chambers's *My Utmost for His Highest*, sat down, and started to read. Those two items often prompt conversation.

On any flight, many men will be seated near you. Many of them flip through their *Playboy* magazines and other pornography, completely unashamed of it. They won't even try to hide the covers. (At the same time, a lot of us Christians feel intimidated even to open our Bibles.)

When I got off the plane, a man sitting nearby asked me, "What were you reading? What was that book you had with the Bible?"

"A few devotional thoughts from a fellow who encouraged preachers all his life," I replied.

"Please give me the name of it," he said, and wrote down the title. I had no more conversation with the man and I don't know his name; he was there and then gone. I do know, though, that when people see a difference in your life, they'll ask questions. They'll ask because you seem to have hope in a world that they trudge through as hopeless.

When you find yourself in such a situation, don't back up. Don't back away. Don't back down. Humbly and honorably step to the front of the line and be able to give a reason for the hope in you. Prepare yourself to tell others of your hope in Christ. Be able to speak from the Bible about your relationship with the Lord.

"But no one *ever* asks me those questions," you say.

I wonder—could that be because you have no fruit in your life? Do you say, "Lord, Lord," but don't do what He says? If so, you can change all that, starting right now.

Your Final Destination

I walked up to an airline counter the other day. A woman looked at my ticket and asked me, "Mr. Hunt, is Atlanta your final destination?"

"Ma'am," I said, "I sure hope not. I don't want to stay here forever."

But if we don't feel comfortable down here on earth responding to Jesus as Lord, then what makes us think we'll feel any more comfortable responding to Jesus as Lord in heaven? What makes us think heaven will even be our final destination?

Eddie Carswell, an original member of NewSong, called me one day after his stepfather died. He was getting ready to visit the cemetery and he couldn't find the verse, "to be absent from the body and to be present with the Lord." Every now and then, I also forget the location of some verse. I told him the text he wanted is found in

2 Corinthians 5:8. He answered, "Brother Johnny, I started studying it in my mind before I located it in the Bible, and God gave me a new song: 'It's not far from here.'"

I'm going to spend eternity with the Lord, and I want to remind you that it's not far from here. How far is it? Just a heartbeat away. Do me a favor and make sure that the Lord you'll greet up there is the Lord you've made a habit of obeying down here.

4

A SAVIOR LIKE NO OTHER

One of my favorite places to visit in Israel is the city of Capernaum. Its ancient ruins sit on the northern shore of the Sea of Galilee, where the city served as the headquarters for Jesus' earthly ministry. I cannot speak about Capernaum without seeing myself walking through its crumbling gates.

One of the things I love about Capernaum is that it had only one synagogue, and the Gospel of Mark says that Jesus preached there. To stand where I know Jesus once spoke just thrills me.

Jesus once healed a paralytic in Capernaum after the man's friends tore the roof off the "house" (maybe the synagogue?) where Jesus was speaking in order to get him in front of the Savior. When they had lowered him into the room, Jesus said to the lame man, "Son, your sins are forgiven you" (Mark 2:5). Some religious leaders sitting nearby immediately took exception, thinking, "Why does this Man speak blasphemies like this? Who can forgive sins but God alone?" (v. 7).

Now, these men had a front-row seat; they saw and heard everything. In Jesus' day, Sadducees and Pharisees always received the most prominent seats, right down front. Something like that still happens today in many places around the world. When I visited Vietnam some years ago, we arrived after the building already had filled up. Dozens of people stood outside, unable to get in. But when we Americans got there, the event organizers met us and took us to our front-row seats.

These religious leaders in Capernaum saw the man's friends taking apart the roof, they witnessed the man getting lowered to the floor with ropes, and they heard Jesus tell the man his sins had been forgiven. Jesus sensed their indignant response and Mark tells us He asked them, "Which is easier, to say to the paralytic, 'Your sins are forgiven you,' or to say, 'Arise, take up your bed and walk'?" (v. 9). Of course, physically it's just as easy to say one sentence as it is the other; but the two statements have vastly different implications. Jesus then continued, "'But that you may know that the Son of Man has power on earth to forgive sins'—He said to the paralytic, 'I say to you, arise, take up your bed, and go to your house'" (vv. 10-11).

Instantly, the man's paralysis disappeared. He jumped up, picked up his pallet, and walked out of the room. Everyone there should have shouted, "Jesus is God! He can forgive sins!" But that's not what happened. While everybody else felt "amazed" and "glorified God," from that moment on, the Pharisees and Sadducees counted Jesus as their enemy.

This story shows that men do not come to God through human wisdom. The religious leaders were right in believing that only God can forgive sins; but when Jesus paired His ability to heal with His ability to forgive, they should have put two and two together and said, "Since that lame man is walking, it proves that Jesus *does* have the authority to forgive. Why…He's God our Savior!" This miracle should have been one of the first incidents to lead these religious leaders to faith, but instead it became one of the first events leading them to oppose and eventually kill Jesus. Instead of embracing Him as their Savior, they left the house plotting how to destroy Him.

Neither their opposition nor their unbelief, however, could change the truth. Jesus had the power and authority to forgive sins, which made Him the Savior. He *still* is, and He always will be.

A Savior Like No Other

One of the most glorious names given to Jesus in all of Scripture is the title Savior. The Bible declares that Jesus "is able to save completely those who come to God through him, because he always lives to intercede for them" (Hebrews 7:25 NIV). This verse magnifies several aspects of Christ's great work of salvation.

Jesus is omnipotent

The fact that Jesus saves at all speaks of His omnipotence. Almighty power throbs in Christ's salvation. No priest or king, politician or psychiatrist, parent or religious leader was ever able to save, not even partially or temporarily. Jesus *only* can save. The Bible says of Him, "Salvation is found in no one else, for there is no other name under heaven given to mankind by which we must be saved" (Acts 4:12 NIV).

I was buying some groceries one day, doing my honey-do jobs. I didn't have much in my cart, but the young woman who waited on me asked if she could take my groceries to my car. As she and I walked across the parking lot, we met a man just bouncing along who stopped and stared at me.

"How you doing?" I asked.

"Good," he replied. He stared some more, and then added, "Excuse me, but are you Johnny Hunt?"

"Yeah," I said.

"Praise God!" he answered. "I've been an atheist all my life, and the other day while riding across Bethany Bridge, God saved me." The memory clearly fired him up. "I'm going to come and tell you about it," he promised.

When I got home, I told my wife the story. "Where's Bethany Bridge?" she asked.

"I don't have a clue," I said. "But I'll tell you one thing: that man will never forget where it is."

The fact that Jesus can visit some little bridge in Georgia and there save a man who's been an atheist his whole life doesn't surprise me. Do you know why? Because Jesus is able. He's omnipotent and saves us with almighty power. He *completely* saves us, past, present, and future. When Jesus Christ saved me, He saved me for forever. My salvation has nothing to do with my ability to serve Him but with His sufficiency to save me. Jesus saved *all* of me for eternity.

Maybe you have a son or a daddy at home, or a mom or daughter, or a friend at work, and you think, *God can't save him,* or *Jesus just can't reach her.* You need to rethink that! Jesus is able.

Jesus operates like no one else

The New King James Bible translates Hebrews 7:25 to say that Jesus "is able to save to the uttermost." I like how one old preacher said it: "He saved me from the guttermost to the uttermost." Jesus plucked me out of the gutter and gave me a prospect brighter than the sun. I was lost in sin, under its power and penalty, and Jesus Christ bought me out of the devil's slave market. He saved me, just as He promises: "For 'whoever calls on the name of the Lord shall be saved'" (Romans 10:13).

And don't forget the prospect of where you're going! We best magnify Jesus' salvation not by what He saved us *from,* but what He saved us *to.* Have you seen the bumper sticker that says "Christians are not perfect, just forgiven"? I might want to add a parenthetical statement: "And for those who don't understand, let me say that I will be perfect one day." *That* is my prospect.

A lady once said to me, "You know, preacher, I'm in the same category you're in. I can't sing, either." I thought, *Thank you very much.* She added, "But I think we're all going to sing on the other side."

Yes, praise God, we will all sing in heaven. But I'm singing on this side too! You don't have to be able to sing to *sing*; you just have to have a song. When I got saved, the Holy Spirit put a song in my heart, and I'm still singing it. Too many people in our churches can sing, but they don't have a song.

Do you have a song? Do you know your prospect? Do you know where you're heading?

Anyone can be the object of Jesus' saving power

Jesus Christ can save *any* sinner from *any* condition—and those He saves, He saves completely and for all eternity. Our Lord emphatically declared, "All those the Father gives me will come to me, and whoever comes to me I will never drive away" (John 6:37 NIV).

Decades ago, when I pastored Long Leaf Baptist Church, one night I went out soul-winning. I dropped by Buddy and Belinda Joyner's house and presented the gospel of Jesus Christ to them. They both got down on their knees and asked Jesus to come into their hearts.

Like any old Baptist boy would do, I returned to the church, eager to share the news. Someone asked, "How's it going?"

"Buddy and Belinda Joyner just got saved!" I said.

"Well, brother Johnny," a man said, "did you know it's not Buddy and Belinda *Joyner*? It's Buddy Joyner, but Belinda's got a different last name. They're living together."

"Is that right?" I said.

"Yeah, so I hate to pop your bubble," he said, "but they didn't get saved. They can't get saved until they break off what they are doing wrong, and then they can come to Jesus."

Don't you believe it! If that were true, no Christian on the planet should ever sing again the old hymn "Just as I am, without one plea." To come to Jesus, you don't *stop* anything. The reason you need Jesus is that you lack the power to change your own life. So you come just as you are. Jesus takes care of the rest.

About three days later, my phone rang. I heard Buddy's voice say, "Can we have breakfast?" I met him at a local restaurant, and he said, "Brother Johnny, I need some help. You didn't know this, but Belinda ain't my wife."

"Well, I heard," I replied.

"I'm really sorry, but for five years we've been living together. We're used to each other's salary helping to pay the rent and all that. But did you know that ever since the other night, after you left, we can't sleep together? She's in one room, I'm in another, and we're in a pickle. We need to know what to do. We can't live like that anymore."

Did some outward law tell Buddy what he needed to do? Oh, no. Jesus took that old, cold stone from Moses's hand and laid it aside, and with His finger He wrote the wonderful law of God on Buddy's heart.

I immediately got on the phone and called one of my wealthy members. "Doug," I said, "I know you have a real big house, and I have a dilemma. Can you give Buddy or Belinda a place to live for a while?"

"I can take either one of them," he answered right away. And that day he took Belinda into his home. I did the wedding about three months later.

Years later, I heard from Buddy. "Belinda sends her love," he said. "We're serving Jesus and have been ever since that night you left our house."

Anybody can be the object of Jesus' saving power. *He* does the saving, not us. No system of legalism, whether Judaic or Christian, ever brought a man to God. Sometimes I witness to someone and he says, "Brother Johnny, I've been coming to your church. I've been doing better lately. I'm going to clean up my act, and then I'll join your church."

You can guess how I respond. "You don't need to clean up your act and join the church," I tell him. "You need to come just as you are, right now, and let Jesus Christ clean up your heart and soul."

Listen, it isn't about you "getting better." You aren't any good and you deserve to go to hell. That's not a message you'll hear often today; we worry more about offending people than about helping them. But I'd rather tell you the truth and offend you than have you sit on the end of a pew and let it rock you to hell.

Christ died for you *because* you were no good. We are all sinners. We've all missed the mark. Jesus took your place on the cross, and that's why we call Him "Savior."

Salvation is completely of the Lord

Is our salvation rooted in our efforts to serve Jesus or in His ability to save us? It's *all* Him. Salvation is of the Lord.

He's the rescuer. *He's* the completer. *He's* the high priest (see chapter 5). *He's* the One who ever lives to intercede for me. *He's* the one who pleads on my side. Every time I sin, Jesus says, "Put it on My account." That's why the Bible says, "The blood of Jesus Christ His Son cleanses us from *all* sin" (1 John 1:7, emphasis mine).

We can no more keep ourselves saved than we can save ourselves in the first place. Constantly, eternally, and perpetually, Jesus intercedes for us before His Father. If you ask some people if they're going to heaven when they die, they'll say, "I hope so." They speak like that because they believe if they get into sin before they die, they won't make it. But that would highlight their ability to obey rather than Christ's sufficiency to save, and God won't have any of that.

He Meets Our Need

Our Savior, Jesus, meets our need like no one else ever could. The writer of Hebrews says that Jesus "truly meets our need—one who is holy, blameless, pure, set apart from sinners, exalted above the heavens" (Hebrews 7:26 NIV).

Jesus fits us like a neoprene glove. He's totally suited to us and meets our needs completely. He "feels" right. I've worn Him long enough to know He's exactly the right Savior for me. Notice five things the writer of Hebrews says about our Savior.

1. Jesus is holy

The Bible describes Jesus Christ as holy. That means He fully satisfies all the righteous claims of a holy God. Who declared Jesus Christ holy? God did.

And what is holiness? Our holy God is set apart from sin, morally perfect, infinitely righteous. The prophet Habakkuk said to the Lord, "Your eyes are too pure to look on evil; you cannot tolerate wrongdoing" (Habakkuk 1:13 NIV). And it's this holy God who says to you and me, "You shall be holy, for I am holy" (1 Peter 1:16 ESV). God demands holiness in the life of every believer.

But how does that help us? How can *we* be holy? In ourselves, we can't comply. In ourselves, we're the opposite of holy. *In Christ*, however, we're holy because Christ in us satisfies all the holy demands of a righteous and holy God. Our salvation doesn't rest on how well we live for Him, but on the fact that He lives in us.

2. Jesus is blameless

Jesus is both upwardly holy and outwardly blameless. No malice or craftiness has ever lived in Him. He is guileless, innocent, and guiltless. Jesus healed, but He never harmed. No one ever has or ever will be able to convict Him of sin.

3. Jesus is pure

Inwardly, Jesus is undefiled and unstained. No sin ever tainted Him and no evil ever corrupted Him. Someone may say, "But during His earthly ministry, wasn't Jesus called a friend of sinners? How can anyone be a friend of sinners and not end up defiled?" Jesus' contact with sinners never defiled His character or warped His conduct. Jesus had lots of contact, but no contamination.

4. Jesus was separated from sinners

This may sound like a contradiction, but it's not. How could Jesus have contact with sinners but still remain separated from them? This speaks of His sinlessness. He is in a different class from everyone else, distinct, unique. But while He stayed separated, He did not remain isolated. Even as He interacted with sinners, He remained separate from them, distinct.

Simon Peter understood this from the very beginning. When Jesus showed up one day at Simon's workplace, the big fisherman allowed Him to preach from his boat. After Jesus had finished, the Lord instructed Peter and his friends to let out their nets into the lake, even though the men had worked the whole night before without catching anything. They complied, and caught so many fish that their nets began to break. Peter immediately sensed how separate and distinct Jesus was, and cried out, "Depart from me, for I am a sinful man, O Lord!" (Luke 5:8 ESV).

Jesus did *not* depart, but instead replied, "Do not be afraid; from now on you will be catching men" (v. 10 ESV). And from that time on, Peter and his fishing buddies "left everything and followed him" (v. 11 ESV). Separated, but together.

Sometimes I go to the race track, where I hang out to talk about Jesus. What a preacher's paradise! Thousands of unsaved people show up, and I come to hand out gospel tracts, books, and tapes and to brag on Jesus. One night, twenty-five thousand people turned out. Several nights, we've had twenty thousand. That's a lot of fish to catch! So I go out to the race track and preach early Sunday morning before I go to church and preach in some worship services.

5. Jesus is exalted above the heavens

Through His resurrection from the dead, Jesus was "declared to be the Son of God in power according to the Spirit of holiness" (Romans 1:4 ESV). While He was always King, in His resurrection He wears the crown of life as the King of kings and Lord of lords. His exaltation above the heavens speaks of His sovereignty:

> Therefore God has highly exalted him and bestowed on him the name that is above every name, so that at the name of Jesus every knee should bow, in heaven and on earth and under the earth, and every tongue confess that Jesus Christ is Lord, to the glory of God the Father (Philippians 2:9-11 ESV).

You could not have a greater Savior!

How Jesus Saves

The Bible lays out a very clear, simple road to salvation. John wrote, "To all who did receive him [Jesus], to those who believed in his name, he gave the right to become children of God" (John 1:12 NIV). Three words in this verse, all action verbs, outline the process of how Jesus saves.

Believe

Did you know that John mentions the name "Jesus" 247 times?

Why mention His name so often? Because to believe in His name is to believe in what His name signifies. It is to believe that Jesus can save you from your sins.

The very name Jesus means "God saves." Before the Lord's birth in Bethlehem, an angel told His foster father, Joseph, "You shall call His name JESUS, for He will save His people from their sins" (Matthew 1:21). Believing in the name of Jesus implies personal surrender and commitment to Him.

May I ask, when have you personally surrendered and committed your life to Jesus Christ? Have you "believed in His name"?

In ancient times, one's name was more than just a personal designation. It was a reflection of one's character and attributes. When we believe in Jesus' name, we yield ourselves to be possessed by the One in whom we believe. When a man says, "I'm giving my life to Jesus Christ," he's expressing his faith in Jesus. He's surrendering himself to Christ, acknowledging the Lord's rightful position and the man's subordinate place before Christ's divine character.

One translation puts it this way: "To those who had yielded him their allegiance, he gave the right to become children of God." People tell me, "Oh, I know all about God." But they don't know Him personally. As a result, Jesus doesn't have their allegiance—everything else does. They give Jesus the leftovers of their time. They give Him little pieces of their talent and scraps (or nothing) of their treasure. Why? Because they know *about* Him, but they don't *know* Him. When a man comes to know Jesus, he surrenders allegiance to Him. All of that is wrapped up in the little word "believe."

Receive

It's not enough to believe that Jesus is the Savior. He must become *your* Savior. And the only way that happens is for you to receive Him.

When my wife gives me a present at Christmas, I believe it's a gift, but I'll never know what that gift is until I open it and receive it as my own. That's what you do when you receive something—you take it and it becomes your personal possession.

A lot of people know *about* God's gift, but have never *received* the gift. Oh, it's been given! But it's meant nothing to them. It's still wrapped and they have no idea what lies inside. They've never taken the time to wrap their hands around it, open it, and receive it. Have you received the gift of Jesus' salvation?

Become

I used to go out at night, handing out gospel tracts. I'd been saved only a little while when somebody bought me fifty orange-colored tracts called *The Four Spiritual Laws*. The final law said, "You must individually receive Jesus Christ as Lord and Savior."

The Bible says you must *individually* receive Jesus. No one else can do this for you. At some time in your life, you must receive Him individually. And when you do receive Him, He gives you the right to *become* a child of God.

The term *right* can be translated "power" or "authority," but don't believe for a moment this means you have the power or authority to become a son of God at will. The word *right* does not refer to the ability to say, "I'll become a child of God anytime I want to." Salvation is of God, which means becoming a child of God is not within your strength or ability.

Salvation is a divine initiative, not a human one. John insisted that God's children are "born not of natural descent, nor of human decision or a husband's will, but born of God" (John 1:13 NIV).

If you think, *I'm not ready to make this decision right now, but when I'm good and ready, I will*, let me explain something to you. Do you know why you're not ready? It's because only God can get you ready to take that step. This isn't a matter of you picking and choosing. Salvation is of the Lord, and He's the one who initiates.

While you're sitting in your favorite chair, minding your own business, He can choose to suddenly touch you. Maybe you didn't intend to do business with Him, but He can step into your world, speak to you, and initiate your conversion. Maybe you're fighting back tears right now. Maybe you're shaking a bit. If so, He's saying to you, "Come to Me, all you who labor and are heavy laden, and I will give you rest" (Matthew 11:28).

Salvation is not of human descent any more than it is of human initiative. It is not "of blood," in the Bible's language. Why not? God has no grandchildren, only sons and daughters.

"But my daddy was one of the finest Baptist preachers this country has ever known," you say. Well, God bless your daddy. But the question is, are *you* a Christian?

Since salvation doesn't come through human desire or by the will of the flesh, that means no amount of wishful thinking can make someone a child of God. One's own efforts simply cannot produce salvation. So, are you a Christian?

"Well, I sure hope so."

That's just wishful thinking. *Hope* so? I *know* I'm a Christian. I've been born again. Jesus has changed my life. I met Him. I know Him. He walks with me, talks to me, reveals Himself to me in the heavens and in my heart. So again, are you a Christian?

"Well, Brother Johnny, you and I believe a little different here, but I'm not a bad person."

I'm not talking about good or bad. No man is good enough to go to heaven on his own merits. Anyone who goes to heaven gets there because of God's grace, not because of his own goodness. Jesus "saved us, not because of righteous things we had done, but because of his mercy" (Titus 3:5 NIV).

If you're a parent, you probably want your children and grand-children to be saved. But if they ever are saved, it won't be because of your will, but because of God's will. Salvation is of divine origin, not of human desire.

My brother had a baby named Frieda, who died tragically by some form of crib death. Afterwards, some religious friends came by to comfort the parents. They meant well, but they asked, "Was the baby baptized? If she was not baptized, she cannot go to heaven." Listen, nobody goes to heaven by human effort. Salvation is not of the will of man. Your parents may have had you baptized as a baby, but that does not make you a child of God. When babies die, they automatically go to heaven because of God's grace, not because of some priest or a preacher or ritual.

Your parents probably wanted you to know God one day, but your infant baptism happened because of their decision, not yours. *You* have to receive Christ. Neither is it enough to go through cate-chism, check off the list, and say, "I believe this about Him, I believe that about Him." It's not what you believe *about* Him, it's *knowing* Him. You have to know Him.

Do you know Him?

Those who receive Christ are granted the privilege of becom-ing children of God, the moment they believe. One snowy Sunday night, my sweet wife and I got in our car and drove less than two blocks to Long Leaf Baptist Church. We went in and sat down on a pew near the front. I already knew I was going to respond to a gospel invitation, so I didn't want to have to walk far. When the preacher gave the invitation to receive Christ, I went down to the front and gave my life to Jesus Christ.

The moment I believed in Jesus and received Him as my Savior and Lord, God granted me the privilege of becoming His child. I didn't "grow into" becoming a child of God. I became one of His children supernaturally, at that very moment. I became a child of God right then, right there, forever.

Our Obligation

Those of us who have believed, received, and now belong to Jesus have an obligation. Remember, Jesus can save only those who come to Him in faith. He is able to save all, but not all will be saved because not all will believe.

While the Bible clearly speaks of divine election—we didn't choose Him, He chose us—I believe it also teaches that a man can say yes or no. One of the saddest verses in the New Testament says, "The Pharisees and the lawyers rejected the purpose of God for themselves" (Luke 7:30 ESV). Yes, you can reject God's purpose for you.

God will save to the uttermost *all* who will come to Him. The late Adrian Rogers once said, "Since we don't know who the elect are, why don't we just go around and witness and nominate everybody?"

While we cannot *make* people believe or obey, our responsibility doesn't end until we have urged them as strongly as we know how to trust in the Savior. A lady said to me one day, "I'm really concerned about one of my loved ones. I'm not sure if he's saved or not."

"Why don't you know if he's saved or not?" I asked.

"I've never asked him," she said.

I believe we have an obligation to ask. Do you know how I know where my dad stands with Jesus? I asked him. My mom is in heaven now. Do you know how I knew where my mother stood with Jesus? I asked her. It's my obligation.

I speak with strangers. I talk to my friends about Jesus. I ask them. I share Christ—and so should you.

So Let Me Ask You Again

Have you ever asked Jesus Christ to be your Savior and Lord? Do you know for sure that you're on your way to heaven? Does Jesus live inside you, empowering you moment by moment to do the will of God?

If you want Jesus Christ to come into your life, then I urge you to receive Him today. Even now, He may be speaking to you, drawing you, working in your heart. Would you like to receive Him? If you do, then I suggest you pray in your heart to God something like the following:

> Lord Jesus, I need you. I'm sorry for my sins. Come into my life and into my heart. I want to individually receive you as my Lord and Savior. Forgive me, cleanse me, save me. Make me into one of Your children. I pray in Jesus' name, amen.

If you prayed a prayer like that, congratulations! Welcome to the family of God.

5

A HIGH PRIEST WHO BREAKS THE MOLD

The Old Testament has no concept of sinful people being cleansed from their sin, only of having their sin temporarily covered. In His forbearance, God allowed the blood of goats and bulls shed in sacrifice to "cover" the sins of His people, until a perfect sacrifice could be made that had the power to totally cleanse guilty men and women.

God arranged for priests to serve as intermediaries between His people and Himself, thus reminding the nation that no sinner could directly approach a holy God. The Lord further stipulated that the priests of ancient Israel had to come from the family of Aaron, and that only the high priest could offer the highest sacrifice under the old covenant. This sacrifice took place only once a year, on Yom Kippur, the "day of atonement" (see Leviticus 16). For one year, God in His forbearance would pass over the sin of the people; but the sacrifice had to take place every year.

When Yom Kippur arrived, the high priest entered the innermost part of the temple, the Most Holy Place, in order to sprinkle the blood of an innocent animal on a golden slab (called the mercy seat) that sat atop the ark of the covenant. Underneath the mercy seat and inside the ark lay the broken law of God—God's way of symbolically showing us that the Messiah's blood covered the broken law. Even though all of us have sinned and so have broken the law, God was willing, even before Christ, to pass over the sin of His people. Of course, the blood of bulls and goats could cover their sin only temporarily, until the final and perfect sacrifice was made.

Because the high priest was as much of a sinner as anyone else, he had to make an offering for himself and his own sins before he could even enter the Most Holy Place (much less make a sacrifice there). On his way to the ark, the high priest had to pass through three areas of the temple. First, he took the blood of an innocent animal and went through a door into the outer court. Then he went through another door into what was called the Holy Place. Finally, he made his way through a thick curtain into the Most Holy Place, the inner sanctum, where the ark of the covenant stood.

Because the high priest was not allowed to sit down as he carried out his solemn duties, the law permitted no chairs in the temple, emphasizing that the sacrifice had to be completed without delay. As soon as the high priest completed his annual task, he left the Most Holy Place and did not return for another year.

This solemn sacrifice on Yom Kippur began with Aaron in Moses' day and continued through the centuries until the Romans destroyed both Jerusalem and the temple in AD 70.

Did you know that eighty-three high priests served God under the Levitical system? Every one of them died. Just like us, they had clay feet. No Hebrew high priest had the power to live forever.

Every high priest who served under the old economy died and was buried.

Not so Jesus! As He did in so many critical categories, Jesus broke the mold.

Jesus Christ, Our High Priest

Do you consider yourself a Christian? If so, the Bible explicitly commands you to "fix your thoughts on Jesus, whom we acknowledge as our apostle and high priest" (Hebrews 3:1 NIV). In other words, you need to make a careful observation, direct your attention to something crucial. God is telling you and me, "Put your mind on Jesus and let it remain there."

While the Bible has a lot to say about Jesus as our high priest, I want to highlight seven characteristics that should change the way we think about our Lord.

1. Jesus is our great high priest

Many religions, instead of having a pastor or a minister, have a priest. The Bible calls Jesus Christ our *great* high priest (Hebrews 4:14). There's no high priest quite like Jesus, the best high priest who ever lived.

Did you know that Scripture never bestows this title of "great high priest" on another? The Bible refers to many priests and high priests, but never has anyone other than Jesus Christ been called our great high priest.

Why is He so great? For one thing, He is not a high priest in the order of Aaron (eighty-three dead men in that category). Instead, He serves as high priest in the order of Melchizedek. Jesus fulfills the ancient prophecy of Psalm 110:4 (NIV), which says of the coming Messiah,

The Lord has sworn
and will not change his mind:
"You are a priest forever,
in the order of Melchizedek."

2. Jesus committed no sin

Unlike every other high priest, Jesus never had to make a sacrifice for His sins, for the simple fact that He never committed any. The Bible tells us that He "was in all points tempted as we are, yet without sin" (Hebrews 4:15). Do you think a harlot ever came after Him? I do. Do you think the enemy ever tried to get Him to tell a lie? Oh, yes. He was tempted in every way that we are, and yet He never sinned.

Certainly, the devil and his helpers did their worst. They loaded their best guns and began their attack. They hit Jesus with every missile from the pit they could muster, and used every shell and every automatic weapon. They brought everything they had, and smoke poured from everywhere. But when the smoke cleared, Jesus looked Satan square in the eyes and said, "Is that all you got, bud?"

I would say that spells V-I-C-T-O-R-Y. Jesus had won! When it was all over, Jesus took everything hell could throw at Him and He ended up the victor. That's our great high priest.

3. Jesus is suited for us

There's nothing like being fitted for something, and the Word of God declares that the Lord Jesus Christ is perfectly suited for us. Hebrews 7:26 says, "For such a High Priest was fitting for us, who is holy, harmless, undefiled, separate from sinners, and has become higher than the heavens." Regardless of our needs, Jesus Christ is sufficient to meet the demands and challenges we face.

4. Jesus is able to save

We serve a High Priest who can present us faultless before God. Hebrews 7:25 says that Jesus "is also able to save to the uttermost those who come to God through Him." Jesus is able to save!

Jesus always completes what He begins: "being confident of this very thing, that He who has begun a good work in you will complete it until the day of Jesus Christ" (Philippians 1:6). Paul adds that Jesus "is able to keep you from stumbling, and to present you faultless before the presence of His glory with exceeding joy" (Jude 24).

5. Jesus is a caring high priest

How wonderful to know that we have a High Priest who personally cares for His family! The writer of Hebrews magnifies this caring aspect when he calls Jesus "a merciful and faithful high priest" who "because he himself suffered when he was tempted, he is able to help those who are being tempted" (Hebrews 2:17-18 NIV). No wonder Peter says, "Cast all your anxiety on him because he cares for you" (1 Peter 5:7 NIV).

6. Jesus sympathizes with us

Many people think of God as far removed from human life and concerns, yet the Bible makes it clear that in His humanity, Jesus experienced our feelings, our emotions, our temptations, and our pain.

Jesus knows what it is to suffer disappointment. He knows what it is to be criticized. He knows what it is to be ridiculed. He knows what it is to be betrayed. He knows what it is to suffer grief. He knows what it is to experience pain. And He knows what it is to suffer death.

When His friend Lazarus died, Jesus wept. Although He knew Lazarus wouldn't remain dead long, Jesus felt deeply moved and touched by the infirmities of His friends.

It's important to note that the Bible calls Jesus a "sympathizing" High Priest, not an "empathizing" one. To empathize would mean that Jesus felt as we do because He did the same things we did, including our choices to sin. To sympathize says, "Although I've never done that and I'll never go there, your pain still deeply moves me." Jesus cleansed sinners while remaining separate from and free of sin. As the sinless Son of God, He didn't empathize and say, "Yeah, I know how you feel because I got drunk one time too." He did, however, sympathize with those who had fallen into sin. Thank God, Jesus is a sympathizer and not an empathizer!

7. Jesus is a bridge maker and mediator

The word *priest* carries the idea of "bridge builder." Only Jesus Christ can build a bridge between God and man. He made a way for us to reach heaven by making Himself into our bridge over troubled water.

As God, Jesus was able to reach up and take hold of the hand of His heavenly Father. In His humanity, Jesus can reach down to us and grab our hands. And as the bridge builder, Jesus Christ brings us and God together...and so changes our lives for eternity.

Jesus' Two Key Roles as High Priest

As our High Priest, Jesus plays two critical roles, each of them equally vital. In one capacity, Jesus puts us in a right relationship with God; in the other, He keeps us in a dynamic relationship with His Father. We need both.

1. Jesus atoned for our sins, once for all

None of the eighty-three high priests who preceded Jesus ever finished the work of atonement. They had to keep returning to the temple, year after year and century after century, to make temporary sacrifices that could never take away sins. Jesus, however, entered the true temple in heaven and offered *one* sacrifice that took care of our sin problem permanently.

How? He offered the perfect sacrifice of Himself.

The Bible tells us, "Unlike the other high priests, he does not need to offer sacrifices day after day, first for his own sins, and then for the sins of the people. He sacrificed for their sins once for all when he offered himself" (Hebrews 7:27 NIV).

Jesus is the only high priest who did not have to make a sacrifice to enter the Most Holy Place. He *was* the sacrifice. Every other high priest in Old Testament days had to offer a sacrifice for his own sins, and only then could he take a spotless lamb and offer its blood on the mercy seat for the sins of others. But Jesus is both the priest *and* the sacrifice. He offered Himself for us.

The blood of Jesus, the God-man, had the power both to meet God's standard of righteousness (infinite perfection) and to wholly identify with the guilty parties (humans). Thus Hebrews 9:12 (NIV) says that Jesus "did not enter by means of the blood of goats and calves; but he entered the Most Holy Place once for all by his own blood, thus obtaining eternal redemption." When Jesus Christ, God's Son, went to Calvary and shed the eternal blood of God on the cross, that blood not only covered our sin, but it washed us clean. If you have placed your faith in Jesus, you're cleansed by His blood. I love how the old hymn says it:

> What can wash away my sins?
> Nothing but the blood of Jesus.
> What can make me whole again?
> Nothing but the blood of Jesus.
> Oh, precious is the flow

that makes me white as snow.
No other fount I know.
Nothing but the blood of Jesus.

Jesus, our great high priest, went just once to Golgotha, where He made a perfect sacrifice for us. On the cross He said, *tetelestai*, "It is finished" (John 19:30). That word had an interesting usage in first-century prisons. I've visited some ancient jails in Jerusalem, and guides say that most prisoners were released because someone had paid for their freedom. The jailer would enter the prison and nail a sign at the top of the man's cell: *Tetelestai* ("paid in full").

When Jesus Christ died on the cross to purge our sins, He did it once and for all. He presented Himself in the heavenly Most Holy Place as our sacrifice, then sat down on His throne at the right hand of God.

Tetelestai, "paid in full."

2. Jesus is always interceding for us

Although Jesus' atoning work has finished for all time, He continues to work on our behalf. We are told that Jesus "always lives to intercede" for "those who come to God through him" (Hebrews 7:25 NIV).

Of course, Jesus couldn't do this unless He lives forever. He couldn't promise to perpetually intercede for us unless He had conquered death—and that is exactly what He did on the cross. Jesus Christ, our great high priest, lives forever. That means that when He makes a promise, He will forever remain alive to make it good. Hebrews 7:24-25 (NIV) puts it all together: "Because Jesus lives forever, he has a permanent priesthood. Therefore he is able to save completely those who come to God through him, because he always lives to intercede for them."

Jesus holds His priesthood permanently. It's unchangeable, unalterable. No one will ever dethrone Him, and thank God He will never resign. He lives forever as our high priest. And where does He perform His intercessory duties? The Bible declares that Jesus "has passed through the heavens" (Hebrews 4:14).

There was a time when we could have followed the tabernacle in the wilderness, or we could have visited the temple in Jerusalem. Neither of them any longer exists. Since the Jewish people have no temple today, there are no sacrifices, no priests, no high priest. The Most Holy Place still exists, but it's in no earthly tent, tabernacle, or temple in Jerusalem. The real thing is in heaven.

When we speak today of going into the Most Holy Place and into the presence of God, we speak of the throne room of our Lord in heaven, where Jesus ever lives to intercede for us. Jesus was both priest and sacrifice—that was His destiny.

Shortly before Jesus left this earth, He prayed to His heavenly Father, "I have brought you glory on earth by finishing the work you gave me to do" (John 17:4 NIV). And what was his work? Calvary. Jesus prayed, "I am coming to you now, but I say these things while I am still in the world" (John 17:13 NIV). Jesus came to earth and did what God sent Him to do, and then went right back to heaven where He came from. So, how does that help us?

The Bible answers, "Let us then approach God's throne of grace with confidence, so that we may receive mercy and find grace to help us in our time of need" (Hebrews 4:16 NIV). The high priestly office of Jesus speaks of a time of nearness. God invites us, "Draw near."

Before the time of Jesus, God simply didn't say, "Hey, typical renegade man who came to faith, come near." Instead, He said, "This mountain is holy. If you so much as touch it, you will die. This ark of the covenant, which represents My presence, only the Levitical priest can touch. If *you* ever touch the ark (or even the wagon on which someone mistakenly carries it), I'll wipe you out."

That same God now says, "Come near."

Suppose a recent convert approaches timidly and whispers, "I'm new. I just started studying my Bible. Who are you?"

God replies, "Abba, Father. Just call me Daddy. And come on, son."

James, the half-brother of Jesus, tells us, "Draw near to God and He will draw near to you" (James 4:8). The Lord Jesus left the throne of glory and went to Calvary that He might one day sit upon the throne of grace.

The Old Testament, before the cross, knew nothing of the throne of grace. Under the old covenant, you and I were condemned to die and were on our way to hell. In the Old Testament, no ordinary Israelite could approach the Most Holy Place, where God sat enthroned. Only the high priest could do that, and then only once a year.

But because of Jesus, you and I can approach the throne of grace *at any time, as often as we wish, for whatever we need.* And God tells us, "Come boldly. Come with confidence." The Lord gives you and me freedom of expression, freedom of speech, and the ability to converse with Him without hesitation.

Just come!

Jesus, Our Advocate

Through His role as high priest, Jesus Christ gives us free access to the Father. That privilege alone ought to amaze us. But the Bible teaches that Jesus does even more. He's not only our high priest; He's also our defense attorney.

The apostle John declared, "My dear children, I write this to you so that you will not sin. But if anybody does sin, we have an advocate with the Father—Jesus Christ, the Righteous One" (1 John 2:1 NIV). The reason we can come to Jesus Christ is because of that adjective, "righteous."

I am not righteous in and of myself, and neither are you. The only righteousness we can claim is that which has been imparted to us, imputed to us, placed into our account by Jesus Christ. We don't go to heaven by our own righteousness; we go to heaven clothed in a robe of righteousness purchased for us on the cross and given to us by grace through faith.

The word translated "advocate" is the Greek term *paracleton.* Four times in the Bible it refers to the Holy Spirit, and once it refers to Jesus. How can it refer to both Jesus and the Holy Spirit? It can do so because the Holy Spirit is God and Jesus Christ is God, and the Bible reveals God as a Trinity, three Persons in one Godhead: God the Father, God the Son, and God the Holy Spirit.

The Holy Spirit convicts us of sin so we'll run to our advocate, and our advocate takes us into a heavenly courtroom where we see at least four individuals.

There's the judge; see Him up there on the bench?

There's the prosecutor; he's the one pressing charges against me.

I have my advocate, my defense attorney, standing there at my side.

And then there's the defendant: me.

God is the judge; the prosecutor is Satan; I am the accused; and the attorney for my defense is Jesus. My advocate will intercede with the judge on my behalf. Don't you just love it when the prosecuting attorney makes his case against you, and then you see your attorney approaching the bench to say something to the judge, as though he knows the judge far better than anyone else? I can almost hear the courtroom scene:

"All right, Almighty God," Satan says, "Johnny Hunt's one of your preachers. You saved him many years ago and he's studied the Bible for over forty years. But did you see how he acted just then? Did you see what he did?" I can hear the devil quote Scripture concerning the penalty for sin: death.

"Yes, Father, this is all true," replies my defense attorney, the Lord Jesus. "Johnny *is* guilty of that sin. But Father, I went to the cross and died for that sin. When Johnny was twenty years old, he placed his faith in Me and I applied My atonement to him. He received My forgiveness. His sins are forgiven. I put My robe of righteousness on him, he's covered by My blood, and he's forgiven because he's My child."

The scene gives me goosebumps…but let me go a step further. What I just pictured was the courtroom of heaven, but in the modern legal world, the defense attorney takes a very different tack. He defends his client on the merits of the defendant's case. The defendant tells him, "Hey, I am guiltless. I did not *do* this crime." That's how defendants on earth want their attorneys to argue for them, based on their innocence.

That is *not* what happens in heaven. When I go into God's throne room, my defense attorney speaks to the judge, defending me, but not on *my* merits. Rather, He bases my defense on *His* merits. As our advocate, Jesus admits we're guilty, but He insists that He's already paid in full for our crimes. He died the death we deserved and rose from the dead so we could live the life He lived.

Why would you not want such a scene playing out *all the time*?

In the modern legal world, no attorney involved in a case can be related to the judge. Neither can the defense attorney be related to the defendant. In our legal system, you can't hire your brother to defend you, and the defense attorney you hire can have no legal relationship to the judge.

But in heaven, the advocate is the Father's Son and the defendant is the brother of the defense attorney (see Hebrews 2:11-12). Not only is my attorney related to the judge, but I'm also related to my lawyer!

Do you see how high the deck is stacked against the devil?

But it's precisely here that you and I can get in trouble. We try to be good enough. We think we can defend ourselves.

We can't.

We need an advocate, Jesus Christ, the Righteous One. He pleads our case before His Father and before our Father.

A Very Different Life

When you know you have in your corner a high priest who cannot die and an advocate who cannot lose, your confidence ought to shoot to the stars. At least three major things ought to change forever.

1. You gain stability in life

Jesus is God in the flesh. In His humanity, He becomes aware of your needs; and in His divinity, He is able to meet your deepest needs. Knowing all this ought to give your life great stability.

Nevertheless, when many men get in trouble or suffer great pain, they tend to run away from God. But why? When you know you have an immortal high priest and an invincible advocate, any trials, tribulations, or disappointments you suffer ought to push you *toward* God.

If you were to ask me, "When has the Lord Jesus Christ felt most real to you?" I would reply without hesitation, "In my times of greatest difficulty."

My dad left when I was seven, so Mom became both Mom and Mister Mom. She was the one who gave me dating money. She was the one who worked two jobs to provide for six children. (I still wonder how she did it, God bless her soul.) She's been with the Son of God for many years, and I look forward to seeing her again.

But what a dark morning I faced after my mom died! A man came to my house and said, "God told me to come by and give you two words: You'll be all right, but God's going to use *God* and *time*." When you suffer a crushing loss, it takes both God and time to heal. I've never lost anyone closer to me than Mom. But during those dark, painful days, Jesus the Son of God, the great high priest, my advocate, was magnificently, wonderfully good to me.

How many men have said, "I just lost my job. How could God do that to me? I'll never go back to church"? Oh, my friend, don't run from Him! Run *to* the mercy seat. When bad news hits, don't make it worse by taking yourself away from the one person who can do you the most good. Draw near.

Jesus is touched with the feelings of your infirmities. He suffers with you. He concerns Himself with what concerns you. God often allows you to go through some valley because He wants to prove His faithfulness to you. He wants some of His children to be able to say, "I know God cares for me, because there was a day I had nothing to eat. Somebody knocked at the door, and I thought, *Who is that?* And standing there was somebody saying, 'God spoke to me and told me to empty my cupboard and bring it over to your house to feed you and your family. I don't understand it, I don't even know who you are or what your need is, but that's what God told me to do.'"

How can such knowledge *not* give you stability in life?

2. You don't need to come to Jesus more than once

When I ask some men, "Have you ever invited Jesus Christ into your heart as your personal Lord and Savior?" they reply,

"Oh, I do that every day." Their answer reveals that they just don't understand.

Jesus Christ is God, you have sinned, and without Him, you are on your way to hell. Jesus died for your sins, and by faith—once for all and forever—you place your faith in the Lord Jesus Christ. You invite Him *once* to come into your life and to be your personal Lord and Savior.

At that moment, Jesus comes into your heart and rescues you, delivers you, and empowers you to become what you ought to be. Do you know how many times you need to ask Him to do that? Just once. Do you know what Jesus does the instant you ask Him to save you? He saves you "to the uttermost," which means forever and completely (see Hebrews 7:25). He never saves any man halfway. He doesn't get you part of the way there and then you have to do the rest. You get it all or nothing at all. That's why you ask Him just once.

Have you ever, for that one time, asked Him to become your Lord and Savior?

3. There's nothing left for you to add to your salvation

You can add nothing to the salvation Jesus supplies, nor can you take anything away from it. Occasionally I'll hear a man say, "It's not that I don't want to become a Christian. I just feel like there's something I have to do."

Listen, there's *nothing* you have to do. Jesus has already done it all. He paid the price. He doesn't need your help. You'd just mess it up, anyway.

Remember that, long ago, God put us in a perfect garden and gave us perfect hearts. What did we do? We messed it up and got kicked out. The only way we could return to the garden is for the perfect one to pay the perfect price—and Jesus did that on the cross.

"I'm Changed! I'm Changed!"

I played pool professionally for four years before Jesus saved me. I still like the game and have a pool table in my house. Most of my sticks cost about $20, although I have one that costs about $150.

Years ago someone asked me to share the gospel with a man who makes high-end pool cues. The four sticks he was making at the time cost $20,000 each, and he'd sold at least one cue worth $50,000. I just wanted to hold that thing! Fifty grand for a pool stick?

After the man showed me around his carpentry shop, I asked if he'd come to the place in his life that he knew for certain he had eternal life. Would he go to heaven when he died? I, and a friend who hadn't been saved long, began to talk to him about Jesus. The late Vance Havner used to say that the most exciting Christian in the world is the man who gets saved before he meets his first theologian. There's some truth to that claim.

"Johnny," my friend said, "let me explain to him how he can be saved."

"Go ahead," I replied.

"When I was younger and was thinking about becoming a Christian," he began, "somebody told me, 'If you really want to become a Christian, you need to do just like you do in business: cut out the middleman. Just forget about Jesus and get right on to God.'" My friend then quoted John 14:1, which says, "Let not your heart be troubled; you believe in God, believe also in Me."

He continued: "I said, 'God, I want you to save me. God, I want you to help me.' But my marriage had fallen apart and I was drinking real bad and I was in a time of despair. I didn't care to live any longer. I didn't even want to get out of bed in the morning.

"One night, while lying in bed, I said, 'God, I ask you in Jesus' name. I come to you in the name of Jesus. Please come into my heart.' And I want to tell you, God invaded my heart in the person of Jesus Christ!"

The more my friend talked, the more excited he got. He grew red in the face, stood up on his tiptoes, and almost shouted, "I'm telling you, I'm changed! I'm changed!"

You can be changed too. That's what can happen when you ask Jesus Christ to become your Lord and Savior—and to top it off, you get a great high priest and an unbeatable advocate in the bargain.

Why wait?

6

HOW TO ABIDE
IN JESUS

Why are you here? For what reason has God put you on this planet?

While a lot of Christian men can quote Jesus' famous words about having life "more abundantly" (John 10:10), they still struggle to figure out why they're here. For many men, that unresolved struggle leads to a crisis of identity.

It doesn't have to be that way.

No Christian man needs to have an identity crisis. Jesus tells us very clearly who we are and why we are here. In short, He declares that He is the vine and we are the branches. We're here to bear fruit to the glory of God.

But how does that work? How do we bear fruit to the glory of God? And what does it mean that Christ is the vine and we are the branches? Let's get some answers...and so get the fruit-bearing started.

Branches in the Vine

Most of what we need to know about bearing fruit for God's glory we learn in John 15. Jesus begins by saying, "I am the true vine, and My Father is the vinedresser. Every branch in Me that does not bear fruit He takes away; and every branch that bears fruit He prunes, that it may bear more fruit" (vv. 1-2).

How do we become a branch in the vine? You and I become a branch by trusting Jesus Christ as our Lord and Savior. We don't initiate it; He does when He brings us under conviction by the Holy Spirit to show us our need for Jesus. If you're a Christian, you are a branch in the true vine, who is none other than the Lord Jesus.

As the life of Jesus Christ comes into you and as you yield to the true vine, you simply rest in Him, as a branch does in its vine. As the sap from the source of your life invades your life, Jesus eliminates old and useless things, much like old, dead leaves fall off a tree. New things grow in their place. Weaknesses get replaced with strengths.

The Bible calls this fruit-bearing. Day by day, God sends moisture up from beneath and the sun from above in order to grow you as a Christian.

"Abide in Me, and I in you," Jesus commanded. "As the branch cannot bear fruit of itself, unless it abides in the vine, neither can you, unless you abide in Me" (John 15:4). He means, "You're going to be a living branch, receiving your substance and the very source of your life through Me. And through that living relationship with the true vine, you will produce fruit."

Not only will you produce fruit, but Jesus makes it clear that your purpose on earth is to produce *much* fruit. "I am the vine, you are the branches," Jesus declared. "He who abides in Me, and I in him, bears much fruit; for without Me you can do nothing" (v. 5). To emphasize His point, He later added, "By this My Father is glorified, that you bear much fruit; so you will be My disciples" (v. 8).

Are you bearing "much fruit" through and for the Savior? If you're not, then you cannot fulfill the purpose for which He put you on earth. Neither can you enjoy the abundant life Jesus promises to those who abide in Him. Your prayer life also suffers. I know this because Jesus also said, "If you abide in Me, and My words abide in you, you will ask what you desire, and it shall be done for you" (v. 7). Are you asking and *not* receiving? If so, the reason may be that you're not abiding.

What keeps us from abiding in Jesus? Certainly, we don't fail because the task is too complicated; it's as simple as remaining connected to the true vine. You don't have to go to seminary to learn how to abide in Jesus. Really, all you have to do is observe a fruit tree growing.

Fruit Trees Don't Grunt

Can you imagine going out to an orchard and hearing the fruit trees grunt? Maybe an apple is growing on some branch, but the apple hasn't yet turned red. The branch is doing all it can to produce more life and sweetness in that apple—but you'll never hear the branch grunt. It simply abides where it is, receiving its sustenance from the tree; and in time, the apple very naturally gets red and juicy.

By faith, you and I have a living relationship with Jesus Christ. You are a *living* branch connected to a *living* vine. And just as a branch gets its life from the vine, so a believer gets his life from Jesus Christ, the true vine.

I have known many believing men who have not grown enough to realize that the genuine source of their life is Jesus Christ. They therefore seek other outlets and other sources to bring them true meaning. None of those other sources ever works because Jesus Christ *alone* is that source. Until these men learn to abide in Jesus, their lives will continue to lack true meaning. Nothing they do will really count for God.

Is it hard to bear fruit? Does it take tremendous effort to abide in Jesus? Frankly, I've never seen a branch struggle. Have you ever walked past a fruit tree and said, "Would you look at that branch over there, struggling to bear fruit! See how the poor thing strains." Of course not. It produces fruit because it's connected to the source.

In an exuberant kind of way, the tree just pushes this life, this power, through that branch. Before you know it, you see leaves. A little later, buds form and flowers start blooming. People smell the fragrance of those flowers, and shortly afterwards, fruit shows up.

Our lives should follow a similar pattern. Someone should be able to look at your life and say, "Would you notice how green that branch looks! There's life there." And then comes the flower, with its sweet fragrance. When we're full of Jesus, we ought to smell, act, and live in ways that attract people. We are living branches growing out of the true vine.

When people begin to smell the fragrance, they move a little closer. Eventually they say, "You're different. You smell different, you look different, you act different, you talk different, you walk different. You go to different places. What is it about you?" When they taste the fruit you've produced, they get what you have—and then they, too, become branches in the true vine.

It is the will of God for every Christian man to be tied into the true source of life, the Lord Jesus, and so bear fruit for the glory of God. Once you accept this simple fact, you're on your way to making your life both meaningful and useful.

The Pruning Process

Those who lack a living union with Jesus Christ cannot bear fruit to the glory of God. They cannot do so because they have no connection to the genuine source of life. Spiritual fruit is the natural result of being connected to the divine life. One can manufacture religious substitutes, but such substitutes always fall far short of God's fruit.

When a fruit tree fails to produce fruit, do you know what a farmer does? He prunes it, cuts it back, until it can start producing. "Every branch in Me that does not bear fruit [My Father] takes away," Jesus said, "and every branch that bears fruit He prunes, that it may bear more fruit" (v. 2). If you're a Christian, you can be sure that one of two things is happening:

- You are producing fruit to God's glory.
- God is pruning you so you can produce more of His fruit.

If you can go out there and do nothing for the kingdom of God, then you may not be part of His kingdom at all. If you're a Christian, either you're bearing fruit or God is at work in your life to enable you to produce fruit (or more fruit). But an extended time of willful idleness never characterizes the life of a genuine believer.

If a branch is doing nothing at all, the only disciplinary action Jesus mentions in John 15 is to cut off the branch and throw it in the fire. Such Christians are "disqualified for the prize," in Paul's terminology (see 1 Corinthians 9:24-27). If a branch refuses to produce fruit, the vinedresser may simply decide to remove it from the earth (see 1 Corinthians 11:27-32).

Why did God save you? So that you might bear fruit in this world. You live on a hungry planet, with people starving for spiritual reality. Very often, when weird movements take place across our nation, you may find yourself thinking, *Maybe they know more about real life than I do.* No, they don't. They're just looking for real life. They're hungry, even starving, for spiritual reality.

Jesus wants to use *you* to show them where to find it.

Bearing Fruit for Others

No branch bears fruit for itself. Branches bear fruit for others to eat.

God wants you to bear fruit because we live in a spiritually hungry world. God has *never* grown spiritual fruit on a branch for its own consumption. Fruit exists to nourish others.

If you are full of the Spirit of God, you are a branch connected to the true vine. The gift of life goes from Jesus Christ to others through you as a branch. Fruit comes through your life, and people around you consume that fruit. The effectiveness of God's work within your life makes them curious and greatly influences them toward the Lord.

As we're united to Jesus and we abide in Him, His life flows through us and in us. In that way, we bear fruit. As we make ourselves available to Jesus, He makes Himself available to us. This is the will of God for every saved man. God wants to use *you* for His glory.

Six Kinds of Spiritual Fruit

Spiritual fruit comes in many varieties. The six kinds of spiritual fruit I'm about to describe are all mentioned in Scripture, but this is no exhaustive list. I see it simply as a helpful place to start.

1. The principle of soul-winning

When a man invited me to church many years ago, little did he know that he'd just invited the guy who would become his next pastor. At the time, I was managing a pool room as a high school dropout and teenage alcoholic, with no direction or purpose in life.

One day a carpenter said to me, "Johnny, I wish you'd come to church and hear the story of Jesus." When I showed up a few Sundays later, Jesus Christ changed my life.

I went off to college and then to seminary. After I graduated, that very church called me back and I pastored there for six of the better years of my life. God brought a lot of fruit during that period.

As I got ready to leave that church to pastor elsewhere, someone checked our church records and discovered that in the half century of the church's history, it had baptized more people the year I came to faith than in any other year. Do you know why? Forty-five of my friends got saved as a result of me getting saved. I began to tell my friends what Jesus had done in my life.

Was it hard to do that? Not if you're connected to the vine. It's simply the principle of soul-winning.

First come the green leaves, then the flower, then the fruit. Paul referred to the process in Romans 1:13, where he told the Roman church of his desire to visit, "that I might have some fruit among you also, just as among the other Gentiles." What kind of fruit did the apostle have in mind? He longed to win Gentiles to Jesus Christ.

Scripture gives us at least five pictures of this soul-winning principle.

A hunter. Proverbs 11:30 says, "The fruit of the righteous is a tree of life, and he who wins souls is wise." The word "win" calls to mind a hunter taking his prey. Sometimes we "track down" a lost soul in order to take him for Christ.

A fisherman. This one comes from Mark 1:17, where Jesus said to Peter and his friends, "Follow Me, and I will make you become fishers of men." Jesus compared evangelism to catching fish. We need to keep a line out. I travel a lot, and when I do, I try to keep a line out. You just never know when you're gonna get a bite or when you may snag something that leads to an opportunity for sharing the gospel.

An ambassador. One of my favorite New Testament passages is 2 Corinthians 5:20, where Paul writes, "Now then, we are ambassadors for Christ, as though God were pleading through us: we implore you on Christ's behalf, be reconciled to God." Here Paul compares an evangelist to an ambassador.

What do we know about ambassadors? They live in a foreign

land, representing their own king or country. If their nation gets into trouble, their king calls them home.

I'm an ambassador for Christ. I live in this world, but it's not my real home. I represent Jesus to those who don't yet know Him. I live in this world, but I am trying not to live as though I am of this world.

In my years as a pastor, sometimes church people would write me unsigned notes. One note asked, "How can you vote no on the liquor referendum, and then play golf at a golf course that serves beer?" The answer is, I am Christ's ambassador, representing Him to those who don't yet know Him. God did not call me to enter a monastery, sit in a corner, and never share my faith with anyone. God's called me to be salt and light in this world. I'm to be a soul-winner.

Don't ever get so spiritual that you say, "I don't go anywhere that does anything wrong." Have you ever read where Jesus went? His enemies called Him a drunkard because He went where the drunkards were, to win them to the Son of God. May God help us to go where the lost world is, and there be salt and light! I'm an ambassador for Christ, and I'm here until my King calls me home.

A harvester. Jesus once told His disciples, "Do you not say, 'There are still four months and then comes the harvest'? Behold, I say to you, lift up your eyes and look at the fields, for they are already white for harvest!" (John 4:35). As He spoke, He and His disciples watched a crowd of unsaved Samaritans coming toward them. *They* were the harvest Jesus had in mind.

A fireman. In Zechariah 3:2, the Lord rebuked Satan and said about a certain man He intended to use, "Is this not a brand plucked from the fire?" I still have a deep conviction that lost people are going to hell and that we need to get out there and pluck them out of the fire. I'm a fireman for Jesus.

Some years ago, a missionary couple from Uganda stayed in our home. Someone asked the husband, "What's it like out there in the bush? Travel maps tell us to stay out of Uganda. You live among people who regularly carry automatic weapons, which they use to kill tourists and visitors. Aren't you afraid for your wife and two little children?"

"Oh, no," he replied. "We're there by the sovereign will of God. God placed me out there." He smiled and then asked, "May I tell you what overcomes my fright?"

His interviewer nodded.

"First of all, God has not given me the spirit of fear. But second, what outweighs my fear is the fact that these men, if they never hear the gospel, will go to hell when they die."

We're firemen, you see.

2. The principle of the sanctified life

Holiness refers to the beauty and the character of God displayed in our daily lives. Holiness means growth in godly behavior, becoming increasingly like Jesus. As we share the life of Christ, we share the character of Christ.

Romans 6:22 says, "But now having been set free from sin, and having become slaves of God, you have your fruit to holiness, and the end, everlasting life." The theme of Romans 6 is victory over sin, and the fruit of this victory is a holy life.

Holiness cannot be manufactured but must come from within, from Almighty God. Jesus Christ is the true vine, sending His life up through the branch. As you yield to Jesus, holiness automatically starts to become part of your life. As a branch of a holy vine, you bear holy fruit. When you respond properly, you fill up with love, joy, and peace.

Every man of God is to be holy and to live a holy life. It is the will of God that you live a sanctified life.

3. The principle of sharing with others

If you plant an apple tree, you're right to assume that one day it will grow, have leaves, flowers, and fruit. If that doesn't happen, you'll find an expert to help you fix the problem, because apple trees are there to produce fruit for sharing with others. Branches exist to bear fruit.

A church I pastored once had to raise $1.2 million within thirty days. We wanted to buy a piece of property we saw as crucial to our mission, but to that point, we typically had income of only $400,000. How would we get that money? We didn't know, but in faith, we believed we would somehow obtain what we needed.

The bank called and said, "Johnny, your church is debt free. Our bank will loan you the money." We had no Plan B. The Holy Spirit had said, "Here's your Plan A: Trust me. I'm going to give you the $1.2 million. And by giving you that money, I'm going to make my name strong in your area."

In the middle of this episode, somebody told me, "Preacher, you're leading the church out on a limb. You know that, don't you?"

When a pastor friend of mine heard this comment, he retorted, "Brother, lead them out on a limb. That's where the fruit is." I've never forgotten his counsel.

Giving to God, and in His name to others, is the result of who we are and what we are. When a branch receives life from the vine, it cannot help but give. The branch *exists* to give. For a branch, living and giving are almost synonymous. This is why the apostle John wrote, "If anyone has material possessions and sees a brother or sister in need but has no pity on them, how can the love of God be in that person?" (1 John 3:17 NIV).

A believing man cannot selfishly hold on to whatever material blessing God may have given him. Can you imagine going through an apple orchard, looking up and seeing a beautiful apple, but when you reach up to grab the fruit, the tree's branches reach out, slap your hand, and say, "We ain't giving you that apple. It's ours!"? How crazy would that be?

Jesus has given you life, and He wants you to share what He gives you. If you're a branch, it makes no sense to say, "No, I want to hold on to it."

If you're not His son, of course, that's a different story. If you're not a branch, then you have nothing to give. A trunk doesn't give fruit; a branch does. You might hang down around the base of some tree, but maybe you've never been grafted into the true vine. Maybe you've hung around the tree because you like the way some of its branches sing. Maybe every now and then you like to hang around an exciting branch that, at least, doesn't bore you. But the truth is, you're just hanging around the tree; you've never been grafted into the vine.

Once God grafts you in, you'll not only rejoice at what God is doing in some preacher, but that preacher will rejoice in what he sees God doing in you as you share your resources with others.

4. The principle of the Spirit

The Bible instructs Christians to develop personal qualities it calls "fruit"—qualities such as love, joy, peace, longsuffering, temperance, self-control, and meekness. The apostle Paul called this cluster of qualities "the fruit of the Spirit" (see Galatians 5:22-23).

I know I can't produce love, joy, peace, and the rest of these qualities on my own. If I'm vitally connected to the true vine, however, and the vine is the source of all love, joy, peace, longsuffering, temperance, self-control, and meekness, then these spiritual qualities will inevitably start appearing in my life.

Since I'm connected to the vine, the vine's life gets sent right on through me as a branch, and in time, my life begins producing spiritual fruit. Qualities such as love, joy, and peace start to bloom and grow in me, and people begin to say, "I like hanging around him. I always feel better after spending some time together. Our conversations encourage me."

As these qualities show up in your life, they emit such a sweet aroma that people who don't yet know Jesus take note. When they start to see fruit growing, they'll want some of their own…and so God's kingdom expands.

The world, of course, has substitutes for these Christian graces, but it cannot duplicate them. Unsaved people can enjoy love, but they can't produce the deep *agape* love that comes only from the heart of Jesus Christ. The world manufactures entertainment and even short bursts of happiness, but it cannot manufacture the deep joy that comes from Jesus Christ. The same is true for each of the spiritual qualities the Bible calls fruit.

Although the world can manufacture faint echoes of spiritual fruit, it can never reproduce the real thing. God produces real apples and genuine cherries; the world can make only wax table decorations.

5. The principle of service

The Bible lists good works as another type of spiritual fruit. Such works don't save you, but a saved man should regularly produce them. Paul told us that we should be "fruitful in every good work" (Colossians 1:10). Jesus Himself instructed us to "Let your light so shine before men, that they may see your good works and glorify your Father in heaven" (Matthew 5:16).

These good works are tailor-made for each believer. Wherever you live, work, go to school, shop, hang out, or spend time, God has tailor-made certain fruit that He wants to produce in your life to meet the needs of starving people in your corner of the world. Men sometimes say to me, "Johnny, I wish I could bring you down to where I work and let you minister to the people there." While I'd love going down to minister to those people, I can think of something much more exciting, and that's *you* going to where you already are and ministering to those people.

If you're a believer, the same Holy Spirit who produces fruit in my life also lives in you, producing the same fruit. Let Him do His work! God has people in your life *right now* who need to taste Christ's fruit through you. I'll never be able to minister to them, but you can.

Almighty God enables you to do unique good works, tailor-made to your situation in life. Ephesians 2:10 tells us, "We are His workmanship, created in Christ Jesus for good works, which God prepared beforehand that we should walk in them." Each believing man has his own ministry to fulfill. We don't need to compete with other believers in the will of God.

6. The principle of the praise of the Spirit

Yet another kind of spiritual fruit in your life is the praise of your lips. Hebrews 13:15 instructs us to "continually offer the sacrifice of praise to God."

A "sacrifice of praise" means that you give thanks to your Lord. While Old Testament worshipers brought the fruit of the field for sacrifice to God, New Testament worshipers bring the fruit of their lips for praise to God.

One of the main reasons God commands us to regularly gather for worship is to praise and thank Him. "Thank You, Jesus," we should be saying. "You woke me up again this morning, gave me a good week, and kept me alive. The obituary columns were full every day this week, but I'm still alive."

God has numbered each of our days (see Psalm 139:16). The only reason you're still breathing is because God gave you the breath to breathe, so praise His name and thank Him for His goodness to you.

What kind of praise should we offer? I can imagine all kinds of praise in our churches, other than anything cold and dead. I've heard people say, "I feel uncomfortable in that church because they applaud. Some folk even holler 'amen' and 'glory!' I think I'll find a church more conducive to my preference of worship." I'd say, go back to Hebrews 13:15 and make sure that your attitude toward worship is based in the Word of God.

Every church ought to be a thankful, grateful, praising body. The words spoken, sung, or even shouted ought to praise and glorify God. At the same time, though, forced praise is empty praise. Just as you don't have to force a tree to produce a certain kind of fruit, so you shouldn't try to force a certain kind of praise in church.

If I were to walk into a church and someone said, "Just raise your hands and praise the Lord," I'd think, *You don't have to force me to do that.* Or maybe at another church someone says, "Notice that the bulletin says we don't applaud here." Others might say, "Please understand, we do not raise our hands here." Why force it, one way or another? Fruit just *is*; you don't force it either way.

Please don't tell me what I can or can't do in His presence. He's God and He owns this world. If He puts it on my heart to stand and shout, then I'm going to stand and shout. You don't force praise into some predetermined mold. I've gone to church some days not feeling well. But when the fruit of praise passed my lips, something changed. I didn't force it, nor did I determine ahead of time what it had to be. But in genuine, unforced praise and thanksgiving, I met God. And through it, He changed my world.

Results vs. Fruit

A big difference exists between results and fruit. For one thing, while results don't necessarily create more results, fruit always has the potential to bear more fruit. Fruit produces seeds that can be planted to produce more fruit, while results often are one-and-done.

Second, Jesus wants our fruit to remain, not disappear. "I chose you and appointed you that you should go and bear fruit, and that your fruit should remain," He said (John 15:16). Results don't always remain, but spiritual fruit *always* remains. I'm interested in producing fruit that remains.

One night years ago I flew to Asheville, North Carolina, to do a joint service for two churches. A man in his fifties got saved, along with a little girl and two little boys. After the service, a young lady approached to speak with me.

"I don't expect you to remember me," she said, "but my mother told me that I shouldn't leave without telling you the story." I noticed some other young women had joined her. "Do you see these girls standing around me?" she asked.

"Yes," I said.

"Do you remember preaching in Southport, North Carolina, in 1987, in the month of June?"

"Yes, I did the state convention. Best I remember, it was a thousand-seat building and we had eleven hundred teenagers there."

"I want you to know that my girlfriends all got saved that week," she continued, "and they're here tonight to thank you. I also want you to know I was already a Christian. I took them with me so they could get saved. God not only saved them, but God called me to full-time Christian service. I just graduated from seminary. It's been eight years since I saw you, and now I'm the children's minister of this church."

That's fruit that remains!

This young woman and her friends were not the "results" of my ministry, but they certainly were "fruit" from the ministry of the true vine. I didn't struggle to see her get saved; I was just a branch, connected to the vine.

If you feel concerned about whether Jesus really drew a certain person to Himself, then write down that person's name and in a year find out where he is. And for the record, I never get as concerned over how many people respond to some message I give as much as I do over how many of them are still walking with Jesus a year later. I want fruit that remains.

Prepare for a Bumper Crop

Jesus came to earth that you might have life and have it more abundantly. So, how can you have that abundant life?

Make sure you're saved. Let no question remain in your mind whether you belong to the true vine. Settle that question for good, and then yield yourself in total submission to Jesus.

Let the Lord do what He chooses to do through your life. Remember, if you're a branch, you can't do a thing on your own. Jesus said emphatically, "Without Me you can do nothing" (John 15:5). But with Him?

Prepare yourself for a bumper crop.

Part 2

TRANSFORMED BY JESUS

7

CHANGED FROM
THE INSIDE OUT

A friend once wrote an article about New Year's resolutions that got picked up by *USA Today*. Approximately 75 percent of the adults surveyed for the article said they believed every person's life had an ultimate purpose and plan. Almost 90 percent of respondents said they thought it was important to pursue a higher purpose and meaning in life, and 67 percent agreed with the statement, "A major priority in my life is finding my deeper purpose."

Do you agree with that statement? Do you believe *your* life has a higher purpose and meaning?

The Bible makes it clear that finding and fulfilling your life's purpose as a Christian man ought to energize you. It ought to launch you out of bed each morning. Everything you and I do should revolve around living out God's purpose for our lives.

But what *is* that life's purpose? Do you know God's purpose and calling for your life? Where is your life heading? Are you moving forward? Do you know where your current direction will take you?

Christian men have no higher calling than to become like Christ. God created you and me to have a growing relationship with Him, and Jesus made this possible by applying His righteousness to our account through His work on the cross.

What would be the downside if you were to become like the One who died for you? How might your life benefit from becoming increasingly like Jesus?

A Certain Destiny

Let's first establish that God's purpose and plan for us really is to become like His Son, Jesus Christ. It turns out, that's very easy to do.

The apostle Paul declared that all Christians are "predestined to be conformed to the image" of God's Son (Romans 8:29). The apostle John declares that our ultimate destiny is to be like Jesus: "Beloved, now we are children of God; and it has not yet been revealed what we shall be, but we know that when He is revealed, we shall be like Him, for we shall see Him as He is" (1 John 3:2). Think of it! When Jesus Christ returns to this earth, all those who have placed their faith in Him will be *totally* and *completely* conformed to His likeness. What a day that will be!

Until that day, however, Scripture declares that God wants us to continually cooperate with His Spirit to move us closer and closer to the way Jesus thinks and acts and operates. Paul told a group of Christian believers that he labored very hard for them, like a woman giving birth, "until Christ is formed in you" (Galatians 4:19). He told some other Christians that "the life of Jesus" should be displayed even in their bodies (2 Corinthians 4:10-11). As we walk with Jesus, Paul declared that we are progressively transformed into the "image" of Jesus, "from glory to glory, just as by the Spirit of the Lord" (2 Corinthians 3:18). He explained that God gave us apostles, prophets, evangelists, pastors, and teachers to help us grow together as Christians, "till we all come to the unity of the faith and of the knowledge of the Son of God, to a perfect man, to the measure of the stature of the fullness of Christ" (Ephesians 4:13).

Believing men are to reflect Jesus' attitudes (Philippians 2:4-5) and His actions (1 Peter 2:21-23). John claims that the man who says he abides in Jesus "ought himself also to walk just as He walked" (1 John 2:6). We are to "imitate" Jesus (1 Corinthians 11:1; 1 Thessalonians 1:6), as the Lord Himself told His disciples after He washed their dirty feet: "I have given you an example, that you should do as I have done to you" (John 13:15).

Do you want to become increasingly like Jesus? That is God's goal for you in this life, and it's also His ultimate purpose for you in the life to come. And how does the Lord plan to accomplish this miracle? He intends to change you from the inside out, using the same divine tool He used to bring you into His family in the first place: grace.

Endowed with Moral Power

God's grace does not merely set you free from the penalty of sin; it also endows you with moral power. It makes a decisive difference for good in your life. Listen to the apostle Paul:

> For the grace of God that brings salvation has appeared to all men, teaching us that, denying ungodliness and worldly lusts, we should live soberly, righteously, and godly in the present age, looking for the blessed hope and glorious appearing of our great God and Savior Jesus Christ, who gave Himself for us, that He might redeem us from every lawless deed and purify for Himself His own special people, zealous for good works (Titus 2:11-14).

Jesus doesn't save you only from your past, but He purifies you to be a part of His own special people, eager to do what's right. God wants you and me to be on fire to do good works.

Every Christian man has been given a radical new nature that enables him to become increasingly like Christ. When God saved me, He not only called me to Himself, He also enabled me by grace to become conformed to the image of Jesus. I need more than God's call; I need His help! And God gives it to me through His grace. He enables you and me to reflect our new nature in Christ through a radically new way of living.

When a man is genuinely saved and given new life in Jesus, a transformation occurs. God changes him from the inside out. A metamorphosis begins, not only of his nature but of his manner of living. The Christian's new nature, new disposition, and the indwelling Holy Spirit all mean a redeemed man simply cannot continue to live in gross sin, bereft of any outward evidence of his new holy and righteous nature. Paul wrote in Galatians 2:20, "I have been crucified with Christ; it is no longer I who live, but Christ lives in me; and the life which I now live in the flesh I live by faith in the Son of God, who loved me and gave Himself for me."

John MacArthur has said, "By his divine grace, Jesus Christ completely reprograms our computers, as it were. He throws away the old disc and deletes the previous programs, all of which were permeated with error and destructive viruses, and graciously replaces them with his own divine truth and righteousness."[4]

The Goal of Grace

Almost a century and a half after its publication, the number one song in religious circles around the world today is still "Amazing Grace" by John Newton, first published in 1779. What makes grace so amazing? What is the goal of grace?

Remember how Titus 2:11-12 puts it: "The grace of God that brings salvation has appeared to all men, teaching us that, denying ungodliness and worldly lusts, we should live soberly, righteously, and godly in the present age." The same grace that saved me also teaches me. Before I ever heard a sermon against getting drunk, the grace of God already had taught me that I was a drunkard. God started preparing me to change my life before I ever heard a gospel sermon.

What does Paul mean that grace "teaches" us? He means that grace instructs us, trains us, disciplines us, educates us, nurtures us, and chastises us. The "teaching" of grace has two sides, one negative and the other positive.

1. Grace teaches us to say no

Before I came to faith, I said yes to a mountain of ugly things. How did I learn to say no? Grace taught me. It not only *told* me, it *enabled* me. Grace teaches us that we must come to a conscious, willful repudiation of all thoughts, words, and actions that oppose true godliness.

The verb "teaches" is in the present tense, indicating a continuing process. No one ever graduates from the school of God's grace. There will never come a time on this earth where you can say, "Thank God, I finally graduated from all that grace wanted to teach me." So long as you breathe, you will continue to receive instruction in Christ's school of grace.

Grace teaches, in part, by warning us. One of the most famous lines of "Amazing Grace" says, "'Twas grace that taught my heart to fear, and grace my fears relieved." One reason why I love the old hymns so much is that many of them were written by great preachers who taught great theology. God saved John Newton out of the miserable life of a slave trader and made him into a preacher and theologian with a broad understanding of God's Word.

Grace also teaches by enabling us. When I was twenty years old, I accepted a man's invitation to visit his church—and immediately I got under conviction. God began dealing with me about my sins and the Holy Spirit began calling me to Himself. It all made me very nervous. A lady standing beside me must have noticed, because she said, "Wouldn't you like to be saved today?"

I really wanted to say yes, but back in those days I was timid and shy, and so I replied, "No, not today."

In the next few moments I heard the preacher say, "There's a man here whom God's speaking to. Let's pray that God will bring him back tonight and save him." Gulp! On the way home, I told my wife that the preacher was talking about me, which led to an interesting conversation.

Back in those days, I loved to gamble, and I won a lot of money playing pool. I would go to the Red Fox Saloon, drink embalming fluid with a bunch of guys, and come home loaded a couple of nights a week. I was completely irreligious. No one in my family *ever* went to church. After that first visit to church, I said to my wife, "Janet, tonight I'm going back to that church, and I'm going to give my life to Jesus Christ."

But one thought plagued me. *What if God doesn't change me? I mean, look at me! If God doesn't change me, I'll come with a Christian label, but I won't have the power to live a new life.*

I knew very well how deeply into sin I'd fallen, and I wanted out. But I also knew I didn't have the strength, on my own, to begin a new, clean life. So I told Janet, "If He doesn't change me, honey, you leave me, because I'll be right back at the saloon." I actually spoke those words.

But guess what happened? That night, I encountered the living Jesus Christ, who saved me and changed me. Since that day, Janet has never once had to come down to the saloon to retrieve me.

Before then, I'd never heard anyone teach the Ten Commandments, but in the first few weeks after my conversion, the grace of God taught me to clean up my language and stop taking the Lord's name in vain (a nasty habit of mine). And He didn't just tell me to clean it up; He empowered me to clean it up.

What does Paul mean that we must "deny ungodliness"? The word "deny" carries the idea of a conscious, purposeful action of the will. It means to say *no!* It's to confess and consciously turn away from anything sinful and destructive and to move toward that which is good and godly. The word "ungodliness" refers to a lack of true reverence for and devotion to God. The original Greek word describes the opposite of godliness; it speaks of defiance toward God's person or hostility toward God's sacred place.

In the church, we hardly ever see defiance toward God's person, but you'll often hear someone say, "I'm a Christian, but I am not going to church." That's defiance toward God's place. If you claim to be a Christian, you'd better learn to get together with God's people, or you'll be one miserable dude when (if?) you get to heaven.

The word "ungodliness" shows up as the adjective "profane" or "godless" in Hebrews 12:16 to describe a man named Esau, the eldest son of Isaac. John Phillips said, "Profane means that there was no sacred enclosure in his life where God could dwell."

If you could open Esau's life and see the spot where Jesus Christ wanted to live, you would not have seen any sacred enclosure where the sacred could dwell. *No place for God!* Can you be in church and have place for lots of religious activities, but have no place for God? Absolutely.

William Barclay, one of the greatest Bible word scholars ever, said, "The word for godless…was used for ground that was profane, in contradistinction to ground that was consecrated. The ancient world had its religions into which only the initiated could come. 'Godless' was a word for the person who was uninitiated and uninterested, in contradistinction to the man who was devout. It was applied to Jews who had become apostates and had forsaken God."[5]

What is an apostate? An apostate is someone who comes very close to making a commitment to Jesus Christ but never quite takes the leap. Eventually he turns away, leaves, and never returns. The term is related to our word *threshold*. Maybe someone is in church, active, and moving toward God. Maybe the man gets as far as the threshold, the place where you enter…and he stops and turns away. That man could be called "godless," regardless of the amount of time he'd spent in church doing religious activities.

Could it be that we have thousands of men in our churches who came to the threshold, but who never quite entered in? When we get to eternity, we'll find out why they never spoke about their faith, or gave, or displayed the fruit of the Spirit in their lives. In fact, they had never crossed the threshold. They had never fully embraced Jesus. They had never fully bought in to the gospel.

They were godless.

Godless describes the man whose mind recognizes nothing higher than the earth, for whom nothing is sacred, and who has no reverence for the unseen. A godless man has no awareness of or interest in God. He is completely earthbound in his thoughts, aims, and pleasures.

Esau's problem was that he treated spiritual things as of no account, and then proved it by selling his birthright to satisfy his appetite. The entire Old Testament might have been written differently had Esau obeyed God. Rather than speaking of Abraham, Isaac, and Jacob, we might be speaking about Abraham, Isaac, and Esau. Although Esau was the firstborn, he cared nothing for its significance. Esau had the right to become the family priest, but the role didn't interest him. He cared nothing about landing in the genealogical tree of Jesus Christ. We trace the family line of Jesus Christ back to Jacob, but could it have been traced back to Esau? As the firstborn, Esau could have inherited a double portion of his father's property, but he preferred immediate gratification instead of waiting for the best. And so the Bible calls him "godless."

Are you sacrificing the eternal for the temporal? Do you care for earth more than for heaven? We have many men in the church who supposedly live for the Lord, but then just check out. In the South, we have a word for those who hang around for a while but then stop living for Jesus. We call them backsliders. So how long can a man remain backslidden?

Suppose a man makes a profession of faith and remains in the church for six months, but then for the next thirty years he lives as a drunkard, a fornicator, a thief, or a robber. In his case, whatever happened to enabling grace? Did God not give him the promise He gave me? Did the man receive something that didn't work? Or did he never really receive it at all?

Suppose another man grew up in a Christian home. In preschool he sang "Jesus Loves the Little Children" in the choir. When he grew older, he got active in Awana, where he could quote scores of Bible verses and learned all about Christian character traits. As a middle schooler, he traveled with a mission group to Cleveland, Ohio, where he gave out gospel tracts on the street. In high school, he joined the senior high choir and took a mission trip to Argentina.

Did attending Awana make that man a Christian?

Did joining the student choirs make him a Christian?

Did going on a mission trip make him a Christian?

Those are all good things, aren't they? Don't we feel good about them? That's the wrong question. The right question is this: Does that man have a sacred enclosure in his life where God lives? All of the other stuff is good, but it's not God.

But what if a man walks down an aisle in response to an evangelist's appeal? Is that man saved? It all depends on his motive. If he really gave his life to Jesus, then his subsequent life will show it. If not, his grace is not amazing; it's pitiful. That man has no sacred enclosure for God.

Do you have a sacred enclosure for God? Deep in your own heart, are you godly or ungodly? Do you look more like Abraham or his grandson Esau?

Esau grew up with great light. It was the duty of every godly daddy to tell his sons the sacred stories so they wouldn't forget how good God had been to them. I can picture Esau as a little boy getting placed on his granddaddy's knee and hearing Abraham say, "Let me tell you about Mount Moriah." God gave Abraham spiritual insight to look into the future, and I'm sure he spoke of it. Esau had every opportunity, as much as any person in his time, of knowing and following God. He didn't come from a godless family. And yet, somehow, Esau did not have a sacred enclosure for God. Despite his godly heritage, Esau was a godless man.

How do you know if a man really belongs to God? If a saved man strays from God, he normally doesn't stray for long because grace teaches, trains, and chastises him. Grace takes him to the woodshed.

But what if that man sins as freely as he breathes and never says, with tears of brokenness, "Look what I'm doing to my Savior"? Then that man has no sacred enclosure for God. He's godless.

Decades ago, when I worried aloud to my wife about whether I could become a Christian, she told me, "Johnny, He'll change you. Go ahead tonight when Mr. Gibson gives the invitation. Go down front, honey, and give your life to Jesus Christ. God will change you." And He did!

I wish I could say that I never sinned after I came to faith, but that'd be a lie. I sin, but I can't sin and be happy about it. I always feel dirty afterward. I can't wait to get right with God.

When God calls you to a new life, He doesn't call you merely to move away from something; He also calls you to move toward something else. It's not just what you deny, it's also what you embrace.

2. Grace teaches us to say yes

A born-again man is no longer under the dominion of Satan and of sin. He's been radically changed and given a new nature. He's called and enabled to live a godly life. God gives him the power to reflect his new nature through a radically new way of living.

When a man trusts Christ, he becomes a witness to the work of Christ in his life. If he should witness to someone how Jesus has changed his life, he will testify not only with his lips, but his life will also do some talking. Observers will see a significant change in him. When a man is genuinely saved and given new life in Jesus Christ, he undergoes a radical transformation. A metamorphosis takes place.

God changes you from the inside out. You begin to feel differently within. You act differently, you think differently, and essentially God makes you into a different person. God gives you His nature, His disposition, and because of the indwelling Holy Spirit, you simply cannot continue to live in rebellion and sin. God's righteous nature becomes a growing reality inside of you.

If you're going to make an impact in your lifetime, it won't be because of what you quit doing; it will be because of what you start doing. The chaff will blow away and the fruit will blossom, once the new man becomes dominant in your life. Titus 2:12 says that every converted man "should live soberly, righteously, and godly in the present age."

What does it mean to live "soberly" or sensibly? We must develop a sound mind. A saved man has control over the issues of his life and exercises self-restraint over his passions and desires. No Spirit-filled man lets himself get out of control, for he is being tutored and taught by grace. He is under the control of Jesus. The believing man is enabled to be conformed to the mind of Christ, which governs his passions and desires.

This doesn't mean that once you place your faith in Jesus Christ, your passions and desires disappear, never again tempting you to sin. Your passions and desires don't vanish, but they do come under the enabling control of Jesus Christ. That's why it's wrong for a man to say, "Wow, I don't know how I just did that." I know *exactly* how he did it. Give me about thirty seconds apart from Jesus Christ and the enabling power of His grace, and I'll do the same thing. I understand why Charles Spurgeon said about men on death row, "But by the grace of God, there go I."

Paul also calls us to live "righteously." Our faith in Christ ought to change our relationships with believers and nonbelievers alike. The term denotes conduct that cannot be condemned. People can talk about you, lie about you, they can even theorize about you, but they can say nothing truly damaging about you, because you have lived a righteous life that cannot be condemned. *Thayer's Greek-English Lexicon of the New Testament* says that the root of this word is "right." God wants us to live right, observing both divine and human laws.

As I thought about this verse from Titus, my wife and I pulled up to a stoplight. No cars were coming and I said, "I'm going to run it."

"You'd better not," she warned me.

Immediately I thought, *If I do run it, I won't be able to discuss this text with integrity.*

The word "righteously" means to conduct yourself in such a way that no one has any reason to condemn you. Had I run that light (which I didn't), and a police officer had seen me, he would have had all the reason in the world to condemn me. Righteousness requires of us a light and a truth in all of our dealings. It means we live with integrity.

I've tried to teach men about integrity, but it's not an easy word to define. A dictionary will tell you it means wholeness, completeness, truthfulness. Thayer says it means whole in every area of your life, complete and truthful in every area of your life.

Maybe a man looks good at church, but he's a shady car dealer at work. He's an excellent lawyer, but he cheats on his taxes. He's a reliable mechanic, but a dishonest student. No, a righteous man is right in *every* area. We are to live in such a way that in no area of our lives or conduct can others rightfully condemn us. People should be able to speak about us without using a comma: "I believe he loves Jesus, *but*…" Why shouldn't they be able to use a period or an exclamation point instead?

The Bible warns us not to "give place to the devil" (Ephesians 4:27), especially since Satan needs only one area to bring us down. We are therefore to live soberly, sensibly, righteously. We're to live as godly men.

If an ungodly man has no sacred enclosure for Jesus Christ in his life, then to be godly means I'm devout. Someone ought to be able to say, "He is a devout Christian, committed to Jesus." We are to *live* godly. The verb speaks of a man's regular manner of life. If you're married, your wife should be able to say of you, "He's a godly man." Listen, if you can be a godly man at home, then you can be a godly man anywhere. But if you're not a godly man at home, then how can you be a godly man anywhere else? What makes you think you can suddenly start to act in a godly way on a business trip? Deep in the spirit of his will, a godly man consciously denies ungodliness. An attitude of supreme devotion to God has replaced his old attitude of indifference.

Finally, Paul says that we are to "live soberly, righteously, and godly *in the present age.*" That means right now. God expects this of us *now.* Those who receive the teaching of the grace of God are enabled to live in this way *at this moment*. His grace in us there-fore becomes a powerful testimony to the saving and transform-ing power of Jesus Christ. When people watch us, they ought to be asking, "What in the world is the difference? How does that man say no?"

God saved us in order that He might demonstrate His glorious grace to others. He produces in us the desire to do what is right and good, thereby giving glory to our Lord Jesus Christ. As that hap-pens, we righteously impact the lives of nonbelievers, in His name. For that reason, the Lord Jesus Christ commanded us to live in such a way "that they may see your good works and glorify your Father in heaven" (Matthew 5:16). *Really?* Absolutely.

Janet's grandmother, Selma Allen, was a wonderful, godly lady. Before my conversion, she persistently kept after me to go to church. Sometimes we would accompany her to a Sunday service. When someone would make an appeal for the morning offering, I'd reach in my pocket, hoping that I had a one dollar bill. I'd think, *Ain't no way I'm giving them a twenty.*

That all changed after I came to faith in Christ. How did I change from trying to make sure I gave God the smallest thing I had to where I want to give him more and more and more? What made the difference? Back then, grace hadn't yet appeared in my life. But when God made His grace known to me and brought me to faith, that same grace began to teach me to do what's right in every area of my life. He's still teaching me, thank God! And His grace will con-tinue to teach me until I see Him face-to-face.

The Priority of Pursuing

Despite all of the apostle Paul's accomplishments, he made it clear that he considered himself still "on the way" in his Christian life. He admitted, "I press on, that I may lay hold of that for which Christ Jesus has also laid hold of me" (Philippians 3:12).

The Greek word translated "press on" was often used of a sprinter. It also referred to a person who acted aggressively and energetically. Paul *pursued* his relationship with Christ with all of his might. Since he wanted to be holy, he pressed on to become more holy. He strained every spiritual muscle to win the prize set before him. And what was that prize?

To be like Jesus.

To become more like Jesus, you have to press on. You have to keep moving when you decide you want to get up early in the morning to spend the first hour of your day with your Lord. That may be a new challenge for you; maybe it's never been part of your routine. But if you want to be more like Jesus, then you need to do some of the same things He did, and one of the things He did regularly was to rise early and spend some unhurried, uninterrupted time with His Father.

What would it take for you to have an unhurried quiet time with Jesus? Would you need to get up fifteen or thirty minutes earlier than usual? I know I need that time with the Lord. It helps me to start off my day right. I journal, I read, I pray. And I don't always feel like doing any of those things. Many times I feel like spending more time in bed. But I press on. I keep moving.

A Total Change Within

God changes us from the inside out. His Holy Spirit takes up residence within us and from there starts a total renovation of our character, our behavior, and our lives.

Where I was a drunkard, God freed me.

Where I was a liar, God gave me truth.

Where I was profane, God made me holy.

God's grace affects my conversation. If I get angry with somebody, I don't talk to him the same way I used to. The Bible says, "Let your speech always be with grace, seasoned with salt" (Colossians 4:6). Grace affects *everything* in your life, enabling you to live a holy and godly life. That's the moral power of grace.

God calls us to demonstrate His saving power in our lives. By this, we show Him to be a loving God; and by this, we glorify Him and draw others to Him. That's what grace does!

I never took a course that taught me how to live sober, but grace taught me.

I never took a course on how not to take God's name in vain, but grace taught me.

I never took a course on how to stop street fighting, but grace taught me.

I never took a course on how to speak to my mother, but grace taught me.

I never took a course on how to treat my wife, but grace taught me. Grace taught me how to treat Janet like a lady. I'm ashamed of the way I treated her before I got saved. The Spirit of God would have quite a time with me if I tried to talk to Janet like I used to before I got saved! But He forgave me. He not only pardoned me of my foul mouth, but He purged me of it. He cleansed me of it and washed away my sin.

The grace of God in Jesus Christ is our teacher. It's our guide, our counselor. The moment we get saved, we immediately come under the tutelage of God through the Holy Spirit and His Word.

Grace is God's primary tool to change us…from the inside out.

8

KEEP THE BALL
IN PLAY

Major League Baseball and its rabid fans keep records on nearly everything that happens in almost every ballgame ever played. One statistic, however, gets only part-time attention, and then only unofficially. If you were to ask, "Who holds the record for hitting the most foul balls in one at-bat?," you'd get several conflicting answers.

Roy Thomas, who played from 1899–1911, unofficially fouled off twenty-two balls in one at-bat, twenty-four in another appearance at the plate, and in yet another at-bat, "maybe" twenty-seven. That's a lot of foul balls!

In the modern era, two players apparently share the unofficial record. On June 26, 1998, Ricky Gutierrez fouled off fourteen times before he struck out. Six years later, on May 12, Alex Cora fouled off fourteen consecutive pitches before hitting a home run on the eighteenth pitch thrown to him.

But no doubt the most interesting (and painful) unofficial record in this category belongs to Richie Ashburn, who played in the big leagues from 1948–1962. As an outfielder for the Philadelphia

Phillies, Ashburn earned a reputation for fouling off pitches in order to prolong his at-bats. In one inning, he fouled off fourteen pitches. One of his foul balls in that plate appearance hit a spectator in the face, breaking her nose. The game continued as medical personnel carried her away on a stretcher—and Ashburn promptly hit another foul ball that struck the poor woman *again*.

Who could blame the lady if she never showed up for another game?

While foul balls in baseball may prolong a difficult at-bat, I don't know of *any* player who'd choose to hit a foul ball rather than get a hit. Two foul balls means two strikes, and if an opposing player catches a foul ball before it touches the ground, the batter's out. Although hitting a lot of foul balls can give a batter more chances to get a hit, and perhaps tire out the pitcher, they're largely a waste of energy.

In life, foul balls have far fewer positive traits. We all hit them occasionally, but they don't help us move forward. They tire *us* out while giving the enemy of our souls a better chance to tag us out. While thinking along these lines in a morning Bible study, I said, "All of us in life have hit foul balls." A man in the audience immediately turned around—it turned out to be Otis Nixon, formerly with the Atlanta Braves—and said, "I've hit a lot of foul balls. It's better than striking out."

True enough…in baseball. In life, though, I pray that God would help us to live more productively than that. Instead of consistently hitting out of bounds, let's learn to keep the ball in play. Let's make it a habit to move our Christian brothers around the bases. Remember, we're in this thing to win—and foul balls simply don't align us with God's Word. To the contrary, they get us off trajectory, and too often they take us out of the game altogether.

From the Outside to the Inside

When I came to faith in Jesus, God saved me and gave me a new nature. The moment I believed, God transformed the inner me. Now, I want the transformation that already took place inside me to become evident on the outside. I want the watching world to be able to see the positive changes in me that the Lord has produced. I want my life to progressively align with the wealth of knowledge I'm gaining from the Word of God.

This outward transformation is made possible by an inner change *in my mind*. I don't always think right. I need God to continually take my foul thoughts, change their trajectory, and give me a line drive in fair territory. The Spirit gives Christian men the power and the desire to transform their minds. A simple formula describes what happens:

Transformed hearts + renewed minds = aligned lives

While the Bible lays out a clear process for renewing our minds (which we'll see in a moment), it also warns us that we have a battle on our hands. Ever since Adam, the natural, carnal mind is at war with God. It refuses to submit to Him and has no interest in obeying His instructions; in fact, it *cannot* obey since it lacks any power to do so. None of us with a mind "set on the flesh" can please God (see Romans 8:5-8). *That's* our problem.

So what's the solution?

Paul writes, "And do not be conformed to this world, but be transformed by the renewing of your mind, that you may prove what is that good and acceptable and perfect will of God" (Romans 12:2). Without renewed minds, we will live our entire lives on earth without ever pleasing the One who made us and redeemed us for His purpose.

The central question is, do you and I want to please God? Do we want to know and do His good, acceptable, and perfect will? If we do, then we need to learn how to cooperate with the Spirit of God in the process of renewing our mind. A renewed mind is a spiritually sensitive mind, and the Bible says, "To be spiritually minded is life and peace" (Romans 8:6).

Who doesn't want *that*?

The How of Renewal

The primary tool God uses in this fight is the Word of God. David said to the Lord, "Your word I have hidden in my heart, that I might not sin against You" (Psalm 119:11). When we put God's Word in our hearts, the Lord uses what's there to bring about remarkable changes in our behavior.

If you want to transform your mind, you must learn how to think biblically. In practice, that means you need to learn to think like Jesus. But how can you think Jesus' thoughts without knowing Jesus' words? In the Gospels, we see Jesus at work and hear Him speak. If we want to become like Him, we have to become intimately familiar with His story as told in Scripture.

As we listen to Jesus' words, meditate on His interactions with others, read of His miracles, and see His power over sin and the devil, in effect, we gaze upon His life. As we are "beholding" Him, we "are being transformed into the same image from glory to glory, just as by the Spirit of the Lord" (2 Corinthians 3:18). The more we behold Jesus' glory, the more we reflect that glory.

In Greek, the word translated "beholding" is in the present middle tense, which means God doesn't *make* you behold Jesus' glory. You don't change because the Lord forces you to change. You change because you continually desire to behold His glory, and that glorious sight changes you. To keep growing in Christ, to continue the process of spiritual transformation, you must keep on beholding Jesus, right up to the time of your homegoing. Our bodies may decline and our physical strength may wane, but the glory of Jesus can continue to shine through our lives.

I long to be further along tonight than I was this morning, and tomorrow I want to be further along than today. I'm still being changed, step by step. I won't get transformed into the likeness of Christ by New Year's resolutions, trying harder, or promising to do better next time. I can change, from one degree of glory to another, only by continuing to behold the glory of Christ Jesus.

Do you want to get in on this? You can—but you have to choose it. The Spirit of God changes us as we willingly surrender and respond to Him in obedience. He does not force us to obey; He empowers us to obey. There is a very large difference! John Piper, commenting on Romans 12:2, put it this way: "What, then, do we do in obedience to this truth? We join the Holy Spirit in His precious and all-important work. We pursue Christ-exalting truth."[6] We *pursue* it. It's a personal, with-all-our-heart pursuit.

Are you pursuing Christ-exalting truth? Are you striving to get to know the Bible, the Word of God? Are you praying that the truth you learn in Scripture enables you to humbly embrace the changes that God wants to bring about in you?

As the Holy Spirit transforms your mind through God's Word, He transforms your living. Over time, you become "fully mature in Christ" (Colossians 1:28 NIV). Oh, you'll still have room for growth. In this life, you and I will never get to the point where we have no room for further spiritual development. Renewal of the mind and conformity to the likeness of Christ take place gradually. It's not as though you get up one morning, spend an hour with the Lord, and say, "Well, there it is! I'm *there*. Praise the Lord, I made it!" No, it's an extended process (the Bible calls it "sanctification") in which the mind gradually gets adjusted to thinking more like Christ.

A Twofold Process

As the process of sanctification unfolds in your life, keep in mind two equal but distinct truths about how it works.

1. *The instant you put your faith in Jesus, God completely dealt with the penalty of your sin.* Jesus suffered both death and separation from God *for you*. That issue is taken care of totally, once and for all. Nothing more can happen there or ever will happen there. You are "in Christ," and that means God sees you as though you're as righteous as Jesus Himself. Some Bible teachers call this *positional truth*.

2. *In your experience on earth, God did not change you once and for all, forever.* When you came to faith, you did *not* immediately become the person you'll be in eternity. That's why the Lord calls you to increasingly live out the eternal life He's already given you. Some Bible teachers call this *experiential truth*.

This twofold reality about sanctification explains why Paul told his Philippian friends, "Work out your own salvation with fear and trembling; for it is God who works in you both to will and to do for His good pleasure" (Philippians 2:12-13). God wants you to work *out* what He's already worked *in*. He doesn't, of course, leave you on your own to do this. He works in you so that you can accomplish His will, thereby giving Him great pleasure through your eager obedience.

Through sanctification, God graciously redirects your worship and affection away from worldliness and toward Jesus' image. I once read an article by G.K. Beale titled, "We Become What We Worship." Have you ever been around somebody who talks all the time about one specific issue? He never stops harping on it. It's always on his mind. When you're around a man like that, you can be pretty sure he's worshiping that thing. It consumes his attention, his time, and his devotion. Eventually, he starts becoming like that thing.

As you become increasingly like Christ—as you become conformed to His image—you are sanctified. In that way, your life becomes less and less about you and more and more about Him.

I sometimes hear men say things like, "I just can't stand Brother Billy. He really gets on my nerves, you know?" Does that look like a foul ball to you? It does to me—and I've hit more than my share. Engaging in that kind of bad behavior puts your mind on the wrong trajectory, and if you stay there, you'll remain in foul territory. Every now and then, God will speak to you and me and whisper to our hearts, "Son, you need to get in fair territory." At those moments, in Christ-honoring humility, we must learn to say, "You're right, Lord, and I'm wrong. Forgive me, and help me to do what pleases You." God can work in our hearts as we embrace godly choices, but He doesn't make us embrace any of them (although He can make things awfully uncomfortable for us until we obey).

When your life aligns with God's Word, you stay in fair territory and your actions bring glory to your Lord. As you stop hitting foul balls, you find your life's calling…and that's when the real fun begins.

Construction Materials for a Christian Mind

Transformed hearts and renewed minds ultimately lead to an aligned life. This process of renewal begins inwardly but manifests itself outwardly. If Christ is working inside of us and is really changing us, His inward work will change us outwardly. We can't keep it inside!

It's ludicrous to talk about being a Christian if the Spirit of God has not invaded your life and begun changing it. It'd be like saying you're an active Major League Baseball player even though you're blind and paralyzed, or that you're going to fly from Atlanta to Boston without your feet ever leaving the ground. The idea is both ridiculous and impossible.

In order to change your behavior on the outside (to match Jesus), you need to first change your thinking on the inside (to match Jesus). You need to construct a biblical mind. How does God build a biblical mind in us? He uses the blueprint of the Bible along with the right building materials. In Philippians 4:8, God lists for us the materials for constructing a biblical mind:

> Finally, brethren, whatever things are true, whatever things are noble, whatever things are just, whatever things are pure, whatever things are lovely, whatever things are of good report, if there is any virtue and if there is anything praiseworthy—meditate on these things.

In considering this list, this saying comes to mind: "You are not what you think you are, but what you think, you are." Scripture leaves no doubt that our lives are the product of our thoughts. It's something like a computer: garbage in, garbage out. Put the wrong thing into someone's mind and out will come the error you put in. Jesus said, "What comes out of a man, that defiles a man. For from within, out of the heart of men, proceed evil thoughts, adulteries, fornications, murders, thefts, covetousness, wickedness, deceit, lewdness, an evil eye, blasphemy, pride, foolishness" (Mark 7:20-22). Notice that "evil thoughts" appear first on Jesus' list. A troubled mind makes a convenient depository for seeds of doubt, despair, and wickedness.

Adrian Rogers put it this way: "The devil had rather get you to think wrong than to do wrong, because if you do wrong but you still think right, you'll get right. But if you do wrong because you think wrong, you'll continue to do wrong because you think you're right."[7] Since the devil wins if he can get hold of your mind, let's take a closer look at the building materials for constructing a biblical mind.

True

When the Bible speaks of truth, it refers not only to the Christian's accurate apprehension of reality, but to every phase of his conduct. I should not only *think* truth, I should conduct my life in a way that reflects truth.

The "belt of truth" holds everything together in Paul's description of the Christian's armor in Ephesians 6. The ancient belt didn't just go around the waist, but extended down to a man's loins. The image speaks of integrity and truth keeping everything together.

You can have everything in the world going for you—you can be intellectual, you can be wealthy, you can have great influence—but if you buy into a lie, you'll have nothing in the end. When a man thinks falsehoods, before long his outer life reflects the inner lies he's accepted.

Noble

The word translated "noble" means honorable, or that which claims respect. The Greek term carries the idea of serious as opposed to frivolous. Believing men shouldn't camp on what is trivial, temporal, mundane, common, or earthly. Rather, they must train their minds to think about whatever is heavenly, worthy of adoration and praise.

Honorable thoughts produce honorable people. When you think dishonorably about a man, you often find yourself telling ugly rumors and lies about him. Someone may say, "But you don't know what he did to me!" May I remind you of what you did to

Jesus? And yet, He forgave you. I'm grateful to God that He did not give me what I deserved.

Years ago, a friend said to me, "We say that we're to love the sinner and hate his sin, but there's one thing wrong with that. The emphasis is on somebody else and not a reflection on ourselves. Why don't we say, 'We are to love the sinner and hate our sin?'" If I'm going to think biblically, it's not what I say about others, but what God has helped me to see about myself. *Then* I can start thinking as Jesus does.

Just

This term is the root of the word *righteous*, or doing what is right. It speaks of a man who faces his duty and does it. It speaks of right relationships and proper action, of fair and equitable dealings with others.

What things cause us to be right with God and with each other? We ought to contemplate them. What is in perfect harmony with God's eternal, unchanging standard as revealed in Scripture? Faithful, believing men dwell on things consistent with God's Word.

To be "just" is the opposite of doing what's convenient. My favorite Bible verse is Proverbs 20:7: "The righteous man walks in his integrity; his children are blessed after him." Am I living toward Christ and others in such a way that my conduct can win God's approval? A just person wants to do the right thing. Are you there? If not, are you willing to get there? Is that a passion of your life?

Pure

The original Greek term refers to all sorts of purity: pure thoughts, pure words, pure deeds. Purity is often defined as "holy, morally clean." Lightfoot says the word suggests "stainless."[8]

Did you know that some thoughts leave a stain that is difficult to erase? At least 35 percent of all downloads on American computers is pornography. Forty million Americans regularly visit porn sites. Every second, nearly thirty thousand users are watching Internet porn. Americans spend more than thirty billion dollars annually on porn, more than received by the entire Christian church in America. Americans spend more on porn each year than they do on Major League Baseball, the NFL, and the NBA combined. In that sort of filthy environment, how can a Christian man keep his thoughts pure?

The ancient Philippians lived in an impure environment where "anything goes" would have made an appropriate slogan. How did they combat it? They had to fill their minds with pure thoughts. Peter told his Christian friends to "gird up the loins of your mind" (1 Peter 1:13). He pictured the thought life as a flowing robe or gown. We're running a race and he said, "Pull up your gown and tie it with a rope so it won't impede your progress."

Moral purity has been a problem since ancient times. Men both then and now were and are under constant attack by a thousand temptations to violate sexual purity. How do you combat it? John says one way is to think of Jesus' return: "And everyone who has this hope in Him purifies himself, just as He is pure" (1 John 3:3). Because Jesus Christ is pure, Christian men must purify themselves. One way they do that is by reminding themselves that Jesus could return at any time.

Lovely

This Greek term is used only here in the New Testament. It could be literally translated "friendly toward." It means pleasing, agreeable, dearly prized, and worth the effort to have and embrace.

Something lovely speaks of that which is full of love. And so I pray, "Lord, help me to construct a mind that will be sweet, gracious, generous, patient, and loving."

Good report

The term means "laudable, well reported of, reputable, spoken of in a kindly spirit." When I leave this world, I want it to be said, "Pastor Johnny was an honorable, respected man of God." I intend to build my life on doing what's right—not what's most popular, not what's most palatable, but what is right. I want to earn a good reputation, and I'll do that as I continue to build a Christlike mind.

Virtuous, praiseworthy

Does your mind every now and then find itself wandering to places that are neither virtuous nor praiseworthy? Maybe it's a fractured relationship or an activity that, if widely known, would cause you a great deal of embarrassment or even shame. Don't let your mind go there.

Instead, fill your consciousness with images and thoughts that, if projected on a screen in front of your loved ones, would prompt them to express gratitude and praise. Why forfeit victory by focusing your attention on corrupt or disgraceful thoughts? Commit yourself to follow Jesus' example and seek the praise of your Father in heaven, especially in your thought life.

Two Critical Bookends

The two bookends of proper thinking are *learning* truth and *implementing* truth. It's not enough merely to know truth or to have curiosity about God's construction materials for a biblical mind. You must implement those materials by meditating on the truth you learn. Dwell on it. Welcome it. Turn it over and over again in your brain.

If you want to build a biblical mind, this is not an option for you. It's a divine command. To meditate on these things means to evaluate them carefully, consider them deeply, ponder them with a view toward putting them into practice.

Christian men must learn to stop dwelling on trivial, temporal, mundane, common, and earthly things, and instead make it a habit to marinate their thoughts on heaven-centered truth. We must train ourselves to think on things worthy of adoration and praise, things that promote godly character. If this begins to happen in your life, you'll act differently from most men. Your behavior will cause you to stand out in a crowd. As a consequence, you will build great self-respect and self-confidence.

When Paul writes, "Think on these things," he again uses a present middle imperative, which means, once more, you have a choice to make. You must *decide* to "think on these things." If you choose not to do so, your mind will go places it shouldn't go. We are responsible for our thoughts and we *can* hold them to a high and lofty ideal.

Imagine a lock and key. The key that unlocks a man's capacity to think biblically is truth. Jesus is truth. The Bible is truth. God has given you truth. The lock of obedience opens only with the key of truth. Many times we find ourselves locked out from the divine resources intended to give us victory simply because we refuse to obey. While it's easier to retain truth than it is to implement it, God wants us to release that truth and so lead us to freedom. Once we take the key (called *truth*) and place it in the lock (called *obedience*), the storehouses of God's resources swing wide open to us.

Again, you must choose. Will you choose to build a biblical mind, or will you say, "I know how I'm supposed to act, but I'm ticked off. I'm hurt." Author Kent Hughes has written, "I have great sympathy for those whose past has been a series of bad choices. I understand that, if over the years, one has chosen the impure and the negative, it is very difficult to change; but as a biblical thinker, I give no quarter to myself or anyone else who rationalizes his present choices by the past."[9]

Don't allow yourself to say, "I'm without hope. I've thought this way for so long that I see no chance of changing." That is simply not true. The Spirit of God can stop the bleeding in your life right now.

He Changes Our Wants

Several years ago, I preached at a friend's church in another state, and someone dear to me whom I hadn't seen in a very long time came unexpectedly to the service. At the close of the evening, I said, "Is there anyone in this room who would like to repent of their sins, ask God to forgive them, and place their faith in Jesus Christ?"

I saw a long arm rise up in the air, attached to a body with a very familiar face.

You can hardly imagine what it meant for me to see my first cousin there, after all those years. I had witnessed to him many times, but he'd never responded. I told the audience, "You can put your hands down." My cousin put his hand down. "Anyone else?" I continued.

His hand shot up again. James Ray wanted to make sure he'd been seen.

That night my cousin gave his life to Christ after a lifetime of alcohol abuse. He and I had been inseparable from five years of age until about age fifteen, remaining best buds that whole time. He'd married young and I had followed suit. After that, we basically went our separate ways and decades had passed. James Ray put his faith in Jesus just after his sixty-first birthday.

A couple of years later, I planned to visit his town again. By then, James Ray had developed cirrhosis of the liver and his kidneys had begun to fail. He weighed about ninety pounds. I called him to say I'd be visiting his area.

"Oh, please come and see me," he said.

"I wouldn't think about coming without seeing you," I answered.

When I arrived at his mobile home, I found him covered in blankets, with the oven on and its door down to help keep him warm.

"James Ray," I said, "tell me what's going on."

"My kidneys are failing and there's nothing else they can do, so I'm going to be leaving any minute."

"James Ray, are you ready to meet Jesus?"

"I am, but I want you to answer some questions for me. Can you take your Bible and tell me what's going to happen when I draw my last breath?"

No one had ever asked me those questions, but I did my best to answer them all. At the end, I said, "James Ray, when you get to heaven, tell my mom I said hello."

As I recall that heart-wrenching scene, my mind flashes back to a friend who got converted while still active with the Hell's Angels. I went to hear him give his testimony, as did a lot of other Hell's Angels—a rough-looking crowd. "If I'm wrong and the Bible's not true," he told us, "I still have lived a better life since I committed my life to Jesus. If I die and it's all over with, I'm still glad I made my decision. But if I'm right and the Bible's true, Romans 8:16 says that once you become a Christian, God's Spirit bears witness with your spirit. He comes to live in us. He changes our wants."

Indeed, God changed the wants of both my cousin and my friend. While my cousin had just as genuine a conversion as my Hell's Angel friend, however, James Ray's "wants" didn't change until almost the very end. A man can be overwhelmingly forgiven on his way to heaven, but that doesn't mean God removes the consequences of the way he's chosen to live for decades.

My friend, you can get past your past and the way you've thought over the years. We are free to have a Christian mind. It is within our reach! And it is our duty.

Will you choose it? Will you choose to keep the ball in play?

9

THE GREATEST POWER
IN THE WORLD

My wife once took me to a NASCAR event and to a chapel service held before the race. I got excited when I found out that the speaker would be James Dobson, the founder of Focus on the Family. He was still recovering from a heart attack that he had thought would take him to heaven.

During his hospital stay, Dr. Dobson said he had a lot of time to ponder what's most important to a man. When you believe your time on earth is growing short, three key issues bubble to the surface:

1. Who do I love?
2. Who really loves me?
3. Will I spend eternity with the ones I love?

As he pondered those three questions, Dr. Dobson realized he didn't know whether his son, Ryan, even knew the Lord. After his release from the hospital, Dr. Dobson felt a consuming passion for his wayward son. The love of God and his own broken heart drove him to make sure that Ryan would spend eternity with him. As father pursued son in the love of God, the Lord did a wonderful work in the life of Ryan Dobson, and today Ryan is a minister of the gospel of Jesus Christ.

This story reminds me that love is an action verb. It *acts* on behalf of those it loves—and if you're a Christian man, God calls you to let the love of God be the driving force of your life.

God's Love: What Is It?

If most people know one Greek word from the New Testament, it's *agape*, a term that refers to self-giving, God-like love. The word suggests the absorption of every part of one's being in one great passion.

Have you ever heard somebody say, "I just want to love God with every fiber of my being"? Well, God loves us with every fiber of His being. Every fiber of His being overflows with *agape* love, and God keeps on loving, even when He disciplines us.

The word has little to do with mere emotion. It indicates a deliberate love, exercised by an act of will. It chooses its object and, through thick or thin, regardless of the attractiveness of the object, goes on loving, continually and eternally. God's *agape* love thinks not of itself but of the objects it loves.

God's *agape* love depends on nothing outside of itself. It's not affected by the worthiness or unworthiness of the one loved. God has chosen to pour into us His love—unconditional, sacrificial, submissive.

God's love is unconquerable, considerate, charitable, and benevolent. It demands expression. It seeks an object to serve and then sacrifices for it. God's love makes it a practice to do good. It doesn't wait to be asked to join an opportunity to do good, but seeks out opportunities to express itself.

Jesus reflected God's *agape* love when He said, "It is more blessed to give than to receive" (Acts 20:35). And so God's love reaches out to those who do not deserve it: "God demonstrates His own love toward us, in that while we were still sinners, Christ died for us" (Romans 5:8). This divine love forgives undeserving people. It knows how to start over and repeatedly sacrifices itself for others. It's a love that genuinely cares.

The love of God endures when all else fails. It is completely indestructible. While other things pass away, His love lasts. It's permanent. It's not going away. It will never dry up, run down, cave in, or blow away. I love the Song of Solomon, which says,

> Many waters cannot quench love,
> nor can the floods drown it.
> If a man would give for love
> all the wealth of his house,
> it would be utterly despised.
> (Song of Solomon 8:7)

Nothing matches God's love. "And now abide faith, hope, love, these three," wrote the apostle Paul, "but the greatest of these is love" (1 Corinthians 13:13).

God's Love: We're to Express It

It should surprise none of us that love is the supreme characteristic that God demands to see expressed in His people. When asked to name the greatest commandment, Jesus replied, "'You shall love the LORD your God with all your heart, with all your soul, and with all your mind.' This is the first and great commandment. And the second is like it: 'You shall love your neighbor as yourself'" (Matthew 22:37-39). It doesn't matter how much you and I know. People want to know that we genuinely care.

The only acceptable love that God ever receives from us is the love that He's poured into us. He pours it in that we might pour it out.

And who do we love? We love both those who love us and those who don't love us. We love our enemies, even those who hate us.

"Well, I can't do that," you say. I agree with you; you can't. But when you allow God to pour His love into you, you'll be surprised at the capacity you gain to love others. I say surprised, not proud, because 1 Corinthians 13:4 insists love is not proud. There is no room for pride in the love of God.

Men who express God's love through their lives don't strut around. Pride short-circuits the effects of *agape* love. Pride *always* precedes loveless living. It can't express genuine love because love requires a focus off of self and on others.

Pride negotiates for its own benefit. Its sense of superiority slices into a man's soul like a surgeon's scalpel. Pride produces both bitterness and resentment because it thinks that by giving free reign to these negative emotions, somehow it pays back the offender. The proud man actually believes that when he drinks the poison of unforgiveness, the person he hates will die.

Love listens; pride talks. Love forgives; pride resents. Love gives; pride takes. Love apologizes; pride blames. Love understands; pride assumes. Love accepts; pride rejects. Love trusts; pride doubts. Love asks; pride tells. Love leads; pride drives. Love frees; pride binds. Love builds up; pride tears down. Love encourages; pride discourages. Love is peaceful; pride is fearful. Love clarifies with truth; pride confuses with lies.

Love and pride are mutually exclusive. Love dies when pride comes alive.

If you struggle with pride, what can you do? The only antidote to pride is humility. Humility is a veritable hotbed of love.

Humility invites love to take up permanent residence in a man's heart. Humility understands that love is reserved for everyone. Love forgives even the worst of sinners, as humility knows it needs help in receiving *agape* love. A humble heart yearns for love from the Lord Jesus Christ.

Love releases the power of God's Spirit in us because the love of God has been shed abroad in our hearts by the Holy Spirit (see Romans 5:5). It edifies and builds up. Love builds up your home. It builds up your marriage. It builds up your life. The love of God takes joy in promoting others.

This kind of *agape* love does not originate in our nature, but comes from the very heart of God. It is supernatural in origin. You do not have *agape* love until you fall in love with God and the Lord instills within your heart His love.

I once attended a Southern Baptist convention where the greatest song performed was sung by the worst voice I'd ever heard. The man had recently been converted and had come to the convention with a choir and orchestra from his church. He'd just left a horrible life of sin, but God had radically changed his life and he wanted to sing about it. He couldn't carry a tune in a bucket, but when he finished, I didn't see a dry eye in the place. I had to dab away tears too.

Is it easy to love others with God's *agape* love? Frankly, no. It's easier to be orthodox than to be loving. I've known some men who had a stranglehold on doctrinal truth, but were as mean as rattlesnakes. It's easier to be active in church than to be loving. If you don't believe me, let me ask a few questions.

Do you ever have trouble loving somebody because you don't think they deserve it?

When did you last get on your knees and pray for your enemies?

Have you ever prayed for those who spitefully used you or who said nasty things about you?

Remember, "love does not envy" (1 Corinthians 13:4). There's no meanness of soul in *agape* love, while jealousy has a viciousness shared by no other sin.

Love "does not behave rudely" (v. 5). It has good manners. It's not blunt or rude or brutal. Love cares about the other person's feelings and takes them into account before it speaks or acts.

One Sunday, in the middle of a sermon, I learned an unforgettable lesson about failing to care for another's feelings. I'd told a story about an exchange between Janet and me, and as I finished, my wife found a mic, grabbed it, came up on the platform, and said to the congregation, "Y'all just heard Pastor Johnny tell a story about us. How many of you'd like to hear my version?" The audience cheered so loud, it embarrassed me. I'd forgotten that love *never* overlooks the other person's feelings. I hope I won't forget again! (Ever since that day, anytime I mention Janet's name in a sermon, I'm fearful of a mic close by.)

Love "thinks no evil" (v. 5). The original term used here was an accounting word for "ledger." Love does not store in memory the wrong against it and retrieve that memory whenever needed. You don't even have a ledger.

Have you ever heard bad news about somebody and rejoiced over the report? Maybe you even said, "It couldn't have happened to a better guy." When you heard that some unpleasant man crashed or his marriage blew up or he'd landed in legal trouble, did you feel good about it? Listen to Proverbs 24:17: "Do not rejoice when your enemy falls, and do not let your heart be glad when he stumbles." Don't throw a party when you hear bad reports about difficult people. If God's love has taken up residence in you, then you want to see the best for everybody.

Love hides the ugliness from public view. It does not drag it out into the light. Aren't you glad for great marriages that can keep some things between themselves and the Lord?

Love "suffers long" (v. 4). That means you have a long fuse, not a short temper. It means that God is building patience into your life. A lot of little things used to bother me about Janet, and in former days, I let her know about them. I've always thought she takes along too much luggage whenever we take a trip. We go overnight and it looks to me like she brings enough for a week. I used to rag on her about it, until love taught me that's just who she is. We've been married just under fifty years, and if my harping strategy had a chance of working, it would have kicked in by now. It hasn't. So I leave it alone.

"Get my luggage," she says.

"Yes, dear," I say. And I think, *Pick it up. Carry it. Don't criticize.*

If you're married, speak to your wife today and say to her, "I'm not going to say anything else about _____." Harping on it doesn't work, but love does. Love may not "cure" her of the habit that bugs you, but it'll sure cure you of being bugged.

Love sees the bright side. It believes the best in people, just like Jesus when he saw Simon Peter, the wavering one. Do you remember what Jesus called him? *Petras,* "rock." What a confidence booster! That was a prophecy, not a statement of then-current fact.

It has been said that the only thing God will reward at the *bēma,* the judgment seat of Christ, is what we've done that was motivated by God's love. If that's true, then what kind of reward can you expect?

Once you genuinely receive the love of your heavenly Father, you can't help but dispense it to others. As you receive love, you become capable of giving it, even eager to give it.

The pinnacle of spiritual development is to love God with our total being and to love our neighbor as ourselves. The strongest men in the world are those who love the most.

This Love Is Strong, Not Weak

Even as Jesus pours His love into us, He also makes us fearless and strong. Paul put it this way: "For God has not given us a spirit of fear, but of power and of love and of a sound mind" (2 Timothy 1:7). The greatest power in *any* man's leadership is love.

Jesus founded His conquering kingdom on love: "For God so loved the world that He gave His only begotten Son" (John 3:16). As a result, millions around the world would willingly die for Him. And just for the record's sake, more have died for Christ in the last one hundred years than in all the nineteen hundred years preceding. That takes strength.

God's love in us is not sentimental emotion, but the outpouring of a man's total being to another in blessing. Maybe one morning you get up and the love of God begins to remind you that a man has something against you. Before you know it, the love of God will say to you, "Call him." It takes real strength to obey. But you reach out with the love of God and you touch him…and then God begins to move. Only then do you realize the real force and power of God's love. You see it in mighty action.

Love outlasts any potent spiritual gift you might have. Maybe you say, "I can't sing now, but when I get to heaven, I'll sure be able to sing!" But heaven will not be about how well you sing. If you think it is, you're missing it. Heaven will be about loving God with a perfected, strong love, and loving one another with God's omnipotent love.

The bottom line is, God magnifies love. At the end of the day, the Lord desires that you and I love Him with a fierce, strong, and growing passion. The only way anyone will ever know if we really love God is if they see us using our gifts and graces to love and serve others. The strongest man on earth is the one who best channels the mighty river of God's love into the lives of those who most need it.

One Fruit, Many Varieties

Just as an apple tree expresses its life in bearing apples, so the Christ follower expresses his life in bearing the spiritual fruit of love. What does a healthy apple tree do? It produces apples. What does a Christian man full of the love of God do? He expresses and bears the love of God.

In the ancient world, the Greeks prized what a man knew, his intellect. The Romans worshiped a man for what he could do, his power. But the apostle Paul stressed what a man is, his character. And so he wrote these amazing words: "But the fruit of the Spirit is love, joy, peace, longsuffering, kindness, goodness, faithfulness, gentleness, self-control. Against such there is no law" (Galatians 5:22-23).

Notice that Paul speaks of the fruit of the Spirit in the singular— the *fruit* of the Spirit, not *fruits*. I agree with many theologians who believe that all eight qualities Paul mentions above are expressions of love. Each of these eight qualities should express themselves through every man who receives God's love. These eight traits are so critical that I want to linger over them, both in this chapter and in the next one. I believe it's that important.

Don't forget that none of us can produce the fruit of the Spirit; only Jesus can do that. While we have the ability to manufacture plastic fruit, no man can manufacture the fruit of the Spirit. Spiritual fruit grows only when a branch remains vitally connected to the vine. In God's family, we are those branches and Jesus is the true vine. As the Holy Spirit pours out the love of God in our hearts (see

Romans 5:5), the fruit of the Spirit grows on us, the branches. The fruit we produce gives nourishment for others, who taste in it the love of God. And so God's kingdom expands.

Joy: Love's Music

Joy is love's music. Tell me something that's sweeter than a home filled with joy. If love is absent, you can forget joy.

God's love can keep a man cheerful in all circumstances. Do you know what the reformers said when they referred to the love of God that brought them joy? They said God gave them a "happy soul."

Is your soul happy? Your soul speaks of who you are, the seat of affection, everything that you represent. Do you have that kind of joy? Jesus told His disciples, "These things I have spoken to you, that My joy may remain in you, and that your joy may be full" (John 15:11). A friend of mine has taped to his desk a saying written by his godly uncle, who served the Lord vocationally for over seventy years and who lived to be just a couple of months shy of one hundred: "Joy is the indisputable proof of the Holy Spirit."

The word translated "joy" in John 15:11 can also mean contentment. When God fills us with His joy, we become content. Are you content? If contentment eludes you, then you lack His joy.

Our self-centered nature has led us to believe that happiness and joy come only when we get what we want. But how many illustrations from real life do we need to see that getting what we think we want does *not* meet our needs? When some of the wealthiest people in the world finally obtain what they've clamored for, they get a divorce. Before you know it, they've walked down the aisle so many times that you've lost count. Is that happiness? Is that joy?

Some men think, *If I could just get that new car* or *a bigger house* or *healthier children* or *a bit of fame*, they'd find contentment, happiness, and joy. But those things never bring joy, because joy comes not from getting but from giving out the love of God. Do you want joy? Then learn to dispense God's love like you're giving out candy.

When the love of God prompts me to give, sometimes I get the holy giggles. Does that sound crazy? Maybe what's wrong with you is that you're in what you call your "right mind," and that kind of mind is about to wreck your life. I wish you could let your hair down!

One Sunday, someone said something terrible to me, and I laughed.

"That's not the response I expected," the man said.

"You'll never make it in this ministry without a sense of humor," I replied. I'm not referring to making jokes or even about having a pleasant outlook on life. This is better than humor; it's joy.

Every time we have the chance to flesh out the love of God to others, our joy cycle revs up all over again. It goes from one wave of joy to another. Why not let God be a source of spiritual refreshment to you and to others?

A farmer once had a helper who filled his buckets of grain only three-fourths full. The farmer said to him, "The buckets are never full until they're running over."

I want God to fill my cup of joy to overflowing. I want my bucket and my heart to overflow with the joy of the Lord. I don't want merely to get by; I want to thrive. A Christian man who never gets filled with the spiritual blessings of God will never run over with joy and so refresh the lives of others.

I like the old acronym J-O-Y. How do you get joy? By living according to the acronym: **J**esus, **O**thers, **Y**ourself.

When Paul tells us to "rejoice always" in 1 Thessalonians 5:16, he uses the same Greek word elsewhere translated "joy." How is it even possible to always have joy? It's possible because joy is not happiness.

While happiness is based on circumstance and happenstance, joy is based on a relationship. I need something that controls me, regardless of my circumstances. I need joy! Someone has said, "Joy is the flag flown high from the castle of my heart, for the King is in residence there."

When Jesus Christ told us in John 15:11 that He wants us to have "full" joy, He immediately added, "This is My commandment, that you love one another as I have loved you" (v. 12). There is a straight line between our love for one another and our experience of joy. As a minister and as a people person, I've observed that at least 90 percent of the time when people lose their joy, they've done so because of a fractured relationship.

As people observe your life, do they see joy or discouragement? If you find yourself constantly asking people, "What are you so happy about?" could it be because you so often feel discouraged?

Habakkuk 3:17-18 features what I call a "hymn of faith." The prophet had seen the coming destruction of his homeland, and he knew that God's fearful time of judgment had arrived. So how did he respond?

> Though the fig tree may not blossom,
> Nor fruit be on the vines;
> Though the labor of the olive may fail,
> And the fields yield no food;
> Though the flock may be cut off from the fold,
> And there be no herd in the stalls—
> Yet I will rejoice in the LORD,
> I will joy in the God of my salvation.

He says, "Everything that I'd hoped for has disappeared. None of the good I wanted has happened. But because of my relationship with God, I still have joy, real joy, wonderful joy."

How did the apostle Paul manage to rejoice when his missionary activities landed him in jail? He rejoiced even in prison because no jail could stop his prayers. No prison warden could cut him off from his living connection to Jesus. Paul had learned to rejoice and be content in every circumstance, not at every circumstance.

Some things bring me no joy. But when I take that circumstance and bring it to Jesus, God can still give me joy. When you get your relationship right with Jesus, you can rejoice in the Lord anywhere and always. Writing from prison, Paul told his Christian friends, "Rejoice in the Lord always. Again I will say, rejoice!" (Philippians 4:4). That's a command, not a suggestion. How can anyone command joy? Only because true joy, deep joy, flows out of a growing relationship with Jesus Christ.

Peace: Love's Agreement

Peace is love's agreement. We can have both peace *with* God and the peace *of* God when we agree that He's right and we're wrong.

Before I got saved, I was at enmity with God. A wall separated me from a relationship with Him. But when I came to faith, Christ Jesus tore down the wall and made me one with others who also have come to know Him. As a result, peace rules in our hearts. We agree with God and with one another.

The word *confession* means to agree with God. When I confessed my sin, repented, and placed my faith in Christ, peace with God became a reality in my life. Peace *with* God comes to every man as a result of a loving relationship with the Savior. It's like making a peace treaty after a war ends. The only way that peace treaty with heaven ever gets signed is to acknowledge that Jesus made perfect provision on the cross so that you and I could be cleansed and forgiven through His sacrifice.

The peace *of* God refers to an inner tranquility you can have, even in the midst of a confusing and disintegrating world. You can have this peace because you know that God remains in charge. The fruit of the Spirit produces peace. I'm at peace with God and I have the peace of God. I have an inner tranquility that God gives me.

One time before a Sunday service, our church's deacons knelt with me to pray. We typically prayed at that time for the service and for me as I prepared to minister the Word, but that morning we knelt and prayed over a dear man in our church suffering with cancer. His numbers didn't look good. We prayed that the peace of God would rule in his heart, overwhelmingly, regardless of his outward circumstances.

If you think, *I might have peace once my circumstances change*, you have a shrunken view of God. Regardless of your circumstances, the love of God can be poured into your heart where God's peace can rule even in the midst of chaos. Despite all kinds of unpleasant stuff happening around you, you can learn to say, as the kids' song says, "I've got the peace that passes understanding down in my heart." This kind of peace is not based on outward circumstances but depends on a living, vibrant relationship with Almighty God.

The Lord pours His peace into you, and it simply has to find expression through your life. Even when the world falls apart, God remains in charge—and that truth brings you peace.

God's peace goes even a step further. It brings peace to others in a world of turmoil. Did you know that God has given you a ministry of reconciliation (see 2 Corinthians 5:18-21)?

Every now and then when I officiate at a funeral, the family of the deceased clearly has no peace. I see turmoil everywhere, with contentious people pulling at me from all sides. How do I respond? I open my Bible and lift up Jesus. And more often than not, I watch as God comes over that place, settles in, and brings His peace. I've never seen anything else like it.

Is that your experience?

How Can I Pray for You?

One day a dear friend and I had lunch at a restaurant. When our server came to our table, I noticed her name tag said "Jennifer." So I said, "Jennifer, we're getting ready to pray to thank the Lord for our food. Anything we can pray for you about?"

She instantly got all choked up. "Pray for me. I'm a single mom with two special needs kids."

"Ma'am," I asked, "have you heard of Night to Shine?" (The Tim Tebow Foundation sponsors Night to Shine, a celebratory prom for special needs young people ages fourteen and older. The nationwide program centers on the love of God.)

Jennifer and I began to talk about her situation. I had ordered club soda with lime, and by the time I left the restaurant, I'd put down three full glasses. Jennifer couldn't do enough to serve me. Every time she walked by our table, she'd say, "God bless you! God bless you!"

The devil's convinced too many of us that if we open our mouths to represent the King who made us, we'll cause offense or make somebody angry. But you can care for someone through praying. You can minister the love, joy, and peace of God to them. I prayed that God would move in Jennifer's heart.

At some point that afternoon, I told her, "Let me share something else with you, Jennifer. My momma was a single mom, raised six kids. Two of them became preachers, both my sisters are serving the Lord. My oldest brother is a deacon in the Methodist church, and I have one brother in prison." I just told her our family story.

When I meet someone in need like Jennifer, I talk about the love, joy, and peace of God. I testify how faithful Jesus is, about how much He loves her and will forgive her, minister to her, and even use her. God can give anyone His love, joy, and peace even in the most trying of circumstances.

How can this happen? Remember, love is an action verb. It's never passive. Love calls you to action, and then goes to work on your behalf and for the benefit of others.

10

DO YOU LOOK LIKE YOUR FATHER?

Most of us have a soft spot in our hearts for family resemblances. We like it when someone says to us, "Boy, I can really see you in your son's face. There's no question who *his* daddy is!"

I've thought about this glee over family resemblances when the Bible calls Jesus "the express image" of His heavenly Father (Hebrews 1:3). I've pondered it when Jesus Himself told His disciples, "He who has seen Me has seen the Father" (John 14:9). And I've wondered why no theologian has ever written a book on the attributes of God solely by using incidents from the life of Jesus Christ. I can't help but think such an approach would make an otherwise abstract topic come fully alive.

As I write, Easter is just a few weeks away. My mind drifts toward Passion Week and Calvary and all that our Savior accomplished for us on the cross. As I dwell on the events of that season, it strikes me that Jesus exhibited *every one* of the varieties of the Spirit's fruit that Paul listed in Galatians 5.

Love, of course, moved God to make provision for our salvation, and love led Jesus to die in our place to make that salvation possible.

God took great *joy* in bringing many sons to glory, and Jesus accepted the shame and agony of the cross for the joy set before Him.

God used Easter to give us *peace* with Him, and the Prince of Peace, Jesus, made it a reality.

In this chapter, I want to briefly discuss the remaining six varieties of the Spirit's fruit—longsuffering, kindness, goodness, faithfulness, gentleness, and self-control—in order to remind us that these qualities must increasingly characterize us as men of God. The more they take up residence in us, the more we look like Jesus.

But as I thought about these qualities, and as I looked ahead toward Easter, it struck me powerfully that even in the last hours before His death, Jesus exhibited every one of the six divine qualities we'll note in this chapter. Consider:

- He demonstrated great *longsuffering* when His disciples kept falling asleep in Gethsemane, even though He'd asked them to join Him in prayer at His most trying hour.

- He displayed stunning *kindness* when He referred to Judas as "friend," even though this disciple-turned-betrayer came to the garden only to deliver Jesus to His enemies.

- He embodied inconceivable *goodness* when He willingly went to the cross on our behalf; no wonder we call it Good Friday!

- He revealed breathtaking *faithfulness* when, while gasping for air, He made provision for the ongoing care of His widowed mother.

- He showed amazing *gentleness* when He told a criminal hanging next to Him—a man who moments before had insulted and scorned Him—"Today you will be with Me in Paradise."

- He exhibited enormous *self-control* when He refrained from calling for legions of angels to free Him. These mighty beings would have wiped out, most eagerly, everyone on the planet in order to save their Lord from harm.

As we briefly consider these six qualities, remember that Jesus Christ perfectly displayed each one in His life on earth, thus perfectly reflecting His Father's divine nature. Now it's our turn. We won't reach perfection, of course; but at least let's get on the road. Through our lives, let's give people a taste of what awaits them in heaven.

Love's Endurance: Longsuffering/Patience

When you love people, you suffer long with them. You develop a longer fuse. You endure slights with unruffled temper. You become long-tempered, patient. Love suffers *long*.

When someone wrongs you, you deal with them patiently. That's not easy. You must firmly resist the old self and graciously accept unjust criticism. A man of God is known for his longsuffering perseverance. The word more literally means "to remain under," which calls for endurance. It refers not to complacent waiting but to a determination that continues even in hard places.

To be longsuffering refers to a victorious, triumphant, unswerving loyalty to the Lord in the midst of trials. Such patience enables a man of God to stick with his calling no matter the cost. When God calls him to do something emotionally difficult, he remains loyal to it. People will say about him, "Now, there goes a patient man."

People are watching. When you persevere, endure, and display a longsuffering spirit, someone will approach you and say, "You modeled the Christian life for me during that hard time. You mirrored what the Word said in such a way that you showed me the character of Jesus. What an encourager you have been for me!"

Not everything Jesus calls us to endure is pleasant. But if we'll stay under it until God is through with us, amazing things can happen. God loves to honor the courage of a man who remains patient while in a hard place.

Love's Service: Kindness

When you serve someone, you express God's love through your kindness. To be kind refers not to sentiment but to service. We express the love of God by acts of kindness done for others. We reflect Jesus' kindness by offering our help even in the small things, thus making someone's life better.

The original Greek word translated "kindness" speaks of a practical warm-heartedness. Through it we show our concern and care. We take care to be friendly.

One way to show kindness is through generosity. We know a family from South America who moved to a closed Muslim country. In that difficult place, they're serving as incognito missionaries within the government. After they moved, something happened in their home country that prevented money from flowing from there to their new place of ministry. When you have no money, serving in one of the world's most dangerous countries, you're in trouble. At the same time, God has given them an incredible platform for ministry. So what can anyone do?

Some of my friends said to one another, "We have to pray. We need to help them somehow." Do you know what kindness does? Kindness goes to the throne of God and says, "King Jesus, what do you want me to do?"

Some Christian men will just forward an email describing situations like this and say, "I think the church needs to do something."

You are the church! Sometimes we have this mistaken idea that the church is "out there" and we're "over here." No, you and I are right in the midst of it. *We* are the church, and if kindness dwells in our hearts, we won't leave needy people to fend for themselves. We'll find a way to help.

In this case, we made sure that somebody willing to put their life in jeopardy by living for Christ in a dangerous country, separated by many hours of flight time from most of their children, would get some help from us. Why? Because the love of God in our hearts prompts us to express that love through kindness.

Jesus came to us from heaven because of His kindness. Nehemiah called God "abundant in kindness" (Nehemiah 9:17). The prophet Joel declared God is "of great kindness" (Joel 2:13). The kindness of God sent us a Savior; God saved us because of His kindness and love (Titus 3:4). Today, the kindness of God sends believers all over the world from their places of safety, helped along by kind individuals, churches, and organizations.

Love is kind. If I'm not kind, I'm not letting the love of God flow through me.

Am I always kind? I wish I could answer yes, but I can't. At times, I have been the opposite of kind. At times, I have not responded as the Spirit of Jesus instructed me. At those times, I didn't let the love of God flow through me.

So what happened? In His kindness, the Spirit of the living God convicted me of my sin, gave me the grace to repent, and said, "Try it again, son."

Love's Deportment: Goodness

Goodness refers to the manifestation of Godlike virtues in a man. We begin to take on those virtues as the Holy Spirit fills us with the love of God, and soon our lives begin to express divine goodness.

Goodness is Joseph fleeing from Potiphar's wife when she tried to seduce him (see Genesis 39).

Goodness is Moses interceding for a rebellious nation when God threatened to wipe it out and start over (see Exodus 32).

Goodness is Joshua sparing the lives of Rahab and her family after she hid the Hebrew spies sent on a reconnaissance mission to Jericho (Joshua 6).

Goodness is Jesus showing compassion to a woman caught in adultery, yet without condoning her sin (see John 8).

Goodness is Peter giving a lame man something very different, but far better, than what the man had requested (see Acts 3).

Goodness is Barnabas befriending Saul and introducing him to the church, even though no Christian wanted anything to do with him (see Acts 9).

Goodness is a high-profile man on his knees, asking God for guidance and strength to do the right thing.

One evening at a program to honor special needs kids in our area, I watched as a man who had sold his company for a lot of money got down on his knees to shine the shoes of the young participants. That's the goodness of God at work.

A friend of mine who eventually succumbed to dementia said, long before his mind started slipping away, "There are no big shots in God's kingdom, and if there are any that think they're big shots, they ought to be shot with big shots." A good man is never too big to bow low.

Goodness is a man on a modest income choosing to serve a needy people group, when he could easily have risen to a more prestigious position had he chosen to promote himself.

Many years ago, I bought a plane ticket to visit four missionary families serving on various Indonesian islands. When I discovered I had cancer, I couldn't go. A friend took my ticket and went in my place. After he returned, he said something I've never been able to get out of my mind. "Pastor Johnny," he said, "the house where they live with their children would be equivalent to a storage house we might have behind our homes." He got emotional and added, "Now, they don't know it. They've not even noticed it." My friend thought we needed to do something about their situation. That's what the goodness of God will do.

Goodness can't help but express itself. You can't keep it inside of you; it has to get out. It spreads all over you and rubs off on everybody you come into contact with. If you're not influencing family and friends through your goodness, it's because you're not letting the love of God be poured out in your heart by the Holy Spirit.

I thank the Lord for the goodness of God expressed to me by so many followers of Jesus. We have a good, good Father! Goodness opposes everything evil and immoral and drives the Christlike person to depend on God to strive to bring about a better world. A man bearing the spiritual fruit of goodness has a strong disposition to hate what is evil. He may pray, "God, help me to hate what You hate and love what You love."

If the fruit of goodness is blossoming in your life, then you have a compulsion to follow after what is good. You have a great desire to gain the wisdom to judge rightly in all things. You have a longing to increase in thoughtfulness and sensitivity in all your dealings with everyone you meet.

The Greek word translated "goodness" in the New Testament never even appeared in secular Greek writing. Neither the Greeks nor the Romans grasped the meaning of *agape* love or of its offspring, goodness. They saw love and goodness as qualities to be avoided, traits that would make a man either feebleminded or weak. But God said, "Goodness is one of my attributes."

If we worship Jesus, His Spirit will infuse us with divine love, and that love will be expressed in goodness. Goodness finds its anchor in the love of God. Goodness produces a deportment that is kind but just, tender but tough, fair but firm.

Could people rightly say of you, "He's a good man"?

Love's Measurement: Faithfulness

Faithfulness means staying true to something. For a follower of Christ, it means staying true to your trust, to your commitment to others, to yourself, and above all, staying true to God.

Faithfulness is Noah building the ark despite the jeers and criticism of his neighbors (see Genesis 6). That kind of criticism has slowed down many a Christian. It's kept many men quiet in a hostile business environment. Many believing students have remained seated while skeptics got up to blaspheme our great God.

Faithfulness is Abraham's willingness to sacrifice his only son because he believed God would deliver Isaac and through him fulfill the Lord's promise (see Genesis 22; Romans 4:20-22; Hebrews 11:17-19).

Faithfulness is keeping your promises. It's paying your bills. It's honoring your appointments. People know that your word is your bond. The attitude of *agape* love behind faithfulness gives vitality and credibility to a man's influence.

Faithfulness accomplishes what fame or force cannot. Manipulation cannot obtain what love-fueled faithfulness can.

The question is often asked, what do you do when faithfulness doesn't work? I'd say, "Increase your dosage." Faithfulness *does* work, although often not on our timetables. Don't give up on God and don't abandon faithfulness in favor of expedience.

Where can you show your faithfulness today? Who in your life most needs to see your faithfulness?

Love's Mood: Gentleness

Gentleness expresses love in a considerate, meek way. The word is closely related to humility. Together, gentleness and humility give enormous strength to your work and ministry.

Men often get the wrong idea about both gentleness and humility. Picture a muscular stallion, broken by its handlers. That horse still has all the strength he ever had, but all those muscles have been brought under the direction of a master. The bit is in the horse's mouth, the reins are in the rider's hands, but that is still one powerful horse.

Gentleness/humility allows you to meet criticism with meekness and a pleasant spirit. It strengthens your soul and honors God. It is love's prevailing attitude, its temperament and disposition. A gentle man knows he's been the object of undeserved, redeeming love, and therefore he doesn't lash out when he's wronged. It's amazing what a gentle man can take.

Somebody once asked the evangelist D.L. Moody, "Are you saying that a humble man doesn't think much of himself?"

"No," Moody replied, "a humble man doesn't think of himself at all." Humility means being nearly unconscious of yourself.

A gentle man is kind, meek, and humble. He sees the minimum of self and the maximum of God. A gentle man, although consumed with the greatness of a noble cause, recognizes that, in and of himself, he makes no contribution to its success. He knows God could accomplish this great thing just as well without him.

Suppose somebody said to Bill, "Bill, thanks for your generous contribution to our initiative. Look what's happening. By the grace of God, we are ready to help more destitute children than ever before in the history of our organization. Your generosity inspired others to give, and now we can expand our work into some of the most needy countries on earth. Even more great opportunities are on the horizon, thanks to you!"

It would be so easy for Bill to throw out his chest and say, "Well, thanks. Last year was a tough year for me, but…" In that moment, I believe the Holy Spirit would likely say to Bill, "What are you talking about? Don't you remember what you read in your devotions just the other day in Malachi 2:2: 'If you will not hear, and if you will not take it to heart, to give glory to My name,' says the LORD of hosts, 'I will send a curse upon you, and I will curse your blessings'? Bill, if you fail to give glory to My name now, I'll curse your blessings. The fact that you were able to give at all wasn't because of you; that was Christ in you. So get on your face and give God the glory for what *He's* done."

How can a man filled with God's Spirit take credit for the Lord's work? A man ruled by the spirit of gentleness takes delight in staying in the background and giving God the glory due His name.

John Bunyan said it better than anyone I've ever read. Listen to these profound words from one of his poems:

> He that is down need fear no fall;
> He that is low, no pride;
> He that is humble ever shall
> Have God to be his guide.

Love's Mastery: Self-Control

A self-controlled man does not let his desires master his life. He allows all aspects of his life to be brought under the mastery of the Holy Spirit. Holy discipline characterizes the life of a self-controlled man.

The Greek word translated "self-control" means "to grip or to take hold of." It indicates that God empowers a man to take control of himself.

I heard Truett Cathy, founder of Chick-fil-A, say, "The reason the average person cannot lead others is that he has not learned to lead himself." Self-control should result in an attitude of humility and caution. It develops strong character and gives a man courage.

How do you develop and exercise self-control? You build it into your life through conscious dependence on God, paired with a life of Spirit-filled discipline. You mind especially the little things. Jesus said, "He who is faithful in what is least is faithful also in much; and he who is unjust in what is least is unjust also in much" (Luke 16:10). When you're faithful in the little things, you demonstrate your capacity and fitness to handle much more.

You can help build your self-discipline if you make some important decisions ahead of time. When my daughters reached the age of ten or eleven, I started teaching them how to remain pure. I told them, "If a boy ever says to you, 'Get in the back seat with me,' don't you dare get back there!" It becomes a lot easier to do the right thing when you make up your mind ahead of time to follow a certain course of action.

When young Daniel found himself in King Nebuchadnezzar's palace, tasked to serve the Babylonian king, he "purposed in his heart that he would not defile himself with the portion of the king's delicacies, nor with the wine which he drank" (Daniel 1:8). Do you think such a decision took self-control, especially when he saw many other young men gladly accept the dainties presented to them? When the right time came, Daniel had a reasonable alternate plan for his overseers. They accepted his suggestion, and at the end of a test period (which Daniel also proposed), he "appeared better and fatter in flesh than all the young men who ate the portion of the king's delicacies" (Daniel 1:15). Daniel's self-control and predetermined commitment to honor his God, even as a young man, led directly to his long and celebrated career in the upper echelons of Middle Eastern power politics.

Make godly decisions ahead of time. On the way to a hard meeting, decide that you need God's help to enable you to navigate the stormy waters. You could pray, "O Lord, clothe me with humility. Fill me with the Spirit of God, help me to exercise self-control, and put a watch on my mouth so that my tongue utters no words that tarnish Your glory."

To exercise self-control requires that you rule over your own spirit. "The devil made me do it" is not only bad theology, it's both false and stupid. Proverbs 16:32 says, "He who is slow to anger is better than the mighty, and he who rules his spirit than he who takes a city." When you control your thoughts, you control your actions. It's amazing what happens when the love of God rules in your heart!

When you allow the Spirit of the living God to help you develop self-control, your whole world changes. You stop making unreasonable demands of others. You give others the benefit of the doubt. A true friend exercising self-control picks up where he left off, even after a long period of not speaking with his buddy. Such a man doesn't say, "Well, *there* you are. Finally! You haven't called. You haven't written. You haven't emailed. What kind of friend are you, anyway?" You might want to say all of those things. You might feel all of those things. But the fruit of the Spirit growing within you allows you to exercise self-control. So what do you say? "Man, it's great to speak with you again! It's been too long."

Proverbs 25:28 says, "Whoever has no rule over his own spirit is like a city broken down, without walls." When you lack self-control, the enemy can invade your space anytime he wants to, raid your goods, and smack you around. How are you going to stop him? You've let the protective walls around you crumble into dust. The love of God doesn't want that to happen, so the Spirit comes into your life, builds self-control into your character, and gives you the strength to persevere.

When the fruit of the Spirit blossoms in your life, even tough times give you the opportunity to shine for God. Through His Spirit, "we also glory in tribulations, knowing that tribulation produces perseverance; and perseverance, character; and character, hope" (Romans 5:3-4). God builds Christian character through perseverance—but what man needs perseverance if he has no problems?

When you exercise self-control in the middle of your troubles, you persevere through them, and as a result, God produces a Christlike spirit in you. Hope breaks forth because you can see God at work within you. You realize that God's Spirit is making you into a better man, a more godly leader, and this realization gives you the hope that great things lie ahead.

Paul told a young pastor, "Exhort the young men to be soberminded" (Titus 2:6). What does a sober-minded person look like? The word suggests the exercise of self-restraint. A sober-minded man develops self-control with the power to govern all his passions and desires. I admit that every time my big mouth has landed me in trouble, the cause was my failure to restrain my passions. I took off the governor.

Suppose you rent a truck to move to another part of the country. You want to get there as quickly as possible, but the truck's owner has installed a governor that will hardly let you reach the speed limit, and it takes forever to get anywhere. Only when you go downhill can you achieve a little speed because the governor restrains how fast you can go.

When we're filled with the Holy Spirit of God, the Spirit serves as a restrainer. In fact, the Scripture even gives Him that name. Writing about the time of the end when God begins wrapping up all of human history, Paul declared, "The mystery of lawlessness is already at work; only He who now restrains will do so until He is taken out of the way" (2 Thessalonians 2:7). When that day comes—the time when the Lord takes out of the way the Restrainer, the Holy Spirit— all hell will break loose. Do you think things look out of control in our nation right now? Just wait until the Restrainer, the Governor, the Holy Spirit, gets removed from this earth. It'll be anything goes.

Self-control allows you to govern all your passions and desires. As the Spirit fills you with His love, and as you cooperate with Him to grow the fruit of the Spirit in your life, you develop self-control, self-discipline, self-restraint. You become sober-minded and you learn to more effectively manage your life.

If you want to become a man of God, you must train yourself to cultivate balance and self-restraint. Do you want God to give you more opportunities to grow, more freedom to explore? There's truth in the old saying: "The more freedom granted, the more self-control needed." Paul wrote, "It is for freedom that Christ has set us free" (Galatians 5:1 NIV).

Many men, however, prefer to live under law: Do this, don't do that, sit here, don't go there. But when you live in freedom, you have more choices to make. What should you do with your free time? How should you set up your schedule? You need a governor, a restrainer, to control your passions and desires. As you abide in the true vine, the spiritual fruit of self-control supernaturally grows. But you have to abide.

Paul put it this way to the out-of-control church at Corinth: "Everyone who competes for the prize is temperate in all things" (1 Corinthians 9:25). To be "temperate" means you exercise self-control. The apostle told his Christian friends that pagan athletes exercised restraint in order to win a race or a match, hoping to obtain a victor's crown made of perishable laurel leaves. Followers of Christ, however, run in the race of life for an imperishable crown.

Paul told them he ran, but not with uncertainty. He fought, but not like a shadow boxer. Instead, "I discipline my body and bring it into subjection, lest, when I have preached to others, I myself should become disqualified" (1 Corinthians 9:27).

To succeed in the Christian life, self-control has to become part of who you are. As the Spirit works in your life, you become increasingly sensible and sound-minded. You gain self-mastery, which directs your behavior.

One time I visited Argentina to speak on leadership. Someone at the conference said to me, "You're here teaching leadership; I'm surprised you're not teaching theology."

"There's a Bible institute here that teaches theology," I replied, "and I've noticed in my travels around the world that the average leader does not get in trouble because of his theology. The average leader gets in trouble because of poor relationships and a lack of understanding about how life works. Many leaders don't know how to relate well and get along with people."

Do you know what I taught that week? I spoke a great deal about self-control, about learning to be sensible and how to gain self-mastery, leading to sound-mindedness and godly behavior. The Old Testament would use the word *prudence* to describe the same issue. To exercise self-control means to develop a quality of mind that keeps your life safe. Self-control produces the kind of security that comes from getting all things under God's control.

When I serve as a guest speaker and a lot of leaders fill the room, do you know what they usually ask after my talk? Most of them ask the same thing: "What's the number one thing that you think leaders need to know?"

I always name the same thing. "Keep it close and clean. Guard your heart, for out of it are the issues of life. Guard it diligently. Develop self-mastery. Don't let your life spin out of control."

The great principle that brings all of this together is Proverbs 29:18, which says, "Where there is no revelation, the people cast off restraint." You might have memorized this verse in the King James version, which renders it, "Where there is no vision, the people perish." The verse means that without a prophetic revelation—without God's Word speaking into a man's heart—that man casts off restraint. He lacks self-control. He has no vision of his future beyond the immediate gratification of his flesh.

Dietrich Bonhoeffer rightly said that the devil is not trying to get you to deny God; he just wants you to temporarily forget God. In that temporary forgetfulness, just for a moment, Satan can tempt you to make a decision that can alter the rest of your life. It can change the way others view you, and not for the better. He can put you on the sidelines.

When we cast off restraint, we throw off the controls, we let loose. We hand over the reins of our life to another. Instead of letting Christ and the Spirit of God control us, we give the reins to someone else. When we give into the temptation to lust, lie, steal, gossip, or whatever else our flesh wants to do, we shelve self-restraint and give in. You will not succeed in life without developing self-control.

The longer I live, the more I'm convinced that *nothing* means as much in a godly man's life as moral purity. It's the truth! And you cannot remain morally pure without developing self-control.

Emulating Beats Delegating

Not very often do I make a tweet-worthy statement, but I did a while ago. Two or three younger guys were standing around when I said something that prompted them to immediately pull out their smartphones and tweet it. I had said, "Delegation is never a substitute for emulation."

Every once in a while, my wife will kiddingly say to me, "All you ever do is go to your office, get on the phone, and tell everybody else what to do."

"It's a gift," I reply. "It's called delegation."

But delegating tasks is never a substitute for emulating Christ. While I definitely get more done by delegating, delegating doesn't much help me to grow more like Jesus.

I want people to see a strong family resemblance between me and my Lord. I want them to say, "Boy, I can really see Jesus in you." If you were to look in a mirror today, how much of Jesus would you see staring back?

Part 3

WINNING IN JESUS

11

FIGHT THE GOOD FIGHT OF FAITH

Andre Ward retired from professional boxing in 2017 as a two-time world champion in the light heavyweight division. He put down his gloves for the last time after compiling a record of 32-0; he hadn't lost in the ring since 1998, when he fought as a thirteen-year-old amateur.

The highlight of his career—the accomplishment he put at "the top of the list," counted as his "highest achievement" and his "crowning moment in boxing"—came in 2004 when he won Olympic gold. No American has managed that feat since then.[10]

Ward announced his retirement on Twitter under the heading, "Mission Accomplished." He wrote, "As I walk away from the sport of boxing today, I leave at the top of your glorious mountain, which was always my vision and my dream. I did it. We did it."

Why did Ward retire at the relatively young age of thirty-three? In a word, the sport took too great a toll on his body. "I am leaving because my body can no longer put up with the rigors of the sport and therefore my desire to fight is no longer there," he explained.

"If I cannot give my family, my team, and the fans everything I have, then I should no longer be fighting."

Ward's decision surprised many observers, but not those who knew him best. He said he chose to step away from boxing to give more time to his family, to his community, to his church, and perhaps to a new career in broadcasting. "Boxing is just a season," he told one interviewer. "This isn't my life. It's what I do, it's not who I am." Nevertheless, he declared he had given the sport "everything I am."[11]

I think that had the apostle Paul lived in our day, he might have thoroughly enjoyed following Andre Ward's career. Paul's writings make it clear the apostle loved watching athletic events, especially boxing and running. I suppose Paul would enthusiastically commend Ward not only for his stellar boxing accomplishments, but for his excellent outlook on life.

The Announcement

Paul announced his own "retirement" in his final letter: "I have fought the good fight, I have finished the race, I have kept the faith" (2 Timothy 4:7). It seems only natural that as Paul faced his death, he should turn retrospective and think back over his long career. He pictured it both as a boxing match and as a long-distance race.

The Fight

Note that Paul does not say he had fought well but that it had been a worthwhile fight. The struggle had called forth his best, worthiest efforts. The original Greek of the sentence reads, "The good fight I have fought." It takes the emphasis off the "I."

Paul made no comment about having done his best in the contest, only that he had fought in the noblest, grandest fight of them all: the ministry of the gospel. No other fight compared to that one. No other mission could rise to greater importance.

The apostle also called it "the" fight, not "a" fight. This suggests Paul believed the Lord had set him apart for a very specific fight. His fight did not look the same as Peter's fight. Timothy had a different kind of fight than either of them. In fact, *all* of us have fights designed specifically for us—different challenges, different highlights, different hardships, different needs. Each round has its own character and feel. While the core of the fight remains the same for us all—making known the gospel of Jesus Christ— how we fight, where we fight, and a host of other details change, often markedly.

The Race

Paul saw his race much as he saw his fight. He did not commend himself for having run the full distance, but simply declared that he had followed the specific course laid out for him by his Lord. Like Andre Ward, he could have tweeted, "Mission Accomplished."

Long before he sat on death row, Paul had said, "But none of these things move me; nor do I count my life dear to myself, so that I may finish my race with joy, and the ministry which I received from the Lord Jesus, to testify to the gospel of the grace of God" (Acts 20:24). Now in a dank Roman prison, Paul knew he was about to finish the divine purpose for which God had placed him on earth. He had finished the race marked out specifically for him.

Do you know the race that God has marked out specifically for you? As God's athletes, a set course has been given to each of us. God Himself has chosen our path and marked out the way He wants us to go. If a man claims he's started the race, but we never see him on the course, is he really in the race? This race demands progression.

It's Your Race Too

Paul chose the analogy of a runner to picture every Christian's spiritual growth. Simon Peter said it this way in the last verse of the final letter he ever penned: "Grow in the grace and knowledge of our Lord and Savior Jesus Christ" (2 Peter 3:18). Both Paul and Peter, in their last written correspondence, emphasized the necessity of growth in the Christian life. How else could we become more like Christ? Like a runner in a race, you and I have to keep going because the ultimate goal is to be conformed to the image of Christ.

Do you *want* to become more like Jesus? I know that you will never remain faithful to the race unless you love where it's taking you. If you don't love where you'll end up, you'll quit. For the Christian, the finish line is unquestionably to become more like Christ. The prize at the end of the fight and the reward at the race's finish line is to be like Jesus.

Do you like that destination? Do you genuinely desire to become more like Jesus Christ?

There's far more to your relationship with God than merely extracting eternal life. Once you're saved, Jesus infuses you with His life, intending it to overrule everything else. From then on, a man of God finds his greatest joy and fulfillment in letting Jesus have His way. Does that sound like you? Regardless of where you are right now, regardless of how well or poorly you've boxed or run to this point, Jesus still wants to fulfill His dream for your life.

You don't know my story, you might be thinking. *Do you really think He has a purpose and a dream and potential for* my *life?* Absolutely! But to make this happen might require a midcourse correction.

I love the Chinese proverb: "If you don't change the direction you're going, you're likely to end up where you're headed." Don't come to the end of your life and say, "This is *not* how I expected my life to turn out." Take a look at the road you're traveling right now.

Peer all the way to the end of the line. If you don't like what you see there, then change your path.

Christ's dream for you includes a compelling life purpose, a continual source of joy and peace, an intimate relationship with His Father, a mind filled with timeless wisdom that only God can give, and a heart overflowing with love for Him and for others. And that's not an exhaustive list.

We've all embarked on a lifelong journey. Our best efforts here will result in an incomplete product, for none of us will be fully transformed until we pass from this life into the next. Today, however, we have the opportunity to shift from a life focused exclusively on success on earth to a life centered on service to God and His creation. That's the match we're fighting, the race we're running. We're called to be Christ followers, not merely Christ admirers. Christianity is not a religion for consumers but a relationship for participants.

Are you in?

The Faith

As the apostle's life on this planet came to a close, Paul said he had "kept the faith" (2 Timothy 4:7). It's as if some valuable treasure had been entrusted to his care for delivery to someone on the other side of the world.

Paul faithfully guarded his Lord's deposit. He carefully stewarded the commission he had received. He would fully agree with Jude, who urged some Christian friends "to contend earnestly for the faith which was once for all delivered to the saints" (Jude 3).

How do we contend for the faith? I once spoke to a weekend conference of eighteen hundred women. One participant asked me during a break, "What would you do, Pastor Hunt, if your husband wouldn't come to church?"

Well, who's the church? *We* are the church. The God who used to live in a temple vacated it because His people desecrated His name. Subsequently, He moved into us and said, "I will never leave you nor forsake you" (Hebrews 13:5). God doesn't plan to ever check out, for the kingdom of God is within us (Luke 17:21).

So I told the woman, "You mean, he won't come to the church where we meet. But *you're* the church, so take church to him. In a sweet, kind, unannoying way, weave your faith into every conversation, every opportunity you have at home. Work it in. Give God the glory." That's one way to contend for the faith.

Another way to contend for the faith is to live it out. Ravi Zacharias is one of the world's foremost Christian apologists and a good friend of mine. He says that the world is in desperate need of *seeing* Christians whose lives change because of their relationship with Christ.

Ravi has spoken on the campuses of many Islamic universities around the world to present his case for Christ. As he watches the crowds listen to his message, he's told me it's as though the Islamic theologians in the audience are saying in their hearts, *I hope what he's saying is true.* They already know that what they've embraced doesn't work.

But can you guess the major obstacle that keeps these men from putting their faith in Christ? It's not theological. These Islamic leaders want to know if this relationship with Jesus Christ can indeed be lived out. They wonder, because when they observe the average professing Christian, they see very little difference between the way he lives and the lifestyle of anyone else.

Paul kept the faith. So must we.

The Prize

Although none of us can earn any part of our salvation in any way, that doesn't mean God saves us so that we can sit around. Paul gives us a wonderful example. He wrote: "By the grace of God I am what I am, and his grace to me was not without effect. No, I worked harder than all of them—yet not I, but the grace of God that was with me" (1 Corinthians 15:10 NIV).

When some false teachers tried to claim that they had more authority and credibility than Paul, the apostle wrote, "I have worked much harder, been in prison more frequently, been flogged more severely, and been exposed to death again and again. Five times I received from the Jews the forty lashes minus one," and then he goes on to detail a long list of his labors for Christ (2 Corinthians 11:23-24 NIV).

Now, at the end of his life, Paul looked forward to receiving a reward for all of this hard work. He had kept the rules and deserved a prize. So he said, "Finally, there is laid up for me the crown of righteousness" (2 Timothy 4:8). Paul had been faithful to God's calling and so he looked ahead with assurance to a rousing commendation from his Lord.

The crown (*stephanos* in Greek) was a victor's crown. God will award the crown "of righteousness" to righteous people who live righteous lives. At the ancient Greek games, officials would display in some public spot the prizes to be awarded the winners. Not only did they honor the winning athletes, but when those winners returned home with their crowns or precious awards, the townspeople gave them a joyous procession and a reception.

Paul has this in mind as he looks ahead to his fast-approaching audience with Jesus, his Lord. He sees the Greek games as a dim foreshadowing of all that victorious Christians can anticipate from Christ. And so he writes elsewhere, "Do you not know that those who run in a race all run, but one receives the prize? Run in such a way that you may obtain it" (1 Corinthians 9:24).

Are you running the race of faith in such a way that you may obtain the prize?

The Referee

If you've ever played a sport, you know that referees don't always make the right call. Almost every year, it seems, an undeserving team wins a game because of a blown call. Officials try their best, but they make errors, just like players and coaches.

Jesus doesn't make those errors. Paul calls Him "the righteous Judge," and He always makes the right calls, every time, without exception. No cheating scandals mar the perfection of heaven, no lack of information leads to faulty judgments. Jesus, the righteous Judge, will give out whatever rewards every believing man has earned.

On "that Day"—the time of our Lord's coming when the judgment seat of Christ will take center stage—every one of us will appear before Jesus to receive the things done in the body, whether good or bad. Salvation will not be in view there but rewards for faithful service:

> Now if anyone builds on this foundation with gold, silver, precious stones, wood, hay, straw, each one's work will become clear; for the Day will declare it, because it will be revealed by fire; and the fire will test each one's work, of what sort it is. If anyone's work which he has built on it endures, he will receive a reward. If anyone's work is burned, he will suffer loss; but he himself will be saved, yet so as through fire (1 Corinthians 3:12-15).

Unfortunately, we don't hear much anymore about eternal judgment or rewards for service. Many years ago, in an interview with Billy Graham, David Frost asked, "Dr. Graham, if you had to do it all over again, what would you do differently?"

I don't remember Dr. Graham's exact words, but in essence he replied, "I would preach more on judgment." Today, if you preach on judgment, someone is likely to say, "You should have told them that God loves them." But no preacher loves his congregation if he fails to preach on judgment. Did you know the Lord Jesus Christ spoke of hell three times more often than He did about heaven?

Back in 1741, Jonathan Edwards delivered a famous sermon that God used to change a whole generation. He called it, "Sinners in the Hands of an Angry God." In our own era, I once heard R.G. Lee preach a sermon he called "Payday Someday." Judgment Day is coming—but we don't have to fear it. Paul looked forward to that Day, because he knew he had fought the fight, run the race, and kept the faith. You can have the same confidence.

The Awards Ceremony

The Bible doesn't give us many details about the heavenly award ceremony where Jesus will present us with our rewards, but you know it'll be spectacular. Unlike the modern Olympics, winners won't get just one day or even four years of notoriety, but an eternity to celebrate what God has done through them.

Back in 1992, as the world prepared for the Barcelona Olympic Games, Reebok launched a massive ad campaign to steal some thunder from Nike, the world's largest athletic gear company. It created a series of splashy commercials featuring U.S. decathletes Dan O'Brien and Dave Johnson under the tagline, "Life is short. Play hard." O'Brien and Johnson were essentially the top two decathletes of that day, and Reebok's strategy focused on which one would win the gold and which one the silver. It saw the pair as "battling it out for the title of world's greatest athlete."

Unfortunately for Reebok, O'Brien didn't even make the U.S. Olympic team, and Johnson suffered a stress fracture in his left foot and managed "just" a bronze medal. Reebok had spent twenty-five to thirty million dollars on the campaign, and it didn't rush to re-sign either athlete for further commercial ventures.

That will never happen with Jesus. As the righteous Judge, He longs to present us with awards of "gold, silver, precious stones" as rewards for our faithful service. If we stumble, He won't pull our contracts. He asks us to work hard, by His Spirit, but He doesn't demand that we work perfectly. We need men in God's race who will run with all their might, shooting for the gold, silver, and precious stones.

Remember, Jesus will never forsake you. He's right there with you as you run your race. When things get tough, think of the awards ceremony to come...and keep running.

The Invitation

Jesus has a crown to give, not only to the apostle, "but also to all who have loved His appearing" (2 Timothy 4:8). Literally all over the place in Scripture, God connects Jesus' return with our living in a godly way.

The apostle John, for example, instructs us to "abide in Him [Jesus], that when He appears, we may have confidence and not be ashamed before Him at His coming" (1 John 2:28). To emphasize his point, he wrote that everyone who puts their hope in Christ's return "purifies himself, just as He is pure" (1 John 3:3).

How often do you ponder the Lord's return? If you thought about it more often, would it help you to keep running your race? What do you expect to receive from Jesus when He parcels out His rewards on that day?

How Well Do You Know Him?

We read Paul's farewell address in 2 Timothy, but in Philippians, we hear clearly the passion of his life, what energized him to the very end. His desire was "that I may know Him and the power of His resurrection, and the fellowship of His sufferings, being conformed to His death" (3:10).

Paul saw getting to know Jesus in a deep, intimate way as the reason for his very existence. There's a vast difference between knowing *about* Him and knowing *Him*! Paul wanted his relationship with Christ to massively affect his daily living. The Amplified Bible, Classic Edition, renders the verse like this:

> [For my determined purpose is] that I may know Him [that I may progressively become more deeply and intimately acquainted with Him, perceiving and recognizing and understanding the wonders of His Person more strongly and more clearly], and that I may in that same way come to know the power outflowing from His resurrection [which it exerts over believers], and that I may so share His sufferings as to be continually transformed [in spirit into His likeness even] to His death.

Paul had a fixed, determined purpose to "know Him." And he wanted to know Jesus in at least three major ways.

1. To know Him intimately

The Greek verb *ginosko* (or *epiginosko*) means to know by personal experience. In this verse it appears in the aorist tense, which speaks of an intimate, personal relationship with Jesus Christ, beginning at some point in the past. Paul had come to know Jesus thirty years before on the Damascus Road, but that knowing had present implications—his major passion to that day. When you come to know Christ, you always want to get to know Him better.

When Old Testament writers wrote about the sexual relationship of a husband and wife, they would say that a husband "knew" his wife. The term described the ultimate human relationship of marriage.

In the New Testament, when Matthew says that Joseph "did not know her [Mary]" until after the birth of Jesus, he used the word *ginosko* (Matthew 1:25). He meant that Joseph never became intimate with Mary until after their marriage and after the birth of Jesus. Again, the word describes the deepest possible human union.

Paul wanted to *know* Jesus in the truest biblical sense; not to know merely by intellect but to know by intimacy. Those who know Jesus Christ only in the sense of head knowledge don't know Him like those who know Him in their hearts. When you know Jesus intimately, your life changes, and so you gain enormous influence in God's kingdom. You desire that everybody comes to know Him.

2. To know Him experientially

The apostle had seen Jesus work in his life in amazing ways. It's quite a thrill to be able to say, "God supplied my needs." You and I have that same opportunity.

During our time in college, my wife and I had nothing. I came out of poverty, I hadn't seen my father in about thirteen years, and my mother was on welfare. We were so broke we couldn't pay attention. Still, I sensed God calling me to the ministry, and Gardner-Webb College accepted my application for admission. I had only a GED, however, and the college couldn't let me in on an academic scholarship. I got in only because I received a one-semester government grant.

One Monday night Janet said to me, "Honey, I know God is going to take care of us, but we're out of groceries." We'd just started attending the Bethel Baptist Church in Shelby, North Carolina. That evening the pastor's wife, Mrs. Ezell, came by our place for a visit. She thanked us for coming to Bethel and told us she hoped that while we attended Gardner-Webb College, we would become part of Bethel's ministry.

"I hope y'all don't mind," she continued, "but we sensed yesterday when y'all were here that there was a need in your life. The Lord spoke to us about it, and so if y'all don't mind, we've got some stuff out in the car for you." They went out to the car and brought in a pile of food. They brought in so many goodies, we had enough not only for us, but since we lived in a whole complex of poor preachers, we went around to them and shared with them our surplus.

God was teaching us that we didn't have to preach only in theory that God takes care of His children. We can testify that He not only sent the ravens to feed Elijah, He has ravens today that He still sends out to supply *you*. It is awesome to know Jesus Christ both intimately and experientially!

Did you know that people watch to see how you respond in foul weather? They want to figure out, *Does he really know God? Does God really come? Does God really take care of His children?*

This hurting world desperately needs encouragement, and you can supply it when you know God both intimately and experientially. It will thrill you to hear someone say to you, "There's no explanation for what I just saw happen in your life, apart from the intervention of Almighty God!"

3. To know His power

Paul wanted to know the *power* of Christ's resurrection. At another time he prayed "that you may know what is the hope of His calling, what are the riches of the glory of His inheritance in the saints, and what is the exceeding greatness of His power toward us who believe, according to the working of His mighty power which He worked in Christ when He raised Him from the dead and seated Him at His right hand in the heavenly places" (Ephesians 1:18-20).

Paul did not pray that God's power be *given* to believers, but that they *become aware of* the power they already have in Christ, and then that they *use* it. If you're a Christian, God already has given you His mighty resurrection power as a possession. Now you need to learn how to appropriate it in your daily life.

Some men don't experience this divine power because they have allowed some sin to become a snare in their lives. Even then, though, the resurrection power of Jesus Christ can set them free. Ephesians 3:20 says, "Now to Him who is able to do exceedingly abundantly above all that we ask or think, according to the power that works in us." God's power is unlimited and far beyond our comprehension.

Will you allow God's power to work through you? You *can* walk in victory: "Just as Christ was raised from the dead by the glory of the Father, even so we also should walk in newness of life" (Romans 6:4). Resurrection power alone has the strength to defeat the power of sin.

What a fresh new day it would be in the churches of America if all the men who claim to be saved would bow before Almighty God and say, "Lord, I have all kinds of desires and ambitions, but I want to surrender myself afresh to the sovereign will of God. I belong to You, I'm made by You and for You. Right now, I surrender to Your will for my life."

Do you need to pray that prayer? If so, I urge you to pray right now, and then tell somebody about it, starting with your family. It's time for that fresh new day to begin in the church of Jesus Christ.

Stand Up!

Too many of us stunt our spiritual growth because we never catch sight of a disciple's full potential. Paul wrote, "That if possible I may attain to the [spiritual and moral] resurrection [that lifts me] out from among the dead [even while in the body]" (Philippians 3:11 AMPC). He means, "Whatever it takes, I will be one who lives in the fresh newness of life of those who are alive from the dead." For Paul, this hope had both future and present implications.

Paul wished to become so much like Christ in the way he lived that people would think of him as a resurrected person now, even before his physical death. The word *resurrection* literally means "to stand," and normally highlighted some contrast, as in "to stand out." To the Greek mind, those who had not been born again were lying down. And to experience a resurrection, a man had to stand up.

If you're dead, what are you? A corpse. Paul is saying, "…that I might stand up among the corpses." This is a present tense reference to the resurrection, not a future tense, and it means to "stand up" or to "stand out."

You could translate the verse like this: "I want to know Jesus and the power of His resurrection and the fellowship of His suffering, that I may give the spiritually dead a preview of eternal life in action, as I stand up among those who are spiritually on their backs." Or like this: "As I walk your streets, as I walk into your houses, as I walk into your stores, as I walk into your offices, as I mingle among the sons of men, I want to be so living for Christ, so outstanding for Him, that you can see that I am a living one among the dead ones."

Harold James was a man who stood up. I cried when I heard he'd died. I loved brother Harold. He got saved at my church many years ago, but before then, he was a corpse, dead in his trespasses and sins. The Lord Jesus Christ changed Harold and made him outstanding in the way he stood up for Jesus Christ.

I never came through the back doors of the church on Sunday without him giving me a hug and a word of encouragement. He never wanted just to shake my hand. During a time of prayer one day after his death, I heard someone say, "God, thank You that Tom came to know Jesus Christ because of the way You changed Harold James."

I will miss Harold for many years to come, but I know exactly where he is. He's already with the Lord Jesus Christ, waiting for the awards ceremony when he'll get a pile of rewards.

I want to so stand up for Jesus Christ that I help others to stand up too. I want to have as many men as possible standing up with me when He comes. I want to know Jesus, as Paul did, in a life-changing, world-shaping way.

May God help us all to stand! One day soon, all of us *will* stand before Him. I pray He helps us to stand now that we may count for something on that Day.

Aim at Greatness

Andre Ward went 32-0 as a professional boxer, but he sometimes got knocked down. He got bloodied. He faced some scary situations. The first time he faced light heavyweight Sergey Kovalev, the big Russian had a record of 30-0-1, with twenty-six knockouts. In 2011, Kovalev so pounded an opponent in the ring that the man died shortly after the bell sounded.

Ward, like a lot of boxers, didn't have an easy life. His African-American mother struggled with cocaine addiction and had little role in his growing-up years. His white father reared him but had a heroin addiction, became homeless, and eventually died of a heart attack. "I know what it is to be biracial when both sides won't accept you and you have that confusion of not feeling accepted," Ward said. "You're left asking, 'Who am I?'"[12]

A man named Hunter became almost a surrogate father to Ward during his teen years, and once told him, "I don't know who you are rolling with, but I know this—God's got his hand on you, son. You ain't gonna get away with anything."

Ward eventually came to faith in Jesus Christ and received a lot of help in learning to live right from his pastor, former NFL running back Napoleon Kaufman. Ward's license plate now reads "SOG," which stands for "Son of God."

"The statistics I was faced with?" Ward said. "I shouldn't have made it. With the grace of God, I did."

In his boxing career, Ward aimed at greatness and achieved it. "I know the great ones that have gone before me who said some of the same things I'm saying and didn't finish strong," he said before his final two fights. "I'm trying to avoid those same demons. I'm trying to shake those ghosts."

I think the apostle Paul would have liked watching this guy. Andre Ward gets it. He gave his best to his boxing career, and now, by the grace of God, he wants to give that same dedication and commitment to his community, his family, and his church. For that reason, I expect Andre Ward has a far bigger awards ceremony ahead of him, greater than anything he's experienced until now.

We could do worse than follow his example.

12

DO WHAT YOU WERE CALLED TO DO

My wife and I visited a Cracker Barrel restaurant one morning several years ago to have breakfast. A man approached our table and said, "I don't want to distract you, but can I just have a minute? I need to tell you a story." And then he started crying.

I thought, *Oh, gosh, I'm going to have a counseling appointment during breakfast at Cracker Barrel.*

"One night at church you told us that we needed to expand our facilities," he continued. "I owned a full gym, and as far as I was concerned, that's all I ever needed to do. But God pressed me to do something else." He explained that he wanted to use his gym to host Upward Basketball, an outreach program for kids. Not long afterward, he began the program, it took off, and later I spoke for him at a national Upward Basketball convention.

As a result, over the past twenty years, more than 6.5 million kids have come through Upward Basketball. It hosts between 400,000 and 500,000 kids each year and operates in forty-six states and seventy-two foreign countries. How did that happen? One word at one meeting touched one man, who so far has touched 6.5 million kids and counting.

Your life matters! God wants to use *you* to touch at least one other person who may touch many others. What if this week, when you're full of the Spirit of God and in the flow of Jesus, you touch one person, whose destiny is to reach many others?

How is your life counting so far? Is anybody going to heaven because of you? Have you enriched anybody's life because your life's been enriched? Is anybody encouraged because you have become an encourager? Regardless of your past, God wants to use you to touch your world.

What's Your Purpose?

God has a specific purpose for each man's life, in addition to our highest calling to become like Christ. My specific purpose is not your specific purpose. Neither is your specific purpose mine. For that reason, I don't allow anyone to transfer their vision or burden to my life.

In my early days, I let people intimidate me into trying to fulfill their vision or take up their burden. But I'm no longer so green; I won't allow that to happen anymore. I try to keep in mind what the apostle Paul said in Philippians 3:12-14:

> Not that I have already attained, or am already perfected; but I press on, that I may lay hold of that for which Christ Jesus has also laid hold of me. Brethren, I do not count myself to have apprehended; but one thing I do, forgetting those things which are behind and reaching forward to those things which are ahead, I press toward the goal for the prize of the upward call of God in Christ Jesus.

Paul had a deep desire to press on, to keep moving toward the purpose for which God had laid hold of him. One thing's for sure: None of us will pursue something for which we lack desire, and Paul had a burning desire to fulfill God's purpose for him. When he said he wanted to "lay hold" of God's call on his life, he used a word that means "to capture." Think of a football player who runs down an opposing player to tackle him, to "capture" his opponent. Like that football player, I'd like to capture some things in my own life, and I won't be satisfied until I accomplish what God calls me to do.

What is God calling you to do? What does the Lord want you to pursue at this stage of your life? Has anyone ever challenged you to run your race as hard as you can?

Jimmy Draper, a former president of the Southern Baptist Convention and president emeritus of Lifeway Christian Resources, wrote a book a few years ago titled *Don't Quit Before You Finish.* Jimmy is now in his early eighties. When I was in my thirties, he said to me, "If the Lord continues to use you, would you bring along the generation following you?"

What does that mean? I wondered.

In time, I figured out what he meant. For me, it meant creating the Timothy Barnabas School of Encouragement and Instruction, designed to help the next generation of preachers coming up behind me. God is allowing me to train guys in their twenties, thirties, forties, and fifties. He's allowing me to reach back four decades, and I don't take that privilege lightly.

God wants to do something special with you too. He's no respecter of persons; He's just looking for your availability. The question is, how energetically have you decided to run the specific race the Lord has assigned just to you?

None of Us Has Arrived

Paul realized that the journey toward Christlikeness begins with

a sense of honesty and sanctified dissatisfaction. Consider what I
journaled one day after I read his words in Philippians:

> Paul's remembering the start of his race. I believe I know
> what went through his mind: *Damascus road, the day He
> got hold of me.* He saw Jesus as the starter of the race and the
> finisher of the race. I love the passage that says, "Wherefore,
> seeing we are also compassed about with so great a cloud of
> witnesses, let us lay aside every weight, and the sin which
> doth so easily beset us, and let us run with patience the race
> that is set before us, looking unto Jesus, the author and fin-
> isher of our faith" (Hebrews 12:1-2 KJV).

Both Paul and the writer of Hebrews used the analogy of a runner
to describe a Christian man's spiritual growth. Paul acknowledged
that he had not yet arrived at his final goal, nor yet accomplished
all in his life that he had been commissioned to do. I'm grateful the
apostle spoke like this, because if you know his writings, his life
challenges, his commitment, his passion, his transparency, his honesty, and his vulnerability, you also know how greatly the church
has always admired him. How many books have been written about
Paul and his extraordinary life? It's staggering. And yet we read these
verses and we say, "You mean *he* was still growing too?"

Indeed he was. Paul insisted, "I'm not yet perfected." One of the
chief marks of Christian maturity is the knowledge that you're not
perfect, that you're still in process. Paul gave us an honest evaluation
of his own spiritual condition.

Where would you say you are in your walk with Jesus? How
would you evaluate your current spiritual condition? Regardless of
the results of your evaluation, I'd remind you that Paul admitted to
the church, and to us, that he had room in his life for further development. At least four qualities and practices characterized the apostle in his pursuit of spiritual development.

Teachable

Are you teachable? None of us knows all that we need to know, and none of us puts into practice everything that we already know. Just like Paul, we must continue to grow in both areas.

I love Sunday school. I look forward every Lord's Day to attending my Sunday school class at 8:00 a.m. I love sitting under a gifted teacher every week and allowing him to speak God's Word into me. Remaining teachable helps me to keep growing in Christ. Learning from others helps me to keep moving forward.

If you want to accomplish what God called you to do, you have to remain teachable. Anybody who thinks they've arrived is dead on arrival. If you're going to keep helping others, you have to keep growing.

Watchful

Scripture instructs us to be "watchful." The word speaks of a well-balanced and self-controlled life. It more literally refers to someone who abstains from strong drink. Watchfulness gives clarity of mind and sound judgment, which alcohol obliterates. So as long as you live and serve the Lord in some capacity, you must maintain a seriousness of purpose.

Are you taking life seriously? Are you taking God seriously? One day you're going to realize that Randy Alcorn had it right when he said that a moment after you die, you'll know exactly how you should have lived.

Enduring affliction

When things get tough—and they will—don't quit. Endurance forms sound character. You don't quit just because your feelings get hurt. You don't quit your marriage just because of marital disagreements. You don't quit going to church because somebody says something ugly to you. You don't quit obeying God when He disciplines you.

Evangelizing

Paul told Timothy to "do the work of an evangelist" (2 Timothy 4:5). In fact, every Christian man has a call to testify to the work of Jesus in his life. If we don't try to win souls to Christ, who will? God has placed you where He can most use you to reach others. You may be the only Christian some people know.

Don't Get Stuck in Your Past

If you want to move ahead in your journey toward becoming more like Jesus, often you must deal with some issues of your past. Paul wrote, "One thing I do, forgetting those things which are behind."

"That's easier said than done," you might say, and you'd be right. But you don't have a choice if you want to move ahead.

I don't want to spend the rest of my life talking about where I got hurt or who injured me. I don't want to waste hours camping on where I messed up or where I got off track. I don't want to talk incessantly about what's kept me from moving on. Like Paul, I want to forget the things that are behind so that I can move ahead. That doesn't mean I must acquire the capacity to not remember. It means that I have the capacity, with Jesus, to no longer allow the past to negatively influence me.

Do you remember Joseph? Before he became Pharaoh's right-hand man, he endured many years of struggle, hardship, and pain. Do you think he strove to forget those years, to force his memory to fail? He actually did the reverse. He said, "I will name my children after my sorrow." Joseph named his firstborn Manasseh (Genesis 41:50). In Hebrew, *Manasseh* means "making forgetful." What kind of a name is that? Joseph didn't leave us wondering. He explained, "It is because God has made me forget all my trouble and all my father's household" (v. 51 NIV).

Joseph didn't want the facts erased from his memory, but he did want God to take the sting out of them so that no bitterness remained behind. In this way, Joseph conquered the temptation to develop a mean spirit. He didn't lie awake at night, watching mental videos of hurt. Instead he said, "Hey, Manasseh, let me give you a hug."

When a second son came along, Joseph named him Ephraim. In Hebrew, Ephraim means "fruitful." After the boy's birth, Joseph declared, "It is because God has made me fruitful in the land of my suffering" (v. 52 NIV).

If you can't bring your past to the cross—the failures and hurts as well as the successes and the triumphs—then you're grieving the Spirit of God. Joseph felt his past deeply and remembered clearly what had happened to him, but he didn't let any of it cloud his present or his future. Joseph owned it all—the good and the bad, the painful and the joyful—while refusing to permit any of it to limit what God wanted to do in his life *now*. To "forget" the past means to refuse to let it negatively influence or affect you.

Accomplishments can hold you back too. I know many men who have allowed their successes to keep them from becoming all that God calls them to be. Forget *all* that stuff. Cut the chains that keep you bound to the past.

When you allow your past to paralyze you—when you focus on the unsavory things you've done or the good things you failed to do—you continue to let those things dominate you. Why would you want something to control you that you don't even like?

Invite your failures to teach you, but don't ever let them terrorize you. Don't allow your past to distract you. Don't permit your past to debilitate your efforts in the present.

Oswald Chambers wrote, "Leave the irreparable past in God's hands, and step out into an irresistible future with him." What does God want you to do that you haven't yet accomplished? Instead of spending all your time regretting what you have or haven't done, get busy doing something interesting that God has in mind for you today.

Winning in the Fourth Quarter

The average lifespan for a man in the United States is 78.6 years. That means the second quarter of your life ends at age 39. At age 58.5, you've entered the fourth quarter. You've moved into the Hotel California; you can check in, but you can't check out.

Two of my mentors died younger than the national average. Adrian Rogers departed at age 74, Jerry Falwell at age 73. Another friend, Wayne Barber of Precept Ministries, was sitting upright in a chair one night in a hotel bedroom, his wife nearby, when he departed this life at 73 years of age.

Most games are won in the fourth quarter, the ninth inning, the third period. That's true in the Christian life as well. We might run well for years, pursuing all the right things. But as we close in on the end of our life, the enemy tries to get us to relax. At a critical time, whatever has been chasing us can catch us and defeat us. If a man of God ever stops pursuing what is right, the thing behind him will catch him and he'll miss his reward at the end of the race.

Whenever the end comes for me—and none of us knows our time—I want to finish with joy, with energy, and with enthusiasm. I don't want merely to limp across the finish line. I want to keep going and live to my last breath for my life's purpose.

All of us were created in God's image and for God's purposes.

The Lord wants to get glory through us. He wants other people to see our good works and give God glory. When we do what is right, God gets the glory through us.

Paul lived his life with that conviction. By the time he wrote 2 Timothy, he knew he didn't have long to live. He wrote, "I am already being poured out as a drink offering, and the time of my departure is at hand" (2 Timothy 4:6). He saw his impending death as a departure, a leaving.

The word translated "departure" is a prisoner's term. It means "to release." From God's perspective, Paul was facing release, not execution. Emperor Nero said, "I'm putting him to death." Jesus Christ said, "I'm bringing him home."

It's also a term used by farmers. It refers to the unyoking of oxen after a long, hard day at work.

It's also a soldier's word. When the moment came for an army to break camp and take down the tents, this term signaled, "It's time to journey."

It's also a seaman's word. It referred to unmooring a ship so it could weigh anchor and head out to sea. Paul knew he was about to set sail into eternity's ocean.

Last, it's a philosopher's word that meant "an unraveling." How many times have our hearts felt disturbed and our minds paralyzed as we puzzled over this life's mysteries? Paul was about to have all those mysteries fully unraveled.

Paul reminds me of Caleb in the Old Testament. When Caleb got ready to finish his race, he wanted the same thing at the end that he wanted at the beginning. Four and a half decades after God sent the rebellious Israelites into the wilderness, the rebels' children prepared to finally enter the Promised Land. Caleb declared, "Today, I'm eighty-five years old, and I am as strong today as when I started. Now give me this mountain" (see Joshua 14:10-12). Do you know who lived on that mountain? Fierce, scary, hostile giants. Caleb was saying, "I want a giant to kill." He didn't say, "I want to buy a motor home and travel around the Holy Land for a few months."

I doubt I'm as strong today as I was forty-five years ago. These days, it takes me longer to recover. I can still take a six-mile walk one day and feel pretty good the next day, but I could never run those six miles. I still have a lot of energy, but not like when I was twenty. Although I doubt I'm as strong as when I started, I know I'm wiser. And so I'm eager to continue the journey.

How long have you been on your journey? What did you want when you first started on the road with Jesus? Every family member saved? Your town turned upside down for God? Something else? If your God-honoring dreams have changed, what diverted you?

Begin with the End in Mind

One of the top leadership statements is that you should always begin with the end in mind. Your age doesn't matter; begin with the end in mind. Jesus pioneered this approach. What the Lord began with, He stuck with.

Did you know that Jesus began His public ministry by getting baptized? Jesus came from Galilee and went straight to the Jordan River to be baptized by John. Why baptism? John had the same question. "I need to be baptized by You," he said to Jesus, "and are You coming to me?"

"Permit it to be so now," Jesus replied, "for thus it is fitting for us to fulfill all righteousness" (Matthew 3:14-15).

This initial act of Jesus' ministry illustrated both the ultimate purpose of His coming and His last act of earthly ministry. Jesus began with the end in mind. When John put Him under the waters of the Jordan, the event illustrated Christ's death; He was buried through baptism. A few moments later, when Jesus arose out of those waters, He pictured His resurrection from the dead.

What would you like to accomplish for Christ by the end of your journey? What end do you have in mind? How might you increase the chance of your success?

Let Your Last Years Be Your Best

A highly influential church leader said to me one day, "The most important span of your lifetime, if you stay healthy and devoted to God, is your seventies. People in their seventies have a more significant impact on the world than anyone else."

Do you know the second most important season of your life, according to my friend? Your sixties.

A couple of years ago I met with a really cool group of guys, all of them wonderful leaders, including a man who runs a successful national ministry. As I prepared for the meeting, I had dinner with this man, who looked at me and said, "I'm sixty-one years old, and I'm struggling with what's going to happen in the next ten years of my life." This man is a phenomenal golfer, something I'm not. He's even won a Senior Tour event. He can flat out play the game—but in a very emotional tone, he said to me, "Johnny, I'm thinking about throwing my clubs away and not playing anymore."

"What's that all about?" I asked.

"I don't know," he said. "I'm just struggling about the next ten years."

Well, that's something, I thought. *I'm getting ready to host a meeting about "The Next Ten Years" with a dozen of the best leaders Jesus has placed in my life. What's going on here?*

I want to capture the latter years of my life for good. The Bible says, "Listen to counsel and receive instruction, that you may be wise in your latter days" (Proverbs 19:20). Your best days ought to be your latter days.

It's not about whether you have the energy you had "back then." It's not about whether you have the physical strength or the stamina or even the eyesight or hearing. It's all about getting to know Jesus better and becoming more like Him. The outward man perishes, and since the Fall, it always has. But I'm being renewed, day by day, in the inward man. So, if I'm getting stronger in the inward man, then what's the Holy Spirit saying to my inward man about these latter days? What does He want me to do?

Over two decades ago I was sitting in the office of Adrian Rogers when he asked me, "How old are you?"

"Dr. Rogers, I just turned forty," I said.

"You're ready to get started, son," he replied.

By that time, I'd already pastored for seventeen years, and I think he knew it. He spoke with unusual wisdom.

God wants to bless your life in order to use it to foster the growth of others. He wants to use whatever success you've known, whatever experience you've had, as a platform to help others succeed.

The song "Find Us Faithful" reminds me to follow the example of my mentors, that I might leave a heritage of faithfulness to Christ. Oh, that those who follow us find us faithful! May our influence inspire others to believe and obey.

What is the Spirit saying to you? How can you listen to counsel *right now* so that in your latter days you may be wise? What can you do today to make your latter days your best days? What do you need to change to become more like Jesus in the final chapter of your life?

The Judgment Seat of Christ

Martin Luther said, "There are just two days on my calendar. This day and that Day." "That Day" refers to the day when "we must all appear before the judgment seat of Christ, that each one may receive the things done in the body, according to what he has done, whether good or bad" (2 Corinthians 5:10). Luther clearly reflected on his journey's end.

Note that we won't be judged on the things we *know* but on the things we *do*. A man can know it all and do nothing. It's not the truth we know that makes a difference but the truth we obey. Jesus won't render His judgment based on who's on your speed dial or who calls you, but based on what you did with your life.

Some of that doing will cost us. Years before he wrote 2 Timothy, Paul said to the Philippians, "If I am being poured out as a drink offering on the sacrifice and service of your faith, I am glad and rejoice with you all" (Philippians 2:17). Those words sound a lot like the ones in 2 Timothy 4:6, with one major difference: In Philippians, they're conditional, hypothetical. The offering might happen and it might not. But in 2 Timothy, the words are both categorical and actual. Paul had reached his journey's end.

In fact, Paul viewed his entire life as a drink offering, poured out in sacrificial service to God. The drink offering, described in Numbers 15, was the final act in an old covenant sacrificial ceremony. Paul was saying, "Here in this last chapter of my life, I want to pour everything out in sacrificial service for Jesus." This thought actually made the apostle glad. Paul expected this final chapter of his life to be the best.

A friend of mine almost died in Vietnam. Although he knew the Lord, he wasn't where he knew he should be. In a foxhole, he cried out, "God, don't let me die in this condition." That man, Bobby Welch, became one of the leading pastors in this nation, president of our denomination, and a passionate soul-winner. He's never forgotten that wartime incident.

If God called you home today, would you be ready? Or would

you not want to die in your present condition? We used to sing a song that said no one should face Jesus empty-handed.

When I was younger, I was bolder. I remember standing one day on a loading dock for Jacoby Hardware. A truck driver I knew walked up to me while I sang an old song about the Lord's return.

"What are you singing there, Johnny?" he asked.

"'What a beautiful day for the Lord to come again,'" I said.

"Oh no, it's not either," he said.

"I thought you said you were a Christian."

"I am, but I don't want Him to come today. I'm not ready for Him to come today."

All of us ought to live as though Jesus could come today. One day soon, He *is* coming, although none of us knows the time of His arrival. I do know, however, that one day you'll meet Him. Even if He doesn't come for you in the clouds, He's going to call for you to give an account of your life. None of us knows that date or time.

Paul's ministry had begun thirty years prior, on the Damascus Road, and would end in a prison in Rome. The moment he exited the race here, he expected to be with Jesus in heaven. Although he spoke of his "departure," to Timothy he said, "But you be watchful" (2 Timothy 4:5). That's a big contrast! As the apostle prepared to leave, he challenged those coming behind him.

As I write, I'm in my midsixties, which means I have more life behind me than I do in front of me. I want God to continue using me, to keep me energized and serving Him. I want to finish well. If I died in Africa and were given an African funeral, do you know what they'd say about me? When a Christian dies there, the believers say, "He's arrived," not "He's gone."

When I die, wherever that happens, I hope my friends say, "Did you hear about Pastor Johnny? He's arrived."

How can your life help the generation coming along behind

you? How does God want you to pour into their life? How can you get ready to finish well? When you "arrive," what do you hope your friends say about you?

Don't Make It Dull

The Christian life is dynamic and glorious and wonderful, but some of us do our dead-level best to make it dull and boring. My friend, wake up to the reality of who God is. Fall in love with Him! When you do, your life will change for good and for His glory.

Do what you were called to do. Fulfill your ministry. Reach your God-given potential. I love the one-liner by Charles Spurgeon: "We have misjudged our God-given capacity." It's easy to miss everything that God can do with just one man who devotes himself to love and serve God. What could God do with you if you devoted yourself to know and love Him?

Since it's a long way from here to wherever God wants to take you, live obediently. When we train pastors at our Timothy Barnabas School, I teach a lesson about how God wants our final years to be our best years. Dozens of preachers have written me to say, "I'd just about retired on the Lord. And now I'm beginning to see that my best years can be out there in front of me."

Yours too.

PLAY TO WIN

An interviewer once asked fifty people, all in their late nineties, "If you could live your life over again, what would you do differently?" Three answers kept rising to the top:

- I would reflect more.
- I would risk more.
- I would do more things that would live on after I am dead.

Leonardo da Vinci reportedly said, "Shun those studies in which the work that results dies with the workers." All of God's workers die, but we have the privilege while we're alive to do a work that never dies.

Do you want to know why I'm so passionate about living for Jesus? It's because I know that what I'm doing never dies. Dwight L. Moody has been with the Lord for 120 years now. He once said, "I am only one, but I am one. I cannot do everything, but I can do some things, and that which I can do, by the grace of God I will do."

Listen, if you're breathing, your best years can still be ahead of you. Rusty Rustenbach said, "You and I live in an age when only a rare minority of individuals desire to spend their lives in pursuit of objectives which are bigger than they are."

When most men die in our era, it will be as though they had never lived. The average Christian man just goes around, content that he has a fire escape policy: "I'm saved. I'm glad I'm not going to hell." I refuse to let that happen! I refuse to die and let it be as though I'd never lived. I have a whole lot of living to do before I get up there and enjoy His life. I want to play to win. I have no interest in just playing.

I recently read a jarring statement by an older writer: "When you get to my age, you have some long days, but you don't have any more long years." Since I have no more long years out there for me, I want to play to win in the years I have left.

Where are you in your walk with the Lord? Do you know Him and love Him more than you did a year ago, or five years ago, or twenty years ago? The mature Christian man honestly evaluates himself and strives to do better. Stewart Johnson said, "Our business in life is not to get ahead of others but to get ahead of ourselves. To break our own records. To outstrip our yesterday by our today. To do our work with more force than ever before."

What may the Lord be calling you to do with the rest of your life? I have no idea, but I love this one-liner by John Maxwell: "You never find out what you can do until you do all you can to find out." In my own life, I did all I could think of to do in order to lead my best friend to faith in Jesus. That's a story worth sharing, even though it happened many years ago.

A Long, Winding Road

When I got saved, my best friend was Donald Pope. I wanted to see Donald saved, so I witnessed to him. I took him to a Billy Graham crusade. I don't remember what Dr. Graham said, because I prayed the whole time that God would save Donald.

But he didn't get saved.

Donald had never heard me preach, and when as a seminary student I became pastor at Falls Baptist Church in Wake Forest, North Carolina, I called him and said, "Donald, I'm preaching in your community now. You ought to come hear me."

"Sure," he said, "Debbie and I will come hear you on Easter Sunday." I got excited and called lots of Christian friends because I believed that God moves in answer to prayer. I told them, "Pray for Donald and Debbie Pope. Pray that God will save them. They're gonna be here on Easter, so pray that God will save them."

The Popes came on Easter and I preached my heart out. At the end of the service, I gave an invitation. Neither of them came forward. I felt greatly disappointed, but I decided to call him that afternoon.

"Donald," I said, "did you enjoy the service today?"

"Man, I really did," he said.

"Well, Donald, I'll just be honest, man. I was praying for you and I was just wondering—did you sense anything when I gave the invitation? Like, maybe you should have come forward and given your life to Christ? Or maybe that you needed what I preached about?"

I never anticipated his response.

"Yeah," he replied, "to be real honest with you, that did happen. I was really moved. I even thought about stepping out."

I got ready to shout "Hallelujah!" and "Praise Jesus!" So I continued, "Well, how do you feel about it?"

"I got over it," Donald said. "I got over it."

Many months later, when I was supposed to be doing some morning hospital visits, I stayed at home. As my wife stepped in the shower, I told her, "I'm leaving." But by the time she got out of the shower, I hadn't left.

"I thought you were leaving," she said.

"I will in a minute," I said. "I don't know why, but I don't feel as if I'm supposed to go right now." Just then the phone rang. It was Donald. For seven years I'd been trying to live my faith before him and tell him about Jesus. I didn't have to guess why he called.

"I'm sick and tired of living like this," he said. "I want you to come over and share Christ with me."

I practically flew over there and led my best friend to faith in Jesus Christ. It's one thing when God changes your life, but when God also changes the people around you—hellions, just like you— it's something special.

Not long afterwards, Debbie felt so thrilled about Donald's decision that she said, "I want to make the same commitment." I baptized them together.

Who in your life needs you to tell them about Jesus? How may God want to use you to bring that man or woman into His family? Do they see the fruit of the Spirit growing in your life? Have they tasted some of that fruit for themselves? Are you becoming increasingly like Jesus, so that they want what you have?

Not only did God save Donald, but He also called my best friend to preach. He went off to Mid-America Baptist Theological Seminary and began an intern program at Belleview Baptist Church, where Adrian Rogers served. Debbie told me that under Dr. Rogers's ministry she came under deep conviction that she had never really been saved. The sense of conviction grew so heavy that after each service, when the Popes got home, she'd tell Donald she wanted to take a hot shower. She needed someplace to cry without her husband knowing.

"I was fearful what would happen if I admitted that I wasn't saved," she said. "I was a minister's wife, and I thought I would get my husband in trouble. How can a preacher start his ministry when even his wife isn't truly converted?"

Debbie stayed in that hard place for some time. Week in and week out, she continued to do the shower thing, until she just couldn't bear it any longer. Finally, one night she told her husband, "Donald, I've never been saved. I made a decision for Jesus just because you did. You've really been changed, but deep in my heart, I've never really been changed."

That night, Donald led his wife to genuine faith in Christ, and the fruit of the Spirit soon began to bud, blossom, and grow in Debbie's life. Before long, she became a heart-and-soul winner. She'd aggravate you with her soul-winning, she got so strong into evangelism. She became an "altar counselor" at church, and when somebody came forward after a service and said, "I'm just coming to move my membership," she'd reply, "Well, tell me your story."

They'd give a report, but she'd press them: "Are you sure of your salvation?" Debbie wanted to hear, in particular, how God had saved them. Many times it turned out the person didn't really know Jesus as Savior and Lord at all—and Debbie would do her best to lead that individual to faith in Christ.

God calls all of us to be ambassadors for Christ. He instructs us to be ready always to give an answer to anyone who asks us why we have such hope. When we anchor our lives in Jesus, when we abide in Him, bear the Spirit's fruit, and day by day allow God to transform us into the image of Christ, we prepare ourselves to have a major impact on the only game that really matters.

Don't play around.

Play to win.

NOTES

1. "Jesus, Be Jesus in Me," by Eddie Carswell, © 1984, used with permission.

2. "*Messiah* Release Date: December 12, 2019," *Wild About Movies*, https://www.wildaboutmovies.com/netflix/messiah/.

3. Denise Petski, "'Messiah': Netflix Orders Religious Drama Series from Mark Burnett and Roma Downey," *Deadline*, November 16, 2017, https://deadline.com/2017.11messiah-netflix-orders-drama-series-mark-burnett-roma-downey-james-mcteigue-direct-1202208898/.

4. John MacArthur, *Titus* (Chicago: Moody, 1996), 114-15.

5. William Barclay, *The Letter to the Hebrews* (Louisville, KY: Westminster John Knox Press, 1976), 183.

6. John Piper, "The Renewed Mind and How to Have It," https://www.desiringgod.org/messages/the-renewed-mind-and-how-to-have-it.

7. I recall this statement from one of Adrian Rogers's radio messages.

8. J.B. Lightfoot, *Philippians* (Wheaton, IL: Crossway, 1994), 155.

9. Kent Hughes, *Disciplines of a Godly Man* (Wheaton, IL: Crossway, 2001), 73.

10. "The Happy Hour: Ward Reveals Why He Retired, What's Next," *NBC Sports*, www.nbcsports.com/bayarea/video/happy-hour-andre-ward-reveals-why-he-retired-whats-his-next-step.

11. Brin-Jonathan Butler, "Andre Ward Fights to Avoid a Boxer's Bad Ending," *Undefeated*, August 4, 2016, https://theundefeated.com/features/andre-ward-fights-to-avoid-a-boxers-bad-ending/.

12. Ibid., and so throughout the Andre Ward story.

Also by Johnny Hunt

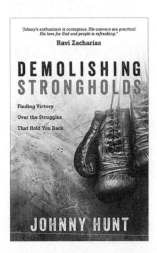

Demolishing Strongholds

Ever wonder how to be a man of God in the trenches of life—in the day-to-day trials and temptations that hound you? It's not impossible! God's promises and strength are real, and you can claim them today.

Whether you feel beaten down by your past failures or trapped in a corner by your current struggles, let hope lift you up. Pastor Johnny Hunt offers the biblical encouragement and guidance that will help you…

- navigate the dangers and discouragements of daily life
- take practical steps toward taming your negative habits
- use your blessings to influence others for God's glory

It's time to learn how to break spiritual strongholds so you can move forward in God's will and become the kind of man you've always wanted to be.

THE
CAMPAIGN MANAGER

THE
CAMPAIGN MANAGER

RUNNING AND WINNING
LOCAL ELECTIONS

THIRD EDITION

CATHERINE M. SHAW

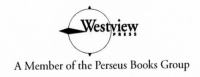

A Member of the Perseus Books Group

Copyright © 2004 by Westview Press, a Member of the Perseus Books Group

Published in the United States of America by Westview Press, A Member of the Perseus Books Group, 3465 Central Avenue, Suite 200, Boulder, Colorado 80301-2877, and in the United Kingdom by Westview Press, 12 Hid's Copse Road, Cumnor Hill, Oxford OX2 9JJ.

Find us on the world wide web at www.westviewpress.com

Westview Press books are available at special discounts for bulk purchases in the United States by corporations, institutions, and other organizations. For more information, please contact the Special Markets Department at the Perseus Books Group, 11 Cambridge Center, Cambridge, MA 02142, or call (617) 252-5298, (800) 255-1514 or email special.markets@perseusbooks.com.

Library of Congress Cataloging-in-Publication Data
Shaw, Catherine M. (Catherine Marie), 1955–
    The campaign manager : running & winning local elections / by Catherine M. Shaw.—3rd ed.
    p.   cm.
    Includes bibliographical references and index.
    ISBN-13 978-0-8133-4222-1 ISBN-10 0-8133-4222-8 (pbk. : alk. paper)
    1. Local elections—United States—Handbooks, manuals, etc.   2. Campaign management—United States—Handbooks, manuals, etc.   I. Title.
    JS395.S43 2004
    324.7'0973—dc22

2004001665A

Typeface used in this text: 10.5-point Kepler 385 Regular 10 Op size

Dedicated to my children, Daniel and Sarah,
who have shared me, nearly all their lives,
with the community I love.

Special thanks to the TCM Campaign Committee
Sarah Golden
Dr. Ruth Schifferle
Rick Shaw and "rickshaw productions"

CONTENTS

List of Illustrations   *xi*

Preface   *xv*

How to Use This Handbook   **1**

The Framework, 1

The Layout, 3

Know the Law, 4

The Ten Commandments of Campaigning, 5

The Cardinal Sins of Campaigning, 5

1. The Campaign Team   **7**

The Campaign Committee, 7

Campaign Committee Packets, 9

The Treasurer, 10

The Campaign Manager, 13

Ten Tips for Campaign Managers, 15

The Campaign Chair or Co-Chairs, 16

Finding Volunteers, 16

Potential Volunteer Sources, 19

Volunteer Sign-Up Sheet, 20

2. The Campaign Brochure   **21**

Campaign Theme and Message
    Development, 22

Polling, 25

Brochure Development, 32

Campaign Slogans, 37

Logo, 41

Layout, 41
Voters' Pamphlet, 50

3. The Volunteer Organization   **53**
Methodology, 53
Phone Banks, 59
Phone Bank Locations, 62
Clerical Workers, 64
Time Allotments for Volunteer Tasks, 66

4. Fund-Raising   **69**
Early Endorsements = Early Money = Early
    Media Buys, 70
Campaign Budget, 71
Direct Mail for Money, 76
Special Events, 81
Holding a Special Event, 82
Candidate Calls to Raise Money, 89
Calling for Money for Ballot Measures, 90
The Campaign Finance Committee, 90
Campaign Finance Committee Packets, 92
Tips for Successful Fund-Raising, 108
Fund-Raising Ideas That Take Less Than
    One Month of Preparation, 109
"Hey, Big Spender," 111
The World's Smallest Brochure: Direct Mail
    That Works, 114
Keeping Track of Donations, 118

5. Lawn Signs   **119**
Logo and General Information, 120
Location, Location, Location, 124
Preparing for the First Day, 125
Field Signs, 128
Maintenance of Signs, 130
Lawn Sign Removal, 131

6. Precinct Analysis: The Sinners, the Saints, and the Saveables 133

The Full-Blown Analysis, 137

Finding the Saints Among the Sinners, 146

The Quick and Dirty Precinct Analysis, 153

Votes Needed to Win, 154

7. Targeting Voters 159

Finding the Likely Voter, 159

Canvassing, 170

Direct Mail, 180

Tracking Polls, 195

8. Media 203

Print Media: Paid and Unpaid, 203

Fielding Questions from the Press, 210

Radio and Television, 226

Choosing Your Media Specialist or Team, 230

Bumper Stickers and Buttons, 245

9. The Candidate 247

The Lay of the Land, 248

Packaging the Candidate, 251

Stay on Your Message, 257

Outsider Campaign vs. Incumbent Campaign, 262

Debates, 265

Fielding Negative Questions, 268

Developing Your Public Speaking Skills, 271

The Write-In and Third Party Candidates, 279

Media and the Candidate, 284

Negative Campaigning, 284

Ten Dos and Don'ts of Attacks, 286

Thank-You Notes, 290

10. The Issue-Based Campaign   293

Initiative and Referendum, 293
Local Preemption, 297
Polling and the Issue-Based Campaign, 298
Speakers' Bureau, 300
Recall, 300
Saving Our Libraries, 303
Building New Schools, 306
Packaging the Issue-Based Campaign, 308
Flies in the Ointment: The Double Majority,
    Independents, and the Super Majority,
    309
The State Initiative and Referendum
    Process, 315

11. Getting Out the Vote (GOTV)   321

The Essentials, 322
Identifying Your Voters: Voter ID, 325
Last-Minute Efforts to Persuade Voters, 328
Poll Watching, 331
Phoning, 335
The Absentee Ballot and Early Vote, 337
Vote By Mail, 340
Organizing the GOTV Effort, 345
Push Polls, 348

12. The Campaign Flowchart   349

Building Your Campaign Flowchart, 350
The Campaign Calendar, 354

13. After the Ball   357

Retiring a Campaign Debt, 359

Afterword   *361*
Appendix: Campaign Web Site Resource Directory   *363*
Index   *383*
About the Author   *399*

LIST OF TABLES AND ILLUSTRATIONS

Tables

Table 7.1	Absentee Voter History in Oregon	161
Table 7.2	Voting Tendencies By Party Registration and Age in 1998	162
Table 7.3	Generation X: Who Are They?	164
Table 7.4	Mobilizing Young Voters: What Works and What Doesn't	166
Table 7.5	How Californians Voted in the Recall of Governor Gray Davis	168
Table 7.6	Women and Minority Vote in 1996 Presidential Election	169
Table 7.7	Minority Vote by Party Registration	169
Table 7.8	Minority Turnout in 1996	169
Table 10.1	States with Citizens' Initiative Authority for Constitutional Amendments and Statutes	318

Figures

Figure 1.1	Example of a Campaign Committee Packet	10
Figure 1.2	Example of a Volunteer Sign-up Sheet	20
Figure 2.1A	Examples of Candidate Photos That Work Well in Brochures	35
Figure 2.1B	Examples of Photos That Work Well in an Issue-Based Brochure	36
Figure 2.2	Don't Swallow the Meals Tax Brochure	39
Figure 2.3	Maxwell for the House Walking Piece	42
Figure 2.4	Example of a Logo for a Campaign to Restore and Expand Ashland's Carnegie Library	43
Figure 2.5	Example of a Logo Using Lettering That Appeals to the American Love of Baseball	43
Figure 2.6	The County Has Changed Brochure	45
Figure 2.7	Youth Activities Levy Brochure	46

Figure 2.8	Youth Activities Levy Brochure, Take 2	47
Figure 2.9	Front of Full-Color Brochure to Elect Dr. Alan Bates, State Representative	48
Figure 2.10	Full-Color Walking Piece for Alan Bates	49
Figure 2.11	Example of Voters' Pamphlet Candidate Statement	52
Figure 3.1	Example of Excel Spreadsheet for Keeping Track of Volunteer Workers	54
Figure 3.2	Example of a 3-by-5-Inch Contact Card	55
Figure 3.3	Example of a 5-by-8-Inch Canvass Activity Card	57
Figure 4.1	Example of a Campaign Budget for a Candidate in a Small-City Race	72
Figure 4.2	Example of a Countywide, Issue-Based Campaign Budget	73
Figure 4.3	Sample Budget Form	77
Figure 4.4	Example of a Remittance Envelope	78
Figure 4.5	Example of Campaign Finance Committee Packet	94
Figure 4.6A	Sample Text for Campaigner Responsibilities Sheet	95
Figure 4.6B	Sample Text for Telephone Campaign Overview Sheet	96
Figure 4.6C	Case for Support Sheet	97
Figure 4.6D	Sample Letter Sent to Supporters	98
Figure 4.6E	Sample Answering Machines Sheet	99
Figure 4.6F	Sample Text for Answers to Frequently Asked Questions Sheet	100
Figure 4.6G	Sample Text for How to Make a Successful Call Sheet	101
Figure 4.6H	Sample Text for "The Ask" . . . Steps for Success Sheet	102
Figure 4.7	Example of a Campaigner Card	103
Figure 4.8	Example of a Donor Card	103
Figure 4.9	Sample Friends I Will Call Sheet	104
Figure 4.10	Sample Letter Welcoming Finance Committee Member to the Campaign	106
Figure 4.11	Sample Thank-You Note from Campaign Finance Committee Member to Campaign Donor	107
Figure 4.12	Front of "The World's Smallest Brochure"	115
Figure 4.13	Sample Fund-Raising Letter Inside of "The World's Smallest Brochure"	116
Figure 4.14	Example of Headings for the Donor Spreadsheet	118
Figure 5.1	Example of a Lawn Sign Using Logo and Theme	122
Figure 5.2	Maxwell for the House Lawn Sign	122
Figure 5.3	Example of a 3-by-5-Inch Lawn Sign Card	127
Figure 5.4	Example of a Field Sign Used in an Issue-Based Campaign	129
Figure 6.1	Sample Spreadsheet Headings for Precinct Analysis	138

Figure 6.2	Example of Tabulating Precincts in Order of Support and Turnout for Similar Election	140
Figure 6.3	Example of a Precinct Targeting Worksheet Filled Out	142
Figure 6.4	Example of Precinct Priorities Worksheet Filled Out	143
Figure 6.5	Example of a Targeting Priorities and Strategy Form Filled Out	144
Figure 6.6	Example of Spreadsheet Headings for Issue-Based Campaign Analysis	147
Figure 6.7	Sample Form for Determining Base Party Support	148
Figure 6.8	Sample Form for Determining Swing Voters	150
Figure 6.9	Sample Form for Determining Average Party Turnout	151
Figure 6.10	Sample Form for Determining the Number of Votes You Need to Win from the Swing Voters	157
Figure 7.1	History of Absentee Voter Performance in Oregon	161
Figure 7.2	A Case for Activating the Right Voters	172
Figure 7.3	Example of a Canvassing Map	174
Figure 7.4	Example of a Canvassing Map Packet	174
Figure 7.5	Example of Simple yet Effective Technique to Help Voters Remember Who You Are	190
Figure 7.6	Example of Direct Mail That Can Reinforce the Opponent's Argument	191
Figure 7.7	Cell Phone Use By Race	198
Figure 7.8	A Winner's Final-Week Direct Mail Piece After a Campaign Marked By Mudslinging	201
Figure 8.1	Example of a Letter-to-the-Editor	206
Figure 8.2	Example of the "Community" Section from a Local Paper	207
Figure 8.3	Example of Candidate Ad Made to Look Like a Newspaper Article	214
Figure 8.4	Example of an Information Ad	215
Figure 8.5	Example of a 2-by-4 Newspaper Endorsement Ad for an Issue-Based Campaign	216
Figure 8.6	Example of an Emotional Ad	218
Figure 8.7	Example of an Emotional Ad	219
Figure 8.8	Example of an Endorsement Ad	220
Figure 8.9	Example of an Endorsement Ad	223
Figure 8.10	Example of a Comparison Ad	231
Figure 8.11	Example of an Establishing Ad	232
Figure 8.12	Example of a Comparison Ad	237
Figure 8.13	Example of an Issue-Based Ad Using Still Photos	239
Figure 8.14	Example of an Ad with Purpose	240
Figure 8.15	Example of a Response/Attack Ad	242

Figure 9.1   A Candidate with a Baby   256
Figure 9.2   Example of a Brochure for a Write-in Candidate   281
Figure 9.3   Example of Stationery for Candidate's Personalized Notes   292
Figure 10.1A Historical Photograph of Ashland's Carnegie Library   305
Figure 10.1B Inside the "Campaign for the Carnegie" Brochure   305
Figure 11.1   Election Day Phone Script   336
Figure 11.2   Example of GOTV Phone Bank Spreadsheet   346
Figure 12.1   Example of a Campaign Flowchart   353
Figure 12.2   Example of a Campaign Calendar for a Non-Partisan
              General Election   355

Boxes

Box 3.1   Example of Phone Instructions and Script for Lawn
           Sign Locations   61
Box 3.2   Example of Phone Bank Instructions   61

PREFACE

Running for local office can be one of the most demanding and exhilarating experiences of your life. Your house will be cluttered and chaotic, your children will be ignored, and your partner, whether involved in the campaign or not, will be stressed. And yet, seeking office or pushing through an issue-based campaign gives you an opportunity to be a leader, to effect change in your community, and to repay something to the city, county, state, or country you love. The campaign experience also offers you an opportunity to grow personally. You will be challenged and stretched as never before. When it's all over, win or lose, you will be a different person, with a different outlook on our political process and a new respect for those who run and serve.

"You have to be smart enough to understand the game and dumb enough to think it's important."
—Gene McCarthy on how politics is like coaching football

When I first ran for mayor of Ashland, in 1988, I had no prior government or management experience. Many felt I should start at the council level and work my way up before taking on the position of CEO of a multimillion dollar municipality. However, having so little experience allowed me to view things with a fresh eye. After three terms and twelve years at that post, the council, the city staff, the community, and I implemented dozens of programs, including open space, water conservation, community composting and recycling, voter-approved air quality standards, wetland and floodplain preservation, wastewater treatment plant upgrades, forest management, and restoration and expansion of the library, fire station, and city offices. We also worked closely with our public school system to find ways to ease their financial burden in the wake of state budget cutbacks. We divested our hospital and acquired a ski resort and an ambulance service. We installed a dark fiber ring in our city, which provides direct-connect, high-speed Internet access and cable TV services. By having community and government work in partnership, we've been able to create and act on opportunities normally available only to large metropolitan areas.

There are over a half million elective offices in the United States. If you have an inclination to serve and a desire to be a leader in your community, do it. Being in a position where you can have a positive impact on your community and bring about change is more rewarding and fun than you can imagine. Ultimately, the only real credentials you need are integrity, a caring heart, and a strong work ethic.

"Politics—good politics—is public service. There is no life or occupation in which a man can find a greater opportunity to serve his community or his country."

—Harry Truman

Since 1985 I have worked on or run many campaigns in my region. Through years of experimentation and collaboration with other seasoned campaigners, I found organizational techniques that worked in political campaigns, and I began to apply them to the campaign process. This book is the culmination of campaign trial and error and will give you the tools you need to organize the efforts of others on your behalf. Whether you are a novice or a seasoned campaigner, you will find information here that will make your efforts more organized and effective.

Good luck, and enjoy the process.

HOW TO USE THIS HANDBOOK

IN THIS SECTION
- *The Framework*
- *The Layout*
- *Know the Law*

R unning an effective local election is more work than you can possibly imagine. It involves recruiting volunteers, raising money (lots of it), running phone banks, creating media presentations, canvassing, and getting out the vote. The candidate or issue must be "packaged" in a believable and compelling way, and resources must be effectively allocated.

This handbook breaks a campaign down into manageable units for easy implementation. If you are the candidate, you will find the necessary tools to coordinate your efforts with those of your campaign manager. If you're the campaign manager, either for a candidate or for an issue-based campaign, this handbook will organize and guide you and your team through the campaign process.

> *". . . the seeds of political success are sown far in advance of any election day. . . . It is the sum total of the little things that happen which leads to eventual victory at the polls."*
> —J. Howard McGrath, Former Chairman, Democratic National Committee

Because implementing each of the components of a winning campaign is easier if you have an understanding of the complexity of the whole process, take time to read this entire handbook before you design your campaign flowchart or draft your campaign plan.

The Framework
In local politics, there are generally three types of political campaigns:

- Partisan candidate races
- Nonpartisan candidate races
- Issue-based

Although some states allow a primary winner who receives more than 50 percent of the vote to take office with no runoff, a partisan race typically has a primary, with winners squaring off in a general election. A nonpartisan race usually has only one election, the general, where the winner takes all. An issue-based campaign, like a nonpartisan race, takes place in one election cycle but, unlike candidate races, depending on the state and locality, can occur in any election.

Issue-based campaigns may either be brought to the voters by the governing body or, in some states, be referred through the citizen initiative process.

"Behind all political success is attention to detail."
—Larry O'Brien, adviser to John F. Kennedy

The "formula campaign" that is the basis for this book is a way of systematically organizing other people's efforts on your behalf. You provide the guidance in setting up systems for phone banks, clerical teams, fund-raising, lawn sign dispersal and maintenance, canvassing, and the get-out-the-vote (GOTV) effort. Within each of these activities, critical organizational work is needed to accomplish a variety of tasks. These tasks include such things as putting together your campaign team and volunteer organization, developing a campaign theme and message, designing campaign brochures and lawn sign art, performing precinct analysis, designing direct mail programs, handling the media, presenting the candidate, designing and following a flowchart, and overseeing campaign clean-up.

After reading this handbook, determine which activities your campaign can implement, and then use the book to assemble the blueprints for completing those tasks successfully. By breaking a campaign down into manageable units and organizing the activities within each component, you will never overload your workforce. Once you have decided what you can or want to do in organizing your campaign, you will need to plot these activities on a campaign flowchart, calendar, or plan. Campaign plans are probably the most widely accepted blueprint design for a campaign. However, I prefer a more visual "campaign flowchart" because it presents a campaign timeline that can be taken in at a glance. Any campaign flowchart or calendar can be converted to a plan. It is just a matter of writing down what's on the chart.

The Layout

Chapter 1, "The Campaign Team," covers both the small, select group that will develop campaign strategies (the campaign committee) and the greater force behind activity implementation, including volunteers, the media team, the treasurer, and the campaign chairs or co-chairs. Chapter 2, "The Campaign Brochure," details the single most important thing the campaign committee will do in the campaign: develop a theme and message. Within this chapter you will also find detailed information on benchmark polling, slogans, logo design, and the voters' pamphlet.

Chapter 3, "The Volunteer Organization," gives you the structure for organizing your phone banks and clerical workers. Chapter 4, "Fund-Raising," helps you raise money in a variety of ways using your volunteer force. Without a certain threshold of money, efforts to get your message to the voters will be hobbled. Chapter 5, "Lawn Signs," covers logo in more depth, as well as the design, placement, and maintenance of signs.

Chapter 6, "Precinct Analysis," is the key to directing campaign resources (money and volunteers) for the most benefit by locating support based on the historical voting trends of neighborhoods. Although a complicated process, precinct analysis is the "open sesame" for finding support, swing voters, persuadable voters, and the votes needed to win, all while avoiding voters who are opposed to your efforts. Precinct analysis can and should be done long in advance of the campaign kickoff.

"Targeting Voters," the topic of Chapter 7, builds on the precinct analysis to help you to find likely voters. The chapter also outlines how to communicate with such voters through direct mail and canvassing.

Chapter 8, "Media," provides examples of and money-saving tips on how to communicate with voters through print, radio, and television. Through the media, candidates and issue-based campaigns gain credibility. Given the expense and the power of this campaign line item, the more you know, the more effective you will be in getting the most out of each media dollar. Chapter 9, "The Candidate," outlines how best to package the candidate to project as positive an image as possible. It also covers negative campaigning, attacks, debates, and dealing with the press in detail. Chapter 10, "The Issue-Based Campaign," covers initiative, referendum, recall, and school and library money issues, along with a couple of "monsters in the night": the double majority and the super majority. Chapter 11, "Getting Out the Vote," covers the all-important voter activation effort that is critical to a winning campaign. The chapter offers tips for last-minute voter persuasion, dealing with the hybrid campaign—that is, the election with both absentee mail voting and poll voting—and tried-and-true methods for the elections that are conducted entirely through vote by mail.

With over a decade of vote-by-mail experience, Oregon has this system down.

"Play for more than you can afford to lose and you will learn the game."
—Winston Churchill

Chapter 12, "The Campaign Flowchart," puts in chronological order all that you will need to do to win. Although creating a flowchart is one of the first things you will do to organize your campaign, without baseline knowledge of the first eleven chapters, it would be more difficult. Also included in this chapter is a campaign calendar, yet another alternative to the campaign plan, that works equally well for organizing campaign efforts.

Finally, Chapter 13, "After the Ball," is simply about winning and losing gracefully, putting your campaign to bed, election night, and retiring a campaign debt (should you have one). Chapter 13 is followed by an appendix containing a Web address reference section.

Know the Law

First things first: Visit the county clerk or city recorder to become familiar with state and local election laws. For example, in my city, you are not allowed to place lawn signs more than six weeks before an election. You are also not allowed to place them on the strip between the sidewalk and the street. Although the homeowner may plant, mow, water, and care for this area, it is in fact part of the public right of way. To place a lawn sign here could be interpreted in one of two ways: either you feel you're above the law or you don't know the law. Either interpretation is a problem if you hope to be in government.

"One thing I know: The only ones among you who will be really happy are those who will have sought and found how to serve."
—Albert Schweitzer

It is against federal law to place campaign literature in and around mailboxes. Even though you bought and installed your mailbox, the federal government dictates how it can be used. The same goes for the little boxes on the side of your home. Publicly owned buildings are maintained, lit, and owned by the taxpayers, so they should not be used for campaign purposes either. And on and on.

The county clerk or city recorder will also draw attention to filing dates that you and your treasurer must know. Missing a campaign expenditure filing deadline will almost always get you media coverage, but not the kind you need or want. Other than the legal materials from the county clerk, the city recorder, or the secretary of state, everything you need to run a successful campaign is included in this handbook.

The Ten Commandments of Campaigning

Honor your base

Stay on message

Money is your savior

Never tell a lie

Aim at the souls that can be saved

Never waste donors' money

Do not commit adultery

Start early

Be prepared in all things

Know who you are

The Cardinal Sins of Campaigning

Being caught in a provable lie

Committing a crime

Having a relationship with a member of your staff

Committing adultery

Declaring bankruptcy

1

THE CAMPAIGN TEAM

IN THIS CHAPTER
- *The Campaign Committee*
- *Campaign Committee Packets*
- *The Treasurer*
- *The Campaign Manager*
- *Ten Tips for Campaign Managers*
- *The Campaign Chair or Co-Chairs*
- *Finding Volunteers*
- *Potential Volunteer Sources*
- *Volunteer Sign-Up Sheet*

For the purposes of this handbook, "campaign team" refers to all those who help organize your efforts. It is made up of the committee, the treasurer, your volunteers, and each of the individual teams that oversee a portion of the campaign. Your media team, for example, may have a liaison to the campaign committee, but it should be viewed as part of your overall campaign team rather than part of the committee itself. Aspects of the campaign team will be covered in this chapter. Campaign efforts that involve large numbers of people and independent efforts, such as lawn sign activities, media projects, brochure development, and fund-raising, will be covered in separate chapters.

The Campaign Committee

The relatively small campaign committee serves two functions: First, it is a support group, both for itself and for the candidate or issue-based campaign; second, it is the primary source of expertise for the campaign. This small, select group will maneuver and steer a campaign while drawing on the resources of the community. The committee should consist of individuals who have different personal strengths and areas of ability.

Your campaign committee is an insiders' group. The candidate, the manager, and each of the members must feel safe in speaking candidly without fear of recrimination. Treat them like insiders and keep them informed of any campaign development. You would never want a committee member to first learn about a problem with the campaign in the newspaper or through the rumor mill. Call or e-mail your committee members often. Welcome their criticisms. Encourage them and support their individual efforts in the campaign. Listen carefully to determine when they might need additional help. Be clear about their tasks, expectations, and time commitment.

"The impersonal hand of government can never replace the helping hand of a neighbor."
—Hubert Humphrey

Take time in choosing the right number of people for a campaign committee. I have worked on countywide campaigns with four committee members (including the candidate), which was too few, and citywide campaigns with twelve members, which was too many. I have found that six or seven committee members for a city with a population of up to 20,000 is perfect. In countywide campaigns a successful committee might also include members from each city who oversee teams within their respective cities.

You want only enough committee members to cover the campaign activities that you have decided to do. Keep in mind that not all campaign activities occur at the same time, so it is often possible to have more than one task assigned to a single committee member. For example, the campaign brochure is written and printed at the beginning of the campaign, whereas the demands on the canvassing coordinator are greatest toward the end of the campaign. On the other hand, fund-raising responsibilities and clerical team coordination are both ongoing tasks and should *not* be combined with any other campaign responsibilities.

Once the campaign starts, meet with the committee each week for one hour. For citywide campaigns where people are not traveling great distances, it isn't a bad idea to meet in the evening after 8:00 P.M., when children have been taken care of and the day's work is done. Up to a point, the later you meet, the better, because people are ready for their day to be done, so they arrive on time and get right down to work. Few people function well after 10:00 P.M., so at 9:30 be ready to call it quits. Try to keep committee meetings to one hour unless it is the first meeting and you're setting up the campaign. For this first meeting, allow additional time by starting the meeting earlier,

or have the meeting at a different time—for example, set up a morning retreat followed by a lunch at which the campaign becomes official. For countywide campaigns, it works well for the committee to meet in a central
location at the end of the workday before dinner.

Campaign Committee Packets

Your committee may quickly break down into specialized campaign functions. Once specialized groups are formed, keep track of their progress by
getting reports back each week. When the committee meets, meetings
should be productive. Always have an agenda. It is important that all meetings begin and end on time.

A campaign committee packet (figure 1.1) is a great organizational tool
for committee members. (The finance committee packets, discussed in
Chapter 4, are assembled in a similar fashion.) Each pocket folder contains
tiered sheets of alternating colors organized by
category for the tasks the committee will undertake in the course of the campaign, such as lawn
signs, canvassing, phone banks, letters-to-the-
editor, and so on. Although one sheet should be
dedicated to listing committee members and all
contact information for each, the remaining sheets clearly outline job descriptions for each campaign duty and indicate who will oversee that particular job. The folders travel with committee members to war room meetings
and contain information that may be distributed there. Helping volunteers
with this kind of organizational framework keeps members happy and
makes your campaign a little more volunteer friendly.

> *"The time to win a fight is before it starts."*
> —Frederick W. Lewis

In addition to the weekly meeting for the full committee, occasionally get
together with the individuals who are responsible for specific campaign
tasks, and bring this information back to the committee. For example, you
may meet with the ad person to hammer out two or three ads and then bring
these to the regular committee meeting to have them critiqued.

Other than the treasurer and the campaign manager, the makeup of the
campaign committee is discretionary, based upon how many people will be
needed to plan and supervise the campaign. You will depend on the people
you invite to join your campaign committee, so they should be capable of
organizing and directing some particular aspect of the campaign. In addition to a treasurer and a campaign manager, your committee must include
one or more people to oversee letters-to-the-editor, canvassing, clerical
work, brochures, the media, lawn signs, phone banks, fund-raising, getting
out the vote, and volunteer workers.

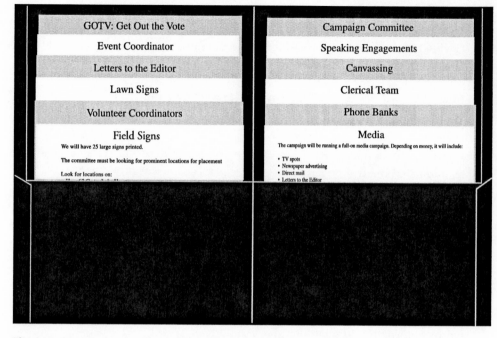

Figure 1.1 Example of a Campaign Committee Packet

The Treasurer

I usually ask a volunteer to serve as the campaign treasurer. I look for someone who is well respected in the community and who will lend credibility to an issue-based campaign or balance a candidate campaign. Selecting the right person for this position is one of the most important things you will do. The name of your treasurer will appear on every campaign publication. He or she will be called from time to time by the press, or even the opposition, and asked questions. Like a vice-president in a presidential election, the treasurer should balance the ticket. For example, if you are a retired senior, select a prominent, involved, young person of the opposite sex. If you are a young progressive man and relatively new to your community, consider an older conservative woman who has been in town a number of years. Find a person who complements rather than merely repeats your strengths. If you're a Democrat, find a respected Republican. If you are working for more taxes for schools, get someone who is conservative and who may have sometimes spoken out against tax increases.

If possible, find someone willing to represent the campaign, discharge the official duties of treasurer, and help in other ways. For example, a treasurer may take on all thank-you notes and keep donor files up-to-date in a database. In one campaign I managed, the treasurer sat in on war room meetings, canvassed, helped with lawn signs, and oversaw data input on campaign donations, but this level of involvement by the treasurer is the exception and not the rule.

"If you want something done, ask a busy person."
—Benjamin Franklin

The treasurer is usually responsible for obtaining and completing the registration forms required for participation in an election. The necessary forms can be obtained from the city recorder's office for city races, from the county clerk's office for county races, and from the election division under the secretary of state for elections to state offices. Don't be afraid to use these offices. The people who staff government offices are extremely helpful and accommodating.

Not all the forms and information in the election packet are necessary or applicable to every race or election. Ask exactly what you need to read, what is required, and when it is required. Ask either the clerk or the recorder for a schedule of the pertinent dates for filing your campaign contributions and expenditures.

"Making the simple complicated is commonplace; making the complicated simple, awesomely simple, that's creativity."
—Charles Mingus

While the filing of these reports is the principal job of the treasurer, it is a good idea for both the candidate and the campaign manager to be aware of them. These tasks should be placed on your campaign flowchart, calendar, or plan as a reminder.

Finally, I now also use a certified public accountant (CPA) in all campaigns. If I can't find one who will volunteer to oversee the reports, I use campaign funds to hire one. Having a CPA on board is actually a great comfort to the volunteer treasurer and helps reduce the overall stress of a demanding campaign cycle. The CPA and the treasurer should work together closely.

Contributions and Expenditures

Your treasurer and the CPA should be sticklers for detail. The opposition will be examining your contributions and expenditures (C&Es) filings for any mistakes to report to the state elections office. If a mistake is found, it is bound to make the local papers. That sort of damage is totally preventable.

After the C&E forms have been filed, local papers generally do a story on who spent how much on what. If you are running a modest campaign and your opposition is funded by outside money, make sure that information makes it to the media. Running a visibly hard-working campaign with modest funds gives people the sense that you are fiscally responsible. That trait is desirable in office, and people will make the connection.

Although it is difficult to work on a campaign where the opposition has unlimited funds, it can also work in your favor. In a small community election that involves no TV ads, there is just so much ad space to buy in the newspaper and just so much direct mail that can be sent to homes without it becoming pretty clear that the election is being bought. In one campaign I ran, we were outspent five to one by the opposition, and we publicized this spending discrepancy to our advantage. When the newspapers ran the usual C&E article, many in the community were stunned by the amount of money coming in from outside interests. Since we had a pretty good idea of how much they were spending, we were ready when the press called for our reaction. Supporters wrote and sent letters-to-the-editor for those who missed the newspaper articles when they first appeared.

In that particular race, the opposition was convinced that the accounting in our campaign was wrong and sent people to the recorder's office on a regular basis to check our C&Es. This is where having a meticulous treasurer pays off. Finally, convinced of foul play, the opposition called the paper and suggested there must be something wrong. When the press called me, I explained that we were in fact spending a normal amount for a small-town race and it was the opposition whose expenditures were excessive. We got another great newspaper story.

Committee to Support

Given the importance of a good treasurer, what do you do if you can't find the right one for you? Not to worry. You have two options. First, you can place a short list of carefully selected supporters (six to nine) at the bottom of all your literature and ads. This "Committee to Support" should represent a good cross-section of the community. Although some of these people might be working on your campaign, this is not your "campaign committee." The primary job of this group is to give your cause credibility by lending their names. Depending on the issue, the "committee to support" may include people in business, environmental groups, real estate, labor, and so on.

Using a "committee to support" works well if you have broad-based support up front; however, it does not work at all if your support is marginal. I once worked on a campaign that was so controversial that I could get only three people to sign their names to the committee-to-support list. Rather than have such a short list, which didn't cover the political spectrum of the city, I dropped the notion of listing the committee. In fact, it helped the campaign to discover the level of controversy so early in the campaign. Information of this sort should not discourage, but rather help set the course.

Let me caution you here. When you are working on a very controversial campaign and have a listed "committee to support" at the bottom of all your literature, you take the risk of opponents to the campaign getting to one or more of those who are listed and undermining your public support. The newspapers also may call these people and grill them on the cause. This can get a little dicey. I find it best to use a "committee to support" for relatively unknown candidates or difficult yet uncontroversial initiatives or measures such as school or public library funding.

> *"Putting a bunch of people to work on the same problem doesn't make them a team."*
> —Gerald M. Weinberg *(The Psychology of Computer Programming)*

Another option you have if the "perfect" treasurer cannot be found is to simply press on. Look for someone who is thorough, honest, easy to work with, trustworthy, and committed to your cause or candidate. Talk to your personal accountant or the person who prepares your taxes. CPAs have great community credibility, and they may be willing to provide report preparation on a pro bono basis or at a reduced rate.

The Campaign Manager

The campaign manager is the single most important position in a campaign. Where other jobs have finite responsibilities and time commitments, the job of campaign manager is open-ended. It is a lot to ask of anyone, especially on a volunteer basis. For this reason it is usually the first and sometimes the only paid position.

> *"Even the highest towers begin from the ground."*
> —Chinese saying

A campaign manager will interact with your volunteers more than any other person in the campaign, so good communication skills are a must, especially phone skills. The duties of the campaign manager vary greatly, depending on the number of individuals working in the inner circle. In general, he or she will do such things as attend coffees, debates, and events with the candidate and set up sign-in sheets while lending moral support. The campaign manager also *must* give candid feedback to the candidate without being indelicate.

If you are running a countywide partisan election campaign, having a manager is critical. You need someone to oversee it all and to be a source of support for the candidate. If you're working on an issue-based campaign, you can serve as the campaign manager with the use of this handbook. Although I believe it is a mistake to run for office without a campaign manager, if you are running for office in a small city, you can probably get away with it. Whether you're serving as your own campaign manager or have hired one, you still need capable people to head up various campaign tasks such as lawn signs, canvassing, and letters-to-the-editor. The most effective campaign teams are those with volunteer team members supervised by a strong manager.

Potential Sources for a Campaign Manager

I highly recommend teachers as campaign managers. They are generally smart, organized, articulate, and personable. They are able to speak to large groups of people and ask for things in simple, understandable ways. They tend to know computers, have a nice collection of presentable clothes, work hard, and are generally politically savvy. They are also likely to be available all summer. If you choose wisely, a teacher who is a campaign manager will force you to get everything ready during the summer so that your fall campaign will go much easier. The drawback of using a teacher is that he or she may be overwhelmed with school responsibilities in the fall and less available to the campaign.

Other potential sources for campaign managers are development directors for local charities, private schools, or nonprofit organizations. These people might consider short-term work for a candidate, and they will have a proven track record. Other leads: people who have worked on other political campaigns, for a United Way campaign, or for a Heart/Lung Association fund drive; and those who have organized local parades, 4-H fair shows, concerts, or county fairs.

In general, a good campaign manager is hard working, organized, intelligent, self-confident, and loyal. And, because appearance is important, this person should reflect the values and style of the candidate or campaign.

Maintaining Control

Recently I was an adviser to a campaign where the manager became problematic; he was parking illegally on city-owned land and then hassling the police with a "do-you-know-who-I'm-working-for?" attitude. To make matters worse, volunteers were complaining to the candidate about the campaign manager being unnecessarily rude. The candidate was at the end of his rope and called me to help find a way to let this volunteer go.

Although a candidate does not need this kind of stress, firing a volunteer manager can bring more headaches than it cures. So short of firing the manager, what can the candidate do?

First, the candidate always has the option of reorganizing the campaign so that the "manager" has less involvement and responsibility. Second, the candidate could deal with the campaign manager and the situation in a clear and straightforward manner. He or she could kindly explain how others were interpreting the manager's actions and how they were reflecting negatively on the campaign and the candidate. Because campaign managers are so closely affiliated with the candidate, there is an assumption that their activities are condoned by the candidate. A problematic situation like this must get immediate attention. Campaigns not only allow the community to see how a candidate will perform both publicly and under pressure but also allow the candidate to get some experience in dealing with awkward situations and people. Once in office, difficult people materialize all the time. If none of this works, the volunteer must be fired.

> *"We've run into a couple of problems, but nothing minor."*
> —Brenda Collier

When running for state legislative office, be prepared to pay the campaign manager handsomely. A good manager will bring many skills to the table and can mean big money to your campaign. Individuals, organizations, political action committees (PACs), and lobbyists want to contribute to "winning" campaigns, and your manager is a big indicator. A strong, experienced, well-organized, hardworking manager will bring an air of confidence to a candidate and campaign team. A candidate should listen to the campaign manager and follow his or her advice.

Ten Tips for Campaign Managers

1. Know the budget and have control of the checkbook.
2. Allow only one person to do scheduling for the candidate. This must be someone who works well with the candidate and is highly organized.
3. Manage the team/consultants and monitor their progress.
4. Hire professionals to develop campaign literature and television/radio spots.
5. Be positive, supporting, and encouraging to the candidate.

6. Raise money—lots and lots of money.
7. Loyalty is more important than experience.
8. Never waste donors' money.
9. Be organized.
10. Do not waste volunteers' time.

The Campaign Chair or Co-Chairs

When working on an issue-based campaign, the messenger is the message. Who heads it up is therefore directly linked to the success of the campaign. Here you have the choice of using either one person serving as a campaign chair or two people serving as co-chairs. Campaign chairs should be noncontroversial leaders in your community and may either serve in "name only" as a figurehead or as the actual campaign co-coordinator. Mostly they are the face of the campaign. They meet the media, they are part of the war room, and they work the endorsement circles of the community—the Rotary Club, the Chamber of Commerce, business leaders, and more. They gain power and stature when they seemingly have nothing personally to gain by the passage of the measure. So avoid using someone as a campaign chair who has a vested interest in the outcome of a campaign, such as a county commissioner for a county tax base.

"Loyalty is more important than experience."
— Bill Meuleman

Choose your co-chairs carefully. Well-respected community leaders with a strong community network are best. Their community relationships are part of the network the campaign will lean on to raise money and activate volunteers. They should balance each other, in gender and in interests. For a county measure, one may be from the rural area with ranching or farming ties, the other from the city with business ties. Selection of your chair or co-chairs is completely dependent on the ballot measure.

If the right chair or co-chairs cannot be found, don't use a campaign chair, but be sure to have top people able to respond to the press and willing to debate the opposition.

Finding Volunteers

Finding and directing volunteers is almost the same for each campaign task. Although the tasks vary considerably, only a small modification is necessary to organize your volunteer force for each specialized campaign activity.

Regardless of the activity, there are seven important things to remember about using volunteers:

1. Don't waste the volunteers' time. Have everything laid out and ready to go the moment they walk in the door. Begin and end on time. Do not encourage late arrivals by delaying the start of meetings.
2. Be prepared with anything they might need. If the task is to stuff envelopes, make sure there are enough stamps, sponges, pens, staples, and other necessities.
3. Call them ahead of time and let them know what they need to bring, such as extra staplers, clipboards, good walking shoes, a truck, etc.
4. Be clear about their tasks, expectations, and time commitments. Give clear written instructions and deadlines. This is especially important for those on phone banks.
5. Pick the right people for the job. Don't ask out-of-shape people to canvass hillsides with a 6 percent grade; don't place counterculture people as canvassers in conservative areas.
6. Keep volunteers informed, and support them. When you call, let them know how the campaign is going. Be sensitive to their schedules.
7. Treat your volunteers as you would highly paid employees.

It is a serious mistake to value volunteer time less simply because it is free. Disorganized campaigns lead to irritated and frustrated workers who may not return if things seem poorly run more than once. Some of the very best volunteers will not come back after even one bad encounter. To avoid such problems, the manager should assemble clerical teams to help set up other tasks, such as stapling lawn signs in preparation for the lawn sign team or looking up phone numbers for phone bankers. This preplanning is vital to creating a volunteer-friendly campaign, helps ensure the success of campaign activities, and allows the campaign to place people in jobs where they will work best.

Matching Volunteers to Skills

Although a small campaign can be run without volunteers, it would be a mistake to do so. When people work for a campaign, they become invested and want to see that investment pay off. Also, involving people in the process brings more interest to government and the political system. There is, however, one caution: If potential workers indicate an unwillingness to do a particular activity, don't make the mistake of begging and pleading to get help in that task.

"Nothing is particularly hard, if you divide it into small jobs."
—Henry Ford

I once placed a woman on the phones who told me she didn't like to phone. I found it hard to believe that in this day and age anyone would have trouble talking on the phone—plus I was desperate. What a mistake. She was painfully uncomfortable calling people she didn't know and projected a poor image of the campaign. I couldn't take her off once I saw my error, because that would have called further attention to the problem, making her more uncomfortable. I left her on the phone for about a half hour and then told her that I had finished my work and asked if she would mind if we shared her phone. She gratefully gave it up. Similarly, if a volunteer reports that he doesn't like to canvass, believe him. It is better for the campaign to have people doing tasks they enjoy.

"In life, as in any game whose outcome depends on both skill and luck, the rational response to bad odds is to try harder."

—Marvin Harris

Here is a tip for placing people who say they would rather not call or canvass: Some who do not like to work phones actually do not like to make "cold calls"—that is, they do not like to call people who may be opposed to the candidate or measure. Quite often, these same people may be willing to make calls to identified supporters, such as in a get-out-the-vote effort. Similarly with canvassers, some do not like to canvass because they dislike knocking on doors and talking to the residents. However, these same people may be willing to do a literature drop, a door hanger, install lawn signs, or other tasks where knocking and talking are not involved.

Supervise volunteers so workers who do not do well on a task are not called a second time to help in the same task. For instance, if a volunteer is struggling at a phone bank, simply note it in the spreadsheet you use to keep track of volunteers or on the volunteer's 3-by-5-inch contact card (see Chapter 3, "The Volunteer Organization"), so that campaign workers will not mistakenly call the person again for that task. Similarly, if an individual is great at a task like phoning, keep him or her away from other campaign activities to avoid campaign burnout. Use volunteers where they excel.

The same kind of supervision is necessary for each volunteer activity. For example, if a canvasser returns without notes for lawn signs, no impressions of voter attitudes, and having only partially covered the assigned area, perhaps canvassing is not the best job for that person. Note this in the volunteer data system. Be sure to make a note as to why, and move that person over to something like lawn sign placement and maintenance. If it can be avoided, do not place volunteers in jobs where they will have a bad time or reflect poorly on the campaign. Attention to these kinds of details helps volunteers be more successful and keeps them returning to help in future elections.

Potential Volunteer Sources

Those involved in grassroots campaigning must find people willing to help. Finding volunteers can initially seem daunting, but remember, the only people you can be certain will not help you are those you do not ask. The following is a list of places to look:

- Your family, friends, and business associates
- Women's rights groups
- Former candidates, office holders, and their volunteers
- Local service groups
- Labor unions
- Teachers or school associations
- Any special interest groups dealing, for example, with the environment, human services, hunting, and fishing

In nearly every election there is an issue so controversial that voters will act solely on the basis of the opposing positions held by the two candidates. These issues create voters who become "ticket splitters" because they allow an issue to influence what would otherwise be a straight-line party vote. Issues that lead to ticket splitting can motivate a voter to work or vote *against* a candidate rather than *for* a candidate.

> *"Nonpolitical issues are the most political."*
>
> —Bill Meulemans

In general, issues that create ticket splitters can translate into both volunteers and money for your campaign. Here is a list of some groups and issues that are more inclined than most to let a single issue influence their votes:

- Veterans
- Sportsmen, fly-fishermen, and hunters
- Environmentalists
- Timber and logging advocates
- Choice
- Land-use advocates
- Seniors
- Tax and antitax groups
- Gay rights and anti–gay rights activists
- Public union employees
- Identifiable work groups such as teachers and firefighters
- Advocates for gun ownership

Volunteer Sign-Up Sheet

In addition to finding volunteers in the groups listed above, you can create a form (see figure 1.2) for sign-ups at coffees, debates, and gatherings once the campaign is under way.

VOLUNTEER SIGN-UP SHEET

Name (please print)	Home Phone	I would like to volunteer for the following (please check all that apply):							
		Canvass Neighborhoods	Phone Banks	Clerical	Lawn Sign Location Address	Donation	Letter-to-the-Editor	Endor. ad?	E-mail

Figure 1.2 Example of a Volunteer Sign-Up Sheet

"Public business, my son, must
always be done by somebody . . . if
wise men decline it, others will not; if
honest men refuse it, others will not."
                                    —John Adams

2

THE CAMPAIGN BROCHURE

IN THIS CHAPTER
- *Campaign Theme and Message Development*
- *Polling*
- *Brochure Development*
- *Campaign Slogans*
- *Logo*
- *Layout*
- *Voters' Pamphlet*

The campaign brochure is fundamental to a campaign. It serves as an introductory piece for candidates and should include photos, a biography, and information that identifies why the candidate would be ideal in public office. If the candidate has previously held office, the brochure is used to underscore past accomplishments and activities and bring them to the attention of the electorate. Unless the campaign plan calls for developing different brochures for the primary and the general election, the brochure should be free of partisan politics, because it travels with the candidate to all public functions.

"Leaders are people who step forward, who influence thinking and action. They emerge to meet the needs."

—William Gore

In an issue-based campaign, the brochure may give a sense of time and history reflecting on past community goals and ideals. An issue-based brochure should clearly explain what is before the voters, delineate the potential impacts of yes and no votes, and include testimonials from important community leaders advocating the passage or defeat of the ballot item.

In either a candidate or an issue-based campaign it is important to develop a theme and a message before writing and printing a brochure, because it is from under this framework that campaign activities will develop and flow.

Campaign Theme and Message Development

Before you sit down to write a brochure, you must develop a campaign theme and message. While political strategists use the words "theme" and "message" in different ways, sometimes interchangeably, for our purposes a "theme" covers the overarching issues that capture the spirit of what voters want, whereas a "message" is a single idea used to bring that theme to the voters.

For example, if you're working on a campaign to fund co-curricular activities for your school district that were eliminated because of budget cuts, your *theme* will likely include the idea of reinstating these programs. However, your *message* will center on the idea that it is no longer enough for students to have a 4.0 GPA if they want to get into a good college or land a better job—they must also be involved in co-curricular and extracurricular school activities. Briefly, your message is "opportunity."

A theme embraces what the voters want and defines the candidate or issue-based campaign in that context, whereas a message is a believable application of the theme to the voters that cuts through to the emotional level. The voters want great schools, which must have a combination of challenging course work and co-curricular activities. You sell these programs for what they are: opportunity for our children. They help students get into competitive universities or land great jobs, they are the reason some kids stay in school, and they represent another layer of preparation that enriches the next generation's future. It all comes back to providing opportunities for youths to excel. It isn't about money; it isn't about how high your property taxes will go. If you're arguing money, you're on "their" message.

When you're selling a bond measure to expand and improve a community asset, such as a library, you are not selling what a great deal the voters are getting, you're selling much more. You know what the voters want: They want a community resource that is enhanced in some way. That's your theme, and you're going to give them what they want.

Your message, however, is about acknowledging those who gave gifts to future generations by building the first library. It is about embracing history and the rich legacy of libraries in our culture. It is about a place where old and young can gather, as they have for a hundred years, to read a book. Your message: "It's about community."

In the presidential campaign of 1992, Clinton had a theme of environmental protection, lower crime rates, education, and universal health care, among other things—things that voters wanted. Each of the issues of the overall campaign theme was then conveyed to the American people through the message "It's the economy." For example, we need to protect our environment to ensure better *jobs* in the future; we need to provide our children with better education if we want a *work force* that can compete on the world market; providing opportunities for everyone to get a college education means *keeping America competitive;* affordable health care allows a family *to get ahead;* high crime rates are destroying our communities and marginalizing *businesses;* and so on. Everything comes back to the message "It's the economy": Addressing the issues that people want will lead to a better economy.

In his 1996 campaign, Clinton's message was "It's the little issues." The theme was similar to that of the 1992 campaign, but with the U.S. economy booming, Clinton's team moved the campaign focus in and personalized it—a very effective approach that has rarely been applied at the national level. In that campaign, education translated into college IRAs, computers in the classrooms, and a million volunteers to ensure that every American child could read by the third grade. Environment became gifts to our grandchildren and ways to recreate with our kids in the summer. Combating crime became distributing 50,000 cell phones to neighborhood crime watch groups. Health care became welfare reform and allowing new mothers to stay longer than forty-eight hours in the hospital. The Clinton campaign assumed that while people care about world peace, worry about the global economy, and dislike political repression in foreign lands, it was personal issues that connected directly with Americans and their lives. By delivering seemingly simple solutions to community and family issues, Clinton presented a clear message of hope in the context of home and community, making the issues tangible.

> *"Leaders can conceive and articulate goals that lift people out of their petty preoccupations and carry them above the conflicts that tear a society apart."*
> —John W. Gardner

A campaign message is how a theme is communicated to the public. It's a story you tell over and over, a story you can tell in a few seconds: "It's the economy"; "This is about opportunity"; "It's the small issues"; "It's hope"; "It's about community." A well-crafted message moves the debate away from which candidate can be trusted to whom the voters trust to do the job. A theme and message articulate the point that the candidate knows *what* job needs to be done. Voters will naturally make the connection that the candidate who knows what needs to be done will be the one more likely to do it.

In an issue-based campaign, a message should tell the voters *why* a task needs to be done. The message should reach them on an emotional level: hope, opportunity, safety, service, preserving our past, planning for the inevitable.

To create a theme and message, your campaign committee must assess the strengths and weaknesses of your candidate or ballot measure. Ask, and answer, the questions of who will vote for your candidate or proposition over your opposition, and why. You must also look for any fatal flaws in your candidate or issue. The campaign message and theme will develop from this process and will become the foundation for your slogan, ads, and media efforts. Once you have a message, do not get off it, and don't let your opponents pull you off.

By taking a critical look at your candidate or issue and listing the strengths and weaknesses, your campaign team is better able to shape and communicate the theme of a campaign through the message. For example, a woman who is energetic, feisty, and steadfast translates into pluses and minuses. The pluses are that she's a fighter, has integrity, is honest, and will fight for the community. The minuses may be that she is pushy, shrill, dogmatic, or overbearing (a word reserved in American society almost exclusively for women).

The charge of the campaign committee is to frame the negative into a positive: Pushy becomes persistent or steadfast; dogmatic becomes directness, which goes with honesty and integrity. All this is communicated through the message that flows from what the candidate represents. For instance, if a community is being overrun by developers and the quality of life is compromised by the inherent impacts of growth, couple a message of thoughtful, planned growth with a candidate's strengths of honesty, integrity, persistence, and willingness to fight for the community. Again, the message is planned, thoughtful growth, and every question answered comes back to this message—all under the umbrella of the theme "quality of life."

Through this process campaigns identify issues that create relationships with the voters and that translate into money and volunteers. For example, people in a particular neighborhood are concerned about development, so the campaign underscores the creation of a park in close proximity to the neighborhood. It is not about stopping growth but rather about mitigating the negative effects of growth. The campaign looks at the impacts growth has on your community and presents approaches that allow growth without compromising quality of life. This in turn will create relationships within your community. For parents and teachers, growth affects class size; for others it's about traffic, open space, or availability of resources, such as water. If you present yourself as antigrowth, you're done; instead lead people to where two worlds can coexist or even enhance one another rather than prophesying what will happen if these two worlds are allowed to collide. In short, planning for growth is good for business, education, resources, neighborhood integrity, and so on.

This concept is important in direct mail, ads, brochure development, speaking engagements, debates, and campaign endorsements, and it will be given further attention in later sections and chapters.

> *"I use not only all the brains I have, but all I can borrow."*
> —Woodrow Wilson

Establishing a strong, succinct, and believable theme and message creates relationships, which in turn creates voters interested in helping and giving.

Very simply, you want a majority to see your side as a better choice than the other side. This is the time to assess the strengths and weakness of your opponent. If your opponent has not defined him- or herself, you can work this process in reverse and define that person for the voters: "My opponent is pro-growth."

The brochure is basic to your campaign. You will walk it door-to-door, mail it to households, and hand it out at debates. The voters who receive it must get the message of your campaign, which will state in subtle and not so subtle ways why people should vote as you want them to. It should also imply why they should *not* vote for your opponent.

Polling

Polling provides a campaign with a snapshot of public opinion. While a benchmark poll looks at where the candidate or a ballot issue is ranked among voters before any campaigning or distribution of information has been done, tracking polls provide ongoing feedback on the impact a campaign has in swaying public opinion.

Benchmark Polls

Conducting a benchmark poll may be the most efficient and accurate way to determine voter concerns before you develop your message. As First Lady Rosalynn Carter remarked, "It is difficult to lead

> *"Public sentiment is everything. With public sentiment, nothing can fail. Without it, nothing can succeed."*
> —Abraham Lincoln

people where they do not want to go." While it is important to have elected officials with strong core values, it is even more important that officials listen to and embrace "where people want to go." Having a clear reading of voter concerns will help your campaign develop and direct a message that will be heard.

It can also inform you about when to keep quiet and which issues to avoid. Generally, a benchmark poll is done in advance of a campaign, and it can be invaluable in developing a campaign strategy, theme, and message.

A good benchmark poll can take as long as thirty minutes per call. It will include questions that lead to information about the following:

- The name recognition of the major candidates
- The favorability of that name recognition
- The voter's knowledge of state and local politics
- The degree of partisanship of the voter
- The issues most important to the voter, by gender, age, and party affiliation
- The education, age, and gender of those who support you and of those who support your opposition
- The income level of those who support you
- Whom the voter will support if the election were held tomorrow (or which direction the voter is leaning)
- Whether the voter intends to vote, is likely to vote, or is unlikely to vote
- What form of message works best, both for your candidate and for the opposition
- What attacks will hurt the most, for both you and your opposition

Polling Messaging with "Push Questions"

Push questions, not to be mistaken with "push polling," "are recognized by all the major associations and leading political consultants as a valid and legitimate research tool for the purposes of testing ad messages and examining the collective viewpoints of electorate subgroups" (Karl G. Feld, *Campaigns & Elections,* (May 2000, p. 63).

"I've got to follow them; I am their leader."

—Alexandre Ledru-Rollin

Push questioning will ask whether a statement is very, somewhat, or not convincing. It will do so for positive questions for both the candidate paying for the poll and that candidate's opponent. It will also test negatives on each of the candidates—and do so equally.

In one section of a benchmark for a state legislative race between our candidate, Democrat Alan Bates, and his opponent, Republican Jane Hunts, we were looking for what the opposition might use against our candidate as well as how negatives might play against his opponent. Of the questions testing the negatives of Alan Bates, this question came out on top:

> Is this a very convincing, somewhat convincing, not very convincing or not at all convincing reason to vote *against* Alan Bates?
>
> *"Alan Bates is opposed to every anti-tax measure on the ballot this fall. He opposes cutting the state income tax, opposes increasing the deductibility of federal tax, opposes allowing voters the right to decide on all new or increased taxes, and opposes amending the state constitution to require government to return the tax kicker."*

This question had a Very Convincing rating of sixteen points, and a total convincing score (the total of very and somewhat convincing) of fifty-two points. The not convincing side weighed in at thirty-seven points.

Of the six anti-Hunts push questions, this one came out at the bottom:

> Is this a very convincing, somewhat convincing, not very convincing or not at all convincing reason to vote *against* Jane Hunts?
>
> *"Jane Hunts has absolutely no government experience. She has never been elected or appointed to any office. In order to effectively represent southern Oregon in Salem, our representative needs the experience Jane Hunts just doesn't have."*

This question came in with a total convincing score of forty-one (of which only nineteen points were for Very Convincing) and with forty-eight points for not convincing. Hmmm. Better think twice about going after Hunts on experience.

Our benchmark poll gave us information about what would or would not work for both Bates and Hunts as positive messaging as well as what would and would not work on attacks.

Getting Data Without a Poll

If your campaign has no money or, more to the point, does not want to spend thousands on a benchmark poll, you can get much of the information a benchmark would give you for free.

Using recent voting history of issue-based campaigns can provide candidates a clear road map of voter opinion—precinct by precinct. For example, in the 2000 general election, Oregon had

"When two people agree all the time, one of them is unnecessary."

—William Wrigley

twenty-five ballot measures before the voters. Among other things, they covered issues involving school funding, gay and lesbian rights, mandatory sentencing, campaign finance reform, drug-related property forfeiture, land use, taxes, powers of the state legislature, tobacco settlement funds, baiting traps, background checks for firearm purchases, and linking teacher pay to student performance. Although some of these measures passed (or failed) in every county, that does not mean they passed or failed in every precinct within the county.

If you're running a campaign in a state that is not as measure-happy as Oregon, potential campaign issues in your voting area can be ferreted out in other ways: letters-to-the-editor, minutes of city council or county commissioner meetings, editorials, general news stories, and county and city elections. Given that issues pop up in candidate elections, reviewing which issues were at the center of those campaigns can be very helpful.

In 2002 I worked on a county commissioner campaign where the candidate had been elected to his conservative city council post on a no-growth platform. Knowing that growth was an issue in my city as well and that the two cities represent opposite ends of the political spectrum, we knew we had an issue that would transcend the county's political schism: growth and the effects it has on our region. Using a tone of "keeping a little of what makes this area special" in his last television ad before the election, we were able to take an issue that everyone cared about and couple it with a pro-environment undertone. This allowed us to go back and lock his drifting base without losing swing voters. This proved to be an important move in this close election. (See figure 8.14.)

Be Creative

Many small communities conduct citizen surveys as a way to track residents' concerns and to assess the job performance of city employees. This is part of the public record and is available for the asking. You can get similar information, minus the job performance of the governing body, at the local Chamber of Commerce. The census also has a wealth of information, and although it doesn't go to the precinct level, it does have helpful information broken down by cities, counties, regions, and states.

Special-interest groups that support your candidate or issue may have recently conducted a poll to track voter support of a particular issue, especially if that issue has been or soon will be placed before the voters. Such polls typically assess support according to voter profile within a region, county, or city.

Benchmark Polls on a Shoestring

If you have no money and are determined to run a benchmark poll, you can do so using volunteers and a professional pollster or a college professor who knows or teaches polling. Depending on the length of the questionnaire, each caller can complete three to five calls per hour.

"You just can't buy your way out of a bad impression."
—Cool Hand Luke

To pull this off you must have three things in order: First, draft the questions for the professional who is oversee-ing the project. I don't care how impartial you think your questions are—they're biased. If you do not have a seasoned pollster reviewing the questions you will spend a lot of volunteer hours on a poll that may or may not give you accurate results and in a worse-case-scenario could lead your campaign in the wrong direction.

Second, have plenty of volunteers who excel on the phone. Let's say you want to conduct a benchmark poll with 300 randomly selected voters. If each caller can poll three people per hour, you need 100 volunteer hours. Should you be lucky enough to land a phone bank location with ten lines and each worker puts in a one-hour shift, that means you need two shifts of ten phone bankers (twenty volunteers) per night for five nights. That's a lot of volun-teers.

Third, obtain (or generate) a random voter list from your county clerk or election office. The clerk's office will sell you a printout with the number of voters you need to reach to achieve a 3–5 percent margin of error (between 384 and 1,100 voters). In my county, 25–30 percent of the lists provided by the clerk's office have phone numbers listed. No matter how many phone numbers are on your lists, do not expect your callers to look up numbers in addi-tion to polling. To fill in all the phone numbers on your lists, do one of three things: set up a clerical team to look up phone numbers; turn the list of regis-

"Imagination is more important than knowledge."
—Albert Einstein

tered voters over to data-entry volunteers and have them drop in phone numbers off the Web; or buy phone lists.

Looking up phone numbers is not a task for everyone, so be sure to ask your volunteers when signing them up if this is something they like to do. Some people are quite good at it, while others are painfully slow. For the work party, make sure everyone has a comfortable chair and table, good lighting, a phone book, and a straight-edge—such as a ruler or a strip of card stock. This is a two-hour shift. Avoid gregarious and chatty volunteers in this task.

Another option is to ask groups endorsing your campaign if they have a list of the registered voters for your area. Many endorsing organizations make this sort of information available to all candidates or issue-based campaigns they support. Often these lists include more information than the county lists, including voting frequency and phone numbers. This should be listed as an in-kind contribution to your campaign.

Creating a Random Voter List for Polling

To generate your own calling list of randomly selected voters, either use the list of registered voters acquired by an endorsing organization, or obtain a list from your clerk's office or elections department. For campaign polling purposes, you really don't need to call nonvoters. So if you are able to obtain a list that indicates whether those listed have voted in recent elections, all the better. Clearly, if someone registered fifteen years ago and hasn't voted since, there is no reason to believe that he or she will suddenly start with your race. Our state is authorized to strike from the rolls anyone who has not voted in the last five elections. Check with the county or the secretary of state's office to determine how often (if ever) the voter rolls are purged in your area.

However you acquire your list, be sure to ask for it in Excel format. (Remember that Excel has only so many cells per page so if you have more registered voters than Excel can handle, break it down into smaller files.) Also make sure there is a heading identifier for each column. If the county uses codes for the column headings, ask for a legend so you can figure out what's what when you begin working with the data.

In our county, every registered voter is identified by an assigned number. Similarly, statewide organizations assign their own numbers. Make life easy on yourself: Whether you're working from county or state lists, never separate this number from the assigned voter. An Excel document created for polling needs only a first and last name, a phone number, and the voter ID number.

The next two things you must do are important so pay attention: First, you must use a process for random selection of voters from the database. Second, you need to make sure that the number of voters selected is proportional to the total number of voters in your election area.

For the first step, insert a column in your Excel spreadsheet, assign a random number within that column for each of the voters, and then sort these numbers numerically. If you don't know how to do this and have no friends with this skill, go to the help menu and type in "random sampling" or something similar until you find what you need. If all else fails, read the Excel manual.

Once you have a random sample of voters, sort it again for phone numbers. You do this for three reasons. First, you only want to call people whose numbers you have: if you have names with no phone numbers, volunteers get confused. Second, you want to be able to organize duplicates for your volunteers. Believe me, you do not want to call a home and ask for Mary and then ten minutes later call the same number and ask for George while a volunteer down the hall is calling the same number asking for one of George and Mary's voting-age children. This, my friend, drives voters crazy. The third reason to sort your random list by phone number is so you can check for balance within the list itself.

Balancing Your Random List

If you are generating your own randomized voter list using Excel, take the time to calculate the percentages of phone numbers within each prefix to be sure that your list reflects the percentages of voters registered within those areas. For example, if voters living in the 488, 482, and 552 prefix area represent 10 percent of the county vote, then make sure those numbers are close to 10 percent of all the voters called.

In the 2002 general election in Oregon, a local television station hired a polling firm from Maryland to conduct a tracking poll about a week before election day. The poll included a community college bond measure, a local school measure, the governor's race, and the voters' opinion on the war with Iraq. After the survey was conducted, I was called and told that the poll indicated voter approval of the community college measure by five points, with 11 percent undecided. After the two money measures went down by fifteen points, I checked around and found that the poll not only indicated that the community college bond measure would pass but that the other money measure would too, and that our county supported the democratic candidate for governor and opposed the war in Iraq. All suspect.

We contacted the polling firm and were told, "Those interviewed were selected by the random variation of the last *four* digits of telephone numbers. A cross-section of exchanges was utilized in order to ensure an accurate reflection of the *state* (emphasis added). Quotas were assigned to reflect the voter registration of distribution by county."

While southern Oregon may be an anomaly, voters within this area vote very differently according to where they live. Some areas are the most progressive in the state while others are the most conservative. By using the *last four digits* of the phone number without taking into account prefixes, which delineate different areas of the county, one might conclude that a disproportionate number of voters in the more progressive prefixes were polled, skewing the results. The clearest evidence that this had happened was in the results of the question about the war with Iraq. That question alone could be a litmus test of the validity of the poll. It is simply not possible that the majority of residents in Jackson County, Oregon, would be opposed to U.S. involvement in Iraq—at any time, much less at the beginning. While some areas in the county would register overwhelming opposition, that would not be true of the majority of the county.

One last step: Be sure your final list reflects countywide gender and party registration.

Polling for Dollars

If you're working on a state legislative race, a professionally conducted poll can mean money for your campaign. Lobbyists and PACs are reluctant to give money to campaigns that "think" they will win. However, show that you're close to your opponent in a legitimate poll, and checkbooks will open. To spend thousands on a poll in hopes of attracting PAC money is risky and works against common sense. Still, it happens, and if the numbers are good, it can pay off. Polls run by volunteers don't count here.

Professionally conducted polling tends to be expensive. To cut costs, you might consider offering to include other candidates in the poll if their campaigns will contribute to the cost. Also, some firms will reduce the price if you provide the workers to make the calls, although this is becoming less acceptable with the large, reputable firms. Again, bear in mind that statewide polling can be an enormous undertaking. However, because it can and should be done before your campaign kickoff, it is often possible to do a benchmark poll without adding much extra stress to a volunteer force or your campaign budget.

Brochure Development

While the campaign committee will help in developing the campaign message and theme, have only one or two people work with you or the candidate in writing the brochure. Obviously you want a good writer who has a couple of free days. The initial writing takes only a few hours, but it is almost always followed by many rewrites. These rewrites should return to the committee to check message and theme, and before it is sent to the printer, the committee must have the final say over the content, theme, message, and "look." Give yourself enough time. If the committee does not like what it sees, you need time to make the necessary corrections before delivering it to the printer.

If you write your own campaign brochure, have someone read it critically when you've finished. The emphasis here is on *critically*. We all love our own words, and our friends are often loath to condemn them. You need someone you can trust, someone who has the political savvy to read your work, correct any errors, and make suggestions.

Pictures

Before you lay out a brochure, the candidate should visit a photographer. I have always been fortunate to work with local professionals who have been willing to contribute their talents to local campaigns. Well-meaning friends with above-average equipment may not get what you want—and, really, nothing compares to professional work. Amateurish photos will hurt your campaign. If a professional will not volunteer his or her time, this is a good place to spend money. If the first sitting does not produce the "right" photo, invest in a second shoot. Also provide the local papers with a photo (usually different shots but from the same sitting) so they will use your photo rather than one generated by their news team. If you e-mail a good-quality photo, it will be particularly easy for the newspapers to use. After your candidate is elected, continue this practice.

When you are campaigning for an issue-based campaign, photos are often easier to come by. For example, if you're working on a school tax base measure, visit the yearbook class at the middle and high school. They save photographs of all age groups and in many activities. For a park program, try the YMCA or the parks department; even city and county offices may have photos, so check there as well. For historic photos of your city or county, try a local historian or historical society. Show what will be accomplished with the passage of this measure through pictures as well as text. Many photographers will let you use their photos in issue-based campaigns as long as their name appears with the photo in a credit line.

Use pictures as a way to break up the text and give the brochure a substantial feel. Most brochures for candidates contain at least one picture of the candidate. This is important to increase name and face recognition. With that recognition comes familiarity, which is psychologically important for the voter. The candidate begins to feel like a friend and a celebrity all at once. You may also carefully select other photos to create an image of who this person is. There may be pictures of the candidate at work, with the family, at play (e.g., batting in a softball game or fly-fishing), with seniors, at a preschool, a public school, a hospital, or a park. Include whatever might both positively connect the candidate with his or her lifestyle and characterize what is important in the community.

Depending on your budget and the size of your brochure, you may just stop with the picture of the candidate. But if you have more, be sure the pictures add to or underscore the story the campaign wants to tell. Put thought into the selection of pictures. Try to show the diversity of your community in the photos: people of all ages and ethnic groups, working class and professionals, men and women. Whether the campaign is doing a studio shot or one of the candidate on the stump, be sure to bring extra clothes for different settings. Brochures that show a candidate at a school, senior center, park, with family, or whatever, are ostensibly intended to show the individual in his or her everyday life over a period of time. However, if the candidate is wearing the same clothes in each shot, it looks contrived and you miss an opportunity to create the feel you want.

One caution here: Avoid photos that picture the candidate standing or sitting coincidentally near a celebrity. Novice campaigners are anxious to show themselves hobnobbing with the elite and will select pictures that show themselves in the general proximity of a celebrity. If you want to use a photo of your candidate with the governor, be sure it is a photo of your candidate with the governor. One brochure I saw had the candidate looking around a plant that was situated behind the governor who was being photographed with other people. This is interpreted for just what it is by the voters.

Some candidates when being photographed with a "name" lean toward or tilt their head toward the celebrity when being photographed ("I'm with him!"). This pose can suggest weakness on the part of your candidate and may have a subtle but negative influence on the voters.

Urge the photographer to take some pictures of the candidate outside. Change the background, walk toward the camera, sit on a bike and lean on the handlebars. (This particular pose, with or without the bike in it, makes a great shot.) Arrange for people to meet you and the photographer for a few shots that can be taken outside, in front of businesses, back-dropped with trees or historic buildings. (See figure 2.1A and B.)

Anxious to show a candidate with all the typical campaign requisites, campaigns will typically use pictures of their candidate at a senior center, in front of a police car, shaking hands with a business leader in front of a factory, reading to children, and on the front lawn with the family. But when a majority of campaign brochures include the same array, your literature will fade into the wallpaper. Make an effort to use the medium effectively and bring spontaneity and motion into your brochure photos. Capture your candidate in a quiet moment reading over papers, through a window at night burning the midnight oil, conferring with a colleague while leaning over a

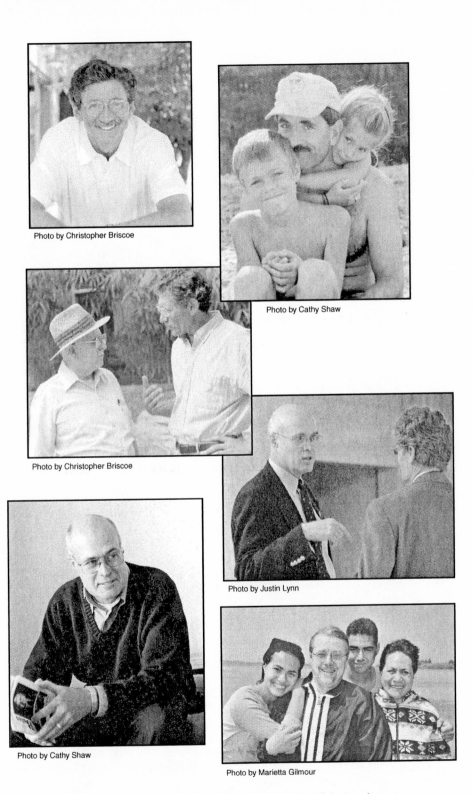

Photo by Christopher Briscoe

Photo by Cathy Shaw

Photo by Christopher Briscoe

Photo by Justin Lynn

Photo by Cathy Shaw

Photo by Marietta Gilmour

Figure 2.1A Examples of Candidate Photos That Work Well in Brochures

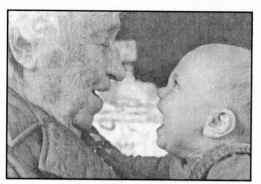

Photo by Cathy Shaw

Photo by Marla Cates

Photo by Cathy Shaw

Figure 2.1B Examples of Photos That Work Well in an Issue-Based Brochure.
When selecting photos for issue-based campaigns, look for ones with movement
and that elicit emotion. The above were used for funding youth sports programs,
water conservation, and state funding for seniors and public schools. The bottom left had the caption: "What future do we offer them?"

desk, and playing with the family from last summer's vacation. This might be where your friend with above-average camera skills can help.

When selecting pictures for either a candidate or issue-based campaign, be sure to look at the whole picture, not just the subject of the picture. In the Campaign for the Carnegie, I selected an interior library photo with a young patron reading in a crowded, cluttered room to demonstrate the dismal state of our library. However, I did not notice that directly behind the subject was a display rack with *Mad* magazines. Luckily the librarians on the committee caught my error.

Campaign Slogans

Years ago, slogans were printed next to a candidate's name on the ballot. At that time, with media playing a lesser role in politics, having a catchy slogan was critical for a win on election day. Slogans can still be very effective, but they require a great deal of thought by the campaign committee. Do not invent a slogan just to have one. Use your campaign message and design a slogan that

> *"Out of intense complexities, intense simplicities emerge."*
> —Winston Churchill

underscores and reinforces it. Sit with your committee, list the strengths of your candidate or measure, and brainstorm possibilities. Once you think you have one, brainstorm on all the ways it could be used against you or hurt your cause. Work through this process until you come up with the right combination.

The slogan is a simple statement about why you should be elected or why the voters should vote for your measure. It should also imply why *not* to vote for your opponent or imply what a no vote may lead to in an issue-based campaign. Your slogan must not depart from your campaign message, and it should evoke a gut emotion. One very effective slogan used in an issue-based campaign in California simply said, "Share the Water." Who can argue with the idea of sharing? It is a friendly thought that is encouraged throughout our lives. It also implies that the water is not being shared.

I was on a campaign that used the slogan "Now Let's Choose Leadership." I was concerned that this slogan would sound patronizing. I was also concerned that those who previously voted for the incumbent, who enjoyed a six-point registration advantage, would feel they were being scolded. Furthermore, this slogan tended to reinforce the perception that our candidate was arrogant.

A Democrat running against an incumbent for the Second Congressional District in Oregon used another problematic slogan. Since the district was formed two decades ago, only Republicans have been elected—three to be exact—and by overwhelming numbers. However, in this particular election, the incumbent had committed so many campaign violations and was misbehaving both in public and in Congress in such a way that it looked as though this Democrat might win the seat.

The Democrat called on me and some other local people to talk strategy in our part of the district, and he also took that opportunity to show us his brochure. Although it was a handsome brochure, it featured a poorly conceived slogan: "It's time we had a Congressman we can be proud of." While I understood that the brochure referred to the incumbent, who was in core meltdown, it overlooked the fact that for more than ten years, Second District Oregonians had voted in huge numbers for a congressman they were very proud of. You can't hope to attract voters to your side of the street by insulting them.

Most important, the slogans in both of these examples imply that the campaign is about the candidate. Effective slogans stem from messages that are about the voters and their communities, not the candidate or, as in these two examples, the incumbent.

For a local restaurant tax to fund wastewater treatment plant upgrades and open-space land acquisition, our opposition used the slogan "Don't Swallow the Meals Tax." This is a clever slogan because it works on different levels: People who swallow something are duped, and then, of course, the tax was on food.

In one open-space campaign, we used the slogan "Parks, Now and Forever." People who opposed the measure saw ours and used the slogan "Parks: *Pay* Now and Forever." A very clever counter slogan. We should have chosen ours more carefully.

In 1997 a group of Oregonians put together an initiative to overturn a previously voter-approved ballot measure allowing physician-assisted suicide. The new initiative was well financed, with billboards and lawn signs everywhere. In the upper right-hand corner of the signs they had the previous measure's number (16) in a circle with a line through it. Next to that was the slogan "Fatally Flawed" and below the slogan was "Yes on 51."

While this was clearly a professional campaign, they mistakenly used a very ambiguous slogan. Basically, it was stating that the previously passed ballot initiative (Measure 16) was "fatally flawed" (physician-assisted suicide) and that a "yes" vote on *this* measure (51) would overturn that one. However, the way the sign was laid out, it appeared that Measure 51, not 16, was "fatally flawed."

During the campaign, I was called by a local organizer to help defeat the referendum. I suggested that the campaign did not need any help, they only

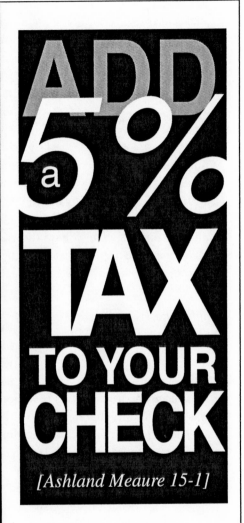

DON'T SWALLOW THE MEALS TAX

[VOTE NO ON 15-1]

Measure 15-1, Ashland's proposed meals tax, is a regressive tax because:

15-1 IS NOT A TOURIST TAX. THE BURDEN OF THE TAX WILL BE PAID BY YOU, THE ASHLAND CONSUMER.

FOOD IS A BASIC NECESSITY. THIS TAX WILL SEVERELY IMPACT STUDENTS, THE ELDERLY, THE POOR, AND OTHERS ON A FIXED INCOME.

IT IS NOT A LUXURY TAX. BECAUSE OF TODAY'S BUSY SCHEDULES, AN AVERAGE OF 48¢ OF EVERY FOOD DOLLAR IS SPENT ON PREPARED MEALS OUTSIDE THE HOME.

IT WILL AUTHORIZE INCREASES UP TO 5% WITHOUT FURTHER VOTE FROM THE PUBLIC.

IT IS CONFUSING, DIFFICULT TO MANAGE, AND COSTLY TO IMPLEMENT.

IT IS SHORTSIGHTED. IF THE STATE LEGISLATURE IMPOSES A STATEWIDE SALES TAX IT COULD NEGATE ANY LOCAL SALES TAXES.

IT WILL PUT ASHLAND ON THE MAP AS THE ONLY CITY IN AMERICA TO IMPOSE A MEALS TAX WITHOUT FIRST HAVING AN OVERALL SALES TAX IN PLACE.

ADD a 5% TAX TO YOUR CHECK

[Ashland Meaure 15-1]

Back   *Front*

Figure 2.2 Don't Swallow the Meals Tax Brochure. Brochure layout: two-panel, front and back. Note that the front and top back of the brochure are visually striking, but the lower, dense, reversed type is hard to read. Also note that this brochure went to press with a typo on the front panel. This is not the responsibility of the graphic designer but rather the campaign team. Avoid this by having a number of people proofread the text.

needed to adopt the same slogan as the opposition: "Fatally Flawed." Because voters naturally associate a negative slogan with a negative vote, every "Yes on 51" lawn sign, billboard, and commercial would become a "No on 51" pitch. Whether they took my advice or came to it themselves, the "No on 51" campaign co-opted the same slogan of the "Yes on 51" campaign, and with very little money it was defeated at the polls— only this time instead of losing by one point, they lost by twenty.

"Leaders have a significant role in creating the state of mind that is society."

—John W. Gardner

As a general rule, you don't want a negative slogan or idea associated with a "yes" vote ("Fatally Flawed"). It's preferable to have a negative slogan, such as in the meals tax example given above, associated with a "no" vote and a positive slogan ("Share the Water") associated with a "yes" vote on a ballot measure or proposition. In the campaign to overturn the measure allowing physician-assisted suicide, the slogan "Yes on 51" campaign expected too much of the voter.

"The aim of marketing is to make selling superfluous."

—Peter Drucker

During my first run for mayor, I used the slogan "Building a Better Community." I chose this slogan because of citywide concerns about growth and development. I wanted a positive slogan that suggested to the voters that more was not necessarily better and that it was a community that needed to be built, not indiscriminate construction.

The following are examples I have pulled from brochures in my files. Using a slogan is optional. Better to omit it than have a bad one.

"It's about people, not politics."
"Experience * Leadership * Commitment"
"The best . . . for the best"
"A voice that will be heard"
"A Strong Voice for [Place]"
"With his experience . . . It makes sense."
"Unbought and unbossed"
"Because nothing counts like results"
"Straightforward, Fair, Effective"
"Tough, committed, fighting for us"
"A New Voice! New Energy!"
"It's time to rotate the crops."
"A leader who makes a difference"

"At a time when experience and dedication are needed most"
"Taking care of [Place]"
"Experience money can't buy"
"This is about governing . . . and I've done it."
"People over politics"
"The Change Will Do Us Good."
"It's Time for a Change."

In the past, when local government was simpler, voters seemed to place little value on experience. Consequently, candidates did not underscore experience in slogans. That does not seem to be true anymore. With government more complicated, no matter what the size of your city or county, people want leaders who have experience and will spend and manage their tax dollars wisely.

Logo

I regularly use the lawn sign image as the logo on my brochures and ads. I think it adds continuity to a campaign, conveying a subtle message that it is well organized and connected. If your race is a difficult one, such as a write-in, a logo can be more important. Write-ins for candidates are covered in Chapter 9.

A logo is like a trademark. It can simply be how the candidate's name is written or, for an issue-based campaign, it can be an image. Figures 2.3, 2.4, and 2.5 present some very effective logos. Obviously, if you have a name like Maxwell, a candidate for the Oregon legislature, you want to take advantage of it in your logo: "Maxwell for the House." In the Maxwell for the House race, we continually had people say "good to the last drop" after hearing her name. It did not hurt that she ran in an area whose residents were predominantly seniors—and undoubtedly still bought their coffee in a can. Spend some time thinking about the name of the candidate and come up with creative ways to link the name with the office being sought, like Audie Bock who used a play on her name in a reelection campaign: "Bock By Popular Demand."

Layout

The layout of a brochure depends on its size, how much you want to say, and the quality and quantity of photos. Unless you know the business professionally, you will need the help of a layout artist or graphic designer. Do not make the mistake of trying to save a hundred bucks by doing this yourself or by using someone just because he or she has a desktop publishing program.

Figure 2.3 Maxwell for the House Walking Piece. Example of a logo using the candidate's name to piggyback onto a positive corporate slogan. We used this walking piece to get newspaper endorsements to homes in the district; the back had photos, a bio, and individual endorsements. (Logo and walking piece design by Crystal Castle Graphics)

A good way to get ideas on layout is to go over past political campaign brochures. Often you can find the look you want and then emulate that look. Some examples of different types of brochures are presented at the end of this section, but your best resource will be the politically experienced graphic designer or layout artist.

COMMITTEE FOR THE CARNEGIE

Figure 2.4 Example of a Logo for a Campaign to Restore and Expand Ashland's Carnegie Library. The logo builds one idea on top of another. (Design by Crystal Castle Graphics)

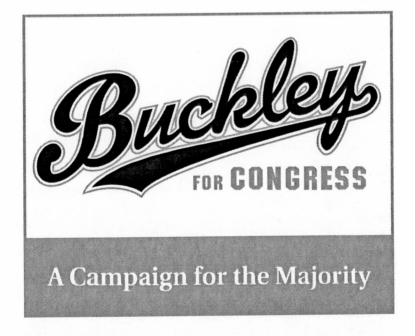

Figure 2.5 Example of a Logo Using Lettering That Appeals to the American Love of Baseball. (Design by Eric Bradford Warren)

Although many experienced campaigners believe that brochure copy should be kept to a minimum, there is the possibility of offending the astute voter with an empty brochure. The challenge is to include enough information without overwhelming the voter with a sea of words. Consider minimizing the impact of the text by placing it in boxes and using bullet points for a candidate's qualifications and experience. Avoid long narratives. A good rule of thumb is that your pictures and graphics should consume as much or slightly more space than the text. No one, even the most sophisticated voter, will read unappealing brochures. Brochures are advertisements, so they must catch the eye and create a "feeling" or positive reaction in seconds.

Use testimonials to get the candidate's message out. To obtain testimonials, I first identify people who support the candidate and might participate in the brochure, and then I try to balance age, gender, party registration, and big names. Once I have a list of people willing to participate, I guide them to cover a specific area I want covered. I then edit or rewrite their missives as needed to fit space, message, and appeal.

Brochures can easily be created on a tight budget. A brochure may be laid out three up on a single sheet of paper so that each sheet yields three brochures. Although each sheet of paper must be cut into thirds, the cost of cutting is less than the cost of folding. Consider using card stock for a three-up brochure. By using card stock, you have the advantage of being able to shove the brochure into doorjambs. Go to a print shop and check out colors and sizes. Clearly, in this small format, text will dominate. However, pictures add very little to the cost and provide an effective visual relief, so they remain important no matter what the final brochure size.

"When I am getting ready to reason with a man, I spend ⅓ of my time thinking about myself and what I am going to say, and ⅔ thinking about him and what he is going to say."
—Abraham Lincoln

Consider using an 8½-by-14-inch paper for a bifold or single-fold brochure. This size lends itself to easy layout and visual impact, and it breathes. As paper size increases, layout becomes easier, but paper costs also increase. Obviously, the size paper you use determines the number of pictures and the amount of text in your brochure, so decide how much you need to say and how much you can afford to say. When the content and layout of the campaign brochure are mocked up, be sure to run it by your campaign committee for final approval.

Figures 2.6 and 2.7 are examples of bifold brochures that were used for local money measures: one for a new county tax base and the other for extracurricular programs for Ashland schools; both are also examples of

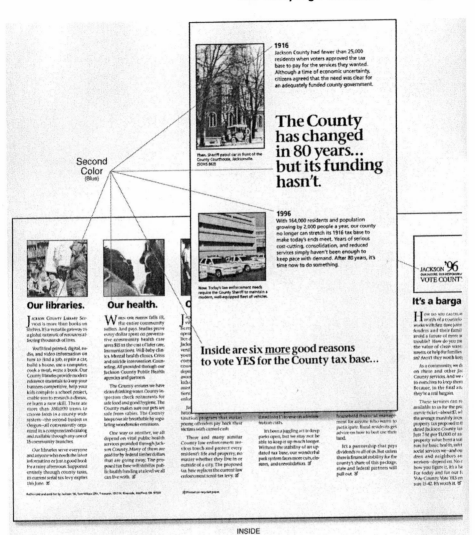

Figure 2.6 The County Has Changed Brochure. Example of a bifold brochure on 8½-by-14-inch paper. Larger pictures with less text would make a better presentation. Also, the front images work against each other here.

what to avoid in a brochure. The county tax base brochure (figure 2.6) had a couple of fundamental problems that should have been corrected. First, the pictures were too small in relation to the text inside the brochure. A greater effort to reduce the amount of text and tell the story more through pictures would have strengthened the piece. Second, the front of the brochure features two pictures (also too small) that should have been selected more carefully. While they were intended to show that government

Questions & Answers

WHAT IS THE CHILDREN'S CULTURAL & RECREATIONAL TAX LEVY -15-3?
The city charter allows the Parks & Recreation Department to propose a two year serial levy that would fund recreational and cultural activities usually provided by the school district. If approved by the voters, the city would collect the money and contract with the school district to provide the activities. The two year levy will restore funds to the Ashland School District budget to accomplish the return of some of the programs now designated for cuts. This is designed to provide interim financing only.

IF THE LEVY PASSES, WILL MY PROPERTY TAXES GO UP?
No. They will still continue downward, as mandated by Measure 5, but just not as much. Each of the next two years, they will drop by $1.53 per thousand, instead of $2.50 per thousand.

WHY HASN'T THE SCHOOL DISTRICT PLANNED AHEAD AND SET ASIDE FUNDS IN ANTICIPATION OF THESE CUTS?
The school district made the decision to use all monies available to continue the very programs we are now wanting to fund with the tax levy.

WILL THE LEVY SOLVE ALL OF OUR FUNDING PROBLEMS FOR THE SCHOOLS?
No. With a 2.9 million dollar shortfall this $800,000 is truly a temporary measure to bring back or keep in place a portion of the essentials, until the state comes up with replacement revenue that would make up the lost funding for the school district.

WHY ARE WE DOING THIS? ISN'T THE STATE SUPPOSED TO HANDLE IT?
The state failed to resolve the school funding crisis brought on by Measure 5. Ashlanders said, "Let's raise our own money and keep it in Ashland so we can save these programs and also regain some local control."

FUNNELING MONEY FOR EDUCATION THROUGH CITY GOVERNMENT SOUNDS UNUSUAL — IS THIS LEGAL?
Yes. Legislative Counsel has researched and confirmed it.

Questions & Answers

HOW WERE THE PROGRAMS TO BE REINSTATED SELECTED?
The list represents the best ideas of the whole community. It was developed by parents of Ashland students, the school board, the city Parks and Recreation Commission, the Booster Club, Ashland Community Coalition, city government officials and the Ashland Schools Foundation. The list was endorsed by school principals.

YOU HEAR A LOT ABOUT "GETTING BACK TO BASICS" AND "CUTTING FRILLS" IN EDUCATION — ISN'T THIS FUNDING DROP A GOOD STEP IN THAT DIRECTION?
No. We are trying to keep the basics: this levy directly protects co-curricular activities that public schools throughout the United States have offered for most of the 20th century: just check your own high school yearbook.

WILL CITY RESIDENTS END UP FOOTING THE BILL FOR THE 20% OF ASHLAND STUDENTS WHO LIVE IN THE COUNTY?
County students will have to pay to participate in these "co-curricular" programs.

WHY DOES IT SEEM LIKE SO MUCH IS GOING TO THE HIGH SCHOOL AND NOT MIDDLE OR ELEMENTARY SCHOOLS?
Remember this is a stop gap measure. If the students now attending high school do not have these programs, we jeopardize their opportunities for college entrance or securing skilled labor jobs. Hopefully, as funding becomes available, many of our excellent elementary and middle school programs will be reinstated.

WHAT HAPPENS IF THE PROPOSED STATE SALES TAX FOR SCHOOLS DOES PASS THIS FALL?
It will not be in time to save the cut programs for the 1993/94, 1994/95 school years. If broader funding sources become adequate again to fund the programs, this levy can be eliminated.

Authorized by United Ashland Committee, Linda and Chuck Butler, Treasurers, P.O. Box 1145, Ashland, OR 97520.

1

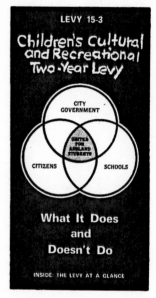

LEVY 15-3

Children's Cultural and Recreational Two-Year Levy

CITY GOVERNMENT

CHILD FOR ASHLAND STUDENTS

CITIZENS   SCHOOLS

What It Does and Doesn't Do

INSIDE: THE LEVY AT A GLANCE

RECREATIONAL AND CULTURAL PROGRAMS AFFECTED BY LEVY	WHAT LEVY DIRECTLY PAYS FOR	PROGRAMS BROUGHT BACK BECAUSE OF MONEY FREED UP BY LEVY	PROGRAMS CUT IF LEVY FAILS	PROGRAMS PARTIALLY FUNDED IF LEVY FAILS	NON SCHOOL RELATED PROGRAMS NEEDED TO COMPLY WITH STATE LAW	AFFECTS HIGH SCHOOL	AFFECTS MIDDLE SCHOOL	AFFECTS ELEMENTARY SCHOOLS	NUMBER OF STUDENTS AFFECTED
RESIDENT OUTDOOR SCHOOL (ROS)	•		•			•	•		280
LIBRARIES (½ of Budgeted Amount)	•			•		•	•	•	3,431
CO-CURRICULUM:									
SPEECH & DEBATE	•		•			•			
DECA (Marketing)	•		•			•			
FBLA (Business)	•		•			•			
VICA (Industrial)	•		•			•			400
YEARBOOK	•			•		•	•		
NEWSPAPER	•			•		•	•		
DRAMA	•		•			•	•		
K-12 MUSIC PERFORMANCES	•		•						
ORCHESTRA						•	•	•	
BANDS						•	•	•	700
CHOIR						•		•	
ATHLETICS:									
SOCCER	•		•			•			
CROSS-COUNTRY	•		•			•			
FOOTBALL	•			•		•	•		
VOLLEYBALL	•			•		•	•		
SWIMMING	•		•			•			
WRESTLING	•		•			•	•		
BASKETBALL	•			•		•	•		650
GOLF	•		•			•			
TRACK	•			•		•	•		
SOFTBALL	•			•		•			
BASEBALL	•			•		•			
TENNIS	•			•		•			
INTRAMURALS	•		•					•	
STUDENT AT RISK PROGRAMS:									
SUBSTANCE ABUSE COUNSELOR		•	•			•	•	•	
CHILD DEVELOPMENT SPECIALIST		•	•			•	•	•	860
YOUTH AT RISK SERVICES		•	•					•	
FOREIGN LANGUAGE	•			•		•			670
TEEN CENTER	N/A	N/A	N/A	N/A	•				
COMMUNITY CENTER ACTIVITIES	N/A	N/A	N/A	N/A	•				

Figure 2.7 Youth Activities Levy Brochure. Example of a bifold brochure. Although this was a very complicated serial levy presented to the Ashland voters, we made matters worse with this brochure. The levy was intended to bring back extra and co-curricular activities that had been cut by a statewide property tax limitation measure. Our idea was to let people know exactly what it would bring back. It was too much information, presented too sterilely. (Design by Brian Freeman, Crystal Castle Graphics)

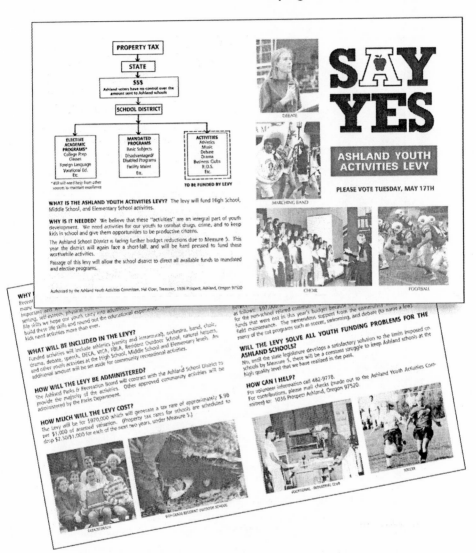

Figure 2.8 Youth Activities Levy Brochure, Take 2. Example of a single-fold brochure on 8$\frac{1}{2}$-by-14-inch paper. After the failure of the first Youth Activities Levy, this brochure was designed to speak more to emotion and less to nuts and bolts. It makes great use of pictures and clearly relays the message: opportunity. (Design by Brian Freeman, Crystal Castle Graphics)

has dramatically changed since approval of the last tax base, they actually tell another story. The historical photo evokes more emotion and reflects back

"We cannot insure success, but we can deserve it."

—John Adams

Figure 2.9 Front of Full-Color Brochure to Elect Dr. Alan Bates, State Representative. As an unknown, we wanted to push people to open the brochure, so the front is intentionally ambiguous. People did just as we hoped. Voters tested on the layout said: "Who's the candidate?" while flipping it open. (Design by Crystal Castle Graphics)

to a simpler, less chaotic time. The current photo, of an ugly, new building, suggests that we would be better off not encouraging that kind of architecture with our tax dollars.

The other example of a bifold 8½-by-14-inch brochure was one we used for the Children's Cultural and Recreational Two-Year Levy (figure 2.7). This may be the worst brochure I have ever been associated with and breaks just about every rule I outline in this chapter. In our defense, it was a complicated proposal that I had thought up just weeks before it was placed in front of the

Figure 2.10 Full-Color Walking Piece for Alan Bates. We wanted it to reinforce the brochure (figure 2.9), which was mailed during the primary campaign. (Design by Crystal Castle Graphics)

voters. It didn't help that the campaign committee had only two members with any campaign experience. That measure failed by just a few hundred votes.

"It's about the right message to the right people at the right time.
—Elaine Franklin

Less than a year later, we came back to the voters with the Youth Activity Levy but used a single-fold 8$\frac{1}{2}$-by-14-inch brochure (figure 2.8). In both brochures, we asked for the same amount of money and sold the same thing: opportunity. But the way the message was delivered in the single-fold brochure is both clearer and more compelling. Ironically, the second brochure is less clear about *where* the money would be spent. This is great information to have. Most voters don't want to be a curriculum committee for the school district at the ballot box. Their preference is to know where the money would be spent (bricks vs. programs), with technical decisions made through the elected school board, school administration, and a citizens budget committee.

Brochures designed for mailing can be reconfigured for a walking piece. One will reinforce the other, and the two can be done at the same time by your graphic designer (see figures 2.9 and 2.10).

Voters' Pamphlet

If your campaign has an opportunity to get in the voters' pamphlet, do it. Many voters pay little attention to campaign propaganda and instead rely on the information passed through the county or state elections office in a voters' pamphlet. Although there is a fee, whatever it is, it's worth it. Candidates and campaigns love to whine about a $300–$500 charge for being in the voters' pamphlet but don't think twice about spending $10,000 on a direct mail piece. Although the value of direct mail is debatable, the value of being in a voters' pamphlet is not.

Getting your candidate or measure into the voters' pamphlet comes with very specific admission criteria, which should be available online from the county, state elections office, or the secretary of state's office (see Appendix 1). Do not "beef up" your résumé in a voters' pamphlet with false information. You might get away with that in direct mail or in advertising, but listing false information in a voters' pamphlet is a felony. That said, there are ways to get the most out of what you have. For example, you attended Harvard as an undergraduate but dropped out before receiving a degree. Later you were accepted into graduate school at Stanford University, solely on the basis of your Graduate Record Examination scores, and there you received a master's degree in communications. Under "education" you would list "Harvard, undergraduate; Stanford, master's in Communication." While voters may assume you received an undergraduate degree at Harvard, you never actually say one way or another. If you completed only a couple of years of undergraduate work at a college or university before heading out into the real world, you would simply list the institution without reference to any degree or year of graduation.

In Oregon the criteria are the same for a primary and a general election voters' pamphlet. Candidates have the option of including a photo, which has to be a certain size. In Oregon the photo cannot be any more than four years old—although election authorities would be hard-pressed to determine whether a picture is more than four years old unless you used the same one in a previous voters' pamphlet. Photos cannot have any identifying props, such as a stethoscope around a physician's neck. This is where you will use your best mug shot. Photos of poor quality get worse when put in the voters' pamphlet, so pay attention to this detail.

"Little things can make as much difference as big things."
　—Malcolm Caldwell

Candidates are given a certain number of words under required and optional categories. Required categories may include occupation, occupational background, educational background, government experience, and community service. Under optional information you may include a statement from the candidate or testimonials from community leaders that say what you need to have said. If you include testimonials, check to see if the elections department requires a signed form from those you wish to quote in the pamphlet. If so, keep in mind that this takes time and must be handled before the voters' pamphlet deadline. Also, it is important to work with those who are drafting testimonials to include in the pamphlet. Even if you list names, they must each have a signed form. Given word count restrictions and the campaign's need to stay on message, the campaign may need to draft the testimonials and run them by the potential signatory. Keeping control over what goes into the voters' pamphlet is extremely important.

"First they ignore you; then they laugh at you; then they fight you; then you win.
　—Gandhi

Primary Voters' Pamphlet

Remember, your objective in the primary is to lock your base. Given that the voters' pamphlet goes to each and every registered voter and is referred to by most, you need to be in there whether you have an opponent or not. While your text should keep partisan material to a minimum, those whose names are included in testimonials may be closely aligned with your party. Each testimonial should bring voters on board, from both the name and the text.

Occupation: Family physician for 24 years in the Rogue Valley; Oregon State Representative 2001 to present.

Occupational Background: Former Chief of Medicine at Rogue Valley and Providence Medical Centers; Director of Valley Family Practice.

Educational Background: D.O., 1977; College of Osteopathic Medicine, Kansas City, Missouri. B.A., 1969; Central Washington State University.

Prior Government Experience: Eagle Point School Board, 1990 – 2001; Governor's Committee for Excellence in Education, Member (1997 – 1999); Oregon Health Services Commission (1989 – 1999, chair: 1997 – 1999).

Military Service: US Army (1965 – 1967); Served in Vietnam.

What others say:

The **Oregon Business Association** ranked Representative Alan Bates among the top ten legislators in Oregon: courageous, smart, thoughtful.

The **Oregon League of Conservation Voters** gave Rep. Bates an 82% pro-environment rating.

The **Oregon Education Association** rated Dr. Bates in the 90th percentile for his advocacy of public education.

"As a freshman legislator, he shined as he forged consensus legislation ensuring a healthy and competitive workers' compensation market in Oregon. It was Dr. Bates who kept the interests of the insured and the small businesses first."
Coalition for Economic Security for Oregon (Small Business Alert, August 2001)

Because of legislation sponsored or strongly supported by Dr. Alan Bates Oregonians will have:
- ✓ increased access to higher education (HB 2521)
- ✓ a patient bill of rights (HB 3040)
- ✓ reduced prescriptions costs for seniors (HB 3300 & SB 819)
- ✓ improved roads and highways (comprehensive transportation package)
- ✓ government made more accountable through annual audits (HB 3980)
- ✓ a cleaner and safer environment (mercury reduction legislation)

"Representative Alan Bates was one of the most effective and respected freshman legislators in Salem this last session. His success was due to hard work, determination, and his ability and willingness to work with both sides of the aisle.

"Alan consistently placed consensus over conflict, compromise over partisanship, and communities over special interest.

"He deserves our support."

Governor John Kitzhaber, MD

Figure 2.11 Example of Voters' Pamphlet Candidate Statement

General Voters' Pamphlet

A statement for the general election voters' pamphlet will look a lot like that for the primary, except for the candidate statement or testimonial section. For the general election you are looking for names and statements that will give voters in the other party permission to jump ship on party and split their ticket. However, you must also speak to those within your party, so look for balance in the big names you use. Figure 2.11 is an example of a Candidate Statement used in the 2002 Oregon Voters' Pamphlet.

3

THE VOLUNTEER ORGANIZATION

IN THIS CHAPTER
- *Methodology*
- *Phone Banks*
- *Phone Bank Locations*
- *Clerical Workers*
- *Time Allotments for Volunteer Tasks*

No matter where you find your volunteers, a campaign must have a system to organize, direct, and assign responsibilities. The system I describe here can be used either with index cards or with a spreadsheet program such as Excel. The methodology as presented in each of these activities really works. If you use it as outlined, you will be able to utilize your volunteers better and run a more effective campaign.

Methodology

Here is how to keep track of campaign volunteers:

Using volunteer sign-up sheets (see figure 1.1), remittance envelopes (see figure 4.4), and lists from other campaigns and support groups, you can begin to amass names of people willing to work, contribute, host a lawn sign, and write letters-to-the-editor. If your campaign is beginning cold, the first thing to do is to contact other campaigns of like-minded people or similar efforts to determine whether those campaigns will give you their list of supporters. Contact all of your friends, local family members, people on committees or organizations in which you participate,

"These things are good in little measure and evil in large: yeast, salt, and hesitation."

—The Talmud

business associates, members of your church and of any clubs you belong to, and members of organizations with similar political leanings. Build a database as quickly as possible.

If you are using a spreadsheet program, list all of your contacts, from your initial cold calls as well as from cards, remits, and sign-up sheets generated by your campaign. This will be your master list. Here are the column names that should run along the top of your master list: last name, first, spouse/partner, street number, street, city, zip, phone. Volunteer work and services categories (which can be filled in with yes or no) include phone work, canvass, clerical, lawn sign, lawn sign install, LTEs (Letters-to-the-Editor), and endorsement ad. Finally a column labeled $ indicates whether a volunteer has also contributed funds, and a column labeled notes may contain brief comments (see figure 3.1).

Although there is a column for donations ($), remember, this sheet is for *volunteer* activities. The $ column simply tracks which of your volunteers have also contributed money. Since states have specific filing requirements for campaign donors, it is important to keep track of donor information

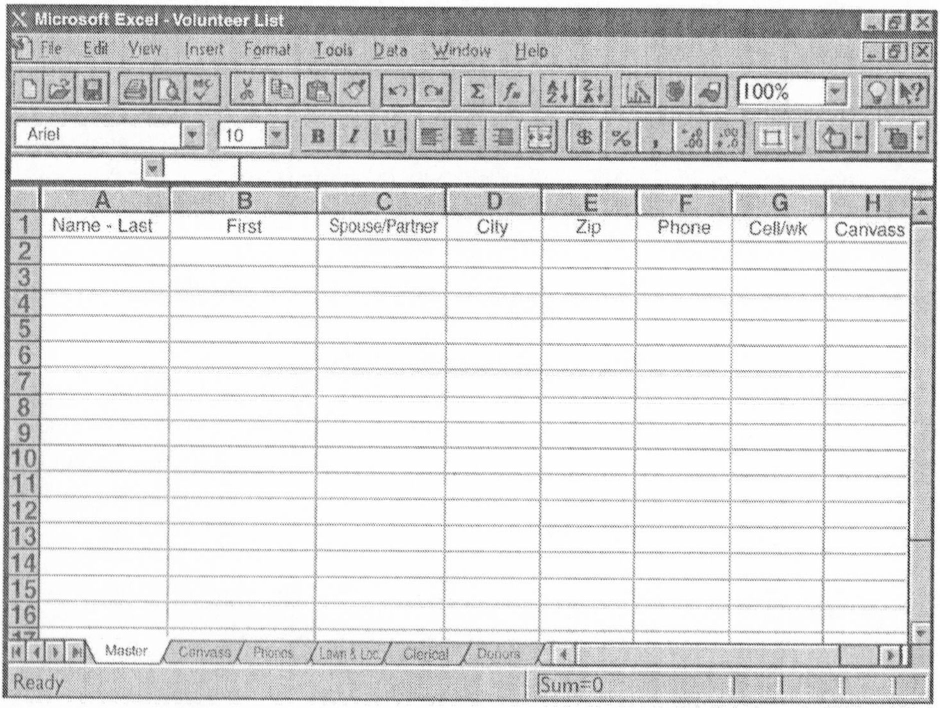

Figure 3.1 Example of an Excel Spreadsheet for Keeping Track of Volunteer Workers

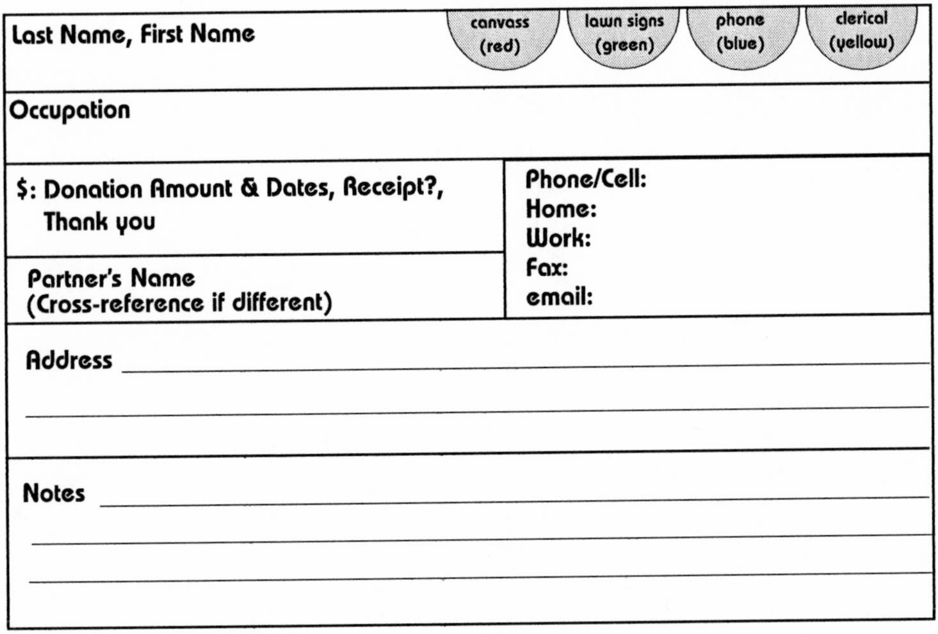

Last Name, First Name	canvass (red)	lawn signs (green)	phone (blue)	clerical (yellow)
Occupation				

$: Donation Amount & Dates, Receipt?, Thank you	Phone/Cell: Home: Work:
Partner's Name (Cross-reference if different)	Fax: email:

Address _____

_____

_____

Notes _____

_____

_____

Figure 3.2 Example of a 3-by-5-Inch Contact Card

apart from your volunteer spreadsheet. An example of a donation spreadsheet can be found in Chapter 4, figure 4.14.

If you are using index cards, place all information for each volunteer on a single card (see figure 3.2). Because index cards cannot be sorted by category as easily as spreadsheet entries, you need a system that will give you volunteer information at a glance. Before I moved all my systems to Excel, I color-coded my cards with colored stickers. Working from the upper right-hand corner toward the left, fold the stickers over the card's top edge so that they look like half circles on each side of your card; this way the color-coding can be seen from the top of the index box at a glance. For each person contacted, an index card will be generated. Keep all cards together in one box.

> "It is one of the beautiful compensations of life that no one can sincerely try to help another without helping himself."
> —Ralph Waldo Emerson

The color-coding indicates which campaign activities the volunteer will work on, such as lawn sign placement, phone banks, canvassing, or clerical work. Use a color scheme that works for you and your campaign, but keep in mind that using more than four colors can easily crowd a 3-by-5-inch card.

The "notes" section of your spreadsheet or card is important. This is where you note such information as "Won't canvass hills"; "Don't call early A.M."; "Don't call after 8:00 P.M."; "Horrible on phones"; and "Has three staple guns." Also use this section to make a note when someone has been rude ("Do not contact again"), so that other campaign volunteers needn't be subjected to it. After hundreds of phone calls, it is impossible to remember such details if a record is not kept somewhere.

Organize Volunteer Activities

Once information is in your spreadsheet or on the index cards, you're ready to set up volunteer activities.

If you are using Excel, follow these directions carefully: The spreadsheet containing the information about the volunteers will say "Sheet 1" in the tab at the bottom of the Excel window. Right-click the "Sheet 1" tab and rename it "Master" or "Raw Data." It is important that one sheet remain intact in case subsequent sorting goes awry and the original information has to be retrieved for the list to be rebuilt. Naturally, as your pool of volunteers grows, you will add names to the Master sheet, and over time you will add notes and make address changes, but you never want to actually sort this list for any activity.

Once you have renamed Sheet 1 as "Master" (or whatever name you choose), go to the top and click on the empty corner in the upper left-hand corner of the sheet, between the row beginning with A and the column beginning with 1. This will highlight your entire master list; now click edit, click copy, click the tab for Sheet 2, click the same empty square in the upper left (now this sheet will be highlighted), click edit, and click paste. You now have a duplicate of your master list that you can sort and play with all you want.

> "You can't have divided authority around a campaign headquarters.
>
> —James Farley,
> Campaign Manager for FDR

If you want to set up a phone bank, highlight everything with text (you cannot use the blank square in the upper right-hand corner this time, because Excell will only sort a defined area). Click data, click sort, and under "Sort by," select the letter of the phone bank column. Then highlight the cells only of those who are willing to phone, and copy them to a third sheet, which you can label "Phones." Go through this list and delete all but the name and phone number(s), and add a column labeled "CB?" (call-back). Obviously, if I am just contacting people to see if they will help in a phone bank, I don't need the information in all the other categories listed on my master list. Before printing this page, be sure to insert gridlines (on the page setup menu), as they make the list a lot easier to read. Also increase the width of the rows, so that you can easily write information as needed. Repeat this process for whatever activity you wish to undertake.

When using the index-card system to organize campaign volunteers, create campaign activity cards with 5-by-8-inch lined index cards set up as shown in figure 3.3. The following process works for activities such as phone banks, clerical work, canvassing, and lawn sign placement or maintenance. Once you have the 5-by-8-inch cards prepared, copy the names and phone numbers from the appropriate 3-by-5-inch cards onto them or a sheet of paper. (The 3-by-5-inch cards should never get far from their box.)

"With their budgets warped towards media spending, candidates and their organizations are led to measure the progress of their campaigns only in terms of dollars raised and tracking polls. Many [candidates] lose due to their failure to organize large numbers of people in their campaigns."

—Morton Blackwell,
The Leadership Institute,
May–June 1998, newsletter

For both spreadsheet and index card systems:

Whatever the activity, have a number of dates lined up for it so that each volunteer is called only once for scheduling. When calling for an ongoing activity such as canvassing, have four or

			ACTIVITY: CANVAS 10/14	
NAME	PHONE #	CB?	9:30AM–12:00	2:30–5:00PM

Figure 3.3 Example of a 5-by-8-Inch Canvass Activity Card

five dates and times, so if one date doesn't work, another may. If a volunteer can do none of the times offered, it is important to determine why and to note that on the card or spreadsheet. If it is a temporary schedule conflict, note when the conflict will be resolved. However, if it sounds as though the volunteer will never do the activity, offer another campaign job. Keep this person on the phone until it can be determined what is going on. If it is clear that he or she will never volunteer, that person's name should be removed from the volunteer list. For now, however, the name remains on your working list with a line through it so that you will remember that you called. If you do not do this, you may forget and call again.

A couple of days before the activity, call back every volunteer who agreed to work and place a check in the "CB?" column. It is best to actually talk to the worker on the call-back, so leave a message only as a last resort. On the call-back, do not ask workers if they still intend to help. Do not even call to remind them directly of the upcoming volunteer activity. They said they would do it, and the tone of your conversation should reflect that verbal commitment. Plus, if they are very organized, they will resent the call. Instead think of this call as a small rattling of the cage and make it about something else: Remind them to bring a clipboard, or ask if they mind doing hills, or check to make sure that they were given the correct meeting place or the correct time. Whatever it is, it's your fault or it's about a small detail that wasn't addressed in the first conversation. You're just checking to make sure the information given previously was correct. If the volunteer has forgotten, the call serves as a reminder. If the person inadvertently made other plans, this is your opportunity to reschedule. Potential no-shows, discovered by a phone call, are incredibly easy to reschedule.

Applying the Methodology

Every campaign consists of basic campaign activities, such as:

- Running phone banks
- Canvassing the voters
- Developing campaign events
- Designing ads or other media
- Organizing clerical support (including thank-you notes)
- Preparing, installing, and maintaining lawn signs
- Raising money

Each of these activities is volunteer intensive. You can apply the techniques described above to find and keep track of volunteers, but each activity requires specific techniques. The method described above will be applied throughout this handbook to organize each activity.

Phone Banks

Phone banks can be used throughout a campaign and are the most efficient way to retrieve information in a short period of time. They can be used to get a head count for a fund-raiser, to get lawn sign locations, to raise money, and to get the campaign more volunteers. If you plan to do a get-out-the-vote (GOTV) effort on election day, you will have to identify (ID) voters who intend to vote for your candidate or cause. This can be done while canvassing, but it is easier and far more efficient to do it by phone. The GOTV effort itself is primarily done by phone. When signing up volunteers, assure them that they will receive training before actually working on the phones.

Generally, I schedule a phone banker to work for one hour and fifteen minutes (fifteen minutes for training and then one hour on the phone). Almost anyone will give up an hour or so for a campaign they believe in, and if it turns out that the volunteer is bad on the phone, an hour is plenty. However, if I am desperate or conducting fast, important calls, as in a GOTV effort, I will put seasoned callers on the phone for up to two hours. A caller who has worked for me in the past will let me know if the full two hours is too long. I then have others scheduled in to replace a caller coming off the phones early.

Have two to three shifts each evening. Volunteers must arrive fifteen minutes before their shift for training. No one likes to go on the phone cold, so people rarely miss training when it's offered and expected. Should time allow, consider doing a role-play with your volunteers—having one volunteer pretend to call another.

Each phone bank should have a "lead." This is the person responsible for unlocking, training, cleaning, and closing up the phone bank. Training begins by handing a phone banker a brochure and an instruction sheet, which should include prepared scripts. If the campaign is using volunteers to conduct a poll, a prepared script must be followed to the letter; however, in all other phone bank activities, a caller who ad-libs will generally do best.

"Let us endeavor so to live that when we come to die even the undertaker will be sorry."

—Mark Twain

Once the volunteers have read the instructions, do a walk-through of what is expected on the phones and explain any peculiarities the phone system may have (such as dialing 9 first). Tell volunteers where the bathroom is, and let them know that you will be providing water. Have a list for the lead of all the details that need to be shared with a new volunteer before he or she starts working the phone.

After a fifteen-minute training session, volunteers begin calling. The first twenty to thirty minutes that volunteers are on the phone, the lead should circulate, answer questions, and take water to people rather than making calls. The lead will have only ten or fifteen minutes between shifts, as the second crew will arrive for training fifteen minutes early, or forty-five minutes into the hour of the previous shift's calls. This way, exactly one hour after the first shift starts, volunteers get a tap on the shoulder from someone on the next shift, and they are off the phones.

". . . it does not require a majority to prevail, but rather an irate, tireless minority keen to set brush fires in people's minds . . ."

—Samuel Adams

Never tell people that you want them for a specific amount of time, then push them to stay longer. This is how a campaign can lose volunteers. When you ask someone to work for you, you have made a verbal contract with him or her for a specific job and a specific amount of time. Don't nudge.

Once the second shift is in place, happily making calls, supplied with water, and all campaign questions asked and answered, the lead must then call all those listed to volunteer on phone banks for the following evening. Giving a quick reminder of place and scheduled time for work avoids no-shows.

Note: Do not expect your phone bank people to look up phone numbers. Use a clerical team of volunteers to do that ahead of time.

Phone Bank Training

The following is an example of what you might prepare for your volunteers who are phoning for the campaign:

> Thank you for your help. Tonight we are cold-calling people who live on arterial streets in hopes of beefing up our lawn sign list. While the lists you're calling have the same party registration as our candidate, they have not been previously identified as a supporter. Just so you know, that may make some of the calls a little harder. Please make a note on your list next to the name of the voter whether he or she will take a lawn sign, and if not, whether that person will be supporting our candidate.

Boxes 3.1 and 3.2 are examples of two approaches for a phone script.

What you ask for will vary according to the phone bank. You could be calling for lawn sign locations, money, volunteer workers, a head count for

"Hello, this is (your name). Tonight I am volunteering to help the Alan Bates campaign. As you may know, Alan is running for reelection to the House, and I was hoping you would consider having one of his lawn signs in front of your home."

If no, thank the caller and ask if Alan can count on his or her support in the upcoming election.

If yes, verify address and ask if there are any special instructions for where and how the homeowner would like the sign placed. Then say:

"Someone will be coming by to place the sign about six weeks before the election. We will also have some maintenance crews checking signs from time to time. However, if you would occasionally check the sign and set it up if it falls over, that would be very helpful. When the sign is placed, there will be a note left on your door so you can contact the campaign should it disappear or be vandalized. Thanks for helping us out."

Box 3.1 Example of Phone Instructions and Script for Lawn Sign Locations

Before You Pick Up the Phone—

1. *Be proud of what you are doing.* You are working for a cause you believe in. You are on the front line of a campaign.

2. *Think about what has motivated you to give up your time to work for the candidate (or ballot measure).* People will ask how a candidate stands on a particular issue. While you cannot speak directly to that, you can share why *you* are working for this individual (or cause).

3. *Identify yourself only as a volunteer working for the campaign.* In general, you want the candidate's name to make it into the consciousness of the voter, not yours, unless, of course, you know the person.

4. *No matter what else happens, get something from the individual before you get off the phone.* "You can't canvass, ever? How about a lawn sign?" "You have a bad lawn-sign location? Do you have a friend who might want one?" "Can we use your name on the endorsement ad?" "Would you make a contribution?" Whatever. You want them in on the campaign with that single call, or to know how they will be voting. (This is helpful information for the campaign.)

5. And thank you for taking the time to help in this important cause.

Box 3.2 Example of Phone Bank Instructions

an event, or voter ID (that is, finding out whether or not a voter supports your campaign). Think about your mission, and prepare a short introduction for the caller.

Phone Bank Locations

It can be difficult to locate enough phones for an effective phone session. I have found that real estate offices work best because people love to have company when calling, and they usually have five or more lines in the same room. Law offices also may be an option, but in the typical office, callers wouldn't be able to see each other. Also, many law offices will be off-limits because of confidentiality concerns. Sometimes campaign headquarters for a bigger race (such as a presidential or gubernatorial contest) will let you use an office. You might also try labor unions and physicians' or insurance offices. In the past, many businesses that supported a cause or a candidate would open their doors for phone banks after hours. However, the advent of caller ID has made it tougher and tougher to find such locations. Still, it never hurts to ask; on one campaign I was running, a Realtor who was working for the opposition let us use his phones because we were friends.

"Make no little plans; they have no magic to stir men's blood. . . . Make big plans, aim high in hope and work."

—Daniel H. Burnham

"There is as much greatness of mind in acknowledging a good turn, as in doing it."

—Seneca

A word of caution on real estate offices: In the last campaign cycle, while we were working phones at a real estate office we had used for years, one of the agents dropped in to pick something up. The next day I received a call from the broker, who said that the agents in his office were apoplectic because one of our callers was from another real estate office, and they worried that this "competitor" could avail herself of secret documents.

Scripts

Wherever your phone bank is located, the important part of campaign phoning is to have an effective message. You should have scripts made up in advance for each campaign activity. While it is preferable to have callers ad-lib, they generally need a prepared script for the first few calls. It gets much easier after that. I also don't have anyone ask, "How are you doing tonight?" The reality is that the volunteer doesn't care, and the person on the other end knows it. When I am calling for money, the calls will be a bit longer and more involved, so I usually start by asking the person who answers if they have a moment to talk. However, with volunteer recruitment, the calls are so short that I just cut to the chase. Here are some sample scripts for typical campaign phone sessions:

"The whole is greater than the sum of its parts."

—Buckminster Fuller

Lawn Sign Location. "Hello, I'm a volunteer working for the Alan Bates campaign for state senate. Tonight we're looking for locations for lawn signs. Will you be supporting Alan in the general election? Great, could we place a lawn sign? Let me verify your address. Someone will be coming by about six weeks before the election to place it. We also have a crew who will be maintaining these signs; however, if it needs some attention, maybe you could help with it. Great. Thanks."

Special Activity. "Hello, I'm a volunteer working for the Alan Bates campaign for state senate. Did you receive the invitation for the campaign dinner this Saturday? The restaurant needs a pretty accurate head count, so we're trying to get an idea of the number of supporters who will be attending the dinner for Alan. Will you be joining us?"

"It is better to wear out than to rust out."

—Richard Cumberland (17th century)

Canvassing. "Hello, I'm a volunteer helping in the Peter Buckley campaign. We are hoping to canvass the city this Saturday with a last-minute door hanger and need about eighty-five volunteers. There will be no door-knocking, just great exercise. Can you help?"

Another. "Hello, I'm a volunteer working for the 'Verger for Senate' campaign. Our notes indicate that you might be willing to canvass. Is that correct?" [Answer] "Great. I have a number of dates for some upcoming canvasses. Do you have your calendar handy?"

GOTV for Absentee and Mail-in Ballots. "Hello, I'm a volunteer from the Jeff Barker campaign. We're down here working on phone banks tonight to turn out as many of Jeff's supporters as possible. As of a couple of days ago, your ballot had not yet been received at county elections; is it possible you still have it at home?"

Voter ID.   "Hello, I'm a volunteer working for the Alan Bates campaign. As you may know, Alan is the Democratic candidate for state senate. Do you know if you'll be supporting him this November?" [Yes, No, Need more info]

Undecided

With any of these scripts, if I call and discover that someone is undecided or leaning, I ask whether the person would like more information from the candidate or campaign committee to help in deciding. Finally, whatever a potential supporter might say, I ask my volunteers to make a note so that the campaign can follow up if need be.

Negative Response

Get off the phone as quickly as possible and make a note for the campaign.

Clerical Workers

The clerical team is an extremely important part of your campaign. Normally you think of people sitting around, addressing, stamping, and stuffing envelopes. While these tasks might make up the bulk of your clerical team's work, you should think of this group in broader terms.

Wherever I can break activities down into more manageable units, I do so. For example, on the day that lawn signs go up, you *cannot* expect your lawn sign team to arrive early in the morning, staple lawn signs, organize lists, and then head out for two hours of stake pounding. Each of these functions is very different and should be treated differently.

"It's not very difficult to persuade people to do what they already long to do."

—Aldous Huxley

Your clerical team can come in days ahead of time to staple lawn signs or bolt them to the stakes, depending on the type of sign you use. They can come in on still another day to help organize the lists, maps, and locations of where those signs are going.

Your clerical team is crucial in keeping your campaign tight and organized. Use them creatively wherever they can help with your workload or with the organization of an upcoming activity. Here are some examples of how the clerical team can be used:

- Staple lawn signs at the corners (if using poly tag)
- Attach lawn signs to stakes (if using corrugated)
- Look up phone numbers for an upcoming phone bank

- Assemble maps for a canvass
- Attach inserts in the brochures for a canvass
- Write thank-you notes for money, lawn sign locations, or to volunteers
- Stuff, stamp, and address a mailing
- Prepare items for a fund-raiser, such as a yard sale or auction
- Set up for a campaign gathering—decorate, print name tags, etc.

To set up a campaign activity requiring clerical workers, contact people who have indicated they will help with clerical work. If you need additional volunteers, try senior groups that support you, the League of Women Voters, and your friends and neighbors. Given how much fun a clerical work party can be, it is usually pretty easy to turn out a crowd.

A clerical work party is a social time in campaigns; it's a time to chat with friends while helping with a cause everyone supports. It's a time to share war stories about canvassing, talk news, gossip,

> *"We are here to add to what we can to life, not to get what we can from it."*
>
> —William Osler

or whatever while having coffee and cookies and doing a mindless task. These meetings are enjoyable and highly productive for the small effort involved.

It is important for people to be comfortable while working and sitting for two or more hours, so be sure to have enough table space for each volunteer. Do not do clerical work in an already cluttered house. Because no one's back is getting younger—and many of the clerical volunteers are older—I take the time to put together a comfortable work area. Avoid having people work on their laps in soft, overstuffed couches and chairs; they will not be as productive. This is akin to cleaning house or doing yard work in flip-flops—you can do it, just not as efficiently.

Have some snacks around—coffee, tea, cookies, and the like—but not on the table where work is being conducted.

Have everything set up. Do not waste your volunteers' time.

Do one activity at a time. If the task is to get out a mailing or to staple lawn signs, do just that. When the task is done—and usually they're done ahead of schedule—don't bring out one more thing for people to do. Remember, as with any other task in a campaign, you have made a verbal contract with your workers. Once they are captive workers in your home, to ask them to work past the designated time or beyond the designated task creates hard feelings. Workers who complete a task early and then go home feel good about their participation and feel that they are helping in a well-organized effort.

Make sure that you have all the necessary materials at each station, so that people are not idle. Have extras of everything you need—staplers, sponges, stamps, envelopes, telephone books, rubber bands, or whatever else the task might require.

Time Allotments for Volunteer Tasks

Below are some general guidelines for what volunteers can do in a designated amount of time. From here, you can calculate how many people you'll need to accomplish a task in the time available. For the task to be completed by a certain date, work your way backward from that date so that you have enough time to complete the task given your resources and task goal—number of calls to make, signs to put up, homes to canvass, and so on.

Phone Banks

"Luck is the crossroads where preparation and opportunity meet."
—Anonymous

In general each volunteer can complete twenty to thirty calls per hour, depending on the nature of the calls. In a GOTV effort, people can make fifty calls during a ninety-minute shift. So, for example, if you want to make 4,000 calls by election day and have only one phone bank location with six phones, you will need people on all six phones, for two ninety-minute shifts, for seven nights. Naturally, if you have more phones or another phone bank location, the number of calling nights goes down and the number of volunteers per shift goes up.

Canvassing

Because Oregon has vote by mail, our precincts are huge, with approximately 3,000 voters per precinct, or 1,400 to 1,500 homes. Precincts typically have about 400 registered voters in 120 to 200 homes. You can use voter lists to get an accurate number of houses in each precinct.

"The feeble tremble before opinion, the foolish defy it, the wise judge it, the skillful direct it."
—Jeanne Roland

Two types of canvassing are used for our purposes here: a knock, and a simple drop without talking.

Knock. Depending on how hilly and tightly compacted a neighborhood is, canvassers can cover ten to fifteen houses per hour. That means that a precinct with 120 to 200 houses would require four canvassers working two to three hours each to cover the distance.

Drop.   A literature drop can be done quite a bit faster than a knock canvass. With a drop, again depending on street grade and the proximity of homes, a canvasser can cover thirty to forty-five homes in an hour.

Clerical (Direct Mail)

A mailing of 500 requires a fifteen-person clerical team working one hour to stuff, stamp, seal, and address envelopes.

"The success of any kind of social epidemic is heavily dependent on the involvement of people with a particular and rare set of social gifts."

—Malcolm Gladwell

Lawn Signs

One lawn sign team—a driver and a pounder—can put up about twelve lawn signs an hour. So, for example, if you have 200 lawn signs to place, you will need sixteen people (eight teams) working two hours each.

4

FUND-RAISING

IN THIS CHAPTER
- *Early Endorsements = Early Money = Early Media Buys*
- *Campaign Budget*
- *Direct Mail for Money*
- *Special Events*
- *Holding a Special Event*
- *Candidate Calls to Raise Money*
- *Calling for Money for Ballot Measures*
- *The Campaign Finance Committee*
- *Campaign Finance Committee Packets*
- *Tips for Successful Fund-Raising*
- *Fund-Raising Ideas That Take Less Than One Month of Preparation*
- *"Hey, Big Spender"*
- *The World's Smallest Brochure: Direct Mail That Works*
- *Keeping Track of Donations*

Although this handbook suggests a number of ways to stretch your campaign dollars, no matter how many volunteers or friends with special talents you may have, eventually you will have to spend money to get your message out. Production and media buys require up-front, cash-in-hand transactions. The U.S. Postal Service will not send direct mail on a promise, and most places that print anything for campaigns require payment when you pick up the product. Although volunteers can cut your debt

"Apart from the ballot box, philanthropy presents the one opportunity the individual has to express his meaningful choice over the direction in which our society will progress."

—George Kirstein

load, the larger the campaign, the more these volunteers become a valuable resource not to be squandered.

The bottom line is that if you want to get your message and your candidate's face into the public view, you must raise and spend a certain threshold of money to be competitive. What that threshold is depends on your race, the voting population, and which campaign activities you intend to implement.

I have worked on campaigns where money was no object and others where every decision was a financial trade-off, and, yes, it's more fun to work on campaigns with ample funds. Most important, money can buy you the opportunity, ability, and freedom to respond immediately to anything coming at the campaign.

While there are always stories of winners being grossly outspent, history indicates that the inverse is more often true, especially as you move up the food chain. According to the Center for Responsive Politics, in the 2002 midterm elections, "just under 95 percent of U.S. House races and 76 percent of Senate races were won by the candidate who spent the most money" ("Money Is the Victor in 2002 Midterm Elections," November 6, 2002).

In the eleven close Oregon House races in the 2002 general election, only four who were outspent survived, and, of those, two of the losers had extenuating circumstances where no amount of money would have delivered the votes.

Both the message and the quality of candidates (or issues) matter when it comes to raising money. However, campaign organization is a major factor in determining whether contributors are willing to "invest" in your campaign throughout the campaign cycle. Relationships that develop as a result of the candidate, the campaign team, your message, and your organization will bring in early money and early endorsements from individuals, companies, political action committees, and formal organizations.

Early Endorsements = Early Money = Early Media Buys

Early money is also a way to communicate to the public that a cause or candidate has the necessary support to pull off a win. Also, throughout the campaign, major donors can serve as another type of communication tool with the electorate. For example, in Oregon, individuals who give more than $50 must be listed separately on the contributions and expenditures forms (C&Es) filed with the secretary of state. If this is true in your state, look for well-respected people whose names can

"Too often leaders are soft on issues and hard on people. We need to be hard on issues and soft on people.
—Charles Maclean,
Philanthropy Now Consulting

draw votes and ask them to give an amount that will get them listed in a prominent way in the local paper, which in turn may bring in money from their friends and business associates. Obviously this amount varies with the type of race. A $250 contribution may be news for a city councilor or alderman in a small town, but not in a large city mayoral race or congressional district race.

Unfortunately, contributions from individual donors tend to arrive late in a campaign, as things begin to heat up. When supporters see the campaign in the paper and on television or hear it on the radio, they know that this takes money. What they may not know is that media time must be bought weeks in advance. *Early money is critical to a successful media campaign.* That is why many candidates take out personal loans to get their campaign rolling.

Know the law: In some states you may not legally begin collecting money until you have filed with the county clerk, city recorder, or secretary of state. However, from the moment you decided to run or work on a ballot measure, you can begin calling and lining up pledges that will come in as soon as you file.

Campaign Budget

It is pretty easy to put together a cursory budget sheet based on the activities you intend to conduct throughout the campaign; all it takes is a few phone calls.

Figure 4.1 is an actual budget sheet from a 1998 city council race, which I updated for 2003 by calling around. While the original brochure was black and white, I have listed costs for a full-color brochure. If your budget is tight, using black and white instead of color will cut the printing costs in half. In 1998, local campaigns were not given the option of being in the voters' pamphlet, which normally carries a fee of $300. This race covered a city of 19,000 people and 8,000 homes. There was no TV or radio advertising.

Figure 4.2 is the budget from a countywide, issue-based campaign. The county covers about 2,000 square miles and has about 180,000 residents and some 100,000 registered voters. Because of the size of the county and limited volunteer help, lawn signs gave way to 4-by-4-foot and 4-by-8-foot field signs placed along highways.

In 2002, hotly contested Oregon House races came in around $225,000 each for the general election. On the high end, a Portland–Metro area campaign bumped up against a half million, and on the low end a couple of races in the outlying areas spent less than $150,000.

SAMPLE CAMPAIGN BUDGET

*(Five week city council race, population 17,000,
one newspaper, no TV advertising)*

Campaign Activity	Cost in Dollars
Brochure	
Layout and design	110.00
Printing (8,000 full color)	2,936.00
Ads (3)	
Layout and design	225.00
Newspaper: 3 ads run three times each	1,500.00
Lawn signs	
Design	100.00
Printing	
(250 @ $2.52 each- 2 color-two sides)	630.00
Stakes (250 @ $20/bundle of 50)	100.00
Hardware	30.00
Voter lists from county for absentee, GOTV	50.00
Direct mail: 1 piece, postcard	
Postage, layout, mail charge	1,240.00
Photocopying, misc. office supplies	60.00
Candidate photo session	165.00
Total	**$ 7,146.00**

Figure 4.1 Example of a Campaign Budget for a Candidate in a Small-City Race

To get an estimate of how much money your campaign will need, consider talking with people who have previously run a similar race. Some will have budgets with predicted and actual money spent. The county clerk or state election office should have C&E forms on file and a little time with these records might give you an idea of where to best allocate your money. The following sections show how you might go about determining a budget for specific campaign activities.

"It's difficulties that show what men are."
—Epictetus, Greek philosopher

Issue-Based Campaign Budget

Direct Mail

   Fundraiser letter–1,000 pieces

Design	$300.00
Printing & mailing	$1,500.00

   General mailer – full color, 50,000 pieces

Design	$300.00
Printing & mailing	$10,000.00

   General mailer – b&w, 50,000 pieces

Design	$300.00
Printing & mailing	$9,000.00

   Targeted mailer–b&w, 25,000 pieces

Design	$300.00
Printing & mailing	$4,000.00

   Walking/info piece – 5.5x11, color, 30,000 pieces

Design	$300.00
Printing	$2,000.00
Precinct analysis	$900.00
Voters' pamphlet	$300.00
Big signs (200)	$5,000.00

GOTV

Voter registration database from County	$100.00
GOTV inactive reports (4x100)	$400.00
Data consultant	$3,000.00

Media advertising

TV ad development: 4 ads @ $1,000 each	$4,000.00
Cable buys	$6,000.00
Network buys	$12,000.00
Radio development, 5 spots @ 250 each	$1,250.00
Newspaper buys	$4,000.00
Ashland	$3,500.00
Medford	$9,000.00

Other advertising

Insert in chamber newsletter	$75.00
Car/Business signs, 500 pieces	$200.00
Campaign Management	$10,500.00
Office supplies	$200.00
Celebration party	$200.00

TOTAL ESTIMATED BUDGET:	**$88,625.00**

Figure 4.2 Example of a Countywide, Issue-Based Campaign Budget

Brochure

1. Find another brochure with a design and layout you like.
2. Get a price quotation from a graphic designer for something comparable that's camera ready.
3. Determine which precincts you will target; using voter registration lists for those precincts, calculate how many brochures you'll need to print. Call a printer and get a price quotation; you can always have more done later, so don't get carried away. Remember that the number of registered voters and that of actual homes are two different things. You need enough brochures so that one will go to each home regardless of how many registered voters live there. To get the actual number of unduplicated households, try calling an electric utility company, the county clerk, or a mail house.
4. Call a photographer and ask how much a photo shoot will cost.

Things that affect the cost of a brochure:

- Color costs; the choices, in descending order of cost, are full-color, spot color, and black-and-white.
- Paper can have a dramatic impact on cost as well as printed quality. Be careful not to use paper that will absorb the ink too much.
- Does it need to be folded or cut? Each of these brings additional charges.

Lawn signs

Use steps similar to those listed above for the brochure. First, determine the total number of signs you will need. I have worked on campaigns with as many as one lawn sign for every thirty homes and others where we had as few as one for every sixty homes. It really depends on whether you can get the locations for signs and whether you're in an urban race or one with an urban/rural mix. Does the race warrant a large number of signs? Again, one way to determine the number of signs you need is to call someone who conducted a similar campaign covering the same geographical area and ask how many signs were put up. While you're on the phone, ask for their list of lawn sign locations.

Once you know the number of signs, get the same number of stakes plus a few more. Signs run around $4.00–$5.00 each with stakes and the miscellaneous stuff you will need for them. Unlike brochures, short runs for signs may take as long as two weeks to print, and they can be costly. For example, in southern Oregon, a run of twenty-five signs costs $13 a sign, whereas the cost per sign for a run of 500 is $2.45. So get enough printed the first time.

If you need hardware or staple guns and staples to attach the signs to the stakes, price these items and list the cost. If you end up using staples and staple guns, be sure to call any friends you have in construction and ask if you can borrow their staple guns. Better yet, ask them if they will help to put up the signs and bring the staple gun to use. *Label all borrowed tools.*

If you have no locations for signs, you can buy lists of registered voters from the county and call those living on arterials for possible locations. Ideally you would get locations from other campaigns, but in my first race for mayor that wasn't an option. Volunteers went down the voter registration list, cold-calling those on arterials—a brutal but very effective technique.

In general, try to think of every little thing you will need to do to complete a specific activity. After you have done these tasks, take an hour or two and call around for some prices.

> "It's not how much money you raise. It's how you spend your money."
> —Jeffrey Gildenhorn, former candidate for mayor of Washington, D.C.

In a small community, a fairly reliable ballpark figure as to the amount of money you will need to raise is $1 per household in the voting district. If you have strong opposition, you will need more (say, $2 per household); if you have weak opposition, you'll need less. Remember, this figure is for households, not voters. The type and number of media buys you plan to make will greatly influence the amount you need. Similarly, the number of direct mail pieces you send will influence the final budget figures. As your target population increases, you will find an economy of scale. For example, an Oregon House race with 40,000 voters will cost anywhere from $3 to $20 per registered voter. A county race of 100,000 registered voters may come in around $80,000 or 80 cents per registered voter. Budgets are more a function of the race than anything else.

Everything you do in a political campaign requires money. While many of the people who work for you will also give you money, the bulk of it will come from people who are not directly involved as volunteers.

I never apologize or feel like I am begging when I ask for money for a candidate or measure. I assume that the potential contributor wants my candidate in office (or wants the benefits of the ballot measure) and is willing to back up that desire with money. When I ask for money, I think of it as providing an opportunity for the voter to get involved at a level other than the voting booth. I also look at a request for money as less demanding than a request for an individual's time. The reality is this: If you can find excellent candidates to serve in office implementing programs that you support, more power to them; do all you can to help get them there.

"The highest use of capital is not to make more money, but to make money do more for the betterment of life."

—Henry Ford

In Oregon, anyone who contributes to a political campaign may file for a state income tax refund of up to $50. If a husband and wife file a joint tax return, they can get a refund of $100. Sadly, only about 16 percent of citizens take advantage of this. The refund tends to level the playing field for grassroots campaigns. If your state has a similar program, find out about it and get this information to your potential donors.

Figure 4.3 is another example of a budget sheet you can use or modify for your purposes. Many local campaigns are too small and underfunded to have a campaign headquarters (other than in your home) or even staff. However, I included a staff section just in case you need it. Feel free to photocopy this page and modify it to fit your budget needs.

Direct Mail for Money

While direct mail can help create a relationship between your campaign and the voter, it is also an opportunity to raise money where those relationships are established. Given that efficient direct mail requires a mailing list of an already identifiable group of voters, I prefer to see which lists I can get and then formulate a letter or piece that will appeal to those voters. Remember, *your direct mail is only as good as the list to which it is sent.* Carefully match your appeal to the people you are targeting.

"My practice is to go first to those who may be counted upon to be favorable, who know the cause and believe in it, and ask them to give as generously as possible. When they have done so, I go next to those who may be presumed to have a favorable opinion and to be disposed to listening, and secure their adherence.

"Lastly, I go to those who know little of the matter or have no known predilection for it and influence them by presentation of the names of those who have already given."

—Benjamin Franklin

In a direct mail piece, you might include a targeted letter, a campaign brochure, and a remittance envelope (figure 4.4). Direct mail can be used simply to align your candidate with an issue such as a concern for jobs where unemployment is high, parks and playgrounds where there are none, or anti-growth in a neighborhood where a big development is planned. Be sure to color-code your remittance envelopes with your direct mail

BUDGET FORM

CAMPAIGN ACTIVITY	AMOUNT	CAMPAIGN ACTIVITY	AMOUNT
Brochure		Billboards or field signs	
Layout & design		Rental space	
Photography		Design & layout	
Printing		Printing	
		Lumber	
Advertising		Staff	
Ad layout		CPA or bookkeeping (contract)	
Photography		Attorney (contract)	
(I would run a separate		Campaign manager & other staff	
print advertising		Salaries	
budget sheet and include		Insurance, taxes	
the number of ads, the			
size of ads and the cost		Television	
of each for the		Production	
number of runs. Put		Buys	
the total for all here.)		(Again, use the ad rep of	
		each station to set up a	
Research		schedule and budget	
		according to exposure you	
Direct mail		want. Put total here.)	
(Do this for each piece)			
Layout and design		Radio	
Printing		Production	
Postage		Buys	
Lists and labels (or)			
Mailing house (they handle		Office supplies	
labels & postage)		Postage, pens, software	
		Telephone, fax	
Polling		Staples, envelopes, etc.	
Benchmark poll			
Tracking poll		Headquarters	
GOTV		Volunteer support	
Voter ID lists		Food, refreshments	
Absentee lists		Staples, envelopes, etc.	
(list it all)			
		Fund-raising expenses	
Lawn signs		Invitations, layout, printing	
Design & Layout		Postage	
Printing		Decorations	
		Prizes	
Misc. printing			
Bumper stickers			
Flyers			
Body badges			
(canvassers & volunteers)			
Letterhead, envelopes			

Figure 4.3 Sample Budget Form

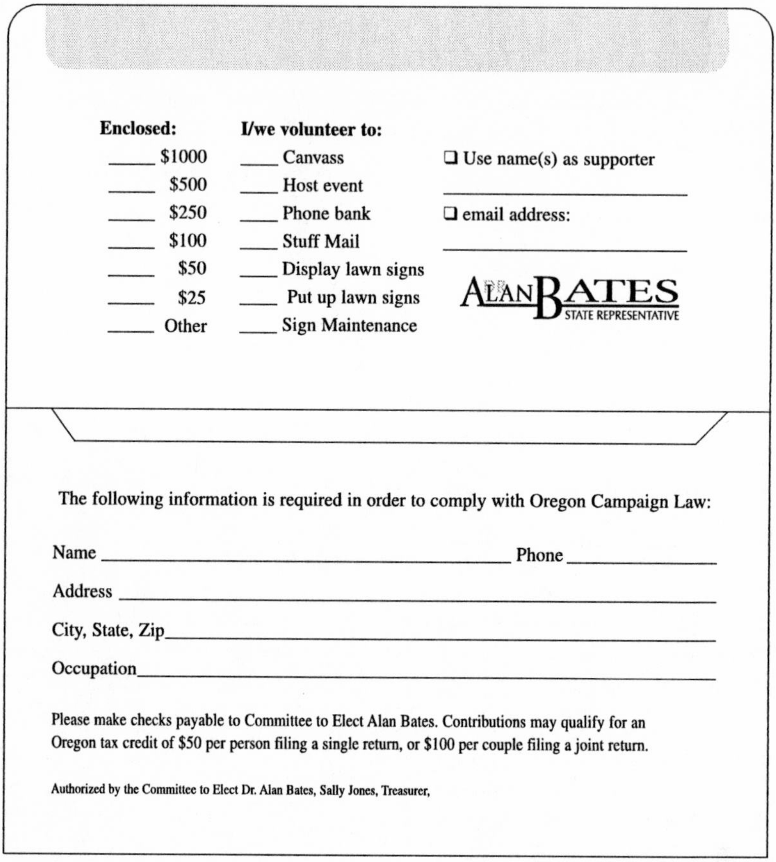

Enclosed:

_____	$1000
_____	$500
_____	$250
_____	$100
_____	$50
_____	$25
_____	Other

I/we volunteer to:

_____ Canvass
_____ Host event
_____ Phone bank
_____ Stuff Mail
_____ Display lawn signs
_____ Put up lawn signs
_____ Sign Maintenance

❏ Use name(s) as supporter

_____

❏ email address:

_____

ALAN**BATES**
STATE REPRESENTATIVE

The following information is required in order to comply with Oregon Campaign Law:

Name _____ Phone _____

Address _____

City, State, Zip_____

Occupation_____

Please make checks payable to Committee to Elect Alan Bates. Contributions may qualify for an Oregon tax credit of $50 per person filing a single return, or $100 per couple filing a joint return.

Authorized by the Committee to Elect Dr. Alan Bates, Sally Jones, Treasurer,

Figure 4.4 Example of a Remittance Envelope. Don't forget to include a line for an e-mail address.

pieces, so you know who is responding to what. That way you get some feedback on which letters are most effective. By running a marking pen along the edges of a stack of remittance envelopes a campaign can cheaply, quickly, and easily color-code envelopes.

Direct Mail Tips for Success

There are all kinds of opinions on the length, the type of paper, and the look of a direct mail piece. While direct mail is used widely to move voters toward a candidate or issue, it can also be an inexpensive and effective way to raise money. Here are some things I've found in soliciting with direct mail.

1. Use quality paper stock and printing. Keep graphics and fonts simple and clean.

2. People in lower economic groups and those with less education respond in greater numbers to a longer "the house is on fire" solicitation. This group gives less money and votes less, so be sure you have targeted correctly before spending lots of money on a multipage solicitation.

   "I have only made this letter rather long because I have not had time to make it short."
   —Pascal, 1656

3. Wealthy, well-educated Republicans respond to letters that are no longer than two pages with lots of "this is what I've done, this is what I will do." A single page will work fine for them.

4. Well-educated, affluent Democrats respond in greatest numbers to short, single-page letters explaining the community needs that you will address and how their contribution will make a difference.

5. Only solicit targeted lists. Most people using direct mail to raise money will send to prospect lists (sometimes thousands of voters) in order to generate a "house list" from those who respond. The first mailing loses money, and subsequent mailings to the "house list" make money. This works well for big campaigns, but local campaigns often cannot send to enough people to generate a large enough house list to make money on subsequent mailings.

6. If you have no targeted lists, spend the money and mail to as big a class of voters as possible to make money on subsequent mailings. For example, mail to everyone in your political party in your targeted precincts.

7. Once people respond to the first mailing, solicit them again. For those responding the second time, solicit them again. After three letters, go back to your house list.

8. A direct mail piece followed up by a phone call from the campaign substantively increases your response rate.

9. Always include a remittance envelope and a P.S. The P.S. should not be a throwaway. This is often the only thing that is read in a fund-raising letter, so make it count.

10. Personalize the letter and envelope if at all possible. Use a size and color of envelope that does not scream junk mail, such as 6 ½ by 5 inches. Have volunteers hand address and use a stamp, even if it's a bulk stamp.

Finding Targeted Mailing Lists

Throughout this handbook are tips and suggestions for establishing relationships with special-interest groups in your community or region. Such alliances can really pay off in mailing-list dividends. Think about who would be most interested in seeing you get elected or seeing your measure passed. Will other candidates or office holders turn over their house lists to your campaign? Consider asking someone who previously ran for the office you are seeking, especially if an incumbent is leaving. Think about other organizations too: Which ones would sell you their mailing lists? Some possibilities of lists that could generate money:

- Teachers, especially if you're working for a school or library bond measure or running for school board
- Environmental organizations such as the Sierra Club, fly-fisherman, League of Conservation Voters, Friends of the River, clean-water groups, greenway organizations, Critical Mass, or any organization that sends a newsletter to a specific group of supporters
- Women's organizations such as Planned Parenthood, National Organization for Women, or Women's Political Caucus
- Your church
- Civic clubs, firefighters, law enforcement groups
- Historic preservation groups

Determine the Amount of Money You Will Need for Direct Mail

1. Decide how many mail pieces you intend to send throughout the campaign.
2. Look at some other direct mail pieces you like and get a cost estimate for layout and design.
3. Decide which groups you are mailing to, and then determine the number of households that will receive the piece. For example, if you want to send a direct mail piece to your top five priority precincts but want to send it only to members of the Green Party, members of the Peace and Freedom Party, Independents, and Democrats, call the county clerk to get a count for each of these group members in those precincts. Because you want a household count, be sure to ask for unduplicated households. Often the clerk's office will download all the necessary information onto a disk for a nominal charge, and you can deliver it to a mailing house where the merge-sort can be done.

4. Use this number to figure your printing and mailing costs for each piece; 50 to 65 cents each is a good ballpark figure. However, economies of scale do count here.

5. Multiply the per-piece cost by the number of direct mail pieces you want to send and add a bit more. That will make up your direct mail budget line item.

Special Events

Special events are campaign-sponsored activities intended to raise money and support for the campaign, such as a coffee at a supporter's house or a campaign-organized luncheon, dinner, or picnic. Although I have had many successful special events for campaigns, compared with the candidate calling supporters directly, they raise very little money and take untold amounts of campaign time. The people who attend are usually supporters who have already given and have every intention of voting for the candidate or cause.

> *"Every experienced campaigner knows that money follows hard work. It is not the other way around."*
> —Margaret Sanger

That said, it is important to stress that fund-raisers are not just about raising money. Special events are also for public visibility and education, for involving volunteers so they are more committed to the campaign and candidate, and for promoting "friend-raising" by strengthening the bonds volunteers and guests have with the candidate.

When approached as an opportunity to advertise the candidate and cement relationships, special events can be worth the necessary resources. But don't underestimate the commitment involved. You need to be cautious about the strain special events put on the campaign committee, the volunteers, and the candidate. If someone other than the campaign committee is sponsoring the event, as is often the case with a coffee, you need to be ready to help that event be a success.

> *"It's nice to have some money, but it's pressing the flesh that's going to win this election."*
> —Jeffrey Gildenhorn, former candidate for mayor of Washington, D.C.

Ensure a Good Turnout

The one thing you must avoid if you schedule a special event is a poor turnout. If it looks like a fund-raising event will have marginal attendance, I invite all my volunteers to attend for free. Numbers are more important than money when holding a special event in political circles. Whatever the attendance, you need to be certain that the people who do attend don't have a bad experience. If people can't find the location, can't find parking, or were inadvertently left off the reservation list, they are likely to blame the campaign. You never want to lose a supporter over an avoidable organizational error at a fund-raising event. Take care of your supporters by taking care of details.

Holding a Special Event

A good rule of thumb for planning special events for fund-raising is that it takes one week of preparation for every ten people you expect to attend. Obviously, this time frame becomes tight in a three-month campaign, but the rule underscores the fact that ample preparation time must be factored in for a successful event. The preparation takes place in four stages.

1. You must *define* the purpose or purposes the event is to accomplish.
2. You must *plan* the event.
3. You must *promote* the event.
4. You must *conduct* the event.

Tips for handling each of these stages are discussed below:

1. Determine the Purpose and Type of Event

Be clear about the purpose of the event. Is it to attract donors, raise money, raise support, thank volunteers and supporters, or just to get the word out on the measure or the candidate? Special events can, of course, have more than one purpose, but you need to focus on one purpose before you can pick the event. Focus on the main purpose when choosing the type of event; then see whether other purposes might be accomplished as well.

"Where there is no vision, the people perish."

—Book of Proverbs, 29:18

Dinners. I have had great results hosting dinners as fund-raising events. I contact a supportive restaurant and ask whether the owner will donate the dinner at cost in the restaurant. I then sell it to the guests at retail. Generally the restaurant can't afford the whole affair, so I go to another eatery and ask whether that owner will donate the dessert, another for a donation of the coffee, a local vintner for the wine, and so on. You can ask a local musician or band to volunteer talent to make the occasion special (consider looking at the high school music department for great talent). Restaurants are often closed on Mondays, making it a perfect night for your fund-raiser.

I have also had great success with intimate affairs at people's homes. In this approach the host produces the invitations and provides the food. If the person hosting the event is new to this sort of thing, it's important to check in frequently and help as needed. These events usually involve a well-known person providing a lavishly catered meal for a well-known candidate at a fairly hefty price. I try, in this scenario, to be selective about whom I invite, although usually the price will select who will attend, and the invitees know that. We have brought in as much as $6,000 in our small area at this type of dinner.

If I am working for a relatively unknown candidate, I do not have a cover charge or a "suggested" donation, for two reasons: First, because the candidate is new to the political circuit, people will stay home rather than give money to a candidate they do not know. Second, I want people to give more than I could possibly charge for such an event. For example, if you charge $100 for a lavish event at someone's home and yet many attendees can give more, the campaign will only get the $100 cover. To lend credibility to my political newcomer, I will bring in a well-known political figure, such as the governor, and will schedule two events back-to-back in two different cities. The first can run from 6:00 to 7:30 in one city and the second from 8:00 to 9:30 in another. To make sure there will be plenty of money flowing, I arrange for one or two people at each gathering to announce that they have just written a check for $1,000 and would encourage all to give as generously as possible. In one campaign we raised $10,000 in three and a half hours with this approach; there was no suggested contribution on the invitation.

> *"Never think you need to apologize for asking someone to give to a worthy object, any more than as though you were giving him an opportunity to participate in a high-grade investment."*
>
> —John D. Rockefeller, Jr.

Coffees. I have found that coffees sponsored by a supporter can be a good special event. I will add, however, that they can also be a miserable failure. To be successful they must, like all special events, be closely supervised. Since the campaign is not the sponsor, the critical factor is who hosts the coffee for you. If the sponsor is a local leader, such as a county commissioner, state representative, mayor, president of a college or university, a business leader, philanthropist, or anyone with a following, there will be a good turnout.

Most people do not really like to go to political fund-raisers such as coffees, so the drawing card should be the combination of the candidate and the host of the coffee. Regardless who hosts the event, the campaign should oversee the invitations and be ready to help with follow-up phone calls to ensure good attendance. A host who invites sixty people only to have three show up may feel humiliated because he or she let you down. Or the host may feel the candidate is responsible for the poor turnout. Either way, the candidate and the campaign manager have been deprived of one more night at home or of time that could have been spent raising money by phone, preparing for a debate, or getting volunteers for a canvass.

A few years ago I started the practice of having one person whose sole campaign job was to oversee coffees. This person should work closely with the campaign scheduler and serves as the campaign's liaison to any host who wishes to sponsor a coffee but does not need to attend war room meetings. The coffee coordinator should be well connected in the community and, ideally, have ready access to lists that may help the hosts in beefing up the invitation list. The coffee coordinator helps with sending invitations, call-backs, and any other tasks that can help the coffee be as successful as possible.

If at all possible, have the candidate call the people invited to the coffee, or at least some of them. This will ensure a donation if they are going, and if they can't make it, it is an opportunity to ask for money or support.

The candidate's call would go something like this:

"Hello, Sam? This is Al Bates. Say, I just got a list of all the people invited to Shirley's coffee, and when I saw your name, I had to take a moment to call and tell you how much I'm looking forward to you being there. It should be a lot of fun. Bring some tough questions for me, will you? Great, see you there."

Using coffees effectively will bring in money, but, more important, they are a great resource for finding campaign workers and lawn sign locations. So if you are going to have them, pay attention to the details and make each one as successful as possible.

Auctions and Yard Sales. Another good fund-raiser is an auction. You and your campaign team can go to businesses and supporters and get a wide variety of donations. For example, ask four different video stores to donate one children's movie, and then put them all together for one auction item. Your campaign volunteers can donate baked goods for the auction. It may work well to have the candidate or the spouse serve as the auctioneer. I have used a popular high school teacher for this task who is funny and can really work the crowd. Be creative and you can have a fun event that actually brings in money. A good auction can bring in as much as $6,000 in a small community.

A yard sale is another option. If you're going to plan one, make it an event. Get a huge yard and lots of donations, old and new. Advertise the great stuff well in advance. Yard sales can be very good fundraising events because almost no money is needed to set one up. However, they require plenty of time. An effective yard sale will take days to set up, two days to run, and two days to put away. Because a big yard sale can be grueling work, be sure not to schedule one during other labor-intensive activities such as canvassing. A good yard sale can bring in $2,000. Since most of the money comes in on the first day, I strongly recommend you advertise it as one day only. Should you decide to do two days, cut the second day so it ends by noon or 1:00 P.M. Be sure to buy pizza for your volunteers for lunch from the proceeds.

> *"I've learned to use the word impossible with the greatest caution."*
> —Wernher von Braun

Involve Attendees.   One event I held in a small community was a dessert bake-off. I called specific supporters in that area and asked them to bring their very best dessert. I charged an entry fee for all but the bakers. The campaign provided the coffee (donated), and I recruited other locals to serve as the judges. I made up ribbons for different awards, such as "Dessert Most Likely to Keep a Marriage Together," and each entry won a prize. Because it was held in a small community, all who attended knew each other. Everyone had a great time, and the only cost to the campaign was the rental of the building.

General Considerations.   Whatever the type of event, the location is a big consideration. Is it big enough? Too big? How about the atmosphere? For indoor events, *never* use a huge hall or room, unless you are expecting a huge crowd. When selecting locations, I look for places where rooms can be closed off in case of poor attendance. No matter how many people come, I want the event to look like it's well attended and successful, leaving attendees with the impression that just the number expected came. In selecting a restaurant for a dinner, try to find one that has a medium-sized room with another adjoining it that can be used or closed off as needed.

> *"One of the symptoms of an approaching nervous breakdown is the belief that one's work is terribly important."*
> —Bertrand Russell

Consider your budget when deciding what type of event to have. Then figure roughly what it will cost the campaign and what income it is likely to generate. You also need to estimate the commitment necessary from the candidate, the

campaign committee, and your volunteers. Don't forget to consider the economic climate in the community. A fifty-dollar-a-plate dinner in a town where
the last factory just closed might not be a very good idea even if it would make
you money. When considering an event, always ask: Does this make sense?
Does it fit? Does it feel right?

2. Plan the Event

Planning an event is an extension of choosing the event. All the considerations
that informed your choice of the event must now be put into an action plan. In
other words, it is time to sort out the de-

"Fatigue makes cowards of us all."
    —Vince Lombardi

tails. For instance, some events will require licenses or permits from local
government. They can be a factor in the
decision to hold an event, but once the de-
cision is made, someone has to make sure the license or permit is obtained.
Similarly, the location, which was a factor in deciding on the type of event, must
now be secured. The theme of the event, whether it is a human services luncheon, environmentalist dinner, or a school auction, now influences the details of
the event.

To run a successful special event, it is critical that you know who your audience is and how to reach it. For example, are you planning a dinner to support
your library? If so, you need to get a mailing list from the Friends of the Library.

Once you know whom you want to reach, you must decide how to reach
them. Printed invitations with a telephone follow-up might work well for a
formal dinner. However, if the event is a yard sale, just advertise it in the
paper or place flyers around town. Whatever the means, people must be assigned to accomplish it. Invitations must be printed; flyers must be designed,
printed, and distributed; ads have to be written and delivered. All this takes
time and people, and you will need to plan accordingly.

A good way to make sure the details are taken care of is to put the event
on a timeline, just like the one for the whole campaign, only smaller. Scheduling in all the tasks and placing the event on a timeline requires someone
who is in charge. That person needs to have volunteers assigned to all aspects of the event. Like the campaign itself, successful special events are the
product of organization. If you assign the leadership of a special event to one
person, provide ample volunteer help, develop a timeline, and plan a budget;
you will have a successful event.

While budgets are an extra step, making one will not only help you get a
handle on expenses but will also remind you of things that need to be done.
For example, listing the cost of the room expense may remind you to check
the date of the event to see what else is going on in the community at that

time. If you're hosting that dinner to support your town library, you don't want to find out right after you printed the invitations and rented the hall that it is on the same night as the American Association of University Women annual dinner at the college. Paying for the ads for your auction may remind you to check whether the hospital auction is on the same weekend. Here is a list of the things that could be included in a budget:

- Site rental
- Food
- Drinks
- Rental (sound system, tables, chairs)
- Printing
- Supplies
- Mailings
- Entertainment
- Professionals
- Parking
- Advertisements
- Decorations
- Insurance
- Fees
- Use permits
- Liquor licenses
- Clean-up
- Awards, door prizes
- Thank-you mailing

Although someone in your organization is in charge of planning the event, when it comes time to implement the plan, provide additional help in the training and staffing of volunteers. Training and staffing requirements must be met before the actual setup begins.

In addition to having trained helpers available, you must plan for the supplies you will need. Often supplies must be ordered well ahead of the event—decorations, for instance—and these should go on your special-event timeline. Also, things that will cost you money—here again, decorations are a good example—are listed in your special-event budget. If you keep going back to the budget and to your expense list, you will be reminded of things you might have forgotten.

Keep in mind that in the planning of an event, some things that do not appear in your budget or timeline may nonetheless be critical. For instance, legal issues such as prohibitions against holding political fund-raisers in public buildings must be considered. On a more mundane but no less critical level, be sure to have duplicates of essential items. If a slide projector is needed for an event, it is wise to have two projectors on hand, or at least two bulbs. How about extension cords and an extra microphone? Also have duplicate lists of all the important phone numbers of the people you are depending on, such as the vendors, caterers, entertainers, staff, and volunteers. These lists will also help you remember all who need to be acknowledged at the end of the event.

3. Promote the Event

To promote a special event properly, you must have a target audience in mind. Consider the income level and age of your target audience. Once these details have been established, consider how best to reach them. Your first task is to determine where to get lists of the people in your target audience. If you have a narrow group in mind, such as teachers, doctors, or human-service advocates, you can often get mailing lists from the special-interest groups these people belong to or support. If your audience is broader, as it would be for a neighborhood bake sale, you can take the list from a general source such as your campaign's county walking list.

"Action is eloquence."
—William Shakespeare

Once you know whom you are trying to contact, you must decide how best to do it. Some possibilities are:

- Invitations
- Flyers
- Radio and television ads
- Press releases
- Posters
- Newsletters
- Handbills or flyers
- Calendars
- E-mail

The content and design of any such announcements must be attractive, professional, and clear. Include the date, place, time (beginning and end), and cost, and provide a map or clear directions for getting there. Note whether any of the cover charge is tax deductible or refundable. For instance, if the event costs $25 for the attendee but your cost per attendee is only $10, then the difference, $15, is a straight campaign contribution. Instead of including the math in the ad, simply put a footnote at the bottom stating what amount of the price is deductible.

4. Conduct the Event

When it is time to conduct a well-planned and well-promoted special event, the most important thing you can do to ensure success is to set up early. Everything should be ready forty-five minutes to an hour ahead of time. As the organizer, you need to keep focused and calm. Your volunteers will take their cue from you, and the message you convey must be calm efficiency. It is a nice touch to have a packet for volunteer organizers with their names on it. Include the overall plan as well as the names of the individuals responsible for each of the volunteer activities. I set up packets similar to the campaign committee packets (see figure 1.1). Although they take a while to write and assemble, volunteers love this format, as it keeps materials well organized.

Once people start to arrive, your focus is on hospitality. How you greet people and work with them will set the tone of the event. Allow adequate time for the candidate to circulate. Do not schedule or allow the candidate to "help" with the operation of the event. The candidate should not be doing things other than meeting the supporters. Name tags will help the candidate when greeting the guests. Be sure to have attendees place the name tag on the right side of their breast so that it can be read discreetly as it moves closer to the candidate's line of sight when he or she is shaking hands.

Remember to thank everyone, even the people who sold you things. Everyone involved—volunteers, guests, and vendors—is forming an impression of the candidate and the campaign, and you need to do everything you can to make a positive impression. That includes a good cleanup, even if you have rented the facility, so make sure there are volunteers who will stay to clean up. As an organizer, never leave an individual to clean up alone. Stay until everything is done.

Candidate Calls to Raise Money

Direct contact by the candidate remains the quickest, cheapest, and most effective way to raise money. It is critical to the success of a campaign. Remember, as the candidate, you are willing to do a job and volunteer your time at a task that few want to do. If people support your core values and ideas, they must show that support by contributing to your campaign, thereby helping you get your name out. Do not sound apologetic. You are doing the community a favor.

While the campaign manager can call for moderate amounts of money, the calls to major donors should be conducted by the candidate or a close family member, such as a spouse, a sibling, or a parent. It is very difficult for people to turn the candidate down on a direct "ask."

Set up some time each day to make the calls. It is important that calls be made from a prepared list that includes phone numbers, addresses, party registration, giving history, personal notes about the prospective donor, and a suggested amount for the ask. Be sure to have accurate information on what name the candidate should use when speaking with the donor: Is it Katherine, Kathy, Katy, Kate, or Kay?

Calling for Money for Ballot Measures

When fund-raising for ballot measures, it is sometimes easier to set up a goal for a specific item, such as a full-page newspaper ad. Let people know what you are trying to buy and how much it will cost so they can contribute accordingly. For example, I might tell people that I am trying to raise $1,500 for a last-minute ad campaign and ask what they can give toward it. If you are going to use a phone bank for fund-raising, use just a few people who are committed and are identified with the measure in the community. Provide each with a list of the people you want to call that includes their giving history along with their phone numbers.

"A great leader is seen as servant first, and that simply is the key to his greatness."

—Robert K. Greenleaf

Since people prefer to sign on to something that's going to fly, I tell potential donors that we are X dollars away from our goal. Keep track as pledged dollars roll in, and if the campaign hasn't received the check within a week, make a quick reminder call.

Voters do not look favorably on candidates who cannot live within their fund-raising abilities, so while waiting for fund-raising to catch up with spending, consider setting up business accounts with as many of your vendors as possible. Although TV and newspapers require that campaign advertisements be paid in full before the ad runs, printers, typesetters, and other vendors may allow you to run an account and pay monthly or at the end of the campaign. Although the money is technically spent, it does not show up on your financial reports until the campaign has received an invoice.

"The palest ink is better than the most retentive memory."

—Chinese Proverb

The Campaign Finance Committee

A campaign finance committee is critical to a successful fund-raising effort, especially if the candidate is running for a county office, a state house or senate seat, a congressional seat, or any statewide office. The committee can handle all of the activities described above, or it can be responsible for telephone follow-up on direct mail solicitations. Depending on who is serving on the committee, it can also be responsible for developing and soliciting major donors. If you are running for an office that covers a fairly large geographic area, you may want more than one finance committee, but within a city, county, or state house and senate district, one will do.

Selecting Finance Committee Members

A great fund-raising committee begins with a strong chair. Your chair should be energetic, charismatic, aggressive, and outgoing and someone who likes asking for money. The chair should have no other campaign tasks during the time of this fund-raising effort. He or she must have great follow-through abilities and a reputation for getting things done. You do not want your campaign to have to use precious time to clean up after a

"Lives based on having are less free than lives based either on doing or being."

—William James

mess has been made, so choose this person carefully and work closely with him or her to make sure things are going according to plan.

The chair, like all members of the committee, should have experience in raising money or in sales. People who have been involved in fund-raising efforts for other political campaigns, charities, nonprofits, churches, civic organizations, academic institutions, foundations, or clubs make excellent committee members. Look also for people who are involved in politics because they feel passionately about an issue, such as school funding, environmental causes, pro-life or pro-choice, labor unions, gun ownership, health care, land use, housing, and so on. Those who have a history with a specific interest group will be able to raise money from others with similar interests.

Look for members who have personal resources, who have a name that means something to your constituency, and who work hard. Too often campaigns and organizations make the mistake of bringing people on board simply because they have a big name. When there are people serving on the finance committee in name only, other members who are working hard may feel resentment, which can cause the committee to break down. While big names work well on the "Committee to Support" outlined in Chapter 1, they should serve elsewhere in a campaign only if they're willing to roll up their sleeves and work in the trenches like everyone else.

Using the Finance Committee for Direct Mail Follow-Up

If you are using a finance committee to increase returns on a direct mail solicitation, begin by sending a letter of solicitation to people who have previously supported the candidate, supported similar candidates, or supported issues embraced by the candidate—especially if they are different from those of the opponent. For an issue-based campaign, send the letter to people who have given to causes or organizations that best reflect the ideals of the ballot measure or proposition.

For local campaigns, which are often strapped for time, money, and human resources, I like to keep the work and scope of the fund-raising effort at a low enough level that it can be managed by a small group of dedicated volunteers and completed within a short time frame. This committee works independently of the candidate's efforts to raise money and, depending on the composition of the committee, may or may not include major donors. It is always preferable to have major donors approached by the candidate or someone close to the candidate. However, if members of the finance committee personally know a major donor, use that connection.

When I chair finance committees, I evenly divide members into groups of three or four and have each team select a name for itself. For example, one could be called the Animals, another the Vegetables, and the third the Minerals. These teams compete with each other for prizes that depend on how many dollars each team brings in. The prizes are usually nothing big but tend to make things more fun—such as coffee from a local coffee house (thanks a' latté). At the end of fund-raising efforts, I have bigger prizes for the team that raises the most money, such as donated pottery or art work. Each of the teams should have a team captain who calls team members on a regular basis and keeps everyone competitive and happy in a friendly way. The team captains report back to the chair.

> *"The first thing you naturally do is teach the person to feel that the undertaking is manifestly important and nearly impossible . . . That draws out the kind of drives that make people strong, that puts you in pursuit intellectually."*
>
> —Edwin H. Land, founder, Polaroid Corp.

Campaign Finance Committee Packets

Providing an effective organizational structure for the campaign finance committee not only results in a more successful effort by committee members but also keeps people coming back to work on other campaigns and efforts. This is really a tough job for people, and while some are better than others, an organized effort on your part helps both the seasoned and the novice fund-raiser to be successful. Creating a packet as shown in figure 4.5 keeps members organized and the campaign contained. Clearly, these are not scraps of paper to leave lying about. They often contain a donor's giving history and personal information.

Details must be attended to in creating these packets just as they must be in preparing packets for the war room. Both the campaign committee and the finance committee are the most important in the campaign. Their members contribute time, resources, energy, and sometimes prestige to your campaign. While the campaign committee provides the organization and leg work, the finance committee helps raise the funds to make everything possible.

In preparing campaign finance committee packets for each member of the committee, include each of the tiered sheets shown in figure 4.5 and detailed in figures 4.6A–H, modified to fit your needs. To give these sheets substance for presentation and durability during the campaign, print them on a heavy paper (no lighter than 80-pound vellum Bristol) and alternate in a two-color scheme—avoid loud or garish colors. Each packet includes eight pieces of paper, in different lengths to create a tiered effect, as well as campaigner cards (figure 4.7), donor cards (figure 4.8), and a sheet that reads "Friends I Will Call" (figure 4.9).

Each of your finance committee members is given a campaigner card (figure 4.7) that will be used to enlist two additional people to assist in the fundraising effort. This method of recruitment increases the finance committee threefold and often brings new faces to a campaign. Campaigner cards can be printed on regular weight paper.

The donor cards are for potential contributors who were mailed a letter of solicitation (figure 4.6D) but have not yet responded by mail. You or the chair will prepare these cards for committee members. To do so, make as many donor cards as there are people who have been solicited by mail, minus the number who already responded, and place a name label in the corner with as much information as you have about the potential donor (figure 4.8). Donor cards must be printed on card stock, because once they are divvied up, committee members handle them a lot while attempting to call from home, the office, or a cell phone while on the way to work.

Once my original finance committee members have enlisted their additional workers (figure 4.7), the candidate should mail a letter to the full committee welcoming them on board, thanking them in advance for their commitment to work on the campaign, and reminding them of the first meeting (figure 4.10). Include with this letter the "Friends I Will Call" sheet (figure 4.9) and a copy of the "Telephone Campaign Overview" (figure 4.6B).

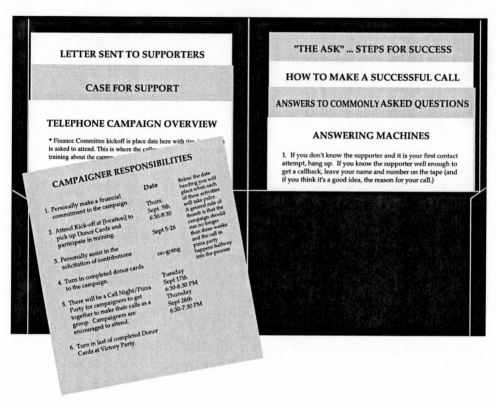

LETTER SENT TO SUPPORTERS

CASE FOR SUPPORT

TELEPHONE CAMPAIGN OVERVIEW

* Finance Committee kickoff is place date here with tim... ...
is asked to attend. This is where the call... ...
training about the camp...

"THE ASK" ... STEPS FOR SUCCESS

HOW TO MAKE A SUCCESSFUL CALL

ANSWERS TO COMMONLY ASKED QUESTIONS

ANSWERING MACHINES

1. If you don't know the supporter and it is your first contact attempt, hang up. If you know the supporter well enough to get a callback, leave your name and number on the tape (and if you think it's a good idea, the reason for your call.)

CAMPAIGNER RESPONSIBILITIES

	Date	
1. Personally make a financial commitment to the campaign.	Thurs. Sept. 5th 6:30-8:30	Below the date heading you will place when each of these activities will take palce. A general rule of thumb is that the campaign should run no longer than three weeks and the call in pizza party happens halfway into the process
2. Attend Kick-off at [location] to pick up Donor Cards and participate in training.	Sept 5-26	
3. Personally assist in the solicitation of contributions	on-going	
4. Turn in completed donor cards to the campaign.	Tuesday Sept 17th 6:30-8:30 PM	
5. There will be a Call Night/Pizza Party for campaigners to get together to make their calls as a group. Campaigners are encouraged to attend.	Thursday Sept 26th 6:30-7:30 PM	
6. Turn in last of completed Donor Cards at Victory Party.		

Figure 4.5 Example of a Campaign Finance Committee Packet

CAMPAIGNER RESPONSIBILITIES

Date

(Below the date heading place when each of these activities will take place. A rule of thumb is that the campaign should run no longer than three weeks, and the call-in pizza party happens halfway into the campaign).

1. Personally make a financial commitment to the campaign.

2. Attend Kickoff at *(location)* to pick up Donor Cards and participate in training.

   Thurs. Sept 15 6:30-8:30

3. Personally assist in the solicitation of contributions.

   Sept 5-Oct. 6

4. Turn in completed Donor Cards to the campaign.

   ongoing

5. There will be a Call Night/Pizza Party for campaigners to get together to make their calls as a group. Campaigners are encouraged to attend.

   Tuesday Sept 27th 6:30-8:30 PM

6. Turn in last of completed Donor Cards at Victory Party.

   Thursday Oct. 6 6:30-7:30 PM

Cut to create a tiered look in the packets.

Figure 4.6A Sample Text for Campaigner Responsibilities Sheet

TELEPHONE CAMPAIGN OVERVIEW

- The finance committee kickoff is (*place, date here with time*). EVERYONE is asked to attend. This is where you will pick up your Donor Cards (approximately 35), get more detailed information and training about the campaign, and meet your team members.
- The Donor Cards will have names of those individuals who have a history of giving to this campaign or similar causes. During the three-week fund drive, campaigners will call these supporters at their convenience.
- There will be three teams consisting of approximately six campaigners and one team captain.
- Teams compete with one another for a variety of awards and prizes.
- Cards are turned in to the captains or the campaign as they are completed. This is done either directly to your team captain or to the campaign office.
- There will be a Call Night/Pizza Party on (*day and date*) for the finance committee to get together to make their calls as a group. Callers are encouraged to attend.
- A party is scheduled for (*day and date*). All remaining cards must be turned in on this evening. The winning teams will be announced and honored. We will all be winners at this point, and so will the campaign.
- Fun **is** a requirement for this campaign, so plan on having a good time for a very good cause.

IMPORTANT INFORMATION
All Donor Cards **must** be returned (even if they haven't been called).
Please do not give Donor Cards to supporters.

THANKS FOR YOUR TIME AND SUPPORT!!!!

Figure 4.6B Sample Text for Telephone Campaign Overview Sheet

CASE FOR SUPPORT

This page is where you most clearly outline what your candidate (or issue-based campaign) stands for. It may be an opportunity to outline the differences between the candidates or to simply make your case without regard to the opposition.

Depending on whom you are soliciting, this sheet may change to accommodate a different focus or emphasis. For example, if you are targeting a Sierra Club mailing list with a letter and follow-up phone call, you may want these notes to include the candidate's stands on environmental issues or past votes if the candidate previously held an office. If you are calling members of a teachers union, you may want to include the candidate's stands on school issues and libraries. For the Chamber of Commerce membership or Rotary Club list, you might focus on the candidate's strengths around business issues. And so on.

It will keep your caller more focused if you match this white paper with the potential donor's interests. You can best determine those interests by knowing the origin of the mailing list.

If you are simply calling a list of general supporters, have a number of important community issues itemized here and your candidate's stands on them. If you're working for an incumbent, list accomplishments while in office.

Figure 4.6C Case for Support Sheet

LETTER SENT TO SUPPORTERS

(This page should include the complete solicitation letter sent to potential donors. Reduce it so it will fit on a single page and still allow room for the above heading.)

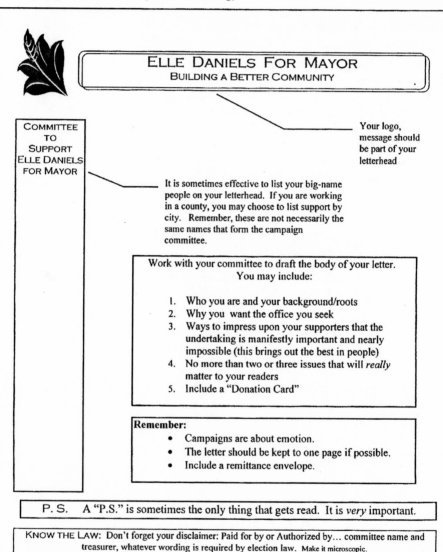

ELLE DANIELS FOR MAYOR
BUILDING A BETTER COMMUNITY

Your logo, message should be part of your letterhead

COMMITTEE TO SUPPORT ELLE DANIELS FOR MAYOR

It is sometimes effective to list your big-name people on your letterhead. If you are working in a county, you may choose to list support by city. Remember, these are not necessarily the same names that form the campaign committee.

Work with your committee to draft the body of your letter. You may include:

1. Who you are and your background/roots
2. Why you want the office you seek
3. Ways to impress upon your supporters that the undertaking is manifestly important and nearly impossible (this brings out the best in people)
4. No more than two or three issues that will *really* matter to your readers
5. Include a "Donation Card"

Remember:
- Campaigns are about emotion.
- The letter should be kept to one page if possible.
- Include a remittance envelope.

P. S.   A "P.S." is sometimes the only thing that gets read. It is *very* important.

KNOW THE LAW: Don't forget your disclaimer: Paid for by or Authorized by… committee name and treasurer, whatever wording is required by election law. Make it microscopic.

Figure 4.6D Sample Letter Sent to Supporters

ANSWERING MACHINES

1. If you don't know the supporter and it is your first contact attempt, hang up. If you know the supporter well enough to get a call-back, leave your name and number (and if you think it's a good idea, the reason for your call).

2. If you don't know the supporter well and it's your second or third taped greeting, rather than give up, leave your name, volunteer status, reason for the call, and phone number:

    Example:

    Hi, this is _____ calling at _____ o'clock on (day of the week).
    I'm volunteering for (name of campaign) *in hopes that you would consider a gift to help support...* (place short message here—it could be the candidate's name and office or it could be something that the candidate stands for that will resonate with this particular donor. For example: management of forest land or fly fishing or choice issues or libraries. This must be worked out ahead of time with your volunteer caller and/or noted on the donor card).

    I've tried to reach you a number of times by phone and although I <u>am</u> giving up reaching you in person, I'm <u>not</u> giving up on the idea that you'll support (name of candidate and office sought). **I'll ask** (name of candidate) **to send you another return envelope. We would be <u>so</u> grateful if you would use it to support** (again, place an issue here that will resonate—appeal to interests over intellect. For example, you might say, "to support better management of our forest resources through [candidate's name]").

    This is an extraordinarily close race with a lot at stake, and we can only win with help from people like you. If you have any questions, please give me a call at _____.

3. On the donor card write that another blank return envelope needs to be sent to the supporter and get it back to the campaign as soon as possible. A nice touch is to include a short handwritten, signed note, such as: "Sorry, I missed you."

4. If leaving a message does not fit your style, perhaps you could send the potential supporter a note and enclose it with an envelope from your folder. Please note on the donor card that you have done so.

GOOD LUCK!!!

Figure 4.6E Sample Answering Machines Sheet

ANSWERS TO FREQUENTLY ASKED QUESTIONS

Sample questions:

Didn't I already give to this candidate (campaign)?

Previous gift information, when available, should be on the donor card or printouts, depending on which you are using. It's OK to give the information to the donor, but volunteer it only when you have a purpose. For example, donors gave $50 to a similar candidate or cause and you want them to increase their gift.

I give money to my PAC at work, and they're already supporting this candidate.

"That's great. However, if we can show that the bulk of our money comes from individuals, such as you, rather than PACs, it encourages others to contribute also. While PAC money will help, we depend on direct support from individuals to pull off a win in November."

I don't know much about either of these candidates. How are they different?

Have two or three key issues that clearly show the difference between your candidate and the opponent and place that here. These key issues should be appropriate for the donor list you are soliciting.

How does this candidate stand on _____?

Think of two or three issues that might come up in a phone solicitation. This is the place to touch on a couple of key issues that might be of concern to the community. However, volunteers should use caution in discussing campaign issues in too much detail. However, for the caller to have more background, your "*Case for Support*" sheet should cover the issues in greater depth.

Who else supports this candidate?

Include a short endorsement list here of organizations and well-known citizens that support the candidate. Prepare here! For example, if you're calling Realtors, don't list an antigrowth group to the potential supporter. Instead it might include members of the Chamber of Commerce, the Rotary Club, or your downtown association. Again, fit the endorsements with the people being called.

Figure 4.6F Sample Text for Answers to Frequently Asked Questions Sheet

HOW TO MAKE A SUCCESSFUL CALL

BEFORE YOU PICK UP THE PHONE:

1. Be proud of yourself for working on the front lines of a campaign. Many talk a good game, but you act.
2. Feel camaraderie with the person you're calling. In nearly every case, the person has previously given to an organization supporting our efforts, directly to our candidate, or to another candidate who embraces ideals similar to our candidate's.
3. Remember what motivates you about *(the candidate or ballot measure)* and why you agreed to pitch in with the campaign.
4. Decide how much you will ask for. If you know the person and their giving capabilities, don't be afraid to be bold. Otherwise you might say that people are giving $50 on average but that any amount would be welcome and put to good use. I often just let the people tell me what they want to give. ("What should I put you down for?" Offering increments of $25, $50, $100 works well.) It is important to get an amount.

MAKING CONTACT WITH THE DONOR:

5. Identify yourself by name and as a volunteer, and ask for the donor by her or his first name.
6. If a couple is identified on the donor card and you don't know which one cares about the campaign, an effective approach is to give your name and say you're a volunteer working for *(name of campaign)* as part of a fund-raising effort to get *(name)* elected. Then ask whether it is X or Y or both who support the candidate. Then ask to speak with that person. Say you'll call back if the person is not then available.
7. Show the donor that you are sensitive to the possibility that your call might come as an intrusion. For instance: ***Do you have a minute to talk now?*** If the answer is "no," ask when it would be convenient to call back. Note the call-back time on the donor card, and then follow through. If the answer is "yes," you're on your way!
8. Refer to the letter sent out by our campaign. Included in your packet is a "Case for Support" paper that will help guide you.

Figure 4.6G Sample Text for How to Make a Successful Call Sheet

"THE ASK" ... STEPS FOR SUCCESS

1. Strategies for The Ask:

    The campaign should have some issues that are important to the donor. For example, if the donor's name came from a NOW list and choice is an important component in the campaign, use this information. Use the information about where the donor's name came from to build a relationship. Whether the source is the Chamber of Commerce, a school union, an environmental group, a women's activist organization, or even the town you live in, use this information.

    Find ways to connect with the potential donor. For example: In a countywide race you may live in the same town as the prospective donor and recognize the last name as a parent with children going to school with your children. *"Hi, I'm a volunteer out working for [name] tonight. As a parent of the Jacksonville School District, I'm supporting [name] because of her leadership within our community schools. Tonight we're raising money to send [name] to the Board of Commissioners, and we're hoping you will join our effort. Would you consider a pledge of $50 toward the campaign?"*

    A very effective technique is to tell the donors how much you are trying to raise for a specific campaign function. For example: *"Hi, I'm a volunteer helping [name of campaign]. We're trying to raise $12,000 for some TV spots that have to be bought now for the November election. Would you be willing to make a pledge or send a gift to support our efforts?"* If they say yes, ask what you can put them down for. If they say no or are curt with you, ask if they would rather be removed from the mailing list.

2. Once you have made the request for money, let the donor respond. Do not distract the donor with nervous small talk. Just be silent. Remember: after the ask, the first one to speak, loses. If the donor declines the ambitious amount you've suggested, ask if he or she would prefer to break the gift down by half and give twice. If that doesn't work, fall back to a more modest amount.

3. If the donor indicates that he or she will probably make a pledge but hasn't decided how much, suggest that the campaign can send another envelope as a reminder, and the donor can send whatever amount he or she feels comfortable with.

4. Finally, verify the address on the donor card, and ask if the donor has any objection to being acknowledged in an endorsement ad. Please note the response on the donor card, and use the card to record any other information that has even the slightest chance of being useful, such as issues that the voter cares about, if he or she wants to work for the campaign or would like a lawn sign.

5. Thank everyone, including turndowns, for their time.

Figure 4.6H Sample Text for "The Ask" . . . Steps for Success Sheet

ELLE DANIELS FOR MAYOR
BUILDING A BETTER COMMUNITY

CAMPAIGNER CARD

Finance Committee Member _____

1st Campaigner's Name _____ Phone _____

Address _____ City _____ Zip _____

2nd Campaigner's Name _____ Phone _____

Address _____ City _____ Zip _____

Figure 4.7 Example of a Campaigner Card (Print three to a sheet of paper and cut to size.)

FRONT:

Daniels for Mayor
PO Box 1
Ashland, Oregon 97520
555-2003

Place donor label here. Include:
Name (include partner or spouse)
Address
Phone number
Email
Giving history

Amount Pledged_____

Payable: Send envelope and information sheet   Turn Down

Pay half now, half later   Contact/Attempts:_____

Other Arrangements   _____

Visa   Mastercard #_____Expiration Date _____

BACK:

Campaigner: Please fill out card, front and back, and return with your weekly reports.
Email address_____
New address (street or box, city, zip)

New Phone number (cell phone?) _____
Out of town; expected return date
Contact later; date to contact
Wrong phone number; present number unknown
If turndown, reason given
Comments

Figure 4.8 Example of a Donor Card (front and back). These are printed on card stock.

FRIENDS I WILL CALL
(Business-Social)

Caller's Name_____

Name		Phone
Address		
City	Zip	Pledge

Name		Phone
Address		
City	Zip	Pledge

Name		Phone
Address		
City	Zip	Pledge

Name		Phone
Address		
City	Zip	Pledge

Name		Phone
Address		
City	Zip	Pledge

Name		Phone
Address		
City	Zip	Pledge

Name		Phone
Address		
City	Zip	Pledge

Name		Phone
Address		
City	Zip	Pledge

__IMPORTANT:__   **PLEASE BRING THIS LIST TO THE CAMPAIGN KICK-OFF SO WE CAN CHECK FOR DUPLICATIONS.**

Figure 4.9 Sample Friends I Will Call

The "Friends I Will Call" sheet is important because finance committee members list *their* friends or co-workers who they believe are supportive of the cause. Obviously this does two things: It increases your donor base, and it gets friends to call friends. This form should be filled out and returned to the campaign before the kickoff party to give the campaign an opportunity to remove any duplicates of names that are already in the mix for a call from the committee. Because many sheets end up arriving on the night of the kickoff (no matter how much you plead to have them back earlier), have a couple of campaign workers on hand to check these lists against your existing donor cards and the other names on the "Friends I Will Call" sheets. Remove duplicates before members begin their calling. This is important because people who hate being called once for a solicitation can get downright nasty on the second or third call in a single evening; plus it makes your campaign look disorganized and committee members go ballistic.

Once donor card duplications have been removed and duplications within each of the lists eliminated, return each "Friends I Will Call" sheet to the volunteer who generated it so that he or she can make contact with those on their list during the fund-raising campaign.

Include in each finance committee packet paper and envelopes so callers can jot a quick thank-you note to the donor after the phone contact (figure 4.11). This provides the added benefit of allowing for a personalized message while the conversation is still fresh in everyone's mind. It's most effective if this is done between calls; if left to the end, it usually does not happen.

This personal and efficient touch works. Use nice paper cut in half and a small envelope (4 1/2 by 5 3/4 inches). Prepare and include a few thank-you notes generated by the campaign for the committee and word them in such a way that they will not need a salutation—only a signature. Whether personal or prepared, completed thank-you notes are paper-clipped to the donor card for mail preparation—don't forget to include a remittance envelope (figure 4.4).

Because callers are more successful when they have plenty of information, finance committee packets should include a lot of detail about the candidate or issue-based campaign. Obviously, callers do not have to read everything in the packet, but those who do are often more at ease in the task. Here, as with canvassing, discourage volunteers from answering specific questions about a candidate's stands on issues. Although a caller can share his or her motivation for volunteering in the effort, specific

"I am deeply touched—not as deeply touched as you have been coming to this dinner, but nonetheless it is a sentimental occasion."

—John F. Kennedy at a political fund-raiser

Dear Bonnie,

Thank you for volunteering as a campaigner for the Daniels for Mayor campaign. This fund-raising effort promises to reach an all-time high in dollars raised and fun to be had.

Please pull out your calendar and write the following dates and times down.

ALL EVENTS ARE LOCATED AT CAMPAIGN HEADQUARTERS
LOCATED AT 525 BEACH STREET

CAMPAIGN KICK-OFF   THURSDAY   SEPT. 15 6:30–8:30PM
CALL NIGHT PIZZA PARTY   MONDAY   SEPT. 27 6:30–8:30PM
TURN IN PLEDGE SHEETS   ON GOING THROUGHOUT MONTH
VICTORY PARTY...LAST OF
PLEDGE CARDS TURNED IN   THURSDAY   OCT. 6 6:30–7:30PM

Now that you have these important dates written down, take a second to look over the enclosed information. I have included a campaign overview to let you know just where we are going with all of this and a "Friends I Will Call" sheet.

Please pay special attention to the "Friends I Will Call" sheet. This important list will accomplish two things. It will help you think of friends and acquaintances you could call who may be interested in supporting Elle Daniels for Mayor. It will also allow us to cross-reference those individuals with the list being called to eliminate the chance of call duplications. Please send it to me as quickly as possible or bring it to the campaign kick-off.

If you have any questions please feel free to contact me at work (number) or home (number).

Thank you again,

Figure 4.10 Sample Letter Welcoming Finance Committee Member to the Campaign

questions can best be answered by directing the donor to call the candidate directly.

It's a nice touch to personalize each of the finance committee packets by putting the caller's name on the front, even if it's in the form of a printed label; it tells the volunteer that he or she is important and is being counted on.

On kickoff night, when each committee member is to receive a packet and a stack of donor cards, the candidate and the campaign manager should be present. The candidate says a few words of thanks and inspiration, and the manager gives an overview of the fund-raising effort.

Callers are to make the calls within a three-week period, usually from home. However, it is a good idea to set up a phone bank party midway. This

Dear Peter,

Just a quick note to let you know how great it was to talk to you tonight and to thank you in advance for your generous pledge.

Without support from people like you we would not be able to pull off a win this November.

Oh, I hope your son did well on his Spanish test.

Thanks again,
Joan

Figure 4.11 Sample Thank-You Note from Campaign Finance Committee Member to Campaign Donor

really gives callers a shot in the arm, and most will complete their calls at this time. In general, people prefer to call in the company of others, and many save their calls for this night—so make it a fun evening with great food and drink.

It is important to remember that the people being solicited in this manner are not major donors. Major donors are contacted by the candidate, his or her spouse, or someone else close to the candidate.

> *"You may never know what results from your action. But if you do nothing, there will be no results."*
> —Gandhi

Potential Sources for Names
The following are individuals and organizations that may be able to provide names or generate lists of names.

candidate   candidate's spouse   contributors to
                          and relatives   other campaigns

finance committee   friends of the campaign   campaign staff
business associates   finance chair   clubs
professional organizations   college class mates   churches
issue groups   the party   unions

Tips for Successful Fund-Raising

1. *Campaigns are about emotion, not intellect.*
2. *Be visionary; present a vision; address opportunity.* People need to feel that investing in a campaign will make life better, both now and in the future. They should feel that your winning will strengthen the community. Make your case larger than the office you seek or the program you hope to fund.
3. *Invite donors to invest in leadership, solutions, and vision.* Through a candidate or a campaign, people are making an investment in their community. Generally, people contribute to a campaign or candidate because they believe that they will get something in return. Describe to the donor, the voter, the citizen what they will get with a victorious election. Use issues that are in front of voters.
4. *Look for early money.* "He who gives early gives twice" (Cervantes). Do not look at fund-raising as though there is just so much money and no more. Money flows like a river; don't think of it like a well or a pond. There's plenty of money if you can show that gifts will be used wisely. This applies to candidates and campaigns as well as schools, libraries, parks, and other issue-based campaigns for money.
5. *Sell ideas and hope, not the candidate.* You're offering something that the voter wants: opportunity, vision, solutions, parks, better schools, less traffic, lower crime rates, cleaner air, whatever. Look at your campaign as the vehicle for the voters to get what they want. Charles Revson, founder of Revlon, said, "In the factory, we make cosmetics. In the stores, we sell hope."

> *"It does not matter so much where we are ... as the direction which we are moving."*
>
> —Goethe

6. *Never think of fund-raising as begging.* If you're a candidate, you're putting yourself out there, at no small sacrifice, to do a job that people want done. If you're working for a ballot measure, you're creating opportunities for a community to realize a vision.
7. *There's a difference between an underdog and a losing effort.* People want to help an underdog but usually will not help finance an effort

they believe will lose. Presenting your campaign as an underdog suggests that people are investing in the American Dream.

8. *Stay on your message.* Your message should always be at the center of every appeal. Incorporate it into the "ask" while keeping the targeted donor's profile and interests as the focus.

9. *Be organized.* Because people equate organization with winning, by showing a strong organizational core you are more likely to get people to give.

10. *Think community.* Community campaigns are the most successful. A community campaign presents issues that people understand. It presents solutions, involves volunteers, and encourages investment in the future. Do not talk about the mechanics of the campaign. A campaign and a candidate don't have needs; the community and the people in it have needs and challenges. The candidate or campaign should represent opportunity, solutions, answers, and the ability to meet those needs.

11. *Don't be afraid to ask for money.* Asking for money is how you fund a campaign.

Fund-Raising Ideas
That Take Less Than One Month of Preparation

1. Personal solicitation.
2. The "Friends I Will Call" sheet.
3. Dinner at a restaurant as outlined above.
4. "Sponsored by . . ." Dinner or brunch at the house of someone well known. This is a variation on a theme of a coffee, but whereas coffees are usually free, a dinner has an admission fee.
5. Theme dinner. These are great fun. First, and most important, you need an incredible friend who is willing to open his or her home and do the preparation of food with other friends. A theme dinner usually will focus on a period in history (such as the turn of the century), an author or set of authors, an important leader, and so forth. For example, you might have an evening focusing on Jane Austin. One friend would research her life and prepare some text that may be read throughout (or between) courses of the meal. Others would prepare the meal that features the types of foods eaten at that time period. A theme dinner can also center on many authors. In this case, your really great friend might prepare favorite dishes of certain authors or dishes featured in books—such as *Like Water for Choco-*

late. We have done this with high school girls and boys acting as the servants (dressed in black and white). You will also need different people to read appropriate passages from books that pertain to the courses being served. As these dinners are a real treat—almost like time travel—and lots of work, charge plenty. Make sure you sell enough tickets to make it worth your while before you head out to shop for groceries and spend days cooking.

6. Small auctions. They are surprisingly easy to conduct. You need volunteers who are willing to approach businesses and friends to get donations for a candidate. Combine donations to make more attractive prizes. Auction a pair of shoes from a local shoe store, or a backpack from a mountaineering supply store; find someone willing to give tennis lessons or golf lessons; ask a historian to donate a tour of your town's historic district; ask a pilot to donate a ride in a private plane; and so on.

7. Softball tournament. This requires lots of work and makes very little money but is great fun and a perfect project for that guy who wants to help, but doesn't quite fit in anywhere else. The admission fees go to the campaign.

8. Birthday party for the candidate. The price of admission in dollars should be the candidate's age in years.

9. Raffle. This requires someone to be completely on top of the event, someone who can really track where the tickets are. You need a big prize and some lesser prizes plus a bunch of people to sell tickets. Again, you can combine things to create a big prize, such as dinner for two, plus two theater tickets, after-theater dessert, and nightcap at a popular spot.

"Men take only their needs into consideration, never their abilities."
—Napoleon

10. A donated weekend in a cabin, at the lake, in the woods, or near a ski resort. Do you know anyone with a condo in Hawaii? If a travel agent supports you, he or she might be willing to forgo the sales commission and help with a really cheap fare that the campaign could afford to pay. Be creative.

"A person is known by his charity."
—Irish proverb

11. An afternoon with . . . Have a local celebrity or author put together entertainment or a reading. How about asking the governor to pop in as he or she is moving through town? Have some great donated pastries and assorted hot beverages on hand.

12. Tasting and toasting. This is a theme coffee with an admission. It is just what it sounds like: wine tasting with finger food and a couple of big names present.

"Hey, Big Spender"

If you've read this far, chances are you don't have millions of dollars to throw at your campaign—maybe not even thousands. So what happens when you head up a ballot measure or pull a petition against big money? Don't worry, there's hope. Big spenders may get a lot of press, but they don't always win. In fact, the Center for Responsive Politics reported that in the 1996 congres-

"We make a living by what we get, but we make a life by what we give."
—Winston Churchill

sional races, only 19 of the 149 candidates who spent more than $100,000 of their own money won—that's less than 13 percent. Similarly, in the 2002 midterm elections, 19 of the 20 U.S. House and Senate candidates who spent $1 million or more of their own funds on their campaigns lost.

While deep pockets can't always buy a win on election day, they can buy name recognition. So, if you're running a campaign against someone with unlimited resources, you'd better have a tight message, a lot of volunteers, a well-organized campaign, and an edge. In this handbook you'll find a number of tips to help you compete with big money. How-

"Big money brings big problems."
—Bill Meulemans

ever, if you know you will be outspent, pay close attention to developing a powerful message and communicating it in effective ways that resonate with the voters.

With the complexities of government more in focus for the voter in recent years, experience is playing a larger role in electing and reelecting candidates. While "I don't know" can initially sound romantic and even charming, it wears thin with the voters as time goes on. Although there are exceptions, candidates who are vague about issues eventually will come across to voters as lacking substance whether they have lots of personal wealth or not.

"Nobody roots for Goliath."
—Wilt Chamberlain

In a special election in 1999, Audie Bock won a seat in the California State Assembly with $40,000, one direct mail piece, a few lawn signs, and 100 volunteers. Her opponent spent $600,000, including $100,000 in the last two weeks on twelve direct mail pieces.

In Nebraska's 1998 gubernatorial primary, Mike Johanns, who was hugely outspent by his two opponents, won using the slogan: "This is about governing . . . and I've done it." This slogan focused on the candidate's experience—something money cannot buy.

By contrast, an underfinanced Republican, Bill Redmond, of New Mexico, was elected to Congress in 1996 in a district heavily populated by registered Democrats not by focusing on his experience but rather on questionable ethical activities of his opponent. And his campaign used one other very effective trick. With a strong Green Party candidate, Carol Miller, in the running, the Redmond campaign sent a direct mail piece to Democrats urging them to vote for her, thereby splitting the Democratic vote.

"A man's real worth is determined by what he does when he has nothing to do."

—Megiddo message

In all these campaigns, the focus on message, a disciplined organization, volunteers, strategy, and communication pulled out not just difficult races, but, in the Redmond and Bock examples, seemingly impossible races, all while being outspent. While Redmond and Bock incorporated negative campaigning, in the Nebraska election Mike Johanns never went negative.

In my town, we effectively fought and won a campaign for a prepared food and beverage tax to pay for an open-space program and wastewater treatment plant upgrades against local restaurateurs, Realtors, and the Oregon Food and Beverage Industry. Although we were outspent five to one, we had an effective message that resonated with the voters and hundreds of volunteers to deliver that message.

Five Reasons Why Personal Wealth Doesn't Translate into Winning Campaigns

1. Many voters feel that money is not an entitlement to hold a public office. Candidates must have substance, a clear stand on issues, and related experience.
2. A candidate who appears to be working hard to get into office will be perceived as someone who will work hard once in office. A candidate who buys everything for support does not always appear to be working as hard as the candidate who can't buy so much.
3. Clear communication will beat money every time. The voter knows that if a candidate can clearly communicate during an election, there's a good chance that he or she will be a good communicator in office.

4. Because there is a perception that candidates with great personal wealth do not need financial support, they have a more difficult time raising money. Money raised is itself a way to communicate with the voters: It tells them who supports a candidate and, in essence, why.

5. Similarly, there is a perception that candidates with great personal wealth do not need as much volunteer help—that they can buy strategists, pollsters, campaign managers, phone bank callers, canvassers, and envelope stuffers. Fewer volunteers on the campaign also means a smaller number of potential supporters from among the friends and family of existing volunteers.

Outside money can also be a liability. There is fundamental suspicion among voters when outside money tries to buy an election. This is most apparent in small communities that take on money measures that poke at large political action groups with unlimited resources to influence the outcome of an election. However, I have also seen allegations of outside money influence used to defeat statewide ballot measures.

So what if you have plenty of money and want to get elected or pass your ballot measure? Here are some tips:

1. If you're working to pass or defeat a ballot measure, remember, the messenger is the message. Carefully choose who will deliver the message to the voters. In the 1998 California general election, the Indian gambling proposition had the out-of-state Las Vegas casinos fighting it while the proponents used Native Americans to promote it. The casinos lost. During a recent tort reform ballot measure, lawyers used victims of drunk drivers rather than themselves in ads. Carefully consider your messenger and use one who evokes an emotion or a positive feeling with the voters.

2. Hit the campaign trail. Don't spend all your time with the high end of society. Get out and meet the public, kiss babies, shake hands, go to malls, get your face or issue out there. Do the walking and talking. If you're independently wealthy and financing your own campaign, you get to spend time with the voters rather than on the phone dialing for dollars.

3. Distance yourself from any legislation or policies that look like they will benefit your business, either directly or indirectly. A good politician will embrace issues that are good for the community, especially the community in the long run. That may not be good for your

business in the immediate future, but it will be good for you as a candidate and office holder.

4. Being rich doesn't mean you shouldn't be informed on the issues, have a tight message, and be able to communicate it well to the public. Get your campaign organized, and don't apologize for your money.

5. Spend your resources as though you don't have a lot. Use lawn signs, newspaper ads, radio ads, and direct mail. Even though you can afford it and it's easier, you should avoid communicating with the voters only through TV ads.

6. Don't run as a businessperson, run as a leader in your community. Talking about your business success can be misconstrued by the voter. Instead relate your business experience to serving in office. While people love to say government should be run like a business, that's not exactly true; streets make no money, sewer and water services make no money. Government is not about making a profit, it's about service to the community—it's business with a heart. Characterize the differences so voters know that you understand what they are.

7. Don't parade your wealth to the voters by saying how much you will spend to win. You never want to appear as though you're buying votes. It's far more important to the voters that you earn them.

8. Most important, always appear to be one with the average person. Integrate this idea as part of your core. Too often, those who are very wealthy project an image of being out of touch with the common person.

The World's Smallest Brochure: Direct Mail That Works

Most direct mailings have a rate of return of 3 to 6 percent without callbacks. Because a campaign does not want to send a direct mail piece to raise funds that costs more money than it brings in, the challenge lies in designing a piece with a higher rate of return that is inexpensive to produce.

"Time is the most valuable thing one can spend."
—Theophrastus (300 B.C.)

People have become very sophisticated at detecting junk mail. To increase the rate of return, the piece must first get opened; second, it must be read (at least in part); and finally, it must be compelling enough to motivate the reader to give. Anything in a business-size envelope (a number 9) with an address label, a bulk stamp, or a meter mark is suspect and apt to be thrown away without being opened. So the first task is choosing an envelope size for the piece that will make it more likely to be opened.

In 1999 the Reform Party created a direct mail piece that went out nationwide to 70,000 recipients. They drew a return rate of 4 percent by using an oversized (5 by 7 inches) courier envelope and an easy-to-read three-page note. The return rate of this piece was double the national average, and they realized a two to one profit (*Campaigns & Elections,* April 2000, p. 54). A mailing that large enjoys an economy of scale that few local elections can attain; in this case, it cost only 67 cents per piece, including postage. The cost of a mailing like this for a short run in a local election could easily be more than twice as much; in fact, postage alone (if using first class) would come in at 57 cents per piece.

While oversized pieces work well with some voters, they do not work at my home. The size that I most consistently open looks like an invitation or a greeting card from a friend; that is, $6\frac{1}{2}$ by $4\frac{3}{4}$ inches. This size is large enough to hold a remittance envelope (without folding) and also will comfortably hold a half-sheet of paper folded in half. Given that a shorter letter is more likely to be read, do not make the mistake of folding an $8\frac{1}{2}$-by-11-inch sheet in four.

REPRESENTATIVE BATES' 2001 REPORT CARD

The Oregon Business Association ranked Representative Alan Bates among the top ten legislators in Oregon: *"courageous, smart, thoughtful."*

The Oregon League of Conservation Voters gave Rep. Bates an 82% pro-environment rating.

The Oregon Education Association rated Dr. Bates in the 90th percentile for his advocacy of public education.

"As a freshman legislator, he shined as he forged consensus legislation ensuring a healthy and competitive workers' compensation market in Oregon. It was Dr. Bates who kept the interests of the insured and the small businesses first."
- **Coalition for Economic Security for Oregon**

Because of legislation sponsored or strongly supported by Dr. Alan Bates Oregonians will have:

- *Increased access to higher education (HB 2521)*
- *A patient bill of rights (HB 3040)*
- *Reduced prescriptions costs for seniors (HB 3300 & SB 819)*
- *Improved roads and highways (comprehensive transportation package)*
- *Government made more accountable through annual audits (HB 3980)*
- *A cleaner and safer environment (mercury reduction legislation)*

Figure 4.12 Front of the "World's Smallest Brochure"

Dr. Alan Bates
State Representative
Oak Street
Ashland, Oregon 97520

Phone and fax: (541) 482-1427
Email: repbates@internetcds.com

Dear Friends,

I wanted to take a moment to thank you for the opportunity to serve Southern Oregon in the legislature. When I first ran for State Representative I never realized how much I would love this work.

Although veteran legislators told me I accomplished more than most freshmen—especially of a minority party—I sometimes felt frustrated watching excellent bills (such as campaign finance reform) die in committee. Still, there were many successes of which I am quite proud. I have included a few in this mailing.

I believe my success was due not only to the support of so many in Southern Oregon who helped me get to Salem, but also those who continued to help throughout the session with emails, phone calls, and letters alerting my office to problem legislation. With 5,000 bills to read we relied on those back home to help. We were not disappointed.

Now, I need your help again. I've been told this area will be targeted in the next election and that I must expect a tough and expensive race. While I am willing to put in the time needed to win the next election, I know that hard work alone is no guarantee. To win, I need your support of both time and money.

Please, take a moment to return the enclosed envelope and, please, consider a contribution today.

Thank you,

PS. Political contributions (up to $50 per person, $100 per couple) are *refundable* on your Oregon tax return. That applies whether you file the short or long form.

Figure 4.13 Sample Fund-Raising Letter Inside of the "World's Smallest Brochure"

Once the envelope is open, it is important that the piece offer plenty of information, be pleasing to look at, and have a weight and feel that says the recipient is important, without looking lavish or expensive.

The challenge then is how to make it all fit in a small format.

To accomplish such a package, my graphic designer and I put together what we call the world's smallest brochure: a half sheet of 8 ½-by-11-inch 80-pound vellum Bristol, folded in half. The front of the piece featured a photo of the candidate and a list of his accomplishments and ratings during his first term in the Oregon House (figure 4.12). The inside had another photo of the candidate and a letter with a P.S. on the state's tax refund policy on political contributions (figure 4.13), each personally signed by the candidate in either blue or green ink (never use black). The back had an endorsement from the governor. Given the space constraints, we skipped the usual business letter practice of including the donor's address in the upper left-hand corner. Some letters had a "Dear Friends" salutation, and on others we used no other identifier than the recipient's first name to make it a personalized letter; this created more work, but was worth it. To keep everything looking sharp, the letter, envelope, and remittance envelope were all printed on white.

To encourage the recipient to turn the envelope over (one step closer to opening it), we had the representative's name and address printed on the envelope flap rather than on the front in the upper left-hand corner.

To test a "Dear Friends" salutation versus a personalized one, I divided the mailing into two parts. The first was sent to 500 people who had canvassed, had a lawn sign, or volunteered time to the campaign in some way. Although some had also given to the campaign, I did not have the donor list at the time of the mailing. This group had a letter that began "Dear Friends," which allowed me to have the whole thing printed, cut, and folded at a local print shop. Using a clerical team of sixteen seniors, we hand addressed, stuffed, sealed, and stamped the envelopes (using bulk, not first-class postage) in one hour and fifteen minutes. The mailing cost $400 (85 cents per piece)—for printing, postage, paper stock, layout, and remittance envelopes.

Because the candidate was a physician, I sent the second mailing to 100 local physicians that he knew, either personally or peripherally, using a letter designed to address their interests. This mailing was identical to the "Dear Friends" mailing except for four things: the text of the letter, the personalized salutation, a first-class stamp rather than a bulk stamp, and a computer-generated "handwriting" font on the envelope. A volunteer printed and stamped the envelopes. One side of the letter was printed at a local print shop, and I used my printer to add the personalized salutation and letter on the other side; I cut and stuffed the letters as they came out of the printer. Increasing the postage from bulk to first class increased the price by 14 cents per piece but saved an enormous amount of time going to the post office and dealing with the bulk mail process. The cost of the second piece was $1 each, for a total of $100.

For the 500 "Dear Friends" letters, the rate of return was 19 percent with an average donation of $61. This $400 mailing brought in $5,745. The mailing with the personalized salutation and first-class postage stamp had a 53 percent rate of return with an average donation of $97. This $100 mailing brought in $5,125. The two mailings combined realized a twenty to one profit. We did not make follow-up phone calls for either mailing.

Keeping Track of Donations

One enormously helpful contribution a volunteer can make to a campaign is to keep the records of donations as they come in. By having these records complete and in one place, your campaign will save money in accounting fees and will have at hand the information needed for filing with the secretary of state or the elections department. Figure 4.14 is an example of headings you can use in a spreadsheet for keeping track.

Name, last	First: (signer name)	Spouse/ partner	Address/PO box	City	Zip	Occupation (signer)	Donation amount	Date received	T.Y.	Phone #

Figure 4.14 Example of Headings for the Donor Spreadsheet. Your campaign must have the occupation of the person who *signed* the check and the date the check was received for filing purposes.

5

LAWN SIGNS

IN THIS CHAPTER
- *Logo and General Information*
- *Location, Location, Location*
- *Preparing for the First Day*
- *Field Signs*
- *Maintenance of Signs*
- *Lawn Sign Removal*

Lawn sign placement and maintenance is a great opportunity to involve people who want to volunteer in a campaign but are not interested in working directly with the public. It is also an ideal activity for campaign workers who you feel might somehow make an unfavorable impression. Although it's a huge time and money commitment, with enough volunteers a well-run lawn sign campaign is an excellent way for a voter to feel involved in a campaign while elevating candidate name recognition or increasing awareness of a ballot issue. Lawn signs also demonstrate support for a candidate or issue within a community. However, that is really all they do. Given the expense and hassle of lawn signs plus the demands on your volunteer base, your campaign committee should consider carefully whether or not to use them. That said, if your opponent is using them, you should too.

In my town, lawn signs cannot be placed more than forty-five days before an election. In anticipation of the big day when all the signs suddenly appear, I ask one person from the committee to be in charge of overseeing the activity. If I am working on a campaign that involves more than one city, I will also have captains in each town who will oversee placement and maintenance in their area.

There are two schools of thought on lawn sign placement. One is not to worry if you don't have a lot of locations at first, since it is what you end up with that counts. In this view, what is important is the appearance of *building* momentum. The other school of thought is: BOOM! Here comes the candidate! Suddenly the name is out, and everyone supports that person. I am an adherent of the latter school. I work like crazy to get as many locations as possible for the big day. I do this to make a big visual impact, of course, but also because this way I only have to organize sign placement once. I know that there will always be additional requests as the campaign progresses, but not so many that a few people can't handle them easily. I always have volunteers whose sole job throughout the campaign is to put up lawn signs as requests come in.

> *"Few things are harder to put up with than the annoyance of a good example."*
> —Mark Twain

As in all campaign-related activities, have everything ready and organized for the teams. Also note that it is especially important that people work in pairs in this activity: one to drive the car or truck and the other to hop out and pound signs stakes into the ground.

> *"To a large degree reality is whatever the people who are around at the time agree to."*
> —Milton H. Miller

Logo and General Information

For our purposes, a logo is your name or ballot measure and a slogan written in a memorable way. Sometimes the name will be written with a star and streamers behind it, or a waving American flag, or stars and stripes. In my first run for mayor, I had one that was quite blocky with the name written in different colored bars. In my second bid, I did another one that was fairly complicated with a backdrop of the city, trees, and clouds. Because I have no imagination and even less talent in these areas, I leave this task to a professional. The going rate for developing a logo in my area is $200–600. Because you will be looking at your logo for months, it's well worth investing time and money into it.

I recently worked on a campaign where we were asked to develop a logo, a walking piece (that is a piece used canvassing), and a brochure. My graphic designer put together an excellent logo, but the campaign committee rejected it. Instead, they developed a similar design using a desktop publishing program. Although the alternative logo looked fine on a small mock-up, it had a fatal flaw that did not materialize until the logo was printed on lawn sign stock and field signs. As this logo increased in size, its readability de-creased. As a result, the lawn signs were difficult to read, and the field signs (4 by 4 feet and 8 by 4 feet) impossible. When I asked the graphic designer about it he told me it was because the new logo included an additional line. This experience is one more reminder to follow the advice of professionals you hire.

Lawn signs, like trademarks, must easily identify your cause or candidate. You need to develop a "look" that distinguishes your campaign from all oth-ers on the landscape. Once you have a logo, try to use it in all campaign liter-ature and advertising.

Regardless of who does your signs and logo, it is a good idea to visit local vendors who print lawn signs. They usually save at least one of each sign they have ever printed. This way you can shop for ideas in style and color combi-nations without any out-of-pocket expenses. When you're designing your sign, keep in mind that using two colors costs a lot more than one but is well worth it (figures 5.1 and 5.2). To save some money, you can get a two-color (or even a three-color) look by having almost a solid color printed over the white stock while leaving the lettering with no color. This produces white lettering on what looks like colored stock. Then use half tones (a mix of the white sign and the solid color showing through) for a design or part of the lettering for the "third" color. The result is very classy.

Weatherproof Stock

Even if money is a big problem, *do not cut costs on your stock.* Get good paper stock that is weatherproof; poly tag or corrugated works well. The corru-gated stock is nice because it is printed on both sides of the same sign, thus eliminating the need to staple signs back-to-back. Stapled signs often come apart and need repair. Also, corrugated can be attached to the stake before pounding it into the ground, which speeds up the work of the crews putting them up. Be sure to use screws *and* washers to attach the sign to the stake.

If you are using poly tag, remember to bring in your clerical team to staple the signs back-to-back. This needs to be done before the signs are put in place. *Do not staple poly tag signs to the stakes before pounding the stakes in the ground. The sign will fall off!*

Have the signs and the stakes in piles of twenty-five when crews arrive. If you have the signs and stakes already counted, you need only assign the area and direct the team to take the appropriate number of bundles of stakes and signs.

Remember, any sign material that is not weatherproof will curl with the first heavy dew or light rain, and your campaign "look" will be one of litter.

Figure 5.1 Example of a Lawn Sign Using Logo and Theme: Campaign for the Carnegie. In an issue-based campaign it is advantageous to connect a positive image with the ballot item. This logo was in red, black, and white and was so well liked that voters who had never had a lawn sign before called and requested one for their yard. (Design by Crystal Castle Graphics)

Figure 5.2 Maxwell for the House Lawn Sign. In the first post–September 11, 2001, general election, we correctly guessed that all political signs would incorporate images of the American flag. To stand apart, we used magenta for the name and slogan and a deep teal for the bar under the candidate's name and the border. As with the Carnegie lawn sign, we received numerous requests for this sign simply because people loved the look.

Political lawn signs are a touchy subject in some communities. Keep lawn signs neat and complete at all times. If you're sloppy about quality, placement, or maintenance, lawn signs may do your campaign more harm than good. But if you do it right, they make your campaign look well organized and well staffed.

Stakes for lawn signs are expensive. To save money, I ask other campaigns to give me their stakes after elections. I then bundle the stakes in sets of twenty-five and lend them to campaigns I support. Call around to those who have run and lost or are not running again and collect stakes. This works especially well if you are running a single campaign in the fall and someone you know lost in the primary election. If you have no luck, try to get a secondary wood products company or nursery to donate them. Still no luck? Ask supporters in the construction industry to make you some. Still no luck? Swallow hard and buy them. Four-foot stakes work best.

You can count on your lawn signs plus stakes costing $4 to $5 each, depending on the size and number of colors. Budget accordingly, and place them carefully.

Obviously, the size of your lawn sign can affect the cost of printing as well as the cost of stock. Lawn signs come in all sizes, so while you're visiting the printer to look at past political signs, check out their sizes as well. A typical sign is 18 by 24 inches, although I've seen some very effective signs that were 9 by 24 inches. Nine by twenty-four works quite well if your candidate has a long name that fits comfortably in that space.

> *"Taxation with representation ain't so hot, either."*
> —Gerald Barzan

In the 1992 presidential campaign, the local Clinton-Gore team used 20-by-30-inch signs in my area. The stock was so heavy that it continually fell off the stake. The team eventually had to go back and place each sign on two stakes. It still looked bad. Finally the team went back again and added a stick across the top of the stakes and then attached the sign on three sides. I would not recommend something that large.

If firefighters or other well-organized groups endorse you, they may have the ability to print lawn signs, with some limitations, such as number of colors or size. It's worth checking; such groups could save your campaign a lot of money. Keep in mind, however, that you would have to post such a contribution under "in-kind" on your contributions and expenditures form.

Another style of lawn sign uses a U-shaped metal rod, like a large croquet wicket, that holds a printed plastic sleeve. This type of sign costs as much or more than the conventional lawn sign, but they're easy to transport, the wickets are practically indestructible, and the sign stock itself does not need to be stapled or attached with hardware to stakes. All the advance work to prepare the signs for placement is eliminated, and the wickets are easy to push in and pull out of the ground; there is no need to carry mallets and staple guns or to look for soft ground. The downside of these signs is that they are not particularly attractive.

"Eliminate risk and you eliminate innovation . . . don't eliminate risk; knowingly take it on."
—Vaughn Keller

Lawn signs should be a work of art. You want the homeowner hosting the sign to be pleased with its look. You know you have a winner when people call and ask for a lawn sign simply because they like how it looks.

Halloween

If you're running a fall campaign, you should be prepared to send your entire lawn sign workforce back out the day after Halloween, which falls just a few days before the general election. You want your campaign to look great right up to the end. Extra effort and foresight are not lost on the electorate, nor are the opposite traits.

I know this may sound obvious, but be sure the signs are put up perpendicular to the street. The point of lawn signs is for people to see them from a distance as they drive by. To get any benefit from lawn signs, you need to attract the attention of voters.

Your "look" and how you present it will determine the success of lawn signs. In a mayoral race some years ago, an outsider ran a really great lawn sign campaign. One of the most distinguishing marks of his campaign was small, undersized lawn signs that he used in place of the normal-sized signs. Neighborhoods began having competitions to see who had the most signs up. Some houses would have ten of these signs on the front lawn. In some areas, neighbors would try to get their entire block covered with the "cute" little lawn signs. Meanwhile, the opponent ran a very traditional campaign using only billboards and, needless to say, lost. Don't hesitate to be creative and bold. You never know what will work. Bold, however, does not mean elaborate. Simple signs with a simple theme are the least offensive and easiest to read, especially at high speeds.

Location, Location, Location

Getting good locations to display your signs is the second half of using lawn signs effectively. Often people who have run for office in previous elections will have a record of where their lawn signs were placed. Try to get such lists and call those people first. This works best when you share a political ideology with a former candidate. Another way is to get a "walking list" (a list of voters, sorted by address, in a particular voting district) for your district from the county clerk. Using a map and this list, note the arterial streets. You can then set up a phone bank to call people living on the favored arterials and ask whether they will allow you to place a lawn sign on their property. This really works.

If the walking lists from the county do not have many phone numbers, set up a clerical team to come in and look up phone numbers ahead of the phone bank. The idea of having a system for organizing volunteers is that you can quickly bring groups of people to bear on problems. Organization allows you to accomplish tasks without overloading your workers.

When possible, try to avoid placing your sign in yards already teeming with political signs and avoid coupling yours with the same signs from other campaigns in hundreds of locations. Keep in mind that voters are highly sensitive to visual cues. They know their neighbors and look to those they respect for help in making decisions about candidates and measures. They are also likely to spot patterns, and although lawn sign patterning is bound to happen, make it a priority to mix things up. By occasionally coupling your signs with those of candidates running in the opposing party, you give voters "permission" to split their ticket.

You will find that supporters will call the campaign and request lawn signs throughout the campaign. It is important to accommodate them. However, this means that your campaign must be discerning about initial lawn sign placement. Hold some back to replace lost or vandalized signs and to accommodate requests. Avoid placing signs on cul-de-sacs or overloading some

"He who gets a name for rising early can stay in bed until noon."
—Irish proverb

streets while others go bare. Let supporters know from the beginning that the number of signs is limited and that the campaign needs to place them in areas of high visibility.

Preparing for the First Day

Setup for lawn sign installation follows the same process as the other campaign activities. After getting locations and making sure that the signs and stakes are ready to go, you need to organize the teams that will put up the signs.

Although I maintain lists of all donors, volunteers, and lawn sign locations on a spreadsheet, I still use 3-by-5-inch cards for my lawn sign teams. I do this for a number of reasons.

Index cards give me the freedom to move a location from group to group easily. For example, an average team can place twenty-five signs in a two-hour time block. However, if a logical area for one team to work has thirty-five locations, index cards allow quick shifting of signs to other teams working in adjacent sections.

Installation instructions can be written for each location at the bottom of the card. For example, some people want to put up their own sign or want the sign stapled to their fence or placed in the hedge. Directives, jotted on the bottom of the card, help the teams be more efficient and keep the home-owner happy.

Installers can also use the card to record information to get back to the campaign should there be a problem.

Further, using index cards and map packets means that lawn sign re-moval after the election is already organized and ready to go.

Begin by printing out, from your spreadsheet, a list of those who have agreed to host a lawn sign. Create a 3-by-5-inch card for each location that includes the address, name, and phone number of the homeowner (figure 5.3). Once the cards are filled out, organize them by addresses that are close to each other. You may be tempted to consider using MapQuest or another online or CD-based mapping program here, but imagine how long it would take to punch in 1,000 addresses for lawn sign locations, the typical number used in a state house race. This task is better tackled with an area map that has an alphabetical listing of streets. Programs like MapQuest may be help-ful for difficult-to-find locations. Alternatively, you can call the homeowner and jot down directions on the bottom of the index card. What you are after in grouping the cards is some kind of logical walking or driving pattern that will allow your placement team to work efficiently. I use groupings of no more than twenty to thirty locations, each of which will take about two hours.

After you have the 3-by-5-inch location cards organized, place the cards for each grouping in a ziplock baggy along with a map with the target area highlighted. Number each packet, and when crews arrive, ask them to sign in and indicate the number of the packet they took. Take a few minutes the night before to record the lawn sign packet numbers in your spreadsheet containing the lawn sign locations. This is helpful if a packet gets lost and also allows you to print out a list for your maintenance people during the campaign.

Placement crews work in pairs. If you are using poly tag signs, the crew needs a staple gun (to attach the sign to the stake), a stapler (in case the sign comes apart at the corners), and a mallet (to pound the stake into the

LAST NAME, FIRST NAME	PHONE NUMBER

ADDRESS

PRECINCT NUMBER

Any special instructions are placed here, such as "Place sign on fence" or "Leave at front door for owner to put up." You may need to leave directions here if the address is hard to find.

Figure 5.3 Example of a 3-by-5-Inch Lawn-Sign Card

ground). If they are placing corrugated signs, they will need only a mallet and maybe a metal pole for making a pilot hole. In either case, it is a good idea to bring along extra signs or repair kits and tools (washers, screws, electric screwdrivers, staple guns, staples, stakes, mallets) in case a sign breaks. If you are using something other than these two types of signs, just remember: Send extras of everything.

Assigning crews is then simply a matter of handing them a baggy with 3-by-5-inch location cards, a map with their area highlighted, and the appropriate number of signs and stakes. Ask as many volunteers as possible to bring tools, or borrow enough ahead of time from friends. *Be sure everything borrowed by the campaign is labeled and returned promptly.*

It is also critical that the volunteers bring back the baggy with the 3-by-5-inch cards. You will need the cards for the maintenance crews to repair signs after Halloween and for sign pickup after the election.

I firmly believe that poorly designed, poorly constructed lawn signs hurt your campaign more than they help it. If you are going to use lawn signs, they are way too expensive and too labor intensive to cut corners on design and production. If you can't raise the money to do them right, don't do them.

That said, there may be times when you must deviate from this rule for strategic reasons. In one campaign, because of lack of funds, we printed only one-third the normal number of lawn signs. Although they were carefully placed to maximize visibility, they soon began to disappear. People who wanted signs were calling, and others were calling to request replacements. We knew it was a close race, and our diminishing number of signs looked as though our support was waning.

So, using the same color of ink as our signs, I hand painted more in my barn on the back of old poly tag lawn signs. In the middle of the night, I placed them throughout the city. I did not want them to be next to each other; rather I wanted to create the impression that homeowners had taken the initiative to paint their own signs and put them up. I wanted the look to be one of individual, rebellious support for our side and angry opposition to the money fighting our effort. We won the election by fewer than 300 votes out of 5,000 cast.

Field Signs

Field signs placed along highways are very effective in campaigns in mixed rural/urban areas. I have worked on campaigns where field signs have been professionally painted by hand and others where they were commercially printed. Naturally, such signs are not cheap. My preference would be to have volunteers paint them for free, but we must be realistic about these things. Not only is this task a lot to ask of anyone, you risk wasting time and losing volunteers if the signs end up looking amateurish and you feel placement would be problematic for the campaign. Regardless of how they are produced, location is the primary concern when using field signs. Figure 5.4 is an example of a field sign.

Field sign locations can sometimes be found by calling Realtors who have parcels listed along highways and in cities. Ranchers, farmers, and owners of large vacant lots who support you will occasionally allow signs to be placed on the corners of their land. If you're running a local campaign during a general election, talk to other campaigns about locations that they have landed.

The volunteer crew putting up field signs must be carefully selected. They should have some construction experience so the structure can withstand wind and the weight of the sign. These crews will need more than a hammer and nails to put up a field sign. Supply them with or ask them to bring posthole diggers, shovels, screws, electric screwdrivers, and additional lumber for supports or bracing. This is a big production.

Know the law: Be sure to contact city and county authorities to find out size requirements and any other regulations on field signs. In the 2002 general election, it suddenly came to light that our county had a size limit on large political signs. Although I'd worked for nearly twenty years in campaigning in southern Oregon, I had somehow missed this, and of the five races I was working on, four were out of compliance in this regard. There was

Figure 5.4 Example of a Field Sign Used in an Issue-Based Campaign. This campaign only used field signs. The sign was a deep red with white lettering and silhouetted people in black. The sign was incorporated into the television spots so that the two could reinforce each other.

some discussion about making candidates and issue-based campaigns remove all signs that were too big, which would have been financially difficult for many of the races. Luckily, two of the three county commissioners were up for re-election, and they had illegal signs themselves. They temporarily changed the law to allow the larger signs.

Another area in which field signs create problems for campaigns is along state highways. Sometimes a state highway right-of-way is as much as fifty feet on either side of the road. Although cities and counties may look the other way when a campaign encroaches on a right-of-way, the state generally does not. To have field signs installed (which can take crews up to an hour per sign) only to have them ripped down by state workers is maddening and wasteful. (When I say ripped down, I mean ripped down. They do not take the time to carefully unscrew each of the sides, nor to be careful in setting your $300 sign in the back of the pickup.) Also, locating your sign among state yards is more difficult than you might think. Save the campaign time and money: Call the state department of transportation and ask about any locations where you are uncertain of the right-of-way.

Maintenance of Signs

Large or small, campaign signs must be maintained once they are up. Depending on the circumstances, you may use the same crew that placed the signs to maintain them throughout the campaign, or you may use a completely different crew. The maintenance crew must travel with a mallet, staple gun, extra signs, stakes, stapler, and so forth in their cars at all times. Ostensibly, maintenance crews are ready to repair any ailing sign they see in their normal daily travels. However, from time to time there may be a need for the crews to travel their assigned placement routes for a more systematic check of the signs.

> "Whatever is worth doing at all, is worth doing well."
>
> —Earl of Chesterfield

As noted earlier, you will need to keep your maps and baggies of 3-by-5-inch lawn sign location cards for your maintenance crews for post-Halloween repairs and for sign removal after the election. However, for ongoing maintenance, use the packet number that you recorded in the spreadsheet, and sort the list according to that number. This way you can print lists or e-mail them to your maintenance workers.

Besides maintenance, there will be the chore of putting up new signs as people call in requesting them or as canvassers return with requests for lawn signs. If there aren't too many, you can assign new locations to the appropriate maintenance crew or have special volunteers to do this chore on an ongoing basis. Believe it or not, having the candidate help with new location installations is great PR. As the campaign progresses, voters increasingly recognize the candidate and will often honk and wave as they drive by. Such a simple thing makes the candidate appear more accessible and "like one of us." In one campaign I worked on, the candidate, a local physician, went out and helped put up field signs on the weekend. He reported that lots of people honked and waved and that some even stopped to help or say hello. A couple of days later when the signs fell down, I got a number of calls from people I did not know asking if they could help get them back up for "Doc." We all laughed about how fast those signs came down, including the candidate, who is a very likeable, self-effacing guy. His initial efforts got him a lot of mileage and brought us some great workers.

> "A problem adequately stated is a problem well on its way to being solved."
>
> —R. Buckminster Fuller

In another campaign there was a street where all the lawn signs disappeared every night. The man who put the signs in that area was also in charge of maintenance and just happened to drive along this street to and from work each day. After the signs disappeared and he replaced them a couple of times, he decided to take them down on his way home from work and put them back up each morning on the way to work. You can't buy that kind of loyalty.

It is best to get requested signs up as soon as possible. However, if there are too many requests, it may be necessary to organize another day for placement. If you do this, be sure to include all of your current locations so that signs can be repaired or replaced if missing.

Lawn Sign Removal

Most localities have regulations requiring that campaign signs be removed within a certain period after the election. Whatever the regulations, your crews should be ready to remove all of your lawn signs the day after the election. If the signs are left up longer, homeowners begin to take signs inside or throw them away, making it difficult or impossible for your crews to retrieve them. Although corrugated signs begin to break down after a few years, poly tag and plastic bag signs seem to last indefinitely, which is money in your pocket for the next election. At a minimum, you will want to retrieve the stakes or wickets for future campaigns. Since you have to get the signs down eventually, you might as well look organized and responsible by retrieving them as quickly as possible.

I like to get the crews set up beforehand for the day after the election. Here again, volunteers work in pairs with maps and the 3-by-5-inch cards containing the addresses. And again, have volunteers sign in and note which numbered packet they took. When they return, you must remember to get your cards and maps back for the next election. This is also a great time to get together a volunteer thank-you party to disassemble your lawn signs, put them away for the next election, and bundle your stakes in sets of twenty-five with duct tape.

6

PRECINCT ANALYSIS: THE SINNERS, THE SAINTS, AND THE SAVEABLES

IN THIS CHAPTER
- The Full-Blown Analysis
- Finding the Saints Among the Sinners
- The Quick and Dirty Precinct Analysis
- Votes Needed to Win

In twenty years of working on campaigns I have found that a precinct analysis is the single best tool in the campaign tool kit. A precinct analysis will tell you:

- The likely voter turnout
- The number of votes needed to win
- Where your base lives
- Where the opposition's strength lives
- Where swing voters live
- Where your base is lazy (nonvoting)
- Where the base of your opposition is lazy
- Which issues the voters care about
- Whether you have a snowball's chance in hell of winning

A precinct analysis gives you accurate direction on where best to spend time and campaign resources to have the greatest impact. It is the best road map you can use to get to a win, and it will save your campaign money, lots of money.

Unlike some campaign activities, a precinct analysis may be conducted months or even years before the campaign, because it is based on voting history. Take advantage of this fact and get it out of the way. It's also cheap. Using this handbook and a few dollars, anyone can conduct a precinct analysis. Although election offices charge a nominal fee for past election records, the information you need is public, relatively easy to obtain, and inexpensive. The only exception would be in counties that do not keep records broken down by party, turnout, undervote, or precinct. For such counties, you may have to go elsewhere to get your data, such as a voter contact service, your party, or a political action committee (PAC) that has endorsed you and tracks voting history. If it is a voter contact service be prepared to pay, but your party or an endorsing PAC will usually provide some voter contact information as an "in-kind" donation to your campaign. If your campaign is too local for PAC or party support, go to a candidate who has such support and offer to include him or her in a precinct analysis if their campaign can get you what you want.

> *"Aim at the souls that can be saved."*
> —Bill Meulemans

> *"Phyllis Schlafly speaks for all American women who oppose equal rights for themselves."*
> —Andy Rooney

Nearly all county clerks or election offices will have past voting records. Some keep the information electronically; some have only abstracts and full printed reports. Some counties will allow you to check out the full reports of an election, but if they don't, pack a lunch and be prepared to spend a few hours down at the election office.

In addition to voting history from election offices, you may also use U.S. census data (www.uscensus.gov) to further profile your voters with demographic and economic data. At the Census Bureau's Web site, go to Publications, then to 2000, and then work your way down the series. The census database will give you demographic information by state, county, and city. The census database is often a great help for local elections, because data are presented separately for each city, apparently irrespective of size. So if your area of concern includes one or more small cities, you're in luck.

Whereas your polling data will tell you who supports your cause by gender, race, age, income, education, and party affiliation, a precinct analysis will give you an idea of how neighborhoods vote on issues and candidates that parallel your campaign. For example, if you are working on a county-wide election and your polling data show that 60 percent of women support your cause, you do not know whether that is 60 percent across the board or

70 percent in one city and 30 percent in another. To make your polling work better for your purposes, ask the polling firm to break down your data by region—or better yet, by precinct. While a poll may tell you where you are on an issue at a given moment in time, a precinct analysis will give you more of a continuum of voter tendencies.

All that said, however, there will be times when a precinct analysis is of minimal help. For example, if you are running a partisan race in an area with a huge registration disadvantage and no voter history of a win from anyone in your party. In this example, a precinct analysis will tell you where your voters are lazy—that is, those in your party who tend to be nonvoters—and it may provide some information on swing voters, depending on the quality of the candidates in the previous elec-

> *"If you would persuade, you must appeal to interest, rather than intellect."*
> —Ben Franklin

tions, but that's about it for candidate history information. Nevertheless, knowing where your lazy support lives can improve your odds come election day. These potential voters can be activated through voter contact, direct mail, canvassing, and phone bank calling. Still, unless your opposition is running his or her campaign from prison, if the voter registration difference is more than fifteen percentage points you are about to launch into an unwinnable race.

Precinct analysis is based on the premise that people who think and vote alike live near each other. Precinct analysis looks for voting trends, specifically precinct-by-precinct voting trends, to give a geographic location of your core supporters. It will tell you where to find high support and low voter turnout for similar candidates or causes in past elections so that your canvassing efforts will activate likely support. This is crucial. You want to invest most of your effort in high-support, low-turnout areas to get out your vote.

> *"No self-respecting woman should wish or work for the success of a party who ignores her sex."*
> —Susan B. Anthony

In every race, there are two kinds of voters: those with their minds made up and those who are either undecided or don't care. For our purposes here, we will divide the first category into two groups—the sinners and the saints—and focus on the third group—the saveables.

The Sinners. These are the voters who will not cast a vote your way, whatever you say or do. You *never* want to give them a reason to vote: Don't canvass, call, or send direct mail to them.

The Saints. These are voters who will vote for you over your opponent no matter what. Although you do not want to completely ignore these voters, you also do not want to waste valuable campaign resources on them. Within the saints group are the high-support/high-turnout voters who need the least attention of all; there is little need to spend much time or money here. However, also within the saints group are the high-support/medium-turnout and high-support/low-turnout voters. These two groups need attention and activation.

The Saveables. These are the voters who do not strictly adhere to party lines, are moved by a hot-button issue, are undecided, or pay little or no attention to politics. These swing voters will often respond to a candidate or issue on the basis of emotion rather than policy or facts. These are the people who say they voted for a candidate because "I liked him," "She's honest," "I could understand him," "She cares about us." For this group it is often form over content. In 1984, polls indicated that more voters supported Walter Mondale's stands on issues than Ronald Reagan's, and yet Reagan was elected in a landslide. The situation was similar in the 2002 contest between Bush and Gore. Voters overwhelmingly supported Gore's policies but he received only a narrow majority in the popular vote.

With precinct analysis, you can determine where the saveables live and then, by further analysis of education, age, and voting history, determine the likely numbers of those who will actually get out and vote. While a precinct analysis will give you important information for canvassing purposes, you must also persuade the likely voters with direct mail and phoning.

Election offices, political parties, and PACs often track voters by turnout. Voting frequency typically will be listed next to the registered voter's name as 4/4, 3/4, 2/4, 1/4, that is, people voting in four out of four of the last elections, three out of four, and so on. They are referred to as fours, threes, twos, and ones. Fours will take very little prodding to get to the polls. The others can be a little trickier to pin down, because some of the occasional voters vote only in presidential elections, some only in general elections, and others in their own individual pattern. However, with a little push, threes and often twos can be activated to get to the polls. This is where your precinct analysis is so critical: You never want to activate voters who are in your low-priority precincts, or you will turn out votes for the opposition. Your goal is to activate likely voters in high-priority precincts who will support your candidate or issue-based campaign.

People who went to the polls only once in the last four elections are pretty tough, and courting those who have never voted is a waste of time and money.

By conducting your precinct analysis early and studying who is most likely to vote, based on issues and past elections, you gain information that helps you shape your campaign theme and message. Obviously, if your message is focused on the large group of voters who are either undecided or disengaged, and you know where they live, you have a better chance of activating them and pulling them over to your cause.

The Full-Blown Analysis

The precinct analysis is a little different for a primary than for a general election. In a primary, candidates of the same party square off, and so the analysis involves looking at past voting records for candidates of that particular party. If the analysis is for a candidate in a general election, compare past voting trends of all parties. If it is for a ballot measure, compare voting histories for similar ballot measures or propositions using the same election cycle (presidential general, special election, midterm primary, etc.). Regardless of the type of election, the materials you need to do a precinct analysis are the same.

"More than any other time in history, mankind faces a crossroads. One path leads to despair and utter hopelessness, the other, to total extinction. Let us pray we have the wisdom to choose correctly."

—Woody Allen

To do a precinct analysis, you will need the actual county printouts of the elections you wish to analyze. Our county keeps election results online for a couple of weeks after the election, and some counties keep them online indefinitely. If your county is in the latter category, download what you need row by row. Most counties use Excel or an Excel-compatible spreadsheet. Getting the data online, on a CD, on a floppy, or e-mailed to you will save a lot of time.

If your county does not have electronic data available, you will need to go to the election office and either enter the information into a spreadsheet on a laptop computer or write it down on paper. If you

"Democracy is the worst form of government except for all the others that have been tried."

—Winston Churchill

do not have a laptop, you may want to create an election data form using the spreadsheet categories provided in figure 6.1 to take with you. Be sure to create at least six blank sheets. Once you have the data recorded on paper, you will need to enter it into a spreadsheet.

You start your precinct analysis by researching past local elections that were similar to the one on which you are working. If you're lucky, you'll be looking at a set of elections that all occurred after redistricting following the

Precinct description	Pre. #	Reg Voters	Vtr TO	% TO	D's Reg	D's TO	D's % TO	R's Reg	R's TO	R's % TO	NAV #	NAV TO	NAV % TO	D undervote	R undervote	

Figure 6.1 Sample Spreadsheet Headings for Precinct Analysis

census. If not, or if precinct boundaries have changed, the election office will have conversion formulas for each of the changed precincts. Another option is to use global information system (GIS) mapping, in which you can lay one map on top of the other to look for patterns.

In general you are looking for a past election that reflects the one you are about to dive into. Ideally your comparison will be for the same office, same gender, in the same party, with similar political ideologies. If you cannot find the same characteristics for the same office, go with gender, party, and ideology for a different office that covers your precincts.

"Illegal aliens have always been a problem in the United States. Ask any Indian."

—Robert Orben

If you are testing the waters for an issue campaign, again the idea is to look for similarities, especially if your campaign is about raising money. Keep in mind that it is critical to use identical election cycles, such as a non-presidential primary, a presidential election year, and so forth. Issue-based campaigns dealing with revenue generally come in two varieties: bricks and mortar, and operation and maintenance. Within these two categories are police, fire, schools, cities, counties, libraries, parks, water systems, special districts, and so on. Issue campaigns that have to do with restricting the power of government, such as term limits, right to die, abortion, and mandatory sentencing, these are a different animal and will be covered in Chapter 10.

Election Data Form

You begin your analysis by going through the election data and transferring it to your spreadsheet (see figure 6.1). The spreadsheet headings should include (going from left to right) the following:

- precinct description (for example, "Airport" or "Phoenix, rural")
- precinct number
- total number of registered voters
- turnout (number) of registered voters
- percent turnout of registered voters
- total number of registered Democrats, turnout of Democrats (number), percent turnout of Democrats

- total number of registered Republicans, turnout of Republicans (number), percent turnout of Republicans
- the same for all other parties
- the undervote for each party, if available

Although the county printout includes more information than you need, you may choose to enter as much or as little as you want. For example, when conducting a precinct analysis for a partisan office, look only at the data pertaining to the office you wish to analyze, or look at voting history for a particular ballot measure or initiative as a way to find pockets of support or non-support. This sort of information can be helpful in identifying areas where certain issues may be more problematic or helpful than other areas.

"Why does a slight tax increase cost you $200 and a substantial tax cut save you 30 cents?"

—Peg Bracken

Sorting the Data

Once you have created one complete spreadsheet of election data, label it as "Master," then select all information on that sheet, click edit, copy, and then paste it onto a second sheet. Never make any alterations to your master data spreadsheet. Should anything go wrong with any of your spreadsheets in subsequent sorting, you will need the original spreadsheet to rebuild scrambled information. Believe me, you do not want to go back to the elections office to reenter data halfway through a precinct analysis.

Spreadsheets such as Excel have features that can be helpful as you copy data from the master sheet to another sheet. In the original spreadsheet, you can enter formulas to have the program calculate percentages as you enter the data. For such calculations to work, however, all the previous components of the formula must be present, which may not be the case when you copy a portion of one sheet to another sheet. You can retain the actual numbers calculated from assigned formulas by using the following steps:

1. On your "Master" data sheet, go to the upper left-hand corner and click the square between the horizontal rows and vertical columns; now everything should be highlighted.
2. Click edit, then copy.
3. Open your second sheet, click any square in the far upper left.
4. Click edit, select "paste special" and click "values" and then "OK." The values (rather than the formulas) of everything you calculated in the previous sheet will be listed and will remain no matter what happens to columns used as part of the value calculation.

Declining Order of Support			Declining Order of Turnout		
precinct	percinct support		precinct	percent turnout	
04	69%		15	77%	
01	66%		02	72%	
08	65%	(5)	08	72%	(5)
02	64%		16	72%	
12	64%		13	70%	
07	59%		11	68%	
10	59%		12	67%	
20	58%		21	66%	
03	57%		01	65%	
05	56%	(10)	05	65%	(11)
06	56%		04	64%	
09	53%		22	63%	
21	53%		19	62%	
13	52%		10	62%	
22	52%		17	61%	
			18	61%	
15	51%				
18	51%		19	60%	
17	49%	(7)	20	60%	
11	46%		06	59%	(6)
19	40%		03	56%	
16	37%		14	54%	
14	36%		07	43%	

Figure 6.2 Example of Tabulating Precincts in Order of Support and Turnout for Similar Election

In your second sheet, sort your data from high to low using the column for "percent of those supporting" the candidate or issue that most resembles yours. Copy all of this and paste it into a third sheet. Go back to sheet 2 and sort the same data, but this time sort from high to low using "turnout" of your party. Copy just the precinct numbers and the results of your sort. Paste these columns on sheet 3 next to your "support sort," or simply list support and turnout on a piece of paper, as shown in figure 6.2. Divide each of the groups into logical groupings of thirds for both support and turnout.

"Children must not be wholly forgotten in the midst of public duties."

—John Adams

Precinct Targeting Worksheet

To fill out the Precinct Targeting Worksheet, you need to decide on a threshold for what constitutes a high level of support for the issue or candidate you have selected as a model for your race. It might be a win of 60 percent, or it might be a win of only 52 percent. This can be a tough call. What you are looking for is the precincts with the best support, comparatively speaking, for that particular election.

The best support will not necessarily be overwhelming support, so you may have to adjust what you'll consider high-, medium-, or low-support areas on a relative basis. Essentially, you are dividing the precincts into those where the issue or candidate that is representative of your issue or candidate did well, fairly well, or poorly. To create a Precinct Targeting Worksheet, use a piece of paper divided into six sections. On the left-hand side, list the precincts from high to low support (figure 6.3).

On the right-hand side, you will list the precincts from high to low turnout. To identify precincts as having high, moderate, or low turnout, divide the difference between the highest precinct turnout and the lowest roughly into thirds. For example, if the lowest precinct turnout in the election was 25 percent and the highest was 75 percent, the turnout categories would be as follows: high turnout, 60 percent and higher; moderate turnout, 45 percent to 59 percent; and low turnout, 44 percent and lower. List the results of this voter turnout analysis on the right-hand side of the Precinct Targeting Worksheet by category, just as you did for support.

Precinct Priorities Worksheet

Once you have support and turnout broken out on the Precinct Targeting Worksheet, you will turn to the Precinct Priorities Worksheet (figure 6.4). This is where you will be listing the precincts from highest to lowest priority for canvassing or get-out-the-vote (GOTV) efforts. This is accomplished by using your Targeting Worksheet to match the categories listed in each of the boxes of the Priorities Worksheet. For example, all precincts that fall in *both* High Support *and* Low Turnout on the Targeting Worksheet would be entered into your first box of the Priorities Worksheet: H/S + L/T. Continue this process until all precincts are listed in boxes on the Priorities Worksheet (see figure 6.4).

What you end up with is a list of precincts listed in order of importance. Obviously, any precinct with low support, regardless of turnout, will be left alone. Your hope is that these people will stay home for the next election. Your job now is to poke all of those people in the high- and medium- support categories in the hopes of increasing the turnout of your support in the next election.

Targeting Priorities and Strategy Form

You will notice that the boxes on the Priorities Worksheet are numbered from 1 to 9. The next step can be done with your spreadsheet or simply on

PRECINCT TARGETING WORKSHEET

* High Support

** High Turnout

H/S*	Support		H/T**	Turnout
(04)			15	
01			02	
08			08	
02			16	
12			13	
M/S			**M/T**	
07			11	
10			12	
20			21	
03			01	
05			05	
06			(04)	
09			22	
21			09	
13			10	
22			17	
			18	
L/S			**L/T**	
15			19	
18			20	
17			06	
11			03	
19			14	
16			07	
14				

Figure 6.3 Example of a Precinct Targeting Worksheet Filled Out

paper. In your spreadsheet, insert a row and place the corresponding numbers of the Priorities Worksheet boxes next to the precinct number. Once
this is done, the spreadsheet can be sorted by these numbers, which will give

PRECINCT PRIORITIES WORKSHEET

(1) H/S + L/T = High Priority	(6) M/S + H/T = Medium Priority
	13
(2) H/S + M/T = High Priority	(7) L/S + L/T = Low Priority
(04) *01* *12*	*19* *14*
(3) M/S + L/T = High Priority	(8) L/S + M/T = Low Priority
07 *20* *03* *06*	*18* *17* *11*
(4) M/S + M/T = Medium Priority	(9) L/S + H/T = Low Priority
10 *05* *09* *21* *22*	*15* *16*
(5) H/S + H/T = Medium Priority	
08 *02*	

Figure 6.4 Example of a Precinct Priorities Worksheet Filled Out. In this example no precincts met the criteria for the first box.

you a list of precincts in order of campaigning importance. The advantage of doing this step in the spreadsheet is that you maintain all precinct information along with the priority listing (figure 6.5). If you're doing it on paper, you can simply list the precincts in descending order of priority and add any information you may want to keep track of from your spreadsheet. You can now assign your canvass or get-out-the-vote teams where they will do the most good. High priority gets done first, then moderate priority. Leave low priority alone.

TARGETING PRIORITIES AND STRATEGY FORM

	Prio-rity	Pre-cinct	Reg. voters	Party density	Rep. Support	Daniels T/O	Rep. U/V	Rep. Precinct location	Campaign strategy
HIGH (7)	2	04	698	35%	69%	64%	8%	*Hills*	*Athletic canvasssers*
	2	01	1,366	39%	66%	65%	14%		
	2	12	1,139	38%	64%	67%	14%		*Senior canvassers*
	3	07	497	25%	59%	43%	9%		
	3	20	982	29%	58%	60%	13%		
	3	03	772	30%	57%	56%	11%		
	3	06	871	28%	56%	59%	23%		*Candidate canvasses*
MEDIUM (8)	4	10	301	40%	59%	62%	11%		*(etc.)*
	4	05	900	35%	56%	65%	18%		
	4	09	930	37%	53%	62%	8%		
	4	21	1,041	40%	53%	66%	12%		
	4	22	283	47%	52%	63%	11%		
	5	08	770	50%	65%	72%	10%		
	5	02	820	36%	64%	72%	17%		
	6	13	107	28%	52%	70%	33%		
LOW (7)	7	19	729	35%	40%	60%	22%		
	7	14	121	50%	36%	54%	21%		
	8	18	499	30%	51%	61%	14%		
	8	17	836	34%	49%	61%	19%		
	8	11	1,219	39%	46%	68%	10%		
	9	15	368	25%	51%	77%	10%		
	9	16	225	48%	37%	72%	21%		

Figure 6.5 Example of a Targeting Priorities and Strategy Form Filled Out

You may be tempted to look over the lowest priority precincts and pull them over to the cusp of a *possible* canvass, but I usually avoid these precincts. Although these are not necessarily the sinners, they tend to vote for the *opposition*. Low-priority precincts are just that: low priority. That said, you can find support within the low-priority precincts (see "Finding the Saints Among the Sinners" in this chapter). This is an area where you should identify those within your party using phone banks and then include them in your GOTV efforts.

For areas of high support and high turnout, you have to ask yourself what your canvassing is likely to accomplish. These are the saints. With limited money, time, and volunteers, do you want to spend campaign resources in precincts where you have both support and a history of high voter turnout? No. That is why these precincts fall into the "medium priority" categories on your priorities worksheet.

I once worked for a candidate who did not fully believe in precinct analysis. I had conducted an in-depth analysis of a number of elections where candidates who embraced a similar political ideology as my candidate ran for office. I also reviewed initiatives that covered issues similar to ones with which my candidate was closely aligned. This candidate had also faced a recall attempt while in office, so I conducted an analysis of a successful recall of an elected official who also had similar political leanings. All pointed to the same precincts for sinners, saints, and saveables. No exceptions. It was clear from the analysis that a handful of precincts would never support the candidate, and given that they were listed as low support *and* low turnout, there was a real concern that if activated they would vote for the opposition.

Notwithstanding the warning, toward the end of the campaign, after all the high- and medium-priority precincts were done, the candidate decided to burn up some restless energy by covering these low-priority precincts. His feeling was that if he personally went to the door, people would be swayed.

"Everything should be made as simple as possible, but not simpler."
—Albert Einstein

Not surprisingly, the low-support precincts turned out to be difficult canvasses. People were rude, and mishaps occurred. The candidate came back demoralized but decided to press on. Ultimately he lost the election by a few hundred votes out of 30,000 cast. After the election, a postmortem analysis showed that the low-priority precincts had turned out in record numbers and voted two-to-one against the candidate.

Precinct analysis tells you not only where your support lives so they can be activated but also where the opposition's support lives so they can be avoided. You never want to activate voters for the opposition.

Ballot Measure Form

An analysis of an issue-based campaign must use previous elections that are similar in type and election cycle. For example, is your issue about raising taxes to build a public building? Restricting the powers of government? Does it primarily affect the general population—such as air quality standards, acquisition of parks, or public acquisition of a business? Does it land in a presidential primary, a midyear general election, or a special election?

"A citizen of America will cross the ocean to fight for democracy, but won't cross the street to vote in a national election."

—Bill Vaughan

Using a spreadsheet program, create a ballot measure form following the example in figure 6.6. Fill in the blanks with data from the elections office. Don't worry about party affiliation.

Finding the Saints Among the Sinners

Within each precinct there are some voters who will never jump party lines (the base party vote), some who will move according to a specific candidate (swing vote), and some who will split their vote on the same ballot (ticket splitters), voting for candidates in different parties usually as a result of a single hot-button issue. To find the number of voters in these categories, you must first predict voter turnout, precinct by precinct.

Predicting Voter Turnout

Because turnout can vary dramatically with type of election, simply averaging the last three elections will not give you a clear prediction of voting patterns for your election. To determine the expected voter turnout, find a similar past election in the same season. For example, is your election in a presidential or non-presidential primary or general election? Is it a special or an off-year election? Whatever it may be, use the same election cycle. Next, compare what was on the earlier ballot with what will be on yours. If the referenced election had a hotly contested governor's race, that will influence the voter turnout. If you are running in a presidential primary and the Republicans hold the White House and have only the president on the ballot, compared with nine candidates in the Democratic field, you can safely assume that Democrats will turn out in larger numbers than Republicans in the pri-

Precinct	Reg. voters	Turnout	Count yes	Count no	Turnout %	% Yes	% No	UV
1	707	552	263	202	78	48	37	
2	680	507	252	188	75	50	37	
3	705	566	305	196	80	54	35	

Figure 6.6 Example of Spreadsheet Headings for Issue-Based Campaign Analysis

mary, even though it is a presidential election. Take such information into consideration and adjust expected turnout up or down accordingly.

In the election you are using for comparison purposes, look at the turnout precinct by precinct for each party. Let's say that in precinct 1, turnout among Republicans was 65 percent, turnout among Democrats was 62 percent, and turnout among nonaffiliated voters was 35 percent. However, in your election, because of controversial issues on the ballot, you predict that voter turnout will be at least ten percentage points higher. So in precinct 1 you will multiply the current number of registered Republicans by 75 percent, the current number of Democrats by 72 percent, and the current number of nonaffiliated voters by 45 percent. Add these numbers together, and that is your predicted turnout for precinct 1. Do the same for all precincts.

If you are uncomfortable with predicting increases or decreases in voter

"Americans know how to find the voting booth when something important is at stake."

—N. Don Wycliff, editorial-page editor, *Chicago Tribune*

participation based on ballot issues, you will be close if you simply multiply the percentage voter turnout of the last identical election by the current number of registered voters. (Keep in mind that in calculations with percentages, the percentage number must be divided by 100. However, if your percentages are formatted as such in your Excel spreadsheet, the program handles this automatically. To format a column as percentages, highlight the column, click format, then cells, and under "category," click percentage.) Even if turnout changes substantially in one direction or the other, the parties will track similarly, within a couple of points. In other words, in a given precinct, you will not see a substantial increase in turnout for one party without seeing a similar spike in the other parties.

Base Party Vote

The base party vote is a useful number and is very easy to calculate. It tells you the number of voters in each precinct that will always vote with their party regardless of how bad their candidate may be. Your base party vote is the number of votes you and your opponent will get no matter what (figure 6.7).

**SAMPLE FORM FOR DETERMINING
BASE PARTY SUPPORT**

A	B	C	D	E=D × C × B
Precinct number	Percentage of votes same party candidate	Current voter registration	Percentage expected turnout	Number of voters who won't leave the party
58	35	655	67	153
59	37	916	73	247
60	38	707	72	193
61	37	676	76	191
62	42	424	66	118
64	45	822	74	274
65	46	693	72	230
66	43	703	67	202
67	37	756	62	173
68	41	740	72	218
69	38	949	70	252
70	36	723	65	169
71	35	1,038	71	258
TOTAL		9,802		2,678

Figure 6.7 Sample Form for Determining Base Party Support

Here's how to find the base party vote:

1. Ask the county clerk for the election results for an election where a candidate of your party was pounded. Since you're going to translate these numbers precinct by precinct, it really doesn't matter if the poor outcome for your party was in the same election cycle. Although it can include more precincts, it must have all the precincts of your campaign area. For example, a heavily lopsided governor's race could be used for county commission seat.
2. List all the precincts in the area where you are running (column A).
3. For each of the precincts, list the percentage of votes the candidate in your party received (column B). Remember, this is a race where your party's candidate lost big.
4. List, precinct by precinct, the voter registration (column C).
5. List the percentage turnout you expect (column D).
6. Finally, multiply the expected percentage turnout by the current number of registered voters, and multiply the result by the percentage

of votes the same party candidate got in the previous election (D × C × B). This will give you the number of people who will vote for your party no matter what.

Repeat these steps with data from an election where someone in the opposing party lost by huge numbers. The result of this tabulation will be the number of votes your opponent will receive simply because of party affiliation.

Swing Voters

Calculating the base party support for both you and your opposition is the first step in calculating the swing vote.

"80% of life is just showing up."
—Woody Allen

Swing voters are those who are registered in one party but are willing to vote for someone from another party. Swing voters are sometimes called "smart voters" because they vote according to issues and information rather than party. However, they also include voters who are persuaded solely by emotion and their impressions of the candidates. Your job is to find them and persuade them that they should vote for your candidate.

To find swing voters you can make a form based on the example in figure 6.8, or you can add columns to your base party vote spreadsheet.

1. As you did for the base party vote calculation, find an election in which the candidate in your party was resoundingly defeated, and then find one in which the candidate from your opponent's party was defeated.
2. List the precinct numbers (column A).
3. List the highest percentage of votes cast for an election in which your party had a big win (column B). (You may also use your opponent's base party support subtracted from 100.)
4. List the lowest percentage received by a candidate in your party in a big loss—that is, your base party support (column C).
5. Use a formula to have your spreadsheet program compute the difference between column B and C (column D). So, if the highest percentage won by your party in precinct 58, for example, was 65 percent and the least your party ever received in that precinct was 35 percent, then the percentage of voters who may swing vote in precinct 58 is 30 percent.
6. List the percentage of the projected turnout (column E).
7. List the most current number of registered voters (column F).
8. Finally, multiply the percentage of swing voters (column D) by your projected percentage turnout (column E) by the current number of regis-

Precinct number	High Democrat win by percent	Low Democrat win by percent	Percent of swing (B − C)	Projected turnout	Current voter registration	Number of voters who could swing (D × E × F)
A	B	C	D	E	F	G

SAMPLE FORM FOR DETERMINING SWING VOTERS

Figure 6.8 Sample Form for Determining Swing Voters

tered voters (column F) (D × E × F). This will give you the number of people who could move from party to party in a given precinct in a given election. It's the same for both Democrats and Republicans. (Note: Do not use an election in which there was a third party candidate.)

Average Party Turnout

Another useful measure is the strength of party turnout, that is, the average number of people in a party that will generally vote in any given election. While this information is most helpful in partisan races, I also use it for ballot measure campaigns. For example, in my area, Republicans are more inclined than Democrats to vote against school funding, tax bases, building improvements, and county operation and maintenance levies. On the other hand, they are more inclined to vote for sheriff patrol, jail upgrades, and juvenile and criminal justice services. Knowing the average of party turnout can help mold your campaign efforts and predict outcomes.

To estimate party turnout for your election, you will need to look at three or more partisan races that had little controversy or big issues pushing one party to turn out in greater numbers than other parties. Choose three very average elections, and follow these steps:

1. List the percentage of the party turnout for each precinct for all three races, and figure the average of each (add them and divide by 3).
2. Multiply this percentage by the current number of registered voters.
3. Multiply the result by the predicted voter turnout (number).

Figure 6.9 is a sample form for making these calculations.

**SAMPLE FORM FOR DETERMINING
AVERAGE PARTY TURNOUT (REPUBLICAN)**

Precinct number	Party turnout 1st election	Party turnout 2nd election	Party turnout 3rd election	Average party turnout (B + C + D/3)	Current Republican registration	Average # Republican turnout (E × F)
A	B	C	D	E	F	G
58	43%	63%	35%	47%	267	125
59	61%	54%	37%	51%	295	150
60	46%	55%	38%	46%	232	106
61	64%	62%	37%	54%	345	186
62	50%	53%	42%	48%	78	37
64	42%	69%	45%	52%	209	109
65	54%	60%	46%	53%	351	186

Figure 6.9 Sample Form for Determining Average Party Turnout

Switch Hitters

A switch hitter, a variant of the swing voter, is a person who will divide his or her vote by switching parties within a given ballot—that is, vote for a Republican in one race and a Democrat in another on the same ballot.

To determine the number of potential switch hitters, again you must look at voting history. Find an election in which a candidate for one party did well while another candidate for the same party did poorly. Again, list the percentages and subtract one from the other. Multiply the difference by the expected voter turnout (current number of registered voters times expected percentage voter turnout). This will give you the number of voters, precinct by precinct, who will not vote straight party ticket. This is helpful information in elections where a strong candidate from another party who appears elsewhere on the ballot is sure to bring out his or her party support.

"Nothing will ever be attempted if all possible objections must be first overcome."

—Samuel Johnson

Undervote

Undervotes (when voters skip a particular candidate or issue on their ballot) generally occur for one of three reasons: don't know, don't like, don't care. If you and your opponent were unopposed in the primary, much of the undervote can be attributed to "don't care." However, within each precinct there will be those who fall into the don't know and don't like categories as well. A high undervote in a primary is a potential problem in the general election, and your campaign should work to avoid it.

Unopposed candidates or campaign teams who think they will save money for the general by not running a primary are misguided. The primary is your opportunity to curry your base, amass volunteers, establish an organization, build name recognition, and test your campaign and volunteer team. If you are running for a state office, it is an opportunity to show the lobby that your campaign is organized and means business. It is also an opportunity to lock your base while getting your message out—all without attacks from opposition that could cause damage in the general.

Running a campaign in an unopposed primary may entail no more than securing locations for lawn and field signs, printing them, and organizing volunteers to put them up, maintaining them, and pulling them down after the election. Add to this one mailing to your party plus a couple of print ads in the local newspaper, and you're out the door. Given that your campaign must print signs, secure locations, and organize volunteers for the general, there is simply no reason not to conduct a primary. If you do not run a primary and your undervote comes in over 50 percent, you have a lot of work to do on your base that could have been managed with a modest primary campaign. If your undervote is over 60 percent, you're in trouble. Save yourself the heartache: Run a primary.

There are two components of an undervote that provide important information for your campaign: your undervote, and the undervote of your opposition.

Your Undervote. Hotly contested general elections usually have undervotes in the 3 to 5 percent range, depending on the type of ballot. (Punchcard ballots have an undervote about three points higher than a scanned ballot does.) However, unopposed primaries are very different from hotly contested general elections.

Coming out of an unopposed primary, you want as low an undervote as possible, but even if you run a primary campaign, be prepared for undervotes in the 20 to 30 percent range. Should high-priority precincts come in with significant undervotes (40 percent or more), you must determine why, so that the problem can be fixed in time for the general election, especially in precincts with potentially high percentages of swing voters. Consider sending a persuasion piece to your party. Look for opportunities within those precincts for coffees. At the very least, send the candidate in for the canvass.

A high undervote in a primary means additional work for you in the general, so put your team on notice.

I once worked for a candidate who ran uncontested in the primary and, to save money, did no campaigning for it. When I came on board for the general, I conducted a precinct analysis on the primary for each candidate and found that the opposition, which ran a modest primary campaign, had a relatively small undervote compared to my candidate, who had undervotes that went as high as 60 percent. The high undervote may have been the result of the perception that the voters thought the candidate was "aloof" and somehow thought he was too good to campaign. His being invisible during the primary only fed this belief.

The Opposition's Undervote.   If both you and your opponent ran unopposed primaries, you now have some great information on your opposition for the general.

After a primary, spend some time with the final results published by the elections office. Abstracts often do not list undervotes, so you must look at the full printout. Ask if the election office can e-mail the results to you or put them on disk—it will save time. When it comes to the opposition's undervote, you are looking for high undervotes in areas where there is a high swing voter potential.

"Our goal is progress, not perfection."
—Williams & Williams

Insert a column on your swing voter sheet and add the actual undervote (provided by the elections department) next to it. Any precincts in areas that were considered off limits that have both a modest swing voter potential and a high primary undervote in the opposing party are back on the table. Your job is to determine whether some of the undervotes in these precincts resulted from voters in the don't like category—they didn't like the candidate their party nominated. It is these voters the campaign should identify. Too often campaigns take time conducting voter identification on members of their own party in precincts that historically vote for their party. Assume you have this support, and instead go behind enemy lines and pull votes from your opposition's base. Identify them, mail to them, and canvass them. With a little effort you can move these voters.

The Quick and Dirty Precinct Analysis

If you do not have the time for an in-depth precinct analysis, there is a condensed method that will give you a pretty good overview, especially if you are conducting a single-city or school-district election. As with the full-blown version, you must research similar elections to find voting patterns. Once you have identified the elections you are interested in, obtain the "summary sheets" or the abstracts for those elections from the elections office. Summary sheets are usually compiled by the county for all elections and list only the vote for, the vote against, and the turnout (number) by precinct. Most counties will fax these sheets to you. If not, ask for copies and pick them up. Don't forget the campaign checkbook.

To do your analysis, take a yellow highlighter and go through the summary looking for precincts that voted correctly—that is, precincts that are likely to support your cause—but had a low voter turnout. These precincts are your number one priority. Once you have identified your high-priority precincts, look for precincts that show support and had a medium or high turnout. These will be on your moderate list. If you see precincts where you are likely to lose big, avoid them.

Votes Needed to Win

There are a number of ways to calculate the number of votes you need to win. One is to simply divide the overall predicted voter turnout (number) in half, and add one more vote to your number. A second way, one that will provide a little more insight, is to calculate the predicted voter turnout by party, by precinct, add these up, and divide by two; again add one more vote to your side.

"What should be done to give power into the hands of capable and well-meaning persons has so far resisted all efforts."

—Albert Einstein

The best way, however, is to know how many swing voters you must gain in each precinct so your campaign can track your numbers as supporters are identified during the campaign.

Calculating Votes Needed to Win from Swing Voters

Calculating the number of swing votes you must win allows the campaign to balance areas of little support with additional swing voters from areas of greater support. Knowing where to concentrate your campaign resources and volunteer energy is the best path to a win. Find your swing voters, find where they live, determine how many are needed for a win, and check them off as you identify voters.

Using the figures calculated earlier in this chapter, you can predict how many votes you will need to win by filling in figure 6.10. The formulas in the headings can either be programmed into your spreadsheet or calculated by hand. The following is a step-by-step overview:

1. Predict the voter turnout (number).
2. Subtract from that the number of swing voters.
3. Multiply that figure by both the predicted percentage you believe you will receive and the predicted percentage you believe your opponent will receive in each precinct.
4. Compute the difference of the votes you will receive from those your opponent will receive.
5. Add this figure to the number of swing voters and divide by two. This plus one more vote is how many swing votes you will need, precinct by precinct, to win the election.

Figure 6.10 is a sample form for making these calculations. In this form:

- Precinct 1 (column A) has 681 registered voters (column B).
- The campaign has projected a 65 percent voter turnout (column C) *based on past election performance.*
- The projected turnout is calculated by multiplying the projected turnout percentage (column C) by the total number of registered voters (column B).
- The campaign also calculated that precinct 1 had a 15 percent swing voter potential. Remember, the swing voter percentage is the difference between an election with a very poor showing for a candidate in a given party and an election with a very high showing for a candidate in the same party, precinct by precinct.

To figure the number of votes your candidate and the opposition will get:

1. First calculate the number of people who will actually vote (multiply total number of registered voters by the percentage turnout: B × C). This goes in column D. (443)
2. Next, calculate the actual *number* of swing voters per precinct (D × E) to get the number of possible votes that are up for grabs: in this example, 66 votes (column F).
3. Subtract the number of swing voters from the number of people who will actually vote (columns D–F). This will give you the actual number of votes that will be divided between you and your opponent based on past voting history percentage. (377)
4. Next, multiply this number by the percentage who will support your candidate (column G, 45 percent) based on past support of a similar

candidate for that precinct. In this example, that gives you 169 votes (column H) in precinct 1 that will probably vote for you ([D – F] × G).

5. Do the same to calculate the number who will support the opposition, but for this number you will multiply the percentage of votes the opposition normally would get (column I, 48 percent) by the expected turnout minus the number of potential swing voters (D – F). That means your opposition will probably pull in 180 votes in precinct 1 ([D – F] × I).

> *"An elected official is one who gets 51% of the vote cast by 40% of the 60% of voters who registered."*
>
> —Dan Bennett

6. Obviously, the difference between the votes you will get and the votes your opponent will get (180 – 169) will tell you how many more votes your opponent will get in this precinct than you (11 votes).

7. Now you need to calculate how many of the swing votes you need to make up the difference and win by at least one vote. Add the difference (11) to the swing votes (66) and divide by 2 (because there are two candidates), which equals 38, to which you need to add one vote to win. That means you need 39 votes of the 66 swing votes to win.

8. The difference between the 39 you need and the 66 swing votes that are up for grabs is 27 votes (column L). Even if your opponent took all 27, you would still win precinct 1 by one vote.

> *"You've got to be very careful if you don't know where you are going, because you might not get there."*
>
> —Yogi Berra

9. Repeat this process with every precinct, and add up the number of votes you will need from the swing voters to win the election.

10. Add this to the total number of votes you think you will get, and that is how many votes you need to win.

When Precinct Analysis Isn't Enough

Campaigns are often so strapped for money that they must be highly focused. Under these circumstances, no matter what your party, if certain areas represent solid support and solid turnout (your saints), you will need to make the assumption that they will vote for you. If they don't, you'll lose anyway, and that will be that. You must feel that you can count on them without spending money or time on getting their vote.

Conversely, there will also be areas that support candidates in the opposing party, election after election. With the exception of the swing/undervote alignment outlined above, these areas should be avoided to keep from

SAMPLE FORM FOR DETERMINING THE VOTES YOU NEED TO WIN

Precinct number	Total registered voters	Projected turnout (%)	Projected turnout (#) (B × C)	Percent swing vote (calculate above)	Votes up for grabs (D × E)	Percent your support	Number your support (D − F) × G	Percent opposition support	Number opposition support (D − F) × I	Votes you need to win (J − H) + F/2 plus 1	Votes left F − K
A	B	C	D	E	F	G	H	I	J	K	L
1	681	65%	443	15%	66	45%	169	48%	180	11 + 66/2 = 38 + 1 = 39	66 − 39 =27
						Total			Total		

Figure 6.10 Sample Form for Determining the Number of Votes You Need to Win from the Swing Voters

activating votes for opposition; it will save volunteer time and campaign money. I recently went to an event where the wife of a candidate for county commissioner came up to me to talk about her husband's loss in the November election. As a Democrat he won Ashland by better than two to one, "and with almost no effort," she said. In another of the county's cities, however, he had lost two to one, "and we canvassed every neighborhood there," she said. As I had never known that city to support a Democrat for a county commission seat (Republicans enjoy a seventeen-point registration advantage), I asked her why they canvassed there. She said, "Because we were such a cute couple." True story.

"If you are not part of the solution, you are part of the problem."

—Eldridge Cleaver

It doesn't matter how swell you think you are, if you spend time, money, or energy in areas where you will lose, that means you are not spending time, money, and energy in areas where you need to win. Work smart: Write off the sinners, trust the saints, and persuade the saveables.

7

TARGETING VOTERS

IN THIS CHAPTER
- *Finding the Likely Voter*
- *Canvassing*
- *Direct Mail*
- *Tracking Polls*

Finding the Likely Voter

Among the best means of finding likely voters are demographic characteristics, such as age, education, race, gender, income, and voting characteristics, including voting history and absentee voter status. According to a 1993 Simmons Market Research Bureau study, college graduates were 33 percent more likely to vote than the average adult, and those with a graduate degree were 41 percent more likely to vote. In November 2002, the Field Institute in California released a study of expected turnout in which it compared the characteristics of the state's voting-age population, its registered voters, and its likely voters (the report is available at www.field.com). The study revealed that those who have no more than a high school education constitute 42 percent of the state's adults but only 24 percent of registered voters (and likely voters), and those with a college degree constitute just 28 percent of the adult population but 42 percent of likely voters.

> *"If it is a blessing, it is certainly very well disguised."*
> —Winston Churchill
> after losing the 1945 elections

Turnout can also be predicted by income level, which correlates with education. According to a 1999 report by the U.S. Census Bureau, people in the workforce with a college degree in 1976 had, on average, an income 57 percent higher than those with only a high school diploma. By 1999 the proportion had increased to 76 percent.

Identifying these voters early and persuading them to support your candidate or measure is critical to a win, because they *will* vote or are *likely* to vote.

Voters who request an absentee ballot have long been among the most likely voters. While the percentage of people requesting an absentee ballot may

"Get your facts first and then you can distort them as much as you please."

—Mark Twain

vary among states and regions, their turnout doesn't. Absentee voters can represent a substantial proportion of the overall turnout. In Oregon, before people could register absentee permanently, those requesting absentee ballots typically ran about 25 percent of all the registered voters. In the 1998 primary election, after voters were given the option to register absentee permanently, 41 percent of the voters registered absentee on a permanent basis (table 7.1). In that election, absentee ballots accounted for nearly two-thirds of all ballots cast (figure 7.1). Absentee voter turnout was 53 percent, whereas turnout among those casting their votes at the polls was only 22 percent. In the 1998 general election, 73 percent of those requesting an absentee ballot returned their ballot. Given the potential percentage of overall voter turnout absentee ballots can represent, your campaign should work them long before the get-out-the-vote (GOTV) effort, with a separate, focused campaign.

The Field Institute reported that in 1978 just 4.4 percent of California's voters chose to vote absentee; by November of 2002 the proportion had in-

"A great many people think they are thinking when they are merely rearranging their prejudices."

—William James

creased to 28 percent. The study also noted that older voters are more likely to be absentee voters. "Of all those voting absentee, 39 percent will be age 60 or older, while just 28 percent of precinct voters will be in this age group." Also of interest is that in any given election, more absentee voters will be Republicans than Democrats (47 percent and 41 percent, respectively) and more will be women (58 percent and 42 percent).

Age, Voting History, and Party

Age is an important factor to consider in determining voter turnout. According to election statistics posted by the Federal Election Commission on their Web site (www.fec.gov), since 1972, when the voting age was lowered to 18, and 50 percent of 18- to 21-year-olds voted, turnout for this age group has been in steady decline. By comparison, those in the 45–64 and 64 and up age groups

Table 7.1 Absentee Voter History in Oregon
(www.sos.state.or.us/elections) Note: In 1998 Oregon voters
approved permanent vote-by-mail elections by 69 percent.

Election	Number of registered voters	Registered absentee	Absentee ballots returned	Voted absentee in election
Primary 1996	1,851,499	20%	66%	36%
General 1996	1,962,155	39%	88%	48%
Primary 1998	1,909,798	41%	52%	63%
General 1998	1,965,736	47%	73%	58%

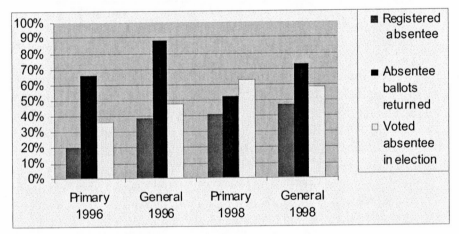

Figure 7.1 History of Absentee Voter Performance in Oregon
(www.sos.state.or.us/elections)

have maintained a consistent voting pattern, with turnout hovering close to 60 percent for twenty-five years. Looking at both the voting history of your district (which indicates who will actually vote) and party registration data becomes helpful in shaping the message and direction of a campaign.

The breakdown of nationwide voter registration in table 7.2 presents a relatively even split of Democrats and Republicans among all age groups except voters 60 and older. However, when voter turnout is broken down by age, party disparity is more pronounced.

After the 1998 election, Mark DiCamillo, the director of the Field Institute, noted that voting rates are correlated with age and education. "The older and more educated you are, the more likely you are to vote." This was borne out in the 1998 November election in California, where

"Campaigns are preparation, organization, execution, and luck."
—Elaine Franklin

Table 7.2 Voting Tendencies By Party Registration and Age in 1998

1998	Nationwide		California	
Age	Percent Democrat	Percent Republican	Percent of voting population	Percent likely to vote 11/98
18–29	48	48	29	13
30–44	49	49	24	20
45–59	50	46	28	37
60 & older	44	54	19	30

SOURCE: Federal Election Commission Web site (www.fec.gov).

people over 60 represented 19 percent of the population but 30 percent of the voters. By contrast, those in the 18–29 age group made up 29 percent of the population but only 13 percent of the voters.

While the 18–29 age group may be evenly divided in party registration, their lack of interest in voting has the effect of adding significant weight to the additional 10 percent party registration held by the GOP for those 60 and older. Of further interest is that of those 60 and older, 75 percent are registered to vote, whereas only 51 percent of the 18–29 age group are registered (www.fec.gov).

Just to demonstrate the voting power of the over-60 age group in this scenario, if all those percentages held for the 1996 election, in which 10 million Californians voted, the 60 and over crowd would weigh in with a million more votes than the 18–29 age group.

Reaching Young Voters

Although this handbook is about directing resources where they will give you the highest return, political consultants, candidates, and campaign managers may want to study young voters in their districts before making any final decisions on what to do with Generation Xers.

During campaigns and while serving in office, candidates and office holders fall all over themselves pandering to seniors and focusing on issues important to our aging population—and with good reason. Seniors have been a powerful political force since they first organized as the Gray Panthers in the 1970s. They often have disposable income, they vote, and they are more likely to volunteer in campaigns. However, as people get older they tend to vote their party and turn out no matter what a campaign does.

"To have doubted one's own first principles is the mark of a civilized man."

—Oliver Wendell Holmes

This is not the case with young voters whose party identification is almost evenly divided among Republicans, Democrats, and Independents or third parties. According to the Campaign for Young Voters, nearly half describe themselves as moderates (www.campaignyoungvoters.org). This is a group that's up for grabs. Although their registration numbers reflect those of the older population, young voters do not have strong party ties and may be the largest of all swing voter blocks—that is, if they can be reached and activated. Equally important for our purposes is to look at how many ways young voters mirror the adult population.

Recognizing Generation X as Us

According to the Campaign for Young Voters, young voters fall into three categories: likely young voters, potential young voters, and unlikely young voters (table 7.3).

Likely young voters are more politically oriented, trust government more, and expect candidates to pay attention to their concerns and to want their vote. They say that voting is important and view elections as a way to have a voice. They are registered and think their vote counts, have parents who involved them in voting at a young age, who voted themselves, and who discussed political issues at home. They are better educated and more apt to be full-time students and to identify with one of the two major parties.

"A candidate or party that can gain the trust and loyalty of young adults now, before their opinions and beliefs are set, can build a generational voting base that will remain for years."
—Campaign for Young Voters

Potential young voters are similar to the likely young voters, except they are typically involved in community projects rather than campaigns. Their passions tend to revolve around volunteer activities in a community and are particularly influenced by candidates who have had similar experiences.

The unlikely young voters are in many ways the opposite of the likely young voters. Their parents didn't vote or discuss politics with them, and they are less likely to be affiliated with institutions such as colleges, churches, and political parties. They are also less likely to be ideological and less likely to be conservatives.

Mobilizing Young Voters

A number of studies have been conducted on how to mobilize the 18- to 25-year-olds on election day. The 2002 Michigan Democratic Party's Youth

Table 7.3 Generation X: Who Are They?

	Likely young voters (30% of all)	Potential young voters (24% of all)	Unlikely young voters (46% of all)
Volunteerism			
% volunteer at least weekly	13%	30%	1%
% volunteer at least monthly	34%	64%	4%
% volunteer at least annually	61%	90%	16%
% never volunteer	22%	3%	66%
Voter registration			
% registered	98%	46%	47%
Parental engagement			
% went to vote with parents	56%	43%	21%
% discussed politics with parents	87%	51%	25%
% parents vote in every election	41%	33%	20%
Core attitudes			
%/(net) can make a difference solving problems	62% (+25)	57% (+15)	31% (-37)
%/(net) say voting is important	81% (+63)	59% (+19)	25% (-48)
% trust other people	47%	47%	33%
%/(net) trust government	75% (+50)	74% (+48)	48% (-2)
% strongly agree elections are a way for people to have a voice	50%	42%	23%
% strongly agree elections are about politicians competing to get elected	48%	49%	56%
%/(net) say political leaders pay a lot/some attention to youth	64% (+30)	55% (+11)	34% (-31)
% strongly agree my vote counts as much as anyone else's	71%	56%	40%
% strongly agree candidates want my vote	56%	50%	32%
Demographics			
% women	47%	59%	45%
18-25: % some college +	63%	51%	41%
15-17: % expect some college +	67%	65%	55%
% ID as partisan (Dem or GOP)	77%	57%	45%
% ID as independent	18%	29%	32%
% liberal	39%	27%	31%
% conservative	32%	28%	15%
% student full-time	33%	35%	17%
% weekly churchgoer	34%	44%	20%

SOURCE: Campaign for Young Voters (www.campaignyoungvoters.org).

Coordinated Campaign and two studies conducted by Gerber and Green in 2001 reported similar findings: Eighteen- to twenty-five-year-olds respond best to canvassing or personal contact from the candidate or campaign (table 7.4). Also of interest is that while phone canvassing was found to increase young voter participation, multiple calls generated no increase beyond single calls. So if you're going to contact these voters by phone, better to do more of them than to make repeat calls to the same voter. Also worth noting in these studies is the lack of impact that direct mail has on young voters. In fact, nothing rates lower. Given the cost of direct mail and the annoyance to the voter created by the sheer volume of campaign mail, this is good news for financially limited underdogs struggling to get their message out.

By largely overlooking 18- to 25-year-olds, candidates and campaigns are perpetuating a vicious cycle: Young people don't vote, so no funds are spent informing them, so they do not become invested, and therefore do not vote. Campaigns spend so much time and money focusing on seniors—who would turn out to vote with little or no campaign effort—but spend almost none targeting the youth vote. Neglection 2000, a project funded by the Pew Charitable Trusts and sponsored by Third Millennium, looked at TV ad placement in four media markets in the 2000 presidential primary. They found that 58 percent were placed in markets for the 50 and over crowd, while only 17 percent were placed with younger voters in mind (*Campaigns & Elections*, August 2000, p. 63).

There are important similarities between what activates the young voter and what activates the sporadic adult voter.

1. Both groups respond best to canvassing, and when younger voters are canvassed by a campaign, they activate adults living in the same house, creating a "trickle up" effect (Green and Gerber, "Getting Out the Youth Vote," December 2001, p. 19; see source note in table 7.4).

2. Young voters identify the voting process itself as part of the problem for low voter turnout, saying it is designed to discriminate against people who move, are overwhelmed with day-to-day concerns, are poorer, or are living on the edge. Priscilla Southwell's 1996 report to the state of Oregon's Vote-by-Mail Citizen Commission, "Survey of Vote-by-Mail Senate Election," showed that those who were younger, worked hourly-wage jobs, were students, were single parents, were minorities, and were registered as independents all turned out in greater numbers in vote-by-mail elections than in polling elections.

Table 7.4 Mobilizing Young Voters: What Works and What Doesn't

Nonpartisan tactic	Mobilizing effect	Dollars/vote	Notes
Door-to-door	8-10%	$12-20	Tested on young voters
Volunteer phone bank	3-5%	$12-20	Tested on young voters
Professional phone bank	0-2%	$140 and up	
Multiple calls	0-1%	n/a	Tested on young voters
Leafleting	0% (party affiliated voters)	$40 and up	7% effect on unaffiliated
Direct mail	0-1%	$40 and up	

Summary of Green & Gerber Findings as Reported in "Mobilizing 18–35 Year Old Voters," by Ryan Friedrichs of the JFK School of Government (04/02). SOURCE: Alan Gerber and Donald Green: "Getting Out the Youth Vote" (12/01).

3. Young voters respond best to candidates who are genuine, speak frankly and directly, and are involved in community activities. These traits are valued by all age groups.

4. Young voters respond best to GOTV phone calls that inform—such as identifying the polling place location (Green and Gerber, "Getting Out the Youth Vote"). GOTV work I've conducted in southern Oregon with older voters mirrors this pattern. As a result, the script of our GOTV calls changes almost daily, and all include some bit of information the voter may not know. "Did you know the county still has not received your ballot?" "This is the last day that ballots can be safely mailed and still make it to the clerk's office by election day." "There isn't enough time to mail your ballot, you will now need to hand-carry it to . . . "

Ethnic and Gender Gaps

Although for many years more women have been eligible to vote than men, it wasn't until 1976 that women actually registered nationally in greater numbers, and not until 1984 that they began to turn out in greater numbers. By 1996, over 7 million more women voted in the presidential election than men. For our purposes, however, it's important to look not only at who votes but also at how they vote when they do.

"Ninety percent of the politicians give the other ten percent a bad reputation."

—Henry Kissinger

In a 1994 survey, Public Opinion Strategies found that white men were markedly more inclined to support Republican congressional candidates over Democratic candidates—51 percent compared with 23 percent. In a 1998 study by the National Election Studies at the University of California, Irvine, analysts found similar numbers, with 53 percent of white men voting for Republican candidates, 37 percent for Democratic candidates, and 10 percent for independents. White women, they found, favored Democrats over Republicans at 48 percent and 42 percent, respectively, and black women overwhelmingly favored Democrats, with 88 percent voting Democratic, 7 percent voting Republican, and 5 percent voting for independents. Although in 1998 the gender gap did not materialize to the degree predicted for the general election, there is no doubt that it played a role.

The low Republican turnout of older white men added strength to those turning out to vote Democratic. Remember, a win isn't based only on who votes for you but also on who does not vote for your opposition. Precinct analysis and looking at voting trends allows you to activate those who will vote your way, persuade those who are inclined to vote your way, and either ignore or not encourage those who will support the opposition. By ignoring the sinners you hope they will forget to vote. By discouraging them (say, with negative information about their candidate), you hope they will undervote the category.

The 2002 Field Institute study of California voters mentioned earlier found the sharpest differences in likelihood of voting among the state's racial and ethnic groups. White non-Hispanics accounted for 51 percent of the state's adults, but 69 percent of the registered voters and 73 percent of the likely voters in the November election. Latinos represented 28 percent of the adult population, but 17 percent of the registered voters and 16 percent of the likely voters.

These proportions held in October 2003, according to a *Los Angeles Times* exit poll on the California recall of Governor Gray Davis (table 7.5). Voting trends among age groups also held in the recall election, with the 18–29 age group accounting for 12 percent of the turnout, the 30–44 age group 30 percent, and the 45 and over age group 58 percent. Educational levels were similarly reflected in turnout of the likely voter, with those

"How few aim at the good of the whole, without aiming too much at the prosperity of part."

—John Adams

having a high school diploma or less constituting 15 percent of the voter turnout, those with some college 26 percent, and those with a college degree 59 percent. The largest disparity among likely voters in the recall election was seen in income levels, with those making more than $60,000 per year accounting for 61 percent of the overall voter turnout.

How the Gender and Ethnic Gaps Affected the 1996 Presidential Race
Table 7.6 presents a breakdown of how people voted in the 1996 presidential election, by gender, race, and party.

Table 7.5 How Californians Voted in the Recall of Governor Gray Davis

	Percent against recall	Percent for Schwarzenegger	Percent for Bustamante	Percent of all voters
Men	41	52	26	49
Women	49	44	35	51
Black	79	18	65	6
White	41	53	27	72
Latino	55	31	55	11
Democrat	75	23	61	46
Republican	11	76	4	39
Independent	46	46	26	12

SOURCE: *LA Times* (www.latimes.com/timespoll.)

The Ethnic Gap

The African-American, Hispanic, and Asian votes can have an impact on the outcome of an election. For example, in 1997, the Asian vote in San Francisco had a large impact in a freeway retrofit measure. In the same year, San Francisco approved funding for a football stadium, largely as a result of the number of minorities voting in predominantly ethnic areas. Whites living in the upper-income sections of the city opposed the measure but ultimately were overwhelmed by minorities hoping for improvements in a marginal neighborhood. Minorities living outside the affected neighborhood indicated that they had supported the stadium in hopes that their neighborhood would be next. Ironically, the very people who supported and voted for the stadium bill are among those least able to afford tickets to see the games.

The Hispanic vote in California, Texas, and Florida also played a large part in the general election of 1998, in which Hispanics and Blacks cast 15 percent of the votes, an increase of 3 percent from 1994. Table 7.7 shows the minority vote by party registration in the 1998 election, and table 7.8 summarizes minority turnout for the midterm election in 1996.

Depending on the demographics of your area, your campaign needs to be aware of the gender and ethnic gap voting potential as well as the fatal flaws

Table 7.6 Women and Minority Vote in the 1996 Presidential Election

	Clinton (percent)	Dole (percent)	Perot (percent)	Percent of all voters
Men	44	44	10	48
Women	54	38	7	52
Black	83	12	4	10
White	43	46	9	83
Democrat	84	10	5	40
Republican	13	80	6	34
Independent	43	35	17	26

SOURCE: How the Gender & Ethnic Gap Affected the 1996 Presidential Race, Federal Election Commission Web site (www.fec.gov).

Table 7.7 Minority Vote by Party Registration

	Percent Republican	Percent Democrat
White	55	42
Black	11	88
Hispanic	35	59
Asian	42	54

SOURCE: "How They Voted Nationwide in November of 1998," *Newsweek*, November 16, 1998, 42.

Table 7.8 Minority Turnout in 1996

	Percent Registered	Percent Voted
White	67.7	56
Black	63.5	50.6
Hispanic	35.7	26.7

SOURCE: 1994 Registration Totals and Turnout, Federal Election Commission Web Site (www.fec.gov).

it can mean for your campaign. Determine the influence of these demographics for shaping message, persuasion, and GOTV efforts.

The Hispanic vote has become the most sought after, for both parties, both in national politics and in states with Hispanic populations large enough to influence the outcome of a close race. I offer the following observations on engaging this important constituency on the basis of having studied for several years in Mexico and Central America, having worked in migrant health in southern Oregon, and having served as ambassador to Ashland's sister city, Guanajuato, Mexico, for over a decade.

First, Hispanics living on the West Coast are largely from points south— Mexico and Central and South America—and they come to the United States primarily for economic reasons. As a result, they tend to want to assimilate into American culture in a very different way than, say, Cuban immigrants. As Raul Damas and James Aldrete have noted, "Cuban exiles who arrived in the 1960s wanted their children to learn Spanish, so the country they lost could remain alive. Recent Mexican immigrants, on the other hand, place major emphasis on their children learning English, because they came here for economic advance-ment" (Damas and Aldrete, *Campaigns & Elections,* June 2003, p. 9).

Second, Americans of Mexican descent are part of a culture that is deeply seated in history. Understanding their history in politics, art, music, and reli-gion is critical to understanding this rich culture.

Third, there is enormous gratitude for non-Hispanics who know and are willing to converse in Spanish, even if it is minimal: Make an effort.

Fourth, Latin cultures are generally physical and demonstrative—Latinos hug, touch, look you in the eye, laugh, and both celebrate and honor family. There is a saying in Mexico that a party is not a party without children. Fam-ilies care for and honor grandparents and children equally.

Finally, a first-generation immigrant is very different from a third- or fourth-generation immigrant.

"This country will not be a good place for any of us to live in unless we make it a good place for all of us to live in."

—Theodore Roosevelt

Candidates should know how U.S. policies have affected people in countries south of the United States. Whether or not you agree with the policies, take the time to understand the historical impact our nation has had on these cultures.

Consider the unnecessary barriers we impose on people from other cul-tures. For example, in Mexico and Central and South America, public trans-portation is cheap and plentiful. However, in most areas in the United States it is virtually nonexistent. On top of that, some states are considering or have passed legislation that imposes restrictions on issuance of driver's licenses to illegal immigrants.

Canvassing

Typically to get a vote, you must ask for it anywhere from three to eight times. Newspaper, television, and radio advertising, direct mail, special events, phone banks, and canvassing are the most common ways to ask for a vote. However, canvassing remains the most effective tool in a campaigner's bag of tricks. In small communities, canvassing is an ideal way to check in with the voting public and can be elevating and gratifying for the candidate. While TV, newspaper, and radio ads target groups, canvassing (like phoning and direct mail) is about targeting individuals—specifically, voters who are inclined to support your efforts.

Canvassing is not generally about changing minds; it's about changing voter turnout in areas that historically have supported candidates and ballot initiatives similar to the one you are promoting. By going door-to-door in areas of high support but of low to medium turnout, you activate your voters for election day.

A dramatic example of the effectiveness of canvassing supportive precincts while ignoring precincts inclined to vote against your efforts is provided in figure 7.2. Identical ballot measures were placed before Ashland voters in 1993 and then again in 1994. Our supporting campaigns were exactly the same, with two exceptions. First, in 1993 both high- and low-priority precincts were canvassed, whereas in 1994, only high-priority precincts were targeted. Second, in 1994 we conducted a voter identification and GOTV effort. The combination of activating only high-support precincts with a GOTV effort worked. The exact same measure that lost in 1993 by 326 votes passed in 1994 by 447 votes.

When low-priority precincts are activated by canvassing, nonsupport increases, as in the 1993 election. However, when supporting voters are identified in low-priority precincts, and when only they are activated in a GOTV effort, two important things happen: First, the overall number of no votes decreases, because nonsupporting voters are ignored, and second, the number of yes votes increases because of GOTV activation. While yes votes increased slightly and no votes decreased in high-priority precincts between 1993 and 1994, the lower turnout combined with the decline of no votes in the low-priority precincts is what won the 1994 election.

Canvassing Leaning Voters

In areas of medium support with low to medium turnout, canvassing can actually pull votes over to your side. All things being equal, the candidate or cause that gets to a leaning voter first and with the best message wins support. Should these voters already be moved by your ads, brochure, debating ability, command of the issues, and good looks, then, as with the first group of high-support precincts, canvassing will serve to activate that support— that is, to remind the voter to vote.

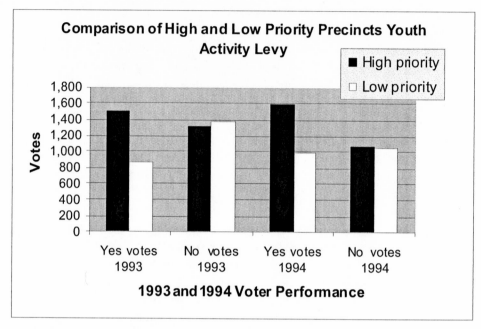

Figure 7.2 A Case for Activating the Right Voters. The difference in the election outcome between 1993 and 1994 is mostly played out in the low-priority precincts, where the biggest shifts occur.

Canvassing is a time-consuming, resource-intensive way to activate sympathetic voters and bring your message to the people. It can also be a great way to get a feel for your chances of winning. In my second bid for mayor, lawn signs for the opposition lined the main street through town, making my prospects seem bleak. However, after I started canvassing, I realized how handily we would win, and therefore felt much more relaxed in all my campaign activities. Canvassing will give you information about voter intentions. It can also help you get additional lawn sign locations in key spots.

If canvassing is done right, you will also get valuable feedback on voter concerns that can help you adjust your ads, direct mail, and debate emphases to meet those concerns. For example, in Ashland's prepared food and beverage tax campaign, a canvasser stopped at a home that already hosted a lawn sign in support of the tax measure. The homeowner told the canvasser that it was fine for the lawn sign to stay, but that she was rethinking her decision to support the tax measure because of all the controversy and seemingly overwhelming support for the opposition citywide. In another campaign a canvasser reported that the base party voters did not know who was running for the office. In both of these examples, thanks to the canvassers, we were able to address the problem, fix it, and win the elections.

Although there are few, if any, campaign activities that have a greater return on investment, it is important to keep in mind that canvassing is not for everyone. Also, some places are too risky for the traditional canvass. Be careful, and know the areas you are going into. Never send someone to canvass alone or go alone yourself, and never enter a house, if for no other reason than that your partner will not be able to find you.

Map Packets

Before volunteers or the candidate can canvass, you must first do a precinct analysis to determine where your high support/low turnout and high support/medium turnout are so you can determine where to expend your efforts. Then you must prepare maps of those areas for your canvassers. After these tasks have been completed, the canvassing activity itself begins. Although I always do the precinct analysis and map preparation myself, I like to divide my city in half and have two canvass coordinators. If you are in a bigger city, you may want to break it down even further. If it is a county, keep breaking it down so that coordinators can oversee manageable units of people and space.

Setting up canvass map packets is a critical element to a successful canvass (figure 7.4). Do not wait to do this with the canvassers when they first arrive, or even the night before. Map packets should be organized in advance, and a generous amount of time should be allotted for the task.

Setting up map packets for canvassing begins with great maps. You can get them from the Chamber of Commerce, Realtors, MapQuest, online from the county, and even the phone book. When possible, use maps from the county clerk's office or the county geographic information system (GIS) department so that precinct lines are identified. In fact, GIS mapping programs (such as ESRI's Arcview and ArcGIS software) are a great option for canvass maps. With GIS programs you can list which doors to knock on according to income, the number of voters living there, how many of the past four elections the occupants have voted in, and more.

If your canvass is a "knock," you can count on canvassers covering anywhere from fifteen to twenty-five homes in an hour and thirty to fifty an hour for a literature drop (no knocking). The time it takes depends on the density of housing and steepness of the terrain. Generally, I use six people working in pairs for about two hours each to complete a precinct canvass of 200 to 400 homes. Larger or more difficult precincts may require eight people for a

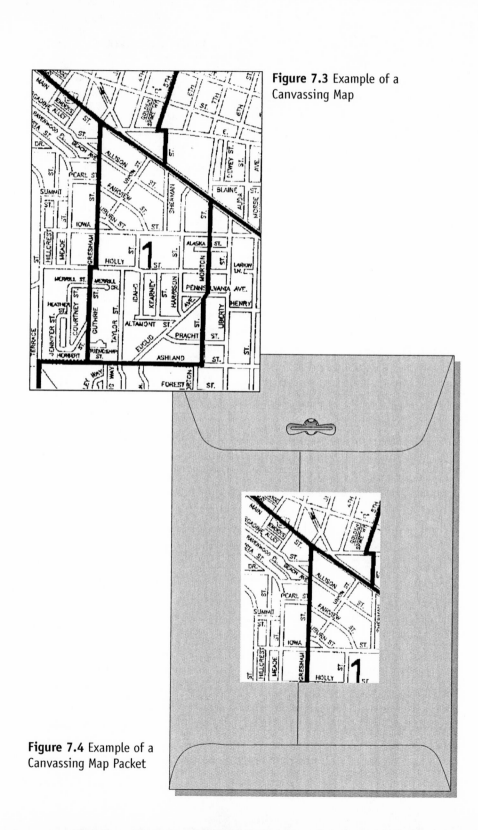

Figure 7.3 Example of a Canvassing Map

Figure 7.4 Example of a Canvassing Map Packet

two-hour shift. If it's your campaign, you should know your precincts better than anyone. If you don't, hop in the car and take a little drive around and get to know them.

Precinct boundaries often run down the middle of a street; that might make sense for the people who draw precinct boundaries on maps, but for canvassing purposes, it's a little silly. When dividing precincts for canvassing teams, it is best to use one team to cover both sides of a normal city street. Doing so may require that portions of two or more precincts be included on the same map. However, efficiency is more important than precinct lines. This rule applies inversely, too: If a precinct jumps a major thoroughfare, do not expect your canvassers to hop across four-lane highways while canvassing.

For each of your teams, make two identical map packets, with the assigned area for canvassing highlighted (figure 7.4). It is sometimes helpful to line up your team maps on a window, or at least side-by-side, to check that streets haven't been missed or been double-highlighted on packets of adjoining canvass areas. Canvassing houses twice wastes both the volunteers' and voters' time and is annoying to both. It's bound to happen, but do your best to minimize it.

No matter how well someone claims to know an area, every canvasser needs to work with a map. No exceptions. That is why two identically highlighted maps must be created for each pair of canvassers. Have canvassers mark off the blocks they complete on their map. This information helps you keep track of both the canvass and canvassers.

Once the maps have been prepared, tape each one to a manila envelope, which will then be used to keep brochures protected in bad weather and looking fresh by the time they reach the doorstep. Manila envelopes are fairly cheap, but they are also easy to find used. If you tell friends and co-workers that you need manila envelopes from their mail trash, you'll have more than you can use in a very short time.

Remember, you have two identical packets. People work in pairs, so the two packets *must* stay together. To make sure the duplicate packets are not separated from each other, fold and place one inside the other or staple the two together. If they get separated, you are bound to have two different teams pick up the same packet and canvass the same area two times, so pay attention to this detail. Also, be sure to number your packets so that you can quickly see if any are missing.

Place the materials necessary for the type of canvass you are conducting into each envelope. If you are doing a get-out-the-vote canvass or using walking lists to contact particular people, this is the packet in which you place those materials. Just put the voter lists and the matching envelope inside one envelope. The canvassers will separate out the walking lists when they divide up how they want to work. You may either place a bunch of brochures into the packet or leave them loose in a box by the door for the volunteers to pick up on their way out. Either way, volunteers should take additional brochures to avoid running out before they have finished their areas.

I often tape a 3-by-5-inch card to the back of the manila envelope. That way, if someone canvasses the home of a strong supporter, he or she can write the information on the card so it can get to the campaign. For example, supporters may tell a canvasser that they want a lawn sign or would like to be in an endorsement ad or to contribute money if the candidate calls. If you do not have time to tape a card to each envelope, canvassers can write on the envelope itself, although in that case you must get the information before the envelope goes out again.

Each canvasser will need a pen, so have plenty on hand. I remind people to bring pens during the call-back before the canvass, but there will be those who forget. It's a nice touch to have your canvassers write on the front of the brochure "Sorry we missed you" for people not at home.

"Only a life in the service of others is worth living."

—Albert Einstein

Walking Direct Mail

Sometimes I staple a personalized message from neighbors in a particular precinct to the brochure. If you do this, you must stuff these brochures inside the canvassing packet to eliminate the risk of canvassers grabbing the wrong brochures. This is an inexpensive way to get a direct mail testimonial to the doors of potential supporters. Having it ready for the canvassers is well worth the effort.

Consider posting a large map of your city or county on a wall where you can mark off areas as they get canvassed. Color-code the wall map according to high, medium, or low canvass priority. As volunteers complete streets, mark them off in different colored inks. That way, volunteers get to see their collective work and feel they are part of a well-run campaign.

Note: Make a duplicate set of the highlighted map. That way you have a complete set from which to prepare map packets for future campaigns or to replace missing packets. Don't give in and use your set when you're in a hurry, or you'll be sorry the next time you need them.

Organizing the Volunteer Force

Have your volunteers arrive fifteen minutes early if they have not canvassed for you before. The moment they walk in, ask them to read the brochure to familiarize themselves with the contents. Generally, I have a plate of cookies, brownies, or some little something to eat, plus juice and water. For morning canvasses, I have coffee on hand if someone asks for it, but I do not set it out; after coffee, people will have to go to the bathroom the minute they get out the door and usually go back home to do it. Coffee or not, urge people to use the bathroom *before* they head out to canvass.

In training canvassers, I tell them never to talk issues. That's for the candidate or the campaign committee to do. However close a canvasser is to the candidate, none can possibly know how a candidate stands on all the issues. When asked a question at the door, canvassers can say, "Why don't you give [the candidate] a call and ask her?" Of course, canvassers can tell people why *they* are out working for the candidate. It might be because of the candidate's stand on the environment, development, timber, air quality, transportation, education, taxes, jobs, libraries, public safety, or human resources. Every person who works for you will have a reason for volunteering. Urge your volunteers to think what that reason is before they head out to canvass. This directive should be part of your precanvassing spiel. Be sure to include things like: "What would motivate you to get out and canvass on a beautiful Saturday when you would probably rather be home with your family?" This is also a nice way to let volunteers know you understand what they are giving up to work for you and that you appreciate it. I also include in my pep talks or training how difficult the odds are of winning the campaign, and how important it is that we, not the opposition, win. This brings out the best in your workers.

Unless otherwise directed by the candidate, the canvassers should not offer to have the candidate call to answer a question. Instead, leave the candidate's phone number and urge the voter to contact him or her. Too often, when a phone call from the candidate is offered, the message doesn't get through or the voter can't be reached, which makes the candidate the bad guy. If a voter truly wants an answer to a question, he or she will take a moment to pick up the phone.

Scheduling the Volunteers

More than anywhere else in the campaign, I try to accommodate volunteers' schedules for canvassing. Generally I set up four time slots for people on a given weekend. However, if none of those times work, I will send volunteers out whenever they can go. Nine times out of ten, there will be someone else who can or must fit into the same time slot, so I can usually provide a partner. If no other volunteer is available at that time, I'll send the candidate or will go along myself. I do this because it's safer for canvassers to work in pairs and because it's good for the candidate or campaign manager to canvass. Not only is it a great stress reducer, but also enables you to become more empathetic about the efforts of your canvassers, get a better understanding of the voters, and demonstrate your willingness to work as hard as the volunteers. Volunteers love to canvass with the candidate or campaign manager.

It is important to accommodate your canvassers in other ways, too. If someone tells me she does not like to walk hills or that she wants to work in her neighborhood, I tell her that I'll set aside a packet for her, and then I make sure I follow through. This further reduces the possibility of no-shows.

A big part of a good canvassing effort is placing the right volunteer in the right precinct. For example, if you have an area with a senior population, place your oldest canvassers in that area. If you have canvassers whose manner of dress is new age or in some way inappropriate for a given neighborhood, put them in a more progressive area or have them work lawn signs. People should canvass their peers.

> *"You can't hold a man down without staying down with him."*
> —Booker T. Washington

Whomever you assign, remember that when they knock at the door, they represent the campaign. Let people know before they canvass that they must present themselves well to the public and look nice, because for that moment they are the face of the campaign. Also, as noted earlier, keep in mind that canvassing young voters will often activate adults in their home.

Sometimes you will have volunteers in areas of swing voters who are overwhelmingly registered with one party over another. (Remember, swing voters are those who do not always vote along party lines but rather tend to vote issues or emotion.) In such cases, try to place a canvasser who has the same party affiliation as the precinct. For example, if you're working for a Democrat and need to canvass a neighborhood that is predominantly Republican, look for "validators" to do the canvassing—which in this example would be other Republicans. That way when someone answers the door and says they always vote party, the canvasser can say: "I know, I'm a Republican and I usually do too, but this election I'm working and voting for the Democrat because . . . "

> *"There are very few people who don't become more interesting when they stop talking."*
> —Mary Lowry

Bad Weather

There are bound to be days of bad weather when volunteers are scheduled for a canvass. When I am working on a campaign, I pray for a rainy drizzle and tell my canvassers to do the same and dress accordingly. When it rains, more people are home, and your campaign gets bonus points for getting out in bad weather. When people open the door, they feel empathy for you and admire your dedication. I have also noticed that volunteers don't mind canvassing in bad weather, which makes sense: If it is a sunny, glorious spring or fall day, wouldn't you rather be out doing something other than canvassing? Up to a point, if the weather is lousy, canvassing is a good thing to do with your time while getting some exercise. However, canvassing in really bad weather doesn't help your cause: Canvassers will hate it, and voters will wonder about the campaign's judgement.

A very effective technique for getting more people to canvass is to ask every person who has agreed to walk to bring a friend. This makes it more fun for those who do, increases your volunteer numbers, and helps reduce the possibility of no-shows. Since canvassing is conducted in pairs, it is an ideal activity for friends or couples.

Canvassers often ask if they can bring their children to help. If the kids are old enough, it should be fine. I started canvassing for my mom when I was in middle school, which is probably too young. I believe in children having a hand in campaigns, not least so that they can celebrate the win with their parents. I especially like to have kids along with canvassers when I'm working for a library or school funding measure. After all, they have a stake in the outcome, and it doesn't hurt for the voters to have a stakeholder at their door. Young children, however, can be a distraction and can really slow a canvasser down. If you are the candidate, you should not tow your kids along, unless of course you're a man with a baby.

> "The reasonable man adapts himself to the world; the unreasonable one persists in trying to adapt the world to himself. Therefore all progress depends on the unreasonable man."
> —George Bernard Shaw

Remember, don't put any campaign literature in or on mailboxes, and be sure your campaign material does not become litter. When residents are not home, volunteers should wedge the brochure or walking piece into doorjambs, screen doors, and trim boards so that it cannot escape into the wind. If it appears that the residents are out of town and campaign literature and newspapers are already littering the doorstep, consider skipping that home.

If you are the candidate, get out and canvass along with the volunteers. Because it is much more effective for the candidate to knock on the door, cover as much ground as possible—but don't overdo it. Pace yourself, and start early in the campaign in order to canvass as many homes as possible. The personal touch really works. However, candidates often get hung up talking with voters, so be sure a partner goes along to help cover the area and prod candidates out of doorways.

Get to Know Your Voters By Where and How They Live

When you canvass, you are moving about in neighborhoods that have supported candidates or causes like yours in previous elections. You can learn a lot by studying the neighborhoods that have popped out as your top- and medium-priority areas. Are the homes historic or modern ranch? Are they well cared for? Is the neighborhood made up largely of working-class or retired people? Minorities, single parents, college students, mill workers? Look for clues as to why these voters may have trouble getting out to vote. Are they simply overwhelmed with life, children, work, school, poverty? As Jim Gimpel, a professor of political science at the University of Maryland has remarked, neighborhoods tell us about the voters who live there. They "reveal housing preferences, spending habits, racial and ethnic composition, lifestyles, levels of geographic mobility, voting habits and other traits relevant to predicting political participation and attitudes" (*Campaigns & Elections,* August 2003, p. 40).

Direct Mail

Whereas canvassing is about activating voters who, according to past precinct voting patterns, are inclined to vote for your candidate, direct mail is about activating voters around specific issues that transcend voting tendencies.

Direct mail can cultivate a relationship between your campaign and the voters based on issues. These issues should resonate with your base vote *and* the swing vote. Again, the goal is to lock in your base vote and move swing voters your way—regardless of party affiliation or prior voting tendencies.

The strategy you use here is the same as you use in an issue-based campaign. With an issue-based campaign, you are looking for ways to package a single issue (such as building a new library) so that voters will identify with it, whereas with candidates you use direct mail to package issues as a way to move voters both away from opposition and toward your candidate. Although there will be specifics on which you and your opposition disagree from the outset, such as taxes, choice, or gun control, the issues that you will use in direct mail are often the result of things said or done by the opposition during the election process. These things may not be readily apparent at the beginning of the campaign, so pay attention. Once the game begins, you are looking for anything that will pry support away from the other side. By offering voters simple, additional information, you're providing a shortcut that will help them make a decision. Direct mail is a way to get a specialized message to individual voters regardless of where they live or how their precincts tend to vote. Although campaigns are relying on direct mail to do more of the communications with the electorate, it is important to keep in mind that it is just one part of a campaign. Direct mail is most useful when it augments the more comprehensive campaign.

Direct mail is more than a letter or brochure stuffed into an envelope. It is the most selective of all media forms, and because of its selectivity, it offers distinct advantages over TV, newspaper, or radio ads. Using direct mail, a campaign can align an exact issue with an exact voter in a specific house. To do this effectively requires research on the part of the campaign. You must know your opponent's stands on specific issues as well as specific issues that will influence specific voters. It requires a well-constructed and wellorganized database. Besides party registration, it is helpful to know voting frequency, age, gender, neighborhood, whether there are children at home, and whether the household is a single-parent household. It can also be helpful to have access to information about whether a hunting or fishing license was issued, if the voter belongs to the National Rifle Association, is a veteran, a union member, a teacher, a police officer, or a firefighter, or works in a medical facility. Basically, you want any information that will help categorize likely voters on the basis of demographics and areas of interest—that is, "universes." For direct mail to be truly effective, you must look for specific universes of people who can be moved by new information that is related to an area of personal interest to them.

> *"Public officials are not a group apart. They inevitably reflect the moral tone of the society in which they live."*
>
> —John F. Kennedy

Direct Mail to Persuade Voters

Through direct mail, you aim to move the leaning voter or to create "switch hitters" or "ticket splitters." Remember, these voters will split the ballot between parties, voting Democratic for one office and Republican for another on the same ballot. They do so because of an issue that is so important that it, and it alone, drives how their vote is cast. Ticket splitters are moved by emotion and issues rather than loyalty to party. Any of the items listed in the "Cardinal Sins of Campaigning" will create "ticket splitters."

The following are examples of issues that could be used to move voters to cross party lines. Each of these examples actually happened in local campaigns.

Military votes: You are running against an incumbent who was one of two no votes in the state senate on a bill designed to protect the job security of

National Guard volunteers after a military rotation. This is information veterans should have.

Libraries: Your opponent voted to close the public library during tight budget years while voting to increase his salary. Friends of the Library, district school teachers, volunteers associated with the libraries, and faculty and students at a local college should know this.

Woman's right to choose: Your opponent voted against sexuality education in the high school curriculum while serving on the school board, and the number of teen pregnancies increased. Supporters of NARAL, the Women's Political Caucus, the American Association of University Women, Planned Parenthood, and the Presbyterian and Unitarian Churches should know this.

Environmental issues (timber, rivers, deserts, parks, and wildlife areas): You are running for county commissioner against an incumbent Democrat who worked outside of her office purview to reduce the acreage of a federally designated monument. The federal designation was the result of nearly two decades of work by local environmentalists. The city representing the incumbent's base polled five to one in favor of the monument as designated. Furthermore, in an effort to reverse the federal designation, your opponent, along with her two fellow county commissioners, skewed numbers on public testimony to make it look as though fewer people supported the designation than opposed it. Getting this information to people in the city of the incumbent's base support and to environmentalists countywide could induce voters to vote against their party or to undervote in the election. Unseating an incumbent generally requires capitalizing on key constituencies that have been alienated.

Lying to the voters: In the above example the incumbent is also vulnerable because of the role she played in misrepresenting data in public testimony. It is not a huge leap to suggest to the voters—whether they are environmentalists or not, whether they support the monument or not—that if she lied to get her way on one issue, she might lie elsewhere to do the same.

State- or area-specific issues: There may be area-specific issues that are not openly addressed in a campaign. For example, in the 2002 Georgia gubernatorial race between incumbent Democrat Roy Barnes and his GOP opponent Sonny Perdue, an underlying issue appeared to be Barnes's replacement of the state flag with one that did not have a confederate emblem dominating it. In Oregon, the mere suggestion that a candidate supports a sales tax is akin to touching the third rail. Voted down by Oregonians in nine elections by overwhelming numbers, a sales tax polled only 35 percent even as Oregon was in economic freefall in 2002.

Flip-flopping: Your opponent tells a school group that she will support a sales tax after emphatically saying she would not in debates. Voters look for consistency in candidates. If a candidate expresses support for an issue while speaking to one group and opposition to the same issue while speaking to another, it will catch up with him. If your candidate genuinely changes his or her mind on an issue, hang a lantern on

> *"The world is moving so fast these days that the man who says it can't be done is generally interrupted by someone doing it."*
>
> —Elbert Hubbard

it. Make it clear why, and turn this potential liability into an asset. ("I am committed to studying issues and basing decisions on sound information. If new information should come to light after I've made a decision, I will weigh it carefully, and if it is in the best interest of my constituency, I may change my mind.")

Other issues that create ticket splitters:

- Air quality
- Traffic (congestion, bikes, pedestrian walkways, mass transit, and so forth)
- Airports, especially general aviation
- Seniors, especially health care issues
- School funding, teacher salaries, and school infrastructure
- Choice
- Unions
- Small businesses
- Land use, development, and parks
- Taxes
- Gun control
- Party switching (candidates who have recently switched party registration)

Although you may intend to use these issues to differentiate yourself from your opponent, your opposition can do the same to you. Your team must carefully examine where you may be vulnerable to losing your base. For example, if the campaign committee counsels a candidate to avoid an issue—say, sales tax—when the candidate is open to the idea, or even supportive of it, there is potential trouble. It is not enough for the campaign committee to tell the candidate to "avoid" an issue, especially if it is bound to be brought up in a campaign; it is their job to help the candidate resolve this internal conflict and to prepare him or her with answers for any questions on the subject.

Ethnic and Gender Gaps

The ethnic and gender gaps play their biggest role in direct mail. Throughout the 1992 presidential contest between Dole and Clinton, the women's vote became the hot issue. What Newt Gingrich laid out, Bob Dole wore around his neck. In 1996, women across America, regardless of income or education, felt an underlying concern about their personal economics. Men tend to worry about problems when they actually arrive, but women look more toward "what ifs." Dole's attacks on "welfare moms" played well to angry white men (whose vote Dole already had) but made women anxious. Many women, working full time while raising children, sometimes without a father, worried that they were just one paycheck away from being a welfare mom.

"Once the game is over, the king and the pawn go back into the same box."
—Italian saying

When Dole went after Medicare and seemed uninterested in shoring up social security, many women worried that they were the ones who would eventually be responsible for taking care of aging parents. When the California GOP went after affirmative action, women again became uneasy. Although women interpreted these types of issues in many ways, they worried about how the general direction Dole and Republicans seemed to be taking would affect them personally. No matter what Dole said to try to win the women's vote, it backfired. Perhaps because of his age, generation, or reference point, he simply did not speak to women's fears, frustrations, and anxieties. Clinton, by contrast, whose father had died before his birth and who was raised by his mother and an alcoholic stepfather, didn't even have to think about it. He just got it. As more and more women, including pro-life Republicans, moved away from Dole, it must have been very disorienting for the GOP.

Similarly, when the California GOP took a hard line against affirmative action and immigrants, the people under attack registered and then voted against Republican candidates in droves. To make matters worse, their turnout doubled and their proportions in the total turnout increased. In Florida and Texas, by contrast, where the GOP had been wooing Hispanics, blacks, and immigrants, Republicans were rewarded in 1998 with votes.

It is always helpful to look at trends to see if they are anomalies or if they indicate substantive changes that can provide your campaign with a road map. For example, as mentioned above, after passage of California's Proposition 187 in 1994, which cut off a variety of state services to illegal immigrants, Latinos began registering and voting in greater numbers. According to Paul Maslin, a Democratic pollster, in the 1980s Latinos made up 7 percent of the California electorate and voted three to two for a Democratic ticket. That amounted to two percentage points for the Democrats. In 1998 Latinos made up 14 to 15 percent of the electorate and voted four to one for the Democrats. That added up to nearly a nine-point lift for the Democrats (E.J. Dionne, Jr., Washington Post Writers Group, *San Francisco Chronicle,* February 2, 1998).

Interestingly enough, in the 2003 recall election of Governor Gray Davis, Latinos, who made up 32 percent of the California population (only 28 percent were adults and only 22 percent were citizens), represented 17 percent of the registered voters. Although their turnout numbers in the recall reflected their overall registration percentage, Latinos reverted to the voting patterns they exhibited before Proposition 187 and supported Democratic candidate Cruz Bustamante five to three.

"The art of persuasion depends mainly on a marshaling of facts, clarity, conviction, and the ability to think on one's feet. True eloquence consists of truth and rapid reason."
—John Adams

It is important to know what is going on within voting groups. This will help you shape your direct mail so that you can either highlight or distance your campaign from a problem. Remember, once a piece of direct mail is in the recipient's hand, it has a life span of about six seconds. For most voters, it's flip, flip, throw, so be sure your front and back covers have all the salient points presented in such a way that the voter is encouraged to open it but also need not actually do so. Also, once the piece is opened, it must contain something to grab the recipient.

Effectiveness of Direct Mail

Direct mail basically has two forms. The first is a letter mailed in an envelope, designed to move the voter by the way an issue is presented in the copy and/or by the effect of the person who sent the letter. Long ago such letters capitalized on the personal relationships the author of the letter had with the recipients. However, they now include mass-mail letters sent from movie stars and current or past office holders from larger or different arenas, including former presidents. The former personal solicitation from one business colleague to another has morphed into something that casts a huge net in hopes of capturing many small contributions. Although direct mail for fund-raising purposes is covered more thoroughly in Chapter 4, it bears repeating here that your piece is only as effective as your mailing list. For smaller, local campaigns that work within tight budgets, each direct mail piece designed to make money must do just that. And the best way to raise funds is to use lists of individuals who have a history of giving to your kind of candidate or issue-based campaign.

The other type of direct mail generally comes as a glossy, full-color, flat or folded, oversized piece of paper that is issue- and voter-specific. This type of direct mail is not about raising money but is similar to fund-raising direct mail in that it goes to targeted voters. This is the most sophisticated medium a campaign can use and should be treated as such.

Let me give you an example. In 1996, I received a direct mail piece from state Senator Gordon Smith, a Republican running for the U.S. Senate, that was intended to hit his opponent, Democrat Ron Wyden. Apparently, in an interview with a Portland newspaper, it emerged that Ron Wyden did not know the cost of a loaf of bread, a gallon of gas in Oregon, or Oregon's unemployment rate, among other things. Personally, I didn't know these things either and couldn't care less that Wyden didn't know. However, there were some who thought he should. The direct mail piece I received from Smith painted Wyden as an out-of-touch Washington politician, and connected his inability to answer these questions with related votes in the House and general trends in Washington.

Two days later, I received another direct mail piece from the Smith campaign. On the front was a photo of Smith walking through grassland with someone else. Both men were looking down at where they were walking, and the picture was slightly out of focus making it seem like early-morning light. It was very evocative. On the bottom it said: "One U.S. Senate candidate shares the values of rural Oregon."

Inside were four photos. The first was of Smith with his family and their horse; the caption read: "A Senator who's one of us." The second was a panoramic view, with the caption: "Defending our property rights." The third was of farmers, with the caption: "A Senator who shares our values." The fourth was a picture of Smith with his son and their bird dog. Both Smith and his son held a gun. The caption on the final picture read: "Standing up for Oregonians."

On the back was a picture and a quotation from the executive director of the Oregon Farm Bureau and a list of endorsing groups. It was an effective piece, but I noticed there were no women in it.

The next day I received yet another piece of direct mail from Smith. The outside was solid blue with white lettering that read: "Have you heard what women say about Gordon Smith?" Inside were pictures and quotes from four women: the president of Crime Victims United in Portland, a mother of two from Salem, a teacher from Silverton (a very cute small rural town), and a small-business owner from an affluent city outside of Portland. Each had appropriate quotations for their special interests: crime, families, education, and a balanced budget. And three of the four talked about how Smith was not like other Republicans within the context of their subject. This piece, by using validators (other women like me), was designed to give me permission to jump party.

I live in a rural part of the state, on two acres, in a conservative county with deep roots in the orchard industry. Many of my neighbors have horses and live on similar-sized lots. My precinct has a high democratic registration, and a mix of people that reflects the full political spectrum in America; voters here will split tickets. Through direct mail, Gordon Smith took his campaign to a home of a single mother in the rural part of the state, hit his opponent with an issue that should resonate with those of us who have to budget our money, and established himself as part of my geographic world and then part of my personal world.

What's important is that these pieces were designed to go after potential swing voters within a well-defined universe to deliver a very specific message, and they did so with specific cues (validators) intended to give the recipients permission to split their ticket. This is really important. When your campaign is wooing swing voters, you must provide validators to give that particular part of the universe permission to stray from party voting. It is really no different than looking for lawn sign locations that couple your candidate with lawn signs of candidates in the other party. All well-run campaigns look for an issue or a cue to present to potential swing voters that will enable them to shift their allegiance from their party.

For example, when the GOP held its convention in 2000, on the stage were people of many ethnicities, more so than at any Republican convention in history. Although many assumed that it was about wooing the black and Hispanic vote, it was actually about giving progressive Democrats permission to jump party. In fact, "despite a display of diversity at the party's national convention and the support of prominent blacks like retired Gen. Colin Powell, Bush drew less than 10 percent of the African-American vote" (CNN.com, December 13, 2000, "Black Democrats Angered by Supreme Court Ruling").

People who tend to be swing voters have specific issues that will move them. Knowing who these voters are and where they live is often enough to bring an issue to them that will make them split their ballots.

For direct mail to be effective you need to work an angle with the voter. In the November 2002 election, an Oregon House candidate mentioned that he would raise taxes on SUVs because of the impact they have on the roads and air quality. The opposition used that opportunity to send a mailing to all soccer moms—women over age thirty-five with school-age children—who voted in two of the last four elections. In another campaign, one candidate made a damaging remark about health care. The opposition sent a direct mail piece to alert people over the age of fifty-five who voted in two of the last four elections.

A few years back, a governor from one of the northeastern states suggested banning disposable diapers because they were adding tons to landfills each year and were considered a health hazard because they contain untreated human waste and could potentially contain live viruses from vaccines. Needless to say, people with small children were not pleased. However, the diaper manufacturers, seeing trouble, immediately introduced biodegradable disposable diapers, which satisfied the governor. When I told this story to a friend of mine with very young children who was a well-educated progressive and a strong environmentalist, she leaned forward, looked me in the eye, and, her voice dropping, slowly said, "*No one* is taking my disposable diapers from me." Truly effective direct mail aims to touch a nerve in a voter that elicits that kind of emotion.

> *"A word once let out of the cage cannot be whistled back again."*
> —Horace (1st century B.C.)

Direct Mail to Hit Your Opponent:
It Takes Research, Opportunity, and Timing

Direct mail can also be based on your research of the opposition. Many candidates hype their background in community service and draw inferences from that experience. So if a candidate claims to be in tune with and committed to education because she served on the school board, your job is to see how well she served. Did she miss a lot of meetings? Was she effective? Likewise, does your opponent claim to be a rancher but keep only a mobile home on a small piece of dirt while traveling extensively throughout the year? Does your opponent claim that you are out of touch yet spend more than half the year at a second home in another state?

In 1999 a direct mail hit piece went out on a state senate candidate, Phil Warren, who claimed to be a farmer. The full-color piece had minimal copy that appeared below each of six simple pictures: a garage door, labeled "A barn"; a push mower, labeled "A harvester"; a square of grass, labeled "A crop"; a poodle, labeled "Animals." The last two pictures were one of the candidate and one of a dollar bill.

Below the candidate, the copy read:

"Phil Warren grows no crops, milks no cows and sells no cattle. So why does he call himself a farmer?"

Then, below the dollar bill, it said:

"So he can get a $42,000 break on his property-tax appraisal. Phil Warren in the State Senate? All fertilizer. No farm" (Crounse & Malchow Inc., *Campaigns & Elections,* June 1999, p. 25).

Pointing out how your opponent has voted while serving in office does not constitute negative campaigning, and juxtaposing actual votes with campaign claims in direct mail can be very effective. However, to do it well, your team must do their homework. Did your opponent claim to support education and yet vote down the school funding package? Did she claim to support people with mental illnesses but vote no on the Health and Human Services budget? Did she vote no on contraceptive parity? Did he receive obscene amounts of money from right-to-life organizations and then vote against a bill that would cover a morning-after pill for rape victims? Is your opponent bought and owned? Show the voters the bread-crumb path.

Know where the opposing campaign's money comes from. For issue-based and candidate campaigns alike, follow the money and follow the endorsements. Look at the principles on which the opposition is basing its campaign—that is, their campaign message. If the voting record directly contradicts the message, you can raise the question of integrity. Campaign themes, like voting records, are fair game.

A voting record is not only a verifiable set of facts, but one that goes to the very essence of why we have elections. Have at least one volunteer dedicated to researching your opponent's voting record. What the research turns up may be useful not only for direct mail but also for debates.

Direct mail should be both clever and simple. Democrat Jeff Barker, a candidate for the Oregon House in 2002, faced Republican Keith Parker in the general election and found that the voters were having trouble differentiating the two because of their similar surnames. To help voters, Barker incorporated a barking dog (figure 7.5), strongly resembling his family dog, in campaign photos. Barker won by 44 votes out of 15,720 votes cast.

Being clever can also backfire. In January 2003, a special election was held in Oregon to backfill falling revenues in the state budget. Opponents of the tax measure said that government, like everyone else, needed to tighten its belt. In response, proponents of the tax measure sent a direct mail piece featuring the gut of an overweight man with a belt cinched about as tight as possible (figure 7.6). The message was to underscore the difficulty schools were having with budget cutbacks as Oregon faced monumental budget

Figure 7.5 Example of Simple yet Effective Technique to Help Voters Remember Who You Are

deficits in the 2003–2005 biennium. However, in the context of the criticism that had been leveled against the measure, one look at the photo brought to mind the opponents' real message: Cut the fat.

Reference Your Comparison Pieces
I usually mail or walk a comparison or persuasion piece to voters the week before the election. During my last run for mayor, I did so, as I had in previous elections for other candidates and issues. Each point I listed about my opponent had been said during one of the five debates we had or was part of

Figure 7.6 Example of Direct Mail That Can Reinforce the Opponent's Argument. Be sure the image you present to the voters is the image you want to communicate.

the public record of his voting history. However, I made a fundamental mistake: I did not reference any of these items. When the piece came out, voters felt it was unfair to bring these quotes up at the last minute when they "did not come up during the campaign." At that late date, no amount of my saying when and where they were said really mattered. I could have avoided this simply by putting dates and events next to each item.

"Washington is a city of southern efficiency and northern charm."
—John F. Kennedy

Direct Mail on a Budget

If you are campaigning in a relatively small area, combining direct mail with canvassing can save a campaign a lot of money and is far more effective than mailing a piece to the voter. Some years back, I ran a campaign where we walked direct mail attached to the brochures. In this campaign, we were trying to get approval for an open-space park program designating where future parks and walking paths would be in our city. Each neighborhood of the city was slated for a park in the plan. So we drafted a specialized campaign piece pointing out what kind of park each specific neighborhood would get and asked four to six supporters from that neighborhood to allow their names to be printed on the specialized piece. Volunteers walked it into the appropriate neighborhood as part of our canvassing effort. With this approach the campaign piece became both a personal letter and an endorsement. We also had neighbors canvassing neighbors, an extremely effective canvassing technique.

"Words that come from the heart enter the heart."

　　　　　—Old saying

In most small towns and counties, specific issues will be important in certain neighborhoods. If you can connect the issues with the neighborhoods, walking direct mail can be very effective and far cheaper than mailing it or printing up three or four different campaign brochures.

Walking direct mail to the door is also a good way to time your mailing. For example, in the above-mentioned campaign for the open-space program, the voters approved the open-space program but turned down the funding proposal. The city council immediately sent another proposal out to the voters, and it went down as well. At this point the entire voter-approved park component would be threatened without a funding package. In a narrow vote, the city council presented the public with a proposal for a prepared food and beverage tax to fund both parkland acquisition and Department of Environmental Quality–mandated upgrades to our wastewater treatment plant.

However, no city in Oregon had a tax on prepared food and beverage, and the industry did not want a domino effect starting in southern Oregon. As a result, our opposition included all but one eating establishment in Ashland, the Oregon Food and Beverage Industry lobby, local businesses, and Realtors who did not want land taken out of the inventory for parks. Again, our campaign had little or no money for lawn signs or advertising, and, because of the controversy, people told us they were reluctant to write letters-to-the-editor.

The weekend before election day, we walked a direct mail piece to every home in the city. In the piece we pointed out nothing more than who was financing the opposition. This tactic worked, probably for two reasons. First, it clearly showed that our side was rich with volunteers: Close to 100 people walked the streets for that canvass. Second, we canvassed the city on the same day that the opposition coincidentally took out a half-page ad that actually reinforced what our flyer said. Given that our measure passed by 150 votes out of 5,000 votes cast, I'm convinced the flyer was the single biggest reason why we won that campaign. This program—both the parks component and the funding mechanism—won state recognition in "Cities Awards for Excellence Program."

"A test of a man's or woman's breeding is how they behave in a quarrel."
—George Bernard Shaw

To save money you might also consider a mailing of postcards. One sheet of card stock can make four postcards, saving your campaign money in paper stock, printing, and postage.

Another option for saving money is to change the size of the universe you are mailing to. If money is short, rather than mailing to voters who voted in two of the last four elections, just mail to those who voted in three of the last four elections. This approach is most effective in non-presidential elections. Still too costly? Select only those precincts with the most swing voters, or mail to the difficult-to-walk rural precincts and then canvass the incorporated areas with volunteers.

"The first and great commandment is, Don't let them scare you."
—Elmer Davis

Remember, too, that as the campaign progresses and your issue or candidate looks like a winner, more money will come in to support your efforts. Even if you have a very limited direct mail budget, chances are that there will be additional opportunities before election day, especially if you target small, distinct universes.

Mail Preparation

If you are mailing fewer than 500 pieces, consider using volunteers to prepare it for mailing. Once you have decided what you are going to do and the direct mail piece has been written and printed and is back at your home or headquarters in boxes, here's what you do:

1. Organize a clerical work team to assemble your direct mail. If there is a letter or brochure, it needs to be stuffed into an envelope along with

other enclosures. If you are mailing out a simple information piece, you can cut costs and labor by printing your message on one side of a single sheet of paper. Have your clerical team come in and fold the piece in half, stamp it, address it, and, if needed, place a return address on it. You do not need to staple the folded sheet, but the piece must be addressed such that the fold is on top and the open edge is on the bottom. Using a bright color here can increase the likelihood that someone will look at it. Keep the message simple. You may also choose to do a mass mailing of invitations to a fund-raiser on half-sheets of 8½-by-11-inch card stock and send them as oversized postcards. This will save the cost and effort of using envelopes, but be aware that postage is the same for an oversized postcard as a letter. However, if it is a nice fund-raiser, don't send a postcard. Whatever the task for your clerical work team, have it all lined up and ready to go when they arrive.

2. Once the mailing is stuffed or folded, it must be addressed. Hand addressing and stick-on stamps really do increase the number of people who will open the piece and look inside. However, if you are mailing to specific precincts, you may prefer labels. If you do, the label should be either clear or the same color as the envelope.

3. As pieces are addressed, they must be kept separate according to zip code. Once things are bundled by zip code, take the bundles to the post office and ask for details on how many they want in each bundle, which post office stickers go on which, and what forms need to be filled out. If lingering at the post office is a hassle, bundle all mail with the same five–digit zip code, in groups of ten or more per pack, with rubber bands. Packs should be no more than two inches thick. Rubber bands should be placed horizontally and vertically. For groups of less than ten with the same zip code, bundle them with other envelopes matching the first three zip code numbers. For example: *97520, 97523, 97540, 97501.* You must know the count of your entire mailing. Make sure that each component of the mailing is exactly the same. For example, I once did a mailing with a number 6 remittance envelope stuffed inside. However, I ran out of the number 6 envelopes and stuffed the rest in a slightly larger one I had on hand. You can't do this. Each component of each piece must weigh the same.

4. Take your bundles to the post office to fill out the paperwork and place the appropriate post office stickers on the front of each bundle. They will provide stickers and forms. Be prepared to stand in line three times. If this is a year-end mailing with Christmas lines, consider sending your mailing first class.

You may wish to hire out the direct mail preparation rather than using volunteers. Take your camera-ready art along with your mailing list, printed in a specific format for labels (call ahead to get the specifics) to a mailing house, and they will take care of everything else, including getting it to the post office.

Often at the end of a campaign, when the committee suddenly decides to create and send another direct mail piece, the grassroots campaign does not have the ability to pull together the people to get the piece out on time. This is a great time to consider a mailing house. Again, if you're activating your base and the swing voters to vote, go to the county and ask for the full registration list for the targeted precincts.

"Americans will put up with anything provided it doesn't block traffic."

—Dan Rather

The mailing house can download which parties you want, eliminate duplicates addressed to the same house, and print the name and address directly on the piece. Be aware, however, that mailing houses are often flooded by last-minute requests from political candidates, which can affect timing.

Direct mail is different from targeting neighborhoods for canvassing in that you are directing your pitch for voter *interest* rather than voting patterns. Also keep in mind that by using direct mail, you can address subjects that, if put in a more public forum, might activate a lot of heated letters-to-the-editor. Well-

"The only thing that saves us from the bureaucracy is its inefficiency."

—Eugene McCarthy

targeted direct mail reaches potential friends of the campaign and lets them know where you (or your opponent) stand and where to send money. Used properly, direct mail can be very effective.

Tracking Polls

Tracking polls are used to fine-tune direct mail and radio and television spots as well as to monitor candidate or issue support. They are generally brief, usually made up of only one or two questions, and they are most helpful when conducted on a regular basis throughout the campaign. However, if you are running a small campaign on a low budget with an overextended volunteer base, a tracking poll may be out of the question.

An alternative would be to piggyback on a tracking poll being conducted for another candidate. This might cost your campaign a little money, but it would be far cheaper than if you were to go it alone. Often, when someone is running for state office, where partisan politics plays a more significant role than in local elections, political parties will conduct tracking polls for their candidates. Also, labor unions, teachers' associations, and PACs might be willing to conduct tracking polls for a candidate or issue their organization has endorsed. Be sure to report this to your treasurer and include it on your contributions and expenditures forms as an in-kind contribution.

"For purposes of action nothing is more useful than narrowness of thought combined with energy of will."

—Henri Frederic Amiel

A tracking poll can be especially helpful in fine-tuning a campaign in a close election and shaping the spin either to increase your support or to erode that of your opposition. Say, for example, that in the final days of a campaign you find that your support among women is shifting away from your candidate. You may then go back to your benchmark poll and, using a high-priority issue for women, generate direct mail to draw back and lock in this support.

A tracking poll may be used to:

- Track candidate or issue support
- Fine-tune a campaign message
- Tell you if a particular campaign event or ad has left you or your opponent vulnerable
- Determine whether negative campaigning, on either your part or that of your opponent, is helping or hurting (this is generally tracked in a quick response poll following an ad)
- Indicate what groups are still undecided

Tracking Polls Without the Poll

If you cannot afford a tracking poll, even as a tag-along, there are some tell-tale signs that will give you an idea about the progress of your campaign and that of your opponent. Here are just a few examples:

Attendance at debates. At the beginning of a campaign, while voters are still undecided, attendance at debates is often high. Once voters have decided how they will vote, they tend to stay home. This phenomenon will vary from city to city. If it happens in a city in which you enjoy support, that's great. If voters are still coming out in droves to hear you and your opponent in an area that does not belong to you, that's bad news for your opponent.

Your opponent, who had been straddling the fence, suddenly moves to the extreme of his or her base. Chances are, when a candidate moves toward the base, it's because information has come in that the base is not secure. Remember, just because you are not polling, that does not mean your opposition is not polling. Trying to lock your base late in a campaign is difficult and can be a sign that a campaign is in trouble.

A week before the general election, canvassers report that people still do not know your candidate. In general, astute canvassers bring back valuable information about your candidate or issue-based campaign. If they report that many people still don't know your candidate, you must find a way to go back and grab your base without losing swing voters. Not ideal, but it can be done.

Polling Trends

Tracking polls that "bounce," predicting winners as losers and losers as winners, are occurring with greater frequency. Karl Feld, a political polling project manager for a Republican data-collection firm, noted in 2000 that "U.S. telephone response rates are dropping to a point that threatens the validity of telephone research" (*Campaigns & Elections,* May 2000, p. 63). Skewed outcomes can be attributed to the use of caller ID, voice mail, and answering machines to screen calls, the self-selection effect determining which registered voters will actually participate in a poll, "push polls," and cell phones.

> *"Candidates have to fight back hard, or else voters don't believe they'll fight for them."*
>
> —Sid Blumenthal,
> former Clinton aide

Slightly more than half of the U.S. population now has a cell phone. Because the cell phone owner pays for minutes of phone use, both for incoming and outgoing calls, Congress passed a law disallowing telemarketers to call cell phones. Furthermore, although overall 3 percent of cell phone users have abandoned land lines, this proportion varies greatly by age. The Yankee Group's 2003 Mobile User Young Adult Survey shows that 12 percent of 18- to 24-year-olds have gone completely wireless, and predicts that another 28 percent will go wireless by 2008. This increase may adversely affect the efficacy of polling data, especially among the 18- to 25-year-old age group in the near future.

Cell phone use among blacks and Hispanics has more than doubled in three years, dramatically outpacing other demographic groups (figure 7.7).

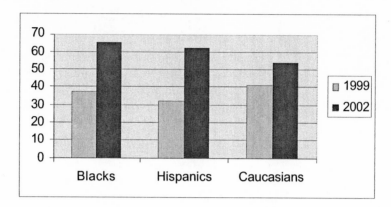

Figure 7.7 Cell Phone Use By Race (Data for cell phone section: Cheskin Research of Redwood Shores, CA; *Concord Monitor;* Connecting with Kids Network; FCC; Frank N. Magid Assoc.; *The News & Observer,* Raleigh, NC; *The News-Sentinel; Pittsburgh Post-Gazette;* PriMetrica Inc; *The Sacramento Bee;* San Jose Mercury News, CA; Scarborough Research; The Statistical Abstract of the United States; Teenage Research Unlimited of Northbrook, Ill; Telephia; US Census Bureau; The Yankee Group)

Should this trend continue, blacks and Hispanics, along with the young adult age group, could be underrepresented in polling data.

Better Not Bigger

Just how effective is direct mail? Most local campaigns will send one to three pieces of direct mail in the course of a nonpartisan election. However, if you are working on a state house or senate seat, direct mail will likely consume a large portion of your campaign budget.

Direct mail for state legislative races is primarily conducted by political consultants, who also advise campaigns on the number of pieces to send, the design, and the appropriate universes to mail to. After the 2002 general election, in which Oregon House Democrats lost eight of the close eleven House races, one consultant told me that Democrats performed poorly because they did not send enough direct mail and needed to go negative sooner and harder.

During the campaign season, I routinely receive phone calls from people in my area asking if I know whom to contact to close the direct mail spigot. I don't know anyone who likes direct mail or anyone who admits to using it in deciding on how to cast their votes. Just as money is a general indicator of a winning advantage for any given campaign, it would seem that the number of direct mail pieces sent or the number of negative pieces sent might also directly coincide with a campaign win. However, I could find no empirical data that would clearly link volume of direct mail or attacks with likelihood of winning. I looked at the eleven close Oregon House races in the 2002 general election to see if any patterns emerged. With information from the Oregon Secretary of State Election Division, Democratic leadership, and political consultants working with Republican candidates, I learned the following.

- *Registration:* Of the seven seats with a Democratic registration advantage, six went to Republicans. Of the three seats with Republican registration advantage, two went to Democrats. One seat with even registration went to the Republican.
- *Money:* Seven of the winners outspent their opponents, and only four who were outspent survived.
- *Volume of direct mail:* Only four of the eleven winning races sent more direct mail than the opposition.
- *Negative direct mail:* Five candidates who won sent more hit pieces, and five who won sent fewer negative pieces. In one race both candidates sent the same number.
- *Ran a primary:* Of those who won, five ran primaries, six did not. Of those who lost, six ran primaries, five did not.

Although these are races in just one state and in one election cycle, hardly a definitive sample on which to base hard-and-fast rules, within this context there is clearly no secret formula for winning based solely on registration, running a primary, number of direct mail pieces sent, or number of negative pieces. In these eleven races, as few as nine direct mail pieces were sent in one race (he won), up to as many as thirty in another (she lost). Altogether, the candidates and their supporters sent an average of nearly nineteen pieces each. One might wonder if at some point direct mail reaches a saturation point, at best numbing the voters and at worst irritating them.

Gender bias: It is only when these close races are grouped by gender that the dots begin to cluster.

- In all the races where Democratic women faced Republican men (five), the women lost.
- In the four races where both candidates were men, Republicans captured only one seat.
- In the one race where a Republican woman faced a Democratic man, the man lost.
- In the one race where two women squared off, the Republican won (although this race had extenuating circumstances).

Taking the first two items, simply because there are more than three races in each, a pattern emerges. In the first item, in which Democratic women facing Republican men lost to the men, money tracked the winner 80 percent of the time. Compare this with the four races with Democratic men running against Republican men, in which money tracked the winner only 50 percent of the time, and in which three out of four wins went to Democrats. In the first group, neither the number of direct mail pieces nor the number of hit pieces tracked a winner or loser. In the races with Democratic and Republican men running against each other, all of the Democrats sent more direct mail and all of the Republicans sent more hit pieces.

What is missing in this analysis may be what lies at the base of a win:

- Timing and nature of negative hit pieces sent against women in the first grouping
- Timing and nature of negative pieces sent against the Democratic men by the Republican candidates
- The universes targeted with direct mail
- The universes targeted by television and radio
- The turnout of the base in underperforming precincts
- Party turnout, performance by precinct, and undervote
- Voter history for women Democrats running against male Republicans

In the 2000 primary, two conservative Republicans (a man and a woman) were squared off in a dead-heat race. The campaign had been unusually acrimonious, and with a seventeen-point Republican registration advantage, the race was really only in the primary. By the end, the woman (Cherryl Walker) had had enough of the mudslinging and went against her campaign consultant's advice and refused to attack her opponent in her last direct mail piece. Figure 7.8 was the final direct mail piece she sent. Featuring her granddaughter and flowers, it was just the breath of fresh air the race needed, and she won.

"When I hear another express an opinion which is not mine, I say to myself, he has a right to his opinion, as I to mine. Why should I question it? His error does me no injury, and shall I become a Don Quixote, to bring all men by force of argument to one opinion?"

—Thomas Jefferson

Figure 7.8 A Winner's Final-Week Direct Mail Piece After a Campaign Marked By Mudslinging. In an Oregon House race, Republican Cherryl Walker broke from the mutual mudslinging that she and her opponent had fallen into. In this simple piece she quickly reminded the district what was at stake.

8

MEDIA

IN THIS CHAPTER
- *Print Media: Paid and Unpaid*
- *Fielding Questions from the Press*
- *Radio and Television*
- *Choosing your Media Specialist or Team*
- *Bumper Stickers and Buttons*

As with other campaign activities, your theme and message must be at the center of all media efforts. No matter what comes at the candidate or the spokesperson for an issue-based campaign, he or she must be disciplined about staying on message.

Print Media: Paid and Unpaid

Newspapers have enormous credibility, and those who read newspapers are the most likely to vote: They are educated, have good incomes, contribute to charities and political campaigns, and tend to be involved in their communities. Don't squander *any* opportunities you have with local newspapers. Thoroughly prepare for interviews, editorial boards, and any campaign events that will be covered by the media.

"The charm of politics is that dull as it may be in action, it is endlessly fascinating as a rehash."
—Eugene McCarthy

Unpaid Print Media

I recently had a candidate announce his intentions to move from the state house to the state senate during an interview regarding the incumbent who was resigning midterm. Needless to say the announcement was buried in the article that covered the real story—a thirty-year incumbent leaving office. If the candidate had waited even one day his announcement would have received front-page coverage. As a campaign manager you must be ready for the candidate who is so excited about running that he gets ahead of himself. In general, a candidate who wishes to seek an office being vacated by an incumbent who has either resigned or died must give an appropriate amount of time and space to the exiting office holder. If this is not done, at best it will cost the campaign money to come back in and fabricate another announcement, and at worst it leaves the public with the impression that the candidate wishing to seek the office is lying in wait politically, is ambitious, or even is arrogant.

The announcement of your candidacy or your issue-based campaign is the first piece in your free media tool kit. Announcements should be timed to have the biggest impact and the best news coverage.

The following tips should help make this exciting day more successful:

Have your campaign team gather as many supporters (cheering throngs) as possible for your announcement: Do it in a public place that is both well known and well liked by your community. Just as candidates seeking state office go back to their hometown and presidential candidates to their home state to announce, you should choose a place that is significant to you and your community.

Know the law: Avoid announcing on publicly owned property such as a school or a civic building, and do not involve people who are on taxpayer-funded payrolls (such as school or city officials) during the workday, even during the lunch hour. While an announcement may be legal on publicly owned property, collecting money for a political cause may not be, and it is typical for people attending an announcement to hand the candidate a check.

Know the schedules of the press: An announcement should be held at a time and place that is convenient for the press, even if it's not for your supporters. Call the local papers and ask what time would work best for them given their deadlines. If you know that some of the media cannot attend, have printed news releases delivered to those who will miss the announcement.

Schedule the announcement at the convenience of television crews rather than newspapers. Getting your face in front of the camera is important, and the print media can be covered with a press packet. Keep in mind that television news crews typically work late at night and are not available until late morning.

If your announcement is too late for the newspaper reporters to attend, provide them with the needed information before their deadlines. You want your announcement to be covered everywhere on the same day. If you are putting together a press packet, include a photo of the candidate and another of the candidate with his or her family, a list of supporters and their phone numbers that the press can call for quotes (don't forget to give these supporters a heads-up), your announcement speech, a bio, and a brochure if you have one.

"Did you ever get to wondering if taxation without representation might have been cheaper?"
—Robert Orben

Find a good date and time to announce a candidacy or to kick off an issue-based campaign: You have to know what else is going on in the community. Avoid major holidays as people don't watch the news or read the papers as much on those days. For the same reason, don't announce on a three-day weekend or on Friday, as fewer people read Saturday's paper and watch Friday evening news. If it is a nonpartisan race with only a general election, announcing in June gives you the opportunity to participate in Fourth of July parades as well as let people know before summer vacations. The objective is to do whatever you can to get your name out in an inexpensive and effective way.

Line up supporters to write letters-to-the-editor immediately after your announcement: Letters should be short and simply say how glad the letter writer is to see that you decided to join the race. The letter writer should also mention one or two things that are central to your theme.

Letters-to-the-Editor

If you don't have the funds for a sustained paid advertising campaign, letters-to-the-editor can carry a campaign until paid advertising begins. Depending on your area, using the letters-to-the-editor section of the local paper can be a very effective media tool. Letters show that a voter cares enough about a candidate or ballot measure to take the time to write a letter and get it to the paper. E-letters are limited in length, which is good. Also, papers tend to run them more quickly than more tra-

"Word of mouth appeals have become the only kind of persuasion that most of us respond to anymore."
—Malcolm Gladwell

ditional letters-to-the-editor, and they are often the lead letters, which gives them prominence.

Once letters are published, they are in public domain, so the campaign can pull great nuggets from them to use in paid endorsement ads as the campaign progresses. Plus, referenced quotes tend to have more credibility.

Assign one of the campaign committee members to oversee letters-to-the-editor. The letters-to-the-editor coordinator should be prepared to write

> # Vote for Daniels
>
> Elle Daniels would be an excellent school board member. Elle has devoted her life to education as a volunteer in the classroom.
>
> We need people in decision-making positions who know first-hand what is going on with our children. Elle Daniels has my vote.
>
> C. Golden,
> Ashland, OR

Figure 8.1 Example of a Letter-to-the-Editor. Letters-to-the-editor are most effective if they are short and appear early in the campaign cycle.

several different sample letters as well as some general instructions and tips to give people guidance, and he or she must be able to constantly remind supporters about getting letters to the papers. It is the most difficult job of a campaign, so choose this person carefully, and do not assign any other campaign tasks to him or her until after the deadline for letter submissions.

Early letters get read. Later in the campaign season, readers become numb and rarely read the last-minute opinions of their neighbors. Also, long letters are not read as much as shorter ones, so remind all who may write on your behalf to keep it short. A good rule is for a letter to cover one subject and to be no longer than one or two short paragraphs. As important as a letter may be, the heading placed above it is more important. Shorter letters mean more boldfaced titles, which will be read, even by those just scanning the page. Finally, short letters are often printed more quickly, and sometimes they are printed after the paper has said, "No more letters." Figure 8.1 is an example of a letter-to-the-editor. Remind supporters to send copies of letters to all of the local papers as you never know who reads what.

Many papers will not print letters received a certain number of days before the election. Get this information for each local paper and include it in the letters-to-the-editor sheet you prepared for your committee (in the campaign committee packet). Most people procrastinate, so keep supporters apprised of the deadline as it approaches. If letters-to-the-editor are a critical component of your media package, their being too late for publication could be fatal to your cause. Because many papers must verify authenticity of mailed letters before they can print them, hand-carrying a letter usually results in an earlier publication. Letters that are typed, e-mailed, and faxed also get printed faster.

Other Free Media Coverage

Many newspapers have a public interest section that serves as a community chalkboard. Find out how often it runs and what the deadlines for submissions are. If your candidate is speaking at the Rotary Club or the League of Women Voters, or if one of your committee members is giving a presentation on your ballot measure, be sure it gets into the community activity section of the paper. Figure 8.2 is an example from a local paper in my town.

I once saw a notice in a community activity section that a particular candidate would be canvassing that week in a neighboring town. It really got my attention. To the average person, something like this highlights the hard work of a candidate who is walking the neighborhood and making herself available to the voters.

COMMUNITY

Dogs need vaccines and licenses

The Jackson County Animal Care and Control Center reminds the public of its on-going license checking program. All dogs over six mouths of age are required to have rabies vaccination and a dog license. Citations will be issued for violators.

In responding to the public's request, the center will be informing the public of the areas that will receive concentrated checking in the near future. The White City area will be the next on the list.

However, people are reminded that officers work all areas of the county. License checking may be done in any area at any time.

The goal of the license checking program is to achieve voluntary compliance, so people are urged to be sure their dogs are vaccinated and licensed.

House candidate to speak

Bev Clarno, Republican candidate for House District 55 will be the featured speaker **Wednesday** at the luncheon meeting of Jackson County Republican Women at J.J. North's in Medford. The luncheon will begin at 11:30 a.m., reservations are requied. For more information call 000-0000.

County fair entry books available

The Exhibitors Entry Book for the Jackson County Fair, July 19-24 and the Harvest Fair and Wine Fest, October 8-9, is now available from local Grange Co-Ops, the Jackson County Library and at the Fair office at the fairgrounds. Anyone interested in entering the fair competitions, both 4-H and Future Farmers of America (FFA), or Open Class must obtain an entry book.

Oregon poet will read in Ashland

Oregon poet and artist Sandy Diamond will be reading from her new book, "Miss Coffin and Mrs. Blood; Poems of Art and Madness," at Bloomsbury Books 7:30 p.m. on Monday.

CORRECTIONS

Christensen runs for city recorder

Barbara Christensen has obtained a petition to run for city recorder in November. Her name was misspelled in Thursday's paper, due to a reporter's error.

Figure 8.2 Example of the "Community" Section from a Local Paper. On this day two candidates got some free ink.

Press Conference

If there is an opportunity to call a press conference, do it. When I was work-ing on our food and beverage tax campaign, the opposition called a press conference to announce a funding scheme for open space that they said would make our tax unnecessary. They gathered together a broad range of local interests to show support for their cause. To counter, we called a press conference as well.

We also had a broad range of local interests represented at our press con-ference. We took advantage of the occasion to point out why the funding proposed by the opposition would fall short of the community's needs. We also went one step further and used the press conference as an opportunity to promote our campaign. We were thus able to pre-vent any damage the opposition's proposal might have caused and to use the opportu-nity to advance our own campaign goals. We kept our campaign message out front.

> *"What we are voting on is far more important than buying cereal. The last thing we should be doing is advertising that dumbs us down."*
> —Cindy Wilson, freelance public relations and marketing specialist

Politics is motion: Take energy that is coming at you and redirect it at your opposition.

In general, don't invite the media to coffees or fund-raisers. If an event is for some reason poorly attended, media coverage could work against your cause. Furthermore, supporters need time with the candidate without the press around. If the media is there, many will have the sense that everything is staged and that those attending are merely props. Do not, however, hesitate to include the media if a big-name politician or movie star is willing to endorse you or your measure on your home turf. I once worked for a candidate who chose to turn down an endorsement and visit from the governor because he felt that the governor was not that popular in our end of the state. That was a mistake. A big political figure can get you the only page of the paper that is not for sale—the front page—not to mention all of the leads on the evening news.

> *"I do not take a single newspaper, nor read one a month, and I feel myself infinitely the happier for it."*
> —Thomas Jefferson

A number of other tricks can be used to get your campaign on the front page of the papers. Challenging your opponent to a series of debates is a time-honored way to get local coverage. Another is to announce that you are chal-lenging your opponent to campaign on a limited budget. If you issue the challenge, you get to come up with the amount; set it at a level you can live with but doubt that your opponent can. If you're an incumbent, this can really work to your advantage. In small-city elections, incumbents are better known and don't need to spend as much as out-siders to get their names out. Because the public tends to think incumbents are compromised, this has the effect of mak-ing them seem more pure. However, one caution here: If you propose a spending limit and your opponent is unwilling to go along with it, you have a problem and should be prepared to drop the idea. Campaigns require an enormous commitment of time and energy by many people, so do not needlessly hobble your campaign with a tight budget when no one else is doing so.

> *"Never argue with people who buy ink by the gallon."*
>
> —Tommy Lasorda

Press Events

Whenever possible, create press events. This is where your research can re-ally pay off. Examine what the opposition is claiming, and then look for in-consistencies in past actions, voting records, and money trails. Dribble this information to the press so that it comes out in increments. Look for where your opposition is getting money and support, and if their sources are incon-sistent with their message, get this information to the press either directly or in letters-to-the-editor. You want to have a game plan—and a "hammer"—ready should your opposition take the hook. For example, you are running against an incumbent who claims to be a clean-air advocate. You point out how his voting record is inconsistent with that claim, knowing full well that his record contains other, favorable clean air votes that he will pull out to make you look silly. That is OK; the hook has been taken. If he doesn't respond, your accusa-tion stands, but if he does, you have a hammer. In this case you hook him with his clean air voting record and then ham-mer him with a history of contributions from polluting companies and other non–air quality votes of his that would suggest that he is bought and owned by these companies. This is where your homework pays off. Hold the opposing campaign accountable to their voting record and their message.

> *"You smile discreetly, you look like you're enjoying yourself, like you're getting ready to get down to serious business. You've got to be careful what you say."*
>
> —Dan Quayle, on how to act with the press

If you find ten inconsistencies with the opposing campaign, use them for ten press releases or press conferences, not one press conference with a list of ten. Use supporters to point out your strengths as well as the problems with the opposition. For example, the Board of Realtors endorses you, an antigrowth candidate. Call a press conference for this announcement and help the Realtors with a reason. In their endorsement they should include not only why they are endorsing you but also why they are *not* endorsing your opposition. Campaigning from a third party is often better because it appears less self-serving.

Take advantage of events that are already happening, like a Fourth of July parade. Plan to attend events that are likely to get media coverage, and let the press know that you will be there. When considering what these events might be, look to your persuadable vote and not your base. Sending a candidate to events that reinforce his or her stand on a particular issue or to an event that is already largely supported by the base takes precious time and energy from the candidate.

"All reformers, however strict their social conscience, live in houses just as big as they can pay for."
—Logan Pearsall Smith

It is also important to look at a possible downside of attending an event: Who will be influenced to vote for the candidate because of his or her participation, and at what cost? One great example of this occurred in 1994 when George W. Bush was running for governor of Texas. He decided to attend the opening day of dove-hunting season to show that he was one of the boys and supportive of a liberal gun policy. Of course the press was invited by Bush's team. When Bush finally did pull down a bird, however, it was not a dove but a bird under protection. This did not play well, and he was fined on top of it. One must question whether this was an appropriate outing for this candidate in the first place. Was this a group of persuadable voters or part of his base? At what cost did he participate?

Fielding Questions from the Press

If the press calls with a question you have not considered or feel unprepared to answer, don't. Explain that you're busy and ask if you can call back in a couple of minutes. Be sure to ask for their deadline, and don't end up crowding it. If the question asked is about a complicated issue and the story will not appear for a couple of days, take the time and do some research before calling back. If the reporter says he or she is on deadline and needs something right away, ask for five minutes. Even a short amount of time can be enough to get your bearings on the issue. Call your media adviser, campaign manager, partner, or a supporter with specific expertise, and come up with an answer. Be creative. Recently a state representative from upstate called because a wastewater pipe had broken in her district and was dumping sewage into a nearby stream. Uncertain about what to say to the press, she called me because she knew that Ashland has its own wastewater treatment system and correctly assumed that I had dealt with such problems while I was mayor.

It's a good idea to write down specific points you want to touch on before returning the call. Make these short and quotable, but deliver them with spontaneity. For example, even though the answer is in front of you, pause from time to time as though you're thinking. It's OK here to throw in a few "uhs" and "you knows."

One important note: If you ask a reporter to "go off the record," he or she must agree, or you are not officially off the record. It does not work to say something and then tell the reporter, "And, by the way, that was off the record," or "Please do not print that." Sometimes, after the interview is over, reporters will engage a candidate or representative of the ballot issue in small talk. You may be thinking that the interview is over, but it's not, so watch what you say. Some argue that nothing is off the record and that a good rule of thumb is to say nothing that you do not want to see in print at the breakfast table. Unless you know the reporter pretty well, that's a good rule to follow.

"If there's more than one person— including yourself—in a room, consider anything said to be on the record and a probable headline in the morning paper."

—John F. Kennedy

If you're upset about an issue, cool down before you head out to face the press. I cannot stress how important this is. Because tempers can flare when you're in the midst of a political campaign, think about how what you say or do will read the next day in the paper, and choose your words carefully. I hear people say that the papers took their comments out of context or distorted what they said, but I have rarely found that to be the case. More often, I have *wished* I had been misquoted.

"Speak when you are angry and you will make the best speech you will ever regret."

—Ambrose Bierce

Top Ten Media Tips

1. As the candidate, you want to project the image of a credible community leader. You must remember that reporters do many interviews and miss very little. What kind of clues are you giving that speak louder than your words? Avoid nervous behavior. Don't click your pen repeatedly, jingle change in your pocket, or twist your hair. Avoid verbal ticks, like "um," "if you will," "you know," and "to be honest." Toeing

the ground—looking down and moving your foot in a half moon with your toe—signals insecurity. So does crossing your feet while standing. Stand with your feet no farther apart than shoulder width. Don't cross your arms. Don't put your hands on your hips. Stand with arms at your sides, or use your hands as a way to emphasize what you're saying. Speak in a clear, firm voice and look directly at the reporter. Keep your hands away from your face at all times.

2. Be sure you know your subject well. Practice with family members or campaign supporters. Discuss talking points around the campaign table and repeat these to yourself until they come out in short, concise sound bites. Reporters do much better if you're to the point and they don't have to do a lot of work to figure out what you're saying.

3. Although you may have the reporter in front of you at that moment, it is the voter who will be reading what you say the next day. Think about your audience and talk to your base and swing voters.

4. I try to keep a positive spin on everything. Reporters like to print controversy, but if that will hurt your cause, do not go there. Remember, you do not have to answer the question being asked. You just have to sound like you're answering it.

5. That said, unless it's your intention, don't answer a question that hasn't been asked. Candidates, especially new ones to the arena, tend to talk on and on. They often will hear one question when another is asked or want to offer up more information than is necessary. Shorter is better, always. Keep on your message and do not let a reporter pull you off.

6. When the press calls, take a moment to think about what you will say, call someone for help if you need it, jot down some notes, and then return the call.

7. In general, return all calls promptly. As a rule, the earlier you're interviewed, the higher up you will appear in an article.

8. Avoid going "off the record."

9. Never speak when angry. Calm down, and then do the interview.

10. You get to select where the interview takes place. Think about the backdrop and whether its visual effect can further your message.

Paid Print Media

Although television is huge, the legitimizing effect of newspaper advertising for a political campaign should not be underestimated. In 2000, the Center for Congressional and Presidential Studies at American University looked at ways voters get their election information. Eighty-six percent of those surveyed saw print media as a very important source for election information, with television close behind at 84 percent.

In general, three advertising formats work well in newspapers: emotional, informational, and testimonial (endorsement). None of these ads are mutually exclusive.

"It's better to recall something you wish you'd said than something you wish you hadn't."
—Frank A. Clark

- Emotional ads are just that: ads that use pictures or images and copy that will elicit emotion in the voters. Children at school, a couple talking privately, a child drinking clean water from a hose bibb, a river, backdrops of your city, congested streets, historic buildings, kids engaged in school activities, seniors, and so forth.
- Informational ads are generally used with issue-based campaigns and are designed to let the voters know some bit of important information, such as the impact a tax measure will have on their yearly debt load.
- Finally, testimonials or endorsement ads use a third person to speak on behalf of a candidate or ballot issue. While those listed or quoted may be movers and shakers in a community, testimonials and endorsement ads can also feature the average person. This approach is especially effective in a candidate race, as it is both more effective and more believable if someone else says you're smart and hardworking than if you say you're smart and hardworking.

Advertising Formats for Newspapers

Between literature drops, lawn signs, direct mail, and advertising, political campaigns have a tendency to look like clutter, a sort of strip mall of democracy. Whenever possible, organize your efforts and give a sense of continuity and neatness to your campaign. Use your logo in all campaign literature, or bring some thread from one medium to another to create continuity for your campaign. If your lawn sign is an especially good design, use it as an identifier in print ads, television spots, direct mail, and badges for canvassers. It's your trademark, and it should be used just as a major corporation would use its trademark.

"Poor ads disengage consumers from the category. They make you feel like the category is not worth entering. Consumers ask, 'Is that all the category of government is?'"
—Joel Drucker, Oakland, California, marketing and communications consultant

CATHY GOLDEN ON INDEPENDENT MANAGEMENT AUDITS

Cathy
GOLDEN
FOR MAYOR

"Ashland city government is long overdue for a management audit by an outside professional firm. It just makes good economic sense.

Management audits consistently pay for themselves in money saved, improved service, and higher staff morale. And they let taxpayers know exactly what they're getting for their money."

Building a Better Community

Figure 8.3 Example of Candidate Ad Made to Look Like a Newspaper Article (Crystal Castle Graphics)

Although there are many formats for newspaper ads, here are a few examples that have helped move campaigns forward in the print media.

"There are two times in a man's life when he should not speculate: when he can't afford it and when he can."
—Mark Twain

Create newspaper ads that mimic a news story in layout. Place the candidate's picture as a fairly prominent part of the ad, with the logo underneath. Select and place a headline with copy alongside the candidate picture. Candidate ads should be no more than three paragraphs long, should cover only one subject, and should include the campaign logo and slogan. Figure 8.3 is an example.

This format can be rotated with five or six different headings and copy. So the voter does not become immune to your ads, change out the candidate picture in each. This format works well as a "two-by-four"—two columns

JUST The Facts

Cultural and Recreational Levy 15-3

If the levy passes, will my property taxes go up?

No. They will continue still downward, as mandated by Measure 5, but just not as much. Each of the next two years, they will drop by $1.53 per thousand, instead of $2.50 per thousand.

Authorized by United Ashland Committee, Linda & Joe Windsor, Treasurers, PO Box 2000, Ashland, OR 97520

Figure 8.4 Example of an Information Ad. This ad uses graphical cues that we typically associate with schools to help the reader identify the ad with the tax measure. (Crystal Castle Graphics)

wide by four inches high. Smaller ads like this are cheap and tend to be placed on top of other ads and directly under newspaper copy. I have seen local races effectively place ads half this size, daily, on each page of the paper. If you have lots of money, you can make the ad any size you want.

A two-by-four lends itself well to informational and endorsement ads. Informational ads for issue-based campaigns should also adopt a uniform look that is recognizable to the public. Figure 8.4 is an example of an ad used in an issue-based campaign for school funding. The font, layout, and design intentionally lead the voter to connect the ad with schools.

"Only those who will risk going too far can possibly find out how far one can go."

—T. S. Eliot

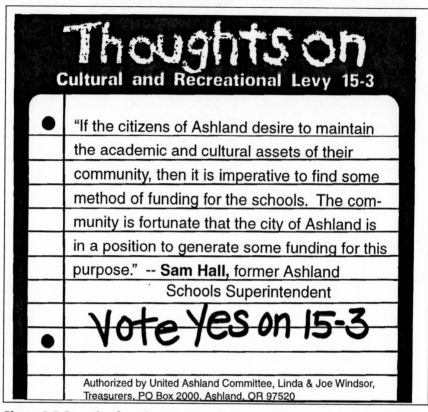

Figure 8.5 Example of a 2-by-4 Newspaper Endorsement Ad for an Issue-Based Campaign. By design, this ad links itself to schools and other ads for the same tax measure. (Crystal Castle Graphics)

Similarly, the endorsement ad shown in figure 8.5 uses the same two-by-four format and visually links itself to other ads advocating for the same school tax measure.

Testimonial or endorsement ads are among the most effective you can use anywhere in a campaign, but they lend themselves especially well to newspaper advertising. Unfortunately, too many campaigns attempt to cram too much into this format. Remember, newspapers are inherently cluttered, so do all you can to help your ads breathe. Keep the pictures simple and memorable. Pictures in small-format ads are difficult to see and work best with a close-up of only one person. Resist the temptation to show the candidate

"Victory goes to the player who makes the next-to-last mistake."
—Savielly Grigorievitch Tartakower

shaking hands with the person lending the quote. Keep all ads as clean and simple as possible.

This format can also be set up with text of a community leader or prominent citizen endorsing the candidate. Be sure to use a picture of the candidate and not that of the person who gave the quote: It's important to get the candidate's face in front of the public at every opportunity.

As the campaign progresses and the candidate gains endorsements, some of these candidate ads can be recycled to emphasize a point. For example, in my first run for mayor, I was characterized as a no-growth candidate. My feeling was that growth itself wasn't the problem, but rather the effects it had on our quality of life. Some would say it is too fine a distinction, but I argued that if we did all we could to mitigate the negative effects of growth, we would probably be OK. One of my small candidate-information ads referred to building moratoria resulting from inadequate planning for growth. Later, when I was endorsed by the Board of Realtors, I enlarged the building moratorium ad and included a banner highlighting the Board of Realtors endorsement. By coupling this endorsement with my advocacy of planning for growth, I took the bite out of my opponent's "no-growth" charge and replaced it with a responsible-growth view. Remember you do not want to get on your opponent's message. Instead lead the voter to your message.

Issue-based campaigns generally do best with ads that tug at emotion. You can and should run some information ads, but in general "information" ads tend to be off message. Expanding a library, adding curriculum options for a school, or acquiring parkland are not about how cheap the projects are but rather about what the projects will do for your community, society, and future generations. There is no price for that. Stay on message: You are not selling 50 cents a pound, you are selling apples, and if voters want apples, they'll buy apples. Your job is to keep them focused on what they're buying, not on how much it will cost.

For example, in Ashland's open-space campaign we ran ads that juxtaposed pictures of open fields filled with grazing sheep with more recent photos showing the same fields filled with housing. The caption urged the voter to help leave some of the community open space untouched by voting yes. Similarly, we ran other ads comparing pictures of wooded hillsides before and after development (figure 8.6).

Ashland's Youth Activities Levy was designed to pick up dropped extra- and co-curricular activities, and we needed to convey the importance of these programs to the future success of our students. To do this we had one ad that juxtaposed two transcripts of the same student. One transcript had fine grades and an excellent GPA; the other had the same grades and GPA, plus a

Figure 8.6 Example of an Emotional Ad (TAO Productions and Crystal Castle Graphics)

list of all the student's ancillary activities, showing involvement and leadership. The caption read: "Which student would you rather hire?" Another ad was identical except for the caption, which said, "Which student is more likely to get into a great college?" In these ads, without a lot of print, we were able to get to the heart of the challenges facing students if they are to get ahead.

"Diplomacy is the art of saying 'Nice doggie' until you can find a rock."
—Will Rogers

When local restaurants opposed a food and beverage tax for funding parkland acquisition and upgrades to the wastewater treatment plant, they argued that the tax was on the tourists who visited our city each year to enjoy the Shakespeare Festival. We agreed. They then said it was a tax on locals. We agreed again. To say this dramatically, we ran an ad with a picture of the city's central plaza on the Fourth of July, when more than 30,000 people

150,000 VISITORS TO ASHLAND A YEAR:

- **FLUSH TOILETS**

- **TAKE SHOWERS**

- **HAVE THEIR SHEETS AND TOWELS LAUNDERED**

This creates considerable sewage flow.

Visitors should share in the sewage solution.

The revenues from Measure 15-1 will come from a good blend of locals AND visitors.

Paid for and authorized by the Good For Ashland! Committee. Hal Cloer, Treasurer, PO Box 0, Ashland, OR.

Photo by Christopher Briscoe

IT'S GOOD FOR ASHLAND! VOTE YES ON 15-1

Figure 8.7 Example of an Emotional Ad. Whenever possible, use what is coming at your campaign and redirect it to the opposition.

drop in for the day. The caption pointed out that 150,000 visitors each year use our parks, have their bedding laundered, and flush toilets (figure 8.7). We took what was coming at us and redirected back at the opposition, implying that tourists, like residents, should help pay for the systems they use.

Endorsements and Endorsement Ads

Endorsements from support groups, editorial boards, and business and community leaders can mean both money and votes for your campaign. As you get endorsements, incorporate them into your brochure, direct mail, and newspaper, television, and radio ads. Craft them into press releases and send them to the local papers and newsrooms.

Endorsement ads or testimonials can take many forms. You can list the names of hundreds of people who support you, hopefully showing a broad cross-section of your community; you can pull quotations and names from

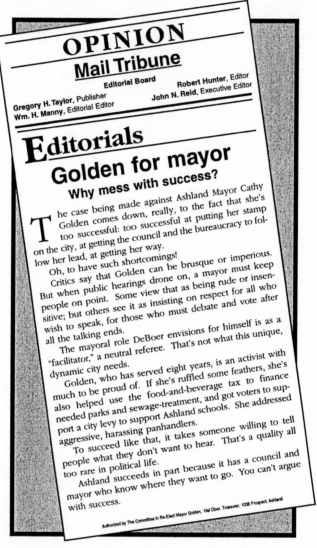

Figure 8.8 Example of an Endorsement Ad. This ad was made more striking by adding shading and placing it at an angle in a box. (Crystal Castle Graphics)

letters-to-the-editor; or you can have a page of logos from businesses that endorse you, with a caption identifying you. Figure 8.8 is an example of an actual ad that included the endorsement of a newspaper's editorial board.

Endorsement ads listing hundreds of names are routinely postponed by campaigns, forcing everyone to scramble in the eleventh hour to amass a list long enough to impress the voters. Whether or not you intend to run this type of ad, you should prepare for one, from the beginning. Ask everyone you talk to if his or her name can be used in an endorsement ad. This will not only make producing an endorsement ad much easier, but it tells you whether the person you are contacting is in fact a supporter and how public he or she wants to go with that support. Some campaigners believe that endorsement ads are ineffective. But when you "hear" that your opponent is doing one, suddenly everything gets dropped while your volunteers start calling lists of people who might be willing to lend their name to an ad. This leaves your workers with the impression that the campaign is disorganized. It also takes time away from other campaign activities at the end of the campaign, when volunteers are stretched to the limit. The last hours of a campaign are precious, so don't needlessly burden yourself: Take care of this as you go.

Ages ago I worked on a campaign in which the candidate said early on that he thought endorsement ads were silly and ineffective and that he did not want to do one. Accordingly, we never collected names. Then, at the end of the campaign, his opponent came out with one of the best endorsement ads I have ever seen. The ad had great pictures of the candidate, a few tasteful lines about America and community, and a full newspaper page of names. And, as if that weren't enough, he bought the back page of the paper for his ad. Even if we had the time and started calling then and there, we couldn't have pulled an ad together that would even approximate what our opposition had done. The ad went unanswered.

When preparing an endorsement ad, keep a separate list of names in a computer or create a field in your campaign database for an endorsement-ad sort. Use the computer to sort names alphabetically to help you find duplicates. However, when it comes time to run the endorsement ad, do not put the names in alphabetical order. A random listing of names pushes people to read through more of them looking for familiar names. Also, random order allows you to put your big names in prominent locations, like at the top of columns or just above a prominent quote. If you know you are going to do an endorsement ad and you are not using a computer, periodically give names to someone who will enter them in a usable format in preparation of the endorsement ad.

In my first mayoral campaign, we ran the endorsement ad on bright yellow paper with a die-cut (hole at the top) so it could hang from doorknobs. On the front at the top was the candidate's logo and the phrase, "Join us in voting for Cathy Golden." Below this was a list of hundreds of names, which continued on the back to cover both sides of the door hanger. The Saturday before the election, about sixty volunteers covered the city in two hours. No matter where voters traveled in the city that day, these yellow endorsement door hangers could be seen.

After the food and beverage tax passed, funding parkland and wastewater treatment plant upgrades, restaurant owners began placing a postcard on every table in every restaurant in town; on one side it asked patrons to let the city know what they thought about the meals tax, and on the other, the card was addressed to me at city hall. Obviously, the idea was to have patrons tell me that they hated the tax. Naturally, some postcards said just that; however, many came in with glowing remarks about Ashland and how happy visitors were to contribute in some small way to the beauty of our community. I saved them all. Eventually, those who opposed the tax pulled a petition and referred it back out to the voters. Once the referral qualified for the ballot and it was clear that we would have to run another campaign, I took the postcards supporting the tax and printed them verbatim in an endorsement ad (figure 8.9).

The avenues with which campaigns communicate with the voters are fairly standard. Lawn signs, advertising, debates, voters' pamphlets, brochures, walking pieces, and direct mail are standards used in political campaigns, whether issue-based or candidate-based. However, the difference between a winning campaign and a losing campaign is really *how* the campaign communicates through these different instruments. In product advertising, there seems to be little concern about whether someone remembers the product because the ad was irritating or because the ad was clever. This is not true in politics. In politics, where the period during which you must attract the voters' attention and move them to support you—and vote for you—is so short, irritating ads can hurt more than help. You want to create ads that have people saying to their family and friends, "Hey, check this ad out, it's really good." Your campaign must "pop" in a memorable way to break out of the clutter.

Years ago I was involved in a campaign for a circuit judge. In the campaign war room was a columnist for the local paper who had been riding me and city hall for years. From time to time I had responded to his missives with editorials that were as hard-hitting as those he had aimed at me. We happened to sit directly across the table from each other one evening in the war room. Everyone in the room who read the local paper knew the history, and I'm sure the tension was palpable. While we were discussing possible newspaper advertising, I suggested that the columnist and I be photographed back to back, arms crossed, looking directly at the camera. The caption would read: "They can only agree on one thing: Phil Arnold should be re-elected circuit court judge." We ran the ad. People in our community loved it and commented on it for weeks.

We *LIKE* the Meals Tax

We've been coming to Ashland since 1970. OSF is the impetus, but we've come to love the charm of your city/area. We make three trips a year into your economy. Since the ambience of the area attracts us, we don't object to contributing to ambience things like park areas, and mundane things like sewers. We're not paying the total cost with our 5% meal tax, just a contribution (maybe $25 a year). It's a small price to pay for the joy we get in return. How would the critics finance these things? And if you don't have them, folks like us wouldn't come. Don't be foolish, there's no free lunch – and we had a picnic in the park last night. 5% was only $1.50.
> – R.S.
> **Eugene, OR**

I applaud the wisdom of your voters in implementing this tax. I hope it continues.
> – B.C.
> **Edmonds, WA**

As frequent summer vacation visitors to Ashland, my wife and I are pleased to make a small contribution to the well being of your beautiful city through the tax. We feel it to be a good idea, not unreasonable.
> – J.R.M.
> **Portland, OR**

Paying 5% on our meals is a small price to pay to help keep Ashland the lovely city it is.
> – T.W. **Talent, OR**

As a frequent visitor to Ashland, I welcome the opportunity to help pay for parks, open space and water treatment. The 5% tax seems appropriate to me.
> – K.R.D. **Corvallis, OR**

I think you would be CRAZY NOT to collect this tax. These services benefit tourists, like us, therefore we should pay for them. This tax should focus more on visitors who put demands on your open space and utilities. Restaurant oriented taxation does that.
> – J.H.J.
> **Winters, CA**

I think the restaurants are foolish to oppose this tax. I support it and think we should have one in Eugene.
> – G.S.
> **Eugene, OR**

Good for you! Deal with your real problems ... I'm glad to chip in my share.
> – M.P.
> **San Luis Obispo, CA**

Although I work at a local coffee shop and am surrounded by opposition to the meals tax, I still support it. Please stick with your aims and goals no matter what pressure the restaurant owners put on you. 'Good Job!'.
> – **Ashland, OR**

We have been annual visitors to Ashland for the past 16 years, and we do not feel burdened to support this sales tax for Ashland's parks and sewers (both of which we USE).
> – R.K.
> **Los Altos, CA**

Save our funding for park acquisition
VOTE NO ON 15-1 and YES ON 15-2
Paid & authorized by the Good for Ashland Committee, Jean Crawford, Treasurer

Figure 8.9 Example of an Endorsement Ad. Again, whenever possible, redirect back to the opposition what they send your way. (TAO Productions and Crystal Castle Graphics)

Brochures that breathe with pictures that have both movement and that elicit emotion will distinguish yours over the opposition's. Lawn signs should be works of art, and slogans clever and memorable. To be creative and memorable in a political campaign costs no more than a campaign that is indistinct in every way.

"The significant problems we have cannot be solved at the same level of thinking with which we created them."

—Albert Einstein

Campaigns are the most fluid segment of the advertising market, and nowhere is it more important for your campaign to adapt to changing circumstances and new information than in advertising. One easy way to differentiate your campaign from others is in timing.

Timing Your Ads

Campaigns typically continue with advertising once they've begun, gradually increasing the number, size, and frequency of ads as the election draws near. However, for challengers there is a strong argument to begin advertising well in advance of the immediate pre-election period when the market is saturated. Early ads allow candidates time to introduce themselves without the distraction of competition with the opponent. Early ads also give a candidate an initial bump in the polls.

This does not mean your campaign should begin advertising in March and keep going until the May 18 primary. Rather you would do ads one week at the end of March and then none until three or four weeks before the election. Television and newspapers may have specials in the spring to encourage people to spend money on advertising. Take advantage of this and jump in.

Your first ads can make the biggest impression. Choose them carefully. If you start and then stop in the final days, it gives the appearance that the campaign is faltering or lacks funds—that is, lacks support, which will make it harder to raise the necessary funds to get to election day. While an early advertising splash helps establish a challenger, if it will seriously cut into your media budget for the final push, you must consider this decision very carefully. Once you hit the final days, your campaign needs to maintain a presence until the end.

A media campaign should work like the fireworks on the Fourth of July. Start with a little at first, then add more and more, climaxing with the finale just before the election. Your money determines when you can *start* advertising, not when you will end. You always end a day out from the election.

Placing your Buys

For newspaper advertising, talk to the person who sells display ads for your local papers. Although newspapers often include ad layout as part of the package and typically do a pretty good job, it is best to have your ad designed by a professional outside the newspaper. It is also worth paying extra to choose where in the paper the ad will be placed. Requesting placement typically adds 15 to 25 percent to the cost of the ad. Salespeople will tell you that it is not necessary to request placement and that they will do all they can to get you what you want for no extra money. This works about half the time. I have found that the personal bias of the editorial team, at least on small papers, gets your ad placed where they want it, not where you want it. If you can afford it, pay for placement.

The best spot for ad placement is opposite the editorial page. Pages 2 and 3 are also good choices. Much farther in and your ad is at risk of disappearing. Don't forget the television listings section. In many papers this section is tabloid-sized, and a full-page ad there costs a third as much as a full-page ad in the regular paper. Plus, people keep the TV section around all week. In my first run for mayor, I ran a full-page ad in the TV section containing the logos of all the businesses that were supporting my candidacy; naturally, the businesses loved the free publicity. My overarching theme was planned, thoughtful growth, so the headline read: "Planning for Ashland's Growth Is Good for Ashland's Businesses."

Don't forget the sports section, local high school newspapers, and college newspapers. Also, consider placing an ad in the help wanted section: "Hardworking, energetic business woman seeks position with the County Commission. Willing to work long hours in community service. Vote [the candidate]." Finally, if you have the money and the space is available, a full-page or half-page ad on the back of the newspaper can work wonders. Ten years ago a woman running for state representative bought the top half of the back page.

> *"True compassion is more than flinging a coin at a beggar; it comes to see that an edifice which produces beggars needs restructuring."*
> —Martin Luther King, Jr

Most of it was a color reproduction of a watercolor by a local artist of the hills surrounding our city. It was the best newspaper ad I had ever seen. She won by a handful of votes.

With all this said about newspaper advertising, it is also important to look at the trends: In 1996, newspapers accounted for 48 percent of where voters received election news, and broadcast networks accounted for 39 percent. In 2000, however, newspapers accounted for 31 percent of where voters got their election news, broadcast networks 24 percent, and cable news 31 percent (Pew Center for the People and the Press, *Campaigns & Elections,* June 2000, pp. 75–80).

A year before the 2002 general election, a local attorney bought the back cover of the phone book for "business" purposes. The cost: $25,000. That spring (about the time the phone book came out) he declared his candidacy for the Oregon legislature. Every day, a hundred thousand people look at his picture, sometimes dozens of times a day—all for just $2,000 a month. He further reinforced his candidacy by using the exact same color picture that filled the back cover of the phone book in all his print ads.

Radio and Television

To be successful in a campaign, it's important to have a mix of media. When you first sit down to assess your preliminary budget, research the cost of radio and television and consider what it can do for your campaign. Generally speaking, candidates for an office in a small town might be well advised to discard radio and television, focusing on mixes of the other media discussed above. However, candidates running for a countywide seat, state senate, state representative, mayor of the county's largest city, or farther up the food chain should consider television and radio.

"The difference between genius and stupidity is that genius has its limits."
—Albert Einstein

According to the study "Americans Speak Out About the 2000 Campaign," conducted by the Center for Congressional and Presidential Studies at American University, 74 percent of those surveyed felt that radio was an important source of political information. Although radio does not have the same presence it once did, many people listen to radio while traveling to and from work, and talk radio is insidious. Stations know their audience numbers and their ratings, so reaching certain segments of the population through radio is pretty easy. Also, the costs of both production and air time are a fraction of what they are in television. Because radio paints a picture with words and sounds whereas television paints a picture with images, I have always treated radio production very differently than television. However, in the 2002 general election, one of my clients used two thirty-second television ads we produced for one sixty-second radio spot. Because the ads were rich with Foley work (background sound) and had strong scripts that could stand alone without the TV images, it completely worked. As a side benefit, the ads playing in two different media reinforced each other.

Radio spots are generally sixty seconds long, which allows the campaign plenty of time to tell a story. In the 2002 primary, a candidate running for circuit court judge ran a very effective radio campaign. He had inadvertently missed the voters' pamphlet deadline and was facing a well-heeled opponent in the primary who was everywhere, including on television. To overcome his opponent's money and organization, the candidate saturated radio stations with a great ad reminding voters that he was the one that *wasn't* in the voters' pamphlet. It was enough to help him barely survive the primary and eventually win in a runoff in the general election.

Television has a vast reach, especially in rural areas, which often have access to only a few local stations and limited cable penetration. In my county we have three local stations, and although anyone living within a city has the option of hooking into cable, only about 60 percent do. More and more residents in the unincorporated areas where cable is not available have satellite dishes, limiting the effectiveness of local ads. Still, the primary access to local news is through the local stations, not cable or satellite.

Television can legitimize a candidate or campaign issue more quickly and effectively than any other medium. However, television is expensive. Raising enough money to have an effective ad campaign, whether you're in an urban or a rural area, can be difficult. Also, whereas you could have friends who are professional photographers volunteering their talents, a sister doing the graphics for lawn signs and newspaper ads, and hundreds of volunteers going door-to-door, television is not something you can leave to people without skill and experience in the medium. Every step, from the creation of the storyboard and script to production, editing, and airing, costs money—and lots of it.

"Rumps in, horns out."
                    —Cow puncher's creed

The advantage of television, like radio, is that the market has been thoroughly researched. There are many sources you can use to research where your swing voters spend their viewing hours, among them Cabletelevision Advertising Bureau, Rocky Mountain Media Watch, Simmons' National Consumer Study (NCS), Nielsen, and Doublebase Mediamark Research. Industry (MRI) tracking firms know who is watching what according to age, education, voting history, income, location, and gender—such as which programs voters who care about health care and voted within the last twelve months will watch.

Here is an example from the 1999 Doublebase Mediamark Research, "Reaching Adult Audiences," on male and female audiences:

- Among the U.S. population of adults aged fifty and over, A&E viewers are 27 percent more likely to vote.

- CNN viewers aged fifty and older are 29 percent more likely to vote.
- The Weather Channel: Median age forty-three, slight audience skew to women.
- The Discovery Channel: 58 percent of prime time viewers are male. Science programming skews more heavily male.
- CNBC, MSNBC, BRAVO, Fox News Channel, Headline News, Travel Channel, TNN, TLC: All have audiences in the thirty-five and older and the fifty and older range that are more "likely" to vote than the population as a whole. Networks such as the Travel Channel may have a smaller audience, but the composition of likely voters is high. Ratings for networks such as TNN and TBS can vary widely by region.

An example from Nielsen on reaching women:

- Lifetime. Lifetime is the No. 1 network with women eighteen and older and women twenty-five to fifty-four in total day, prime, and weekend viewing.
- HGTV. During the daytime, almost an 80 percent skew toward female viewers, during prime audience is 66 percent female.

Reaching men:

- ESPN: 74 percent male viewership (MRI, Spring 1999).
- ESPN II: 80 percent male viewership. Viewers have higher household income than ESPN viewers (MRI, Spring 1999).
- The History Channel: 69 percent male skew during prime time.
- Golf Channel: 78 percent male audience; average age 47 (Claritas/ Prizm Profile), 70 percent watch during prime time.

Reaching older voters:

- CNN's *Larry King Live* and *Inside Politics*
- Lifetime's *Intimate Portrait*
- A&E's *Biography*

What is helpful for the campaign is that by using industry resources you can develop and run ads that speak to an audience that is more likely to vote and one with highly specific demographics. Knowing who watches what helps a campaign avoid overtargeting a particular demographic group.

You can take demographic research one step further by going to marketing sites on the Web to study where products are being targeted within the consumer market. For example, although some states reflect this trend more than others, right now middle-class America is spending a lot of money fixing up their homes, which would speak strongly for advertising on the Home and Garden channel. With this type of information, your campaign can choose the right programming to reach your target voters as well as to tailor your ads to reflect what is important in the voter's life. Ads that embrace the idea of neighborhoods, community, and timeless values that speak to the homeowner may be well received in today's market.

"Politics is short, very focused. To compete with all the commercial advertising you have to punch through."

—Leo McCarthy,
Former Minnesota Lt. Gov.

Cable Television: A Better Buy

In larger media markets where network television is prohibitively expensive for local campaigns, cable remains affordable—and advertising on cable offers a bonus as well: According to Nielsen Media Research, cable viewers are, on average, 4 percent more likely to vote than are viewers in homes without cable, and at least two cable networks have adult viewerships that are 25 percent more likely to vote than their broadcast counterparts. Also, according to Rocky Mountain Media Watch, cable news shows have 20 percent more "hard news" and 15 percent less advertising clutter than do network news shows.

In southern Oregon a campaign can buy a thirty-second spot on cable for about $10. In the Portland Media Market, where house races could not afford to advertise on network television, nearly all of the close house races in the 2002 general election advertised exclusively on cable.

Fat-Free TV Advertising

In smaller media markets, television is a relatively affordable asset in your media budget. In the 2002 general election, we advertised on four daytime network stations, nearly every hour for one week, for the same price as developing and sending one direct mail piece. But to keep television affordable, attention to detail must be practiced at every level.

Although the bulk of production for television should be left in the hands of a professional, the more you know about the process, the more input you'll be able to have in creating the finished product. There are a number of ways to stretch your campaign dollars if you decide to use television advertising.

It's important to do as much front-end work as possible. Research the candidate and the opposition. Anyone creating your ads should know both the strengths and the weaknesses of your candidate. While the strengths may be accentuated in ads that establish a candidate, your media specialist should also have a clear idea of where the candidate may be vulnerable. Once attacked, the media consultant may have to respond by delivering a finished product to the television stations within hours. Knowing your candidate's weaknesses allows you to begin the groundwork for response ads before they are necessary. If the need never materializes, all the better.

"The press always has the last word."
—Tom Olbrich,
campaign media adviser

Your campaign should also research the strengths and weaknesses of the opposition. Even if you do not intend to run negative ads, by researching the opposition's flaws, you can juxtapose your candidate's strengths with your opponent's weaknesses and never mention them. They become implied. "Jane Doe will not miss important votes" *implies* that her opponent has (figure 8.10).

It's a good idea at this time to gather as much background information about your candidate as possible in the form of newspaper articles, childhood and current family photos (especially ones that help underscore an image you want to project), career history, and a list of names and phone numbers of close family and friends that the media consultant can contact. To give a producer as many options as possible, collect newspaper clippings for the opposing candidate, as they can often be used in ads. Your efforts to gather information saves the campaign time and money and usually results in a better product. In the 2002 general election, we were called in late in the cycle to do a few television spots for a local race. Although we had some footage of the candidate from a forum we attended, it wasn't enough, so an appeal was put out in the community for any video on the candidate. One local resident had video of all the candidates in the Ashland Fourth of July parade. Although the quality was marginal, converting it to black and white and slowing the motion gave it a timeless quality, and it added a great deal to the ad (figure 8.11).

Choosing Your Media Specialist or Team

Before you begin to interview producers for your ads, check to see what level of expertise already exists within your campaign team. With the advent of digital video, there are a lot more consumer-savvy hobbyists who may speak the same language as the producer you hire. Your team might have people with the skills and equipment to shoot your own ads—but a word of caution: Making television-quality video is not the same as shooting home video. Look

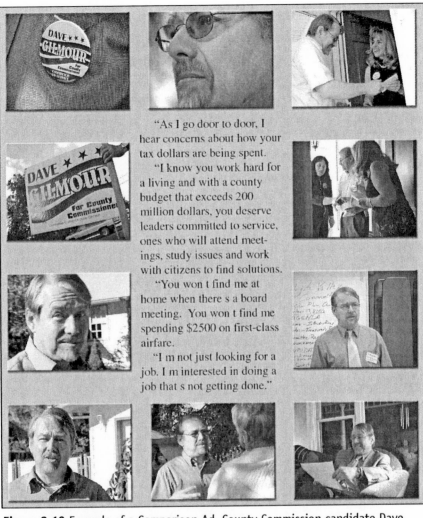

"As I go door to door, I hear concerns about how your tax dollars are being spent.

"I know you work hard for a living and with a county budget that exceeds 200 million dollars, you deserve leaders committed to service, ones who will attend meetings, study issues and work with citizens to find solutions.

"You won t find me at home when there s a board meeting. You won t find me spending $2500 on first-class airfare.

"I m not just looking for a job. I m interested in doing a job that s not getting done."

Figure 8.10 Example of a Comparison Ad. County Commission candidate Dave Gilmour was running with an eight-point registration disadvantage against a popular incumbent. The incumbent had been somewhat remiss in the use of public funds and had received damaging press regarding drug and alcohol abuse and marital problems. We felt going straight after the incumbent's personal problems would be needlessly unkind and could backfire. Instead we used images to portray the two candidates' differences: Gilmour was to project a healthful image (walking door-to-door), a sound family relationship (his daughter and his son narrated two of the three ads), and the ads spoke to integrity, referencing only his opponent's indiscretion with use of tax dollars. (rickshaw productions)

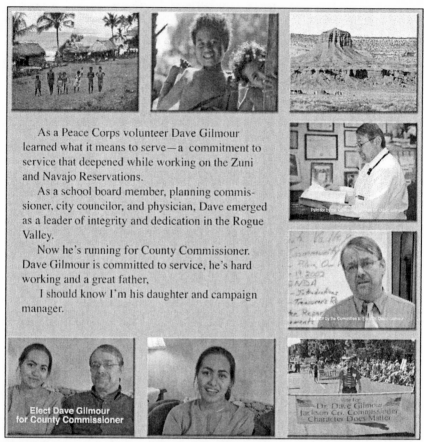

As a Peace Corps volunteer Dave Gilmour learned what it means to serve—a commitment to service that deepened while working on the Zuni and Navajo Reservations.

As a school board member, planning commissioner, city councilor, and physician, Dave emerged as a leader of integrity and dedication in the Rogue Valley.

Now he's running for County Commissioner. Dave Gilmour is committed to service, he's hard working and a great father.

I should know I'm his daughter and campaign manager.

Elect Dave Gilmour for County Commissioner

Figure 8.11 Example of an Establishing Ad. All ads should tell a story, but your first one should tell a story of the candidate. Effective ones reveal who the candidate is and not only touch on history but also tug at emotions. (rickshaw productions)

at samples from whoever you use, whether it's someone you hire or a volunteer, before you commit your hard-earned media dollars. Volunteer producers can also be found at local cable access stations where fledgling producers may be willing to work for the experience and exposure. Again, with television, free is great, but quality is more important. A bad or poorly crafted television spot can hurt your case.

As an aside, the local community access station is often hungry for programming and may be willing to produce shows with a candidate at little or no charge. Such productions can provide some outstanding material for your producer to use in an ad or a portion of an ad.

More than likely, you'll need to hire someone to produce your ads. So, what do you look for? First check around from the last campaign and look at locally produced spots. You can usually find out who produced particular ads simply by asking the candidates or their teams. Second, watch local commercials that are currently airing. Do any of them stand out? Check for the use of graphics, logos, and type of ad. Has the producer layered the ad with rich visuals and Foley (sound) work? Can you see a difference in quality? By simply calling or visiting local stations, you can find out the names of producers whose ads stand out. Third, ask for copies or demos of a local production team's work. Give preference to agencies that specialize or have experience in campaign ads, but don't ignore new talent in the form of some of those local commercials you liked. New producers are like new restaurants: They keep their prices down and give excellent service. Just make sure the food is good. That new producer may bend over backwards to give your project all the attention it needs, but he or she still needs the skill and equipment to give it broadcast quality.

Judge all demos on style, quality, and overall look. At this point you're looking more for a feeling than content. When it comes to content, hopefully you'll be very involved in writing the script. Look for film-like softness, lighting, and movement. Do the demos include subjects in motion? A car ad may look great but that doesn't mean the same agency can shoot a candidate going door-to-door. Look for producers who like to shoot outdoors and use natural lighting. You will pay more for on-location shoots than studio shoots, but it is worth it.

> *"If Hitler invaded Hell, I think I would find a good word to say about the Devil in the House of Commons."*
> —Winston Churchill, in response to criticism for siding with Stalin during WWII

Next, interview the top three to five producers on your list. Before you get to the nitty-gritty of production schedules and rates, spend some time talking about your candidate or cause. Can the producer understand why this is important to you? Why this candidate or issue-based campaign needs to win? Make sure the producer thoroughly understands your message and theme. Leave plenty of room for discussion, brainstorming, and give-and-take. A good producer has probably been thinking in images the whole time and should have some immediate ideas for you. However, don't commit to anything just yet. The most important decision for you is whether or not this is a person who can work for and with your candidate or cause. This is especially important given that shooting film and video is stressful, expensive, and deadline driven.

Next, share all the possible materials you have (photos, newspaper clippings, and so forth) and ask the producer to send you a proposal with a budget breakdown. Ask for treatments and pricing for one, two, and three ads. You may later use this information for negotiating prices. If the budget includes crew, find out if the producer can or is willing to make use of your volunteers to reduce costs.

"Wisdom oftentimes consists of knowing what to do next."
—Herbert Hoover

Local stations may also pitch you their own studio production at a fraction of the cost of local producers. Buyers beware, though: These ads are usually in a cookie-cutter, talking-head format with a studio backdrop. This format is best reserved for a candidate who is responding to an attack or for featuring local stars or incumbents with clout who are willing to publicly endorse a candidate or cause. If the talking-head format can stand on its own for your particular application, it can be a very effective and an inexpensive ad to produce. In 2000 I worked on a local campaign where the candidate had the backing of Governor Kitzhaber, who has an excellent television presence. Although the governor said he would cut some ads for us, it was difficult to get everyone's schedules lined up for a shoot in southern Oregon. Eventually the scripts were written in Ashland and e-mailed to the governor in Salem, where we had arranged for a shoot in a studio that was located close to his home. A member of our campaign committee met the governor at the studio, and they did two or three takes on each of the scripts for about $200 for the cameraman. The video was then brought to a local production company in southern Oregon, where music, logo, and disclaimer were added to complete the ads for another $100.

There are plenty of occasions for the media team to attend events that include both candidates, providing a venue to capture footage of each. Seizing opportunities of this nature allows your campaign to study both candidates and pick up material for additional ads.

Streamline Production:
Ten Tips to Save Money and Improve Your Television Spots
Many producers don't press for multiple takes or worry much about mistakes made during filming out in the field, because most can be fixed in production. However, minimizing the amount of time the editor spends on your ads saves money.

1. As a candidate, if you're delivering a speaking part, know your part, and be fully prepared. Never use a TelePrompTer: People can tell. It makes the candidate seem insincere and the message seem contrived.

It also suggests that the candidate can't be trusted to speak well without a prepared text.

2. Bring an appropriate change of clothes if needed—that is, if your ad creates or re-creates events and settings that are quite different and supposedly took place over time. For example, if your ad contains a shot with the candidate at a day care center, another at a business, and another with seniors, the piece will look contrived if the candidate is wearing the same outfit in each shot. Recently, I saw an ad for a woman in Washington State running for Congress. The ad began with her talking to the camera while walking through a hilly outdoor area in a skirt, a pink silk blouse, and white pearls. It was bizarre. My first thought was that she was out for the day to make ads and this is what she wore. Sure enough, in nearly every subsequent shot, she had the same pink blouse and white pearls. How much trouble can it be to bring a change of clothes? If you are going from woods to senate chamber, dress appropriately for the settings.

3. If the ad involves testimonials, impress upon those involved that they need to know what they will say, and provide them the lines. E-mail the scripts to people well before the shoot to provide enough time for them to learn the lines. When it comes to a shoot with testimonials, schedule all of the people at a location that can take on many different looks. Be sure you do not have to deal with traffic noise.

4. Find locations that convey message and image. Think about these ahead of time, and share your thoughts with the media specialists.

5. Consider using photos with a voice-over. Still photographs of the candidate as a child, at work, as a parent, as a spouse, fly-fishing, and so forth, can be a very effective way to evoke a feeling of intimacy with a candidate. Don't forget to add newspaper stories to increase the credibility of the accomplishments mentioned.

6. Get enough baseline footage so that more ads can be cut without sending the crew out again.

7. Try using just music and no voice-over. Because TV is so noisy, if a thirty-second ad appears with only music, everyone looks.

8. Consider using stock photos and film clips. For a relatively small cost, your campaign can purchase stock images to convey a message or create an emotion. This is especially important when your ad covers delicate issues such as domestic violence. Rather than send a professional photographer to an old-growth forest or a wastewater treatment plant that uses wetlands for polishing, why not purchase this footage? Images of the great halls of government, people shaking hands, crowds, a child with the American flag, piles of money, orchestras, you name it,

are already available and professionally done. The Image Bank is one source, but there are others.

9. Send a professional photographer to early campaign events. Use these images for ads.

10. The script should be written for a 29-second read. Although you are buying a 30-second spot, the spots are actually 29.5 seconds. Too often campaigns compensate for long scripts by having the narrator read faster. Remember the quip, "I would have written you a shorter letter if I had the time"? Take the time. This is a little like backpacking. Lay out everything you're going to take and then reduce it by half, and then half again.

Great Ads Don't Just Happen: Be Creative, Organized, Focused

In television and radio campaign advertising, there are generally three types of ads: establishing, comparison, and response/attack. Whatever the format of your ad, certain overriding principles apply to all:

1. A good ad begins with a good script. It is not enough to simply have a presence on television. Television ads must have an objective. The first question to be asked and answered before a script is drafted is: "What is our objective with this ad?"

   If your objective is to establish the candidate, that is, tell a story about who he or she is, your ad must stay focused on that aspect of the candidate. An establishing ad, for example, should really tug at emotion; it's a voyeuristic glimpse into the candidate's personal life, past and present. It's a time capsule of what this potential community leader will bring to the table in terms of experience and core values. Is she a fighter? Has he volunteered for country or community? Has the candidate had unique challenges in life that have shaped who he or she is?

   The media team must look at the candidate's bio and decide what should stay and what should go. An establishing ad is a good place for the old photos you had the candidate dig up; it is also an excellent venue for stock photos (figure 8.12).

"Endeavor to speak truth in every instance; to give nobody expectations that are not likely to be answered, but aim at sincerity in every word and action—the most amiable excellence in a rational being."

—Ben Franklin

Figure 8.12 Example of a Comparison Ad. In the Maxwell for the House campaign, the Democrats drafted Shayne Maxwell after the primary, setting her considerably behind schedule. With this late start, with little money, in a conservative district, and with a seventeen-point registration disadvantage, we knew the first ad had to be bold. It also had to establish the candidate and draw comparisons with her and her well-heeled opponent. (rickshaw productions)

2. Use language that reflects that of your voters. Don't talk over people's heads, and don't talk down to them. Talk about issues the way real people would talk about them.

3. Show clear comparisons between the candidates. This can be implied, as shown in figure 8.10, or it can be more direct, as in figure 8.12.

4. Make ads believable, whether you are attacking your opponent or promoting your objectives. Be both specific and realistic about promises and programs you want to bring to the voters once elected. Be sure your goals are achievable. Making unrealistic claims or promises insults people's intelligence.

5. Use a "stealth" approach. All media buys for political campaigns are on public record, and you can be sure the opposition is checking your buys just as you should be checking theirs. Lead the opposition to believe that you're struggling for media buys. Lock in some great spots and then backfill with smaller-rated (less expensive) availables just before they air.

6. Let others do your bidding. Using family or prominent, respected community leaders can be an effective tool for an outsider to establish credibility. Using on-the-street people can show that an incumbent is still connected to everyday people.

7. Use black and white. What color does for direct mail, black and white does for TV. It's an effective tool to get noticed and to create mood, intimacy, and a sense of history for the candidate or issue-based campaign.

8. Ads should be easily distinguishable from one another. In the 2002 general election we were brought in to help a candidate who was in a deadheat race for circuit court judge. His ad company had cut four ads, each with the candidate sitting in a large leather chair talking directly to the camera. Although each ad had a different script, they all looked as though they were identical. Given that the opposition was making age an issue, our client could have met that criticism without actually acknowledging it by showing images of himself fly-fishing knee-deep in a river. Instead what he got were four ads that looked exactly the same.

9. Use still photography and create motion by zooming and by panning pictures. By mixing childhood photos with more current images, you can tell a story about the candidate in a controlled, evocative way. Still photos work well for issue-based campaigns (figure 8.13).

10. Carefully select the ad's music. Although an abundance of copyright-free music is available, unfortunately most of it is pretty bad. The Music Bakery has the best selection, but many online services are available. Most do not expect payment for a piece until you download it for use. Selecting music takes a lot longer than you can imagine, so allow yourself plenty of time.

Hundreds of men and women found that Rogue Community College allowed them to pursue their dream and prosper in a now very uncertain economy.

RCC's expansion plans provide exactly what we need at the right time: a technical training center so our workers can learn new skills without relocating.

By voting for Measure 17-85 you support the economy of this region.

Support RCC. Vote yes on Measure 17-85.

It's a vote for all of us.

Figure 8.13 Example of an Issue-Based Ad Using Still Photos. This ad juxtaposed still, black-and-white photos with the brilliant red field sign used in the campaign. The producer brought the field sign to life in the last frames of the ad by cutting out each of the characters in the still photos and layering them on top of the silhouettes featured in the field sign. Using captivating music, the ad ran for ten days with no voice-over, to pull the viewer in and pop the ad from all the other political clutter. We then came back with the identical ad and a voice-over. Because of the nature of the community college bond measure, we chose a student who had a great deal of experience in public speaking and an engaging voice that, although deep, had a "youthful" quality to it. (rickshaw productions)

11. Use professional equipment, good camera operators, proper lighting, and thoughtful settings. The settings should all have a purpose. You're spending a lot of money and time, so don't cut corners here (figure 8.14).

12. Make video look like film. Many in the industry prefer to use film because it creates a more reflective feel. Few campaigns, especially local ones, can afford this. However, lighting can go a long way toward softening images and creating a film-like look. Ask your production company what techniques they can use to soften video.

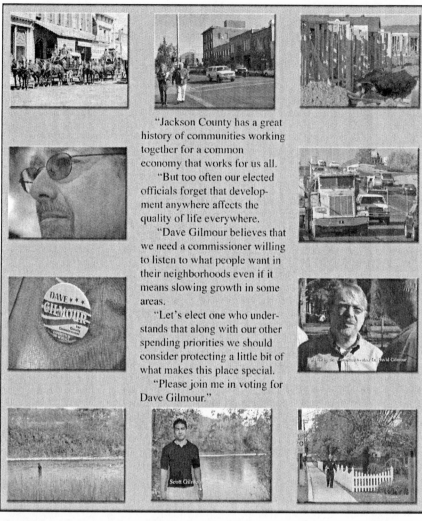

"Jackson County has a great history of communities working together for a common economy that works for us all.

"But too often our elected officials forget that development anywhere affects the quality of life everywhere.

"Dave Gilmour believes that we need a commissioner willing to listen to what people want in their neighborhoods even if it means slowing growth in some areas.

"Let's elect one who understands that along with our other spending priorities we should consider protecting a little bit of what makes this place special.

"Please join me in voting for Dave Gilmour."

Figure 8.14 Example of an Ad with Purpose. Late in the Gilmour for Commissioner race, canvassers reported that voters still did not know Dave Gilmour. We knew we had to go back in and lock his base without losing any swing voters. To do this we took an issue that was problematic across all communities in southern Oregon—development—and used it as the anchor for the ad. By incorporating progressive environmental images embraced by Gilmour's base with countywide concerns about development, we accomplished our objective. The voice-over was done by the candidate's son. (rickshaw productions)

13. Use motion. When a candidate speaks directly to the camera, have him or her moving forward, either to a stationary camera or to one

that moves with the speaker. This conveys the message that the candidate is someone who is going places: moving forward.

14. In general you can defend yourself on television and radio, but attacks are best made through direct mail. In the 2002 general election we were helping a Democratic candidate who was being outspent seven to one, had very little money, and had a huge registration disadvantage. However, tracking polls showed her closing in on her opponent, and as his double-digit lead dwindled to the margin of error, he went on the attack through a direct mail piece sent by Oregon Right to Life. With only a few thousand dollars in the bank, responding through direct mail was not an option for us, so we generated a television ad that brought back to the forefront the unprecedented nasty primary the Republican had run against the incumbent he unseated. "He's at It Again" (figure 8.15) aired for a week in closely targeted television markets. However, in doing so, we made a couple of mistakes. First, Oregon Right to Life had used a mailing list targeting the house district as well as a select group of Republican voters. The television ad, however, went out to a much broader audience and gave our opponent a reason to use TV ads and automated phone calls to defend himself in a very believable way. Because most people in the district had not seen the right-to-life hit piece, it looked as though we had gone negative on him rather than the other way around. Second, attacks must be answered in the same medium in which they were made, which we could not do because of financial constraints. We would have served the client better in this case by leaving the charge unanswered.

Placing Your Buys on Television

Production companies that make your ads will often do the buys as well. The time is sold to them at a 15 percent discount, which is where the real money is made. Buying is a complicated prospect, but if you're willing to do the research and have a good sales rep at the local station, you should be able to do it and save the campaign money that can go into more buys. However, congressional or statewide races would be foolish to do this in-house. If your opponent is paying big bucks to have a professional firm make the buys, tell the sales rep you want everything she or he buys. It isn't very scientific, but it gets the job done.

> "It's the responsibility of the media to look at the president with a microscope, but they go too far when they use a proctoscope."
> —Richard M. Nixon

Figure 8.15 Example of a Response/Attack Ad (rickshaw productions)

Although there is a price break for political candidates, the trade-off is the risk of getting bumped by someone who is willing to pay the full price. Usually ad reps will let you know if you need to bump up to keep a spot you reserved, but not always. Sometimes you will be moved to a "comparable," that is, a spot with similar demographics. If you're working on an issue-based campaign, there may not be any break for TV ads. If that is the case, add at least 20–50 percent to your television budget buys. That said, in 2002 when I was helping a school tax measure I talked to a sales rep of one of our three local stations and argued that "local" issue-based campaigns were quite different from statewide initiatives, which often came fortified with millions in special-interest money. Convinced, the station gave us the same break that candidates received. I then called the other stations and told them what their competition was doing for the community and got similar breaks across the board.

"The suspense is terrible. I hope it will last."

—Oscar Wilde

Because most campaigns run their media with greater frequency as the election approaches, open time slots for media buys become scarce. In television programming, as with radio, there are just so many available seconds in the hour. Unlike a newspaper, which can add more pages, television and radio have limited amounts of time to sell. Depending on the popularity of the show, the time when you might consider a buy can be even more restricted. If you do not secure your media buys early, there could be nothing available as the election deadline draws near.

That does not mean you have to deliver finished products the day you buy ad time. All the production work can be done later. But it does mean that in August or September if you're going to buy thirty seconds on *60 Minutes* for November, you must have the cash in hand. This is where early endorsements and early money pay off.

If you know which voters your campaign needs to target, and exactly what message you want to get to what age group and income, one of the most predictable highways is television. Local station sales reps know their programming and will lead you to the best reach and frequency. So if your targeting turns up a specific demographic profile as likely to support you, your television ad rep will tell you where to place your ads and how many times they will need to air for the targeted voter to see them; he or she will also know how many times a viewer will see the ad given the number of gross rating points (GRPs) you buy. For example, a purchase of 600 GRPs, a typical buy for political campaigns in October, translates to 89.6 percent of television viewers seeing the ad 6.7 times each, according to David Townsend, who heads Townsend, Raimundo, Besler & Usher, a political consulting and public affairs firm in Sacramento, California.

"Television allows you to be entertained in your home by people you wouldn't have in your home."
—David Frost

A thousand GRPs, a typical purchase the week before an election for a hotly contested seat, means that 94 percent of the people watching will see the spot about 11 times each. If you're running a campaign in Nebraska, which is a relatively inexpensive television market, you will pay about $110 per GRP in a statewide race. That translates to $100,000-plus for the final week of the campaign. If you live in California, however, the same 1,000 GRPs will cost you better than $2 million. Compare these to a local campaign in a rural area where viewing is restricted to a few stations. For example, in southern Oregon and comparable small communities across the nation, 1,000 GRPs will cost less than $40,000. Since 1,000 GRPs in a small market would be overkill, a fraction of that buy may be all you need to achieve a presence and establish credibility. This means in small markets, television becomes a very affordable tool.

In any television market, as GRPs increase, so does the number of times a viewer might see the ad. Obviously, the more GRPs, the greater the number of people reached and the greater the frequency with which they are reached. For example, according to the Television Bureau of Advertising, Inc., "A total of 100 GRPs in one week, placed in all time periods, can reach 56.7 percent of all people or homes an average of 1.8 times. Raise the figure to 200 GRPs and reach can go to 73.5 percent for an average frequency of 2.7 times."

Buy Smart

I once worked for a candidate who had a background in television production. He knew quite a few people in the business and headed up the media team. He also produced excellent local ads. One night I was home watching David Letterman, and one of the candidate's ads came on. When I asked the candidate why he'd placed an ad in this time slot and on this show, he said that he watched David Letterman, as did *a lot* of his friends. Folks, the objective of this exercise is not to have friends at work say, "Hey, I saw your ad last night"; the objective is to influence targeted voters. If you have to woo your base, you're going to lose anyway. Assume that they will vote for you, and spend your money on media to influence the all-important swing voters.

> *"Political ads are giving Americans a choice between bad and awful, distorting and undermining debate, increasing campaign costs and driving voters from the polls."*
> —Curtis Gans, Committee for the Study of the American Electorate

There are a few ways to reach your targeted audience and hit that critical mass if dollars are short. Television costs are based on the size of the audience: The bigger the audience, the higher the cost. However, purchasing less expensive time slots, when the audience is smaller (smaller-rated), may allow your campaign to air your ads more frequently for less money and still meet the reach and frequency you desire.

If you know you will be advertising on television but really don't have the funds to keep a critical presence for more than a week, buy your television time starting with election eve and work your way back. As money becomes available, you can buy ads for more and more days preceding the election. Also, by purchasing the time closest to the election first, you don't run the risk of that highly coveted time being unavailable later. Smaller-rated "avails" (availabilities) are usually the last to go, so there may even be some opportunity for in-fill close to election day, but don't count on it. Buy early.

Consider producing ten-second ("dime") spots that use the images of a thirty-second spot ("thirty"). A dime can reinforce a thirty, and it will get a candidate's name and a quick message before the voters. Be aware, however, that a dime saves the campaign only about 25 percent in production and buys, and that cable often will not use dimes.

"We all learn by experience but some of us have to go to summer school."
—Peter De Vries

Rules and Regulations

The following are general rules and regulations as they apply to political advertising. However, be sure to get media packets from your local stations and familiarize yourself with individual station requirements.

You must be a qualified candidate for public office or an authorized campaign organization to promote a person's candidacy for office. Political action committees and noncandidate campaigns (issue campaigns) do not fall under the political advertising guidelines.

Reasonable access for political "use" will be provided to all legally qualified federal candidates during the forty-five-day period before a primary or primary runoff election and the sixty-day period before a general or special election.

While candidates may request specific programming, the station reserves the right to make reasonable good-faith judgments about the amount of time and program availability to provide to particular candidates.

All ads must comply with the visual sponsorship identification requirements of the Communications Act. In other words, they must all have a disclaimer. The disclaimer ("PAID FOR BY . . . ") must last at least four seconds and be at least 4 percent of screen height. Who or what follows the disclaimer depends on who paid for the ad and whether the candidate authorized it or not.

Any spot for a political candidate or on behalf of an announced candidate must include video and/or audio use of the candidate's image or voice.

In many areas political ads may not be placed just before, during, or just after news programs.

"Man is the only animal that laughs and has a state legislature."
—Samuel Butler

Bumper Stickers and Buttons

Bumper stickers are an inexpensive way to familiarize the community with your name or ballot measure. Whereas bumper stickers are used predominantly in large city, county, state, and federal races, they can be quite effective in the small election simply because they continue to be a novelty there.

This is one application for which I would relax my strong recommendation to place your campaign logo on all your materials. Bumper stickers are small and hard to read, so clarity is what is important. On a bumper sticker, ideally you want your candidate or measure before the voters, nothing more. In one campaign where we used bumper stickers, we placed the logo along with the name. Even though the logo was modified, it was still difficult to read.

"This is now in general the great art of legislation at this place. To do a thing by assuming the appearance of preventing it. To prevent a thing by assuming that of doing it."
—John Quincy Adams

A bonus with bumper stickers is that they are occasionally left on cars if a candidate wins, giving the community the impression that the individual is well liked in office. People who like to display bumper stickers are often willing to kick in a dollar or two to buy them.

Three points of caution on bumper stickers. First, should you decide to print bumper stickers, be sure to print them on removable stock. If people know the stickers will easily come off after the election, they'll be more inclined to place one. Second, urge people to drive courteously while displaying your name on their cars. If they are rude on the road, the only thing the other driver will remember is the name on the bumper sticker. Finally, keep in mind that use of bumper stickers, like lawn signs, is an untargeted campaign activity.

Buttons are walking testimonials or endorsements. If supporters actually wear them, it further serves the goal of getting your name in front of the voting public. My experience is that very few people put them on each day, and they tend to be added clutter and expense for the campaign. However, since all canvassers should have some sort of official identification with the campaign, this is what I recommend:

At a stationery store, buy a box of the type of plastic name holders used at conventions and meetings. Ask the graphic design artist who put together the lawn sign logo to make a miniature version of it, sized to fit the plastic badges. Also ask the designer to lay out as many of these as will fit on a sheet of paper. Reproduce on brightly colored card stock as many as you think you will need, keeping the original to make more throughout the campaign. Cut out your miniature lawn sign logos and slide them into the plastic holders. After the campaign, you can reuse the plastic name badges.

9

THE CANDIDATE

IN THIS CHAPTER
- *The Lay of the Land*
- *Packaging the Candidate*
- *Stay on Your Message*
- *Outsider's Campaign vs. Incumbent's Campaign*
- *Debates*
- *Fielding Negative Questions*
- *Developing Your Public Speaking Skills*
- *The Write-In and Third Party Candidates*
- *Media and the Candidate*
- *Negative Campaigning*
- *Ten Dos and Don'ts of Attacks*
- *Thank-You Notes*

Once you declare your intention to run for office, you become part of the public domain. You are fair game for just about any criticism people might feel inclined to level at you. Should someone write a letter with an outright lie in it, you essentially have little recourse. You can defend yourself, but unless you can prove malice, you cannot sue. Some political analysts think candidates should ignore attacks and lies. However, far more think that unanswered allegations imply truth. Either way, it is a problem. You can defend yourself, but when you decide to run, you give up your right to whine. It is great preparation for holding elective office.

This chapter is about projecting a positive image before the voters and thereby minimizing the potential nit-picking that the public might do. You will also find suggestions on how to redirect negative questions at your opponent, turning the ammunition back on him or her. For a candidate, this is not a time to be defensive. Take criticism as a gift and an opportunity.

Before declaring my intention to run for mayor, I was at a picnic with my family in a nearby city. The Historical Society was sponsoring the event on a glorious summer evening on the lawn in front of a historic museum situated in a turn-of-the-century gold-rush town. The speaker was the Oregon secretary of state, who within a few years would be our first woman governor. I remember being wowed by her speech and filled with pride at the prospect of joining ranks in the elected arena with women of her capability.

> *"A mayor does not create a new vision of a city from the inner workings of his own mind. Rather, he collects it from scattered hopes and buried dreams of people he has listened to in the course of his own political journey."*
> —Ray Flynn, former mayor of Boston, in his 1984 inaugural speech

As I was eating, a friend shared a comment she had just heard about me. A woman had said, "How can Cathy ever hope to run a city if she can't leave her children at home?" I was stunned, enraged, offended, and more. But once I calmed down, I thought about her criticism. If she felt this way at an *outdoor picnic,* imagine the criticism having my children at a more formal event might draw. Rather than react in a defensive way, I realized that my actions were more potent than my words. If I were elected, I could lead by example and thereby serve as a role model for young women in the community. However, if I moved off my campaign message to beat up potential voters on the double standards that exist in society, I might never hold a position of leadership, serve as a role model, and accomplish the programs that prompted me to run in the first place. I did not let the criticism distract me. I also chose not to drag my children through the political process with me. I would add that children need a family life of their own and are better off not serving as political props.

> *"If you get to be a really big headliner, you have to be prepared for people throwing bottles at you in the night."*
> —Mick Jagger

The Lay of the Land

Each elective office has specific powers and duties associated with it. For example, the Ashland City Charter says that the mayor is the chief executive of the municipal corporation and will closely oversee the workings of city government. Laced throughout the document are other stipulated duties associated with the office, such as appointment of department heads and duties in relation to the city council. The charter sets up a strong-mayor form of government.

Before running for mayor of Ashland, I spent a great deal of time familiarizing myself with council business and city documents, but I never actually read the powers of the office of mayor. Then, within my first six months in office, the city council set about stripping the powers of the office. Their intention was to do it through a simple resolution, which, unlike an ordinance, does not need a public hearing and cannot be subject to a mayoral veto. As they put it, they didn't want to "take" the powers, they merely wanted to "share" them with me and to "help" me do a better job. I was young, just thirty-five, and felt both attacked and betrayed. No help came from the administrator, who was probably equally concerned about my ability and wanted the department head appointment power to fall under the jurisdiction of his office. Furthermore, no support came from fellow councilors, who in fact had initiated the coup and wanted equal say on city board and commission appointments.

Many department heads, who did not want to work for a woman, especially one as young and inexperienced as I was, aligned with the administrator even though they technically worked for the mayor. Word came back that many at city hall were saying disparaging things about me, including name calling—my favorite was "the meddling housewife." I represented an upset and a change of the status quo—the problem wasn't necessarily that I would wreak havoc on the city or that the existing system was working all that well. There is just a general suspicion, especially in government, when moves are made from the known to the unknown. The overall proposed action would result in moving Ashland from a strong-mayor form of government to a weak-mayor form of government, all without going to a vote of the people.

Things heated up quickly. I did not want to go down in history as the mayor who lost the powers of the office. I floundered in meetings as I tried to find footing. I simply could not figure out how to stop the train. Then another southern Oregon mayor told me he thought his city's charter was modeled after Ashland's, and if they were the same, what the city council was doing was illegal. He said, "Read your charter." Simple, obvious, good advice. I did just that.

At the next meeting, armed with information, I held my ground, recited the powers of my office and threatened to take the council's actions to a vote through the initiative process if they persisted. They backed off. Four tumultuous years followed, during which time three department heads and the city attorney went. By the time I left office, twelve years later, there had been a complete changeover in all department heads and the administrator and I went from a relationship of suspicion to one of trust, understanding, and mutual respect.

Before you run for office, know the powers and duties of that office; attend meetings and familiarize yourself with the lay of the land. Wouldn't you prefer to know before you run whether you're suited for the kind of work that goes with the office? You should also know something about the system: how land use laws work, how property and other taxes are distributed, the revenue stream, the expenditure stream, and which follows which.

In the 1998 California primary, gubernatorial candidate Al Checchi gave a speech to the Democratic Leadership Council, which was followed by a question-and-answer period. At some point he stated that all property taxes went to the state. Knowing this to be false, reporters followed up, asking Checchi to explain. Again he said the state claims all real estate taxes. Two more follow-up questions, and Checchi did not change his assertion. He did not know something as basic as how property taxes were distributed and yet he wanted to be governor. Details, such as this, are not missed by the press or the voters.

"There is no conversation so sweet as that of former political enemies."
—Harry Truman

It's also important to know the lay of the land of your community. Recently, an Ashland candidate appeared in a debate at the Rotary Club. Prior to making a point, he asked if there were any businesspeople in the room. He was not joking.

So what do you do if you make a mistake? Own up to it. A while ago, the Southern Pacific Railroad divested some very important real estate in the heart of our city. We had hoped for a portion of it to create a pocket park; however, the option to buy was quickly secured by a developer. The neighborhood was upset. After many calls from the city trying to cut in line without success, I gave up. I explained to the neighbors that it was hopeless and that we needed to look elsewhere for a park. However, they would not give up. Finally, somehow, they got the parcel for the park. Sometime later, at a council meeting, I was chastised by this group for giving up and calling the situation hopeless. I had to admit it was the best crow I ever ate, and I acknowledged the group for their success where I had failed.

More recently former Mayor Willie Brown of San Francisco attacked a *San Francisco Chronicle* reporter for exaggerating a problem regarding vandalism and drug abuse on the part of homeless people. When later reports corroborated the reporter's allegations, the mayor apologized and said he wished he could retract his words.

Many people are propelled into the public arena as a spokesperson for an issue that has the electorate enraged. Often, in the heat of the fight, these individuals decide to take on public office to further champion the cause. A word of caution for such individuals: Single-issue candidates generally make bad elected officials. Government has become a complex business that needs office holders who are engaged and attentive to the many facets of the public corporation. Too often, single-issue candidates have trouble with the wide array of duties of a given office and, once elected, sit disengaged until the governing body hits a topic that connects with their issue. It can be unsatisfying and frustrating for the office holder, fellow office holders, and the community.

Finally, another thing to keep in mind is that while you are a candidate, you should never work on other campaigns, either issue or candidate based. Voters are suspicious of candidates who appear to be manipulating an outcome in too many arenas. Your only task is to get yourself elected; once in office, work on as many campaigns as you please.

Packaging the Candidate

A political candidate is selling a lot more than political views. People are looking for an individual who will represent their community, city, school, or county in a professional way. Elected officials fulfill the role of continually answering to the public trust. If the community believes in the candidate, then they'll believe that their money is in good hands. To meet voter expectations, the candidate must always look the part.

If you have a spot on your clothing, no matter how small, change. You should not have any holes in your clothes; your shoes should be polished and your clothes buttoned, and the buttons should not be pulling or strained from a poor fit.

Because people associate weight loss with happiness and success, an overweight candidate may choose to diet and lose weight during the campaign. It's actually helpful to be disciplined in all things while campaigning, and a good diet helps keep stress levels down and appearance at an optimum. Canvassing can really help in this area. Whatever improvements can be made in your appearance and dress, make them. Attention to appearance will project a positive image, and you will look and feel the part. You and your campaign cannot afford to cut corners on your personal appearance and dress. A crumpled look may be endearing at home, but not on someone running for public office. Inattention to personal appearance translates into inattention to detail and incompetence.

Dress in a consistent style. This gives the community the impression that you are stable and know who you are. Do not do things out of character. We all remember the picture of Michael Dukakis in the military tank. Cowboy hat and boots worked for Ronald Reagan but not for Bill Clinton. When Bob Dole began dressing in khakis and running shoes in an effort to appeal to younger voters in his 1996 bid for the presidency, he looked silly. Somebody got to Bill Clinton, who began his first term in office jogging in shorts and a T-shirt that hung below the bottom of the shorts. By his second run, he had moved to the golf course, a more presidential activity. While off the course, he was rarely seen in anything other than a black suit. He was The President and looked the part of a president. One candidate in eastern Oregon who wore Pendleton shirts changed to three-piece suits midway through the campaign because his numbers were sagging at the polls. After his makeover they went down further. Behave and dress in a way that is consistent with who you are.

> *"The Constitution gives every American the inalienable right to make a damn fool of himself."*
> —John Ciardi

Recently, a candidate for a mayor's race in a large metropolitan city countered accusations that he was "uptight" by jumping into the shower with a couple of radio disc jockeys. It backfired. Voters want stability in office and are apt to run from candidates who act out of character or unpredictably. If someone accuses you of being uptight, say, "Maybe I am, but might I suggest that is exactly the kind of person we need right now." Then move back to your message, redefining uptight in terms of your strengths and with specific examples of what the city needs and how you will meet the challenge.

Image Over Ideology

The uninterested, undecided, and persuadable voters will decide on a candidate based on who they think the candidate is (image) over what the candidate says (ideology). In 1984, polls indicated that more Americans embraced the ideology of Walter Mondale over that of Ronald Reagan, and yet they voted for Reagan in overwhelming numbers. People in this important and elusive group are making their decision on the basis of a feeling they have about each of the two candidates.

> *"If you look good and dress well, you don't need a purpose in life."*
> —Robert Pante

Ideology comes into play with your base support. While a candidate may craft theme and message to get at the persuadable voter, he or she must not forget the base and what issues are important to this group. If there is any hesitancy on the part of the base to support the candidate, it must be addressed quickly and within the parameters of your theme and message. So in creating theme and message, leave room for this possibility. For example, again, in the 1996 presidential race, California's environmentalists were upset with Clinton's policies on the issues they cared about most—so much so, that many were threatening a move toward the Green Party candidate, Ralph Nader. To lock these voters in, Clinton set aside 1.7 million acres of southern Utah, the Grand Staircase–Escalante National Monument, under the Antiquities Act. For Clinton, Utah was a lock for the GOP. There was nothing he was going to do or say that would move that voter base to him, so the giveaway cost him nothing there while locking in his electoral rich California base and drawing in much-needed campaign workers from the environmental community.

"I Yam What I Yam." —Popeye

People running for office often are embarrassed about their résumés and anxious to beef them up in an effort to present a more credible image as a community leader.

What may feel like a painful biographical note to the candidate can actually be an asset. For example, if a candidate is embarrassed because she dropped out of high school, she is overlooking the possibility that having earned her GED followed by working her way through college carries more weight because of her early struggles.

Candidates and campaigns committees who are tempted to embellish personal history should think long and hard before doing so. It's a crime to place any false statement into the voters' pamphlet, and only takes an accusation by the opposition to activate an investigation.

In 1994 Wes Cooley was elected to the Second Congressional District of Oregon. During the campaign, he had claimed in the voters' pamphlet that he was a member of Phi Beta Kappa. When that statement was found to be false, the secretary of state gave Cooley the benefit of the doubt and let it go. However, in his reelection bid, two years later, he made more claims. He listed "Army Special Forces, Korea," among his qualifications, although he was never in Korea. During the investigation he claimed that it was a top-secret mission and all very hush-hush. It didn't let up. Because of his constant denials, the press took on the investigation and in so doing turned up far more than the Korea fabrication. He failed to get building permits for home improvements, the contractor had not been paid, and he and his wife were secretive about their marriage date so that she could continue to collect benefits as a Marine's widow. Cooley backed out of the race and later was indicted.

What is particularly instructive about this story is that more voters could probably relate to someone who was simply drafted and never went anywhere than to someone who claimed to be part of a secret special mission. More people do average things than the opposite. More have attended state-owned universities than private, graduated without honors than have, and most never made the football team. Don't miss the opportunity to build relationships with the average citizen by instead trying to make yourself look "more qualified."

"Voters want fraud they can believe in."

—Will Durst

Manners Matter

As important as dress and appearance are, there is more to looking the part of a serious public servant than that. The candidate must adopt the kind of manners a mother would be proud of. Do not eat with your mouth open, pick your nose, clean your ears, or floss in public. Cover your mouth when you yawn. A few years back, a candidate running for office called and asked to meet with me to "touch bases." During our forty-five-minute meeting he must have yawned five times, and not once did he cover his mouth. I cannot remember what we talked about, but I remember his uvula.

When appearing as a dinner speaker, you should eat only moderately at the event or, better yet, have a light meal beforehand. You cannot afford to have a stomach upset from nervous energy and certainly can't afford to burp through the speech. One candidate I worked for would eat a full meal at the head table before rising to give his speech. During the speech he would need to burp, but for some reason this guy always burped by turning his head sideways. I watched as he did this a couple of times and noticed the audience turning their heads with the candidate's. In general, eating and greeting don't mix well for candidates, which is ironic given that food and drink are often the bait used to pull potential supporters to a political event.

Avoid drinking alcohol while running for public office. Besides the fact that alcohol adds empty calories and affects ability to deal with stress, people have tons of issues around alcohol and it's not worth the grief or uncertainty of how drinking, even as little as one glass of wine, will play. Similarly, if you're a smoker, keep it closeted.

Bring along a sweater or light jacket to cover up possible nervous perspiration. Wear deodorant and clean shirts. Previously worn clothes can carry body odor that might be activated with nervous perspiration. Go light on perfume and aftershave. Do not chew gum. Bring breath mints, but don't be a candidate who pulls out the little bottle of breath freshener and squirts it mid-sentence. In fact, avoid all public grooming: hair combing, lipstick, and the like. Also, avoid problems by thinking ahead. For instance, when I get nervous, my mouth gets dry, so I always go to the podium with a glass of water.

As I said before, a woman candidate should leave her children at home. Not only does that enable her to be more focused, it also meets the voters' need to see her in a professional role. It is difficult for many people to accept a woman as a leader if the only image of her they have includes children clinging to her. This is absolutely *not* true for men. In fact, men are given bonus points for being seen with their children. Society assumes that men are professional, and seeing a man with his children gives the voters the idea that they are getting a glimpse into his private life. He seems warmer (figure 9.1).

Groomers

Given the importance of image, it's a good idea to have a "groomer" for the campaign. As a candidate, I generally recruited a friend whose only campaign job was to let me know how I looked and to make suggestions on what I should wear and how to better project my image. In all three of my campaigns for mayor, I had a groomer who proved to be invaluable. In my second run for mayor, I was to be on television in a debate with my two male opponents, and my groomer advised me to dress conservatively. Both of my opponents showed up dressed very casually and looked less than professional to the television audience. The show repeated seven or eight times throughout the campaign cycle.

"You'd be surprised how much it costs to look this cheap."
—Dolly Parton

The next campaign debate was covered by the media but not broadcast live. My groomer predicted that my principal opponent, having looked casual for the televised debate, would try to make up for that mistake by dressing conservatively for this one. He advised me to wear my hair differently and dress in a brightly colored dress that I had rarely been seen in. The idea was that I should stand out to the live audience.

I did as I was told. My opponent, as predicted, wore a three-piece black suit and appeared quite intense, severe, even funereal. I had time before the debate to say hello and chat with members of the audience and to enjoy myself. My appearance was friendly, and I was clearly having a good time. My opponent did not smile and seemed out of place, strapped in his television

Photo courtesy of SOHS

While Jeff Golden chats with supporters, daughter Sarah Beth gets an eyeful of photographer.

Golden celebrates wir

New commisioner's daughter accompanies him

Candidates each bring their own style and special approach to politics, sometimes they carry a lot of political baggage.

But only Jeff Golden carries a baby on his back.

For much of Tuesday evening – ev live TV interview – the Ashland D wore a baby backpack that held hi daughter, Sarah Beth, born a year ; giving.

Figure 9.1 A Candidate with a Baby. When it comes to children, there is a double standard in society that carries over into campaigning. Whereas women are penalized for campaigning with their children, men are rewarded.

armor. The difference between us was dramatic, and the debate proved to be a turning point in the campaign.

When I work for other candidates, I usually assign a groomer as well. I look for a man or woman with an eye for fashion and detail. If my candidate needs a haircut, I try to get him or her the best available. Have the campaign pick up the cost of a studio photo shoot. The groomer and I will often discuss the kind of look we want out of the shoot and share those ideas with the candidate and the photographer. For example, if I have a candidate who smiles very little and is somewhat hesitant, I look for a photo where he or she leans into the lens. Whatever may be a weakness of your candidate in personality or appearance, your photo shoot is an opportunity to make it look otherwise. Many believe that a photo starting low, looking up at the candidate, projects power and one from above angled down, the opposite. Personally I think nostril shots are unflattering and don't use them. I like the photographer to work with the camera coming straight on. See figure 2.1A for examples of candidate photos that work well.

A groomer must be willing to attend debates and observe the candidate's behavior. I usually like to talk with the groomer after an event to discuss how delivery can be improved; we then talk to

"Non-verbal cues are as or more important than verbal cues."
—Malcolm Gladwell

the candidate and discuss adjustments. All such suggestions, however, should be cushioned with lots of praise. Candidates' egos can be fragile, and you don't want them to be self-conscious at the next event.

Pick and choose your events carefully. Do not say yes to every coffee or speaking-engagement offer that comes your way. As campaign manager, think ahead about where you intend to spend time and energy, and go where the votes (and money) are. Take into consideration your candidate's personality. For example, minimize the amount of time in public for the candidate who is awkward in a crowd. Also, remember that candidates who go to events of strong supporters often get in trouble. This is especially true late in the cam-

"Enlightenment will be extinguished. . . unless applied. . . to the machinery of political and legislative action."
—Margaret Sanger

paign cycle, when candidates are tired and let their guard down. Part of your job is to keep your candidate from saying something stupid, and sometimes the easiest way to do that is to keep him or her away from gatherings where it is more apt to happen.

Stay on Your Message

Don't let your opponent pull you off message. Ever.

The candidate's image is important, because voters need to be able to identify with him or her. However, the candidate and the campaign team must know who will support the candidate and why. The reason that people vote a specific way will become the basis for your campaign message. Develop that message to build relationships between the candidate and the voters. A benchmark poll can really help here.

List all the candidate's positives and why the team feels that voters will support this individual. That list might include programs the candidate has been involved with, stands on controversial issues, votes in previous offices, vision, character, and experience. It might be nothing more than a clear list of issues and beliefs that the candidate embraces.

You must also develop a list of issues and concerns that might hurt the candidate's support. (There should be a fair amount of overlap between the lists of positives and negatives.) It is this list that you will use in preparing the candidate for negative questions and in formulating strategies to defuse negative perceptions. For example, if the candidate has an image of being slick, the team sends him to neighborhood meetings where he can be seen as one of the crowd. This requires a candidate who is open to observation and criticism, and a close campaign team to develop the campaign message.

"No man ever listened himself out of a job."

—Calvin Coolidge

Once you have developed your campaign message and strategy, stick to it. When your opponent hits you, respond and move the discussion right back to your message. When appropriate, go after your opponent's campaign inconsistencies and weaknesses.

The campaign team will work only as hard as the candidate or campaign leader. So work hard. Keep in mind that the public, besides looking for a community representative and leader, is observing everything during the campaign: your stand on issues, your presence and composure, your appearance, how you handle stress, and your ability to answer their questions. In particular the public is looking for how well you react under pressure and how hard you work to get into office. That will tell them something about whether they can expect you to keep your head and work hard once you are in office.

Staying on message can be particularly hard for candidates under attack. It's important to respond to attacks, but how you do translates into whether you're on your campaign theme and message or have moved over to that of your opponent. In a recent local campaign for district attorney, the incumbent's opponent was accusing him of running an inefficient office. The incumbent had an increasing caseload with a stagnant tax base. The challenger had left the DA's office a few years before to go into private practice and now wanted back in as boss.

The incumbent, being the *first* to speak at the debate, stood and said: "I would take issue with anyone who says I'm not running my office efficiently." Boom, he was on his opponent's message. The following day the debate was covered in the local paper. The headline: "DA denies allegations of mismanagement."

How could this have been handled differently? First, the DA could have laid out to the audience the dramatic increase in caseload, decrease in staff, and marginalized tax base that, with inflation, translated to less, not more, real dollars. He could have suggested that his opponent left his job at the DA's office because of a workload that pales in comparison to the current one. He could have compared tax dollars expended per case today and in the past. He could have talked about the increasing complexity of some crimes being committed, requiring additional court time, legal process, and resources. In short, he could have promoted his achievements while preempting any criticism that his opponent might be tempted to wage and done it all without sounding defensive. He would be safe under the umbrella of disclosure.

While looking professional, minding your manners, working hard, and being on message, you must find some way to minimize stress. One way is to listen to your campaign manager. Another is to do nothing that, once done, will lead you to tell a lie.

One dramatic example of a lie gone bad occurred a few years back when a county commissioner was undergoing a recall in another part of the state. The recall looked dead, even though its proponents were able to gather the signatures and actually get it to a vote. It was a vote-by-mail election, and, as is often the case in vote by mail, the computer spit out a few ballots where signatures did not quite line up. One of these was the wife of the county commissioner targeted in the recall. The local elections office, in conjunction with the secretary of state's office, asked the county commissioner if the ballot had, in fact, been signed by his wife or someone else. The commissioner said his wife did indeed sign it. They checked again, and it still came out as a no match. They asked the commissioner and his wife again. Both said she signed it. The secretary of state's office continued to press. Finally the commissioner confessed to signing his wife's ballot because she was in the hospital and directed him to do so. While the commissioner had easily beaten the recall, he now had to resign, and was charged with and convicted of a Class C Felony. Obviously he shouldn't have signed the ballot to begin with, but had he said from the get-go, "My wife asked me to take care of it for her while she was in the hospital, isn't that OK?" the secretary of state would very likely have said, "No, don't do it again" and dropped the matter.

If a candidate is caught in a lie while on the campaign trail, it is sudden death. As one of the ten commandments of campaigning and one of the cardinal sins, being caught in a provable lie is about the worst thing that can happen to a candidate.

In the 2002 general election in Oregon, a Democratic candidate for the house was to attend and speak at a Coalition for School Funding Now meeting. The campaign between the Democratic challenger and the Republican incumbent had been very friendly, and in fact it had been the incumbent who had suggested that his opponent jump in the race and run against him. As a candidate, the Democrat was a dream: She was involved in schools, church, community groups. She was well organized, articulate, and hardworking. She had a supportive extended family and a great campaign team. She was such a good candidate that in a poll conducted in the last days of the campaign, she was ahead of the incumbent by twenty points.

Needless to say, the campaign was confident of the election so when the Coalition meeting was in conflict with another gathering, the candidate and her campaign manager split the duties, with the manager attending one while the candidate attended the Coalition meeting. Unfortunately, the candidate, who had a full work and volunteer schedule without a campaign, got away a little late. She then misread the directions, got lost on the way to the meeting, and arrived later than comfortable for all concerned. As a result, the candidate was flustered and off center, and the coalition group was irritated.

After the meeting, the state Republican Party sent a direct mail piece to the district saying that the Democrat was in favor of a sales tax to resolve Oregon's budget shortfall. Since the allegation was attributed to the Coalition for School Funding Now meeting, the campaign committee asked the candidate if she had said *anything* that would lead the other party to believe that she supported a statewide sales tax. The candidate, who had been repeatedly schooled by her committee never to talk about a sales tax, said no. Just to be sure, the campaign manager called a couple of people she knew had attended the Coalition meeting and asked them if the candidate had said she supported a sales tax during any part of the meeting. They said no.

The candidate and her campaign committee were outraged at the attack and so, along with the Democratic campaign office, registered a complaint with the secretary of state's office. The investigation uncovered an audiotape made by a staff member of the Republican Majority Office who had attended the Coalition meeting. On the tape the candidate could clearly be heard saying that she would support a sales tax if all other avenues were exhausted and if it included a reduction in the state income tax. The comment was made after an audience member and school advocate repeatedly pressed the candidate to make a stand on a sales tax. The twenty-point lead disappeared as the tape hit the airwaves, and the Democrat lost the election by 92 votes, out of 11,418 votes cast.

Set aside the whole sales tax issue: If the voters do not understand a lie, they will not forgive it. Being caught in a provable lie is a cardinal sin; it's death to a campaign. While the general response would be to focus in on the mistake made by the candidate, there were many leading up to it that should not be overlooked either.

First, it is not enough for a campaign committee to tell a candidate never to discuss a topic. While that can be the directive, there should also be a "what if" scenario that the committee works out with the candidate. In the above example, a red flag for the committee would be that the candidate personally was not against a sales tax. If the candidate holds an opinion that could cost support if openly expressed, the issue must be addressed in the war room. The team and the candidate should have covered all appropriate responses should this occasion ever arise, such as: "Once elected I will look at every revenue stream just as I will look at every expenditure. Without the opportunity to first examine where we are spending money, it would be premature for me to talk about revenue streams to remedy the budget deficit." Further, I have sat in many war rooms where a difficult issue was brought up for discussion and had the candidate say, "We don't need to go over that; I have an answer." Whenever a candidate says this, ask to hear the answer.

Second, there should always be a committee member present at public forums. Even if it cannot be the campaign manager, there must be someone who can go with the candidate or meet the candidate at an event. What typically happens in the final days of a campaign is that good candidates who are really very trustworthy are left to cover ground on their own. But things happen, and you need someone from the committee to help communicate with the war room.

Third, candidates must allow enough time to get to an event. It is the obligation of the campaign committee to get clear directions and a phone number to call should any mishaps occur en route. Ask a volunteer to drive the route if it is new to the candidate and call in directions and distances. Print out a map and directions from a program such as MapQuest for the candidate. Whatever it takes, getting to an event should not be stressful for the candidate.

Fourth, once the candidate is late, he or she should still take some time to gather composure and acknowledge to the group that she has made them wait. In other words, center the audience. Start with a personal and warm story. Something that happened on the campaign trail that the group would love to hear. If you don't, you run the risk of having hecklers—especially among your saints. In politics, teams love to eat their own.

Fifth, a candidate must be aware of what he or she says and not hang the committee out to dry. In this example, if the candidate had remembered what she said, she could have brought this back to the committee and damage control would have been implemented. Unfortunately, candidates are so overloaded that their memories cannot be trusted. (See the second item above.)

Sixth, supportive groups need to cut a candidate some slack. People running for office are spending insane amounts of time to secure positions that typically result in a pay reduction while they serve—not to mention huge amounts of time away from family. For a member of a group supportive of a candidate to choose to press and press and press an inflammatory issue is both stupid and counterproductive.

Finally, one must question why a candidate who, as a school official, was loved throughout the education community accepted an invitation to speak at a Coalition for School Funding Now meeting in the first place. Going to the saints pulls time and energy from other activities—and might even cost you the election. That said, candidates love to speak to groups who are supportive. So much of campaign work is difficult and stressful, and attending a meeting of "friends" feels good. The flip side is that when candidates go to supportive groups in the final days, they are often very tired, they let down their guard, and they say something they shouldn't. It happens all the time.

A follow-up on this last point: I have found that support groups can be some of the hardest on a candidate. They still want "their" time with the candidate and frequently make requests for the candidate to attend non-fund-raising events put on by their saints. For example, toward the end of the 2002 general election cycle our district office received a call from the campaign for the Democratic gubernatorial candidate. The campaign wanted to know if the state representative I work with could attend a Jackson County Democratic Central Committee meeting in place of the gubernatorial candidate. Folks, if you're a member of the "team," give candidates a break; make as few demands on their time as possible. Your job is to give money, write letters, volunteer, deliver the votes, and help the candidate woo the saveables.

> *"The question, 'who ought to be boss?' is like asking 'who ought to be the tenor in the quartet?' Obviously, the man who can sing tenor."*
>
> —Henry Ford

Outsider Campaign vs. Incumbent Campaign

Outsiders

If you are in government already, you are an insider; if not, you're an outsider. Insiders and outsiders typically run very different campaigns, because the voters expect the insider to defend what government is doing and the outsider to challenge it with a fresh outlook. In reality, however, skillful politicians who have been in office for years have, when the need arises, waged outsider campaigns against first-time candidates. Insider or outsider status is as much a state of mind as a fact. Whatever the actual status of the candidate, insider and outsider campaigns require distinctly different strategies.

> *"People that are really very weird can get into sensitive positions and have a tremendous impact on history."*
>
> —Dan Quayle

To run an outsider's campaign, you must first legitimize yourself through establishment endorsement (no matter how tangential the endorsement might be). The public record the incumbent has amassed while in office actually defines that person—but in terms of image, not specifics. If you're an outsider, it's important for your team to define the test the voters will apply. Obviously you want to stay away from experience, since an incumbent would easily pass that test. Your best hope is to define the test the voters will apply as that of "time for a change." Ultimately, as an outsider, it is more important that you present sound reasons for why an incumbent should be cast out of office than for why you should be elected.

Attacks on the system are effective if they plant seeds of doubt about how things are being done or where attention and public money are being focused. You cannot just throw complaints against a wall to see what sticks. You have to know what you're talking about. Research how things have worked or not worked and explain them to the voters. Remember, you must sound like a potential office holder rather than a malcontent. That requires offering solutions, not just criticizing. This is where your homework really pays off.

Before my first run for mayor, I went to the local college library, checked out ten years of city council minutes, and read them all. I also checked out every current report on every system in which the city had hired a consultant. I read the city's comprehensive plan and the downtown plan. This put me at a decided advantage: Because it was so fresh in my mind I could recall the information more quickly than my opponent, who had been a sitting city councilor for ten years. Incumbents who live through the events compiled in such reports while in office will find it difficult to recall the details, and they make matters worse by believing they can. Typically, an incumbent will underprepare for an election.

Incumbents
If you are an incumbent, you must show that the average citizen still supports you and show how, working cooperatively with other elected officials,

you have made a positive contribution. In other words, your campaign should make the test applied by the voters that of "experience and accomplishment." This is a strong theme when voters have a grasp of the complexities of government. Again, your public record defines who you are. But avoid looking at each vote individually. This definition is more about image than specifics. Although you may not actually use the word, stick close to a theme of "proven" leadership. Make your record the focal point of the campaign by using examples that the average person will understand and that apply to the day-to-day lives of those being served. Avoid speaking in governmentalese—that is, using acronyms and jargon that only those in government would know.

Whether you are the incumbent or the challenger, you should list all personality characteristics of both the office holder and the challenger, both strengths and weaknesses. Your objective is to contrast your strengths with your opponent's weaknesses.

Your Opponent

You may breathe a sigh of relief when you discover that you are unopposed in your election or groan when you find that at the last minute someone has filed to run against you. However, an opponent in any campaign is a blessing. Without an opponent, your race will be ignored by the press, and the programs and issues you want to get before the voters will be that much more difficult and expensive to get there. If you are involved in a hotly contested race, the press will more likely provide front-page coverage, which greatly reduces the amount of advertising you will have to buy.

If you have a primary race in which you are unopposed, you may never build the momentum and party support that are necessary to win the general election. Do not lament if someone declares against you. Thank your lucky stars and organize a great campaign. Bring forward programs you want to begin or to maintain, and use the election as a mandate to muscle these into place. Use the campaign as a reminder of who you are and what you stand for and as a rallying point to get people behind your efforts.

"What is noble can be said in any language, and what is mean should be said in none."

—Maimonides

Some voters need something to vote *for*, while others need something to vote *against*. Voters who are more motivated by one candidate's negatives than the opposition's positives lie at the heart of negative campaigning. Average voters watch the debate unfold in the paper and on the news and listen to see who makes sense and who doesn't. Others get outraged by a candidate's track record or by inane arguments from the opposition and decide to vote for your cause although they normally would not. Without the missteps and misstatements of your opposition, you might never get the necessary support to push your campaign over the top.

Debates

Don't use debates to attack your opponent; rather use them to tell what you know and would do once elected.

Debates can be turning points for a campaign or amount to nothing. I've seen amazing mistakes made during debates that had little or no effect on the campaign and seen other items that should have gone unnoticed blow up. There are a number of ways you and your campaign committee can minimize the risk factor and make a debate work in your favor. Small precautions include familiarizing yourself with the room before the event and making sure that some friendly faces are in the audience. However, preparation is your best tool for positioning yourself. When you are well prepared, political debates are surprisingly easy and great fun. As a political candidate, you should welcome the showiness of debates, the pressure, and the opportunity to get your opinions in front of voters. When you have successfully positioned yourself as a candidate, people recognize who you are and what you do. You make sense to them.

"Sometimes when you look in his eyes you get the feeling that someone else is driving."

—David Letterman

The central rule of debating is that the voters should know more after the debate than they did before. Come armed with lots of information. In my third run for mayor I had the advantage of being well versed in city matters—and even though I was the incumbent, I studied like crazy to prepare for all six of my debates. In the first debate, I was shocked at how uninformed my opponent was in city matters. He had seemingly done little or nothing to prepare for the event. I thought, boy, this is going to be easy. But with each debate that followed, my opponent took, verbatim, statistics and anecdotal examples that I had used in previous debates and presented them to each new audience as though they were his thoughts and his research. It really threw me. I couldn't say, "Hey, you sound just like me," or "That's exactly what I said last week," without sounding like I was petty, whining, accusatory, or on the attack. Every debate was before a new audience who had never heard either of us, so they assumed he was delivering his spiel, not mine. In hindsight, I should have had a campaign supporter at each event who would, as the pattern unfolded, call him on it.

"I will never apologize for the United States of America—I don't care what the facts are."

—George Bush

To get ready for a political debate, choose eight to ten subjects that are of interest to you and/or the community. You should include among them issues that are part of your campaign platform. For each of the subjects you have chosen, list the information and points that you feel are relevant on one side of a 5-by-8-inch index card. Use only one card per subject and only one side of the card.

For example, development in the forest interface is of great concern in my community. As an incumbent, I would list on a card all that government (with my help) has done to limit development in these fire-prone areas as well as fire mitigation implemented on existing structures. On the right side, I would list remaining concerns of fire danger and what government still needs to do to make the forest and the community safer. If I were running an outsider's campaign, for the same subject I would list all that is being done, how that is not enough, what has gone wrong (being specific), and exactly what I would do to correct the course. This information is just listed on the card, not written out. The idea is to be very familiar with the information before the debate and to use the cards to focus what you want to talk about, not exactly what you will say.

Once you have the subject cards filled out, choose a separate color for each card and color a single stripe along the top of each card in a particular color. For example, your card for budget issues might be red; for forest interface, brown; for park issues, green; for recycling, yellow; for air quality, blue; for transportation, black; and so on. Once the cards are color-coded, the appropriate card can be found at a glance. By color-coding in advance, you can avoid disorienting yourself looking through all the cards to find the one you want. Once you have the card you need for a particular subject on top of the stack, you can glance at it while looking around the audience. When looking at the cards, you should appear to be collecting your thoughts rather than reading.

Do not kid yourself that you can guess all the subjects or questions that will be asked in a debate. You will undoubtedly prepare for areas that are never addressed and have nothing for areas that are covered. Even so, with the preparation done ahead of time, you will be much more relaxed and "on" during the debate. Be sure to bring extra blank cards to jot down thoughts during the debate. This will help you remember on rebuttal what you want to say.

Familiarize yourself with any ballot measures coming before the voters or any initiative petitions being circulated. Either the press or your opponent may ask you about your position on these issues, so have a clear idea of where you stand and why.

The importance of your image and how you present yourself cannot be overstated. Smiling and speaking clearly and slowly enough so those in the audience can hear and understand is very important. A certain amount of tension surrounds a campaign in general and a debate in particular, and people will notice how you deal with that tension. Be aware that your image gets projected in a hundred ways.

Below are some of the more famous examples of debate situations in which one candidate appeared to greater advantage than his opponent—either by chance or design.

"There was a gap between what went on in his mind and what came out of his mouth."

—James M. Cain

Before a 1960 Kennedy-Nixon televised debate, Kennedy's team checked out the studio location for the debate a few days earlier and found it set up with a drab, gray background. To contrast with the background, Kennedy was told to wear a dark-blue suit and spend some time under a sun lamp. The hope was that he would project an image of youth and vigor. Kennedy was also told to look directly at Nixon when Nixon spoke, and to look directly at the cameras (his audience) when he spoke. This would show that Kennedy had respect for what people had to say, even his opponent, and that he could communicate with the nation. Kennedy's advisers also found out that Nixon had hurt his leg while campaigning, so they requested that the two candidates stand. During the debate, Nixon looked tired. He was poorly made-up, and he was ill. He shifted about because of his leg pain, and he perspired under the hot lights of the studio.

In the second debate between Ford and Carter, Ford was asked about the Soviet sphere of influence in Eastern Europe. He responded saying there was no Soviet domination in Eastern Europe.

In the Reagan-Carter debate in 1980, the president said he asked Amy, his daughter, what she thought was the most pressing issue facing the world, and her response was nuclear weapons. The opposition assumed correctly that Americans would be uncomfortable with teenager Amy Carter as a presidential political adviser and made it a campaign issue. In the same debate, Reagan scored big points by crossing the stage to shake hands with the President.

In the Reagan-Mondale debate, President Reagan said, "The nation's poverty rate has begun to decline, but it is still going up." Comments like this brought the factor of his age to the race, but only briefly.

In the Bush-Dukakis debate, Dukakis was asked whether he would change his mind about capital punishment if someone raped and killed his wife, Kitty. Dukakis's response lacked passion and emotion. Some said he framed his answer no differently than if he were asked whether he preferred a dill pickle to relish.

And finally, a defining moment in the Gore-Bush race had to be the first debate in which Al Gore harrumphed and rolled his eyes at responses given by George W. Bush. Just as looking respectfully at Nixon while he spoke gave Kennedy an advantage, the inverse caused Gore to falter and ultimately struggle for the remainder of the campaign.

Fielding Negative Questions

Think of everything as a gift or opportunity.

You will very likely get nasty questions and innuendos during a debate. Look at such questions as an opportunity to show how well you respond under fire. People know that being subjected to negativity is part of serving in public office, and they will want to see how you handle it. Never be defensive. If possible, be humble and self-effacing; if you can come up with a little joke that turns the attack to your advantage, so much the better. Find anything that uses the ammunition of the opposition and redirects it at them. If you redirect attacks, it is important to do so with class, without sounding defensive, and with poise. This is your opportunity to sound smart. Being quick on your feet is not a function of IQ but of preparedness, confidence, and poise.

Grace Under Pressure

Your campaign committee should help you list everything that is a weakness: every vote, every misstatement, every missed meeting, all of it. They should also list everything on which your candidate may appear vulnerable: past voting records, who is paying for the campaign, special-interest support, inconsistencies in statements and deeds. Once this level of homework is done, you will be much more comfortable.

In general, there are four options for responding to an attack:

1. I did not do it.
2. I did it, *but* it's not like you think.
3. I did it, I'm sorry, I won't do it again.
4. Attack the source.

If you are attacked and do not respond, you are presumed guilty, especially if the attack is considered fair. When you do respond, you should do so on the same level as the attack. For example, if you were attacked in a letter-to-the-editor, respond with a letter-to-the-editor.

Fatal Flaws

One way to prepare yourself for attacks is to sit with your campaign team and brainstorm on every possible negative question that might come your way. Practice responding to questions concerning your weaknesses. Listing the "fatal flaws" of a candidate or measure allows discussion within your support group where the team can deliberate on the best possible responses. These responses may be placed according to topic on your 5-by-8-inch cards for handy reference during the debate. Even if the attack is not *exactly* what your team predicted, this level of preparation lends comfort, poise, and organization to the candidate, resulting in better responses in high-pressure situations.

Here are examples of how to capitalize on negative questions. In my second bid for mayor, I responded to criticism of city budget increases by explaining that I was the only member of the budget committee who voted no on the last budget. Later in the campaign, my opponent pointed out (during a debate) that when this same budget came before the city council for final approval, the council vote was split. He went on to point out that I failed to cast the tie-breaking no vote and instead voted yes. Why, he asked, if I was so opposed to the budget during the budget process, was I unwilling to vote no at the council level?

Until that moment, I had forgotten that the budget came before the council when two members were away and two (for odd reasons) voted no. That left only two voting yes. As mayor, I was to cast the deciding vote. As I went to the podium to respond, I pulled out my color-coded budget card.

"I really didn't say everything I said."
—Yogi Berra

From the card, I was able to outline the exact issues on which I had concern as a budget committee member. After relating those concerns to the audience, I explained that I lost my appeal to the budget committee to delve into those issues further and explained that the committee ultimately adopted the budget. Having been outvoted at the committee level, I suggested to the audience that it would be disingenuous to veto, in effect, the budget by casting a no vote in a tiebreaker. I therefore voted to put in place the will of the majority of the committee and council, even if I personally disagreed with some budget provisions.

Because I was prepared, my opponent gave me what I could not get on my own: the opportunity to show that I had good reasons to vote against the budget during the budget process and that once outvoted, I was able to set aside my differences with the budget committee. As an incumbent, I was able to demonstrate that I was still willing to challenge the process and yet be a team player.

At another debate one opponent brought up a program that I had initiated to use volunteers to clear fuel (dead and dying brush) from the forest interface. He cited how the program had been a miserable failure and had placed the city at risk of potential litigation because of possible worker (volunteer) injury. I picked up my forest card and took the microphone. I said that while the outcome of the program had been different from what was first envisioned, it raised community awareness of the need to mitigate fire danger. Moreover, the voters needed to make a decision for the future: Did they want leadership that never tried anything out of fear of failure or leadership that solved problems creatively at the risk of an occasional partial success?

> *"Earlier today the senator called a spade a spade. He later issued a retraction."*
>
> —Joe Mirachi

By using this attack as a gift, I was able to direct attention to the limited success of the program and then shift back to my message, which was strong, creative leadership: leadership willing to take risks.

Another approach to leading or negative questions is the "Yeah, so?" response. For example, the opposition might say, "Since you became mayor, the city has acquired more and more programs that should be run by the private sector." Your "Yeah, so?" response might be, "I'm sorry. How is this a problem? The proof is in the pudding. We are extraordinarily successful at providing a broad range of outstanding programs, programs that our community may never have enjoyed if left to the private sector. And we do so while saving the taxpayers money." While you may not use these exact words, this is the tone: "Yeah, so? What's your point?"

In Debates, Attacks Can Backfire

Hitting your opponent with a negative during a debate is somewhat unpredictable. Do it carefully. Here is an example of how it can backfire: I worked for a candidate whose opponent, an incumbent, was receiving lots of PAC money. My candidate wanted to hit the incumbent for taking special-interest money. Because the campaign team had heard rumors that the incumbent had a story to die for whenever he was hit on PAC money, the campaign team felt an attack was dangerous.

At the next debate, however, our candidate went after the credibility of the incumbent based on the PAC money coming in. Our candidate implied that the incumbent was bought and owned because so much of his money came from PACs and so little from citizens. True to the rumors, the opponent stood up and said that when he was first elected, a supporter who had given a three-thousand-dollar campaign contribution visited his office at the capital. According to the story, the contributor was looking for a particular vote on a bill and felt that the size of the campaign contribution warranted this vote. Our opponent went on to say that after hearing the demand, he went to the bank, took out a personal loan, and returned the money to the contributor. He concluded by saying that no one owned his vote.

In about thirty seconds our opponent not only killed the whole PAC money attack, but showed that he was poor like everyone else in the room—he had to take out a personal loan to pay off the contributor—and that he had integrity. In hindsight, this attack would have taken on new meaning if our campaign had been able to point out exact figures on campaign contributions and accompanying votes that appeared to follow PAC money.

In debates you just never know how your opponent will turn an attack around. So, unless armed with concrete information, avoid rehearsed attacks. If, however, your opponent leaves himself open, seize the opportunity. For example, a few years back a Democrat and a Republican were facing off for a U.S. Senate seat. The Democrat had been criticizing the Republican for using federal superfund money for cleanup of industrial waste in his family-owned business. During a debate, the Republican, who was worth millions, was challenged by the Democrat to pay back the money to the taxpayers. The Republican stood and said, "I'll pay it back just as soon as you pay back the honoraria you said you would never take when you ran for Congress." The Democrat in a very flustered voice said, "Why, why, you've insulted my integrity!"

This is an opportunity that doesn't come along very often. The Democrat should have seen this coming and been ready. He missed an opportunity to reach into his pocket to pull out a checkbook and say, "Deal! I'll pay back all the money I received for giving speeches. You get out your checkbook and do the same for the federal cleanups, which amounts to $XYZ. And, while you're at it, make it out to the federal deficit, because the only way we're going to get our arms around it is if those that *have* stop taking from those that *don't*." While the Democrat had received thousands in honoraria, the Republican had received millions—an easy exchange.

Developing Your Public Speaking Skills

Before my very first debate as a candidate I was genuinely excited about what was ahead of me. I was charged up and armed with enough information to handle any question thrown at me. Afterward I thought I'd done a great job. So when someone from the audience handed me a slip of paper, I was certain it would be the name and address of a potential campaign volunteer. The note said: "You said 'um' 48 times during your speech and the question and answer period that followed. Why don't you join us at Toastmasters?"

Unless you're a top-notch public speaker—either a natural or an actor, you need to get some skills and you need to get them quickly. Even after three campaigns and twelve years in public office, I still got nervous before a speech; it didn't matter how perfunctory it was or how young the audience. But remember, it isn't what you say that's important but rather how you say it. Given how quickly people form opinions of candidates, the candidate who gets some early help in giving speeches will have a longer shelf life than the candidate who receives none. Training in public speaking does not need to take a whole lot of time and can ultimately make the journey much more enjoyable.

The following describe three simple things the candidate and team can do to improve speech-giving, debates, and public appearances.

1. The On-Camera Interview. Have a friend or campaign worker with a video camera, ideally one that approximates those used by newspeople, ask the candidate questions that might come up in the process of running for office. The team can go over questions ahead of time, but the candidate should not know them. That said, do not spend a lot of time worrying about the questions; the objective of this exercise is not to see how well your candidate answers but rather how well she handles herself. In addition to general questions, ask some that are personal and a little borderline, like, "How do your children feel about you running for office?" and "Do you think being Hispanic will help or hurt your chances?" The interview can run, say, fifteen to twenty minutes.

After the interview, the candidate and someone with experience in public speaking should go over the video. Ask the debate coach at the high school, a newsperson, a friend who will be honest, or someone involved in public speaking. Look at everything:

- What's behind the candidate? Remember, for interviews, the candidate can almost always choose the backdrop and setting. If a reporter wants to interview you, they generally come to you. Always look around and see what will be behind you. If seated, choose your chair carefully; do not sit in overstuffed chairs, which can affect delivery and make a candidate look slumpy. You want a setting that will further the image you want to project. Choose the wicker furniture on the front porch, the horse corral, a park, a garden, or the living room. If you are outside, remember that the sun must be in your eyes, so orient yourself accordingly.

- Look at the candidate's clothes, mannerisms, eyes, hair, everything. Does the candidate have verbal tics, scratch his chest, toe the ground, stroke his chin, fluff his hair, or jut the chin? Does she hold her hand to her cheek when seated? Does she do a "pretend" yawn? Tap her foot?
- Finally, does the candidate answer the questions in a direct manner?

In this exercise, it does not matter if the interviewer is in the picture, so the person behind the camera can be the one asking the questions. When we do this for candidates, the camera is set on a tripod with the interviewer asking questions while running the camera.

> *"The Republican Party stands for: Anti-bigotry, anti-Semitism, anti-racism."*
> —George Bush

2. Mock Debates. Mock debates are really fun and very helpful for a candidate. To do a successful one, you must have a moderator, an opponent, and an audience. High school government teachers, newspaper reporters (though not those who will be covering the campaign), and people who are politically active and involved make the best audience. Your objective is to have seven or eight people who are well versed in public speaking and politics, are smart, and can communicate suggestions without offending the candidate. Rearrange the furniture in the living room so that it looks more like a classroom. Use bar stools for the real and the pretend candidate to perch on. The moderator should be armed with questions that most certainly will come up in a campaign. This is the time to focus on your questions. Let all involved know that everyone will be in character throughout the mock debate. The moderator should be dressed up, and whoever is playing the opposition candidate should study how that candidate dresses, moves, answers questions, and attacks in real life. This does not take long: Read the literature and watch him or her on a commercial, interview, or public appearance, and you're there.

> *"Well, I would—if they realized that we—again if—if we led them back to that stalemate only because that our retaliatory power, our seconds, or strike at them after our first strike, would be so destructive that they couldn't afford it, that would hold them off."*
> —Ronald Reagan, when asked if nuclear war could be limited to tactical weapons

Have everything in place when the real candidate and the pretend opponent arrive. Establish guidelines and time the answers, just as they would be in a real debate.

After the debate, questions are taken from the audience and answered by both the real candidate and the pretend opponent. If the campaign is concerned about how the candidate will respond to a question, this would be the time to have someone in the audience persist in asking it.

This is followed by a frank discussion of the candidate's performance, of which questions posed problems, and what made the candidate defensive. Cover body language, the brevity and clarity of answers, hair style, and clothes: everything.

Most public speakers are best when they have a command of the material and can talk off the top of their head. However, if you are working with a candidate whom you have told time and again not to read speeches because he or she is horrible at it, be sure to send the debate questions ahead of time. In general, candidates read because they feel uncertain of their ability. If you provide the questions ahead of time and a clear directive that reading is not a choice, the candidate will prepare content and only fret about delivery. Helping a candidate gain confidence works best if specific aspects of a debate or speech are isolated and worked on one at a time. You don't teach someone to swim by throwing him in the deep end.

"He can compress the most words into the smallest idea of any man I ever met."

—Abraham Lincoln

Be sure to have someone videotape the mock debate so the candidate and team can review it later.

Recently we set up a mock debate for a novice candidate. The candidate was given questions ahead of time, and the audience was also prepped. I served as the moderator, and my husband, Rick Shaw, who headed up the television media team, volunteered to role-play the opponent. In preparation for his part, Rick read direct mail, white papers, the brochure, and newspaper ads and studied the mannerisms and dress of the opponent. Rick was the opposition in nearly every way—vaguely answering questions and subtly going after our client as we had seen the opponent do in real debates. The reporter who attended was smart and direct with questions, as were a U.S. history teacher from the high school, a teacher from the middle school, and an assortment of people from the war room.

The whole debate took over two hours, including the question-and-answer period that followed. It was very successful except for one thing: The candidate was furious with Rick after the debate, in much the same way opposing candidates are in real elections—so much so that she never watched the video of the mock debate.

However, at the next debate, when the "real" opponent (who, by the way, was dressed identically to my husband, right down to the American flag on his lapel) seemingly reenacted what had occurred at the mock debate, our candidate was brilliant. Her response to a demeaning comment made by her opponent brought the conservative crowd to a round of boisterous applause. She was so good and her opponent so bad that we cut an ad of that debate by simply juxtaposing the two for thirty seconds.

3. Attend Public Appearances with the Candidate. One way to help candidates find their feet is to start with coffees before they head out on the debate trail. A coffee can be well attended with lots of unknown faces, but it will almost always be a forgiving crowd.

Have at least two committee members attend the first coffee and let them know you want feedback. I will often ask the groomer to attend the first coffee, and if I am the campaign manager, I will make notes as my candidate is speaking.

Things to watch for:

"I would feel that most of the conversations that took place in those areas of the White House that did have the recording system would in almost their entirety be in existence but the special prosecutor, the court, and I think, the American people are sufficiently familiar with the recording system to know where the recording devices existed and to know the situation in terms of the recording process but I feel, although the process has not been undertaken yet in preparation of the material to abide by the court order, really, what the answer to that question is."
—Ron Ziegler, former White House press secretary, answering a reporter's question about the Nixon White House taping system

- Are responses to questions clear and brief?
- Does the candidate scan the room, or fixate on just a few faces?
- Does the candidate toe the ground or look at his or her shoes?
- Does he play with change or keys in his pocket?
- Does her voice drop so that those in the back cannot hear?
- Does she ramble?
- Given an answer, is it clear that the candidate does not know a certain subject area?
- Do verbal ticks distract from content of answers?
- Does he lean against the wall?
- Where are the candidate's hands? They should be used to reinforce what is being said, not stuffed in pockets or laced behind the back.

- Does he cross his feet while standing? This is a sign of insecurity and an attempt to make yourself smaller.

A few years back, I was running a campaign for a very capable, well-educated, professionally successful candidate. However, after a debate, I was called by the groomer whom I had asked to attend to observe the candidate in action. She did not have much to say about his dress but told me that his answers were rambling, that he continually said he agreed with his opponent, and that his opening and closing statements were weak.

I immediately called the candidate on his cell phone and asked if he could exit the freeway and return to my home. Although the candidate and I had previously gone over all issues and discussed possible answers, he had not yet made debate cards as he had been instructed. So for two hours we revisited the issues and made debate cards together. (Note: This is *not* something you can do *for* the candidate.) In addition to issue cards, we discussed how no candidate should ever say he agrees with his opponent and why. Finally, we prepared opening and closing statements. No matter how great your candidate is, this kind of coaching is invaluable to his or her success. For the campaign manager, getting the candidate's speaking and debating skills in order is every bit as important as printed materials, ads, lawn signs, and letters-to-the-editor. As the candidate left my home, he said it was the best two hours he had spent since the beginning of the campaign. After that he became focused and had a level of comfort I had not seen before.

"Experience is a hard teacher. She gives the test first, the lesson afterwards."

—Anonymous

Below are a few things the candidate can do to make speeches and debates more effective.

1. Arrive a few minutes early, but before leaving your car, go over your speech one last time. You will neither have the time nor the inclination to do it once inside.
2. Arrive in the room a little early to get a feel for the audience and the setting.
3. When asked a question, answer it (or appear to be answering it). I have an unfortunate tendency to drift into a stream-of-consciousness thing. One thing reminds me of another and another and another. Avoid that.
4. Have fun. Remember you are on stage. This is your moment. Enjoy it. Smile a lot.

5. Lose the verbal tics: Um, you know, basically, if you will, quite frankly, to tell you the truth, and like all can distract from your presentation. For the campaign manager, just calling attention to a candidate's inclination to use certain words or phrases is enough to change the candidate's behavior. Every moment does not have to be filled. Silence can be a time to gather power. Never underestimate its force.

6. Have some notes about what you are going to say, even if it is a short speech and one you have given a million times. I was once asked to speak at the local outdoor Shakespearean Theater, which had a standing room capacity of around 1,000. I had never spoken to such a large group, under lights, or on a stage like that. I walked out and could not remember one line of my two-minute, memorized speech. Not one. I stood there for what seemed like an hour waiting for it to come to me. Nothing. Finally with no hope of it coming back, I looked down at my notes. The first line triggered the speech, and out it came. Even if you think you won't need them, bring along some notes.

7. Make your speech fun for others to hear. Include something in it to make them feel proud or appreciated. Throw in some self-deprecating humor. I once watched a candidate give a speech at a Rotary Club meeting. She got up bemoaning the fact that one more lumber mill had closed. It would have been much more effective if she had stood up and said, "In Jackson County, small business is big business." She could have followed that up with examples, using members sitting in the room—all testimonials of our economic strength. She also could have pointed out how the success of communities like ours is dependent on the volunteerism and commitment of organizations such as the Rotary Club. Again, give examples. People really hate to hear candidates whine. Avoid it.

One speech I gave as mayor was to the Annual Conference of the Engineers of Oregon. I am the daughter of an engineer, and until recently I was convinced that my son would also be an engineer. One night, when I got home from work quite late, my son, six at the time,

"From you. And let me say something about the tenor of that question. I look around this room and I see privileged people. It's easy to sit back and criticize government efforts to help ordinary people, but helping them is our responsibility."

—Robert F. Kennedy, at an elite medical school, responding to a student who asked him where he was going to get the money for the solutions he proposed to fix a deeply troubled country called me to his bed (I thought) for a kiss goodnight. Instead he pulled one of the most bizarre contraptions I'd ever seen out from under his bed and said, "If I could just have a little piece of electrical tape . . ." I told this story to the Engineers of Oregon with the tone of "You don't know how your mothers suffered," and then pulled three or four examples of my son's handiwork from a bag. It was great fun. It was a room full of people who grew up with contraptions under their beds waiting for a piece of electrical tape.

8. Add history to speeches. Some people know the background of their town, but many don't. Call seniors or local historians for ideas.

9. Focus on friends in the audience. I gave a speech once while I was in the middle of a really horrible campaign for a city money measure with which I was personally aligned. In the audience was one of the opponents, making faces and otherwise distracting me. It had to be the worst speech of my career. Now I look for friendly faces and focus on them.

10. Use quotations, jokes, and anecdotes. Although there are exceptions, I usually do not tell jokes but rather incorporate jokes as funny stories within a speech. This is where self-deprecating humor works.

    For example, at a speech to the Oregon Nurses Association, I came on after two women who were not nurses but rather children of nurses. Although I had not thought of this while I wrote my speech, I said that I too was the daughter of a nurse: an operating room nurse. I told them that OR nurses are the only people I know who wash their hands before and after they go to the bathroom. Even my mom laughs at this, because it's true. Give people something of yourself.

    Collect quotations and incorporate them wherever possible. There are many books available that offer food for thought in quotations. I have mentioned more than 300 books in this book. Look for them and incorporate them in your speeches. Modify them so they are your own words or fit the moment.

11. Share experiences that happened to you on the campaign trail. "The other day while I was canvassing . . ." can be an effective way to make known that you canvass and care what voters think, plus it provides an opportunity to communicate an important idea that is part of your platform.

12. Save correspondence that is entertaining and incorporate it in your speech. My favorite was a letter from a supporter telling me I needed to wear more makeup. I never reveal the author's name in this situation.

13. Target your audience with the campaign message.

14. Give your speech to yourself in the mirror or have a supporter video-tape a speech and have the campaign team watch and critique it.

15. Avoid "word stir-fry"—that is, avoid confusing people with unprepared, incoherent speeches or answers to questions. It makes those listening think you do not know what you're talking about.

Speaking Engagements

Look for opportunities to speak before groups. You need to get your name and face known to the public if you are a candidate, and you need to get your cause before the public if you are working for an issue-based campaign. That said, it is just as important to protect the candidate's time from too many activities with marginal returns. Look for speaking opportunities where the audience should be receptive to your campaign message, and focus on the saveables.

The Write-in and Third Party Candidates

The Write-in Candidate

After the sudden death of a city councilor just weeks before the general election of 1998, a few of us got together to help a write-in candidate.

This turned out to be a great campaign. There were lots of volunteers, plenty of money, great ads, well-placed lawn signs, an excellent brochure, and a solid candidate—one who was both hard-working and willing to do anything her campaign committee asked, from walking districts to modifying her "look." She had been actively involved in city politics and had served on volunteer boards and commissions, she was smart and well spoken, and she did her homework. She got strong endorsements from both local newspapers. She was also a very progressive Democrat.

The opposition really ran no campaign other than two or three ads and about as many lawn signs. The opponent was a conservative Republican, which, in terms of registration in the city, comes in third behind Democrats and non-affiliated voters. We made no mistakes during the campaign, and still we lost.

> "(They) leave the impression of an army of pompous phrases moving over the landscape in search of an idea; sometimes these meandering words would actually capture a straggling thought and bear it triumphantly, a prisoner in their midst, until it died of servitude and overwork."
>
> —William McAdoo, regarding President Harding's speeches

Write-in campaigns, under the best of circumstances, are tough to win. Can it be done? Absolutely. There are examples everywhere of people pulling it off. Washington State elected a congresswoman on a write-in ticket. Write-ins are really no more work than a regular election. However, depending on the ballot type, voting for a write-in is more complicated for the voter. In the case of this write-in candidate, our county was using a punch-card ballot, requiring voters to do more than just write a name next to a position (figure 9.2).

"I have always found paranoia to be a perfectly defensible position."
—Pat Conroy

First things first:

1. You must know the ballot type used by your county and what it looks like.
2. Find out precisely how a write-in vote must be cast at the ballot box. Does the voter have to put down the full name, the position of the office (for example, County Commissioner #3)? Exactly how must it be written? Does punching the opponent's number on a ballot invalidate the vote?
3. Know the law. Are the laws for financial disclosure the same for a write-in as for a candidate on the ballot?
4. Know when the absentee ballots are mailed. You must both identify support and turn out your absentees on or before election day. This is crucial for a win.
5. Know what percentage the absentees are of those who vote—not the registered voters, but those who actually vote. For example, although 25 percent of all registered voters may request and vote absentee, on election day they may represent 50 percent or more of the voter turnout.
6. Run two campaigns: one for absentees and one for walk-ins.
7. In your campaign literature and advertising, illustrate and reinforce what voters will see on their ballot.
8. Get your candidate on the speaking circuit with the opponent(s).
9. Conduct all other business as you would for any other campaign, keeping in mind item 7 above.

You might think this sounds convoluted, but write-in campaigns are actually more fun than running a regular campaign. No one really expects a write-in to win, so everyone is rooting for you. Also, because write-in

Figure 9.2 Example of a Brochure for a Write-in Candidate. Write-in candidate Cate Hartzell had a difficult challenge to overcome in her attempt to win an election: the ballot. Each county has a ballot that is particular to that area. Some lend themselves well to a write-in, some do not. To overcome the challenge in this campaign, a facsimile of the ballot was placed on all campaign materials: the brochure, ads, lawn signs, and direct mail. Still, hundreds of citizens filled their ballots out incorrectly in an attempt to vote for Cate. (Design: Crystal Castle Graphics)

campaigns are so rare, the media gives the campaign more attention with feel-good stories *during the news,* especially if the candidate is working his or her tail off in an obviously well-organized effort. This kind of campaign creates a sense of urgency that brings out the best in volunteers, so they really go the extra distance for the campaign.

It is usually difficult to raise money for a candidate who appears to be losing; however, with a write-in, people don't perceive being behind as the fault of the candidate but rather of circumstances beyond the candidate's control. As a result, if you have a strong write-in candidate, it is surprisingly easy to raise money.

"I don't care if he did it or not, just get him to deny it."

—Lyndon Johnson

Finally, because people know the odds are long on a write-in winning, when you lose, your efforts get far more attention than they would in a more traditional race. Depending on the kind of campaign you run, the candidate ends the race with more stature, power, and respect in the community than before the campaign, and, ironically, is not portrayed as "the loser."

In our write-in race, we had a punch-card ballot, which may be the most difficult type of ballot to work with. On some ballots there is a place to write the name of the candidate right next to the position they are seeking. On the punch-card ballot, now made famous by the state of Florida, our voters had to write "city council," the position number of the council seat, and the candidate's name in an area completely separate from where the actual punch position was on the ballot. They also had to remember not to punch the corresponding number of the opponent on the ballot itself. The name had to be the same on all write-ins. For example, in this case the write-in's first name was Cate. However, even if people spelled her last name correctly, if her first name was spelled with a K rather than a C, the clerk told me she could not accept it.

To visually reinforce what was required of the voter, we re-created a ballot to use as our campaign logo and put it on everything: lawn signs, the brochure, and direct mail. Still, according to the county clerk, the voters made so many mistakes—such as failing to put the proper council position or any position on the ballot, writing only the position number without specifying "city council," and so on—that hundreds of write-in votes did not count.

Third Party Candidates

As in all campaign activities, a third party candidate can be a blessing or a curse. If you're a third party candidate, you will benefit most by presenting the Republican and the Democrat as one and the same. You and you alone provide an alternative. To win as a third party candidate, you must be able to pull votes from both major parties, all age groups, and all income levels.

Most often, third party candidates act as spoilers by splitting the vote of one party and thereby increasing the likelihood of a win by the other. Voters registered as independents will track the party of greatest registration within their precinct, so the candidate running as an independent has little claim to any voter and will pull votes from either the Democrats or the Republicans, depending on how he or she stands on the issues. In 1990 a very conservative independent went on the gubernatorial ticket in Oregon. He ran on an anti-choice, anti–sales tax, anti–land-use-planning platform and successfully pulled conservative votes from a very popular moderate Republican, which effectively gave the Democrat the win.

In New Mexico, Republican Bill Redmond won a congressional seat in 1996 in a district registered heavily Democratic by using a third party candidate to pull support from his Democratic opponent. Redmond's win was due primarily to three strategies: target the Democrat with negative ads, boost the Green Party candidate to split the Democratic vote, and turn out the Republican base. Redmond's campaign even sent literature to registered Democrats *for* the Green Party candidate.

In 1999, in California, Audie Bock became the first Green Party candidate elected to state office in the United States. Her rise began with the resignation of Congressman Ron Dellums (D–CA), who left office in the middle of his fourteenth term. A special election was held to fill his seat in the U.S. House for the remainder of his term, and another to fill that of California state Senator Barbara Lee, who won Dellums's seat. Yet another special election was held to fill the 16th District assembly seat of the successor to Lee's senate seat, Don Perata.

Two Democrats weighed in for the sixteenth District: former Oakland Mayor Elihu Harris, who had also served twelve years in the California State Assembly, and Frank Russo, who also had a long list of party credentials behind his name. No Republican entered the fray, as this district had a Democratic registration advantage of 51 points. Because California law forced the top vote-getters of each party into a runoff if no one received a majority of total votes cast in an open primary, either Russo or Harris had to pull in more than 50 percent of the votes to lock the win.

Seeing a potential opportunity for a runoff, the Green Party recruited Audie Bock and hoped that neither Democrat would garner the necessary votes for an outright win, thereby forcing a runoff between the Democrat and Green Party candidate. That is exactly what happened. Harris beat Russo but attained only 49 percent of the vote.

In the runoff Bock ran on a platform that focused on the Democratic Party machine and suggested that the machine was responsible for the series of special elections, beginning with the midterm resignation of Congressman Dellums. While the Harris campaign packed up the headquarters in Oakland and Harris went to Sacramento to select furniture for his new office, Audie Bock hit the streets. Her team of forty primary volunteers grew to 100 who walked, phoned, and targeted voters. She had 500 lawn signs and enough money for one mailer—a postcard.

Harris's consultant ran a late poll and became so concerned that he dropped a dozen mail pieces in the last two weeks. But it was too much and too late, and the last-minute flurry served only to reinforce the Bock campaign theme urging voters to shun big-party politics. Having spent only $40,000 against Harris's $600,000, Audie Bock won by 327 votes with 30,000 cast (David Beiler, "Green, Lean, and Keen," *Campaigns & Elections,* September 1999, pp. 22–27).

Media and the Candidate

You and your campaign team may suspect bias on the part of the local media, and you may even have those suspicions confirmed, but there is no way to use something like this while campaigning. Complaining about the press makes a candidate look weak—and it's political suicide. The best revenge is to win.

Although I'm amazed when I see candidates go after the media, especially presidential candidates, who should know better, it's understandable why they do. In recent years the media, especially in talk radio, has become more vicious and combative. They can be merciless in their treatment of elected officials—who have volunteered their time to serve the community—and then wonder, editorially, why so few throw their hat in the ring for the next election cycle.

"You never get ahead of anyone as long as you try to get even with him."
—Lou Holtz, Arkansas football coach

Although candidates should respond to attacks from the opposition, they would do best to ignore any bait that the press floats on the pond. That said, if the editor of your local paper is coming after you, call supporters to come to your defense in letters-to-the-editor.

Negative Campaigning

Negative campaigning is inherent in the process. After all, you are running because you embrace issues or values that differ from those of your opponent. You are working on a campaign—whether for a candidate or an issue—for a reason, and as you define that reason, you define both your campaign and that of your opposition. The inverse is true also.

Although the thought of being attacked in public can cause panic for a candidate or campaign team, remember that it is yet another opportunity to get your message out and to show how you comport yourself under pressure. Do it with grace, and an attack can actually help.

"Whatever else there may be in our nature, responsibility toward truth is one of its attributes."

—Arthur Eddington

In listing the strengths and weaknesses of a candidate or issue-based campaign, you are preparing for the inevitable attack. Candidates who have reviewed all possibilities with the committee and drafted responses will have confidence and strength under fire. By preparing, the committee and the candidate can deal with attacks immediately, succinctly, and deftly. If no response comes from your side, an attack often gains credibility.

If your campaign goes negative, keep in mind that numerous studies conducted on the impacts of negative campaigning indicate that only four areas consistently fall in fair territory when it comes to attacks: actual voting records, *current* ethical problems, business practices, and money received from special-interest groups. Finally, do not think you can win in a direct mail war; your campaign must be smarter and have scores of volunteers assisting your efforts.

"In politics as in sport, you take a grave risk when, instead of playing to win, you play not to lose. Running not to lose [means] running on your résumé rather than your vision . . . people don't elect résumés. They elect candidates with an agenda."

—Former U.S. Congressman Les AuCoin in a letter to Democratic gubernatorial candidate Ted Kulingoski

So what do you do if you are attacked? In 1999, the University of Maryland conducted a study, the Campaign Assessment and Candidate Outreach Project, that looked at the impacts of negative campaigning on voters. Charges that voters considered unfair placed the attacking candidate in serious trouble, whether the opposition responded or not and regardless of whether or not voters considered the counterattack fair.

Charges that were deemed fair (such as a voting record) caused problems for the candidate being attacked, especially if he or she did not respond or did so in an unfair manner. The best outcome for the candidate under attack is to counter with a "fair charge" in return (*Campaigns & Election,* October 1999, pp. 20–25).

"You better start swimmin' or you'll sink like a stone."

—Bob Dylan

Ten Dos and Don'ts of Attacks

1. Resist starting a campaign with an attack.
2. Define yourself before going on the attack, especially if you're running against an incumbent who is respected by the voters.
3. Have a focused message.
4. Avoid mixing a lot of unnecessary arguments together.
5. Avoid mixing positive and negative issues within the same ad or directional piece.
6. Avoid misleading or unconvincing arguments.
7. Avoid inconsistent claims: *Anything* questionable will lead the voter to doubt *everything.*
8. Do your homework so you can back up any charges you make and be prepared for a counterattack. I have worked on a number of campaigns where research has turned up very damaging information on our opposition. However, in each case, the committee decided that we would use it only if we were attacked first; because my candidates were not attacked, we never used the damaging information.
9. Be sure that any attacks are believable and fair.
10. Time your attack carefully. An attack launched too early in a campaign may not have the intended impact, and one launched too late may not have enough time to sink in with the voters.

Campaign committees must prepare the candidate for the possibility of negative attacks. Just as a team prepares the candidate for debates, the team also anticipates anything that may come at the candidate by listing all possible scenarios and then preparing responses for the candidate and committee should they come under fire. While it is typical for political parties and special-interest groups, such as environmental organizations, business lobby groups, trial attorneys, unions, grocery PACs, and the like, to conduct negative campaigns against candidates and issue-based campaigns, none of them compare to Citizens for a Sound Economy (CSE) and Right to Life organizations (RTL). I have worked on scores of candidate and issue-based campaigns, many of them heated, and many featuring negative campaigning, but nothing you read or experience can prepare your team fully for these two organizations.

> *"Be a listener only, keep within yourself, and endeavor to establish with yourself the habit of silence, especially in politics."*
>
> —Thomas Jefferson

Whether Republican, Democrat, ultraconservative, or progressive, you may well face one or both of these organizations in a campaign. If a decision is made to get you out of office, target you in an open seat, or come after your issue-based campaign, you need to be prepared.

Lobby for Hire: Citizens for a Sound Economy (CSE)

If CSE has not come to your state, hang on: They're on their way, and they're well funded. CSE was founded by David Koch, executive vice president of Koch Industries, an oil and gas conglomerate out of Wichita, Kansas, who ran on the Libertarian ticket for vice president in 1980. His brother, Charles Koch, co-founded the libertarian Cato Institute. CSE presents itself as a grassroots organization advocating for the poor, underrepresented taxpayer. However, the reality is really quite different. In November 2003, Steve Law of the *Statesman Journal* in Salem, Oregon, reported:

"This amendment does more damage than it does harm."
—Louisiana state legislator during a floor debate

> Citizens for a Sound Economy, a little-known national group, emerged in Oregon during the 1999 legislative session, when it lobbied for a telephone deregulation bill sought by phone monopoly US West. Months later, leaked internal documents revealed the self-described "grass roots" group received $1.25 million from US West in 1998.

Investigative reports also showed Citizens for a Sound Economy:

- Got $1 million from Philip Morris while opposing cigarette tax hikes.
- Took money from Microsoft and lobbied Congress to curtail federal antitrust enforcement.
- Secured money from the Florida sugar industry while opposing an environmental restoration plan for the Everglades.
- Received oil and gas industry money while opposing a potential energy tax.

The Washington, D.C.–based group is the dominant player in a referendum drive to overturn a $1.2 billion tax increase approved by the 2003 (Oregon) Legislature to balance the state budget. Its platform: cut taxes, reduce the size of government, and prune business regulations.

"Americans for Tax Reform president Grover Norquist convenes leaders of the group weekly to coordinate their work," said Ann Beaudry, strategic planning director for People for the American Way. That liberal group tries to monitor and counteract some of the work of its conservative counterparts.

Citizens for a Sound Economy's approach is to mobilize grass-roots activists in selected states to push an agenda set largely in Washington, D.C. The group actively worked to defeat a tax increase on the ballot in Alabama in September (2003).

The group's main lobbying arm, Citizens for a Sound Economy Inc., reported $3.6 million in income in 2002 and assets of $2.2 million, according to tax forms filed with the Internal Revenue Service. A companion group, Citizens for a Sound Economy Educational Foundation, reported income of $4 million in 2002, and assets of $5.6 million. In 2001, the foundation reported spending $2.3 million on its state chapter activities.

Such groups are allowed to delete names of funders before making the tax filings available to the public. The foundation's 2001 tax filing listed nine large donations, ranging from $100,000 to $750,000, for a total of $3.1 million. The donors' identities were whited-out.

Past leaks to publications and interest groups have provided the most detail about the group's financial backers, supplemented by publicly available reports of foundation grants.

A 2000 report by the Ralph Nader–affiliated group Public Citizen listed $7.2 million in corporate donations to Citizens for a Sound Economy in 1998, based on leaked internal documents. The oil and gas industry collectively contributed the largest sum: $2.3 million. US West was the single largest donor, contributing $1.25 million.

Soon after, Citizens for a Sound Economy's Oregon representative was lobbying for US West's priority bill in Salem. In that period, US West was being routinely criticized by Oregon businesses and state utility regulators for poor customer service.

Yet Citizens for a Sound Economy literature described the group as "the voice of consumers for free enterprise."

"I think it ends up being a marriage of convenience between radical right political forces and corporations who share that agenda," said Beaudry. "You end up with thinly veiled people lobbying on behalf of these corporations and you can't follow the money trail."

Because the organization is so secretive, it's unknown, for example, if any tobacco industry money is going to the Oregon referendum campaign. If the campaign overturns the tax package passed by the 2003 Legislature, that automatically rescinds a longstanding 10-cents-per-pack cigarette tax. (Steve Law, "Activist Group Brings Money, Draws Concern, *Statesman Journal,* November 2, 2003)

What is not reported in this article is that the lead lobbyist for CSE in Oregon was previously a lobbyist for Oregon Right to Life (ORTL).

Right to Life

If you have never worked for a candidate or run a campaign against Right to Life but are about to, fasten your seat belt; you're in for a bumpy ride. Little will prepare you for the vitriolic attacks from Right to Life. In a 2002 newsletter sent to members, Oregon Right to Life indicated that they would target "safe" Republican seats and move the party farther to the right. In one race I worked on, a very conservative Republican was targeted by Oregon Right to Life because she crossed party lines and voted for a bill that would require health insurance companies to pay for *contraception* for women. Contraceptive parity was already mandated by the courts in Washington State and was moving through Oregon's judicial system, so this should have been a nothing bill. But ORTL made it a litmus test and targeted three Republicans in the primary. The force with which they applied their strategy suggested that this was not just about these three legislators voting their conscience; rather it was a lesson for future legislators who might mistakenly think they work for the voters.

"A candidate does not always need party infrastructure and a lot of campaign money to win—if he or she can get the public's attention. Regardless of economic conditions, people want government to regard them as the boss, not some party chief or big contributor."

—David Beiler

Most remarkable about these elections was the unabashed twisting of voting records and a new low in negative campaigning, with some of the most disturbing attacks ever witnessed by those of us in the field; "distressingly nasty" was how our region's largest newspaper described it. Through half-truths, exaggeration, and outright lies, they unseated every republican incumbent they went after.

In the general election, ORTL targeted six Oregon races. The only two that survived the assault were those where candidates connected the dots for the voters. If you are targeted by extremist organizations like these, your best bet is to do just that: Connect the dots for the voters by showing them who is funding the opposition.

A Word of Caution

In 2000, a friend of mine was running for office. One night she was on her cordless phone talking with her campaign manager when suddenly her next-door neighbor and the campaign manager of her opponent came on the line. Their voices were as clear as if she were on a conference call; she easily recognized both men, and they called each other by name. Amazingly, they were talking about her race and in the conversation revealed some very damaging information they had dug up about her. Apparently, someone had come forward and relayed some ancient history to the opposing campaign; the conversation included who came forward and a detailed account as related by the informant. The discussion revolved around whether and how to drop the dirt so that the voters would know before casting a ballot.

My friend's neighbor, an unhappy man in general, had been actively opposing her candidacy and was desperate to break the news. He strongly urged the campaign manager to leak it. It was my friend's opinion, based on the tenor of the voices and what was said, that her neighbor was more interested in personally hurting her than in winning the race for her opponent. The opposition's manager was reluctant to move forward with a hit piece. My friend hung up before hearing the decision on what to do with the information.

It was the wildest story I had ever heard. When campaign committee people are talking strategy on the phone, urge them to stick to land lines and avoid cordless phones and cell phones. You just never know who will be listening.

Thank-You Notes

With the introduction of computers and desktop publishing, a printed thank-you note does not carry the same weight as a handwritten thank-you note from the candidate. Most people know that computers can not only generate a personalized thank-you note but also print the candidate's signature. While a campaign should send a thank-you note/receipt for a contributor's tax records, if you are working with a candidate who is willing to scratch a few lines in his or her own handwriting, it really goes a long way. Besides thank-you notes for contributions, it is important to send notes to volunteers who have gone above and beyond the call of duty and to anyone who hosts a coffee or facilitates a campaign event.

Because thank-you notes are fairly expensive to send, I look at them as an opportunity to strengthen a relationship between the donor and the candidate. To do this, I put together a printed, personalized thank-you note for the candidate to sign but will look for some small thing that the candidate can add to the note after it is printed. I will go through the lists of contributors with the candidate to identify those he or she knows personally. This doesn't take long and can be done over the phone. I make a note on the photocopied checks of contributors the candidate knows so that I can keep those notes apart from the rest. If I personally know the contributor because of his or her involvement with the campaign, I attach a Post-it to the thank-you note indicating what I want the candidate to jot on the bottom. For example, if the campaign receives a contribution from someone who also baked all the cookies for a coffee earlier in the campaign, I instruct the candidate to acknowledge that effort one more time in the contribution thank-you note: "Still thinking about those great desserts you brought to the coffee last month. Hope all is well and thanks again."

When responding to contributions from a targeted mailing, I will include in the body of the thank-you letter information that the contributor may want to know because it pertains to his or her field of interest. I also try to make these a little gossipy, so the contributor feels more a part of the inner circle. In other words, acknowledge the contribution, but give the donor a little more. This is especially important with anyone who gives more than $100. Only a small portion of a thank-you note is about the gift. The real power of a thank-you note is to curry the donor for the next "give" so that subsequent contributions will increase. In local elections, personal communication with donors is about investing them in the campaign in more ways than just money.

In all preprinted thank-you notes, be sure to have the candidate sign in an off-color pen. Because blue and black ink are often used in computer-generated signatures, green is best. However, you can get away with blue if you use a pen with a slightly thicker point. Avoid colors like pink, red, or purple.

For thank-you notes that do not need a contribution receipt, I have special stationery that I print from my computer. On the front is a picture of the candidate on the campaign trail or a collage of the candidate in different settings. I usually ask my graphic designer to put together the layout and then e-mail it to me so that I can print them out as needed. However, if

Figure 9.3 Example of Stationery for the Candidate's Personalized Notes (Design: Crystal Castle Graphics)

your design will use just one photo, it is pretty easy to drop it in yourself (figure 9.3).

To generate this stationery, lay it out in landscape format so that each sheet of paper will make two note cards, and use paper that is slightly heavier, such as 80-pound Vellum Bristol, with matching preprinted envelopes (the ones you used for your world's smallest brochure mailing work well). To help the candidate, it is a good idea for the campaign manager or someone from the committee to make a short list of who might receive a personalized thank-you note. Have the envelopes preaddressed and stamped so that the candidate need only jot a note before the notes are stuffed, sealed, and mailed.

10

THE ISSUE-BASED CAMPAIGN

IN THIS CHAPTER
- *Initiative and Referendum*
- *Local Preemption*
- *Polling and the Issue-Based Campaign*
- *Speakers' Bureau*
- *Recall*
- *Saving Our Libraries*
- *Building New Schools*
- *Packaging the Issue-Based Campaign*
- *Flies in the Ointment: The Double Majority, Independents, and the Super Majority*
- *The State Initiative and Referendum Process*

Initiative and Referendum

The initiative and referendum process arose out of the fundamental controversy about whether government should come directly from the people or through representatives to the various levels of government. Although some direct democracy existed in the early years of U.S. government, during the first hundred years it was almost exclusively representative. It wasn't until the late 1800s, when dissatisfaction with government and distrust of the state legislatures became prevalent, that citizens enacted the initiative process. Primarily a western-state phenomenon, the initiative process began in reaction to laws that benefited a few powerful interests rather than the body electorate. Its effect was to enlarge the role people have in policy decision making.

Ironically, today it has become a tool for special-interest groups with agendas related to natural resources, morality, minority rights, taxation, and so forth. As Oregon's former Secretary of State Phil Keisling said, "At key moments in our history, the initiative has held up a mirror to who we are as [a society], reflecting our pettiness as well as grand visions, our mean-spiritedness as well as our generosity, our perils and possibilities as a political community."

"To be successful, grow to the point where one completely forgets himself; that is, to lose himself in a great cause."

—Booker T. Washington, American educator (1856–1915)

The state initiative process enables citizens to bypass the legislature and directly place proposed statutes and constitutional amendments on the ballot by gathering signatures. Each of the twenty-four states with citizens' initiative authority has different criteria to activate the process (see table 10.1, at the end of the chapter). Before you begin an initiative campaign, contact your local elections office or secretary of state's office to learn all the necessary details.

The referendum process, by contrast, serves as a check on the governing body by forcing adopted legislation to a vote of the people, allowing them to accept or reject it. The signature requirement for referring legislation out to a vote is usually less than the initiative process.

Increasingly, the initiative process is being used to amend state constitutions in an effort to keep legislative bodies from tinkering with a voter-approved initiative. The result is that state constitutions and city and county charters are needlessly cluttered. However, in defense of this practice, in the 2003 legislative session alone, Oregon Republicans tried to undo a number of voter mandates. One of them, a measure to increase the minimum wage in the state, had received voter approval just three months before the house majority advocated undoing the law at the behest of the business interests that funded their campaigns. Another attempted to undo a ban on the use of bait and traps for cougars and bears that had previously been affirmed by voters on *two* occasions. Also, each session, legislators revisit voter directives related to reproductive rights.

"I pay my taxes gladly. Taxes are the price of civilization."

—Oliver Wendell Holmes

Initiative and referendum processes are also available in many local jurisdictions, and their requirements and scope usually mirror state requirements. Local initiatives can be very useful tools for school districts, libraries, and municipal and county government.

In a local initiative, although most of the guidelines are established by state statutes, the percentage of signatures that need to be gathered varies by locale. Voters may also refer (through referendum) any legislation passed by the local governing body to the voters. As with the state, the number of signatures required is some percentage of the number of people who voted in a specific election—for example, 10 percent of those who voted in the last mayoral election.

The local referendum process differs from the initiative process only in the number of signatures required for qualification and in a time limit; that is, it must be referred within a certain number of days after adoption by the governing body. However, if enough people are opposed to a law, it can, in essence, be repealed through the initiative process at any time. Because both the initiative and the referendum process circumvent the legislative body, they have some inherent problems. If you're not working in conjunction with the local elected officials, be prepared: They have more tricks in their bag.

Who drafts the ballot title may have a decided advantage. Some titles are prepared in such a way that you cannot tell whether a yes vote is actually a yes or a no (for example, "yes, repeal it" vs. "yes, don't repeal it").

Also, some states have limitations, such as allowing only a single subject to be covered in a measure. Meeting this limitation can be a little more difficult than it sounds. Often citizens are anxious to throw in a couple of ideas, each of which may strengthen the other and are quite related, and then, after collecting the signatures or running the winning campaign, find that their wording covered more than one subject. It really isn't for the local governing body to determine whether you have more than one question. If you intend to do all this work, hire an attorney—a good attorney.

There are many restrictions on initiatives and referendums. For example, in Oregon local government cannot put land use matters to a vote, only legislative matters. So before spending a lot of time and money, learn what your parameters are.

Another caution: Those signing the petition must be registered within the jurisdiction of the area that will be affected by the proposed legislation. For example, if your school measure is to be voted on by those within your school district, then only those registered within the school district will qualify as signers on the petition. Similarly, if your proposed legislation affects your city, then only those registered within the city limits would qualify. In other words, only those affected get to weigh in on the discussion.

Also, in a statewide initiative or referral, the people whose signatures are on the petition must be registered in the county in which they signed the petition. This requirement stems from the fact that signatures are verified at the county level where voters are registered.

Be sure to get at least 10 percent more signatures than is required for qualification.

Competing Measures

Competing measures have two forms. The first, which results from a legislative body responding to a qualifying initiative, is designed to give voters an alternative to the citizen-drafted law. In this case, the governing body places before the voters legislation that is linked in some way to an initiative or referral generated by the public. A competing measure is a powerful tool that can be used effectively. For example, as I mentioned earlier in this book, in 1993 Ashland voters approved a prepared food and beverage tax to fund an open-space land-acquisition program and state-mandated upgrades on our wastewater treatment plant. It was a divisive campaign that had local restaurants, Realtors, and the state food and beverage industry on one side and the parks commission, environmentalists, and citizens buckling under potentially astronomical utility bills on the other. Although proponents were outspent five to one, the voters approved the tax by a narrow margin. Opponents decided to immediately refer it back to the voters.

In the meantime, the state legislature decided to place a statewide sales tax for school funding before the voters. The timing was such that the referral of the meals tax would appear on the same ballot as the sales tax proposal. I assumed the proponents of the food and beverage tax repeal would use the scare tactic of suggesting that the food and beverage tax would be added to a statewide sales tax. Although a statewide sales tax was unlikely to pass, given that it had been defeated at the polls eight times already, Ashland had always been supportive of such a tax. While the voters might approve a 5 percent local food and beverage tax, few would stand still for a 10 percent tax that would result from the two combined. To head off this predicament, the city placed a competing measure on the ballot along with the food and beverage tax referral. The competing measure said that (1) if the state sales tax passed, Ashland's food and beverage tax would be repealed, and (2) if people voted in larger numbers for the competing measure than for the repeal of the tax, it would override the referendum on the food and beverage tax. Citizens chose the competing measure over an outright repeal of the tax. The statewide sales tax went down by around three to one, with Ashland supporting it two to one.

Just a note: Measures approved by voters, no matter how narrow the margin, are rarely overturned when re-referred. Voters historically come back on the referral and reaffirm previous intentions by even larger margins.

The other type of competing measure occurs when two or more unrelated money measures appear on the same ballot. They can come from the same governing body, such as two county measures requesting funding through the property tax, one for juvenile services, the other for adult detention, or from different governing bodies placing money measures on the same ballot, such as a county, city, school, or special district.

These days, counties and cities often place competing measures on ballots, because so many needs are falling by the wayside. However, doing this increases the likelihood that all will fail. For example, in November 1998, our county placed three bond measures before the voters, and all went down. The reason is fairly simple. Among voters, there are those who vote no on *any* new taxes, and those who will vote yes on some. Of the

"A life spent making mistakes is not only more honorable but more useful than a life spent doing nothing."
—George Bernard Shaw

yes voters, some will vote for more than one money measure, and some will choose between the measures, effectively splitting the yes vote. They compete with each other.

That counties and cities would place two measures on the ballot at the same time might suggest that some muddled thinking was involved. However, there are situations where it cannot be helped. For example, your school district is trying to pass a bond measure for a new gym, the city needs money for new fire stations, and the county needs the library system upgraded. Three different governing bodies, all with the right to place items on the ballot, separately create a competing-ballot measure scenario. Ideally they would be talking to one another and work together to spread these items out, but that doesn't always happen.

"It doesn't make sense to talk about successful corporations in a society whose schools, hospitals, churches, symphonies, or libraries are deteriorating or closing."
—Clifton C. Garvin, Jr.

Further complicating the survival rate of competing measures occurs when initiative-driven legislation is placed on the ballot that will inflame one group over another, such as legislation dealing with gun control, reproductive rights, or sexual orientation. Issues of this sort will bring out a voter who might otherwise stay home, and as long as they're at the voting booth, they'll weigh in on your issue-based campaign.

Local Preemption

State legislatures love to preempt local government. Having served twelve years as a mayor and witnessing two Oregon legislative sessions as chief of staff for a state representative, I find it remarkable that an assembly that could not organize a sock drawer would have the cheek to prevent local governments from solving issues within their jurisdiction. However, moneyed interests have discovered that fighting targeted taxation and legislation is much easier in a statewide arena, where money is king. For example, in 2002 two statewide grassroots initiatives on the Oregon ballot went down in flames: One, a proposal for universal health care, was outspent 32 to 1, and the other, which would have required labels on genetically modified foods, was outspent 61 to 1. The latter prompted the agricultural industry, which dumped $5 million into defeating the food labeling measure, to get legislators to introduce a bill prohibiting local government from implementing any food labeling laws.

During my last term in office, the city of Ashland, which owns the electric utility, brought in high-speed data services and cable television as part of the electric utility system upgrade. By doing so, the city was able to provide high-speed, direct-connect Internet access to schools, libraries, and the university for pennies. It was also a boon for our software industry and graphic design businesses. Although the private sector had no intention of providing high-speed data services until the city stepped up, they urged the Oregon legislature to introduce legislation prohibiting other cities from doing what Ashland had done—and tried to make the law retroactive in an effort to undo Ashland's system. Government participation in the creation of this kind of infrastructure is no different from when it participated in state highway systems or rural electric development in days gone by, and it may be one of the best tools for strengthening local economic development. However, when moneyed interests knock on legislators' doors, those answering are often willing to do the bidding for special interests on the house or senate floor.

> *"If you're doing what's right, the bullets bounce off."*
> —Cathy Shaw

Polling and the Issue-Based Campaign

Political consultants and pollsters generally agree that an issue-based campaign must begin with the support of at least 60 to 70 percent of voters. While this is certainly the case for any issue in which something is requested of the citizens, such as a tax increase or restrictions on where cows can graze, issues that *restrict government,* such as term-limit legislation or mandatory sentencing for certain crimes, track a different polling pattern.

In my experience, legislation proposing to restrict government need only show a voter preference in initial polls to successfully pass on election day.

For example, a poll looking at proposed legislation to reintroduce term limits in Oregon showed voter support at 56 percent and opposition at 30 percent. At first glance it looks like this proposal does not meet the 60 to 70 percent threshold for passage. But comparing the support and opposition numbers shows almost a two to one voter preference for term limits. The other thing to consider is the "hard" support and "hard" opposition of the proposed issue-based campaign. In this term-limit example, the hard numbers in favor (definitely for) came in at 35 percent, and the hard numbers in opposition (definitely against) came in at only 20 percent. These numbers suggest that term-limit legislation would be approved by a proportion similar to the Oregon 1992 constitutional amendment, which passed with 69.6 percent.

Things to consider before embarking on an issue-based campaign:

1. It must be simple and straightforward.
2. It must have voter appeal and speak to emotion. Remember, you are selling an idea, not a person, so there are some inherent challenges. Issue-based campaigns that sell hope and opportunity tend to do best.
3. It must be self-serving. The voter must feel that he or she will personally get something upon passage: a park, better schools, a library, reduced taxes, or a shifted tax burden (e.g., to tourists or the wealthy).
4. It must have populist appeal for fund-raising purposes. Remember: Money is thy savior.
5. Timing is everything. Will you be in an off-year election, when fiscal conservatives vote, or in a presidential year, when more progressive voters turn out?
6. What else will be on the ballot? Have other groups placed initiative legislation on the ballot that will induce one segment of the population to turn out more than another?
7. Will your issue-based campaign hurt or help candidates you want to support or need to keep in office?
8. Is there enough time to make your case to the voters, and do you have people willing to head up the campaign?
9. Who will be drafting the ballot title and summary—a friend or a foe?
10. What are the polling numbers? If you're working on a losing campaign from the beginning, you will finish the race exhausted and will have actually set your cause back.
11. Who will carry the measure? Who will carry the opposition? The chair, speakers' bureau, endorsers, and opponents of an issue-based campaign are often the biggest clues voters have for supporting or rejecting an issue-based campaign.

12. Finally, an issue-based campaign designed to raise taxes must answer four questions: (1) How high will (can) the tax go? (2) Where will it be spent? (3) When will it go away? (4) Is there a logical connection between what is being taxed and where the new revenue will go, such as a cigarette tax to fund health care? If there is not a logical connection, your campaign must make one. For example, in the meals tax, we pointed out that tourists and residents alike used city parks and flushed toilets, so both should help improve these systems.

Speakers' Bureau

When organizing campaigns for ballot measures, set up a committee of supporters whose sole job is to serve as speakers; collectively, they are the speakers' bureau. If it is a countywide proposition or measure, the speakers' bureau might be quite large. In an individual city, it may be as small as two. Whatever the size, their job is to seek opportunities to speak and to make sure someone is there from the committee to explain the ballot measure and answer questions in a knowledgeable way. These should be people with little political baggage.

A speakers' bureau is a terrific way of publicly involving big-name people who want to be aligned with a campaign. It is also good for the ballot measure. Whereas an election with a candidate depends on that candidate and his or her stands to build relationships with the voters, ballot measures often encompass only one idea.

"I should have dropped the Math and English Departments and study hall. Then no one would have known about it."

—James Taylor, College of Southern Idaho president, reacting to outcries against his dropping three sports and five coaches to solve a financial crisis

Often with a ballot measure, the people who attach their name to it create the relationship. You might have the president of the college, the president of the Rotary Club, the mayor, the leaders of every church, and so on. Each will bring a following. Their names have come to represent something in the community, and it is their reputations that draw the vote.

Recall

As with the initiative and referendum process, recalls require a number of signatures of registered voters equal to a specific percent of those who voted in a specific election. For example, the number of signatures for a recall for a state office might be equal to 8 percent of the number who voted in the last election for governor, whereas a recall of a city official might be 10 percent of those who voted in the last mayor's election. Once a petition is pulled, it must be filed within a specific time (depending on the state or local statues), and a special election must be held within a specific number of days after verification of the signatures. In Oregon the whole process can last no more than 140 days: 90 to gather the signatures, 10 to have them verified, and 40 to organize the special election. You cannot begin a recall process until someone has been in office for six months after his or her *last election.* This goes for those who are in their second or third term of office as well.

From my experience, recall attempts are often prompted by one specific action that, coupled with the personality of the office holder, means trouble. The recall attempts often focus on strong, smart, outspoken women and strong, smart, soft-spoken men with an overriding theme that the office holder doesn't know who butters his or her bread. If you find that you are the subject of a recall, remember: You only need to survive; they need to conquer. A failed recall attempt generally leaves the office holder in a politically stronger position than before. Whether you believe enough signatures will be gathered is really not the point. Once the attempt has begun, do not hang your head: Fight back. There are lots of people who do not believe in recalls—76 percent of black voters in California, for example, according to data from the 2003 recall of Governor Gray Davis.

Fighting a recall is no different from running a regular campaign. As soon as you hear of an attempt being waged against you, organize a campaign committee. If the organizers of the effort against you claim that you are supported by only one segment of the population, or one community in the county, then be sure that you have representatives from each and every city and people from all walks of life. If you're being thrown out because of your connection with special-interest groups, then be sure they are nowhere to be seen in the campaign; show broad-based support.

Begin by fund-raising. You want to amass a war chest that will scare the opponents before they file the papers. Depending on the circumstances, fund-raising events for office holders subjected to a recall are often surprisingly easy and raise lots and lots of money. A bonus is that because you're undergoing a recall while serving in office, no one expects you to do more in the campaign than just showing up. So enjoy: Raise money, support, and marginalize your opposition as the small-minded, self-serving people they are. If you cannot find a way to say this yourself, have it said by others in letters-to-the-editor, again and again and again.

If you're thinking about recalling an elected official, stop and reconsider. Recalls are almost never warranted. They generally take on the atmosphere of a public flogging and execution. Recalls also scare off other qualified, honest, hardworking people, the kind of people we need, from serving public office. If you're mad enough to want to recall an office holder, get over it and run a candidate or run yourself in the next election.

A Petition Is Pulled!

Whether fighting a recall, an initiative, or a referendum, once a petition has been pulled there are lots of things you can do to prepare for the inevitability that the petitioners will get the required signatures. Do not make the mistake of waiting to see if it actually happens. If you do, the momentum will be with the petitioners, and you will not have enough time to mount a viable campaign. Remember, the best way to prevent signatures from getting collected is to organize, fund-raise, and line everything up for a full-on frontal assault. You want petitioners to believe that you're really enthused, delighted, and looking forward to the possibility of going toe to toe with them.

Here's what you do:

1. Organize a campaign committee.
2. Send at least one mailing explaining what is going on.
3. Set up phone banks and begin voter identification work immediately in all swing precincts. Knowing who is opposed to the recall or referendum and getting them out on election day will be critical to survival.
4. While you're on the phone, secure lawn sign locations and names for an endorsement ad. It will be important to show broad community support for your side. Secure field sign locations as well.
5. Whether local or statewide, when it comes to referrals and recalls, voters are hugely influenced by their neighbors and community. The best way to fight a recall or referendum is to focus in close. The battle is waged neighborhood by neighborhood. Show individual support if you're facing a recall, and show individual opposition (rebellion) if your tax measure is being targeted.
6. Establish a speakers' bureau and put them on the circuit immediately.
7. Do not let petitioners define you. If your efforts are backed by unions, they should stay in the closet. If your efforts are backed by big business, keep them at a distance.
8. You must define the opposition and communicate that those referring the tax measure are self-serving outsiders supported by big money. Have proof.
9. As soon as a petition is pulled, start fund-raising, especially if their campaign is being bankrolled by special-interest groups. If the law does not allow fund-raising until petitions are verified, then ask for

pledges you can call in the moment the opposition qualifies for the ballot.

10. Line up letters-to-the-editor. Remember, while they are gathering signatures, you are too—signatures for letters and endorsement ads. As a campaign, review these letters and decide when they go to the paper(s). Letters need a mix of emotion, pragmatism, and ridicule of the petitioners. Keep 'em short.

11. Get TV and radio ads made.

12. If you're fighting a recall, sing long and hard on accomplishments and service, but make the messenger the average person. If you're fighting a referendum, do not fight the actual referral, but rather promote what is being referred. If it's about taxes for schools or the disabled, you are selling hope, opportunity, independence, and investments in our future.

13. Know your audience and ask sales reps in both television and radio to set up schedules for buys. You don't actually have to buy, but you want to know the cost, penetration, reach, and frequency that will get you what you need.

14. Design your lawn signs and brochures, and have the camera-ready art at the respective printers with a directive to wait for your phone call.

15. The moment the petitions are filed and certified, you want to be able to make five calls and quickly move the whole process into high gear.

Saving Our Libraries

For some reason, voters too often look at library funding as a frill. Unlike new wastewater treatment plants or water pipelines, both of which can be funded through revenue bonds, libraries have suffered under taxpayer revolts and lack of understanding. If your mission is to get money to build a new library or to remodel and expand an existing one, there's plenty of hope.

Library campaigns must be set up a little differently from other bond measures, in part because it is more difficult to convince people of the need. There are basically three steps involved and a number of choices within each of those steps.

1. Establish a committee to examine needs, opportunities, and direction. Your first step is to get a select group of community members together to usher your project through. Although some may end up working on the campaign, that is not the purpose of this committee. Its members' job is to serve as liaisons with the community and the project. Assemble people who represent the many sides of your community and are

well respected in their circle. You may select an individual from the immediate neighborhood, a businessperson, representatives of influential city boards or commissions (such as planning and historic), a builder, a librarian, a member of the Friends of the Library group, and a liaison to the city council. It is also important to have city or county staff there for guidance and administrative support. It doesn't matter if not all the committee members are 100 percent on board for the project at the beginning; it's actually better if opinions are spread. Don't worry, people will come around or the project won't fly anyway.

2. Once you have the committee in place, working with the local government, hopefully municipal, you will need to select an architectural team. The architectural team should be committed to community process and inclusivity. You want architects who are interested in what the community wants, not what they think is best for the community. Through community visioning, in which citizens are invited to attend a half-day workshop, a clear idea of what people want will emerge. From this the architects can draft architectural renderings and come up with a money figure to place before the voters (figure 10.1B).

3. Obviously you want your governing body to place this on the ballot for you. If they don't, see the section above on the initiative process, and consider running for office next time someone in the governing body is up for reelection. Using the money figure generated by the architectural team and backed by your committee, the council should place the matter before the voters. You now have two months to convince people.

    Here you might consider who gets to vote on this issue. In my area, those who live in the unincorporated areas—that is, outside of city limits—tend to vote no on such things, so I prefer to leave them out of the district and limit the vote to the city. It's also much easier to turn out the vote if it's just citywide. Don't forget, those who use the library the most live close to it.

If you think you'll have trouble convincing the city council to place the measure on the ballot or you want additional public input and direction, consider having your Friends of the Library group print fliers with questionnaires and canvass the city. One part of the flyer can be dedicated to what the community proposed in the visioning process, and another part could invite community members to join the Friends of the Library group. You would be surprised at how much money you can bring in with this small effort. Keep

Figure 10.1A Historical Photograph of Ashland's Carnegie Library. This photo was used on the front of the "Campaign for the Carnegie" brochure. (Photo courtesy of Terry Skibby, Ashland Historian)

Figure 10.1B Inside the "Campaign for the Carnegie" brochure we used this image to show voters what they were buying. In issue-based campaigns, use a mix of the old with the new. Civic buildings reflect who we were as well as who we are. As Winston Churchill said: "We shape our buildings, and then our buildings shape us."

in mind, however, this money and effort can never touch your campaign. It must be kept separate and distinct.

"This nation cannot afford to maintain its military power and neglect its brainpower."
—John F. Kennedy

If the cost estimate of your library project comes in on the high side and sticker shock among voters is a concern, here are some suggestions to get the price down:

1. Have local donors or organizations financially sponsor different rooms, fixtures, floors, rugs, and so forth. Determine how much the children's, young adult, and reference section will cost, and ask civic groups to fund a room with a promise of having their name placed over the door. Go to likely organizations that might pick up the computer component.
2. Have either local organizations or the historical society consider funding and placing all the art work for the library. Have the walls tell the story of your historic library or town through pictures.
3. Determine whether there is state-owned furniture warehoused somewhere that could be used for the public library.
4. If it's a historic structure, are there local, state, or federal historic renovation grants available for some portion of the remodel?
5. If your library's funding is dependent upon patronage, consider investing in a great video collection that people can access for free.

Building New Schools

The biggest obstacle that public school districts have in passing measures for operation and maintenance money or construction bonds is that schooling has evolved beyond the kind of education much of the electorate received. As a result, many voters see computers in the classroom as a luxury, extracurricular activities such as debate and business programs as unnecessary, and connection to the World Wide Web as a frill. I can't tell you how many times I have heard how we need to get back to the basics of reading, writing, and 'rithmetic. The reality our students face has to do with screen-based literacy, collaborative learning, and critical thinking.

"All who have meditated on the art of governing mankind have been convinced that the fate of empires depends on the education of youth."
—Aristotle

In order for voters to support the changes needed in our schools, we must educate the populace to understand that our schools are no longer training students for trades and specific jobs. Instead, students are and need to be trained to work with people, to be flexible in an ever-changing job market, and to think creatively and freely with access to data. Most of the jobs for today's elementary school students do not yet exist.

The bulk of America's schools were built in the early 1950s or earlier and either are falling apart or are inadequate for the electronic demands of the computer age. The task of rebuilding them or constructing new ones, on top of all the other costs of public education, is almost overwhelming to taxpayers, leaving them immobilized. In Ashland, however, we have had great luck in this sphere. Here are some tips for success based on our experience.

> *"Education makes a people easy to lead, but difficult to drive; easy to govern but impossible to enslave."*
> —Baron Henry Peter Brougham

1. Again, set up a committee that represents a good cross-section of the community. The last time we proposed major improvements to our schools, we started out with about forty citizens, all invited, who then worked in focus groups to design a plan and figure out a dollar amount that would work for our community. However you decide to do it, just remember to start broad and continue to widen involvement all the way to the campaign.

2. An architect will need to be selected. Obviously, you can't use a large group to select this individual or team, but this is a really important step and needs the right people. Too often in an effort to save money and make public buildings salable at an election, we cut corners. We should construct civic buildings with materials that suggest permanence, are compatible with the community, and will be objects of civic pride. It costs no more to build a beautiful building than an ugly one. Look closely at what the architect has designed before. Do the buildings all look the same? Have past contractors had trouble working with the architect? Do a lot of research and homework here, or you'll be sorry.

> *"We are continually faced with a series of great opportunities brilliantly disguised as insoluble problems."*
> —John W. Gardner

3. If you think you'll have trouble getting this sort of thing to pass districtwide, ask the council to float it to city residents.

Packaging the Issue-Based Campaign

In an issue-based campaign, the message is the messenger. You want those in your community who have broad support and leadership standing to usher your project through. I have touched on issue-based campaigns throughout this handbook, but there are many specifics that bear emphasis.

1. Set up a Committee to Support of movers and shakers that is separate from your campaign committee—people whose name will appear on ads, in direct mail, and on the brochure.

2. Find the right chair (or co-chairs) for this committee: someone who embraces the many sides of your community. This is an opportunity to use an individual who will bring along the saveables, not the saints.

3. Remember, with schools and libraries you are selling opportunity. You are not asking people to fund needs. This means you must educate the electorate on the changing world. The idea that I talked about earlier contrasting two high school transcripts of straight-A students, only one of which lists extracurricular activities, resonates with voters. It asks voters to ensure the success of their children and grandchildren. There is also an element of self-interest to consider. As an aging society, we must position ourselves to improve the education of those who will take care of us in our old age.

4. Talk about libraries as information hubs once again. Our libraries have become as historic on the inside as on the outside, and the pathways and opportunities they can open to a community, young and old, are often overlooked, even by librarians.

5. In designing libraries, be sure to have areas that can be used after hours for community needs apart from the books. These areas might include meeting, reading, and study rooms as well as computer labs that members of the community can use to become more computer literate.

6. Conduct a precinct analysis that closely tracks who has voted for similar measures. If you are looking for funding for a library, look at census data to determine who has school-age children, then target those areas. Remember, schools are moving more toward training our students to work in groups, and these groups need to gather somewhere to do projects and research. What better place than the public library?

7. Acknowledge the changing face of libraries and schools. For example, because of the Web and CD-ROMs, reference sections are actually getting smaller.

8. Use teachers, PTAs, and parents to volunteer for this effort.

9. Pay close attention to any fatal flaws. For example, in a nearby school district a bond measure for schools failed because voters discovered that it included money to pave the parking lot. At no time did the committee tell the voters that federal track-out laws require paving if remodeling occurs.

10. Have a speakers' bureau of people who can speak to civic groups. This should not be teachers or librarians, who have a vested interest in the bond passing.

11. Create a strong theme and message and stick to them. Remember, a theme is strategic not tactical. Aim at the souls that can be saved, and use the theme as a focus point for your campaign team and Committee to Support.

12. In campaigns, timing and context are everything. In general, the further away from a presidential election, the more conservative the vote. Time your election to fall in a presidential year, rather than a midterm or special election. Find out if there will be other issue-based campaigns that will compete with yours. To have a ballot on which only one money issue is presented to the voter allows that single issue to get lots of light, air, dialogue, debate, and media attention. Plus, it gives those working for them a chance to turn out the support without another election poking a sleeping dog somewhere else.

Flies in the Ointment: The Double Majority, Independents, and the Super Majority

The Double Majority

In November 1996 Oregon passed an initiative that included, among other things, a criteria requiring at least a 50 percent turnout of the registered voters for money measures affecting the property tax. The author of this initiative felt that too many money measures were placed on the ballot during obscure special elections when officials knew turnout would be low. The only exception to this rule is during even-year general elections when the double majority would not apply.

The challenge became one of turning out at least 50 percent of the vote, not just a majority of support. Opponents quickly figured out that if they stayed home, their no-show status worked more in their favor than if they actually cast a no vote. Their challenge became one of not voting and urging their friends to stay home as well so the tax measure would be defeated before votes were even counted. An added bonus was that people who had not been purged from the voter rolls after they moved or died suddenly got a de facto vote.

In March 1997 the city of Ashland needed to pass a flood restoration bond after the New Year's Day flood to raise the necessary local matching dollars for Federal Emergency Management Agency funds. Having never run a campaign under the double-majority rule, the get-out-the-vote (GOTV) campaign was set up as outlined in Chapter 11, except that phone banks were run for six nights instead of seven. Still, it was the longest and most ambitious GOTV campaign we had conducted in the city.

During the six nights of calling, we easily made it through 80 percent of the registered voters. At that time, retrieving phone numbers from the Internet was prohibitively slow, so huge clerical teams were assembled to look up phone numbers of registered voters. Throughout the calling, volunteers hit scores of nonvoting college students, people who had moved, local kids away at college, and about ten dead people still on the voter rolls. (One vote, one person . . . for eternity.) All in all, about 10 percent of the voter rolls were unavailable to vote. That meant we needed to turn out between 55 and 60 percent to meet the 50 percent requirement under the double-majority rule.

"Human history has become more and more a race between education and catastrophe."

—H. G. Wells

The final numbers showed the bond passing by 55 percent; however, the bond ultimately fell short by 150 voters to make the necessary 50 percent turnout requirement. In May, after working with the county to purge deadwood from the registration rolls, we returned to the voters with beefed up phone banks and an additional night of calling. This GOTV formula has worked for six out of seven double-majority elections I've worked on since that time. The one in which it did not work added one more piece of information about double-majority elections: independents (also referred to as nonaffiliated voters, or NAVs).

Independents

In the 2002 midterm primary, we failed to meet the 50 percent turnout threshold on a countywide college bond levy. This campaign had a great GOTV component, and for seven nights eighty-five volunteers called registered voters. Approximately one-third of the 100,000 registered voters in the county were contacted and reminded to vote. With each night of calling, the Republicans and Democrats tracked turnout numbers similar to those of previous elections. However, independents did not. Independents turned out in such low numbers that it was impossible to make up their poor showing with party loyalists to get to the 50 percent mark.

After twenty years of precinct analysis, I have found independents to be anything but. They consistently track the party of greatest registration in about the same percentages, *when* they vote. Although turnout numbers reflect those of the two parties, they will lag behind anywhere from 14 to 30 points. In other words, if there is a high party turnout in a given precinct, independents will also turn out in higher numbers, but not to the same extent. If they are embedded in enemy territory, in low-priority precincts, leave them alone. If they are in precincts of high turnout and high support, they will behave accordingly. In any precincts where there is 50/50 registration of the two major parties, the independents should be identified, because half of them will move with one party and half with the other. Left to their own devices, most will move in the direction of their neighbors, with some sitting on the extremes of either end.

However, when it comes to non-presidential primary elections, when even party loyalists underperform, independents stay home in huge numbers. They do so because they are often not allowed to participate in the primary elections of either party. If you are working an issue-based campaign under double-majority constraints, there is little you can do to meet the required 50 percent turnout in a midterm election unless the campaign covers a small area (city or school district) with an active electorate. Save your money. You will win the vote but lose because of turnout. Ironically, these same campaigns, coming back for a second shot in the midterm general election, lose because of support. It is almost as though everyone who stayed home in the primary votes no in the general. A postmortem on the primary will not give you solid predictors for the general, because the primary support numbers simply do not carry over. To predict these elections, you must take another general midterm election for an issue-based campaign that lost in a primary.

"The absence of alternatives clears the mind marvelously."
—Henry Kissinger

The upside of a double-majority election is that if 50 percent turn out, it almost always results in a win. Apparently, protax voters are simply less motivated to vote than antitax voters. The introduction of a double-majority requirement has been great: It creates a sense of urgency on the part of the protax voter as well as the volunteers needed to prod them, and it has the added benefit of scaring away competing measures. One small caveat is that double-majority elections work best in cities.

Keep the Vote Within City Limits

Those living in the unincorporated areas can be the most conservative of American voters and often want little or nothing to do with what government has to offer. They have wells and septic drain fields, and many heat exclusively with wood or some other fuel shipped directly to their homes. Oh, they love to drive on paved roads, use libraries, have the sheriff and fire patrol appear promptly, and they want their kids to attend great public schools, but when it comes to being taxed, they're a loud and strong no vote. People living in cities, however, tend to want what government offers and are willing to tax themselves to get it. If you have an opportunity to run an election under the double-majority rule without the unincorporated vote, do it.

The resounding no vote of the unincorporated voter can keep city residents from getting what they want. There's a disparity in how we pay taxes: County residents pay only for county services, city residents pay for both, so what? If you want programs for your school district or library system and can keep the vote within the city limits, your chances of passage increase significantly. Here are five reasons to keep the vote within city limits for programs benefiting both those in and out of town:

1. The assessed valuation (per acre) is greatest within the city, so even if you include county residents in the overall funding scheme, it won't have a huge impact on the cost per thousand dollars of the property tax.
2. People within city limits have a higher voter turnout than those in the county, so you're already ahead if you have to meet a double-majority rule.
3. It's easier to run an election and bring in votes within city limits because of the population density.
4. The percentage of people favoring taxes for *anything* is higher within city limits than in the county.
5. By holding your voting district to the city limits you eliminate a greater proportion of nonsupporters because of the voting tendencies of those living in unincorporated areas.

Avoid Competing Measures and Think Creatively

There are all kinds of things that have to go to a countywide vote or a vote larger than the city, but schools and libraries aren't among them. Be creative. If you're an elected official, you are in a unique position to help constituencies realize programs that they want in the community. When roadblocks are placed in your way, keeping your community from having great schools, open spaces, and libraries, don't take that road. Find another path.

For years community leaders in our county had been advocating for upgrades to the county library system. Each library had unique challenges for meeting long-overdue improvements to the point that a systemwide upgrade would easily run tens of millions of dollars. The county commissioners were reluctant to put it to a vote prior to other county improvements they felt were more important. The county Friends of the Library group also seemed hesitant as a countywide vote could ultimately be turned down by the voters, leaving them with dilapidated buildings that no longer could house the incoming books or the volume of patrons availing themselves to the system.

The Ashland Friends group was dogging the county to move forward to no avail. Finally they came to me and asked if the city could help. As the Ashland branch was actually owned by the city, we were in a unique position to help. Following the first meeting with the Friends of the Ashland Library it was clear that there was a general mistrust between the Ashland group and the county. There were concerns that Ashland would not get from the county the quality of renovation that the local community wanted and that Ashland would be put on the end of the list after areas that were walking in lock step with the county.

I proposed that the Ashland renovation move ahead of the countywide upgrades. However, the county wanted no part of this proposal. They felt that Ashland voters would not support county system upgrades on top of the Ashland branch renovation and expansion. They also felt that without a strong Ashland vote, the countywide tax measure would have more difficulty surviving an election. Those in the Ashland contingent were concerned about a countywide measure passing period, with or without Ashland, and were further concerned about meeting a countywide double-majority requirement which would be very difficult. Meanwhile the commissioners were not moving.

To get everyone what they wanted we moved Ashland's city library upgrades to be voted on ahead of the county vote. However, should the bond measure pass in the city, we agreed to hold off on issuing bonds to pay for the project until the county had an opportunity at the polls. This had many benefits. First it got us off of our knees begging the commissioners to do something as a citywide initiative required only the Ashland city council to vote to place the tax measure before the voters—an easy prospect. Second, it would guarantee Ashland voters that a specific amount would be spent on our branch and that the renovation outcome would reflect what citizens had agreed upon in the community visioning process. Finally, for those who did not want to pay twice, holding off on issuance of bonds for the project negated those concerns. To underscore this, we agreed to communicate with the voters that a vote for the county system upgrades would result in lowering the debt load for the Ashland improvements with our taxpayers. The latter is important because the first vote held in the city would mean that only city residents would pay for upgrades while folding our improvements into the county bond would mean that those surrounding the city would also share in the tax burden.

In this way, we locked in how much money would be spent in Ashland and exactly what the upgrades would look like.

In the spring the city bond measure passed easily and with an ample double-majority turnout. In the fall, when the county put the whole system before the voters, it was approved and the double-majority requirements were also met. Eighty-five percent of those casting a ballot in Ashland voted for the countywide upgrades, more than 20 points higher than typically vote for county library measures. Given that the second vote actually lowered Ashland's tax on the library upgrade, one would have to wonder what the 15 percent who voted no were thinking.

"Experience is not what happens to a person, it is what a person does with what happens."
—Aldous Huxley

The worst thing we could have done would be to place an Ashland library upgrade before the voters at the same time as a countywide library upgrade, where the two would become competing measures. Although these two sides had plenty of history and suspicion of each other, ultimately we were able to craft an agreement that met all concerns. And given that the city would hold off on floating the voter-approved bonds only until the next election, it pushed the county commissioners into action.

The Super Majority

The super-majority rule, applied to tax measures, requires that either two-thirds or 60 percent of those voting approve the measure before it may take effect. Here your objective is dramatically different from when your constraint is a double majority. The best defense you have to pass anything with a super majority is to place your money measure on an election with the lowest voter turnout possible and no competing measures. Then you must identify your supporters and have a top-notch GOTV effort to get them to the polls or to mail their absentee ballots.

A few years back, in Marin County, California, supporters of a school facility plan used an interesting tactic to pass their bond measure under the super-majority rule. The supporters of the measure determined that those 65 and older were both a no vote and likely voters. To move this age group over to the yes column, the bond measure excluded them from having to pay, but did not exclude them from the vote. The campaign then worked hard to turn out the 65 and over age group, who had nothing to lose by voting yes. The facility plan passed.

Given that many seniors are two generations away from having children in public education and that they have probably paid enough, this seems like a happy compromise.

The State Initiative and Referendum Process

There are three types of initiatives:

1. *Direct initiative:* The completed petition places a proposed law or amendment directly on the ballot, bypassing the legislative process.
2. *Indirect initiative:* The completed petition is submitted to the legislature, which then may enact the proposed measure or one substantially similar to it. If the legislature fails to act within a specified time, the proposal is placed on the ballot.
3. *Advisory initiative:* The outcome provides the legislature with a nonbinding indication of public opinion.

There are four kinds of referenda:

1. *Mandatory referendum:* Requires the legislature to refer all proposed amendments to the constitution as well as measures regarding tax levies, bond issues, and movement of state capitals or county seats.
2. *Optional referendum:* The legislature may refer to the citizens any measure that it has passed. This is often called a referral.
3. *Petition referendum:* Measures passed by the legislature go into effect after a specified time unless an emergency clause is attached. During that interval, citizens may circulate a petition requiring that the statute be referred to the people either at a special election or at the next general election. If enough signatures are collected, the law is not implemented, pending the outcome of the election. The signature requirement is usually lower and the time allowed to gather signatures less than for a straight initiative.
4. *Advisory referendum:* The legislature may refer a proposed statute to the voters for a nonbinding reflection of public opinion.

Initiative and Referendum Procedures

1. Preparing the Petition

    Preparing the initiative petition and organizing the collection of signatures is the responsibility of the chief petitioner(s). The text of the proposed measure is drafted by the chief petitioner(s), with legal assistance if desired, and filed with the secretary of state for state initiatives and the local election office for local initiatives.

2. Filing the Petition

    Any prospective petition must include the names, addresses, and signatures of the chief petitioner(s), a statement of sponsorship signed by a certain number of registered voters and verified by county election officials, a form stating whether or not the circulators of the petition will receive payment, and the complete text of the proposed measure.

> *"Here may the youth of this extensive country forever look up without disappointment, not only to the monuments and memorials of the dead, but to the examples of the living."*
>
> —John Adams of the nation's new Capitol

3. Obtaining the Ballot Title

    State statutes usually provide strict timelines for moving a filed petition through the process to obtain a ballot title. For statewide initiatives, all petitions are filed with the secretary of state, and two additional copies are sent to the attorney general, who prepares a draft of the ballot title.

4. Preparing the Cover and Signature Sheets

    The chief petitioner(s) must submit a printed copy of the cover and signature sheets for approval prior to circulation. The cover sheet must include names and addresses of the chief petitioner(s), the proposal itself, the ballot title, and instructions to circulators and signers. The cover sheet must be printed on the reverse of the signature sheet and contain instructions to signature gatherers. Notice of paid circulators must be included. Signature sheets must never be separated from the cover sheet and the measure's text.

5. Circulating the Petition

    As soon as approval is obtained from the election officer, the ballot is certified and may be circulated for signatures. Usually you can withdraw the petition at any time. Any registered voter may sign an initiative or referendum petition for any measure being circulated in a district where the registered voter resides. All signers on a single sheet must be registered voters residing in the same county.

6. Filing the Petition for Signature Verification

There's a deadline for signature verification statewide (usually four months) and locally (usually less time).

7. Filing Campaign and Expenditure Information

Within a specified period after filing petition signatures for verification, the chief petitioner(s) must file a statement of contributions received and expended by them or on their behalf.

Before a political committee receives or expends any funds on a measure that has reached the ballot, the committee treasurer must file a statement of organization with the secretary of state, and subsequent contributions and expenditures must be reported. Sometimes this must be done even if a petition is withdrawn.

Table 10.1 States with Citizens' Initiative Authority for Constitutional Amendments and Statutes. This table summarizes the initiative process in other states.

STATES WITH CITIZENS' INITIATIVE AUTHORITY
for Constitutional Amendments and Statutes

State, Date Adopted	Constitution Signature Basis	Statutes Signature Basis	Amend or Repeal by Legislature	Restrictions
Alaska, 1959	Not allowed	10% of votes in general election from 2/3 of districts	After two years can repeal or amend	No revenue measures, appropriations, acts affecting judiciary, local, or special legislation. No laws affecting peace, health, or safety
Arizona , 1910	15% of vote for governor	10% of vote for governor	Yes	One subject only; legislative branch only
Arkansas, 1909	10% of eligible voters	8% of eligible voters	2/3 vote in each house	Limited to legislative measures
California, 1911	8% of vote for governor	5% of vote for governor	With voter approval	One subject only
Colorado, 1910	5% of vote for secretary of state	5% of vote for secretary of state	Statutes, yes Constitution, no	One subject only
Florida, 1972	8% presidential election; 8% from ½ from each congressional district	Not allowed	Amend, yes Repeal, no	One subject only
Idaho, 1912	Not allowed	10% of vote for governor	Yes	No provisions
Illinois, 1970	8% of vote for governor	Not allowed	No provisions	Limited to legislative branch; structural and procedural subjects only
Maine, 1908	Not allowed	10% of vote for governor	Yes	Any expenditure in excess of appropriations is void 45 days after legislature convenes

(continues)

Table 10.1 (continued)

State, Date Adopted	Constitution Signature Basis	Statutes Signature Basis	Amend or Repeal by Legislature	Restrictions
Massachusetts, 1918	3% of vote for governor; no more than 25% from one county	3% of vote for governor; no more than 25% from one county	Yes	Not for religion and judiciary, local, special legislation, or specific appropriations
Michigan, 1908	10% of vote for governor	8% of vote for governor	Yes, by 3/4 of each house	Applicable to statutes that legislature may enact
Mississippi, 1992	Qualified elector, 12% of vote for governor, 1/5 from each congressional district	Not allowed	Yes, with voters' approval	No modification of bill of rights, modification of public employees' retirement or labor-related items
Missouri, 1906	8% of vote for governor, 8% from each of 2/3 of congressional districts	5% of vote for governor, 5% each from 2/3 of congressional districts	Yes	One subject; not for appropriations without new revenue; not if prohibited by constitution
Montana, 1904	10% of vote for governor, 10% from 2/5 of state legislative districts	5% of vote for governor, 5% from 1/3 of state legislative districts	Yes	One subject; not for appropriations; not for local and special laws
Nebraska, 1912	10% of eligible voters, 5% each from 2/5 of counties	7% of vote for governor, 5% each from 2/5 of counties	Yes	Limited to matters that can be enacted by legislature; no more often than every three years
Nevada, 1904	10% of total votes in last general election, 10% each from 3/4 of counties	10% of total votes last general election, 10% each from 3/4 of counties	After 3 years	No appropriation or require an expenditure of money unless a sufficient tax is prohibited
North Dakota, 1914	4% of resident population	2% of resident population	After 7 years except by 2/3 vote in each house	Not for emergency measures, appropriation for support and maintenance of state departments and institutions

(continues)

Table 10.1   (continued)

State, Date Adopted	Constitution Signature Basis	Statutes Signature Basis	Amend or Repeal by Legislature	Restrictions
Ohio, 1912	10% of vote for governor, 1.5% of each from 1/2 of counties	3% of vote for governor, 1.5% each from 1/2 of counties	Yes	One subject; not for property taxes; legislation only
Oklahoma, 1907	15% of votes cast for office with highest number of votes	8% of votes cast for office with highest number of votes	Yes	Single subject; legislative matters only
Oregon, 1902	8% of vote for governor	6% of vote for governor	Amend and repeal, Yes	Single subject; legislative measure only
South Dakota, 1898	10% of vote for governor	5% of vote for governor	Yes	Except laws as necessary for immediate preservation of public peace, health, or safety, support of state government and existing public instruction
Utah, 1900	Not allowed	10% of vote for governor, 10% each from 1/2 of counties	Amend, Yes	Legislative matters only
Washington, 1912	Not allowed	8% of vote for governor	After 2 years, 2/3 of each house	Legislative matters only
Wyoming, 1968	Not allowed		Amend, yes; repeal after 2 years	No earmarking, make or repeal appropriation create courts, define jurisdiction of courts or court rules, local or special legislation defeated initiative within 5 years, or legislation prohibited by constitution.

SOURCE: Oregon League of Women Voters, 1996.

11

GETTING OUT THE VOTE (GOTV)

IN THIS CHAPTER

- *The Essentials*
- *Identifying Your Voters: Voter ID*
- *Last-Minute Efforts to Persuade Voters*
- *Poll Watching*
- *Phoning*
- *The Absentee Ballot and Early Vote*
- *Vote By Mail*
- *Organizing the GOTV Effort*
- *Push Polls*

Make no mistake; everything you have done up to this point is about the GOTV effort. Everything. You've canvassed, mailed, advertised, phoned, raised money, and delivered your message again and again and again. Why? To move voters and activate your base for support on election day. But voters get busy: Kids get sick, cars break down, food boils over, an old friend calls. . . . In short, life gets in the way, and somehow 8:00 P.M. rolls around and best intentions to vote are out the window. Now, after months of campaigning, your job, your one and only job, is to remind, remove obstacles, and motivate your support to do their civic duty.

"[Push polls] breed cynicism about politics, and we believe they contribute to declining response rates for polls."

—Michael Traugott,
American Association for
Public Opinion Research (AAPOR)

While canvassing is about activating people who you *think* will vote favorably, a GOTV effort is about activating voters who you *know* will support your cause. With your base you know because of registration, neighborhood, and historical voting patterns. With everyone else, you know because your campaign has personally contacted them and has been told. Identifying how the swing and undecided voter will vote is called voter ID. Getting your support out on election day is called GOTV.

"One thing the world needs is popular government at popular prices."

—George Barker

Whether voter ID is conducted while canvassing or during phone bank calling, the campaign must keep track of voter intentions (supportive, somewhat supportive, undecided, somewhat opposed, opposed) and secure a current phone number for election night.

The Essentials

Activating Your Base

Regardless of whether your campaign conducts voter ID, you must activate your base to increase voter turnout. Although your base vote has not received the same level of attention as potential swing voters, they have not been neglected either. Your base support, that is, party loyalists, have received some direct mail, have lawn signs, and have seen and heard your ads. In some cases, they have even been canvassed. When it comes to the GOTV, this group is extraordinarily important. Your precinct analysis has told you who among your base will vote with very little effort from the campaign and who needs to be reminded before election day.

"Persistence in the face of adversity is what wins an election."
—Patricia Schifferle, former Assistant to the Speaker, California

Those who need a little prodding can actually be quite different depending upon their context. With these voters there are generally two groups. The first are those who live in areas of equal or slight registration advantage (up to 10 points) but are disengaged. The second group is also disengaged, but they are embedded in neighborhoods where their party (and that of the candidate) is greatly outnumbered.

For our purposes, you will have three strategies for your base:

1. Your hard-core voters, those who traditionally have high turnout rates, will need little effort from the campaign. Although it is a good idea to canvass them with a drop piece on election day, if time, money, volunteers, and logistics are a problem, this activity could be dropped.

However, it will be important to track the returns from these precincts, because you are really counting on them. If it looks as though their turnout will be down, the campaign should be ready to activate them with GOTV phone calls.

2. For your lazy yet loyal voter (high support/low to medium turnout) your campaign has canvassed, mailed, called, and canvassed them again. Now you need to stay on them like a fly on compost. If you're in a state that doesn't use vote by mail, your GOTV team will closely watch the polls and absentee lists to make sure these voters do their duty. If they don't, you will need to call them. These are the voters you must continue to activate in the days leading up to the election; remind them that voting early helps your volunteer efforts, and emphasize that their vote and their vote alone will make the difference in a win. For the precincts that are loaded with lazy voters, organize canvass teams to go in and rattle their cage on election day. In vote-by-mail elections, send canvassers in to pick up ballots and return them to the drop boxes for the voter.

3. The third group is a little trickier. Voters registered in your party who live behind enemy lines will need very specific attention, as they are often the most difficult to activate. These voters should be treated like swing voters: They must get direct mail from the campaign, and they should be canvassed by the candidate. It is critical that these voters be part of your voter ID effort, as they are the least predictable of your entire party. Your swing analysis will tell you what percent will always vote party. Voter ID will tell you, by name, whom you can count upon. I recently worked on a campaign for a Democrat where nearly all the support was in areas of heavy Republican registration. During the GOTV, all party voters were called, but more than a third of them said, "Why are you calling me? I'm a registered Republican and always vote Republican." Since we were working from county registration lists that clearly indicated that their registration was Democrat, it was a little disorienting. The good thing about this group is that if you identify them as supporting your opponent and then do not contact them again, they tend to be nonvoters.

Swing Voters

The next group of voters your campaign will identify are those who live in precincts with high numbers of swing voters. Recall that the precinct analysis has told you exactly which precincts they live in and how many of them you need to win. Because the campaign must have a clear reading of who will be supporting you, who is undecided, and who will not move, use the candidate, volunteers registered in the opposing party, and your best can-vassers to knock in these areas. Your campaign must keep track of the voters who say they will support you and send persuasion mail to the undecided. After the persuasion piece has been mailed, the campaign should follow up with a phone call to determine whether the voter's support can be counted on. If the answer is yes, two questions are asked: (1) Will you take a lawn sign? And (2) Can we use your name on an endorsement ad?

You want the swing voter to go public. These two simple and inexpensive "public" contributions to the campaign will guarantee a vote. Depending on the reason, if the voter says no to both of these questions, you should assume that on the issue of support, you have been told what you want to hear rather than given a guarantee.

The Pleasure of Your Company

It's always a good idea to be aware of other ballot issues that may affect your turnout or that of the opposition. If no other campaign is conducting a strong GOTV that will help you, do not let anything keep you from running a comprehensive one for your campaign. In a close election a GOTV is the difference between winning and losing.

If you're involved in an election where a controversial measure is also on the ballot, there may be a high voter turnout that significantly affects your efforts. For example, a few years back I was working for a progressive Demo-crat who was on the ballot with two ballot measures intended to limit the rights of a targeted minority. Our campaign had a well-organized GOTV, and we had conducted voter ID from September through November. The com-mittee working in opposition to the two ballot measures also had a great GOTV effort, which helped ours even more. The state Democratic caucus was running tracking polls, and we knew we were neck and neck with our opponent. We also knew from polling that the two ballot measures were going down statewide. What we had not anticipated was the precincts of the sinners turning out in huge numbers to vote yes on these ballot measures, and, as long as they were there, they voted against our candidate as well.

Unfortunately, we realized too late that we spent far too much time iden-tifying and getting out the vote where the proponents of the two ballot mea-sures were also working. Had we left this portion of the electorate to the other campaign, more volunteer time and energy could have been freed up for voter ID and GOTV of our persuadables.

Disorganized and uncoordinated GOTV efforts can enrage hard-core vot-ers. In Ashland, largely because of the statewide passage of the double-majority requirement in 1997, we have had a GOTV machine that rivals any in the state. Voters are conditioned to vote early if they do not want to be bothered with activation calls during the week leading up to the election. However, in the 2000 general election, other well-meaning campaigns, specifically those working for candidates running for state and federal office, duplicated the efforts of hundreds of volunteers working on our campaign. Making matters worse, a local teacher, anxious to involve students in the electoral process, conducted yet another GOTV effort. As a result, voters were called three or more times in a single evening. It was ugly.

This kind of voter harassment must be minimized if at all possible. To avoid it, conduct cooperative GOTV efforts with other campaigns, or, at the very least, call and see what other campaigns intend to do. Call all campaigns that may inadvertently duplicate your efforts and carve up the county so that there is no overlap in calling areas. Contact high schools and let leadership and government teachers know how, when, and where their students can help.

Identifying Your Voters: Voter ID

Whether identifying voters by phone or by canvassing, you will need walking lists. These lists can be generated from the CD-ROM of registered voters you bought from the county, directly from the county itself, from a voter contact service, or from an organization that is endorsing your efforts.

No matter where you get your walking lists, you must first conduct a precinct analysis to know where to focus your voter ID efforts. Since you do not want to waste time on households where registered voters do not participate, prepare your lists so that only the two out of four voters—those who voted in two (or more) of the past four elections—are listed. These lists will need to be organized by precinct and then by street and street number.

The lists should be prepared so that streets are separated by page. Across the top of each page have: "Supporting," "Leaning support," "Undecided," "Leaning no support," and "Not supporting," or use a number rating system correlated with these categories from one to five that corresponds to the categories from "supporting" to "not supporting."

Once you have the walking lists, you will ID voters by canvassing, phoning, or both.

Canvassing for Voter ID

If you intend to ID voters while canvassing, you need to organize the walking lists to coincide with and match your canvassing maps. This is a lot more work than you might imagine. *Do not let just anyone help you with this task!* If you do, you'll spend days undoing and redoing. Once you match a walking list to a canvassing map, place the list *inside* the canvassing envelope.

If you are canvassing to ID voters, you will need twice the number of canvassers normally required, *or more*. At the door, each of your canvassers must ascertain whether the house will be in favor, opposed, undecided, or leaning in some way. If voters are leaning toward support or undecided, your campaign should be ready to follow up with litera-

"There is no knowledge that is not power."

—Ralph Waldo Emerson

ture or a phone call to bring them into your camp. If no one is home, you must have clean-up teams going out to re-knock or do the voter ID at phone banks to determine how people intend to vote.

The idea here is to identify individual voters who support your candidate and compile a list of these supporters so that your campaign can track them on election day and remind them to vote if it looks like they might be a no-show.

Voter ID by Phone

Although it puts a heavy burden on the phone bank team, I tend to prefer voter ID by phone, for a number of reasons:

1. For some canvassed areas, only 40 percent of the households have anyone at home during the canvass. That means that the remaining homes have to be recanvassed or called anyway.
2. It is generally easier to get phone volunteers than canvass volunteers, and canvassing for voter ID eats up people.
3. Although canvassers can read body language and facial expressions to determine voter intent, voters are often more forthcoming on the phone about their support, especially if they support your candidate or issue-based campaign. It's sometimes hard for voters to tell candidates or volunteers face-to-face that they will be supporting the opposition.
4. Voter ID by canvass will sometimes net individuals who are not registered to vote.

Whether by phone or canvass, your goal should be to target 10–15 percent of the total number of votes you need to win. As the area and voting population increases, your voter ID ef-

"Winners never quit and quitters never win."

—Bob Zuppke, Illinois football coach

forts must also expand. Always start with the precincts that will give you the most return for the effort. For voter ID, that means going into swing voter precincts to look for swing voters and calling your embedded party registration living behind enemy lines.

If you are conducting voter ID by phone, you can use walking lists. Be sure to include phone numbers if it is your intention to use the same lists for both types of voter ID. Should you decide to identify all voters by phone and use canvassing only for activation and persuasion, you might as well prepare your calling lists in a format that will work best at the phone banks.

Pull precincts where you want to ID voters and sort by last name alphabetically and by phone number. If you sort only alphabetically, you risk repeating calls to households where people have different last names. If you sort by name and phone number, you improve your chances of catching and organizing duplicates in a way to prevent repeat calls.

To identify your supporters, systematically call every registered voter in the identified precincts. Remember, you are first calling areas that have a high swing voter tendency, so you will be calling as many voters as you can reach. Often, county lists do not have all of the phone numbers listed, so you may need to set up clerical sessions to look up phone numbers before your phone banks begin. Don't forget to check Web directory services. Phone banking to identify supporters goes much quicker than canvassing.

In your first round of phone calls, your campaign has a couple of choices: You can conduct blind calls or persuasion calls. In a blind call, volunteers ask questions about the candidates or issues but do not reveal for whom they are working. In a persuasion call, the caller immediately lets the voter know which organization is behind the calling effort. I prefer the persuasion call simply because it saves time by eliminating one step. If you start with a blind call and the voter is undecided or has a question about one of the candidates, your volunteer cannot field the question or attempt to persuade. Your campaign must be ready to follow that call with direct mail or another call from the campaign to try to persuade the voter.

If the first call is a persuasion call and your volunteer finds an undecided voter, he or she can immediately provide information that may help move the voter to support your candidate or cause. A campaign can also use an endorsement group to draw voters in a persuasion call, such as the National Rifle Association, a clean air coalition, teachers, nurses, and so forth. You can also use people from within a particular precinct to call their neighbors: "Hello, is this George? Hi, I'm Shirley Smith, I live just down the street from you. . . ." Indirect supporters can be very persuasive.

"To do great and important tasks, two things are necessary: a plan and not quite enough time."
—Anonymous

Last-Minute Efforts to Persuade Voters

1. Mail or walk a door hanger to your high-priority precincts reminding them to vote.
2. To swing precincts, mail or walk a persuasion piece that features an individual or group that normally would not support your cause or candidate (validators) to encourage voters to split their ballots.
3. Mail pieces designed to give information to the voters such as polling places, how to mark a ballot for your write-in candidate, whom to call if a ballot needs to be picked up, or whom to call for a ride to the polls. These are very effective and often rise above other direct mail clogging mailboxes in the last week.
4. While mail is easier, showing that your campaign is rich with volunteers can be far more effective, especially given the huge amounts of political mail seen in the last days of a campaign. Any big canvassing effort is bound to draw positive attention.
5. The night before election day, move lawn signs from one location to another. People get desensitized to lawn signs, but if a new one goes up in a neighborhood or, better yet, ten new ones appear, voters will notice.
6. Attach helium-filled balloons to lawn signs located on busy streets.
7. Hand paint specialty signs for a specific neighborhood and place them the day before the election. "Elect Mayor Daniels for a central bike path." "For more parks, elect Daniels." You want a personalized message for just that neighborhood that will present the look of an upwelling of new support. (I have used the reverse side of old lawn sign stock for this.)
8. Have the local paper place a 3-inch-by-5-inch Post-it note on the front page of the paper reminding people to vote for your candidate or cause. Use a yellow Post-it, red ink, and a style and size of font that looks like handwriting yet is very easy to read. Our local paper has done this from time to time for local businesses—usually for oil changes. The first time I saw one, I could not believe how it popped out at me as I unfolded the paper in the morning. So we did one for a GOTV on a double-majority issue-based campaign in the 2003 primary. Although the Post-its must be printed somewhere else, our local paper will do the insert for $142 per thousand. It is very effective.
9. Some local papers that place the daily in a plastic bag will sell advertising space on the bags. Like the Post-it note inside the folded paper,

this "message on a bag" goes to people who subscribe to and presumably read the newspaper—some of the more likely voters. Check with the newspaper to see if it can use different messages for different cities or areas within your voting district.

Avoid Untargeted Activities

A GOTV effort is most effective in elections where there is voter apathy and low voter turnout is expected. Through the GOTV, you bring up the turnout of one segment of the population while leaving the support for the opposing camp alone. Still, every candidate I have worked for has wanted to stand at the entrance of the county fair, set up a table on the plaza in the heart of the community, wave signs at commuters, or hand out flyers in front of a grocery store. Unless you are conducting an untargeted activity such as this in a community where your candidate has overwhelming support, it can actually work against your GOTV effort. Remember, getting-out-the-vote is about getting *your* voters to the polls, not all voters. Unless it is a double-majority election, reminding *everyone* that they need to vote is counterproductive.

One might also argue that there are far better ways to use the candidate's time than standing on a corner during rush hour. Personally, I like to keep the candidate busy and out of my hair on election eve and election day. It's a great time to have him or her on the phone for GOTV or canvassing a high-priority precinct. It is also an excellent time for the candidate to call and thank supporters for their donations and volunteers for their time.

The GOTV: A Raft in a Hurricane

There comes a point in a campaign where you and your team have done everything you could possibly do. You have run a tight, well-organized campaign and raised enough money to get a clear, resonating message across to the voters. You may have been outspent by an opposition that had better television ads, brochures, press, and direct mail. But as the election draws near and you prepare for the GOTV, remember that both your campaign and your opponent's are headed into the same storm. If your efforts have

"Let me tell you the secret that has led me to my goal. My strength lies solely in my tenacity."

—Louis Pasteur

placed you within striking distance, the GOTV is a great equalizer, often making the difference between a win and a loss. In the end, the odds are best for the team that is better prepared.

Although there are many who would disagree, I have found that by the final three weeks of a campaign most voters have made up their minds.

While campaigns send copious amounts of direct mail, especially toward the end, if you have not made your case by then, no amount of money or direct mail is going to change that. Don't misunderstand: There will still be voters struggling with the decision of whom to vote for, which is one reason a comparative piece is best left until last. However, by the end of a campaign, the effort is really about who can rally the most troops out of the bunker, regardless of how many happen to be in there. Effective last-minute direct mail pieces are more about relocking your base and rallying your troops to get out and vote than about moving voters from one bunker to another. Although there may be last-minute revelations that will swing campaigns twenty points, those are the exception, not the rule.

After the recall of Governor Gray Davis in California, voters were surveyed and asked (among other things) what impact the last-minute allegations of sexual harassment charges had on their support of Arnold Schwarzenegger. The surveys "showed that more than two-thirds of the voters had made up their minds more than a month before the election. As a result, the intense publicity in the last week of the campaign about accusations of Mr. Schwarzenegger's unwanted sexual advances appeared to have had little effect on how women—and others—voted" (Katherine Seelye and Marjorie Connelly, "Signaling Voter Unrest, Schwarzenegger Cut Deep into the Democrats' Base," *New York Times,* October 9, 2003).

In the last month before the 2000 presidential election, polling numbers showed Gore and Bush bouncing in and out of the lead. At the time this was attributed to voter whim. However, after analyzing fifty-two polls conducted by seven polling firms, Donald Green and Alan Gerber found that the "preferences toward the candidates changed little" and that "the failure of certain polls to predict the closeness of the actual vote reflects sampling bias, not the electorate's capricious preferences" (Green and Gerber, "What Causes Polls to Fluctuate?" Yale University, August 2001).

After the 2002 general election in Oregon, one political consultant attributed Democratic losses in house seats with close registration numbers to insufficient direct mail and a general unwillingness among Democrats to send hit pieces. However, on closer examination of the eleven close house races, only four of the winning races sent more direct mail pieces, and only five of the winning races sent more negative pieces than the opposition (data gathered from the political consultants involved in house races for both Democrats and Republicans, and the Oregon secretary of state).

While each race has its unique signature requiring specific action, the overriding features of losing campaigns are that they (1) did not communicate a clear message and (2) did not give due attention to the GOTV among last-minute campaign demands.

From day 1, all communication with the voter should be about two things: getting your base to care enough to vote, and moving swing voters and undecided voters to your camp. Keeping track of who moves (voter ID) and getting your base plus those who have moved to the polls (GOTV) is what wins elections, not copious direct mail.

As the final week before the election approaches, everything about the campaign should shift so that attention can be directed to the GOTV effort. That does not mean media, direct mail, or solicitation stops; however, everyone on the team must be focused on filling the phone banks. Like fundraising, GOTV should have its own team leader and timeline. To run a successful GOTV, a campaign must:

1. Have 10–15 percent of the registered voters identified, including, hopefully, most of those outside of the party base in identified precincts of swing voters.
2. Have enough volunteers and phone lines to contact both identified voters and base party voters living in precincts with high support and low and medium turnout.
3. Have a well-organized data system, with someone other than the GOTV coordinator or the campaign manager supplying the campaign with calling lists generated from registration rolls. In vote-by-mail states, this person would also be responsible for getting daily updates from the clerk's office of inactive voters (those who have not yet returned a ballot) for the week leading up to the election.

Once you have identified your supporters, your campaign must track them to see if they've voted. Tracking for vote-by-mail elections, early voting, or absentees can be done electronically. If you are tracking voters at the polls you have a couple of choices: One is poll watching and the other is working your list by phone and asking voters if they have cast a ballot.

"I wanted to look nice if we won, and if we lost this would be nice to be buried in."

—Bob Borkowski, assistant coach, on why he showed up for a game in a black pinstriped suit

Poll Watching

Poll watching is a labor-intensive campaign activity that requires plenty of preparation. It cannot be put together at the last minute, so prepare ahead of time. Find someone who will oversee this activity, and support that person with your volunteer base. Each poll watcher will need lists of people who have been identified as supporters sorted alphabetically and by precinct. Ideally you would use a list of all members of the candidate's party, with supporters highlighted, although a list that includes only your identified supporters is fine.

Things to Do for a Successful Poll Watching Effort

1. Before the election, ask your county clerk or election official what is required of poll watchers. Are there forms that must be filled out and returned? Does the clerk require training conducted by his or her staff? In my area, before the introduction of vote by mail, it was legal for poll watchers to review the poll book, as long as they didn't interfere with the work of the election board. However, in some areas poll watchers can only listen for names as they are being called out.

"It's not so important who starts the game, but who finishes it."
—John Wooden, former UCLA basketball coach

2. Provide poll watchers with an alphabetical list, a clipboard, pencils with good erasers, and a cell phone. It is also a nice touch to send them out with a folding chair or stool. It's a good idea to provide each poll watcher with more than one list so that when volunteers come to retrieve the list to start calling no-shows, time isn't burned transferring names.

3. Place your poll watchers in high-priority precincts (that is, where high numbers of your supporters have been identified), and direct them to note which of your ID'd supporters have voted throughout the day.

4. As the name of the voter is called out, the poll watcher will check the list of supporters to see whether that individual is among those who have been positively identified.

5. Relay this information back to phone banks, and approximately four hours before the polls close, supporters who have not yet voted get a call from a volunteer urging them to get down to the polls.

6. Regardless of what you think about the outcome of the election, tell the phone bank volunteers to impress upon the voters how important it is that they get to the polls, that you predict a *very* close election, and that every vote will count. The supporter who hasn't yet voted must have a sense of urgency to get to the polls and vote.

7. Offer rides to get supporters to and from the polls. If there is a sleeping baby or child, a volunteer may offer to stay in the voter's home while the parent votes.

With the poll watcher, the phone bank, and the transportation effort, you will have a lot of people involved, and you may find that the best hope for pulling it off is to combine efforts with other campaigns.

Format for Poll Watching

There are two basic steps for the poll watching process:

1. Volunteers observe the voters all day—from the time the polls open to two hours before they close—in selected precincts to see who votes. Those who vote are marked off the list.
2. Two hours before the polls close, the final poll watcher of the day takes the precinct list to preassigned phone banks. There, callers divide up the sheets and call all identified supporters who have not yet voted and urge them to get to the polls before they close.

    Note: If your poll watcher wants to stay at the polls longer, he or she can call in names by cell phone to the phone banks.

Precinct Captains

Each precinct where poll watching is to take place must have a precinct captain who is responsible for the precinct team. Each captain has three specific duties:

1. Before election day, phone numbers must be looked up and written on the precinct lists, and your identified vot-

    "The important thing in life is not the triumph but the struggle."
    —Pierre de Coubertin

    ers must be highlighted on the lists. It is best to assemble a clerical team for this activity. If the voters' phone numbers cannot be found, run a line through their names as though they had already voted.

    If your campaign has not identified supporters before election day and the intent of your poll watching is to call all supporters in your highest-priority precincts, then be sure to put a line through the names of those who have voted absentee.

    In the process of writing phone numbers, be sure not to separate the precinct sheets. This task should be completed no later than the Friday before the election.
2. The captain is responsible for recruiting four poll watchers and one standby. These five people need to be certified, trained, and supervised. Poll watchers should meet with their team captain the weekend

before the election. Signed certificates for each poll watcher should be provided to the precinct captains at that time. Your county clerk or county elections office will supply you with all the information and forms you may need.

3. The captain must be present at his or her precinct when it opens at 8:00 A.M. and supervise the precinct on and off throughout the day.

Poll Watcher Responsibilities

1. Arrive a few minutes early at the polling place.
2. Give your signed certificate to the election judge, who is a member of the polling board.
3. Do not engage in conversation with the election board. You may, of course, answer questions, but do not discuss other topics with the board.
4. As voters arrive and give their names to the board, listen for the name and then cross it out on your list as they are voting.
5. Two hours before polls close, the final poll watcher should take the precinct list to the designated phone bank.

In close elections, the poll watchers and phone banks that follow will often supply the margin of votes needed for a win on election day. However, because of the amount of organization required and the labor-intensive demands of this activity, few campaigns conduct poll watching anymore. *If at all possible, do it. Voter ID, poll watching, and GOTV make the difference between winning and losing in a close race.*

"Anything worth doing is worth doing frantically."

—Jane Tower

Regulation of Persons At the Polls

As in all aspects of a campaign, it is important to know the law; however, in poll watching, it is imperative. The polling place has special regulations that cover everything from how close individuals may stand to the polls if they are not voting and are not certified poll watchers to what topics may be discussed by those present. The campaign manager should contact the county clerk well beforehand and get the regulatory information to the precinct captains in written form.

Authorized poll watches are allowed in the polling place and must sign a specific section of the front cover of the poll book. Only as many poll watchers are allowed as will *not* interfere with the work of the election board.

Poll watchers must have written authorization from one of the following:

1. For the purpose of challenging electors at the polling place, either from the county clerk or a political party
2. For the purpose of observing the receiving and counting of votes, from a candidate

> *"The only thing that hasn't changed is our ability to think differently."*
> —Albert Einstein

Poll watchers *may:*

- Take notes
- Have access to poll books, so long as it does not interfere with the work of the board
- Challenge persons offering to vote at the poll
- Challenge entries in poll book
- Wear campaign buttons

Poll watchers *may not:*

- Campaign in any way
- Circulate any cards, handbills, questionnaires, or petitions
- Fail to follow the instructions of the election board
- Take poll books off tables

All members of the poll watching effort should familiarize themselves with the specific election law violations.

Phoning

Let's suppose that you do not have enough people to watch the polling places all day. Don't worry. I recently worked on a campaign where we came up with an approach that was very effective and less labor intensive than poll watching.

> *"Democracy is a contact sport."*
> —Ray McNally of McNally Temple Associates Inc., in Sacramento, California

For this process you will need a good precinct analysis. Remember, your precinct analysis will tell you where your support is and show you where people have voted for candidates or causes similar to yours in the past. Your precinct analysis will also tell you where people live who will *never* vote for your cause or candidate. If it is clear that a precinct has traditionally voted against campaigns such as the one you are working on, don't canvass them, don't call them, don't activate them. Forget them for the GOTV effort. Instead, look for precincts that have been split: those that have narrowly supported or narrowly defeated past campaigns similar to yours. These are the precincts you should call to ID voters. Then on election day call only the *identified* yes voters, even though they may have already voted (figure 11.1).

As for those remaining precincts that have overwhelmingly supported past campaigns similar to yours, it is not so necessary to ID the voter. You know they will tend to vote your way.

On election day, while your people are going down the list of supporters in the marginal precincts calling the *identified* yes votes, they can call *all* of the voters in the high-priority precincts for an issue-based campaign, and for a candidate race, all who are registered in your party. If your campaign has time before election day, you may want to ID the voters in the high-priority

---

ELECTION DAY PHONE SCRIPT

Hello, this is _____ .

I am a volunteer worker for *(name of the campaign).*

I am calling to remind you that the polls will remain open until 8 P.M., and also to encourage you to vote. This will be a very close election, and we really need your support for *(name of person or ballot measure)* to win.

Your polling place is located at _____ .

Will you need transportation to the polls?

> ## If transportation is needed, they can call the following numbers:
>
> _____
>
> _____
>
> _____
>
> _____

Figure 11.1 Election Day Phone Script

precincts as well, but this is not as important. Look at the phone calling on the day of the election as your one last canvass in high-priority precincts. If your precinct analysis is accurate, you will turn out strong support that might have stayed home otherwise. *Remember, here you are not changing minds, just the turnout.*

When a caller reaches someone who has already voted, that person's name should be crossed off the list so that he or she will not be called again. For those who have not voted, it is up to you to decide whether you want to call them again later. If the election is close, you may want to urge them one more time to get down to the polls. However, in general, more than one call a day is an annoyance and is counterproductive.

One important note: *Don't duplicate calling lists for phone banks.* Each phone bank caller or phone station needs a separate and unique calling list.

The Absentee Ballot and Early Vote

Voting absentee used to be a service to the voter who was temporarily out of the area or unable to get to the polls. However, in many states, it has now become the vote of convenience. As ballots become longer and more complex, the busy and conscientious voter is choosing to vote absentee. In a recent California election, it took some voters more than an hour to complete their twelve-card ballot.

With long, complicated ballots, you run the risk of voter fatigue. Voter fatigue occurs when voters actually lose interest in voting as they spend more and more time working through their ballot. Because local elections are at the end of ballots, down-ballot candidates and issues are often overlooked. If your candidate or measure is way down on a ballot, encouraging voters to register and vote absentee at home may help minimize the undervote for those races.

"If the only tool you have is a hammer, you tend to see every problem as a nail."

—Abraham Maslow

There are a number of reasons it is to your advantage to register as many of your supporters as possible to vote absentee or early:

1. Often campaigns don't heat up and get nasty until the final three weeks. As voters are becoming more and more disillusioned with negative campaigning, their response is to stay home on election day rather than vote against the candidate slinging mud. If a candidate or party has a huge percentage of the turnout locked in before things get nasty, they're at a decided advantage.

2. If you know who will vote absentee or by early vote, then your campaign can concentrate on these voters well before election day, closer to when they actually will vote.

3. Nasty weather can affect voter turnout on election day.

In the 1998 midterm election, nearly half of the registered voters in Oregon requested absentee ballots. Of those who requested them, 73 percent returned them (see table 7.1). Of those who did not request absentee ballots, only 41 percent turned out to vote. The absentee ballot represented over 58 percent of the total voter turnout.

Although in the 1998 general election Oregon voters approved vote by mail for all elections, they could already register as permanent absentee voters in 1997. The lists of absentee voters were available from the county clerk for a small charge, and about 40 percent of the names also had phone numbers listed. Having lists of those who will make up nearly 60 percent of the overall voter turnout is very helpful and means that with a little effort any campaign can reach a large group of likely votes, ID whom they intend to support in the election, send persuasion mail to the undecideds, and make sure that those supporting your efforts return their ballots by election day.

"Vote early and vote often."

—Al Capone

In many states the option to register absentee is open to anyone for the asking up to the day before the election. Those who request absentee ballots within the three weeks before an election are the most likely to actually vote. Your county elections office may be able to provide updated lists of those requesting absentee ballots as the election draws near. When someone makes the request, that voter should be immediately contacted by the campaign.

Most states that have absentee voting require that the voter make that request before each election, although in some states, such as California, a voter who has a permanent disability can register to vote absentee always, unless they miss an election. Some states require that a reason for the absentee ballot be given before each election.

Some states have "early vote." With early vote, the registered voter may go to a designated polling place between certain hours and vote just as though it were election day. Depending on the state, it can take place anywhere from four to forty days before an election. As with absentee voting, early vote gives a campaign an opportunity to lock in votes before the election. However, it does require that a campaign peak twice: once for the early vote and/or absentees and once for election day. Direct mail, advertising, canvassing, and everything else must happen earlier for these voters.

Voters love the convenience of absentee and early vote, and those who use these options tend to be among the most likely of the likely voters. For example, in 1996, early vote represented 40 percent of the voter turnout in some districts in Texas.

Whether your state or county has early vote or absentee voting:

1. Check past elections to determine the number who requested or took advantage of this option. For those who requested absentee ballots, look at the percentage who returned their ballot and determine what proportion of the overall voter turnout these voters constituted. Note that this information may already be on the secretary of state's Web site, so check there first. (Web addresses for all elections departments can be found in the appendix of this handbook.)

2. See whether a list of those who requested absentee ballots is available to your campaign through the county clerk or election office.

3. Inquire about updated lists of those who actually vote absentee or early as the election draws near. That way you will not be continually contacting those who have already returned their ballots, burning up campaign money and time.

4. If the lists of absentee voters do not include phone numbers, set up a clerical team to look them up.

5. If you are in a state that offers early vote, hound your supporters to vote early.

"Poll" Watching for Absentee Ballot Requests

Absentee ballots present some unique challenges to the grassroots campaign. Here is an inexpensive way to deal with absentee ballots if lists are not available from the county elections official.

Assign the task of the absentee voters to a team. One person must be willing to go the county clerk's office on a daily basis to find out who has requested absentee ballots. This person keeps a running list. The requests must be checked on a regular basis because voters who request absentee ballots will often fill it out and return it within a very short time frame. Once you know which voters request an absentee ballot, you must try to persuade

> *"You may be disappointed if you fail but you are doomed if you don't try."*
> —Beverly Sills

them to vote for your candidate or cause. Forget the precinct analysis for absentee voters. For this group, you are not hoping that those who don't support you will *not* be voting. You know for a fact that most *will* vote. To persuade these voters, you have a number of choices.

1. Use direct mail to persuade.
2. Send volunteers or the candidate out to canvass these voters at home.
3. Have the candidate, a friend, or a prominent citizen call.
4. Send a personalized letter from the candidate or from a well-known, well-respected local leader of the same party affiliation as the voter.
5. Use some combination of all these techniques.

Vote By Mail

Currently seventeen states are either using or considering using vote-by-mail elections. Vote by mail was originally introduced to Oregonians in 1981, and by 1987 most counties in Oregon conducted vote-by-mail elections for local elections. The cost savings to taxpayers and the increased voter turnout are the two most tangible benefits of vote by mail. According to the Oregon secretary of state's office, the cost savings of the 2000 vote-by-mail primary election over the 1998 primary precinct election was nearly $600,000. "In general, the cost of conducting all-mail elections is one-third to one-half of the amount required for polling place elections" (Priscilla Southwell, "Five Years Later: A Re-Assessment of Oregon's Vote By Mail Electoral Process," 2003).

The principal argument against vote by mail is the potential for voter fraud. However, after more than a decade of using vote by mail, Oregon has had only four cases of fraud resulting in prosecution. One that I personally know about occurred when a husband signed his wife's ballot because she was in the hospital. Getting people to vote at all in America is more an issue than voters committing a felony by voting twice for a candidate they support.

Real voter fraud, the kind that can have tangible results, is far more effective when placed in the hands of those who know what they're doing; a husband signing a ballot for his hospitalized wife is not in this category. The 2000 general election in Florida, where impediments seemed to have been contrived to prevent voter participation, represents the kind of election that needs attention more than vote by mail.

Black voters in Florida and around the country turned out in record numbers on November 7. Since then, many have complained that Florida election officials removed large numbers of minorities from state voting rolls, wrongly classifying them as convicted felons—and accused Florida officials of using police to intimidate voters in some areas. [Jesse] Jackson cited the reports of students from historically black colleges in Florida, who have said they went to the polls carrying voter identification cards and were told they were not on the voter rolls.

The Florida Supreme Court had ordered a hand recount of all ballots where mechanical counts had registered no vote for president. Many of those "undervotes" came from majority-black precincts, heavily Democratic, where aging punch-card ballots failed to record votes for president in mechanical counts. (CNN.com, "Black Democrats Angered by Supreme Court Ruling," December 13, 2000)

With little evidence of fraud, opponents are now claiming that vote by mail represents one more step in the progression of isolation in American society. Although this view is certainly understandable, and isolation is indeed cause for concern, a better solution might be to ban drive-up windows (as we did in Ashland for the same reason) than to come after vote by mail.

Although higher turnout and huge savings to the taxpayer are strong endorsements for vote by mail, vote by mail also increases voter turnout among minorities, single parents, students, people who are paid by the hour, independents, young voters, and people who have moved within the last two years—all segments of society that are underrepresented for various reasons (Priscilla Southwell, "Survey of Vote-by-Mail Senate Election," April 1996).

Vote by mail also makes life easier for the GOTV effort for candidates and issue-based campaigns, which in turn helps communities secure funding for schools, parks, libraries, and needed improvements for government buildings. For state and local governments to provide the option of both absentee and poll voting with tax dollars is a costly luxury we should relinquish.

In mail-in elections, as with absentee voters, the county mails all ballots to the homes of registered voters within a specific voting district. In order to give voters ample time to review the ballot items, ballots are mailed about three weeks before the final election date when they must be at the county clerk's office for tabulation.

"Trust in Allah, but tie your camel."
—Arab proverb

For the purposes of your campaign team, the difference between a mail-in and poll voting lies primarily in the timing of your election and the mechanics of a GOTV. In a conventional election, canvassing continues up until election day, and nearly all of your ads appear in the three weeks before the election. With a mail-in election, the campaign must peak when the ballots are mailed, not the day they are due back. This means that all canvassing should be completed by the weekend following the Friday that ballots are mailed, and ads must start to run at least a week before the ballots leave the county clerk and peak during the first week voters receive them.

"It's far easier to start something than to finish it."
—Amelia Earhart

Even though many voters will return their ballots immediately, your campaign should maintain a presence in the media until the day the ballots are due. You must be prepared to spend more money on ads to span the period from before the ballots are mailed to the voters up to election day.

GOTV and Voter ID

A GOTV effort for a mail-in election is remarkably easy and painless. With vote by mail, counties keep track of who has returned their ballots as they're received, and for a nominal charge they will print or e-mail a list of those who have voted (activity list) or those who haven't voted (inactivity list). For a GOTV effort, you want to know who has *not* voted. Some county elections departments, however, are not equipped to separate the active and inactive lists. For these counties, your data person will have to remove the active voters from the lists as they come in from the county.

Although you want to conduct voter ID throughout the campaign, as the election draws near your team will have to buckle down and make sure that all supporters within targeted precincts are identified.

Here is what you do:

1. Print a list of registered voters in your high-priority/swing precincts (you determined these when you did your precinct analysis).
2. Have a clerical team look up phone numbers. Don't forget to check Internet sources for local phone directories.
3. Find phone bank locations and set up phone banks to begin calling the voters in your favorable precincts to ID them for support of your candidate or ballot measure.
4. If the voter is undecided and needs persuasion, this is the time to do it.
5. Follow up all undecided voters with direct mail and phone calls from friends, colleagues, co-workers, the candidate, or prominent citizens. Stay on the undecided voters until you know where they stand.

6. ID voters who should be supportive of your candidate or cause in lower-priority precincts based on party affiliation, age, income, and education. Be sure to keep track of whether their support is yes, no, or maybe.

7. Follow up maybe's in the lower-priority precincts and leave the no's alone everywhere.

It's in the Mail

Once ballots are mailed, all campaign efforts shift to the GOTV. Hopefully the GOTV coordinator and the field director or volunteer coordinator has a pretty full roster for each night of the phone banks.

> *"The people who win elections are those with the guts to keep on running when nobody else gives them a prayer."*
> —Christopher Matthews,
> *San Francisco Examiner*

If not, it is now the campaign committee's responsibility to help get people to the phones. All of my committee members work at least one evening of phone banks, and I train them to supervise the activity. Although some consultants believe that phone banks should begin when the ballots are mailed to the voters, I like to give voters a chance to get their ballot in without a phone call. Although calling during the first week after ballots have been mailed will give you an initial spike on your ballots received list, any benefits that are realized by phoning early equalize by election day. More important, calling the first week after ballots are mailed puts a campaign at risk of running out of

> *"The wise don't expect to find a life worth living; they make it that way."*
> —Anonymous

volunteers and steam when you really need them—in the last week. This can be disastrous in a double-majority election, where 50 percent of all registered voters must return a ballot before ballots are counted. In terms of a GOTV effort, the last week is the most important, so fill those volunteer seats first.

Ten days before the ballots are due to the clerk, order an inactivity list (alphabetically by precinct) either from the county or from your data person. Again, if your county does not separate those who have and have not voted and no one on your team can remove those who have voted from the lists, line up a clerical team to highlight which ones have not yet voted; this will make calling a little easier for your phone bank team.

Set up another clerical team to look for voters who have said they will be supporting your candidate or cause and have not yet returned their ballot.

This is also a good time to transfer the looked-up phone numbers from the first list you were calling.

Set up phone banks to call and activate supporters who have not yet returned their ballots.

At this point your GOTV effort is two-pronged; not only will you call voters who have been identified as supporting you, but also you will make the calls to turn out your base.

To do this, print out lists of the voters in precincts where the base is supporting but not reliable on turnout. These voters will be called first. Precincts with a voting history of high support and high turnout are called next, to give them a chance to get their ballot in, thereby saving your campaign time. Finally, come back in for a second pass on the lazy base voters.

Each caller can contact fifty voters in a ninety-minute shift. Because you know how many callers you have for each night and how many inactive voters are in each precinct, it is not necessary to print all inactive voters in all precincts—you will need just enough of them to keep your banks busy each night. The next night, you can print out lists for new precincts with that day's active voters already removed. Remember, call only base and identified supporters.

In an Oregon House race I worked on in 2000, forty volunteers called 2,000 registered voters each night for seven nights straight. Still, those 14,000 phone calls did not reflect even half of the 35,000 registered voters, and many voters were called two and three times. While a GOTV effort in a state without vote by mail will focus primarily on support that has been identified, vote by mail allows your campaign to begin its efforts in precincts where your party historically underperforms and to continue all the way to those precincts of high support/high turnout before going back in to work the high-support/low- to medium-turnout precincts. By working through precincts, campaign work is really cut to an efficient level.

For your base voters who are located in low-support/low-turnout precincts, if you have not ID'd them before the GOTV, you can sometimes conduct GOTV and voter ID in the same phone call.

First, you must determine whether the voter on the other end of the phone is supportive. I do this by simply asking. If the voter is not supporting, get off the phone. Don't worry about activating no votes. For those called who say they are supporting your cause but, for whatever reason, still have their ballots, offer to pick them up. In this case, ask the voter to tape the ballot to the screen door or tuck it into the doorjamb, so a volunteer can quickly pick it up without knocking. I've found that most people don't want you to pick up their ballot. Nearly three-quarters of the people we call who are supportive and still have their ballots, instead say that they'll drive it immediately to a drop-off box. Because I can never be sure that a voter's good intentions will be enough, I push the voter just a bit more and say, "Hey, we have someone driving right by your house to get another ballot, let us save you the trip." If they say, "No, I'll do it," then I let it go.

> *"Spend the time to make the foundation right or you will pay in time and money all the way to the roof."*
>
> —Tony Nunes, builder

For the final two nights, Monday until 9:00 P.M. and Tuesday until 6:00 P.M., have phone banks going full tilt, and have runners lined up. More runners are needed for Tuesday than for Monday night. Runners are people whose sole job is to go out and pick up ballots as phone banks turn them up. It's best to use two runners per car so the driver doesn't have to park. The driver stops, the passenger hops out and retrieves the ballot from the screen door or the doorjamb, and off they go. Use runners efficiently: Divide the voting district into logical areas so that runners don't wind up spending an hour to pick up four ballots. As soon as a phone volunteer has a ballot to pick up, put the address and name on a card or piece of paper and route them. Continue to do this until a driver returns and there are enough ballots to pick up in another area. It is best for runners to have cell phones so that ballot locations can be called to the car as they come in.

> *"Out of the strain of the Doing, Into the peace of the Done."*
>
> —Julia Louise Woodruff

On election night, with the polls closing at 8:00, pack it in at 6:00 or 7:00, depending on how many ballots need to be picked up. At this time, all callers become runners. The phones shut down and everyone goes out to pick up the last of the ballots.

Organizing the GOTV Effort

Although phone-bank systems are described in Chapter 3, some repetition would not be amiss here. The importance of having fully staffed phone banks on a GOTV effort cannot be overemphasized. In the example above of three phone banks going each night (one had two shifts of ten and two had one shift of ten), if each shift were short just one caller each night, that would amount to 200 calls per night or 1,400 calls over the course of the GOTV effort. To give you an idea of the impact this can have on the outcome of a race, consider that of seven close house races in Oregon's 2002 general election, all were won or lost by 2,700 *combined*, out of 280,000 voters. Even if you think you will win big, organize a strong GOTV effort. Remember, it is not enough to win; you want to shove the win down the opposition's throat. While George W. Bush proved you do not need a voter mandate to do what you want once in office, that is not the case for down-ballot candidates. For these candidates, a big win means power after the oath and the potential of scaring away opponents in the next election. For issue-based campaigns, a decisive win will tend to dissuade opposition from referring the measure back out to the voters.

Make a spreadsheet listing all volunteers for the GOTV phone bank. The first column contains their names, and the next, their phone numbers. Then have a smaller column with "CB?" (for "called backed?") as the column header; later, a check mark is placed in this column on the printout after a volunteer has been called back and confirmed that he or she will be there for the next day's phone bank. Next are seven columns with dates, one for each night of phone banking. Each phone bank will have its own spreadsheet, listing only the volunteers who will be calling from that location.

Below the dates I list the starting times of the phone banks. For example, the first bank usually runs from 6:00 to 7:30 P.M. and the second from 7:30 to 9:00 P.M. (figure 11.2).

The names on the spreadsheet are kept in alphabetical order. If your lists are short, this detail is less important, but in the example of the phone bank with two shifts of ten for seven nights, the campaign will have 140 volunteers working the GOTV in one location alone. As volunteers let the campaign know if they can do the early or late shift, the time slot is circled in red so that the lead or supervisor can easily see it. It is a good idea to include a blank sheet for people who volunteer to call after the GOTV begins. Each night of calling must have a lead person or a supervisor. The lead's duties are as follows:

1. Arrive a few minutes early and open the phone banks.
2. Have paper cups for water and red pens for marking precinct lists.

NAME	NAME (LAST)	Place lead names here for each night PHONE #	CB?	LEAD NAME Wed. 11/1		Thur. 11/2		Fri. 11/3		Sat. 11/4		Sun. 11/5		Mon. 11/6	
				6:00	7:30	6:00	7:30	6:00	7:30	6:00	7:30	6:00	7:30	6:00	7:30
				6:00	7:30	6:00	7:30	6:00	7:30	6:00	7:30	6:00	7:30	6:00	7:30
				6:00	7:30	6:00	7:30	6:00	7:30	6:00	7:30	6:00	7:30	6:00	7:30

Figure 11.2 Example of a GOTV Phone Bank Spreadsheet

3. Bring enough phone bank instructions so that each caller in each shift will have a set.

4. Bring targeted precinct lists with inactive voters—this is provided by the campaign

5. Have the master copy of all volunteers participating in the GOTV. (I have a satchel with cups, pens, and the GOTV master calling list inside. I secure the precinct calling lists before the phone banks start and either deliver the lists to the leads or have the leads pick them up, at which time the satchel is passed off as well. In outlying phone banks, I have the GOTV coordinator organize everything except the voter lists to call. These are e-mailed to the coordinator early enough for him or her to print them before the phone banks start.)

6. Welcome the volunteers and give instructions (provided by the campaign).

7. Have callers begin, and then circulate and answer questions.

8. Fill water cups and distribute one to each volunteer, refilling if necessary.

9. Once questions subside, call ALL volunteers for the next evening's phone banks, using the master lists for the GOTV phone bank and checking off the CB column for each confirmation. Afterward, look over the CB column; any last-minute cancellations must be communicated to the campaign as soon as possible so the spot can be filled.

10. The next shift arrives fifteen minutes early for training. Begin anew, providing instructions to the next team.

11. At exactly 7:30, the next crew pulls the first shift off the phones and takes over at their desk, continuing to call down the sheets provided for the first shift.

12. Again, circulate, answer questions, pick up old water cups and distribute new ones, and be available for as long as necessary.

13. Once questions subside, get on the phone and make GOTV calls until 9:00 P.M., when the banks close.

14. Clean up all remnants of the work crews: cups, pens, lists, and so on. The pens and the master call list are returned to the satchel along with any unused cups.

15. Lock up and get the satchel to the next lead or back to campaign headquarters.

A couple of years back, I ran GOTV for an issue-based campaign where the system was set up as outlined above. On the third night of phone banks my lead called and told me that three callers had not showed up for the first shift and four for the second. As this had never happened before, I contacted the lead from the previous night's phone banks and found that she had become busy with personal business and never made the calls to remind the next evening's volunteers as instructed. GOTV calling—especially on a double-majority election—is so tight that we had to set up a separate phone bank to make up for the seven callers we lost on that one evening. It is important always to call your volunteers and remind them of the location and time; if a lead does not get to the job, he or she must let the campaign know so that someone else can do it in time to ensure a full contingent at the next day's phone banks.

One other GOTV war story: In 2000 I was running a campaign for a candidate for the Oregon House. We had phone banks set up at a real estate office we had used for many campaigns. However, just before the GOTV, we were informed that the campaign needed to find another location. It turned out that the local Board of Realtors had endorsed our opponent, and we were out. It's always a good idea to have a backup location just in case.

Push Polls

"Push Polls" are nothing more than a telemarketing technique disguised as a real poll to fool the voter. They are used primarily as a tool for a GOTV effort. They are called push polls because they are designed to push a voter away from one candidate and toward another. With push polling, specific voters are targeted and given false and intentionally damaging information under the guise of a legitimate poll; of course, there is no intent to conduct real research. Do not confuse push polls with push questions, covered in Chapter 2. Unlike push questions, where candidates are equally tested for negative and positive campaign issues and themes, push polling questions are biased and designed to have a negative impact on only one of the candidates. They hurt the industry and legitimate polling firms.

Whereas a benchmark or tracking poll selects voters randomly, a push poll targets undecided or swing voters. As Karl Feld, of Western Wats Opinion Research Center, describes them, "Questions used in push polls often sound similar to those used as push questions to test campaign messages in legitimate polls. This is done intentionally to camouflage the true nature of the push poll" (*Campaigns & Elections,* May 2000, p. 63).

Should your campaign be the victim of a push polling effort by the opposition, call the media immediately for a press conference. Calling attention to this kind of misleading and underhanded campaigning is your best defense.

12

THE CAMPAIGN FLOWCHART

IN THIS CHAPTER
- *Building Your Campaign Flowchart*
- *The Campaign Calendar*

You are almost all the way through this handbook and can now decide, given your time, resources, and volunteer base, what campaign activities you are capable of doing well. You are now ready to create a campaign flowchart, which actually marks the beginning of your campaign. For our purposes, a campaign flowchart is identical to a campaign plan except it is a linear model that is placed on a wall rather than in a three-ring binder. If you are working on a state campaign where party members are unfamiliar with a campaign flowchart and instead want a campaign plan, you can convert your completed flowchart to a campaign plan by simply writing down each of the activities, beginning with the election and working backward to the first day of your campaign.

> *"Simply reacting to the present demand or scrambling because of tensions is the opposite of thoughtful planning. Planning emphasizes conscious, disciplined choice."*
>
> —Vaughn Keeler

To make a campaign flowchart, start by listing the tasks you need to complete before the election. These might include canvassing, brochure development, media, phone banks, fund-raising, and lawn signs. Your choices, of course, are dictated by your resources and the type of campaign you are running. For instance, you may not be able to afford direct mail even though you'd love to do it, or you may have decided you do not want to do lawn signs because they are unnecessary in the ballot measure campaign you're working on.

Once you have the list of campaign tasks, all you need to do is transfer them onto your campaign flowchart in the proper sequence. A mock-up of a campaign flowchart is included in this chapter.

Building Your Campaign Flowchart

A campaign flowchart (plan or calendar) is an essential tool in any successful campaign. Flowcharts keep the campaign organized and provide you and your team with a visual plan of the whole campaign. I have also found that the chart can have a calming effect on the candidate and staff because it clearly outlines exactly what needs to be done and when. Dedicate a specific color for each activity so it can be easily traced throughout the campaigning process.

To construct your flowchart, you will need a long, unbroken wall and the following items:

- Five or more Post-it pads in assorted colors
- Butcher or freezer paper
- At least six different colored marking pens
- A yardstick
- Masking tape
- One or two key campaign people (no more) to help you think

If possible, pull in someone who has worked on other campaigns to help you. Although an experienced campaigner is an invaluable aide in building the flowchart, you can also use the table of contents of this book.

To begin your chart, unroll about ten feet of butcher paper and tape it up to a wall. On the far right of the chart, on the bottom, place the date of the day after the election. On the far left, on the bottom, place the date of the beginning of your campaign. It may be the date that you start your flowchart or the date when your first "formal" campaign activity, such as your announcement, is to take place. Draw a single line along the bottom between the two dates.

"The final days are the longest."
—Bill Meulemans

Divide the line into fairly equal monthly or weekly parts by drawing in all the dates between the day your campaign begins and the day it will end. Next, using a Post-it of a different color for each campaign function, begin brainstorming with your helpers and slapping up on the butcher paper the appropriately colored Post-it above the date that you want to do that particular campaign function. For example, if lawn signs are represented by green Post-its, put one that says "Take down lawn signs" on the day after the election, because you know that your crew will have to take down lawn signs on that day.

Work your way backward from the end of the campaign, making decisions as you go. For instance, you know you will need to repair lawn signs the day after Halloween, so put that on a green Post-it above November 1. Lawn signs usually go up one month before the election, so put that up next. You'll need a work party to get the signs stapled if you're using poly tag. This is a clerical function, so choose a different color that will be used for all clerical work. Write on the Post-it "Staple lawn signs," and put it up somewhere in the week before the signs are to go up.

Keep working your way back, thinking through each of the campaign activities you have on your list. Review the chapters and headings in this manual. Think in terms of the progression of an activity and all the subactivities needed to support it.

To continue the lawn sign example, you will need stakes before you can start putting up signs. Decide on a date that doesn't conflict with other lawn sign activities, such as stapling the signs, and write "Get stakes" on the Post-it. Ask yourself by what date the signs must be printed and write "Print lawn signs" on the Post-it. Naturally, before they can be printed, you must have them designed and camera ready. You might want to allow two weeks for this. So, two weeks before the lawn signs are due to go to the printer, affix a Post-it that says, "Design lawn signs." Continue in this fashion for each and every function. Some functions will flow into others. For instance, fund-raising goes everywhere. The clerical team supports a number of activities, some of which may be happening at the same time. Use an arrow from the clerical line down to the appropriate activity line to show the connection. Should dates start to bunch up, move your activity dates around and keep track of them with your Post-its.

Spread Out the Activities

With this method, time periods with too much campaign activity become immediately apparent. For example, if you find by the concentration of multicolored Post-its that brochure development, two direct mail pieces, and a phone bank for an event are all happening at the same time, you may consider moving something to another time slot. Brochure development could move up and be done sooner, and the direct mail pieces may be handled (just this once) by a mailing house, or they may be prepared earlier or later. Your Post-its are mobile for a reason, and you want to take advantage of this during this campaign planning activity. Spread out the activities so you and the volunteers do not get overworked or burned out. If nothing can move, you will know to line up extra help to organize the work.

> *"A perfection of means and a confusion of aims seem to be our main problem."*
> —Albert Einstein

By using colored Post-its for every function in a campaign on the chart, you build a visual representation of the campaign. The process is simple: Just take whatever it is that you want to do, give it a color, and work your way back from the date that you want to see that function completed to the point where that task must start in order to be completed on time. Some of the functions will end when others begin. For example, your brochure must be ready in time for canvassing. If canvassing will take you two months, working each day after work plus weekends, then your brochure must be back from the printer by this time. Therefore, the Post-its for "Brochure development" and "Printing" will end on the flowchart before canvassing activities start (see figure 12.1).

The Activities
Here is a partial list of activities that should be represented on your flowchart:

- Ads—print, radio, and television
- Lawn signs
- Field signs
- Coffees, fund-raisers, special events
- Letters-to-the-editor
- Direct mail
- Brochure development
- Canvassing and precinct analysis
- Phone banks

Once all your Post-its are up and where you want them, you are ready to put together your permanent campaign flowchart. Take another ten feet of butcher paper, your colored marking pens, and a yardstick. Lay the butcher paper on the floor in front of the Post-it flowchart. If there is room, you can hang the new chart on the wall directly below the old one. Now all you have to do is write in and make permanent your campaign commitments on the dates listed. Follow your color scheme. For example, if lawn signs were in green Post-its, use a green marking pen for lawn signs on the flowchart.

"Time is nature's way of keeping everything from happening at once."
—Woody Allen

Above the various dates, write the activity that is on the Post-it for that date, then draw a line in the same color to the next date or activity, and so on, until you have transferred everything from the Post-it chart. By using colored lines, you will be able to follow a particular activity at a glance across the whole campaign. Look at the accompanying example of a typical general election race (figure 12.1).

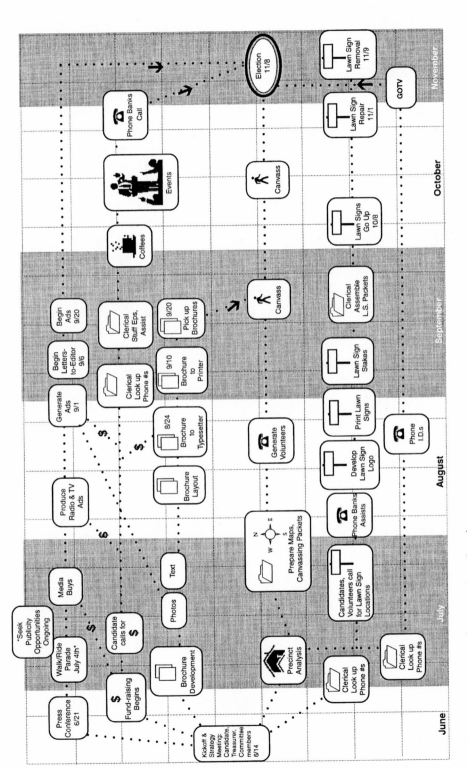

Figure 12.1 Example of a Campaign Flowchart

The Campaign Calendar

As noted earlier, many campaigns lay out the activities and duties of the process in a campaign plan. Nearly every book on campaigning makes reference to campaign plans and provides examples of how to set them up. I have tried to write and use them before and found that they are for a different type of person. Although I prefer a campaign flowchart, I have also had great results using a campaign calendar. A campaign calendar has a decided advantage: Smaller, monthly versions can go into your campaign committee packets for your team to use on an ongoing basis.

All you need for a calendar is a large sheet of tag board, a straightedge, and a pencil. Again, you will map out your activities from election day backward, but on a large calendar that the committee can see. I start with pencil, and then once things are set, go over it in ink. However, if time does not allow that, just get it down as quickly and easily as possible, and hang it up.

You can also simply transfer data from your campaign flowchart to a calendar. It is also helpful to create a calendar in Excel placing all activites under the dates on which they occur. These calendars can be e-mailed to your committee or printed up for the weekly meetings.

Sunday	Monday	Tuesday	Wednesday	Thursday	Friday	Saturday
15	**16** Committee working on Brochure wording Lawn Sign to Graphic Designer	**17**	**18**	**19**	**20** → Lawn Sign to Printer	**21**
22 8PM Campaign Team Meets	**23** Brochure copy to Graphic Designer Call for Volunteers to put up Lawn Signs	**24**	**25** Review Brochure with Committee	**26**	**27** Pick-up Brochure from Graphic Designer	**28**
29 8PM Campaign Team	**30** Brochure to Printer	**1** 11AM Ground breaking for Senior Center 4PM Opponent on Ken Linbloom Show KCMX Call for $	**2** 10AM Temple Emek Shalom Ribbon Cutting Golden Class: Meet the Candidates Candidate call for $	**3** Pick-up Lawn Signs from Printer Organize Lawn Sign Cards	**4** Clerical Party to Staple Lawn Signs - Bundle Stakes	**5** 8-10AM Lawn Signs Go up 12 - firefighters 2 - Carole, Ken 2 - Bill Street Canvass?
6 Canvass 8PM Campaign Team Meets	**7** Candidate Calls for $	**8** 5:30-7PM Chamber of Commerce - Meet the Candidates, AHI	**9** 12 noon LWV Lunch at the Mark 5-6 Canvass $ Calls	**10** Canvass Ashland Mine 6:30-10PM Kathleen Brown Dinner SOWAK, Red Lion	**11** 12 Noon Welcome Leadership Conference 4-6 Canvass	**12** 10AM Canvass 3-6PM Make informercial SOU for Cable Access $ Calls
13 Canvass 12-3 3-5 Canvass 8PM Campaign	**14** 5-6 Canvass $ Calls	**15** 7AM Lithia Springs Rotary Debate 5 min. + Q&A $ Calls	**16** 4 PM Office Hours 5-6 Canvass $ Calls	**17** 10AM Meet the Candidates 1023 Morton St. DEBATE - AAUW/LWV	**18** Letter-to-Voters Ad to Graphic Designer 4-6 Canvass Kennedy Roosevelt Dinner	**19** 10-1 Canvass 4-6 Ribbon Cutting of Environmental Center Design and Write Experience Ad
20 10AM Crop Walk 12-3 Canvass 3-5 Canvass 8PM Campaign	**21** Experience Ad to Grahic Designer Camera-ready Letter-to-Voters Ad to paper 4PM Ken Linbloom Radio Show	**22** 7PM Cable Access Debate	**23** 5-6 Canvass	**24** Camera-ready Experience Ad to paper Run Letter-to-Voters Ad Noon Rotary Debate	**25** Run Letter-to-Voters Ad again 4-6 Canvass	**26** Bob Miller 2-1001 Welcome Lions Club AHI 10-1 Canvass 3-5:30 Canvass Letter-to-Voters Ad again Call for EndorsementAd
27 12-3 Canvass 3-5 Canvass 8PM Campaign Meeting	**28** Run Experience Ad Layout Endorsement Ad Canvass	**29** Run Experience Ad Camera-ready Endorsement Ad to paper Canvass	**30**	**31** Run Experience Ad	**1** Run Endorsement Ad Lawn Sign Team Clean-up 4-6 Canvass	**2** Run Endorsement Ad Canvass 10-1 3-5:30 Canvass
3 12-3 Canvass 3-5 Canvass 8PM Campaign Meeting	**4** Run Endorsement Ad	**5** - ELECTION DAY -	**6** Lawn Signs come down			

Figure 12.2 Example of a Campaign Calendar for a Non-Partisan General Election

13

AFTER THE BALL

"When the fall is all that's left, it matters."
—Lion in Winter

IN THIS CHAPTER
- *Retiring a Campaign Debt*

There are many things you must do to put your campaign to bed, win or lose. However, before taking down your lawn signs, bundling your stakes, paying your bills, finishing reports for the state, closing out bank accounts, and reassembling your house, you must first face election night.

On election night, if you are not in a well-known location with other candidates and their volunteer teams, you should let the press know where they can find you. I have held campaign parties in restaurants and at my home. I prefer the latter. In the last days of the campaign, I let my volunteers know that I will be home and throwing a party in honor of them and a great campaign. I live in a small town, so people call and stop by all night. It is difficult to stay home and watch returns alone if you have been involved in a campaign, especially a winning one. Most people drop by to share the excitement, even if it is just for a few minutes. My home is open.

If your campaign was one that covered an area larger than one city, you need to go to a more central and public location. Again, tell all your volunteers where you will be and invite them. Spend election day or even the weekend before the election calling and personally thanking volunteers; this is also a good time to remind them of the election-night gathering. Don't wait to thank them until after the election. If you lose, volunteers are anxious to talk and reflect and comfort, and you are anxious to sit alone on the floor of a dark closet with the door closed.

"Always let losers have their words."
—Francis Bacon

There is no preparing for a loss, and I'm not sure people *ever* get over it. It will change your life, just as winning will. But win or lose, you must be prepared to face the media and do it with class.

In one election on which I worked, I sat with the candidate as the first big returns came in. The shock that went through us as we realized we were losing is indescribable. I remember cameras pointing at our faces. There is something predatory and morose about our society when it comes to watching a leader fall. We had expected a win and were not prepared for what was before us.

"The two happiest days of my life were the day we moved into the White House and the day we moved out."

—Betty Ford

The next day, our pictures were in the paper. I looked for shock, disbelief, upset, disappointment. None of it was there. We just sat, stunned, looking at the huge TV screen in the restaurant. In the story that followed, the candidate thanked his volunteers, his campaign team, and his supporters. He thanked everyone for a chance to serve. The end.

Win or lose, that is the speech. You must be graceful and appreciative. If you win, you must be humble, acknowledge the efforts of your opponent, and immediately begin mending fences that might have been broken during the process. Win or lose, you thank your family, volunteers, supporters, and the community for support. If you lose, there is one more call you must make, and that is to your opponent. Congratulate that person and say that you are on board to help make his or her time in office as successful as possible.

In my second bid for mayor, we won handily, by nearly two to one. On election night my house was full of friends and volunteers. Well-wishers phoned. Everyone brought something to eat or drink. Then a reporter called and said that one of my opponents was convinced that he had lost because of a damaging letter-to-the-editor that accused him of criminal wrongdoing twenty years ago. The reporter said my opponent had suggested that I was responsible for the letter.

"In every thing one must consider the end."

— *The Fables of La Fontaine*

Although I had nothing to do with the letter and the accusation was without merit, it made me feel like the campaign wasn't over.

Have you ever watched a game where the coach for the losing team says basically it's no wonder we lost—we made mistakes or didn't play our best? While it may make that person feel better, it makes the losers feel guilty and the winning team feel slighted.

Be graceful. If you lost, say you put together a great effort but that your opponent put together a better one. Give your opponent a little of the limelight if you won and a lot of the limelight if you lost. Don't blame your loss on an insufficient campaign effort. That translates to "My volunteers are responsible for my loss." The most common feeling among volunteers of a losing campaign is, "What a waste of time that was." Say that you had a great campaign team that put in countless hours and that the whole thing was a ball—challenging, instructive, and fun from beginning to end. Take heart in the fact that you have come to know yourself and the democratic process better.

Should you ever run for office again, you will be glad you acted magnanimously.

Retiring a Campaign Debt

I counsel all candidates to spend within their means. Lending money to your own campaign sends the wrong message to the voting public. A campaign that is chronically short of funds is a sure sign of one that is in trouble. Nevertheless, it happens, and when it does, it is up to you, the candidate or the campaign manager, to retire the debt.

Never walk away from debt with businesses that have provided services to your campaign. Graphic designers, print shops, photographers, and such are trying to make a living, and generally they are very well connected with the community in which you live and hope to serve. In politics, nothing is more important than your reputation. But short of taking a second mortgage out on your home, there are a few things you can do to ease your debt. Win or lose, it is tough to retire a campaign debt. However, if you win, you tend to have more options.

1. If you have run for the state assembly and have won, go through the contributions and expenditures form for all those who gave to your opponent but not to your campaign. Contact those representing "moderate" interests and ask them to match the contribution given to your opponent. It should be obvious which among them will double dip, and it should be obvious which ones you do not want listed on your finance form.

2. Win or lose, you should be able to go to your most faithful donors. Send an appeal to your donor list, explain that you are doing all you can to retire your debt, and ask for some help.

3. Call major donors and ask for contributions. Set up a time each day to make these calls.

4. Reactivate your finance committee.

AFTERWORD

You are now prepared to begin on that time-honored path of a political campaign. Campaigns are enormously fun and exhilarating. If you do everything right, you are almost assured a win. Just a few reminders before you begin:

1. Know the law.
2. Stay on your campaign theme and message, and you will be in control.
3. Deliver that message to your targeted voters: Aim at the souls that can be saved.
4. Redirect negative campaigning at your opponents and use it as an opportunity to restate your message.
5. Work hard and others will work hard for you.
6. Be humble and listen more than you speak.
7. Know who you are before others find out.
8. Smile. Always look as though you're having a great time.

> *"The great use of life is to spend it for something that outlasts it."*
> —William James

Win or lose, you will emerge from the process a different person, a leader within your community.

Appendix

CAMPAIGN WEB SITE RESOURCE DIRECTORY

(SOURCE: *Campaigns & Elections*, June 1999, pp. 35–45)

Search Engines

AltaVista
www.altavista.com

AOL
www.aol.com

Excite
www.excite.com

Go2
www.go2.com

Google
www.google.com

HotBot
www.HotBot.com

Infoseek
www.infoseek.com

Keyword.Com
www.keyword.com

Lycos
www.lycos.com

Metacrawler
www.go2net.com/search.html

"The ax handle and the tree are made of the same wood."
—Indian proverb

MSN Internet Search
search.msn.com

Snap
www.snap.com

Starting Point
www.stpt.com

Yahoo!
www.yahoo.com

Advocacy Groups and Issues

Accuracy in Media
www.aim.org/main.htm

Action on Smoking and Health
ash.org

Alliance for Better Campaigns
www.bettercampaigns.org

Alliance for Justice
www.allianceforjustice.org

American-Arab Anti-Discrimination Committee
www.adc.org

American Association of Retired Persons
www.aarp.org

American Civil Liberties Union
aclu.org

American Israel Public Affairs Committee
www.aipac.org

American Pro-Life Web
www.plnweb.com/index.html

Americans for the Environment
www.afore.org

Americans for Tax Reform
atr.org

Amnesty International
www.amnesty.org

Campaign for Tobacco-Free Kids
www.tobaccofreekids.org

Children's Defense Fund
www.childrensdefense.org

Citizens United
www.citizensunited.org

Coalition for the National Tobacco Settlement
www.tobaccosettlement.org

Concord Coalition
concordcoalition.org

Digital Democrats
www.webcom.com/~digitals

English First
www.englishfirst.org

Fairness and Accuracy in Reporting
www.fair.org

Friends of the Earth
www.foe.org

Gay and Lesbian Victory Fund
www.victoryfund.org

Gun Owners of America
www.gunowners.org

Human Rights Watch
www.hrw.org

Lawyers Committee for Human Rights
www.lchr.org

Leadership Conference on Civil Rights
www.civilrights.org

Log Cabin Republicans
www.lcr.org

"When we're elected, we'll take care of people like you! Okay, boys, throw him out!"
—Richard Nixon to a heckler (*The Almanack of Poor Richard Nixon*, World Publishing Company, Cleveland and New York)

Marie Stopes International
www.mariestopes.org.uk/campaigns_advocacy.html

National Arts Leadership Council
www.artstozoo.org/artslynx/issues.htm

National Association of Socially Responsible Organizations
www.nasro-co-op.com

National Coalition Against Legal Gambling
www.ncalg.org

National Community Action Foundation
www.ncaf.org

National Council of Senior Citizens
www.ncscinc.org

National Organization for Women
www.now.org

National Right to Life
www.nrlc.org

Nature Conservancy
www.tnc.org

Project for the Future of Equal Justice
www.equaljustice.org/statead.htm

Project for Public Spaces
www.pps.org

Safari Club International
www.safariclub.org

Taxpayers for Common Sense
www.taxpayer.net

Washington Office on Latin America
www.wola.org/index2.htm

Women Against Gun Control
www.wagc.com

World Wildlife Fund
www.wwf.org

Media and Publications

ABC
www.abc.com

American Spectator
www.spectator.org

Associated Press
www.ap.org

Atlantic Monthly
www.theatlantic.com

Brill's Content
www.brillscontent.com

Campaigns & Elections
www.campaignline.com

Capitol Watch
www.capitolwatch.com

CBS
www.cbs.com

CNN AllPolitics
cnn.com/allpolitics

Congressional Quarterly
www.cq.com

C-SPAN
www.c-span.org

The Drudge Report
drudgereport.com

The Economist
www.economist.com

E-Vote.org
www.evote.com

The Harvard Political Review
hcs.harvard.edu/~hpr

"In this world there are only two tragedies. One is not getting what one wants, and the other is getting it."

—Oscar Wilde

The Hill
www.hillnews.com

Intellectualcapitol.com
www.intellectualcapitol.com

Liberty Journal
www.libertyjournal.com

Mother Jones
www.mojones.com

MSNBC
www.msnbc.com

Nando Times
www.nandotimes.com/politics

The Nation
www.thenation.com

National Journal
www.cloakroom.com

The National Review
www.nationalreview.com

NBC
www.nbc.com

The New Republic
www.thenewrepublic.com

News Hour with Jim Lehrer Online
www.pbs.org/newshour

Newsmax
www.newsmax.com

Newsweek
www.newsweek.com

Original Sources
www.originalsources.com

Policy.com
www.policy.com

The Political Pages
www.campaignline.com

Political Science Quarterly
epn.org/psq.html

Politics 1
www.politics1.com

Reuters
www.reuters.com

Roll Call
www.rollcall.com

Slate
www.slate.com

Time Magazine
cgi.pathfinder.com/time

U.S. News & World Report
www.usnews.com

US Newswire
www.usnewswire.com

Washington Times' Insight
www.insightmag.com

The Weekly Standard
www.weeklystandard.com

Yale Political Quarterly
www.yale.edu/ypq

Newspapers—Circulation Dailies

The Arizona Republic
www.azcentral.com

The Boston Globe
www.boston.com/globe

Cleveland Plain Dealer
www.cleveland.com/plaindealer

The Dallas Morning News
www.dallasnews.com

The Detroit Free Press
www.freep.com

Minneapolis Star Tribune
www.startribune.com

Newark Star-Ledger
www.nj.com/starledger

New York Post
nypostonline.com

Philadelphia Inquirer
www.phillynews.com

San Francisco Chronicle
www.sfgate.com

Government Agencies

Federal Communications Commission
www.fcc.gov

Federal Election Commission
www.fec.gov

Library of Congress
thomas.loc.gov

U.S. Census Bureau
www.census.gov

Public Information and Political Research

Center for Responsive Politics
www.crp.org

Democracy Net
www.dnet.org

Democracy Place
www.democracyplace.org

E-Policy Network
epn.org

Pew Center for the People and the Press
www.people-press.org

Politics Online
www.politicsonline.com

Public Service

Project Vote Smart
www.vote-smart.org

Media and News

Evote.com
www.evote.com

Opposition Research

Investigative Research Specialists, LLC
www.researchops.com

State & Local Politics

Alaska
www.juneau.com/guide/politics

California
www.calvoter.org/cvf/home.html
www.calnews.com
www.capitolalert.com
www.politicalaccess.com
www.rtumble.com
www.clemens.org/suspects.htm (San Francisco)

Connecticut
www.nutmegpoliticalreport.com

District of Columbia
www.dcwatch.com

Georgia
www.votecentral.com
www.billshipp.com

Hawaii
www.hookele.com/vote/intro.html

Illinois
www.uis.edu/~ilissues

Iowa
www.iowapoliticalhotline.com

Massachusetts
www.erols.com/massvoter
www.the-election.com

Michigan
grebner.com/hats.htm

Minnesota
www.e-democracy.org
mn-politics.com
www.checksandbalances.com
www.opensecrets.org/mn

Nebraska
www.lincolnconnection.org/nepolitics

New York
www.pathfinder.com/NY1/news/headlines
www.nyc.dnet.org

North Dakota
www.prairiepublic.org/features/VIP

Texas
political.com

Wisconsin
www.madison.com/wsj/index.html

Schools and Educational Programs

American University Campaign Management Institute
auvm.american.edu/~ccps

Campaign and Election Seminars
www.campaignline.com

Graduate Programs at Suffolk University
www.suffolk.edu

Graduate School of Political Management, George Wasington
University
www.gwu.edu/~gspm

Regent University School of Government
www.regent.edu

University of Akron, the Ray C. Bliss Institute of Applied Politics
www.uakron.edu/bliss

University of Florida, Graduate Program in Political Campaigning
web.polisci.ufl.edu/campaign.html

University of Maryland, Department of Government and Politics
www.bsos.umd.edu/gvpt

The University of Pennsylvania
Annenberg School for Communication
www.asc.upenn.edu

State Election Offices

Alabama
www.sos.state.al.us/election/index.cfm

Alaska
www.gov.state.ak.us/ltgov/elections/homepage.html

Arizona
www.sosaz.com/election

Arkansas
www.sosweb.state.ar.us/elections.html

California
www.ss.ca.gov/elections/elections.htm

Colorado
www.sos.state.co.us/pubs/elections/main.htm

Connecticut
www.sots.state.ct.us

Delaware
www.state.de.us/election/index.htm

District of Columbia
www.dcboee.org

Florida
election.dos.state.fl.us/index.html

Georgia
www.sos.state.ga.us/elections/default.htm

Hawaii
www.hawaii.gov/elections

Idaho
www.idsos.state.id.us/elect/eleindex.htm

Illinois
www.sos.state.il.us

Indiana
www.state.in.us/sos/elections

Iowa
www.sos.state.ia.us

Kansas
www.kssos.org/elewelc.html

Kentucky
www.kysos.com/INDEX/main/elecdiv.asp

Louisiana
www.sec.state.la.us/elections/elections-index.htm

Maine
www.state.me.us/sos/cec/elec/elec.htm

Maryland
www.sos.state.md.us

Massachusetts
www.state.ma.us/sec/ele/eleidx.htm

Michigan
www.sos.state.mi.us/election/elect.html

Minnesota
www.state.mn.us/election

Mississippi
www.sos.state.ms.us/elections/elections.asp

Missouri
www.sos.mo.gov/elections

Montana
sos.state.mt.us/css/ELB/Contents.asp

Nebraska
www.nol.org/home/SOS/Elections/election.htm

Nevada
sos.state.nv.us/nvelection.htm

New Hampshire
www.sos.nh.gov/electionsnew.htm

New Jersey
www.state.nj.us/lps/elections/electionshome.html

New Mexico
web.state.nm.us/elect.htm

New York
www.elections.state.ny.us

North Carolina
www.sboe.state.nc.us/index.html

North Dakota
www.state.nd.us/sec/Elections%20Division.htm

Ohio
www.state.oh.us/sos/elections/index.html

Oklahoma
www.state.ok.us/~elections

Oregon
www.sos.state.or.us/elections/elechp.htm

Pennsylvania
www.dos.state.pa.us/bcel/site/default.asp

Rhode Island
www2.corps.state.ri.us/ELECTIONS/elections_division.htm

South Carolina
www.state.sc.us/scsec

South Dakota
www.sdsos.gov/elections

Tennessee
www.state.tn.us/sos/election.htm

Texas
lamb.sos.state.tx.us/elections/index.shtml

Utah
elections.utah.gov

Vermont
vermont-elections.org/soshome.htm

Virginia
www.sbe.state.va.us

Washington
www.secstate.wa.gov/elections

West Virgina
www.wvsos.com/elections

Wisconsin
elections.state.wi.us

Wyoming
soswy.state.wy.us/election/election.htm

Guam
gec.guam.net/index.html

Puerto Rico
www.ceepur.org

U.S. Virgin Islands
www.gov.vi/aandd.htm

National Parties

Democrats

Blue Dogs
www.house.gov/tanner/blue.htm

College Democrats
www.collegedems.org/cda

DCCC
www.dccc.org

Democratic Governors' Association
www.democraticgovernors.org/dga

Democractic Leadership Council
www.dlcppi.org

Democratic Legislative Campaign Committee
www.democrats.org/hq/dlcc.html

DNC
www.democrats.org/index.html

DSCC
www.dscc.org

New Democrat Network
www.newdem.org

Progressive Caucus of the U.S. House of Representatives
www.dsausa.org/pc/pc.caucus.html

Young Democrats of America
www.yda.org/yda

Republicans

College Republican National Committee
www.crnc.org

National Federation of Republican Women
www.nfrw.org

NRCC
www.nrcc.org

NRSC
www.nrsc.org

Republican Governors' Association
www.rga.org

Republican Liberty Caucus
www.rlc.org

RNC
www.rnc.org

Other Parties

American Reform Party
www.americanreform.org

Communist Party
www.hartford-hwp.com/cp-usa

Democratic Socialists of America
www.dsausa.org/dsa.html

Freedom Socialists
www.socialism.com

Green Parties
www.greens.org

Labor Party
www.thelaborparty.orgLibertarian Party
www.lp.org

Reform Party
www.reformparty.org

Democratic State Parties

Alabama
www.aladems.org

Alaska
www.alaska.net/~adp

Arizona
www/azdem.org

Arkansas
www.arkdems.org

California
www.ca-dem.org/dems/cadems.nsf/index

Colorado
www.coloradodems.org

Connecticut
www.ctdems.org

Delaware
www.deldems.org

Florida
www.florida-democrats.org

Georgia
www.georgiaparty.com

Hawaii
www.hawaiidemocrats.org

Idaho
www.wepak.net/~iddems

Illinois
www.ildems.com

Indiana
www.indems.org

Iowa
www.iowademocrats.org

Kansas
www.ksdp.org

Kentucky
www.kydemocrat.com

Louisana
www.lademo.org

Maine
www.mainedems.org

Maryland
www.clark.net/pub/mddem

Massachusetts
www.massdems.org

Michigan
www.mi-democrats.com

Minnesota
www.dfl.org

Mississippi
hometown.aol.com/msdempartypolitics/index.htm

Missouri
www.missouridems.org

Montana
www.mcn.net/~mtdemocrats

Nebraska
www.nebraskademocrats.org

Nevada
www.nvdems.com

New Hampshire
www.nh-democrats.org

New Jersey
www.njdems.org

New Mexico
dpnm.org

New York
www.nydems.org

North Carolina
www.ncdp.org

North Dakota
demnpl.org

Ohio
www.ohiodems.org

Oklahoma
www.okdemocrats.org

Oregon
www.dpo.org

South Carolina
www.scdp.org

Tennessee
www.isdn.net/tdp

Texas
www.txdemocrats.org

Utah
www/utdemocrats.org

Vermont
homepages.together.net/~vtdems

Virginia
www.vademocrats.org

Washington
www.wa-democrats.org

West Virginia
www.wvdemocrats.com

Wisconsin
www.execpc.com/democrat

Wyoming
members.aol.com/wyodem/dems.html

INDEX

Absentee voters
  finding likely voters, 160–161
  Getting Out the Vote, 337–340
  write-in candidates, 280
Advertising
  ads for recall attempts, 303
  budgeting for, 73, 77
  choosing a media specialist,
    230–234
  creating good television ads,
    236–241
  endorsement ads, 219–224
  flowchart, 352
  good timing, 224
  placing newspaper ads, 225–226
  placing television ads, 241–245
  radio and television, 226–230
  rules and regulations governing,
    245
  See also Lawn signs; Media
Advisory initiative, 315
Advisory referendum, 315
Ad with purpose, 240
Affirmative action, 184
African-American voters. *See* Black
  voters
Age as voter factor, 160–162
Alcohol consumption, candidate's,
  254
Aldrete, James, 170

"Americans Speak Out About the
  2000 Campaign" study, 226
Analysis. *See* Precinct analysis
Answering machines, 99
Area-specific issues, 182
Asian-American voters, 168
The Ask, 102
Attacks, responding to, 258–259
Attitude, campaign manager's,
  14–15
Auctions as fund-raisers, 84–85, 110

Balancing the ticket, 10–11
Ballot measures, 90, 146–147
Ballot types, 280, 282
Barker, Jeff, 189
Barnes, Roy, 182
Baseball, 43
Base party vote
  direct mail, 180
  Get Out the Vote, 322–323, 344
  opponent's security with, 197
  predicting voter turnout, 146–149
Bates, Alan, 26–27, 48–49, 52, 116
Beaudry, Ann, 288
Begging, fund-raising as, 108
Behavior of the candidate, 251–252
Benchmark polls, 25–26, 29–30, 257,
  348
Birthday parties as fund-raisers, 110

Black voters
accusations of voter fraud,
340–341
cell phone use, 197–198
party affiliation, 167–168
recall election, 301
2000 election, 187
Blind calls, 327
Bock, Audie, 41, 111–112, 283–284
Body language, 211–212
Bricks versus programs, 50
Brochure
brochure development, 32–37
budgeting for, 71–72, 74, 77
campaign theme and message
development, 22–25
direct mail, 114–118
flowchart, 352
importance of, 21–22
layout, 41–50
photos, 33–37, 45, 47–48
polling, 25–32
recall attempts, 303
thank-you notes as, 291–292
write-in candidate, 281
Brown, Willie, 250
Budget
as election issue, 189–190
challenging your opponent's
budget limits, 208–209
direct mail, 80–81, 192–193
preliminary planning for, 71–76
retiring campaign debt, 359–361
sample budget form, 77
special events, 85–88
television advertising, 229–230,
234, 242, 244
timing your advertising, 224
tracking polls, 195–197
See also Finance

Bumper stickers, 245–246
Bush, George H. W., 267–268
Bush, George W., 136, 187, 210, 268,
330, 346
Bustamante, Cruz, 185
Buttons, 246
Buying votes, 113–114

Cable television, 229
Calendar, 354–355
Campaign Assessment and
Candidate Outreach Project,
285
Campaign calendar, 2
Campaign chair or co-chairs, 16
Campaign committee
brochure development, 32
campaign chair or co-chairs, 16
campaign manager, 13–16, 257
campaign message, 24–25
for recall attempts, 302
makeup and functions of, 7–9
preparing for a debate, 268
slogans, 37
treasurer, 10–13
See also Volunteers
Campaign debt, 359–360
Campaigner card, 93, 103
Campaigner Responsibilities Sheet,
95
Campaign finance committee. *See*
Finance/campaign finance
committee
Campaign flowchart, 2
Campaign for Young Voters, 163
Campaign manager
choosing a manager, 13–15
projecting the candidate's image,
257
ten tips for, 15–16

Campaign message
  examining your opponent's
    message, 189
  for library and school campaigns,
    309
  fund-raising, 70, 109
  importance of, 22–25
  importance of message over
    funding, 113
  importance of sticking to,
    257–262
  newspaper ads, 217
  slogan and, 37
  using in speeches, 278
Campaign plan
  campaign calendar, 2, 354–355
  campaign flowchart, 2, 349–353
Campaign team. *See* Campaign
    committee; Treasurer;
    Volunteers
Campaign theme, 22–25
Campaign treasurer, 10–13
Candidate
  announcing candidacy, 204–205
  canvassing, 113, 179–180
  canvassing follow-ups, 177
  case for support, 97
  debates, 265–271
  establishing and comparison ads,
    231–232
  giving up privacy, 247–248
  image, 251–257, 267, 271–279
  importance of sticking to your
    message, 257–262
  insider versus outsider campaign,
    262–265
  knowing the duties of the office,
    248–251
  lying, 253–254, 259–261
  media coverage and bias, 284
  negative campaigning, 284–290
  projecting the proper image,
    251–257
  public speaking skills, 271–279
  stance on issues, 182–184
  television advertisements, 230
  thank-you notes, 290–292
  third party candidates, 282–284
  untargeted activities during
    GOTV efforts, 329
  write-in candidates, 279–282
  young voters' response to, 166
Canvassing
  bad weather, 178–180
  direct mail and, 195
  effectiveness, 170–171
  effectiveness with young voters,
    165
  flowchart, 352
  for voter ID, 325–326
  GOTV and, 321–322
  leaning voters, 171–173
  map packets, 173–176
  matching volunteers to skills, 18
  phone scripts for, 63
  projecting the candidate's image,
    251
  time allotment for, 66–67
  undervote, 153
  vote by mail, 341–342
  walking direct mail, 192–193
Capital punishment, 267–268
Cardinal sins of campaigning, 5
Carnegie Library campaign, 37, 43,
    122, 305
Carter, Amy, 267
Carter, Jimmy, 267
Carter, Rosalynn, 25
Case for Support sheet, 97
Cato Institute, 287

Celebrities, 34, 208
Cell phones, 197–198, 290
Census Bureau, 134
Center for Congressional and
    Presidential Studies, 226
Center for Responsive Politics, 70,
    111
Certified public accountant (CPA),
    11–12
C&E's. *See* Contributions and
    expenditures
Checchi, Al, 250
Children
    incorporating into public life, 248,
        255–256
    involving in canvassing, 179
Children's Cultural and Recreational
    Two-Year Levy, 45, 49
Churches, as source of mailing lists,
    80
Citizens for a Sound Economy
    (CSE), 286–289
City limits, 312
Civic clubs, as source of mailing
    lists, 80
Clerical teams
    directing volunteers, 17
    direct mail preparation, 193–195
    mail-in ballots, 343–344
    organizing activities for, 64–66
Clinton, Bill, 23, 123, 184, 252–253
Close elections, 145–146, 334
Coffees as fund-raisers
    developing public speaking skills,
        275–276
    flowchart, 352
    importance of, 83–84
    media presence, 208
    thank-you notes for, 291
    variations on the theme, 111

Cold calls, 18
Committee to Support, 12–13
Community interests, 113–114
Comparison ads, 231, 237
Comparison pieces, 190–191
Competing measures, 296–297,
    312–314
Confidentiality issues, 62
Constitutions, state, 294, 318–320
Contact cards, 55–56
Contraceptive parity, 289
Contributions and expenditures
    (C&E's)
    as source of budget information,
        72
    initiative and referendum, 317
    large donors, 70–71
    need for accuracy, 11–12
    third-party candidate, 284
Controversial campaigns, 13, 324
Cooley, Wes, 253
Cordless phones, 290
Corporate donations, 287–289
Costs
    direct mail pieces, 114–115
    lawn signs, 121, 123
    libraries, 306
    precinct analysis, 133–134
    radio advertising, 226
CPA. *See* Certified public accountant
Crime, candidate's committing, 259
CSE. *See* Citizens for a Sound
    Economy
Cuban Americans, 170
Cultural and Recreational Levy,
    215–216

Damas, Raul, 170
Data base. *See* Spreadsheet
Davis, Gray, 167–168, 185, 301

Debates
  attacking your opponent, 259–262
  fielding negative questions,
    268–271
  importance of image, 255–256
  mock debates, 273–275
  process and purpose of, 265–268
  projecting the candidate's image,
    257
  public speaking skills, 271–279
  television coverage of, 208
  use as tracking polls, 196
Debt, 359–361
Dellums, Ron, 283–284
Demographic data
  canvassing neighborhoods, 180
  direct mail effectiveness, 181
  finding likely voters, 159
  precinct analysis, 134
Development as campaign issues,
  40–41
DiCamillo, Mark, 161
Difficult people, 14–15
Dinners as fund-raisers, 82–83, 109
Direct initiative, 315
Direct mail
  budgeting for, 72–73, 77, 192–193
  characteristics of successful
    pieces, 78–79
  comparison pieces, 190–191
  effective use of, 185–188
  finding mailing lists, 80
  flowchart, 352
  fund-raising, 76–81, 185–186
  last-minute mailings, 330
  mail preparation, 193–195
  packaging issues, 180–184
  success of, 114–118
  targeting ethnic groups and
    women, 184–185
  targeting your opponent, 188–190
  time allotment for, 67
  type of campaign, 198–199
  using the finance committee for
    follow-up, 91–92
  walking direct mail, 176
Discrimination against minorities,
  170
Dole, Robert, 184, 252
Donations. *See* Fund-raising
Donor cards, 93, 103
Doublebase Mediamark Research,
  227–228
Double majority, 309–310, 314
Dukakis, Michael, 252, 267–268

Early money, 70–71, 108, 243
Early voting, 337–340
Eating in public, 254
Economy as campaign theme, 23
Education
  as campaign theme, 23
  level of voters' education, 159, 167
  school bonds, 306–307
Election data form, 138–139
Election day
  losing the election, 357–359
  phoning identified voters,
    335–337
  poll watching, 331–335
Emotional advertising, 213,
  218–219
Endorsements, 216–217, 219–224,
  324. *See also* Testimonials
Environmental issues, 182
  as campaign theme, 23
  Clinton's response to, 253
  effective direct mail, 188
Environmental organizations as
  source of mailing lists, 80

Equipment
  for a campaign flowchart, 350
  for poll watchers, 332
  lawn sign placement, 126–127
  See also Packets
Establishing ads, 232, 236
Ethical issues, 285
Ethnic gap, 166–170, 184–185, 187
Excel spreadsheet. *See* Spreadsheet
Expenditures. *See* Contributions
  and expenditures
Experience, value of, 111

Federal Election Commission, 160
Feld, Karl, 197–198, 348
Field Institute, 159–160, 167
Field signs, 71, 128–129, 352
Filing dates, 4–5
Finance
  benchmark polls on a shoestring,
    29–30
  brochure layout, 44
  campaign finance committee,
    10–13, 90–108
  funding polls, 32
  photos for the brochure, 34
  voters' pamphlet, 50
  See also Budget; Fund-raising
Firefighters organizations, 80, 123
Fiscal responsibility, 12
Flip-flopping on issues, 183
Flood restoration bond, 310
Florida ballots, 341
Flowchart, 349–353
Food and beverage tax. *See* Meals tax
Food labeling laws, 298
Ford, Gerald, 267
Fraud, 340–341
Frequently Asked Questions sheet,
  100

Friends I Will Call sheet, 93, 104–105
Friends of the Library group, 304,
  306, 313
Fund-raising
  campaign finance committee,
    90–108
  candidate calls, 89–90
  committee members'
    responsibility, 8
  countering big money, 111–114
  direct mail, 76–81, 185–186
  early money, 70–71
  estimated needs, 75
  for a write-in candidate, 282
  for ballot measures, 90
  ideas that take less than one
    month, 109–111
  keeping track of donations, 54–55,
    118
  local funding versus outside
    money, 12
  media presence at events, 208
  need for, 69–70
  phone scripts, 63
  polling for dollars, 32
  recall attempts, 301
  special events, 81–89
  thank-you notes for, 291
  tips for success, 108–109

Gender gap, 166–170, 184–185,
  199–200. *See also* Women
  voters
General elections
  ethnic gap, 168–169
  flowchart for, 353
  Native American gambling
    proposition, 113
  partisan and nonpartisan races, 2
  precinct analysis, 137

undervotes, 152–153
voters' pamphlet, 52
Generation X, 162–166
Geographic information system
 (GIS), 173
Gerber, Alan, 330
Get Out the Vote effort (GOTV)
 absentee ballots and early voting,
  337–340
 activating your base, 322–323
 budgeting for, 73, 77
 combining with canvassing, 171
 double majority elections, 310
 importance and organization of,
  345–348
 last minute persuasion, 328–331
 mail-in ballots, 340–345
 phone banks, 59
 phone scripts for, 63
 phoning identified voters,
  335–337
 poll watching, 331–335
 purpose of, 321–322
 push polls, 348
 super majority, 314–315
 swing voters, 323–324
 targeting young voters, 166
 time allotment for, 66
 voter ID, 325–327
Gilmour, Dave, 231–232, 240
Gimpel, Jim, 180
Gingrich, Newt, 184
GIS. *See* Geographic information
 system
Golden, Jeff, 256
Gore, Al, 136, 268, 330
GOTV. *See* Get Out the Vote effort
Grand Staircase-Escalante National
 Monument, 253
Green, Donald, 330

Green Party, 253, 283
Groomers, 255–257, 275–276

Halloween, 124
Hardware, budgeting for, 75
Harris, Elihu, 283–284
Hartzell, Cate, 281–282
Health care initiatives, 298
Hispanic voters, 167–170, 184–185,
 197–198
House list, 79
Humor, 278
Hunts, Jane, 26–27

Ideology versus image, 252–253
Image of the candidate, 251–257,
 267, 271–279
Immigration issues, 184
Inactivity list, 343
Income tax deductions for
 campaign contributions, 76
Incumbents
 campaign slogans, 37–38
 importance of sticking to
  campaign message, 258–259
 lying to the voters, 182
 preparing for a debate, 265–268
 running the campaign, 262–265
 special-interest money, 270–271
 winning on smaller budgets,
  111–112
Independent voters, 167, 310–311
Index cards
 lawn sign placement, 125–127
 organizing volunteer activities
  and information, 55–58
 preparing for a debate, 266
Indirect initiative, 315
Informational advertising, 213, 215
Initiative process, 293–297, 315–320

In-kind contributions
  phone lists, 29–30
  precinct analysis, 133–134
  printing lawn signs, 123
Insider. *See* Incumbents
Internet, 298, 306
Issue-based campaigns, 2
  advertising, 217–219, 239
  brochure, 21, 33, 36
  budget, 71, 73
  campaign chair, 16
  campaign manager, 14
  campaign message, 24
  case for support, 97
  competing measures, 312–314
  double majority, 309–310
  importance of a big win, 346
  independent voters, 310–311
  initiative and referendum,
    293–297
  library campaigns, 182, 303–306,
    308, 313
  logos, 41
  packaging the campaign, 308–309
  polling, 298–300
  precinct analysis, 138
  preemption, 297–298
  recalls, 300–303
  school bonds, 306–307
  slogans, 37–40
  speakers' bureau, 300
  unincorporated vote, 312
  volunteer sources, 19
Issues
  canvassing, 177
  direct mail, 180–184, 188–190
  Get Out the Vote effort, 324
  precinct analysis, 133
  preparing for a debate, 265–268
  single-issue candidates, 251

  ticket splitters, 181–182, 186–188
  women voters, 184–185

Jackson, Jesse, 341
Johanns, Mike, 112
Junk mail, 114–115

Keisling, Phil, 294
Kennedy, John F., 267
Knock canvassing, 66–67, 173, 175
Koch, Charles, 287
Koch, David, 287

Latino voters. *See* Hispanic voters
Law, Steve, 287
Law enforcement groups as source
    of mailing lists, 80
Lawn signs
  budgeting for, 71–72, 74–75, 77
  campaign flowchart, 351
  canvassing and, 172
  choosing the materials, 121,
    123–124
  endorsement ads, 224
  field signs, 128–129
  flowchart, 352
  for recall attempts, 303
  Get Out the Vote effort, 324
  location and maintenance of, 75,
    124–125, 130–131
  logo selection, 120–121
  organizing volunteers, 64, 125–128
  phone script for lawn sign
    locations, 61, 63
  post-Halloween placement, 124
  relocation before election day, 328
  removal of, 131
  time allotment for, 67
  to use or not to use, 119–120
  using in ads, 213

Law offices, 62
Laws, election, 4–5
Layout of the brochure, 41–50, 72, 117, 291–292
Lazy voters, 135, 323
Leaning voters, 171–173, 181
Lee, Barbara, 283
Legal issues
    advertising regulations, 245
    announcing candidacy, 204
    election laws, 4–5
    field signs, 128–129
    poll watching, 334–335
    write-in candidates, 280
Legislature, initiative process, 293–294
Letter Sent to Supporters, 98
Letters-to-the-editor, 205–207, 284, 302, 352, 358
Libertarian Party, 287
Library campaigns, 37, 43, 122, 182, 303–306, 308, 313
Literature
    drop and knock canvassing, 67
    for write-in candidates, 280
    littering, 179
    See also Advertising; Brochure; Direct mail; Newspapers
Lobbyists, 32, 287–289
Local initiatives, 294–295
Logo
    bumper stickers and buttons, 246
    importance and creation of, 41–50
    on lawn signs, 120–121
    using in ads, 213
Losing gracefully, 357–359
Lying, 253–254, 259–261

Mail-in ballots, 66, 259, 340–345
Mailing lists, sources for, 80

Mandatory referendum, 315
Manners, candidate's, 254–255
Mapping programs, 126, 173
MapQuest, 126
Maps, 173–176
Maslin, Paul, 185
Maxwell, Shayne, 41–42, 122, 237
Mayoral duties, 248–250
Meals tax, 38–39, 112, 172, 192, 218–219, 222–223, 296
Media
    bias against a candidate, 284
    budgeting for, 73
    choosing a media specialist, 230–234
    covering a write-in candidate, 281–282
    covering the losing candidate, 358
    free media coverage, 207
    need for early money, 70–71
    of contributions and expenditures, 12
    paid print media, 212–219
    press conferences, 208–209
    press events, 209–210
    push polls, 348
    radio and television, 226–230
    tips for handling the press, 210–212
    undesirable coverage, 4–5, 12
    unpaid print media, 203–205
    vote by mail, 342
    See also Advertising; Debates; Direct mail; Newspapers; Television
Message. See Campaign message
Messenger, 113
Midterm elections, 70
Military votes, 181–182
Miller, Carol, 112

Mistakes, making, 248–251
Mock debates, 273–275
Mondale, Walter, 136, 252, 267
Money trail, 189
Mudslinging. *See* Negative
    campaigning

Nader, Ralph, 253
Name recognition, 189, 220–221
National Election Studies, 166
Native Americans, 113
NAVs. *See* Independent voters
Negative campaigning
    difficult campaigns, 112
    doing it right, 284–290
    handling negative questions
        during a debate, 268–271
    refusing to engage in, 200–201
    Right to Life organizations, 289
    television ads, 241
Neglection 2000, 165
Newspapers
    budgeting for ads, 72
    Get Out the Vote efforts, 328–329
    letters to the editor, 205–207
    making good use of interviews
        and articles, 203–204
    placing your ads, 225–226
    use of advertising, 212–219
Nielsen Media Research, 229
Nixon, Richard M., 267
Nonaffiliated voters (NAVs). *See*
    Independent voters
Nonpartisan candidate race, 2
Nonvoting base, 133

On-camera interviews, 272–273
Open-space campaigns, 38
Opposition
    calculating swing votes, 155–156

candidate's image, 255–256
comparison ads, 231
comparison pieces, 190–191
composing television ads, 230
congratulating the winner, 358
debates, 196
direct mail targeting opponent,
    188–190
importance of sticking to your
    message, 257–262
issues, 183–184
mock debates, 273–275
personal malice against a
    candidate, 290
precinct analysis, 133
press events to challenge
    opponent, 209–210
pros and cons of an unopposed
    race, 264–265
recall attempts, 302
taking a stand on issues, 180–181
undervote, 153
See also Debates
Optional referendum, 315
Oregon Right to Life (ORTL), 289
Organization, importance of, 109
Organizations as source of mailing
    lists, 80
ORTL. *See* Oregon Right to Life
Outside money, 113
Outsiders, 262–265

Packets
    campaign committee, 9, 10 (fig.)
    campaign finance committee,
        92–108
    for canvassing, 173–176
    lawn sign placement, 126
    letters-to-the-editor, 206
Parker, Keith, 189

Parties and celebrations
  birthday parties as fund-raisers, 110
  donor campaigns, 95–96
  wine-tasting parties, 111
  work parties for clerical workers, 65
Partisan candidate race
  campaign slogans, 37–38
  choosing a campaign manager, 14
  precinct analysis, 135
  primary and general elections, 2
  women's voting patterns, 166–167
Party affiliation
  canvassing for swing votes, 178
  finding likely voters, 160–162
  minority vote, 169
  third-party candidates' treatment of, 282–283
Party turnout, 150–151
People for the American Way, 288
Perata, Don, 283
Perdue, Sonny, 182
Personal habits, candidate's, 254–255
Personal malice, 290
Personal wealth, 112–113
Persuasion calls, 327
Persuasion pieces, 190–191
Petition referendum, 315–317
Petitions, 295–296, 300–303
Pew Charitable Trusts, 165
Phone banks
  benchmark polls on a shoestring, 29–30
  campaign finance committee, 90–108
  candidate calls for fund-raising, 89–90
  creating a random voter list for polling, 30–32

direct mail follow-ups, 79
  duplicating calls, 325
  flowchart, 352
  fund-raising for ballot measures, 90
  Get Out the Vote effort, 345–348
  How to Make a Successful Call sheet, 101
  keeping track of information, 56
  mail-in ballots, 344–345
  matching volunteers to skills, 17–18
  midway party, 106–107
  organizing volunteer activities, 56–57
  phone lists, 29–30, 60, 125
  poll watching, 332
  scripts for, 61–63, 99, 166, 336
  targeting young voters, 166
  telephone campaign overview, 96
  time allotment for, 66
  tracking polls, 197–198
  voter ID, 326–327
Photos
  brochure layout, 33–37, 45, 47–48
  creating television ads, 235
  in thank-you notes, 291–292
  projecting the candidate's image, 256–257
  targeting your opponent, 188–189
  use in direct mail, 186–187
  using in newspaper ads, 214–215, 217
  voters' pamphlet, 51
Physician-assisted suicide, 38, 40
Pictures. *See* Photos
Polling
  budgeting for, 77
  creating a random voter list, 30–32

Polling *(continued)*
  importance and function of,
    25–32
  issue-based campaign and,
    298–300
  last-minute voter surveys, 330
  polling trends, 197–198
  tracking polls, 195–200
  versus precinct analysis, 134–135
Poll watching, 331–335, 339–340
Postage costs, 117–118
Postcards, 193
Powell, Colin, 187
Precinct analysis
  absentee voters, 340
  ballot measures, 146–147
  base party vote, 147–149
  benefits of, 133–134
  condensed method, 153–154
  data sorting, 139–140
  direct mail on a shoestring,
    192–193
  election data form, 138–139
  flowchart, 352
  issue-based campaigns, 308
  party turnout, 150–151
  phoning identified voters during
    GOTV, 335–337
  Precinct Priorities worksheet, 141,
    143
  Precinct Targeting worksheet,
    140–142
  predicting voter turnout, 146–147
  swing voters, 146, 149–150
  switch hitters, 151
  Targeting Priorities and Strategy
    form, 141–146
  tracking independents, 311
  undervotes, 151–153
  voter ID, 325

  votes needed to win, 154–158
  women and minorities' voting
    patterns, 167
Precinct captains, 333–334
Precinct Priorities worksheet, 141, 143
Precinct Targeting worksheet,
    140–142
Preemption, 297–298
Presidential elections, 167–168. *See
    also* General elections
Press conferences, 208–210
Press events, 209–210
Primary elections
  partisan and nonpartisan races, 2
  precinct analysis, 137
  pros and cons of an unopposed
    race, 264–265
  tracking independents, 311
  undervotes, 152
  using radio advertising, 226–227
  voters' pamphlet, 51
Printing, budgeting for, 77. *See also*
    Brochure; Lawn signs
Print media. *See* Media; Newspapers
Professionals, hiring
  campaign manager, 15
  layout artist, 41
  logo design, 120–121
Psychology of elections, 33
Public Citizen group, 288
Public Opinion Strategies, 166
Public speaking skills, 271–279
Punch-card ballots, 280, 282, 341
Push polls, 321, 348
Push questions, 26–27

Quotations, using in speeches, 278

Radio, 226–227, 303
Raffles as fund-raisers, 110

Reagan, Ronald, 136, 252, 267
Real estate offices, 62
Recall elections, 167–168, 185, 259, 300–303
Recycling sign stakes, 123
Redmond, Bill, 112, 283
Referendum, 293–297, 315–320
Referrals, 296
Reform Party, 115
Remittance envelopes, 78–79
Reproductive rights, 182, 289–290, 294
Research
  budgeting for, 77
  effectiveness of television, 227–229
  opponent's voting record, 189
  precinct analysis, 133–134
  preparing an outsider's campaign, 263–264
  preparing for a debate, 265–266
  preparing for a negative attack, 286–290
Response/attack ad, 242
Restricting government, 298–300
Résumé, candidate's, 253–254
Right to choose, 182
Right to Life organizations (RTL), 286, 289–290
Risk-taking, 270
Rocky Mountain Media Watch, 229
RTL. *See* Right to Life organizations
Russo, Frank, 283

Safety issues in canvassing, 177–178
Saints (decided voters), 135–136
Salutation, 117
Saveables (swing voters), 135–136.
  See also Swing voters
School campaigns, 306–307

Schwarzenegger, Arnold, 330
Senior citizens, 162, 228, 315
Sexual harassment, 330
Shaw, Rick, 274
Signs. *See* Lawn signs
Simmons Market Research Bureau, 159
Sinners (decided voters for the opposition), 135, 324
Slogans, 37–41, 112
Smith, Gordon, 186–187
Smoking, candidate's, 254
Softball tournament as fund-raiser, 110
Speakers' bureau, 300, 302, 309
Speaking engagements, 279
Special events, 81–89
Special interest groups, 293–294, 302
Special-interest money, 270–271
Speeches. *See* Debates
Spending. *See* Contributions and expenditures
Splitting the vote. *See* Vote splitting
Spreadsheet
  generating a phone list for polling, 30–32
  GOTV phone bank, 346
  lawn sign placement, 126
  matching volunteers to skills, 17–18
  organizing volunteer activities and information, 53–56
  precinct analysis, 137–138
  sorting election data, 139–140
State initiatives. *See* Initiative process
Super majority, 314–315
Supreme Court, U.S., 340–341
Surveys, 28. *See also* Polling

Swing voters
  calculating necessary votes,
    154–156
  canvassing tactics, 178
  direct mail, 180–182
  Get Out the Vote effort, 323–324,
    326–327
  personalizing direct mail, 186–187
  precinct analysis, 133, 136, 149–150
  predicting voter turnout, 146
  television ads targeting, 244
Switch hitters, 151

Targeting Priorities and Strategy
  form, 141–146
Targeting voters
  age, voting history, and party
    affiliation, 160–162
  canvassing, 170–180
  direct mail fund-raising, 76, 78–79
  ethnic groups and women,
    166–170
  finding mailing lists, 80
  know your neighbors, 180
  per capita funds, 75
  promoting special events, 88
  push polls, 348
  television ads, 243
  young voters, 162–166
  See also Canvassing; Direct mail;
    Get Out the Vote effort
Taxes
  as area-specific issue, 182
  campaign slogans, 38–39
  Citizens for a Sound Economy,
    287–289
  deducting campaign
    contributions, 76
  issue-based campaign for raising
    taxes, 299–300

  meals tax campaign, 38–39, 112,
    172, 192, 218–219, 222–223, 296
Teachers
  as auctioneers, 84
  as campaign managers, 14
  as source of mailing lists, 80
Telephone use. *See* Phone banks
Television
  choosing a media specialist and
    composing ads, 230–234
  importance of a media mix,
    226–230
  placing television ads, 241–245
  principles for creating good ads,
    236–241
  recall attempts, 303
  taking advantage of free air time,
    204–205
  targeting young voters, 165
  tips for advertisements, 234–236
Ten commandments of
  campaigning, 5
Testimonials
  buttons as, 246
  creating television ads, 235
  different formats, 219–224
  getting out the campaign
    message, 44
  in the voters' pamphlet, 51
  newspaper ad formats, 213
  voters' pamphlet, 52
Text of the brochure, 44–46
Thank-you notes, 107, 290–292
Themes
  campaign theme, 22–25
  for library and school campaigns,
    309
  theme dinners, 109–110
Third Millennium, 165
Third party candidates, 282–284

Ticket splitters
  direct mail, 181–182
  issues that create, 183–184
  personalizing direct mail,
    186–187
  predicting voter turnout, 146
  switch hitters, 151
Time management
  campaign calendar, 354–355
  campaign flowchart, 349–353
  volunteers' time, 16–17, 66–67
Tobacco industry, 287, 289
Townsend, David, 243
Tracking polls, 195–200, 348
Training
  phone banks, 59–62
  public speaking, 271–279
Transportation efforts, 332–333
Treasurer, 10–13
Typos in the brochure, 39

Undecided voters, 64, 327
Underdogs, 109
Undervotes, 151–153, 341
Unincorporated vote, 312
Untargeted activities, 329
US West, 288

Validators, 187
Vision, importance of, 108
Volunteers
  benchmark polls on a shoestring,
    29–30
  blaming them for your loss, 359
  canvassing, 176–180
  clerical workers, 64–66
  dealing with difficult volunteers,
    14–15
  direct mail preparation, 193–195
  election night, 357

falling down on the job, 347–348
  finding and directing, 16–18
  for library and school campaigns,
    309
  Get Out the Vote phone banks,
    344
  keeping track of donations, 118
  lawn signs, 119–120
  matching skills to activities, 56
  organizing, 53–59
  phone banks, 59–64
  poll watching, 331–335
  potential sources for, 19–20
  sign-up sheets, 20
  special events, 81–89
  thank-you notes for, 290–291
  time allotments for tasks, 66–67
Vote by mail. *See* Mail-in ballots
Voter apathy, 329
Voter concerns, 25
Voter fatigue, 337
Voter fraud, 340–341
Voter harassment, 325
Voter identification, 325–327,
  342–343
Voter lists, 30–32, 72
Voters' pamphlet, 50–52, 71
Voter turnout
  characteristics of likely voters,
    159–160
  double majority, 309–310
  ethnic groups and women,
    184–185
  mail-in ballots, 341
  precinct analysis, 133, 136, 140
  predicting, 146–147
  tracking independents, 310–311
  write-in candidates, 280
  See also Get Out the Vote effort
Vote splitting, 112, 283

Voting history and patterns
  ethnic groups, 185
  precinct analysis, 134, 138
  providing voter opinion without
    using a poll, 27–28
  targeting voters, 160–162
  women, 166–167
  See also Precinct analysis
Voting record, candidate's, 189,
  285

Walker, Cherryl, 200–201
Walking lists, 125, 325, 327
Walking piece, 49, 73
Warren, Phil, 188
Weather conditions, 178–180, 338
Weight loss, 251
Wine-tasting parties, 111
Winning gracefully, 357–359
Women's organizations as source of
  mailing lists, 80

Women voters
  effectiveness of television
    advertising, 228
  gender gap, 166–170, 184–185,
    199–200
  importance of direct mail,
    184–185
  personalizing direct mail,
    186–187
  polling analysis, 199–200
  women's issues, 182
Word stir-fry, 279
Work parties, 65
World's Smallest Brochure, 115–116
Write-in candidates, 279–282
Wyden, Ron, 186

Yard sales as fund-raisers, 84–85
Young voters, 162–166, 197–198
Youth Activity Levy, 47, 50, 171–172,
  217–218

ABOUT THE AUTHOR

Cathy Shaw served three terms (twelve years) as mayor of Ashland, Oregon. First elected in 1988, she was the youngest person and the first woman elected to her city's highest post.

She currently works as a political consultant and as a member chief of staff in the Oregon legislature.

She has managed local campaigns for nearly two decades with a success rate of 84 percent. Combining the power of elected office with campaigning expertise, Cathy has successfully managed campaigns to pass innovative taxing measures for funding public education, recreation, parks, and open-space programs.

Outspent in every election, sometimes as much as five to one, Cathy has developed and perfected techniques to combat big money and to engineer seemingly impossible wins. She has been a frequent guest speaker and instructor for political science classes and campaign schools.

Cathy is available for teaching at campaign schools as well as for telephone and on-site consultations. Please contact her by e-mail: cshaw@internetcds.com. For questions regarding the television ads shown in the media section, please contact Rick Shaw by e-mail: rickshaw@internetcds.com.

Animals That Live in the Forest

Porcupines

by JoAnn Early Macken

Reading consultant: Susan Nations, M.Ed.,
author/literacy coach/consultant

 Gareth Stevens
PUBLISHING

Please visit our website, www.garethstevens.com. For a free color catalog of all our high-quality books, call toll free 1-800-542-2595 or fax 1-877-542-2596.

Library of Congress Cataloging-in-Publication Data

Macken, JoAnn Early, 1953–
    Porcupines / JoAnn Early Macken.
      p. cm. — (Animals that live in the forest)
    Includes bibliographical references and index.
    ISBN-10: 0-8368-4485-8 ISBN-13: 978-0-8368-4485-6 (lib. bdg.)
    ISBN-10: 0-8368-4492-0 ISBN-13: 978-0-8368-4492-4 (softcover)
    1. Porcupines—Juvenile literature. I. Title.
  QL737.R652M24 2005
  599.35'97—dc22   2004057215

This edition first published in 2005 by
Gareth Stevens Publishing
111 East 14th Street, Suite 349
New York, NY 10003

Copyright © 2005 by Gareth Stevens Inc.

Art direction: Tammy West
Cover design and page layout: Kami Strunsee
Picture research: Diane Laska-Swanke

Picture credits: Cover, © Joe McDonald/Visuals Unlimited;
p. 5 © Alan & Sandy Carey; p. 7 © Lisa & Mike Husar/TeamHusar.com;
pp. 9, 17 © Tom and Pat Leeson; p. 11 © Lynn M. Stone; pp. 13, 21
© Michael H. Francis; p. 15 © Joe McDonald/Visuals Unlimited; p. 19
© David Cavagnaro/Visuals Unlimited

Printed in the United States of America

4 5 6 7 8 9 10 09 08 07

Note to Educators and Parents

Reading is such an exciting adventure for young children! They are beginning to integrate their oral language skills with written language. To encourage children along the path to early literacy, books must be colorful, engaging, and interesting; they should invite the young reader to explore both the print and the pictures.

Animals That Live in the Forest is a new series designed to help children read about forest creatures. Each book describes a different forest animal's life cycle, eating habits, home, and behavior.

Each book is specially designed to support the young reader in the reading process. The familiar topics are appealing to young children and invite them to read — and re-read — again and again. The full-color photographs and enhanced text further support the student during the reading process.

In addition to serving as wonderful picture books in schools, libraries, homes, and other places where children learn to love reading, these books are specifically intended to be read within an instructional guided reading group. This small group setting allows beginning readers to work with a fluent adult model as they make meaning from the text. After children develop fluency with the text and content, the book can be read independently. Children and adults alike will find these books supportive, engaging, and fun!

— Susan Nations, M.Ed., author, literacy coach,
and consultant in literacy development

A baby porcupine is born in spring. Its eyes are open. It has hair and teeth. In less than an hour, it can walk.

5

The baby, called a **porcupette**, drinks milk from its mother. In a few days, it can climb up a tree. Its sharp claws help it climb.

In a few weeks, it eats grass and other plants. By fall, a young porcupine is ready to be on its own.

Porcupines find their
food by its smell.
They eat tree bark,
twigs, and leaves.
Their sharp front teeth
keep growing.
Chewing keeps them
from growing too long.

Porcupines eat mainly at night. During the day, they sleep. They often sleep in trees.

13

Porcupines have three layers of hair. The top layer is long. The short bottom layer keeps them warm in winter. The middle layer is hard and sharp. The hard, sharp hairs are called **quills**.

An angry porcupine
raises its quills. It may
make a warning
sound. It turns its back.
It swings its tail.

If the tail slaps an enemy, the quills come out. They stick in the animal's skin. They hurt!

19

Porcupines are active in winter, even where snow falls. They may stay up in trees for days. Porcupines are at home in the forest.

21

Glossary

porcupette — a baby porcupine

quills — hard, sharp hairs

layers — **levels that lie over or under each other**

For More Information

Books

Porcupines. Lola M. Schaefer (Heinemann)

Porcupines. Welcome to the World of Animals (series). Diane Swanson (Gareth Stevens)

Prickly and Smooth. Animal Opposites (series). Rod Theodorou and Carole Telford (Heinemann)

Prickly Porcupines. Pull Ahead Books (series). Shannon Zemlicka (Lerner)

Web Site

Natureworks: Common Porcupine
www.nhptv.org/natureworks/porcupine.htm
Porcupine facts and pictures

23

Index

claws 6

climbing 6

eating 6, 8, 10, 12

enemies 18

eyes 4

hair 4, 14

porcupettes 4, 6, 8

quills 14, 16, 18

sleeping 12

tails 16, 18

teeth 4, 10

walking 4

About the Author

JoAnn Early Macken is the author of two rhyming picture books, *Sing-Along Song* and *Cats on Judy*, and six other series of nonfiction books for beginning readers. Her poems have appeared in several children's magazines. A graduate of the M.F.A. in Writing for Children and Young Adults program at Vermont College, she lives in Wisconsin with her husband and their two sons. Visit her Web site at www.joannmacken.com.

Surpassing Shanghai

Surpassing Shanghai

An Agenda for American Education Built
on the World's Leading Systems

Edited by

Marc S. Tucker

HARVARD EDUCATION PRESS
CAMBRIDGE, MASSACHUSETTS

Library of Congress Control Number 2011928626

Paperback ISBN 978-1-61250-103-1
Library Edition ISBN 978-1-61250-104-8

Published by Harvard Education Press,
an imprint of the Harvard Education Publishing Group

Harvard Education Press
8 Story Street
Cambridge, MA 02138

Cover Design: Sarah Henderson
The typefaces used in this book are ITC Stone Serif, ITC Stone Sans, and Helvetica Neue.

Contents

Acknowledgments   vii

Foreword   ix
     Linda Darling-Hammond

INTRODUCTION   1
Researching Other Countries' Education Systems:
Why It's Indispensable but Tricky, How We Did It, Why This
Time It's Different
     Marc S. Tucker

PART I: Countries with High-Performing Systems—A Sampler   19

CHAPTER 1
Shanghai: How a Big City in a Developing Country Leaped   21
to the Head of the Class
     Kai-ming Cheng

CHAPTER 2
Finland: Superb Teachers—How to Get Them, How to Use Them   51
     Robert B. Schwartz and Jal D. Mehta

CHAPTER 3
Japan: Perennial League Leader   79
     Marc S. Tucker and Betsy Brown Ruzzi

CHAPTER 4
Singapore: A Journey to the Top, Step by Step   113
     Vivien Stewart

CHAPTER 5
Canada: Looks a Lot Like Us but Gets Much Better Results   141
     Jal D. Mehta and Robert B. Schwartz

PART II: How the United States Can Match the Best Performers   **167**

CHAPTER 6
How the Top Performers Got There: Analysis . . . and Synthesis   169
Marc S. Tucker

CHAPTER 7
An Action Plan for the United States   211
Marc S. Tucker

About the Editor   221

About the Contributors   223

Index   225

Acknowledgments

Marc S. Tucker served as general editor of this book. Betsy Brown Ruzzi served as project director, and Jackie Kraemer and Jennifer Craw assisted her with the data displays. Harry Spence commented on the final draft, and Suzie Sullivan proofread the book.

This book originated in the manuscripts submitted by the National Center on Education and the Economy (NCEE) to the Organisation for Economic Co-Operation and Development (OECD) in connection with NCEE's collaboration with OECD on a report on the nations that have consistently outperformed most others, or made rapid progress, in the PISA studies on student achievement.

In the summer of 2010, after the research for the report had begun, NCEE convened a meeting of the authors and other experts in Bar Harbor, Maine, to react to the researchers' initial findings and to contribute to the further development of the conceptual scheme put forward by Marc Tucker as a possible basis for the work. The attendees at that meeting included all of the authors of this book as well as Michael Day, Training and Development Agency for Schools, Manchester, England; David Hopkins, Institute of Education, University of London; Richard Hopper, OECD; Jackie Kraemer, NCEE; Barry McGaw, Graduate School of Education, University of Melbourne; Elizabeth Pang, Ministry of Education, Singapore; David Mandel, NCEE; Pasi Sahlberg, CIMO, Finland; Andreas Schleicher, OECD; Susan Sclafani, NCEE; Suzie Sullivan, NCEE; and Siew Hoong Wong, Ministry of Education, Singapore.

The authors wish to express their particular appreciation first to U.S. Secretary of Education Arne Duncan, for initiating the request to the OECD that set this train in motion, and then to Andreas Schleicher, for choosing NCEE as its collaborator on the original report. Without them, this book would never have happened. We are also indebted to Susan Sclafani, who served as project director for the NCEE contribution to the original report and author of one of the chapters in that report.

Our thanks go to Caroline Chauncey, editor-in-chief at Harvard Education Press, for her infectious enthusiasm for this book and the effort she made to get it into print quickly.

We are also grateful to the individuals who were interviewed at length either for the original report or for this book.

Foreword

This extraordinary book could not be more timely or more important. Following what is widely perceived as several decades of decline, the United States public education system is currently engaged in a tsunami of "reform" that, more than ever before in our history, drives national and state efforts around a limited menu of change. In 2011, this menu includes an increasingly short set of ideas that have become the starting point and, frequently, the ending point as well, for dialogue among policy makers:

- Frequent high-stakes testing using multiple-choice measures tied to rewards and sanctions for students, teachers, and schools.
- Expansion of one-off entrepreneurial school models operated by charters, contract schools, performance schools, and educational management organizations.
- Alternative routes into teaching and leadership that minimize preparation and reduce access to knowledge about curriculum, instruction, and assessment.
- Efforts to improve teaching by eliminating tenure, ranking teachers against one another, instigating competitively allocated merit pay, and firing those whose students' scores are lowest.

This menu is as noteworthy for what it ignores as it is for what it includes. *Not* on the menu are most of the strategies discussed in this book, which highlights how high-performing states and nations have dramatically changed education and improved student outcomes. Furthermore, none of these jurisdictions—Finland, Japan, Ontario (Canada), Shanghai (China), or Singapore—is focused on the pursuit of narrow test results, market-based reforms, a deskilled teaching force presumably motivated by threats of firing, or a competitive approach that sets up some schools, teachers, and, consequently, students as winners, while setting up others as losers.

While there is considerable talk about international test score comparisons in U.S. policy circles, there is too little talk about what high-performing countries actually *do*:

- Fund schools equitably, with additional resources for those serving needy students
- Pay teachers competitively and comparably

- Invest in high-quality preparation, mentoring and professional development for teachers and leaders, completely at government expense
- Provide time in the school schedule for collaborative planning and ongoing professional learning to continually improve instruction (typically 15–25 hours per week)
- Organize a curriculum around problem-solving and critical thinking skills
- Test students rarely but carefully—with measures that require analysis, communication, and defense of ideas

Increasingly these assessments include challenging projects, investigations, and performances, much like what leading educators have created in innovative public schools in the U.S.—schools that struggle to survive on the margins of a system that currently does not value the kind of serious learning they pursue.

In sum, as this book vividly illustrates, high-performing states and nations are focused on building coherent *systems* of teaching and learning, focused on meaningful goals and supported with universally available, strategic resources. This collection makes clear that, if we actually want to create high-quality schools for all children in the United States, our strategies must emulate the best of what has been accomplished in public education both here and abroad.

In *The Flat World and Education*, I examined America's educational challenges and the lessons that can be learned from successes in schools, districts, and states that have dramatically improved their performance, as well as those that can be learned from nations which were once inequitable and relatively low-achieving, but now support high levels of achievement for virtually all of their students. Many of the countries I studied are also represented here, and the lessons drawn point in the same direction.

It is noteworthy how similar the strategies of thoughtful, systemic reforms have been both here and abroad. Leaders have set meaningful goals focused on higher order learning; supported intensive learning among educators; redesigned schools to better support learning for both children and adults; built capacity within systems for developing and sharing knowledge; and tackled longstanding inequalities in access to resources.

At the same time, a striking difference between U.S. examples of productive change and those of other nations is that, in the U.S. tradition of pendulum politics and disposable ideas, few of the most successful reforms have been sustained for more than a few years. By contrast, nations that have soared to the top of the international rankings have been making steady progress with a clear vision of educational improvement, often over many decades. They have done this with the guidance of strong, professional ministries of education that are well-informed by research and best practices and buffered, to a greater extent than here, from political whims.

The United States has a constant love affair with "reform," which has become an ever-present—but discontinuous and dysfunctional—process. We need to stop "reforming" and become smart and honest about what kinds of educational strategies actually work—and we need to stop chasing silver bullets and shibboleths if we are to create genuine educational opportunity for all students. Those involved with educational change have learned over and over again the harmful effects of ever-changing, top-down, poorly informed reforms: They demoralize staff, frustrate communities, disrupt progress, and leave participants feeling helpless, rather than hopeful.

Thus, part of the challenge for American policymakers and educators is to create an education governance structure that is less politically vulnerable and more strongly steered by professional knowledge and research, as well as an understanding of successful practices around the world. This book will contribute substantially to that understanding.

Another part of the challenge is to finally acknowledge and address the inequalities that are the Achilles heel of American education. With far more children living in poverty in the United States (one in four) than in any other industrialized nation, and far more lacking basic supports—housing, health care, and food security—than in any of these nations, U.S. schools in communities of deepening severe poverty have a very different challenge than those in any other developed nation. Furthermore, whereas high-achieving nations fund schools centrally and equally, the United States spends much more on the education of affluent children than it does on poor children. Both segregation of schools and inequality in funding have increased over the last two decades, leaving a growing share of African American and Latino students in highly segregated, apartheid schools that lack qualified teachers, up-to-date textbooks and materials, libraries, science labs and computers, and safe, adequate facilities. As Marc Tucker points out in the initial chapter of this volume:

> The most successful education systems spend their money very differently from the way the United States does. They uniformly invest the most money on the students who have the steepest climb up to reach high standards. Unlike us, they do not make the amount of money available to educate their children dependent on the wealth of the local community. And they go to considerable lengths to directly assign their best teachers to schools serving disadvantaged children, or create strong incentives for them to do so. The United States generally does the opposite.

In addition to a more thoughtful curriculum and assessment system, stronger educator training, and better designed schools, we will need what has been described in Finland as a commitment to "reciprocal, intelligent accountability," in which schools are accountable for learning outcomes and education authorities are accountable to schools for making expected outcomes possible by providing adequate resources, investments in educator learning, and support for continual learning for the system as a whole, as well as for individual practitioners and schools.

Given the critical importance of education for individual and societal success in the flat world we now inhabit, inequality in the provision of education is an antiquated tradition the United States can no longer afford. If "No Child Left Behind" is to be anything more than empty rhetoric, we will need a policy strategy that creates a twenty-first-century curriculum for all students, and supports it with thoughtful assessments, access to knowledgeable, well-supported teachers, and equal access to school resources. This book explains how we can learn from others to construct a uniquely American approach to this critical mission.

Linda Darling-Hammond
Charles E. Ducommun Professor of Education,
Stanford University

Researching Other Countries' Education Systems

Why It's Indispensable but Tricky, How We Did It, Why This Time It's Different

Marc S. Tucker

This book answers a simple question: How would we redesign the American education system if the aim were to take advantage of everything that has been learned by the countries with the best education systems in order to build a system better than any that now exists anywhere?

That question is important because a growing number of countries are outperforming the United States on the most respected comparisons of student achievement while at the same time spending less on education per student.

One would think that this disparity might have created great interest among American researchers in figuring out how they do it. But that is not the case. Only a handful of American education researchers have participated in international efforts to compare the performance of American students to the performance of students in other countries and to find out why we lag so far behind our competitors. The United States is, by far, home to the largest group of education researchers in the world. But the vast majority of them do their research right here in the United States. They are looking under the wrong bed for the answer. They need to be looking where the superior performance is, where countries are getting much better results at lower cost.

The contributors to this book are all associated with the National Center on Education and the Economy (NCEE), either as staff members or as members of the International Advisory Board of the NCEE's Center for International Education Benchmarking. For twenty-two years, the NCEE has been researching the education systems of the countries with the highest student performance. We have taken what we have learned about the world's most successful practices and policies and used that information to design technical assistance programs for disadvantaged students, academic standards and assessments for use in the nation's schools, and policy proposals for states. Sadly, we quickly learned that it did not help our cause to tell people that the ideas on which our work was based came from other countries. We discovered that, until recently, Americans have been convinced that there was little to learn from other countries in the field of education, that many have been suspicious of ideas developed elsewhere.

But that seems to be changing. In the spring of 2010, the Organisation for Economic Co-operation and Development (OECD) secretary general Angel Gurria and U.S. education secretary Arne Duncan met to discuss the release of the 2009 Programme for International Student Assessment (PISA) report in December 2010. They agreed that it would be very useful if, in addition to generating the report on the 2009 PISA results, the OECD would also produce another report on strategies used by the countries that had, year in and year out, topped the league tables on the PISA surveys as well as those used by the countries that had made the most progress on the surveys.

This was a signal moment—the first time that a U.S. secretary of education had ever expressed such interest in the strategies employed by other nations to surpass the United States on the PISA league tables, much less asked the OECD for a report on the subject. Following that meeting, Andreas Schleicher, director of the PISA surveys at the OECD and counselor on education to Secretary Gurria, asked the NCEE if it would be willing to work collaboratively with the OECD headquarters staff to produce the report on a very demanding schedule. The report, *Strong Performers and Successful Reformers: Lessons from PISA for the United States,* was released on December 7, 2010.

This book is based in part on *Strong Performers.* But where *Strong Performers* did not explicitly compare U.S. policy and practice with the policies and practices of the countries with the best-performing education systems or make any policy recommendations, this book does both. Whether or not the readers agree with the recommendations we make, they will be able to see where these proposals come from, and it will be much easier to grasp the implications of the policies used by our most successful competitors for the United States.

We are deeply grateful to the OECD and to Andreas Schleicher for encouraging us to produce this version of the report that we all collaborated on so productively. Their intention was not to produce a report that graced analysts' shelves but, rather, to stimulate debate on the central issues of national education policy, drawing on the enormous resources of the OECD and the PISA database. They encouraged us to produce a version of the report that would, in our judgment, accomplish that goal.

WHAT IS PISA?

The Programme for International Student Assessment of the OECD compares outcomes for fifteen-year-old students on measures of language literacy, mathematics, and science among the seventy countries that collaborate in the PISA system. The assessments do not measure a particular curriculum but, rather, whether students can apply the knowledge they have gained and the skills they have mastered to real-world challenges found in the modern industrialized world. Thus, the purpose of the assessments is to inform countries on the degree to which their students are prepared by their education for life. The PISA assessments are administered every three years and are reported on one year after each administration.

In addition to data on the common measures of student achievement (see figures I.1–I.3), PISA collects a wealth of background information that can be correlated with the assessment data to shed light on which features of education systems are associated with which outcomes. It shows, for example, which countries are producing high outcomes at low cost and which are producing equally good outcomes at much higher cost; in which countries social class is a good predictor of high achievement and in which countries

Figure I.1 Reading performance on PISA 2009

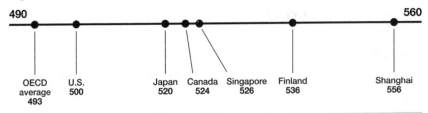

Source: OECD 2010. *PISA 2009 Results: What Students Know and Can Do.* Vol. 1.

Figure I.2 Math performance on PISA 2009

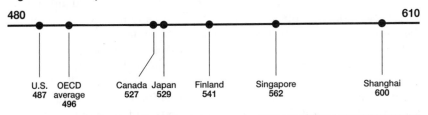

Source: OECD 2010. *PISA 2009 Results: What Students Know and Can Do.* Vol. 1.

Figure I.3 Science performance on PISA 2009

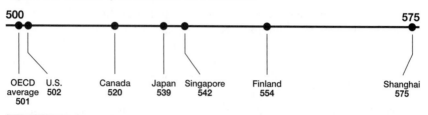

Source: OECD 2010. *PISA 2009 Results: What Students Know and Can Do.* Vol. 1.

that is not the case; and which countries get both high mastery of the set curriculum and the ability to apply what they have learned to the kinds of problems they have not seen before and which countries do not. Examining this data, countries can compare the achievements of countries in the PISA sample to their own, paying particular attention to those that do the best job on the goals they think most important.

Because PISA assesses regularly, countries can see who is improving and who is not. Because the same measures are used everywhere, contending parties can accept the PISA data and analysis as impartial. Because so many countries are included, any given country can find others like themselves.

WHY INTERNATIONAL COMPARISONS ARE IMPORTANT

Not so long ago, we used to compete economically with the person, community, province, or state next door. Now, as Thomas Freidman pointed out in his now-iconic book, *The World Is Flat: A Brief History of the Twenty-First Century,* world labor markets have been swiftly integrating worldwide. It is more likely that we are competing with people with similar skill levels halfway around the world than with people just over the state or provincial line. Workers in countries with relatively high wages are competing directly with other people with much the same skills who will work for less in what amounts to one integrated worldwide labor market. The same thing is true for people with low skills. The obvious question is why should global employers pay more for workers in one place than in another? Why not employ the lower-paid worker if their skills are much the same?

The effect of this dynamic is to raise wages in less-developed countries and depress wages in the most-developed countries. But these changes in the global economy do not affect all workers in these countries equally. The process of job automation is proceeding much faster than the process of offshoring jobs just described. The effect of automation—and more generally of the progress of technological change—is to reduce the demand for people who are only capable of doing routine work and to increase the demand for people who are capable of doing what Peter Drucker called "knowledge work." If the work is routine, chances are it can be reduced to an algorithm. If it can be reduced to an algorithm, it can probably be incorporated into a software program. And if it can be incorporated into a software program, it can probably be automated. There are, of course, some jobs that must be done by human beings and some jobs that can only be done close to the customer; but once those jobs are exempted from the calculation, the vast majority of jobs are subject to the dynamics just described.

The cost of automating jobs is steadily declining. Jobs worldwide are going to the countries that can provide the skill levels required to do any particular operation at the lowest offered price. As this happens, wages in those countries will rise. In turn, it becomes more and more worthwhile to automate jobs in those countries, because the difference between the cost of automating those jobs and the cost of a human being doing those jobs will decline to zero ever more quickly (and it is only one step beyond that when it is cheaper to employ the machine than the human being).

Over time, more and more routine work will be done by machines and more and more human beings will be doing "knowledge work" that cannot easily be routinized. A high proportion of nonroutine work is professional work. So, more and more people will be doing professional work. High-wage countries will find that they can maintain their relative wage levels only if they can produce workforces made up largely of people capable of doing knowledge work for a living. But having a lot of knowledge and high skills will not be enough for workers in the highest-wage countries, because they will be competing with people who have much the same skills and knowledge and are willing to work for less. They will be paid at the top of the world scale only if they can invent the future, which will require world-class levels of creativity and innovation as well as world-class skills and knowledge.

This is actually a description not of a possible future but of the economic dynamics that are currently in play. Right now, in the high-wage countries, demand for highly skilled people is increasing faster than the supply, and demand for low-skilled workers is decreasing just as fast, thus pushing wages for high-skilled workers up and wages for low-skilled workers down. Jobs are moving rapidly to countries that can offer the skills needed for any particular operation at below-market rates. And the rate of automation of jobs is steadily increasing in both high-wage and low-wage countries.

These dynamics are placing increasing pressure on governments to provide an education to their citizens and their children that will enable them to earn a decent living in this environment and to offer their children a life at least as rewarding as their own. That means pressure to create education systems that offer participation to everyone (not just a favored few), that are globally competitive on quality, that provide people from all classes a fair chance to get the kind of education on which success is now based and do all this at a price that the nation can afford. The aim is no longer just to provide a basic education for all, but to provide an education that will make it possible for everyone to have a reasonable chance at the jobs available for knowledge workers: jobs that require very high skill levels, the ability to solve complex problems of a sort no one has seen before, to be creative, to synthesize material from a wide variety of sources and see the patterns in the information that others cannot see, to work with others in productive ways, to take a leadership role when necessary, to be a good team member when needed, and to do all of this with a high ethical standard.

Some people have described these skills as twenty-first-century skills, but that is not the case. These were the very skills that the best of the English public schools, like Eaton and Harrow, were expected to develop in the future leaders of Britain who constituted their student bodies in the 1890s. The difference is not the skills. The difference is that any country that wants to have a very high general wage level will now have to provide these skills to *all* their students, not just a small elite.

It is precisely because there is a growing consensus on these points that seventy different nations came together and agreed on the criteria for a common assessment. It is because there is such a consensus that the nations involved want so badly to know how they are doing against criteria of this sort, individually and in relation to each other.

HOW IS THE UNITED STATES DOING?

For a country that once led the world's education league tables, the answer is "not well."

Even though the United States spends more per pupil than any other country in the survey, except Luxembourg, its students perform average in reading and science and below average in mathematics. Students in countries that spend less than half what we spend are achieving at higher levels. (See figures I.4–I.5.)

Figure I.4 GDP per capita (US$)

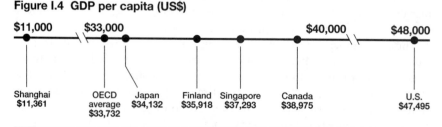

Source: OECD 2010. *Strong Performers and Successful Reformers in Education: Lessons from PISA for the United States.*

Figure I.5 Percent of GDP spent on primary, secondary, and non-tertiary education

2.8%		4.0%

Japan 2.8		Finland 3.6	
Singapore 2.8	Canada 3.5	OECD average 3.6	U.S. 4.0

Sources: OECD Education at a Glance 2010, year of reference 2007 (U.S., Finland, Canada, and OECD average). UNESCO Institute for Statistics: Statistics in Brief year of reference 2008 (Singapore).

Many in the United States distrust these figures, believing that other countries educate only their elites while we educate everyone. But this is not true. Some 25–30 percent of our students drop out of high school. That proportion is smaller—typically much smaller—among the top-performing countries. Increasingly, it is the United States that is educating only our elite and our competitors who are educating everyone.

American teachers will point out that performance problems are to be expected with so many immigrants and so many children from so many different backgrounds speaking so many languages. But countries like Canada, with even greater proportions of students born outside that country, are showing much higher performance levels for all children, including immigrant children. In fact, the reading performance of children without an immigrant background in the United States is only marginally better than the performance of all students. It turns out that Canada, New Zealand, Australia, and Hong Kong, all with percentages of immigrant students equal to or greater than the United States, all outperform the United States in reading. (See figures I.6–I.7.)

We repeatedly hear that, were it not for the poor and minority kids in our big cities, U.S. student performance would be right up there with the best performers. American schools, it is said, are okay, only excepting those that serve our lowest-income students, mainly in the cities. But that is not true.

Figure I.6 Percent of students with first or second generation immigrant status

0%				25%

Finland 2.5	OECD average 10.3	Singapore 14.4	U.S. 19.4	Canada 24.4

Source: OECD 2010. PISA 2009 Results: Overcoming Social Background. Vol. 2.

Figure I.7 Percent of students with an immigrant background speaking another language at home

Source: OECD 2010. *PISA 2009 Results: Overcoming Social Background.* Vol. 2.

It certainly is the case that our low-income and minority students do poorly compared to the international benchmarks. But even our suburban schools score only very slightly above the OECD average.

Even our top performers are not doing so well. PISA divides reading performance into six bands. One and one-half percent of our students score in the top band, better than the OECD average of 0.8 percent. But Australia, Canada, Finland, Japan, New Zealand, Singapore, and Shanghai do better, with proportions ranging from 1.8 to 2.9 percent. Only 2 percent of our students reach the highest point on the PISA mathematics scale, compared to the OECD average of 3 percent, and countries above that go all the way to 27 percent (Shanghai). Only 1 percent of American students come in at the top level for science, the OECD average, but the percentage for Singapore is 4.6 percent, for Finland 3.3 percent, for New Zealand 3.6 percent, for Shanghai 3.9 percent, and for Australia 3 percent. (See figures I.8a–c.)

One might think that, given our experience, we would be better at educating disadvantaged children than the best-performing countries. But that does not seem to be true. PISA has classified as "resilient" students who are in the bottom quarter of the PISA index of economic, social, and cultural status but who score in the top quarter on the PISA achievement measures. The United States comes in below the PISA average on this measure, with twenty-seven countries outperforming us, among them Mexico and Turkey.

A variation on this theme is the assertion that there are many states in the United States that perform as well as the best countries in the world. But that is not true. Wisconsin, settled mainly by Scandinavians and among the best performers among American states, performs substantially below Finland.

It is certainly true that poverty among American schoolchildren impacts their ability to learn in school and that poverty in the United States among children is increasing and that our schools cannot be held accountable for that. But it turns out that socioeconomic status is a better predictor of education achievement in the United States than in most other OECD countries. Socioeconomic status predicts 17 percent of the variance in student performance in

Figure I.8a PISA reading student scores (2009)

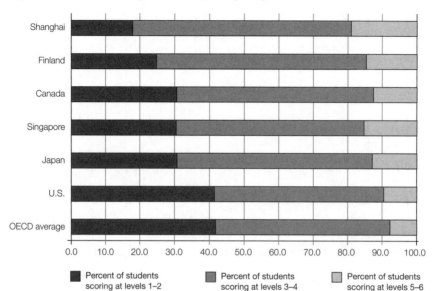

Percent of students scoring at levels 1–2 · Percent of students scoring at levels 3–4 · Percent of students scoring at levels 5–6

Figure I.8b PISA math student scores (2009)

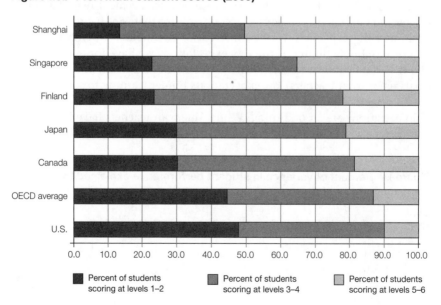

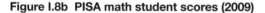

Percent of students scoring at levels 1–2 · Percent of students scoring at levels 3–4 · Percent of students scoring at levels 5–6

Figure I.8c PISA science student scores (2009)

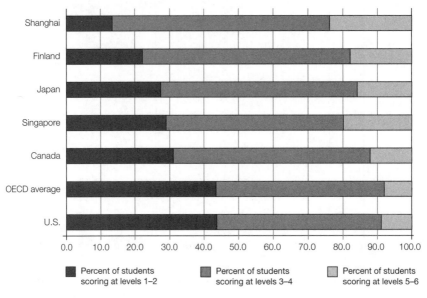

Source: OECD 2010: *PISA 2009 Results: What Students Know and Can Do.* Vol. 1

the United States but only 9 percent in Japan and Canada. That means that poverty is making a bigger difference in student achievement here than elsewhere, and our schools can be held accountable for that. (See figure I.9.)

Among the explanations often offered for the mediocre performance of American school children is the low expectations we have for our students. The PISA data confirm this hypothesis. In Finland, 6 percent of school principals report that teachers' low expectations hinder learning to some extent, but 23 percent of American principals do so.

Expectations are an odd thing. While American teachers have low expectations for their students, it turns out that the PISA data show that Ameri-

Figure I.9 Percent of variance in student performance explained by socioeconomic status

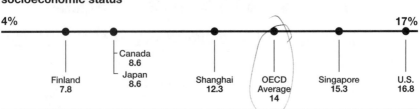

Source: OECD 2010. *PISA 2009 Results: Overcoming Social Background.* Vol. 2.

can students rate themselves better students than students in countries in the highest-performing countries rate themselves. OECD speculates that this may be because our students are often complemented on performance that is substandard when measured against the best performers. By expecting less, we make our students comfortable with achieving less when there is every reason to believe that they could be achieving much more.

One would think that being a big spender on education would mean that we spend more money than other countries on teachers' compensation. But that is not the case. When the OECD looked at teachers' compensation in terms of how teachers are paid compared to other professions requiring the same level of education, only three OECD countries pay their teachers less than we do in the United States. So the money is not spent on our teachers; much of it seems to be put into our buildings. Only three OECD countries spend more on capital outlays than we do in the United States.

Overall, OECD finds that the only resource that correlates with student performance is teachers' salaries. It also finds that countries that prioritize teachers' salaries over class size get better results. The United States has done just the opposite, prioritizing reduction of class size over teachers' salaries.

Being a big spender, it turns out, does not put the United States in the position of providing disadvantaged students with the resources they need to succeed. The opposite is true. Half of the OECD countries actually provide more teachers per capita to their disadvantaged students than they do for their average students. Among all the OECD countries, only Israel, Slovenia, Turkey, and one other country provide more resources to schools enrolling students from wealthier families than they do to schools serving students from poorer families. That other country is the United States.

This is just one aspect of a disturbing pattern related to school finance. The most successful education systems spend their money very differently from the way the United States does. They uniformly invest the most money on the students who have the steepest climb up to reach high standards. Unlike us, they do not make the amount of money available to educate their children dependent on the wealth of the local community. And they go to considerable lengths to directly assign their best teachers to schools serving disadvantaged children, or create strong incentives for them to do so. The United States generally does the opposite.

THE METHODOLOGY

The preceding section was largely based on data from the OECD PISA surveys, which have produced by far the largest and most sophisticated database on global education performance, policy, and practice ever assembled. It is a matchless resource.

But like all such databases, it has certain limitations. It cannot tell you what a given country was trying to achieve, what obstacles it perceived as being in its way, what strategy it chose to address those obstacles and achieve its ends, what the relevant political issues were at the time, how allies were strengthened and opponents mollified or eliminated, which premises turned out to be right and which wrong, how the unexpected was dealt with, how the goals changed along the way, what tradeoffs were made and why, what happened when governments changed, how continuity of purpose was maintained, what cultural factors turned out to be strengths to build on and which weaknesses had to be overcome on the way to success, and so on. Questions of this sort have usually been addressed when comparing countries' education systems using national case studies. But these studies have their own limitations, not least the fact that there was, until recently, no way to compare outcomes on common measures across countries, much less intermediate variables, such as school finance systems or instructional or accountability systems. Often, these international case studies have been descriptive studies focused on one program in one country, or one program in several countries, without common measures of the outcomes. It is very hard to learn much about which factors are decisive in the design of effective national education systems that way.

The work on which this book is based represents a blend of two very different but complementary research techniques. One is the survey methodology employed by PISA. The other is industrial benchmarking.

Industrial benchmarking gained currency at the close of the 1970s and the early 1980s when Japanese firms began to challenge large multinational U.S. firms globally. Many American firms did not survive that challenge. But many that did survive did so because of their use of the benchmarking techniques they employed. The aim of the American firms was to learn enough from their competitors to beat them at their own game. To do this, they identified their most successful competitors in their own industry. But they also identified the companies that led the world in each of their major business process areas (e.g., accounting, sales, inventory). They collected all the information they could possibly find about their competitors in the business press, in major academic studies usually conducted and published by business school faculty, and through papers presented by their competitors in industry journals. After they had learned everything they could possibly learn in this way, they did their best to visit their competitors' work sites, sending their own leading experts to examine manufacturing techniques, forms of work organization, training methods—anything they thought might contribute to their competitors' success.

When this research was complete, they would analyze all the information and analysis they had gathered. Their aim was not to replicate anything they had seen but to build a better mousetrap by combining the best ideas they had seen elsewhere with their own ideas to make something that would be superior to anything they had seen anywhere.

What they discovered, of course, was that the methods, protocols, techniques, and strategies they had seen were all, in one way or another, built to address a particular set of circumstances. The firm doing the research rarely faced the same set of circumstances. So the firm doing the research had no need to incorporate in their design some of the workarounds that another firm had had to invent to get around some particular challenge in their own environment. Of course, it was equally true that the firm doing the research might have to build their own workarounds to deal with problems that other firms did not face. The important point here is that firms doing the research were not interested in replicating anything because they were trying to build something superior to anything they had seen and because they did not want to incorporate unnecessary workarounds into their own designs.

The dominant research methodology in education is not built on the industrial benchmarking model but, rather, on the clinical research model used in medical research. In that arena, the aim is to identify the most successful drug or procedure available for any particular presenting disease. The method typically used to do this research is experimental designs in which subjects are randomly assigned to treatments. This method is preferred in order to ensure that there are no systematic differences among the groups assigned to different treatments. That being so, the observer can attribute differences in results for the individuals to the different treatments they received. Treatment A can be said to have "caused" result B.

The aim of the research presented in this book is to ascribe differences in student achievement between one country and another to certain features of those countries' education systems or to all the features in one country's education system as opposed to others. Presumably, one could do so with confidence by randomly assigning entire national populations to the education systems of another country or to certain features of the education system of another country. But no population of any country would allow such a thing to happen. Random assignment is not an option here.

But even if it were an option, it would not work anyway. The people who run national, state, and local education systems are much more like firms competing with one another than doctors trying to identify the most powerful drug available to treat a particular disease. They are not at all likely to replicate in its entirety and with perfect fidelity a particular complex solution to an education problem. Education is highly value laden. Systems develop for historical reasons that reflect the values and preferences of parents, students, administrators, politicians, and many others. These things are constantly changing. The result is that the decision makers are like the heads of firms doing benchmarking research: they will take a little from here and a little from there and add something of their own—always. It is simply impossible to replicate and then completely stabilize the implementation of any complex educational system or subsystem at scale. Such an approach will not work, either in theory or in practice.

In such a case, the purpose of this research is not to fully specify a complete method but, rather, to produce resources for decision making by political leaders, educators, parents, and others. It is intended to suggest directions that policy might take based on the experience of countries whose education systems have proven to be exceptionally successful.

But, the observer might ask, on what basis will those recommendations for policy direction be made? How can the researchers, using industrial benchmarking techniques, say with any confidence that this or that policy or practice caused this or that result in any given country or situation if controlled experiments cannot be used to establish the causal relationships involved?

The answer lies in the use of a multiplicity of mutually reinforcing methods of research. PISA combines advanced forms of educational assessment with sophisticated survey research methods. In this way, an extensive web of correlations can be drawn between certain dimensions of student performance and a large range of factors that could conceivably affect that performance. Various forms of statistical analysis can then be used to apportion the relative influence of a variety of factors in determining variations in student performance.

But, as we pointed out above, these analyses do not reveal the fact that new political leadership reframed the issues in education policy in such a way that an old policy gridlock was broken and new reforms were made possible. They leave no record that a country that thought it was doing very well discovered almost overnight that it was not and mobilized its whole education establishment to change the previously unchangeable to radically improve its education outcomes. To find these things out, one must go and visit the country in question; read its newspapers; talk to its policy makers, experts, ordinary citizens, journalists, and educators; read its history; examine its economic context; and much more.

PISA data provides invaluable clues for such an investigation. Broken trend lines and other anomalies in the data will cry out for explanation. So will unbroken trend lines beg for explanation when they vary dramatically from those of seemingly similarly situated countries. These methods of investigation are complementary. The PISA data can not only guide the benchmarker toward the most interesting questions, but it can also prevent the benchmarker from making otherwise understandable mistakes by closing off lines of inquiry that he might otherwise pursue. Similarly, the deep on-the-spot investigations of particular countries by the benchmarkers will lead to new questions that can be incorporated in future surveys undertaken by PISA.

All of these forms of research have been employed in the preparation of this book. The conclusions drawn are based on instances in which all these lines of data and analysis converged.

A THEORETICAL FRAMEWORK

This book represents a certain interplay between empiricism and theory. One always makes choices in doing research of this sort, deciding to ask some questions and not others. The choice of questions is guided by guesses about causation. Those guesses are in turn based on ideas, or models, one has about how the world works. Those models are a kind of theory. The theories, in turn, are only as good as their capacity to develop a picture of reality that is convincing, based on the data collected. When empirical data falsify a theory, because they do not conform to it, then a new theory is needed that fits the facts better and has more power in predicting what the observer will find the next time he or she does research on the same topic.

In this case, the initial theoretical framework for the research grew out of decades of experience on the part of the researchers. But it was in turn influenced by the research itself. Halfway through the research program, a three-day conference was held in which the researchers met with one another and with other experts to consider what was being learned and to see what tentative conclusions might be drawn that might lead to a theoretical construct that might guide the researchers in their continued work. Thus, the theoretical construct that follows is both the guide for the research and the product of the research.

The purpose of this book, as noted above, is to identify the factors that appear to make the most important contributions to superior performance. But what does "superior performance" mean? There are two answers to that question.

First, we defined countries as high performing if almost all of their students are in high school at the appropriate age and if the top 10 percent of performers place among the countries whose top 10 percent are among the best performers in the world with respect to their mastery of the kinds of complex knowledge and skills needed in advanced economies as well their ability to apply that knowledge and those skills to problems with which they are not familiar. Student performance is only minimally predicted by their socioeconomic status, and spending per pupil is not at the top of the league tables. Put another way, we are defining superior performance as high participation, high quality, high equity, and high efficiency.

One might suppose that there is one best way to organize a national or state education system to achieve world-class status. But the evidence suggests otherwise. First of all, countries, like students, cannot simply leap to the end of the development process. Countries in the early stages of economic development have very low levels of literacy among both students and teachers and very little to invest in education. To succeed, they must invest a lot in a small elite who can run their country and the rest in teachers who may have only two years more education than the students they will teach. Because teacher quality is so low, they must tell their teachers exactly what to do and exactly how they want it done, and they must use Tayloristic methods of administrative control and accountability to get the results they want.

At the other end of the economic development spectrum, the most advanced countries are discovering that the only way they can compete in the global economy is to provide to everyone the kind and quality of education that they had once provided only to a small elite. To do that, they are finding that they must recruit their teachers from the same pool out of which their top professionals have been recruited. But such people will not work in schools organized as Tayloristic workplaces using administrative forms of accountability and bureaucratic command and control systems to direct their work. To attract the people they need, these countries must transform their schools into a work organization in which professional norms of control replace bureaucratic and administrative forms of control.

Most developed countries have systems that lie somewhere along this spectrum. As their goals move from the delivery of basic skills and rote learning to advanced, complex skills, they find that they have to have teachers with better and better education, and they begin to alter their forms of work organization accordingly, moving toward more professional forms of work organization, more professional forms of accountability, and more developed forms of professional practice. These are fundamental differences in education system design, and they have important ramifications in every aspect of the education system.

It is possible to represent the ideas above in the following way:

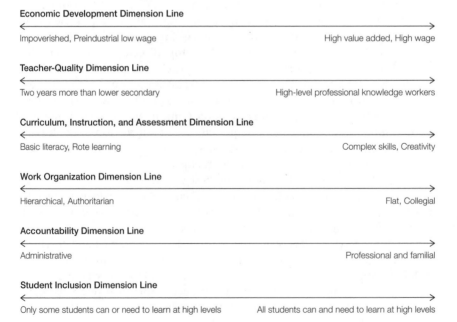

Economic Development Dimension Line

Impoverished, Preindustrial low wage ← → High value added, High wage

Teacher-Quality Dimension Line

Two years more than lower secondary ← → High-level professional knowledge workers

Curriculum, Instruction, and Assessment Dimension Line

Basic literacy, Rote learning ← → Complex skills, Creativity

Work Organization Dimension Line

Hierarchical, Authoritarian ← → Flat, Collegial

Accountability Dimension Line

Administrative ← → Professional and familial

Student Inclusion Dimension Line

Only some students can or need to learn at high levels ← → All students can and need to learn at high levels

The advantage of this form of representation is that it suggests that progress along one of these dimension lines can move, at least to some degree, independently of the others. And there may be some penalties attached to that phenomenon. That is, nations whose systems attempt to promote complex learning and creativity without moving teacher quality to the right side of that dimension line may be in trouble. Nations that try to move teacher quality to the right side of the dimension line without also moving the work organization to the right side of the dimension line may also be in trouble. And so on. In this construct, there is nothing inevitable about the movement from left to right, nor is it necessarily the case that policy makers will see the need for coherence in the policies in play at any one time. But there is a price to be paid for lack of coherence.

In the chapters that follow, the reader will find evidence for these dimension lines and for the construct as a whole and, at the same time, will find each country described in terms that are consistent with the dimension lines.

THE ORGANIZATION

In the following five chapters, reports are presented on five countries that have enjoyed sustained records of superior performance. The history and culture of these countries are briefly described to provide a context for the description of the education system. The chapters then describe the main elements of the education system as they bear on the reasons that might lie behind the success of each country. These elements generally include standards, examination systems, instructional systems, school finance, teacher quality, gateways through the system, incentives that affect student motivation, and so on. Recent developments are highlighted and conclusions are drawn concerning the lessons the United States might learn from that country.

The countries in this section include Canada (with a focus on Ontario), China (with a focus on Shanghai), Japan, Finland, and Singapore. We chose these countries to provide a variety of strategies, all of which have led to excellence. Canada shares a border with the United States and operates in a very similar political context but gets very different results. The chapter on China focuses on Shanghai, which, measured for the first time in 2009, emerged as a star performer. Shanghai provides a window into the impressive education accomplishments of a county now taking a prominent position on the world stage. In Japan we see a country that started at the top of the range and has stayed there. This chapter tells the story of how they did that. When PISA reported that Finland topped the charts some years ago, no one was more surprised than the Finns. But they have stayed at the top of the charts, and this chapter tells us where that staying power came from. Singapore is no larger than most of the world's cities and smaller than many. But it is a country that has risen from the bottom of the charts to the top in record time.

In the last chapter we compare what we found in the target countries, point by point, to the United States and propose an agenda—of policy and practice—for the United States to help it catch up to, and perhaps even outpace, these education leaders.

REFERENCES

Drucker, P. 1968. *The Age of Discontinuity: Guidelines to Our Changing Society.* New York: Harper & Row.

Organisation of Economic Co-operation and Development (OECD). 2010. *Education at a Glance 2010.* Paris: Author.

Organisation of Economic Co-operation and Development (OECD). 2010. *PISA 2009 Results: Overcoming Social Background—Equity in Learning Opportunities and Outcomes.* Vol. 2. Paris: Author.

Organisation of Economic Co-operation and Development (OECD). 2010. *PISA 2009 Results: What Makes a School Successful?* Vol. 4. Paris: Author.

PART I

Countries with High-Performing Systems—A Sampler

CHAPTER 1

Shanghai

How a Big City in a Developing Country Leaped to the Head of the Class

Kai-ming Cheng

Despite China's emergence as one of the world's most influential economies, relatively little is known in the West about China's educational system and how its students learn. The prevailing impression is that students in China learn by rote and that much in the schools is about memorization and cramming for examinations.

This chapter seeks to give a picture of education in China using Shanghai as an example. Student learning is the focus, and other dimensions—such as teaching and teachers, school facilities, and systemic strategies—are understood as context. Of course, China encompasses a whole spectrum of economies, societies, and cultures, and while generalizations are possible, diversity and disparity are the national rule. Hence, although Shanghai does provide a very powerful window into China, it does not represent all parts of the country.

THE CULTURAL CONTEXT

China has a long tradition of placing a high value on education. This began with the Civil Examination system, established in AD 603 and exported to Japan and Korea later in the seventh century. It was a very competitive yet efficient system for selecting officials, one known for its rigor and fairness. The exams evolved over many dynasties before their abolition in 1905.

The system had three tiers of examinations: county, provincial, and national levels. The general mode was an essay test, which found the candidates confined for days in an examination cell, given good food, and required to write essays of political relevance. To do this, they had to be familiar with the classics, basically the *Four Books* and *Five Classics*, and refer all arguments to these works—hence, the requirement for rote learning. Good calligraphy and writing styles were also basic requirements. The final test was usually held in the Examinations Department, which was often part of the imperial setup. Whoever gained the appreciation of the emperor, who was virtually the chief examiner, would be the champion, followed by a few runners-up. These winners were appointed to various levels of officialdom according to their exam results.

A few attributes of this system have sustained it over many centuries. First, it was simple, requiring only performance on the examinations. Teachers were afforded only by wealthy families, so no formal institutions such as schools existed apart from the examination. It was basically a self-study system, or a "self-motivated distance learning system," in contemporary jargon. It was low-cost at both government and household levels because it involved only an examination, and the textbooks (the standard classics) were common in household collections. Apart from gender bias, which was not limited to examinations, there were no entrance requirements, so it was thought that family background would not matter. Indeed, Chinese folklore over hundreds of years, reflected in novels, operas, dramas, and all other art forms, includes stories about scholars from poor families who endured years of hardship and poverty, became champions in the Civil Examination, were appointed ministers, married princesses, and enjoyed glorious homecoming celebrations.

However, the Civil Examination was generally perceived as a very difficult goal to achieve. The acute competition produced only a few winners among tens of thousands of candidates every year, The rather open-ended examination essay and the unavailability of model answers created a kind of unpredictability and, hence, immense psychological pressure. The only thing the candidates could do to study was digest the classics and try to guess what the examiner appreciated. The examination preparation was hard work, and there was no end to this hard work.

The Civil Examination gave almost all families, regardless of socioeconomic status, high hopes for the future of their children (the boys), and such hopes translated into diligence and adaptability. This cultural tradition belongs to the entire Chinese population. However, it also led to the emphasis—an almost exclusive emphasis—on examination results, without respect to genuine learning or knowledge. In a way, for more than sixteen centuries, generations of young Chinese were trained only to face the challenges of examinations.

This cultural respect for "education" thus carries a special meaning for China: education (that is, examination preparation) has long been viewed as

Shanghai's education system

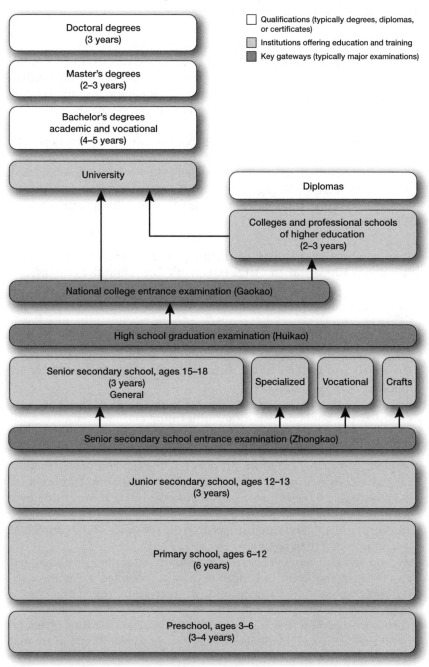

the sole path for upward social mobility, as the only hope for an individual's future. Some results of this way of thinking include:

- Education is regarded as the major means up the social ladder. This is intertwined with the supreme status given to civil servants, the officials. Because of the Civil Examination, only scholars could historically become officials. A circular causality is at work here, where social status, officialdom, scholarship, and education have become synonymous in people's minds.
- Despite the meager opportunities for moving to the top, the hope and belief in chances of success mobilized the entire population to submit to examination, or education. This is augmented by the assumption that working hard, and nothing else, pays off. While other factors, such as family background and innate ability, are not controllable, working hard is something anyone can do.

Some corollary observations may help explain the culture of education in contemporary China and, to a large extent, in other "chopstick" cultures:[1]

- Success in examinations is seen as the only respectable success in China, unlike in other societies where military capacity (such as with the samurai in Japan) or economic wealth can also attract social respect.[2]
- Achievements in education are measured by examination success or by credentials and their social consequences, rather than by knowledge acquisition in the modern sense.
- Reading, learning, and education are taken as synonyms. Reading is regarded as the only effective means of learning and memorization—"All are low but reading." Hence the tradition of rote learning.
- The reality, however, is that test scores were decided subjectively by the emperor or the chief examiner, the ones holding supreme power. Successful essays conveyed ideas that would appeal to authority. This tradition may help explain the cultural aspect that favors political correctness over scientific objectivity.
- Teachers, students, and parents agree that the relevance of the curriculum is less important than the test score.
- As most research results concur, motivation in education in China (and also in Japan and Korea) is basically extrinsic, prompted by family or social expectations. In most cases, intrinsic motivation, or genuine interest in the subject matter, is absent.
- This also underpins the fundamental source of examination pressure. In all the "chopstick" societies, all kinds of private tuition and tutorial schools exist that do little else but prepare students for examinations.

- The Civil Examinations tradition also explains the culture of hard work and tolerance of hardships. "Only those who could tolerate the bitterest among the bitter would come out as a man above men," the saying goes.
- This tradition also underpins the belief that effort is more important than innate ability. "Diligence could compensate for stupidity" is a common Chinese belief, a view not shared by many other cultures.

The social emphasis on education has always made it easy for Chinese societies such as mainland China, Hong Kong, and Macao to develop their education systems, as popular support is constant for expansion of education to more people. However, genuine attention to quality learning is often a challenge to education reformers in these societies.

THE NATIONAL CONTEXT

Shanghai is the largest city in China, with a population of 19 million, of whom 14 million are permanent residents and 5 million are temporary. In addition, around 7 million are mobile (without a Shanghai home). The city is one of four municipalities (the others are Beijing, Tianjin, and Chongqing), cities with the status of a province. In 2009, Shanghai's GDP was US$11,563 per capita. While its population and land account for 1 percent and 0.06 percent of the nation, respectively, it contributes one-eighth of China's income. In 2009, the contribution of the service sector to economic growth in Shanghai was around 60 percent, the highest in mainland China.

Although Shanghai has an edge over other parts of China in terms of education, it is nonetheless an integral part of the national system. This system has undergone several stages of development: the rather rigid Russian model of the 1950s, the period of "renaissance" in the early 1960s, disastrous damage during the Cultural Revolution (1966–1976), rapid expansion during the 1980s and 1990s, and the move toward "massive" higher education in the twenty-first century.[3] With the exception of the Cultural Revolution period, education in general has trended upward both in scale and quality.

The Cultural Revolution (1966–1976)

It is essential to understand the context in which education reform began in the early 1980s. The death of Mao Zedong in 1976 marked the end of the Cultural Revolution, which Mao had launched in 1966 as a national political campaign to eliminate all "bourgeois" influences in the country's "super-structure" (as opposed to the economic infrastructure), such as music, drama, opera, novels, and other fine arts, and to make sure their replacements were rooted in proletariat ideology. Activities in all these art forms restarted from zero, using a few prototypes created from proletariat ideology. It became a social campaign, and intellectuals were the most vulnerable.

Among the revolution's many disasters was the closing of conventional schools, which were replaced with schools led by political teams of workers, peasants, and soldiers and a revamped curriculum designed to reflect class struggle. Several attempts to resume traditional schooling had little effect. Higher education institutions were suspended, replaced by new institutions admitting only workers, peasants, and soldiers without regard for academic merit. Professors and intellectuals were sent to factories, villages, and remote places to be "re-educated" (i.e., they had been trained in the bourgeois tradition, and now had to be reeducated by the proletariat). The concept reflected a utopian ideal of egalitarianism, but the reality was economic stagnation, a society of "equal poverty," as people in China have recognized in hindsight. It is no exaggeration to say that China had to rebuild the entire education system in the late 1970s and early 1980s amid the ruins of the Cultural Revolution.

The Reconstruction of Education (late 1970s–1980s)

In 1978, at the end of the Cultural Revolution, Deng Xiaoping's economic reform gave peasants land and allowed them to keep their crop surpluses. Commercial activities started back up again. Schools resumed normal activities. A milestone was the resumption of university admissions in 1977 (with double intake) and 1978, when most of those enrolled were mature students who had been deprived of learning opportunities during the revolution.

In the same years, peasants who could earn incomes were eager to build schools of their own in the villages. This led to a decision in 1980 to allow local nongovernment financing of schools, which paved the way for a major reform and decentralization of education in 1985. As a way of mobilizing community resources, the traditional high values placed on education became evident and schools cropped up everywhere. The target of universal primary education was achieved in just a few years.

In 1986, China enacted the *Law of Compulsory Education*, which required every child to complete nine years of formal schooling, six years of primary school and three of junior secondary school.[4] By the mid-1990s, China had basically achieved this goal.

In 1982, China for the first time established its degree system for higher education, following the Western model. At about the same time, in 1980, cities like Shanghai, with considerable nonstate enterprises, saw new types of vocational schools that did not guarantee or assign jobs. This was a significant step away from the strict manpower control that was an integral part of the planned economy. By 1997, formal assignment of jobs to graduates disappeared from all levels of the education system.

It was not until 1988 that China moved away from uniform national textbooks to experiment with diversity in texts, which, in line with cultural tradition, were the most essential instrument for student learning and were provided by the state (almost free of charge). In turn, textbook diversification opened a window for diverse interpretations of the centralized syllabuses.

The Quantitative Expansion

China has recently finished the stage of extending basic education to additional people. Official statistics (2009) show a net enrollment of 99.4 percent at the primary school level, the envy of many countries. The gross enrollment ratio for junior secondary school was 99 percent, and for senior secondary level, both general and vocational, it was 79.2 percent.[5] The general (academic) senior secondary schools enroll 52.5 percent of students at this level, putting about half of senior high school students in the academic stream. However, the figures may conceal regional disparities.

The 1985 reform decentralized local school finance and governance, which led immediately to huge regional disparities because of the differences in local economies. After several back-and-forth adjustments, the 2006 *Revised Law of Compulsory Education* established subsidies from the central government to regions of varied economic capacities.[6] This marked the government's determination to sustain universal basic education and paved the way for more energetic reforms.

If the highlight of the 1980s and 1990s was expansion of basic education, the highlight of the first decade of the twenty-first century was expansion of higher education. Starting in 1998, China broke away from its long-standing policy of restricting higher education to an elite few. In 1999, all institutions were required to increase intake by 50 percent. This was followed by further jumps of 25 percent in 2000 and 22 percent in 2001.

Despite government intentions to pause after that, higher education now has its own momentum, and nongovernment initiatives such as private institutions and self-financing programs are flourishing. The result is that the higher education population grew from fewer than 6 million students in 1998 to 29.8 million in 2009. Although the enrollment ratio remains at a low 24.2 percent, China still has the largest number of higher education students in the world, more than India's 11 million and almost double the 15 million in the United States.

This has immense implications. On the one hand, there is visible graduate unemployment, particularly in major metropolitan areas. Analysts often argue that this is mainly due to graduates' unwillingness to take low-income jobs or work in less developed regions and that it should not deter further higher education development.[7] Indeed, the job situation does not appear to hamper parents' and young people's aspirations for more higher education. Yet, on the other hand, the rapid expansion has created a new level of desire for academic studies, prompting remarkably high enrollment in general (academic) senior secondary schools and lowering enrollment in vocational schools.

In all these expansions, private institutions emerge in great numbers. In terms of percentage and student populations, they are still the minority, but the trend is irreversible. It is also notable that private institutions in mainland China are called *minban* schools, which means "community" schools or, more accurately, "nongovernment" schools. The nomenclature is justifiable, because in China the notions of public and private are blurred. For example, many private schools are headed by former government officials, or government departments may run private schools for income.

The quantitative picture would not be complete without including China's complex structure of lifelong learning, which includes full-time sabbatical study, evening spare-time programs, distance learning programs, and self-study examinations. Such courses often lead to formal credentials such as certificates and diplomas and, at times, degrees. Operators range from extension arms of major higher education institutions to individual professional and private for-profit enterprises. At the other end of the lifespan, the recent reform document that lays out education plans to 2020 shows that China is moving to introduce universal preschool education. This is likely to pose new challenges given the nation's diverse conditions and concepts about early childhood development.

Teachers and Teaching

Teachers have always been a major issue in China. Educational expansion in the 1980s immediately led to an enormous shortage of teachers. Many young people with some education (such as primary or junior-secondary) were branded intellectuals during the Cultural Revolution and sent to rural villages, where, as the most educated in the village, they became minban (community) teachers. While some were competent and popular, most were untrained, underqualified, and underpaid. A policy in the 1980s aimed to retrain these teachers and put them on the public payroll. Success there, however, led to an exodus of teachers to the cities for better living and working conditions.

Village schools now often resort to hiring even less qualified teachers, using the "supply teachers" category that is meant for temporary substitutes. It is a structural problem that has yet to be solved. The disparity in competence among China's teachers is perhaps a driving force behind the development of a system of organizing teaching.

The situation in cities is more positive. Since 1997, when universities began to charge fees, a state policy has granted early admission to teacher candidates. Hence, normal (teacher training) universities enjoy priority admissions and attract better students. In major cities such as Beijing and Shanghai, where the economy is more open and incomes fluctuate, teaching stands out as a preferred occupation with a stable income. Because of improvement in teachers' salary scales, teaching has become a preferred occupation.

Still, teachers' salaries in mainland China are not very high. Extra income may come from additional assignments beyond normal responsibilities, from private tutorials or invited talks, or from school "bonuses" (e.g., sponsoring fees collected from students from other neighborhoods or whose test scores are below the official admissions cutoff).

Class sizes in mainland China are generally large; the national norm is fifty students. However, in rural areas, where good schools are few, it is not unusual to see classes of more than eighty or even one hundred. Parents often indicate a preference for better schools and better teachers over smaller classes. However, in major cities, recent drastic declines in population have forced local governments to adopt smaller class sizes so as to minimize teacher layoffs. This has significantly reduced teachers' workload and created room for student activities that would have been impossible in large classes.

China has also developed a rather rigorous framework and system of teaching. At the grassroots level, subject-based teaching-study groups engage in daily study and work on improving teaching. For example, a physics teacher of Senior-Secondary 2 (SS2) in a teaching-study group typically teaches twelve to fifteen classes per week of only one program (e.g., SS2 Physics) and nothing else. The teaching-study group holds scheduled meetings, often with related personnel, such as laboratory assistants, and commonly creates a detailed lesson plan for the following week. Teachers are expected to teach according to the scheme, which is then translated into more detailed lesson plans by and for individual teachers.

The lesson plan serves not only as a play for the teacher to act out during the lesson, but it also documents the teacher's professional performance. In many cases, teachers are watched by officials considering promotions or awards. Teachers may also be observed by peers (e.g., teaching a new topic), by new teachers (learning from more experienced teachers), by senior teachers (mentoring), or by the principal (monitoring or constructive development). Sometimes teachers are expected to teach demonstration lessons (called public lessons) for a large number of other teachers to observe and comment on. In short, a Chinese teacher sees a lesson as a performance and puts in many hours of preparation to cover the standard forty-five-minute period. This structured organization is not only a means of administration but also a major platform for professional enhancement in all grassroots units.

Such protocols are taken for granted throughout China. Observers may see them as quality assurance, but they also serve as professional development and pedagogical advancement. The steps are built into teachers' career ladders, which have four grades. Promotion up the grades often involves giving demonstration lessons, contributing to the induction of new teachers, publishing in journals or magazines about education or teaching, and so forth.

Almost all education officers, at both the municipal and district levels, started as school teachers and then distinguished themselves either as teachers or school principals. This perhaps explains their devoted attention to teaching and learning amidst all their administrative and political chores. They have also managed to maintain this focus while overcoming the normal teachers' mind-set and navigating a policy arena that goes well beyond education.

Continuous Curriculum Reform

Reform has been a sustained concept in Chinese education since the early 1980s. Milestones include the 1985 decentralization of finance and administration; a 1988 move to encourage local production of textbooks (rather than requiring a uniform national set); a spectacular expansion in higher education in 1999 with a major redesign of entrance exams; legislation in 2002 to encourage private schools; and policy moves in 2006 to alleviate disparity in financial support for education.

The most recent reform is a national campaign to improve education in the next decade. It calls for universal preschool education, overcoming educational disparity, and respect for diversity and individual needs. It is generally regarded as a strategic plan to move into an era of quality, equity, and individuality in education.

However, examinations have long been the focus of any reform attempt. Teaching and learning, especially in secondary schools, still follow the examination syllabi, and school activities are oriented toward exam preparation. Subjects such as music and art, and in some cases even physical education, are often not offered because the exams do not cover those subjects. Students work long hours every day and into the weekends, often taking additional exam-prep classes. As noted earlier, private tutorials, most of them profit-making, are widespread, almost a household necessity. In the past two decades, national policy has sought to move the system away from an examination orientation but hasn't yet seen any real success. The most recent effort is the move to "reduce students' workload," which will be a major task in the coming decade.

Some provinces forbid students from taking formal classes on weekends. There is a general belief that exam emphasis jeopardizes students' genuine development and is detrimental to the entire population. But few effective solutions have emerged. Educators jokingly describe the situation: "High-sounding appeals to promote quality education, down-to-earth preparation for examinations." Nevertheless, committed reformers expend great effort to reform the national curriculum. A major document called in 2001 for the following changes:

- To move away from pure knowledge transmission—to move from learning knowledge and skills toward learning attitudes and values
- To move away from discipline-based knowledge—to introduce more comprehensive and balanced learning experiences

- To move away from pure "bookish" knowledge—to improve relevance and interest in curriculum content
- To move away from repetitive rote learning—to increase student participation, real-life experiences, capacity in communications and teamwork, and ability to acquire new knowledge and to analyze and solve problems
- To deemphasize the screening and selective functions of assessments—to emphasize formative and constructive functions
- To move away from centralization so as to allow adaptation to local relevance and needs.

Concrete changes included a reorganization of the disciplined "subjects" structure according to life-relevance and progression in learning; introduction of integrated content linking natural sciences and humanities; creation of elective arts modules as a compulsory part of the curriculum; change of formats from fact regurgitation to problem analyses and solutions; and so forth.

The reform discourse is now clearly one of *student learning.* This carries a strong connotation of constructivist learning as a main underpinning, the idea first introduced by cognitive psychologists that learning is fundamentally a process in which the students use information from the environment (including the teacher) to construct their own knowledge base, adding new knowledge, piece by piece, to a framework that the students are continually constructing to interpret and understand their world. Building curriculum and instruction around this idea represents not just an improvement of an existing conventional curriculum but an overhaul of the basic concept of curriculum, and hence it challenges basic assumptions about education. It is not just doing more and better what has traditionally been done but doing it differently.

Understandably, this approach has faced strong opposition from some in the academic establishment. They argue that it damages the integrity of the disciplines and will hinder the nation in producing new scientists. The constructivist interpretation of learning has also generated debates: not everyone agrees that it should be the core assumption of curriculum reform. Some frontline teachers have resisted these ideas, finding the new curriculum difficult to handle in preparing their students to do well on the public examinations. Nonetheless, these reforms are gaining ground inch by inch.

EDUCATION IN SHANGHAI

If Beijing is China's political center, Shanghai is all business. Shanghai is also the country's most international and open city, a legacy of its prosperous and colonial past, before the change of government in 1949. It was among the first ports that international powers forced open in the mid–nineteenth century.[8] After 1978, at China's opening and move toward the socialist market economy, Shanghai took on a new role on almost all fronts, including education. It is, therefore a fit example for our study here.

The Cultural Heritage

Shanghai may be China's most cosmopolitan city, but cultural traditions about education still prevail there. Popular support of education means the city has had little difficulty in launching universal education. However, it also struggles with undue examination pressure.

Shanghai was among the first cities to achieve universal primary and junior-secondary education and almost-universal senior-secondary education. Preschool enrollment was 98 percent in 2009, which surpassed the new national goal for 2020. More than 80 percent of the city's higher education age cohort attended school in one way or another, compared to the national figure of 24 percent. In other words, all those who would like to attend higher education are admitted. (See appendix A for rankings of Shanghai on key education and economic indicators.)

In 2009, Shanghai counted sixty-one official higher education institutions plus quite a few private ones yet to be officially recognized. This is higher education oversupply for Shanghai residents, but Shanghai institutes also admit students from all over the nation.[9] Indeed, Shanghai has always attracted the best students from the national pool of candidates, second only to Beijing. And if not for the places reserved for Shanghai students, the city could have hosted more and better candidates from the entire nation. Meanwhile, graduates from Shanghai institutions are allowed to stay and work in Shanghai, regardless of their home towns. For that reason, many education migrants now move to Shanghai mainly for the education of their children.[10]

Shanghai's high position on the aspiration ladder has made the city's local students more keenly competitive, even with their very generous admissions quota. Reformers had thought that when the system became less selective, undue competition would also be reduced. This does not seem to have happened.

This phenomenon, common to many "chopstick" societies, has varied explanations. One is that Chinese perceive society as a vertical hierarchy and always seek to enter the best institution despite broader access to higher education in general.[11] By the same token, parents want their children to be ranked highest in their classes, and anything less than 100 marks is perceived as undesirable.[12] Another interpretation is that cultural tradition cherishes hard work, which for students is "study" (or "reading books," in the ancient tradition) and "responsibility." Parents and teachers do not feel comfortable if students have much free time.

This cultural heritage also has positive effects. Shanghai is the home of several experimental programs aimed at quality education as a goal rather than exam success. Given the status of examinations in Chinese culture,

Shanghai has opted to modify the exams to serve reform. The Chinese saying is that public examinations are the baton that conducts the entire orchestra; so rather than remove the baton, reformers modify the baton so that it conducts better music.

In 1985, Shanghai was given the privilege of organizing its own higher education entrance examination. Generally, exam changes match reform expectations; for example, integrated papers are now required that cross disciplinary boundaries and require students to solve real-life problems. Some exam questions provide students with information not covered in the syllabi, testing their comprehension and ability to apply what they know to problems they have not seen. Multiple-choice questions have basically disappeared.

Student Engagement

A fundamental influence of China's cultural heritage is students' intense engagement in learning. Typically in a Shanghai classroom, students are fully engaged, and inattentive students are not tolerated. In a lesson I observed—by no means unique—students at Junior-Secondary II covered fifteen problems about parabolas in forty-five minutes, including blackboard demonstrations by selected students. This seriousness and responsible behavior is taken for granted in Chinese society.

Homework is also an essential part of Chinese learning and governs students' lives after school. Parents expect students to do homework every evening and are prepared to devote family time to it, again part of the ancient tradition. In fact, homework can be such a burden that many local authorities have stipulated the maximum number of hours of homework schools are allowed to assign. Shanghai is among the first areas to impose such limits as a municipal policy.

The intensity of students' engagement goes well beyond the schools. A comprehensive remedial system of tutorial schools caters to the demand for exam preparation. Although formal statistics are lacking, it is estimated that more than 80 percent of parents send their children to exam tutors. Such schools are mostly for-profit, operate after school or on weekends, and tend to use small groups. Teachers are not totally against such schools either, because they also think passing exams is the prime aim of student study. Even parents who oppose exam cramming often send their children to tutorial schools as a kind of insurance. Even very strong students attend to achieve higher scores.

Students are further obliged to take part in all kinds of other learning activities. A Shanghai municipal requirement says every student should engage in at least one hour per day of physical education: morning exercises before class; an "intermission exercise" midmorning; and/or other physical activities after school. Some schools practice "eye exercises," which involve massage for acupressure points to prevent eyesight deterioration.

Extracurricular activities are offered in sports and the arts, where students are expected to learn organization and leadership. They take turns at "daily duties," such as cleaning the classrooms and corridors. They are organized to visit rural villages or deprived groups as a matter of social or service learning. All these activities are coordinated by the municipal education authority.

Apart from the remedial system, the supplementary system of programs outside schools gives young people experience in music, fine arts, sports, martial arts (*gungfu*), and other subjects the schools don't offer. Private providers make a good profit out of such classes. The most popular are piano, flute, ballet, and Chinese calligraphy and painting. Parents are prepared to invest in these expensive activities.

Students are often overwhelmed by all these demands on their time. That perhaps explains the call in the national 2020 planning document for a "reduction of student workload." Shanghai is already much more moderate in this regard than many other places in China: good schools often refrain from holding classes during evenings and weekends, and parents do not normally press for heavier workloads. The logical conclusion of all this activity is that students learn more, even though what they learn and how they learn are under constant debate. Critics see young people as learning by being fed knowledge in imposed structures, seldom left on their own to learn in their own way. They have little direct encounter with nature, for example, and little experience with society in general. While they have developed the skills, they may not have learned how to learn.

Curriculum Reforms

Central to Shanghai's reputation as an education reform pioneer is reform in curriculum. Building on the seriousness and intensity of students' engagement in learning, curriculum reform concerns what to learn and how to learn it: to overcome "exam orientation" in schools so as to build "quality education." It has had three prongs: reorganizing curriculum and textbooks, reforming pedagogy, and redesigning examinations.

Reorganizing the curriculum and textbooks began in 1988 with an attempt to change subject-centred curricula to allow students to select courses of personal interest. A three-block curriculum was established, which was made up of compulsory courses, elective courses, and extracurricular activities. Accordingly, new textbooks and teaching materials were produced and phased in. In 1997, new textbooks were issued to all students in Shanghai.

The second phase of curriculum reform sought in 1998 to integrate the natural sciences with the humanities, the national curriculum with a school-based curriculum, and knowledge acquisition with active inquiry. The purpose was to transform students from passive receivers of knowledge to active participants in learning. Traditional subjects were reorganized into eight learning domains:

language and literature, mathematics, natural sciences, social sciences, technology, arts, physical education, and comprehensive practicum. Schools were encouraged to develop their own curricula specific to local conditions. Museums and other "youth education bases" that purport to enrich students' learning experience have now become crucial sites for the new curriculum.

The curriculum has three components: the *basic* curriculum for all students, which includes mainly compulsory courses; the *enriched* curriculum, which aims to develop students' potential and is made up of mainly elective courses; and *inquiry-based* curriculum, which is comprised of mostly extracurricular activities. With guidance from teachers, the inquiry-based activities ask students to identify and carry out research topics based on their experiences. Such independent projects help students learn to think creatively and critically, to participate in social life, and to promote social welfare.

To share good practices of curriculum design, development, and implementation, a Web-based platform was constructed and put into use when the new curriculum went into effect throughout Shanghai in 2008.[13] Included on the Web site are resources for curriculum development and learning, success stories, and research papers.

Reforming the pedagogy is an effort to change classroom reality. One very significant change involved the slogan "return class time to students," a call for increasing student activity in classes, as opposed to teachers lecturing. This was a fundamental change in the definition of a good class, which once meant well-designed presentations by the teachers. Videos once concentrated on teachers' activities; now, model classes are filmed using two cameras, one focusing on the teacher and the other on the students. Teachers are now also evaluated by the time they give to student participation and how well they organize student activities. Another slogan is "to every question there should be more than a single answer." This overturns the old orthodoxy of exam preparation and of teachers' absolute authority over the information they convey. These changes add up to a sea change in classroom pedagogy.

The use of slogans is a Chinese tradition. Slogans are carefully crafted to capture the essence of the proposed change and to be easily understood by grassroots teachers, especially in rural schools, where most theories are still foreign ideas and then to become a campaign. The use of slogans is also based on the idea of constructive conformity: teachers do not mind imitating other teachers' good practices, and, indeed, creative practices are meant to be copied. This is very different from the meaning of creativity in, say, the United States, where practices are called creative when they are different from others.

Redesigning the examination is the third crucial element in Shanghai reform. In 1985, as noted earlier, Shanghai received permission to create its own higher education entrance examination. This heralded a trend of exam decentralization, which was key to localized curricula. It also allowed Shanghai to be comprehensive in reforming its curriculum.

Since 2001, the entrance examination has had the form of 3 + x: the three core subjects of Chinese language, English language, and mathematics plus the x of any other subject(s) individual institutions or faculties require. The x may be a paper-and-pencil exam, an oral exam, a test of practical skills, or so on. It may cover one discipline, one kind of ability, or several disciplines or abilities. Individual institutions decide on the weighting of the four components. For example, at Shanghai University for Science and Technology, the three core subjects contribute to 40 percent of the candidate's overall scores and the x component 60 percent.

To reduce exam pressure further, Shanghai allows some admissions based on school recommendations. Selected institutions, presumably the stronger, also can set their own admission criteria and entrance examinations. More recently, students are allowed to do self-recommendations.

Overall, curriculum reform involves broadening students' learning experiences, enhancing subjects' relevance by relating them to broader human and social issues, and concentrating on the development of capability rather than accumulation of information. Over the years, teachers' threshold qualifications have been significantly elevated. In particular, great importance has been attached to strengthening all teachers' knowledge of the subjects they will teach, including primary school teachers. At the secondary level, all teachers are expected to have undergraduate degrees in the subjects they will teach. At the primary level, teachers are expected to teach either mathematics and science or Chinese and social studies, and they are expected to at least minor in the areas that they plan to specialize in. All teachers in secondary schools are degree holders with professional certification, and many teachers have master's degrees. Shanghai was the first district in China to require CPD (Continuous Professional Development) for teachers. Every teacher is expected to engage in 240 hours of professional development within every five years.

Overcoming Disparity

In recent years, China has joined the international community in realizing the importance of overcoming disparity and inequality in education (and in society at large). This is significant since the initial education reforms were based on a breakaway from the extreme egalitarianism of the Cultural Revolution. Deng Xiaoping, architect of the reform, created the concept "let a few become rich first," arguing that disparity was an incentive to the growth of national wealth and a cure to national poverty. However, further developments in recent years have led to disparity issues significant enough to catch governments' attentions. Shanghai was among the first to detect and attempt to tackle the disparity problems.

Key schools. China has long had the concept of key schools, those selected to be given additional resources and better teachers. National key schools are very rare now, but they persist at provincial and district levels. Some key universities with privileged resources exist, but the term is no longer used for them. The key schools admit better students who then are more likely to be selected into higher-level key schools or universities. Parents do not question the system; they think only of ways their own children might get into the key schools. Because of this demand, selective public examinations became the norm to allocate students. This is another reason for the prevalent examination pressure. There had always been a national policy intention to eliminate the notion of key schools. Shanghai was the first to echo such an intention and abolished the notion of key schools at the primary level as early as the 1980s.

Neighborhood attendance. In 1994, Shanghai was the first city in China to introduce neighborhood attendance for primary and junior-secondary schools, in effect further eliminating key schools at these levels. This caused some uneasiness among parents, who were bewildered that their children could no longer compete for admission to the better schools. Their pressure led to a compromise ruling that students could choose schools in other neighborhoods by paying a sponsorship fee. It is the Chinese version of school choice, a hot issue in the United States. Chinese parents see the additional fees as fair, however, because preferential admissions could otherwise go to children of parents with political or personal connections.

Neighborhood attendance also disconcerted teachers who were not used to teaching classes of mixed abilities. Now, however, teachers seem proud of being able to handle diverse children, realizing that this is common in other societies. Neighborhood attendance has allowed removal of exams at the end of primary schooling, releasing teachers, parents, and students from examination pressure. As an immediate result, innovations and creativity flourish in primary schools. Policy makers often see this as an essential reason Shanghai is a champion of curriculum and pedagogy reforms.

Migrant children. Neighborhood attendance prepared schools to face the challenges of migrant children, who became a major national problem in the late 1990s. In the 1980s, migrant workers from rural villages looking for work flooded the cities. Most are now low-wage factory or construction workers; but others brought small businesses to the urban market, and in general migrant workers have contributed immensely to China's economic growth. But the cities did not want to spend local taxpayer money to educate migrant children, and parents opposed sharing their own children's schools with migrant children.

Around thirty million of China's school-age children now belong to migrant families—20 percent of the student population. About twenty million live with their parents in cities, but the other 10 million have been left behind in villages without parental care. Both categories pose serious educational as well as social problems and have become a major issue on the government's agenda and in its 2020 education plan.

Shanghai, because of its industrial and commercial economy, is understandably a principal recipient of migrant workers. In 2006, 80 percent of migrant children were of school age, and those in Shanghai schools made up 21.4 percent of the student population at the basic education level.[14] Since 2002, national policy has been based on two principles: "education of migrant children is mainly the responsibility of the recipient city," and "migrant children should be educated mainly in public schools." This has been received variously in different cities.

Shanghai is among the cities that have dealt with migrant children with reason and compassion. The city's spectacular economic growth can be attributed to the contribution of migrant workers, and it followed that their children should be treated well. As one interviewee put it, "Shanghai has historically always been a city of migrants. Children of the migrants today will stay on and become bona fide citizens of Shanghai. How they are treated today will determine how they feel toward and contribute to the future of Shanghai."

An article in a recent issue of *Shanghai Education*, the popular teachers' magazine, argued that mixing urban and migrant children has positive effects on both. The migrants bring frugality and perseverance, while urban children from one-child families could be quick in mind and broad in knowledge but spoiled in their personalities. "Bilateral integration" would therefore benefit all of them, the article said. The arrival of migrant children is also helping solve the problem of an acute decline of school-age children among permanent residents due to China's one-child population-control policy.

Conversion of weak schools. Although basic education is free and compulsory in Shanghai, the quality of public schools still varies greatly. To reduce this disparity, the city has adopted several strategies. One is to *convert weaker schools into stronger schools.* Since the 1980s, several rounds of renovation tried to put schools in sound physical condition. In the mid-1990s, the one-child policy began to show demographic results, which gave the government an opportunity to further improve the schools. A total of 1,569 schools were either reorganized or closed, three-quarters of all schools in Shanghai. A third wave of school renovation started in 2002, and one-third of the city's junior-secondary schools benefited.

The second strategy for reducing disparity is *financial transfer payment*. Since 2006, all students receiving compulsory education have been exempted from tuition and miscellaneous fees. Since 2007, they have received free texts and exercise books. But statistics showed that per-student expenditure in rural areas was only 50–60 percent of that in the city. The strategy became to set a minimum standard for spending per student and to transfer public funds to deprived areas. During 2004 and 2008, over US$500 million was transferred to rural schools to build new facilities and laboratories, update older ones, purchase books and audiovisual materials, and increase teacher salaries.

The third strategy is to *transfer teachers* from urban to rural areas and vice versa. It was often difficult for rural schools to recruit and retain qualified teachers. To reverse the situation, the government transferred a considerable number of teachers from urban public schools to rural schools, along with some outstanding urban principals. Principals and teachers were also transferred from rural to urban schools, on the theory that they would return to the rural schools and enrich them with their new urban experiences.

The fourth strategy is to *pair off* urban districts with rural districts. In 2005, nine urban districts signed three-year agreements with nine rural districts. They exchange educational development plans and discuss problems such as teachers' capacity building. Teachers' Professional Development Institutes share curricula, teaching materials, and good practices. Some ninety-one schools paired up as sister schools, and a substantial number of teachers participated in exchange programs. The first round of the three-year pairing off program ended in 2008, and the second round is under way.

The fifth strategy is *commissioned administration*, a kind of school custody program in which the government commissions "good" public schools to take over the administration of "weak" ones. Under this scheme, the successful school appoints its experienced leader (such as the deputy principal) to be principal of the struggling school and sends in a team of experienced teachers. In 2007, the Shanghai municipal government asked ten of its good schools to take charge of twenty rural schools under two-year contracts, with city government bearing the costs. The arrangement not only benefits the poor schools; it also gives good schools more room to promote their teachers.

The sixth strategy is to establish a *consortium of schools,* where strong and weak schools, old and new, public and private are grouped into a consortium, or cluster, with one strong school at the core. The Quibao Group is an example of the consortial model which hosts six schools in both the public and private categories.

CHALLENGES AHEAD

Outside observers might see Shanghai's education development and practice as very effective. However, none of the participants interviewed for this study felt satisfied with its quality. They agreed that significant improvements have taken place in student learning: students are now exposed to a much broader knowledge base and are trained to integrate their knowledge and tackle real-life problems; they also become used to identifying questions of interest to themselves and are accustomed to undertaking open-ended explorations. These changes are markedly different from the traditional Chinese pattern of rote learning regurgitated in examinations.

However, as one experienced educator expressed it, the changes resulted chiefly from organized and structured top-down reforms, either through the examinations or policy shifts. Students are still not given much autonomy; outstanding schools are still rare, and examination pressure still prevails. He has little expectation of fundamental change in the near future, because in comparison to injustice from abuse of power or payments of money, examination scores are seen to be "scientific," "reliable," and, hence, "fair." And the dictates of the examinations have left students with little time and room for learning on their own. "There is an opportunity cost in terms of time and space," said the educator. "Students grow within narrow margins" and are still not fully prepared for lives and work in the future.

WHAT CAN BE LEARNED FROM SHANGHAI?

Shanghai belongs to an organized society and approached education reform in an organized way. But it would be inaccurate to describe the Shanghai reform as completely top-down. Unmistakable and remarkable initiatives did emerge from the grassroots, and the municipal government not only designed the reform but intervened in the process, for example, by running schools and improving teaching. Nonetheless, several broad principles of a successful national reform effort can be deduced from the foregoing examination of the Shanghai experience.

Clear and ambitious goals, widely supported, are essential to success. Aiming high is key to Shanghai's approach. There is always a statement about education, one conceived on a high moral ground. In the 1990s, Shanghai used the slogan "first-class city, first-class education." Although the definition of "first-class" remained vague, the concept still drives development of education reform and keeps it atop the policy agenda.

This sustained emphasis on education quality, from the highest government levels on down, carries enormous implications. It attracts attention and support. It underpins the allocation of substantial government resources to education and helps mobilize community resources. Meanwhile, with the understanding that good education cannot be achieved only with teachers, the statement is itself an appeal for support from all parts of society.

A recent example is China's *Outline of the Medium and Long-Term Plan for Education Reform and Development*, the blueprint for education in 2020 and beyond. The initial "consultation" draft, published in February 2010, took more than eighteen months to produce. The process involved thousands of professionals and experts and more than twenty-three thousand seminars and forums for brainstorming and was accompanied by technical reports totaling more than five million words. It received 2.1 million submissions from all walks of society. Even the draft for consultation was the result of forty revisions of the first draft. Further revisions then included provisional plans for interpretation and implementation.

The exercise was chaired by Prime Minister Wen Jiabao, a very prestigious sponsor, and went through the State Council, receiving endorsement from the Central Committee of the Chinese Communist Party and eventually the Politburo, just to make sure of its high political priority. Such a strong effort in legitimacy building guaranteed that the reform movement would carry huge momentum.

Reform must engage the cultural heritage. We now must ask which of the factors we observe are due to cultural heritage and which are due to policy interventions and practices. They are intertwined. If we attribute everything to cultural causes, we can learn very little, because cultural elements refer to norms, beliefs, and assumptions that are hardly transferable. And despite deep cultural influences in values surrounding education, Shanghai's policy interventions had visible consequences. Cultural roots cannot explain all the changes—moving from elite to massive popular education, from an emphasis on teaching to an emphasis on learning, from fact memorization to development of learning capacities, and from economic needs to individual needs. Although the emphasis remains on education, the change in the orientation of the entire education system is not part of the culture. In fact, many such changes involved struggles *against* the culture.

The key here is that reform itself is a cultural value. Shanghai has been very conscious of the cultural traditions surrounding education, and, indeed, much reform effort arose from the parallel tradition of courage in self-criticism. The dismal reality of what had been going on in formal education was plain for all to see, and widely acknowledged. In a way, many of the reforms sought to deal with adverse effects of the culture. This cultural sense of reform is shared by Singapore (see chapter 3 in this volume), which started its education reforms in the late 1990s, and by reformers in Japan and South Korea in the mid-1980s.[15] The degree of success in these reforms vary, but intolerance of the ill effects of cultural heritage was common.

Such a sense of reform in Shanghai could be part of the legacy of the Cultural Revolution. Shanghai was never hesitant in changing the status quo. But the sense of reform is not the same as a sense of improvement. Improvement could aim at doing more and better what the system has been doing all along. Reform aims at paradigm shifts and doing things differently in order to cope with changed expectations; it entails an awareness that further development of education requires an understanding that education has to

catch up with changes in society, a fundamental issue. Reform is about setting new goals and aiming at a different plane. Otherwise, any improvement
only reinforces what isn't working. This is perhaps the problem with education policies in many other systems. Often, worries concentrate on students'
underperformance in visible areas such as language and mathematics but
pay no attention to the possibility that the entire curriculum and pedagogy
are obsolete.

Instruction and learning matter. It is easy to forget that structure, policy,
standards, and finance make no difference unless they affect the instruction students get and what they ultimately learn. And *learning* was the core
concern in Shanghai's education reform. In other systems, reform may
tackle systemic planning or finance or school management or accountability without looking at the causes, environments, and processes of student
learning. Management systems are important to examine, but only in a
framework that aims at enhancing student learning. In this case, Shanghai
succeeded by moving away from the tradition in which education had become identified with the examination process, which was revered without
much understanding of the process of learning.

The core position of *learning* becomes evident only when one understands
the recent changes in one's society and, hence, the need for change in the
function of education. In a typical industrial society, existing school systems
emerged when education's prime function was to prepare manpower and
provide credentials as labels for workers who would fit into the sectors and
layers of the manpower structure. Such a function is now diminishing as the
pyramidal structure of the workplace collapses and is replaced by small work
units where individuals have to face clients, solve problems, design products or solutions, endure risks, and face moral and ethical dilemmas. Knowledge and personality are of prime importance, and education has to prepare
young people with such knowledge and personality for a precarious future.
In short, the attention to learning is not so much a matter of puritan educational ideals but, rather, an awakening to future social needs.

Attention to social change and attention to learning are two sides of the
same coin. Hence, genuine reform in education has to start with an analysis
of society and its changes. Seen from this perspective, the attention to learning is actually "back to the basics." It was because of a mechanistic workplace
and industry's need for division of labor that education also became a mechanistic institution. It was there where genuine learning was neglected.

Shanghai has made a tremendous effort to understand human learning.
This has required, among other things: (1) a critical mass of scholars who
concentrated on the sciences of learning; (2) a framework based on learning
that shapes the curriculum; (3) professional discussions among educators in
the form of debates, seminars, forums, conferences, and experiments, where

theories of learning are interpreted and translated into grassroots practices; (4) effective methods of dissemination (such as Shanghai's slogans) among grassroots teachers; and (5) perception management to convince parents and the media of the value of the changes. All these dimensions have had to be strategically coordinated and synchronized, and this in turn required champions who are committed to the mission of learning.

A common element here is the conflation of learning, study, and education. That means it is often essential to roll out education reforms in phases. The beauty of a top-down campaign is that it can set milestones and phased targets, so that reforms do not linger in bureaucratic hands that might turn them into administrative routines. Overlooking this need could explain some of the failures of education reforms elsewhere that, despite a dramatic start, quickly revert to conventional approaches.

A coherent, comprehensive approach is essential. Shanghai's comprehensive approach to education reform means first that reform does not concentrate only on certain aspects of education. Reforms in curriculum and changes in pedagogy are just components. No single factor causes immediate improvement in student performance, even if that is our only aim. Students are complex human beings, and their educational achievement can improve only when all the complex contextual factors are considered and changed. Education works, and students learn within a holistic ecology.

Second, comprehensive reform in Shanghai perceived education as the development of the student as a whole. Again, students' academic achievements are not separate from the other aspects of their personal development—affective, physical, cultural, spiritual, and so on. Extracurricular experiences, for example, are treated as an essential element of students' holistic development and not seen as competing for schedule time and funding in a zero-sum game. Students are expected to participate in all activities and develop all-around.

Third, reform in Shanghai sought to mobilize all sectors of society. Shanghai promoted its reform as "first-rate city, first-rate education," part of a broader aim of building a world-class city competitive in the global arena. Hence, the reforms not only received priority on the government agenda but were sold as a high priority for everyone. This kept politicians, parents, employers, and the media, as well as educators, involved in the reform.

A capable center is required, with the authority and legitimacy to act. The Shanghai system is part of China's overall system, developed almost independently by China and shaped by the communist leadership. The city is divided into districts, each of which runs its schools on local finance. However, the municipal government retains its policy-making and coordinating authority and maintains strong monitoring to ensure parity among schools. Decentralization dominates the literature about education planning and governance, but it may deserve a closer critique. Centralization may not be a virtue, but finding a balance between central and local control, choosing a degree of decentralization, is something all governments must handle carefully. Education is no exception.

Gateways are very important. Alongside the single governance authority is Shanghai's single powerful public examination (at two levels). Reformers have rightly seen attitudes toward the public examinations as being a major hurdle in liberating students for broader learning experiences. But the exam does provide a basic structure for learning, especially the imparting of knowledge, without which Shanghai schools and teachers and even parents would feel bewildered. It might be simplistic to argue that public examinations are a necessary evil, but ways might be found to explore their positive function.

The PISA exercises and reformed public examinations in Shanghai and Singapore all provide experimental ground for using exams in a positive way, monitoring the output of education *as a system* or ensuring the quality of student learning, again *as a system*. No convenient replacement would serve the same functions. That said, the objectives and modes of public assessments have to be revisited and reformed to make sure that they capture state-of-the-art know-how.

For example, simple multiple-choice tests may now be obsolete because they give little information about students' learning; graded tests in many cases are replaced by pass/fail or yes/no assessments; public examinations may be coupled with school-based assessments; one-off examinations could be augmented by comprehensive and time-sensitive student portfolios; and so forth. Many such dimensions are being tried out.

Accountability matters. "Accountability" is pervasive in education policy literature, but procedures of quality assurance are not the same as the assurance of quality. If we set a low standard, any assurance mechanism will only give us low quality. Then, quality assurance works only in a culture that values high quality at every point, so that the norm is active involvement in creating quality—something "I should do" rather than waiting to be told "you should."

In Shanghai, there is no shortage of performance indicators and appraisal mechanisms, and no phobia about using such technicalities. The educational system is also basically transparent. While parents are not used to intervening in school activities as they do in many Western societies, they still have very powerful influence over schools, either through their choice of schools or through the media, which run constant reports on school events and quality findings (often on discrepancies). The vibrant cybercommunity has added to the already-strong pressure on schools to maintain a high quality of education, and information flows both ways between schools and parents on cell phones.

Principals and teachers therefore face a constant daily struggle to balance administrative accountability, client (student and parent) accountability, and professional accountability. Dealing with this larger environment beyond the school is not seen as an extra chore but as an integral part of professional responsibilities.

CONCLUSION

Shanghai students consistently perform well in international comparisons. Yet the city has been dissatisfied with some of the problems caused by its cultural heritage and has sought to overcome them by aiming high and aspiring to champion performance in education, as in many other areas of social development. This ambition is augmented by prospering economic and financial sectors. However, leaders see their human resources as the only resources they can rely on, and hence they have made substantial investments in education.

This is a virtuous circle. The spectacular reforms in Shanghai's education system have made possible a no-less-than-spectacular economic success, which has in turn made it possible to continue to ratchet up educational quality. The cultural heritage has played an important role in these successes, but that heritage has been constantly modernized.

China, of course, entered the global economy very late in the game but has been moving at breakneck speed ever since. Still, one can find almost everything somewhere in China, from preindustrial agricultural methods to some of the world's most advanced industrial production sites.

This chapter reflects this compressed development pattern in its account of China's recent educational system history. The Chinese experience appears to be taking place worldwide as the economy globalizes. If the rate of these changes appears faster in China than elsewhere, that merely means the changes are not over yet.

NOTES

1. *Chopstick* refers to South Korea, Japan, Mainland China, Hong Kong, Macao, Vietnam, and North Korea.
2. In ancient China, the general understanding of the social hierarchy from high to low was scholars to farmers to artisans to, finally, merchants.
3. "Massive" is defined by an enrollment ratio of over 25 percent. The enrollment ratio in 2009 was 23 percent, very near the massive threshold.

4. Despite minor variations, 6+3+3 is the basic pattern for primary, junior-secondary, and senior-secondary schooling. Vocational schools normally operate at the senior-secondary level.

5. I use the gross enrollment ratio here because of age staggering at that level.

6. The central government provides up to 80 percent subsidy toward student unit cost in underdeveloped provinces, 60 percent in provinces of medium economies, and no subsidy in developed provinces.

7. This is the argument, for example, of Weifang Min, party secretary of Peking University and a leading economist of education, which he made at the World Bank conference of 2007 in Beijing.

8. This was due to the Nanking Sino-British Treaty of 1842, which followed China's defeat in the Opium War.

9. These percentages are comparable with South Korea and Japan, where the number of places in higher education exceed the number of high school graduates. However, those are nations, and Shanghai is a city.

10. Institutes in Shanghai belong to different categories of relationships with the central and municipal governments, with different degrees of sponsorship and different mixes of admission quotas between local and national candidates.

11. To contain such education migrants, migrant children who attend basic education in the hosting city (e.g., Shanghai) must return to their places of origin for application to higher education institutions. In other words, they cannot occupy a seat reserved for Shanghai children.

12. The best presentation of this assumption is from Fei Hsiao-tung, a student of Malinovsky and China's first renowned anthropologist. He says that Chinese see society in a "hierarchical configuration" that is vertical and structured, as opposed to the Western view of society in an "association configuration" that is flat and ad hoc. This was best presented in Fei's lecture series *Earthbound China* (1947), which, unfortunately, is among the few of Fei's works that have not been translated.

13. The following three sections are modified from the paper "Educational Reform and Development in Shanghai," by Xiaojiong Ding of the Shanghai Academy of Educational Research, written especially for this study.

14. Japan started quite a few reforms in education, perhaps the most significant of which came out of the National Council of Educational Reform of 1986. The reform called for internationalization and individualization, ideas very much against Japanese cultural tradition. South Korea launched a few reforms in the 1980s, which went against the elitist tradition in calling for equalization of secondary schools and mass admission to higher education.

REFERENCES

Ji, L. 2010. "From Integration to Fusion." *Shanghai Education* 7, no. 4A: 12–19.

Ke, J. *The Project of Standardization of Primary and Secondary Schools Was Completed in Three Years and 1569 Schools Were Upgraded.*

Http://sh.sina.com.cn/news/20030102/08432422.shtml.

Http://wljy.sherc.net/kgpt/.

Shanghai Ministry of Education. 2001. *Guidelines for Curriculum Reform in Basic Education (Draft)*. Shanghai: Author.

Shanghai Ministry of Education. 2010. *The State Plan for Medium and Long-Term Development and Reform of Education*. www.gov.cn/jrzg/2010-07/29/content_1667143.htm.

Shanghai Municipal Education Commission. 2004. *Shanghai Education Yearbook 2004*. Shanghai: Shanghai Educational Publishing House.

Shanghai Municipal Education Commission. 2008. *Shanghai Education Yearbook 2008*. Shanghai: Shanghai Educational Publishing House.

Shanghai Municipal Education Commission. 2009. *Shanghai Education Yearbook 2009*. Shanghai: Shanghai Educational Publishing House.

Shanghai Municipal Statistics Bureau. 2010. *2010 Shanghai Basic Facts*. Shanghai: Shanghai Literature and Art Publishing Group.

Stevenson, H. W., and J. W. Stigler. 1992. *The Learning Gap: Why Our Schools Are Failing and What We Can Learn from Japanese and Chinese Education*. New York: Summit Books.

INTERVIEWS

Bai Bin, Chinese teacher and principal, Wen Lai Middle School; PISA school coordinator in 2009 field trial

China Pu Dong Cadre College, various interviews

Ding Yi, vice principal at a middle school affiliated with Jing 'an Teacher Education College, Shanghai

Gu Ling-yuan, professor, master teacher, and former vice director of Shanghai Academy of Educational Sciences

Li Xiao-yu, Chinese teacher and vice principal, Qibao High School, Shanghai

Lu Jing, associate professor and vice director, Shanghai Institute for Basic Education Research and Shanghai PISA Centre, Shanghai Academy of Educational Sciences

Qiu Zhong-hai, master teacher and master principal, Shanghai Qibao High School, Shanghai

Shen Zu-yun, director, Shanghai Educational News Centre

Shi Ju, mathematics teacher, Wen Lai Middle School, Shanghai

Tan Yi-bin, master teacher, teaching researcher in Chinese, and assistant director, Shanghai Teaching Research Institute; PISA 2009 reading expert group, Shanghai

Wang Hong, Chinese teacher, Wen Lai Middle School, Shanghai.

Wang Jie, associate professor and director of Teacher Education Centre, Shanghai Academy of Educational Sciences

Wang Mao-gong, director, Education Bureau, Xuhui District, Shanghai

Xu Dian-fang, director, Shanghai Teaching Research Institute

Xu Feng, politics teacher and vice principal, Wen Lai Middle School, Shanghai

Yin Hou-qin, vice director-general, Shanghai Municipal Education Commission

Zhang Min-sheng, professor, Shanghai Education Society; former vice director-general, Shanghai Municipal Education Commission

Zhang Min-xuan, professor and vice director-general, Shanghai Municipal Education Commission, PGB and NPM of Shanghai PISA 2009

Mr. Zhou, vice principal, Wen Lai High School, Shanghai

Zhou Ming-jun, English teacher, Wen Lai Middle School, Shanghai

Zhu Jian-wei, director of Education Bureau, Minhang District, Shanghai

APPENDIX A

Reading performance on PISA 2009

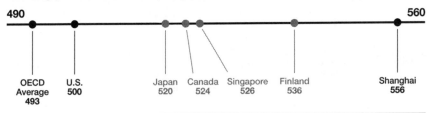

490   560

OECD Average 493 • U.S. 500 • Japan 520 • Canada 524 • Singapore 526 • Finland 536 • Shanghai 556

Math performance on PISA 2009

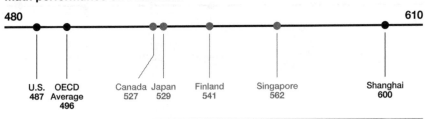

480   610

U.S. 487 • OECD Average 496 • Canada 527 • Japan 529 • Finland 541 • Singapore 562 • Shanghai 600

Science performance on PISA 2009

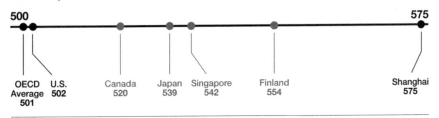

500   575

OECD Average 501 • U.S. 502 • Canada 520 • Japan 539 • Singapore 542 • Finland 554 • Shanghai 575

GDP per capita (USD)

| $11,000 | $33,000 | | $40,000 | $48,000 |

Shanghai
$11,361

OECD
Average
$33,732

Japan
$34,132

Finland
$35,918

Singapore
$37,293

Canada
$38,975

U.S.
$47,495

Percent of variance in student performance explained by socioeconomic status

4%   17%

Finland
7.8

Canada
8.6

Japan
8.6

Shanghai
12.3

OECD
Average
14

Singapore
15.3

U.S.
16.8

Source note: The source materials for these five charts can be found on the individual graphs in this book's introduction.

CHAPTER 2

Finland

Superb Teachers—How to Get Them, How to Use Them

Robert B. Schwartz and Jal D. Mehta

Prior to 2000, Finland rarely, if ever, appeared on anyone's list of the world's most outstanding education systems. This was partly a function of its relatively small size and geographical isolation, but also because its path to education reform and improvement has been slow and steady, proceeding gradually over the past four decades rather than as a consequence of highly visible innovations launched by a particular political leader or party. While it has always done well on international tests of literacy, in five different international mathematics or science assessments between 1962 and 1999, Finland's performance was never better than average.

With the publication of the first PISA results in 2001, however, Finland is now rightfully seen as a major international leader in education. It has consistently ranked in the very top tier of countries in all PISA assessments over the past decade, and its performance has been especially notable for its remarkable consistency across schools. No other country has so little variation in outcomes between schools, and the gap within schools between the top- and bottom-achieving students is extraordinarily modest as well. Finnish schools seem to serve all students well, regardless of family background or socioeconomic status. For this reason, Finnish schools have become a tourist destination, with hundreds of educators and policy makers annually journeying to Helsinki to try to learn the secret of Finland's success. (See appendix B for rankings of Finland on key education and economic indicators.)

As is too often the case when educators are confronted with evidence of success in other jurisdictions, the response of some international observers is to focus on those aspects of the Finnish success story that are so particular to its national history or culture that there couldn't possibly be anything for others to learn from Finland. These skeptics point out that Finland is culturally homogeneous—true, but there are now schools in Helsinki where nearly half the students are immigrants. They observe Finland's overall economic health, with its flourishing information technology sector, but neglect to note that its average per-pupil expenditure is well below that of the highest-spending countries, including the United States. They note that teaching is now the most popular profession among Finnish young people, attracting the top quartile of high school graduates into its highly competitive teacher training programs, without asking whether this has always been so or whether the country took special steps to upgrade the status of teachers and teaching.

As we will demonstrate below, the evolution of Finland's education reform story is in fact closely intertwined with the country's economic and political development since the Second World War, and cultural factors are clearly an important part of the Finnish success story. However, they are by no means the whole story. There are Finnish education policies and practices that others seeking to emulate Finland's success might study with profit.

HISTORICAL AND POLITICAL CONTEXT

Finland is a relatively young country, having only established its independence in 1917.[1] Finland had to fight long and hard to preserve that independence through World War II. For a nation with a population of less than four million, the cost of the war was devastating: 90,000 dead, 60,000 permanently injured, 50,000 children orphaned. Additionally, as part of the 1944 peace treaty with the Soviet Union, Finland was forced to cede 12 percent of its land, requiring the relocation of 450,000 Finnish citizens. A Soviet military base was established on a peninsula near Helsinki, and the Communist Party was granted legal status.

The first postwar elections in 1948 produced a parliament in which the seats were almost evenly divided among three political parties: the Social Democrats, the Agrarian Centre Party, and the Communists. In the 1950s, the Conservatives gained sufficient strength to also be included in major negotiations. Multiparty systems typically require the development of a political consensus in order to move any major policy agenda forward, and one priority around which such a consensus developed was the need to rebuild and modernize the Finnish education system.

The 1950 Finnish Education System

The education system that the new postwar parliament inherited was highly unequal and more reflective of the needs of a predominantly rural, agricultural society than of a modern industrial society. Although the country was still in fact 60 percent rural as late as 1960, the urbanization process really began right after the war and over the next decades accelerated to the point where Finland is now two-thirds urban.

Finland's education system

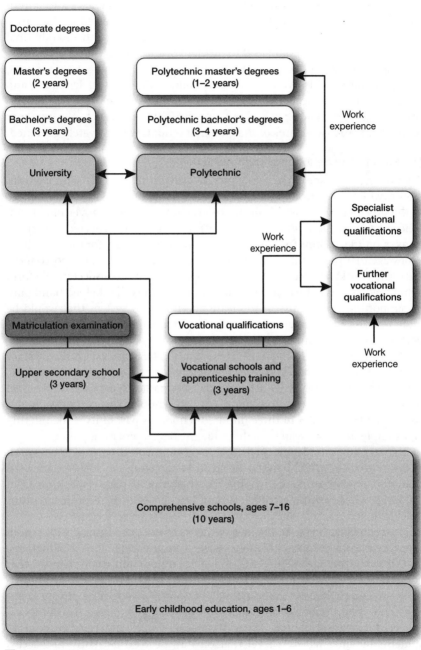

Doctorate degrees

Master's degrees
(2 years)

Polytechnic master's degrees
(1–2 years)

Bachelor's degrees
(3 years)

Polytechnic bachelor's degrees
(3–4 years)

Work
experience

University

Polytechnic

Specialist
vocational
qualifications

Work
experience

Further
vocational
qualifications

Matriculation examination

Vocational qualifications

Work
experience

Upper secondary school
(3 years)

Vocational schools and
apprenticeship training
(3 years)

Comprehensive schools, ages 7–16
(10 years)

Early childhood education, ages 1–6

☐ Qualifications (typically degrees, diplomas, or certificates)

▨ Institutions offering education and training

▨ Key gateways (typically major examinations)

In 1950, most young Finns left school after six years of basic education, for only those living in towns or larger municipalities had access to a middle grade education. There were two types of middle grade education: civic schools, run by some municipalities, which offered two or three additional years of schooling and could lead to further vocational education if you were fortunate enough to live in a town large enough to support such a school; and grammar schools, which offered five additional years of schooling and typically led to the academic high school (*gymnasium*) and then to university. Only about a quarter of young Finns in 1950 had access to the grammar school path, and two-thirds of the grammar schools were privately governed.

The Push to Create a Comprehensive School

Over the next decade there was explosive growth in grammar school enrollments, which grew from 34,000 to 270,000. Most of this growth took place in the private schools, which in the 1950s began to receive government subsidies and come more under public control. This growth reflected the aspirations of ordinary Finns for greater educational opportunity for their children, a message that the country's political leaders heard as well. In the postwar decade, the Eduskunta, the Finnish parliament, created three successive reform commissions, each of which made recommendations that helped build public support and political will to create an education system that would be more responsive to the growing demand for more equitable educational opportunities for all young people in Finland.

The first of these commissions, launched in 1945, focused on the primary school curriculum and offered a compelling vision of a more humanistic, child-centered school, in contrast to the Germanic, syllabus-driven model of schooling that characterized most Finnish schools. This commission also conducted field studies in three hundred schools as part of its work, offering an example of how research might guide the development of policy.

The second commission, launched in 1946, focused on the organization of the system and advocated for the creation of a common school grades 1–8 that would serve all students. This report produced such opposition from the universities and the grammar school teachers that its recommendations quickly died.

A decade later, however, the idea of the common or comprehensive school resurfaced in the recommendations of the Commission on School Programs, and this time the idea gained traction. The commission recommended that compulsory education in Finland should take place in a nine-year municipally run comprehensive grade 1–9 school, into which existing private grammar schools and public civic schools would ultimately merge. This proposal triggered a very substantial debate about core values and beliefs. Could all students be educated to a level that only those who currently had access to grammar schools were expected to achieve? Did the society really need all young people to be educated to a high level? Did all young people really need to know a third language in addition to Finnish and Swedish (a requirement of grammar schools), and was it fair to expect this of them? Over the next several years, these debates continued, but as Finland's ambitions grew to become more economically competitive, and as the demand for social and economic equality grew, pressure on legislators grew to move forward with the recommendation to create the new comprehensive school. Consequently, in November 1963, by a substantial margin, the parliament finally enacted legislation to create a new basic education system built around a common, comprehensive 1–9 school.

THE EVOLUTION OF TODAY'S FINNISH EDUCATION SYSTEM

The reason for dwelling at some length on the political evolution of the comprehensive school idea is that most Finnish analysts believe that the comprehensive school (*peruskoulu*) is the foundation on which all subsequent reforms rest. As Pasi Sahlberg, director of the Center for International Mobility and Cooperation, and perhaps the foremost interpreter of Finland's education story to the outside world, put it, "The comprehensive school is not merely a form of school organization. It embodies a philosophy of education as well as a deep set of societal values about what all children need and deserve."

The transition from a parallel form of school organization to the single comprehensive system was challenging and, consequently, was phased in slowly and carefully. Implementation did not begin until 1972, initially in northern Finland and only gradually spreading to the more populated municipalities and towns in the south. The last southern municipality to implement the new comprehensive system did so in 1979.

Jukka Sarjala, who spent twenty-five years in the Ministry of Education (1970–1995) before becoming director-general of the National Board of Education, described the task he faced as the person in the ministry with lead responsibility for planning the implementation of the new law:

> My challenge was to develop a plan that guaranteed that this reform would ultimately be implemented in every Finnish community. There were lots of municipalities that were not eager to reform their system, which is why it was important to have a legal mandate. This was a very big reform, very big and complicated for teachers accustomed to the old system. They were accustomed to teaching school with selected children and were simply not ready for a school system in which very clever children and not so clever children were in the same classes. It took several years, in some schools until the older teachers retired, for these reforms to be accepted.

A major vehicle for addressing the anxieties of veteran teachers and resolving some of the difficulties inherent in merging the formerly parallel sets of schools into a unified system was the development of a new national curriculum for the comprehensive school. The process for developing the curriculum engaged hundreds of teachers and took place over a five-year period (1965–1970). One important decision that allayed the fears of some of the critics of the comprehensive school was to allow some differentiation in the upper grades to accommodate perceived differences in ability and interests, especially in mathematics and foreign languages. Schools could offer three levels of study in these subjects: basic, middle, and advanced, with the basic level corresponding to what had been offered in civic schools and advanced to what had been offered in the old grammar schools. This form of ability grouping persisted into the mid-1980s, when it was finally abolished.

Perhaps the most significant and long-lasting consequence of the shift to the comprehensive school was the recognition that if the underlying vision of a school that could serve all students equally well regardless of family background was going to be realized, this would require a teaching force with a very high level of knowledge and skills. To quote Pasi Sahlberg again:

> In the early 1970s policy-makers realized that if we were to successfully implement this very ambitious comprehensive school reform, bringing all Finnish students into the same school and expecting them to master the same curriculum, it would require not only different systems of support but a very different level of understanding and knowledge from each and every teacher.

This recognition led to the development of a sweeping set of reforms that significantly raised the bar for aspiring teachers by moving teacher preparation from the three-year normal school into the university and ultimately requiring all teachers, primary through upper-secondary, to obtain a master's degree as a condition of employment. The design and content of the new teacher preparation programs are described in more detail below.

A third major effect of the implementation of the comprehensive 1–9 basic school was to greatly heighten demand for upper-secondary education. In 1970, only 30 percent of Finnish adults had obtained at least an upper-secondary diploma. That percentage is now over 80 percent; and among those aged 24–35, it is 90 percent. This extraordinary growth is in part due to a radical set of reforms enacted in 1985, in which the traditional lock-step structure of the academic upper-secondary school was replaced with a much more flexible, modular structure that injected significantly more choice into the system. In recent years the modernization of the academic secondary school has been mirrored in the vocational secondary school, which has been significantly strengthened and expanded to the point where it now enrolls 42 percent of graduates from the comprehensive school. One reason for the increasing popularity of the vocational secondary option is that Finland has in recent years created a set of polytechnic colleges, thereby creating a pathway into tertiary education for vocational students. Consequently, 43 percent of young Finns in their twenties are enrolled in tertiary education, well above the OECD average of 25 and the highest percentage in Europe.

THE INFLUENCE OF FINLAND'S ECONOMIC DEVELOPMENT ON EDUCATION REFORM

The story of the evolution of the Finnish education system over the past two decades is inextricably linked to the development of the modern Finnish economy. If the rise of the comprehensive school in the 1970–1990 period needs to be seen in the context of the development of the Finnish welfare state and the national push for much greater social and economic equality, the less visible but equally profound changes in Finland's schools over the past two decades need to be seen in the context of the deep changes taking place in the Finnish economy.

Two major events occurred in the early 1990s that triggered a significant shift in the economic development strategy promulgated by Finland's government and private-sector leaders. The first was the initiation of the accession process that led to Finland's acceptance into the European Union in 1995. With the collapse of the Soviet Union (a major trading partner), Finland had no choice but to diversify its export strategy and begin to move away from its historic reliance on timber and other traditional industries. The second and more powerful stimulus for reform was a major economic recession in the early 1990s touched off by a collapse of the financial sector, reminiscent of the banking crisis the United States recently experienced. Unemployment in Finland approached 20 percent, the GDP declined 13 percent, and public debt exceeded 60 percent of the GDP.

The government used this crisis as an opportunity to develop a new national competitiveness policy designed to support private-sector innovation and focused heavily on the development of the telecommunications sector, with Nokia as the central player. In a remarkably short time, Finland managed not only to dig itself out of recession but to reduce its historical reliance on its natural resources and transform its economy into one based on information and knowledge. Investments in research and development provided the fuel for this growth. In 1991, only five Finnish workers out of 1,000 were in the research and development (R&D) labor force. By 2003, this number had increased to twenty-two, almost three times the OECD average. By 2001, Finland's ranking in the World Economic Forum's global competitiveness index had climbed from fifteenth to first place, and it has remained at or near the top in these rankings ever since.

The impact of this new focus on innovation and R&D not only led to the development of new partnerships between tertiary education and industry in Finland, but it also had a profound effect on the primary and secondary education sector as well. Finnish employers sent very strong signals to the schools as to the kinds of knowledge, skills, and dispositions young people needed in order to be successful in the new economy. Finnish industry leaders not only promoted the importance of math, science, and technology in the formal curriculum, but they also advocated for more attention to creativity, problem solving, teamwork, and cross-curricular projects in the schools. An example of the kind of message corporate leaders were delivering to the schools is this statement from a senior Nokia manager Pasi Sahlberg interviewed during this period in his role as chair of a task force on the national science curriculum:

> If I hire a youngster who doesn't know all the mathematics or physics that is needed to work here, I have colleagues here who can easily teach those things. But if I get somebody who doesn't know how to work with other people, how to think differently or how to create original ideas and somebody who is afraid of making a mistake, there is nothing we can do here. Do what you have to do to keep our education system up-to-date but don't take away creativity and open-mindedness that we now have in our fine peruskoulu.

Implicit in the Nokia manager's comment is his belief that comprehensive schools were already paying attention in their approach to instruction to developing at least some of the traits that employers in the new Finnish economy were seeking. In fact, it is hard to imagine how an information- and knowledge-based economy could have grown up so quickly in the 1990s if the Finnish schools had not already been producing graduates with the kind of flexibility and openness to innovation that industry was now demanding. The development of these kinds of qualities is at least as much a function of the culture and climate of schools as of the formal curriculum.

THE CULTURE OF FINNISH SCHOOLS

What are Finnish schools actually like? While it is important to note the key legislative landmarks that have created the policy framework within which Finnish schools have become world-class over the past decade, these hardly provide a full explanation for Finland's remarkable success story. After all, Finland is not the only northern European country to have abolished tracking and created a unified basic school structure. Other countries have revamped and upgraded their teacher education programs and have taken steps similar to Finland's to modernize secondary education. So what does account for Finland's success?

One way to address this question is to detail some of the most salient characteristics of Finland's comprehensive schools as these have been described by our Finnish informants. The first thing to note is that these schools offer more than education. These are full-service schools. They provide a daily hot meal for every student. They provide health and dental services. They offer guidance and psychological counseling and access to a broader array of mental health and other services for students and families in need. None of these services is means-tested. Their availability to all reflects a deep societal commitment to the well-being of all children.

A second, related characteristic is the role of the special education teacher. Finland prides itself on its commitment to inclusion. While 2 percent of Finland's children are deemed sufficiently handicapped to be placed in special schools, and another 6 percent are in special education classes, Finnish educators believe that if schools focus on early diagnosis and intervention, at least 90 percent of students can be helped to achieve success in regular classrooms. Its principal mechanism for supporting struggling students in a timely fashion is the "special teacher," a specially trained teacher assigned to each school whose job is to work closely with the class teachers to identify students in need of extra help and to work individually or in small groups with struggling students to provide the extra help and support they need to keep up with their classmates.

The attention to the needs of individual children is not left solely to the discretion of the regular class teacher to identify a problem and alert the special teacher. Every comprehensive school has a pupils' care group, as described by Riitta Aaltio, principal of a 360-student primary school in Kerava, just outside of Helsinki. The group meets at least twice a month for two hours and consists of the principal, the special education teacher, the school nurse, the school psychologist, a social worker, and the teachers whose students are being discussed. The parents of any child being discussed are contacted prior to the meeting and are sometimes asked to be present. Aaltio describes the group's function as follows:

> In each meeting we usually have enough time to discuss two classes of pupils with their class (i.e., homeroom) teacher, plus any "acute cases." First, we talk about the class and how things are going in general. If there are any concerns—learning, teaching, social climate or some problems with individual students we try to decide what kind of support we can provide. If we believe a pupil needs professional help beyond what we can provide at the school, we help the family get that kind of help, be it medical, psychological, or social. These measures are available to all students—social background makes no difference—because health care, like education, is free in Finland. This functional support system is a very important part of our education system. It helps explain why we have such small gaps in student achievement.

When we shift from describing the special support available to students in need to the role of the regular class teacher (grades 1–6) or subject teacher (7–9), we find teachers who exercise an enormous degree of professional discretion and independence. While there remains a national curriculum in

Nalond Core

Finland, over the past twenty years it has become much less detailed and prescriptive. It functions more as a framework, leaving individual teachers latitude to decide what they will teach and how. Teachers select their own textbooks and other instructional materials. Because the only external testing in comprehensive schools is done on a sampling basis in grades 6 and 9 and is designed to provide information on the functioning of the system as a whole, assessment in Finnish schools is a classroom responsibility. Not only are teachers expected to assess their own students on an ongoing basis, using the assessments that accompany the curriculum materials or designing them on their own, but a major focus in Finnish classrooms is on helping students learn how to assess their own learning. In Principal Aaltio's school, this emphasis begins as early as first grade.

Finnish classrooms are typically described by observers as learner-centered. As the emphasis on student self-assessment would suggest, students are expected to take an active role in designing their own learning activities. Students are expected to work collaboratively in teams on projects, and there is a substantial focus on projects that cut across traditional subject or disciplinary lines. By the time students enroll in upper-secondary school (grades 10–12), they are expected to be able to take sufficient charge of their own learning to be able to design their own individual program. Upper-secondary schools are now mostly individualized. There is no longer a grade structure; each student proceeds at his or her own pace, with the modular structure allowing students to start new courses every seven or eight weeks.

The focus on helping students take increasing responsibility for their own learning is not accidental; it reflects a key value undergirding the national curriculum for the comprehensive school. Here is a representative excerpt from the preamble of the National Core Curriculum for Basic Education, from a section on the "Learning Environment":

> The learning environment must support the pupil's growth and learning. It must be physically, psychologically, and socially safe, and must support the pupil's health. The objective is to increase pupils' curiosity and motivation to learn, and to promote their activeness, self-direction, and creativity by offering interesting challenges and problems. The learning environment must guide pupils in setting their own objectives and evaluating their own actions. The pupils must be given the chance to participate in the creation and development of their own learning environment.

FINNISH SUCCESS FACTORS

As with all education systems that achieve good results, Finland's success is a function of the interaction of several different factors that work together to create a coherent approach that supports consistent systemwide perfor-

Success

mance. Some of these factors are cultural. As Sahlberg points out, Finland's history and geography—"caught between the huge kingdom in the west and the even bigger empire in the east"—compelled it to put the nation's interest first and not allow education policy to become victim to partisan politics.

> We are a small nation that the rest of the world sees as a strange place that speaks a language nobody else understands. Over the last half-century we developed an understanding that the only way for us to survive as a small, independent nation is by educating all our people. This is our only hope amid the competition between bigger nations and all those who have other benefits we don't have.

While Finland has jealously guarded its hard-won independence, in many areas of social policy it has been much influenced by its Scandinavian neighbors, especially Sweden. As noted above, the idea of the comprehensive school emerged in Finland as part of a larger movement in the 1960s for more social and economic equality, and over the next two decades the Finns adopted many features of the Swedish welfare state. Consequently, Finnish schools are embedded in a society with strong social safety nets and a broad and deep commitment to the healthy development and well-being of children, as reflected in Principal Aaltio's description of the pupils' care group in her school.

Another reflection of the society's deep commitment to its children can be found in its school buildings. In the period following World War II, municipalities and towns all over Finland embarked on a major effort to rebuild schools that had been destroyed and build new ones where none had existed. Consequently, most children in Finland attend schools that are quite small, small enough for each child to be known by all the adults in the school. While the schools are not intended to be architectural statements, they are typically light, airy, and functional. Their small size allows for a degree of personalization and individual attention that is one of the hallmarks of Finnish education.

Finnish society is also characterized by a degree of social cohesion and trust in government that is partly a function of size and relative cultural homogeneity but also reflective of the national temperament. Social cohesion and trust are difficult factors to isolate and quantify, but they clearly are part of the explanation for why teaching has become such an attractive profession for talented young people in Finland, at least on a par with medicine and law. Olli Luukkainen, president of the union that represents all Finnish educators, comments on the trust factor in discussing the status of teaching in Finland:

> Teachers in Finland are very independent. They can decide almost everything: how they will teach, what they will select from the basic (national) curriculum, when they will teach each particular topic. The fact that teachers

have so much independence and respect influences young people as they are deciding what program they will follow in the university. If they choose teacher education they know they will be entering a profession that enjoys broad trust and respect in the society, one that plays an important role in shaping the country's future.

While the trust that teachers enjoy in Finnish society can be seen as a causal variable in helping to explain how Finnish primary teacher education programs are able to attract ten applicants for every slot, it can also be viewed as an effect of the quality of the preparation of Finnish teachers. In other words, Finnish teachers have earned the trust of parents and the larger society by their demonstrated ability to use professional discretion and judgment in the way they manage their classrooms and respond to the challenge of helping virtually all students become successful learners.

The quality of teachers and teaching lies at the heart of Finland's educational success, and the factors responsible for producing that quality can be found at the intersection of culture and policy. The role of policy in enabling Finland to create a world-class teaching force can be seen not only in the 1979 decision to move teacher preparation into the universities and make it substantially more rigorous, but in the subsequent decisions of Conservative governments in the 1980s to devolve increasing levels of authority and responsibility for education from the Ministry of Education to municipalities and schools. This movement was largely an expression of ideology, of a growing skepticism in the West about the role of central governments and their ability to know what works best in the field; but the effect of these decisions was to extend even greater responsibility and trust to educators in the schools.

Prior to devolution, the ministry had two primary tools for regulating the quality of education: the national curriculum and a national school inspectorate. As mentioned above, the national curriculum over time has become much less detailed and prescriptive—there are now only ten pages for all of basic school mathematics—and the current version acknowledges that the curriculum plan adopted by each municipality will incorporate locally developed priorities and be reflective of community aspirations and values. Even more striking, the inspectorate has now been abolished, leaving only the periodic sampling of student learning in grades 6 and 9 as the ministry's vehicle for assessing and monitoring school quality.

If one had to retroactively ascribe a theory of action to those responsible for designing the reforms that have followed from the establishment of the common school in Finland, it would go something like this:

> If we can somehow manage to recruit highly talented young people to enroll in our teacher preparation programs and then redesign those programs to equip all incoming teachers to differentiate instruction, diagnose learning problems, and assess student progress; and if we can create the conditions in

schools that allow teachers to exercise professional judgment and discretion in selecting materials and designing instruction tailored to the needs of their students; and if we can create school cultures in which teachers take collective responsibility for the learning and well-being of their students; and if we can create in every school mechanisms that provide access to extra support for children and families most in need; then we can be reasonably confident that virtually all students in virtually all schools will thrive.

Because this theory of change rests so heavily on the quality of the teaching force, let us now turn to the role of teacher preparation in Finland.

TEACHER RECRUITMENT AND PREPARATION

Teaching has long been a respected occupation in Finland, but until the teacher education reform act of 1979, there was little sense of teaching as a field with a sufficient knowledge base to require much advanced training. After completing upper-secondary school, prospective primary and middle grade teachers enrolled in a *seminarium* (the Finnish equivalent of teacher college) for two or three years of mostly practical training and then moved straight into the classroom. This model of preparation was hardly unique to Finland. Its premise was that as long as students had a solid foundation of subject matter knowledge from their upper-secondary schooling, they could be taught enough about pedagogy, child development, and classroom management in two or three years to become effective teachers. The normal schools presumably screened their applicants to ensure that they had the requisite character and personality traits to become teachers, but their admissions criteria were understandably much less rigorous than those of the universities.

All this changed with the movement of teacher education from the teacher colleges into the university and, especially with the decision to require even primary school teachers to obtain a master's degree before receiving a license to teach. As was the case with the creation of the comprehensive school, this decision was not without controversy. University leaders initially resisted the idea that teaching was anything more than a semi-profession and feared that advocates for other semi-professions, like nursing and social work, would now clamor to have their training programs obtain university status. Their real worry was that the admission of teacher education candidates would lead to a dilution of academic standards and a consequent loss of status.

Over time, however, as the new university-based teacher education programs were designed and built, these fears were not borne out. In fact, university-based teacher education programs are now highly selective. In 2010, more than 6,600 applicants competed for 660 available slots in primary school preparation programs in the eight universities that educate teachers. The admissions process has two stages. The initial paper screen is based on the applicant's Matriculation Exam score, upper-secondary school record, and out-of-school accomplishments. Those who survive that screen must then take a written exam based on a reading of an assigned text on pedagogy; be observed in a teaching-like clinical activity in which their interaction and communication skills can be assessed; and, finally, undergo an interview to assess, among other things, the strength of their motivation to teach.

The teacher education programs for prospective primary and upper-grade teachers are somewhat different in structure but not in rigor. Primary grade teachers major in education, but they are expected to minor in at least two of the subjects included in the primary school curriculum. This means, for example, that they are studying mathematics in the math department, not in the education department. Upper-grade teachers major in the subject they will be teaching, but they do substantial work in education as well, either in an integrated five-year program or in a concentrated fifth year after they have completed their work in their subject field.

Teacher education in Finland has at least four distinguishing qualities. First, it is heavily research based. Teacher candidates are not only expected to become familiar with the knowledge base in education and human development, but they are required to write a research-based thesis as the final requirement for the master's degree. Upper grade teachers typically pick a topic in their subject area; primary grade teachers typically study some aspect of pedagogy. The rationale for requiring a research-based project is that teachers are expected to engage in disciplined inquiry in the classroom throughout their teaching career.

A second distinguishing characteristic is a strong focus on developing pedagogical content knowledge. Traditional teacher preparation programs too often treat good pedagogy as generic, assuming that good questioning skills, for example, are equally applicable to all subjects. Because teacher education in Finland is a shared responsibility between teacher education faculty and academic subject faculty, there is substantial attention to subject-specific pedagogy for prospective primary as well as upper-grade teachers.

A third strength, implicit in the discussion of the role of the special teacher, is that all Finnish teachers are trained to diagnose students with learning difficulties and to differentiate their instruction based on the learning needs and styles of their students. Finally, and perhaps most important, there is a very strong clinical component in Finnish teacher education. Linda Darling-Hammond, a leading American scholar and practitioner of teacher education, describes this aspect of Finnish teacher preparation:

> Teachers' preparation includes both extensive course work on how to teach—
> with a strong emphasis on using research based on state-of-the-art practice—
> and at least a full year of clinical experience in a school associated with the
> university. These model schools are intended to develop and model innova-

tive practices, as well as to foster research on learning and teaching . . . Within these model schools, student teachers participate in problem-solving groups, a common feature in Finnish schools. The problem-solving groups engage in a cycle of planning, action, and reflection/evaluation that is reinforced throughout the teacher education program and is, in fact, a model for what teachers will plan for their own students, who are expected to use similar kinds of research and inquiry in their own studies. Indeed, the entire system is intended to improve through continual reflection, evaluation, and problem-solving, at the level of the classroom, school, municipality, and nation.

In summary, then, raising the bar for entry into teaching made this an even more attractive career option than it had been in an earlier era, enabling teacher preparation programs to select from the top quartile of secondary school graduates. And the significantly lengthened and strengthened preparation of teachers has equipped them to exercise the increasing degree of professional autonomy and control that the government has vested in them. The autonomy and trust that teachers enjoy has only enhanced their status in the society, thereby ensuring that teacher preparation programs will continue to have a steady flow of highly talented and motivated applicants.

The Work of Teachers

One of the most striking facts about Finnish schools is that their students have fewer intended hours of instruction than students in any other OECD country. This means that Finnish teachers teach fewer hours than their peers in other countries. In lower-secondary schools, for example, Finnish teachers teach about 600 hours a year—800 forty-five-minute lessons, or four lessons per day. By contrast, U.S. middle school teachers teach about 1,080 hours, or six 50-minute daily lessons. Leave aside the important question of how Finnish fifteen-year-olds manage to outperform peers in other nations who in some instances experience the equivalent of three more years of schooling. The relevant question here is what Finnish teachers are doing when they are not engaged in classroom teaching.

With the professional autonomy Finnish teachers enjoy comes very substantial responsibility for tasks that in other systems are typically handled more centrally. Chief among these are curriculum and assessment. As described above, the national curriculum is really a framework rather than a roadmap, leaving teachers an enormous amount of discretion to interpret that framework, select their own textbooks and other curriculum materials, and then design their own lessons. In some schools, the process of curriculum development is undertaken collaboratively by teams of teachers, while in smaller schools the responsibility might fall largely on each individual teacher.

The National Curriculum document offers some broad guidance on assessments, but again, the principal responsibility for building systems to continuously assess the progress of students falls on classroom teachers. Teachers are also expected to be in close communication with the parents of their students, and many schools have an elaborate structure of staff committees to deal with various aspects of school life. Although Finnish teachers in theory are allowed to leave school when they are not teaching, teaching is clearly a full-time profession.

When it comes to professional development in Finland, the situation seems highly variable. This is in large part because Finnish schools are primarily funded at the municipal level, and municipal authorities attach varying degrees of importance to professional development. Municipalities are required to fund three days of mandatory professional development for each teacher, but some municipalities do much more. On average, Finnish teachers report spending seven days a year on professional development, some of which is done on their own time. Some larger municipalities organize common professional development activities for all their schools, while others allow each school to design its own program.

According to Olli Luukkainen, this highly variable approach to professional development is a weakness of the Finnish system:

> Our system of continuing education and professional development for teachers is not good enough. It differs too much from one part of the country to another and one group of teachers to another. Teachers in vocational schools, for example, have much better support for continuing education than do primary teachers.

Recently, however, the union and the Ministry of Education and other partners have come together to develop a national program to try to provide more equitable access to professional development, especially for teachers in more disadvantaged schools. The ministry has allocated US$30 million to support this program, with the intention of doubling the funding by 2016.

QUALITY ASSURANCE

Perhaps the most frequent question asked of Finnish policy makers is, "How, in the absence of annual external assessments and any form of outside inspection, do you ensure that all students in all schools are receiving a quality education?" This question comes most frequently from visitors from countries like the United States and the United Kingdom, which invest heavily in external accountability systems designed to produce more equitable outcomes but whose results pale in comparison to the Finnish system.

Beyond the periodic sampling assessments administered in grades 6 and 9, there is no national mechanism for monitoring the performance of schools. There is a national Evaluation Council, but its role seems to be focused more on the evaluation of national policies than the performance of schools. There is a National Matriculation Exam taken at the end of upper-secondary school by those seeking admission to university, but its function is to certify what the student knows, not to assess the quality of his or her school.

There is no obvious, single answer to the quality-assurance question. Rather, the ability of Finnish schools to produce high achievement with so little variation between or within schools is the result of the confluence of factors, cultural and educational, outlined throughout this chapter. One factor cited by Principal Aaltio is, paradoxically, the heavy Finnish emphasis on assessment. While the Finns do not assess for school accountability purposes, they do an enormous amount of diagnostic or formative assessment at the classroom level. When asked how she knows how well the students in any particular class are learning, Aaltio's answer is that there is so much assessment data at her disposal that there is no way she would not know if a teacher was failing to teach her students. She also reports that, in her school at least, the parents keep a close eye on how their children are progressing and alert her if there are problems. And there are also the twice-monthly meetings of the pupil's care group to bring class as well as individual problems to light.

Accountability in the Finnish system is built from the bottom up. Teacher candidates are selected in part based on their ability to convey their belief in the core mission of public education in Finland, which is deeply moral and humanistic as well as civic and economic, and the preparation they receive is designed to build a powerful sense of individual responsibility for the learning and well-being of all the students in their care.

The next level of accountability rests with the school. Again, the level of trust that the larger community extends to its schools seems to engender a strong sense of collective responsibility for the success of every student. While every comprehensive school in Finland reports to a municipal authority, authorities vary widely in the quality and degree of oversight that they provide. They are responsible for hiring the principal, typically on a six- or seven-year contract, but the day-to-day responsibility for managing the schools is left to the professionals, as is the responsibility for ensuring student progress.

Given the very substantial level of autonomy that schools enjoy, one might expect that the system would focus the same kind of attention on recruiting and developing a corps of highly effective principals as it does on preparing teachers. However, there is little evidence of this. As in many countries, the role of the school principal in Finland is changing. But the very independence of teachers in Finland poses some special challenges, at least as seen by Jouni Valijarvi of the University of Jyvaskyla, lead researcher for the analysis of Finland's PISA results.

> Historically, the principal in Finland has simply been head teacher, first among equals as a member of the teaching staff with the added responsibility of representing the faculty to the rest of the society. But given the degree

to which school budgets have been decentralized, the job is now much more demanding, for principals now have financial responsibility along with responsibility for the care and well-being of the students. Because Finnish teachers are highly educated and are accustomed to being in full control of their own classroom, we have no tradition of principals actively visiting classes to monitor the quality of teaching in their schools. In fact, given our small school sizes, most principals are themselves teaching at least a few hours a week, so their role is a mixed one, with confusing and sometimes contradictory demands.

While some universities, including Valijarvi's, have now mounted professional development programs for principals, this does not seem to be seen as a major problem or need.

CHALLENGES AHEAD

The big question all high-performing systems need to face is whether or not the policies and practices that have enabled their current high performance will be sufficient to sustain them in a rapidly changing, globalizing world. In the case of Finland, this question is a particularly intriguing one, for the big policy shift that most observers credit with undergirding Finland's current level of performance took place forty years ago. Unlike many other high-performing countries, Finland's reforms have evolved slowly and carefully over decades, have enjoyed broad and sustained political support across many changes in government, and are so intertwined with deep cultural factors that they are firmly institutionalized in the fabric of everyday life in schools. They are not the result of bold new policies or big programmatic initiatives that one can identify with a particular government or political leader. Rather, they are now almost taken for granted as the way schooling is done in Finland.

Given its history and development, what particular challenges might the future hold for Finland's education system? One is hardly unique to Finland, and that is the challenge of successfully absorbing increasing numbers of children of immigrants into its schools. This is a problem many European nations have struggled with, some more successfully than others. Although children of immigrants only make up about 3 percent of Finland's students, this percentage is growing, and there are already some schools in Helsinki where nearly half the students are immigrants. Until now Finland has been committed to providing immigrant children the option of continuing to learn in their native language. This could be a problem going forward, as Jouni Varijarvi observes:

> Traditionally we have stressed that immigrant students can be taught in their own language. We have done this for reasons having to do with our own history, when we were part of Sweden and wanted the right to be

taught in Finnish. Even today, when Swedish is the native language of only 5 percent of our population, we have extended them the same right to be taught in their language. But when you have a growing number of languages, it may not be possible to continue to be able to provide this right to be taught in your own language. And then there is this larger question of how to balance respect for your native language with the importance of learning the Finnish language to be able to function in Finnish society. We have been critical of Sweden for its insistence that newcomers integrate into Swedish society, but given the expense and difficulty of finding enough teachers to teach all immigrant children in their own language, we may be forced to move in this direction as well.

A second question one might ask about Finland's future has to do with the extraordinary degree to which its system relies on its continuing ability to draw its teachers from the top end of the talent pool. Can one imagine circumstances under which teaching might begin to lose its allure among young Finns? Professions undergo cycles in which their relative status in a society can rise or fall. Suppose, as some observers fear, the pendulum begins to swing back to somewhat more centralized control of schooling in Finland. If other countries begin to surpass Finland on PISA or other international measures of performance, will there be calls for the education ministry to step in and take a stronger hand in guiding Finnish education? If that were to happen, would young people continue to find teaching so attractive?

A third, less speculative, question concerns the future of the current upper-secondary divide between academic and vocational education. While there seems to be a strong societal consensus that supports the division of upper-secondary education into tracks, at least one respected and deeply experienced former education official wonders whether the principle of the common comprehensive school might someday be extended into upper-secondary education. Jukka Sarjala asks whether in the future the needs of academic and vocational education students will really be so different from one another:

> If we ask what foreign-language skills young people will need in the future, won't everyone need at least English in addition to Swedish, and many people in different lines of work might also need French or German or Russian. And what about mathematics? Won't everyone need some form of advanced mathematics? Wouldn't it make sense to combine academic and vocational programs in the same institution while allowing students to develop their own individual programs?

Current upper-secondary school policy does in fact allow students to take courses in both institutions. But as a practical matter, this option is really available only to students who live in communities where both types of schools are offered and conveniently located. Jouni Varljarvi believes that the rising popularity of vocational education among young people is likely to create increasing pressure at the municipal level for greater collaboration between the two types of schools:

> Many academically oriented upper-secondary schools are having trouble today attracting students. Because they are funded based on student enroll-ment, in some smaller municipalities this is a serious threat to their survival. We are now starting to see some of these schools close, a brand new phe-nomenon in our system. At the same time a growing number of very tal-ented students are leaving comprehensive school and choosing vocational studies, thereby increasing the popularity of vocational schools. In the com-ing years this will mean that unless the academic schools learn to collabo-rate on a deeper level, many more are likely to close, since most of our 450 academic upper-secondary schools are very small and cannot sustain a con-tinuing loss of students.

A final worry or challenge is one best articulated by Pasi Sahlberg at the end of his unpublished manuscript, "Finnish Lessons." In his view, the Finn-ish reform movement over these last several decades has been animated by what he calls "the Big Dream," a unifying vision of a more equitable soci-ety in which even students in the most isolated rural schools would receive a strong enough educational foundation in the first nine years of school-ing to equip them for further education and in which young people from all walks of life would be prepared to live and work together through a com-mon schooling experience. Is there now a need for a new vision, one more reflective of the changes taking place in today's society and more responsive to what young people will need in the coming decades, a vision powerful enough to fuel the next generation of reforms?

WHAT CAN BE LEARNED FROM FINLAND?

For all of Finland's perceived advantages of size, relative cultural homogene-ity, and (in recent years) economic strength, it is important to remember that as recently as 1970 only 14 percent of Finnish adults had completed upper-secondary school, and as recently as 1993 Finland was in near economic col-lapse. Finland's ascent into the very top tier of educational performance was by no means inevitable: it was at least as much the result of a set of policy decisions deliberately taken, implemented thoughtfully, and sustained over a very long period of time as it was of factors endemic to the country's cul-ture and history.

Commitment to education and children matter. The commitment to educa-tion and to the well-being of children has deep roots in Finland's culture and provides the bedrock on which the comprehensive school movement rests. One of the striking things about Finland's reform story is that once a political consensus was established almost fifty years ago that it would be in the best interests of all children to educate them together in a common school system, that consensus has remained intact across numerous changes of government.

Cultural support for universal high achievement matters. The underlying belief behind the creation of the comprehensive school was that all children could be expected to achieve at high levels and that family background or regional circumstance should no longer be allowed to limit the kinds of educational opportunities open to children. It is important to note, however, that the Finns have a significantly broader definition of "high achievement" than do countries in which the definition rests solely on performance in two or three subjects on standardized tests. The Finns pride themselves on offering a broad, rich curriculum to all students, even those who choose the vocational pathway in upper-secondary school.

Teacher and principal quality matter. Many countries pay lip service to the importance of attracting and retaining a high-quality teaching force, but few have pursued this goal as single-mindedly as Finland. While teachers have always enjoyed a degree of respect in Finnish society, through a combination of raising the bar for entry into the profession and granting teachers greater autonomy and control over their classrooms and working conditions than their peers enjoy elsewhere, Finland has managed to make teaching the most desirable career choice among young Finns. Consequently, teaching is now a highly selective occupation in Finland, with highly skilled, well-trained teachers spread throughout the country. This fact more than any other accounts for the high level of consistency across Finnish schools.

Finland does not seem to have paid the same kind of attention to the recruitment, training, and ongoing development of principals, but it is hard to believe that Finnish schools could perform so well without solid leadership, especially given the degree of autonomy that Finnish schools enjoy.

Accountability matters. Accountability clearly matters in Finland, but it is almost entirely a professional model of accountability. The strongest manifestation of that accountability can be seen in the degree to which Finnish schools are organized to take collective responsibility for struggling learners. Finnish teachers are trained to identify children who are having difficulty and to intervene before these children get discouraged and fall too far behind their classmates. The proximity of help in the form of a specially trained intervention specialist—the special teacher—in every school means that the regular classroom teacher has easy access to support and that struggling children are much less likely to go unnoticed or to fall through the cracks. The small size of Finland's schools is an important factor here, as is the coordination of resources embodied in the pupils' care group. Again, this combination of elements helps explain why the gap between the top- and bottom-performing schools and students in Finland is so narrow compared with virtually all other nations.

How money is spent matters. Finland is by no means the highest spender per pupil among OECD countries, so money cannot be an important factor in explaining Finland's success. Teacher salaries are in the middle range for European countries. Schools are quite small in size, but they have minimal administrative overhead. Even in larger schools, principals are expected to teach, and the resources of the school are tightly focused on the classroom. Because of their commitment to the inclusion model, the costs of special education are significantly lower than in countries that rely more heavily on separate classrooms for special education students. Finally, because Finnish schools are mostly a function of municipal government, there are no separate school districts and no intermediate education units sitting between the municipalities and the ministry. Therefore, except for the costs of the Ministry of Education and the several national boards, virtually all of the money spent on education in Finland is focused on schools and classrooms.

Instructional practice matters. The decision three decades ago to move teacher education into the universities and upgrade the rigor and length of the training was made largely in response to the challenge of meeting the needs of diverse learners in a common school. Part of the challenge was equipping teachers to diagnose learning difficulties and design timely interventions. But the larger challenge, especially with the abolition of tracking in 1989, was helping them learn to differentiate instruction sufficiently well to engage all students in heterogeneously grouped classrooms. By all reports, Finnish teacher preparation programs focus intensively on helping teachers develop these skills, especially in the extended clinical portion of their training under the supervision of master teachers in the university-run model schools.

School organization matters. This, of course, was *the* central insight that has driven Finland's reform agenda over the past several decades. Virtually all observers and Finnish policy makers credit the decision to create a common comprehensive school, eventually untracked, that would serve students together from all walks of life as the single most important education policy decision taken since Finland established its independence in 1917. All the other policy decisions that, taken together, help account for Finland's dramatic ascent to a position of international leadership in education in the last decade flow from that basic organizational decision. Obviously, creating the comprehensive school structure in itself was no guarantee of improvement. Rather, it has been the steady, thoughtful way in which the new structure has been implemented—especially the investments in recruiting and developing a teaching force committed to the values that underlie the comprehensive school and capable of meeting the needs of diverse learners in that setting—that is mostly responsible for the extraordinarily high and equitable achievement of Finnish students.

Dimension lines of the national economic development schema. In many ways, what is most distinctive and impressive about Finland is the degree to which its education system has developed in close alignment with its economy and social structure. As described above, the story of the development of Finland's education reforms cannot be told without reference to the development of the welfare state in the 1960s and 1970s and the high-tech, information-based economy of the last two decades. On the various development dimensions outlined in the introduction to this book, Finland is at the farthest end of the continuum. Its economy is driven by continuing investments in innovation and research and development. Finnish teachers are drawn from the top quartile of upper-secondary graduates. Teachers are highly professional knowledge workers and are treated as such. Accountability is almost entirely professional, as evidenced by the elimination of the inspectorate and the absence of external assessments. The curriculum framework and instructional guidance is designed to encourage an inquiry-based approach to learning.

Finnish schools work to cultivate in young people the dispositions and habits of mind we associate with innovators: creativity, flexibility, initiative, risk-taking, the ability to apply knowledge in novel situations. Some skeptics attribute Finland's consistently high performance on PISA to the degree of alignment between the kind of learning PISA measures and values and the goals of the Finnish education system. There is clearly some truth to this observation, but this hardly constitutes a criticism of the Finnish system. The Finns are not the least bit apologetic about their focus on preparing people for an economy in which innovation and entrepreneurship will continue to be drivers of progress.

FINAL OBSERVATIONS

Two final observations are related to the degree to which the Finnish education system is aligned with and reflective of qualities in the larger culture. The first has to do with the very nature of education reform in Finland. Most governments enact education reform through new programs—smaller class sizes, more ambitious external assessments, increased professional development. Reforms like these take the basic features of the system as given. The Finnish reforms, by contrast, especially the creation of the comprehensive school, created a sector that functioned in a radically different way. It is the shape of this new sector, not continued programmatic initiatives from a central government, that accounts for Finland's success. One critical observer suggested that Finland doesn't really have a reform strategy, by which he meant that there were no central initiatives that the government was trying to push through the system. From a longer-term, more sectoral perspective, however, Finland did and does have a strategy, one that has propelled it to the top of the international rankings. Other countries might benefit from adopting this perspective on their reform work.

The second observation has to do with the importance of trust. Trust, of course, cannot be legislated. Consequently, this lesson may be the least useful to others wanting to learn from Finland, especially if one views trust as a precondition for the kinds of deep institutional reforms embodied in the development of the comprehensive school. But in the case of the relationship between teachers and the larger society, one can argue that trust is at least as much a consequence of important policy decisions as it is a preexisting condition. Given the respect that teachers have historically enjoyed in Finland, there was a solid base to build on. But the combination of much more rigorous preparation coupled with the devolution of much greater decision-making authority over things like curriculum and assessment enabled teachers to exercise the kind of professional autonomy other professionals enjoy. This grant of trust from the government, coupled with their newfound status as university graduates from highly selective programs, empowered teachers to practice their profession in ways that deepened the trust afforded them by parents and others in the community. The fact that there seems to be very little interest in Finland in instituting the assessment and external accountability regimes that have characterized the reform strategies of many OECD countries, most prominently the United States and the United Kingdom, is perhaps the best evidence of the fundamental trust that seems to exist between the educators and the community. Given the extraordinary performance of the Finnish system over the past decade, this is a lesson others might want to study.

NOTE

1. The historical material cited in this report draws heavily on P. Sahlberg's unpublished manuscript, *"Finnish Lessons: What Can the World Learn from Educational Change in Finland?"*

REFERENCES

Aho, E., K. Pitkanen, and P. Sahlberg. 2006. *Policy Development and Reform Principles of Basic and Secondary Education in Finland since 1968.* Education Working Paper Series. Washington, DC: World Bank. www.pasisahlberg.com/downloads/ Education%20in%20Finland%202006.pdf.

Darling-Hammond, L. 2010. *The Flat World and Education*. New York: Teachers College Press.

Finnish National Board of Education. 2008. *Education in Finland*. www.oph.fi/download/124278_education_in_finland.pdf.

Finnish National Board of Education. 2010. *Structures of Education and Training Systems in Europe*. http://eacea.ec.europa.eu/education/eurydice/documents/eurybase/structures/041_FI_EN.pdf.

Grubb, W. N. 2007. "Dynamic Inequality and Intervention: Lessons from a Small Country." *Phi Delta Kappan International* 89, no. 2. www.pdkintl.org/kappan/k_v89/k0710gru.htm.

Hargreaves, A., G. Halasz, and B. Pont. 2007. *School Leadership for Systemic Improvement in Finland*. OECD. www.oecd.org/dataoecd/43/17/39928629.pdf.

Sahlberg, P. (2010). "Finnish Lessons: What Can the World Learn from Educational Change in Finland?" Unpublished manuscript.

Sahlberg, P. (2010). Web-site. www.pasisahlberg.com.

INTERVIEWS

Riitta Aaltio, principal, Kerava Primary School, Kerava, Finland

Sakari Karjalainen, Department for Education and Science Policy, Ministry of Education, Finland

Hanna Laakso, senior adviser, International Visits, National Board of Education, Finland

Timo Lankinen, director general, National Board of Education, Finland

Olli Luukkainen, president, Trade Union of Education in Finland (OAJ)

Ray Marshall, Professor Emeritus of Economics and Public Affairs, LBJ School of Public Policy, University of Texas at Austin

Pasi Sahlberg, director-general, Centre for International Mobility and Co-operation (CIMO), Finland

Jukka Sarjala, former director-general, National Board of Education, Finland

Jouni Välijärvi, Institute for Educational Research, University of Jyvaskyla, Finland

Henna Virkkunen, minister of education, Finland

APPENDIX B

Reading performance on PISA 2009

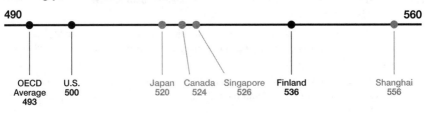

490   560

OECD   U.S.   Japan   Canada Singapore Finland   Shanghai
Average   500   520   524   526   **536**   556
493

Math performance on PISA 2009

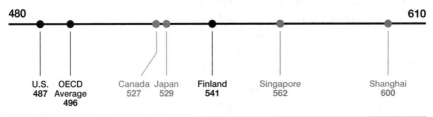

480   610

U.S.   OECD   Canada Japan   Finland   Singapore   Shanghai
487   Average   527   529   **541**   562   600
        496

Science performance on PISA 2009

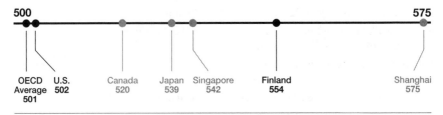

500   575

OECD   U.S.   Canada   Japan   Singapore   Finland   Shanghai
Average **502**   520   539   542   **554**   575
501

GDP per capita (USD)

$11,000 $33,000 $40,000 $48,000

Shanghai   OECD   Japan   Finland   Singapore   Canada   U.S.
$11,361   Average $34,132   **$35,918** $37,293 $38,975   **$47,495**
        Average
        $33,732

Percent of GDP spent on primary, secondary, and non-tertiary education

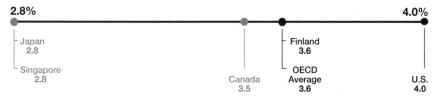

2.8%

Japan
2.8

Singapore
2.8

Canada
3.5

Finland
3.6

OECD
Average
3.6

4.0%

U.S.
4.0

Percent of students with first or second generation immigrant status

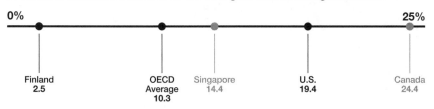

0%

Finland
2.5

OECD
Average
10.3

Singapore
14.4

U.S.
19.4

25%

Canada
24.4

Percent of students with an immigrant background speaking another language at home

1%

Finland
1.9

Singapore
11.3

U.S.
11.5

Canada
11.6

12%

Percent of variance in student performance explained by socioeconomic status

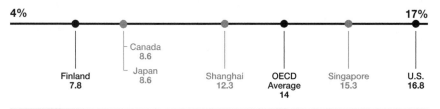

4%

Finland
7.8

Canada
8.6

Japan
8.6

Shanghai
12.3

OECD
Average
14

Singapore
15.3

17%

U.S.
16.8

Source note: The source materials for these eight charts can be found on the individual graphs in this book's introduction.

CHAPTER 3

Japan

Perennial League Leader

Marc S. Tucker and Betsy Brown Ruzzi

The performance of Japan's students relative to those in the other OECD countries in mathematics and science is legendary, and their comparative performance on the PISA reading survey, though not in the very top ranks, is nonetheless impressive. There is nothing new about this consistently superior performance. Japan has placed at or near the top of the international rankings on all such surveys since they began. (See appendix C for more information on the economic and education rankings in Japan.)

Some seasoned observers report that average Japanese high school graduates who enter colleges compare favorably in terms of what they know and can do to average American college graduates. Less generous observers report that they compare favorably to American college students with two years of college. Other observers note that many Japanese high school graduates know more about the geography and history of many other countries than do natives of those countries.

One is tempted to believe that these comparisons are the result of measuring the achievement of only a small elite of students, but that is not the case. Ninety-four percent of the age cohort completes high school in Japan.

The result is that newspapers in Japan routinely write their articles on the assumption that their readers can understand sophisticated statistical tables and abstruse topics in science. Factory managers assign to teams that include recent high school graduates manuals that assume a knowledge of calculus.

The advantage of this level of knowledge and skill to a country, in both citizenship and economic terms, is incalculable. The question addressed in this chapter is, How did they do it? And the corollary to that question is, What can other countries learn from Japan that might transcend the cultural differences?

A HISTORIC PERSPECTIVE

Japan is, of course, an island nation. And it is a mountainous one. The proportion of arable land to population is among the lowest in the industrialized world. Its people huddle in the mountain valleys and along its coasts in densely populated enclaves. For century upon century, it was never clear when the crops would fail, but it was always a distinct possibility. It is also a nation that is subject to more than the usual frequency of natural disasters, like typhoons and earthquakes. And, finally, these islands contained very little in the way of natural resources.

The effect on the Japanese of living in such a hostile environment for a very long time has been profound. It has given them a feeling that they were always on the edge of disaster, and the only thing that could stave it off was very strong cooperation among the people who lived in the enclaves between the mountains. They knew, too, that, because of the lack of natural resources, the only resource they really had was their wits. It is hardly surprising, then, that the result was to frame a culture in which great value is placed on education and skills, on the one hand, and on the group and on social relations within the group on the other hand.

In Japan there is a shared belief that, if the individual works tirelessly for the group, the group will reciprocate with everything at its command; but if one flouts the group, one can expect very little from society. There is no country in which a higher value is placed on education than in Japan. According to Teiichi Sato, adviser to the minister of education, "The tradition of placing importance on education goes back all the way to feudal times."

In the Tokugawa era, for about 250 years up to the mid–nineteenth century, Japan was at peace. Prior to the Tokugawa era, Japanese culture was a warrior culture, and the samurai had the highest social status in the nation. When peace came, they retained their social status and put away their swords to become the bureaucrats who ran the country. Largely isolated from the outside world, Japan prospered and enjoyed a high culture. By 1850, at least a quarter of all Japanese were literate, putting Japan about even with Europe. But it lagged behind the European nations in technology and finance.

Toward the end of the Tokugawa era, Japan's government was beset by endemic corruption and incompetence. When American admiral Matthew Perry's "Black Ships" appeared in 1853, Japan was wholly unprepared to resist Perry and his demands that it open up to trade on terms favorable to the West. The tottering Tokugawa regime was overthrown in 1868 by a rebellion led by lower-ranked bureaucrats who were disgusted at the incompetence of the dying regime and felt the need to overthrow it if Japan were to survive as an independent state. The emperor was restored to the throne in the Meiji Restoration.

Japan's education system

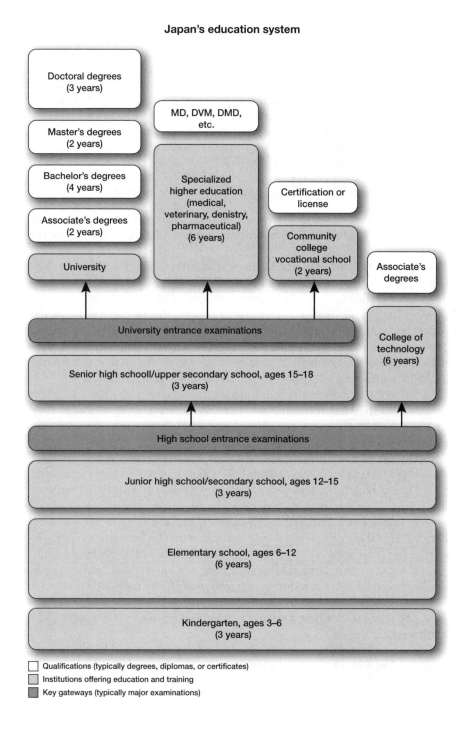

Doctoral degrees
(3 years)

Master's degrees
(2 years)

MD, DVM, DMD,
etc.

Bachelor's degrees
(4 years)

Specialized
higher education
(medical,
veterinary, denistry,
pharmaceutical)
(6 years)

Certification or
license

Associate's degrees
(2 years)

Community
college
vocational school
(2 years)

Associate's
degrees

University

University entrance examinations

College of
technology
(6 years)

Senior high schooll/upper secondary school, ages 15–18
(3 years)

High school entrance examinations

Junior high school/secondary school, ages 12–15
(3 years)

Elementary school, ages 6–12
(6 years)

Kindergarten, ages 3–6
(3 years)

☐ Qualifications (typically degrees, diplomas, or certificates)
▨ Institutions offering education and training
■ Key gateways (typically major examinations)

Robert Fish of the Japan Society describes the leadership goals at the time:

> They were determined to do whatever was necessary to establish a relationship of equals with the Western nations that had entered and humiliated Japan. The new government sent an enormous delegation to the Western nations to rewrite the unequal treaties that had been imposed on Japan. Nearly half of the leadership of the new government took to the seas. And they were astonished at what they saw. Realizing that advanced education, science and technology had made possible the industrial strength that had made the "opening" of Japan to the West possible, these Japanese officials came back to Japan determined to match the achievements of the West in education, science and technology and upgrade their military.

With almost total consensus across leaders from all sectors, the Japanese were determined to modernize their country in order to survive in the new world order.

In the field of education, the Japanese scoured the West for ideas that they could adapt to the pressing needs of Japan. They have continued to benchmark their competitors to the present day, one of the most important reasons for their great success in this field. Tokugawa Japan had not neglected education, and the "temple schools" found all over Japan at the end of the Tokugawa era, as well as the elite schools created for the children of the samurai bureaucrats, provided a strong base on which the new leaders could build the world-class education system they were determined to have.

 Meiji Japan borrowed the administrative scheme for its new education system from the French (centralized and very orderly). From Germany they took the idea of an entire educational system built around a few elite national universities. England provided a model (in public schools like Eaton and Harrow) of schools built around strong national moral principles. And the United States provided a powerful pedagogical model in the teachings of John Dewey, which the Japanese found very congruent with their own idea of a school being responsible for developing the whole child as a family does.

The new government, moving quickly to make a modern nation-state, decided to mandate universal education and, with the education system, to abolish the kind of rigid class distinctions that it believed had helped cripple the old regime. Every Japanese citizen needed to be as well-educated as possible. There was to be no tracking or segregation of students by ability or social class in Japanese compulsory education. This turned out to be a critical decision, one that laid the base for what would become one of the world's most meritocratic societies.

In the 1880s, a reaction set in. The Meiji government had been so determined to implement ideas from elsewhere in the world that it had aroused deep fears that the essence of what it meant to be Japanese would be lost. The

Imperial Rescript of Education, released in 1890, was a ringing declaration of the primacy of Japanese values as a paramount guide in the continuing construction of the new compulsory education system. Emphasizing the Confucian virtues of loyalty, respect for one's elders, and good relationships with family members, spouse, and friends, the document reminded its readers of the importance of modesty and moderation and of the obligation to educate oneself to the fullest, to obey the constitution, and to observe the laws. Ever since the Rescript was issued, Japanese education policy has been anchored at one end by a drive to benchmark the world's best education systems and to bring them back to Japan and, at the other end, by a very strong need to make sure that the result is firmly grounded in traditional Japanese values.

After World War II, under U.S. occupation, Japan introduced nine years of compulsory education for the first time, providing financial assistance for those students who needed it, and made it possible for every high school graduate to take the college entrance examinations. Formerly, only a limited number of special high school graduates were allowed to take these examinations. These policies reinforced the drive to a thoroughly meritocratic system that had begun with the Meiji Restoration.

The Japanese System and Society

It is impossible to understand the Japanese education system without looking a little more closely at the influence of traditional values on Japanese society.

The sense that Japanese have of living on the edge of disaster may have caused them to construct a set of shared values that tend to place the welfare of the group above that of the individual. Some Japanese social scientists believe these circumstances have led to the high value Japanese place on the concept of group harmony, the need they feel to be welcomed and supported by the group. This sense of being enveloped by a group expressing uncritical love is called *wa*. Wa is not only the route to happiness, but it is a vitally important concept in Japanese society. Wa is sought at every stage of life, first with one's mother, then with the rest of one's family, then with friends at school, and then with other friends in college or with superiors in the workplace.

In such an environment, an individual would expect to gain esteem by doing things that the group values, and, if those actions threaten group harmony, social sanctions tend to follow. If one loses the respect of the group and is ostracized, then establishing wa with other groups can be more difficult. Breaking group harmony and suffering social sanctions can have wide-ranging repercussions. So most Japanese work hard to maintain good relations with all the groups they belong to.

Mothers in Japan often do not work as much outside of the home as mothers in Western countries do, mainly because the esteem in which a mother is held in Japan is a function of how well she is perceived to have attended to the education of her children. Mothers are expected to sacrifice for their children, and, in return, their children are expected to perform well in school.

In Japan, the reputation of a school depends on the academic performance of the students and on their behavior, and the society holds the faculty of the school responsible for both in a way that has no parallel in the West. If a student violates the law, the law enforcement authorities call her homeroom teacher and mother and all of the faculty members and apologize for her behavior. Knowing this, the student develops a strong sense of obligation to the faculty to do her best to perform well academically and to stay within the limits of the law when not in school. Indeed, the same idea applies to a students' relationship to the other students at the school. To fail to do well is to let the group down. To let the group down is to violate a deep social code, and most members of this society will work very hard not to let the group down but to do as well as possible, always working toward higher goals, because that is the way one earns acceptance and gains status in this society.

The same values permeate the workplace. People work very hard in Japan because that is how they earn the respect and admiration of their colleagues. Japanese do not work hard for personal distinction but, rather, for the good of the group. An individual does not slack off in Japan not only because the boss is watching but also because his colleagues at the same or even lower ranks are also watching. If one gives one's all, this version of the family— the firm—will give back. In an extension of this notion of "family," Japanese firms often provide housing, trips, education, and even funeral expenses to their employees.

In many societies, advancement depends mainly on connections and clans. Not so in Japan. Japan is one of the world's most aggressive meritocracies. Children from wealthier families do get better jobs, but this is not because of connections; rather, this is because they can spend more money on their children's education.

In Japan, people typically work their entire lives for the firms they joined on leaving school or university. Although this is less true than it was formerly, it is still the dominant pattern in Japan. To a degree that is virtually unique in the world, access to employment in a particular firm is a function of which educational institution one attends prior to joining the firm. And, to a degree that is also very unusual on the world stage, which firm one is hired into is a function of which high school or university one comes out of. In turn, which high school or university one matriculated from is based entirely on how a student does on her high school or university entrance exams.

When we said earlier that a mother is judged primarily on her success in supporting her son's or daughter's education, this means that, in practice, she is judged by first the high school her child gets into and then by the university he or she is admitted to. The rankings of all these institutions are not a matter of dispute; they are known to everyone.

Thus, advancement in Japan is a function of merit, and merit is determined by examination. This ought not to work, because there is much that is important and not measured by examinations, particularly examinations like those used in Japan, which emphasize memorization and the accumulation of facts and the mastery of procedures rather than analytical thinking or creativity or the capacity for innovation. But it does work. It works because Japanese employers are mainly interested in three things: applied intelligence, the capacity to learn, and the capacity to work hard and persist in the face of difficulty.

Because the Japanese tend to work for the same firm or government agency all their lives, their future employer is not particularly interested in the narrow job skills they bring to the job. Employees are likely to have many jobs during their time with the firm, many of which were not conceived of at the beginning of their tenure. Because Japanese firms generally believe that they will employ people for a long time, they are willing to invest heavily in their continuing education and training. It is not uncommon for a firm to send new university recruits overseas during their early years to take a graduate program or to intern in a foreign plant. So what is most important to Japanese firms is whether the person they are hiring is highly intelligent and ready to learn whatever they need to learn.

But the word *intelligent* has a different meaning in Japan than it does in the West. This may be one reason why Western-style intelligence tests to screen prospective employees are not widespread in Japan. Japanese employers want to know not just whether a job candidate is smart but whether he can do something with his intelligence. Employers are interested in applied intelligence. Japanese exams are designed to find out how much applied intelligence students can demonstrate, the degree to which they can use their intelligence to do something of value. But there is something else at work here, too. It is impossible to do well on Japanese exams without working very hard over long periods of time. This takes discipline and persistence, two values that rank very high on the Japanese value hierarchy. Many countries talk about the importance of "learning to learn," but Japan has done much more than just talk about it. It has built an education system around it.

Three points are relevant in summing up this section. First, in this steadfastly meritocratic society, the high school entrance examination and the university entrance exams are the surest gateway to status in Japanese society. Second, there is the belief, shared widely by the Japanese, that how well one does on such exams is much more a function of how hard one works on one's studies than how smart one is. Third, whether you succeed on the exams does not reflect just on you but also on your mother, the other members of your family, and your teachers. They will share the responsibility if you fail, but you do not want to fail because you do not want to disappoint them.

All this is taking place in a society that decided in the latter half of the nineteenth century that education held the key to its future and has never wavered in that conviction since then. Is it any wonder that Japan has done very well?

With this background in mind, we will now look more closely at the specific features of the Japanese educational system for more clues to the reasons for its outstanding performance.

KEY FEATURES OF THE EDUCATION SYSTEM

Curriculum, Standards, and Assessment

Many observers regard the Japanese curriculum as the glory of the Japanese education system. It is set by the Ministry of Education, Culture, Sports, Science, and Technology (MEXT) with input from the Central Council for Education. In reality, the key figures in setting the curriculum are university professors and ministry staff.

Ryo Watanabe, director of International Research in the National Institute for Education Policy Research, believes that "Japanese students have done so well on PISA because of the curriculum. Japan has national curriculum standards, or courses of study that define the content to be taught by grade and subject and, every ten years, it revises this curriculum. Throughout the country, teachers teach based on the national curriculum standards."

In theory, the curriculum that comes from the Ministry of Education is just guidance. But the prefectures also get their funds from the ministry, and the "guidance" is generally closely followed. Even though the guidance itself is long and detailed, the ministry also publishes booklets to explain it in even greater detail, subject by subject, by school level. It is revised on a regular schedule.

Until recently there was very little flexibility in the Japanese curriculum, and very little time in the school day for anything but the official national curriculum. In ordinary Japanese high schools, roughly 70 percent of total available time was devoted to just five subjects: Japanese language, social studies, math, science, and foreign language (mostly English). The remaining hours were devoted to gym, music, art, homeroom, and other elective subjects.

We will describe recent changes to the curriculum later on in this chapter, but suffice it to say here that, even with the recent liberalization, there is still less choice for students in the Japanese curriculum than is typically available in any Western country. This, combined with the very large difference in the amount of time spent in school (in favor of the Japanese), means that Japanese students, not distracted by a great welter of ancillary courses, are very focused on the core subjects in the curriculum and have much more time to go farther in these core subjects than do students in most other countries.

And this is a very demanding curriculum. It is also very thoughtfully put together and highly coherent, in the sense that it progresses step by step in a very logical fashion from year to year, concentrating in any one year on the topics that must be mastered in order to master what will come the next year. There is nothing extraneous to distract the student or teacher, but what is essential is given plenty of time. Each topic is carefully developed. In mathematics and science, the emphasis is on the underlying concepts, which are presented clearly and straightforwardly. One might say that this curriculum is narrow but very deep.

The curriculum requires mastery of a great deal of factual material. Students have to memorize the different kinds of coal mined in countries on the other side of the world, the location of rivers in equally obscure places, the dates of events that occurred long ago outside of Japan. Students routinely achieve mastery of topics in mathematics and science that secondary school students in other countries never reach.

The faithful implementation of this curriculum in every corner of Japan makes it much easier for everyone to hold the system accountable for results. The fact that all students are expected to master this very challenging curriculum, that there are not different curricula for different students, and that all students are expected to proceed through this curriculum at the same pace adds to this transparency. "Attention is also given to the whole person," said Jim Stigler. "Music, art and physical education are highly valued and students don't do this for just a bit of time, they really learn how to do these things and do them well."

Suffusing the whole curriculum is the moral education agenda of the Japanese government. Although there are courses on moral education, this agenda extends far beyond them. Even in high schools, where there are no specific courses on moral education, the national curriculum emphasizes that all activities at high schools should take into consideration the connection with moral education. Everywhere one looks in the schools there is evidence of the effort to reward hard work and persistence, to praise students who take on a challenge, to engage students in serving their school and fellow students and taking responsibility for helping others, and to reward modesty and giving others credit for what you have done. In many different ways, students are taught to respect their elders and their teachers, to do what is right, to be orderly and planful.

Textbooks in Japan are very lean and compact compared to their counterparts in other industrialized countries. They are very inexpensively produced paperbacks. There is an inexpensively produced paperback for each semester for each subject, each fewer than a hundred pages. The central feature of these textbooks is their attention to the core concepts underlying the course.

Teachers do not pick which parts of the text they will use; they are expected to teach the entire textbook, which is the surest sign that all Japanese students are taught to the same standards. Until recently, the ministry had to approve all textbooks used in Japanese schools. Its role in textbook review has recently been significantly curtailed to only making sure that the texts are neutral in content and that they treat the correct topics for the grade level they are aimed at. But given the clear, detailed, coherent nature of the Japanese curriculum, it is not surprising that the textbook companies still stick very closely to the national curriculum.

Until a few years ago, according to Ryo Watanabe, there were no national tests in Japan. But when Japan became concerned about the possibility of being overtaken in education accomplishment by the Koreans and Chinese, the government instituted a national test of every student at the sixth- and ninth-grade levels, but it has since decided to administer the test only to a sample of students in order to monitor the performance of the system.

Instruction

At first glance, the Japanese approach to instruction violates the most commonsense principles. The classes are large, by Western standards, with thirty-five to forty-five students in a class, and most instruction is whole-class instruction. There is less instructional technology than in many other countries and fewer instructional aids of other kinds. Students are not separated into ability groups, and many students who might in other countries be assigned to classrooms only for special education students are, in Japan, assigned to these heterogeneous regular classrooms.

Yet, some of the highest student performances in the world emerge from these classrooms. How do they do it? Most important, the primary goal of Japanese teachers is student engagement. Many people outside Japan imagine Japanese schools as quiet, intense places where students scribble notes on what the teacher is saying as fast as they can copy it into their notebooks. But that is not the reality. Visitors to Japanese elementary schools report that the level of noise is often well above that found in Western classrooms. Students can often be heard excitedly talking with one another as they tackle problems together. The visitor walks down the halls of these schools and sees students acting in plays, playing musical instruments alone and in ensembles, and working through a tea ceremony. The sound of laughter and intense conversation fills the school.

The more engaged the students are, and the more students who are engaged, the happier Japanese teachers are. One might wonder how it could be possible for one teacher to engage thirty-five or more students in a wildly heterogeneous classroom when it is so hard for teachers in many other parts of the world to engage twenty-five students in more homogeneous classrooms. The answer is a major key to the success of Japanese education: Japanese teachers spend little time on drill or on lecturing to their classes. The drill is done at home or in "cram school."

Central to the Japanese approach to classroom instruction is its idea of a lesson. Japanese teachers put a great deal of thought into their design for the way each lesson will unfold, from the standpoint of maximizing student engagement.

The lesson will often begin with the presentation of a practical problem. Harold Stevenson and Jim Stigler, in their classic *The Learning Gap*, describe the beginning of a fifth-grade mathematics class:

> The teacher walks in carrying a large paper bag full of clinking glass. Her entry into the classroom with a large paper bag is highly unusual, and by the time she has placed it on her desk, the students are regarding her with rapt attention . . . She begins to pull out items . . . She removes a pitcher and a vase. A beer bottle evokes laughter and surprise. She soon has six containers lined up on her desk. The children watch intently.
>
> The teacher . . . poses a question: "I wonder which one would hold the most water?"

The rest of the class is devoted to answering that question. The students decide that the only way to answer it is to fill the containers with something. They decide on water. They fill up buckets with water and the teacher asks what they should do next. Eventually the students decide that they should identify a small container and then find out how many small containers full of water it will take to fill each of the containers the teacher brought to class. They settle on a drinking cup. The teacher then divides the class into smaller groups. Each fills its cups, measures how many cups it takes to fill the containers, and records the results in a notebook. The teacher then records the answers in the form of a bar drawn to scale under each of the containers she brought to class. When she is done, the bars form a bar graph. She never defines terms. She did not use the class to illustrate a concept or procedure she had already put on the blackboard.

As Stigler says,

> The lesson almost always begins with a practical problem [either of the sort just described] or with a word problem written on the blackboard . . . It is not uncommon for a . . . teacher to organize an entire lesson around a single problem. The teacher leads the children to recognize what is known and what is unknown, and directs the student's attention to the critical parts of the problem. Teachers attempt to see that all the children understand the problem, and even mechanics, such as mathematical computation, are presented in the context of solving the problem. Before ending the lesson, the teacher reviews what has been learned and relates it to the problem she posed at the beginning of the lesson.

The point of a Japanese teacher's questions is not to get a right answer but to make the students think. The point of the lesson is not to cover the ground for the test—there is no test—but to stimulate real understanding.

Another very important feature of Japanese instruction, which also bears on the way Japanese teachers use whole-group instruction, is their approach to mistakes. In many Western countries, mistakes are something to be avoided. Those students who produce right answers quickly are rewarded, and those who do not are often ignored or punished. Not so in Japan.

Often, when a Japanese teacher is conducting a class, she will present a problem and ask her students to work on it. As they do so, she walks up and down the rows looking at the approaches taken by the students. After a while, she will call on several children to go to the front of the classroom and copy their work onto the blackboard. Some of those that she picked will produce the right answer and some will not. She will ask the class to offer their views on the approach picked by the student at the board. If a student thinks it will not work, that student is asked why and must give an answer that is grounded in mathematical reasoning. The students discover that some answers are wrong for interesting reasons, and those reasons are discussed at length. Sometimes they discover that there is more than one approach to answering the question posed and they then discuss why some solutions are more efficient than others but why others might be more interesting. In this way, they arrive at a much deeper understanding of the mathematics that underlie the solution to the problem and become much more adept at using mathematics to solve problems than students who are simply taught procedures by rote.

Engagement is the method and deeper understanding is the aim of Japanese lesson development.

Organization. Every Japanese student has a homeroom teacher and spends an hour a day in homeroom. The homeroom becomes that student's family in the school. Japanese homeroom teachers at elementary schools teach all subjects except specialized subjects like music and crafts. These homeroom teachers typically follow their classes through the grades for several years. They are required to visit the families of the students in their classrooms regularly. Students often go to their teachers' homes on their teachers' birthdays. In the upper grades, the teachers are expected to provide academic and career and job counseling.

Students are not put in special classes for the gifted, nor are students pushed ahead by a grade or more if they are perceived to be exceptionally able. Similarly, students are not held back by a grade or more if they are having difficulty. The job of the teacher is to make sure that all students are keeping up with the curriculum framework, and that is what they do. Teachers meet frequently with one another about students who are having difficulty and provide as much individual attention to those students as they can within the regular school day. It is not unusual for students who are not doing well in certain subjects to get extra instruction after school.

Teachers at elementary schools maintain communication with parents by means of a notebook that students shuttle between school and home. Even if a student is having a problem other than academic performance, the teacher will communicate the nature of the problem to the parents, who are expected to provide appropriate support at home. If that is not sufficient, the teacher will advise the parents to consult other services available at municipal offices.

This entire approach is aided by the belief that effort, not ability, is what primarily explains student achievement. So if a student is behind, it is not because she is not good at school work; it is because she is not working hard enough, and the system has a solution for that. This approach is also aided by the idea that many people, not just the student, are responsible for the poor performance of that student, and poor performance by that student reflects badly on those people, too—which motivates both parent and teacher to do everything possible to make sure the student gets back on track.

Time. Time is an important factor in explaining the high academic performance of Japanese students. Until recently, Japanese children went to public school six days a week. They have six weeks of vacation during the summer, less than students in many other parts of the world, and students are assigned to complete special homework for each core subject and do their own research during vacation time. Many Japanese students also spend considerable time in various schools that provide private instruction after the regular school day. These run the gamut from schools meant to help catch-up students who are behind, to schools meant to open the door to more advanced study than is available in the public school at any given grade level, to schools that offer extracurricular activities, to one-on-one or small-group tutoring for some combination of these purposes. In addition, Japanese schoolchildren have several hours of homework a day. Very few Japanese children hold paid jobs, even during high school.

The combined effect of all this additional study is Japanese students who, by the time they finish high school, have the equivalent of several more *years* of schooling than, say, the typical American student. Not only that, but, because of the briefer vacation, over the summer they lose much less of what they have learned the previous year as they begin the next school year.

But we should not view this extra schooling entirely through the lens of instructional time. Observers believe that one reason Japanese students seem more engaged when they are in class than do students in many other countries is that they are given more breaks from class than those students. Several times a day, students in compulsory school get to go outdoors, play, do exercises, and blow off plenty of steam. It is not all work and no play for Japanese students. Nonetheless, they do hit the books more than students in many other countries, and it shows.

Parent involvement. We have described the close relationship between the parents (usually the mother) and the teacher and the notebook that is carried by the student daily between school and home, which is used by both parties to chat about the child's education, problems that are arising, and how they might be dealt with. And we have also described how the fact that homeroom teachers are expected to follow their students through several grades builds closer bonds between teachers and parents and a feeling of accountability on the part of the teacher toward the parent, as well as the fact that these teachers take on many of the responsibilities of parents.

It is also the case that, during the U.S. occupation of Japan after World War II, the Americans required Japan to start Parent-Teacher Associations of the kind that are common in the United States. In the ensuing years, these organizations have grown less strong in the United States, but they have grown stronger in Japan and provide parents with a real voice in education policy and local practice. They have an organization not only at the school level but also at prefectural and national levels, with a seat on the Central Council on Education.

We know of no country with stronger parent involvement in the education of their children than Japan.

Teacher quality. Surely one of the most important keys to the quality of education in Japan is the quality of its teachers. In many industrialized countries, teaching stands at the boundary line between professional and blue-collar work. It is often the case that the new teacher is the first member of the family to have a college education, an emblem of the family's breakthrough from the lower middle class to the middle class.

But when the Meiji Restoration got under way in Japan, and the state modernized the education system, most of the teachers were samurai, members of Japan's upper classes. This was because most of the schools prior to the Meiji Restoration were samurai schools, and in the Confucian tradition, great honor went to the teacher. So, as the modern era began and classless schools were created for the first time in Japan, those schools were staffed in significant numbers by members of the upper classes. So from that time forward, teaching has been a desirable occupation in Japan.

According to Teiichi Sato,

After WWII, as incomes began to rise across the board, the government worried that respect for teachers would decline. Prime Minister Tanaka decided to raise compulsory school teacher salaries to 30 percent higher than other public servants. While this has gradually eroded, teachers' salaries are on par with other civil servants. This made a difference in the quality of teachers ever since.

Teachers are still, by law, among the highest paid of Japan's civil servants. When they start their service, they are paid as well as beginning engineers. But it is not the pay alone that attracts competent young people to teaching. It is primarily the regard in which teachers are held.

Teaching is a prestigious job in Japan. The country's Confucian history and the role of the samurai in staffing the schools during the Meiji Restoration are important contributors to the regard in which teachers are held, but they're not the whole story. In Japan's meritocratic system, these factors would not get teachers very far if it were not for the fact that Japan's teachers have vaulted their students to the top of the world's league tables. Ultimately, it is performance that matters most in Japan, and Japan's teachers have performed. The result is that there are seven applicants for every open teaching position. It is a highly desired job.

Attending a university or junior college's ministry-certified teacher education program is the typical path to becoming a teacher in Japan. Programs for students wanting to teach in the lower grades focus more on pedagogy than programs for students wanting to teach in the upper grades, where more of the focus is on the specific subject a student is interested in teaching. A practicum is a common part of all teacher education programs. Japan also has some national teacher training universities with model schools attached to support teacher training for new teachers.

Prefectures, like other employers in Japan, are prepared to make major investments in their new employees to make sure they have the necessary skills to succeed. Like other employers, they assume that these new employees come to them with the necessary applied intelligence but do not assume that they have the needed job skills. So, they take responsibility for providing an induction program that provides a sustained opportunity to apprentice to master teachers with a lot of experience before being expected to perform as a full-time teacher. The induction period lasts a full year, and the master teachers are given a full year off from their teaching jobs to supervise their apprentices. Once a teacher is inducted into the regular teaching workforce, the law requires teachers to take certain specified additional training (e.g., after ten years of service). Teachers can also apply for paid leaves to enroll in master's degree programs at graduate schools. And the Ministry of Education offers various training programs for prefectural trainers at its national center.

But the most interesting aspect of teacher development in Japan is the teacher's subsequent career on the job. We have already described the central importance of the design of the lesson in Japanese instruction and now come to the central importance of "lesson study" in the development of the Japanese teaching profession.

Here again, Stevenson and Stigler's *The Learning Gap* tells the story.

> [From the time they begin their career right to its end, Japanese teachers] are required to perfect their teaching methods through interaction with other teachers . . . Experienced [teachers] assume responsibility for advising and guiding their young colleagues. Head teachers [principals] organize meetings to discuss teaching techniques . . . Meetings at each school are supplemented by informal district-wide study groups . . . [Teachers work together designing lesson plans.] After they finish a plan, one teacher from the group teaches the lesson to her students while the other teachers look on. Afterward, the group meets again to evaluate the teachers' performance and to make suggestions for improvement . . . Teachers from other schools are invited to visit the school and observe the lessons being taught. The visitors rate the lessons, and the teacher with the best lesson is declared the winner.

This practice is entirely consistent with the way teams work in private industry. It is also entirely consistent with the Japanese focus on relying on groups to get work done. But it has a profound effect on the practice of teaching. Indeed, it is the best hope for the continual, sustained improvement of teaching practice. It brings the work of teaching out from behind the closed door of the classroom and the individual teacher and opens it up for inspection and critique by that teacher's colleagues.

There is very strong teacher accountability in Japan, but that accountability does not come in the form of formalized accountability to the bureaucracy but, rather, from intimate and very real accountability to one's colleagues. In Japan, because one does not want to let the group down, teachers work hard to develop superior lesson plans, to teach them well, and to provide sound and useful critiques when it is their colleague's turn to demonstrate their lesson plans.

Cost and finance. The Japanese spend less on their schools than a number of other OECD countries do, but they get better results. One reason is that they spend their money differently. Japanese schools are built to ministry designs. They are perfectly functional but very plain. They are not architectural symbols of community pride and lack many of the special features found in schools in other advanced industrial countries. School administration is typically confined to a principal, an assistant principal, a janitor, and a nurse. There is no cafeteria. The students take turns serving their teachers and fellow classmates the midday meal out of a central kitchen, and the teachers and students eat in the classroom. The students are also responsible for cleaning their classrooms. As noted above, textbooks are very simply produced in paperback format and are much smaller than in many other industrialized countries. At every point, the Japanese have made sure that the money they spend on educating their children is spent as much as possible on teachers and on instruction, so it is no surprise that a much greater proportion of total funding is spent on these factors than is the case in many other countries.

Equity. We have already pointed out that there is no tracking in Japanese schools, that classes within schools are designed to be as heterogeneous as possible, that no student is held back or vaulted forward one or more years, and that all are expected to master the same demanding curriculum. That is a powerful formula for equity if *equity* is defined in terms of outcomes. What is particularly impressive about this approach is that the outcomes are at the top of the range of possible outcomes worldwide.

There is a widely shared belief in Japan that the greatest good for the greatest number will be achieved with these policies, and research bears this out. Japanese classes are set up so that students who are achieving more will help those who are achieving less, within a group, within a classroom and within a school. This is consistent with Japanese values, and, as a practical matter; it contributes greatly to the generally high level of Japanese achievement. The research literature shows that both older students and younger students, and those who are doing very well and who doing less well, are helped by this approach, because the students who teach and tutor learn as much or nearly as much in the process of tutoring as others do in receiving the tutoring.

Japanese teachers and principals can be, and often are, reassigned to different schools by the prefectures. Fish remarked that "teachers and administrators are transferred regularly every few years so the same people are not in the same schools all of the time—there is a lot of leveling among schools." This is done, among other reasons, to make sure that the distribution of the most capable teachers among schools is fair and equitable.

All these and many other factors, including school finance, make for a high degree of equity in Japanese education. But the reader should note that there is no immigration policy in Japan because there is virtually no migration into Japan. The very small number of people regarded as immigrants in Japan, mostly Koreans and Chinese, are not counted in the national education statistics. But they make up less than 2 percent of the Japanese population. The Burakumin, the one group thought of as a minority group in Japan, are indistinguishable from other Japanese but are the descendants of a very low caste occupational group and are often discriminated against.

Accountability. The Japanese have virtually none of the trappings of formal Western accountability systems. The only tests are the entrance exams for high school and university. They do not need formal accountability systems, since everything hinges on which high school you went to, if you are not going to university, or which university you went to. Everyone knows the rankings of these institutions, and everyone knows the record of each compulsory and middle school in getting their students into the right high schools and universities. These are published in the newspapers regularly. The newspapers are full of statistics for each school, much like the statistics for popular sports teams in other parts of the world. Magazine articles are written about changes in the rankings and what they mean and why they happened. Other stories are written about students who succeeded against all odds on the exams and others who did not.

But that is only half the story. As pointed out earlier, in Japanese society, the burden for the fate of the student is shouldered in large part by the family, the teachers, the faculty, and even the classmates of the student. A teacher's reputation among her peers rests on the success of her students in a way that has no parallel in many Western countries.

The system of homeroom teachers provides another level of accountability. Because these teachers follow the students through the grades and are involved in their students' lives outside of school, and because they are in constant communication with the parents, they are accountable to the parents in a way that has no parallel in countries where teachers do not follow students through the grades and are responsible for only one or a few subjects.

"It's always about what students are learning, agreeing on that, and holding yourself accountable and each other accountable by engaging in meaningful reviews of how students are doing," says Stigler. This is a system with a great deal of accountability, but it is not a system of administered accountability.

Student motivation. Some countries provide very strong incentives to students to take tough courses and to study hard in school, others do not, and many are somewhere in between. Japan is firmly a leader in the first camp, and most observers believe that this factor is a major contributor to Japan's high place in the international education league tables.

The Japanese system creates clear, powerful, and tangible rewards for student academic success. In the short term, these come from parents, whose praise is highly valued by children. In the middle term, they come in the form of admission to the right high school or university, which is of paramount importance to the student and to everyone around her. And, finally, in this highly meritocratic society, they come from the value that employers and the society at large place on academic achievement.

In many societies, how one does in school does not matter very much in terms of how others you care about view you. In Japan, how your siblings, your parents, your friends, your teachers, your employers, and your colleagues view you typically depends on how well you do and have done in school. This is not a country in which your best friends are likely to thumb their nose at school and to view you as suspect if you do well there. It is a country in which what other people think of you matters very much.

All of this, of course, contributes mightily to "exam hell," the well-known pressure cooker that young people in Japan go through at exam time. People elsewhere in the world talk about the high suicide rate of young Japanese people going though exams and vow never to institute anything like that in their own country. In fact, as we shall see, the Japanese themselves say they would like to put an end to this high-stress situation.

But the suicide rate among young people in that age cohort is significantly higher in the United States than it is in Japan. And, in the surveys of students that the OECD has conducted, Japanese students tell the researchers that they are happier in school than students in most other OECD countries say they are. It turns out that the image that much of the rest of the world has of Japanese students as "grinds" who are under relentless pressure to produce and who are somehow robbed of their childhood in the process is not a view that is shared by the Japanese students themselves. It is possible, it seems, to construct a system in which students are highly motivated to succeed in school without depriving students of a happy school experience.

It is, however, certainly true that, for Japanese students, much in their life depends on what their teachers are teaching, and they know it. No surprise then, that they learn it.

HOW THE SYSTEM IS CHANGING: CHALLENGE AND RESPONSE

No country's education system stands still for very long, even one with as distinguished a record as Japan's. Over the last two decades, there has been a rising chorus of criticism concerning education. It is, of course, very much within the Japanese tradition to be self-critical. Indeed, self-criticism is highly valued as a contributor to continuous improvement. Nonetheless, we believe that other nations have something to learn from those criticisms and the government's response to them.

Two things in particular have worried the Japanese: a possible deficit in the realm of creativity and innovation, on the one hand, and, on the other, the hot breath of competition for top honors on the international league tables for student achievement.

Creativity and Innovation

Many experts from Western nations visited Japan shortly after the Third International Mathematics and Science Study (TIMSS) came out in 1995. Japan was among a handful of East Asian nations that had topped the charts. The Western experts had come to sit at the feet of the winners to understand how they had done it. But their hosts were not crowing. They were not so sure that they had won what was most important. They worried that, although they had done better on the TIMSS assessments than any other country, it might not translate into success in the business arena. Where, they asked, are our Nobel Prize winners? Where are our Bill Gates and Steve Jobs? Where are the people with the kind of breakthrough ideas that create a new Microsoft or Apple or even whole new industries? Maybe, they said, we should find out how the Western nations teach creativity.

But the Western nations do not teach creativity. They put more value on the individual than on the group, whereas the Asian nations place a higher value on the group. In Asia, the saying goes, the nail that sticks out gets hammered down.

The idea that what is responsible for Western creativity is the emphasis on the individual can be uncomfortable to many Asians. They value social order highly and see the high crime rates and general social disorder in many Western nations as simply unacceptable. And it might be said that many people from the West are not willing to pay the price the Asians pay for the high levels of student achievement they get if it means giving up "the personal freedoms" they enjoy.

But it is possible that this analysis is much too oversimplified and unidimensional. It may be true that because Asians typically defer to their elders and superiors publicly even if they have private reservations about their judgment, wait to take their moment in the sun until their superiors are gone, do not like to criticize others openly, prefer to be modest rather than sing out their achievements, value a contribution to the group more highly than a solo achievement, and hammer down the nail that stands out, Asians are not so likely as people from some Western countries to make breakthroughs and chart whole new courses for their industry or even create new industries.

Yet, Japan has built a workforce of uniformly high caliber—one of the best-educated, most flexible, fastest-learning workforces in the world. The reward is a nation that is brilliant at continuous improvement of products and processes and capable of very high-quality production on a vast scale. Who is to say which is more important: the occasional breakthrough or the continuous improvement of almost everything almost all the time?

And even this analysis may give too much weight to the criticism that Japan is short on creativity and innovation. After all, Japan places very high on the Global Innovation Index, falling just behind South Korea and the United States in the 2008–2009 report.

But the Japanese answer to the criticism seems to be that they want high student achievement as measured by such assessments as PISA. They also want a greater measure of capacity for creativity and innovation, but they will try to get what they think they do not have enough of while giving up little or none of what they have already achieved.

The creativity issue, while important, was not the only education challenge on the minds of the Japanese over the last decade or so. There were many more.[1]

Not least was

a spreading tendency among youth to neglect society. This tendency is not totally unrelated with young people's declining association with society. It can be traced partially to a social trend placing too much emphasis on individual freedom and rights . . . At home children have their own private room and...mobile phones and other information equipment allow them to avoid getting closely involved with family members . . . There seems to be increasingly less time spent in peer groups outside and more time spent playing video games at home. This phenomenon of the thinning socialization of children is thought to be leading to a decline in young people's sense of respect for rules and models and further aggravating their tendency to neglect society or recede into a "world of solitude."

This worry combined with great anxiety in Japan over what they saw as an alarming decline in the "educational functions" of the family, leading to bullying, disruptions in the classroom, student absenteeism, and even violence in the schools. While the incidence of these kinds of student behavior were small relative to their frequency in many Western countries, their increased presence in Japan was very alarming to the society.

But there was more:

The standardization of education due to excessive egalitarianism and the cramming of too much knowledge into children has tended to push aside education geared more to fit the individuality and capabilities of children . . . making classroom lessons boring to children with a quick understanding and difficult for children who need longer to understand.

And, finally, the Japanese, very much aware of the degree to which their future depends on their ability to continue to generate and exploit advanced technologies, were no less alarmed at what they saw as a real threat to their continued dominance in this crucial field. They noted that Japan's students continued to do as well as ever in international comparisons of student achievement in math and science but that their students appear to like science less than other students in other countries with high math and science achievement, and they liked it less and less the further they had gotten in their schooling.

These concerns, steadily growing over many years, led to major new education policy initiatives in the early years of the twenty-first century, captured in the passage of the first new Fundamental Education Law in sixty years and a sweeping piece of education reform legislation dubbed by many as Zest for Living. The legislation has many elements. We briefly summarize the most noteworthy.

Concerns about lack of creativity and the results of what the Japanese saw as excessive standardization did not lead to an increased emphasis on individual achievement at the expense of the group, because, as we have seen, the Japanese were concerned that severe problems were already in view due to the breakdown of their traditional values, so they coalesced instead into a reaction against their previously strict insistence on uniformity, specificity, and direction from the top. They turned some of the functions of the Ministry of Education over to lower levels of government, reduced the number of credits that must be earned from required courses from thirty-eight credits to thirty-one credits, increased the amount of time given to electives by a comparable amount, went from a six-day school week to a five-day school week (though the schools are still open on Saturdays for extracurricular activities and extra school work for those who want it), and changed the curriculum guidelines to reduce the emphasis on rote learning and memorization and increase the emphasis on experimentation, problem finding, and problem solving.

They made it possible for their best students to enroll in university early and take college courses in high school. They introduced the use of criteria other than one's score on the college entrance exams to be used in determining entrance to a university.

Schools were given greater discretion over their budgets and personnel. New measures were taken to evaluate teachers and, especially, to commend and reward excellent teachers while transferring "teachers with questionable track records to non-teaching positions."

Though the required curriculum was shrunk overall, an important new required course was added, the Period of Integrated Study. The aim of this course is to

(1) foster children's ability and quality to find a theme, think, judge and solve a problem on their own; and (2) enable children to think about their own life, urging them to explore subjects with creativity and subjectivity and to solve problems through their own ways of learning and thinking. To this end, the Period of Integrated Study actively introduces experiential learning such as experience in nature, social life experience, observations, experiments, field study and investigation as well as problem-solving learning to learn about cross-sectional, comprehensive subjects like the environment, international understanding, information, health and welfare as well as subjects that interest students.

With respect to the challenge in math and science, the Japanese felt the need to (1) put more emphasis on experiential, problem-solving learning through observations, experiments, and project studies; (2) reach out to universities, research institutes, and museums for help in engaging students' interest in science; and (3) make the images of leading scientists and engineers more visible and appealing to students thinking about what careers they might pursue.

Overall, we see a general loosening up of what many perceived to be a very rigid system. But the overall structure is still very much in place, and the move toward more freedom was cautiously made. And all the while there was the acknowledgment that something needed to be done about the slide away from Japanese values, not just among the students but in Japanese families, where the principal responsibility for Japanese education lies.

So the Japanese government rewrote the Japanese Fundamental Law of Education, the first revision since the end of World War II. The first Fundamental Law, laid down in 1947, put forward four principles:

1. The idea of education seeking the "accomplishment of character building"
2. Equal opportunities of education and equality of the sexes
3. A democratic and single-track school system
4. Free, compulsory education under the 6-3 school system

Implementing these principles took many years, but the result was the much-admired system we have described.

The new Fundamental Law on Education, passed in 2006, declared that much had changed since the last law was decreed. And that was clearly true. Life expectancy for males had gone from 50 years to 79, for females from 54 to 85. The fertility rate had dropped from 4.5 to 1.3 children per woman. The high school attendance rate had gone from 43 percent to 98 percent. The university attendance rate had climbed from 10 percent to 49 percent. From a world in which 49 percent were employed in agriculture and 30 percent were employed in manufacturing and related industries, in Japan, fewer than 5 percent were employed in agriculture and more than 67 percent in manufacturing and related industries. Everything had changed.

Everything but Japanese values. The new law reaffirmed those values. In doing so, and in determining the ways in which education policy would change to enable Japan to adapt to the needs of the next century, it reaffirmed the characteristic Japanese approach, so evident in the Meiji reforms, of working hard to be as aware as possible of what those countries with the best education systems were doing to adapt to changing requirements and bringing back those ideas that seemed to be attractive and adapt them to Japanese requirements while, at the same time, reaffirming and being ever faithful to Japanese values.

It will take time before the Japanese know whether the new policies are delivering the results they hoped for. They continue to worry that other nations are catching up to and might surpass them. They worry about slipping on the OECD PISA rankings. When it appears that that might be happening, critics say that the reforms should be revoked, while others advocate patience.

WHAT CAN BE LEARNED FROM JAPAN?

The question for the reader is what can be learned from the Japanese experience. Everyone knows that we cannot abstract a feature from another country's education system and expect it to work the same way in our own country. But we also know that we find many good ideas in other countries that will work much better in our own country than what we are now doing. The trick is to be able to identify principles and practices that will travel well.

The biggest hazard in doing that is the fact that so many of a system's features work the way they do because of the way they are related to other features of the same system. Keeping a student in school for more hours will not work as well in a system with poor instructional practices as it does in a system with effective instructional practices. Recruiting better teachers will not work very well if they flee schools that are oppressive to work in. And so on.

With these cautions in mind, we will share some observations about what might be learned from the Japanese experience. It is true, by the way, that many features of the Japanese system can also be found in other East Asian countries, particularly those that share a common Confucian heritage. But some are uniquely Japanese.

Another point is worth making here. The list of lessons learned from Japan is useful for analytical purposes, but it obscures a very important aspect of the Japanese educational system. The deeper purposes of the system go way beyond the development of students' cognitive capacities to the development of a society that is based on ethical behavior, meritocratic advancement, and social cohesion. So, when the point is made below, for example, that incentives are important, they are structured the way they are in Japan not just to promote learning in the narrow sense but to promote the values just mentioned. The entire system is aligned not just to produce high student achievement but to help the whole country realize the values it holds most dear.

A nation is not likely to have a top-ranked education system unless it believes that its children and its education system are the keys to its future. Japan's total commitment to children is not just a rhetorical priority (which it is almost everywhere) but a concrete and enduring one for which individuals and the nation as a whole are prepared to make real sacrifices. It is the main reason that Japan has access to a first-rate teaching force. It is the reason that Japanese students are superbly supported at home. It the reason that the schools are well resourced. This commitment is the foundation of the Japanese system.

A nation is not likely to have a first-rate education system unless it makes a determined effort to benchmark what its best competitors are doing constantly and in detail. The second reason for Japan's success is its commitment to continuous international benchmarking of education systems. From the first embassy of the Meiji government to the present, Japan has succeeded in no small measure because of its determination to know what the best performers are doing and to adapt the best of what they find to the Japanese setting, weaving it together into a coherent and powerful whole.

Incentives count for everyone, but especially for students. Students in Japan, from the earliest age all the way through their working life, have very strong incentives to take tough courses and work hard in them. In some ways, this is the core story of the Japanese education system. If those incentives were not present, the outcome would be very different. It is worth noting that other countries provide equally strong incentives for their students to take tough courses and work hard in school, but they do not have students who are as happy in school as Japanese students are. These two factors together make for a nation full of people who want to learn all through their lives.

Curriculum matters. The Japanese have paid more attention to the details of their curriculum than have most other countries, and they have insisted that the intended curriculum actually be taught. That curriculum is coherent, focused on a carefully chosen core, logically sequenced, concentrated on conceptual understanding of the subjects studied, and set to a very high level of cognitive challenge. The result is that Japanese high school graduates have a level of mastery of the subjects taught that would be admired in college graduates in many Western countries.

Effort and expectations matter. Because the Japanese, like most East Asians, believe that academic achievement is more a matter of effort than natural (genetically endowed) ability, they demand that the effort be made, and they have high expectations for all their students. It turns out that the students of whom they expect a lot—which is everyone—produce a lot. It is hard to argue with their belief that it is effort, not natural endowment, that matters most.

The spending of available resources matters. The Japanese spend less than other industrialized nations but get more for their money. There are many reasons why this is so, but one of them is how they allocate the money they spend: less than other nations on school construction and facilities, non-teaching staff, central office specialists and administrators, full-color glossy textbooks with lots of illustrations, and so on, and more on teachers.

Organized instruction matters. Teachers all over the world would prefer to teach fewer students, but Japanese teachers, at least in certain subjects, believe student performance will be better with bigger classes because in bigger classes students will be pursuing a wider range of problem-solving strategies from which other students can learn; because in some classes the variety of ideas students offer can be used to spark a lively discussion; and because in science classes, for example, there will be a wider range of outcomes from lab experiments that also can be used to explore problem-solving strategies as a way to promote deeper understanding of the topics under study. Their approach to whole-class instruction is not unique. Other East Asian countries use it too. But Japanese teachers teaching large classes have more contact time with each student than is possible in countries with much lower student/ teacher ratios, and that in turn makes it possible to have large class sizes. This means that Japanese teachers have more time to plan, to work with other teachers, to work one-on-one with students who need individual help, and to engage in lesson study, all of which also improve the outcome for students.

Attention to individual differences is important, but labeling students may be counterproductive. Our description of the Japanese approach to classroom instruction makes it clear that the Japanese, like many other East Asian peoples, work hard to adjust instruction to meet the needs of the individual students in the school. That appears to work well when the underlying assumption is that all, or very nearly all, students are expected to learn to high standards. But in many Western countries, the idea that students should get different educations is code for treating students differently based on their imputed ability. In that case, the underlying assumption is often that student achievement is the function of a student's inherited learning capacity and that capacity varies widely. The result in such cases is that some students, who could be achieving at much higher levels, do not do so because they are given a very diluted curriculum. The extreme case of this is the case of special education students. Like most East Asian countries, Japan has roughly half the proportion of the student cohort assigned to special education, as is the case in some Western countries. Some in the West have decried this as inattention to students who need and deserve extra help. That may be true in some cases, but there is a lot of evidence that many students assigned to special education classes in the West have very low levels of achievement despite being the recipients of much more spending, simply because their teachers have very low expectations for their achievement.

Attention to the steady improvement of practice by the teachers themselves may be a powerful engine for improvement of student performance. Japan as a nation is a laboratory for the idea of continuous improvement of practice. The incarnation of that idea in Japanese schools is lesson study. This practice undoubtedly contributes in important ways to the high quality of instruction in Japanese schools. There is no reason that it could not be used all over the world.

Careful attention to school-to-work transition may be crucial to economic performance. Japan has an unusual and highly effective system for moving students into the workforce. It depends on the idea of lifetime employment, which makes it worthwhile for employers to invest heavily in the continued education and training of people entering the workforce right out of high school or university. The system produces low rates of youth unemployment and students who are accustomed to working hard. It also produces workers who are used to working as loyal team members, working collaboratively with others, showing up on time, and working against deadlines. And it produces students who know how to learn and are eager to learn and who come to work with a prodigious set of skills. Although the system of lifetime employment is currently under threat in Japan, any nation interested in workforce development should be interested in learning how this system works in detail.

Attention to the moral dimension may have a lot to do with many societal outcomes through life. Again and again, the Japanese have asserted that the most important dimension of their system is the moral one, by which they mostly mean their conception of how people should behave and how they should relate to one another. Whenever the Japanese have become afraid that their interest in learning from the rest of the world would make them un-Japanese, they have once again reasserted the primacy of their values. It is not hard to imagine how this sort of attention to common moral standards can affect many aspects of social life, from business ethics to health care, from a sustainable environment to crime. Some countries do this explicitly, some implicitly, but it is worth considering what might happen to a country that does not attend to the moral issues at all.

There are different ways to "do" accountability. Some countries will look at Japan and think that it has no formal accountability system because it does not have national tests. But there is very strong accountability in Japan. Students are accountable to teachers and parents. Teachers are accountable to each other in a system in which all the teachers in the school know just how good or bad the other teachers' teaching really is because of the lesson study system. Everyone knows how the high schools and universities are ranked, and so everyone knows how to rank the institutions and teachers who prepare students for those high schools and universities. And the performance of the students on those entrance exams and of the schools that prepared them for those exams is there for all to see—in a world in which those results matter a lot. Japan proves that there are different ways to design a system for high accountability.

One may or may not like any specific feature of the Japanese system, but they are all well worth considering carefully. This is a country with very high levels of high school and university attainment, as well as measured academic achievement. Its students enjoy school more than most. It has produced one

of the world's best-educated and most productive workforces. It has exceptionally low crime rates and a very strong social order. It has high rates of citizen participation and a citizenry that has an unusually sophisticated grasp
of the issues it votes on. Parents in Japan participate in their children's education and partner with teachers to an unusual degree. The country has one
of the world's most admired curricula. Although the Japanese are not resting on their laurels, the methods they have used to build this system should
surely be considered by any country that wants to match their achievements.

JAPAN AND THE DIMENSION LINES OF THE NATIONAL
EDUCATION DEVELOPMENT SCHEMA

Japan clearly ranks among the world's most advanced industrial economies.
It is a leading center for the development and application of the most advanced technological systems and a leading source of such systems for the
rest of the world. Those were among the goals it set for itself when the Meiji
Restoration was launched, and those who launched it embraced from the
start the thesis that those aims would not be achieved without a first-rate,
highly inclusive, aggressively meritocratic education system.

In some ways, though, the Japanese skipped some of the steps in the more
usual education progression described in the introduction to this volume and
have not taken others. They skipped the typical slow upgrading of the quality of teachers in the system, having inherited a system from the Tokugawa
era in which the samurai class staffed the schools. They also skipped the typical slow progression from a system of school organization based on the usual
feudal orders to one that ultimately makes it possible for students from every
social class to gain access to elite education opportunities.

Japan was also ahead of many other nations in embracing at least some aspects of modern industrial work organization, especially with respect to the
way teachers work with one another in teams to improve instruction and the
professional norms of governing teachers' work.

But it is also true that Japan has been reluctant to embrace devolution
of authority to schools as aggressively as some other countries and that it
also found it harder to create schools that develop independent, creative students. This may be a function of the clash between the demands of a creative
culture in which individual initiative is highly valued and the Japanese culture, in which the approval of the group is typically sought before aggressively advancing one's own ideas. So Japan is a fascinating case of sustained
achievement produced on a trajectory that is at the same time similar to but
distinctive from the more measured development of the education systems
of most industrial countries.

NOTE

1. Some of the educational challenges described use quotes from Ministry of Education White Papers and reports of the National Commission on Educational Reform.

REFERENCES

Arani, M., and T. Fukaya. 2009. "Learning Beyond Boundaries: Japanese Teachers Learning to Reflect and Reflecting to Learn." *Child Research Net.* www.childresearch.net/RESOURCE/RESEARCH/2009/ARANI.HTM.

Auslin, M. 2009. "Can Japan Thrive—or Survive?" *American Enterprise Institute for Public Research* 1, no. 2: 97–110.

Channel News Asia. 2010. "Japan Ruling Party Banks on Firebrand Female Minister for Votes." Channelnewsasia.com, July 8. www.channelnewsasia.com/stories/afp_asiapacific/view/1068283/1/.html.

CIA World Factbook. 2010. *Japan: Country Background Information.* www.cia.gov/library/publications/the-world-factbook/geos/ja.html.

Crowell, T. 2010. "Japan's New Prime Minister Faces the Voters." *Asia Sentinel*, July 6. www.asiasentinel.com/index.php?option=com_content&task=view&id=2579&Itemid=176.

Ito, H., and J. Kurihara. 2010. "A Discourse on the New *Kai'entai*: A Scenario for a Revitalized Japan." *Cambridge Gazette*, March 17, 1–15.

Jansen, M. 2000. *The Making of Modern Japan.* Cambridge, MA: Harvard University Press.

Kaneko, M. 1992. *Higher Education and Employment in Japan: Trends and Issues.* International Publication Series No. 5. Hiroshima: Research Institute for Higher Education.

Kaneko, M. 1997. "Efficiency and Equity in Japanese Higher Education." *Higher Education* 34, no. 2: 165–181.

Lehmann, J. 2010. "Corporate Japan is a Little Lost in Communication." Taipeitimes.com, April 17. www.taipeitimes.com/News/editorials/archives/2010/04/17/2003470763.

Mizukoshi, T. 2007. *Educational Reform in Japan: Retrospect and Prospect.* http://unpan1.un.org/intradoc/groups/ public/documents/apcity/unpan011543.pdf.

Ministry of Economy, Trade and Industry. 2010. "The New Growth Strategy: Blueprint for Revitalizing Japan." METI Cabinet Decision, June 18. www.meti.go.jp/english/policy/economy/growth/report20100618.pdf.

Ministry of Education, Culture, Sports, Science and Technology (MEXT). 2005. *Redesigning Compulsory Education: Summary of the Report of the Central Council for Education.* Tokyo: National Education Policy, Author.

Ministry of Education, Culture, Sports, Science and Technology (MEXT). 2010. *Elementary and Secondary Education.* www.mext.go.jp/English/shotou/index.htm.

Ministry of Education, Culture, Sports, Science and Technology (MEXT). 2010. *Ministry of Education, Culture, Sports, Science and Technology 2010*. Brochure. Tokyo: Author.

Monahan, A. 2010. "Japan Data Show Fragile Economy." *Wall Street Journal*, July 9. http://online.wsj.com/article/SB10001424052748703636404575353664100091340. html.

Newby, H., Weko, T., Breneman, D., Johanneson, T., and P. Maasen. 2009. *OECD Reviews of Tertiary Education—Japan*. Paris: OECD.

Organisation of Economic Co-operation and Development (OECD). 2010. "Japan: Country Note." In *Economic Policy Reforms: Going for Growth*. Paris: Author. 122–123.

Organisation of Economic Co-operation and Development (OECD). 2010. "Japan— Economic Outlook 87 Country Summary." *OECD Economic Outlook no. 2*.

Organisation of Economic Co-operation and Development (OECD). 2010. *Supporting Japan's Policy Objectives: OECD's Contribution*. Paris: Author.

Qi, J. 2009. "Globalization, Citizenship and Education Reform." Paper presented at the American Educational Research Association, San Diego, CA.

Rohlen, T. 1983. *Japan's High Schools*. Berkeley: University of California Press.

Siegel, A. 2004. "Telling Lessons from the TIMSS Videotape: Remarkable Teaching Practices as Recorded from Eighth-Grade Mathematics Classes in Japan, Germany, and the U.S." In W. Evers and H. Walberg (eds.), *Testing Student Learning, Evaluating Teaching Effectiveness*. Palo Alto, CA: Hoover Press. 161–194.

Stewart, D. 2010. "Slowing Japan's Galapagos Syndrome." *HuffPost Social News*, July 21. www.huffingtonpost.com/devin-stewart/slowing-japans-galapagos_b_557446.html.

Stevenson, H., and J. Stigler. 1992. *The Learning Gap*. New York: Touchstone.

White, M. 1988. *The Japanese Educational Challenge: A Commitment to Children*. New York: Free Press.

Wieczorek, C. 2008. "Comparative Analysis of Educational Systems of American and Japanese Schools: Views and Visions." *Educational Horizons* 86, no. 2: 99–111.

Wong, A., Yeung, D., Montoya, S., Olmstead, S., Litovitz, A., Klautzer, L., Kups, S., and A., Raab Labonte, 2010. *Japanese Science and Technology Capacity: Expert Opinions and Recommendations*. RAND Technical Report. www.cgi.rand.org/pubs/technical_reports/TR714/.

INTERVIEWS

Robert Fish, Education Specialist, Japan Society

Steve Heyneman, Professor of International Education Policy, Vanderbilt University

David Janes, director of foundation grants and assistant to the president, U.S.-Japan Foundation

Teiichi Sato, adviser to the Ministry of Education, Culture, Sports, Science, and Technology (MEXT), Japan; and former (administrative) vice minister of MEXT, Japan

Andreas Schleicher, head of Indicators and Analysis Section, OECD Education
    Directorate

Jim Stigler, Department of Psychology, University of California, Los Angeles

Ryo Watanabe, director of International Research and Co-operation, National Institute
    for Educational Research, Japan; and adviser to MEXT (and former administrative
    vice minister), Japan

APPENDIX C

Reading performance on PISA 2009

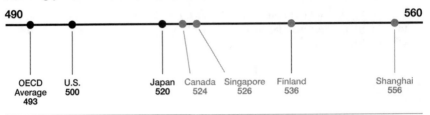

Math performance on PISA 2009

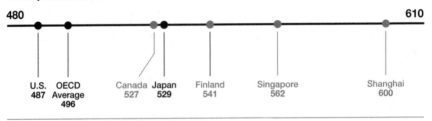

Science performance on PISA 2009

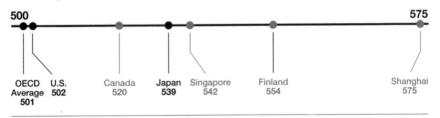

GDP per capita (USD)

Percent of GDP spent on primary, secondary, and non-tertiary education

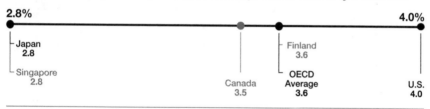

Percent of variance in student performance explained by socioeconomic status

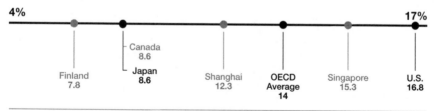

Source note: The source materials for these six charts can be found on the individual graphs in this book's introduction.

CHAPTER 4

Singapore

A Journey to the Top, Step by Step

Vivien Stewart

When Singapore became independent in 1965, it was a poor, small (about 700 sq km), tropical island with few natural resources, little fresh water, rapid population growth, substandard housing, and recurring conflict among its ethnic and religious groups. At that time, there was no compulsory education and only a small number of high school and college graduates and skilled workers. Today, Singapore is a gleaming global hub of trade, finance, and transportation; it is one of Asia's great success stories, a transformation "from third world to first," in the words of Lee Kuan Yew, in one generation.

All children in Singapore receive a minimum of ten years of education in one of the country's 360 schools. Singapore's students placed first in the world in math and science on the Trends in International Math and Science Study (TIMSS) in 1995, 1999, and 2003 and fourth in literacy, as measured by the Progress in International Reading Literacy Study (PIRLS). They continue their excellence as one of the top-performing countries in the 2010 PISA results. Singapore was rated as one of the best-performing education systems in a 2007 McKinsey study of teachers and was rated first in the 2007 IMD World Competitiveness Yearbook for having an education system that best meets the needs of a competitive economy. At the higher education level, the National University of Singapore was ranked thirty-fourth in the world and fourth in Asia in the *Times Higher Education Supplement* Rankings of World Universities in 2010. (See appendix D for additional economic and education rankings for Singapore.)

So how has this "little red dot on the map," as Singaporeans frequently refer to their country, a nation that is not even fifty years old, emerged from a backwater undeveloped economy into a world economic and educational leader in such a short period of time? What education policies and practices has Singapore employed? And are the lessons from Singapore's experience relevant for other countries? This chapter attempts to provide some answers to these questions, but, first, it looks at the broader context.

Under British colonial rule, from 1819 on, Singapore developed as a major seaport at the mouth of the Malacca Straits on the shipping lanes between Britain, India, and China. During this period, it attracted large numbers of immigrants, primarily from southern China and India. At the time of its independence from Britain in 1959 and then its separation from Malaysia in 1965, Singapore had no assets other than its deepwater port. There was no real economy and no defense, and tensions simmered with neighboring countries. Moreover, it had to import most of its food, water, and energy. The Republic of Singapore seemed an unlikely candidate to become a world-class economic and educational powerhouse.

The risks facing this nation at birth—the sense of political and economic vulnerability to larger countries and global changes—created a sense of urgency that influences policy to this day. Lee Kuan Yew, the first and longtime leader of Singapore, set two overarching goals: to build a modern economy and to create a sense of Singaporean national identity. He recruited the best and brightest people into the early government and sought to promote economic growth and job creation. In the 1960s, the emphasis was on attracting labor-intensive foreign manufacturing to provide jobs for its low-skilled workforce. In the 1970s and 1980s, a shift to more skill-intensive manufacturing led to an emphasis on technical fields. Since the mid-1990s, Singapore has sought to become a player in the global knowledge economy, encouraging more research- and innovation-intensive industry and seeking to attract scientists and scientific companies from around the globe. The results of the government's economic policies have been stunning: rapid economic development to developed-country levels and a per capita income estimated at S1$50,000 (ca. US$38,000) in 2009. One of the so-called Asian Tigers, Singapore is a free market, business-friendly, and globally oriented economy shaped by an active and interventionist government.

The government of Singapore is a highly efficient, honest, and flexible meritocracy with a strong focus on integrated strategic planning and detailed execution. "Dream, Design, Deliver" aptly characterizes its approach to policy development and implementation. Small size and political stability (the same People's Action Party has ruled Singapore since its independence) have kept the vision of making Singapore a great global city constant but have also enabled it to be versatile in responding to rapidly changing environments. With a small, limited domestic market, Singapore has had to become highly integrated with the global economy. To survive several global recessions and the ever-present uncertainties of the global economy, continuous innovation has been essential.

With respect to Lee Kuan Yew's second goal of nation building, early race riots led to a profound commitment to creating a multiracial and multiethnic

Singapore's education system

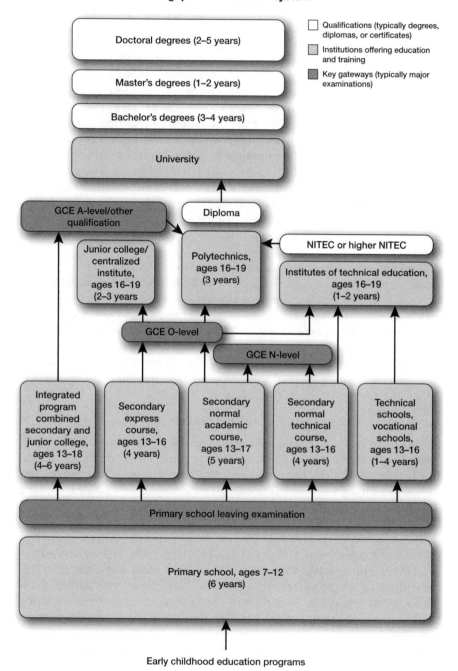

society. Singapore had multiple religious groups (Buddhist, Muslim, Taoist, Hindu, Christian), multiple ethnic groups (Singapore's population is about 76 percent Chinese; 15 percent Malay; 7 percent Indian and European, and 2 percent other), and no common language. Nor did it have a common school system or a common curriculum. A series of measures were put in place over time to make a reality of the Singapore pledge: "One united people regardless of race, religion or language." Singapore recognizes and teaches four official languages—Chinese, English, Malay, and Tamil, although English is the language of government and, since 1978, the medium of instruction in schools. Two years of compulsory national service unite different ethnic groups, as does the policy of integrating each group in the government-built housing, where most Singaporeans live, to avoid the racial and ethnic segregation that afflicts many countries. Schools play a major role in inculcating Singaporean values and character; civic and moral education play a major role in schools. Honesty, commitment to excellence, teamwork, discipline, loyalty, humility, national pride, and the common good have been inculcated throughout government and society.

Lacking other resources, human resources were and are today seen as the island republic's most precious asset. From the beginning, education was seen as central to building both the economy and the nation. Its job was to deliver the human capital to be the engine for economic growth and to create a sense of Singaporean identity. The economic goals of education have given education policy a very pragmatic bent and placed a strong focus on scientific and technical fields. Singapore's education system has evolved over the past forty years in tandem with the changing economy.

HOW SINGAPORE BECAME A LEARNING NATION

Over a forty-year period, Singapore has been able to raise its education level from one similar to that of many developing countries to one comparable to the best in the OECD. The current system did not emerge full-blown but has developed through adaptation to changing circumstances and ideas in three broad phases.

Survival-Driven Phase (1959–1978)

According to then Prime Minister Lee Kuan Yew, the aim of Singapore education in its early days was to "produce a good man and a useful citizen." This first phase of education has, in retrospect, been named the survival-driven phase. In the late 1950s, 70 percent of the GDP was from entrepôt activities. This was not enough to sustain, let alone grow the economy. There was high population growth and significant unemployment. The government decided that there was a need to expand the industrial base and, because of the small size of the domestic market, to make it export oriented. It set about trying to attract foreign manufacturers that needed low-skilled labor (e.g., textiles, garments, wood products) both to provide jobs and to gain expertise.

Prior to independence, only the affluent in Singapore were educated; most of the population of two million was illiterate and unskilled. Therefore, the focus of this "survival" period was on expanding basic education as quickly as possible. Schools were built rapidly. Teachers were recruited on a large scale. The schools that had been established by different ethnic groups were merged into a single Singaporean education system. A bilingual policy was introduced so that all children would learn both their own language and English. A textbook agency was created to provide textbooks. The expansion was so rapid that universal primary education was attained in 1965 and universal lower secondary by the early 1970s. By the end of the survival-driven phase, Singapore had created a national system of public education.

However, the quality of education was not very high. In the early 1970s, out of every 1,000 pupils entering primary grade one, only 444 reached secondary grade four after ten years. And of these, only 106 gained three or more passes in the O-level examinations. A significant report by Dutch economic adviser Albert Winsemius estimated that in the years 1970–1975, Singapore would average a shortage of 500 engineers and 1,000 technical workers per year and would have a severe shortage of people with management skills. The oil crisis of 1973 and the increasing competition from other countries in Asia for low-skill, labor-intensive industry led to a growing realization that Singapore's comparative advantage was eroding and that it needed to transition to a higher-skill economy. A large number of policy changes and changes of ministers of education in this period, however, caused confusion. Teacher morale was low, and there was considerable attrition. Although there were attempts to expand vocational education, it had low status and was viewed as a dumping ground. In 1978, a watershed report, the Goh report, highlighted the high "wastage" (dropout) rates and low standards and ushered in the next phase of reform.

Efficiency-Driven Phase (1978–1996)

During what is now called the efficiency-driven phase of Singaporean education, the focus shifted. The government's economic strategy was to move Singapore from a third-league, labor-intensive economy to a second-league, capital- and skill-intensive country. So in January 1979, a New Education System was introduced. Singapore moved away from its earlier one-size-fits-all approach to schooling to create multiple pathways for students in order to reduce the wastage rate, improve quality, and produce the more technically skilled labor force needed for the new economic goals. Streaming (tracking) based on academic ability was introduced, starting in elementary schools, with the goal of "enabling all students to reach their potential while recognizing that all students do not grow academically at the same pace." Students could have more time, for example, to complete different stages of schooling.

The multiple pathways included three types of high schools: academic, which prepare students for college: polytechnic, which focus on advanced occupational and technical training and can also lead to college; and technical institutes, which focus on occupational and technical training for the lowest one-third of the students. The Curriculum Development Institute of Singapore was established to produce high-quality curricula for the different pathways. While streaming was unpopular when it was introduced, dropout rates did, in fact, decline significantly: by 1986, less than 3 percent of students left school with fewer than ten years of education. The range of efforts to raise standards also yielded results: performance on the O-level English examinations went from a 60 percent failure rate to a 90 percent pass rate by 1984, and by 1995 Singapore led the world in math and science on TIMSS.

As Singapore sought to attract companies with a more sophisticated technological base (e.g., silicon wafers, computers), a major goal of this second phase was producing technical workers at all levels. Concerned about the low status of blue-collar jobs, Singapore began investing significantly in the Institute for Technical Education (ITE) in 1992. With a number of campuses around the city, the ITE provides high-quality technical and vocational education in beautiful high-tech facilities with amenities comparable to those of universities. Each technical field is advised by industries in that sector to keep it current with changing demands and new technologies. New programs can be built for multinational companies looking to locate in Singapore. There has been strong market demand for ITE graduates, and it is possible for the top graduates to go on to polytechnics and then to university. As a result of these changes, the image and attractiveness of vocational education vastly improved. At the top end of the technical workforce, the number of university and polytechnic places was also expanded during this period to increase the pool of scientists and engineers.

Ability-Based, Aspiration-Driven Phase (1997–Present)

By the early 1990s, the efficiency-driven education system had yielded clear results. But, as became clear during the Asian financial crisis of 1997, the world economy was shifting, becoming a global knowledge economy. The competitive framework of nations was being redefined and national progress would increasingly be determined by the discovery and application of new and marketable ideas. The growth of the global knowledge economy required a paradigm shift in Singapore's education system, with a new focus on innovation, creativity, and research.

As Singapore intentionally navigated toward the global knowledge economy, the government-run Agency for Scientific and Technical Research (A*Star), which provides generous funding for research and aims to attract top scientists and scientific companies, took a lead role. One million foreign nationals with scientific, technical, or managerial skills have been encouraged to work in Singapore in international corporations and higher education. Singapore's three universities, and especially the National University of Singapore, have research partnerships with leading universities around the world with a focus on selected fields, including bioinformatics, information sciences, and medical technologies.

At the school level, Singapore created a new educational vision in Thinking Schools, Learning Nation, a major milestone in Singapore's education journey which recognized that "a nation's wealth in the twenty-first century will depend on the capacity of its people to learn," according to then Prime Minister Goh Chok Tong. "Thinking Schools" represented a vision of a school system that can develop creative thinking skills, lifelong learning passion and nationalistic commitment in the young. "Learning Nation" is a vision of learning as a national culture, where creativity and innovation flourish at every level of society.

Over a number of years, Thinking Schools, Learning Nation encompassed a wide range of initiatives designed to tailor education to the abilities and interests of students, to provide more flexibility and choice for students, and to transform the structures of education. It revised career paths and incentives for teachers and upgraded teacher education. Curricula and assessment changes put greater emphasis on project work and creative thinking. With three successive master plans, the Singapore government made a major resource commitment to information and communication technology (ICT) as an enabler of new kinds of self-directed and collaborative learning. The Ministry of Education created a broader array of subject matter courses for students and encouraged a portfolio of different types of schools, including specialized arts, math and science, and sports schools as well as a number of independent schools. "We need a mountain range of excellence, not just one peak and inspire all our young to find their passions and climb as far as they can," said Tharman Shanmugaratnam, then minister of education.

The Ministry of Education also made major changes in the management of schools. Moving away from the centralized top-down system of control, schools were organized into geographic clusters and given more autonomy. Cluster superintendents, who had previously been successful principals, were appointed to mentor others and to promote innovation. Along with greater autonomy came new forms of accountability. The old inspection system was abolished and replaced with a school excellence model. It was felt that no single accountability model could fit all schools. Each school, therefore, sets its own goals and annually assesses its progress toward meeting them in nine functional areas and four "enablers" as well as in academic performance. Every six years, there is an external review by the School Appraisal Branch of the Ministry of Education. Greater autonomy for schools also led to a laser focus on identifying and developing highly effective school leaders who can lead school transformation.

In 2004, Prime Minister Lee Hsien Loong introduced the idea of Teach Less, Learn More as the next step under the Thinking Schools, Learning Nation umbrella. Its aim was to open up more "white space" in the curriculum so as to engage students more deeply in learning. Despite the system's widely recognized successes, students were still seen as too passive as learners, as overloaded with content, as driven to perform but not necessarily inspired. Teach Less, Learn More aims to

> touch the hearts and engage the minds of learners by promoting a different learning paradigm in which there is less dependence on rote learning, repetitive tests and instruction, and more on engaged learning, discovery through experiences, differentiated teaching, learning of lifelong skills, and the building of character through innovative and effective teaching approaches and strategies.

The Ministry of Education made further moves in this direction in 2008 with an envisioning exercise that led to Curriculum 2015. According to Ho Peng, director-general of education in the Singapore Ministry of Education, this review asserted that the Singapore education system had strong holding power and important strengths in literacy, math, and science that should remain, but it needed to do better on the soft skills that enable future learning. In addition, "The overload of information has put a premium on the ability to do critical analysis. Working across cultures will require language skills and a larger world view." A review of primary schools in 2009 focused on the question of how each child's learning can be driven by their innate curiosity and love of play. Art, music, and physical education are also being enhanced in the curriculum. Finally, Curriculum 2015 reemphasized that education must be rooted in values. "Without a moral and ethical compass, all learning will come to nought. We must rebalance content, skills and character development to achieve a more holistic education," said former education minister Ng Eng Hen.

Current Education Structure

So, in the Singapore education system of today, students receive six years of primary education, and four to five years of secondary education, followed by two years at junior college, polytechnics, or the ITE.

Primary education consists of a four-year foundation stage during which all students follow a common curriculum that emphasizes English, "mother-tongue," and mathematics. Science is introduced beginning in primary grade 3. Other subjects taught in primary school are civics and moral education, social studies, health, physical education, and music. Streaming, which has been a key feature of the Singapore education system, was designed to allow students to progress at their own pace from primary grade 4 on. However, in 2008, streaming was abolished in upper-elementary schools and replaced with subject-based banding. At the end of primary grade 6, all students sit for the Primary School Leaving Examination in English, math, mother-tongue, and science. Based on the results in this examination, students are admitted to an express (60%), normal academic (25%), or normal technical (15%) course in secondary school.

Students in the express course follow a four-year program to the General Certificate of Education (GCE) O-level. Students in the normal academic course follow a four-year course to GCE N-level and may sit for O-levels in year five. The normal technical program prepares students for articulation into technical education and the ITE after a four-year program leading to the GCE N-level. In recent years, more choice has been offered to students in secondary school with a wider range of subjects at O-level and elective modules. Some students may skip O-levels entirely in order to engage in broader learning experiences that develop their leadership potential and capacity for creative thinking. There is now more horizontal mobility among courses, and students who do well are allowed to transfer between tracks. Schools specializing in sports, art, and math and science are also available as well as a small number of independent schools.

After ten years of general education, students go to postsecondary education, junior colleges (30%), polytechnics (40%), or ITE (20%). Academically inclined students can take A-levels during this period and then proceed to university. Students may also take diploma courses in technical or business subjects at polytechnics. Students with GCE O- or N-levels can take skill-based certificates in technical or vocational subjects at ITE. Outstanding ITE graduates can also go on to polytechnics or universities. About 25 percent of a cohort goes on to university in Singapore (the number of places will rise to 30 percent in 2015). Many students also attend university abroad.

KEY SUCCESS FACTORS IN SINGAPORE'S PERFORMANCE

Singapore has pursued its vision of a high-quality education system over a long period of time and has accomplished significant improvements at each stage of its journey. What are some of the key features that have helped Singapore become so successful?

Primacy Placed on Education for Economic and National Development

The wealth of a nation lies in its people.
—Prime Minister Goh Chok Thong (1997)

The high value placed on education as the key to economic development and national cohesion in a country with no national resources can be seen consistently in the statements of Singapore's senior leaders since the founding of the republic. But the statements about "nurturing every child" are not just political rhetoric. They have been accompanied by willingness at each stage to invest considerable financial resources in education. Education spending rose to 3.7 percent of the country's GDP in 2001, second only to defense.

The linkage of education to economic development is tight and comes from the top of the government. As Singapore moved from an entrepôt to a low-wage, labor-intensive manufacturing economy, to more capital- and skill-intensive industry, to its current focus on knowledge-intensive industrial clusters, the education system was expected to ramp up its production both of the quality of education and of specific skills to make Singapore globally competitive.

Singapore has perhaps a uniquely integrated system of planning. The Economic Development Board plays a central role and coordinates with the Ministry of Manpower. The Ministry of Manpower works with specific industry groups to identify critical manpower needs and project demands for future skills within a work skills framework. These are then fed back both into preemployment training and continuing education and training. In other countries, labor and education markets make these adjustments slowly over time, but the Singapore government believes that its manpower planning approach helps students move faster into growing sectors, reduces oversupply in areas of declining demand more quickly, and targets public funds more efficiently for postsecondary education. The Ministry of Education and the institutions of higher and postsecondary education then use these skill projections to inform their own education planning, especially with respect to the universities, polytechnics, and technical institutes.

In short, the ability of the government to successfully manage supply and demand of education and skills was and continues to be a major reason for Singapore's competitive advantage. As Singapore seeks to become a global scientific hub, it is bringing together all aspects of the government—the finance ministry, economic development board, manpower planning board, education ministry, urban and environmental planning bodies, housing and immigration authorities—to create the next platform for Singapore's growth.

Alignment Between Policies and Practices

One of the most striking things about Singapore is that the same clear focus on the same bold outcomes, on careful attention to implementation and evaluation, and on orientation toward the future are heard everywhere—in the Ministries of Manpower, National Development, Community Development, and Education and in the universities, technical institutes, and schools. "Milestone" courses bring together top officials from all the ministries to create a shared understanding of national goals. And a focus on effective implementation runs throughout the government. "Dream, Design and

Deliver" is an apt characterization of Singapore's approach to public administration. Because of the value placed on human resource development and the understanding of its critical relationship to economic development, the leadership of the Singapore government provides a very clear vision of what is needed in education. This means that the Ministry of Education can then design the policies and implement the practices that will meet this vision.

At the institutional level, both policy coherence and implementation consistency are brought about by the very close tripartite relationship between the Ministry of Education, the National Institute of Education (NIE), the country's only educator training and professional development institution, and the schools. The ministry is responsible for policy development while the NIE trains educators and conducts research. The NIE's research is fed back to the ministry, and this evidence is used to inform policy development. Since NIE professors are regularly involved in ministry discussions and decisions, it is relatively easy for the NIE's work to be aligned with ministry policies.

For example, the move from a purely knowledge-transmission model of education to one that emphasized creativity and self-directed learning, as outlined in Thinking Schools, Learning Nation and Teach Less, Learn More, was advanced through ministry policy directives, through the regular monthly meetings of cluster superintendents with principals, and through the frequent professional development opportunities for teachers. The government also funded the Centre for Research on Pedagogy at the NIE, which examined current teaching practices in Singapore classrooms, piloted new approaches, and fed back needed changes to the ministry. Recently, the NIE has revamped its teacher education model to focus on producing teachers who themselves have such twenty-first-century literacies and can create learning environments that enable their students to develop them. Changing pedagogy is always difficult, but in Singapore there is much less of a gap between policy and classroom delivery, between the intended and the actual curriculum, than elsewhere.

According to David Hogan, senior research scientist at the NIE, this degree of institutional alignment is very unusual in global terms. Singapore is a "tightly coupled" system where the key leaders of the ministry, the NIE, and the schools share responsibility and accountability. Its remarkable strength is that no policy is promulgated without a plan for building the capacity to meet the new demand. And while there is variation in performance within schools, there is relatively little variation between schools. By contrast, loosely coupled systems have a much harder time bringing about reform initiatives and are often characterized by an endless parade of new, sometimes conflicting, policies without the capacity to meet them. The teacher preparation programs in universities are also often not in alignment with the reform policies. Consequently, practitioners become cynical and wait for successive reform waves to pass. There are usually also large discrepancies among schools in the extent to which reforms are carried out.

In recent years, Singapore has loosened its tight coupling somewhat. More autonomy has been given to schools so as to encourage more innovation, and the NIE has the independence appropriate to an institute in a modern research-oriented university. However, the alignment among the curriculum, examinations and assessments, incentives for students to work hard, and accountability measures for teachers and principals is still strong and makes policy making and implementation much easier and more effective than it is in a loosely coupled system, like the United States.

In trying to understand Singapore's success, it is important to remember the scale of Singapore. Singapore is a very small national education system—more like a city or a small state in other countries, with approximately 522,000 students and 360 schools. Lee Sing Kong, director of the NIE, likens it to "turning around a kayak rather than a battleship." The stability of the government and the broad popular consensus about the instrumental purposes of education also make it possible to pursue policies for a long enough period to see if they have any impact.

Commitment to Equity and Meritocracy

Meritocracy was a cornerstone philosophy of Lee Kuan Yew's government from the beginning. He believed it was the most efficient way to run a government and the only way to create a peaceful multiethnic society. The system of education that was in place during colonial times—highly elitist and separated by ethnicity and religion— was anything but that. He sought to replace it with a universal state-funded system in which talent and hard work would prevail.

At the time of independence, there were large attendance and achievement gaps between the Chinese population, on the one hand, and the Tamil and Malay populations, on the other. These gaps threatened the political stability of Singapore as well as its economic development. In the first education phase, the survival phase, rapid expansion of schooling led to universal elementary and lower secondary education by the early 1970s. In the second phase, the practice of streaming was introduced to reduce the high dropout rates, and although controversial, it was successful in doing so. Today, with a secondary school (tenth grade) graduation rate of 98 percent, the gaps in educational attainment have been substantially reduced. Still, there is more work to be done. In the TIMMS results, for example, Singapore has very high mean achievement scores in math and science, but there is also a long tail to the achievement distribution. On other measures, too, socioeconomic status (SES) has a significant impact on achievement.

According to Lee Sing Kong, the measures Singapore has taken to reduce the achievement gap have been both social and educational. Believing that the causes of underachievement lie in social structures such as single-parent families, Singapore has developed a system of local Town Councils and Community Councils that identify families in need and that can provide a range of different kinds of assistance, including financial assistance. In addition, each of the ethnic communities, Malay, Indian, and Chinese, has a self-help community organization. These organizations are funded by members of each community and support children in need. As an example, Malay children perform less well in math and science than other groups, so the Malay community organization is working with schools to improve their children's performance in these subjects.

When asked whether Singapore's housing policies have an impact on the achievement gap (80 percent of people live in government-built but self-owned apartments and ethnic groups are deliberately mixed in each housing block), Lee said that he did not know of any empirical studies but thought that it seemed plausible that being in a community with high expectations for academic achievement would have an overall positive effect on children.

On the educational side, children who do not perform well on reading tests in the first grade are provided systematic intervention Learning Support Programmes, where teachers work with these children for thirty minutes per day in small (six to eight students) groups so that they do not fall behind. About 12–14 percent of children need such support in reading. The curriculum includes phonics and English language development, since many of the children speak languages other than English at home. Learning Support Programmes also exist in math. In addition, while most preschools in Singapore are privately funded, the government funds preschool education for low-income students to help prepare them for school.

In recent years, Singapore has abolished streaming in elementary schools and replaced it with subject matter banding. It has also created more opportunities for students to move horizontally between tracks at the secondary level and beyond, in order to create more flexibility in the system and to recognize late bloomers. Another remarkable feature of the Singapore education system is the value, attention, and resources it devotes to lower-level achievers, not just high achievers. This focus on "leveling-up" so that the lowest track gets very high-quality training exemplifies the multiple pathways approach. The resources devoted to vocational and technical training are immense, and the system is perhaps the best in the world—a significant reason for Singapore's success story.

Singapore has a small population (4.7 million in 2010), with only 522,000 students in elementary and secondary schools. So every child is valued. The goal of the education system, therefore, is to nurture every child, no matter what their ability or achievement level. The ecology of education reform rests on these shared values. Parents want good opportunities for their children, high levels of social mobility, and rising levels of income. The government has delivered those, so, overall, parents share the belief in the fairness of the system. As former minister of education Tharman Shanmugaratnam said, "We have avoided the large disparities in educational standards seen elsewhere, between schools for the privileged and those for the masses. We have achieved high standards across a spectrum of abilities, allowing a large proportion of Singaporeans to proceed to high-quality post-secondary and tertiary education."

Focus on Strong Math, Science, and Technical Skills

Singapore's solid foundation in math and science in the elementary grades seems to be fundamental to students' later success. At the primary and secondary levels, math and science are core subjects. Math begins when students enter school in primary grade 1, and science is taught from primary grade 3 on. Students have specialist teachers in math and science from upper-primary on. From upper-secondary on, there is a range of specialized math courses at higher levels for those students who are interested. At the tertiary level, more than half the programs are oriented toward science and technology.

The Singapore approach to math is distinctive and has become well-known because of the students' success. Developed in the 1980s after reviewing math research developed around the world, and refined several times since, the Singapore national math curriculum is based on the assumption that the role of the math teacher is to instill "math sense." In a Singapore classroom, the focus is not on one right answer; rather, the goal is to help students understand how to solve a math problem. Textbooks are much slimmer than they are in the United States. The Singapore Model Method also makes extensive use of visual aids and visualization to help students understand mathematics. The heavy emphasis on visuals also makes the approach useful for language-minority children, since many of Singapore's students are learning English in school as a second language. Teachers cover far less material but cover it in depth: the goal is to master math concepts. The mathematics in the Primary School Leaving Examination (grade 6) is approximately two years ahead of that in most U.S. schools. Singapore math also blurs the distinction between algebra and geometry. These concepts are integrated into basic math instruction before students reach high school. Singapore teachers are all trained in how to teach the national math curriculum and meet regularly to fine-tune exercises and hone lessons.

The Singapore national science curriculum in primary and lower-secondary grades focuses on developing the idea of science as inquiry through three domains: knowledge, understanding, and application; skills and processes; and ethics and attitudes. To interest students in viewing science as useful, inquiry projects are based on the roles played by science in daily life, society, and the environment. Cocurricular activities such as math and science fairs, competitions, and learning trails (applying math and science subjects in outdoor settings) are designed to generate interest among students. The DNA Centre at the NIE develops hands-on activities for learning life sciences, and the government science agency, A*STAR, exposes students to research done by working scientists.

In many countries, technical education is looked down on as a dead-end option, as being of low quality, and, typically, as falling behind the changing needs of employers. But vocational education has been an important pathway in Singapore's journey to educational excellence. In 1992, Singapore took a hard look at its own poorly regarded vocational education system and decided to transform and reposition it so that it was not seen as a place of last resort. Law Song Seng led the creation of the Institute for Technical Education (ITE), which transformed the content, quality, and image of vocational education. Its goal was to build a world-class technical education institution that is "effective, relevant and responsive to the knowledge-based economy." ITE's founders brought in leadership with a broad vision and staff committed to caring for students. They completely revamped the curriculum and workforce certification system, developed courses in new industries, and consolidated existing technical campuses into three mega campuses with a sophisticated technology base and close ties to international corporations.

To combat the societal prejudice against less academically inclined students, the ITE promoted and rebranded its kind of "hands-on, minds-on, hearts-on" applied learning. The result has been a doubling of enrollment since 1995, and ITE students now constitute about 25 percent of the post-secondary cohort. More than 82 percent of enrollees complete their training and are placed in jobs. Pay levels for ITE graduates have also been strong, so the ITE track is now seen by students as a legitimate way to a bright future. Part of the reason for the success of the technical education at ITE is that students get a strong academic foundation early in their schooling so they can acquire the more sophisticated skills being required by leading-edge employers. ITE received the first Kennedy School/IBM award for innovation and has been recognized worldwide as a global leader in technical education.

Human Resource Management System

In the earlier phases of Singapore's educational development, when there was rapid expansion of the schooling system, Singapore did not have a high-quality teaching profession, contradicting the widely heard statement that high-quality teachers are due simply to a kind of historical cultural respect for teaching. The high quality of Singapore's workforce today is the result of deliberate policy actions, especially dating from the 1990s on. Since then, high-quality teachers and school leaders have formed the cornerstone of the education system and are a major reason for the high performance of the education system.

Rather than focusing on just one element, Singapore has developed a comprehensive system for selecting, training, compensating, and developing teachers and principals, thereby creating tremendous capacity at the point of education delivery. Key elements of that system are:

Recruitment. Prospective teachers are carefully selected from the top one-third of the secondary school graduating class by panels that include current principals. Strong academics are essential, but so are commitments to the profession and to serving diverse student bodies. Teachers receive a stipend equal to 60 percent of a teacher salary while in training and commit to teaching for at least three years. Interest in teaching is seeded early through internships for high school students, and a system for encouraging midcareer entry also exists, since it is seen as a way of bringing real-world experience to students.

Training. All teachers receive training in the Singapore curriculum at the NIE at Nanyang Technological University, either in a diploma or a degree course, depending on their level of education at entry. There is a close work-ing relationship between NIE and the schools, wherein all new teachers are mentored for the first few years. Since the NIE is a single institution whose primary purpose is training all Singapore teachers, there are no divisions between arts and sciences faculty and education faculty, so the conflicting priorities that plague many Western teacher education programs are less significant and there is a stronger focus on pedagogical content knowledge.

Compensation. The Ministry of Education keeps a close watch on occupa-tional starting salaries and adjusts the salaries for beginning teachers to ensure that teaching is seen as equally attractive as other occupations for new graduates. Teacher salaries do not increase as much over time as those in private sector jobs, but there are many other career opportunities within education for teachers. Teaching is also regarded as a twelve-month position. There are retention bonuses, and high-performing teachers can also earn significant amounts in performance bonuses.

Professional development. Recognizing the need for teachers to keep up with the rapid changes in the world and to be able to constantly improve their practice, teachers are entitled to one hundred hours of professional develop-ment per year. This may be undertaken in several ways. Courses at the NIE focus on subject matter and pedagogical knowledge and lead toward higher degrees. Much of professional development is school based, led by staff de-velopers whose job it is to know where there are problems in a school (e.g., with a group's math performance) or to introduce new practices such as proj-ect-based learning or new uses of ICT. Each school also has a fund through which it can support teacher growth, including the development of fresh perspectives by going abroad to examine aspects of education in other countries. Teacher networks and learning circles encourage peer-to-peer learning, and the Academy of Singapore Teachers, opened in September 2010, further encourages teachers to continuously share best practices.

Performance appraisal. Like every other profession in Singapore, teachers' performance is appraised annually by a number of people and on sixteen different competencies. Included in this Enhanced Performance Management System is their contribution to the academic and character development of the students in their charge, their collaboration with parents and community groups, and their contribution to their colleagues and the school as a whole. Teachers who do outstanding work receive a bonus from the school's bonus pool. This individual appraisal system sits within the context of great attention to the school's plan for educational excellence, since all students in Singapore have multiple teachers, even in primary school.

Career development. Throughout Singapore, talent is identified and nurtured rather than being left to chance. After three years of teaching, teachers are assessed annually to see whether they have the potential for three different career paths: master teacher, specialist in curriculum or research, or school leader. Each has salary increments. Teachers with potential to be school leaders are moved to middle-management teams and receive training to prepare them for their new roles. In turn, middle managers are assessed for their potential to become assistant principals and, later, principals. Each stage has a range of experiences and training to prepare candidates for school leadership and innovation. Singapore has a clear understanding that high-quality teaching and strong school performance require effective leaders.

Leadership selection and training. Leadership matters. Inferior leadership is a key factor in teacher attrition in many countries. Singapore's approach to leadership is modeled on that found in large corporations. The key is not just the training program but the whole approach to identifying and developing talent. This differs from the U.S. or U.K. approach, for example, in which a teacher can apply to train as a principal or school head and then apply for a position in a school. In Singapore, young teachers are continuously assessed for their leadership potential and given opportunities to demonstrate and learn, for example, by serving on committees and then being promoted to head of department at a relatively young age. Some are transferred to the Ministry of Education for a time. After these experiences are monitored, potential principals are selected for interviews and go through leadership situational exercises. If they pass these, then they are eligible to go to the NIE for six months of executive leadership training, with their salaries paid. The process is comprehensive and intensive and includes a study trip and a project on school innovation in another country.

When asked why Singapore uses the "select then train" rather than the "train then select" model, Lee Sing Kong said that while the U.S./U.K. approach is feasible, it carries a higher risk. Singapore is very confident that it can consistently have the best possible leaders for its schools and that there is a wide range of inputs in their selection.

By putting its energy in the front end of recruiting high-quality people and giving them good training and continuing support, Singapore does not have the massive problems of attrition and persistently ineffective teachers and principals that plague many systems around the world. Teaching has developed into a competitive and well-regarded occupation. It is considered an honor to be a teacher in Singapore.

Finally, another critical aspect of the human resource capacity of the Singapore system is the civil service. Lee Kuan Yew's philosophy of governance was to recruit very high-quality people into public service. Singapore has an extremely competent civil service, including in the Ministry of Education. Top civil servants are carefully selected, well-trained (many at the best universities in the world), pragmatic, hard-working, and well-paid. They have a global outlook, paying attention to education developments around the world, and are accustomed to using data and evidence in their decision making. And they have the clear responsibility for the efficiency and effectiveness of the Singapore education system.

Continuous Improvement over Time

While in recent years Singapore has devolved considerable authority to schools, it is still a centrally driven government system. In many countries, government bureaucracies are sclerotic and move about as fast as molasses. But Singapore has inculcated an attitude and developed mechanisms for continuous improvement. In addition to the ties to economic planning that drove the major shifts in educational goals from one of the three major phases to the next, there are a multitude of smaller changes and improvements being made seemingly at all times.

Officials from the Ministry of Education and faculty from the NIE are in the schools often and have a good informal handle on what is going on, unlike the remoteness of government departments and universities in many countries. They also pay a great deal of attention to data, such as the School Cockpit and Student Hub data systems.

There is now also a high level of investment in research relative to the size of the country. Following the announcement of the policy direction Thinking Schools, Learning Nation in 1997, a national education research agenda was developed to which SI$50 million was devoted. Since then, a wide range of different types of research has been carried out, with research design decided by researchers, not the government. One major set of studies has been carried out by David Hogan, former dean and now senior research scientist at the Centre for Research on Pedagogy and Practices at the NIE. This six-year effort aimed at understanding the extent to which modern pedagogical practices were being used in Singapore classrooms and at piloting interventions to demonstrate how to move classrooms from a predominantly knowledge-transmission model to a twenty-first-century model where students engage in complex knowledge construction. This research does not just sit on a shelf; it is regularly fed back into the ministry's deliberations.

Singapore has also made extensive use of international benchmarking as a tool for improving quality and introducing innovations in its education system. Staff of the education ministry, NIE, and the schools all participate in visiting other systems and exploring international best practice. Typically, the visits and study focus on very specific issues and on what works and doesn't work in implementing particular policies. For example, Singapore math was developed from reviewing math research and practice from around the world. Recently, Ministry of Education personnel visited the United States and other countries to examine Mandarin teaching to nonheritage speakers. Ministry staff members have also visited a number of countries to examine new kinds of assessments, including Hong Kong, Australia, Scotland, and Sweden. NIE professors are constantly looking at research, curriculum, and pedagogy in other countries, and, as a result, Singapore classrooms incorporate a wide range of pedagogical styles. Principals and master teachers are also encouraged to examine innovations in other countries and to explore how they could be adapted for use in Singapore schools. A couple of years ago, a *Washington Post* reporter covered a visit by a group of Singapore principals to several schools in northern Virginia. "Why," she asked, "since Singapore is best in the world on the TIMMS international math and science assessments, was a group of Singapore principals visiting science classes in northern Virginia schools?" The attitude of Singapore educators is that there is no perfect system in the world. There are pockets of excellence in many places; and the key is how to adapt them to the local context and implement them well.

Whenever Singapore seeks to create a new institution, it routinely benchmarks its planning to the best in the world. If Singapore is not in a position to create a world-class institution in a particular field, it will try to import the expertise, as it did, for example in its recent partnerships with Duke University to create a new medical center and with Yale University to create a liberal arts college. All Singapore educational institutions—from the National University of Singapore ("a global university centered in Asia") to individual schools—are being encouraged to create global connections in order to develop "future-ready Singaporeans."

Future Challenges

While all these features have helped to make Singapore's education system world-class, no system should rest on its laurels, and Singapore educators are certainly not complacent. As a small country in an information- and innovation-driven globalized economy, it is always vulnerable to the actions of larger players. The education system is now being looked to to provide the kind of high-skilled creative, flexible workers needed for the twenty-first-century economy. And the education system is responding through a wide variety of initiatives flowing from the Thinking Schools, Learning Nation paradigm shift. However, it is a significant challenge to change a traditional content-heavy curriculum that is reinforced by high-stakes assessments that parents believe in and support through extensive tutoring.

The assessment system does indeed set high standards, but it also constrains innovation. The Singapore Ministry of Education recognizes the need to change, but there is, as yet, no agreed on set of measures of the new kinds of complex, "twenty-first-century" skills. Just as important, it is difficult for teachers who have been trained in a teacher-dominated kind of pedagogy to fundamentally change their practice. And Singapore leaders also worry that as the economy continues to grow and change, and as these new demands are being placed on teachers, it may get harder to recruit the kind of top-flight people into teaching that are needed to support the new kinds of learning.

Finally, the economic changes associated with globalization are increasing the level of inequality in Singapore, as in many other countries. And while Singapore has closed achievement gaps to a significant degree and focused on raising those on the bottom, there is still a stronger correlation between SES and achievement than Singapore education leaders would like.

Still, Singapore has, in Linda Darling-Hammond's words, "built a system in which students are routinely taught by well-prepared teachers who work together to create high-quality curriculum, supported by appropriate materials and assessments that enable ongoing learning for students, teachers and schools alike."

WHAT CAN BE LEARNED FROM SINGAPORE?

Singapore is both a" rapid improver" and a "continuing high performer." To those who believe that large-scale change in educational performance is not possible, Singapore has shown several times over that significant change is possible. Singapore has developed a high-quality system in terms of educational retention, quality, equity, and efficiency. To become and remain high-performing, countries need a policy infrastructure that drives performance and a capacity for educators to deliver it in schools. Singapore has developed both. Where Singapore stands today is no accident but, rather, the result of several decades of judicious policy and effective implementation. In the spectrum of national reform models, Singapore's is both comprehensive—the goal has been to move the whole system—and public policy driven.

While the small scale and tightly coupled nature of the education system in Singapore may make its approaches seem inapplicable elsewhere, in fact, Singapore is the size of many states/provinces or large cities in other countries, and many of its principles and practices are applicable to countries of a different scale and governance structure, although their implementation would have to take a different form. Some of the key lessons learned from Singapore follow.

Vision and leadership matter. Leaders with a bold long-term vision of the role of education in a society and economy are essential to creating educational excellence. Changing any system takes five to ten years, so where there are frequent changes of political leadership, a guiding group needs to be created to keep the vision moving forward, rather than having a change of direction with every change of government or minister.

The alignment of the design of a country's education system to its economic development goals matters. The strong link between education and economic development in Singapore has kept investment in education a central priority; made education policies highly pragmatic; and led to high-quality math and science and also world-class vocational/technical education, an area where most countries fail. It has also kept education dynamic, *expecting* to change as conditions change rather than being mired in the past. While the tightness of the link may not be possible in less-planned economies, bringing together economic and education policy makers and business and education leaders to continually assess changes in economic conditions and how education and economic development could better work together would strengthen both.

The coherence of the education system and the alignment of its constituent elements with each other matter. In many countries there is an enormous gap between policies and their implementation at the school level. In Singapore, whenever a policy is developed or changed, there is enormous attention to the details of implementation—from the Ministry of Education, to the National Institute of Education, to cluster superintendents, to principals and teachers. The result is a remarkable fidelity of implementation and relatively little variation across schools. While different mechanisms would be needed in larger, more multilayered or decentralized systems, finding ways to bring greater alignment and to make all the parts work together to produce results in classrooms is essential to creating greater gains in other nations' systems.

Clear and ambitious goals; rigorous, focused, and coherent standards; and gateways marked by high stakes matter. Singapore's education system is extremely rigorous.

The academic standards set by its Primary School Leaving Examination and Singapore's own O- and A-levels are as high as anywhere in the world. *Rigor* is the watchword. Students, teachers, and principals all work very hard toward these important gateways. All students have a strong early foundation in the core subjects of math, science, and literacy in two languages.

Curriculum, instruction, and assessment to match the standards matter. Singapore does not just establish high standards and then leave it to individual teachers to figure out how to achieve them. Serious attention to curriculum development has produced strong curricula in math, science, technical education, and languages, in particular, which teachers are well-trained to teach. Having been very successful as a knowledge-transmission education system, Singapore is now working on curriculum, pedagogy, and assessments that will lead in the direction of a greater focus on high-level, complex skills.

High-quality teachers and principals matter. In earlier times, Singapore often had teacher shortages and was not always able to attract the highest-quality people into teaching. In the 1990s, Singapore put in place a comprehensive and intensive human resource system to obtain high-quality teachers and school leaders that could meet its ambitions for its students. The system rests on active recruitment of talent, accompanied by coherent training and serious ongoing support. Education policies in Singapore today are less focused on structure and more on maintaining and increasing the quality of the education professions. In 2007, it introduced the GROW package, measures to promote teacher growth, recognition, opportunity, and well-being.

A capable center with authority and legitimacy to act matters. The Ministry of Education in Singapore is staffed by knowledgeable, pragmatic individuals who are trained at some of the best universities in the world. They function in a culture of continuous improvement, constantly assessing what is and is not working using both data and practitioner experience. They respect and are respected by professionals in the schools. Around the world, countries vary in whether the locus of authority is at the national, state/province, or local level, but whoever is vested with strategy and authority would do well to emulate the competence and capacity of the Singapore Ministry of Education.

Accountability matters. Singapore runs on performance management. Teachers, principals, ministry staff, NIE faculty, students—all have incentives to work hard. For teachers and principals, serious attention is paid to setting annual goals, garnering the needed support to meet them, and assessing whether they have been met. Data on student performance is included but so too are a range of other measures of contribution to school and community and judgments by a number of senior practitioners. Reward and recognition systems include honors and salary bonuses. Individual appraisals take place within the context of school excellence plans. No country believes that it has got accountability exactly right, but Singapore's system uses a wide range of indicators and involves a wide range of professionals in making judgments about the performance of adults in the system.

Meritocratic values matter. Undergirding the whole system is the belief that education is the route to advancement and that hard work and effort pay off for students of all ethnic backgrounds and all ranges of ability. The government has developed a wide range of educational and social policies to advance this goal, including early intervention and multiple pathways to education and career. The success of the government's economic and educational policies has brought about immense social mobility that has created a shared sense of national mission and made cultural support for education a near-universal value.

Eagerness to learn from other countries and an orientation toward the future matter. The design of Singapore's education system owes a lot to lessons from other parts of the world. Focused and universal use of international benchmarking and, more recently, significant funds for research have enabled Singapore to move up the value chain and foster a culture of never standing still. This is a system that recognizes the rapidity of change around the world and that has the capacity and inclination to learn and adapt. Singapore fosters a global outlook for everyone—teachers, principals, and students, who are expected to have "global awareness and cross-cultural skills" and to be "future-ready." In the words of Tan Chorh Chuan, president of the National University of Singapore, Singaporeans must be ready to "scale new heights in a changed world."

CONCLUSION

While the deep details of Singapore's education system remain particular to Singapore, the lessons from its education journey to excellence are generalizable to other settings. Success requires a clear vision and belief in the centrality of education for students and the nation; persistent political leadership, alignment between policy and practice, and a focus on building teacher and leadership capacity to deliver reforms at the school level; ambitious standards and assessments; broad support in the population; and a culture of continuous improvement and future orientation that benchmarks educational practices against the best in the world.

REFERENCES

Asia Society. 2007. *Learning in a Global Age: Knowledge and Skills for a Flat World.* New York: Author.

Asia Society and Council of Chief State School Officers. 2010. *International Perspectives on U.S. Policy and Practice.* http://asiasociety.org/education/learning-world/what-can-america-learn.

Darling-Hammond, L. 2010. *The Flat World and Education.* New York: Teachers College Press.

Goh, K. S. 1979. *Report on the Ministry of Education 1978.* Singapore: Singapore National Printers.

Hong, K. T., Y. S. Mei, and J. Lim. 2009. *The Singapore Model Method for Learning Mathematics.* Curriculum Planning and Development Division. Singapore: Ministry of Education.

Lee, S. K., C. B. Goh, B. Fredriksen, and J. P. Tan. (eds). 2008. *Toward a Better Future: Education and Training for Economic Development in Singapore since 1965.* Washington, DC: World Bank.

Low, E. 2010. *Educating Teachers for the 21st Century: The Singapore Model.* Singapore: National Institute of Education.

Ministry of Education, Singapore. www.moe.gov.sg.

National Institute of Education. www.nie.edu.sg.

Ng, P. T. 2008. "Developing Forward-Looking and Innovative School Leaders: The Singapore Leaders in Education Program." *Journal of In-Service Education* 34, no. 2: 237–255.

Mullis, I. V. S., M. Martin, J. Olson, and D. R. Berger. (eds). 2007. *A Guide to Math and Science Education around the World.* TIMSS Encyclopedia, vol. 1. http://timss.bc.edu/TIMSS2007/encyclopedia.html.

Sclafani, S., and E. Lim. 2008. *Rethinking Human Capital in Education: Singapore as a Model for Human Development.* Washington, DC: Aspen Institute.

Singapore Examination and Assessment Board. www.seab.gov.sg.

State of the University 2009. Singapore: National University of Singapore.

Stewart, V. 2011. *Improving Teacher Quality Around the World: The International Summit on the Teaching Profession.* http://asiasociety.org/education/learning-world/.

Yew, L. K. 2000. *From Third World to First.* New York: Harper Collins.

INTERVIEWS

David Hogan, principal research scientist, National Institute of Education, Singapore

Lee Sing Kong, director, National Institute of Education, Singapore

Low Ee Ling, associate dean, National Institute of Education, Singapore

Elizabeth Pang, program director, Literacy Development, Curriculum Planning, and Development Division, Ministry of Education, Singapore

Ho Peng, director-general, Ministry of Education, Singapore

Representatives from the Economic Development Board, Housing Development Board, Ministry of Manpower, National University of Singapore, Ministry of National Development, NUS School of Science and Math, Victoria High School, Chongfu Primary School, Assumption Pathway School, Institute of Technical Education, National Institute of Education, A*Star, Keppel Offshore and Marine, and Marshall Cavendish

Siew Hoong Wong, director of schools, Ministry of Education, Singapore

APPENDIX D

Reading performance on PISA 2009

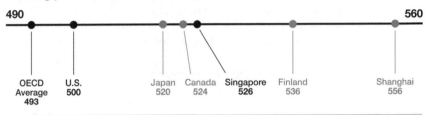

Math performance on PISA 2009

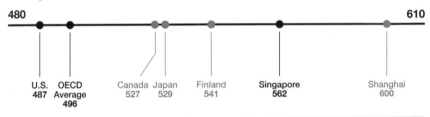

Science performance on PISA 2009

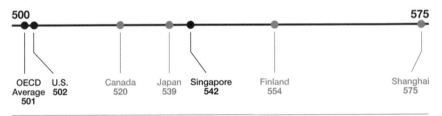

GDP per capita (USD)

Percent of GDP spent on primary, secondary, and non-tertiary education

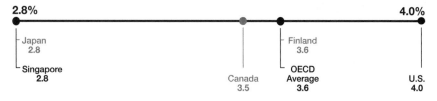

2.8%   4.0%

Japan
2.8

Singapore
2.8

Canada
3.5

Finland
3.6

OECD
Average
3.6

U.S.
4.0

Percent of students with first or second generation immigrant status

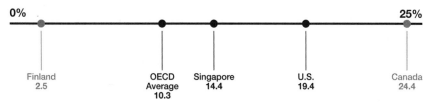

0%   25%

Finland
2.5

OECD
Average
10.3

Singapore
14.4

U.S.
19.4

Canada
24.4

Percent of students with an immigrant background speaking another language at home

1%   12%

Finland
1.9

Singapore   U.S.   Canada
11.3   11.5   11.6

Percent of variance in student performance explained by socioeconomic status

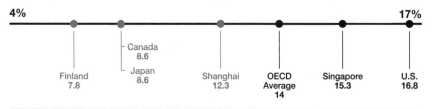

4%   17%

Finland
7.8

Canada
8.6

Japan
8.6

Shanghai
12.3

OECD
Average
14

Singapore
15.3

U.S.
16.8

Source note: The source materials for these eight charts can be found on the individual graphs in this book's introduction.

CHAPTER 5

Canada

Looks a Lot Like Us but Gets Much Better Results

Jal D. Mehta and Robert B. Schwartz

Canada is a relative latecomer to the top of the international rankings. Unlike Japan and Korea, it was not a clear leader in international assessments in the 1980s and 1990s, and it was only after the release of the PISA rankings in 2000 that Canada found itself in that role. These results have been confirmed in subsequent administrations of the PISA tests, which have revealed that Canada has strong mean results as well as less dispersion among its high and low socioeconomic status students than do many other nations. (See appendix E for additional economic and education rankings for Canada.)

Understanding the reasons for this strong performance is not easy for two reasons. First, Canadian education is governed at the provincial level with a limited to nonexistent federal role, and so each of the ten provinces and three territories has its own history, governance structure, and educational strategy. Second, because Canada is a newcomer to educational success, there has not yet been the array of visitors, scholars, and other interested observers who could generate the kind of secondary literature that could be used to try to tell a story of Canadian success as a whole. Given those limitations, this chapter endeavors to describe the features of the system and what is known about the reasons for its success and also provide an in-depth look at the recent educational strategy of the nation's largest province, Ontario.

This chapter aims to spur further investigations into the work of additional provinces, which would allow for a more definitive assessment of the reasons for Canadian success in future years. This question is especially important because Canada has achieved success within a highly federated system that features significant diversity, particularly with respect to issues of language and country of origin. Given that many of the other PISA leaders are relatively small and culturally homogeneous countries, Canada could provide a model of how to achieve educational success in a large, geographically dispersed, and culturally heterogeneous nation.

UNDERSTANDING THE CANADIAN SYSTEM

The most striking feature of the Canadian system is its decentralization. It is the only country in the developed world that has no federal office or department of education. Education is the responsibility of its provinces and territories. Four of those provinces hold approximately 80 percent of Canada's 5 million students: Ontario (2 million), Quebec (1 million), British Columbia (610,000), and Alberta (530,000).

Responsibility within the provinces is divided between the central provincial government and more locally elected school boards. The provincial government is responsible for setting curriculum, determining many major policies for schools, and providing the majority, if not all, of the funding for schools (funding patterns vary some across provinces). The minister of education is chosen by the premier from among elected members of the provincial legislature and then becomes a member of the ruling party's cabinet. The deputy minister is a civil servant who carries much of the operational responsibility for the workings of the department. Tensions can exist between the civil servants in the province's Department of Education who generally, by training and inclination, are sympathetic to the views of educators and elected officials who may have a broader reform agenda.

Local school boards are elected. They employ staff and appoint principals and senior administrators. They also set annual budgets and make decisions on some programs. Over time, the number of districts has shrunk considerably through processes of consolidation. In Alberta, for example, at one point there were more than five thousand districts; by the end of the twentieth century, there were fewer than seventy. There is no interim level of administration between the provinces and districts in Canada; provinces and districts work directly with one another on provincewide initiatives.

Teachers are unionized in Canada, and the unit of collective bargaining varies across provinces. Some bargain at the local level, some at the provincial level, and some are mixed. Teacher training takes place in universities, although the standards for certification have traditionally been set by the provinces. In 1987, British Columbia was the first to make its teachers self-governing, granting to the British Columbia College of Teachers exclusive responsibility for governing the entry, discipline, and professional development of teachers. In 1996, Ontario followed suit, creating an Ontario College of Teachers; on its thirty-one-member governing council sit seventeen teachers elected by the college and fourteen members appointed by Ontario's minster of education. In both cases, more traditional bread-and-butter issues continue to fall under collective bargaining and are separate from the work of these self-regulating bodies.

The Canadian system has also gained distinction internationally for its efforts to balance respect for diversity of language and religious affiliation with provincewide educational goals. With respect to religion, Section 93 of the

Canada's education system

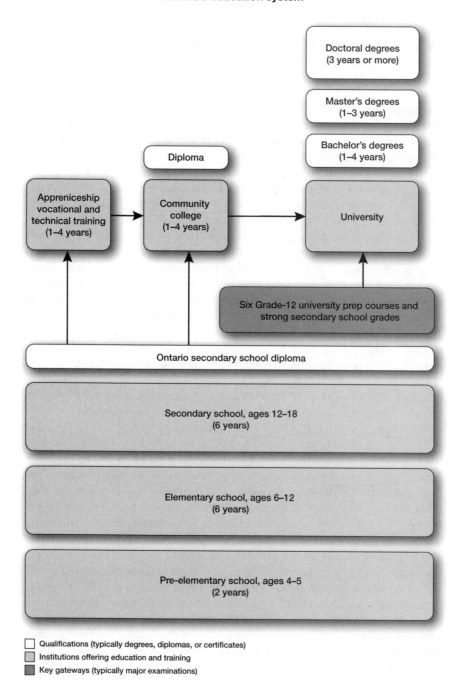

Doctoral degrees
(3 years or more)

Master's degrees
(1–3 years)

Bachelor's degrees
(1–4 years)

Diploma

Appreniceship
vocational and
technical training
(1–4 years)

Community
college
(1–4 years)

University

Six Grade-12 university prep courses and
strong secondary school grades

Ontario secondary school diploma

Secondary school, ages 12–18
(6 years)

Elementary school, ages 6–12
(6 years)

Pre-elementary school, ages 4–5
(2 years)

☐ Qualifications (typically degrees, diplomas, or certificates)
▨ Institutions offering education and training
▨ Key gateways (typically major examinations)

Constitution Act of 1867 sought to protect parents' rights to send their children to Protestant and Catholic schools using public money, subject to provincial control over funding and teachers. This structure means that these schools and school boards in Canada are within the public system and under partial control of the Ministry of Education and not in the private sector. These schools were named *separate schools* in Canada West and *dissentient schools* in Canada East. There is variation across provinces in exactly how these arrangements have evolved. In some provinces, like Alberta, Ontario, and Saskatchewan, public and separate/dissentient schools exist; in others, like Manitoba and British Columbia, parents seeking a Catholic or Protestant education have to send their children to private schools, though even these often receive some degree of public funding.

While initial education struggles in Canada centered around religious differences, in more recent years language has shown greater salience. Section 23 of the Canadian Charter of Rights and Freedoms protects parents who speak a minority language (English or French) with the right to receive primary and secondary instruction in their native language as well as access minority-language educational facilities if sufficient numbers warrant. There has been some controversy over how many minority-language students are required to invoke this right; in Quebec it has generally been interpreted to mean only one, whereas in Nova Scotia fifty was judged too few for the creation of a French school. Courts have also had to adjudicate what it means to have minority-language educational facilities, with some seeing that as requiring only separate programs within existing schools and others as necessitating whole separate schools. The aggregate result of the protection for both language and religious rights is that in some provinces, such as Ontario, as many as four separate systems of public schools can exist within one province (English, English Catholic, French, French Catholic).

Students in Canada are grouped by ability in ways that are very similar to the U.S. system. Elementary school–aged children are often placed in ability groups within heterogeneous classrooms. Students in secondary schools are placed into tracks, or streams, based on perceived ability levels. Most high schools have tracks such as general, advanced, vocational, or university entrance. These practices have faced criticism for not sufficiently challenging students in the lower tracks, but sorting by perceived ability persists.

The thumbnail history of Canadian educational reform in the postwar period is similar to that of the United States and much of the industrialized world. Strong economic growth in the 1950s and 1960s, combined with increasing demand for schooling, led to rapid increases in spending on schooling between 1950 and 1970, with much of the energy focused on school construction and teacher hiring. Because of the increased demand for teachers, teacher wages rose considerably over this period. Schools and teachers were given more autonomy as to what to study, and the inspection functions of provincial ministries were delimited or eliminated. At the same time, provinces were taking increasing financial responsibility for schooling: localities paid 64 percent and provinces 36 percent in 1950; by 1970 the ratio had largely reversed, with provinces paying 60 percent and localities 40 percent. By 1997, eight of the ten provinces had taken 100 percent responsibility for funding.

The postwar boom of the 1950s and 1960s gave way to hard economic times in the 1970s, and the final three decades of the twentieth century saw Canadian education seeking a way to cut costs while increasing educational outcomes. Globalization and the arrival of the knowledge economy increased the importance of schooling as a matter of economic competitiveness. A neo-liberal emphasis on efficiency pervaded the system, and support for greater choice, growing support for private schools, and increased state accountability became the order of the day. While all four leading provinces increased the role of centralized testing and curriculum planning in the 1980s and 1990s, some of these efforts combined greater centralized accountability with more school-level control under a tight-loose philosophy of school improvement. The emphasis on testing in Canada was extensive compared to most European systems but not nearly as prominent as it was in the United States.

The first decade of the twenty-first century saw a set of educational reform efforts, at least in Ontario, that both built on but also differentiated itself from the reforms of the 1980s and 1990s. These reforms continued the emphasis on centralized standards and assessments that characterized the earlier reforms but coupled them with a strong effort to try to build capacity among teachers and to generate teacher buy-in to the improvement strategy. While the earlier strategy of testing grew out of an increasing skepticism about the quality of education and a more general distrust of government, the new strategy identified this distrust as one core problem it sought to address and aimed to generate a virtuous cycle of greater performance leading to higher levels of trust, which in turn generated more energy for continued improvement.

REASONS FOR PAN-CANADIAN SUCCESS

When asked to explain Canada's strong nationwide PISA results, several Canadian officials and knowledgeable observers could only offer informed hunches, given the absence of any meaningful role of the national government in education. These hunches fell generally into three categories: Canadian culture; the Canadian welfare state; and three policy-specific factors: teacher selectivity, equalized funding, and provincial curricula.

In terms of culture, observers noted that parents in Canada were generally supportive of their children's education and could be seen as assets to the schools. Comparative PISA data on the leisure reading habits of Canadian students suggests that Canadian students are more likely than any other children in the world to read daily when they are not in school. While culture is notoriously diffuse and difficult to measure, further exploration of its potential influence seems warranted because it could help explain the similarity of results across provinces that differ in their educational strategies.

Despite its provincial educational structure, Canada does have a strong national welfare state, which came out of the crisis spurred by the Great Depression and grew in the 1960s. Observers suggested that this has had two important educational consequences. First, children and their parents have access to national health insurance, and adults are protected from the vicissitudes of capitalism by a strong social safety net. While child poverty rates in Canada are fairly high by international standards (Canada had the seventh-highest child poverty rate of twenty-three countries measured), variation across provinces in child poverty rates are correlated with PISA outcomes (i.e., Alberta has the lowest rate at 11.2 percent and the highest PISA scores).

Second, the idea of a welfare state and a common good is much more firmly entrenched in Canada than in its more individualistic neighbor to the south. The idea that health care and other social services are a right and not a privilege carries over into education, where there is a broadly shared norm that the society is collectively responsible for the educational welfare of all of its children. The combination of this norm with the protections afforded by the welfare state creates a climate in which school success for all students is expected. As Harvard professor Richard Elmore, who has worked for years with Canadian schools, says,

> While the structure and artifacts of the Canadian system look about the same as the American one (professional learning communities, resource rooms for data driven instruction), the culture in which this work takes place is entirely different. Canadian teachers feel that the state has done its part by delivering the students to the schools ready to learn, and that they, in turn, have a deeply felt obligation and responsibility to ensure that the students do indeed get educated.

In terms of policy, observers noted that there was relatively little active coordination across the provinces. The Council of Ministers of Education (CMEC), which is the forum through which the education leaders in the respective provinces can meet for coordination purposes, was consistently described as limited in its impact because it acted only when all of the ministers agreed, which was infrequently. Yet, according to Ontario's current deputy minister, Kevin Costante, CMEC serves an important information-sharing function and enables good ideas and practices to spread across provincial lines.

> Despite the jurisdiction being at the provincial level, we follow one another and copy one another extensively and freely, so that when you go to Alberta or British Columbia or Nova Scotia the actual school systems don't look all that much different. And something that starts to work here, we find it gets

copied pretty quickly in the other provinces. And we are great plagiarizers ourselves. So if we see something working in British Columbia or somewhere else, we will take it up. There is a formal mechanism for doing this—the Council of Ministries of Education of Canada. The ministers meet twice a year. Sometimes it can be a bit of a frustrating forum, but the most valuable part is really the information sharing that goes on. We don't frankly do a lot of work together, although there is some. But it really is a sharing of what works and then people picking it up.

Despite this lack of a national role, a number of respondents suggested that the provinces were not that dissimilar in some of their key policies. The reason given was what scholars in other contexts have called "isomorphism," or the desire to acquire legitimacy by looking roughly at the practice of other similar organizations. Despite the lack of a national coordinating body, a number of our respondents said that, in broad strokes, the provinces were not as dissimilar as we might expect. As Neil Guppy, a professor of sociology at the University of British Columbia and an author of a textbook on Canadian education, told us:

> My own take is that autonomy is overblown—many of the textbooks used by the provinces are identical, our teacher education programs are very similar, the arrangements of schooling (kindergarten, elementary, middle, high) are very similar, unionization is similar, school administration personnel shuffle between provinces with little problem, etc. To my knowledge all universities treat student grades from each province as substitutable even though we do not have SAT or national exams. Imitation from, and monitoring of, other jurisdictions is high. In most English speaking provinces you are likely to find as much variation between rural and urban as you are province to province.

Three common policy factors (in addition to the welfare state and cultural reasons) were highlighted as potentially important to pan-Canadian educational success. The first is the establishment of a common curriculum within each of the provinces. Curricula are developed by the respective ministries of education in a process of extensive consultation with groups of teachers and subject matter experts. In some provinces, these curricula are fairly detailed, whereas in others they serve more as guidelines of what should be learned when. While there is certainly wide variation in the degree to which these curricula actually penetrate classroom practices, they do provide basic guidance as to what should be learned by which students at what ages. In recent years, some of the smaller provinces in the west have moved toward coordinating these efforts to establish greater uniformity across provinces, similar to consortia of states in the United States working together toward Common Core standards. Recent PISA results have shown that Alberta is the highest-scoring province, and the Alberta ministry ascribes this success in part to the quality of its curriculum.

The second factor potentially determining the country's success is the high degree of selectivity in choosing teachers. The 2007 McKinsey report on PISA leaders emphasized that one factor that differentiated PISA leaders from those further down the chart was the degree to which teacher education programs were able to draw their students from the top of the talent pool. Ben Levin, former deputy minister in Ontario and a widely cited scholar on Canadian education, said that Canadian applicants to teachers colleges are in the "top 30 percent" of their college cohorts. One Canadian teacher we interviewed explained that it was difficult to get into a teachers' college in Canada, although, he pointed out, "everyone knew that there was a loophole—you could always cross the border to the United States. Anyone can get credentialed there." The education within these teacher training institutions is seen by some to be of high quality. Levin estimates there are perhaps fifty in all of Canada, as opposed to hundreds across the United States, which allows for greater monitoring of training quality. Other respondents agreed that teacher selectivity was high, but they were more skeptical of the quality of the training institutions.

The third factor is equalized funding. Because funding has shifted to be entirely or almost entirely at the province level, the provinces are able to provide funding to offset the greater neediness of some of their students. Funding from the provinces to districts is generally split into three categories: block grants based on number of students; categorical grants, which are either used to fund particular programmatic needs (i.e., special education) or to help districts meet the greater challenges some districts have in providing basic services (i.e., more geographically dispersed districts need more funds for transportation); and equalization funding, which is used in the districts that retain some local funding in order to equalize the poorer districts.

These factors represent the views of a small sample of Canadian officials and observers; this is how they understand their own success. But these explanations are not very satisfying; there is clearly more research and analysis needed. There are many countries and states/provinces within countries that have centralized curricula without yielding these kinds of results. There is also an extensive literature debating the importance of funding, which, in very broad strokes, suggests that money can help but that it all depends on how you spend it. The teacher selectivity argument carries more weight because it is one of the few factors that more generally differentiates PISA leaders from the rest. In general, the major features of the Canadian system don't look that different from many other systems that do not do as well on the PISA, and thus it is particularly difficult to know the sources of their success.

Similar structures can actually house very different types of work depending on the culture in which they are situated. Curriculum, funding, and teacher talent are resources that provinces and schools can draw on to create high-quality schooling if they are inclined toward collaboration and are willing to take internal collective responsibility for student outcomes. We explore one example of this practice in Ontario. But before getting to that, it is important to address one other factor that does in fact differentiate Canada's performance: the education of immigrant children.

IMMIGRANT EDUCATION

One of the most striking things about the Canadian results is their success with immigrant children. By some estimates, Canada has the highest rates of immigration per capita in the world. It is a country about which former prime minister William Lyon MacKenzie King famously said, "If some countries have too much history, we have too much geography," referring to the way in which Canada is a relatively young nation with travelers from all over the world. Canada takes in about 250,000 immigrants per year (in a country of approximately 34 million). Given the size of the land area, the relative paucity of people, and low birth rates, immigrants are seen in Canada as an important and needed resource. All of the major political parties currently support either sustaining or increasing rates of immigration; there is no popular support for restricting immigration.

Patterns of immigration have shifted over time. Up through approximately 1970, the majority of immigrants came from Europe; over the past forty years, the most have come from Asia and the developing world. In 2007, the leading countries of immigration were China and India (ca. 28,000 each), the Philippines (20,000), and Pakistan (10,000). Smaller groups of immigrants come from the United States, the United Kingdom, Iran, South Korea, Colombia, Sri Lanka, France, Romania, Russia, and Algeria, each of which sends more than 3,500 immigrants per year. In total, these patterns of immigration mean that there are 40,000 newcomers to public schools each year. Eighty percent of these students are non–English speaking, and 90 percent will go to school in Montreal, Toronto, or Vancouver.

Immigration in Canada is organized into three classes: refugee populations, family class sponsorships, and imported workers who fill a need in the Canadian economy. In 2008, approximately 150,000 of these immigrants were economic, 65,000 were family class, and 22,000 were refugees. The fact that 60 percent of immigrants are selected on the basis of their ability to make an economic contribution means that a large class of highly educated immigrants is settling in Canada. In total, 23 percent of current Canadian workers are born abroad, but 49 percent of doctorate holders and 40 percent of those with master's degrees come from other countries.

PISA results suggest that within just three years in the system, Canadian immigrants average a 500 on the PISA exam, which is remarkably strong by international standards. For comparison's sake, on the 2003 reading PISA,

Canadian first-generation immigrants scored an average of more than 510 on the PISA, ranking second (as compared with less than 460 in the United States and less than 430 in France). Canada is also one of very few countries where there is no gap between its immigrant and native students on the PISA. (By contrast, in the United States the gap in math is 30 points, in France more than 50 points, and in Germany 80 points). Second-generation Canadians perform significantly better than first-generation Canadians, suggesting that the pattern is one of progress over time. Finally, Canada is one of only two countries (along with Australia) where there is no difference in performance between students who do not speak the language of instruction at home and those who do.

Interviewees ascribed this success to three factors. First and most importantly, because the majority of immigrants are selected on the basis of their ability to contribute economically, many immigrant children have highly educated parents. A 2006 OECD report found that, on average, first-generation Canadian students had parents with as many or more years of education as native-born parents. These advantages in terms of parental education and socioeconomic status also translated into school resources; in the same study, Canada was one of a few countries where immigrant students had access to equal or greater resources than native-born students. Specifically, student-teacher ratios, physical infrastructure, classroom climate, and teacher morale were on average higher for immigrant students than for native students in Canada.

Second, Canadian multiculturalism provides a distinct philosophy that seeks to both respect the importance of native cultures and incorporate immigrants into a distinctively Canadian identity. In practice, this has meant that immigrant students are, for the most part, placed into classes with native students in English and French; native-language instruction primarily takes place in nonprofits and other workplaces outside of schools.

Third, in some of the provinces that have had the largest influx of immigrants, an explicit policy strategy has sought to support the success of these students. In British Columbia, for example, students participate in the regular curriculum, but the ministry provides funds for additional language support if a series of criteria are met. These include (1) evidence that the student lacks proficiency and will not reach it without additional support; (2) an annual instruction plan that meets the needs of the student; (3) a teaching specialist participating in the creation and review of the plan; (4) the school providing pull-out and in-class support for the student as well as support and training for the affected teachers.

All in all, Canada has a positive and reinforcing cycle when it comes to immigration and educating immigrant students. It is an attractive destination for immigrants, and immigrants are welcomed as part of both a cultural commitment and an economic necessity. The majority of immigrants who come to the country are selected to fill economic needs, which means that they are not seen as a threat or as competition for jobs, which increases the political support for their continued entrée. Immigrant students as a group are demographically similar—with respect to parental education and socioeconomic status—to native-born students, and they attend schools that by all measures are relatively equal. Philosophically, they are welcomed as part of Canada's commitment to multiculturalism, and some programs are in place to supplement students' learning of English and French, although the emphasis is largely on immersion. Overall, this combination of factors creates a fairly welcoming environment for relatively advantaged immigrants, and they correspondingly fare extremely well by international standards.

TURNING TO ONTARIO

From 2003 to 2010, Ontario was a world leader in pursuing a sustained strategy of professionally driven system change. Initiated by Premier Dalton McGuinty with his election in 2003, the Ontario strategy has achieved widespread results in increasing elementary literacy and numeracy, improving graduation rates, and reducing the number of low-performing schools. A constellation of elements came together to produce this strategy.

The Ontario Context

Ontario is the largest province in Canada, with an area of four hundred thousand square miles and a population of approximately thirteen million, which is 40 percent of all Canadians. It is a highly urbanized province, with 80 percent of students located in metropolitan areas. In terms of diversity, 27 percent of Ontario students are born outside of Canada and 20 percent are visible minorities. Toronto is one of the most diverse cities in the world

There are four sets of locally elected school boards in Ontario, meeting Canada's constitutional requirements for public support of minority languages and religious minorities:

- Thirty-one English school boards serve about 1.3 million students
- Twenty-nine English Catholic school boards serve about 560,000 students
- Eight French Catholic school boards have 60,000 students
- Four French school boards have 13,000 students

This means that any given area of the province will be served by four boards, so there is some degree of choice in the system. There are about five thousand schools in the public system; there is no public funding for private schools.

Programmatic Initiatives and Results

There were two major initiatives pursued by the Ontario Ministry of Education over this time period. The first focused on elementary schools, the second on high schools.

The first was the Literacy and Numeracy initiative. The aim here was to increase reading and math outcomes in elementary schools. Through a deep-capacity building strategy, this initiative succeeded in raising the average passing rate on provincial exams from roughly 55 percent (2003) to roughly 70 percent (2010) in reading, math, and writing in grade 3. Similar gains of about ten to twelve percentage points are apparent in the same subjects in grade 6.

The second was the Student Success initiative, whose goal was to increase the high school graduation rate. The thinking behind this program was that the road to dropping out of high school starts early; by tracking students who have failed one or more courses in the ninth grade, it is possible to identify potential dropouts early. By funding a student success officer in each school and creating credit recovery programs through which students could make up the parts of courses that they failed, the graduation rate has increased from 68 percent to 79 percent.

Background Conditions for Success in Ontario

Ontario benefited from a set of background conditions that helped facilitate much of its success.

Politically, the McGuinty premiership benefited by following a Conservative government that was extremely unpopular with teachers and others working in the education sector. That Conservative government is generally credited with having created a provincewide curriculum and instituting an accompanying assessment and accountability framework, but it also alienated the education community in the process by cutting funding, reducing professional development time by half, running television ads demonizing teachers, and increasing support for private schools. During this period, fifty-five thousand students left the public system, and polls suggested that more than 15 percent of public school parents were actively considering private school options. There were several teacher strikes, including a two-week work stoppage protesting government legislation in 1997. Morale was extremely low, and the relationship between the government and teachers was highly acrimonious. Union leader Rhonda Kimberly Young, former president of the Ontario Secondary School Teachers Federation, characterized the years before the McGuinty government took over:

> Then we got the Conservatives and they came in on what they called a common sense revolution which was that there was going to be a miracle. They could lower everybody's taxes. They could cut waste. They could get more with less—better quality at lower cost. Unfortunately, they were able to sell this idea to the voters. When they took office Mike Harris was the premier and the first education minister that he appointed was a high school dropout. We saw that as fairly indicative of their approach to education. [That they were not] going to be looking at pedagogy, research and those sorts of

things but rather were coming in with a hammer . . . We will show you what can be done in education—just let us put in a business model. In 1998 we had a provincewide walkout—it was a political protest.

In this highly polarized environment, the Liberal Party made an early decision to make education the central issue in the next provincial election. As opposition leader, McGuinty made a major policy speech in 2001 committing the party to a quite specific set of reforms, including class-size reductions, should they be elected. This speech was followed up by the development of a very detailed education platform with sixty-five policy proposals. So by the time the Liberals took office in 2003, they believed they had a strong reform mandate.

McGuinty's first education minister, Gerard Kennedy, came in with a running start, for he had been the opposition party's education critic, or shadow minister. As he recounted in his own words, he came into office unusually well-prepared:

> During my time as critic I visited lots of schools and school boards all across the province. I spent a lot of time in lunchrooms with teachers, in meetings after school with parent groups, and I sat down with student councils whenever I had the opportunity. I met with every key stakeholder group not only to build relationships but to engage them in the development of our policy agenda. I must have met with 6,000 people during that period.
>
> We needed to create a new political consensus on education. The current level of politicization of the system was taking a huge toll on public confidence. In the preceding eight years of Conservative government hundreds and hundreds of hours of school had been lost to strikes and lockouts, and this level of disruption was at the core of public discontent with the system. We felt we had to change that dynamic if we were going to have any chance of successfully moving our reform agenda. We needed to reestablish trust between the government and the profession, and between school boards and teachers.

In addition to Minister Kennedy's leadership role, the McGuinty government benefited from the advice and leadership of a deeply knowledgeable and experienced school reformer, Michael Fullan, a University of Toronto expert who had written widely and lectured around the world on school reform. He became McGuinty's special adviser on education and helped recruit Ben Levin, another deeply knowledgeable academic and practitioner, as deputy minister. All of these figures shared a relatively similar vision of capacity-building system change, which helped anchor and sustain the reforms in the years that followed. McGuinty also visited England to learn about somewhat similar British reforms, and the Ontario strategy drew on the British strategy with some important modifications.

Financially, funding in Ontario had shifted in 1997 so that 100 percent of school funding came from the province. Thus, while the system does have multiple levels, provincewide funding increased the leverage of the ministry.

THE THREE PARTS OF THE ONTARIO STORY

Sustained Political Leadership

All accounts of Ontario are clear on the sustained leadership of Premier Mc-Guinty as having been fundamental to the success of the reforms. McGuinty ran on a platform of becoming the education premier, and through his election in 2003 and reelection in 2007, he kept a sustained focus on educational improvement. McGuinty was personally involved in the reforms and, over the course of his tenure, met repeatedly with key educational stakeholders to emphasize the importance of the reforms. Fullan, who was the architect of the strategy, said of McGuinty:

> The premier is key, obviously. If Premier McGuinty had left it would have been a different story. I said to him in the first term, when you get reelected . . . [don't] lose the plot, fail to keep the sustainability and focus on it. And the week after he got re-elected, he said to me, "Not only am I not going to lose the plot, I'm going to intensify it, become even more committed and more confident and more impatient."

In contrast to the kind of spinning wheels that often stall school reform efforts as systems lurch from leader to leader, or in contrast to situations where education falls off leadership's agenda after an initial bout of enthusiasm, McGuinty maintained an active, sustained, personal, and consistent focus on education for his two-term premiership. Deputy Minister Kevin Costante, who took office in 2009, recalls receiving a call from McGuinty on the day he took office, who told him, "Don't get distracted. There will be a lot of people asking you to do all sorts of nice things out there, some of which may be perfectly good but will not add to our student achievement agenda. I want you to keep focused on the student achievement agenda." And just in case the new deputy thought he might have an opportunity to coast on the achievements of the past several years, McGuinty charged Costante with developing and implementing a new full-day kindergarten program for four- and five-year-olds in six hundred schools by September 2010.

Limited Goals

From the beginning, central to Ontario's theory of change was that school systems are easily distracted and drawn into many questions and controversies that have little or no relationship to improving student learning and educational attainment. It also believed that creating systemic change across several layers of government and five thousand schools would require a very limited number of goals that would serve as a focus for coherent effort. McGuinty made two central commitments that guided the work of the ministry: increasing literacy and numeracy in elementary schools and increasing the high school graduation rate. His administration also set ambitious but, it hoped, not unrealistic long-term numerical targets for each of these goals: to improve the provincial passing rate in literacy and numeracy from 55 percent to 75 percent and to increase the graduation rate from 68 percent to 85 percent.

Building the Structure, Culture, and Capacity for Sustained Improvement

To achieve these goals, the education ministry leaders had a seemingly simple but actually quite complex theory of action. This work was informed by a careful reading of the failings of previous initiatives documented in the implementation literature. Most top-down initiatives, they concluded, were unable to achieve deep and lasting changes in practice because: (1) the reforms were focused on things that were too distant from the instructional core of teaching and learning; (2) the reforms assumed that teachers would know how to do things they didn't know how to do; (3) blizzards of conflicting reforms asked teachers to do too many things simultaneously; and (4) teachers and schools did not buy into the reform strategy. To achieve sustained change, then, would require: (1) strategies directly focused on improving the act of teaching; (2) careful and detailed attention to implementation along with opportunities for teachers to practice new ideas and learn from their colleagues; (3) a single integrated strategy and one set of expectations for teachers and students; and (4) support from teachers for the reforms. Both province and district policies would need to be crafted with all of these goals in mind.

Creating the climate. Of all of these points, the last one—gaining teacher support—was perhaps most important to the new strategy. Improve skills across five thousand schools would require a continuous and sustained effort on the part of hundreds of thousands of teachers to try to improve their practice. This, they thought, could only happen if teachers were "onside" (to use their word) with the effort.

To this end, the ministry drew a sharp contrast between its capacity-building approach to reform and the more punitive versions of accountability used in the United States, and, to a lesser extent, in Britain.[1] They chose to downplay the public reporting of results, and they emphasized that struggling schools would receive additional support and outside expertise rather than be punished or closed.

Politically, it is clear that the ministry acted extremely skillfully to win over teachers, schools, and unions to their vision of reform. The appointment of Gerard Kennedy, who was a vigorous critic of the previous administration, was widely seen as a move supportive of public education and as sensitive to the needs of teachers. The deputy minister met quarterly with the major teachers unions, superintendents organizations, and principals associations to discuss ongoing reform strategies. The ministry also created the Ontario Education Partnership Table, where a wider range of stakeholders could meet with ministry officials two to four times a year. The Partnership Tables then led to Working Tables, where smaller groups of stakeholders worked more closely on particular issues.

Key to these efforts was the signing of a four-year collective bargaining agreement with the four major teachers unions in 2005. In this agreement, the ministry was able to negotiate several items that were consistent both with their educational strategy and with the unions' interests. Specifically, McGuinty had pledged to reduce class size in elementary schools, which created 5,000 new jobs. The ministry and the unions also wanted 200 minutes of weekly preparation time for all elementary school teachers; this created 2,000 new positions in music, arts, physical education, and languages. The agreement also provided money for the hiring of a student success position (full- or part-time) in each school. Thus, this agreement pushed forward the educational agenda and created a sustained period of labor peace that allowed for a continued focus on educational improvement.

Creating the structures for deep implementation. To achieve these results, the ministry created a deep implementation strategy. With respect to the Literacy and Numeracy initiatives, it created a new one-hundred-person secretariat that would be responsible for building the capacity and expertise to do the work. This was separate from the ministry and thus was able to start fresh without the usual bureaucratic obstacles. It also required that teams be created in each district and each school in order to lead the work on literacy and numeracy. By so doing, it paired external expertise with sustained internal time and leadership to push the initiative. Avis Glaze, who was responsible for leading the Literacy and Numeracy Secretariat, said that the effort succeeded in part because of its field base.

> We recruited a new team of people who had deep experience in the field—teachers, principals, subject matter specialists—people who were deeply respected by teachers and schools, and were not seen primarily as representatives of the department. This mini-organization was largely based in the field—we had 6 regional teams plus one French language team, each of 6–8 people. This means that the majority of the people in the Secretariat were actively working in the field, building relationships with schools, principals and teachers, rather than in the home office back at the Ministry.

The ministry also tried to ensure that reform was really a two-way street rather than simply something that came from the top down. As Fullan describes it, one of the lessons learned from the British model was to avoid mandating from the top.

Michael Barber in the English strategy eventually called their strategy . . . "Informed Prescription." So the idea of Informed Prescription was that you do your homework at the center, you get informed and then you pretty much prescribe the curriculum and the instructional methods and use of time, including such things as the literacy hour. By contrast, when we set up our Secretariat, we said to the field, to our 72 districts, don't worry, we are not going to come up with Informed Prescription and start advocating particular usages. Rather, what we are going to do is join in partnership with you in the field, the sector, and identify good practices and consolidate those and spread them. They might eventually come to have a certain kind of status that comes close to being non-negotiable, but we are not in the business at the center of telling you what to do. We are in the business of jointly co-discovering it, so that's what we did and that's how we did it.

For the Student Success initiative, the government pursued a different strategy. Rather than sending out a team from the ministry, it gave the districts money to hire a student success leader to be responsible for coordinating efforts in the district. The ministry also gave money for the district leaders to meet and share strategies. Again, each high school was given support to hire a provincially funded student success teacher and required to create a Student Success team to track data on which students were likely to dropout and design appropriate interventions.

An important element in the development of the Student Success strategy was the creation of a new programmatic initiative in the high schools called the High Skills Major. The objective here was to take high school students who were not engaged by the traditional academic curriculum and give them a different menu of courses without replicating the problems of tracking that had plagued such efforts in the past. By working with employers, the High Skill Major program created packages of more hands-on courses that helped students gain skills and led to employment opportunities. More than 20,000 students are now enrolled in 740 High Skill Major programs in 430 schools.

The ministry also had a clear theory of comparative advantage in terms of who should do what with respect to the reforms. The role of the ministry was to set clear expectations and targets, to provide funding, to create a working collective bargaining agreement that would support improved teaching and learning, to provide external expertise, and to intervene with support in struggling schools. The role of the district was to align its personnel and hiring policies with the overall strategy and to support the schools as they went through continuous processes of learning. Much of the real action necessarily had to happen at the school, which was where teachers worked in communities to think through problems of practice and to learn from one another. While the mission and sustained pressure derived from the top, there was a clear recognition that it was at the school level where change had to happen and that the role of other actors in the system was to support the learning and change that had to happen there.

WHAT IS NOT IN THE STRATEGY: ECONOMIC VERSUS SOCIOLOGICAL THEORIES OF ACTION

Missing from the strategy are elements that are common in a number of other reform efforts, particularly in the United States: punitive accountability, performance pay, and competition among schools. Very broadly speaking, the architects of the reforms seem to take more of a *Homo sociologicus* than a *Homo economicus* view of reform. The problem is more a lack of knowledge than a lack of will; and to the degree that motivation is at issue, the key is not individual economic calculations but, rather, the chance to be part of successful and improving schools and organizations.

The theorists that the architects draw on tend to be organizational theorists like Peter Drucker and Edwards Deming rather than economists, and the key challenge is to create layers of organization directed toward systemic improvement. This means that the key ideas are less about "hard" concepts like accountability and incentives and more about "softer" ideas like culture, leadership, and shared purpose. There is also little emphasis in the Ontario strategy on "getting better people"; rather, the idea is that you have to work with what you have and work to upgrade their skills. In all of these respects, the Ontario model challenges more market-based theories of reform.

WHAT CAN BE LEARNED FROM CANADA?

The Ontario strategy is perhaps the world's leading example of professionally driven system change. Through consistent application of centrally driven pressure for higher results, combined with extensive capacity building in a climate of relative trust and mutual respect, the Ontario system has been able to achieve progress on key indicators while maintaining labor peace and positive morale throughout the system.

So what can we learn from it?

Commitment to education and children matters. The strong cultural commitment to the importance of education seems to be an important underlying national value that helps explain Canada's overall strong performance despite the absence of any visible national governmental role in education. The commitment to the welfare of children, as expressed in the strong social safety net, helps explain why Canada's achievement gaps, while still worrisome, are nowhere near as profound as those in the United States.

Cultural support for universal high achievement matters. The extraordinary per-formance of Canada's immigrant children is largely a reflection of the high expectations immigrant families have for their children and of the fact that those high expectations seem, by and large, to be held by educators as well. Because Canada has historically seen its immigrants as important assets, as crucial to the continuing development of the country, and because its im-migration policies reflect those values, schools see their role as integrating children into the mainstream culture as rapidly as possible. If anything, the value placed on high achievement for immigrant children seems to have positive spillover effects onto the expectations for native-born children, rather than vice-versa.

System coherence and alignment matter. This is one of the big lessons from Ontario's reforms. Although some observers complained about the sheer number of initiatives launched by the McGuinty government, it is apparent that the Ontario reform designers worked hard to develop and implement a systemic response to the problems and challenges they inherited. An important, often underestimated, barrier to achieving system coherence is the lack of a shared understanding among key stakeholders about how key governmental leaders see the problems of the system and what lies behind the policies and programs they have designed in response. The McGuinty government worked tirelessly to build a sense of shared understanding and common purpose among key stakeholder groups, and, as a consequence, their two major systemic initiatives—the Literacy and Numeracy Secretariat and the Student Success/Learning to 18 strategy—enjoyed broad public un-derstanding and support.

Teacher and principal quality matter. Ontario's reforms rested heavily on the confidence the government had in the quality of the province's teaching force. The decision by the Literacy and Numeracy Secretariat not to follow England's informed prescription model but, rather, to put seed money out into the field to encourage local experimentation and innovation sent a strong signal that teacher-generated solutions to weaknesses in reading and math performance were likely to be more successful than solutions imposed from above. The fact that teaching has historically been a respected profes-sion in Canada, one that continues to draw its candidates from the top third of secondary school graduates, meant that the government had a solid basis for believing that its trust would pay off. Given the teacher bashing engaged in by the previous government, this show of trust in the competence and professionalism of the teaching force was an essential ingredient in repairing the rupture that had developed between the profession and the government.

Ontario has also paid special attention to leadership development, espe-cially for school principals. In 2008, the government initiated the Ontario

Leadership Strategy, based on a framework that spells out the skills, knowledge, and attributes of effective leaders. Among the elements of the strategy are a strong mentoring program that has now reached over forty-five hundred principals and vice principals and a new provincewide appraisal program for school leaders.

A single capable center with authority and legitimacy to act matters. The Ontario story is very much a story of strong central leadership coupled with a major investment in capacity-building and trust-building with the field. The combination of skilled, sustained political leadership from the premier and a succession of capable ministers, and very strong professional leadership from Ben Levin and his successors in the deputy role, accounts for a big part of Ontario's success. While the initial decision to create the Literacy and Numeracy Secretariat outside the bureaucracy suggests that the political leadership did not have confidence that the ministry could carry out such an ambitious, high-profile initiative, one of Levin's key goals was to make the ministry more attentive and responsive to the field, and by all accounts he and his successors have made progress in that regard.

Professional accountability matters. Ontario has managed to balance administrative and professional accountability in an admirable fashion. The McGuinty government made no attempt to dismantle or weaken the assessment regime put in place by the previous government, and it has consistently communicated the message to the field and the public that results matter, as defined by performance on the provincial assessments. However, its response to weak performance has consistently been intervention and support, not blame and punishment. One of its major successes in the early years was to reduce dramatically the number of low-performing schools, but in doing so its strategy was to flood the schools with technical assistance and support, not threaten to close them (as often happens in the United States). The underlying assumption of Ontario's leaders seems to be that teachers are professionals who are trying to do the right thing and that performance problems are much more likely to be a product of lack of knowledge than lack of motivation. Consequently, teachers seem to own more responsibility for performance than is often the case in countries with a more punitive approach to external accountability.

Making education part of a larger strategy matters. Canada is an interesting case. It is more reliant than many advanced industrial countries on commodities and agricultural production. Yet this country, especially its four most populous provinces, can certainly be counted among the most advanced of the industrial nations. Although it has more resources in the ground than most industrial countries do, it behaves as if it did not when it comes to its conviction that high education levels for everyone are essential to its economic future. In that sense, it looks very much like Singapore and Finland, even though its economic profile is very different.

Similarly, Canada fits the education profile of a country that is counting on its human resources for its prosperity. It recruits its teachers from the top third of the cohort. It seems, at least from the example of Ontario, to have struck a nice balance between a top-down and bottom-up approach to reform. It has clearly moved as far as any other nation has moved toward trusting its teachers and treating them like professionals. While schools have a fair amount of discretion, they operate within a clear provincial framework of standards, assessments, and accountability. In some ways the system is quite traditionally organized. Students are tracked by ability, and yet there seems to be a strong focus on students most at risk of failure, as evidenced especially by the Student Success Initiative. In that sense, Canada has adopted the view that its future cannot be assured unless all students are performing at high levels, and the Canadians have specific policies designed to ensure that outcome. Canada's postsecondary enrollment rates are now among the highest in the OECD community, a clear reflection of the growing public realization that education beyond high school will be increasingly essential in a knowledge-based economy.

FINAL OBSERVATIONS

The Canadian model demonstrates that success can be achieved without a national strategy. This runs counter to the instincts of many of those who sit in policy seats and seek to effect change, but the fact is that Canada has achieved success on PISA across its provinces despite a limited to nonexistent federal role. The best explanation for this is some form of isomorphism, or the idea that more powerful than regulation is the idea that different units want to look legitimate and thus will not differ much from one another. The power of ideas and the possibilities of diffusion can be sufficient forces to generate good practice. Ironically, some Canadian leaders, including Gerard Kennedy, are trying to mount a more national strategy today, arguing that education is too important to be left entirely to the provinces.

Too often in education policy discussions the choices are frequently framed as reform versus the status quo. The implicit idea is that there are two sides: external reformers pushing for progress and existing forces, comprised primarily of teachers, administrators, and unions, resistant to progress. The Canadian experience suggests a more complex analysis, one in which teachers are a critical constituency that can be swayed. On the flip side, the more the teachers perceive the state as the hammer, the more likely they are to entrench themselves in a unionized rather than a professional association. The Ontario experience suggests that by treating teachers as professionals and including them at the table, the ministry was able to build considerable goodwill, which they saw as a critical resource for long-term and sustainable change. This did not mean that the government was naïve—they were quite aware of the bread-and-butter aspect of union negotiations—but they were able to direct that energy toward win-win issues like providing more professional development time. Ultimately, the Ontario government created a sustainable strategy that created a clear push for improved performance in a way that did not alienate teachers and instead included them.

NOTE

1. For a comparative international look at accountability, see Jonathan Supovitz, "Can High Stakes Testing Leverage Educational Improvement? Prospects from the Last Decade of Testing and Accountability Reform," *Journal of Educational Change*, 10, no. 2 (2009): 211–227.

REFERENCES

Bussierre, P., and F. Cartwright. 2004. *Measuring Up: Canadian Results of the OECD Pisa Study*. Ottawa: Statistics Canada.

Bussierre, P., T. Knighton, and D. Pennock. 2007. *Measuring Up: Canadian Results of the OECD Pisa Study*. Ottawa: Statistics Canada.

Canadian Language and Literacy Research Network. 2009. *Evaluation Report: The Impact of the Literacy and Numeracy Secretariat; Changes in Ontario's Education System*. Ontario Ministry of Education. www.edu.gov.on.ca/eng/document/reports/OME_Report09_EN.pdf.

Davies, S., and N. Guppy. 1997. "Globalization and Educational Reforms in Anglo-American Democracies." *Comparative Education Review* 41, no. 4: 435–459.

Fullan, M. 2010. *All Systems Go: The Imperative for Whole System Reform*. Thousand Oaks, CA: Corwin Press; Toronto: Ontario Principals Council.

Guppy, N., and S. Davies. 1998. *Education in Canada: Recent Trends and Future Challenges*. Ottawa: Statistics Canada.

Leithwood, K., M. Fullan, and N. Watson. 2003. *The Schools We Need: Recent Education Policy in Ontario; Recommendations for Moving Forward*. Toronto: Ontario Institute for Studies in Education.

Levin, B. 2008. *How to Change 5,000 Schools: A Practical and Positive Approach for Leading Change at Every Level*. Cambridge, MA: Harvard Education Press.

Levin, B., Glaze, A., and Fullan, M. 2008. "Results Without Rancor or Ranking: Ontario's Success Story." *Phi Delta Kappan* 90, no. 4: 273–280.

Manzer, R. 1994. *Public Schools and Political Ideas: Canadian Educational Policy in Historical Perspective*. Toronto: University of Toronto Press.

McKinsey and Company. 2007. "How the World's Best Performing School Systems Come Out on Top." E-resource. www.mckinsey.com/App_Media/Reports/SSO/Worlds_School_Systems_Final.pdf.

Organisation of Economic Co-operation and Development (OECD). 2006. *Where Immigrant Students Succeed: A Comparative Review of Performance and Engagement in PISA 2003*. Paris: Author.

Pascal, C. E. 2009. *With Our Best Future in Mind: Implementing Early Learning in Ontario.* www.ontario.ca/ontprodconsume/groups/content/@onca/@initiatives/documents/document/ont06_018899.pdf.

Pedwell, L., B. Levin, B. Pervin, M. J. Gallagher, M. Connor, and H. Beck. 2011. "Building Leadership Capacity Across 5,000 Schools." In T. Townsend and J. MacBeath, eds., *International Handbook on Leadership for Learning*. Dordrecht, the Netherlands: Springer Press.

Tibbetts, J. 2007. "Canadian 4th Graders Read up a Storm." *The Gazette* (Montreal), November 29, A2.

Statistics Canada. 2008. *Report on the Demographic Situation of Canada*. Table A-4.1. www.statcan.gc.ca/pub/91-209-x/2004000/part1/t/ta4-1-eng.htm.

Statistics Canada. 2009. *Facts and Figures 2008: Immigration Overview.* www.cic.gc.ca/english/resources/statistics/facts2008/permanent/01.asp.

Ungerleider, C. 2008. *Evaluation of the Ontario Ministry of Education's Student Success/Learning to 18 Strategy*. Ontario Ministry of Education. www.edu.gov.on.ca/eng/teachers/studentsuccess/CCL_SSE_Report.pdf.

Young, J., B. Levin, and D. Wallin. 2007. *Understanding Canadian Schools: An Introduction to Educational Administration*. 4th ed. Toronto: Nelson.

INTERVIEWS

Kevin Costante, deputy minister of education, Ontario

Leona Dombrowsky, minister of education, Ontario

Richard Elmore, Anrig Professor of Education Leadership, Harvard Graduate School of Education

Michael Fullan, Professor Emeritus of the Ontario Institute for Studies in Education, University of Toronto; special adviser to the premier and minister of education, Ontario

Avis Glaze, former CEO of the Ministry of Education's Secretariat for Literacy and Numeracy, Ontario

Keray Henke, deputy minister, Alberta

Gerard Kennedy, member of Parliament; former minister of education, Ontario

Benjamin Levin, professor and Canada Research Chair of Education Leadership and Policy, Ontario Institute for Studies in Education, University of Toronto; former deputy minister of education, Ontario

Rhonda Kimberly Young, former resident of the Secondary School Teachers Federation, Ontario

APPENDIX E

Reading performance on PISA 2009

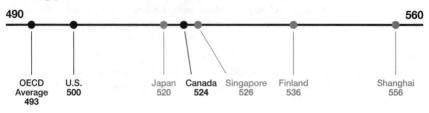

Math performance on PISA 2009

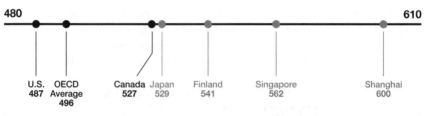

Science performance on PISA 2009

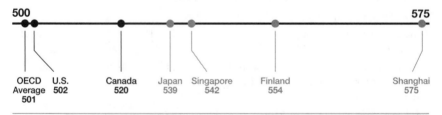

GDP per capita (USD)

Percent of GDP spent on primary, secondary, and non-tertiary education

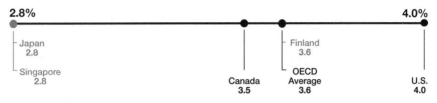

Percent of students with first or second generation immigrant status

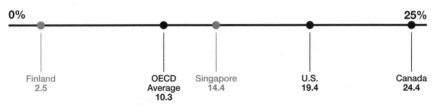

Percent of students with an immigrant background speaking another language at home

Percent of variance in student performance explained by socioeconomic status

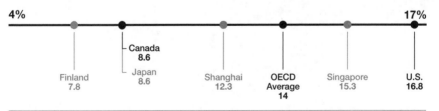

Source note: The source materials for these eight charts can be found on the individual graphs in this book's introduction.

PART II

How the United States Can Match the Best Performers

CHAPTER 6

How the Top Performers Got There

Analysis . . . and Synthesis

Marc S. Tucker

A century ago, the United States was among the most eager benchmarkers in the world. We took the best ideas in steelmaking, industrial chemicals, and many other fields from England and Germany and other countries and put them to work here on a scale that Europe could only imagine. At the same time, we were borrowing the best ideas in education, mainly from the Germans and the Scots. It was the period of the most rapid growth our economy had ever seen, and it was the time in which we designed the education system that we still have today. It is fair to say that, in many important ways, we owe the current shape of our education system to industrial benchmarking.

But, after World War II, the United States appeared to reign supreme in both the industrial and education arenas, and we evidently came to the conclusion that we had little to learn from anyone. As the years went by, one by one, country after country caught up to and then surpassed us in several industries and more or less across the board in precollege education. But few Americans paid any attention to their achievements.

Senior U.S. policy makers didn't take much notice until Secretary of Education Arne Duncan asked the OECD to produce a report on the strategies that other countries had used to outpace us, and then called an unprecedented meeting in New York City of education ministers and union heads from the countries that scored higher on the education league tables than the United States. Now, once again, the United States seems to be ready to learn from the leading countries.

In this chapter, I stand on the shoulders of giants, asking what education policy might look like in the United States if it were based on the experiences of our most successful competitors. I rely on the research reported throughout this volume as well as on that conducted by the OECD, by other researchers, and, over two decades, by the NCEE.

The policy agenda presented here is not a summary of what all the nations studied in the preceding chapters do. There are few things that all of the most successful countries do.

But companies that practice industrial benchmarking do not adopt innovations only when all of their best competitors practice them; they adopt them when the innovations of particular competitors appear to work well and when they make sense for the company doing the benchmarking in the context of their own goals and circumstances. Their hope is that by combining the most successful innovations from individual competitors in a sensible, coherent way, and adding a few of their own, they can not only match the competition but improve on their performance. That is the approach I have taken here.

Here I offer a contrast between the strategies that appear to be driving the policy agendas of the most successful countries and those that appear to be driving the current agenda for education reform in the United States. I conclude that the strategies driving the best-performing systems are rarely found in the United States and, conversely, that the education strategies now most popular in the United States, with the notable exception of the Common Core State Standards, are conspicuous by their absence in the countries with the most successful education systems.

Many will be quick to point out exceptions to my characterization of American practice. In fact, examples of excellent practice in almost every arena of importance can be found in the United States. But my aim here is not to focus on isolated examples of good practice but, rather, on the *policy systems* that make for effective *education systems* at scale. For this is where the United States comes up short.

No doubt, the complete transformation of the whole system of policy and practice I suggest will seem an overwhelming prospect to many people. So I turn to Canada as our best example of a country that might be used as a source of strategies for making great improvements in the short term. It seems quite plausible that, while the short-term plan is unfolding, the nation might embark on the longer-term agenda suggested earlier—ranging from finance equity to all the elements of the teacher quality agenda and beyond—which would lead to even greater improvements.

Bear in mind that although there are useful roles that the U.S. government can play in improving dramatically the performance of our schools, I believe the main player has to be the state governments. So when speaking of changing the system, it is the states, not the national government, I have in mind.

So we begin by identifying broad themes, principles, policies and practices that appear to account for the success of some of the best-performing systems in the world.

THE BROAD THEMES

While it is important to begin by identifying the broad themes, principles, policies, and practices that appear to account for the success of some of the best-performing systems in the world and analyzing the strategies used by these countries, it is easy to lose sight of the forest when looking at the trees. For the big story is really about the convergence of two major developments: the trajectory of global economic development and the workforce needed to teach our children in the current stage of global economic development.

The nations featured in this volume already are, or want to be, very-high-wage countries. They have all recognized that it will be impossible to justify high relative wages for skills that are no greater than those offered by other people in other parts of the world who are willing to work for less, because we are all competing with each other now. Only those who can offer the world's highest skill levels and the world's most creative ideas will be able to justify the world's highest wages. These nations have also realized that this formulation means that very-high-wage nations must now abandon the idea that only a few of their citizens need to have higher-order skills and creative capacities. This is a new idea, the idea that all must have an education formerly reserved only for elites. It leads to abandonment of education systems designed to reach their goals by sorting students, by giving only some students intellectually demanding curricula, by recruiting only a few teachers who are themselves educated to high levels, by directing funding toward the easiest to educate and denying it to those hardest to educate. It is this fundamental change in the goals of education that has been forcing an equally fundamental change in the design of national and provincial education systems.

The second big development follows from the first. No nation can move the vast majority of students to the levels of intellectual capacity and creativity now demanded on a national scale unless that nation is recruiting most of its teachers from the group of young people who are now typically going into the nonfeminized professions. Recruiting from that pool requires a nation not just to offer competitive compensation but also to offer the same social status that the nonfeminized occupations do, the same quality of professional training, and the same workplace conditions. Doing all that will change everything—the standards for entering teachers colleges, which institutions do the training, who is recruited, the nature of the training offered to teachers, the structure and the amount of teachers' compensation, the way teachers are brought into the workforce, the structure of the profession, the nature of teachers unions, the authority of teachers, the way they teach, and much more.

If these really are the core lessons we are to learn from the countries that are outperforming the United States, then much of the current reform agenda in this country is irrelevant, an unfortunate detour from the route we must follow if we are to match the performance of the best.

WHAT THE TOP PERFORMERS DO AND WE DON'T DO

In the introduction, I defined a high-performing national education system as one in which the best students' achievement is world-class, the lowest-performing students rank not much lower than the best students, and the system produces these results at a cost well below the top spenders. In short, the top performers are nations with education systems that are in the highest ranks in terms of quality, equity, and productivity.

In this chapter, I summarize some of the key factors contributing to first-class performance in each of these three categories. I hasten to point out, however, that this schema is rather artificial. System features described under any one of these categories more often than not contribute to outcomes in others. System effects abound. Nonetheless, I hope this schema will prove useful to the reader.

But before I get to the factors that most affect quality, equity, and productivity, it is important to examine international benchmarking as a key strategy for improving national education systems.

Benchmark the Best

Every one of the top performers is very conscious of what the other top performers are doing, though some benchmark more aggressively than others. The reader will recall that the modern Japanese school system owes its very existence to trips taken by the new government when the Meiji Restoration took place, when the Japanese government resolved that the only way it could catch up with the West was to aggressively research its educational institutions and adopt and adapt the best of what they found. Japan has continued to research the education programs of the leading countries as a major input into its education policy making. The Singaporeans may be the most determined and disciplined benchmarkers in the world, not just in education, but across all fields of social policy, and their efforts have paid off. Finland, too, has always made a point of researching the best performers when developing education policy. Ontario premier Dalton McGuinty traveled abroad to visit other countries before settling on his new education policies for Ontario. And in China, the Hong Kong government actually hired an Australian who had done state-of-the-art work in several countries on curriculum, standards, and assessment when it was looking to reform its standards and assessment system.

Many Americans think that they have benchmarked other countries' education systems when they have merely worked up equivalency tables showing which scores on key American assessments correspond to certain scores on the national assessments used in other countries. But that is not what international benchmarking in education means for the countries that have been doing it for years. For those countries, to benchmark another country's education system is to compare broad goals, policies, practices, and institutional structures, as well as relative standing on common measures, in order to understand what another country is trying to achieve, how it has gone about achieving it, what it would have done differently, what mistakes it made and how it addressed them, which factors most account for its achievements, and so on. Benchmarking is a wide-ranging research program that never ends, because no country's education system stands still for very long.

Countries that base their education strategies on the careful study of successful strategies employed by the leading nations are not as likely to go down blind alleys wasting large amounts of resources on initiatives that fail to pay off as are countries that base their strategies on untested theories, which is what the United States has tended to do over the years. What follows is a distillation of what the researchers affiliated with the National Center on Education and the Economy have learned since 1989 from the countries with the best education systems, with a particular focus on the countries, provinces and cities highlighted in this volume.

Design for Quality

GETTING THE GOALS CLEAR

Reading the official documents from the ministries of the top-performing countries, and listening to the top officials in those countries, one cannot help but be struck by the attention that is being given to achieving clarity and consensus on the goals for education in those countries.. All of these top performers now realize that high wages in the current global economy require not just superior knowledge of the subjects studied in school and the ability to apply that knowledge to problems of a sort they have not seen before (the sorts of things that PISA measures) but also social skills, personal habits and dispositions, and values that are essential to success. The Asian countries in particular are concerned that their students may not have as much capacity for independent thought, creativity, and innovation as their countries will need.

Although all these countries are concerned about developing the unprecedented levels of cognitive and noncognitive skills required by the global economy, they are no less concerned about social cohesion, fairness, decency, tolerance, personal fulfillment, and transmission of values that they feel define them as a nation. In many cases, these discussions of national goals have laid the base for profound changes in the design of national education systems, providing a solid foundation in national opinion for the kind of political leadership needed to redesign institutions that are—and should be—very hard to change. Not since the formation of the National

Education Goals Panel in 1990 has there been a focused discussion of American goals for its students of the sort that many of these other countries have had more recently.

INSTRUCTIONAL SYSTEMS AND GATEWAYS

Virtually all high-performing countries have a system of gateways marking the key transition points from basic education to upper-secondary and upper-secondary to university and from basic education to job training and job training to the workforce. At each of these major gateways, there is some form of external national assessment. Among the countries studied here, only Canada does not have such a system. And among the top ten countries in the PISA rankings, Canada is the only outlier.

The national examinations at the end of upper-secondary school are generally—but not always—the same examinations that the universities in that country use for admissions. In many countries, these examinations are the only thing taken into account in determining who is admitted to which university and to the programs or schools within the university. It is also true, in many of these countries, that the scores on exams determine admission to upper-secondary programs designed, in turn, to prepare students for admission to university. The content of the upper-secondary exams is usually determined by the university authorities and is closely tied to the content of the upper-secondary curriculum.

It is also typically true that there is a different upper-secondary program available to students who have successfully completed their basic education by the end of grade 9 or 10 that is intended to provide training for students who will either enter the job market or go on to a polytechnic school for advanced technical training. The standards for the examinations at these gateways are typically set by the state in close collaboration with representatives of the industries that will employ the graduates and, in some cases, with representatives of the labor organizations in those industries.

In these systems there is very close alignment between the upper-secondary curriculum, the upper-secondary exams, and the university requirements. There is also very close alignment between employer's requirements and the skills students acquire to prepare for work in the industries in which they seek jobs. And finally, in these systems, regardless of which path they decide to take in upper-secondary education, students must all meet a common basic education standard aligned to a national or provincial curriculum before moving on to upper-secondary school.

In countries with gateway exam systems of this sort, every student has a very strong incentive to take tough courses and to work hard in school. A student who does not do that will not earn the credentials needed to achieve her dream, whether that dream is becoming a brain surgeon or an auto mechanic. Because the exams are scored externally, the student knows that the only way to move on is to meet the standard. Because they are national or provincial standards, the exams cannot be gamed. Because the exams are of a very high quality, they cannot be "test prepped"; the only way to succeed on them is to actually master the material. And because the right parties were involved in creating the exams, students know that the credentials they earn will be honored; when their high schools say they are "college and career ready," colleges and employers will agree.

But the power of this system does not end there. In the countries that have some form of this system, the examinations are set to national standards and are directly derived from a national curriculum. Teachers in those countries are taught to teach that curriculum. It is also the case that these countries work out a curriculum framework, which means they decide, as a matter of policy, what topics should be taught at each grade level in each of the major subjects in the curriculum. In this way, they make sure that each year the students are taking the material that will be prerequisite to the study of the material they are supposed to master the following year and that all students will be ready for advanced material when it is offered. Further, in these countries, the materials prepared by textbook publishers and the publishers of supplementary materials are aligned with the national curriculum framework.

Thus, the standards are aligned with the curriculum, which is aligned with the instructional materials available to teachers. And the examinations are also aligned with the curriculum, as is the training that prospective teachers get in teacher training institutions.

In all of the countries studied for this volume, the national curriculum goes far beyond mathematics and the home language, covering, as well, the sciences, the social sciences, the arts and music, and, often, religion, morals, or, in the case of Finland, philosophy. In most of these countries, few if any of the upper-secondary school examinations are scored by computers, and much of the examination is in the form of prompts requiring the student to work out complex problems or write short essays. They do this because the ministries in these countries have grave doubts about the ability of computers to properly assess the qualities they think most important in the education of their students.

Perhaps most important, the curricula and examinations in each of these countries, save Canada, were set not just to a very high standard but to a particular kind of standard. Their students did well on the PISA examinations because they demonstrated high mastery of complex content as well as the ability to apply that knowledge to practical problems. Shanghai, Japan, and Singapore have in recent years all engaged in multiyear massive revisions of their curricula to see if they could strike the right balance between high-level content mastery, problem-solving ability, and the ability to demonstrate a capacity for independent thought, creativity, and innovation. Finland, having produced an elegant curriculum specification years ago for every level of its school system, has been working to make that document less detailed in an effort to find the right balance between specificity and flexibility for its teachers.

The level of detail at which the national standards and curriculum are specified varies widely. In most of the East Asian countries, they are fairly detailed, while in Finland, as just noted, they have been getting progressively briefer. In all cases they are guidelines, and in no case do they get down to the level of required lesson plans. They typically give teachers considerable latitude with respect to the specific materials used, pedagogy, and pace.

It is important to point out that, in this realm, the United States has something that these other countries do not have, and it is not entirely clear that it is a good thing. The idea of grade-by-grade national testing has no takers in the top-performing countries. These countries do national testing at the gateways only, and some don't even do state or national testing at every gateway. Typically, there are state or national tests only at the end of primary or lower-secondary education and at the end of upper-secondary school. Schools and the teachers in them are expected to assess their students regularly as an indispensable aid to good teaching, but the assessments given between gateways are not used for accountability purposes, as the basis of teacher compensation, or to track students.

This very powerful, and successful, instructional system has few parallels in the United States. For a long time, Americans have preferred "curriculum-neutral" tests to those aligned with the curriculum, virtually guaranteeing that students would be measured on a curriculum the teachers had not taught. Schools of education had no obligation to teach prospective teachers how to teach the national or state curriculum, because there was no such thing. Because the states had no curriculum frameworks, textbook manufacturers put a vast range of topics in their textbooks, knowing that any given topic might be taught by teachers at many different grade levels, and gave each of those topics only cursory treatment because so many topics had to be included in the text. The federal government now requires tests in English and mathematics at many grade levels and has tied important consequences to student performance on those tests, thus heavily biasing the curriculum toward the teaching of these subjects and away from the teaching of other subjects that top-performing countries view as critical. Whereas these countries have placed a high value in their national policies on the mastery of complex skills and problem solving at a high level, the United States has in recent years emphasized mastery of basic skills at the expense of mastery of more advanced skills. And we continue to prefer tests that are largely based on multiple-choice questions and that are administered by computers.

The new Common Core State Standards for mathematics and English and the work being done by the two assessment consortia will begin to address some of these issues. But even when that work is done, the United States will still be at an enormous disadvantage relative to our competitors. We will have tests in these two subjects that are still not squarely based on clearly drawn curricula. The two consortia are betting heavily on the ability of computer-scored tests to measure the more complex skills and the creativity and capacity for innovation on which the future of our economy is likely to depend. No country that is currently outperforming the United States is doing that or is even considering doing that, because they are deeply skeptical that computer-scored tests or examinations can adequately measure the acquisition of the skills and knowledge they are most interested in. If the United States is right about this, we will wind up with a significant advantage over our competitors in the accuracy, timeliness, and cost of scoring. If we are wrong, we will significantly hamper our capacity to measure the things we are most interested in measuring and will probably drive our curricula in directions we will ultimately regret.

In any case, if the interstate consortia continue to measure performance only in mathematics and English (with the eventual addition of science), we will have no multistate curriculum and assessments in the other subjects for which many other countries have excellent assessments. It is unclear to what extent there will be strong curriculum and related instructional materials available to support the new tests in math and English, to say nothing of the other subjects in the broader core curriculum or subjects that cut across the curriculum. Nor is it clear to what extent our schools of education will assume responsibility for preparing teachers to teach the curriculum that emerges from the new Common Core State Standards efforts.

None of this is intended to take away from the enormous achievement that is represented by the Common Core State Standards. But it is important to recognize that the development of the kind of complex, coherent, and powerful instructional systems described in the foregoing chapters took many years to develop and improve. There is little doubt that these instructional systems now constitute one of the most important reasons for their countries' excellent performance. Implementation of the Common Core State Standards will still leave the United States far behind in what is undoubtedly one of the most important arenas of education reform, so it will be essential to continue, to expand, and to expedite work on developing our instructional system.

TEACHER QUALITY

What Is "Teacher Quality"?

There is a good deal of discussion now about teacher quality, but it is not clear that there is much consensus about what is meant by that term. It is possible to derive a tripartite definition of teacher quality from the experience of the five countries we studied: a quality teacher must possess a high level of general intelligence, a solid mastery of the subjects to be taught, and a demonstrated aptitude for engaging students and helping them understand what is being taught.

Some U.S. law firms recruit only from a handful of top universities; others are happy to take graduates from the local night school. The former firms recruit from the most elite universities not because they believe those universities do a better job of teaching the specific skills they are looking for but because they are using the university selection system to screen the candidates for other qualities they care very much about. They are looking for people of outstanding general intelligence who also have the drive, tenacity, and capacity for hard work that it takes to get into and survive the top law schools. They know that such people will quickly learn on the job what they need to know to do the specialized work they will be assigned. They know that, everything else being equal, they can count on such people to outperform their competitors on a wide range of assignments. They will be able to function with less supervision. They will produce better work. They will rise up the ladder of responsibility faster. The Japanese call this bundle of qualities "applied intelligence." Companies of all kinds in all industries will go as far up the applied intelligence scale as they think they can afford to in order secure a competitive advantage in their markets.

When a country is in the preindustrial stage or in the throes of a mass production economy, few workers will need advanced skills, and most students will not need much more than the basics. But, in advanced postindustrial economies, a much larger portion of the workforce needs to grasp the conceptual underpinnings of the subjects they study in school. They need more advanced knowledge. They need to be fluent at combining knowledge from many different fields to solve problems of a kind their teachers never anticipated. They can only do this with a much deeper and more advanced knowledge of the subjects in the core curriculum than used to be the case. And deep subject matter knowledge is not enough, either. They will have to be able to synthesize established and new knowledge quickly, analyze problems quickly, and from odd angles, and synthesize the knowledge they need in unusual ways to come up with creative and often unique solutions. In many cases, they will need good aesthetic taste as well.

But the students will not have the knowledge, skills, and other attributes they need if their teachers lack them. The top-performing countries are making strenuous efforts to greatly improve the subject matter knowledge of their teachers as well as their ability to analyze and synthesize what they know.

However, one may be good at physics and still be a poor physics teacher. To be good at teaching, one has to be able to connect with students, to engage them, inspire them, communicate easily with them, get inside their heads and figure out what they don't understand, and, ultimately, find a way to help them understand it. And it is not all about conveying content. It is also about helping students understand what the "right thing" is and why it is important to do it when doing so is not easy. It is about persuading a student that she has what it takes to go to college, or to stay in high school when her dad just went to jail and she is living on the sidewalk. It can be about being a friend, a mentor, and a guide.

Most of the countries studied here have made strenuous efforts to raise the quality of their teachers in each of these dimensions. The strategies they have used are sometimes very similar and sometimes very different.

Quality of the Pool

Organizations that care about the quality of their workforce know that the single most important factor in that calculus is the character of the pool from which it recruits. No private firm, much less an entire industry, would prefer to recruit its professional staff from the least- able college graduates if it could do better than that.

Three things directly affect the quality of the pool from which a nation recruits its teachers: (1) the status of teaching in the eyes of the potential recruit relative to the status of other occupations to which he or she aspires, (2) the compensation offered relative to other possible choices, and (3) the conditions of work, or the degree to which the way the work is organized, makes it look more like professional work or like blue-collar work.

It turns out that the countries with the most successful education systems are using a whole set of connected strategies to address all of these factors at the same time that they are addressing the need to get the teachers with the highest possible applied intelligence, the deepest content knowledge, and the best teaching ability.

Standards for Entry to Teacher Education

The logic for raising standards for getting into teacher education programs is the same everywhere. Low standards for entry means that people who could get into professional programs perceived as hard to get into see teaching as attractive only to people who do not have the skill or ability to do anything else, so they do not want any part of them. If these schools and programs are easy to get into, the message in the college or university is that they are low status, and so higher education faculty who can get higher status jobs in their institutions do not want to teach in the education programs. Raising the standards for admission will attract a higher quality of applicant and, at the same time, discourage lower quality applicants, and it will also attract a higher quality faculty, which also attracts a higher quality applicant.

So at this stage of the process, when applicants for teacher education programs are being considered for admission, quality means scores on common, highly regarded measures of general intelligence, such as, in the United States, the ACT and the SAT; high scores or grades in courses in the subjects the applicant plans to teach; and high scores on indicators that show the candidate has the personal attributes needed to connect with, inspire, and support children of the ages he or she plans to teach.

The Japanese have had high standards for entry into the teaching profession since the days of the Meiji Restoration more than a century ago, and Shanghai has raised their standards for entry into higher education programs intended to prepare teachers. In Singapore, young people for a long time have taken A-level exams to get into teachers college. These are very difficult end-of-course examinations built on the English model. Low scores on these exams used to be sufficient for aspiring teachers, but, in recent years, that is no longer true, and scores in the middle of the range are now required. Alternatively, the candidate can now present a polytechnic diploma, which is roughly equivalent to a high-level college degree in the United States. This is an even finer screen, because the polytechnics are in the top of the status hierarchy of the Singapore higher education system. In addition, the successful candidate must also survive a demanding interview conducted by a panel including National Institute of Education faculty chaired by a serving or retired principal. The panel is charged with finding out whether the candidate has the passion, commitment, communication skills, empathy, and disposition to be a good teacher. Only one out of eight applicants survives this whole process.

In Finland, applicants for admission to teachers college who are accepted must survive a two-stage review. The first stage is a document review. To make it through this stage, they must score very high on the national college entrance exams, have a high grade point average on their high school diploma, and have a strong record of out-of-school accomplishments while in high school. In the second phase they must complete a written exam on assigned books in pedagogy, interact with others in situations designed to enable a skilled observer to assess their social interaction and communication skills, and survive interviews in which they are asked, among other things, to explain why they have decided to become teachers. They are admitted to a teacher education program only after they have passed all of these screens. Only one out of ten applicants for entry into Finnish teachers colleges is admitted.

Thus, two of the countries with the highest scores on the 2009 PISA have both instituted rigorous measures used to determine entrance into teacher preparation programs intended to assess all three of the components I used to define teacher quality. The effect of these rigorous measures is to limit Singapore's intake to the top 30 percent of high school graduates and to limit Finland's intake to the top 20 percent.

It is a different story in the United States. The College Board reported in 2008 that when high school graduates going on to college were asked what their intended major was, those who had decided on education scored in the bottom third on their SATs. Their combined scores in mathematics and reading came in at fifty-seven points below the national average.

This should not surprise us, because in the United States most schools of education at both the undergraduate and graduate levels are widely regarded as being very easy to get into. Their status within the university is typically among the lowest of all schools and departments. Not so long ago this was also often the case in the best-performing countries—that is, until they began their march to their present much higher rankings.

There is, of course, an exception to this broad generalization: Teach for America, a program that enrolls very high-performing graduates of many of the most elite colleges in the United States and then assigns them to teaching positions in schools serving disadvantaged students. But the proportion of openings for new teachers every year in the United States filled by Teach for America participants is vanishingly small, and, in any case, most of these high achievers have no interest in continuing as career teachers after they have satisfied the initial requirement. Teaching is viewed by many Teach for America participants as the equivalent of a tour in the Peace Corps, not as a serious career opportunity. The experience of Teach for America makes it plain that it is possible to attract the very best and brightest to teaching, but Teach for America does not itself provide a path to staffing our schools with highly capable teachers for the time and in the numbers needed. Teach for America is not an alternative to building schools of education that can attract first-rate candidates and teach prospective teachers what they will need to know to be successful in our schools.

It has not always been this way. There is reason to believe that the standards for admission to teacher education programs in the United States were once considerably higher. In fact, there is reason to believe that the problem with the American teaching force is not that it has long been of low quality and must now be raised but, rather, that the United States greatly benefited for the better part of a century from having a teaching force largely made up of college-educated women whose choice of career was largely limited to nursing, secretarial work, and teaching and of some minorities whose career choices were similarly constrained. Many women chose teaching because it would allow them to be home when their children came home from school. Because career choices were so limited, the American public reaped the twin blessings of a highly capable teaching force willing to work for below-market wages under poor working conditions. Those who accepted that deal are now leaving the workforce in droves. There are now more women than men in the professional schools preparing young people for many of the most prestigious professions, and they are taking advantage of those opportunities. The United States is now about to get the least-capable candidates applying to our education schools when we need the best.

When we had higher quality candidates applying to our teachers colleges, the colleges could afford to be more selective. That is why there is good reason to believe that the standards for entry into teacher education have been sliding. When the baby boomers were leaving college, many people predicted that the coming baby dearth was going to result in great reductions in the size of college student bodies as the size of the whole cohort declined dramatically. However, while the size of the cohort certainly declined, the size of student bodies did not. The data suggest that the colleges made a fateful decision to lower their standards in order to fill their classrooms. There is every reason to believe that this happened in our teachers colleges in just the same way it happened in other colleges, but it was also at this time that opportunities for women and minorities greatly expanded, which would mean that the quality of applicants in teachers colleges would have suffered from both of these causes, not just one. Furthermore, analysts are now noticing a large falloff in applications for admission to teachers colleges all over the country, a result of the financial crisis. Potential candidates, who used to view teaching as almost immune from the business cycle and therefore one of the most secure of all occupations, are noticing that teachers are being laid off in very large numbers and now see teaching as a very risky bet.

Taken together—highly qualified college educated women and minorities abandoning teaching as a career, the drop in admission standards following the baby boom, and the decision by many capable students to avoid teaching because of the widespread teacher layoffs—we can see the danger ahead for the United States. All we need to do to acquire a very poor teaching force is do nothing. Inaction, not action, will bring about this result. It is critical that this trend be reversed. We cannot afford to continue bottom-fishing for prospective teachers while the best-performing countries are cream skimming.

Attracting Top-Flight Students

Most of our competitors have formal policies that peg teachers' compensation to the top ranges of their civil servant compensation system or to the compensation of other professionals, such as engineers, in the private sector. Their aim is to make sure that young people making career choices see teaching as offering compensation comparable to that offered by the more attractive professions. Finland's teachers appear to get paid a little less, relatively speaking, than teachers in the other top countries, but, because salaries for everyone are very flat in Finland, as compared to most other countries, and the status of teachers is so high, they still get excellent candidates.

At the International Summit on the Teaching Profession convened by Secretary Arne Duncan in New York City in March 2011, Singapore's minister of education observed that the goal of compensation policy ought to be to "take compensation off the table" as a consideration when able young people are making career decisions. There was wide agreement on that point among the ministers of the other top-performing countries.

The United States, however, is far from the Singapore minister's standard. According to the National Association of Colleges and Employers, teachers earn a national average starting salary of $30,377. That compares with $43,635 for computer programmers, $44,668 for accountants, and $45,570 for registered nurses. And none of these occupations is among the leading professions, which provide starting salaries that are even higher. Not only do teachers make markedly less than other occupations requiring the same level of education, but census data show that teachers have been falling farther and farther behind the average compensation for occupations requiring a college degree for sixty years. The average earnings for workers with college degrees are now 50 percent higher than average teachers' salaries, which is a very long way indeed from the Singapore education minister's standard.

Making sure that initial and average compensation for teachers is competitive is essential. But there are other issues having to do with compensation and financial incentives for choosing teaching as a career that other nations have addressed and we have not.

Shanghai, for example, has waived its charges for tuition for teacher education and offered early admissions to students applying to teacher education programs. This has made teaching a very attractive career choice, especially for students from the poorer regions who have strong academic backgrounds. Although the compensation for teachers in China is low by international standards, teachers in that country can make substantial additional income from tutoring. And the government also offers bonuses to teachers willing to teach in rural areas. The result of these and other initiatives has now made teaching the second- or third-most-popular career choice in China.

But it is obvious that if compensation is not adequate, raising standards for admission to teacher preparation programs in universities, raising the standards for licensure, and refusing to waive those standards in the face of teachers' shortages will simply guarantee shortages of teachers into the indefinite future.

It turns out that total compensation of teachers is more competitive than cash compensation taken by itself, because American teachers' compensation, like that of civil servants generally, is heavily weighted toward retirement benefits. Costrell and Podgursky report that in 2008 employer contributions to teachers' retirement plans was 14.6 percent of earnings, compared to 10.4 percent for private professionals, this difference having more than doubled in the four years since the data were first collected. The problem with this is that while it provides a strong incentive for experienced teachers to stay in teaching longer than they might otherwise, it makes teaching unattractive to young people who are more concerned about supporting new families than they are about their retirement.

The trajectory of cash compensation is also important. Most American teachers top out quickly. And even when there are adjustments for differences in the quality of teaching, which is rarely done, they are very small. Countries that are restructuring teachers' careers are adjusting compensation as teachers ascend career ladders within the profession and in administration and as they take on more authority and responsibility. Some countries—again, Singapore is a good example—are even paying bonuses of up to 30 percent to teachers who are found to be particularly effective on a wide range of measures. And many of those countries, not just China, are paying more to teachers who are willing to work in outlying areas or who have qualifications that are in short supply.

Institutional Settings

As late as the 1970s, Finnish teachers were prepared in relatively low-status colleges dedicated to teacher education. Now, all their teachers are educated in the country's major universities. This was not accomplished by simply allowing the former teachers colleges to become universities but by sending prospective teachers to institutions with the highest status in the postsecondary system.

Years ago, prospective teachers in Singapore were also trained in a separate and relatively low-status college for teacher training. Then Singapore created the National Institute of Education (NIE) to train its teachers. More recently, the government incorporated the NIE into Nanyang Technological University, a top-tier institution in Singapore's higher education system. Nanyang has partnerships with many of the world's most highly regarded research universities and is ranked as having one of the best business schools in the world. NIE is now a major research institution in its own right and, at the same time, is a very high-status component of Singapore's postsecondary education system.

Thus, many of these top-performing countries have not only greatly raised their standards for getting into higher education institutions preparing teachers but most have moved teacher education out of their lower-tier institutions and into their top-tier institutions. This has had the effect of further raising the status of teaching, improving the quality of faculty, improving the quality of research on education, facilitating the dissemination of high-quality research to prospective teachers, and creating a teaching force that is less likely to put up with old forms of work once they become school teachers.

Teacher education in the United States is no longer done in normal schools, but it is generally done in second- and third-tier, relatively low-status institutions, many of which were formerly normal schools. When it is done within major universities, it is typically accorded the low status associated with the other feminized occupations. While graduate study in education is often done in the major research universities, many of the institutions that offer professional training in school administration and education research do not offer professional training to school teachers. This is very similar to the profile that many of the leading countries abandoned ten or more years ago.

Content of Teacher Education and Induction

I've combined here two functions usually thought of quite separately: what prospective teachers are taught about their craft before entering service and what they are taught immediately after entering service. The reason I have done that is that some top-performing countries rely heavily on preservice teacher education to teach the skills of the craft and others put much more emphasis on the use of apprenticeship-style instruction in the workplace, after the teacher has been hired, to convey the essential craft skills.

Consider first the approach taken by Finland. The Finns require all of their teachers, including their primary school teachers, to have master's degrees. Primary teachers major in education, but they must minor in at least two of the subjects in the primary curriculum. These minors are taken not in the education schools but in the arts and sciences departments of the university. Upper-grade teachers must major in the subject they will be teaching. Their education in pedagogy is either integrated into their five-year program or provided full time in the master's year, after the student has completed a bachelors program with a major in the subject that person will teach. Candidates who already have such a master's degree must get another master's degree in teaching. There are no alternative routes to entering the teaching force in Finland. Clearly, the Finns place a very high value on having teachers who have really mastered the subjects they will teach and on giving teachers the skills they will need to teach those subjects well once they arrive in the classroom.

Now consider the approach taken by Shanghai. In Shanghai, 90 percent of the teacher preparation program is devoted to mastery of the subject the prospective teacher will be teaching. A school mathematics teacher in training is expected to take the same undergraduate mathematics curriculum as undergraduates who will go on to do graduate work in mathematics—a very demanding curriculum. It is clear that the Shanghai authorities are at least as determined as the Finns that the teachers who go on to teach a subject know as much about its content by the time they complete their undergraduate program as do those people who will go on to work (as physicists or chemists or mathematicians) in the field. And this is also the case for their future elementary school teachers as it is for their secondary school teachers.

The comparison with American policy and practice on the same point is very telling. Whereas elementary school teachers in these two other countries specialize in math and science or in social studies and language, Americans preparing to become elementary school teachers do not. Most American elementary school teachers know little math or science, and many are very uncomfortable with these subjects. That is hardly true of their counterparts in Finland or Shanghai. And some of our secondary school math and science teachers know a good deal less than their counterparts in those countries.

It is also true that once someone becomes a teacher in the United States, irrespective of the arena in which she is trained, she can be assigned to teach a subject in which she was never really trained at all. An anecdote related to this point is worth telling. Some years ago, Bill Schmidt, among the most distinguished Americans who have been benchmarking the performance of the leading nations over the years, and who led the American team working on the Trends in International Mathematics and Science Study (TIMSS) research program, was in a meeting with his other colleagues from the countries designing the tests and research studies. One of the Americans made a pitch for including a background question in the research instrument that would have asked how many teachers of mathematics and science in each country were teaching subjects they had not been prepared to teach. There was an expression of astonishment from the representatives of all the countries, except those from the United States. It simply was not done. Teachers were not permitted to teach outside their subject. There was no need to ask this question. The topic was never raised again. Evidently, among all the industrialized countries, only the United States allows its teachers to teach subjects they have not been highly trained in.

The cumulative result of these differences is a much greater likelihood that, from the first grade to the last, schoolchildren in Shanghai and Finland will be taught by teachers who have a better command of the subjects they will be teaching than will schoolchildren in the United States. The consequences of this are incalculable.

The question of policy and practice concerning the standards to be met by teachers with respect to pedagogy is a very important issue in both Finland and Shanghai, but the strategies for achieving excellence in this important arena are very different in these two countries.

The Finns place most of their faith in developing the pedagogical skills of their future teachers while they are still in preservice training. Obviously, the Finns believe it is very important for prospective teachers to get a strong background in pedagogy before entering the teaching force. They provide a strong background in the research underlying teaching, and they also provide their teachers with strong research skills. All teacher candidates have to complete a research-based thesis. Prospective teachers are expected to learn a lot about subject-specific pedagogy. There is considerable emphasis in the teacher education curriculum on the development of the candidate's skills at diagnosing student problems and learning how to choose the right solution for those problems based on the relevant research. And there is a very strong clinical element in the program, including a full year of practice teaching done under the close supervision of a master teacher.

Whereas the Finns take five years or more to educate a teacher and divide that time almost equally between content training and pedagogical training, the Chinese devote 90 percent of the available time during preservice training to deep mastery of the subject the prospective teacher is preparing to teach. The remaining time available for teacher education—only 10 percent of the total—is devoted to a program of instruction in education theory, the psychology of learning, and teaching methods that has not changed in many years and that many observers think is out-of-date.

At first glance, it would appear that the Finns believe in the importance of substantial instruction in pedagogy and the Chinese do not. But that is not the case. In Shanghai, a new teacher is expected to spend the first year of employment as a teacher under the intense supervision of a master teacher. The master teachers are relieved of all or most of their classroom responsibilities in order to allow them to play this role. These master teachers often sit in on every lesson taught by the new teacher and provide intense coaching. And, in turn, the new teacher will also observe the master teaching many lessons.

Recall that the Finns have decided that it is essential that their prospective teachers learn as much as possible about how to diagnose the nuances of the difficulties students experience in mastering difficult material, as well as how to identify the right techniques and methods to address those problems. They put a lot of effort into building their prospective teachers' skills in this arena before they enter service. The Chinese are no less concerned than the Finns that their teachers master the art of teaching, but they have a very different strategy for accomplishing this aim. They put most of their faith in a very demanding apprenticeship strategy that begins as soon as the teachers college graduates are hired.

Both countries devote significant resources to the development of the pedagogical skills of their recruits. It is certainly true that American schools of education teach methods courses. But American teachers complain constantly that what they learn in these courses is of very little value when they enter real classrooms. By all accounts, the efforts of the Finns and the Chinese to give their prospective teachers and beginning teachers much better-supported initial classroom experience—at the hands of master teachers who can build their skills in recognizing specific problems that students have in learning the subjects they will teach and figuring out which research-based techniques are appropriate to address those problems—is key to those countries' success.

The careful attention to the development of skills in diagnosis and prescription, in the development of effective lessons, in the adjustment of instruction to the actual needs of students under the extended and intensive guidance of master teachers has no counterpart in the American experience. Little attention is typically devoted to detailed instruction in diagnosis and prescription, except, in some instances, in the case of special education. The typical clinical experience of American candidate teachers is usually of poor quality, too brief, unconnected to the rest of their instructional program, and provided by classroom teachers who cannot, on the whole, reasonably be called "master teachers." Once graduated from teachers colleges and hired by their first school district, American teachers are typically put in a sink-or-swim situation with little or no support from experienced teachers or supervisors and often in the most demanding classroom situations. Once again, the contrast with the experience of their Shanghai and Finnish colleagues could not be more stark.

It is worth pointing out, however, that the training of American medical doctors rests firmly on the very elements just described as the basis of the training of Finnish and Shanghai educators. American medical doctors are supposed to have a thorough background in the sciences that underlie medicine, physiology, and pathology. Their training is essentially clinical in nature and is provided by master practitioners. The heart of the training is a form of apprenticeship known as "rounds" and "residencies." The most important aspect of their training is developing skills in diagnosis and prescription based on a firm knowledge of the relevant research. This training takes place not in third-tier, low-status institutions but in professional schools in top research universities. While most of these features have been adapted to the needs of professional teaching by most of our top competitors, none yet typifies American practice.

Licensure and Standards for Entry

When teacher shortages develop in the United States, the government's response is almost always to waive the regulations defining the minimum qualifications for teaching in public schools. When there is a shortage of civil engineers, we do not say that it is no longer necessary to make sure that civil engineers have the qualifications needed to design safe bridges. Neither do we decide that doctors no longer need to meet the minimum requirements for licensure if there's a dearth of doctors. If there is a shortage in those fields, or in virtually all truly professional fields, compensation increases until the market clears and the shortage disappears.

There is no clearer sign of society's lack of respect for teachers and teaching than its view that, in the end, what really matters is having a warm body in front of their children, irrespective of that person's qualifications to teach. The best-performing nations do not do this. They do not have to. They have many more fully qualified applicants for teaching positions than positions available.

Curriculum and Continuing Professional Development

Most Americans would not naturally combine these two topics—but that may be part of our larger problem, because it does come quite naturally to educators in many of the top-performing Asian countries.

Consider the Japanese practice of lesson study. In Japanese schools, the faculty works together to develop new lessons or redesign existing lessons to make them more engaging. Once developed, that lesson is demonstrated by one of the teachers and critiqued by the others and revised until the faculty is happy with it. Thereafter a particularly capable teacher will demonstrate it for others and, in turn, critique their practice when they teach it. Throughout, the development process calls on the latest research. Teachers who get very good at leading this work are often called on to demonstrate their lessons to other schools and even to teachers in other districts and provinces. In this way, instructional development and professional development are merged and the professional development becomes an integral part of the process of improving instruction in the school as informed by the latest and best research. In fact, Japanese teachers are taught research skills in their preservice training so that this local, teacher-led development process is supported by the kind of research skills needed to make sophisticated judgments about the effectiveness of their local development work.

In the United States, teachers are generally the objects of research rather than participants in the research process itself. The topics for professional development are often chosen by administrators in the central office rather than by teachers seeking to improve their own practices on terms of their choosing. Because the topics chosen for professional development are typically not the topics the teachers would themselves have chosen, they often perceive the professional development they get as not particularly helpful.

The Japanese model is certainly not the only model used in the top-performing countries, but it suggests the possibilities that come to mind when teachers are viewed as highly competent professionals who are expected to take the lead in defining what good practice is, advancing that practice, and keeping up-to-date on the latest advancements—which is exactly what happens in professions that are led by members of the profession rather than by those who are administratively responsible for their work.

All over the world, well-run companies and government agencies give a lot of thought not only to how they can source their staff from the most capable pool possible but also how they can offer their best people attractive careers in the agency or company, careers of increasing responsibility and authority, and the increased compensation and status that come with those jobs. Typically, they carefully groom their most promising staff for the next steps on the ladder, giving them at each stage the training they will need for the next job, providing mentors who can help them develop the right skills, and so on.

That is what Singapore does for its professional educators. Having done its best to make sure that they have a very talented pool from which to source their teachers, it recruits the best and then provides top-level training for them. But it does not end there. Education policy makers have carefully structured several distinct career lines that are available to the new recruits. For each career line, they have designed programs of training that are matched, step by step, to each rung of the ladder. The system selects those people for further training who have the best qualifications, get the best ratings, and have done the best in the training for the next position. In this way, Singapore carefully nurtures its talent pool, reserving the most expensive training for the people best prepared to use it well.

When teachers in Singapore are first hired, they become eligible to choose among three possible career ladders. One leads to the position of principal master teacher through the intermediate steps of senior teacher, lead teacher, master teacher, and, finally, principal master teacher. That is the teaching track. Teachers who want a career in administration proceed through subject head/level head, head of department, vice principal, principal, cluster superintendent, deputy director, director, and, lastly, director-general of education, the top spot. That is the leadership track. And there is another track, the senior specialist track, that is designed to describe the trajectory of a career in the Ministry of Education in various specialized areas such as curriculum and instructional design and education research and statistics. Highly qualified candidates for advancement in this system may be offered scholarships for advanced study in Singapore and in leading universities all over the world. They may be deliberately rotated among carefully selected assignments in the schools to give them the kind of experience the ministry is looking for.

It is fair to say that neither the United States nor any of the individual states has policies designed to create a high-quality pool from which we select candidates for teacher training. We often simply take whoever shows up. The pool is self-selected. With rare exceptions, we do not have well-defined paths for teachers who want to advance their careers but stay in teaching. Nor, obviously, have we defined the training and further education that candidates for advancement on that nonexistent path must complete in order to be eligible for advancement. Indeed, unlike the Singapore government, we have not defined what qualities we are looking for in teachers that would qualify them for advancement.

This section on teacher quality is one of the longest in this chapter, and it is easy to lose the thread. But there is one. We see two images, one of teaching in the United States and the other of teaching in the countries with the world's most effective education systems. And they are very different.

The prevailing view in the United States is that our teachers need not come from the more able strata of the college-educated population. We behave as if we believe that only a few weeks of training is needed to do what they have to do, a sure sign that we do not believe teaching is a profession at all. If they do get more training, it can certainly be done in very low-status institutions; and if they do not get much training, it's no big deal. If there is a shortage of teachers, we quickly waive the very low standards we insist on in boom times. We congratulate ourselves on offering $10,000 signing bonuses to teachers when we worry about the qualifications of the ones we are getting, and then we wonder why we cannot attract a better quality of candidate or simply more candidates. We do little or nothing about starting salaries that will not permit a young teacher to support a small family in the style to which college graduates are accustomed in this country. In most places, teaching continues to be a dead-end career, with no routes up except those that lead out of teaching. We make teachers the objects of research rather the people who do research. We talk a lot about getting rid of the worst teachers—as if that was our biggest problem—but not at all about doing what is necessary to get better ones, thus accomplishing little but the destruction of teacher morale. And we do all of this while talking a lot about teacher quality.

So it should surprise no one that we have a teacher quality problem.

When we look at the countries topping the education league tables, we see that teaching is not just referred to as a profession but is actually treated as one. Those countries are willing to compensate teachers in the same way they compensate people in the professions that, until recently, have been heavily dominated by men. They take their professional training seriously. It is lengthy and done in high-prestige institutions. The standards for getting into those institutions are very high, and the competition to get into them on the part of top-notch students is equally stiff. The training programs mimic the way doctors and other highly regarded professionals are trained. They are carefully mentored by very capable people when they are hired. They are at the heart of the process of improving the system, not the object of that process, and their career prospects depend on their professional contribution. It would appear that the top-performing countries are far along in a process of converting their teachers from blue-collar workers to professionals on a par with the other professions. So is it any wonder that these countries are experiencing much better results than the United States?

Of course, if teaching moves away from a Tayloristic work organization and takes on the attributes of a true profession, that will have implications for our teacher unions and their contracts. American labor law is firmly grounded in the mass production model of work organization and assumes that workers and management will be locked in eternal conflict. The National Labor Relations Act assumes that conflictual relationship and sets out the rules under which it will work. But, although that act of Congress was intended to apply only to the private sector, it was eventually applied to the public sector by most states, and that resulted in the work rules and contract provisions that are now giving this country so much trouble. Those rules can and should be changed. As the states decide to pay teachers like professionals and provide teachers the kind of professional responsibility and autonomy that other professions have, the teachers will need to be willing to write contracts that move away from the blue-collar model and toward contracts that embrace a professional model of work organization, in which teachers take responsibility for raising teaching standards to world-class levels, for the performance of students, for working as many hours as it takes to get the work done, for evaluating the work of their colleagues, for recommending termination for teachers who do not measure up to high standards, and so on.

Teachers will have to give up seniority rights of assignment and retention and other hallmarks of the blue-collar work environment, and they will have to accept the proposition that some teachers will be paid more than others and have different responsibilities in recognition of their superior performance. That is part of what it means to be a professional. In exchange, of course, they will earn once again the high regard of the public and their peers, be paid like engineers and architects and doctors and enjoy the same high status in the community and their country that their colleagues in the top-performing countries enjoy.

PRINCIPAL QUALITY

In much of the rest of the industrialized world, school leaders are called "head teachers" because they continue to teach while they manage. Typically appointed because of their superior teaching ability, they are still viewed as teachers but with additional responsibilities.

This is not the case in the United States probably because schools in most other countries are smaller than our schools, but also perhaps because American schools typically have less discretion, especially in the suburbs and cities, and report to district central offices that are larger, often much larger, than their counterparts in most other countries. Having an intermediate layer of administration that is both larger and closer produces much more detailed and frequent requests and demands for information and compliance than school heads in most other countries experience. That, too, makes school leadership a full-time job.

One result of this difference is that few of the countries with the most successful education systems have separate licensure for school heads or specialized training for them, although that is beginning to change as many of the leading countries are now realizing that they may be able to improve their systems even further by attending more to the selection, training, and licensure of school heads.

Singapore, an exception to the general rule, takes the training of school principals very seriously, offering a separate, defined career path for teachers who seek school and district leadership positions. Candidates for principal positions must take a six-month training program consisting of coursework, supervised practice, and mentorship, all monitored against clear definitions of the qualities that the Singapore government is looking for in their principals. The mentoring component of the program takes place during two sessions, each a month long. Aspiring principals shadow principals who have been hand-picked by the ministry for their outstanding leadership qualities. The process is mediated by a faculty member from the National Institute of Education.

INSTRUCTION

Focusing on the relative effectiveness of different instructional strategies is important in its own right, but it is also important because of other factors affecting student achievement.

The chapter on Japan describes an approach to instruction that can reasonably be described as whole-class instruction or large-group instruction, but definitely not lecturing. We related how the teacher sets an assignment for the class, walks up and down the rows of students working the problem, picks out students using very different strategies for solving the problem, and asks the students who devised those strategies to come to the board, one by one, and describe their approach to the problem. The aim is not to focus on the right solution but to provoke an extended class discussion of the various strategies used to get to a solution. This discussion of the strategies employed by the students is intended to help them understand why the right solution works, to help them reach a deeper understanding of the conceptual underpinnings of the topic under study. Because the success of this technique depends on identifying a good variety of solution strategies, teachers in Japan want large class sizes, not small ones. This approach to instruction is characteristic not only of Japan but of many other East Asian countries as well. (Of all the strategies available to improve student performance, decreasing class size is among the most expensive and least effective. Instructional strategies that improve the outcome by increasing class size can release very large sums of money that can also improve student achievement, thus creating a very large multiplier effect.)

But the instructional methods used in Finland are different from those used in Japan, especially at the high school level. While the Japanese are putting a relatively new emphasis on learning as distinguished from teaching—on promoting more student initiative in the learning process—Japanese teachers are still expected to stay pretty close to the national curriculum as promulgated by the ministry, and that curriculum is pretty clearly spelled out. Finland, however, has been pressing hard in recent years toward a teaching and learning style in which the student takes increasing responsibility for the learning process. The Finns have been paring down the length of their curriculum guidance and providing many more choices with respect to what is studied by modularizing the curriculum at the upper-secondary level and letting the students assemble their own curriculum.

This trend in curriculum is accompanied by a complementary trend in learning and instructional style away from whole-group instruction and toward problem- and project-based learning pursued individually and in teams. To the extent that Finnish students select and design their own projects and decide how to go about addressing them, this becomes student-directed learning in which the teacher becomes a facilitator rather than director of the learning process, and the object of instruction becomes not only the acquisition of subject-based knowledge and skill but also the ability to frame problems to make them more amenable to solution, to identify possible sources of information that bear on the problem at hand, to analyze that information, to synthesize what has been learned, to frame a solution, and then to communicate the solution. What has just been defined is a disciplined learning process intended to enable the learner to come up with sophisticated and creative solutions to novel problems. Increasingly, this is the object of Finnish education. It requires teachers whose great skill is not so much the development of great lessons but is stimulating, facilitating, mentoring, and partnering with students in the learning process, teachers who can create learning environments that are more like workshops than classrooms, whose intellectual skills and knowledge are deep enough and flexible enough for them to follow and lead their students in very unpredictable directions.

But we hasten to add that self-directed problem- and project-based learning can easily turn into a poor substitute for deep mastery of the underlying subjects in the curriculum. When the student lacks a firm command of the nuances of the core subjects in the curriculum, project- and problem-based curricula often result in very shallow knowledge gained in the classroom. What makes it work in Finland is the fact that these pedagogies and learning methods rest on top of solid mastery of the core subjects in the curriculum that Finnish students acquire in the lower grades.

Design for Equity

SCHOOL FINANCE

Local control of school finance has been an emblem of American education for a very long time and is a deeply ingrained feature of our system. In essence, in many states, groups of citizens have been allowed to gather together to form their own education taxing districts. The result is that wealthy parents, by forming their own taxing districts, can drive their tax rates very low while benefiting from very high tax yields. At the other end of this spectrum, people who cannot afford very much for housing end up congregated together in districts where they must tax themselves at very high rates to produce a very low yield. In such a system, the children of the wealthiest families get the best teachers and the best of all the other available education resources, and the families with the least money get the worst teachers and the worst of everything else as well.

Not one of the top-performing countries has a school finance system that works this way. Every one of them has been moving away from local control, if they ever embraced it, and toward systems designed to distribute resources in ways intended to enable all students to achieve high standards. That does not mean equal funding for all students. It means differential funding. It means unequal funding designed to come as close as possible to ensuring high achievement across the board.

One interesting case is Shanghai. Until recently, China had a system of "key schools," which were open only to Communist Party members and operated as a national system of elite schools at a much higher per-pupil cost than the average Chinese state schools. This system of key schools is being dismantled.

Perhaps the most interesting case from an American perspective is Canada. Two decades ago and more, elementary and secondary education in most of the provinces was funded much the way it is in the United States, with each community raising much of the money locally, with the provinces providing additional sums intended to moderate the disparities in per-student funding that such a system inevitably produces. But about twenty years ago this began to change. Conservative governments, in response to complaints from citizens about skyrocketing local tax rates, initiated a move to steadily reduce reliance on local taxes and to increase the portion of the total budget paid for by the province. Now, in the biggest provinces, little if any of the money for public education is raised locally. All or almost all comes from the province. Not surprisingly, the gross inequities that came with raising money locally are gone too, and Canada, like the other top-performing countries, is moving toward a funding system intended to promote high achievement among all students—which means putting more money behind hard-to-educate children than behind children who are easier to educate.

SECONDARY SCHOOL ORGANIZATION

When we look far enough back into the histories of most industrial nations, we usually come to a time when their primary schools were comprehensive (in the sense that students from all social classes were mixed together in all, or almost all, the classrooms) and the upper grades were not. As secondary education developed in most countries, separate schools were created for three groups of students: the children of the working class, the children of the artisans and shopkeepers, and the children of the nobles (or, later, the professionals, and the owners and managers of the larger enterprises).

In some countries, secondary schools were comprehensive in their enrollment. But, as in the United States, there were different tracks within those comprehensive schools for the children of different social classes, so the result for the students was the same as in those countries that had different schools for students from different social classes. Depending on the country, the break between the comprehensive lower schools and the tracked upper grades might come as early as the end of grade 4.

In the Scandinavian countries, after World War II, the period of comprehensive basic education for all students was extended to the point that most of these countries now have common schools through grades 9 or 10. Students from all backgrounds attend these schools, and they all get the same curriculum. In these and some other countries, it is not until a student is sixteen that education paths begin to diverge.

Inevitably, as the previously separate education programs are merged and the decision to give all students substantially the same education is made, there is a national discussion about the standard against which that education will be set. In the countries with the high-performing education systems, that argument was almost always settled by a decision that the standard would be the same standard that was formerly applied only to the students in the top track.

As we saw earlier, this battle took place in Japan more than a century ago. Singapore abandoned tracking in its primary schools, but the standard for its lowest track just above primary school is still well above the average standard of performance for the OECD nations. The United States calls its high schools comprehensive schools, but it still offers different courses set to very different challenge levels to students from different social backgrounds. The implementation of the Common Core State Standards might change that, but for now few American high schools expect most of their students to reach a global standard of academic achievement by the end of grade 9 or 10—which is exactly what the top-performing countries are expecting of their students.

FIXED STANDARDS, FLEXIBLE SUPPORT

In countries that expect their ninth or tenth graders to achieve at internationally benchmarked levels, typically very few students are left behind and very few are pushed ahead by more than one grade a year. Virtually all but the special education students make a grade of progress for each year they are in school, against very demanding standards. This requires very different supports for students than a system, like the United States', that is designed to operate by sorting students out along a long performance curve. In a system in which almost all students are expected to perform at high levels, the standard is fixed and the support varies to the extent needed to make sure that all students get to the finish line.

As already noted, this means that financial resources are allocated so that students who need more help are given more financial resources so they can get that help. It also means that the students who are farthest behind get the best teachers, as is the case in Singapore. It is also the case in Singapore that the students who need help get more time, meaning after school, on weekends, and during the summer.

In Finland and many Asian nations, teachers are carefully trained to diagnose very quickly and accurately students who are beginning to fall behind, and they are given the skills needed to figure out what those students need to get back on track quickly. In a sorting system, those skills are not very important, but in a system intended to get virtually all students up to a high standard and to keep them there, year after year, they are essential.

LOW-PERFORMING SCHOOLS

Sometimes it is not the student that is underperforming, but the school. This appears not to be a problem in Finland, where the variation in school performance is among the lowest in the world. Shanghai addresses this problem by requiring schools performing well to take responsibility for managing schools that are not performing as well by assigning high-performing staff members in high-performing schools to work in lower performing schools and by posting key staff members in low-performing schools to temporary assignments in high-performing schools in order to gain the skills they need before sending them back to their home school. Shanghai has also graded its schools by academic performance and the physical condition of its schools and shut down those in which both performance and physical condition did not justify continuation, sending the students and faculty to other schools as it built new facilities to replace those in poor physical condition. Other Asian cities and nations have similar policies.

Design for Productivity

MANAGEMENT PARADIGM

For many years, American policy makers have alternated between the search for quality and the quest for equity. What we are discovering is that other countries have figured out how to get both in greater measure. It would be natural for American educators to sigh and whisper that it would be wonderful to have both, but there is no more money. Perhaps the most important discovery is that other countries have not only figured out how to get greater quality and far more equity, but they have figured out how to do that while spending substantially less than we do. They have done it by adopting a very different way to organize the work of schooling.

The chief management guru of the early twentieth century was Frederick Winslow Taylor. His counterpart for the latter half of the century was Peter Drucker. Their messages were very different.

Taylor codified the methods of scientific management. Writing at the apogee of the mass production system, Taylor lived in a world in which goods and services once available only to the royalty and nobility were becoming increasingly available to Everyman, courtesy of very complex, very expensive machines that could turn out vast numbers of identical parts at remarkably low cost. Prior to the mass production system, most finished products of any complexity were produced by craftsmen, one at a time, each object requiring great skill. But in the mass production system, many fewer people—mainly the engineers who designed the machines and processes—needed high-level skills. Most other workers—from the people who minded the machines, to those who assembled the parts into finished products, to the clerks and the farm hands—required only basic literacy. Taylor declared that the way to run the system most efficiently was to observe many people doing these low-level tasks, figure out who did them most efficiently, and then make sure that everyone did it that way. Workers were just like the interchangeable parts they assembled. One was as good as another. Skill was not terribly important. Management just needed to make sure someone was doing the work and doing it efficiently.

The mass production method affected American industry more profoundly than that of any other major country. It was at its zenith when the current form of American education was set in place. Though industry has long since moved on, the organization of work in American education has not.

Peter Drucker, in the 1970s, opined that the age of mass production had reached its limit. The future, he said, belonged to firms and nations that embraced knowledge work and knowledge workers. By "knowledge work and knowledge workers," he meant something like "professional work and professional workers." Advanced industrial societies, Drucker said, would be able to maintain a high standard of living only if most of the workers were doing work that depended on them having a very high level of knowledge and the ability to apply that knowledge, case by case, to the challenges they faced every day. The challenges would be different, and so they would require a great deal of discretion as they figured out how best to respond to each challenge.

Taylor's methods would not work in such a situation. Workers would no longer be interchangeable. They would have to be managed in the same way professionals are managed and for the same reasons. Rather than telling the workers just what to do and how to do it, managers would have to hire and train high-quality staff, set the goals, support the workers in every possible way, and then get out of their way. The workers, who would themselves be the experts in the work, would have to figure out how best to meet the challenges they faced and would have to hold each other accountable for delivering top performance.

In the world of knowledge work, excellence would be rewarded. Blue-collar factory workers, Drucker said, expected an honest day's pay for an honest day's work. But knowledge workers expected an extraordinary day's pay for an extraordinary day's work, like professionals in any field.

In varying degrees, all of the countries with high-performing education systems have been moving toward the management paradigm offered by Drucker. Few embraced Taylor's system in its schools as avidly as the United States did. But Taylor's paradigm is still alive and well in American schools. It still influences our conception of teachers' work, the way we organize our schools, the way we talk about accountability, the way management in our schools relates to our unions, the way we respond to teacher shortages, the status of teacher colleges in our education system, and much, much more. Recall that most of our current teaching work force is made up of women and minorities who signed up for teaching at a time when college-educated women and some minorities had a very narrow choice of careers. When they retire, the United States is very unlikely to get the quality of teachers we need in the quantity we need them until we replace the Tayloristic paradigm of work organization with the model advocated by Drucker.

This is, of course, just what the top-performing education systems have been doing for years. The cases of Finland and Ontario are textbook examples of moves to forms of work organization in which teachers are treated much more like professionals and much less like blue-collar workers, cases in which management has been exercising progressively less control and providing progressively more support and getting better and better results as a consequence.

ACCOUNTABILITY AND AUTONOMY

Accountability is one example of the point just made. In Tayloristic management systems, the workers at each level are accountable to their supervisor. In many situations, the worker is simply responsible for putting in an honest day's work for the requisite time on the clock. In others, the worker is paid by the units produced. In professional workplaces, however, while there is some element of accountability to the supervisor, there is usually a major component of responsibility to professional colleagues for the quality and quantity of work performed. In professional workplaces, the workers are expected to put in whatever time it takes to get the work done. They feel a strong sense of responsibility to their colleagues to do their level best and they know that, at the end of the day, it is their colleagues, along with their supervisor, who will play a major role in determining their career prospects and very likely their compensation, both of which will depend on very nuanced judgments about their professional contribution to the work of the organization.

We can think of Tayloristic workplaces as emphasizing vertical accountability and professional workplaces as emphasizing lateral accountability. In Tayloristic workplaces, it is always very clear who the workers are and who management is. In professional workplaces, it is often the case that the professionals are organized as a partnership and that the workers are also the managers as well as the owners. Even when this is not the case, there is typically a strong element of lateral accountability in professional workplaces, and it is usually also the case in professional workplaces that the workers are also managers, though they may not also be owners.

These differences in accountability between Tayloristic management systems and professional systems are a function of the nature of the work. If the work can be done by semi-skilled people who are essentially interchangeable and whose work is most efficiently managed by supervisors who are in a position to direct the work in detail by virtue of their superior knowledge, then a top-down system of accountability will probably work best. But if the work is of the kind that Drucker was interested in, then the people in the best position to make the judgments about the way the service will be delivered will be those who are actually doing the work, and they will have to have a wide range of discretion in determining how it will be done. The incentives that work in a Tayloristic workplace will not work in a professional workplace. Professionals, as Drucker pointed out, are much more motivated by the need to excel in the eyes of their professional colleagues and to meet professional norms. They will do whatever it takes, knowing that, if they don't, they could lose not only their job but also the respect of colleagues whose respect they greatly value.

The other side of increased lateral accountability is increased professional autonomy. When there is one best way to get the work done, the job of management is to make sure it gets done that way. But when the best way to get the work done is a function of a particular situation, then the professional must be free to make the decision as to how the service will be delivered to the client. One way to frame this is to say that management has little choice in that situation but to trust the professional to know what to do and to do it.

But schools are small societies, not collectives in which each professional is an individual entrepreneur. Some teachers are better at one aspect of the overall work than another, just as some attorneys are better at bringing in new clients and others are better at research and writing and still others are better at litigating. The law firm works best when these different skills and abilities come together in one team. The senior members of the workforce are in the best position to judge the contributions of each member of the team. Each has plenty of professional autonomy, but each is responsible to the other members of the team for the quality and timeliness of their work. And so it is with a school.

There is a general trend among the countries with the most successful education systems away from Tayloristic models and toward the kinds of accountability systems associated with professional work. The Japanese emphasis on earning the respect of the group puts great pressure on Japanese teachers to be accountable to the rest of the faculty for the effort they put into their work and the quality of that work. In recent years, the Japanese education ministry has, somewhat cautiously, begun to provide progressively less explicit direction to the schools and to provide greater degrees of freedom to school faculties with respect to how the curriculum will be implemented, as well as on other matters. There are similar trends in Singapore and China.

The Finnish reforms in the 1970s resulted in a much-admired and rather detailed specification of the Finnish curriculum. But since then there has been a steady reduction in the detail with which the curriculum has been specified, and the ministry has abolished the Finnish inspectorate. All this has happened in a country in which there are no national examinations of all the students, so that neither schools nor teachers can be held accountable for their performance on the basis of data from such examinations. All of these policy positions are a measure of the high degree of trust that the Finns have in their teachers. At the same time, the high performance of Finnish students is a testament to the degree to which Finnish professionals hold each other accountable for the quality of their work and the effort they put into it.

The Canadian province of Ontario is another case, much like Finland, in which the current administration has abandoned the policies of its predecessor in favor of one providing great discretion to teachers and trusting them to do the right thing—and getting great improvement in student performance in return.

INCENTIVES

The way incentives are structured can make a big difference in the relative productivity of systems. Perhaps the best example is the effect on student motivation of the use of external examination systems as gateways by the best-performing nations. In countries with external examination systems used as gateways, students have strong incentives to take tough courses and work hard in school. In the United States, unless a student is headed for a selective college, he or she quickly realizes that, even if the objective is to get into an open-admissions college, it makes no difference whether the student gets good grades or a D-minus; the result is the same—entrance to a nonselective college. The effect is to send a message to our students that high school is a place to hang out with friends: As long as you show up, you will do as well as you would if you take school seriously. What they do not know, of course, is that, if they have not done well enough to succeed in their initial credit-bearing college courses, they will have to take remedial courses, for which they will receive no credit while piling up debt. By the time they learn that, it is too late.

American policy makers assume that all school faculty have positive incentives to adopt research findings that show X works better than Y. But that is not true if they think that adopting X may arouse the anger of some vocal group in the community. Administrators are almost certain to get into deep trouble if they take high-cost contracts away from local contractors in order to give them to lower-cost national contractors, even though doing so would save a lot of money that could be used for instruction. Actually, the faculty has stronger incentives for avoiding trouble than for doing what works for students. School people have no incentive to meet the needs of minority and low-income students if their performance improves and the money is taken away. If school administrators find a way to deliver the same services for less money, their reward is to have their budget reduced. Education school deans report that if they propose to raise standards for admission in their schools, the arts and sciences faculty may veto that move because it might mean fewer students in their departments. Some minority students in inner-city schools who decide to work hard in school are turned into pariahs for "acting white." Some teachers who do whatever it takes for their students are ostracized by their colleagues for violating the union contract. Teachers who teach complex skills to their students that are not measured on the standardized test are sometimes penalized because they are not sticking to the schedule for teaching much lower basic skills. These are all examples of positive incentives for lowering, not raising, achievement. Our education system is rife with such perverse incentives.

Other, high-performing education systems typically have far fewer perverse incentives than the American system does. The case chapters have already pointed out that all students, not just those going to selective colleges, have strong incentives to take tough courses and study hard in the top-performing countries. Teachers in Japan have strong incentives to work hard and perform at high levels because of the value that all Japanese work groups place on that behavior. The Singaporeans provide substantial bonuses to teachers to do outstanding work. Teacher colleges in the best-performing countries are not expected to be "cash cows" for the arts and sciences schools in those countries. And so on.

Generally, if you don't like the performance of the education system, it is easy to blame the actors. But the chances are that you would behave just the way they are behaving if you were experiencing the same incentives. If you want better performance from the system, one of the first places to look for opportunities is the structure of incentives in that system. If you find a lot of perverse incentives—incentives to produce the behavior you do not want—then change the incentives. The United States' best competitors have done just that.

SCHOOL-TO-WORK TRANSITION

Investing more in education is a sort of bet, a bet that giving students a better education will result in certain outcomes. Among those outcomes is that they are more likely to be able to support themselves and their families and enjoy a good standard of living. But there is no direct connection between being well-educated and earning a good living. Students need to make an effective transition from school to work, and that process is more complicated than it might at first appear.

Among other things, it involves turning academic skills into the kind of skills that are needed to do particular jobs, which always involves more learning, a part of which usually takes place on the job under the supervision of an experienced hand. It involves having an opportunity to get that experience, which usually requires access to an informal network of people who have jobs, internships, or apprenticeships to offer. And it involves the acquisition of many skills and kinds of knowledge that are not included in the usual school syllabus.

Some countries have systems to effect such transitions, and many do not. The United States is among the latter. Many of our high school and college graduates have few, if any, family connections to people who can and will offer them the first rung on the ladder, the chance to acquire the initial experience needed. Many lack the specific skills, attitudes, and dispositions needed to succeed in those jobs. The result is very high youth unemployment rates, a high rate of youth delinquency and crime, and ruined lives.

Finland and Singapore both have multiple pathways that are highly developed and successful at delivering occupational skills at the upper-secondary level. Japan reaches much the same goal through its system of having designated high schools that supply high-prestige employers with high-quality candidates, who are then provided high-quality on-the-job training. These systems are very different from one another, but each is a vital component of that country's system for providing a rewarding future for all its children and a capable workforce to drive its economy. The point here is that a country may have a high-quality precollege education system and still have a low-quality workforce if it fails to create a sound school-to-work transition system.

A SINGLE CAPABLE CENTER

Every high-performing country the National Center on Education and the Economy has studied has a unit of government that is clearly in charge of elementary and secondary education. In Canada, those units of government are not at the national level (the national government has even less responsibility for the schools than the federal government does in the United States) but at the provincial level. In Finland, Singapore, and Japan, it is the national ministries of education that are in charge. In China, Shanghai has unusual independence from the national Ministry of Education, for very different reasons.

In many of these countries, educators view a position in the education ministry as the capstone of a distinguished career. The ministry sees itself, and is seen by others, as having great legitimacy as the keeper of the whole system, the agency responsible for defining the future course of education and for leading the national discussion as to the best shape for that system. It is often the case that these ministries do not have to issue many regulations because their informal guidance is so respected.

In such countries, the ministry has an obligation to concern itself with the design of the system as a whole, with the structure of incentives that design provides to everyone affected by it, with the coherence of that design, and with the ability of that design to address the problems the country faces.

No unit of government in the United States occupies such a position. No one expects or wants the U.S. Department of Education to play that role for the United States. Certainly, no city school district plays the role just described. But it is also true that no state department of education has a role comparable to that of a typical national ministry of education.

That is not because our state departments of education lack the constitutional authority to play that role. Most departments are required by their state constitutions to provide a "thorough and efficient education" to their citizenry. But two centuries of practice have vested a great deal of authority in local boards of education, to a degree that has no parallel in most other countries, and that authority was essentially delegated from the state a long time ago.

The result is that no level of government in the United States thinks of itself or is thought of by others as the place where the buck stops, the place where responsibility ultimately resides for the effectiveness and efficiency of the system as a whole. And the result of that is that education reform in the United States takes a different form than it typically does in the countries with the most effective education systems. When compared with other countries, the United States appears to see education reform as a process of adding programs to the corpus of programs already in place. We endlessly initiate new programs in the announced hope that they will somehow prevail, but the reality is that they gain favor with early adopters and rarely go much further. Where other countries carefully consider new policies and work hard to integrate them with existing ones in ways that will increase rather than decrease system coherence, the United States simply adds another program and hopes for the best.

SYSTEMS, COHERENCE, ALIGNMENT, AND TRADEOFFS

After twenty-two years of research on the factors that account for the success of the countries with the best education record, I find myself convinced that seven things account for the lion's share of the difference:

1. Aggressive international benchmarking
2. Quality teaching force
3. Use of aligned instructional systems and external examinations that measure complex thinking skills
4. Deciding to get all students to those standards
5. Use of professional systems of work organization instead of blue-collar models
6. Funding systems that put the most funds behind the students who are hardest to educate
7. Coherence in the design of the overall education system itself

If I were forced to reduce the list even further, I would choose the second and last of these.

Coherence of system design is that important. Why this is so is not immediately obvious. Our education research tradition has taught us to think in terms of the effectiveness of individual initiatives. We use statistical techniques to create a virtual environment in which we can simulate the effect of the intervention of interest on the outcomes of interest, everything else being equal. Then we wonder why the effects of even the most powerful interventions are almost always trivial.

The reality is that the outcomes we care about in education are the result of myriad variables, all interacting in ways we cannot possibly visualize or simulate in our computers, to produce the outcomes we see. Each program we evaluate with our sophisticated research techniques can actually be considered in real schools and school systems as one among many variables affecting the outcomes we care about. If no one thinks of themselves as responsible for the design of the overall system, then we should not be surprised that any single initiative or program, no matter how well conceived and executed, has a relatively small effect on student achievement. Because so many things affect the outcome in ways that no policy maker has thought very much about, it is to be expected that altering one variable cannot affect the outcome very much at all, one way or the other. The one thing that could have a very large effect—the design of the system itself—is no one's responsibility.

Visiting the average school is a bit like an archeological exercise, unearthing layer upon layer of initiatives carefully deposited in the school over the decades of its existence—a text that the social studies text selection committee liked ten years ago when it was all the rage, an instructional method that Jack and Judy brought back from their professional development program during the last administration, that technique that the central office was onto six years ago and caught the fancy of our then-principal who moved on last year and was replaced by a principal with a very different agenda. But none of it ever really goes away. Legislators add law after law, the courts make their decisions, the state department issues regulation after regulation—all of it is added on until it looks like the sedimentary rock in the road cut on the interstate going out of town.

It is little wonder that our systems are full of negative and perverse incentives. No one ever thought about how all of these layers of law, regulation, court decisions, textbook choices, professional development programs, and much, much more fit together, and so it is little wonder that they do not fit together. The texts do not align to the curriculum, which are not aligned to the assessments, which are not aligned to what teachers are taught in teachers colleges, which is unrelated to the curriculum frameworks, which do not exist.

As Americans, we can only imagine what might happen if we had an education system in which the parts and pieces were constructed to fit together in a sensible way, so that they reinforced each other rather than spent their lives fighting with each other. This is the end result of living in a country that was founded by people who deeply distrusted government and believed that education was one arena in which local decisions would be best, because local people knew best what their children would need to be successful.

The reality is that local control is mostly honored in the breach. Textbook manufacturers control the curriculum actually taught, to the extent that anyone does. Districts must choose among national tests made by national testing companies. The curricula of schools of education are more influenced by the curricula of other schools of education around the country than by the state in which they are chartered. Local control is a chimera. But no one else is in control either.

Our forefathers and foremothers never imagined a world in which the sons and daughters of local citizens would be competing for jobs directly with the sons and daughters of people who lived on different continents in a very complex global economy that would require highly complex education systems designed and overseen by people with rare expertise. But that is the situation we now face, and our educational institutions are not well-equipped to cope with it.

To talk with the people who run the Singapore education system is to hear a tale in which the designers worked much as an engineer would work to build an ever more effective system, step by step, element by element. That is actually just what they did, rising from third-world status fifty years ago to front-rank status today. Similarly, wave after wave of visitors have descended on Finland to find out what key policy initiative vaulted them to world-class status while no one was looking only to find out that there was no single policy initiative the Finns took to get where they are. Like the Singaporeans, the Finns, it seems, worked in a logical way, while governments came and went, in small increments over the same fifty years to take an education system designed to support a small rural economy to world leadership in just five decades. At each stage, these countries had education systems that were genuine systems.

It is only when we consider the education system as a coherent whole that it becomes possible to analyze and deal with the tradeoffs that are inherent in any system.

Consider Japan, where the overall ratio of students to teachers is much the same as it is in the United States, but the classes are considerably larger, leaving much more time for teachers to plan and develop more effective lessons and to work with individual students and small groups of students.

Consider Finland, where the government has provided its teachers with greater autonomy and accountability as the quality of its teachers have improved. Reducing the detail with which the curriculum is specified, virtually eliminating test-based accountability, and closing down the inspectorate would make no sense at all if the Finns had doubted the quality of their teachers. But it all became necessary when they managed to produce one of the highest-quality teaching forces in the world. It is essential for a high-performing country to trust its teachers, but it had better have teachers it can trust.

The most important tradeoffs undoubtedly lie in the area of system effects having to do with investments in quality.

The American mass production system was primarily concerned with driving cost down as low as possible. Quality was secondary. American production lines would produce a lot of parts and finished products that needed to be thrown out or remanufactured. But, in the latter half of the twentieth century, the Japanese, borrowing American ideas that did not get a hearing in the United States, started to reengineer their manufacturing systems to ensure that quality was built in at every stage of the process, with the result that the finished product met high quality criteria with little wastage produced along the way. They actually showed that it is less expensive to build quality in at the very beginning than to compensate for the lack of quality at the end of the production line.

Part of the price paid by the American education system for being built on the mass production model is that we tolerate an exceptionally high rate of wastage. Only in our case, what is being discarded is young people. We see this in the very high percentages of young people who are not fluent readers by the time they leave elementary school, the very high rates at which students drop out of high school, the appalling rates at which those who enroll in college need remedial work when they get there, and the equally appalling rate at which they drop out and never receive a degree.

That does not happen in the countries with the best-performing education systems. These countries have learned how to build in quality before birth and extending throughout the entire education process. One illuminating example will suffice. The United States is now bottom-fishing for its teachers, sending them to low-status training institutions, preparing them poorly for teaching, not supporting them in their initial years while they are learning their craft, and compensating them poorly. It should not surprise us that a significant number of teachers do not do a good job, nor should it surprise us that many want out. Close to a third of those who trained as teachers are gone within three years, and close to half are gone in less than five years. These rates are significantly higher than for other professions.

Imagine what would happen if they stayed for ten years, on average, instead of three to five years? We would need fewer than half as many slots in our teacher colleges. We could afford to upgrade their training substantially and still have money left over, which we could use to provide them with better support when they get their first job, and there might even be money left over to raise their pay. We might be able to get a world-class teaching force for the same money we are paying now—in much the same way that our automobile companies found out that they could produce higher-quality cars for the same money it cost to produce low-quality cars.

Consider another take on the same theme. Most of the top-performing countries are getting their students through the common curriculum by the end of the lower secondary school, or about age sixteen. We shoot for the doing the same thing by the *end* of upper-secondary education. Suppose we set our system up to match the students' achievement. We could save the cost of the junior and senior years of high school. Of course, we would not really save it because we would need the extra money to make the improvements needed to get all our students to the goal line by the time they are sixteen. But the reality is that 30 percent of our students drop out, and a substantial fraction of the rest leave high school with no more than an eighth- or ninth-grade level of literacy. Our competitors have dropout rates in the neighborhood of 10 percent or less, and their students leave with average literacy rates far higher than ours. So we could get much better results than we are getting now for the same money by taking the money we are wasting on the last two years of high school and spending it wisely in the earlier years, as our competitors do.

The reason I believe that high-quality staff, equitable funding, and coherent systems are the key to highly successful education systems is that these points lead to all the others. Any country that recruits its teachers from the higher ranges of the applied ability distribution will quickly find that, in order to keep them, it has to train them in high-quality, high-status universities; support them well once they're hired; offer them decent pay and professional work environments; and, not least, trust them to do the right thing.

Any country that really strives for coherence and that seriously researches the best practices of the leading countries will in time be forced to adopt high-quality curriculum-based examinations and use them to define a few important gateways, to develop strong curriculum frameworks, to fund their schools equitably, and to make sensible tradeoffs as they make decisions about how their money will be spent. Any country that moves toward a system of truly equitable school finance has made the crucial decision to get all of its students to high standards. These key practices, if informed by serious international benchmarking will, in time, lead to all the others.

THE DOG THAT DID NOT BARK

In one of Arthur Conan Doyle's best-known Sherlock Holmes stories, the decisive clue is a dog that did not bark. In this case, the dog that did not bark is the dominant elements of the American education reform agenda.

It turns out that neither the researchers whose work is reported on in this book nor the analysts of the OECD PISA data have found any evidence that any country that leads the world's education performance league tables has gotten there by implementing any of the major agenda items that dominate the education reform agenda in the United States, with the exception of the Common Core State Standards.

We include in this list the use of market mechanisms such as charter schools and vouchers, the identification and support of education entrepreneurs to disrupt the system, and the use of student performance data on standardized tests to identify teachers and principals who are then rewarded on that basis for the value they add to a student's education or who are punished because they fail to do so. Among the strategies now on the front burner in the United States, only the effort to develop internationally benchmarked student achievement standards and high-quality examinations appears to have a parallel in the program of the nations with the best student performance.

This is not to say that none of these initiatives will lead to significantly improved performance at scale. It is only to say that none of the countries that have the best records of performance have employed these strategies to get there.

It is important here to make it clear that many countries are interested in current efforts in the United States to identify through research what makes for good teaching and for a good teacher. They understand that such information would be very useful in creating criteria for admission to high-quality teacher education programs, for designing those programs, for producing better criteria for licensure, for creating better professional development programs, and for evaluating teachers. But they worry that using standardized- test data as a major basis of evaluating and rewarding teachers will create perverse incentives of many kinds, and they also worry that there is much in student performance that is important that standardized tests are unlikely to capture and that great student performance is the result of the work of many adults working in collaboration rather than individual teachers working alone.

CHAPTER 7

An Action Plan for the United States

Marc S. Tucker

So what does all this mean for the United States? In this final chapter, I take the analysis I presented in the last chapter and answer the question this book opened with: What would the education reform agenda of the United States be if it were based on the strategies used by those countries whose students achieve at the highest levels in the world?

In building on the key ideas of the previous chapter and reframing the language, I have devised an action agenda. To be clear, this is not an agenda for the United States; it is an agenda for individual states.

Benchmark the Education Systems of the Top-Performing Countries

- Make sure you know what the leaders are trying to achieve, the extent to which they achieve it, and how they do on common measures.
- Compare your state to the best performers, paying particular attention to countries that share your goals.
- Conduct careful research on the policies and practices of the best-performing nations to understand how they get those results.
- Benchmark often, because the best never stand still.

Design for Quality

- Clarify your goals and get public and professional consensus on them.
- Create world-class instructional systems and gateways.
  - Define a limited number of gateways—not more than the end of basic education, end of lower-secondary, and end of upper-secondary (matched up to college-entrance and work-ready requirements).

- Create standards for each gateway, making sure they are properly nested and are world-class.
- Create logically ordered curriculum frameworks (topics for each year for each subject) for the basic education sequence.
- Create curricula (broad guidelines, not lesson plans) for each school level leading up to the gateway exams (the level of detail should be inversely related to the quality of teachers).
- Create exams for each gateway based on standards and curricula.
- Train teachers to teach those curricula well to students from many different backgrounds.

- Develop a world-class teaching force.
  - Raise standards for entry into teacher education to internationally benchmarked levels—including standards for general intelligence, level of mastery of subject matter content, and ability to relate to young people—with rigorous selection processes.
  - Move teacher education out of second- and third-tier institutions and into the major research universities.
  - Insist that teachers at all levels have a depth and breadth of mastery of the subjects they will teach comparable at the bachelor-degree level to that of the people who will go on to graduate education in those fields.
  - Make sure that prospective teachers have excellent skills in diagnosing student problems and prescribing appropriate solutions.
  - Design the teacher preparation program on a clinical model, with plenty of clinical experience under the constant supervision of master teachers in real settings.
  - Raise the criteria for teacher licensure to internationally benchmarked levels and never, under any circumstances, waive the licensure standards in the face of a teacher shortage.
  - Make sure compensation for beginning teachers is and remains comparable to compensation for the other nonfeminized professions; add the amounts necessary to attract capable teachers to hardship locations and specialties in shortage; tie amounts to steps on the career ladder.
  - Provide for an induction period for new teachers of at least a year, during which time they are supervised by master teachers who are released from full-time teaching for this purpose.
  - Construct multiple career pathways for teachers, one of which is into school administration, another of which is within teaching, and all of which provide for merit-based advancement with increasing responsibility and compensation.

- Set up a system for identifying teachers who have been in service for a few years who have the attributes likely to enable them to be strong candidates for one of the career pathways; groom them for advancement by offering them free advanced training tied to the steps on the career ladder; provide mentoring and other forms of support and continue that support as long as they continue to be promising candidates for advancement.
- Explore the development of approaches to instruction that would enable the state to get world-class results with larger class sizes. Class size is important because it is the fundamental driver of teacher cost, and teacher cost is the fundamental driver of the cost of the entire system. Japan has shown how it is possible to increase class size and increase student performance at the same time. Perhaps that method would work in the United States, perhaps not. It is important to find out if it does and, if it does, to make as much progress on this front as possible.

Design for Equity

- Move toward full state adoption of responsibility for school finance and toward implementation of a weighted pupil finance system, which would calculate the amount due each school entirely on the basis of a uniform state formula. The formula would provide funding to any public school chosen by the parents and the student, with the same base funding behind all students in the state and with additional amounts going to students who need to be brought up to the high state academic standards. Among the students bringing more money to the school would be those from low-income families, students from families that do not speak English at home, and those who have some form of disability.
- Develop a system in which all schools, from kindergarten through the end of lower secondary school, are truly comprehensive; open to all children of all races, ethnicity, gender, and socioeconomic status; and are untracked and committed to bringing all students up to the same high standards, regardless of background.
- Make sure that schools have the same high expectations for all students and that they provide the additional supports required by students who need them to achieve those standards (which is why a weighted student formula for school funding is necessary).
- Identify schools that are not succeeding in bringing all their students to high standards and close those schools. Distribute the students to high-performing schools, send key staff from better-performing schools to take leadership positions in the low-performing schools, and send key staff

from low-performing schools for training in the high-performing schools, or have the managements of high-performing schools also take responsibility for managing the low-performing schools.

Design for Productivity

- Adopt as a conceptual framework for the reform program the goal of reframing teaching from a feminized occupation performed in a Taylorized work organization to professional work (or knowledge work) performed in a form of work organization appropriate for professionals, as per Peter Drucker.
- Look for opportunities to build quality into the education system from the beginning rather than coping later on with the high rate of wastage.
- Examine the total state budget for opportunities to make better tradeoffs between major budget elements in favor of higher productivity.
- Do what is necessary to redesign the state department of education so that it has the capacity and status needed to drive the state education system to excellence.
- Examine the state's school-to-work transition system to see if it is truly world-class, so that it gives all young people access to high-quality work experience and on-the-job training, access to networks of people who are offering good jobs, and access to further schooling designed to provide high-quality education and training leading to industry-recognized occupational certification.
- Make sure your systems are coherent and aligned.

BUT THAT'S IMPOSSIBLE! REALISTICALLY, HOW CAN WE GET STARTED?

Sure, you say. All this sounds sensible, and you have explained that it is all being done somewhere by somebody. But it simply cannot be done here, in these United States, or at least in my state, in the foreseeable future. Too many vested interests, too deep a commitment to local control, too many teachers colleges to be shut down, too many objections from unions, too few master teachers available, just too much!

It has taken from thirty to one hundred years to build the national and provincial education systems on which these recommendations are based. None was built in one or two decades. If the United States is to catch up, it will have to get started soon, and it will have to work very hard at it for a long time.

But what do we do while waiting for the long-term payoff?

We have not mentioned Canada much until now, because this is where it fits best in the discussion. The government of Ontario did not predicate its reform program on replacing its current teacher workforce with a new workforce. It didn't think it needed to. Leaders asked themselves how they could get much better results from the workforce already in place. The answer they came up with was to make peace with the teachers unions, which had been demonized by the previous administration, and with the teachers, who had been so badly demoralized, and invited them to join them in thinking through a reform program that would improve student performance. They insisted on high standards, but they listened hard to what the teachers had to say about the support they needed to raise student achievement to those standards. They decided that the highest leverage strategy available to them was to build the capacity and professional skill and commitment of their in-place teaching force. They focused on what it would take to build capacity at every level of the system to deliver, and, wherever possible, they supplied it. These education leaders made a point of trusting teachers, and the teachers returned their trust.

Earlier Canada redesigned its school finance system to create a far more equitable one. It is impossible to overstate the importance of this policy change. On that foundation, leaders built an education system, province by province, that put the nation as a whole comfortably among the top ten performers in the world.

These measures did not result in equal improvements at all student ability levels. There was broad and substantial improvement for the students in the bottom half of the achievement distribution but much less among those who had been doing better before these measures were introduced. And there was considerable improvement on measures of basic skills but nowhere near as much on measures of higher-order skills. This is exactly what can be expected of such an approach. With the same teachers in place, and with a strong effort to build capacity in the teaching force, it is not surprising that the most improvement would be among those students who, before the initiatives, had been doing least well.

By building the capacity of the current teaching force, the Ontario government took the distribution of student performance and moved the left end of the performance curve toward the middle, while the middle and right portions of the curve did not change much. Their next challenge will likely be to move the entire curve to the right, so that the performance of all students improves substantially and the performance of the students who perform least well is not far from the best-performing students, who would then be performing at world-class levels. That is precisely how I defined world-class performance at the beginning of this chapter. To get that, Canada will have to adopt the other features of the agendas of their top-performing peers.

And this is exactly what my coauthors and I think makes sense in the United States. Start with the Canadian agenda while at the same time beginning to work on those parts of the larger agenda that seem possible at the outset. The strategies chosen would be different for different states, depending on what is politically possible, what the state's strong points are, and the nature of its weak points. But working over time in this way strikes us as plausible in the real world.

Bear in mind, we are not suggesting that it is possible to shortcut the steps the best-performing countries have taken on the way to the top of the league tables. Canada, like many of the other top performers, has moved the preparation of its teachers into the universities. In order to teach in Ontario schools, high school graduates must complete a degree program in the subject they wish to teach and another year-long (at least) degree program in professional education. This includes elementary school teachers, who must specialize in one or two subjects in the elementary curriculum. Secondary school teachers must have academic credentials in at least two subjects , and candidates who think they might want to be a subject specialist must take an honors degree. High school students must have 3.2 to 3.3 grade point averages on a scale of 4 to get into the institutions offering the first of these two degrees. There are fewer universities per capita in Canada, and the universities in which teachers are trained have a higher status than their opposite numbers in the United States. And finally, teachers in Canada are paid better than American teachers.

It might be fair to say, then, that the Canadian benchmark before it embarked on the current round of reforms was above where the United States is now—but within reach. An American state could reasonably set an agenda for reaching toward the Canadian starting line, then Canada's current state, and then the more distant configuration of public policies for education adopted by the very best performers in the world. That is a very ambitious agenda, but it is doable in stages.

WHAT THE FEDERAL GOVERNMENT CAN DO

No one wants a national education system in the United States. Even if one wanted to mandate that a state adopt an agenda of the sort described above, it would not work. The kinds of systems described here would not be faithfully implemented in a state that was opposed to them, no matter what compliance mechanisms were used. Nor is it very likely that all states would want to embark on such an agenda. That logic suggests that a federal government interested in the adoption of such an agenda would be well-advised to provide assistance to states that would really like to implement such an agenda but that, in the current environment, lack the resources needed to do so.

The agenda laid out here is consistent at many points with the markers that the Congress and the Obama administration have already put down. Secretary Duncan has reversed half a century of history by actively calling attention to the achievements of the countries that are outpacing us in education and by doing something to learn how they do it. Race to the Top was designed and passed in a form that encourages the kind of comprehensive and coherent planning advocated here, rather than the digging of postholes encouraged by categorical programs. Through the Common Core State Standards work, a major step toward the implementation of the kind of internationally benchmarked standards embraced by all high-performing countries was initiated by the states, and it has received the enthusiastic support of the Obama administration. And the initiative to use Race to the Top funds to support the development of tests matched to the standards should move the United States much closer to the kinds of powerful, cohesive instructional systems the top-performing countries have. Further, the president's call for making all high school students college- and career-ready and for setting a goal of once again leading the world in college completion is a big step toward developing the kind of consensus on education goals that characterizes the countries with the best education performance. The administration has also proposed a number of initiatives on teacher quality that are consistent with the strategies other countries have taken to ensure a strong supply of high-quality teachers in the years to come.

So the stage is set. The time has come to build on these beginnings and to embrace aggressively a comprehensive agenda that is squarely based on the principles that lie behind the success of those countries that rank highest on the world's education league tables.

This book was written on the eve of reauthorization hearings for the Elementary and Secondary Education Act. My coauthors and I suggest that a title of that revised act be written that would create a competition among states for funds that would be used to implement the agenda described in this chapter. We would make sure that there was considerable latitude for the states in the way they approached their design for implementation. It might be appropriate for the federal government to conduct activities intended to broadly familiarize the states with the strategies being employed by the countries with the most successful education systems before such a competition takes place. People familiar in detail with those strategies (including representatives of the countries at the top of the league tables), people who have researched those countries, and people familiar with each states' current situation might be involved as reviewers of the state proposals. After the first round of grants is made, the government might wish to sponsor additional rounds.

We would be leery of mandating specific design features in the announcement of such a program, much less implementation schedules and deadlines. States should be free to build on their existing strengths and to minimize their weaknesses as they build their strategies. Their strategies need to reflect their politics and their history. The review process ought to be less a compliance check than an assessment of a state's determination and their capacity to take full advantage of the path blazed by the countries with the most successful education systems. Let the states convince the readers that they understand what has happened in these countries and are prepared to do what is necessary to adapt and profit from that experience in their own unique ways.

WHAT THE STATES CAN DO

The real power to act lies with the states. Whether or not the federal government chooses to take an active role, the states have all the authority they need to move in the direction outlined here. This is certainly a very ambitious agenda. It is inconceivable that it could be successfully implemented without capable and determined leadership to produce a wide consensus for the main outline of the work. In almost every case described in this book, there was an individual or a political party that provided unusual continuity of leadership for this agenda over a long period of time. That is not easy to achieve in the United States, but it's not impossible either.

The claim that this agenda has on my coauthors' and my attention is simply that it has worked. It has worked in countries as different as Singapore and Finland, Japan and Canada. It is not a Republican agenda or a Democratic agenda. It is neither conservative nor liberal. While it requires major changes in the way we do things in the United States, it demands changes more or less equally of all parties. The changes it calls for are as dramatic as the changes made in government during the Progressive Era. But let the record show that the United States made those changes. And we can make these, too, if we choose to do so.

REFERENCES

Allegretto, S., and L. Mishel. 2008. *The Teaching Penalty: Teacher Pay Losing Ground.* Washington, DC: Economic Policy Institute.

Asia Society. 2010. *Canada: School Improvement Without Rancor and Rankings.* New York: Author.

Auguste, B., P. Kihn, and M. Miller. 2010. *Closing the Talent Gap: Attracting and Retaining Top-Third Graduates to Careers in Teaching.* New York: McKinsey.

College Board. 2008. *2008 College-Bound Seniors: Total Group Profile Report.* New York: Author.

Costrell, R., and M. Podgersky. 2009. "Teacher Retirement Benefits." *EducationNext* 9, no. 2: 59–63.

Economic Policy Institute. 2004. *How Do Teachers Wages Compare? Methodological Challenges and Answers.* Washington, DC: Author.

Education Trust. 2008. *Core Problems: Out-of-Field Teaching Persists in Academic Courses and High-Poverty Schools.* Washington, DC: Author.

Franke, R., S. Ruiz, J. Sharkness, L. DeAngelo, and J. P. Pryor. 2010. *Findings from the 2009 Administration of the College Senior Survey: National Aggregates.* Los Angeles: Higher Education Research Institute, University of California.

Gitomer, D. 2007. *Teacher Quality in a Changing Policy Landscape: Improvements in the Teacher Pool.* Princeton, NJ: Educational Testing Service.

Heilig, J., and S. Jez . 2010. *Teach for America: A Review of the Evidence.* East Lansing, MI: Great Lakes Center for Education Research and Practice.

Higher Education Research Institute. 2010. *Findings from the 2009 Administration of the College Senior Survey (CSS): National Aggregates.* Los Angeles: Graduate School of Education and Information Studies, University of California.

Hurley, E. 2006. *Teacher Pay 1940–2000: Losing Ground, Losing Status.* Washington, DC: National Education Association.

Lykins, C., and S. Heyneman. 2008. *The Federal Role in Education: Lessons from Australia, Germany, and Canada.* Washington, DC: Center on Education Policy.

Markow, D., and M. Cooper. 2008. *The MetLife Survey of the American Teacher: Past, Present and Future.* New York: MetLife.

Ministry of Education. 1997. *Towards Thinking Schools.* Singapore: Author.

Ministry of Education. 2001. *Guidelines for Curriculum Reform in Basic Education.* Beijing: Author.

Ministry of Education, Culture, Sports, Science, and Technology (MEXT). 2010. *Education Reform for the 21st Century, National Council of Education Reform and the Process of Its Reform.* Tokyo: Author.

Ministry of Trade and Industry. 1986. *The Singapore Economy: New Directions.* Singapore: Author.

National Association of Colleges and Employers. 2010. *Salary Survey.* Bethlehem, PA: Author.

National Center for Education Statistics (NCES). 2006. *Characteristics of Schools, Districts, Teachers, Principals, and School Libraries in the United States: 2003–04 Schools and Staffing Survey.* Washington, DC: Author.

National Science Foundation (NSF). 2010. *Science and Engineering Indicators: 2010.* NSB 10-01. Arlington, VA: Author.

Norrie, K., and S. Lin. 2009. *Postsecondary Education Attainment and Participation in Ontario.* Toronto: Higher Education Quality Council of Ontario.

Ontario College of Teachers. 2011.*Thinking About Teaching.* Toronto: Author.

Ontario Focused Intervention Partnership 2007–2008. 2007. PowerPoint presentation. Literacy and Numeracy Secretariat, Ontario Ministry of Education. www.decs.sa.gov.au/quality/files/links/Powerpoint_Results_Without.ppt.

Orland, M. 2011. *School Turnaround Policies and Practices in Australia, Canada, England, and New Zealand: Overview and Implications.* San Francisco: WestEd.

Sclafani, S., and E. Lim 2008. *Rethinking Human Capital in Education: Singapore as a Model for Teacher Development.* Washington, DC: Aspen Institute.

About the Editor

Marc S. Tucker, president of the National Center on Education and the Economy (NCEE), created the National Institute for School Leadership, America's Choice, Inc., and the Commission on the Skills of the American Workforce. He was also the director of the Carnegie Forum on Education and the Economy, which created the National Board for Professional Teaching Standards. Among numerous book and report publications, Tucker is the coauthor of *Thinking for a Living: Education and the Wealth of Nations* (Basic Books, 1993, with Ray Marshall) and coeditor of *The Principal Challenge: Leading and Managing Schools in an Era of Accountability* (Jossey-Bass, 2002, with Judy Codding).

About the Contributors

Kai-ming Cheng, professor and chair of education and senior adviser to the vice chancellor at the University of Hong Kong, Hong Kong, China, trained as a mathematician and worked as a school teacher and principal. Recently appointed to China's State Advisory Committee on Curriculum Reform, he was also appointed as a member of the Hong Kong Education Commission, where he was instrumental in the comprehensive reform of that education system that began in 1999.

Linda Darling-Hammond is a former president of the American Educational Research Association and member of the National Academy of Education. She served as executive director of the National Commission on Teaching and America's Future. While at Stanford University, Darling-Hammond has launched the Stanford Educational Leadership Institute and the School Redesign Network.

Jal D. Mehta, assistant professor of education at the Harvard Graduate School of Education, is currently working on a manuscript, *Between Justice and Order*, about repeated efforts to rationalize American schooling across the twentieth century. He is also writing a book, *The Chastened Dream*, about the evolving relationship between social science, social policy, and social progress.

Betsy Brown Ruzzi is vice president and director of the Center on International Education Benchmarking at the National Center on Education and the Economy (NCEE). At NCEE she was the associate director of the New Commission on the Skills of the American Workforce and helped create the National Institute for School Leadership. Prior to joining NCEE, Ruzzi worked for a number of members of Congress.

Robert B. Schwartz, Francis Keppel Professor of Practice of Educational Policy and Administration and academic dean at the Harvard Graduate School of Education, has played a variety of roles in education and government over the past four decades, including high school teacher and principal, foundation officer, and president of Achieve, Inc.

Vivien Stewart, senior adviser for education and chair of the Asia Society Confucius Classrooms Initiative, was the director of education programs at the Carnegie Corporation of New York and has also been a senior adviser on education for the United Nations.

Index

action plan for U.S.
  benchmarking the best, 211
  Canadian model, 214–216
  design for equity, 213–214
  design for productivity, 214
  design for quality, 211–213
  federal government's role, 216–218
  states' role, 218
Agency for Scientific and Technical
    Research, Singapore (A*Star),
    118–119
Alberta, 146, 147
applied intelligence, 178
assessments and accountability
  elements of best practices, 211–212
  in Finland, 66–67
  grade-by-grade national testing in
    U.S., 176
  instructional systems and gateway
    exams use, 174–177
  in Japan, 24, 85, 86–88, 95–96
  in Shanghai, 21–22, 24, 35–36, 44
  in Singapore, 119–120, 129, 132,
    134–135

Canada
  central leadership importance, 160
  cultural support of education,
    145–146, 158, 159
  education as part of a strategy,
    160–161
  education policies as a success factor,
    146–148
  education system described, 142,
    144–145
  education system flowchart, 143
  immigrant education, 149–151

lessons learned, 158–161
minority-language accommodations,
    144
model overview, 161–162
Ontario's system (*see* Ontario)
PISA rankings, 141
professional accountability, 160
school funding, 145, 148–149, 195
system coherence and alignment, 159
teacher and principal quality, 159–160
teacher training, 142, 148
welfare state structure as a success
    factor, 146
Center for International Education
    Benchmarking, NCEE, 1–2
Centre for Research on Pedagogy, Singa-
    pore, 123
China. *See also* Shanghai
  Civil Examination system, 21–22, 25
  class sizes, 29
  constructivist learning, 31
  content of teacher education and
    induction, 187
  culture of education, 24
  curriculum reform focus, 30–31
  disparity in competence amongst
    teachers, 28
  framework and system for teacher
    training, 29–30
  teachers' salaries, 28–29
Civil Examination system in China,
    21–22
Common Core State Standards, 170,
    176, 177, 209, 217
Costante, Kevin, 146, 154
Council of Ministers of Education,
    Canada (CMEC), 146

Cultural Revolution, China, 25–26
Curriculum 2015, Singapore, 120
Curriculum Development Institute of
    Singapore, 118

Darling-Hammond, Linda, 64–65, 129
Deng Xiaoping, 36
Drucker, Peter, 5, 198
Duncan, Arne, 2, 182–183

Education Partnership Table, Ontario,
    156
education spending. *See* school funding
Elmore, Richard, 146
equity in education
    low-performing school attention,
        197
    school finance, 194–195
    secondary school organization,
        195–196
    standards and flexible support,
        196–197
examinations. *See* assessments and
    accountability

Finland
    assessments and accountability,
        66–67, 71–72, 201
    background, 52
    challenges ahead, 68–70
    commitment importance, 70–71
    comprehensive school system
        creation, 54–55
    culture of schools, 58–60, 61–63, 71
    education system flowchart, 53
    education system in 1950, 52, 54
    growth in upper-secondary education
        attendance, 56–57
    instructional system, 72, 193–194
    lessons learned, 70–73
    national curriculum development, 56
    national economic picture and educa-
        tion, 57–58, 73
    nature of the reforms, 73–74
    new teacher preparation programs
        development, 56
    PISA ranking since 2001, 51

school organization, 72–73
school-to-work transition approach,
    203
special education approach, 59
spending decisions, 72
standards for entry into teaching, 180
success factors, 61–63, 73–74
teacher education and induction, 184,
    185, 186–187
teacher recruitment and training, 62,
    63–65
teachers and principal quality, 71
teachers duties, 65–66
trust in the system as a success factor,
    61, 74
Friedman, Thomas, 4
Fullan, Michael, 153, 156–157
Fundamental Law of Education, Japan,
    101

Glaze, Avis, 156
Goh report, 117
Guppy, Neil, 147
Gurria, Angel, 2

High Skills Major, Ontario, 157
Hogan, David, 123, 130
homework
    student engagement in Shanghai,
        33–34
    student motivation in Japan, 96–97
Ho Peng, 120

immigrant education
    in Canada, 149–151
    in Finland, 68–69
    international comparisons, 7, 8
    in Japan, 95
    in Shanghai, 37–38
    in United States, 7, 8
Imperial Rescript of Education, Japan, 83
Institute for Technical Education, Singa-
    pore (ITE), 118, 127
international benchmarking
    characteristics of top performers, 172
    designing for equity (*see* equity in
        education)

designing for productivity (*see* productivity in education)

designing for quality (*see* quality in education)

economic themes motivating other countries, 171

by Singapore, 131

as a strategy for improvement, 12–13, 172–173

study methodology (*see* study methodology)

value in using, 169–170

international comparisons of education systems. *See also individual countries*

academic performance, 7–10

automation's effects, 4–5

distribution of finances and performance, 11

immigrant population and performance problems, 7, 8

impact of low expectations, 10–11

pressure on governments to educate children, 5–6

shift to knowledge work, 5

socioeconomic status as a predicator of education achievement, 10

spending patterns and academic achievement, 11

spending per pupil, 6–7

teachers' salaries correlated to student performance, 11

wages vs. skill levels globally, 4

International Summit on the Teaching Profession, 182–183

ITE (Institute for Technical Education, Singapore), 118, 127

Japan

accountability and assessments, 95–96, 105–106

cost and finance, 94–95

creativity and innovation challenges, 97–101

cultural changes causing concern, 99

culture and education, 80, 83–86, 102, 105

curriculum, standards, and assessment, 86–88

curriculum tied to professional development, 189–192

education system creation, 82–83, 106

education system flowchart, 81

equity for populace, 95

incentives for students, 103

instructional system, 88–90, 103–104, 193

international benchmarking, 102–103

legislation addressing curriculum, 100–101

lessons learned, 102–106

level of knowledge and skill typical of graduates, 79

merit-basis of advancement, 85

organization, 90–91

parent involvement, 92

political history, 80, 82

reaffirmation of traditional values, 101

resources, 103

school-to-work transition approach, 104–105

societal commitment to education, 102

special education approach, 104

standards for entry into teaching, 180

student motivation, 96–97

teacher professional development approach, 104

teacher quality, 92–94

time spent learning, 91–92

traditional values' influence, 83–86

valuing the group over the individual, 97–98, 201

workforce strengths, 98

Kennedy, Gerard, 153, 155–156, 161

King, William Lyon MacKenzie, 149

Law of Compulsory Education, China, 26

Law Song Seng, 127

Learning Gap, The, 89, 94

Lee Hsien Loong, 120

Lee Kuan Yew, 116, 117, 130

Lee Sing Kong, 124–125, 130
Levin, Bob, 148, 153
Literacy and Numeracy initiative,
    Ontario, 152, 156
Luukkainen, Olli, 61, 66

McGuinty, Dalton, 151, 152, 153, 154
moral education in Japan, 87

National Center on Education and the
    Economy (NCEE), 1–2
National Education Goals Panel (1990),
    174
National Institute of Education, Singa-
    pore (NIE), 123, 184
National Labor Relations Act, U.S., 191
Ng Eng Hen, 120

OECD (Organisation for Economic
    Co-operation and Development), 2
Ontario
    accountability and autonomy, 201
    central leadership importance, 154, 160
    commitment to education and chil-
        dren, 158
    conditions facilitating success,
        152–154
    context, 151
    cultural support, 159
    economic versus sociological theories
        of action, 158
    education as part of a strategy,
        160–161
    focus on specific goals, 154–155
    lessons learned, 159–161
    pace and focus of reforms, 214–216
    professional accountability, 160
    programmatic initiatives and results,
        151–152
    strategy of sustained improvement,
        155–158
    system coherence and alignment, 159
    teacher and principal quality, 159–160
Organisation for Economic Co-operation
    and Development (OECD), 2
Outline of the Medium and Long-Term Plan
    (China), 40–41

Period of Integrated Study, Japan,
    100–101
PIRLS (Progress in International Reading
    Literacy Study), 113
PISA. *See* Programme for International
    Student Assessment
productivity in education
    accountability and autonomy,
        199–201
    central leadership, 203–204
    incentives for students and teachers,
        201–203
    management paradigm followed,
        197–199
    school-to-work transition approach,
        203
    Tayloristic workplaces, 198, 199, 200
professional development
    curriculum tied to in Japan, 104,
        189–192
    in Finland, 66
    professional accountability in Canada,
        160
    separated from curriculum in U.S., 189
    for teachers in Shanghai, 36
    for teachers in Singapore, 128–129,
        190
Programme for International Student
    Assessment (PISA)
    about, 2, 3–4, 8–9, 10
    data on immigrants in Canada,
        149–150
    Finland's ranking since 2001, 51
    limitations in survey data, 11–12
    Singapore's ranking, 113
Progress in International Reading
    Literacy Study (PIRLS), 113

quality in education
    instructional systems and gateway
        exams use, 174–177, 193–194
    principal quality, 192–193
    setting clear goals and, 173–174
    teacher quality (*see* teacher quality)

Revised Law of Compulsory Education,
    China, 27

Sahlberg, Pasi, 55, 58, 70
Sarjala, Jukka, 55, 56, 69
Sato, Teiichi, 80, 92
Schleicher, Andreas, 2
Schmidt, Bill, 186
school funding. *See also* teachers' salaries
  in Canada, 145, 148–149, 195
  design for equity, 213–214
  in Finland, 72
  international comparisons, 6–7, 11
  in Japan, 94–95, 103
  in Singapore, 122
  spending patterns and academic
    achievement, 11
  in U.S., 6–7, 11, 194–195
Shanghai. *See also* China
  about, 24
  assessments and accountability, 44–45
  central leadership importance, 43–44
  challenges ahead, 39–40
  class sizes, 29
  coherent and comprehensive
    approach use, 43
  constructivist learning, 31
  content of teacher education and
    induction, 185, 187
  cultural heritage supporting educa-
    tion, 24, 32–33, 41–42
  Cultural Revolution, 25–26
  curriculum and textbooks reorganiza-
    tion, 34–35
  curriculum reform focus, 30–31
  disparity in competence amongst
    teachers, 28
  education system flowchart, 23
  examination redesign, 35–36
  expansion of access to education,
    27–28
  goals set for success, 40–41
  instruction and learning importance,
    42–43
  key schools concept, 37
  lessons learned, 40–45
  lifelong learning structure, 28
  migrant children's education, 37–38
  neighborhood attendance, 37
  pedagogy reform, 35

post-revolution education reconstruc-
    tion, 26–27
  strategies to strengthen weak schools,
    38–39
  student engagement, 33–34
  teachers' compensation, 28–29, 183
  training framework and system, 29–30
Shanmugaratnam, Tharman, 119, 125
Singapore
  alignment between policy and prac-
    tices, 122–124
  assessments and accountability,
    119–120, 129, 132, 134–135
  background, 114, 116
  central leadership importance, 134
  coherence of education system,
    133–134
  commitment to equity and meritoc-
    racy, 124–126, 135
  continuous improvement commit-
    ment, 130–131
  curriculum tied to professional devel-
    opment, 190
  education system features, 120–121
  education system flowchart, 115
  education system rankings, 113
  education viewed as a national
    priority, 121–122
  future challenges, 131–132
  international benchmarking, 135
  lessons learned, 133–135
  math, science, and technical skills
    focus, 126–127
  phases of education system, 116–120
  principals' training, 192–193
  quality in teachers and training, 134,
    184
  school-to-work transition approach,
    203
  success factors, 122–130
  system aligned with economic devel-
    opment, 133
  teacher recruitment and training,
    127–130
  teachers' salaries, 128
  vision and leadership importance, 133
  vocational education, 127

spending on schools. *See* school funding
Stevenson, Harold, 89, 94
Stigler, Jim, 89, 94, 96
Strong Performers and Successful Reformers,
    2
Student Success initiative, Ontario, 152,
    157
study methodology
    clinical research model basis of educa-
        tion research, 13
    complexities inherent in education
        research, 13–14
    dimensions of education, 16–17
    identifying superior performance,
        15–16
    industrial benchmarking model, 12–13
    limitations in survey data, 11–12
    theoretical framework, 15

Taylor, Frederick Winslow, 198
Tayloristic workplaces, 198, 199, 200
teacher quality
    attracting top students, 182–184
    content of teacher education and
        induction, 185–188
    curriculum tied to professional devel-
        opment, 189–192
    defined, 177–179
    institutional settings, 184–185
    licensure and standards for entry, 188
    practices in successful countries, 191
    professional development and (*see*
        professional development)
    quality of entrants and, 179
    standards for entry and, 179–182
    teachers' unions and, 191–192
teachers and training
    in Canada, 142, 148
    in China, 28–31
    core changes needed, 171
    elements of a world-class teaching
        force, 212–213
    in Finland, 56, 62, 63–66, 180, 184,
        185, 186–187
    in Japan, 92–94, 189–192
    in Singapore, 127–130, 184
    in U.S., 180–182, 184–188

teachers' salaries
    correlated to student performance, 11
    correlation to quality of new teachers,
        182–184
    in Finland, 72
    in Japan, 92–93
    in Shanghai, 28–29, 183
    in Singapore, 128
    in U.S., 183–184
teachers' unions, 191–192
Teach for America, 181
Teach Less, Learn More, Singapore, 120,
    123
textbooks in Japan, 87–88
Thinking Schools, Learning Nation,
    Singapore, 119, 123, 132
Third International Mathematics and
    Science Study (TIMSS), 97–98
Tokugawa era, Japan, 80
Trends in International Math and
    Science Study (TIMSS), 113, 186

United States
    academic performance, 7–10
    action agenda for individual states (*see*
        action plan for U.S.)
    content of teacher education and
        induction, 184–188
    curriculum separated from profes-
        sional development, 189
    distribution of finances related to
        performance, 11
    federal government's role in educa-
        tion, 204, 216–218
    immigrant population and perfor-
        mance problems, 7, 8
    impact of low expectations, 10–11
    industrial benchmarking history,
        169–170
    lack of attention to teacher selection
        and retention, 190
    licensure and standards for entry, 188
    perverse incentives inbedded in the
        system, 202
    practices that have led to improve-
        ments, 209
    reliance on computer-scored tests, 177

school finance model, 194–195
school-to-work transition approach, 203
secondary school organization, 196
socioeconomic status as a predicator of education achievement, 10
spending per pupil, 6–7
standards for entry into teaching, 180–182
state governments' role in education, 218
summary of shortfalls in system, 205–209
system versus other countries', 205
Tayloristic workplaces as the model for schools, 199

teachers' compensation, 183–184
teachers' salaries correlated to student performance, 11
unprecedented use of grade-by-grade national testing, 176
view of teacher quality, 190–191
U.S. Department of Education, 204

Valijarvi, Jouni, 67

Watanabe, Ryo, 86, 88
Winsemius, Albert, 117
Working Tables, Ontario, 156
World Is Flat, The (Friedman), 4

Young, Rhonda Kimberly, 152